P9-COP-849

GREAT APACHE CHIEFS
COCHISE AND GERONIMO

EDWIN R. SWEENEY AND ANGIE DEBO

MJF BOOKS

NEW YORK

Published by MJF Books
Fine Communications
Two Lincoln Square
60 West 66th Street
New York, NY 10023

Library of Congress Catalog Card Number 96-76475
ISBN 1-56731-091-5

Cochise: Chiricahua Apache Chief Copyright © 1991 by the University of Oklahoma Press,
Norman, Publishing Division of the University.
Geronimo Copyright © 1976 by the University of Oklahoma Press, Norman, Publishing
Division of the University.

This edition published by arrangement with the University of Oklahoma Press, Norman,
Publishing Division of the University.

Manufactured in the United States of America on acid-free paper ∞

MJF Books and the MJF colophon are trademarks of Fine Creative Media, Inc.

10 9 8 7 6 5 4 3 2 1

COCHISE

Chiricahua Apache Chief

by Edwin R. Sweeney

To my wife Joanne and my three daughters, Tiffani, Caitlin, and Courtney, with love, and Dan Thrapp for paving the way.

CONTENTS

CONTENTS

ILLUSTRATIONS

Figures

Maps

ACKNOWLEDGMENTS

I am indebted to many persons who have helped me during my research. I would like to take this opportunity to give them my sincere thanks.

Thanks to the Arizona Historical Society, where much of my early research was performed, and to Mrs. Lori Davisson, research historian, who has been particularly helpful with information; to Joe Park, former microforms librarian at the University of Arizona library, who directed me to the Apache material contained in the Sonora State Archives at the Arizona Historical Society; to Simeon "Bud" Newman of the Special Collections Library at the University of Texas at El Paso for his assistance with the Janos material in their holdings; and special thanks to Cynthia Radding of Hermosillo, Sonora, who helped me gain access to important documents in Sonora's state archives.

Allan Radbourne of the English Westerners' Society gave important help, sharing his vast knowledge of the Chiricahua and Western Apaches. I would also like to thank my good friend Dan Aranda of Las Cruces, New Mexico, for accompanying me to several sites, and to his wife, Joyce, for hospitality extended to me and my family.

Several field trips were made more enjoyable in the company of my brother, Kevin Sweeney, of Stoughton, Mass.; Rick Collins of Tucson; Ron and Rebecca (Becky) Orozco, formerly of Cochise, Arizona; Alicia Delgadillo, my tour guide for Cochise County, who is the director of the Fort Sill Chiricahua–Warm Springs Apache Research/Resource Center located in Cochise's stronghold; and one of the nicest persons I have met, Bill Hoy, former ranger in charge at the Fort Bowie National Historic Site, now of Bowie, Arizona, whose door was always open.

I am grateful to Susie Sato of the Arizona Historical Foundation at Arizona State University in Tempe; Susan Ravdin of Bowdoin College, who helped with the General Oliver Otis Howard Papers; Vivian Fisher of the Bancroft Library at the University of California at Berkeley; and Robert B. Matchette, Dale E. Floyd, and Michael E. Pilgrim of the Military Archives Division of the National Archives.

Others who have made contributions for which I am grateful are Bill and Joyce Griffen of Flagstaff; Leland Sonnichsen of Tucson; Harwood Hinton of the University of Arizona in Tucson; Lynda Sanchez of Lincoln, New Mexico; and Morris Opler of Norman, Oklahoma. Thanks are due to Herb Hyde, my editor; to Sarah Nestor, Managing Editor, University of Oklahoma Press; to Don Bufkin, for preparing the maps; and to Karen Hayes of Portal, Arizona, for providing photographs.

I am also grateful for the help and support of Bill Schaefer of Saint Charles, Missouri; Ruth McGarry of Malden, Massachusetts; and my mother, Mary L. Sweeney, of Stoughton, Massachusetts.

Two writers were inspirational in my decision to research Cochise, and I don't hesitate to say that I feel blessed to have met both of them. The late Eve Ball, the Chiricahuas' oral historian, provided encouragement, information, and suggestions. I am eternally grateful to Dan L. Thrapp, the authority on Apache–U.S. military affairs, for his advice and endless encouragement. His constructive comments greatly improved the manuscript.

Finally, thanks to my wife Joanne for never doubting my purpose.

EDWIN R. SWEENEY

Saint Charles, Missouri

INTRODUCTION

As the most powerful chief of the Chiricahua Apaches in recorded times, Cochise was a significant figure in nineteenth-century south-western history. One of the greatest of all American Indian leaders, he was a much-feared yet in many ways admirable man who dominated Indian-white relations on an expansive frontier. He was a chieftain who lived and prospered by war and died in peace after a sometimes pivotal role in a turbulent border region where he was frequently at odds with powerful forces of two nations. Therefore it is somewhat perplexing that until now there has been no thoroughly researched and objective study of him, his career, and his influence.

Cochise was a complex and interesting man with a fine mind, an impressive physique, and unusual talents. He was an accomplished orator in the manner of his people, and an individual of character and honor (the latter by his own standards, which were not those of contemporary American society). His considerable natural abilities, honed to the keenest edge, enabled him to deal on equal terms with governors and generals as with all others. Most whites who met him in peace or truce seemed as impressed with his quiet dignity and supple intelligence as they were with his thoroughly autocratic sway over his people—in itself a most singular phenomenon in Apache culture and tradition.

During the course of a century, information about Cochise's life, deeds, and times has become so distorted and romanticized through legend and myth that sometimes it bears scant resemblance to the truth. By today's somewhat gentler standards, even the basic facts often appear stark and harsh until it is understood that Cochise must be judged not by our precepts, but by those of a barbaric, violent, often cruel, and frequently merciless world. Through his understanding and the rules he fashioned to guide his conduct, he emerges from his milieu as a man of recognizable integrity and principle, a wholly worthy leader of a warrior people.

Certainly Cochise was no saint by white standards (no fighting Apache was), and be it conceded that there were precious few white saints in the Apachería of Cochise's day. This Indian was the paradigm of the Chiricahua fighting leader: an efficient raider and war chief who was bold enough and sufficiently influential to attract plenty of followers on both the band and tribal levels. He won and held continentwide fame in his own times. Only Geronimo's name is more recognizable today, and Geronimo, a far lesser man, did not compare with Cochise by any logical measurement, either in his own day or in history.

Among Cochise's contemporaries were other great Apaches, of course. Cochise did not establish political alliances like those conceived and molded by Mangas Coloradas, his father-in-law, who was the dominant Eastern Chiricahua leader for some twenty years before his death (or execution) at the hands of white soldiers in 1863. Nor did Cochise evince Victorio's skills in the art of guerrilla warfare. His fame was not based on a single whirlwind raid as was that of Nana, Victorio's lieutenant, and he did not possess the military genius of Juh. Yet each of these men was Cochise's ally at one time or another, and although they were not of the same band, each willingly fought under Cochise or at his side. All respected his leadership ability; his fierce, uncompromising hatred toward his legion of enemies; and, above all, his courage in battle and his wisdom in counsel.

Some whites who met Cochise employed the James Fenimore Cooper image of the noble red man in describing him. He was tall for an Apache, built much like his youngest son, Naiche, and resembling him in appearance. No photograph of Cochise has turned up, although at least one reportedly was taken, but from the many accounts of people who spoke with him or engaged him in battle we have some idea of his appearance. He stood about five feet, ten inches tall, one officer remarking that he "looked more than his height on account of his somewhat slender build, and his straight physique." [1] Another found him as "straight as an arrow, built, from the ground up, as perfect as any man could be." [2] Still others described him as "powerful and exceedingly well built" [3] or "of manly and martial appearance, not unlike our conception of the Roman soldier." [4] He weighed about 175 or 180 pounds, according to one estimate, [5] making him a man of heavyweight proportions by nineteenth-century standards. His hair was jet black, although laced with gray in his later years; it was worn, in the traditional Apache style, to his shoulders. He had well-proportioned features, a high forehead, a strong Roman nose, and prominent cheekbones. A white who sat in on a New Mexico council with Cochise reported that his "countenance displayed great force of character," although it seemed rather sad or perhaps meditative in aspect. [6] Alexander Duncan ("Al") Williamson, a sutler at Fort Bowie in 1873–74 and whose customer the chief was, said that "Cochise never smiled. He was severe and grave of aspect." [7] Another observer said Cochise seemed "anything but the most dreaded, warlike, and barbarous savage," [8] and Brigadier General Oliver Otis Howard, who conferred with Cochise and finally brought him to a lasting peace, echoed this view, writing that Cochise's "countenance was pleasant, and made me feel how strange it is that such a man could be a notorious robber and cold-blooded murderer." [9]

Although Cochise was recognized for the weight he placed on truth and openness, still there were times when his word, given to an enemy, seemed disingenuous, especially when he felt wronged or had been treated treacherously. He often mentioned his respect for truth, telling an Indian agent in 1870: "I want the truth told. A man has only one mouth and if he won't tell the truth he [should be] put out of the way." [10] Cochise once told an army officer: "I want to talk straight. . . . I have no split tongue." [11] In a conversation with his friend Thomas J. Jeffords, first and only agent of the Chiricahua Reservation in southeastern Arizona, he said that "a man should never lie. . . . If a man asks you or I a question we do not wish to answer, we could simply say, I don't want to talk about that." [12] In fact, Cochise used this stratagem in several conferences with Americans to avoid answering questions or to change the subject. He was particularly reticent about discussing certain activities about which whites showed curiosity and about which he did not wish to talk.

Cochise's insistence on integrity was demonstrated when the Chiricahuas were in council with Anglos at Cañada Alamosa. Victorio and Loco were questioned about a southern New Mexico stock raid they knew all about but were reluctant to discuss. They appeared ready to deny all until Cochise abruptly "told them to tell the truth. I can say that they appeared to be much relieved" to learn how he thought they should respond, reported an army officer who was present.[13]

Other whites reflected their appreciation of the manner in which Cochise handled the truth as it appeared to him. Fred Hughes, who assisted Jeffords on the reservation, said Cochise "kept his word till the day of his death."[14] First Lieutenant Joseph Alton Sladen, who as Howard's aide accompanied the general on his peace mission to the chief, wrote that not only Cochise but all his people seemed infused with honesty. After spending ten days in the Apache camp he remarked that "in their relations with us they were thoroughly honest. . . . During the [period] I spent in their camp not a single article . . . was lost or stolen."[15]

On occasion, Cochise also could exhibit fair-mindedness. An incident illustrating this occurred in 1860 when an American named John Wilson killed in a duel a warrior who was said to have been a protégé of Cochise. The outcome caused excitement among the Indians until Cochise intervened. "It was a fair fight [and] no blame could be attached to anyone," he ruled.[16] That settled the matter.

Toward his immediate family and the extended family group Cochise "was more affectionate than the average white man. He showed nothing of the brutish nature generally attributed to him," a close observer reported.[17] Just as Victorio's most trusted advisers included his sister, Lozen, so did Cochise respect the advice of his own sister, a woman fifteen years his junior and "in whom he seemed to have great confidence and [she] from her independence and force seemed to justify this faith." The fact that life in his Dragoon Mountains Apache camp was ordinarily a warm and friendly place surprised the few whites who were fortunate enough to visit it. Sladen remembered that the Indians there were "always cheerful, demonstratively happy, and talkative . . . brim full of fun and joking, and ready to laugh heartily over the most trivial matters. They were especially fond of playing practical jokes of a harmless nature upon each other."[18]

No Indian ever went hungry if there was food in camp. Generosity was a marked trait of the Apaches, particularly of a leader among them, and Cochise strongly exhibited it, for he was a good hunter and provider. Sladen related an incident in which a young warrior returned empty-handed from a hunt. The chief called for his own horse, picked up his rifle, and rode away. Hours later he returned with an antelope, which was immediately "divided up and distributed amongst the people present."[19]

Nor was compassion completely foreign to him, although he usually did not display it, as white survivors of battles with him would attest. Amelia Naiche, his granddaughter, told me about a massacre in which a little white boy survived. Most of the Apaches, including Geronimo, favored killing the child, but Cochise lifted him onto his horse and protected him. According to legend, he raised the boy and later gave him his freedom.[20]

The chief was not without blemishes, of course; he was as normal as anyone else in that regard. By nature he was kind and considerate among his people, but he also was subject to abrupt mood changes, a trait most clearly evident when wrongs against Indians were discussed. His own people, too, could incur his wrath; they knew it and were wary of doing so. At times they treated him with fear, though ever with the utmost respect. Asa ("Ace") Daklugie, son of Juh, remembered that as a child he was warned against even looking at Cochise's wickiup lest it be interpreted as disrespect.[21] Like many Apaches, Cochise was not averse to a good drunk, and when under the influence he sometimes became violent, even beating his wives and sister, and abusive to others who crossed his path. Sladen mentioned a time when he "heard screams from Cochise's wife and sister. I saw them fleeing in terror from his bivouac. He was striking and scolding them." During this affair "the Indians showed very plainly that they were alarmed, and soon all got out of sight if not out of the sound of his voice." It may have been during such a binge that his spunky younger wife twice bit him severely.[22]

Despite such lapses, Cochise won devotion from his followers;

they regarded his word as law. His seemingly absolute rule amazed Fred Hughes:

> It was astonishing also to see what power he had over this brutal tribe, for while they idolized him and also worshipped him no man was ever held in greater fear, his glances being enough to squelch the more obstreperous Chiricahua of the tribe.[23]

Sladen, too, was amazed by the chief's practically unheard-of influence among his followers. Anthropologists who have studied Apache culture believe that the "leaders," or chiefs, had "no absolute control" over their followers, that the "authority of the leader is far from absolute,"[24] but with the greatest of chiefs—Mangas Coloradas, Victorio, and, above all, Cochise—control came very close to being absolute. Sladen described the arrival of the captains, or subchiefs, from a raid. They would report to Cochise and the "chief would occasionally ask a question or grunt an approval." On one such occasion Cochise became visibly upset about a warrior's report and his voice "grew louder until he worked himself into a violent passion. He rose to his feet . . . and as the returned warrior [also] rose . . . the chief dealt him a violent blow upon his head."[25] Another observer said Cochise possessed what no other chief was able to boast of: supreme control over his bands. "A private soldier would as soon think of disobeying a direct order of the President as would a Chiricahua Apache a command of Cochise."[26]

Like that of Mangas Coloradas, Cochise's influence extended to various Apache bands besides his own.[27] For example, an army officer reported the following incident on the Cañada Alamosa Reservation of New Mexico. Some Chihennes under Victorio and Loco came in to receive their rations and a few of the Apaches found or traded for whiskey and became drunk. Loco and Victorio cooled the initial crisis, but a drunken warrior returned, gun in hand, apparently eager to make further trouble. At this juncture Cochise appeared, took in the situation, and "gave a yell so quick and shrill . . . its effect was instantly apparent. Some sixty or eighty of his own immediate band rushed upon . . . the offending Indian . . . and seized him and escorted him out." Cochise, in name chief of only the Chokonen band, ordered Victorio and Loco of the Chihennes to leave until everyone sobered up, and they did so.[28] Captain Frederick W. Coleman, an experienced officer who was thoroughly acquainted with the Apaches, said that other Chiricahua chiefs were "mortally afraid of Cochise [and] when he is around they are exceedingly small fry."[29] An army surgeon affirmed that Cochise "was the only Indian chief that I ever knew that could enforce instant obedience to a given command."[30]

Fred Hughes also discussed Cochise's influence among Chiricahua bands. "Although the Indians of the Tularosa [Chihenne] were of a different [band] from that of Cochise," he said, "there is no doubt that he could call upon them and control them whenever he saw fit." Hughes felt that the Nednhis, too, "were afraid of Cochise," as well they might be. In November 1872 after hearing a report (later proved false) that the Nednhis had harmed his friend Tom Jeffords, Cochise told Arizona Governor Anson Safford that if the rumor proved true, he "intended to kill every one" of them.[31]

Cochise's influence among non-Chiricahua Apaches was less pervasive, of course, yet because he was an able and successful war leader, members of Western Apache bands until the mid-1860s joined in some of his forays, and he had close ties with the White Mountain (Coyotero) band, particularly its eastern group. Although he seems to have had little if any contact with the Mescalero Apaches east of the Río Grande, many of the smaller bands west of the river provided plenty of recruits for his enterprises. Cremony said other Apaches thought him "invincible and [so] flock[ed] to his support,"[32] and Dr. John White, who in 1874 studied the Western Apaches, considered him to be the only chief "who really exercised control over any of the Apaches" except those in his own band.[33]

It was Cochise's reputation as a war chief that clearly placed him above other Apache leaders. Born about 1810, he had matured during a relatively peaceful period of Apache-Mexican affairs. While he was in his early twenties, however, relations deteriorated and treachery and war replaced tranquility and peace. The Johnson and Kirker massacres (1837 and 1846) left indelible impressions on Cochise, who may have lost family members in them.

Asa Daklugie thought Cochise became chief "when he was a very young man. That meant that his ability as a fighting man was well established and that he was respected by his people."[34] This was essentially the case in that Cochise was a war leader at an early age.

He was, however, overshadowed by more influential and important men until he assumed leadership of his group about 1856–57. He became the leader of the Chokonen band about one year later, which coincided with Anglo arrival in southeastern Arizona. Although apprehensive about the newcomers, he perceived a golden opportunity to receive American rations and gifts while still being able to raid into Mexico. The precarious relationship became strained in late 1859 and early 1860 before it gradually degenerated and hit rock bottom when he was mistreated by an American officer, Lieutenant George N. Bascom, at Apache Pass in February 1861.

After the Bascom affair, with Mangas Coloradas aging, Cochise emerged as the dominant Chiricahua chief on a tribal basis and the most celebrated Apache of the next decade. Two years later, Mangas Coloradas was treacherously murdered. All of this resulted in a fierce and abiding hatred and an ingrained distrust of Americans which lasted for well over a decade. Cochise remained committed to his war until he determined that life as a free Apache was no longer possible. Perhaps in a bit of an oversimplification, he said of Bascom's act: "I was at peace with the whites, until they tried to kill me for what other Indians did; I now live and die at war with them." [35] And fight he did. From 1861 through 1872, except for a few brief stays on the reservation in the early 1870s, Cochise fought the whites like no other Apache. Apache antipathy toward Mexicans was legendary, but Cochise's hatred of Americans exceeded his hatred of Mexicans during the 1860s. For almost a decade he spurned peaceful contact.

The Cochise wars of the 1860s differed significantly from the more celebrated Victorio and Geronimo wars of the 1870s and 1880s. For the first five years (or essentially until the Civil War ended), Cochise remained the aggressor, taking the fight to the few remaining whites in Arizona and boldly attacking ranches and travelers. Throughout this period his people were able to camp and range as his ancestors had. Although forts were established and ranches were worked, the Chiricahua Apaches retained control of most of southeastern Arizona. Cochise's people frequently lived in the Chiricahua Mountains, within a day's ride of Fort Bowie, or in his strongholds in the Dragoons, some fifty miles east of Tucson. The few times he felt pressure from U.S. troops, his access to Mexico was usually open. There were some years when he lived south of the border as much as he did north. By the late 1860s, his war inevitably had become a defensive conflict. Mexican and American counterstrikes led him to retaliate as hard as he could, for he knew no other way.

A powerful warrior, Cochise was renowned for his ability with weapons. James Tevis did not think "Cochise ever met his equal with a lance," while John C. Cremony claimed that "no Apache warrior can draw an arrow to the head, and send it farther, with more ease than he."[36] In his prime, Cochise embodied the essence of Apache warfare. Except when he was surprised or when his family was endangered, an Apache fought only on his terms when success seemed certain. There were a few exceptions, however. When fighting for revenge, he threw caution to the wind and took chances that he normally would not take. Most war parties were organized with this intent.

To all this Cochise brought his own audacious and warlike presence. Although he was never a "red Napoleon" or a military genius, in his day there was no better fighting Apache. He was not a leader who stood in the background while his men fought. In fact, few Apache chiefs were cast from that mold. He led by example. In every single action in which he participated and of which an eyewitness account has been left behind, there is one striking similarity: Cochise led his warriors into battle. This constant leads me to conclude that he, like Geronimo, had a vision telling him that he would not be killed in battle, a feeling shared by at least one American who met him during the 1870s.[37]

Yet this bravery should not be interpreted as foolhardiness. The traditional Hollywood assault against circled wagon trains or enclosed forts (in fact, none of Arizona's territorial posts was completely walled) rarely, if ever, occurred; it was too dangerous and too risky. An Apache valued his life just as much as any white man. He wasn't recklessly brave; in this he differed from the Plains Indian, whose society encouraged the counting of coup on live enemies. An Apache admired stealth: he wanted to dispatch of his foes as quickly as possible without risk to himself. Of course there was some hard skirmishing at times but usually little loss of life, which is easily explained when one understands the nature of an Apache fight. General George Crook pointed out that in most Apache fights a hostile was rarely seen. All you saw were puffs of smoke from the rocks; you rarely saw an enemy. This was the case in many of Cochise's fights, but in other ways he was an atypical Apache, especially in the early years of his war when he was the aggressor and fought for revenge. He showed no mercy to his enemies, who, if captured, were tortured to death in a slow, painful, and inhumane way.

Cochise's survival skills were legendary. For twelve years he successfully eluded troops and volunteers from four states and two countries. His allies were his ancestral mountains and the territorial boundary line, which he used adroitly, leapfrogging back and forth when heavily pressured. His rancherías were almost impossible to surprise, although it was done from time to time. His camps were strategically located in areas which could be defended easily and which offered a haven for safe retreat. His camp overlooking the San Pedro Valley on the slopes of the West Dragoons was a fine example, for if they were threatened, the Indians could easily move higher into the mountains. Sladen marveled at its location:

> Troops must have come up in plain view for some miles and they could easily have been repulsed in any attempt to climb the steep face of the mountains below us, while the scattered rocks and boulders gave ready shelter to the Indians above
>
> The path above us would have afforded a passage to . . . shelter to the women and children, on the other side of the mountain, or if necessary, our entire party could have safely retreated over the ridge onto the other slope of the mountain.[38]

Cochise continued such precautions even after he made his final treaty, thereby revealing that he never completely trusted Americans because of the Bascom affair.

To Cochise's survival skills must be added one more factor: luck. Perhaps it was the element the Apaches called power, of which Cochise had his share. Asa Daklugie referred to it, but the way in which it related to Cochise is somewhat ambiguous. Not being Apache, I would be the first to admit that I do not fully comprehend its concept and significance. To me, the extraordinary thing about Cochise's life was the fact that he was at war with either Mexico or the United States for much of forty years; was involved in countless raids, skirmishes, and fights; was surprised and attacked in his camp on occasion; was wounded several times; and allegedly was killed on a dozen occasions, give or take a few. Yet he survived, which was a testament to his stubborn persistence in the face of white subjugation. Finally, he accepted the hard reality that peace was his only option and succeeded in obtaining a reservation in his country, where he died a natural death. Was it fate, luck, or power? Who knows?

There was little middle ground among southwesterners regarding the Apaches during the last half of the nineteenth century. Many had lost family members or friends to an Apache arrow or bullet. Typical of this dichotomy in perception was a government survey conducted by two Arizona pioneers, both very familiar with Cochise's people. Sidney Delong, post sutler at Fort Bowie and an Anglo who subscribed to the extermination policy as the panacea for the Apache problem, described the Chiricahuas as "savages, with all their vices; intractable; treacherous; not truthful; dishonest; not hospitable; cowards." Chiricahua Apache agent Tom Jeffords, who had a unique friendship with Cochise, described the Indians as "gentle, docile, truthful, honest, hospitable, chaste, courageous." [39] By Apache standards, Jeffords's views were on the mark. Most whites, however, were not familiar with Cochise's people and would have endorsed Delong's opinion.

I have tried to portray Cochise as a leader of unusual ability and influence who played a leading role in the tumultuous period of Chiricahua Apache history between 1830 and 1874. On the whole, he seems to have performed better than any other Apache.

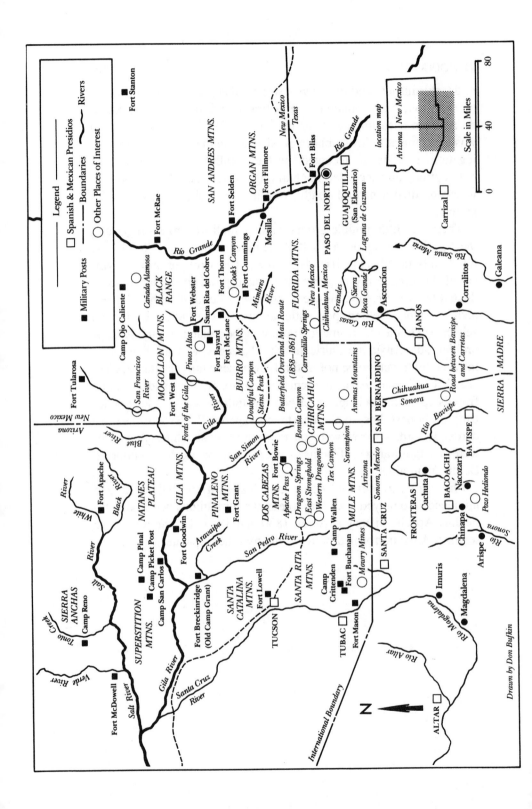

Chapter 1

THE EARLY YEARS

The Apaches were a warlike and nomadic people who roamed the Southwest, preferring to live in rugged, inaccessible mountains but equally at home in the harsh desert. There are two schools of thought on derivation of the word *Apache*. The first holds it may be from the Yuman word *e-patch,* loosely interpreted to mean "man." The second and more likely possibility has it originating from the Zuñi word *apachu,* which means "enemy." The Apaches called themselves *tinneh, dine, tinde,* or *inde,* which translates to "man" or "people."[1] These migrants to the Southwest from the Mackenzie River Valley of western Canada were members of the Athapaskan linguistic family, which is divided into three geographic divisions: Northern, Pacific Coast, and Southern. The Apaches belonged to the Southern. Anthropologists and historians disagree about the date of their appearance in the Southwest, some believing they had arrived by the late sixteenth century and others, notably Jack D. Forbes, arguing they were living in New Mexico and Arizona in the 1400s.[2]

The Southern Athapaskans known as Apaches are divided into seven major groupings. The Jicarilla, Lipan, and Kiowa-Apache tribes form the eastern division, and the Navajo, Mescalero, Western Apache, and Chiricahua tribes comprise the western division. The word *Chiricahua* probably was derived from the Opata Indian word *chiguicagui,* meaning "mountain of the wild turkeys." The Chiricahuas are the focus of this study.[3]

The Chiricahuas consisted of four bands. The easternmost, labeled by Morris E. Opler the Eastern Chiricahuas, were known to Mexicans and Americans as the Mimbres, Copper mines, Warm Springs, Mogollons, and the all-encompassing Gilas, names describing geographic locations where they lived. Their territory was west of the Río Grande in New Mexico, and they lived in the Cuchillo, Black, Mimbres, Mogollon, Pinos Altos, Victoria, and Florida mountain ranges.[4] Their leaders from the 1820s through the 1870s were Mano Mocha, Fuerte, Cuchillo Negro, Itán, Mangas Coloradas, Delgadito, Victorio, Nana, and Loco. To the Apaches, they were the Chihennes, or Red Paint People.

The second band, called by Opler the Southern Chiricahuas, was known to Mexicans and Americans as the Janeros, Carrizaleños, and Pinery Apaches, each in reference to specific areas they inhabited. The mountains along the U.S.-Mexican border served as their homeland, although they also roamed deep into the vast Sierra Madre in the Mexican states of Chihuahua and Sonora.[5] Occasionally they wandered across the border into present-day southeastern Arizona and southwestern New Mexico. The Janeros people were so named for their friendly relations at Janos, a small town in northwestern Chihuahua. Their leaders from 1820 through the 1870s were Juan Diego Compá, Juan José Compá, followed by Coleto Amarillo, Arvizu, Láceris, Galindo, Natiza, and Juh. The Carrizaleños lived south of the Janeros people near Carrizal, Chihuahua. Their most prominent leaders in the 1820s and 1830s were Jasquedegá and Cristóbal. In the 1840s, Francisquillo, Francisco, and Cigarrito assumed leadership, followed by Cojinillín and Felipe in the 1850s. Both groups were hit hard by Mexican campaigns from the 1830s through the early 1860s, when the Carrizaleños were virtually wiped out as a distinct unit. To the Apaches, they were the Nednhis, or Enemy People.

Opler named the third band, the one of which Cochise was a member, the Central Chiricahuas. Their homeland was southeastern Arizona, particularly the Dragoon, Dos Cabezas, and Chiricahua mountains.[6] They also ranged north to the Gila River, east into southwestern New Mexico, and south into the Sierra Madre. The mountains along the U.S.-Mexican border gave them sanctuary from Mexican and American troops. From the 1820s through the 1870s their leaders were Pisago Cabezón, Relles, Matías, Tapilá, Yrigóllen, Miguel Narbona, Carro, Posito Moraga, Esquinaline, and Cochise, who rose rapidly in the mid-1850s to become the leading chief of his band. To Anglos of the nineteenth century and to the Apaches of today, this was the band first referred to as Chiricahuas, known to the Indians as the Chokonens.

The Chiricahuas recognized one other band, the Bedonkohes, during historical times. Their territory was northeast of the Chokonens and northwest of the Chihennes in the vicinity of the Gila River and Mogollon Mountains. The notorious Geronimo was born into this branch. The smallest of the Chiricahua divisions, the Bedonkohes were assimilated into one of the other bands in the early 1860s, the majority opting to follow Cochise after the death of Mangas Coloradas.[7]

The bands identified one another as related, having "linguistic and cultural bonds which identify them as one people." The tribal relationship was expressed in many ways: the three peoples were usually at peace with one another, visiting was frequent, and social dances, puberty rites, and marriages were reasons for assembling. The band served as the political unit of the tribe, and an individual remained a member of the one into which he or she was born, except when a man married outside his band. In this case, it was Chiricahua custom for the man to live with his wife's people, and his offspring were known by the affiliation of her band.[8]

Each band consisted of three to five local groups, each made up of several families who camped together near a geographic site from which they usually took their name. For example, during Cochise's life, camps, or rancherías, were scattered throughout Chokonen country, perhaps in the Dragoon, Chiricahua, and Peloncillo mountains. Unlike the band, the local group was not a stable unit. The relationship between members was based primarily on residence and could be severed because of food scarcity, epidemics, internal conflicts, or the death of a leader.[9]

Cochise towered over other leaders because in historic times he commanded allegiance from every Chokonen local group. In contrast, during the same period of the 1860s, the Chihennes recog-

nized at least three local group leaders—Loco, Victorio, and Nana—
and the Nednhis recognized at least two, Natiza and Juh. Chiricahua
local groups often consisted of one or more rancherías, usually separated by some distance and scattered up and down high mountain
valleys. These clusters, called extended family groups, were related
through the maternal chain. A Chiricahua informant described the
extended family as "a group of homes occupied by relatives. At the
very least an extended family is a father and mother, their unmarried
children, and the families of their married daughters." The sub-
groups were known by the names of the family leader.[10]

Into one of the Chokonen local groups Cochise was born. When
and where are not definitely known, although writer Frank C. Lockwood believed that Cochise was born in the Chiricahua Mountains
about 1815.[11] Samuel Woodworth Cozzens, a Mesilla lawyer, and
army surgeon Bernard John Dowling Irwin, both of whom apparently met Cochise about 1860, had different estimates of his age.
Cozzens thought the chief to be about forty-seven,[12] and Irwin
guessed about thirty.[13] The latter estimate is clearly too low when
one considers that an Apache identified as Chis, or Chees, almost
certainly Cochise, was mentioned in 1835 as the leader of a party
that was raiding in Mexico. Furthermore, Cochise was on the Janos
ration lists in 1842 and 1843, at which time he had a wife and possibly a child. For what it is worth, during the 1860s, when he avoided
American contact, sometimes he was referred to as Old Cochise,
perhaps a term used more to show respect than to indicate age. In
the late 1860s and early 1870s there were numerous estimates of his
height, build, and age. In February 1869 an eyewitness thought Cochise to be about fifty.[14] In another interview recorded by an army
surgeon (they were usually good observers), he was thought to be
fifty-eight in 1871,[15] while still another credible report, this one
from Arizona Governor Anson P. Safford, who visited Cochise in
November 1872, put his age about sixty.[16]

Apache accounts are sparse but in agreement. Asa Daklugie believed Cochise about seventy at the time of his death in 1874.[17]
Gillet Griswold's study of the Chiricahua Apaches supports Daklugie's statements, estimating Cochise's birth date at about 1800.[18] I
do not feel that the evidence supports such an early date; my best
guess would place Cochise's birth about 1810, probably in northern

Mexico or southeastern Arizona. It is quite conceivable that he was born in the Chiricahua Mountains as asserted by Robert Humphrey Forbes on the basis of information furnished by Thomas J. Jeffords, Cochise's best-remembered white friend.[19]

Cochise's parents were Central Chiricahuas, or Chokonens, and his father was a leading man at the band level. A common legend, developed by Anglos because Apache oral history seldom recalled individuals or events beyond one generation, has Cochise descended from a long line of leaders. Whether this is true is another matter;[20] again, Apache sources are lacking. Cochise himself claimed that his grandfather had been the leader of all Apaches, probably meaning the Chiricahuas.[21] But this may have been translated or recorded in error; he probably meant his father. Asa Daklugie believed that Cochise was related in some manner to Juan José Compá, a Chiricahua leader of the 1830s. His opinion cannot be dismissed lightly; however, Juan José Compá was not a Chokonen and any relation was probably through marriage instead of blood.[22]

The best contemporary information about Cochise's father was provided by James Henry Tevis,[23] a station keeper at Apache Pass who became well acquainted with Cochise in the late 1850s. Tevis wrote that Cochise's father was the head chief of the Apaches (referring to the Chokonen band) who perished at the hands of duplicitous Mexicans. "The Mexicans invited Cochise's father and some of his noted warriors to a feast," he wrote, "and, by treachery, got him and his warriors drunk and killed them." It was a scene repeated several times in Chiricahua-Mexican relations.[24] In 1875 the *Arizona Citizen* published a biographical article on Cochise, giving a version similar to Tevis's.[25] An incident like the one Tevis described did take place in the summer of 1846 when notorious scalp hunter James Kirker[26] and other mercenaries slaughtered 148 Chiricahuas near Galeana, Chihuahua. Among the dead was the Chokonen leader Relles[27] and perhaps Pisago Cabezón,[28] the most prominent Chiricahua in the first forty years of the nineteenth century. The none-too-reliable James Hobbs, who was a member of Kirker's party, described the incident years later and identified Cochise as one of the leaders of the band butchered by Kirker.[29]

At this date it is extremely unlikely that these discrepancies ever will be reconciled.[30] His father may have been Relles but more probably was Pisago Cabezón. In any event we know that Cochise's father was a leading man at the band level and that as his son Cochise was expected to assume a leadership role, although leadership was not inherited. It was earned, through one's actions and accomplishments; if these were combined with wisdom in counsel, the individual might become a chief. The son of a great chief, however, had an advantage in that he no doubt had received excellent training as a young man and normally would be more prepared than most to follow in the footsteps of his father.[31]

Cochise was born in a peaceful period as far as relations between the Chiricahua Apaches and Mexico were concerned, yet this had not always been the case. For much of the eighteenth century, there had been war between most Apache bands and the Spaniards, who had adopted one policy after another, ranging from extermination to colonization, in an attempt to pacify the incorrigible Apaches.[32] The conflict continued into the 1780s, with, according to Spanish estimates, six hundred Apaches (including some Chiricahuas) attacking Tucson on May 1, 1782, and occupying areas beyond its walled presidio before the garrison drove them off, claiming about thirty enemy killed. Two years later a Spanish force surprised a band of Chokonens at Dos Cabezas, killing nine men, three women, and four children and recapturing a Pima woman taken in the attack at Tucson.[33] Finally, in 1786, recognizing the failure of its diverse policies, the royal crown issued yet another order, called the *Instrucción*.

The new order was based on Spanish experience of the previous quarter-century, which now accepted that extermination alone was impracticable; victory might be achieved by persuading the hostiles to live in peace near Spanish presidios, or forts. The *Instrucción* recognized that the Indian's economy consisted of gathering, hunting, and raiding, with the last also an important part of his society. Perhaps the way to pacify him was to turn him away from his culture, but first he must be subdued through unremitting war. After all, "a bad peace was better than a good war." The *Instrucción* addressed the fundamental issue of attempting to understand Apaches and proved to be the beginning of a forty-year period of generally peaceful but tenuous relations between the two races. It succeeded because it took a realistic, pragmatic approach in addressing the Indian problem.[34]

By the early 1790s most of the Chiricahuas had been compelled to sue for peace, which was granted under the condition that they live quietly in designated areas. This they did, settling at the presidio of Janos[35] in Chihuahua and eventually at other locations along the frontier. Almost at once the Spaniards introduced a systematic policy that was intended to disrupt and destroy the Apache social system. On the one hand, they issued rations of corn or wheat, meat, brown sugar, salt, and tobacco to a reported six thousand Apaches at an annual expense of twenty-three thousand pesos. On the other, they furnished gifts of guns, liquor, clothing, and other items with the duplicitous intention of making the Apaches totally subservient to and dependent on the Spaniards. The guns were inferior and prone to break down, necessitating the services of a Spanish gunsmith to repair them. Furthermore, it was hoped that the Apaches would neglect their bows and arrows, which they used more effectively than firearms. Intoxicating liquors were dispensed freely so that the Indians would acquire a taste for them. "It was at once a highly sophisticated, brutal and deceptive policy of divide and conquer, of peace by purchase, of studied debilitation of those who accepted peace and of extermination of those who rejected it," writes Max L. Moorhead. However cruel and immoral, he concludes, "it was . . . a practical policy and one which offered both races the opportunity for survival."[36]

At first the conditions were confining to the Apaches, who were accustomed to coming and going as they pleased. Eventually they were allowed to leave their peace establishments, provided that permission had been granted. Most historians agree that peaceful relations continued for the remainder of the Spanish period, that is, until 1821, and there is evidence to conclude that it prevailed until 1830. William B. Griffen estimates that perhaps two-thirds of the Chiricahua Apaches were involved with this system. He concludes that the presidio system was essentially a success because the cost in controlling the Apaches was far less than the damage hostiles would have caused and the tremendous expense that punitive military campaigns would have incurred.[37] Consequently, Cochise's people had

been at peace for fifteen to twenty years by the time of his birth.
Frank C. Lockwood characterizes the period as a "nearer approxi-
mation to peace [between Apaches and Spaniards] than at any previous time. . . . It was during these years of respite that mines were
opened and successfully operated, churches built and beautified,
and ranches prosperously conducted."[38]

Cochise was born during this season of amity. His immediate
family eventually included at least two younger brothers, Juan and
Coyuntura (Kin-o-Tera), and at least one younger sister. He probably had other brothers and sisters whose names were not remembered. One or two months after birth, when his parents were sure he
would live, he received a name suggested either by the midwife or
by an unusual event that distinguished his birth; the name bestowed
upon him at that time is not known. It was probably as a young adult
that he received the Apache name *Goci,* literally translated as "his
nose," because of his prominent Roman nose.[39] This information,
provided by Morris E. Opler, seems more plausible than the accepted historical statement that Cochise's name meant "wood" or
"a quality or strength in wood." Another explanation has the name
bestowed upon him because he once supplied firewood to the
Apache Pass stage station. This, too, seems improbable because
there are references to Cochise in Mexican records dated some
twenty years before the station was established.

Apache society was ritualistic; there were ceremonies and supernatural help to explain virtually all aspects of everyday life.[40] There
were strong emotional ties to one's birthplace, and upon returning to
the site, a child or even an adult might roll on the ground to the four
directions. When a child was a few weeks old, his mother or maternal grandmother pierced earlobes so that he would "hear things
sooner" and obey quicker. Ever present in Chiricahua parent-child
relations was discipline, and obeying one's parents was always emphasized early in life.

A baby spent the first six or seven months of his or her life in a
specially constructed cradle; a shaman performing the cradle ceremony, usually the fourth day after birth. The cradle was constructed
of oak, ash, or walnut, with sotol or yucca stalk used for the supporting back pieces and buckskin covering the frame. In each phase
of construction the shaman prayed that the child would have a long,

good life. In addition, he attached amulets, such as bags of pollen or turquoise, to the cradle to protect it. The mother added her own good-luck charms, perhaps the right paw of a badger or the claws of a hummingbird, to protect the baby from malevolent forces. In the cradle ceremony, which was held early in the morning with the members of the local group attending, the cradle was held to the four directions, beginning with the east and proceeding clockwise to the beginning, at which time the baby was put inside. Then a feast or social dance was held.

As a child grew, several rituals were performed to ensure that the individual followed the same steps in life as the mythical Apache culture heroes. The moccasin ceremony usually was held when the child was about seven months old, although it could take place as late as the age of two. As in all Chiricahua ceremonies, a shaman or individual who knew the rules directed the celebration, and, like the cradle ceremony, it also served as a social gathering. After the infant, called Child of the Water, took four ceremonial steps, the shaman saying a prayer after each, a great feast was held.

The next ritual was the spring hair cutting, usually held the spring after the moccasin ceremony. Pollen was applied to the child's cheek and head and "then his hair, with the exception of one or more locks, is closely cropped." The hair was allowed to grow back soon after. Most Chiricahuas paid very close attention to the grooming of their hair, a particular Cochise observed throughout his life.

As a young child, Cochise learned about Chiricahua religion, which focused on the supernatural and "emphasizes the virtues of humility and gratitude." When a child is "old enough to understand his parents, they begin to teach him to be religious, to use religious words and to know Life Giver, Child of the Water, and White Painted Woman." The Chiricahua youth also acquired knowledge about other cultural heroes: the Mountain People, supernaturals living in the interior of sacred mountains, who protected the tribe and were "potential sources of supernatural power." He heard the familiar coyote stories, about the adventures of the wily coyote, an inveterate trickster, which had a moral or a lesson to be learned. All of this was intended to prepare the boy for adulthood.

Parents instructed their children about appropriate behavior. As a leader's son, Cochise received better training than most youths. In the words of a Chiricahua: "More pains are taken with such children; they are kept out of mischief more. They should not resent things easily. They are supposed to be better bred. Quarreling should be beneath them. But, above all, the child is taught respect. He was told, Don't steal from your own friends. Don't be unkind to your playmates. If you are kind now, when you become a man you will love your fellow men." To correct improper behavior, a child was brought into line with threats; and if this didn't work, the parent could whip the child, although this was an extremely infrequent occurrence. So it was that Cochise acquired the traits and characteristics of a good leader, for good training usually meant a boy would turn out to be a good man. Yet supernaturalism dominated each step in the child's development, the parents constantly striving to protect their children with ceremonies, rituals, and good-luck charms.

When he was about six or seven years old, Cochise probably took his first step in training. A male relative, possibly his father, grandfather, or paternal uncle, gave him a bow and arrows so that he could join other boys in hunting small birds and animals. Boys separated from girls at this age and began playing games, such as hide-and-seek, foot racing, tug-of-war, and wrestling, all emphasizing speed, agility, and strength. Horsemanship was also practiced. "Children from seven years of age and on would go and learn by themselves when the older people didn't even know about it. There were always some gentle horses for the boy to ride." Ubiquitous in all stages of Chiricahua life were ceremonies, shamans, prayers, songs, and sacred objects.

Physical fitness, self-discipline, and independence dominated the next stage of preadolescence. The elders encouraged a boy to take care of his body, for "no one will help you in this world. . . . Your legs are your friends." The boy began to hunt more, primarily birds and squirrels, and by these experiences acquired important skills, such as stealth, patience, and perseverance, to secure his prey. To guarantee continued success in hunting, he was advised "to swallow whole the raw heart of the first kill." A boy this age also became experienced with horses; he learned how to care for them and how to ride expertly. In his early teens, more responsible scout and guard duties were assigned. Physical endurance and stamina also were important, and we can presume that Cochise learned well because a "leader's son never fails to make good, for he is trained and advised from boyhood to manhood."

About the age of fourteen, a boy was ready to begin training as a warrior, becoming a *dikohe,* or novice. When a boy was old and mature enough, he volunteered, his family cautioning him that dangers and hardships lay ahead. Training now assumed a more intense and formal tone. Whereas up to this juncture the extended family group was responsible for the boy's training, now the local group assumed responsibility. Frequently, many young men of the same age were assigned to a shaman who knew about war. The training became more vigorous than before: physical events, such as wrestling, slingshot fights, small bow-and-arrow contests, and races dominated, and discipline and obedience were stressed constantly.

Chiricahua boys developed in many ways. They were assigned tasks to teach them obedience and prepare them for the physical hardships of a warrior. For example, in the late fall or early winter when ice had formed on lakes, they were told to disrobe and jump in. But perhaps the skill that was emphasized most was running. Boys were ordered to run up hills and return just as quickly; races and games were organized to sharpen competitive instincts. During these contests, future warriors and leaders were conspicuous by their actions. From these Cochise emerged, disciplined and physically tuned, ready to participate in the four raids required to become a man.

The youth was now ready for the final phase of the *dikohe* period; when he heard that a raid or war party was being organized, he volunteered for duty and a shaman prepared him for it. The primary concern was the individual's behavior during the raid and his obedience to his leaders. If the *dikohe* acted in an undesirable manner or exhibited signs of dishonesty, cowardice, or gluttony, or was unrestrained and had sexual intercourse during one of the first four journeys, he would be labeled for the rest of his life as unreliable. The *dikohe* accompanied the warriors to learn from them; to do menial camp chores, such as cooking and preparing the warriors' beds; and to stand guard. The novices were protected from danger, for injury to them would reflect on the party's leaders.

During the four raids, the warriors called the *dikohe* Child of the Water. He wore a ceremonial hat for protection and learned special words that were taught him for the occasion.[41] In addition, he had other restrictions: he must drink through a tube and eat all food cold. After the fourth raid, unless there was sharp criticism of his performance, the youth joined the ranks of the warriors. Certainly this was Cochise's status by the time he reached his midteens, and he must have performed exceptionally well during the four raids. Now he could smoke, marry, and have all the privileges of a warrior. And he would have many opportunities to gain recognition as a warrior because the long period of peace between the Chiricahua Apaches and Mexico was ending.

Chapter 2

LITTLE WARS

As Cochise matured, relations between the Chiricahua Apaches and Mexico changed significantly. The Mexican Revolution, which began in 1810, forced Spain to divert troops, resources, and funds from the northern presidios to the interior to quell the rebellion. As a result, frontier garrisons were reduced to skeleton strength and soldiers went unclothed, unfed, and unpaid. Affairs worsened after Mexico won her independence in 1821. The revolution had drained public treasuries and depleted the funds required to maintain the presidios and the Apaches.[1] This situation did not happen all at once. Some rations were furnished to Chiricahua bands living near Janos, Fronteras[2] in northeastern Sonora, and Santa Rita del Cobre[3] in southwestern New Mexico.

The federal government in Mexico City permitted the presidio system to decline during the early 1820s. Troop discipline continued to deteriorate, salaries were slashed again, and hard currency was unavailable.[4] Consequently, the Apaches received even less assistance, and some minor raiding occurred. Citizens were called upon to donate cattle and grain to appease the discontented Indians, which served to increase animosity between the two races.[5] At this time, Juan Diego Compá[6] and Pisago Cabezón combined to lead their groups at Janos; Fuerte[7] and Mano Mocha[8] led the Chihennes at the copper mines. In December 1821, 1,423 Apaches received rations in Chihuahua: 442 at Janos (Chokonens and Nednhis), 210 at San Buenaventura (Nednhis), 347 at Carrizal (Nednhis), and 424 at San Elizario (Mescaleros). Although some 1,000 cattle were allocated to feed these bands, the number proved inadequate and some of the Indians went hungry.[9]

Finally, in 1824, the Chiricahuas bolted from their peace establishments—certainly because of the dwindling rations—and sporadic raiding began. Chokonen and Nednhi groups fled Janos, as did the Chokonens living at Fronteras under Matías[10] and Teboca.[11] Although we cannot be sure that Cochise was a member of this group, we can say that most of the Chokonens resumed hostilities.

That summer, a band that had left Fronteras was reported living in the Dos Cabezas Mountains a few miles north of Apache Pass, a favorite camping area of Cochise's local group. That fall, Chiricahua leaders planned several raids against the frontier, apparently unsure of raiding the more prosperous and populous interior districts. Raiding parties struck near Fronteras, Bavispe, and Tubac with relatively slight success: some stock was taken and a few Mexicans were killed. Their raids, however, evoked memories of what Apache terror once was.

Authorities at Fronteras conceded that the depredations were committed by Chiricahuas who had been living at peace. The situation could easily have erupted into a full-scale war, which seemed to Mexicans the Indians' intention. A peaceful Apache at Janos revealed that Teboca's Chokonens had joined Fuerte's and Mano Mocha's Chihennes in southwestern New Mexico and planned an incursion into Mexico. Furthermore, hostile Chiricahuas were lurking in the Enmedio Mountains to ambush travelers between Janos and Fronteras.[12]

Sonora attempted to quell the uprising, planning an offensive composed of troops from Fronteras and militia from Santa Cruz, Bavispe, and Bacoachi. From Arispe, reinforcements were dispatched to Fronteras, but lack of arms, ammunition, and mounts grounded the campaign before it got under way.[13] Yet in November Sonoran soldiers defeated a Chiricahua party; this, combined with the onset of winter, caused the Indians' enthusiasm for combat to wane. On November 12 near Agua Prieta, a small force from Fronteras managed to overtake hostiles and wound several Indians who had raided Cuquiarachi.[14] The next month, Juan José Compá and three other leaders requested an armistice at Santa Rita del Cobre and most of the fighting was over.[15] During 1825, Chiricahua bands returned to their establishments at Santa Rita del Cobre, Janos, and Fronteras, but there is no way of knowing what role Cochise played, if any. Possibly, he could have served as a *dikohe*.

There was a precarious truce for the next few years. Rations were slashed again in early 1828, forcing the Indians to move into the Chiricahua, Enmedio, and Animas mountains to plant, prepare mescal, and hunt for subsistence. Pisago Cabezón raised a few crops at Alamo Hueco, but many of the Indians again had become disaffected about the lack of rations. Nonetheless, through 1829 groups of Apaches remained at Janos under Pisago and Juan Diego Compá, Fuerte and his band remained at Santa Rita del Cobre, and a group of Chokonens under Matías and Teboca remained encamped near Fronteras.[16]

Yet Mexican officials ignored this festering Apache discontent. In early January 1830, Pisago Cabezón, Juan Diego, and other leaders met with the military commander of Janos and made several requests. First they wanted their rations, now reduced to corn alone, to include a portion of meat; they also requested an interpreter and farming tools. Their appeal was forwarded to Chihuahua City, and the response was to the point: although some farming implements were issued and an interpreter hired, rations could not be increased; Mexican troops would receive first priority.[17] This insensitivity can best be explained if one considers that these public officials, living in safety at Chihuahua City, may well have discounted the Apaches as a force to be feared. Yet in reality the Indians had prospered and become more dangerous during their years at peace: many leaders understood Mexican tactics, many Indians could read and write Spanish, many of them had become adept in the use of Mexican weapons. Although statistics are not available, their number must have increased because few warriors were lost to war.

In any event, Apache raiders quickly dispelled the notion. Without food, some Chiricahuas began raiding, for no Apache willingly went hungry. The more militant bands, perhaps including Cochise, had begun depredating in Sonora during the winter of 1830, hitting hardest the districts of Altar, Arispe, and San Ignacio.[18] In late February a great trail of Apaches, with stolen stock from Sonora, was reported at Alamo Hueco, a rendezvous site for the three Chiricahua bands. Sensing widespread hostilities, the commander at Janos was directed "to severely punish any Indians absent without permission."[19]

Unbeknownst to whites and Indians, the forty-year period of controlling the Chiricahua Apaches with the presidio system was ending. In late 1830, Apaches living at San Buenaventura (either a Nednhi or Chokonen group) bolted their establishment for the Sierra Madre. There was little food and an epidemic swept through the area, sickening the entire garrison at San Buenaventura with a fever.[20] Hostiles swept into the interior of Sonora and Chihuahua, raided ranches, and ambushed unsuspecting travelers. Their success no doubt inspired and incited those factions which had been reluctant to sever relations with Mexico. Still, in early 1831, Pisago Cabezón's and Juan Diego's bands were still at peace and on January 31 received their last issue of Mexican rations. Shortly thereafter they fled, perhaps to avoid contracting smallpox, now prevalent at Janos. West at Fronteras, Chokonen bands under Teboca and Matías deserted in late June, citing lack of rations. Cochise remembered this period: "After many years the Spanish soldiers were driven away and the Mexicans ruled the land. With these little wars came, but we were now a strong people and did not fear them."[21]

Hostilities in the spring of 1831 were extensive in that, unlike past uprisings, almost every Apache band under Mexican influence participated. Mexico quickly learned that the hungry Apaches, better armed than those in the revolt of 1824, were still a formidable force. Presidio life had destroyed neither their social organization nor their warlike society. Cochise, now a young warrior of about twenty-one, had developed into a tall, well-built man. Physically, he had a more commanding presence than most of his peers: at five feet ten inches, he was some five inches taller than the average Chiricahua. He usually was associated with the more bellicose groups throughout his life, so we can speculate that he was at the forefront of the 1831 raiding and getting his first taste of victory and loot.

As the Chiricahuas had expected, Sonora and Chihuahua took

countermeasures. In late June 1831 the former organized a force of four hundred men to wage war against the hostiles. However, equipment and other problems pushed the expected departure date from September to October or November and the expedition, if indeed it ever got under way, made no inroads in punishing the hostiles.[22] By October 16, 1831, Apache devastation had become so widespread that José Joaquín Calvo, the hard-line commanding general of Chihuahua, declared war on the hostiles and began preparing for an offensive into Apachería like those of the 1780s.[23]

Raids continued during the first five months of 1832, ostensibly with the severity of the previous summer. Chihuahua was hit hard and forced to request one hundred Opata Indians from Sonora because it lacked "sufficient forces in order to contain the rebellion of the Indian Apaches who were at peace and who every day commit more murders." The Chihuahuans planned to employ the Opatas at Janos in conjunction with quick-striking troops under the command of Captain Mariano Ponce de León. Ramón Morales, the hawkish military commander of Sonora, recommended that the request be denied because of the "critical circumstances which the frontier of this state [Sonora] finds itself." Furthermore, he caustically pointed out, his small force of presidio troops was inadequate to protect Sonora and the one hundred Opatas could not be spared. The governor rejected Morales's arguments and ordered him to dispatch the reinforcements, reasoning that "this objective is beneficial, not only to that state but to this."[24]

Meanwhile, the Chiricahuas were active in the triangular area of Fronteras, Bavispe, and Janos. On March 26, 1832, they attacked the horse herd at Fronteras, forcing Morales to send reinforcements. A week later they captured the mail between Bavispe and Janos, thereby collecting important military information because many Apaches, including Juan José Compá,[25] were literate. About a month later they raided Turicachi and killed a man. These events prompted Ramón Morales to press the governor for four hundred men for a drive into Apachería: one hundred would establish a base camp at San Simon in present-day southeastern Arizona, and the rest would continue north, particularly into the Mogollons of New Mexico, where, it was believed, the hostiles were based.[26]

Chihuahua acted before Sonora did and on May 23, 1832, scored a decisive victory over the allied Chiricahuas near the Gila River a few miles south of the Mogollon Mountains in New Mexico.[27] The hostiles, estimated at three hundred warriors led by Pisago Cabezón, Fuerte, and Mano Mocha, were whipped soundly in an eight-hour battle by 138 men under Captain José Ignacio Ronquillo. The fighting was characterized by alternating charges back and forth until the Mexican troops routed the Indians. According to Ronquillo's windy report, between May 21 and May 23 his troops killed twenty-two Chiricahuas and wounded fifty, some in hand-to-hand combat. The Mexicans lost three men killed and twelve wounded.[28] Again Cochise's involvement is uncertain, but the presence of many Chokonen and Chihenne leaders and his close relationship with Pisago Cabezón make it quite possible that he took part in the fight, which proved to be an intimidating lesson for the Apaches.

This defeat and Sonora's victory against Western Apaches at Arivaipa Canyon (where seventy-one warriors reportedly were slain)[29] compelled the humbled Indians to sue for peace in the summer of 1832. Believing the Indians conquered, Calvo accepted their proposals and on July 28 dictated preliminary surrender terms to Colonel Cayetano Justiniani, an experienced and Apache-wise officer. An obstinate Calvo, however, advocated conditions which had been functional and successful during another era. Essentially, the treaty of 1832 paralleled that of 1810, in which peace had been granted to defeated Mescalero Apaches with no Mexican assistance; the Indians were assigned specific areas where they were to subsist by hunting and planting. Calvo's treaty of 1832 assigned the Mescaleros and Chiricahuas three zones: the Mescaleros from San Elizario to the Sacramento Mountains; the Chihennes from Santa Rita del Cobre to the Negrita Mountains, with the Mogollons included; the Chokonens and Nednhis from Janos north to the Peloncillo and Burro mountains.[30]

Calvo arrived at Santa Rita del Cobre in mid-August. Present were the Chiricahuas (Chokonens), Mogollons and Mimbres (Chihennes), Janeros and Carrizaleños (Nednhis). The treaty, signed on August 21 by twenty-nine leaders, demanded that the Apaches relinquish all stolen stock; this of course was impracticable and few if any animals were returned. Yet they did accept Calvo's concept of three zones with a chief, or general, responsible for the activities in each. The generals were Juan José Compá for the Janos area, Fuerte for the Copper Mines, and Aquién[31] for the Sonoran frontier. The truce did restore order to the frontier, but it was flawed in some respects. First, Calvo maintained his penurious and hard-line policy that the Apaches somehow should subsist without raiding because rations were not part of the agreement. Second, he erred in not having representatives from Sonora present. His provincial plan had small chance for ultimate success, although the immediate situation improved in some ways.[32]

The treaty of 1832 shifted Chiricahua headquarters from Janos to Santa Rita del Cobre, the isolation of which encouraged clandestine commerce. Robert McKnight,[33] a naturalized Mexican who owned the mines, had been present during the negotiations, along with some Americans, among them James Kirker. Their pernicious influence paved the way for a flourishing but illicit trade, with Kirker and McKnight serving as middlemen. Quite simply, the Apaches raided into Sonora and Chihuahua and returned to Santa Rita with their loot, which they traded for food, guns, and whiskey. "The Americans trade guns and ammunition to the Apaches at Santa Rita del Cobre" was a charge heard often.[34] Wrote one historian of the treaty of 1832: "The stage was set to trigger the largest boom in the history of *cambalache* [illegal trade] along the far southwestern frontier."[35]

The truce was destined to fail from the beginning. Lack of subsistence forced most of the Indians to live in the mountains, free from Mexican control, and during the winter of 1833 they resumed their marauding in earnest. Some of Pisago's young men (of whom Cochise was one) raided Janos in February 1833 and in the spring full-scale hostilities erupted at Bavispe, Santa Rita del Cobre, Carrizal, and Janos.[36] For Cochise's people, a three-year war ensued, and it took an enormous toll in lives and property in Mexico.[37]

The first few months after the outbreak, the Chiricahuas, better armed than ever before (primarily because of the illicit trade), swarmed over northern Sonora with impunity. Ranches, towns, and even large cities, such as Arispe and Ures, were raided. From the beginning of hostilities through October 1833, some two hundred citizens were killed.[38]

The new year dawned with similar prospects. On January 8,

1834, a large Chokonen war party surrounded Fronteras and ran off some fifty horses. Cochise may have been present because the two dominant band leaders, Pisago Cabezón and Relles, led the raid. Furthermore, the Apaches struck with audacity, a characteristic of the Chokonens. Two of the other leaders who were recognized were Félix and Tutije, a fast-rising war leader. Captain Bernardo Martínez and a force of presidio troops pursued, confident of routing the Indians if they could overtake them, but a half-mile east of Fronteras the Chiricahuas swarmed from the hills and almost surrounded the command, killing Martínez and three others within sight of the presidio. Afterward they continued south, cleaning out the ranch of Narivo Montoya and then murdering two citizens en route to Bacoachi, where they wiped out another party of six men. Not satisfied with their plunder, they continued southeast to Chinapa, a favorite Chokonen target, which they boldly occupied, running off every head of stock before retiring northward.[39] Fights like these allowed a young warrior to make a name for himself, and Cochise did not squander such opportunities.

The Chokonens returned north to their rancherías in the Chiricahua and Mule mountains, their subsequent movements uncertain. A Tucson rumor had it that Apaches from the Janos and Fronteras regions had joined the Coyoteros (Western Apaches) who were planning to attack Tucson, but no one knew for sure. It was also rumored that the hostiles had firearms, which of course was impossible, and that they numbered six hundred warriors, which was equally absurd. But there were scattered hostilities. On March 30 near the Babocomari ranch they ambushed and killed Captain Leónardo León of Tubac and routed a small force; it was learned that Matías's Chokonens were responsible. The next month, Montiju, a warrior from Matías's group, appeared at Fronteras with startling information: some four hundred Apaches had rendezvoused at Batepito, eighteen miles northeast of Fronteras, where two of the principal leaders, Matías and Tutije, argued about the target. The latter wanted to attack Fronteras, but Matías, who once had lived in peace near Fronteras, demurred, advocating a strike in the interior.[40]

The threatened attack on Fronteras did not materialize, and it was not until three months later that anyone realized what had happened.

In early July a woman who had been captured in the raid at Babo-comari ranch escaped from Matías's camp in the Chiricahuas and somehow made her way to Tucson. According to her, after the argument at Batepito, the bands divided, half under Pisago Cabezón and Tutije heading for the Mogollons and the others, under Relles and Matías, remaining in the Chiricahuas to make mescal. Although she denied that the Coyotero or Pinal Apaches had joined the Chiricahuas, she did confirm that the hostiles were conducting a brisk trade at Santa Rita del Cobre and warned that their next targets would be Tubac and Santa Cruz. Messengers were dispatched to the two places immediately, warning them to prepare for the Apaches. This disturbed Tubac's residents, for the town had no walls or artillery and not many armed citizens, and its water supplies were so scant that the prospect of an Indian siege was unnerving.[41]

That summer Sonora planned an offensive which the Chokonens probably got wind of because in mid-July several leaders appeared at the deserted Opata mission of Cuchuta, twelve miles south of Fronteras, and requested peace. According to Relles, some fourteen leaders would come into Fronteras at the end of July 1834. For some reason the Indians reneged, perhaps because the band was divided and the militant faction saw no benefit to negotiating; they had been at war for eighteen months, and neither Mexican state had mustered an offensive.[42]

Sonora also opposed peace despite the philosophy of Ignacio Mora, who had become commanding general in September. Mexican officials denounced his plans of sending emissaries to the hostiles, who had gone unpunished. Sonora required vengeance, so a campaign was planned and drastic measures adopted. Salaries of public officials were slashed and the savings were used to raise troops. As an added incentive, the volunteers would be allowed to keep plunder. These proposals were delayed, however, when frustrated presidio troops rebelled against Mora. Finally Manuel Escalante y Arvizu, the restless governor described "as a bold man who enjoyed adventure," turned his administrative duties over to Vice-Governor Ignacio Bustamente temporarily and took command for a climactic strike into Apachería.[43]

In late September 1834, Escalante y Arvizu put a force of 442

Apache Pass. Favorite camping site of Cochise's band prior to Anglo arrival in the Southwest. View from Overlook Ridge looking north. (*Photo by Karen Hayes*)

men in the field. Guided by several Opata Indians and seven tame Apaches enlisted from Tucson, the detachment, plagued by hunger and desertions, reached Puerto del Dado (Apache Pass) on October 15. Here the Opatas refused to continue and promptly deserted despite Escalante y Arvizu's threats of execution. To this point the command had found thirteen rancherías, abandoned since the previous summer. Three were discovered in the Chiricahua Mountains and two at Apache Pass, one near the springs and the other in the canyon, two of Cochise's favorite campsites. The Chokonens were believed to have moved north to the Mogollons and the Gila River.[44]

From Apache Pass the command followed an Indian trail north. On October 24 in the foothills of the Mogollons they surprised hostiles returning from a foray into Chihuahua. The Chiricahuas were led by Tutije and Vivora.[45] After a brief but hard fight, Escalante y Arvizu somehow succeeded in capturing "the wicked chief" Tutije and killing two other warriors. The next day the Mexicans withdrew with their important prize, since Tutije was considered to be an important war leader among the Chiricahuas. Escalante y Arvizu, evidently a man who believed in swift retribution, intended to make a point with the other militant leaders. Taking Tutije to Arispe, he paraded him through the streets. Furthermore, instead of using him as a hostage to secure peace, the governor decided to make an example of him, publicly hanging him in the streets of Arispe.[46]

The execution was intended to deter future raids and to teach the Chiricahuas a lesson, but it did neither. In fact, in late 1834 some Chihenne and Chokonen chieftains, including Pisago Cabezón, had sent word to Chihuahua that they wanted peace,[47] but news of Tutije's execution incensed several leaders and they decided to continue hostilities, for revenge must be had. Among those who remained at war were Pisago Cabezón and a young Chokonen daredevil who was beginning to make a name for himself, one who had attracted a small following of young Chokonens: Chis. Only the Nednhis and some of the Chihennes were seeking peace.

Accordingly, on February 12, 1835, Juan José Compá and several other leaders appeared at Santa Rita del Cobre to discuss conditions. They left after a lengthy conference with the sagacious Colonel Cayetano Justiniani, who reported the results to Calvo. Justiniani's account reflected his pragmatic understanding of Apaches, who had agreed to terms and even pledged to join Chihuahuan troops in their defense against the Comanches, an inveterate foe of the Mexicans. The only obstacle was the article which required the return of all stolen stock. Unable to enforce this condition, Justiniani prudently recommended its elimination, reasoning that "the Indians claim that they have very little left," which he discredited, but "in order to compel its return it would take a force of 800 men well mounted and provisioned for four months."[48]

During the conference, the Mexican officer pressed Juan José as to the disposition of the hostiles who had boycotted the talks. Juan José refused to speak for the absentees and said he did not know whether they would make or even wanted peace. Justiniani asked whether the peaceful Apaches would make war on those who remained hostile, one of Calvo's treaty conditions, emphasizing that there would be no armistice unless the Chiricahuas agreed to this article. The Indians held a lengthy conference and agreed "to make war on any of their fathers, sons or brothers who should refuse to accept the good that was offered them." At this point a reference to Cochise appears. Juan José revealed that the hostiles were raiding in Sonora and that one party, led by Chees, or Chis, had left the San Francisco River on a raid into Mexico. This undoubtedly was Cochise and indicates that he had been successful in war since the outbreak in 1831. For a young warrior to attract a following, he must have proved himself an able leader in raids and war. Other raiding parties under Pisago also were out, and Juan José mentioned them because he felt that they should have one last opportunity to accept the treaty. If they refused, he declared, his followers would attack the hostiles, which, of course, was purely lip service.[49]

The agreement was signed on March 31, 1835, by sixteen leaders who represented the moderate faction of the three Chiricahua bands. Because only half the Chiricahuas were represented, the judicious Justiniani was less than sanguine about the prospects for a stable or enduring peace without first gaining the consent of Pisago Cabezón and Fuerte. They were unquestionably the leaders of the hostiles, and both were said to be adamantly opposed to any agreement until they had avenged Tutije's death. Recognizing this, Justiniani cautioned his superiors that the treaty "cannot be considered complete because the Mescaleros and twelve other capitancillos were absent." Those not present included Pisago, Fuerte, Mano Mocha, Teboca, and Vivora.[50] Chees is conspicuously absent, indicating that Cochise probably was in Pisago Cabezón's following.

The other important issue was to gain the participation of Sonora; consequently, Justiniani dispatched Matías to Ures. Sonora, however, was in no mood to negotiate and refused to recognize the treaty. José María Elías González[51] and Bustamente scoffed at the idea of making peace: "A thousand times they have asked for peace and frequently have abused the indulgences which we have granted them, because their requests have had no basis in a true desire for peace, but only to lull us into thinking that the end of the war has come."[52]

Throughout the spring and summer of 1835, Juan José Compá tried to induce Pisago Cabezón and the hostiles to come in, but to no avail. Chokonen groups believed camped near San Simon raided

Bavispe, Janos, and Galeana in April and May. According to Juan José, Pisago had organized two war parties, one against Sonora and the other against the Navajos in New Mexico. Justiniani passed this information on to his superiors, who forwarded it to Elías González at Arispe.[53]

Elías González had been planning an offensive, which departed Fronteras on June 12, 1835, under the direction of his cousin, Captain Antonio Comadurán, a capable field officer familiar with the Western Apaches because of his service at Tucson. His force, consisting of 402 men and two small howitzers, established a base camp at San Simon, from which his troops scoured the territory to the north, yet little was accomplished. The Chiricahuas had detected and easily eluded the intruders. Pisago had moved his people north into the rugged San Francisco Mountains and Gila River country. As a result, Comadurán's command returned to Sonora without achieving anything and the hostiles grew even more confident.[54]

A few months later the Sonoran legislature adopted harsh measures in an attempt to check the onslaught. Recognizing the ineffectiveness of their military establishment, the lawmakers declared war on the Apaches and called on each village and town to take the offensive. Citizens were required to donate funds and supplies to provision these parties. The legislature provided another incentive by authorizing a bounty of one hundred pesos for the scalp of each Apache male over the age of fourteen. Only force would compel the Chiricahuas to return to peace; if not, the alternative was extermination.[55]

A month after the September decree, the hostiles suffered a severe blow when a Sonoran detachment under Elías González found them in force in eastern Arizona. On October 27, 1835, the Mexicans surprised a ranchería and killed ten warriors, including a son of Pisago Cabezón. The Sonorans recognized many warriors who had once lived at Fronteras and Bavispe. Elías González was surprised at the discipline and tactics employed by the Chiricahuas during the fight and attributed it to the influence of Anglo-American traders, who he believed directed the Indians; two Apaches in Tucson corroborated his report. Probably he was referring to James Kirker, who, it was rumored, had joined the hostiles at this time.[56]

By late 1835, Chokonen groups had returned to the Chiricahuas.

News of their activities can be discerned from the statements of a fifteen-year-old captive who escaped from Matías's group. He testified that Matías had eight more captives and a large amount of stolen stock in his possession and confirmed reports of the clandestine trade being conducted at Santa Rita del Cobre, even naming Juan José Compá, whose ephemeral truce had ended abruptly in September, as one of the ringleaders. The Americans bartered powder and guns for stolen stock, according to the boy. Finally, alluding to the sentiment of the Chokonens, he reported that all Apaches wanted war and talked about more raids along the frontier.[57]

Events in late 1835 and early 1836 supported the lad's testimony. On December 18 hostiles killed a man at Cuchuta. The next week they raided Galeana and in early January wiped out a party of five vaqueros at Hacienda de San Pedro, which probably forced its abandonment.[58] Depredations continued in the spring of 1836. A large Chiricahua war party struck near Fronteras in April and killed four citizens before continuing into the interior for more raids.[59]

That spring, Elías González received information which appalled him. According to reports, an enormous force of Navajos, Utes, and Apaches was planning an expedition into Sonora, in particular against Bavispe and Santa Cruz. As with most Chiricahua war parties, revenge again was the motive, this time to avenge the death of Pisago Cabezón's son and the execution of Tutije. Although this force did not materialize—the three tribes were not allies—the report apparently was taken seriously.[60]

The deteriorating condition of the frontier forced Elías González to reappraise Sonora's position. In an abrupt policy reversal, he rationalized that a peace plan was his only option. After all, Sonora had received no aid from Mexico City and the two campaigns of 1835 had accomplished little. His state had neither the money nor the manpower to defeat or even curtail the hostiles. The militaristic policy had failed.[61]

Like Sonora, the Chokonens looked favorably on an armistice. They had been at war for some four years; stock had been accumulated, honors won, and they had proved themselves capable foes of the Mexicans. Pisago Cabezón sounded out the military commander at Santa Rita del Cobre in May and June of 1836 but nothing of substance was resolved. Consequently, Cochise's people turned to Sonora. On August 30, five Chokonen leaders—Relles, Matías, Marcelo, Eugenio, and Miguel[62] (probably Miguel Narbona)—met at Elías González's home at Arispe and agreed to fifteen articles of peace. Both parties promised to reconvene at Fronteras in October to consummate the arrangement.[63]

Elías González had considerable experience, knowledge, and ability in dealing with the Chiricahuas. He became cautiously optimistic about the Chokonen peace solicitations, primarily because Pisago Cabezón had also expressed such desires. He recognized that Sonora must provide subsistence to obviate Chiricahua raiding, so on September 27 he wrote the governor, explained his plan of issuing rations, and asked for advice. The governor's response failed to address the problem but did endorse what Elías González was trying to accomplish; however, the source of funds to finance the operation was largely ignored.[64]

Undaunted, Elias González reached Fronteras in late October and, surprisingly, met Pisago Cabezón. He had just arrived from Santa Rita del Cobre, where, a few weeks earlier, citizens had turned on some peaceful Chiricahuas, killing one woman and two men. The deaths were especially brutal; one man was killed in cold blood and the other two Indians were "beaten, stabbed, speared and shot to death." The two warriors were said to have married into Pisago's family. Incensed, Pisago decided to open talks with Sonora. The entire Chokonen band was present or camped nearby, including Cochise, though it seems doubtful that he participated in the talks. To his surprise, Elías González discovered that Chihenne chiefs Boca Matada (Thick Lips) and Caballo Ligero (Fast Horse) were present and had consented to the articles. The Sonoran leader assigned the Chokonens to live at Cuchuverachi, some ten miles south of San Bernardino, and appointed Marcelo general. He gave the Chihennes the territory from Santa Lucía to the Gila River and named Boca Matada general. Yet neither party could have expected the peace to endure; rations were not a part of the agreement, and the Chiricahuas had not made peace with Chihuahua. More ominous, most of the Chihennes and Nednhis were still hostile.[65]

To remedy this, Elías González sent Pisago Cabezón to Santa

Rita del Cobre on a dual mission. First, he would try to negotiate a truce with Chihuahua; second, he would try to persuade the hostile Chihennes and Nednhis to make peace. Pisago and Caballo Ligero did meet with Robert McKnight and Captain José María Arze, who informed Calvo of the proceedings. Calvo instructed Arze to make a tentative peace until formal talks could be held, but by the time Arze arrived at the mines, the impatient Apaches had left. On January 26, 1837, the captain reported that the Chiricahuas had resumed hostilities, raiding Santa Rita del Cobre and fleeing west. Therefore, he wrote, "I have inferred that they do not wish peace." [66]

Actually, most of the Chokonens and some of the Chihennes had decided to live in the area stipulated by the treaty. Fuerte was the one exception, chooisng to remain aloof in the Mogollons. The Chokonens encamped near the present Arizona-Sonora line; Marcelo was camped at Embudos Canyon, [67] a few miles southeast of Cuchuverachi; and other groups, under Relles and Matías, were living at Sarampion, which was in the lower Peloncillos due east of the southern Chiricahua Mountains.

After a few months of peace it became clear that Chihuahua's inability to consummate an agreement would cause trouble. In February a Chokonen war party raided that state and returned to Sonora with some five hundred head of stock. Immediately after that, buoyed by success, thirty warriors left for a foray into Chihuahua. Marcelo could not control his young warriors; within days the Sonoran frontier was hit. [68]

On February 18, 1837, Teboca, a first-class hostile, with a few of his young men and two incorrigibles from Sayo Siza's group (San Juan and Rapado) surrounded several men about seven miles from Fronteras, stripped them, and stole five horses and two hundred cattle. The citizens' testimony clearly identified the Indians involved in the shakedown. Luiso Romero declared: "I know the chief Teboca very well. . . . I have seen him at this presidio several times when he has come here for peace." José Escalante informed the prefect of Arispe, who immediately requested additional information, implying that he hoped the Indians had not been abused. [69]

Escalante assured the prefect that the Apaches had been treated well, but they have "laughed at our friendship." At the same time,

the military commander at Fronteras wrote Elías González supporting Escalante's version. After weighing these statements, Elías
González summarily declared that all Chiricahuas not at Fronteras
by March 19 "would immediately thereafter be considered declared
enemies." His decision was not an impulsive one, for he had received several reports about Apache raiding parties. Apaches had
continued to harass the San Bernardino ranch, stealing much stock.
Thus, he concluded, "there is no longer any doubt that the previously mentioned Apaches have broken the peace treaties." He suggested joint punitive action with Chihuahua against the hostiles.[70]

Elías González's intuition proved correct. Most of the Chokonens
fled, especially those who had been raiding in Chihuahua. Relles
and Matías brought their followers to Fronteras but remained in
touch with relatives who left. Marcelo and Vivora ignored the order
and joined the hostiles under Juan José Compá. Cochise's whereabouts were not positively known. He probably left with the hostiles
and may have been in the vicinity for the Johnson massacre, which a
Chiricahua described as the first in "a series of treacherous attacks
made upon us by whites or Mexicans."[71]

The Chiricahuas had begun raiding in March 1837 when they
killed two men escorting a wagon train from Janos to Santa Rita del
Cobre and struck in the Janos–Casas Grandes region, where their
depredations "were preventing agriculture."[72] In Sonora "the frontier towns were helpless" to take action. Governor Escalante y Arvizu issued another timeworn proclamation, declaring: "These ferocious indigents . . . have multiplied their incursions committing all
the atrocities to which they are inclined by their natural bloodthirsty
character." The government was "destitute of resources" and required assistance in food, arms, and money. "War to the death to
the enemy" was the proclamation.[73]

A few weeks after this declaration, Apaches raided the Noria
ranch, which was some thirty miles north of Moctezuma, killing
several people and capturing some women and children. It was
about this time that Charles Ames and a group of Missouri mule
buyers arrived at Moctezuma in the hope of purchasing mules, but
there were none because the hostiles had cleaned out the area, Ames
conferred with John Johnson,[74] an Anglo living in Sonora, and they

decided to pursue the Apaches. Governor Escalante y Arvizu had granted Johnson permission to track down hostiles; whether it was oral, in writing, or just a tacit approval based on the governor's proclamation of early March mattered little. Johnson's compensation would be half of all stolen stock recovered, which satisfied the American's requirements. So the scenario was set: Johnson, seventeen Anglos, and five Mexicans left Moctezuma on April 3. At this point there was no evidence to indicate that Escalante y Arvizu sent Johnson out specifically to get Juan José Compá, as some reports asserted. It was purely happenstance that Johnson eventually came across Juan José's band and not another. Either way, the results would probably have been the same.

Johnson's party followed an Apache trail to Fronteras, where he arrived on April 12 and conferred with the commanding officer, Antonio Narbona.[75] Narbona attempted to dissuade him from continuing by pointing out that the Apaches far outnumbered his small party. Nonetheless, Johnson opted to go on, and Narbona gave him a small cannon or swivel gun. His decision was not as reckless as it seemed. Anglo-Americans were generally on good terms with the Chiricahuas. With a pack train of loaded mules, Johnson hoped the Apaches would perceive him as another Anglo trader, and common sense dictates that this was the case, given the ease by which he made contact with the Indians.

On April 20, Johnson arrived at Agua Fría Springs, located somewhere in the Animas Mountains in southwestern New Mexico, a range that bordered the territory of the three Chiricahua bands. Several rancherías were in the vicinity. Juan José Compá's and Juan Diego Compá's Nednhis were present, as were Chokonens under Marcelo and Vivora. The Apaches should have been somewhat suspicious, for most of the clandestine commerce had taken place along the Mimbres or at Santa Rita del Cobre. Nonetheless, the two groups talked, Johnson claiming they were going to Santa Rita, and agreed to trade, although the Anglos and perhaps the Apaches had treachery in mind. Either that day or the next, the Apaches sold Lautura García,[76] who had been a captive for an undetermined amount of time. According to Johnson, she told him the Indians planned to ambush his party en route to Santa Rita del Cobre.

Friday, April 21, passed without any problems. A profitable trade ensued, with the Apaches receiving whiskey and other sundries in return for their stolen mules. Juan José conceded that he would continue hostilities, but in the months to come he claimed that he would attempt a truce with Sonora; he also boasted that Relles, the Chokonen leader living near Fronteras, reported to him on troop strength and movements. According to Johnson, Lautora García had warned him that Juan José was scheming to lead the Americans into an ambush, yet in her testimony at Moctezuma she failed to mention any Apache double-dealing. In fact, she declared that in the short time she was a captive she could not understand "their language or their customs." She characterized relations of the first two days as having "passed with much friendship." April 22 would be different, although the Chiricahuas seemingly had no reason to suspect the contrary.[77]

That evening and early on the morning of April 22, Johnson and his party plotted their treachery; the five Mexicans refused to partake and left during the night. Early the next morning, the Chiricahuas returned to trade and Johnson sprang his surprise. Lautora García testified that while trading "pañocha and piñole, and when the Apaches were all mounted, the Americans fired the cannon charged with metallic scraps" and made an enormous carnage in human bodies. Lautora García was uncertain about the number of casualties, saying only that many were wounded. The fact that the Indians were mounted indicates that they were either just arriving or just leaving. Regardless, the attack caught them by surprise. After the first blast, the seventeen Anglo marksmen finished off the deed. When the slaughter was over, twenty Apaches lay scattered on the field, including Juan José Compá, Juan Diego Compá, and Marcelo; certainly many more were wounded and, more important, indelible psychological scars were left, which deepened the chasm of distrust between Chiricahuas and all white men.[78]

After the butchery, Johnson quickly retreated to Janos. On April 24 he wrote the governor of Chihuahua and furnished details of his "battle" with eighty Apaches:

> As I recognized their superior numbers, I delayed my attack from the 20th until 10 o'clock in the morning of the 22nd, not feeling it possible to wait for a longer time on account of the acts of mistrust

and treachery that I observed from their preparations . . . despite the dangers and obstacles that stood in its way . . . as a result there were left on the field of battle twenty dead Indian renegades, including the three chiefs, Marcelo, Juan José and Juan Diego, whose scalps I have presented to the commander of this presidio [Janos].[79]

Johnson's report was noteworthy for what it did not contain. For example, he failed to mention anything about the cannon, nor did he explain how he killed twenty Apaches without loss to his party.

From Janos, Johnson returned to Moctezuma via Bavispe, where, according to one report, he left the scalps of the three Chiricahua chiefs. At Moctezuma his official report was submitted to authorities; at the same time, Lautora García gave her version. This account was forwarded to Sonora's commanding general, who shuffled it to the governor of Sonora, who passed it along to the minister of war and navy in Mexico City. The deed done, Johnson was compensated with one hundred pesos, seemingly closing the incident.[80]

Many accounts of the Johnson affair, as it became known, were published in the nineteenth century, and each progressively added its own unsubstantiated details. Rex Strickland's article in *Arizona and the West,* based largely on Johnson's official report, sheds immense light on a previously ambiguous incident. It clears up the conjecture as to where the massacre took place, the number of Apache casualties, and some of the circumstances surrounding the attack, yet Strickland's assessment that this new information "reduces the event to its relative trivial dimensions" would have been passionately disputed by Apaches who knew of the event in the nineteenth century.[81]

The perfidious massacre would not be forgotten; to the Apaches, its ramifications were both immediate and enduring. As for Cochise, he probably was not present but might have been in the vicinity. He certainly became aware of the tragedy and joined other Chiricahuas to avenge Johnson's deed. Fifteen years later his father-in-law, Mangas Coloradas, bitterly recalled the incident:

At another [time] a trader was sent among us from Chihuahua. While innocently engaged in trading, often leading to words of anger, a cannon concealed behind the goods was fired upon my people and quite a number killed.[82]

Mrs. Eve Ball and Jason Betzinez mention the incident. From their accounts it is clear that the Apaches perceived the Johnson affair as one of the worst things ever perpetrated on them, at least until James Kirker got into the act a few years later.[83]

Not all parties in Mexico applauded Johnson's deed. From Mexico City came concerns about the incident, although they were not focused on the inhumanity of it. The minister of war and navy asked Elías González to explain why Sonora permitted an armed party of foreigners to make war against the Apaches. By foreigners he obviously was referring to Americans, with whom Mexico now had uneasy relations over the Texas question. Elías González was ordered to make a "positive and official report" and was admonished that "armed men who are not in your command cannot operate in the territory of this Republic." Governor Escalante y Arvizu responded, and his answer, politically motivated, deliberately distorted the facts. On July 20, 1837, he wrote Sonora's commanding general:

> Your lordship knows very well that it was not a company of armed adventurers that carried out this campaign, as has been falsely reported at the highest level of the government. It was rather several Americans, many of them intermarried and living as neighbors.

Up to this point Escalante y Arvizu was stretching things, but his next statements border on the absurdity:

> However they [Americans] were not going to pursue the Apaches alone, but rather as support troops for a party of Sonoran patriots who had offered to do it at their own expense. Only through mischance and error were the latter prevented from participating in the fighting done by these foreigners together with five Mexicans.

The reply was clearly intended to close the investigation and appease authorities in Mexico City, who Sonora justifiably felt were too far removed to understand the realities of the situation. The governor concluded his report by assuring them that he "would never allow in [Sonora] a gathering of armed adventurers . . . this is especially true considering the current state of the relationship existing between the Republic and the nation to which belong the individuals who have performed this service."[84]

Apache reaction to Johnson's deed was predictable, as it was after Kirker's slaughter at Galeana in 1846, Carrasco's clandestine attack at Janos in 1851, Lieutenant George N. Bascom's egregious handling of the incident at Apache Pass in 1861, and the California Volunteers' cold-blooded killing of Mangas Coloradas in 1863. In all occasions the natural and only Chiricahua response was revenge, hopefully on the parties responsible, but, as one individual expressed it, "they go after anything, a troop of cavalry, a town. They are angry. They fight anyone to get even."[85]

Chapter 3

TURBULENT TIMES

The Chiricahua sword of justice materialized immediately after the Johnson affair. Near the Gila the Indians reportedly wiped out a group of twenty-two trappers known as the Kemp party and soon after that massacred a wagon train of twelve men en route to El Paso from Santa Fe.[1] That fall they struck northwest Chihuahua. On September 25, 1837, they captured a young boy named Felipe de Jesús Fuente from Galeana; three days later they attacked a party near Casas Grandes, killing two citizens and wounding four others. On October 1 they stole eighty cattle and eleven horses from Ramos, a hacienda some fifteen miles south of Janos, then raided Janos itself, perhaps because Johnson had retreated there after the carnage. On October 26 the Chiricahuas ambushed two men and two women harvesting crops, and six weeks later a large war party killed a judge and eight other people at Ramos, which forced its abandonment.[2]

These raids convinced Mexico that the Chiricahuas must be stopped. That fall Chihuahua Governor Simon Elías wrote Sonora Governor Manuel Escalante y Arvizu and proposed a joint campaign specifically to punish the Chiricahuas. His plan called for a four-hundred-man force to campaign for six months, using Santa Rita del Cobre as a base. This constant pressure would compel the Chiricahuas to sue for peace, or so the two governors believed. Like so many others, the plan never got off the ground; lack of money and political instability forced postponement.[3]

As 1838 dawned, Simon Elías continued to press for a large army to penetrate Apachería and subjugate the hostiles, but conflicts between rival political factions forced these plans to be scaled down. In Sonora, new Governor José Urrea, a veteran of the Alamo and other historic battles of the Texas revolt against Mexico in 1836, recognizing that the northern presidios must forsake their defensive posture, put two experienced and competent officers in charge of the northern command. Lieutenant Colonel José María Martínez was given command of the presidios of Tubac, Santa Cruz, and Tucson, which in turn was reinforced with troops from Altar, and Captain Ignacio López was placed in charge of the presidios of Bacoachi, Bavispe, and Fronteras. These two commanders, in conjunction with national troops under the intrepid José Ignacio Terán y Tato,[4] were ordered to carry the war into Apachería and keep scouting detachments in the field at all times.[5]

The commands were soon in action. Toward the end of January 1838, Apaches burned the Bacanuchi hacienda near Bacoachi. Immediately Captain Francisco Narbona pursued, killing two hostiles before they vanished into the mountains. About the same time at Santa Cruz, Apaches stole six hundred cattle and were pursued, although unsuccessfully. In February, Urrea ordered his new commanders to scout Apachería. Martínez's command reconnoitered Western Apache territory but was impeded by heavy snows in the mountains; nonetheless, he managed to destroy one ranchería. Meanwhile, in Chokonen country, one hundred warriors ambushed López's detachment, but the Mexicans drove them to the mountains and out of Sonora, or so they reported, before returning to Fronteras.[6]

As it turned out, many of the Chokonens had moved east into Chihenne territory, though not as a consequence of Sonora's efforts. Early that spring Pisago Cabezón called a tribal council, with the leaders concluding to send two war parties against Mexico. The first group of two hundred warriors would be commanded by Tapilá,[7] an up-and-coming Chokonen war leader. Armed with rifles and ammunition purchased from Anglo traders, this band, said to have been accompanied by James Kirker, roared into Sonora and swept down the western slopes of the Sierra Madre. The second group, under Pisago, planned to waylay the wagon train which brought provisions to Santa Rita del Cobre.[8]

In recent years the mines had become unprofitable to operate. Moreover, since the Johnson attack, small Apache raiding parties had annoyed the diggings. No full-scale attack had taken place because Apache war parties found other targets more profitable, and more vulnerable, in Sonora and Chihuahua. Pisago's objective, as with most war parties, was revenge and plunder, in this case the supply train's livestock and provisions.

On March 26 the Chiricahuas moved south by way of the Florida Mountains to Carrizalillo Springs, where Pisago prepared to ambush the whites before they reached the springs. On March 30, Ambrosio Tachan's wagons were moving unsuspectingly through the pass when, about 3 P.M., the Indians swept down on the cattle herd, which was ahead of the main party. The escort and several Americans pushed forward but were unable to do much; the Indians reportedly numbered four hundred—three hundred mounted and one hundred on foot—although this estimate seems too high. The whites halted abruptly and the confident Apaches fell back to the springs, daring their adversaries to attack. There was sporadic gunfire the rest of the day and throughout the moonlit night, but there were no casualties.

Early the next morning, Chato Pisago, son of Pisago, approached the whites, stating that he wished to parley. Pascual Mora ventured out and talked with Chato, who declared that Pisago wished to speak with a citizen from Janos. After a few tense moments, Gabriel Zapata, trusting the Indians, left the wagons and met Pisago Cabezón.

A few years later George W. Kendall met a Chiricahua chief who might have been Pisago. He described the Indian as "middle height, strong and well built, some sixty-five or seventy years of age, and with hair as white as snow." Zapata recalled that

Pisago came down and the two Indians [Chato and Pisago] together greeted and embraced me. After speaking about several things in a friendly manner Pisago said, "I want peace, I don't want to fight." I answered saying that although I was only a servant of the hacienda I would risk my life and that should they let the wagons and the people pass, I would remain with their band until he should receive a guarantee of protection from either Don Roberto [Robert McKnight] or from the Governor. Pisago agreed to this.

The agreement was short lived and somewhat questionable, for this was a major war party intent on revenge and loot. In any event, Bernavé, a renegade Mexican who once lived at Santa Rita del Cobre, reminded Pisago of the recent atrocities inflicted by whites on the Apaches. First he cited those Indians killed in the Johnson massacre and others who had been "beaten to death with sticks" at Santa Rita del Cobre. Furthermore, since the wagons belonged to Robert McKnight, "the greatest rascal there is," they "should not pass, nor the Americans," insisted Bernavé. Pisago took this under advisement and conferred with his leaders. A short time later he returned with other chiefs, including Manuel Chirimni, who wanted to kill Zapata, but this Pisago would not permit. He allowed Zapata to return with the Indians' demand to "abandon everything and they would not be attacked." Either that day or the next (April 2), the whites abandoned the entire train of ten wagons and its supplies and returned to Janos, arriving there with only twenty-two horses.[9]

Shortly after Pisago seized its provisions, the Chiricahuas attacked Santa Rita del Cobre, killing several citizens and wounding a few others. With the miners desperate for supplies, another train with a seventy-man escort was dispatched from Galeana on May 6. A few Apaches were seen, but no trouble occurred. It was the last supply train to the mines; sometime in late June the diggings were deserted and the public property was transferred to Janos.[10]

No evidence has been found to support John C. Cremony's account that "every man, woman and child" who left the mines was cut off and killed "except for four or five."[11] Two contemporary accounts, one by Frederick A. Wislizenus, who journeyed through northern Mexico in 1846–47, and the other by John Russell Bartlett, an associate of Cremony, left behind reliable versions obtained from citizens. Neither mentioned anything about a wholesale slaughter. Wislizenus wrote that the mines "had to be abandoned on account of hostile Indians, who killed some of the workmen, and attacked the trains."[12] Bartlett was more specific, obviously referring to Pisago's fight at Carrizalillo Springs. He described the ambush in which the Indians took the wagons, mules, and horses, "first giving each who accompanied the train a mule to carry him away. At the same time they sent word to the inhabitants of the Copper Mines that they would allow no further supplies to reach them and, furthermore, would destroy them whenever an opportunity offered, [therefore] the people determined to abandon the place." [13]

In Sonora the situation was just as perilous in the late 1830s. Its presidios, poorly equipped and sparsely garrisoned, were incapable of preventing raids or of mounting offensives, and political instability continued to disrupt affairs. The two rival groups, Gándara's and Urrea's, continued their fight for control of the state rather than focusing their energies on the Apaches. [14] Despite some insignificant Mexican successes (in the summer of 1838 troops killed four warriors near Santa Cruz and a chief and two warriors near Fronteras), the Apaches controlled the frontier, with little resistance from Sonora. [15]

The summer of 1839 was no better. The Indians' audacity increased to the point where they murdered a man inside a house at Santa Cruz and in August ambushed and killed two soldiers outside the corral at Bavispe. [16] Finally, in November 1839, Gándara's and Urrea's forces stopped fighting each other long enough for Manuel María Gándara to lead a campaign to the Mimbres River in southern New Mexico. Gándara's troops killed seventeen warriors, including, he believed, Pisago Cabezón (which proved to be untrue), and confiscated nineteen American rifles. [17] The expedition had little effect and in 1840 the Chiricahuas continued their depredations in Sonora. Authorities continued to blame Sonora's impotence on the turmoil caused by internal conflict. "Since the beginning of the Revolution of 1838, the troops of this department have been occupied in defeating it, leaving few troops to fight the Apaches." [18]

In the late 1830s, Chihuahua suffered heavily from renewed Chiricahua raiding. Affairs were at a low ebb: mines were abandoned, haciendas deserted, and public roads had become increasingly unsafe. Recognizing that presidio troops were no match for the mobile, quick-striking Apaches, its government, influenced by businessmen, opted for a course of action differing from that of its neighbor to the east. Stephen Courcier, once Robert McKnight's partner at Santa Rita, had become one of the wealthiest and most influential men in Chihuahua. He urged the governor to organize a private army of mercenaries to kill as many Apaches as possible—hopefully every hostile living. On April 9, 1839, Courcier called a meeting of the "Society to Make War," appointed the ubiquitous James Kirker to organize the group, and called for public donations of one hundred thousand pesos to support it. Kirker, described as a "blue eyed, gray haired and gray whiskered man . . . short and stout," accepted the position without reservation.[19]

He was a logical choice; he knew the Apaches and was thoroughly acquainted with their territory and their favorite camping areas. Equally important, he was an opportunist usually prepared to take the side most profitable to him; this time it meant Chihuahuan pesos. He was an efficient and unscrupulous businessman who understood the equation that scalps plus confiscated plunder equaled cash. When Apaches were not available, it was alleged that he scalped Mexican peasants and turned their hair in for the bounty. After all, to distinguish between Apache and Mexican hair was virtually impossible. During the 1830s he had played both sides: Anglo against Apache and most recently Apache against Mexican. Now he would reverse the latter role and join the Mexicans against the Apaches. In early April, Amado de La Vega wrote to each prefect, announcing the program and requesting contributions.[20] Although the scheme was considered somewhat extreme, pubic support was enthusiastic and unanimous. On June 14, Angel Trias, president of the municipal council of Chihuahua City, issued an ordinance levying a tax on merchants to support Kirker's outfit.[21]

Kirker's force consisted mainly of American trappers, traders, and Delaware and Shawnee Indians. Over the next year he did succeed in garnering many scalps, some Mexican and some Apache, in addition to having several brushes with Cochise's people. In early 1840 he surprised Pisago's camp, reportedly killing ten warriors and capturing twenty individuals.[22] That spring, Francisco García Conde, Chihuahua's new governor, described as "a portly, handsome man," promptly canceled Kirker's contract on humanitarian grounds. He allegedly ignored Kirker's claim for thirty thousand pesos in unpaid bounty, infuriating Kirker, who exacted compensation by stealing six hundred of Conde's horses and selling them in Santa Fe, or so the story goes.[23]

Kirker's first stint in the scalp-hunting business had caused few casualties as far as the Chiricahuas were concerned. What was more significant, at least in the Apaches' perception, was the organization of a well-armed, well-provisioned, and fearless mercenary group which campaigned in Apache country. This was the only effective way of fighting Apaches, who, it should be pointed out, spent very little time making war. The Chiricahuas put little stock in planting because group campsites varied from season to season. In spring the Indians gathered fruits, vegetables, and mescal and in autumn they harvested nuts and berries. Therefore, the presence of a significant enemy force scouting their country had the potential to disrupt this element of their fragile economy.

The Chiricahuas continued at war throughout 1840 and 1841 as Apache dominance reached its highest point since the 1780s. The Indians were better armed and mounted than ever before. On top of this, their war parties frequently consisted of one hundred or more men, a far cry from their earlier hit-and-run guerrilla tactics. Chihuahua could not stop them, and in Sonora, the Chokonens' primary raiding area, conditions were even worse.

The frontier towns pleaded for additional troops, guns, and ammunition to protect themselves. The alternative, they warned, was abandonment of crops and homes. The continual Apache raids led to poor harvests in both 1840 and 1841 because most citizens were afraid to work their crops. On September 10, 1840, a raiding party stole some stock near Bacoachi. Twelve men, led by Justice of the Peace José Narbona, marched in pursuit. The Apaches were waiting and it was a rout, not a retreat. Narbona and five others were killed. Two weeks later at Cuquiarachi, some twenty-five miles northeast of Bacoachi, Apaches, probably Chokonens, slaughtered six citizens as they worked in their fields. These tragedies compelled many citizens to desert their homes for new lives, some as distant as California.[24]

In the spring of 1841, Captain Antonio Narbona, a capable officer well known to the Chiricahuas, was named commander of the frontier presidios. He had only seventy troops to cover the area from Altar to Fronteras, a distance of some two hundred miles, so of course he could do little. Raiding parties hit Bacoachi more than once that spring; no citizen dared to leave the town's security to work his crops. Narbona did his best, but scant resources meant infrequent success. His requests to superiors produced ambivalent responses from staff officers, who made weak promises of future aid and imaginary campaigns.[25] As 1841 ended the Chiricahuas definitely held the upper hand. They had retaliated with vigor and in

Cuchillo Negro. This important Chihenne chief was painted by John Mix Stanley in 1846. (*Courtesy National Museum of American Art, Smithsonian Institution, gift of the Misses Henry, 1908*)

force since the Johnson massacre, all three bands uniting in a common cause to seek revenge. It was during this period that a powerfully built Chihenne leader came to the fore. His name was Mangas Coloradas.

Mangas, who was born in the early 1790s, was literally a giant among his people, standing six feet four inches tall and weighing two hundred and fifty pounds. As with Cochise, little is known of his early life, although stories and legends abound. He first appeared in documents in 1842, when he was identified as the leader of the hostile Mogollons, probably the branch of the tribe the Chiricahuas called Bedonkohes. Since his status was not achieved overnight, he was undoubtedly known by another name prior to this time. His Spanish name, meaning "red sleeves" or "roan shirt" (either because he wore shirts with red sleeves or because the blood of his victims splattered his shirt), may have been acquired during the tumultuous period after the Juan José Compá massacre. What name he went by before this is not known, but it is possible that he was related to or known as Fuerte, the dominant Chihenne leader from 1815 through the 1830s. Fuerte, whose name implied a strong physique, lived near the Mimbres and Santa Rita del Cobre before disappearing about 1840, when Mangas Coloradas came to the fore. It is possible that Mangas was in the shadow of such Chihenne leaders as Fuerte and Mano Mocha and succeeded them as their influence waned. By 1840 these chiefs were aging and Chihenne leaders like Mangas, Cuchillo Negro, Itán, and Delgadito began to attract followings on the local-group level. In late 1842 a report from Janos noted that Mangas had relatives among the Apaches who were at Fronteras and those living in the Chiricahua Mountains. Cochise certainly would have been in one of these groups.[26]

Cochise must have accompanied Mangas Coloradas on many of the latter's incursions. In the late 1830s or early 1840s he married a daughter of Mangas and Tu-es-seh named Dos-teh-seh ("something at the campfire already cooked"), who was his principal wife throughout his life.[27] Chiricahua custom required a man to live with the local group or band to which his wife belonged; in Cochise's case, perhaps following a brief six- to eight-month trial period, he returned to live with his Chokonens because his status among his people made him too valuable to be gone very long. According to one anthropologist, "the sons of prominent men were obliged to stay close at home."[28] In any event, the relationship between Cochise and Mangas Coloradas developed and was nurtured in the years that followed.

For reasons not altogether clear, in early 1842 many Chiricahua leaders decided to make peace with Mexico. The venerable Pisago Cabezón and the aged Mano Mocha were the leading proponents of an armistice; Mangas Coloradas led the dissenting minority. Many Chiricahuas simply had grown tired of war and peace offered a respite from the five-year conflict: they could mend fences and forestall Mexican campaigns. Consequently, in early April 1842, Mano Mocha appeared at Janos and requested an end to hostilities. After a short council, Captain Pedro Madrigal issued him a pass for safe conduct to Chihuahua City to speak with the governor.[29] Some sort of preliminary agreement was reached, for by the end of April other groups arrived at Janos to discuss terms. On May 11, Chihuahua's commanding general appointed a peace commissioner to consummate a treaty.[30]

As a result, on May 23, Pisago Cabezón sent Vicente, two warriors, and seven women to Janos. The next day, however, they departed abruptly, fearing "they would be betrayed, just as happened at El Paso."[31] This excited Janos's citizens and soldiers and they braced for hostilities. Captain Madrigal must have heaved a sigh of relief when the Chokonen chief Manuel returned to Janos in early June and again emphasized his desire for an armistice.[32] Prospects looked so favorable that *La Luna,* the official state newspaper, editorialized: "It is probable, it is necessary, it is useful, and it is urgent." Accordingly, in late June, Governor García Conde left the capital to conclude the agreement, arriving at Janos on June 27.[33]

The treaty was signed on July 4, 1842, with Pisago Cabezón, Ponce,[34] and other leaders representing the Indians, who consented to cease hostilities, to deliver all captives and stolen horses, to establish their rancherías near Janos, and to make war on the hostile Mescaleros. In return, García Conde, recognizing that the peace treaties of 1832 and 1835 had failed because of Mexico's refusal to issue rations, agreed to feed the Indians. He authorized weekly rations, which consisted of three *almudes* of corn (about two and one-half liters), tobacco, sugar, and meat. Afterward, García Conde went south to San Buenaventura, where Torres and Cristóbal were waiting; they agreed to the same conditions. Significantly, Sonora was not mentioned, possibly because groups of Chokonens had been negotiating at Fronteras.[35]

In mid-July a few Indians filtered into Janos, and in early August other Chokonens arrived, including Pisago. A force commanded by Colonel Elías González had forged into northeastern Sonora on a search-and-destroy mission directed at hostiles under Mangas Coloradas, and its presence concerned Pisago, who asked Madrigal at Janos for protection. Madrigal promptly dispatched four soldiers to warn González to stay out of Chihuahua. Satisfied with these actions, Pisago brought thirty warriors, fifty-five women, and eighty-six children to Janos in August. Cochise did not come in, apparently remaining with Mangas Coloradas at Alamo Hueco.[36]

In all likelihood Cochise had spent part of 1842 in the neighborhood of Fronteras. Many Chokonens under Esquinaline,[37] Teboca, and Yrigóllen[38] had been encamped near there since early 1842, waiting to hear whether Sonora would grant them peace and assistance. Their patience had waned by late summer. Sonora's campaign, coupled with the prospect of rations at Janos, persuaded Teboca and Esquinaline to join Mangas Coloradas at Alamo Hueco; Yrigóllen moved southeast to San Buenaventura. Cochise and about ten warriors eventually split from Mangas Coloradas and joined Pisago's followers at Janos. Cochise first drew rations on October 17, 1842, with his wife joining him on October 24 and October 31. In all probability, this was Dos-teh-seh, daughter of Mangas Coloradas, who may have sent his son-in-law to ascertain Mexican treatment of the Indians. Cochise remained at Janos until early November, and his name was absent from the ration rolls until the following July.

Janos, Chihuahua. Ruins of the presidio where Cochise received rations in 1842–44 and 1857. (*Photo by Dan Thrapp*)

In light of subsequent events it would seem likely that he returned
to his father-in-law and reported favorably on affairs at Janos, for
Mangas, who had steadfastly opposed peace, did an abrupt about-
face and decided to negotiate.[39]

The great Chihenne sent word in late 1842 that he wished to talk.
Chihuahua resonded quickly, inviting him in for a parley. At Janos
the peace commissioner, Vicente Sanchez Vergara, succeeded in
gathering an authoritative representation of chiefs and held talks
with Mangas Coloradas, Itán, Cuchillo Negro, and Teboca in late
January or early February. If Cochise was present, he was in the
background. The Chiricahua leaders promised to bring in their
people that March to conclude the armistice.[40] As a result, Chihuahua's commanding general, Mariano Monterde, left Chihuahua City
and reached Janos on March 25 or 26. Mangas arrived on the
twenty-eighth and conferred with Monterde for the next four days.
Monterde recognized that the Indians were extremely apprehensive
because of past Mexican treachery, alluding to the Johnson affair,
Kirker's scalp-hunting expedition, and the unprovoked attack at
Paso del Norte. Yet as the proceedings developed, Monterde became impressed with the Indians' punctuality, their sincerity, and
the importance with which they viewed peace.

Mangas agreed to the same conditions Pisago Cabezón had ac-
cepted some nine months before and before departing agreed to send
Apache emissaries to Sonora to meet with Governor Urrea. Ac-
cordingly, Negrito, the venerable Matías, and Marcelo (another of
Pisago's sons), accompanied by Captain Vergara, went to Ures in
mid-May and then on to Guaymas, which they reached on June 2.
Here they conferred with Urrea, who agreed to peace as long as the
Apaches refrained from depredations in his state. In essence, if the
Apaches left the Sonorans alone, Sonora would reciprocate.[41]

This ephemeral period of good relations was not destined to continue. Ironically, the truce was already doomed by the time the agreement was made. While the Mexican-Apache peace party was negotiating with Urrea, troops at Fronteras murdered six Chokonen men
for no apparent reason. The incident was indicative of the volatility
of relations between the two races. In late May, Western Apaches
(referred to as Coyoteros to distinguish them from Cochise's Chiri-

cahuas) stole some stock at Fronteras. At the time of the raid, seven Chiricahua men were at the presidio. They volunteered to help the soldiers and after a short pursuit succeeded in recovering most of the stock. At this point, for some inexplicable reason, the Sonoran troops turned their weapons on the Apaches; only one escaped. These cold-blooded murders demanded an Apache response, so Mangas and Pisago retaliated by attacking Fronteras and killing two citizens and wounding one. The militant Chiricahuas were once again at war with Sonora.[42]

Notwithstanding the renewed hostilities with Sonora, many Chiricahuas continued to live in peace at Janos, but the hostiles continued to find refuge and a market for their spoils. Although Janos's authorities knew where the stock and loot came from, they apparently made no attempt to stop it, even rationing those Apaches who returned with the blood and spoils of their victims. Though many of the Chiricahuas had kept their agreements at Janos, the hostiles gave the whole group a bad reputation, at least in the eyes of Sonora.

Cochise was active during this time, stopping in at Janos (his name spelled *Chuchese,* as it would be by Arizonans twenty-five years later) for rations on July 24, 1843. The next week he was not present, but an Indian woman named D-Tosa, perhaps a corruption of Dos-teh-seh, with a child (perhaps his eldest son, Taza, born about 1842) did receive rations. Also present was a woman named María de Chis with two sons. Whether she was another wife of Cochise will probably never be known. He was a polygamous man, so it was possible that they were his relations who were killed before Anglo contact. He disappeared for the next four months, probably joining Mangas and Pisago in southwestern New Mexico. If so, he had a hand in the bloody events of 1843, when Chiricahuas began raiding ruthlessly into Sonora and retreating to Janos to dispose of their booty.[43]

In Sonora, the energetic Elías González would not stand still. On July 20 he wrote Monterde to advise him that he was planning an expedition against the hostiles. An apprehensive Monterde admonished Elías González to punish only those hostiles found in Sonora. Furthermore, he warned, he would consider it a serious crime if any Sonoran troops trespassed into Chihuahua. Monterde at once instructed Captain Madrigal to inform the Janos Apaches of Sonora's campaign, at the same time emphasizing that Chihuahua intended to live up to its end of the treaty.[44]

Savage raids continued throughout 1843, and many appeared to be the work of Apaches drawing rations at Janos. In late September, Sonora's governor complained to Mexico City about the raids, but there was no response. A few months later a Fronteras citizen wrote the prefect of Arispe a despairing letter, which the prefect forwarded to the minister of war in Mexico City. The letter charged that prior to Chihuahua's peace treaty in June 1842 the Apaches

> used to steal both in that Department and in this one in order to sell in New Mexico, with which they were not at war. Since then it is only Sonora that bears the burden of their depredations. . . . Since the towns of Chihuahua are so close by, in a very short space of time the barbarians come over to our towns and commit murders and robberies. Evading the vigilance of our troops, with the quickness of lightning they go back to their camps, where they are protected and defended from punishment by the Commander of Janos.[45]

Federal officials demanded a response from Chihuahua. On January 13, 1844, Monterde, who seemed preoccupied with justifying every move he made, vehemently denied the allegations. In fact, he asserted, his administration had stopped the bloodshed and had effectively destroyed the age-long practice of Apaches raiding into one state and seeking refuge in another. He also pointed out that in the spring of 1843 he had sent Apache leaders to Sonora, where they had made peace. He tersely remarked that Sonora's problems began shortly after soldiers at Fronteras treacherously murdered several Chiricahuas near that presidio. Since then, those Apaches, not the ones living in peace at Janos, had retaliated against Sonora. He closed by citing examples of Apache cooperation in returning stolen stock and assisting troops against the hostiles. It was true that many of the Chiricahuas living at Janos under Manuelito, Chinaca, and Láceris had not been raiding in Sonora; unfortunately for them, beginning in the summer of 1843, they became guilty by association when many of the hostile Chokonens, including Cochise, arrived with Sonoran loot and irregularly received rations.[46]

Conditions intensified in the fall when many Chiricahuas relocated to Janos from Galeana, where smallpox had broken out. Yrigóllen arrived the first week of October, and a month later Coleto Amarillo, a prominent Nednhi leader, began drawing rations. That fall, rations were issued to perhaps eight hundred Chiricahuas. Cochise was at Corralitos from November 27 through December 25 with a group under Relles and Ponce, who was said to have been a good friend of Cochise. Also present were two men named Collotura (Coyuntura) and Juan, both married, both probably brothers of Cochise.[47]

Compounding the lethal arrival of smallpox was another long-standing problem: inadequate rations. The previous spring, Madrigal had reported that his supply of rations was nearly depleted. This forced him to request assistance from residents, which increased tensions between the two parties; any incident could lead to war. In November 1843, Madrigal told his superiors the Indians had become surly and had abused several citizens. This, he wrote, could be attributed to the "lack of military personnel and insufficient rations." By early 1844, affairs had quickly got out of hand once more. Some 600 to 700 Indians were present throughout December, but only 200 remained on January 15, 1844, the number falling to 120 the following week. Most had left because of the smallpox epidemic; a few had contracted the disease and in February several men died, including two minor leaders, Chinaca and Chato Pisago.[48]

By February most of the Indians still healthy had returned to the mountains in northeastern Sonora. From here Mangas Coloradas and Pisago Cabezón led several campaigns against Sonora during the first seven months of 1844. Mangas's first strike occurred on February 7 when a large Chiricahua war party attacked the horse herd at Fronteras, wounded three soldiers, and carried off more than two hundred head of stock. The next month, Mangas Coloradas and Yrigóllen assaulted the vulnerable presidio at daybreak, killing one man and wounding another before withdrawing into the hills. Captain Teodoro de Aros led a force of twenty-nine men, all on foot, after the Indians. About a mile from the fort the overeager Apaches attacked, setting off a skirmish which lasted some five hours before the Indians broke off the fight. The Mexicans lost one man dead and three wounded, including the captain. Several Indians were wounded, among them Yrigóllen and Posito. Mangas's plan failed because several overzealous warriors revealed themselves before the Mexicans had become entrapped; a few minutes more and the entire command might have been annihilated.[49] The Chiricahuas, however, apparently learned a lesson.

After the fight at Fronteras, the hostiles continued into the interior for more raids. In late April another sanguinary encounter occurred in the Oputo Mountains. While retiring north, some Chiricahuas unexpectedly encountered eleven Sonorans and in a sharp clash killed eight and wounded the other three. The Indians later conceded that six warriors were killed, although a rumor that Cuchillo Negro was one of the dead proved false. They returned to the Fronteras vicinity and on April 28 at 8 A.M. surprised Cuquiarachi, riding brazenly through its streets and surrounding the town. By eleven o'clock they had killed several men and had captured three children and one man. At that point the typical parley ensued and the captives were ransomed. Among the Apache representatives were Mangas Coloradas, Relles, Pisago Cabezón, Yrigóllen, Chepillo,[50] and Miguel Narbona. All except Mangas were Chokonens. His presence and that of Pisago Cabezón are strong evidence for Cochise's involvement. The Indians, loaded with plunder, headed for Janos, killing seven more Sonorans along the way.[51]

The next incident convinced Elías González, who believed in swift retribution, that he had to act. Sometime in July 1844 a large Chiricahua war party massacred Ensign Manuel Villa and twenty-eight men near Santa Cruz. Mangas apparently led the Apaches, who successfully implemented the time-worn decoy tactic, a strategy which rarely worked because it required discipline and coordination unusual in Apache warfare. That it did succeed was a tribute to Mangas's status in the Chiricahua Tribe; no other leader could have pulled it off. The war party succeeded in decoying the Santa Cruz force away from the presidio and into the trap. The Mexicans, surrounded before they knew what hit them, were wiped out. Elías González soon determined to take matters into his own hands and snuff out the illicit trade at Janos.

To achieve this, he decided on a campaign against the Janos Apaches. In August he attacked Chiricahua rancherías near Corralitos and Janos, butchering some eighty Indians, most of them

women and children. Many innocent Chiricahuas (although some of
the men in these rancherías had been raiding) perished in Elías
González's attack; many innocent Mexicans would be killed in retaliation.[52] The attack stunned the Chiricahuas; most bolted into
southern New Mexico and Arizona, where they regrouped and
planned their revenge. Naturally it was war, and Cochise must have
been in the middle of it all.

In December 1844, Mangas Coloradas called a council and local
groups gathered in the Chiricahua and lower Peloncillo mountains to
plan a campaign against Sonora. The goal was captives, perhaps to
trade for those held by Sonora.[53] Reports in early 1845 revealed that
Apache bands raided deep into Mexico. *Revista Oficial,* the state
newspaper of Chihuahua, reported that "peace was enjoyed for
thirty-one months, war now exists."[54]

In May 1845, Chihuahua scored an important triumph against the
Chokonens living in northeastern Sonora. On May 8 a small raiding
party pilfered 117 cattle from Corralitos; fifteen days later, Apaches
ran off some oxen there. On May 28 they audaciously entered the
corral at the Barranco mines and drove away twenty-three horses.
Ensign José Baltazar Padilla, an experienced Indian fighter, with
twenty-seven troops and fifty-two citizens, left in pursuit. Padilla
followed the trail northwest to the Espuelas Mountains in extreme
northeastern Sonora, where he found a large Chokonen ranchería
estimated to have a hundred warriors. On June 1 he surprised the
Indians and after three days of hard fighting finally withdrew, having
suffered four soldiers killed and nine people, five of them citizens,
wounded. His force killed fourteen Indians and captured a woman
and a child. Whether Cochise was present is not known, but in view
of events that followed, there is little doubt that he was in the area.[55]

The Indians moved north into the Chiricahuas and decided to solicit peace with Chihuahua. Accordingly, on June 30, 1845, there
appeared at Janos three Chokonens sent by Yrigóllen. Manuelito,
Naque, and Matías (the sons of Yrigóllen and Matías were leaders in
Cochise's band in the 1860s). Nothing definitive came of the talks at
the time, but six months later the Chiricahuas resumed negotiations
with Chihuahua, which seemed anxious to explore their proposals.[56]

The pattern of peace, uprisings, and war countered by Mexican

campaigns and Chiricahua submissiveness seems difficult to comprehend, yet an examination of previous relations reveals that the
Indians had lived peacefully and somewhat prosperously under the
presidio system. A whole generation of Chiricahuas matured in it,
and many of their leaders (Relles, Matías, Teboca, Yrigóllen) recognized the benefits of living at peace. The Chiricahuas were not an
agricultural people, and their many years of close Mexican contact
had left them somewhat dependent on the border towns and northern
presidios for trade, whether for arms, ammunition, liquor, or food.
In addition, they may have heard rumors of Chihuahua's intent to
recall Kirker, which was done in early 1846.

The Chokonens and Nednhis feared Kirker, recalling all too viv-
idly his activities in the late 1830s and early 1840s. Therefore, in
the spring of 1846, further peace gestures were made, with the entire Chokonen band apparently involved. According to one account,
Cochise probably had a hand in these events, which would irrevocably alienate the Chokonen band for many years to come. Discussions began on May 25 with a meeting between Relles and the commander of the San Buenaventura presidio, Ensign Carlos Cásares, a
sincere, sensitive, and idealistic officer sympathetic to the Apaches'
plight. Cásares, who saw it as an extraordinarily challenging assignment, held initial talks with Relles, Vicente, and Francisquillo.
They claimed that Chato, Maturán, and Láceris[57] (a Nednhi leader
coming into prominence) shared the same feelings but were apprehensive about coming in, probably because of Kirker's recent
activities.[58]

More Chiricahuas came to San Buenaventura on June 12, led by
Láceris and Carro,[59] an emerging leader in Cochise's local group.
They acknowledged that Janos had been their former establishment
but now they wished to settle at Casas Grandes. Two days later José
Chato and his band of fifteen warriors made peace, even though
Cásares noted that "it is well known that they have committed serious depredations in Namiquipa." Yet Cásares wished to forget the
past and was willing to give peace another try. His sincerity and
understanding imbued the Chiricahuas with trust, and they placed
confidence in what he said. He adamantly refused to issue any rations until the Chiricahuas released every one of their captives. On

June 22, Vicente brought in a captive from Namiquipa; Aceves and Esquiriba had other prisoners they agreed to bring in. Cásares's uncompromising policy had paid dividends.[60]

On June 24 he wrote the commanding general of Chihuahua about the Chiricahuas:

> It is necessary to treat the Indians with gentleness and prudence, never lacking in both. It is also necessary to sustain them and that they comply religiously with the rules, at the same time punishing vigorously those who continue hostilities.

He was much concerned about an issue which was ever present in Apache-Mexican relations but usually not addressed: Apaches trading stock and rations to citizens for liquor and arms. Unlike other commanders, who tacitly condoned and ignored this practice (and reaped some of its rewards), Cásares wrote that he planned to "cut off this pernicious abuse and to establish laws necessary for the public welfare." Unfortunately for both him and the Apaches, his honorable intentions remained unfulfilled.[61]

On June 26, 1846, two days after Cásares wrote the commanding general, James Kirker and twenty-five men left Chihuahua City with the permission of Governor José María Irigoyen, whose instructions, or lack of them, virtually gave Kirker a free hand when operating against hostile Apaches. Irigoyen diplomatically wrote the commanding general at Coyame to solicit his approval; animosity between Kirker and the military had resurfaced, and Irigoyen wished to avoid problems. The commanding general, who was receiving reports from Ensign Cásares about the prospects for peace, concurred with the governor's actions but prudently attached important conditions concerning Kirker's mission:

> [This] operation should be left to the free will of those conducting them. However, I do require that these [parties] do not trample on the law nor kill pacified Indians nor accept foreigners in their ranks.

On July 6 the governor's secretary forwarded a copy to Kirker, but by the time Kirker received it (if indeed he did) irreparable harm had been done.[62]

Kirker hustled up his own fighting force as he moved north. His march began innocuously enough, covering fifty miles northwest to Encinillas, where he picked up forty-nine volunteers. On June 29 he found sixteen dead cattle butchered by Apaches whose trail, according to him, led to Galeana. The next day, thirty-three volunteers deserted because Kirker could not pay them.

On July 1, instead of heading for Galeana, Kirker continued due north to Carrizal. Two days later he moved east, following a hostile trail (or so he claimed) which led to Apache rancherías near Galeana. On July 5 the clandestine plan began to come together. Kirker sent messengers to Juan Ortiz at Galeana and subprefect Manuel de La Riva, who told Kirker the people of his district and those from Janos had decided to attack the Indians living at Galeana because of recent depredations and murders. Early on the morning of July 6, José Ponce arrived at Riva's home and declared that he had killed eighteen Indians at San Buenaventura, thus breaking the truce. This news was music to Kirker's ears. He asserted that they would all "perish at the hands of the ten chiefs with their hordes of warriors" unless the allied Mexicans took action. In an obvious exaggeration, he said "it was kill or be killed . . . more than one hundred times had the Indians been treasonous to us." These statements were pure rationalization, fabricated to justify his own conduct. Consequently, Kirker's forty-four men joined José Morales and some citizens from Janos under José María Zuloaga and set out to kill as many Indians as possible.[63]

It was a double-cross as far as the Chiricahuas were concerned, one of the most egregious deeds ever carried out against them—far worse than Johnson's slaying of Juan José Compá some nine years earlier. Kirker's dispassionate report on the affair lacked details, as did Cásares's emotional account of July 7, but George Frederick Ruxton visited Chihuahua City a few months later and saw Apache scalps on display. He left behind an account which corroborated the Apache recollections of Jason Betzinez and Mangas Coloradas. All three versions agree that the Apaches were invited to a feast and came, under the protection of a treaty, to Galeana. Mescal or whiskey flowed freely that night, Ruxton writing that Kirker was the supplier (though this seems unlikely), so that by the early morning "nearly everyone was lying in a drunken stupor," according to

Apache accounts. That morning Kirker and his compatriots, in cahoots with the citizens of Galeana, killed the inebriated Chiricahuas in their sleep. Virtually all were slaughtered, and their scalps were mounted on poles. In referring to the incident, Mangas Coloradas said that "my people drank and became intoxicated, and were lying asleep, when a party of Mexicans came in and beat out their brains with clubs." Reportedly, 130 Chiricahuas, consisting of Chokonens and Nednhis, were murdered by Kirker's party.[64]

On July 7 a distraught Cásares wrote a letter stating that Kirker, together with citizens from Galeana, Casas Grandes, and San Buenaventura, had surprised and attacked the Apaches, killing 130 without regard for sex or age. He disputed Kirker's claim that the Chiricahuas had committed a robbery at Encinillas which the Apaches claimed was committed by another band. Cásares predicted correctly that the affair would have "far reaching ramifications. . . . All hope for peace is gone." The Apaches, he warned, would take revenge.[65]

Kirker's deed influenced Chiricahua-Mexican relations for several years. Most of the Indians killed seem to have been Chokonens from the bands of Yrigóllen, who lost family members; Carro; and Relles, who was a victim of the slaughter. The Nednhi band, made up of Láceris's Janeros and Francisquillo's Carrizalleños, also suffered losses but not as severe as those of Cochise's people. James Hobbs, who was present, wrote that Cochise was involved and he may have been, given the circumstances.[66]

The double-cross at Galeana, as the Chokonens remembered it, left indelible impressions on Cochise. He may have lost family members, perhaps even his father, who reportedly perished in the same manner as those at Galeana. Undoubtedly it intensified his hatred of Mexicans, and after this he became increasingly aloof to whites, taking his cue from the militant Chiricahuas under Miguel Narbona and Mangas Coloradas.

The Chiricahuas remembered the affair as perhaps the most revolting attack in the annals of Apache-Mexican relations. More than a hundred years later Jason Betzinez referred to it as the "ghastly butchering of our families" and one of the "bloodiest conflicts in which Apaches were ever involved."[67] It would be remembered forever, and its aftermath was predictable. Kirker had in fact laid the foundation for war because all of those Apache losses had to be avenged.

The Chiricahuas took their revenge that fall. According to Betzinez,

> the chiefs considered for a long time the action which they should take to pay back the Mexicans . . . the desire for vengeance burned more fiercely as the days and weeks passed. Finally Baishan [Cuchillo Negro] . . . called a council of the chiefs of several bands. Among those who responded were Cochise, Chief of the Chiricahuas [and] Mangas Coloradas . . . and others whose names I do not recall.

The war party, which consisted of 175 warriors and several novices, started out in late fall 1846. Although there is no corroborating evidence, Betzinez says the Chiricahuas attacked Galeana (he confused Galeana with Ramos, a deserted hacienda near Janos), occupied the town, and killed many of its occupants. "Those who increased their reputations in the battle," he writes, "were Cochise, Mangas Coloradas, Benito and Geronimo."[68] Cochise undoubtedly would have participated in an expedition of this nature, although not as leader of his band; he would have followed Yrigóllen, Tapilá, and Miguel Narbona. By now, though, he had become a leader in his local group.

Chapter 4

GALEANA AVENGED

Besides having to confront the Chiricahuas, who were "all stirred up" by the Kirker massacre, in late 1846, Mexico was forced to focus on another enemy: the expansionist Yankees from the north. Fighting between the two countries had erupted on April 25, and the following month Congress declared war on Mexico.

It was not until Brigadier General Stephen Watts Kearny[1] and his Army of the West occupied Santa Fe on August 18 that Sonoran and Chihuahuan officials became cognizant of the American threat. In September, after establishing a government at Santa Fe, Kearny and three hundred men set out to take California. Guided by the consummate scout and mountain man Kit Carson, Kearny cut his route through Apache country. By October his force had been reduced to one hundred men because he sent two-thirds of his command back to Santa Fe when he was informed that California had been taken by John Charles Frémont. He met Mangas Coloradas and other Chiricahua leaders when he arrived at Santa Rita del Cobre, where one of the chiefs went so far as to offer his services against the contemptible Mexicans. Kearny's mission, however, was to reach California, so he continued on the Gila Trail, ignored Tucson and its detachment of Mexican troops, and proceeded to California.[2]

Kearny's expedition was soon followed by the fastidious Captain Philip St. George Cooke[3] and his Mormon Battalion of 340 men, which had left Santa Fe on September 19. Guided by two experi-

enced scouts, Pauline Weaver[4] and Antoine Leroux,[5] Cooke's men
forged a new route, one which would be followed by many overland
travelers in the 1840s and early 1850s until the more direct route via
Apache Pass became known. His force, which actually trespassed
into northern Mexico, greatly alarmed Sonora's leaders, especially
when irrefutable evidence indicated that the Americans and Chiricahuas had made peaceful contact. Rumors of a potential Apache-
Anglo alliance left Sonorans aghast, although this was a remote possibility. Not only did the Chiricahuas distrust the Americans, but the
latter were intent on reaching California and had no interest in ally-
ing themselves with the wild Apaches, whom they viewed with
contempt.

Cooke's command encamped at the deserted San Bernardino
ranch on December 2. The Chokonens were wary and had to be persuaded to come in. A few days earlier, he had assured the Chokonen
chief Manuelito[6] that "the men he called Americans, and who led
the Mexicans to war against the Apache, were men who had run off
from their own country and become Mexicans," an obvious reference to Kirker and Johnson. With these consolations, Manuelito
brought "a superior chief and several others" in from the mountains
to meet Cooke. The superior chief was probably either Yrigóllen or
Miguel Narbona. For many, perhaps Cochise, this was their first
look at American soldiers. Cooke explained his intentions and
offered to trade for mules. Noted for his discipline and organization,
the officer was unimpressed with the Chokonens:

> They are poor, dirty Indians, but are generally dressed in cotton
> shirts and many in trousers. They have fine moccasins, which have
> boot tops. They ride fine horses, which they prefer to mules, and are
> armed with very formidable-looking lances [and] with guns and
> bows. They are ugly and squalid, [and] wear their hair generally long
> and in various fashions. They wear a kind of leather skullcap, now
> and then ornamented with feathers and chinpieces. They seem to
> understand Spanish.[7]

A few days later the Americans continued west toward Tucson and
occupied the town on December 17 (the Mexican troops had temporarily withdrawn). After a short stay Cooke marched to California,
having left a letter at Tucson for Governor Gándara suggesting that
the two countries join forces to fight Apaches.[8]

With the war going on, the Apaches focused their attention on Mexico and, according to Hubert Howe Bancroft, "caused great distress. More settlements were destroyed and even the suburbs of Ures were assailed."[9] Reports from the frontier bespoke a deteriorating military situation, one which would continue for the remainder of the decade. For the most part, Chiricahua raiders enjoyed a wide selection of targets with relative impunity. Cochise, following the lead of his local-group leader, the warlike Miguel Narbona, was certainly in the middle of it all.

Little is known of Miguel Narbona's early life. In fact, Chiricahua informants of Mrs. Eve Ball knew nothing about him; in addition, the sparse oral history available from the Apache perspective does not mention him. The reason seems twofold. First, Miguel Narbona died about 1856, before Anglo entrenchment in southern Arizona, so he was virtually unknown to Americans. Second, and just as important, was the fact that Apache death taboos prohibited mention of the deceased by name.

Fortunately, Merejildo Grijalva, a captive of Miguel Narbona, has shed some light on this intriguing chief with whom Cochise was so closely associated. According to Merejildo, Miguel was captured as a young boy by Mexican troops under Captain Antonio Narbona, Senior, from whom he took his surname. Miguel remained with the Narbona family for almost a decade, becoming educated and Christianized. At the age of eighteen he escaped and rejoined his people. By this time, for some inexplicable reason, he had developed a fierce, lifelong hatred of Mexicans. According to Merejildo, his "daring and prowess won him high position in his band." His insatiable desire for Mexican blood apparently was the result of his years in captivity and subsequent Mexican acts of betrayal upon his people. He was the one Chiricahua leader not involved in any peace discussions after the Kirker massacre. Yrigóllen was the principal Chokonen leader of the late 1840s and early 1850s; the war leader, however, was Miguel Narbona, whose bellicose, intractable personality dominated the militant Chokonens. Wherever Yrigóllen was, Miguel Narbona usually could be found; likewise, wherever Miguel Narbona was, Cochise usually could be found.[10]

In early March 1847 a large Chokonen-Nednhi war party under Miguel Narbona, Yrigóllen, Teboca, Esquinaline, and Láceris surprised twenty Mexicans some four miles southwest of Fronteras. Within minutes the attackers had killed fourteen men and captured two others, including Corporal Juan Chacon. Relief parties from Fronteras and Cuquiarachi were dispatched, with Antonio Narbona riding at the head of the latter group. An interesting confrontation must have occurred when Narbona parleyed with an Indian who told him that the Chokonens might attack Fronteras.[11] The Indians continued into the interior for further depredations. Upon their return north, near Bacoachi, they happened across eleven persons, five men and six boys, whom they waylaid, killing ten of them. Once again they had avenged the Galeana double-cross.[12]

In early April the Chokonens reappeared at Fronteras. On April 5 several Indians led by Yrigóllen, some carrying white flags, appeared suddenly in the hills east of the presidio. Deciderio Escalante, Antonio Narbona, and Captain Mateo Calvo y Muro cautiously went out and parleyed with Yrigóllen, who claimed that every Chokonen leader favored peace. In the light of recent raids, this statement puzzled Escalante. Nonetheless, he communicated their wishes to the governor, but in reality he favored military action, not amelioration of relations. Nevertheless, Elías González was ordered to open negotiations.[13]

The Apache-wise officer arrived at Fronteras in late April. After several councils he finally deduced why the Indians had requested peace: from their contact with the whites, several Chokonens had contracted measles and the disease had infested the band. The prospects of Sonoran retaliation at this time disturbed the Indians. Elías González had no qualms about killing Apaches (witness the eighty men, women, and children killed at Janos and Corralitos in August 1844), but in his words, "considering the present difficulties and the circumstances in which we find ourselves, it seems prudent to me to concede it." Like all Mexicans, he dreaded the prospects of an Apache-American alliance.[14]

The truce was short lived. Apparently some of the Chokonens became healthy because they soon resumed hostilities. First they raided Fronteras, then Cuquiarachi, where they seriously wounded one person and captured a young boy.[15] From there they vanished into the Chiricahuas, where they camped during the summer of 1847, safe from a Sonora still occupied by the American threat. In fact, for the rest of 1847, Chiricahua bands do not seem to have caused much mischief. The Chokonens were relatively quiet, perhaps recuperating from the measle epidemic and deliberately avoiding northern Sonora, where troops had been concentrated in anticipation of an American invasion.[16]

That fall Sonora mounted two expeditions against the Chiricahuas. Although the results were less than spectacular, they stirred up the hornets again just the same. In September, Antonio Narbona swung out of Fronteras at the head of a mixed force of 120 cavalry and infantry. Six days later, on September 13, his force camped at Apache Pass and the following day discovered and ransacked a deserted ranchería, probably in what is known today as Goodwin Canyon. The next day, scouts found another ranchería and four freshly butchered cattle, indicating that the Chokonens were near. Narbona's suspicions were confirmed when his men discovered an Indian woman hidden in the rocks. Frustrated that their prey had eluded them, the Mexicans dispassionately murdered her. Given the Chokonens' actions of the previous spring, where they had showed no mercy, it was a decision that Narbona could justify, yet he himself would eventually pay the price.

Later that same day, several Chokonen chiefs, including Miguel Narbona, shouted at Antonio Narbona from the mountains that they wanted peace and would meet the Mexicans early that evening at San Jacinto Springs, evidently somewhere in the Chiricahuas. Needless to say, the Chokonens reneged on their promise, and Narbona's party returned to Cuquiarachi on September 22. Although Narbona conceded that the results of his scout were disappointing, he commended his men for a good performance. The senseless killing of the Indian woman, however, was a blunder and could have been avoided. Shortly after Narbona's campaign, another Sonoran expedition from Moctezuma captured several members of Yrigóllen's family. These two scouts provided the incentive for a Chokonen response.[17]

In December 1847 the Chokonens had their revenge and their plan worked exactly as designed. Their objective was to wipe out Cuquiarachi and get even with their longtime adversary Antonio Narbona. Cuquiarachi, founded in 1654, was a small village a few miles southwest of Fronteras. Bartlett passed through it a few years later and wrote that the fields "skirted the roads, the rows of pomegranate trees in full bloom, and the orchards of peach, pear and mulberry, all betokened a high state of cultivation." For days the Chiricahuas harassed the town, brazenly threatening Narbona's life. Finally, on December 23, they stormed the village and overwhelmed its residents. Narbona fought gamely but was slain on the porch of his house. Before the assault ended, seven more men and six women had perished and six children had been captured. All of Sonora mourned Narbona's death, but the surviving citizens of Cuquiarachi were especially devastated. Their spirits drained and their will gone, six weeks later they took what possessions they could carry and left Cuquiarachi to the Apaches and the snakes.[18]

About the time Cuquiarachi was being abandoned, a large war party composed of Chokonens, Chihennes, and possibly some White Mountain Western Apaches united for an expedition into Sonora. Their target was the small town of Chinapa, like Cuquiarachi a mission settlement established in 1648. Apaches had raided frequently in recent years, but this time they intended to clean it out, according to the testimony of Manuel Bernal, who was captured during the raid but escaped shortly thereafter. On February 18, 1848, the Apaches surprised Chinapa and burned it to the ground, killing twelve Mexicans, wounding six, and capturing an astonishing forty-two people, mainly women and children.

Miguel Narbona led the Chokonen faction and boasted of recent raids into Chihuahua, indicating that he and most likely Cochise were active there. According to Bernal, the Indians were "all stirred up" by the massacre at Galeana and "would find a way to get revenge." Furthermore, the Apaches were angry because of Sonora's campaign the previous fall (the attack on Yrigóllen's camp). Yrigóllen, whose ranchería was tucked away in the Chiricahuas, planned to exchange the Chinapa captives for his relatives. Initially, Bacoachi officials were uncertain about Bernal's testimony, primarily because Apaches normally did not take adult male prisoners; usually, torture or death was their fate.[19]

In June 1848 there occurred an incident that had lifelong ramifications for Cochise. On June 20 some Mexicans were herding cattle near Turicachi, some fifteen miles south of Fronteras, when they espied a band of Apaches driving a large herd of horses and cattle.

Miguel Narbona and Cochise were returning from a raid when the Sonorans turned the tables and ambushed the unsuspecting Indians, killing two and wounding several others. Three Mexicans were wounded slightly. Next morning the Chokonens, under Cochise and Miguel Narbona, appeared in force at Fronteras; they surrounded and captured five citizens at the *ciénaga* near the presidio. The sentinel at the top of the church saw a cloud of dust and sounded the alarm. Two parties were dispatched, the first consisting of eight citizens and the second, under Eusebio Gil Samaniego,[20] numbering fifteen. When the whites reached the scene, the Chokonens defiantly stood their ground. Soon after, the two old adversaries parleyed. Miguel Narbona, Cochise, and a few other warriors represented the Chiricahuas; Samaniego, with an equal number of citizens, represented the whites. The Apaches ransomed their five captives, although what Samaniego gave in return was not mentioned. Next the

Fronteras, Sonora. Ruins of the presidio where Cochise was imprisoned in 1848. (*Photo by Dan Thrapp*)

inevitable skirmish occurred, probably initiated by the Chiricahuas, seeking to avenge their fatalities of the previous day. In any event, an Indian identified as Negrito Cucchisle (Cochise) was somehow captured and "put in irons and shackled." A blast from the presidio's cannon wounded Miguel Narbona, killed his horse, and put the rest of the Indians to flight.[21]

The evidence points to Cochise as the individual who was captured. First of all, Fronteras, located within the lower limits of Chokonen territory, was a place he frequented regularly throughout his life. Further support comes from the identification of Miguel Narbona, whom Cochise succeeded as chief of the Central Chiricahuas, or Chokonens. In addition, the captive's immense status within his band was revealed when the Indians subsequently exchanged eleven Mexicans to obtain his release. Finally, the definite reference to a *capitancillo,* meaning "little chief" or "subchief," Cochise's position at this time, plus the specific reference to Cucchisle, leaves me to conclude that the captured Chokonen was indeed Cochise. He remained a prisoner for some six weeks, during which time his feelings toward Mexicans became more acrimonious.

The next six weeks were tense for Fronteras residents. Shortly after the skirmish with Miguel Narbona, Captain Calvo y Muro wrote Gándara about the lamentable state of affairs there. The Chokonens, cognizant of the small garrison, had established their rancherías within five miles of the presidio. Their intent, Calvo y Muro thought, "was to watch over everything and every person who passes from here" in order to take captives to exchange for Cochise. Furthermore, his men, inadequately fed and scantily clothed, were constantly on the alert. As a result, morale had deteriorated to a dangerously low level. Of his fifty-six men, eight were on detached duty at Ures, two were mail carriers between Fronteras and Bavispe, eight were sick, and seven were in the guardhouse. This left but thirty-one men for scout duty and other necessary tasks. For this reason, twenty-five troops from Bacoachi were ordered to reinforce Fronteras and a load of provisions and fifty firearms were sent, probably from Bavispe.[22]

The Chokonen siege of Fronteras continued throughout July 1848. Citizens feared to work their fields, and small parties dared not venture from the safety of the fort. In late July, Miguel Narbona, looking for a chance to take prisoners, turned the screws even tighter, moving his camp to within one mile of Fronteras. No supplies were coming to or leaving the fort, and by August 7 the inhabitants had been reduced to eating tortillas, the only food available. Finally Calvo y Muro allowed a party of twenty-three soldiers and citizens to leave the presidio to obtain provisions. Miguel Narbona and Posito Moraga were ready. They allowed the whites to reach Cuchuta before surrounding them and killing or capturing everyone except Jesús Escalante, who was wounded and escaped to Fronteras.

In response, Captain Calvo y Muro reluctantly dispatched a relief party to Cuchuta, where they spotted the Apaches. José Yescas, a soldier who was trusted by the Chiricahuas, conversed with Chino, who said Posito Moraga would bring Corporal Serapio Olguin, four soldiers, and six civilians to exchange for Cochise. The deal was done on August 11. Never again would Cochise allow himself to be taken.[23]

While the ransom negotiations were taking place, a force of troops under Ensign Saturniño Limon[24] entered Fronteras under cover of darkness, hoping to surprise the Indian rancherías in the vicinity. He departed August 13 and was beset with trouble immediately. For almost a week his force scouted the Embudos and other mountain ranges, but the slow-moving troops were no match for the nimble Chiricahuas. Running short of provisions, Limon returned to his supply train at Batepito, planning to provision his force before sweeping north into the Chiricahuas, where the Indians were thought to have gone.

Again he seemed hampered at every turn. At Batepito, hungry national troops had plundered the supply train. Next they decided to mutiny and refused to continue, and if that wasn't enough, Limon received more startling news: the inhabitants of Fronteras had abandoned the presidio for Bacoachi. Completely frustrated, he blamed the fiasco on the people of Fronteras, charging that they had warned the Apaches of his campaign, but this, of course, was an oversimplification. In reality, the constant Chokonen presence during the summer of 1848 compelled the citizens to conclude that prospects at Bacoachi had to be better than their precarious existence at

Fronteras.[25] So it was that the Chiricahua siege, implemented primarily because of Cochise's imprisonment, forced the shutdown of Sonora's oldest presidio.

West of Fronteras at the presidio of Santa Cruz, conditions had reached a similar and equally critical stage. Summer Indian raids had terrorized the neighborhood, and on September 8, Apaches assailed the town, stole seventy cattle, and killed ten horses and three mules. The military commander warned that his presidio would suffer the same fate as Fronteras unless more troops and provisions arrived. Indeed, several men had deserted because of the deplorable conditions.[26]

Governor Gándara did not recognize the plight of the northern frontier until Fronteras was abandoned. Two months earlier, the minister of war and navy in Mexico City had requested information about the Apache problem. Ignoring the realities of the situation, Gándara responded with idealistic optimism, which the situation certainly did not warrant. He contended that if Sonora's six presidios were adequately equipped, fully garrisoned, and led by competent officers, the Apaches would be subjugated within three months. Just in case this was not accomplished, he diplomatically added that victory could be achieved only if the Apaches "don't find protection on the other side of the Gila," territory ceded to the victorious United States in 1848. In truth, Gándara neglected the fact that, for the most part, the Chokonens had remained south of the Gila and within his jurisdiction throughout the 1840s.[27] Yet the governor's viewpoint found unexpected support in Mexico City. Mariano Arista, secretary of war and navy, shared Gándara's beliefs. He proposed a string of forts and settlements across the northern frontier; however, when drawing up his plans, he failed to consider the Apaches' complete domination of northern Sonora and Chihuahua.[28]

Gándara's report evidently evoked a response from Mexico City because the November 3, 1848, issue of *El Sonorense* announced that the indefatigable and incomparable José Mária Elías González had been named the military inspector of Sonora. "This is proof that the Supreme Government has not viewed with indifference the horror in Sonora", editorialized *El Sonorense*.[29]

The Chiricahuas scored another important victory only a few

weeks after Elías González assumed command. In mid-November, Chino appeared at Bacoachi and said a contingent of warriors would come in to make peace. The Chokonens had no intention of return-ing (they distrusted Captain Calvo y Muro), and Chino's visit was simply to gather military intelligence and trade for whiskey. A few weeks later, Calvo y Muro did scout Turicachi, but the Indians were believed to have moved into the Peloncillos or Chiricahuas.[30]

As Calvo y Muro had surmised, the Chokonens had moved north, hiding their families in the Chiricahuas before heading west against their next target, the presidio of Tubac, which at this time consisted "of a collection of dilapidated buildings and huts."[31] Apparently the presidio was not garrisoned, the townspeople relying on Santa Cruz and Tucson for protection. On December 9 the war party struck, killed nine citizens, and created so much terror that the remain-ing occupants abandoned the town. The majority relocated to San Xavier, others to Tucson, some to El Soni, while the remainder marched to California with some of Tucson's citizens.[32] Elías González was furious when he heard the news and on January 23 ordered Captain Antonio Comadurán to send twenty soldiers to re-occupy Tubac. Comadurán cautiously demurred, informing his rela-tive that Tubac's population had scattered and that those who had remained in the vicinity were too frightened to return. Furthermore, when news of the orders leaked to his soldiers stationed at Tucson, eight men deserted rather than regarrison the abandoned presidio. Comadurán concluded his argument by depicting Tucson's current state: it lacked food, morale had hit rock bottom, and everyone was afraid the Indians might attack Tucson itself.[33]

By the end of 1848 the Chiricahua Apaches had made the resi-dents of northern Sonora their tenants, extracting rent in subsidies of horses and cattle. When these began to diminish, they convinced their residents that voluntary eviction was better than starvation and death. Meanwhile, optimistic Mexican officials believed that Apache incursions had reached their highest level. They hoped that Elías González's experience and leadership, combined with more federal assistance, would enable Sonora to recapture some of its lost pride and territory.

Besides the Chiricahuas, Elías González had another problem: the lure of gold in California was draining the state of troops and men. The adventurers absconded with many of the government weapons intended for use against the hostiles, and many left their dependents behind; now they were more exposed to Apache raids than ever before.[34] From Tucson in January 1849, Captain Comadurán speculated that the fear of Apaches and the lure of gold in California could cause the total collapse of the frontier settlements.[35]

The spring of 1849 was active for Cochise's people. Although he was not specifically mentioned, his band leader, Miguel Narbona, and Mangas Coloradas were prominent in the region, and almost certainly Cochise enhanced his reputation as an up-and-coming war leader. In March 1849, Miguel Narbona led a Chiricahua war party against the small mining town of Banamichi, situated on the Sonora River some five miles north of Huepac. On March 9 shortly before the noon siesta, an estimated one hundred warriors assaulted the Feliz ranch, which was about a mile from Banamichi. The men were spread out and going about their normal duties when the Indians attacked the ranch, which was populated "by honest and hard working families." Within minutes, in the words of an eyewitness, "all of the people of the ranch were killed," captured, or wounded. It was Chinapa revisited. The Apaches killed seven men and two women and wounded five men. The remaining ten women and four men were captured, along with several small children, including Marijenia Figueira, who was liberated by American troops fifteen years later.[36] The Chiricahuas set fire to the ranch and the surrounding houses.

One mile away the justice of the peace at Banamichi helplessly surmised that "there were some casualties because the savages had burned the houses." Nonetheless, he was unable to send out a scouting party because a few weeks earlier most of the men, some thirty in all, had rushed to the California gold fields, and those who remained were aghast at the thought of encountering Indians. Therefore he sent a frantic note to the prefect of Ures, who in turn dispatched National Guard troops under Rafael Buelna to investigate. By the time Buelna arrived, the Chiricahuas had rounded up their captives and were headed north along the Sonora River, killing two more people and capturing two others at Motopori, five miles north of Banamichi. Later the same day the war party passed near Sinoquipe, but authorities there were helpless; their people lacked arms, provisions, and the heart to go out after "*los Apaches barbaros.*"[37]

Miguel was not finished. His captivity had left him with deep antipathy toward Sonorans; he was the most belligerent, the most incorrigible, and the cruelest among a people noted for ruthlessness toward their enemies. He killed to supply his seemingly insatiable desire for Mexican blood; perhaps he actually believed that the Chiricahuas could drive the Mexicans from northern Sonora. He became obsessed with this thought as the victories, beginning with Cuquiarachi in December 1847 and continuing with Chinapa in February 1848, Fronteras in August 1848, and Tubac in December 1848, continued to accumulate. Without a doubt, he was the most feared Chokonen war leader during the 1840s and early 1850s.

As for Sonora, never was vigorous remedy more urgent, but the ailing government lacked that capacity. In April the Chiricahuas made plans to attack two of Sonora's remaining northern presidios. On April 8 one hundred mounted warriors surprised Bavispe, killing four adults, capturing four children, and burning the surrounding fields.[38] Three weeks later Miguel Narbona, Yrigóllen, Posito Moraga, and Teboquita raided Santa Cruz, whose population of two or three hundred individuals scarcely ventured outside the presidio's walls except in large numbers. A large body of hostiles suddenly appeared north of the town early on Sunday, April 29. The Indians nearly surrounded one family, but prompt response from the congregated citizens drove them away. The next day, two parties of brave citizens left the presidio to work their fields, each a few miles away, one to the north and the other to the south. The Chiricahuas lay waiting and within minutes seven hard-working men lay dead. Saturniño Limon immediately dispatched two parties of ten men, one under Corporal Dionicio Aldecoa and the other under Juan Abad Telles,[39] with instructions to march to the river and aid their neighbors. With the relief party at the scene, the Chokonens withdrew, having carried away most of the town's stock. Afterward, Limon wrote that "more than eighteen men with their families have prepared to emigrate for the interior and the rest of them are searching for their stock. For your consideration I must say to you that circumstances are critical with respect to this garrison."[40]

As the Chokonens returned to their rancherías in northeast
Sonora, José Terán y Tato, whose brother had recently been killed
by Apaches, left Moctezuma with a force of 118 men and one piece
of artillery. Marching north, his command was augmented by 70
men from the towns along the way. On May 10 he arrived at Bavispe
and three days later departed for the Pitaicache Mountains, about
twenty-five miles east of Fronteras. Near here, at Rusballo, he surprised a small encampment (actually an extended family camp) and
killed or captured the entire group. Eusebio Gil Samaniego, who
had participated in the capture of Cochise, lanced to death San Juan,
a notorious warrior, and another man and captured nine Indians.
The prisoners revealed that they were part of Yrigóllen's band and
were en route to Janos to trade. They also disclosed that other
rancherías were in the Enmedio Mountains and that Mangas Coloradas was thought to be either in the Chiricahua or Florida ranges.
Yrigóllen and Miguel Narbona were camped along the San Bernardino River. Cochise, we can assume, was with Mangas or Miguel
Narbona.[41]

The Chokonens retaliated quickly. Six days later Yrigóllen, Miguel Narbona, and Tapilá raided Bacoachi, wounded two people,
and captured four children. Captain Teodoro de Aros with thirty
troops and citizens pursued them west for a few miles, and then the
Indians counterattacked, killing two soldiers and two citizens and
capturing one soldier (Julian Romero) and one citizen (Félix Montoya). After the fight the Apaches raised a white bandanna. Captain
de Aros and three men parleyed with Yrigóllen, Casimiro, and a few
others. He tried to persuade the Indians to release their six prisoners, but they refused, instead promising to return within three
weeks to exchange captives. The Mexicans returned to Bacoachi,
and the Chiricahuas marched victoriously north toward Bavispe,
planning to exchange captives.[42]

Ten days later the Indians appeared at Bavispe, where they presumed that their relatives captured by Terán y Tato were held. The
Chokonen leaders announced that they had prisoners to exchange,
but because only one Indian was held at Bavispe the Apaches relinquished only one captive named Francisco Duran. The commander,
probably Captain Reyes Cruz, may have made some promises be-

cause the Chiricahuas said they would return within twenty days to exchange more prisoners, the same yarn given Captain de Aros at Bacoachi. This time they appeared as promised but in a fighting mood. At sunrise on June 22 one hundred mounted warriors stormed the presidio, killing one old man, severely wounding another, and carrying off a young boy. They fled north and then broke east into Chihuahua. Despite the few casualties, the Chokonens achieved their objective. With Tubac and Fronteras deserted and morale at Santa Cruz deteriorating, the residents of Bavispe may also have considered abandonment. According to Bavispe's commander, the Apaches' presence had forced the people "to live in constant fear." [43]

Meanwhile, throughout the winter and spring of 1849, Elías González was occupied with drawing up plans to counteract the Apaches' victories. He envisioned a grand Sonoran offensive that would march into Apachería and take war to the hostiles. He certainly had the support of most Sonorans as they rallied behind their popular leader. Local prefects, judges, and ministers pledged money, mounts, supplies, and volunteers for the campaign, which was scheduled to begin in September. [44]

Before those plans could be put in motion, Elías González concentrated on regaining a foothold in northern Sonora. In May he announced his intent to regarrison Fronteras and after that Tubac; if possible, he hoped to coordinate the offensive with Chihuahua. That summer he transferred a troop from Altar to Tucson, sent 50 infantry from the Fronteras company (stationed at Bacoachi) to Tucson, and placed the troops at Santa Cruz under Captain Comadurán. Elías González explained clearly to Comadurán that his primary objective, besides killing Apaches, was to regarrison Tubac. Comadurán's campaign was to occur about the same time Captain de Aros and 118 troops scouted the mountains near Fronteras. [45]

Elías González's much-talked-about offensive was launched from Bacoachi on September 23, 1849. Dividing his force into three divisions, he took one force, which would enter present-day southwest Cochise County, Arizona, and scouted the ranges in that area; Captain Agustín Moreno with 80 troops and the supply train would journey northeast and establish a base camp at Sarampion in the Peloncillos; José Terán y Tato took the third branch of 130 national troops, which would reconnoiter the mountains in northeast Sonora before going to Sarampion at the end of September.

None of these forces enjoyed a particularly auspicious beginning. Elías González's command was plagued with problems. Twelve soldiers deserted within the first four days, and fourteen were left behind at Santa Cruz because of sickness. From the hacienda de San Pedro, his troops marched northeast toward the Chiricahua Mountains, arriving there on September 27 in a driving rainstorm. The next day, twenty-seven men came down with a fever, although one has to suspect that some of these illnesses may have been induced by the prospect of meeting Apaches. On September 29 they reached Apache Pass and found a deserted ranchería, which they thought had been abandoned since the previous July. Still no Apaches were seen; consequently, Elías González decided to suspend operations and join the supply train. He cut through Apache Pass and proceeded south along the eastern face of the Chiricahuas, arriving at Sarampion on October 1.

The pack train was nowhere in sight. The commander waited for a day, then broke camp, taking the route by which the supply train should have come. At San Bernardino he met an American wagon train en route to California via Cooke's route. The Americans told the officer they had seen Apaches along the Mimbres but none since that time. Finally, on October 5, Elías González's command crossed the present-day boundary and stumbled onto Captain Moreno's supply train near the Caguillona Mountains, a small group of hills with a dependable spring some fifteen miles north of Fronteras.

Moreno had remained there because several members of his command were sick. The next day, last rites were administered to eight men who were seriously ill. After two weeks the Sonoran offensive had met with disastrous results: sickness and desertions had hindered the command and the severe weather, and rough terrain had exhausted the stock. The Chiricahuas had avoided the campaign by moving north to the Gila River and Burro Mountains.[46]

Despite these setbacks, Elías González was not ready to give up the hunt. The dogmatic commander desperately needed a victory of any kind; he needed to give the hostiles a show of force. On October 6 he resumed the march, heading north toward the Chiricahuas.

He must have heaved a sigh of relief the second day out when his scouts captured a Chokonen warrior near San Bernardino. The prisoner furnished Elías González with definite information regarding the Chiricahuas' movements. All of the hostiles except Triqueno's group had retired north toward the Burro Mountains because of an epidemic within the bands.[47]

Based on this information, Elías González headed for the Burros, where he arrived October 13. Here he encountered John Coffee Hays,[48] who was in Chiricahua country hoping to make a peace treaty with the Indians. Yet the Apaches were too suspicious of the Americans and eluded them, Hays believed on account of "Americans employed by the Gov. of Chihuahua expressly to fight Indians."[49] After leaving Hays, Elías González finally caught his prey. Guided by Negrito, a Nednhi unjustly imprisoned at Janos the previous June, Elías González found at least two rancherías and succeeded in killing the Nednhi leader Cochi and ten other warriors. In addition, the Mexicans captured five persons and recovered some stock. The Sonoran leader was surprised at the light resistance until the Apache prisoners disclosed that the warriors were absent on a campaign against Janos. With this intelligence, Elías González decided to terminate the campaign in southern New Mexico and move toward Janos, hoping he could surprise the hostiles as they returned to their base camp.

The Apaches had left Janos by the time the Sonoran army reached it. Accordingly, Elías González decided to return to Sonora, thus officially ending his grand offensive. On the surface the results seemed less than spectacular. Although he had failed to strike an important blow against the Chiricahuas, he had forced the hostiles once again to consider Sonora as an enemy to be reckoned with.[50]

The Chiricahua war party against Janos had been organized to avenge Chihuahua's new extermination policy. Cochise's people had more or less avoided Chihuahua throughout 1849, although several had continued trading at Janos. These peaceful contacts had convinced Captain Baltazar Padilla that a truce might be made if Yrigóllen, Posito Moraga, and Carro could be induced to come in.[51] He realized that the militant Chokonens under Miguel Narbona, Teboca, and Cochise entertained no such thoughts. Padilla's hopes vanished on May 25, 1849, when Chihuahua adopted the so-called

Fifth Law, which essentially declared war against all hostiles and encouraged the slaughter of Apaches by bounty hunters. Any individual, regardless of nationality, could enter into a contract with the state to exterminate Apaches. Scalp bounties were fixed at 200 pesos for each warrior killed, 250 pesos for each warrior captured, and 150 pesos for each female or any male Indians under fourteen captured. Eager mercenaries materialized overnight, all hoping to capitalize on Chihuahua's new law.[52]

The scalp hunters enjoyed success until the hostiles withdrew from reach. Then, late that summer, the Apaches retaliated. Their raids extended to the suburbs of Chihuahua City and forced the closing of mines and the evacuation of ranches. An American businessman living in Chihuahua City attributed the depredations to revenge for the scalp hunters' deeds.[53]

In September 1849, Padilla closed the door on peace, at least for the short term, by destroying the ranchería of the Nednhi chief Soquilla[54] in the Florida Mountains a few miles southeast of Deming, New Mexico. Padilla's force killed Soquilla and eleven others and captured nineteen, who were subsequently imprisoned at Corralitos.[55] The Chiricahuas were naturally concerned about the fate of their relatives; accordingly, on October 11 a war party estimated at 150 warriors attacked the horse herd at Janos and ran off every head. A short time later the aggressors withdrew and hoisted a white flag. Padilla went out to parley with Chokonen leaders Yrigóllen, Manuelito, and Posito; Nednhi leaders Coleto Amarillo,[56] Láceris, and Arvizu;[57] and Itán, a Chihenne leader. All of the Indians were well armed and some were drunk, which produced a volatile atmosphere. Padilla convinced Arvizu and Manuelito to come in and talk; the others were too apprehensive. The Indians offered to exchange captives plus the stolen stock for their people; Padilla decided to write his superiors for instructions.

At this crucial moment, twenty-six whites, primarily Americans, freshly arrived from Santa Rita del Cobre, changed the odds. They were within half a mile of Janos when a large group of Apaches—four hundred according to the Americans, two hundred according to Padilla—suddenly appeared. With the presidio's proximity, the whites were not unduly alarmed, which proved to be a fatal mistake for several of its members. A Mr. Thompson recalled:

This was at a place where danger was least expected. A few who were in advance dismounted and prepared to defend themselves, but the Indians gave them to understand that they were friendly that the Apaches and Americans were amigos—that they did not want to fight. They then allowed them to approach, when they commenced shaking hands in the most friendly manner, and even going as far as to take several in their arms and hug them affectionately. After separating them as much as possible they suddenly seized the bridles of the horses and told them they were all prisoners, and then immediately marched them off towards the mountains. The little party finding itself deceived, tried to get together to make resistance, but the Indians took good care to prevent that by surrounding each man with seven or eight warriors.

When they reached the mountains, the Apaches proceeded to strip the Americans, cut open their packs, and steal their horses.[58]

About 5 P.M. Arvizu arrived at Janos and offered to exchange the American captives for the Indians held at Corralitos. After he left, however, the Apaches received news of Elías González's attack in the Burro Mountains. At this point a quarrel arose, with one faction demanding revenge on the captured Americans. Coleto Amarillo counseled against killing the prisoners, noting their importance in obtaining the release of their people. Through his intervention, "the mercy of God and darkness of night," most of the American party, naked and bruised, escaped to Janos. Seven men were not so fortunate; the next day, they were found lanced to death.[59]

Cochise's involvement in this incident is not known. With Miguel Narbona and Mangas Coloradas evidently not present, it would be difficult to speculate what role, if any, he played. Both leaders were in Chihenne country in late 1849, however, attempting to ascertain the disposition of the recently arrived Americans. Cochise was most likely with them.

Chapter 5

CHOKONEN ACTIVITIES 1849–56

The end of the United States–Mexican War in 1848 brought something new to the Chiricahua world: American troops in New Mexico, now a territory of the United States. In 1848 the newcomers had several clashes with Indians; most of the fighting, however, occurred in the north against the Jicarillas and Utes.[1] That summer, troops were garrisoned on the outskirts of Chiricahua territory. Captain Enoch Steen[2] and a company of First Dragoons were stationed at Doña Ana, five miles north of Las Cruces, and Steen had a few minor brushes with raiding Chiricahuas in 1849 and again in 1850.[3] These incidents helped to convince the suspicious Chiricahuas to avoid the unknown (Americans) and resume dealing with the known (Mexicans).

Although Chiricahua bands may have wanted good relations with Americans, small raiding parties occasionally harassed southern New Mexico. On December 27, 1849, a band of Chihennes under Josecito captured two boys, named Teofilio and Mateo Savanillo, from Doña Ana. Immediately the party returned to its home base near Santa Rita del Cobre and dispatched Itán to negotiate. En route, Americans reportedly attacked the party, killing and wounding several. Itán and the others limped back to camp, where the incensed Apaches organized a war party to avenge their losses.[4]

The honor of leading the group went to Miguel Narbona. Early on the morning of February 2, 1850, fifty-six Chiricahuas raided Doña

Ana and drove off every head of stock, killed one man, and wounded three others. The Apaches' audacity surprised the American troops, for the Indians had come so close that the troops saw them from their quarters. Captain Steen pursued with a force of dragoons and infantry, but the raiders were already six miles ahead when he started. Steen anticipated that the hostiles would head for the Gila; they struck toward San Diego Crossing. He divided his force. He took a detachment and crossed the Jornado del Muerto,[5] and Lieutenant Laurence W. O'Bannon with twenty-five men marched northwest to cut off the Indians before they reached the Mimbres Mountains. North of San Diego Crossing, O'Bannon's party overtook the Apaches and in a brisk fight wounded at least three warriors and possibly more. One soldier was wounded. After a hard march, in which most of his mounts broke down, Steen's party encountered thirty to forty warriors, "all mounted and dashing about on their horses and cursing us in bad Spanish, calling us to come over and fight them." Even though his force had dwindled to seven men, the Apaches, respecting the Americans' firepower, rode away and avoided a senseless encounter.[6]

These skirmishes, perhaps the first Chiricahua encounters with American troops, left the Indians with a healthy respect for the newcomers. Unscrupulous Mexican traders contributed to the Indians' apprehensions about Americans by spreading rumors that the latter intended to kill all Apaches. As a result, the Chiricahuas again turned to northern Mexico. They also had concluded that an armistice would be beneficial, especially because both Mexican states continued to hold Chiricahua prisoners. The distressed Chokonens and Chihennes had hoped to secure the release of their relatives through negotiations and most groups favored this strategy but not all; Miguel Narbona and Mangas Coloradas characteristically opposed peace at all costs.

Indian peace overtures began in February 1850 when a Chokonen named Antonio came into Bacoachi to request a truce. Because of recent raids, Captain Manuel Martínez promptly imprisoned Antonio but released a woman to return to the Chiricahua leaders. On February 27, Chino, four warriors, and several women arrived, bringing a letter from Posito Moraga[7] offering to exchange their captives for those taken by Terán y Tato the previous May. Martínez forwarded the missive to Elías González, who in turn sent it to the governor, the pragmatic commander recognizing that it would be the first serious Chokonen discussions with Sonora since the treaty of August 1836.[8]

Elías González at once marched to Bacoachi to deal with this important subject. On March 5, 1850, a suspicious and sullen Posito Moraga came in and agreed to return in four days with all of his prisoners, yet he failed to fulfill his promise because he distrusted Sonora and feared a repeat of the Kirker massacre of 1846. Elías González, however, held the trump cards, offering to release his Apache prisoners if the Chokonens would do the same. Finally on March 19 the big catch, Yrigóllen, came in with his captives and the deadlock was broken. Yrigóllen had realistically concluded that acommodation was a necessary alternative to war and agreed to five conditions of peace. Despite this, Elías González was not overly sanguine, admonishing the governor that the Chokonens required time before they "got over the fear that our people are lying in wait to double cross them, as happened at Galeana in the state of Chihuahua and as in fact happened elsewhere." Furthermore, the conditions of the treaty were totally impracticable because they required the Apaches to sustain themselves by hunting and gathering. Elías González knew it was ludicrous to expect the Apaches to remain at peace for any significant length of time without rations.[9]

The Chokonens under Miguel Narbona, Teboca, and probably Cochise were in New Mexico with Mangas Coloradas when Chino first proposed peace. Within a few weeks, they too left Chihenne country for northern Sonora and cast offers of peace. Whether they had any serious intention of ceasing hostilities, however, was another matter.

Teboca himself came into Santa Cruz on March 16 and discussed a truce. After a two-hour conference he left, ostensibly to bring in Mangas Coloradas, who was reported to be in the vicinity. Elías González became cautiously optimistic, characterizing Teboca as "one of the Indians who most resists pacification, although very trustworthy when it comes to any agreement he makes."[10]

He soon received another report that the Chiricahuas, recalling the Kirker massacre, would not reestablish themselves near presidios but would prefer to live peacefully in the Chiricahua Mountains. Unfortunately for both Sonora and those Chokonens peacefully inclined, the Indians were divided into factions: Posito Moraga and Yrigóllen apparently wanted a truce; Teboca and Esquinaline appeared to be leaning toward it; Mangas Coloradas and Miguel Narbona were staunchly opposed. In all likelihood Cochise followed Mangas's lead and had a hand in the bloody raids of 1850–51.[11]

While Yrigóllen and Posito Moraga refrained from raiding, Elías González was overwhelmed with reports of Apache depredations. In early April, Indians killed one man and two women and captured two children from Granados, east of Moctezuma. Near Moctezuma they ran off the horses of Captain Sebastian Reyes. At San Ignacio and Magdalena, Chiricahuas murdered several men and women and captured a young girl. Mangas's band boasted of these killings to an American party they had met and probably traded with.[12] Elías González received other ominous messages. The prefect of Moctezuma echoed the thoughts of most Sonorans, writing that he was "never persuaded that the Apaches' solicitations were in good faith."[13] At Bacoachi, Captain Martínez was unnerved by the testimony of a former captive, José María Mejias, who declared that the Apaches' objective was "to continually wear out this town [Bacoachi] until they can force its depopulation," almost certainly a threat from the tongue of Miguel Narbona.[14]

These events notwithstanding, on April 22, 1850, Elías González concluded a treaty with the moderate Chokonens with rations the key element, which he agreed to issue beginning July 1. Collecting these Indians, many of them hostile and many of them suspicious, was no easy task and he had misgivings, realizing that they had two months to kill before rations were issued. His years of dealing with the Indians had left him cynical: "The outcome cannot be foreseen with complete certainty due to the audacity, double crossing and unreliability of the Indians."[15] Of course the Chiricahuas had the same thoughts toward the Mexicans.

Although Yrigóllen and Posito seemed to favor a cease-fire, the militant faction remained opposed. In early May 1850 a large Chokonen and Bedonkohe war party killed and plundered its way south. The final target was the small village of Soyopa on the Yaqui River

about thirty miles southwest of Sahuaripa, which they assaulted on
May 25, 1850, killing twelve, wounding seven, and capturing nine
before finally returning north. Yrigóllen, who had remained quiet,
sent word that Mangas Coloradas and the Chokonen chiefs Teboca,
Esquinaline, and Triqueno led the war party.[16]

Meanwhile, at Ures, with the resurgence of hostilities, Governor
José de Aguilar wrote Mexico City on June 22 and again on June 28
to plead for federal assistance. On July 25 he reiterated his concerns
about the Apache problem, hoping that officials in Mexico City
would take some action. "The frontier is deserted," he wrote, "the
prosperity lost, and the lands which had been cultivated reflect only
the shadow of what they had been and the graves of many victims
sacrificed to the fury of the savages."[17] As the Indian war intensified, Sonoran officials accused, indicted, and convicted Apaches
living in peace near the presidio of Janos under a treaty consummated on June 24, 1850.

In the spring of 1850, at the time the Chokonens were negotiating
with Sonora, Chihenne and Nednhi bands had completed an armistice at Janos. In June Chihenne leaders Delgadito, Itán, Ponce, and
Pluma and Nednhi leaders Coleto Amarillo, Láceris, and Arvizu
met with Chihuahuan representatives Antonio Guaspe and Alejo
García Conde. Conde believed that the Indians were "disarmed and
whipped" and were compelled to sue for peace because their New
Mexico market had been negated by the American presence. Conde
wisely realized that rations were vital to any successful treaty; without them, he feared a repeat of past uprisings.[18] Significantly, Mangas Coloradas and most of the Chokonens remained aloof, although
he did authorize the Chokonen Aguirre, a brother of Yrigóllen, to
speak for him.[19] In late August, Yrigóllen, the only major Chokonen
leader who had expressed interest in accepting Chihuahua's proposal, disillusioned with events in Sonora, finally brought his group
to Janos. The remainder of Cochise's band continued depredations against Sonora, skirmishing with troops near Turicachi on August 26.[20]

In September, Miguel Narbona and Mangas Coloradas led another war party against Sonora. First they struck the Santa Cruz–
San Ignacio area, cleaning out ranches of their stock. Near Imuris

they butchered at least eight citizens before fleeing to Arizona. Believing that peaceful Apaches at Janos were responsible, Elías González wrote Juan José Zozaya at Janos, warning him that his troops would pursue to wherever the trail led—even Janos itself.

One force under Terán y Tato followed hostiles north to the Chiricahuas, Apache Pass, and then on to the Gila. He believed he was pursuing Miguel Narbona and Teboca's followers. Beyond the Gila lay American territory, so Terán y Tato returned to Sonora and on October 30 at Cuchuta jumped Posito Moraga and Triqueno's ranchería, killing two warriors, five women, and one child and taking two prisoners, both members of Triqueno's family.[21]

As 1850 ended, a year in which Apaches reportedly murdered 111 Sonorans, the federal government in Mexico City tried to remedy Sonora's Apache problem and appointed as commanding general and inspector of the military colonies an energetic, capable, but controversial individual who thought himself omniscient: Colonel José María Carrasco.[22] Carrasco replaced the popular Elías González, who had dealt as effectively as possible with the Chiricahuas. The latter had reinvigorated and reinforced the frontier presidios and had carried out coordinated offensives, but the lack of money, resources and the usual chaos in politics had hampered his efforts.

Before Carrasco arrived, a Chiricahua war party invaded Sonora. According to official reports, the Indians divided into two groups, each with at least 200 warriors, and ravaged the state. Mangas led one and Yrigóllen and Posito Moraga the other. In mid-January the Apaches retired north, driving some thirteen hundred cattle and horses before them. Captain Ignacio Pesqueira[23] gathered a force of 100 nationals from Bacoachi and Arispe and headed for Pozo Hediondo, some twenty-four miles southeast of Bacoachi, where he arrived on January 19. At 8 A.M. the next day, Pesqueira detected a cloud of dust and took up pursuit. Three hours later he overtook the Indians, who had taken a defensive position on high ground. What he lacked in judgment he made up in valor as his soldiers charged up the slopes and dislodged the enemy, who fled with Pesqueira's force on their heels. Shortly after, an estimated 250 warriors under Mangas Coloradas counterattacked Pesquiera's party, for whom the fleeing Apaches had been a decoy. The Indians swarmed around the

Merejildo Grijalva. Captured by Chiricahuas in 1849, he escaped in 1859 and became a scout and a thorn in Cochise's side. (*Courtesy Arizona Historical Society, Tucson*)

Ignacio Pesqueira. Future governor of Sonora, he led the troops annihilated at Pozo Hediondo in January 1851 by Mangas Coloradas. (*Courtesy Arizona Historical Society, Tucson*)

Mexicans and in a three-hour battle killed or wounded almost half the Mexicans, including every officer. The survivors retreated to a hill and dug in.

At 4 P.M. another party of two hundred warriors under Yrigóllen and Posito Moraga arrived, augmenting the Apache force to a reported four hundred warriors, although this seems too high. The Apaches repeatedly assaulted the Sonorans. At 6:30, Pesqueira withdrew to another hill, relieved that night had finally arrived and with it a lull in the fighting. The fight was a classic, full of excitement and heroism on both sides and with all the color and drama of a battle between whites and Indians. Total Mexican casualties: twenty-six killed and forty-six wounded,[24] perhaps the most successful Chiricahua victory of the nineteenth century. The Apache casualties are not known, as no account from their perspective exists, but according to a Mexican eyewitness the Sonorans killed or wounded seventy Apaches—probably an exaggeration.[25]

As to Cochise's involvement, the circumstantial evidence normally would be sufficient to conclude that he was probably there. In this case, however, there may be other reasons to support his presence. Merejildo Grijalva may have been referring to the Pozo Hediondo fight when he said one of Cochise's earliest successes came in the early 1850s during a raid that extended as far south as Hermosillo, as did the war party that fought Pesquiera. Cochise returned at the head of his warriors, driving 150 horses and mules. He kept none for himself, instead distributing them among his followers.[26]

Geronimo remembered a big "revenge fight" in Sonora. He mentioned that Cochise, Mangas Coloradas, and Juh united to fight Sonoran troops near Arispe. There are striking similarities between Geronimo's account and Sonoran reports of the battle. The fight occurred east of Arispe with troops from there and Bacoachi involved. Geronimo recalled that the troops were from Arispe. Hard fighting and heavy casualties were reported in both versions, and both accounts say Mangas Coloradas led the Indians. Furthermore, I know of no other engagement like this in the early 1850s, which was when Geronimo's fight occurred. Because he dictated his memoirs some fifty years after the fact, it was perhaps only natural that he made Cochise leader of the Chokonens when in reality Miguel Narbona and Yrigóllen were the band leaders in this battle. But if Geronimo's recollections can be trusted, Cochise was there and, like Geronimo and others, enhanced his reputation during the fierce battle.[27]

The Chiricahua victory at Pozo Hediondo incensed Carrasco, who arrived shortly after the defeat. He immediately criticized Elías González and Terán y Tato and a running feud developed, which did little to alleviate the burdens of all concerned. Carrasco at once announced plans to avenge the defeat. By mid-February he had come to a decision: the Apaches at Janos must be punished and he would do it. Accordingly, he led a Sonoran army into Chihuahua and in the early morning of March 5, 1851, surprised several rancherías in the neighborhood of Janos, killing twenty-one Apaches (sixteen men and five women) and capturing sixty-two, among them six warriors. Among the slain was the principal Chokonen chief Yrigóllen and the Nednhi leader Arvizu.[28]

We can only speculate on Cochise's role at this time. Yrigóllen's local group was the only Chokonen unit to make peace at Janos; the remainder of the band and Mangas Coloradas's Bedonkohes continued at war. Undoubtedly Cochise remained with the hostile faction. In fact, just as Carrasco was entering Chihuahua, Miguel Narbona and some fifty Chokonens were striking along the Sonora River at Sinoquipe and Bamori, where they killed several people. One of the victims, before dying, claimed that Miguel Narbona was wounded in the fight. After this, learning that Carrasco was planning a second campaign, the Chokonens retired into present-day Arizona and New Mexico.[29]

Carrasco's second expedition failed to accomplish much, although he did surprise a Nednhi ranchería. Soon afterward he parleyed with three Chokonens near Fronteras (reoccupied in September 1850) and agreed to make peace, providing the Indians obeyed some twenty-eight articles. The Apaches accepted immediately; their sole interest was to obtain the release of the sixty-two prisoners captured at Janos. Unfortunately, Carrasco came down with cholera and died, leaving relations up in the air. Despite this, by late July some four hundred Chokonens had complied with his terms and were camped near Fronteras. In August, Chepillo and Chagaray (both subordinates of Yrigóllen) traveled to Ures to visit their imprisoned relatives, among whom was Chagaray's wife. When nothing was resolved, the two leaders returned to Fronteras, gathered up their followers, and returned to the Chiricahua and Animas mountains; the Chokonens were again at war. No doubt they had a hand in the depredations of August, when Apaches killed fifty-nine Sonorans, bringing the total to more than two hundred in 1851. Sonora announced it would retaliate.[30]

José María Flores succeeded Carrasco as commanding general. He concluded that a major campaign, Sonora's third of 1851, was warranted and necessary, so he made plans for simultaneous operations both north and south of the Chiricahua Mountains, hoping to deprive the Indians of using that area as sanctuary. By late September he had gathered more than 300 men, which he divided into two units. He commanded the first, consisting of 172 presidio troops and two pieces of artillery; the capable José Téran y Tato headed the second division of 150 national troops. A base camp was to be established at San Simon,[31] some fifteen miles northeast of Apache Pass.[32]

In October 1851 the entire command began marching for San Simon. En route Terán y Tato sent out a patrol under the Apache-wise officer Captain Eusebio Gil Samaniego. On October 13, Samaniego's force discovered a ranchería (which proved to be Posito Moraga's and Triqueno's) at Carretas and killed four warriors, two women, and one boy and captured six women and three children. Posito Moraga's wife and relatives of Triqueno were among the captives. Samaniego rejoined Terán y Tato's command south of the Chiricahua Mountains, which they scouted before reaching San Simon on October 21.[33]

Here Flores split his force. He continued north and scouted the Gila country before proceeding into Western Apache territory, where he encountered Indians, killing five warriors and capturing four others. The second division, consisting of Terán y Tato's nationals, scouted east to the Burro Mountains in New Mexico, then southwest along the eastern slopes of the Chiricahuas to the Pitaicache Mountains in Sonora. In the Pilares Mountains in late October, they discovered the Chokonen ranchería of Tapilá, "a most terrible Apache" and killed eight warriors, captured five, and recovered thirty-seven animals.[34] So it was that Sonora's third campaign against the Chiricahuas was brought to a close. With Apache prisoners, Terán y Tato predicted that the Indians would soon solicit peace in order to exchange their prisoners for those held by Sonora. The Chiricahuas did not disappoint him.

In late October, Tapilá, Chepillo, and Chagaray showed up at Bavispe, wishing to exchange prisoners. Details were sparse. According to Mexican accounts, the Sonorans became wary when the Indians arrived, already drunk and obnoxious. In self-defense the Mexicans were forced to kill Tapilá, Ponesino (a brother of Chepillo), and a brother of Chagaray; undoubtedly there was more to this than was reported. These were devastating losses for the Chokonens. Tapilá was a leading war chief, so his death would have to be avenged. Cochise's people moved into the Chiricahua Mountains, where in early 1852 the Chihennes, Bedonkohes, and Chokonens convened for talks to avenge their losses of 1851.[35]

Sonora again took the offensive in 1852. The first campaign got under way in March when Terán y Tato and Captain Miguel Escalante left Santa Cruz for a march into Chokonen territory. On March 18 at the Perilla Mountains in extreme southeastern Arizona they were joined by thirty dragoons under Captain Teodoro de Aros. Late the next afternoon a group of Indians arrived from the Chiricahuas, making signs that they wished to parley. Two Apaches, Delgadito (Chihenne) and Casimiro (Chokonen) conversed with Ensign Manuel Gallegos[36] and agreed to bring in other leaders to talk.

The next morning a party of Chiricahuas estimated at 180 warriors arrived, making signs to parley. Gallegos met them with proposals from Captain de Aros. A blanket was placed between the two lifelong adversaries, with de Aros joining Gallegos and the Chokonens represented by Casimiro, Esquinaline, Miguel Narbona, and at least two of Teboca's sons. Delgadito and a son of Mangas Coloradas (probably Cascos) were also present, as were other Apaches, possibly Cochise and his brother Coyuntura. The meeting took place somewhere north of the Swisshelm Mountains and a few miles west of the southern Chiricahuas. Here "a truce was made with the Apaches, in respect of their superior numbers."

While the two parties were in parley, another large group of Apaches was seen coming from the Chiricahuas. Suspecting treachery, the Mexicans terminated the talks and returned to their camp. Shortly thereafter, Delgadito reappeared and again talked with Gallegos. Earlier that month Mexican troops had attacked his ranchería in the Caguillona Mountains and had captured several of his band. He wanted to make an arrangement for his people who were being held in confinement at Fronteras, but Gallegos had no authority to promise anything; instead, he told Delgadito that they had to leave to find water and grass. The next morning, the Mexicans moved along the foothills on the western side of the Chiricahua Mountains, took a short siesta, and continued on to Bonita Canyon[37] in the Chiricahua Mountains, where they camped.

That evening they noticed Indian fires above the canyon. Consequently, Escalante sent out a small scouting force, who reported that the slopes were crawling with Apaches. At dawn the next morning, March 22, 1852, three hundred to four hundred Chiricahua warriors attacked the Mexican force at Bonita Canyon. They came from all directions, most of them mounted, and wounded Captain de Aros in their first charge. Escalante and de Aros rallied their men, who poured an effective fire on the rampaging Indians. With the element of surprise gone, the Apaches withdrew, maintaining a brisk but ineffective fire for the next two hours. The fight lasted two hours and thirty-six minutes. The Chiricahuas had killed three men and wounded ten, six seriously. De Aros estimated the Indians' loss at twelve dead and thirty wounded. After the fight he moved his force to Apache Pass before he returned to Sonora without any more encounters.[38]

This fight was soon followed by an important triumph over the Nednhis. A 230-man Sonoran force under Captain Miguel Lozada and Captain Eusebio Gil Samaniego found Coleto Amarillo's ranchería in the vicinity of the Florida Mountains, where Padilla had killed the Nednhi leader Soquilla two and one-half years earlier. On March 27 the Sonorans surprised the camp and killed 7 warriors and 21 women and children, captured 16 Apaches, and took 39 mules and horses and 24 head of cattle. Among the dead were Coleto Amarillo and El Chinito, "known for their atrocities in Sonora and Chihuahua."[39] It was a devastating blow to the Janeros local group of the Nednhis; the loss of two important leaders compelled the Indians to move from Mexico's grasp and effect an agreement with the Americans in New Mexico. The remainder of the 1850s was characterized by this behavior: when the Chihenne and Nednhis wore out their welcome with the Americans, they leapfrogged the border into Chihuahua. For the most part, Cochise's people remained in southern Arizona beyond the reach of Mexican troops.

The early 1850s was a time of dramatic change in the leadership of the Chokonens. In 1851 they lost three of their principal leaders; Yrigóllen and Tapilá at the hands of Sonorans and Teboca probably in the same manner. No one leader emerged to dominate the Chokonen band as Pisago Cabezón had in the 1830s and, to a lesser degree, Yrigóllen had in the 1840s.

During the early 1850s, the Chokonen local groups were broken down as follows: the one headed by Posito Moraga, Triqueno, and Teboquita normally lived in the area bounded by Arizona, New Mexico, Sonora, and Chihuahua, with the Pitaicache Mountains their favorite camping area; another, under the leadership of Chepillo, Esquinaline, Yrinco, Aguirre, and Parte, lived in the southern Chiricahua, Animas, and Peloncillo mountains (this was Yrigóllen's old band, and philosophically it was more moderate than the other two); Miguel Narbona, Carro, and Cochise continued to lead the third group of Chiricahuas, whose favorite camping areas remained Apache Pass and the Chiricahua and Dragoon mountains.

As Miguel Narbona and Carro aged and their influence waned, Cochise emerged as leader. One Chiricahua explained: "Ability in war and wisdom make the leader. It's easier to get to the front if you are a good fighter. . . . The leader is not chosen, he is just recognized." [40] This described Cochise's position as he approached his prime in the early to mid-1850s. There were no pacifists among Chiricahua leaders; for a warrior to emerge as chief, he had to combine great fighting skill with wisdom and a deep sensitivity to the lessfortunate members of his group.

From 1852 through 1856, Cochise's Chokonens continued to war on Mexico. Although not specifically mentioned in any of the Mexican reports, Cochise definitely participated in many of the war parties which ravaged Mexico at this time. Even the notorious Miguel Narbona, well known in Sonora, was mentioned but sparingly after 1852. Cochise's war parties left few survivors to identify their assailants. Each winter he joined Mangas Coloradas on expeditions against Mexico, and each year his reputation within the band grew when his warriors returned with large amounts of booty and livestock.

In early 1853, Chokonen groups migrated south to the Chiricahuas and northern Sonora. That March, Mangas Coloradas organized the annual winter expedition against Sonora. After raiding deep into the interior, the Apaches made their ritualistic last stop at Fronteras. On April 11 the war party came across five boys tending their sheep south of the presidio; they dispassionately killed each, then swept through Fronteras and galloped away with most of its stock toward the San Bernardino Valley.

Captain Mendoza rounded up a force of twenty-five men and later that day unexpectedly encountered Mangas's rear guard. A hard fight ensued, with both sides taking casualties before the Sonorans limped back to Fronteras. All told, the Mexicans lost four soldiers killed and two soldiers wounded. The Apaches lost eight dead and several wounded, according to Mendoza's report. Mangas Coloradas acknowledged that he lost three warriors in this encounter.[41]

Two Chokonen war parties invaded Sonora in the summer of 1853. They overwhelmed everything in their path, slaughtering women and children indiscriminately. One party was led by Posito Moraga and Triqueno, the other by Carro, Casimiro, and Yaque. The first raided along the Sonora River; the second hit the small town of Granados. One June morning forty citizens of Granados left their homes to work their crops; the Chiricahuas were waiting and sprang upon them from every direction, killing nine (five men and four children) and capturing one woman and two children. Next they continued south to Tepache, where they ran off several mules and oxen. For the next three weeks they terrorized settlements along the western slopes of the Sierra Madre. The two war parties finally united at Tecoripa, eighty miles southeast of Ures, and routed a party of twenty nationals, killing a captain and three others. The next day, three miles north of Cumuripa, about two hundred Indians destroyed Hacienda de Cieneguita and killed twelve people, wounded two, and captured one.[42] José Vega was seriously wounded but lived to tell his story to Captain Pascual Cota of Cumuripa's National Guard. Cota led a reluctant and jittery group of nationals to the scene of the disaster. His men, however, appalled at the devastation, refused to follow the Apaches. A disgusted Cota vowed that he "would never again lead citizens against the enemy."[43]

The following winter, the Chiricahuas sent another war party against Mexico. Mangas Coloradas, Delgadito, and Miguel Narbona led this incursion into Sonora from the Chiricahuas. Although the foray had been in the planning stages for some time, the Chokonens had only recently become incensed because of an encounter in Sonora. In late January 1854, three prominent men, including Casimiro, were murdered at Bavispe under conditions which suggested foul play.[44] The Chiricahuas avenged these killings and more. Throughout February they pillaged their way south, hitting the districts of Sahuaripa and Alamos. The governor notified towns to mobilize against the hostiles as they returned north, but the Indians easily eluded pursuit.[45]

A few months later another war party was organized, this time under the Chihenne chiefs Delgadito and Costales[46] in conjunction with Miguel Narbona. This band penetrated south to Alamos, where an estimated 200 Apaches attacked the outskirts of the city. By late May, Delgadito and Costales had retired to the Oputo Mountains, and Miguel Narbona was reported at Turicachi. On June 1, Miguel and 50 Chokonens harassed citizens at the *cienaga* near Fronteras. They stole sixteen mules and horses and carried off a boy before heading for the Teras Mountains. Miguel had chosen an advantageous time for this raid: only hours earlier, 135 men had left the presidio to scout the Chiricahua Mountains, where the Indians were finding refuge because of the recent Gadsden Treaty between Mexico and the United States.[47]

The Gadsden Treaty was negotiated in the last days of 1853 when Mexico sold a large tract of land to the United States, pushing the Sonora and Chihuahua borders south to the present boundary.[48] The United States Senate ratified an amended version of the treaty on April 25, 1854. At the time of the sale, according to Hubert Howe Bancroft, there was little concern in either Sonora or Chihuahua because the land sold was essentially Apache country and generally uninhabited,[49] yet the agreement had significant ramifications in the ongoing Chokonen-Sonora conflict. Mexican forces were not supposed to penetrate north of San Bernardino and the present border. Eventually Cochise's people became aware of this and continued to find sanctuary in the Chiricahua Mountains, along the Gila River, and in the Mogollon Mountains.

Initially, most Mexicans viewed the Gadsden Treaty with ambivalence, but implicit threats of Yankee expansionism and explicit threats from American filibusters, coupled with the incessant Apache raids from north of the line, gave Sonorans an increasingly apprehensive feeling toward most North Americans. After the treaty, the Chiricahua Tribe continued to raid into Mexico at will. This exasperated Mexican officials, who accused American settlers and government officials of trading arms and ammunition to Apaches in return for stolen Mexican stock, a charge that undoubtedly had some validity and was repeated countless times during the next decade.[50]

During the mid-1850s there emerged a casual pattern of Chiricahua raids into Mexico followed by retreats to U.S. territory and security. An example of this occurred in the spring of 1855 when a large party of Chokonens and Chihennes joined forces for a raid into Mexico. The Chihennes, living near Santa Rita del Cobre, went west to Apache Pass, where they enlisted a large group of Chokonens, probably under the leadership of Cochise. On their way south, they picked up another group in the lower Peloncillos, probably at Sarampion. Once in Mexico, they split into smaller parties, the Chokonens concentrating on Sonora and the Chihennes under Josecito, Costales, and Itán raiding into Chihuahua.[51]

The Chokonens hit their favorite target, Sonora, before they slipped from Terán y Tato's grasp back into Arizona. The Chihennes returned to their camps along the Mimbres River, where they found that the Americans were ready to make another treaty—the third in the past four years. The major difference in this agreement was that the Americans, for the first time, convinced the Apaches to cede large tracts of land. Many of the Chihenne leaders signed, but Mangas Coloradas demurred.[52]

The mid-1850s was undoubtedly a prosperous time for Cochise and his people. Although living primarily in U.S. territory, they had little contact with Americans, mainly because of the scarcity of traffic and lack of settlements in their country. Cochise's people were not a party to the treaties made in 1852, 1853, and 1855 in New Mexico by the Chihenne and Nednhi bands. This leads to a question: Did the Anglos know of the Chokonens, and if so they recognize them as a distinct band?

The Chokonens, who were to become known to Americans as the Chiricahuas in the late 1850s, were living in southern Arizona, yet references to any band identified as Chiricahuas before 1850 are scarce. The Mexicans generally lumped southern Apache bands, basically the Chiricahua Tribe, into one generic group and called them Gilenos. Historian Ralph Smith, who has done extensive research on Apache activities in Mexico prior to 1858, wrote that he had not "encountered a single mention of the term Chiricahua to identify an Apache tribe or band in . . . the [eighteen] thirties or forties." [53] Mexican archives do contain scattered references to the "Chiricahua" Apaches from 1830 through 1850, but on the whole these references are vague, sparse, and immaterial.

According to Merejildo Grijalva, who lived with Cochise at the time, during the 1850s the Chokonens ranged over an enormous territory: from the Gila River and Mogollon Mountains in Arizona south to the Sierra Madre in Mexico. He recalled that he first met Americans at Stein's Peak, probably in the fall of 1858 or perhaps earlier. The point to be made is that during the 1850s the Chokonen band was living in Arizona within its historic local-group territory. Although some of its leaders were known to Americans, the Indians were not known or referred to as Chiricahuas. Two reports identified Chokonen chiefs as Mogollon Apaches. The first mention was by Captain Joseph Horace Eaton in a report dated December 23, 1855, from Fort Thorn, New Mexico, and the second was by Dr. Michael Steck,[54] agent for the Chihennes, whose sincerity and honesty were unique in a government bureau noted for corruption.

In late 1855 the Chiricahuas raided Mesilla. Eaton pursued the hostiles but could not overtake them before they disappeared into the Burro Mountains. At San Vicente he met with José Mangas, brother of Mangas Coloradas, and Casco, a son of Mangas Coloradas. These two individuals, with whom Cochise was well acquainted, informed Eaton that Chaynee, a Mogollon, had led the hostile party, which was camped near the Gila. In the same report, Eaton shed some light on the Chokonen band, probably having obtained the details from either Steck or José Mangas. The Mogollon chiefs, Eaton wrote, are "Miguel, El Carro, Juan Apache, El Fresco and Capitan Chaynee, fighting men number some say 300, Dr. Steck says not over 150." [55]

Eaton had unwittingly identified the leaders of the Chokonens, who at this time were living in the northern limits of their range. These chiefs were well known to Mexicans: Miguel was Miguel Narbona, El Carro was Carro and El Fresco was probably Francisco, a close associate of Cochise who actually was a leader among the Eastern White Mountain Apaches, a non-Chiricahua band. The identities of Juan Apache [56] and Chaynee are not known.

Further evidence that the Chokonens were sometimes misidentified as Mogollons may be discerned from Dr. Steck's report of September 19, 1856, in which he named Esquinaldine (Esquinaline) as the "principal chief of the Coyoteros" and said two of the subordinate chiefs were "Chagari [and] Cochil." [57] Chagaray was a prominent Chokonen leader and Cochil might well have been Cochise, who may have been a subordinate of Esquinaline at this time.

In any event, few Americans understood the breakdown of Apache bands in the 1850s and 1860s. On several occasions Cochise was referred to as a Coyotero or Pinal, which to twentieth-century students would indicate Western Apache, a distinct tribe from the Chiricahua. As far as Anglo references to Apaches as Chiricahuas, it came into vogue in the late 1850s when Americans established a stage station at Apache Pass. In fact, Steck identified Esquinaline, the same Indian he called a Coyotero two years earlier, as a Chiricahua (or Chokonen) when he first met Cochise's people in late 1858.

With the identity of the Chokonens solved, it must be assumed that they raided New Mexico periodically. Steck recognized this and on the last day of 1855 recommended that the army mount an expedition against the Apaches living near the headwaters of the Gila, who he supposed were the culprits. In early January 1856, depredations in the vicinity of Mesilla were attributed to Apaches living in the Mogollons. Mangas Coloradas admitted that some of his people had participated and that he was unable to restrain them. Steck feared his Chihennes would be unfairly charged for some of these raids; consequently, the military began preparations for an expedition into the inaccessible and almost impregnable Mogollon country. [58]

The campaign, commanded by Captain Daniel T. Chandler, consisted of troops from Fort Craig and Fort Thorn. Steck accompanied the expedition, which struck a large trail of stolen sheep and followed it northwest into the Mogollon Mountains. Here they surprised a ranchería, recapturing 250 sheep and 21 horses and mules. The attack stunned the hostiles, who had not expected pursuit. The soldiers killed one Apache and wounded three or four others, two of whom later died from their wounds according to Refugio Corrales, an Apache captive who was at the fight. This was the camp of El Cautivo, Bedonkohe or Chokonen leader with whom Cochise was closely associated.[59]

In late April 1856 the Chihennes left their homes in New Mexico and joined Cochise's Chokonens for a series of sanguinary raids into Sonora and Chihuahua. According to a Mexican captive, the war party was led by Mangas Coloradas, Delgadito, and one who would strike terror in the hearts of southwesterners for nearly a quarter-century: Victorio. One group under Delgadito and Victorio concentrated on Chihuahua. The second consisted of Chokonens and Bedonkohes under Mangas Coloradas, his son Cascos, and most likely Cochise, who had evolved into a Chokonen war leader by this time. They left Sonora in a state of frenzy most of May. Their goal was horses and captives, for which there was a ready market along the Mimbres and Río Grande, where the Apaches could trade them for guns, ammunition, and whiskey.

Casco's party caused much damage. During the first three weeks of May, the Chiricahuas besieged Bacerac, stealing stock and preventing farmers from working their fields. Fifteen miles north lay Bavispe, whose troops were hunting for Apaches along the border, leaving it virtually defenseless. On May 24 the Indians surrounded it, killed one man, and captured his son. The Apache scourge was worse than anyone had ever seen, reported Bavispe officials.[60]

Meanwhile at Chinapa, some seventy-five miles west of Bavispe, another war party (probably the Chokonen element) virtually decimated the town. Chinapa had a pathetic history of being hit by Chiricahua war parties; in early 1848, Chiricahuas under Miguel Narbona had killed, wounded, or captured most of the town. On May 27, 1856, Apaches burned and destroyed most of the town and killed several of its citizens. The prefect of Arispe informed the governor of the gory attack: "Today the town of Chinapa does not exist. Yesterday at 3:00 P.M. a citizen of that town presented himself to me and expressed in these terms: The Apaches have finished, they have captured Chinapa."

The prefect immediately gathered a force of eighty-five men and marched to Chinapa, arriving there at 11 P.M. and discovering "a most dreadful silence, everything burning in flames and blood splattered everywhere." The party cautiously examined the area and stumbled over three bodies. Not a sound was heard until a barking dog drew the rescuing parties attention to a stone house where many of the women and children, with ten men, had taken refuge. The exit was smoldering, but only the door was burned. The survivors furnished details of the bloody disaster. The Apaches had arrived about eight o'clock, taking one woman prisoner and killing her husband. For the next five hours they went door to door and burned each house. They finally left about one o'clock.[61] The Chokonens withdrew to their rancherías in the Chiricahua Mountains.

Despite their successes in the summer of 1856, some Chiricahua groups were willing to make peace with Chihuahua. Many had become disenchanted and apprehensive about living in U.S. territory. First, members of the Nednhi band arrived at Janos, followed by some Chokonens under Chepillo and Esquinaline, then some Chihennes under Itán and Delgadito. During the spring and summer of 1856, Cochise's following remained camped in the Chiricahua Mountains, making mescal and organizing raiding parties into Mexico.[62] It was about this time that Miguel Narbona died (details are vague) and only Carro and Esquinaline of the old-line Chokonen leaders remained. In the prime of life physically and intellectually, Cochise was recognized as the war leader within his band. Soon he would be the dominant Chokonen chief.

Chapter 6

DOUBLE TREACHERY IN MEXICO

During the mid-1850s Americans began to make their presence felt in Arizona. In 1856 American soldiers replaced Mexican troops at Tucson, and ambitious American capitalists rejuvenated the mining region of Tubac. Cochise scarcely noticed their arrival as the Chokonens remained undisturbed by these groups to the west. East of them, however, was a different story. In 1857 American troops, responding to Apache depredations in New Mexico, launched a large-scale offensive known as the Bonneville campaign. It struck Apaches, including some Chiricahuas, but most of the Indians had heard of the expedition and slipped into Mexico, where they hoped to remain until affairs calmed down and American troops returned to their posts. Once below the border, they planned to resume friendly relations at either Fronteras or Janos. Initially Cochise remained aloof, awaiting the results of these meetings. Finally, in the summer of 1857, he cautiously brought his followers into Janos and then Fronteras.

Several Chokonens had been negotiating off and on at Janos for the past two years, although Cochise apparently was not involved. In the summer of 1855, Yrigóllen's old group under Yrinco,[1] Aguirre,[2] and Parte[3] sent emissaries to Janos, but no treaty was consummated.[4] The following summer Yrinco again solicited peace at Janos and to prove his sincerity joined Mexican troops in pursuit of hostiles under the venerable Babosa.[5] They overtook the raiders in

the mountains west of Janos and recovered the stock.[6] Soon thereafter Esquinaline and Chepillo left the Chiricahuas for Janos, also
hopeful of making a truce.[7] Only those Chokonens under Cochise
and Carro remained in Arizona, opposing an armistice for the time
being.

Soon after the Chokonen request for a cease-fire, a few Chihennes, dissatisfied with American treatment in New Mexico, arrived at Janos. Their discontent had festered because of the paucity
of rations and assistance provided by the Americans. Relations
became further strained when an American officer attacked Delgadito's ranchería in April 1856, killing one woman and wounding
several women and children. Steck protested, but his report was discredited by Colonel John Garland, who claimed the Indians were
appeased when compensation was provided. After all, they were
only Apaches.[8]

The Chihennes had another motive: they hoped to obtain the release of Nalze, a son of Monteras who was captured by Padilla's
troops in May 1855. Accordingly, on July 30, 1856, Itán, Láceris,
and Monteras requested a truce at Janos and turned over Prudencio
Aralos, whom they had captured some three months before. Captain
Padilla requested instructions from José María Zuloaga,[9] recently
appointed Chihuahua's peace commissioner. Zuloaga sanctioned the
release of Nalze in the "best interests of humanity," obviously
hoping that the Chihennes would make peace. Soon after, however,
to show his appreciation, Monteras and a small band ambushed
three men on the road from Barranco, killing one and wounding the
other two. Then his band murdered another man near Casas Grandes
before returning to Steck's agency in New Mexico.[10]

Surprisingly, Monteras's actions did not impede negotiations.
Some Chokonens continued to press for an armistice, joined by a
few Chihennes and Nednhis who had decided against returning to
New Mexico. On August 15, 1856, Steck explained to Governor
David Meriwether of New Mexico that some of the Chihennes had
made a treaty with the towns of Janos and Corralitos. "Their reason," wrote Steck, "was that a year ago the people of Janos had
captured an Apache [Nalze] and about three months ago the Apaches
captured a Mexican; a treaty was then concluded in order to exchange captives."[11] On August 19 the official newspaper of Chihua-

hua, *El Eco de la Frontera,* reported the possibility of a peace "as thirty-six of them are now living near Corralitos and will accompany Commissioner Zuloaga to Chihuahua City to make a formal peace with the Governor." [12]

The Indian commission that was to confer with the governor encountered an unexpected delay; two incidents upset the conciliation. In late August, Luis García pursued into Chihuahua a band of Apaches who had been raiding in Sonora. Only through the intervention of the people at Janos were hostilities averted. This incident excited the Indians, who recalled Elías González's and Carrasco's attack, and disturbed Chihuahuan authorities, who found García's actions "criminal and against the dignity and interests of this state." [13] The second event occurred lightning quick and without warning and temporarily stalled negotiations. On September 2 at the siesta hour, Mangas Coloradas and thirty to forty warriors boldly raided Janos, galloping away with more than one hundred head of stock. Padilla recognized several hostiles, including El Cautivo and other Chokonens. Cochise is not mentioned but may have participated in that Mangas led the raid and Cochise was closely associated with El Cautivo. [14]

In all likelihood Mangas was cognizant that a small party of Chiricahuas under Esquiriba was bargaining at Janos but was disinterested in the results; he and Cochise opposed any talk of peace. Yet the raid infuriated and embarrassed Padilla, who imprisoned Esquiriba's party (thirteen individuals, including four men). Employing a strategy which had worked in 1850, Padilla and Zuloaga decided to use the captives as ransom to force Mangas to return the stock and to lure other hostiles into Janos. [15]

Padilla and Zuloaga knew the imprisonment of Esquiriba's group was unjustified because he did not belong to the same band of Chiricahuas that carried out the raid. Moreover, neither Esquiriba nor any members of his band could compel Mangas's party to return the stolen stock, which was the condition set by Padilla for the prisoners' release. Both Padilla and Zuloaga knew better; they had more experience and more contact with the Chiricahuas than any other whites on the North American continent, either Anglo or Mexican. They understood that there was no one supreme chief among the Chiricahuas, no one man whose word was promptly accepted and obeyed by the autonomous bands. This is precisely why, at every peace conference, the Mexicans designated one leader to act as general and another to serve as his second in command. They hoped the white man's political organization would serve to control and influence the independent Apache bands and local groups. History had proved this impracticable, but the Mexicans could not conceive of handling the Chiricahuas in any other way.

Padilla's and Zuloaga's plan worked in one respect. After a few months of parleying, the Indians, who were assisted by a concerned Dr. Steck, came into Janos. On December 31, 1856, the Nednhi leaders Láceris and Felipe, with a party of eleven warriors and fourteen women, arrived at Janos to reopen negotiations.[16] Láceris was from the Janeros local group of Nednhis, who for the past few years had been living along the Mimbres River in New Mexico. Felipe was a Carrizaleño Apache, a local group of Nednhis which lived almost exclusively in Chihuahua; the Carrizaleños had been at war with Mexico since the summer of 1855. For the past eighteen months, Chihuahuan campaigns had proved somewhat effective; one in September 1855 and another in March 1856 had succeeded in scattering the local groups of Felipe and Cojinillín.[17]

The Indians remained at Janos for three days before agreement was reached. Láceris (probably Esquiriba's brother) traveled to Chihuahua City, arriving there about January 19, 1857, and conferring with commanding general José Merino. The general was impressed with Láceris's sincerity and concluded the treaty. The conditions were neither as complicated nor as unrealistic as past treaties, the main points being that the Apaches would release their captives and that the Mexicans would issue rations. When convinced of the Indians' good intentions, Merino would authorize Padilla to free Esquiriba's party.[18]

Láceris brought his Nednhi band of 184 individuals into Janos. In February 1857, Padilla began issuing rations to the Chiricahuas and afterward wrote Merino about the auspicious beginning. The armistice soon attracted more Chiricahuas. In March, Felipe brought in his Carrizaleño group of 98, increasing the number of peaceful Apaches to 282, and events in New Mexico and Sonora soon drove the Chokonens and Chihennes into Janos.[19]

Having heard rumors of the Bonneville campaign, the Chihennes were the next group of Chiricahuas to forsake U.S. territory for Janos. In mid-March, Steck reported that the Chihenne chiefs "and most of their people had gone to Janos to make a treaty." [20] In reality, American treatment of the Apaches had left much to be desired, although the sincere and competent Steck had done all in his power to keep them content. The Indians were unhappy about their rations; Mangas Coloradas had complained to Steck more than once about the lack of them. Almost as important was the cavalier American treatment of Apaches, which caused the Chihennes to wonder whether the grass might be greener in Mexico. Beginning with Chandler's wanton attack in April 1856 and continuing through the winter of 1857, the Chihennes had several encounters with Mexicans and Americans in southwestern New Mexico.

Not all of the incidents were unprovoked. During the first three months of 1857, nine Chihennes were killed in engagements with Americans, making their decision to move into Mexico a little easier. By the spring of 1857, Delgadito and fifty members of his group joined in the peace at Janos; Mangas and the other Chihennes would wait and see.[21]

Cochise's Chokonens had been camped in the Chiricahuas since early 1857, undecided about their next course of action. In February 1857 a local group had attempted to make peace at Janos, but the overture was rejected. Yaque,[22] an inveterate raider and killer, had arrived with several hundred sheep stolen in New Mexico, perhaps implicating him in the cold-blooded murder of Zuñi agent Henry Linn Dodge[23] the previous November. In any event Padilla was uncertain about feeding Yaque's band and wrote Zuloaga for instructions. Zuloaga officially replied that any Indians who had raided in either New Mexico or Sonora must not be rationed.[24] Yet this response apparently did not prevent Yaque from trading his sheep. In March, two citizens from Janos told Steck the Apaches were "carrying on a brisk trade of mules and horses and [had] sold 600 sheep." [25]

The large number of hostiles along the border produced a volatile atmosphere, and Zuloaga and Padilla realized that they had to persuade the Indians to join in the precarious truce. In the spring of 1857 several events occurred, any one of which could have forced the skittish Apaches to bolt. In April a force of 150 Chihuahuan volunteers reached Casas Grandes, planning to attack the Indians, who they claimed had been raiding in the interior. It was of little concern to these volunteers that Láceris's people were innocent; they wanted Apache blood or scalps. Fortunately for all concerned, Padilla had received word of their arrival and immediately dispatched a terse note to Esmeregildo Quintana, who was leading the volunteers, admonishing him that any attack would be "treasonous and disgraceful and should be suspended." Padilla's decisive actions averted a potential crisis.[26] After this, Zuloaga and Padilla redoubled their efforts to bring in all the hostiles living at Alamo Hueco, but to no avail. Mangas Coloradas and Cochise were still taking a wait-and-see approach.

In late May another incident led to more turmoil, which Sonora erroneously blamed on the Janos Apaches. Details are vague, but apparently a few Chokonens had gone into Janos, perhaps to visit relatives or to trade booty. Padilla ordered them seized and placed in the guardhouse, hoping to coerce the hostiles in. Instead this enraged the Indians, who at once raided the ranches of Miguel Samaniego and Agustín Acuña near Bavispe, running off twelve mules and a horse and capturing two children. From Bavispe, Captain Cruz wrote Zuloaga and blamed the raid on the Indians at Janos. Zuloaga insisted that the hostilities were likely the work of those bands living at Alamo Hueco under Mangas Coloradas, Carro, Esquinaline, and Cochise. "These bands," added Zuloaga, "have not agreed to peace and I am doing all in my power to convince them to make peace." Zuloaga also believed that the two captives would be used to trade for his prisoners at Janos.[27]

By late June the hostiles had reached a decision; with the Bonneville campaign scouring the heart of their territory, the Chiricahuas again turned toward Mexico. Mangas's followers opted for Janos and Cochise's Chokonens sent emissaries to Fronteras for the second time in four months. The previous February, Pablo, a son of the old-time Chokonen chief Matías, had come in requesting peace for the entire Chokonen band and Sonora had named a peace commissioner, but nothing of note occurred.[28] By March the Chokonens had retired to the Chiricahuas, where they were reported to be harvesting mescal.[29] In July, Pablo again entered Fronteras and parleyed with Captain Gabriel García. The Apache claimed to speak for several groups, which, we can infer, included those of Cochise, Esquinaline, Chepillo, and Colchon, and pledged to return in mid-July with the entire Chokonen band to consummate a truce.[30] García's plan, which included rations, was endorsed by both the state and federal governments, but again the Chokonens failed to come in, ostensibly having had second thoughts about trusting Sonora. Some joined their Chihenne and Nednhi relatives at Janos, while others raided Sonora before eventually joining Mangas at Janos.[31]

The raids began in mid-July and the state government offered empty rhetoric to appease local authorities. The prefect of Arispe declared that the Apaches' peace proposals were a smoke screen: "It was their cunning and accustomed slyness so that they could harvest their acorns and commit their accustomed robberies."[32] The *Alta California* quoted Sonoran Acting Governor José de Aguilar relative to the Chokonen overtures made by "some of their principal warriors, now on the frontier between Fronteras and Janos . . . desiring a cessation of hostilities, and anxious to form a treaty of peace; but no confidence . . . [can] be placed in these savages and robbers; they had so frequently made treaties and as often violated them, that they were no longer to be trusted." De Aguilar recommended a war of extermination against the Apaches, even though Sonora was in no position to take any offensive.[33]

In the meantime, more and more Chiricahuas visited Janos to receive rations and whiskey and to dispose of their stolen stock. Sometime in July, Mangas Coloradas, Victorio, Sargento, and Riñon brought in their Bedonkohe and Chihenne followers.[34] Their groups numbered more than three hundred and according to one report swelled the Indian population to more than one thousand, although official Janos records indicated there were about six hundred.[35]

Cochise and his followers showed up in August, probably to dispose of stolen stock and plunder.[36] These wilder Chiricahuas, or broncos, were a destabilizing influence. Zuloaga and Padilla might have decided to take this opportunity to do away with as many Chiricahuas as possible. Again details are sparse, but it seems likely that Mexican officials deliberately issued poisoned rations to .the Apaches. Cochise, fearful of contaminated rations and aware of a rumor that troops would be sent to exterminate the friendly Apaches, returned to the Chiricahuas and security.[37]

After a band council in early September, the Chokonen leaders decided to reopen negotiations at Fronteras, hoping at least to postpone a Sonoran offensive. As proof of their good faith, they returned a captive taken in one of their raids near Matape.[38] By late September, Cochise and most of the Chokonen band of 680 individuals showed up at Fronteras wanting rations. This created enormous problems for the Fronteras commander, Captain Gabriel García. To begin with, he had received no instructions from his superiors; second, he barely had adequate provisions to feed his small garrison, notwithstanding 680 Indians. He sent urgent appeals to the governor imploring him to provide rations for the Apaches until the arrival of the peace commissioner.[39]

More than anything, García wished to take steps before the Americans struck an alliance with the Chiricahuas. The Sonoran government was acutely sensitive to American expansionism, although the arrival of American troops in southern Arizona in 1856 had brought about an ephemeral period of improved relations. It was first hoped that the Americans would prove to be a barrier between Mexico and the Apaches, who had driven out most of the Mexican settlers along the border by 1857. Knowledgeable Mexicans thought they were better off to have the Apaches under their care rather than across the border in the United States, where they could find refuge after their raids into Sonora.[40]

Sonora's new governor, Ignacio Pesqueira, was far from prepared to deal with the Chiricahuas' proposal. Internally, chaos prevailed as skirmishes between rival political parties (Pesqueira's and Gándara's) continued; externally, the federal government in Mexico City was providing less and less assistance. While it once had provided six hundred thousand pesos a year for the state (collected within Sonora for customs duty, paper, and tobacco taxes) to fight Apaches and Yaquis, by 1857 it had diverted most of this money to finance its own needs. These problems were further compounded when Pesqueira was forced to shift troops south of Ures to suppress a Yaqui rebellion. Therefore, at the time of Pesqueira's inauguration, the state was in deplorable condition socially, economically, and militarily.[41]

Pesqueira was absent when García's urgent letter explaining the peace proposals arrived. When informed, the governor promptly named Rafael Angel Corella, a battle-hardened officer who had been wounded in the Pozo Hediondo fight, peace commissioner. Pesqueira's selection of Corella was puzzling in that the latter despised Apaches, having buried the victims of their raids on more than one occasion. The year before, he had led the relief party to Chinapa, finding, in his words, "corpses of men, women and children who were completely nude, and the ground saturated with blood." He preferred fighting instead of feeding Apaches and subscribed to the old frontier axiom that the only good Indian was a dead Indian.[42]

Pesqueira instructed Corella to impose fifteen articles on the Apaches before ratifying an armistice, so as usual, the treaty was full of fallacies, with the Sonorans aiming to domesticate and civilize the Chokonens. The articles covered all aspects of Apache life, and the last decreed that if the Apaches failed to live up to any of the fourteen previous articles, the treaty would be voided and the Indians "severely chastised." Any man who thought the Indians would settle down to farming was simply unacquainted with their background and culture. If Corella had had the opportunity to present these demands to Cochise's people, they would have had a good laugh around the campfire. Although the Indians may have agreed to the terms in principle, they never would have put them into practice.[43]

Before meeting the Apaches, Corella reported to Pesqueira:

> When the savages solicit peace at Fronteras the people believe this is the end of their suffering; but quickly they realize that they have been deceived; that this belief is an illusion . . . these same Indians continue committing their accustomed depredations.
>
> Our experience of many years, your excellency, has made us aware of this astute enemy, experience that we have bought with the lives of our many sacrificed victims; these savages have no good will.[44]

Meanwhile, at Fronteras, Cochise, weary of waiting, left the area in early October. Captain García wrote that the Apaches had left without his knowledge and that Esquinaline had sent his sister to advise him that they had retired only to gather acorns, berries, and other food staples. García pessimistically wrote that the Apaches had either resumed raiding or had gone to Bavispe, where an Apache woman named Lucía had solicited peace. The officer was dubious about the Chokonens' intentions, although Esquinaline's sister "assured me with her life that the Apaches will return." [45]

At 10 A.M. on October 9, 1857, an Apache warrior, his wife, and his two children approached Fronteras. The man might have been Cochise's brother Coyuntura and the woman Coyuntura's wife, Yones. Cochise frequently used his sister-in-law as a messenger because she was probably somewhat conversant in Spanish. The warrior willingly furnished details about the recent activities of the Chokonens, revealing that Cochise was camped with El Cautivo and had sent him to inform García that the Chokonens had retired to Guadalupe Canyon near the San Bernardino River. Many families were infected with a fever, he said, and several Indians already had perished in the epidemic, probably the result of contaminated rations from Janos. Cochise had sent him not only to reiterate his desire for peace but also to deter a potential Sonoran offensive, although none was planned at the time. An incredulous García asked, "If all the Apaches were so sick, who were committing the depredations in the interior?" To this the warrior responded that "they had not lost their passes given to them at Janos and that those committing these depredations must be from the bands living at Janos. This was the information given to them by Colchon, whom they had left a few days before." He also revealed that while "at Janos they were always very sick. Several women and children had died and at least ten men. The survivors had moved to gather acorns that had been previously stored. Also that Nabecilla [a Chokonen man] had gone to gather some gold hidden in the Chiricahua Mountains, which he would take and trade to Captain Padilla at Janos." [46]

Steck corroborated the Chiricahuas' belief that they had been poisoned at Janos. On November 21, 1857, he wrote his superiors that Mangas Coloradas had sent him word offering to return from Janos and live in peace:

> [These Apaches] . . . have suffered much from disease and many of them have died from their own story the mortality has been very great scarcely a family returns but has their hair cropped short, the badge of mourning for some near relative. They believe they have been poisoned and I have but little doubt that many of them have as reports have reached here from the citizens of Janos that many of them have been poisoned and the symptoms as described by the Indians re-

semble those of poisoning by arsenic—probably administered in their rations—whiskey as that formed a part of them.[47]

Steck reported later that more than sixty Chihennes had fallen victim. Cochise's Chokonens had suffered a similar fate.[48]

Meanwhile the Chiricahuas awaited Corella's peace commission, which arrived at Fronteras on November 5. Soon thereafter, Colchon's wife appeared at Fronteras as a representative of three local groups (Colchon's, Cochise's, and Esquinaline's) that were living in the Pitaicachi, Enmedio, and Animas mountains. She acknowledged that several Apaches were still very sick and that ten Chokonen men had died (probably forty to fifty individuals in all), including the prominent Carro and a minor leader named Tinaja. Furthermore, she claimed, Esquinaline planned to honor the peace agreement and settle at Cuchuverachi, a deserted ranch twenty miles northeast of Fronteras. She also said the Americans had communicated with the Chokonens—probably a reference to messages Steck had sent the Chihennes asking them to return to New Mexico, which may have included an invitation to the Chokonens.[49]

Corella's conference with Colchon's wife was ostensibly unsatisfactory. Wary of Corella and his "peace" contingent of seventy troops, the Chokonens remained in the hills. Their actions delighted Corella, who was itching for a fight. He enthusiastically reported that the Apaches had resumed raiding in earnest, though he cited no specific incidents. He therefore requested new orders to pursue those who have "taken up arms against the state." Not all agreed with Corella, however. In mid-November the perspicacious José María Elías González again urged that the state provide rations before the Chiricahuas made peace in Arizona. Captain García endorsed this thought the following month, but no government assistance was in sight.[50]

Mangas Coloradas and Delgadito had returned to Steck's agency by early December. Only the groups under Victorio, Láceris, and a few other minor leaders remained at Janos until early January 1858. They, too, finally returned to New Mexico, their ranks decimated because of the poisoned rations at Janos.[51]

Cochise apparently spent the winter of 1857–58 in southeastern Arizona, away from Mexican control. From here his people resumed their old raiding patterns into Mexico, encountering only token resistance. As long as they depredated below the border, they were left alone by American troops, who were too few and too scattered to give the Apaches any trouble. At Fort Buchanan an American officer allegedly remarked that he would make an agreement to sell arms and ammunition to the Apaches to help them in their raids below the border. When they returned to American soil, they would find a ready market for all of their stolen stock.[52]

The next news of Cochise's people arrived in late April 1858. On the evening of April 28 a small party of two women and two warriors appeared at Fronteras soliciting peace for the ranchería of Lucas, who, with Colchon, had succeeded Posito Moraga as leader of a local group. Lucas was camped near Batepito with some forty warriors. Two days later at 8 A.M., the influential Chepillo surprised the garrison at Fronteras and spoke for his ranchería of fifty warriors in the Chiricahuas. There was no mention of Cochise's whereabouts, but his local group was probably living in the Apache Pass and Stein's Peak vicinity, where Apaches were seen by overland parties.[53]

In May 1858, Cochise was probably raiding in Sonora, having been summoned by Mangas Coloradas. A few months earlier, a company of Sonoran nationals from Cucurpe had clashed with some raiding Chiricahuas and had killed two sons of Mangas, possibly including Cascos.[54] As a result, Mangas organized an avenging war party and Cochise, with his wife Dos-teh-seh losing two brothers, probably joined him and led the Chokonen contigent. They again found Sonora virtually defenseless as prefects of several districts begged the governor for assistance. According to Sonoran reports, more than five hundred Apaches plundered the state "under the pretext of avenging the deaths of Mangas Coloradas' sons." This same account reported that Mangas had declared he would continue killing until three hundred victims were sacrificed, although one would question the anonymous source of this statement. The districts of Moctezuma and Sahuaripa were among the hardest hit. On their return north the Indians raided the ranch of the peace commissioner, Rafael Corella, before running off the horse herd at Fronteras.[55] The Chihennes returned to New Mexico and the Chokonens to the Chiricahua Mountains, where an overland party supposedly met Cochise, who was again considering relations with Fronteras.[56]

Why Cochise was a party to the several peace negotiations at Fronteras in 1857 and 1858 is difficult to comprehend. The most important reason seems to have been his apprehension of Americans, in particular American troops, but one thing is clear: the Chiricahua Apaches were not constantly at war with all groups. For their own self-preservation, they maintained friendly relations with some Indians (for example, the Zuñis in northwestern New Mexico, with whom they traded for guns and ammunition, and the Navajos in the same region, with whom they occasionally traded for blankets) and with some Mexican towns in northern Sonora and Chihuahua.

This balance of power shifted with the arrival of Americans in the Southwest, particularly when ranches, settlements, and forts were established, making the Anglos a force to reckon with. Moreover, as with any society, there were leaders within it who were more peaceably disposed (Esquinaline and Delgadito) and others who were more belligerent (Cochise and Mangas Coloradas). Yet even these war chiefs realized that it was not practical to fight everyone, that they needed a place to dispose of stolen plunder, that their number had decreased because of continued war with Mexico, and finally that American troops had proved themselves to be more than able adversaries. Unprovoked American attacks on the Chihennes had left an impression on the wilder and more suspicious Chokonens, leaving them disinclined to confront the Americans. Stated simply, the message is this: the Chiricahuas, although fierce warriors and highly efficient raiders, did not kill every Mexican or American they happened to come across. These Apaches valued their property, family relations, and lives as much as any other people might. Therefore, they continued to solicit peace at Fronteras because they wished to avoid contact with the uncertainty to the north (Americans) and to a lesser degree the Chihuahuans to the east.

As in the previous fall, the entire Chokonen band was involved, with Cochise's group the last one agreeing to participate in negotiations. In early July 1858 an Indian woman showed up at Fronteras and requested peace for the entire band. She returned on July 11 with five warriors and five women. At this meeting she revealed that

she had talked with Cochise, who also favored an end to hostilities.[57] The Apaches left the next day, promising to return within
four days to conclude the agreement. Sonora's state newspaper, *La
Voz de Sonora,* declared that the Apaches' motives were simple:
"They know that within a few days a campaign against them is to
begin and for this reason they asked for peace." Furthermore, "the
governor knows very well the treacherous manner of this tribe and
will not be deceived." Its prophecy was correct; this time the Chokonens would be the ones deceived.[58]

On July 14, 1858, the stage was set for the Indians' appearance at
Fronteras. Frustrated by previous overtures which never came to
fruition and exposed to Apache hostilities, the Fronteras officials
came up with an ingenious plan to slaughter the Apaches, one which
had been successful in the past and which the Apaches should have
suspected. Although there is no doubt that the Apaches suffered
losses (both Mexican and Indian accounts place the number of
Apache men killed at substantially the same), there are the inevitable discrepancies between white and Indian accounts of the affair.
According to Captain García, the Mexicans were compelled to protect themselves because the Chiricahuas entered the presidio looking for trouble. He claimed that when the Chokonens arrived, many
were already drunk, although this seems to defy explanation and is
somewhat dubious, given the Apache version. The Apaches contradicted Escalante's report, claiming that the Mexicans liberally furnished them with mescal and then turned their weapons on the unsuspecting Indians. He asserted that the conflict was initiated by a
drunken Chokonen who had wounded a soldier, at which time he
"gave orders that all Apaches who were drunk, and especially the
one who wounded the soldier, be conducted to the guard house until
they sobered up."

The Chokonens refused to go, and a general melee erupted in the
streets of Fronteras. Colchon attacked and killed one soldier and
wounded another before he was cut down by the troops. The soldiers eventually gained control of the fight as the Chiricahuas fled.
At once García "marched to their ranchería, carrying as guide one
of the Apache prisoners." The troops overtook some of the inebriated warriors and succeeded in surprising the Apache camp near
Cuchuta. All told, twenty-six Apache men and ten women were

killed. Besides Colchon, two other chiefs were killed. The Mexicans captured "ten carbines, twenty lances, seven horses, three mules and two burros." Escalante closed his report by asking for reinforcements because the Indians "will avenge this and attack me in great numbers within six or eight days." [59]

This report was obviously biased on several points. As has been said, the Chiricahuas certainly did not arrive at the peace conference already drunk. The Mexicans had probably prepared an elaborate feast and supplied the Indians with all the liquor they wanted. Only in this drunken stupor could the Chokonens have been so easily entrapped and slaughtered. In fact, a Chiricahua may have referred to this incident to Morris E. Opler: "The Chiricahua would make peace with the Mexicans. Then the Mexicans would give them liquor, get them drunk, take them in their houses and cut off their heads. Then the war would start again." [60] Two months later the Apaches told Americans at Stein's Peak that they "had been intoxicated and then killed," admitting to twenty-five fatalities. [61]

Why the Chiricahuas lay prone to Mexican treachery is best summarized by Dan L. Thrapp, authority on Apache-military relations:

> Stories of such slaughters of drunken Apaches occur so frequently during the frontier years that one must accept them as basically true, but one can only speculate how they were engineered so often as the Apaches report, and why the Indians fell into the same old trap with such regularity. Perhaps peaceful relations between Mexicans and Apaches were as common as war, and for purposes of trade and perhaps other reasons a tenuous relationship always existed; the occasional massacres were abuses of this relationship, rather than chance incidents in a long period of generally hostile dealings between the peoples. [62]

The massacre at Fronteras was a severe blow to the Chokonens. The loss of three leaders, twenty-three warriors, and ten women wiped out more than half of a local group. The remaining warriors eventually acknowledged Cochise as their leader at the band level.

Ironically for the Mexicans, the massacre forced the Chiricahuas into the hands of Americans, the one thing Sonorans most feared. After the slaughter, the Chokonen groups returned to southern Arizona, from whence runners were dispatched to Mangas Coloradas, inviting him to join the Chokonens for a foray against Fronteras. A Chiricahua war party was usually organized to avenge deaths. Its objective and scope differed from those of a raiding party in one element: the revenge factor. The objectives of the raiding party were both economic and political, with the stolen stock and plunder serving as a necessary part of their subsistence and giving the warrior an opportunity to enhance his prestige. In contrast, the organization and objectives of a war party revolved around vengeance. Stock and plunder were desired, of course, but they were secondary to revenge. A war party set out to punish a specific ranch, town, district, or state. While a raiding party could have as few as five warriors and usually no more than twenty, the number in a war party could range from thirty or forty to two or three hundred.

Late that summer, warriors gathered at Stein's Peak to prepare for their retaliatory attack against Fronteras. Led by Cochise and Mangas, the party totaled some two hundred warriors. In early September, Sylvester Mowry reported that he met at Stein's Peak with José Mangas, a brother of Mangas Coloradas, who boasted that the warriors were going on an excursion to Fronteras "to wipe out the town." Mowry added that "all of the men had collected at Steins Peak when I passed."[63]

Before departing, the Chiricahuas probably had a war dance, held "only when they go out for revenge and fighting." The dance, in which only the warriors participated, was known as fierce dancing and started at least four nights before the expedition was to begin. It was repeated each night. The overtone of the war dance was serious. Warriors danced and prayed for good fortune. They wished to meet their enemy and kill him; they hoped to capture food and plunder. The war dance allowed the warrior to prepare himself for battle, to work himself into a fighting pitch. Social dances followed the war dance, and at daybreak the participants would retire to sleep. The same ritual continued for three more days, and the war party left on the fifth or sixth day.[64]

The Indians left Stein's Peak about September 12, with Cochise and Mangas Coloradas leading. The entire camp gathered to see them off, with the women calling out encouragement. Scouts were sent out to the front, flanks, and rear. During the march, the men of each cluster, or extended family group, followed their own local group leader. By the evening of September 15 the Chiricahuas, safely in the mountains east of Fronteras, prepared for the attack, which would take place the next morning.

Whether by design or not, the Chiricahua war party had chosen an opportune time to attack. Of the seventy men stationed at the presidio, thirty dragoons were out with Captain Eraclio Escalante on a scout to the Magallanes Mountains, thirty miles northwest of the presidio, and twenty infantrymen had gone to Bacoachi for supplies. Therefore, on the morning of September 16, 1858, only twenty soldiers remained at the fort and several of them were protecting the citizens working their fields. The Apaches attacked at 9 A.M., but the move was ill advised and poorly coordinated. All of the Mexicans were able to reach the safety of the presidio except one, Sergeant Simon, who was killed. The Chiricahuas fought until the citizens and troops "fought them off with rifles and spades and fired three cannon balls to disperse them." Cochise and Mangas retreated into the hills. The element of surprise gone, the Apaches called off the fight, content to wait for another time. Their losses are not known. Why they had made such a poor showing is difficult to comprehend except for their well-grounded fear of cannon fire. Cochise himself had reason to be wary: the cannon may have contributed to his capture at Fronteras ten years before.[65]

After being repulsed at Fronteras, the Apache war party divided. Mangas Coloradas and his Chihennes returned to Stein's Peak in a foul mood; they demanded and received twenty sacks of corn from Butterfield Overland Mail Company stage station personnel. Cochise and his Chokonens, intent on revenge, proceeded into Sonora, raiding, plundering, and killing before returning to the Chiricahuas.[66]

By October, Cochise had returned to Apache Pass, secure from the reinforcements stationed along Sonora's northern border. Intending to discourage American expansionism and impede Apache incursions, Lieutenant Colonel José Juan Elías announced plans to regarrison the frontier with a force of 500 men distributed as follows: 150 to Fronteras, 100 to Bavispe, 100 to a temporary fort on the San Pedro, 75 to Santa Cruz, 50 to Imuris, and 25 to serve as scouts. To gain public support, another Apache campaign was planned and donations were requested. Unlike the previous fall's drive, citizens from Ures and Hermosillo responded by dipping into their pockets for some three thousand pesos, proving that people would pay for exterminating Apaches but not for pacifying them.[67]

In late October, Elías received a report from Fronteras that the Apaches were organizing another war party from Santa Rita del Cobre, where the Americans were providing them with arms and ammunition. Their target was Fronteras, no doubt, because of the July massacre. As a result, Elías left Ures with forty-six men and one piece of artillery bound for Fronteras. He stopped at towns and ranches to receive contributions and recruit volunteers. His march provided him with a vivid picture of the deplorable state of the frontier north of Arispe. He passed Chinapa, which Apaches had burned to the ground twice in the past eleven years and was now deserted. Bacoachi was almost a ghost town, for many families had left to seek refuge in the center of the state. Elías promised that the government would provide security and protection to all; in addition, the prefect of Arispe pledged seed, tools, and stock as an incentive to any hardy citizens who wished to repopulate Chinapa.[68]

Elías arrived at Fronteras about November 10. He strengthened the garrison to 150 men and appointed Captain Cayetano Silva Escalante, a dogmatic campaigner, commander of the National Guard. He also adopted an aggressive policy of keeping patrols in the field, which soon paid off. On December 13, Escalante's command attacked a ranchería in the Otates Mountains, killing 18 Indians and taking 4 prisoners. The Indians confessed that they had come to Sonora on a campaign, although Apache war parties normally did not bring their women and children. Probably they had migrated south for the winter and Escalante had attacked the base camp while the warriors were out raiding. This report, in addition to Steck's information, makes it appear likely that the Chihennes or Bedonkohes were the victims of this attack, in which 16 of the 18 killed were women and children, suggesting indiscriminate killing—not an unusual practice for this time or the "civilized" twentieth century.[69]

Escalante ordered several other expeditions to scout the mountains usually inhabited by the Chiricahuas. By early December he concluded that the Apaches had moved north of the border to U.S. territory. Here the Indians discovered that small parties of Americans had built square adobe stage stations at their usual haunts at Stein's Peak in the Peloncillo Mountains and Apache Pass between the Chiricahua and Dos Cabezas mountains. At one of these places, the first recorded meeting between Cochise and Americans occurred. He was ready to deal with the Anglos.

Chapter 7

APACHE PASS

By 1858, Cochise had emerged as the principal leader of the Chokonen band. Other headmen, such as Esquinaline and Chepillo, continued to lead local groups, though smaller than Cochise's. The
band, however, lacked centralistic leadership. The venerable Mangas Coloradas still retained ample influence, on a tribal basis, to
mobilize large war parties into Mexico, but during the next three
years he relinquished this position to Cochise, now the ablest of the
militant Chiricahua leaders.

When the Anglos began to make their presence felt in southeastern Arizona, in particular the chaparral-covered hills and ravines of Apache Pass, it was Cochise with whom they dealt. They
found a chief who desired peace, not so much because he feared
their military might at this time, but because relations with Mexico
had broken down. He could not afford to have enemies on both sides
of the border.

Those who met Cochise in the late 1850s recognized him as the
principal Chokonen chief and were impressed with his stature.[1]
Samuel Woodworth Cozzens, who claimed to have met him at
Apache Pass in 1859, described him as a "tall, dignified-looking Indian."[2] James H. Tevis, who may have had more contact with Cochise than any other American before 1861, depicted him as "fine a
looking Indian as one ever saw. He was about six feet tall and as
straight as an arrow, built, from the ground up, as perfect as any

man could be. He only had one peer in physique, Francisco, chief of the Coyoteros. I don't suppose that Cochise ever met his equal with a lance." [3]

Cochise's first reported Anglo contact occurred in the fall of 1858 at either Apache Pass or Stein's Peak, and he attended his first official meeting in December 1858 when he conferred with Indian agent Dr. Michael Steck at Apache Pass. These peaceful encounters were significant because they signaled the beginning of a new Chokonen attitude: a willingness to interact with Americans. The willingness was a product of two related events. First there was the growing American presence in southern Arizona, which was manifested by the development of mining activities in the Tubac area, the construction of Fort Buchanan some forty-five miles southeast of Tucson, and the emergence of the Butterfield Overland Mail Company, whose route cut through Cochise's country. Second, Sonora strengthened its northern presidios in the late summer and early fall of 1858, partly to protect itself from American expansion and partly to forestall Apache raiding. Finally, the souring of Chiricahua-Mexican relations, beginning with the Carrasco affair in March 1851 and culminating with the massacre at Fronteras in June 1858, forced Cochise to consider friendly relations above the border.

The Americans' arrival in southern Arizona had not gone unnoticed by Cochise. In fact, there had been a few minor skirmishes between his people and the whites. In June 1857, Captain Richard Stoddert Ewell,[4] a seasoned veteran of the Southwest, jumped a ranchería in the Chiricahua Mountains and captured twenty horses. The next night, the dispossessed Apaches retaliated, recapturing their stock and stealing two cavalry horses.[5] Although Ewell failed to mention Apache casualties, in all likelihood Indian blood was spilled. One month later, on July 20, 1857, Apaches (probably Chokonens) ambushed a small wagon train at Apache Pass and killed two men named Short and Irving, wounded two women, and stole twenty head of cattle. The hostiles were supposed to have suffered the loss of four or five warriors. When news reached Fort Buchanan, Captain Edward H. Fitzgerald, twenty soldiers, and twenty citizens left in pursuit but found no trace of the hostiles, who apparently had slipped across the border into Mexico.[6]

For the next year the overland route through Chokonen country was noticeably free from depredations. Between June 1857 and September 1858, James E. Birch's Jackass Mail Route made some forty trips through Chokonen country without a single hostile encounter, primarily because most of the Chiricahuas were living in northern Mexico at this time.[7] By the fall of 1858, for reasons previously discussed, Cochise had become resigned to establishing relations with the Americans, and if William Hudson Kirkland's reminiscences are correct, in October 1858, Cochise showed that he wished peace.

Kirkland was one of Arizona's earliest pioneers, having settled in the Sonoita Valley in the mid-1850s. On October 24, 1858 (although Kirkland later remembered the incident as having occurred in the early 1860s), he was hauling wood from the Santa Rita Mountains when Cochise and twenty-five Apaches surrounded him and two of his men. Cochise punched him in the back with the blunt end of his lance and ordered the white men to prepare a meal for them. Kirkland recalled that "I didn't know I could cook, but, by God, I found I could cook pretty well." After eating, Cochise let the whites go.[8] A short time after this incident, Cochise established a relationship with the whites at the Stein's Peak or Apache Pass stage stations, which had been constructed as part of the Butterfield Overland Mail Route. The Butterfield Overland Mail Company, which succeeded James E. Birch's Jackass Mail Route, was the culmination of an expanding nation's need for a transcontinental mail system.

By late summer 1858, 141 stage stations were strung between St. Louis and San Francisco along a 2,800-mile route. They were about 20 miles apart, although sometimes the interval was only 9 miles but could be as much as 60. By 1859 there were 200 stage stations. Normally, two to four employees manned each station, although some had as many as eight. The mail company, which employed two thousand men at the peak of its operation, instructed its employees to keep their distance from the Indians and to avoid trouble as much as possible. At the same time, it admonished them to be prepared for Indian attacks and treachery. Consequently, each of the stage stations had a small arsenal of Sharps rifles, plus experienced men who knew how to use them. In September 1858, one year after the company received the contract, the Butterfield Overland Mail Route was operational.[9]

One of the more dangerous sections along the route lay between

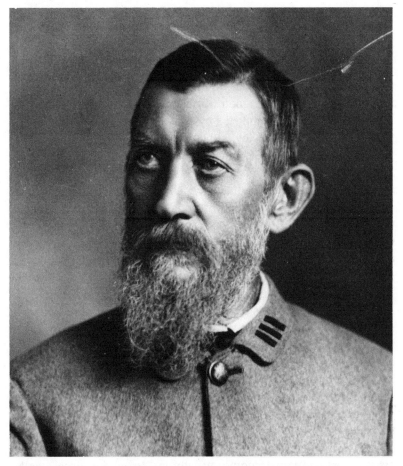

James H. Tevis. A station keeper at Apache Pass in 1858–59, he knew Cochise well and his comments were less than flattering. (*Courtesy Arizona Historical Society, Tucson*)

Mesilla and Tucson in the heart of Chiricahua territory. Nine stage stations threaded this isolated stretch, giving employment to one hundred men and costing about one hundred thousand dollars a year to operate, with Giles Hawley providing competent direction of activities.[10] Three stage stations (later expanded to five) were situated in Chokonen country about equidistant from one another, and each

was to play an important role in future events. The Stein's Peak station was on a bold uplift at the eastern mouth of Doubtful Canyon in
the Peloncillo Mountains. Thirty miles to the southwest was the
Apache Pass establishment, deep in the defile separating Dos
Cabezas and the Chiricahua Mountains. The third station was forty
miles to the west at Dragoon Springs, just north of the Dragoon
Mountains. All were completed by early September under the direction of William S. Buckley, although the Dragoon Springs station
was finished under tragic circumstances. All of the Arizona and
New Mexico stage stations had large square enclosures with adobe
or rock walls, and each had a dependable water supply.[11]

Evidently some of Cochise's first contacts with stage personnel at
the Stein's Peak and Apache Pass stage stations were less than cordial. Anthony Elder, in charge of the Apache Pass station, whipped
and chastised a Chokonen warrior after Cochise allegedly raided the
stock of the Santa Rita Mining Company. According to James H.
Tevis, who succeeded Elder, Cochise threatened revenge, forcing
Elder's superiors to transfer him to a position in charge of overland
supply. Tevis's reminiscences contain obvious mistakes in chronology and facts and an exaggerated account of his own exploits,
but they cannot be disregarded. He knew Cochise well, and his
letters to the *Weekly Arizonian* in the spring and summer of 1859 are
some of the best source material about Cochise at this time.[12]

During 1859 and 1860, Cochise's local group could usually be
found camped at Cochise Canyon (later called Goodwin Canyon),
about one mile north of the stage station at Apache Pass. From here
his warriors continued raiding, usually in Mexico but occasionally
some overzealous young men stole stock from ranches north of the
border, apparently against his orders. In early December 1858 he
joined Mangas Coloradas for an incursion into Sonora. By mid-
month "only the sick and disabled" warriors and the women and
children remained at Apache Pass. By the twenty-sixth he was back
in the pass and probably was instrumental in returning some mules
stolen from the stage station by a few Chokonens. In fact, one chief
(perhaps Cochise) declared that the Indians "would not molest the
whites" as long as they did "not interfere with their incursions into
Sonora."[13]

In New Mexico, Apache agent Steck was informed that the

William H. Kirkland. This early Arizona pioneer unexpectedly met Cochise in October 1858 in the Santa Rita Mountains in southern Arizona. (*Courtesy Arizona Historical Society, Tucson*)

Chokonens had established their rancherías at Apache Pass. Possibly Mangas Coloradas told him about their presence; if not, the stage station personnel at Apache Pass may have done so. The previous summer, New Mexico's superintendent of Indian affairs, James L. Collins, had written Steck requesting information about the Indians living in Arizona. In his reply, the good doctor separated the Mogollon band from Cochise's Chokonens, the first time, to my knowledge, that this was done by Americans. Wrote Steck: "The Mogollon band of Apaches range in the Mogollon Mountains, the

Buras [Burro] Mts, the Head waters of the Gila and the country between Gila and Mimbres and as far south as the Republic of Mexico.
This band has about 125 warriors and five hundred women and children [this was probably the Bedonkohe band]." Furthermore, he
pointed out, "to this band should be added the Band who live on the
Cierra Larga [Peloncillo], Chilihuihui [Chiricahua] Mountains and
the country between these mountains and the Gila. They will number about 150 warriors and five hundred women and children [this
was the Chokonen band or Cochise's Central Chiricahuas]." The
two bands "are identically the same people are intermarried and
make common cause of any difficulty and in their expeditions for
plunder, go together." [14] Steck understood that Cochise's people
were distinct from the Mogollons.

On December 23, 1858, Steck left Fort Thorn for his first visit to
Arizona. He had written Tevis asking him to notify the Chokonens
of his plans. En route he rationed the Chihennes at Santa Rita del
Cobre, finding them quiet and satisfied. From there he followed the
mail route west for 170 miles and arrived at Apache Pass on December 30. Here he "found a Band of Apaches called Jeneros or
Chilicagua [Chiricahua] Mountain Apaches with their chiefs Chees
[Cochise], Es-ken-el-a-ne [Esquinaline] and Fresco [Francisco?],
fifty men 120 women and about four hundred children, totalling six
hundred." Steck believed that "this band of Apaches . . . have
committed no depredations upon the route [to California] for near
two years." To encourage their continued "good behavior," he
issued them rations. Among the presents distributed were several
head of cattle, 20 *fanegas* of corn, 211 blankets, 100 yards of
manta, and 200 brass kettles. Cochise no doubt was pleased with
the gifts and perceived this as a golden opportunity: he could raid
into Mexico at will and live in safety at Apache Pass; he would receive rations from Americans occasionally as long as he caused no
trouble. [15]

Next the indefatigable Steck continued west to Fort Buchanan,
hoping to meet Western Apache bands. He conferred with Captain
Ewell, who told him that on January 4 the Apaches had stolen some
horses from the vicinity of the Sonoita and Santa Cruz rivers. As a
result, they decided to visit the Chokonens at Apache Pass, but before doing so they had more pressing matters: they met and rationed

the powerful Pinal and White Mountains Apache bands before journeying east into Chiricahua territory and arriving at Apache Pass on
January 25, 1859.

In the presence of Ewell's dragoons, Cochise was conciliatory
and returned the stolen stock. He also released a Mexican captive
recently taken from San Ignacio, Sonora. Steck reminded Cochise
and the other chiefs of the serious consequences if they continued to
raid and concluded that "the chiefs seem well disposed and promise
to exert themselves to maintain peace." [16]

Steck and Ewell had done their job well, providing the right mix-
ture of gift giving and saber rattling. As long as the Indians kept the
peace in Arizona and New Mexico, citizens, military officers, and
government agents were content. This attitude, reciprocated by
Mexicans when the Apaches lived in Sonora and Chihuahua, was
not as hypocritical as appears. To begin with, the Americans were
not yet formidable enough to prevent Apache raids into Mexico; in
addition, many southwesterners looked condescendingly at the
Mexicans, whom they viewed with much antipathy and contempt as
tensions between the two countries remained high. Although humane individuals such as Steck did not condone such actions, in reality he was powerless, as was the military, to prevent Apache raids
into Mexico.

The agent returned to New Mexico in early February, having
promised Cochise that he would return in a few months with more
presents. Collins congratulated him and urged him to visit Arizona
frequently. Accordingly, in mid-March 1859, Steck again went
there and parleyed with the western Apache bands at Cañon del
Oro, twenty-five miles northwest of Tucson. Here, in the presence
of Ewell and John D. Walker, the brilliant and eccentric agent for
the Papagos, Pimas, and Maricopas, a treaty was negotiated. The
Apaches agreed not to molest Americans or their property, and
Steck promised to distribute rations in return.

Steck's plan did not sit well with some citizens. *The Arizonian,*
the first newspaper published in Arizona, disagreed with a policy in
which the army and Indian agents went into Apache country to
make peace. Instead, it advocated that "when troops go into an Indian country, they should go to fight. If Indians want peace, let them
come after it!" Magnanimously, the *Arizonian* did agree that if the

Pinals kept their word, occasionally the government should furnish
them with a supply of corn and beef.[17]

With the conclusion of the Pinal treaty, Steck retraced his steps to
Apache Pass and on April 1 met with Cochise. Assisted by Tevis
and the latter's personnel, he distributed rations to the local groups
of Cochise, Esquinaline, and Old Jack,[18] estimating the strength of
the three groups at one hundred warriors. Tevis described the scene:

> [The Indians] were formed in a circle in front of the station. . . .
> First, Cochise, Old Jack, Esconolea and the medicine men; in the
> next row, warriors; in the third row, young boys under the warrior
> age; in the fourth row, the chiefs' families: and in the back, the fami-
> lies of the warriors.[19]

After receiving presents, Cochise made plans for another campaign
against Fronteras. First his people consumed the corn ration, pro-
cessing it into tiswin, a weak alcholic beverage which, when consumed after fasting, quickly put the drinker in a state of intoxication. An observer noted that "one drink of tis-win . . . would make
a jack-rabbit slap a wildcat in the face."[20]

On April 6, Cochise called a council, which all the warriors attended, drinking tiswin and discussing their next move: an attack on
Fronteras to avenge the massacre of the previous July. A scouting
party of ten warriors had just returned and reported in favor of an
attack. Cochise had invited Francisco,[21] a powerful Eastern White
Mountain ally whose one hundred men would bring the total of
the expedition to three or four hundred warriors, although Tevis
doubted the Indians could raise that many. The attack was delayed
until Francisco and his followers arrived and the tiswin had been
consumed.

For the next two weeks the Chokonens were exceedingly perverse
and continually drunk. They constantly annoyed Tevis, who wrote
that "there has not been a day . . . that we have not had trouble with
them," primarily because they were not allowed in the station.
Without Steck's or Ewell's presence, Cochise was in an obnoxious
mood and tried to intimidate the few whites, rationalizing that the
station was on Apache land and the government owed him compensation. He soon learned that strategies employed against Americans

were more difficult to implement than those normally carried out with ease against Mexicans. Tevis summed up the relationship between the isolated Americans and the wild Chokonens: "When any government train is here they are as gentle as lambs, but as soon as the train leaves, the devil seems to let loose among them." Fortunately for Tevis, Francisco arrived and on April 24 the war party departed for Sonora. Only two warriors and the noncombatants remained at Apache Pass.[22]

On April 27 at 8 A.M. Cochise, Elías,[23] and sixty warriors surrounded several citizens working their crops near Fronteras. The Apaches assaulted the first man they came across, shooting and lancing him to death. Once the alarm sounded, most of the workers escaped to the presidio and their surrounding homes, but a few were not so fortunate. José Nicolas Lillas was irrigating his land when he found himself trapped; he submitted and was bound immediately. The Indians also captured two boys, the first a son of Rafael Villa, a soldier at Fronteras, and the other a son of the town blacksmith. There was only one reason they were not killed immediately: Cochise had bigger fish to fry. After the initial assault, he and his warriors withdrew to the mountains east of the town.[24]

Cochise's next tactic showed that the Apaches were just as treacherous as the Mexicans, no matter who started it all. To draw his adversary away from the presidio, Cochise displayed a white flag and placed his prisoners in a position where they could easily be seen. The captive Mexicans' pleas could be heard by their rescuers, who must have been apprehensive about meeting the same Indians they had trapped and whipped only nine months before. Nonetheless the two parties held a parley, with Cochise offering to release his hostages in exchange for whiskey, pinole, and tobacco. As he was negotiating, his warriors moved into position for an ambush. The Mexicans sensed this and, "realizing the parley was a fraud," fled toward the presidio, the Apaches on their heels. The move proved fatal to Lillas; he was killed instantly. The Indians rounded up the loose stock and returned to the hills, from whence a wounded warrior took the two boys to Apache Pass. Tevis paid ten sacks of corn as ransom to obtain their release.[25]

The war party followed an old Indian trail to Moctezuma, which they planned to take by surprise. En route they ambushed and killed three men bound for Arispe. Their Moctezuma plans were upended and in the ensuing skirmish the Mexicans mortally wounded Cochise's "favorite warrior," who was not identified but probably was a close relative. Believing he had fallen into a trap, Cochise picked up the injured warrior and retreated to a secure position in the mountains. After conferring with Francisco, he decided to return to Apache Pass; Francisco elected to continue the campaign. The wounded warrior died on the return trip, canceling the great feast Cochise had confidently given orders to prepare. To avenge the fatality, Cochise declared that he would kill twenty Mexicans, which he undoubtedly meant.[26]

By the early summer of 1859, Cochise realized that peace with Americans was precarious. Conflicts between the newcomer whites and the native Apaches were inevitable, of course, because their beliefs, values, lifestyles, and cultures differed so profoundly that clashes could not be avoided. From the time the Chokonens first met Steck in December 1858, there prevailed a tenuous truce, interrupted from time to time by Chiricahua stock raids, which the Indians did not ordinarily consider an act of war.

Cochise must have wanted peace, if only nominally, but it held a different meaning for Americans. The Apaches were accustomed to agreements like those they established with Sonora and Chihuahua, where their raids were condoned and even tacitly encouraged as long as they occurred in another district. So Cochise no doubt saw advantages in making peace with the Americans. First there was the matter of presents, or rations, which, unbeknown to him, would arrive semiannually instead of weekly, as the Mexicans distributed them. Second, the Apaches might be able continue their forays into Mexico and perhaps find a ready market for their plunder at Apache Pass. American nonintervention was dictated by the fact that the nearest U.S. military post was a hundred miles away and the American agent who would supervise the Indians was two hundred miles away. Consequently, Cochise virtually had a free hand, so that an occasional stock raid in Arizona might go undetected.

Important was Cochise's relationship with those Americans with whom he came into contact: Agent Steck, Captain Ewell, and station keeper Tevis. The Chiricahuas wanted the gifts Steck distributed, and they probably feared and respected Ewell's dragoons.

At any rate, Cochise's people behaved when in Steck's or Ewell's presence, although they showed less deference to Tevis and his employees. Tevis himself never trusted Cochise, whom he described in a less than flattering manner:

> [Cochise was] a very deceptive Indian. At first appearance a man would think he was inclined to be peaceable to Americans but he is far from it. For eight months I have watched him, and have come to the conclusion that he is the biggest liar in the territory! and would kill an American for any trifle, provided he thought it wouldn't be found out.[27]

Tevis, who had a tendency to exaggerate, did not think much of Cochise's character, but Apaches scorned a liar and Cochise's integrity within his tribe was beyond reproach. At this stage in Cochise's life, Americans had not yet gained his total respect, so to them his deportment was honesty when it suited him.

What, then, was the relationship between Cochise and the Anglo-Americans? The legends and myths established in these early years must be discussed and analyzed. It has been written, for example, that Cochise "allowed" the mail line to operate through Chiricahua country. Be it noted that the Butterfield Overland Mail Company established its route without asking Chiricahua permission. Although Cochise could have attacked and perhaps wiped out the stage stations at any time, he undoubtedly was aware of the advantages of peace and may even have considered the possibility of troop retaliation. He often seemed to hold the station personnel at Apache Pass in contempt, sometimes blustering against their operations. More than once Apaches piled rocks across the route to impede movement of the stagecoaches, although whether Cochise himself had anything to do with it is not known; the matter has generally been ignored by historians and writers. Two oft-repeated stories would seem to support Cochise's early friendliness toward the white interlopers: that he supplied the stage station with wood and hay, perhaps under contract, and that he prevented attacks on the stagecoaches, in the spring of 1859 even killing four Apaches who dared violate this forbearance.

Both stories lack documentary evidence to support them, which is not unexpected of course. The station had to obtain hay and wood somewhere, and it would be routine for Cochise's women to bring it in—as was done in similar circumstances elsewhere—with no record of such an agreement being preserved. Cremony does not mention the practice, nor does Tevis. John G. Bourke wrote in 1891, however, that "old-timers have often told me that the great chief, Cocheis, had the wood contract for supplying the 'station' . . . with fuel."[28] In his 1915 *History of Arizona,* Thomas E. Farish wrote that Cochise "had a contract . . . for supplying [the Apache Pass station] with wood," although he fails to cite his source.[29] This information, which might be factual, has been accepted by Woodworth Clum, Paul I. Wellman, Ralph Hedrick Ogle, and other writers down to the present day.[30] As far as Cochise's purportedly killing four Apaches who had caused trouble along the mail route, there is absolutely no shred of evidence to support this tale, which apparently was fabricated by John P. Clum. Although Cochise and Esquinaline both offered to overlook the mail route, there is no record of their fighting other Apaches to protect the Butterfield operation.[31]

Cochise seemed friendly, on the surface at least. He reportedly told his warriors that if the mail were left alone, the white soldiers would adopt a laissez-faire attitude toward other things,[32] a sort of Anglo adaptation of the Mexican viewpoint. In addition, on more than one occasion, Cochise returned stolen stock; a chief becoming aware that this had been done might, if he were sufficiently forceful and respected, demand the animals from the thieves and do what he wished with them. In Cochise's case, it was to return them to their proper owners.

One such incident occurred early in the summer of 1859. Cochise had just returned from Sonora and learned that a few weeks earlier there had been a raid for which he doubtless would be blamed. Consequently, he decided to visit Fort Buchanan, or so Tevis reported.[33] Shortly afterward a band of about twenty Indians stole eighty to ninety horses and mules from the Sonora Exploring and Mining Company near Patagonia, the raid being reported to Captain Isaac Van Duzer Reeve at the fort. Reeve blamed the Chokonens and ordered Ewell to follow their trail. It was wiped out by a heavy rain, but Ewell too concluded that the thieves were Cochise's people—as indeed they were. The leader of the party was Parte.[34]

Probably a few men from Cochise's group were implicated. When

they returned with their loot, he insisted that it be returned; some
may have resisted. Merejildo Grijalva, who was with the Chokonens
at the time, said Cochise became so incensed that he not only seized
the livestock but killed a warrior who defied his doing so.[35] He sent
two of his men to Fort Buchanan with eleven of the animals. On
July 21, Captain Isaac Van Duzer Reeve wrote his superiors:

> This morning two Chiricahui Indians of Chees' [band] came in &
> brough [sic] (11) eleven of the stolen animals.
> This band was encamped on the San Pedro & Chees, having heard
> of the robbery sent and took these animals & sent them in.
> He sent word that he would try and get all that had been stolen. He
> says they were stolen by a band of Chiricahuis headed by a chief
> named "Parte" that they supposed when they took them that they
> were in Sonora and that the animals belonged to Mexicans!

Reeve added that "Chees appears to be acting in good faith,
prompted somewhat, I doubt not, by my visit to the Chiricahua
Mountains in search of a site for a post."[36]

Reeve may have assessed correctly Cochise's respect for his
troops, but then too the chief may have thought Ewell could trace
the animals to his band, hence his prudent decision to return them.
Cochise's desire to avoid Anglo conflict seems to have been confirmed in a conversation between Grijalva and Fred Hughes, an assistant to Tom Jeffords and later clerk of the Chiricahua Reservation. Grijalva said that in the late 1850s the Chiricahuas, although
continuing their raids into Mexico, "had strict orders from Cochise
never to lay hands on anybody or anything within the boundary of
the United States."[37] This philosophy seems evident in an 1865 report in which Cochise conceded that during this period he was unable to keep his warriors from raiding but it was not his desire to be
at war with Americans.[38]

Throughout the summer of 1859, Cochise maintained friendly
relations with Americans. After restoring the stolen stock, he and
most of the Chokonens headed straight for the upper Chiricahuas to
gather acorns and piñon nuts for winter. These staples were almost
as important as mescal in the Chiricahua economy, and it was common for a family to gather five hundred pounds for future use. Only
Esquinaline's following remained at Apache Pass, where in mid-

August he met Samuel Cozzens, a lawyer from Mesilla. In his youth Esquinaline had been a bold warrior who led his tribesmen on many raids against Mexico; now, in his mature years, he had learned moderation and wisdom. Cozzens described him as "rather a good looking specimen of an Apache, about 60 years old and speaks Spanish, very imperfectly, however."

Cozzens had more to tell. He said Esquinaline's local group and "that of Jack, one of the Coyotero Apaches, are now at war. An engagement took place near here a few days ago in which several on both sides were killed and wounded." It was later ascertained that eight to ten warriors were killed in the fight. Cozzens ended his letter with the revealing statement, if true, that "the Chiricahua Indians declare themselves friendly to whites, and willing to protect the mail company." This statement was repeated by Cochise three months later.[39]

By October 1859, Cochise had returned to Apache Pass, intending to spend the winter in the vicinity of Cochise Canyon. On November 6, Steck arrived with rations, which were distributed to some four hundred Indians. He found the Chokonens "very friendly and were gratified for their presents." Cochise returned three stolen animals to Steck and "promised to watch over the interest of the Overland Mail and travellers upon the great thoroughfare to California that passes directly through his country." Perhaps he was sincere in his offer, but the turn of events made it meaningless.[40]

Steck returned to his agency in late November. The harmonious relations he had established with Cochise were beginning to deteriorate, mainly because of Chokonen stock raids north of the border. Captain Reeve, in command of the temporary camp on the San Pedro, was ordered to mount a campaign against Cochise's people, but he was concerned about the mixed signals given to the Indians:

> Department special orders Number 121 suggests a scout against the Chiricahua Indians. Since the publication of that order the Indian agent, Dr. Steck, has visited these Indians, has distributed presents to them, met with and treated them in all respects as faithful friends. It is well known that they have often stolen during the past half-year. . . . They are responsible for about 24 animals stolen in July last from the Arivaca Mine, belonging to the Sonora Exploring and Mining Co.—also 5 animals stolen from Patagonia mine. I cannot

make an expedition against these Indians with the means left in my possession after another scout against the Pinals; and shall therefore await further instructions.[41]

A report from Tucson told of increasing raids below the border, some of which originated from Apache Pass: "These Indians [Chokonens] are almost continually on the warpath, they are better armed than the Pinals, having a great many firearms which have been given to them in exchange for their spoils steeped in the blood of Sonora."[42] Apparently, Cochise's people had found a market at Apache Pass to dispose of stock and booty from Mexico.

In late 1859 and early 1860, several events militated against a continuation of the precarious armistice between Chiricahuas and Anglos. First, in late 1859, Merejildo Grijalva, with Tevis's assistance, escaped to Mesilla and found employment with Dr. Steck.[43] The causes of Merejildo's disenchantment with the Chiricahuas have been widely discussed, focusing on two theories: that the Apaches killed five of his brothers and that he fell in love with and married an Apache girl who was killed by her tribesmen.[44] Neither yarn seems plausible. More than likely, Merejildo had simply become weary of life with the Indians and wanted a change of scene.

Even more serious were three other incidents that occurred in late 1859 and early 1860; these marked the beginning of Chokonen-Anglo hostilities. On three occasions Americans were compelled to kill Chokonen men, two of them in the act of stealing livestock.

In late November 1859, Chiricahuas ran off some mules from the ranch of Thomas Smith of Sonora, thirty miles below the border. Smith pursued the raiders with some of his men, overtook them near Santa Cruz, and in a running fight killed three and recovered his stock.[45] After he returned to Apache Pass, the leader of the raid, an "old chief," confessed that he had thought it was Mexicans in pursuit of him or "he would not have stopped to fight." The old chief may have been Cochise, who at the time was sometimes referred to that way, but more than likely it was Plume.[46]

Pressure was felt most immediately by the Apache Pass stage people. From Tubac it was reported on January 14, 1860, that the "friendly Indians at Apache Pass had given intimations of extensive preparations for a total extermination of the Overland Mail line through their country, to be followed by a descent upon the settlements," a gloomy prediction frequently echoed in the frontier press, although an Indian attack on a white settlement north of the border was rare indeed. The writer, lawyer Thompson Turner, a sometime newsman, continued that "if they decide upon this step, they can with ease massacre the men at the stations and seize the exchange horses." Even if Turner had never seen a wild Apache—and there is no evidence he had done so—his passing along this Wild West gossip probably seemed valid to his middle western readership.[47]

Tevis described a similar attempt. Cochise had craved revenge, he said, after Americans on the Sonoita River near Patagonia killed a Chokonen in the act of horse stealing. Cochise, Tevis added, was so incensed that he ordered his Indians to kill anyone who went for water at Apache Springs, but Tevis may well have been exaggerating because no one was killed for doing that and Tevis himself, through his own intrepidity, defied Cochise's order and obtained water from the springs when it was needed.[48]

In any event, Cochise's smoldering animosity toward Anglos burst forth again in early 1860. On January 18, less than a week after the Apaches had threatened the Apache Pass station again, Chokonen raiders seized forty head of stock from Mexicans between San Simon and Apache Pass, although none of the Mexicans was hurt, it was reported.[49] Ten days later a station keeper named John Wilson killed one of Cochise's Mexican captives, a boy named José, in self-defense. Tevis recalled that Cochise "growled considerably" about the outcome, but the former explained that "Wilson was in the right so that was the end of it."[50] Nonetheless, the Chokonens "assembled in large numbers" and threatened to attack the station before Charles Hayden's freight train arrived, which diverted their attention. The Indians surrounded it, killed one yoke of oxen and lanced three other animals. Hayden's men refused to depart for Patagonia unless they got protection, so Ewell was prevailed upon to send them an escort.[51]

Even other Indians began pointing at Cochise's people. The Pinal Apaches, talking peace with the Americans, asserted that the Chokonens, with some help from the Coyoteros, had done nearly all of the stealing thereabouts, and even if they were dissembling, in part, some credence must be given their words. By mid-March relations between Apaches and Anglos were so impaired that Ewell reported the Indians to be depredating everywhere and "no tribe that I know of Apaches is guiltless."[52]

Cochise had plenty of outlets for his growing belligerence, if that is what it was. In the late winter of 1860 he led a war party into Sonora, striking terror as he went. He was not alone. During a one-month period, Apaches slaughtered more than fifty Sonoran men, women, and children, and no doubt many of the killings could be laid at his wickiup door. The hostiles' efforts were concentrated southeast of Ures at Soyopa, Tonichi, Sahuaripa, and Alamos. At Tonichi and Soyopa, Indians killed thirteen Mexicans before vanishing into the inaccessible Sierra Madre. A particular sanguinary combat between the two longstanding foes took place toward the end of March. Cochise, with about one hundred warriors, was returning from Sonora and was about seventy miles below the Arizona border when the Indians ambushed and killed four travelers on the road between Cucurpe and San Ignacio. The next day a party of fifty nationals under Angel Elías pursued the Chiricahuas to the summit of a hill, up which the courageous troops, at Elías's urging, charged. The Chiricahuas swarmed out like angry hornets, killing eleven men at close range; almost all were lanced to death. A wounded man was left on the battlefield to a fate of certain death, perhaps by torture. Cochise added seven more victims later that day.[53]

A week later, on April 7, the Chokonens returned to Arizona and stole some stock from the Dragoon Springs stage station. According to Samuel Cozzens, who was there at the time of the raid, the Americans suspected Cochise. The next day, Cozzens inquired of Cochise about the incident and the chief's ambiguous reply caused him to conclude that Cochise had led the raid, which he probably had.[54]

Meanwhile, back in Arizona, the Chokonens were raiding Tubac again and threatening a major outbreak. In mid-May a "friendly Apache" reminded the station keeper at Apache Pass that "it was the intention of the Indians to clean out the station."[55] Two weeks later, Cochise's Chokonens ran off the entire herd of the Santa Rita Mining Company near Tubac. Captain Ewell trailed the thieves to the Chiricahua Mountains and in early June parleyed with the leader, in all likelihood Cochise, and compelled him to return some of the stolen stock, the Apaches claiming to have eaten the re-

Richard Stoddert Ewell. Pictured here as a Confederate general, Ewell was a popular and efficient officer who met Cochise on more than one occasion before the Civil War. (*Courtesy Arizona Historical Society, Tucson*)

mainder. They proposed, however, to provide compensation and asked the officer to return in late June to receive the balance.

On June 25, Ewell and a detachment of seventy-five men, including assistant surgeon Bernard John Dowling Irwin, left Fort Buchanan for Apache Pass. Five days later they met the Chokonens, who returned some of the required stock but the agent of the Santa Rita Mining Company refused to receive five animals as "not being of sufficiently good quality." At the time of Ewell's first visit, Apaches had stolen mules at Tubac, although the chief, probably Cochise, "disclaimed all knowledge of it" and may have been correct. The Apache leader did concede that a robbery had been committed by the Chihennes and that the Chokonens overtook this party and seized two of the mules in order to hand them all over to Ewell. The remainder of the animals had been traded to Mexicans or had died along the route, he said. The two mules indeed proved to be among those stolen from Tubac and Ewell restored them to their owners. In Ewell's opinion, "the perpetrators of this Tubac robbery . . . were strongly in favor of its having been done by these same Indians [Chokonens]." [56]

Cochise insisted that the mules were the best he could offer. An incredulous Ewell decided to examine the Chiricahua Mountains in search of Apache stock because "it is generally supposed that these Indians have large herds of fine stock." After eight days of fruitless searching, the officer concluded that the Indians possessed little or no stock and that he "was satisfied that they had done all in their power to meet the demand." Chokonen raiding inevitably led to Anglo distrust of Cochise's people and the gradual acceptance that if stock were stolen, the Chokonens were guilty. [57]

Ewell's report to headquarters was unusually long for him. Apparently there were some "amateurs" at Apache Pass who disagreed vehemently with his handling of the affair, and Ewell felt they would misrepresent it. Letters written to the *Alta California* and *Missouri Republican* were scathingly critical of "Old Baldy" for holding a parley instead of attacking the Chiricahuas. [58] In his report Ewell defended his policy of negotiating. After all, he had received some of the stolen stock, and any attack would have been in violation of a truce. He concluded by pledging that in the event of another theft he would not ask for restitution but would leave the fort "at night, and attack them when unprepared and try to make an effective blow." He did not get another chance to meet the Chiricahuas. He was ordered to Fort Bliss, Texas, to appear as a judge at a court-martial, after which he went to Virginia on sick leave. On May 7, 1861, he resigned his commission and joined the Confederacy with the rank of lieutenant general.[59]

Ewell's visits merely intensified the growing animosity between the two races. Immediately after his first visit on June 17, 1860, a large number of Chokonens appeared at the Apache Pass station, well armed and ominously painted, to tell the Anglos to quit under the timeworn threat of being cleaned out.[60] Yet portentous from Ewell's second meeting was the report that only 150 Chokonens remained at the pass. Many had cleared out to Janos and Corralitos in northern Chihuahua, where, it was reported, 10 Chiricahua leaders had solicited peace on June 12.[61] This report was the first indication that some of the Apaches again were ready to deal with Mexico, although the Chihennes remained in New Mexico and the more militant Chokonens under Cochise stayed in Arizona to await the results of their relatives' efforts in Mexico.

In June one Chokonen local group had begun discussions with Chino (who had been at Apache Pass), representing Yaque's local group. Their main complaint with the Americans was the infrequent amount and distribution of rations and presents; hence they looked for greener pastures in Mexico. At Janos they resumed negotiations with their sometime adversary and sometime friend José María Zuloaga, who was virtually the economic and political czar of northwestern Chihuahua.[62]

Zuloaga was a pragmatic man who adapted to circumstances. He owned the Corralitos mines and so had a vested but precarious interest in Apache relations as long as the Indians left his area alone. He tacitly encouraged depredations in the United States, Sonora, and even the interior of Chihuahua. Stolen stock and plunder seemed to find their way with suspicious frequency into his possession. Sonoran and American officials accused him of trading arms and ammunition for stolen livestock, yet he was unyielding when he had the upper hand and negotiated from a position of strength (Esquiriba's imprisonment in September 1857 is a case in point). A resourceful man, he understood that his existence depended on com-

ing to terms with the Chiricahuas, furnishing rations when necessary, and providing a market for stolen stock. Where the animals
came from, or how they were obtained, was of little concern to him.

Notwithstanding his growing reputation, the governor of Chihuahua authorized Zuloaga to make peace. The latter triumphantly announced: "It is our good fortune that we did not request peace, they
[Apaches] have solicited the peace and they must abide to the conditions." He also wrote Pesqueira in Sonora that Apaches living in
security across the border continued to raid and murder in Mexico
and suggested that the only way to control these bands was to keep
them under close scrutiny; and the only way to protect the people on
the frontier, he said, was to declare an armistice. Zuloaga obviously
sensed an opportunity to remove the Apaches from American influence and back to Mexico, a tug of war which existed from the end of
the Mexican War in 1848 through the Geronimo wars of the 1880s.
Furthermore, he hoped, Pesqueira would join him and eventually
create in Sonora establishments where the Apaches could receive
rations. He believed that fifteen hundred Chiricahuas eventually
would come in for rations.[63]

Cochise remained at Apache Pass throughout the summer and fall
of 1860. He too was growing disenchanted with Americans, particularly with the trivial amount of assistance provided by the government. The semiannual rations had arrived on March 31 and were
quickly consumed. There would be no more until November, a lapse
of almost eight months. By August even the pacific Esquinaline had
deserted Apache Pass for Fronteras, where on the last day of the
month a woman from his camp requested a truce, saying the Chokonens were dissatisfied with the Americans at Apache Pass. She also
had been sent by several other leaders, among them Parte (at the
time living near Janos) and Delgadito, who had fled New Mexico
because of white encroachment.[64]

Sonora eagerly accepted the Chiricahua offer. Captain Gabriel
García requested instructions from Pesqueira, who replied favorably: "Fronteras is a satisfactory place to administer the peace . . .
treat the Apaches, who have asked for peace, well."[65] As a consequence, by early October a small band of forty-six Indians under
Esquinaline and Delgadito had settled near Fronteras to test the
waters. To prove their sincerity, they turned their weapons over to

García, although these undoubtedly were only their unserviceable or obsolete firearms.[66] Both sides had learned from experience not to trust the other completely.

While all this was happening, Steck completed his arrangements for an Apache reservation to congregate the Mescalero and Chiricahua tribes at Santa Lucía Springs, in the heart of Mangas Coloradas's country in southwestern New Mexico. He had first considered the idea the previous November. Complaints from Apache Pass about Chokonen disturbances probably affected his decision to put the Mescaleros and Chokonens with the Chihennes, in whose territory mining activity was increasing. The previous March, Steck had gone East for personal reasons and while there had conferred with the commissioner of Indian affairs about his plan. The reservation would be fifteen miles square and would include a rich and fertile valley large enough to accommodate several Chiricahua groups, who Steck estimated at 300 men and sixteen hundred women and children, plus the Mescaleros, who Steck counted as 120 men and 600 women and children.[67] Subsequent developments forced Steck to change his plans and the Santa Lucía Springs reservation never became a reality.

Cochise probably would have objected to relocating in Chihenne territory. By the fall of 1860 many Chiricahua groups had become increasingly hostile, and some had relocated to northern Mexico. Even Steck felt the brunt of Apache raids. In mid-October 1860, Apaches reportedly drove off his mules while he was en route to Santa Lucía. Other reports from Tubac and Fort Buchanan suggested that the Apaches depredated because they were starving. More ominously, however, their activities had become more than just the occasional stock raids; they had killed a few Americans. Lieutenant Colonel Pitcairn Morrison, Fort Buchanan's new commander, wrote to his superiors and complained about the depredations; his want for troops, especially cavalry; and his lack of a good guide. He concluded: "I cannot see any other course to pursue than to feed [the Indians] or exterminate them."[68] Conditions deteriorated further in late 1860 when Steck was elected delegate of the Territory of Arizona, as Mowry had been before him, but pending formal organization of the territory, neither man was seated.

Before leaving for Washington, Steck probably met Cochise on

November 10 at Apache Pass, where the Chiricahuas reportedly received their semiannual supplies. Little is known of Cochise's activities at this time, but growing Apache resentment of Americans was evident in the number of Indians appearing at Janos and Fronteras to make peace, among whom were many of Cochise's associates. A month after receiving Steck's rations, Cochise sent a clear signal that he also wished relations with Fronteras. On December 9, Chiquito Teboca, his family (two women, four children, and two men), a Chiricahua woman named Yones and the woman's nine-year-old son arrived at Fronteras seeking peace and rations for Cochise's following.[69] Yones was the wife of Coyuntura, whose reputation was high among the Chiricahuas: "[He] was never known to go out on an expedition with his command of 18 Indians without bringing back stock. . . . He was more dreaded in Sonora than the captains of any other band of Apaches."[70] García received an affirmative reply from Pesqueira; if Cochise could prove his sincerity, he would be rationed.[71]

Ironically, if Pesqueira's reply had come sooner, a whole era of American-Apache conflict and Apache vengeance raids might never have occurred and Cochise's Chokonens might have remained in northern Sonora. This is not to suggest that the Apaches' already strained relations with the Americans might not have resulted in eventual conflict. Raiding probably would have continued under any circumstance, but it might not have been as severe as the devastation that hit Arizona in the spring and summer of 1861. In any event, Cochise did not wait for the governor's reply. By January 1861 he was back at Apache Pass, destined to be involved in one of the most significant and controversial incidents in Apache-Anglo relations, the Bascom affair.

Chapter 8

CUT THE TENT: THE BASCOM AFFAIR AT APACHE PASS

As 1861 dawned, Cochise had already spent more than three-quarters of his life in relative obscurity, as far as the non-Chiricahua world was concerned. He was approaching fifty and had two wives (he took a third some years later). According to Chiricahua accounts, his first and principal wife, Dos-teh-seh, bore him two sons: Taza, born in the early 1840s, and Naiche, born about 1856. By his second wife, who was of Chokonen blood but whose name was not recalled, he had two daughters: Dash-den-zhoos and Naithlotonz, both born in the late 1850s or early 1860s. A report from the San Carlos Reservation in 1886 does not concur with twentieth-century Apache recollections; it said Cochise had two widows at that time. By one he had had two children, who died; by the other he had had Taza, Naiche, and two daughters.[1]

Cochise made sure that his sons received a proper education. The older of the two, Taza, nearly twenty, had completed his novice training and was much like his grandfather, Mangas Coloradas, in build. At maturity he carried two hundred pounds on a five-foot ten-inch frame.[2] As the first-born son, he received particular attention. According to Asa Daklugie, Cochise "groomed him for the position" of Chokonen chief. Consequently, Cochise taught Taza "every trail, every source of water, and every secret cache known."[3] A Chiricahua informant explained the development of a leader to Morris E. Opler: "Most of the leaders I knew were sons of leaders. The chief's children get special advice and act in a different way. Because he is trained in a good way right from the start, the leader's son usually turns out to be a real man."[4]

In addition, Cochise passed his medicine power (a resource which took many forms, from having the ability to cure sickness to finding the enemy) along to Taza. During the 1860s and the early 1870s, Taza evolved into a good fighting man and succeeded his father as chief in June 1874. Pneumonia struck him down two years later in, of all places, Washington, D.C.[5]

In contrast to Taza, Naiche was much like his father in appearance. At maturity he stood five feet eleven inches and was considered to be the best-looking man in the tribe.[6] After his father's death he supported his brother's decisions, and when Taza died, he assumed leadership of the Chokonens who remained on the reservation. In September 1881 he fled from the San Carlos Reservation and, allied with Geronimo, led the last of the incorrigible Chiricahuas, who finally surrendered in 1886.

The Bascom affair, which spawned open hostilities between Cochise's people and the Americans, is difficult to reconstruct for several reasons. To begin with, several of the participants' accounts were recorded many years after the event: William Sanders Oury's in 1877, policeman Oberly's in 1886, assistant surgeon Bernard John Dowling Irwin's in 1887, and Captain Daniel Robinson's in 1896. Inevitably, chronology and facts were sometimes distorted, especially in the accounts of Oury and Irwin, both of whom missed the first week's activities. Oury, who reached Apache Pass eleven days after the initial hostilities, left behind a most unreliable account. Irwin's recollections were also lacking in some areas, but his memory was better than Oury's. Fortunately, we have the narratives of two eyewitnesses, policeman Oberly and Captain (then Sergeant) Daniel Robinson, both of whom were present from beginning to end. Oberly's account, often discarded as worthless, is upon close examination sometimes in accord with Robinson's, which was a contrast to every other version. Robinson was not only an eyewitness but a participant in much of the affair. His recollections contain excellent descriptions of the first Bascom-Cochise meeting, Cochise's subsequent escape, the Cochise-Bascom parley of February 5, and the fight at Apache Springs on February 8.[7]

Next, the contemporary accounts furnished by driver A. B. Culver and William Buckley provide but a brief synopsis of what took place before they arrived on February 6 and February 7, respectively. Their reports are reliable but limited because they were not present for the important events of February 4–6. Another concurrent account was written in November 1861 by a soldier, stationed in Arizona, who may have been present for part of the affair. This trustworthy account, which was published in the *Missouri Republican* nine months after the event, contained a vivid description of Cochise's escape and a harsh condemnation of Bascom's actions and judgment (considering it was written by a soldier).[8]

We also have Lieutenant George Nicholas Bascom's official reports of February 14 and February 25. Neither is entirely satisfactory because he attempts to justify his actions. Each contained errors in chronology, and both were ambiguous and perhaps duplistic in some respects, obviously to cover up his egregious mishandling of the incident.[9]

Finally, we have the Apache perspective as articulated by Geronimo, Jason Betzinez, and the published writings of Mrs. Eve Ball, whose version was based on accounts provided her by Chiricahuas. Cochise gave what was perhaps his most detailed version to William F. Arny in October 1870.[10] The Apaches knew the incident as "cut the tent," a reference to Cochise's means of escape. Although Geronimo's version placed Mangas Coloradas in the tent (an obvious error in translation), the remainder of his account is surprisingly accurate. Unlike Betzinez and the Apaches who conferred with Mrs. Ball, Geronimo recalled correctly that Cochise killed his prisoners first. Cochise himself spoke very little of the events at Apache Pass because Apaches normally did not dwell on the past because of death taboos, yet for the remainder of his life he steadfastly maintained that Bascom's mistreatment was responsible for the conflict.

The Bascom affair began rather innocuously. On January 27, 1861, two parties of Apaches raided the ranch of John Ward[11] eleven miles south of Fort Buchanan. One group stole twenty head of cattle, while the other seized a twelve-year-old boy named Félix[12] within three hundred yards of the house. The timely arrival of two Americans thwarted further hostilities. They sent a message to Fort

Mickey Free. Captured by Western Apaches, he was the youth whom Bascom demanded from Cochise. Free was a scout and interpreter during the Geronimo Wars of the 1880s. (*Courtesy Arizona Historical Society, Tucson*)

Buchanan and the next morning First Lieutenant George Nicholas Bascom,[13] a brave young officer with no Indian experience, and a detachment of infantry and dragoons (who had just arrived from Fort Breckenridge) examined the trail but found nothing. Later that day they returned to the fort, ostensibly satisfied that the tracks led toward the San Pedro River and then into Chokonen country; hence Cochise's people were suspected.[14]

Public opinion supported this belief. Evidently John Ward thought the raiders were Cochise's people. Reporting from Tucson, Thompson Turner summed up the matter succinctly: "It is generally believed that his captors are the Apache Pass Indians."[15] As it turned out, the Chiricahuas had nothing to do with the raid, which, according to one historian, was probably the work of Western White Mountain Apaches.[16] Here, in chronological order, is what happened.

Tuesday, January 29, 1861

Department headquarters in Santa Fe had furnished instructions regarding the action that the commanding officer at Fort Buchanan should take in the event of Indian hostilities. This morning, Lieutenant Colonel Morrison adopted these orders, which said he was "to pursue and if possible chastise such marauding parties . . . you are authorized to do whatever you think is proper."[17] Furthermore, he was undoubtedly aware of Captain Ewell's pledge, made some six months before, that if Cochise's band raided again he would not ask for restitution but would instead "strike a blow."[18]

With these circumstances in mind, Morrison issued Order No. 4, Headquarters Fort Buchanan, instructing Lieutenant Bascom to "pursue the Indians and recover a boy made captive by them." Assistant surgeon Irwin recalled that Bascom was to "follow the trail until the cattle were found and recovered." If the trail led to Cochise, Bascom was to "demand the immediate restoration of the stolen property." If the chief refused, the young lieutenant "was authorized and instructed to use the force under his orders in recovering it." These orders reveal that Morrison authorized Bascom to use whatever means he deemed necessary to punish those responsible and to recover the boy.[19]

Unfortunately for all concerned, public opinion had indicted and

Lieutenant George N. Bascom. Although he was commended by his superiors for his decisions at Apache Pass, Bascom's actions began the Cochise War. (*Courtesy National Archives*)

convicted Cochise's people because of previous Chokonen raids in
the Tubac area. But the Chokonens had never taken captives, only
stock. If Morrison had gone by recent history, he would have dispatched troops into Western Apache country, for these were the Indians who were known to have taken white prisoners. Instead, perhaps based on information provided by the same individuals whom
Ewell had contemptuously called amateurs, Morrison sent soldiers
into Chiricahua country. Bascom and fifty-four men of the Seventh
Infantry, mounted on mules, were accompanied by John Ward,
who, quite naturally, was "directly interested in the results." The
detachment moved east toward Apache Pass.

Wednesday, January 30, to Saturday, February 2

Bascom's command marched slowly into Chokonen territory toward Apache Pass. According to one account, he followed the hostiles' trail,[20] but this seems dubious in that the Ward boy was later
reported to have been taken to the Black Mountains in Western
Apache territory. Nonetheless, Bascom continued across Sulphur
Springs Valley, heading for the narrow defile between the Dos
Cabezas and Chiricahua mountains. He probably spent the evening
of February 2 at the Ewell Springs stage station, some fifteen miles
west of Apache Pass.

Cochise, camped in his winter headquarters at Cochise Canyon,
probably was informed by one of his scouts that troops were approaching. Their presence was neither unusual nor alarming. Ewell's
command had been there twice in the past six months, and troops
from Buchanan and Breckenridge regularly escorted wagons through
the pass.

Sunday, February 3

The column reached Apache Pass near midday. A few miles west
of the stage station, Bascom met thirteen troopers under the command of Sergeant Daniel Robinson, a sandy-haired man of medium
build,[21] who was returning west after escorting a wagon train to Fort
McLane. He furnished Bascom with information about the Indians
and the location of their rancherías. Robinson's command joined
Bascom's and together they continued toward the stage station,[22]

Bascom campsite. View from the west slope of Siphon Canyon looking northeast across drainage into the probable site of Bascom's first camp, which lies in the center of the picture on the far side of the drainage. (*Photo by Karen Hayes*)

where they met Butterfield Overland Mail employees James F. Wallace[23] and Charles W. Culver, both said to be on good terms with the Indians.

While Bascom conversed with them, Robinson and John Ward questioned two women, "one old and the other young and comely [Juanita]," both apparently part or full-blooded Mexicans. They said they knew nothing of the Ward boy and were told to go to Cochise's camp and tell him that the soldiers wished to parley. About midday, Bascom continued up Siphon Canyon and pitched his tents about one mile from the stage station.[24]

Cochise received the message but did not come in immediately; he may have been awaiting the return of his own runners, whom he had dispatched to the Western Apaches to obtain information on the Ward boy.[25]

Monday, February 4

Early that afternoon, Cochise still had not come in and Bascom was growing impatient. About midafternoon he retraced his steps to the stage station and asked Wallace to go to Cochise's camp to reiterate the lieutenant's desire for a meeting. Wallace hesitated, then went reluctantly. In his absence a freighter wagon train passed eastward and camped near Bear Springs, some two miles beyond the stage station. This was the Ortiz train under Romualdo Torres, en route to Las Cruces.[26]

At the dinner hour Cochise arrived. That he did not anticipate any problem was borne out by whom he brought along: his brother Coyuntura; two or three warriors, believed to be nephews; his wife; and two of his children (according to Apache history, one of them was Naiche). "After the customary greeting of How, How," Cochise, Coyuntura, and another warrior went into Bascom's tent to talk; Ward acted as interpreter.[27] During or after eating, Bascom began questioning Cochise about the raid. Cochise denied Chokonen involvement and said the Coyoteros had the boy in the Black Mountains. If Bascom would wait ten days, he would do all in his power to restore him. Bascom agreed to this proposition, according to his report, but in view of subsequent actions, one would have to question whether he actually assented to this or whether he fabricated a story to save himself embarrassment.[28]

Cochise's pledge was obviated by Bascom's next move. Through Ward he told Cochise that his people would be detained as prisoners until the boy was returned. What happened next is the subject of controversy even today. According to Bascom, he released Cochise, who had promised to obtain the boy,[29] yet every other Anglo version, whether it be an eyewitness (Oberly, Robinson), someone involved in the event who arrived later (Culver, Irwin, Oury), or a letter written to the *Missouri Republican* nine months later by a soldier who may have been present, agrees on one point: Cochise escaped. None of these independent reports even hints that Bascom allowed Cochise free passage. In fact, five of the six Anglo accounts state that Cochise escaped by cutting his way out of the tent, and two of these men were present at the time. Culver's account is the only exception. He arrived two days after the incident, and he said Cochise "effected his escape, after a desperate rush through the guard."[30] A military report made two months later also seems to contradict Bascom. Captain Gurden Chapin wrote that Cochise "was wounded by troops from this post at Apache Pass in February," which must have occurred at the time of his escape unless it happened during the subsequent fighting.[31]

The Apaches' story rebuts Bascom's version. Mrs. Eve Ball's informants told her that "Cochise offered to investigate, determine the offenders, and help restore the child. When he was told he was to be a prisoner, he cut a slit in the tent and escaped." Geronimo recalled that Cochise escaped by "cutting through the tent." Cochise told William F. M. Arny in October 1870 that "he cut his way through the tent was fired at by the soldiers and escaped." In 1872 he told an army officer that "with his knife he slashed the back of the tent, and . . . fled up the hill and escaped."[32]

Most accounts agree that Cochise bolted after he learned that he was to be held prisoner. Sergeant Robinson, who was a short distance from the tent, had this to say:

> Finally it was suggested that the sub-chief [Coyuntura] should go and find him [Ward boy] and that Cochise must remain as a hostage. This ended the talk. As quick as lightning both drew forth concealed knives, cut open the tent and darted out, Cochise to the front—at whom the interpreter fired. The sub chief (escaping through the rear) tripped and fell and was captured.[33]

Cochise had reacted instinctively, slitting the tent and scrambling through the astonished soldiers, who, according to some accounts, had surrounded the tent in compliance with Bascom's orders. "Shoot them down," shouted Bascom, to which John Ward responded, quickly snapping off a few shots at Cochise. These were the first of some fifty rounds fired at the Chiricahua chief, who apparently was wounded in the leg or thigh before he reached the top of the hill with his coffee cup still in his hand, he later told an American.[34] Cochise's relatives were not so fortunate; all were captured, and according to Robinson and Buckley, at least one warrior was killed.[35]

An hour later Cochise reappeared on the top of a nearby hill and asked to see Coyuntura. Bascom responded with a volley and Cochise "raised his hand and swore to be revenged." Cochise reminded the whites that "Indian blood was as good as white mans blood; that he and his tribe had been falsely accused; that for the injuries inflicted on him . . . he would have revenge." After making these threats, Cochise disappeared behind the hills.[36]

That evening Bascom broke camp and retraced his steps up Siphon Canyon to the stage station, mainly because its building and corral offered protection for his men and stock. At dusk Apache signal fires could be seen from the surrounding peaks. Despite this, the Americans were not too concerned; they had "twenty days' rations on hand, some forage and a fair supply of ammunition."[37] Yet the odds of restoring order were poor, especially if one Chokonen had indeed been killed. Of more significance, Bascom continued to insist upon the return of the Ward boy, who was in the possession of Western Apaches, a different tribe over whom Cochise had neither authority nor control.

Tuesday, February 5

Early this morning the Chokonens "assembled in force on a hill 600 yards south of the station." After a short time the Indians began to disperse, leaving a white flag, which was soon acknowledged by Bascom. A lone warrior approached, saying Cochise wished to parley midway between a ravine and the station, and Bascom agreed. Each party consisted of four individuals: Bascom, Sergeants Smith and Robinson, and John Ward comprised the American party; Cochise, Francisco, and two other warriors represented the Apaches. The two groups met in Siphon Canyon some 100 to 150 yards from the station, yet nothing of consequence could be settled despite Cochise's efforts to convince Bascom that he did not have the boy. According to Robinson's account, Cochise pleaded for the release of his captive friends. Bascom replied that they "would be set free just so soon as the boy was restored." Again Cochise denied having the boy.[38]

At this juncture the Butterfield employees (Wallace, Culver, and a man named Welch or Walsh), who were thoroughly acquainted with the Chokonens, left the stage station, hoping to take matters into their own hands and appease the Indians. Bascom immediately ordered them back, although he had no jurisdiction over civilians, declaring that he would not exchange his Apache prisoners for them if they were captured.[39] Nonetheless, the three courageous but naïve Americans continued, but they made the mistake of going into a ravine and were seized. Seeing this, Cochise and Francisco broke for cover and the Apaches opened fire on Bascom's unarmed party, slightly wounding Sergeant Smith, who had been carrying the white flag. Meanwhile, in the ravine, Welch and Culver managed to knock down their captors and flee towards the station. Culver was shot in the back but was picked up and brought to safety. Welch made it to the corral, where he was killed, in all likelihood by soldiers who mistook him in the excitement for an Indian.[40] The remainder of the Apaches, generously estimated by Bascom at five hundred, including Mangas Coloradas, kept up an intermittent fire. Robinson believed that several Apaches were killed or wounded. That evening the whites could see the Indians' "signal fires blazing from the peaks" and could hear "a war dance . . . in one direction and in another the weird cries of the squaws were distinctly heard wailing over their dead."[41]

The few casualties on both sides plus the fact that each were holding prisoners, who could be exchanged for each other, gave rise to hopes that more hostilities could be averted. In one respect, however, the capturing of Cochise's family would have left him with an indelible distrust of Americans. Even if his relations were eventually exchanged, it would have been a pretty sure bet that open hostilities would have followed.

Wednesday, February 6, Noon

Although the morning passed quietly without any sign of Indians, Cochise was watching from the hills. He allowed Sergeant Robinson to lead a party of soldiers and their stock to the springs, some six hundred yards from the station. The Americans anticipated a fight because the trail to the springs led through a winding ravine, an ideal place for an ambush. However, Cochise had no such plans; he was hoping to avoid trouble and perhaps settle things without more bloodshed.[42]

About midday Cochise appeared on a hill overlooking the station (probably Overlook Ridge), leading Wallace, who had "his arms bound behind his back, and a rope around his neck." [43] The chief again asked that his family be freed and offered to exchange Wallace and sixteen government mules. Again Bascom refused and became even angrier when Cochise explained that the mules had been stolen "from a government train, of course." [44] Furthermore, he may have been indignant at Wallace because the civilian had defiantly disobeyed his orders the day before. Bascom clung adamantly to his position that he would release Cochise's family only when the Ward boy was restored. According to some accounts, Sergeant Reuben F. Bernard briefly intervened and tried to dissuade Bascom from his course, urging him to trade the Indians for Wallace. His suggestions, if indeed he was present, fell flat. [45]

Two legends about this meeting should be addressed because they have become so steeped in Arizona history that they are accepted as fact. The first is that Bascom refused to trade because Cochise was holding four prisoners and offered to exchange only Wallace. In fact, Bascom knew nothing of the other three prisoners because Cochise did not have them at this time. If he had had other captives, he would have included them in his proposal to liberate his family. Four whites would have been more enticing to Bascom than one. [46] The second legend, frequently told but not mentioned by any of the eyewitnesses, says Cochise was so infuriated by Bascom's refusal to trade that he or one of his warriors dragged Wallace behind his horse "at full length by the neck" to his death. This did not occur because Wallace later returned. [47]

Wednesday, February 6, Afternoon

Shortly after three o'clock the stagecoach from the east arrived at the western mouth of Apache Pass; it was some eight hours ahead of schedule. It had left the San Simon station before noon, and its occupants were unaware of any danger. At a narrow part of the canyon, perhaps at a place that is today called Tevis Rocks, Cochise's warriors had barricaded the road with hay and rocks, intending to set the hay on fire when the stage got there. Its early arrival foiled the plan. [48] Instead, while the westbound stage approached the station, Cochise had his eyes on Sulphur Springs Valley, from whence five wagons were approaching the mouth of Apache Pass.

Wednesday, February 6, Early Evening

Cochise had been following the progress of José Antonio Montoya's wagon train, loaded with flour for Las Cruces. Montoya had no reason to suspect danger as he and his men began the ascent from Sulphur Springs Valley to the summit of Apache Pass. He had probably made this trip on several occasions, and his only concern was what to give the Apaches in the event they asked for handouts. No one knows for sure the sequence of events, but this is probably what happened: Cochise and a large party of Apaches appeared in a ravine a few hundred yards east of the summit. The Indians may have approached the whites making signs of friendship. Then, at a signal from Cochise, they suddenly surrounded the train, capturing nine Mexicans and three Americans named Sam Whitfield, William Sanders, and Frank Brunner. All of the mules were taken. Having no use for the Mexicans, Cochise had them tied by their wrists to the

Wagon-train massacre site. This gently rolling terrain afforded a good campground for the Mexican wagon train captured by Cochise after Bascom seized his relatives. (*Photo by Karen Hayes*)

wheel spokes and tortured. Next the Indians burned the wagons and killed the Mexicans, but the Americans were taken to his camp in the hope that he could trade them for his family.[49]

That evening he instructed Wallace to write this message: "Treat my people well and I will do the same by yours, of whom I have three [four]." Cochise obviously wished to exchange the four whites for his family. The note, left on the hill and "fastened to the brush," was not retrieved until at least two days later, according to one account. In his report, Bascom implied that he received the note that evening. If he had, his couriers, who left the following day, would have included the information in their reports at Tucson and Fort Buchanan. Instead, the note was not obtained, either because Bascom feared a trap or did not know of its existence. Thus he was unaware that Cochise held four whites until it was too late.[50]

Thursday, February 7

Cochise evidently felt that his four prisoners were not enough. He therefore prepared to ambush the eastbound stage, which had left Tucson the morning of February 5 and would reach Apache Pass early this morning. The whites were not cognizant of the recent hostilities and the last thing they expected was an Apache attack, considering the darkness and the proximity of the stage station.

As they reached the summit of Apache Pass they were stunned by a volley of shots which broke the silence of the night, wounding the stage driver, King Lyons, killing one mule, and wounding another. At once William Buckley, the superintendent of the route, jumped from the stage to aid Lyons. The first thing he saw was the burned Mexican train and the charred bodies. After putting Lyons in the stage, Buckley took the reins and forged on toward the stage station, still almost three miles away. About a half-mile away, the Chokonens had torn away part of a small stone bridge, probably thinking that if the first attack failed, the coach would almost certainly capsize. A determined Buckley whipped the mules and forced them to jump the bridge; the stage's momentum carried it across. The rest of the route was just as perilous because the Indians had put rocks in the road and the passengers were compelled to push the stage over the incline as the Chokonens maintained sporadic fire from the hills.

Bridge abutments. Cochise's men tore away part of the stone bridge hoping the stage would capsize. (*Photo by Karen Hayes*)

The coach finally arrived at the stage station about 2 A.M., thereby frustrating Cochise's attempt to take more prisoners.[51]

To everyone's surprise, not an Apache was seen. Robinson recalled that "everything around us was as still as a graveyard."[52] That morning the mules were watered, and the day passed uneventfully, which must have been a blessing for Bascom's command. Why Cochise did not appear to exchange prisoners is not known. He may have felt that Bascom's obstinacy would make any conference fruitless, and it is possible that, in the words of Geronimo, because Bascom did not reply to Cochise's note, the latter interpreted this as a refusal to trade, "so we killed our prisoners, disbanded, and went into hiding in the mountains."[53]

It is possible, though unlikely, that the four Americans already had been tortured to death. The action of the past few days undoubtedly had resulted in Chokonen fatalities. If so, they may have been avenged by female relatives who vented rage on the prisoners. This was the Chiricahua way, and it is possible, though unlikely, that the torture had been carried out without Cochise's consent.

Thursday, February 7, Evening

No Apaches were seen all day. Cochise had broken camp, removing his noncombatants south into the Chiricahuas. Nonetheless he had decided to take his relative by force if possible. That day he and his warriors prepared for the next day's fight: first a war dance, then the preparation of protective garments and amulets, special prayers asking for success, and finally preparing the bows, arrows, and guns for war.

During the day it was clear to all at the stage station that help was required. Bascom needed a doctor for the men who had been wounded during the previous day's skirmish, and Buckley required additional men to escort the stage. Therefore, shortly after dark, a small party of soldiers and A. B. Culver, who had arrived with the stage from the east and was the brother of the wounded Charles Culver, left to obtain reinforcements. The mules' shoes were wrapped with blankets to dampen sound and prevent detection. Surprisingly, the party had no trouble and gained Sulphur Springs Valley without incident. The soldiers arrived at Fort Buchanan late the following evening; Culver reached Tucson about the same time, having made the 125-mile trip in twenty-four hours.[54]

Friday, February 8, Morning

By now everyone had begun "to think they [Apaches] had left the country."[55] Indeed many had, at least the women and children, but Cochise, now allied with Francisco's and Mangas Coloradas's groups, had returned, intent on making one last effort to free his people. Geronimo, who was present, furnished a simple but honest account of Chokonen activities after Cochise cut his way out of Bascom's tent:

> In a few days after the attack at Apache Pass we organized in the mountains and returned to fight the soldiers. There were two tribes [bands]—the Bedonkohe and the Chokonen Apaches, both commanded by Cochise.[56]

Cochise's attack was well planned. The first assault would take place at Apache Springs after the soldiers had finished watering their stock. He hoped Bascom would weaken his defenses at the stage station and send reinforcements to repulse the diversionary first strike. If Bascom took the bait, a large body of warriors would storm the station from the east and free his family. The scheme was sound and bold.

Sergeants James Huber and Daniel Robinson drove the stock through the ravine to the springs. The advance party was led by Robinson, who felt confident that no Apaches were in the vicinity because it had snowed the night before and "no marks or signs" were observed. He "stood on a knoll above the spring" and "the signal was given to send up the animals." On the previous two mornings, the stock had been watered in two shifts; this time, to Robinson's consternation (he called it a misunderstanding), every animal was sent, a grave mistake by Bascom. Still, as the last animal had its fill, no signs of Indians had been seen.

This changed quickly. Just as the return trip was begun, Robinson observed "a large party of Apaches [two hundred, according to Bascom] moving at a swinging gait" from upper Siphon Canyon and threatening to cut the herd and its escort off from the station. Wrote Robinson:

> They were in war dress . . . naked and painted . . . and they were
> singing a war song. . . . They were coming so open and boldly that
> they no doubt expected to sweep all before them without much
> trouble. . . . We opened fire at once . . . [and] forced them to change
> their course so as to leave the way open to the station.

The soldiers responded quickly, directing several well-placed vol-
leys, wounding several wariors, and repulsing the Indians, who retired in the same direction they had come. The respite was brief. A
few minutes later the Chiricahuas swung to the soldiers' right flank
and gained the heights overlooking the springs.[57]

At the first volley, Bascom sent out a small relief party under the
capable command of Lieutenant John Rogers Cooke, who had arrived with the eastbound stage. Cooke rendezvoused with the soldiers at the springs and took command. By this time every animal
had been driven off into the mountains, and the soldiers, now afoot,
were unable to pursue. During the attack a large group of Apaches,
probably under Cochise, appeared opposite the station, looking for
a chance to take it by surprise. Bascom reacted quickly, however,
and diverted his men to the front to repel the attack, which seemed
imminent. To his credit, his decisive response definitely saved many
lives, both red and white. An assault at this time would have been
costly and uncharacteristic of Apaches, who, it should be remembered, very rarely fought unless they were supremely confident of
success. The Chiricahuas fell back out of range.[58]

The fight was over. Bascom lost forty-two mules and the mail
company fourteen. Mail employee King Lyon was killed and Sergeant Robinson was wounded. Bascom estimated the Indian casualties "with certainty but five Indians killed, but think there were
twelve to fifteen more killed or badly wounded. This includes all
since my arrival at the Pass." The Chiricahuas later acknowledged
at Fronteras that three warriors were killed, and Geronimo remembered that several men were killed. Although the whites scarcely
could have known it, they would see no more Apaches. With reinforcements streaming in from the west, the bands split up, with
Francisco and Mangas Coloradas heading for the Gila and Cochise
and his Chokonens for Sonora, but not before they tortured to death
the four American prisoners, leaving their mutilated remains where

they could be found by the whites. This decision effectively slammed the door on negotiations and eventually led to the death of several Chokonens, including Cochise's brother and two nephews.[59]

Saturday, February 9

Unbeknown to the whites, the siege was over. This morning, in a blinding snowstorm, assistant surgeon Irwin left Fort Buchanan with fourteen soldiers and one civilian, James Graydon, taking with him medical supplies for the wounded. They would camp that evening at Dragoon Springs.[60] Also on this day at Tucson, William Sanders Oury dispatched a messenger to Fort Breckenridge, informing the troops there of Bascom's plight.[61]

Cochise's Chokonens were also on the move. A few stragglers arrived at Fronteras with news of the outbreak, specifically mentioning that a few Indians had been bayoneted and alluding to the hostilities of February 4. In the days that followed, many more Chiricahuas took refuge in the mountains north and east of Fronteras, from whence they descended on the isolated presidio and began drawing rations.[62]

Sunday, February 10

Irwin's reinforcements left Dragoon Springs early this morning, traveling the Overland Mail route. At Playa de los Pimos, which was located south of present-day Willcox, Arizona, Irwin espied some Apaches driving a herd of cattle stolen from Mexico. He pursued and "succeeded in capturing the party consisting of a Coyotero Chief and two warriors" and several head of stock, although one might question how Irwin's party could capture the Apaches, who knew nothing of the difficulties at Apache Pass, unless by ruse. It is generally believed that these Indians were Coyoteros, unrelated to Cochise's Chokonens. Yet it is possible that they were Chokonens or at least Chiricahuas. Irwin, like most Americans, could not differentiate one band from another.[63]

Some two days earlier, some Chiricahuas had conversed with a few citizens outside Fronteras. The Indians said they belonged to the bands of Cochise and Mangas Coloradas and were heading south for a raid into the interior.[64] One might question their veracity, however, for they might have just returned from an incursion. Irwin may have jumped this group. Cochise said repeatedly that the war began when Bascom hanged six warriors (Irwin's three and Bascom's three), thereby implying that the three captured by Irwin were Chiricahuas.

Late in the afternoon Irwin's relief party reached Apache Pass and marched to the station without incident. Although Irwin wrote that the Apaches were off chasing other troops, in reality no Indians were present except for a few scouts.[65]

Monday, February 11, to Monday, February 18

For the first three days, Bascom's command had remained at Apache Pass, totally inactive and ostensibly believing they were bottled up. In reality, the only Indians present were scouts, who certainly would not have sought a fight. Yet, inexplicably, Bascom had not sent out any scouting parties, electing instead to await reinforcements from Fort Breckenridge. They arrived on February 14: sev-

Oak tree at the western edge of Apache Pass near the location where Cochise's relatives were hanged. The actual tree was cut down about 1930. (*Photo by Karen Hayes*)

enty soldiers of Companies D and G, First Dragoons, commanded by Lieutenant Isaiah N. Moore. In all likelihood, Sergeant Reuben F. Bernard arrived with this detachment.

On February 16 and 17, Moore and Bascom led a command of 110 men and scouted the mountains in search of Apaches. None were found.[66]

On February 18, Irwin found the bodies of the four Americans—Wallace, Whitfield, Sanders, and Brunner—all horribly mutilated and "riddled with lance holes." Oury recognized Wallace's body by the gold fillings in the teeth. The corpses were buried some three hundred yards from the charred Mexican wagon train near four large oak trees.[67] Why Cochise left the bodies where they would be found is a question only he could answer, but leaving them there sealed the fate of his relatives. Most of the civilians, soldiers, and officers advocated execution of the six Apache men. According to some accounts, Bascom demurred but was overruled by Lieutenant Moore, who told Bascom that he would assume full responsibility.[68]

Tuesday, February 19

The commands of Bascom and Moore left Apache Pass for their home forts, the former leaving Sergeant Patrick Murray and thirteen men to guard the mail station. As they made their way west through the pass, Bascom had the interpreter explain his intentions to the Indians.[69] Oberly said the Indians asked to be shot instead of hanged and requested whiskey.[70] Both requests were denied. The Indians then accepted their fate and "sang their death songs,"[71] although one man "begged piteously for his life." Another warrior, probably Coyuntura, "went to the gallows dancing and singing, saying that he was satisfied as he had killed two Mexicans in the last month."[72] Robinson recalled that "the dragoons furnished the lariats; one end was thrown over the boughs of the trees, while the Indians placed under them were hoisted so high by the infantry that even the wolves could not touch them." The hanging took place on four oak trees under which Wallace and the other whites were buried.[73] The women and children were released, although Cochise always believed that a card game had decided their fate—a little-known story also mentioned by Oberly.[74] Bascom's and Moore's commands reached Fort Buchanan and Fort Breckenridge on February 23.

Monday, February 25, 1861

On this day both Moore and Bascom wrote their official reports of the outbreak. Moore's, written from Fort Breckenridge, was brief and factual;[75] Bascom's, drawn up at Fort Buchanan, was longer, ambiguous, and duplistic.[76] He omitted several things which would have been a source of embarrassment. It is also conceivable that his report was written with Lieutenant Colonel Morrison's blessing, although we will probably never know for sure. Morrison, then sixty-five years old, was awaiting departmental approval of his request for a leave of absence and may not have wanted any controversy to hinder it. Bascom, after all, had followed orders, but the results were not what they had hoped for.

An analysis of Bascom's report reveals several errors of omision, obviously an attempt to cover up the blunders that resulted from his poor judgment. No other officers were present during the first four days, so his report is the only one dealing with this crucial period, at least from the contemporary military perspective. If Morrison heard post scuttlebutt critical of Bascom's actions, he must have ignored it. It is also possible, however remote, that he accepted Bascom's report implicitly. To begin with, Bascom failed to mention Cochise's escape and his subsequent wounding, which was common knowledge at the post. He also neglected to mention that his own soldiers probably killed Welch at the stage station; he said only that one of the station keepers was killed (implying the Apaches did it), but other accounts indicate that his own soldiers were the marksmen. Next, he implied that he received Wallace's note on the evening of February 6. In truth, the note was not recovered until at least the eighth and perhaps later. Finally, he did not mention that the loss of the mules at Apache Springs was the result of his poor judgment.

The Bascom affair was a prodigious Anglo blunder, but Cochise must bear some responsibility for not controlling his rage or that of his people in the torturing of his four white prisoners, his only bargaining chips. His decision has caused much discussion among historians, perhaps more than anything else he ever did. Why indeed? There is no simple answer, and in his later years he was reluctant to discuss the matter. Perhaps he had already written them off, believing his people would be killed regardless of his actions. It is also possible (although remotely, in my opinion) that the prisoners were killed without his approval. To Cochise, the hanging of Coyuntura and his two nephews meant war.

But what of Bascom? He was commended by department headquarters. And what of the troops? Referring to the Bascom-Cochise incident, a soldier wrote nine months later: "Tread on a worm and it will turn—disturb a hornets nest and they will sting you. — So with savage Indians: misuse them and you make them revengeful foes." [77]

Chapter 9

THE WAR BEGINS

After his relatives were executed, Cochise hated Americans with an abiding and impenetrable passion, perhaps more fanatically than any other Apache. It mattered little that only a few whites had actually wronged him; he hated them all. The loss of Coyuntura distressed him deeply, for Apache brothers were very close, even inseparable if they were in the same local group. It is conceivable that he married Coyuntura's widow, Yones, because Coyuntura's children were blood kin. One of them might have been Chie, or Chee, who was said to have been raised by Cochise.

Initially, Cochise raided and killed to avenge his brother's death; later, as his rage abated, he continued to wage war, and eventually it evolved into a bloody cycle of revenge and retaliation. Throughout the 1860s, American forces were unable to subjugate him as he demonstrated that he had indeed become an implacable foe. Essentially he believed that his people had not begun the fighting and were undeserved victims of American treachery. In February 1869 he told Captain Frank Perry: "I tried the Americans once and they broke the treaty first, the officers I mean. This was at the Pass." [1]

The following year he visited Camp Mogollon (later renamed Fort Apache) and the Cañada Alamosa Reservation in New Mexico to discuss peace. At Camp Mogollon in August 1870 he told Major John Green that "he did not begin the war . . . and only fought for revenge and self defense." [2] Two months later at Cañada Alamosa he confessed to William F. M. Arny that he "had been guilty of murders and thefts . . . since 1860 [1861] when he was treacherously seized and six of his braves hung and he escaped by cutting his way through his prison." [3]

In 1871 and 1872, Cochise granted interviews in which he steadfastly insisted that the war had begun because of the hangings at Apache Pass. He told Brigadier General Oliver Otis Howard in October 1872: "The worst place of all is Apache Pass. There, five [six] Indians, one my brother were murdered. Their bodies were hung up and kept there till they were skeletons. I have retaliated with all my might." [4]

Arizona accounts of the early 1860s supported Cochise's statements about why the fighting began. In May 1861, Captain Gurden Chapin wrote:

> The Chiricahuas, Coyoteros, Pinals, and Coppermine Indians are all at war with us. They have since the action at Apache Pass in February last stolen upwards of one hundred mules and a large number of cattle. They have killed one soldier, several drivers and others on the overland route . . . [they have] also killed several white men, wagonners and farmers. [5]

Another chronicler who was in Arizona when it occurred wrote in November 1861 that the Apache war began with the Bascom affair. Since that time, he said, Cochise had been "the enemy of the white race." [6] John C. Cremony, who arrived in Arizona in 1862 with the California Volunteers, declared that since the confrontation Cochise "has been one of the most bitter, most active, and unrelenting of foes, losing no opportunity to destroy life and property." Cremony, who had a propensity to exaggerate, did not do so in this case. [7]

Other informed Arizona residents from the mid-1860s through the early 1870s echoed these statements. In 1865, N. S. Higgins, who was researching the Western Apaches, heard of the Bascom affair from an old Arizona pioneer who had known Cochise. After the outbreak, he said, Cochise had been "the dread of this country." [8] In the fall of 1867, Arizona pioneer William Oury told William A. Bell at Fort Bowie that after the Bascom affair Cochise "and his entire band fled back once again to their mountain fastnesses never more to come in contact with the white man, unless in the execution of their unquenchable revenge."[9] One year later, Lieutenant Colonel Thomas C. Devin wrote that the incident "aroused him [Cochise] to make war."[10] Captain Reuben F. Bernard attributed Cochise's war to the tragedy at Apache Pass, as did another writer, who said in 1870 that ever since, Cochise "and his tribe have sought and found vengeance."[11]

Twentieth-century writers also say the Bascom affair ignited Cochise's war. To Paul I. Wellman, "it was war to the knife now between Cochise and the white man."[12] Frank C. Lockwood: "His [Cochise's] fury knew no bounds."[13] Historian Robert M. Utley summed up the situation succinctly. After the Bascom affair he said, Cochise possessed "an implacable hostility toward all Americans and [this] spurred him to wage upon them a bloody warfare that lasted for a decade."[14] Although Cochise vowed vengeance, there is no basis for the version put forth by Woodworth Clum, and accepted by some historians, that "ten Americans must die for each Apache the Americans have killed."[15] The Chiricahuas' version, as recorded in several accounts, all say Cochise's war began in February 1861.[16]

At department headquarters in Santa Fe, civil and military authorities moved to quell a full-scale Apache outbreak. James L. Collins,[17] the superintendent of Indian Affairs in New Mexico, unfairly blamed the uprising on Dr. Michael Steck, claiming that if the agent had been present to issue rations, the Apaches would have been content and "the present difficulty would have been, beyond question, prevented." Collins's view was a classic example of the naïveté with which white officials viewed the Indian problem. Steck's presence would not have prevented the hostilities; furthermore, the Indians were upset about the infrequency and paucity of rations, for which the agent could not be faulted. In late February, Collins insisted that Steck be ordered back to his agency, but at this point conditions had deteriorated so much that even the efforts of the influential agent would have been fruitless.[18]

As the Bascom affair was winding down, department headquarters in Santa Fe opted for punitive operations against the Mescaleros and Chiricahuas. On February 10, 1861, it ordered simultaneous campaigns against the Apaches on both sides of the Río Grande. Lieutenant Colonel George Bibb Crittenden was directed to punish the Mescaleros east of the river, and Major Isaac Lynde was instructed to "actively prosecute war against the Apaches from the vicinity of Fort Floyd."[19] When news of the Apache Pass incident reached Santa Fe, the department commander ordered two additional companies of the Seventh Infantry to Fort McLane, which "with the present garrison of Fort McLane, Buchanan, and Breckenridge it is hoped will be sufficient to enable you to sustain vigorous operations . . . at once against the Apaches." Lynde was given a free hand to organize the campaign as he saw fit and was told that headquarters would furnish the necessary resources.[20]

Major Lynde, however, vacillating as always, seemed unable to decide on anything except to remain where he was. This was a stark contrast to Crittenden's campaign, which was "promptly and energetically conducted" and forced the Mescaleros to sue for peace.[21] In fact, after receiving reports from Fort Breckenridge and Fort Buchanan, Lynde concluded that his troops lacked provisions to conduct a campaign. The only meat on hand at any of the three posts was bacon; furthermore, at Fort Buchanan, the mules were "completely broken down and unfit for the field." Lynde argued that "the present force was barely adequate to provide protection" and concluded that "it would be useless to attempt to operate against these Indians."[22]

Actually, any American offensive probably would have accomplished little, for the Chiricahuas had scattered and were relatively quiet. Mangas had headed north to the Gila, but not before he, perhaps with Cochise, cleaned the San Simon stage station of stock.[23] Geronimo recalled that the Indians "went into hiding in the mountains," and "after this trouble [Bascom] all of the Indians agreed not to be friendly with the white man any more."[24] As for Cochise, he plunged south into Sonora and established camp near Fronteras, where some Chiricahuas under Esquinaline, Teboca Chiquito, and Delgadito were living.

Cochise had been in touch with them. The presence of his "broncos" definitely unnerved the Fronteras authorities, who were uneasy, awaiting an explosion. In early February a few of Cochise's Chokonens spoke with some Mexicans near the abandoned town of Cuquiarachi. The Indians' actions intrigued the commander at Fronteras: "I don't know what the intentions of these Indians was in coming to these residents without harming them but I think it was probably for the purpose of finding out about the peace treaties that the other Indians have." Because most of the troops at Fronteras had been sent south to fight the Yaquis and Mayos, the Indians were not followed. This angered Governor Pesqueira, who responded that "in such cases the residents are called together and they have always shown the greatest willingness to help." [25]

On February 9 a few wounded warriors from the fights of either February 6 or February 8 straggled into Fronteras and told of the conflict at Apache Pass. On March 5 additional details were furnished by Teboca Chiquito and Remigio, who said Cochise's followers were agitated because Coyuntura and a warrior named Garanon had been killed. Allied with Francisco's band, the Chiricahuas had raided a train and had stolen more than 150 head of stock, probably implicating them in the February 16 raid at San Simon. The presence of Cochise's followers alarmed even the so-called peaceful Apaches. Delgadito fled Fronteras by the end of February, although it was not clear whether he joined the hostiles or relocated to a safer area to avoid the trouble Cochise's people usually brought. [26]

Once established in northern Sonora, Cochise planned his retaliation, which, for the Apaches, could hardly have come at a more opportune time. Affairs in Arizona were coming apart at the seams. Just as Sonora was vulnerable to Chiricahua raids in the 1840s, so did Arizona prove to be in 1861. The first big blow to the Anglos fell in March, when financial hardship and the imminent Civil War closed the Butterfield Overland Mail Route in Arizona. Many experienced men lost their jobs and left the territory. Quite naturally, Cochise believed that he had forced the abandonment.

The last Butterfield stage from the west reached Mesilla in mid-March and reported that the Indians "had returned in great numbers to Apache Pass." [27] This was almost certainly Cochise. The Chiricahuas tried the white-flag gambit at the stage station, but its personnel were not fooled. Subsequently the Chiricahuas hoisted a black flag, indicating no quarter asked or received. [28]

Despite the increase in Apache signs, no significant hostilities were reported, yet a portending unrest was felt. Both Morrison and Chapin conceded that Cochise was living below the border at Fronteras, beyond their control.[29] Although Sonoran reports failed to mention him, this should not be taken as conclusive evidence that he was not present, inasmuch as some activities were never reported. Cochise or his representatives definitely were at the presidio from time to time. Living near it, he had the option of raiding on either side of the border. Finally, in April, he commanded a Chokonen war party consisting of warriors from all three local groups. With Yaque, Parte, and perhaps Remigio, the Chokonens swept north on a campaign against the Americans.[30]

The first reprisal, a typical Cochise-led encounter, occurred in late April: an ambush of a party of whites traveling through Doubtful Canyon near a place the Indians called Tsisl-lnoi-bi-yi-tu (Rock White in Water), otherwise known as Stein's Peak. *Mesilla Times* of May 11, 1861, reported what happened:

> Nine men are missing, and it is feared have all been massacred although there exists some hope that some of them may be retained as prisoners. The Savages inflicted upon some of their victims a horrible torture, and exhibited a refinement in cruelty unparalleled in the catalogue of Indian barbarities. From the expressman Mr. Price, we gather the following particulars: A provision wagon left Tanks station on April 23, Edward Donnelly and Patrick Donaghue in charge, to put a load of flour at the San Cimone Station. They started on their return but never reached the Tanks. The next day two expressmen, Messrs. Paige and O'Brien left the Tanks westward bound and never reached the San Cimone Station and have not since been heard of. On the 27th a coach left the Tanks for the West, in which were five persons Mr. J. J. Giddings, Superintendent of the San Antonio and San Diego Mail Company, Michael Nies [McNeese], Road Agent and Anthony Elder, Samuel Neely and Mr. Briggs, employees of the Overland Mail Company. Two of the mules which left in the coach returned to the Tanks Station badly bruised, and had evidently been in a severe struggle. This circumstance aroused the suspicion of all and our informant went the next day to Fort McLane and applied for an escort of troops to investigate the matter. A Lieutenant and sixteen men were dispatched who on Monday near Steins Peak, met a train of W. S. Grant, Army Contractor, who gave them information of their having a fight with Cochise and his braves and confirmation of the fears that the coach had been captured by the Indians at or near Doubtful Pass [Grant's train had reached Stein's Peak about dark]. . . .

They found scattered along the ravine, newspapers and other mail matter, pieces of harness, etc. The roof of the station (which was some time since abandoned) had been burned, the corral wall had been thrown down, and the Indians had formed a breastwork around the springs. Near the station the bodies of two men were found, tied by the feet to trees, their heads reaching within eighteen inches of the ground, their arms extended and fastened to pickets, and the evidence of a slow fire under their heads. The bodies had been pierced with arrows and lances. They were so disfigured as to render recognition impossible.[31]

The Apaches killed nine men, with Cochise's fury manifesting itself in the torture reserved for those captured alive. According to Oury's account, Cochise and some sixty warriors, whom he placed in ambush at the springs (located a short distance northwest of the station), ambushed Giddings' party "just at dawn of day, as they were approaching the station at Stein's Peak." The driver (Briggs) and Anthony Elder, who had had a run-in with Cochise in late 1858, evidently were killed in the first fire. The uncontrollable mules "ran for about a mile and a half to the foot of the mountains, where the coach was capsized and everything brought to a standstill." According to a Mexican living with the Chiricahuas, the fight between the surviving whites and the Indians continued for the rest of that day, with the Apaches sustaining heavy losses and Cochise himself being wounded in the hard battle. Neely was killed soon after. By the end of the day, the two survivors, Giddings and McNeese, short of ammunition, may have attempted to parley with Cochise. McNeese had been the agent at Stein's Peak and evidently knew Cochise. His decision was a grave mistake. Like Wallace, he trusted that his earlier friendship with Cochise might mean something; his fate, like Wallace's, was the same. Cochise was in no mood to negotiate, and the two whites, said an eyewitness, were "captured and burned alive, head downward." [32]

Cochise had made a nice haul, if we can believe George H. Giddings's claim against the government for restitution. When Giddings received the news of his brother's death, he recruited twenty-five men and marched to Stein's Peak, where he found the ruins of the station and what remained of two stagecoaches. The Chiricahuas al-

Stein's Peak. Located at the eastern end of Doubtful Canyon, this was the site of Cochise's ambush of Gidding's party in April 1861. (*Photo by Dan Thrapp*)

legedly destroyed or seized property valued at $8,335, including thirteen Colt pistols and thirteen Sharps rifles.[33]

The fight had given the Indians new confidence. Cochise followed it with another hard encounter, but this time the Anglos fought him to a standstill. On April 27, 1861, a freight train departed Fort Buchanan for the Río Grande. A detachment of twenty-one troops served as escort, bringing the total of able-bodied whites to about forty. On May 3 they encamped at the abandoned San Simon station (about eighteen miles northeast of the Apache Pass station) and turned the stock out to graze. Suddenly Cochise and about thirty warriors swept down and stampeded the herd, driving it north toward Stein's Peak. At once Jud Jones took five men in pursuit and almost overtook the hostiles. A running fight ensued for the next four or five miles, some of it hand to hand. A warrior threw his lasso over a Mexican, who immediately tied it "around the horn of his saddle and wrenched it from the Indian."

Cochise was in the forefront as usual, boldly charging the whites, before the fight became "a personal contest, [and] the chief Kachees stepped out and called on Jones, upon whom he dispatched four six-shooters." The shots missed, revealing that Cochise's skill with his native weapons far exceeded that with a six-shooter. Although Jones recaptured some of the stock, the Indians got away with seventeen head. According to Jones's report, the whites killed three Chokonens.[34]

Two weeks later, Cochise planned a strike against the soldiers at Fort Buchanan. On May 16 at Monkey Springs, about two miles south of the fort, a group of Chokonens surprised a small army party, killed one soldier, Private Salliot, and fled with two mules, a rifle, and a revolver. Troops followed the trail for three miles before the Apaches scattered. Antonio, an experienced scout, identified the arrows as Chokonen. A few weeks later, Cochise struck again, this time perhaps in conjunction with Francisco. Charles Mowry and three men left the Patagonia mines for Fort Buchanan. Halfway there, Apaches jumped them, killing a man and wounding the driver. Mowry somehow escaped.[35]

The commanding officer of Fort Buchanan, Captain Gurden Chapin, wanted to launch a campaign against Cochise, but his hands were tied. He informed department headquarters that depredations were being committed by Chiricahuas living under the pernicious influence of Mexicans at Fronteras. Consequently, he said, he had petitioned Governor Pesqueira for permission to enter Sonora "for the purpose of chastising the Indians." Pesqueira diplomatically refused, saying the request required federal approval and an incursion would jeopardize the peace at Fronteras. Pesqueira, who was suppressing a rebellion of the Yaqui and Mayo Indians at the time, probably denied Chapin's request because he distrusted the Americans and because he had no troops to protect the northern frontier.[36]

The commander at Fronteras, Captain Gabriel García, shared Chapin's apprehension; Cochise's presence in northern Sonora was just as alarming to him as it was to Chapin. Just as important, however, was the resurgence of Chihuahuan scalp hunters to the east, which pushed the Chiricahuas in from that frontier. In early May,

Yaque, Parte, and Taces brought their people to the presidio and were rationed even though they had been raiding, almost certainly with Cochise.[37]

On May 10 a Nednhi chief discussed peace conditions, which led to the arrival of a large local group under Galindo,[38] the Janeros headman. Sonoran troops from Bavispe had surprised his band, killing one and capturing another at Embudos Canyon on May 1. As a result, he brought in his band, which consisted of thirty men, fifty-four women, forty boys, and twenty-two girls, and agreed to live at Santa Rosa, some eight miles north of Fronteras. But García continued to fear the presence of the broncos, meaning Cochise's followers, who were bound to create problems and influence younger warriors who were anxious to acquire loot and prestige by raiding.[39]

A week later, clearly referring to Cochise and the recalcitrant Yaque, Captain García reiterated to Pesqueira that the large number of recently arrived Chiricahuas had put the presidio, which numbered but thirty soldiers, in a state of alert. "The peaceful Apaches declare that the broncos are very bad and that they have no confidence in them and fear them." Apparently, some of Cochise's people had tried to incite the peaceful Apaches, brazenly boasting that they intended to kill farmers working their crops. Teboca Chiquito warned citizens to be on their guard.[40]

This time, however, Cochise's quarry was Americans, not Mexicans. In his April and May fights, his strength was thought to be somewhere between thirty and sixty men. In June, that figure doubled, indicating that he may have been joined by the Nednhis or other warriors from Mexico and perhaps by some White Mountain Apaches under Francisco. In June, Cochise returned to Arizona and directed another large war party on a destructive sweep through the Santa Cruz Valley. First the Chokonens cleaned out the stock of the San Pedro station, stealing forty-four mules.[41] Next they proceeded west along the northern Whetstone and Santa Rita mountains before abruptly swinging south to the Santa Cruz River. Here he led his war party of eighty to one hundred on a whirlwind rampage through the valley. At the Canoa Inn, the Chiricahuas murdered four men and virtually destroyed the ranch. When Raphael Pumpelly and Charles Poston reached the scene, they were stunned. Pumpelly described the disaster:

The sides of the house were broken in, and the court was filled with broken tables and doors, while fragments of crockery and ironware lay mixed in heaps with grain and the contents of mattresses. Through the open door of a small house, on one side of the court, we saw a naked body, which proved to be the remains of young Tarbox. . . . As in the case of many of the settlers, the first Apaches he had seen were his murderers. Under a tree, beyond a fence that divided the court, we found the bodies of the other American and a Papago Indian who, probably driven in by the Apaches, had joined in a desperate struggle that had evidently taken place. These bodies were pierced by hundreds of lance wounds.[42]

Arizona pioneer Pete Kitchen lost about four hundred head of cattle in the raid. He later recalled that Juh and Cochise led the Apache force, which he thought numbered five hundred to six hundred men (a gross exaggeration) and said he followed their trail into Mexico.[43]

Cochise continued raiding. On June 20 a band of Indians believed "to have been Chiricahuas" attacked the cattle herd of a Mr. Thompson about fourteen miles south of Fort Buchanan and stole every head. Thompson had a brush with the raiders and thought he had killed two warriors. Two days later at dawn "the bold war chief Cochise" led a force estimated at more than one hundred warriors and ran off a herd grazing about a mile south of the fort. The Chiricahuas killed one soldier and one Mexican, then fled, with "one party driving the mule herd towards Mexico, and the other [headed by Cochise] with the beef herd in an opposite direction towards the Whetstone Mountains."

Bascom, Irwin, and nine troopers, guided by Antonio and James Graydon, were in the saddle by 9 A.M. in pursuit of Cochise's party. After a twenty-mile march, Bascom's presence forced the Indians to kill most of the cattle. Near the Whetstone Mountains a group of warriors on foot reinforced Cochise's raiders. Realizing he was outnumbered, Bascom retired to open ground. In the meantime, Cochise had recognized him and made several whirlwind charges, to no avail. The Chiricahua chieftain "called out . . . in English, taunting, and cursing." The soldiers repulsed each assault and Cochise withdrew, having suffered four killed and three wounded; the troops had but one wounded. Bascom's party returned to Fort Buchanan late that day.[44]

Chapin reiterated to his superiors in Santa Fe that the aggressors were Cochise's Chokonens allied with Francisco's Coyoteros. He praised Lieutenant Bascom's conduct and digressed to say he desperately needed cavalry. Infantry, he said, "cannot be brought efficiently into service."[45] Headquarters sent no reinforcements. With the outbreak of the Civil War and the invasion of New Mexico by Confederate forces, the army decided to abandon southern Arizona's only two posts. Fort Breckenridge was evacuated and burned on July 10; Fort Buchanan was evacuated and burned on July 23.[46]

This decision signaled the end of ranching, mining, and all other economic pursuits around Tubac and the mining area. Once prosperous, it had been hit hard by Apache raids and now had no protection. Mines, ranches, and small settlements were hastily abandoned. The final blow fell on either August 3 or August 4. Tubac, where many of the miners and ranchers had taken refuge, was attacked by about one hundred Apaches, who killed two men and took all of the stock. The citizens finally halted the attack and the Apaches left, reportedly losing seven to ten killed.[47] Some historians think Cochise led the raid, and its characteristics (large party, bold attack) certainly were symptomatic of his kind of action, yet he almost certainly was not there; Western Apaches probably were responsible.

By late summer 1861, southern Arizona was virtually uninhabited except for Tucson and a few isolated mines. The Apaches again ruled, their confidence inflated by the departure of the soldiers. The *Tucson Arizonian* described the abysmal scene in southern Arizona:

> Our prosperity has departed. The mail is withdrawn; the soldiers are gone and their garrisons burned to the ground; the miners murdered and the mines abandoned; the stockraisers and farmers have abandoned their crops and herds to the Indians, and the population generally have fled, panic struck and naked in search of refuge. From end to end of the territory, except alone in Tucson and its immediate vicinity, there is not a human habitation.[48]

Although Cochise had been extremely active from late April through June, his Chiricahuas had taken losses in every engagement. He lost a few and perhaps several warriors in the Stein's Peak fight in April, and in early May he lost at least three more in his fight with citizens near San Simon. Thompson believed he killed at least two Chiricahuas in June, and then Lieutenant Bascom reported at least three dead and others wounded. It should be noted that white accounts tended to inflate the number of Indian dead. Even so, Cochise had not escaped unscathed, a prominent historian asserting that "the operations of Cochise probably would have been checked in an early stage had not the Civil War intervened . . . and the troops withdrawn."[49]

Cochise probably interpreted the white exodus on the basis of his experiences in Sonora, where ranches, mines, towns, and presidios had been abandoned as a direct result of Chiricahua raids. Undoubtedly, then, he concluded the same thing when southern Arizona was deserted. At least we may infer this from a statement he made ten years later: "At last your soldiers did me a very great wrong, and I and my whole people went to war with them. At first we were successful and your soldiers were driven away and your people killed and we again possessed our land."[50]

About this time Mangas Coloradas's Chihennes went to war in New Mexico. Most of the Chihennes initially had refrained from joining Cochise's retaliatory raids, a fact corroborated by Cochise in his later years. They certainly had ample justification to commence hostilities, however. In the spring of 1860, "yellow iron" was discovered at Pinos Altos in the heart of their country, and the predictable gold rush on a small scale ensued.[51] Wrote an observer: "All wild with the fever—everything that can leave has gone out. The Overland stages have lost many of their men."[52] Naturally the Chihennes were disturbed, yet they could do little to deter white men obsessed with getting rich.

Conflicts were inevitable with the Indians pilfering stock, or so the miners charged. Finally the unrest culminated in yet another treacherous action by whites against the Chiricahuas. In December 1860 a party of miners led by an old Cochise acquaintance, James Tevis, attacked some Apaches near old Fort Webster, killed four Chihennes, and captured thirteen others. This wanton assault, described by Dan L. Thrapp in *Victorio and the Mimbres Apaches*, put the majority of the Chihennes on the defensive, at least until the whites freed their people, but it was not forgotten.[53]

Some of the Chihennes lingered along the Mimbres throughout January, hoping their people would be released. Mangas and his

Bedonkohes had moved into Chokonen country, having become disenchanted with affairs in New Mexico. In mid-February, as the
Bascom affair was winding down, Victorio, Riñon, and Chabnocito
cautiously approached Fort McLane (Fort Floyd having been renamed such on January 18, 1861) and conferred with Major Lynde.
The officer was eager to mend relations and avert hostilities because
he had been ordered by headquarters to "use every effort to dissuade
and prevent the settlers from inflicting unnecessary outrages upon
the Indians at the same time keeping the Indians from becoming
hostile or aggressive." Convinced of their sincerity, Lynde released
the hostages, pointing out that

> three sub chiefs of the Apaches came here and professed to be
> friendly to the Whites and promised to do all in their power to keep
> peace and prevent any depredations by the men of their bands, and I
> think they are sincere. I delivered up to them the captives taken by the
> men from the mines, who have been in confinement here since that
> time. Chabnocito promised to send for Mangas Coloradas, the Head
> Chief of the Apaches, and thought he could induce him to come in
> and make peace. The three sub chiefs mentioned above are of the
> Bands residing on the Mimbres and vicinity.[54]

Lynde's actions evidently appeased the Chihennes, who remained
at peace during the first four months of 1861. Acting agent Pinckney
Randolph Tully[55] rationed them on February 18, March 8, March
28, and April 18, when plans for raising crops were discussed. On
March 26, Estevan Ochoa wrote Steck claiming that the Western
Apaches, Chokonens, and Mescaleros were the bands doing the depredating. The Chihennes evidently had not yet begun raiding.[56]

Mangas Coloradas squashed Tully's hopes of keeping the Chihennes peaceful. Perhaps because of the alleged whipping at Pinos
Altos, perhaps because he realized the whites were steadily poach-
ing his country, or perhaps because he felt bound to join Cochise
and drive out the Americans, Mangas went to war. According to one
report, he "threatened extermination to all whites within the limits
of his range."[57] In May 1861, while Cochise was occupied in Arizona, Mangas began raiding the Pinos Altos–Fort McLane vicinity.
His first target was a Mexican train near Pinos Altos, which the
Apaches jumped, killing one man and running off the mules.[58] Two

weeks later they cleaned out the stock at Fort McLane, prompting Tully to write Collins: "What has led to this outbreak I am at a loss to know. They have had their rations regularly issued to them." [59]

By early June the allied Chiricahuas had all but closed the road between Mesilla and Tucson. Agent Lorenzo Labadie arrived at Mesilla en route to Tucson, where he was to investigate the condition of the Apache *mansos,* or tame Apaches. He discovered that affairs had deteriorated so much that he was unable to procure transportation to Tucson. He notified his superiors that Indian hostilities had forced citizens to abandon their fields and miners to desert their diggings. This was probably the origin of the *Santa Fe New Mexican's* report that the Pinos Altos mines had been abandoned, a rumor also picked up by the *Missouri Republican.*[60] Pinos Altos was far from deserted. These rugged, gold-crazy individualists provided a good deal of southern New Mexico's protection for the next several months, engaging in several brisk fights with the allied Chiricahuas.

The Chihennes continued raiding. On June 3 at Cook's Peak they ambushed a train belonging to Ellsburg and Ambury, killing two Mexicans and stealing two mules. In mid-June they raided Pinos Altos and on June 18 struck a hay camp some three miles from there, killing John Gillem and wounding another man. A state of war now existed between Americans and the Chiricahua Tribe.[61]

Indian agent and physician Michael Steck returned to New Mexico in mid-July, but the conflict had become general and he reluctantly conceded that "I am unable to do anything. . . . It may be many months before the presence of an agent will be needed here."[62] He was right, except it was years, not months.

The situation deteriorated rapidly as Cochise gained new allies. In early July he moved east to join forces with Mangas Coloradas and drive the remaining whites from Chihenne territory. This was when he emerged as a war leader at the tribal level. Historian James McClintock notes that Cochise now "had the ability to gather together more fighting men than any Apache chieftain of modern times." He proved it again and again during the next year.[63]

In July and August 1861, Cochise and Mangas made their temporary headquarters in the vicinity of Cook's Peak, called by the Apaches Dziltanatal ("Mountain Holds Its Head Up Proudly").

Here they hoped to cut off the Pinos Altos miners from Mesilla. Cook's Springs, about eighteen miles north of present-day Deming, New Mexico, had a dependable water supply, which made it a mandatory stopping spot for troops and travelers. It was thought to be the most dangerous point in southern Arizona and New Mexico except for Apache Pass, wrote Brigadier General James H. Carleton in 1865.[64] In fact, if actual encounters and casualties were tallied, it would have far exceeded those committed at Apache Pass and Stein's Peak. Between 1861 and 1863, Apaches ambushed and killed about one hundred whites here, which, for a change, may not have been too much of an exaggeration.[65] Travelers left behind grim and morbid descriptions of the area. "Passed many human bones along the road,"[66] a soldier wrote in his diary, while another observed: "Place all along is graves, broken wagons . . . piles of rocks denoting a grave . . . a human skull with face."[67]

It was into Cook's Canyon in July 1861 that a party of seven Americans rode. Former employees of the Butterfield Overland Mail Company, they were known as the Free Thomas Party, which consisted of Freeman Thomas, Joe Roescher, Mat Champion, Robert Aveline, Emmett Mills, John Wilson, and John Portell. All were said to have been experienced frontiersmen who were "picked for the dangerous duty they had to perform." Their job was to transport the mail to California. The whites left Mesilla on the morning of July 20; by the next evening they had reached Cook's Canyon, where they were waylaid by a party of Apaches probably numbering between one hundred and two hundred.[68]

All available evidence indicates that Cochise was there, though he may not have been in overall command, given Mangas Coloradas's presence. According to William S. Oury's account, the attack surprised the Americans, but Thomas quickly responded and ordered the driver to leave the road for high ground. This achieved, they stripped the coach of guns, ammunition, water, and other essentials and sent the team down the hill, hoping this would satisfy the Chiricahuas. It did not. Next morning, the Indians renewed the fight, which settled into a sniping duel with the besieged Americans, who had constructed a breastwork of rocks, about two feet high, at the top of a small hill.

At this point it becomes difficult to reconstruct the sequence of events. Various stories reflect the imagination of the writer rather than the facts. What we do know, from accounts of those who arrived on the scene shortly after the fight, is this: the Indians poured a devastating fire on the entrenched Americans. Daguerre and Thabault, who arrived a few days after the fight, described the scene:

> All about this wall the ground was strewn with battered bullets. Every rock and stone within many yards, which could have partially secreted an Indian, had bullets lying near. One small tree, some 150 yards from the wall, had the marks of eleven balls in it.

The Indians eventually killed all seven men; four bodies were found within the breastworks, two some 50 yards in the rear and the other, presumably John Wilson, 150 yards away. According to some accounts, Mangas Coloradas left after the second day, but not before taking heavy losses. Other accounts claim that Cochise was wounded before his men finished off Thomas's party the next day.[69] When Daguerre and Thabault discovered the horrifying scene a few days later, every body had been stripped, the arms of most had been broken, and all had bullet holes through the head. Tevis came across the remains and recalled that "the buzzards had picked the eyes out of the bodies."[70]

Although they had suffered casualties, Cochise and Mangas reportedly bore witness to the courage of the seven Americans. Mangas allegedly admitted to Jack Swilling that the Americans had killed twenty-five warriors and crippled many more; moreover, according to Mangas, if his Apaches had been as brave "as these few white men, he could whip the world."[71] In contrast to Swilling, Oury went to the other extreme and claimed that Cochise confessed he lost 175 warriors, Cochise also paid tribute to the seven Americans, declaring that "with twenty-five such men he would undertake to whip the whole United States."[72] Both accounts overstated Apache losses, and Oury's was perhaps apocryphal. It was inconceivable that Apaches, even fighting for vengeance, would have exposed themselves to a loss of that magnitude.

The Chiricahuas retired to northern Chihuahua after the fight. Oury said Cochise told of his role in the battle at Corralitos. Keith Humphries, a historian in the Las Cruces area, heard a story in the 1930s from Natividad Padilla, who said he was at Janos when the

Chiricahuas ventured in to seek treatment for a wounded son of Cochise, probably Taza, shortly after the Cook's Canyon fight. The Apaches traded their victims' gold watches for ammunition.[73] A report from Fronteras at this time also confirmed the Chiricahuas' presence in Chihuahua: "The Apaches have been trading their plunder taken from the Americans at Janos and Corralitos."[74] After a short rest, the allied Chiricahuas departed, their thirst satisfied, bellies filled, and ammunition restored, thanks to the generosity of their sometime friend, sometime enemy, José María Zuloaga. Toward the latter part of August they returned to New Mexico and assumed their temporary headquarters in the hills around Cook's Peak.

About this same time, a group of Americans comprised of ranchers from the Tubac, Sonoita Creek, and Tucson area were abandoning their homes for more civilized parts. The recent attacks by Cochise's Chokonens and the Western Apaches, plus the abandonment of Fort Buchanan, had compelled these courageous individuals to leave while they still had their lives. Known as the Ake party (named for Felix Grundy Ake, a fifty-year-old farmer), the wagon train consisted of six double wagons, two buggies, and one single wagon when it reached Tucson. Here it was reinforced by several other people, including Moses Carson,[75] who was a half-brother of the celebrated Kit and was himself a brave and experienced Indian fighter. The caravan left the Sonoran desert on or about August 15, heading east, and was made up of twenty-four men, sixteen women, and seven children. They carried many of their possessions and herded several hundred head of cattle, sheep, goats, and horses. They were, in effect, an open invitation to Cochise and Mangas.[76]

Ake had hoped to accompany the soldiers who evacuated Fort Buchanan to the Río Grande, but when they reached the rendezvous site at the Cienega, about twenty miles east of Tucson, they discovered that the troops had already departed. Nonetheless, Ake opted to continue, believing that his party was large enough to discourage an Indian attack. Indeed, Apache ambushes on parties this size were rare, if not unheard of, in U.S. territory.

The eastbound whites saw no Indians along the route, although at Apache Pass they observed "ropes and some bones and rags a-hanging" at the Bascom execution site. Forging on to the Mimbres, they encamped and heard that some two hundred Apaches had wiped out nine Mexicans at Cook's Canyon, which Ake's party was scheduled to traverse the next day. Ake and his men were dubious of the report, believing it had been fabricated. The next morning, the wagon train left for Mesilla before sunrise, hoping to reach Cook's Canyon before the torrid summer sun took its toll.[77]

That morning, Cochise's scouts espied the small wagon train, which he knew would continue on to Cook's Springs. Eyewitnesses estimated the number of warriors at more than two hundred; all were hidden on both sides of the hills, which ran parallel to the road. The whites trudged into Cook's Canyon with Phillips's wagon in the front, followed by Ake's wagon and then the rest. The ambulance in the rear contained most of the women and children. Despite the warnings about Indians, neither scouts nor skirmishers had been deployed, so the whites were woefully unprepared for an attack.

Cochise and Mangas launched the attack as the last wagon entered the mouth of the canyon, and then, "without no warning at all, the Indians come hellity-larrup, just a-swarming outen the rocks." Mariano Madrid, a teamster, said the hostiles some "dressed like soldiers [and] armed with cap guns." They immediately stampeded the cattle and sheep herds. As the stock fled up the hill, Ake, Wadsworth, and several of the mounted men counterattacked and repulsed the Indians, but not without cost: James May was killed, Wadsworth wounded fatally, Thomas Farrell wounded, and Thomas Redding (or Reden) suffered a broken leg, which, however, did not prevent him from continuing the fight. As the wagons were circling, Redding and the mounted men "charged again and again . . . and held them off from getting right down in the wagons." Finally all of the wagons were circled except two: the lead one, which the Phillipses were forced to abandon, leaving behind everything but their money, and the rear one, carrying most of the women and children, which had reversed direction at the first volley and fled west. Several men, including Sam Houston, a nephew of the noted Texan, escorted it to the Mimbres.[78]

Several Apaches plundered the Phillips wagon while the remainder maintained a withering fire from the hills, finally killing the brave Redding. With the protection of the wagons, the whites responded and inflicted some damage. One woman, a daughter of Ake married to George Davis, courageously "stood behind a wagon and loaded guns all day." [79] Moses Carson fought "like hell, brave as a lion and quick as a cat, with his white head dodging around." The fighting subsided early in the afternoon when Mariano Madrid killed one last Apache. The Indians then disengaged and withdrew with their plunder. According to one report, they had stolen four hundred cattle and nine hundred sheep. [80] The whites retreated to the Mimbres.

Meanwhile, the women and children had reached the settlement along the Mimbres and sent a dispatch to Pinos Altos, where a company of Arizona Guards under elected officers Captain Thomas J. Mastin, Lieutenant Thomas Helm, and Lieutenant Jack Swilling were stationed. Although they had been mustered into Confederate service, their primary duty was to fight Apaches and "to reopen the road between Mesilla and Tucson, [and] especially to rout the savages from Apache Pass." [81] The next day a group of thirty-five men started in pursuit, but instead of going to Cook's Canyon they "made a straight shoot for the Florida Mountains in the hope of catching up with the Indians, and knowing that they could not travel very fast with the sheep, we might have a chance to overtake them." [82]

Mastin's hunch paid dividends. The Guards were secreted in ambush as the Indians approached the foothills of the barren Florida Mountains. The whites immediately charged the Apaches, whom Hank Smith estimated at eighty, and in a running fight retook several pack mules and cattle and routed the Chiricahuas, killing eight according to one report. Mastin pursued them back toward Cook's Canyon, where the Indians made a halfhearted attempt to regroup. A minor brush occurred with no further casualties. [83]

Mangas and Cochise had scored impressive victories in late July and August, but the ambush carried out by the Arizona Guards at Florida Mountains had dampened their celebration. Naturally it would be avenged.

Chapter 10

CAPITAN GRANDE

In early September 1861, Cochise and Mangas returned to northern Mexico, where they discovered that relations at Janos had become strained. Joaquin Terrazas, a tireless and inveterate Indian fighter, had led a scout which killed eleven Apaches in late August. This offensive made Janos too hot for the Chiricahuas and this, combined with the lethal arrival of smallpox (which eventually infested the Río Grande Valley), forced Cochise and most of the Chiricahuas back into their mountain sanctuaries along the border.[1] From here they were bound to cause turmoil on both sides of the line. That fall, Cochise was reported in the Animas Mountains, where, according to Apaches at Corralitos, he had organized yet another war party, intending to attack either Fronteras or Janos. Neither was hit because the Americans remained his priority.[2]

Knowing that Mexico offered him refuge, Cochise began cultivating relations at Fronteras. He had been in contact with Remigio, who had succeeded Esquinaline as leader of that small Chokonen local group and who now joined Cochise in mid-September for a campaign in New Mexico. Once again the Chihennes and Bedonkohes were united for an attack on the hated miners at Pinos Altos. It was a tribal venture.[3]

Cochise and Mangas might have achieved their objective had it not been for the arrival of Captain Mastin and fifteen Arizona Guards shortly before the attack. Mastin had been sent to Pinos

Altos by a lean, blue-eyed Indian hater, Confederate Lieutenant Colonel John Robert Baylor,[4] whose feelings epitomized frontier thought that the only good Indian ws a dead Indian. In September, Baylor sent instructions to Mastin, giving him a free hand to deal with the Apaches. The instructions were tantamount to genocide, if that was what Mastin wished. Even if the Chiricahuas solicited peace, Baylor ordered Mastin to "kill them anyway he could; and did not care whether he made them drunk, poisoned them, or shot them on sight."[5]

The Chiricahuas were in the vicinity of Cook's Springs on September 26, hidden in ambush for Charles Hayden's wagon train. Yet the presence of Mastin's command, which escorted the train through the canyon, probably convinced Cochise, who recalled the success of the Arizona Guards a month earlier, to call off the attack. Accomplishing this, Mastin's group marched toward Pinos Altos and camped near the site of present-day Hurley.[6] At 10 P.M. the sentinel heard voices that he thought were Indians. The camp was aroused immediately and the Guards prepared to defend themselves, but no attack came. After an hour's wait, Mastin pushed on to Pinos Altos, arriving there at daybreak and drawing supplies at Roy and Sam Bean's store. As the Guards split up for their own camps, the Chiricahuas emerged from the hills and attacked.[7]

The initial assault apparently was a surprise, although today residents will say that the Apaches were lined up shoulder to shoulder at the top of the hills overlooking the town. Hollywood would have loved that scenario, but Cochise and Mangas failed to take this ostentatious display into account. In reality, the two leaders had a carefully conceived and coordinated plan. The number of Indians involved has never been determined with accuracy, although there may have been nearly two hundred. Early on the morning of September 27, 1861, they struck simultaneously at the mining camps that spread out from the main town. Many of the miners were cornered in their diggings and were unable or too frightened to venture out; the remainder fought from their log homes.

Hank Smith and three men rushed to his cabin at Whiskey Gulch and eventually drove the Indians away. Soon afterward, he retreated to the main camp and found the Chiricahuas and whites in "hand to hand combat." Early in the fight the Indians attempted to set fire to many of the log homes, a tactic employed successfully in Mexico, but these experienced and intrepid miners were well armed and could not be dislodged. Fierce fighting continued through the morning. By noon the battle was concentrated around Bean's and Roman's supply stores in the center of town. It was here that Captain Thomas Mastin was mortally wounded. At Roman's store two other men were killed. Finally, about 12:30 P.M., the Guards fired the cannon at Roy and Sam Bean's store. Nails and buckshot splattered, routing the aggressors, who had a well-grounded fear of this weapon. The miners counterattacked and "never gave them a chance to concentrate again." Thirty minutes later the fight was over.

Both sides had heavy casualties. The Indians left ten bodies on the battleground and were believed to have carried off twenty more killed and wounded. The whites lost five dead (Mastin, Private J. B. Corwin of the Arizona Guards, and three civilians) and seven wounded. Though the numbers suggest a victory for the whites, in the days that followed many of the whites deserted the mines for either Santa Fe or Mesilla.[8]

The encounter at Pinos Altos was but another in a series of hard-fought engagements between the Chiricahua Apaches and the remaining whites in New Mexico. It had been a show of force, a warning to the whites. The Indians had seized the offensive behind the two greatest Chiricahua leaders of the mid-nineteenth century. A Chiricahua war leader "would go before [his men] in battle, and perform great feats to spur them on,"[9] so we may assume that Cochise was one of them and that Mangas Coloradas was the other.

After the Pinos Altos fight the Indians left the area. Mangas and his followers probably moved northwest to the remote Gila country; Cochise and his Chokonens plunged into Mexico, perhaps near Fronteras, where Remigio and many warriors who had joined him in the fighting had made peace. It was a logical decision. To the north he had fought several pitched battles against the Americans and he and his band needed a rest. To the east, Chihuahuan troops were making life miserable for the Apaches. In particular, their efforts temporarily closed the Janos-Corralitos market, where the hostiles usually found refuge to dispose of their plunder for food, liquor, and ammunition. Terrazas's campaign had been followed in late September by a scout from Paso del Norte which jumped a band near Lake

Guzmán, killing seven Apaches and capturing sixteen. In one of these fights a brother of Mangas Coloradas was killed, perhaps Phalis Palacio or another relatively unknown man named Chaha.[10] Hence Fronteras appeared to be a viable alternative; at the least peace discussions would suspend any campaigns in that state, if any were planned.

With this in mind, in late October 1861, Cochise sent Yones to Fronteras to request a truce. The report filed by the commander was important because it revealed Cochise's status within the Chiricahua Tribe:

> Today at two in the afternoon an Apache woman, the wife of the late chief Coyuntura, came in and asked for peace in the name of the chief Chis [Cochise]. She was accompanied by eight women from those settled here. This chief has requested peace several times, but it has not been granted him because of the people at Janos. . . . But today it has been granted to him since they now are united and say that he is the big captain. He is at the *head of them all,* according to what is said by the Indians when they come to get their rations. More-over, they also say that he has all the warriors stationed from Mesilla to Sarampion waiting for the enemy [Americans] to come and make a campaign against him. This Indian should report within twenty days and have a force of only ten men.[11]

Two points merit analysis: first, that the Apaches considered him the *capitán grande,* or "big captain," and second, that he was the chief of all the warriors from Mesilla to Sarampion, in the Peloncillo Mountains, indicated that Cochise, with Mangas aging, had become the dominant leader within the Chiricahua Tribe. At his father-in-law's request he had brought his Chokonens into Chihenne territory and together they had proved to be formidable foes of the remaining whites in southern New Mexico. This leads to the second point: that Cochise was anticipating an American campaign because of his actions since the Bascom affair.

The report was forwarded to Governor Pesqueira, who ordered Cayetano Sanchez, the prefect of Moctezuma, to "make an effort to overcome all difficulties that may occur to achieve this very important goal."[12] A thankless task it was. While Pesqueira advocated a peace policy, he failed to address how Sanchez and the garrison at Fronteras were to support the Chiricahuas. In the end Cochise stayed away.

Cochise kept his base of operations in northern Mexico for the last few months of 1861. In late November it was reported from Corralitos that he had gathered a large force and was planning to attack either Janos or Bavispe. In early December hostiles assaulted a party near Bavispe and killed Sergeant Miguel Enriques and a corporal. Then they invaded Sonora and extended their depredations further into the interior, though Cochise's role, if any, is not clear.[13]

A large contingent of Chiricahuas continued to receive rations at Fronteras in early 1862; for many, this would lead to death. Smallpox spread like wildfire, and many Chiricahuas fell victim. According to *Estrella de Occidente,* the disease decimated Apache bands in both Chihuahua and Sonora. By February 11 at Fronteras alone, thirty-two Chiricahuas had died (seventeen warriors, seven women, and eight children). Among the dead leaders were two of Teboca's sons (Chiquito Teboca and Vicente Teboca), Parte, and Vivora, an old chief who was present at the capture of Tutije in 1834 and the Juan José Compá massacre in 1837. *Estrella de Occidente* smugly editorialized: "We hope that more Indians die to decrease the numbers of this horrible tribe."[14]

Fortunately, Cochise had kept his local group clear of Fronteras. By the end of 1861 he had his eyes set on southern Arizona, where only two settlements of consequence remained: Tucson and the Mowry, or Patagonia, mines. "The whole of Western Arizona is now a scene of desolation" reported the *Missouri Republican,*[15] and another traveler grimly added that "little mounds of stones, with rude wooden crosses over them, were visible all along the roads."[16] In August 1861, Sylvester Mowry, owner of the mines, had implored the secretary of war in Washington to send troops and other assistance. His letter depicted the deteriorating situation in the once prosperous region: "Every farm and rancho is abandoned, the people having taken refuge in Tucson, Tubac or followed the troops. The loss of property is immense. I am holding my place at great expense. In fact it is a garrison. . . . I am constantly prepared for a fight." Furthermore, declared Mowry, hoping to get Washington's attention, the "Arizona Apaches . . . openly boast that they have driven the Americans, soldiers & all, out of the country."[17]

Mowry had good reason to be concerned about Arizona's plight. According to a Mexican captive living with the Chokonens, Cochise "had constant information of everything at the Mowry mines during the year that the troops were withdrawn." The chief was very anxious "to break it up" and force abandonment. Somehow, probably from Mexicans at Fronteras, he had threatened Mowry that "he would wipe it out as he had all other American settlements." [18]

Mowry, who compared Apaches to rattlesnakes and felt they should be treated as such, recalled that "the Apaches made a great combination of all their forces and sent me word through Cachees, their great fighting captain and a man of signal ability, they were going to take my place." As a result, the American capitalist "made a perfect garrison of the mines—surrounded the houses with high walls loopholed for fighting—armed all my men who work with a gun in one hand and tools in the other." [19] This, he believed, would deter Cochise from attempting a direct assault, since the cost in Apache lives would have been prohibitive.

In late 1861, with smallpox rampant in northern Mexico and Chihuahua on another scalp hunt, Cochise shifted his headquarters to Arizona. Chokonen local groups probably camped during the winter of 1861–62 in the Huachuca, Dragoon, and Chiricahua mountains. From these locations his scouts maintained a close watch on the Mowry mines. A large war party drove off 181 cattle, near Tucson, which may have been Fritz Contzen's herd grazing at San Xavier. A few Americans and one hundred Papagos overtook the Indians, killed a few, and wounded several others. [20] Whether Cochise had a hand in this is not known, but he probably had a role in the next incident. In early December, Indians wounded two men near the mines, one of whom may have been early Arizona settler Thomas Gardner. If so, Cochise was definitely involved, and his actions revealed he would resort to any means to kill an enemy, especially an American. The story was evidently first told by Thomas Jeffords, which lends credibility to the incident.

In the early sixties, returning to the mines [Mowry] one day from Santa Cruz, whither he had gone for provisions mounted on a spirited horse with but one companion, he saw two Indians approaching on horseback. He soon recognized Cochise, who made the peace sign

Thomas Gardner. Pictured here in his later years, Gardner was wounded by Cochise about December 1861. *(Courtesy Arizona Historical Society, Tucson)*

and rode up apparently for a parley. He carried his cocked gun across his horse in front of him. Maneuvering for a favorable position, he shot without raising his rifle. Gardner fell shot clear through the body just in front of the spine; Cochise snatched for the rein of the coveted horse, but the animal galloped away pursued by the Indians. Gardner recovered from his wounds.[21]

After this encounter Cochise again tried to assemble a force to put pressure on Mowry's mines, attempting "in every way to make a combination with the other bands to attack the mines." Notwithstanding his reputation as a war leader, he was unsuccessful. The Chokonen and Nednhi groups living in Mexico were incapacitated by smallpox and Mangas's Chihennes were discussing a truce at Pinos Altos in New Mexico. As a result, only Cochise's immediate followers undertook forays against the Americans in southern Arizona.[22]

In the winter and spring of 1862, Cochise and his warriors ambushed several parties coming or going to the mines. Toward the end of February in a canyon halfway between the Mowry mines and Santa Cruz, Sonora, he waylaid Elliot Titus and a companion known as Delaware Joe (said to be a Delaware Indian). They were traveling along the road when the Indians opened fire, killing Delaware Joe in the first volley. Within seconds Titus's horse was killed, but the imperturbable American made for the other end of the canyon, fighting "very bravely and coolly for several hundred yards, doing much execution with his shotgun and revolver," according to the Chiricahuas. Titus had almost reached safety when an Indian in his rear shot him through the thigh. Realizing that escape was impossible, he put a bullet through his brain, fulfilling a pledge "that he would kill himself rather than be taken alive." In respect for Titus's bravery, Cochise reportedly ordered his warriors to leave the body alone. Titus's "beautifully mounted" revolver was taken by Cochise and became part of his arsenal.[23]

Some five or six weeks later Cochise was again prowling in the neighborhood of the mines. Consequently, Mowry requested help from Captain Sherod Hunter,[24] who, with some seventy-five Confederate troops, had occupied Tucson on the last day of February 1862. The people in Tucson welcomed the command, regardless of affiliation, hoping it would furnish some protection against the Apaches. Mowry wrote of those dangerous days: "If the Devil would have helped me fight Apaches, I would have asked his help at any price except my soul."[25] Hunter's stay was hardly noteworthy, and he did no Indian fighting. He tactfully refused Mowry's request, declaring "that the precarious position in which I am placed will not permit me to take my command immediately to your assistance."[26]

A scout by Hunter's command might have driven the hostiles off. Instead, toward the middle of April, Cochise's Chokonens annihilated a small party en route to Santa Cruz from Mowry's mines. Wrote Mowry:

> I had sent seven peons with a cart and yoke of oxen to Santa Cruz. . . . Sent also an explorer as escort . . . a few miles from Santa Cruz a large body of Indians killed them. A woman and child were also killed. Body of the child was hung to the cart wheel. Indians stole a yoke of oxen, a colts revolver, rifle, 6 shooter and several hundred dollars in silver bullion.

With the abundance of Indian sign, only Mowry could explain why he sent such a small and relatively unarmed party with only one man as escort. A larger force might have repulsed the Indians.[27]

Cochise directed this cruel and brutal massacre and rode the chestnut mare he took for the next few years.[28] It would appear that he was waging a war of attrition against Mowry's stronghold, and he might well have succeeded had not volunteer troops from California, sent to drive the Confederates from Arizona and New Mexico, arrived on the scene.

Hunter left Tucson on May 4, 1862, when he heard the California Volunteers were coming. The next day at Dragoon Springs, Cochise and Francisco jumped the rebels, killing four men and running off thirty mules and twenty-five horses. José Mendibles,[29] a captive of the Western Apaches who was present at both this fight and the Bascom affair, declared that Francisco was present, undoubtedly with his ally Cochise. After this encounter, Hunter's force forged ahead to New Mexico and arrived there without further trouble.[30]

During the spring of 1862, Cochise had been in touch with his Chihenne relatives in New Mexico, who had their own problems to deal with, namely Baylor's Confederate troops. In January, Baylor had received reinforcements under the command of Brigadier General Henry Hopkins Sibley,[31] who had moved his troops from Fort Fillmore to Mesilla. About this time, some Chiricahuas ran off one hundred horses belonging to Sibley's troops. Baylor, itching for revenge because Mescalero Apaches had massacred fourteen Texans the previous August, marched out, "accompanied by many native-born citizens of Arizona and New Mexico." The Indians drove the stock into Chihuahua; Baylor's force dogmatically pursued the trail into Janos and then Corralitos, where he trespassed into Zuloaga's home and captured nine Chiricahuas. Then he practiced what he preached. Believing "it justifiable in killing the Indians and recovering the animals," Baylor dispassionately executed the adults (one man and three women) and captured the children. Apparently they were Chokonens from the group of Miguel Yrigóllen, now a captain in Cochise's band.[32]

In late February or early March the Chihennes, probably including Mangas, talked peace at Pinos Altos. According to William Fourr, Mangas was in the area at this time. Baylor issued an infamous order which reeked of duplicity, brutality, and insensitivity and was born of ignorance. From Mesilla on March 20, 1862, he instructed Captain Thomas Helm, commander of the Arizona Guards at Pinos Altos:

> I learn from Lieutenant J. J. Jackson that the Indians have been in to your post [Pinos Altos] for the purpose of making a treaty. The Congress of the Confederate States has passed a law declaring exter- mination to all hostile Indians. You will therefore use all means to persuade the Apaches or any tribe to come in for the purpose of making peace, and when you get them together kill all the grown In- dians and take the children prisoners and sell them to defray the ex- pense of killing the Indians. Buy whiskey and such other goods as may be necessary for the Indians . . . I . . . look to you for success against these cursed pests who have already murdered over 100 men in this Territory.[33]

Fortunately for Mangas, he avoided the mines and a few months later joined Cochise in an attempt to repel the advances of the California Column, which, the Indians believed, had come to punish them.

The California Column was organized to counteract the Confed- erate invasion of New Mexico. The volunteers, numbering 2,350 troops, were under the command of Brigadier General James Henry Carleton, an experienced and energetic officer who had served in New Mexico. Carleton's objectives were to drive the Confederate forces from Tucson and the Mesilla Valley, to reoccupy the aban- doned southwestern forts, and to reestablish federal rule in Arizona and New Mexico. By the time he arrived the rebels had been effec- tively defeated. Besides guarding against a Confederate invasion, his role for the remainder of the war would be to make Arizona and New Mexico a safe place for travelers, to provide security for miners and ranchers, and to revitalize commerce. The Apaches were the major obstacle to the achievement of these goals and Carleton, like Baylor, felt that most Indians were animals and deserved killing.

On May 20, Colonel Joseph Rodman West,[34] whose giant ego dwarfed his diminutive stature, and the first elements of the Califor- nia Column occupied Tucson. On May 24, Carleton ordered Fort Breckenridge and Fort Buchanan reoccupied. By June 5, most of the column had reached Tucson. Hoping to restore order, Carleton declared martial law three days later. Furthermore, he arrested "nine of the cutthroats, gamblers and loafers who have infested this town to the great bodily fear of all good citizens." Tucson rapidly became a law-abiding town.[35]

Isolated in Tucson and unaware of the strength of his enemy forces stationed along the Río Grande, Carleton decided to communicate with Brigadier General Edward Richard Sprigg Canby,[36] who had driven Sibley's command out of New Mexico in late March, two previous attempts having proved unsuccessful. Expressman John Jones, Sergeant William Wheeling, and a Mexican guide named Chávez were selected for this dangerous mission.

The trio left Tucson on June 15. Traveling primarily by night and resting by day, they approached Apache Pass in the late afternoon of June 18. A mile or two west of the pass, the whites saw Apache smoke signals and hastened through the canyon. A few miles east of the pass they saw Apaches who "jumped up from their hiding place in the brush." Jones's party dismounted and the Indians "mounted their horses and came on at a gallop." Chávez was wounded in the hip and could not remount. Jones recalled:

> The Mexican begged us not to leave him. We told him we could not save ourselves. We mounted up and started. The sergeant, I think, never got from among the Indians. They followed after me on horseback yelling, saying "now let's have a race. Mucha buena mula, mucho bravo Americano." I shot one in the side, shot another in the shoulder; six pursued until sundown.[37]

Miraculously Jones got through to the Río Grande, where he was captured by Confederate troops. Nonetheless, he somehow sent word to Canby that "the Column from California is really coming."[38]

Two days after Jones's party left Tucson, Carleton ordered Lieutenant Colonel Edward E. Eyre and a force of 140 men of Companies B and C, First California Cavalry, to make a scout of the area between Tucson and Mesilla. Eyre's command reached Apache Pass at 6 A.M. on June 25 and encamped at the abandoned stage station. Fresh Indian signs were seen, "but no attention was paid them as it was thought that the Indians would not dare come near so formidable a force as ours."[39] This imprudence revealed itself in the command's comportment, with one soldier recalling that "horses were scattered everywhere."[40] Shortly before noon, four shots were heard near Apache Springs and Indians were seen on the hill where the first Fort Bowie later was built. Immediately the volunteers prepared for a fight, at least until Lieutenant Colonel Eyre arrived. He had been ordered to avoid engagements with the Indians if possible. Even though he was told that three men were missing, he hoisted a white flag and the so-called Pemmican Treaty ensued.[41]

Cochise was wary and more than an hour passed before he could be induced to come within range to talk. By this time, seventy-five Indians were present, "their lances flashing in the sun and their bows and rifles sticking above the bushes and rocks." Finally, Cochise and a dozen warriors held a parley with Eyre and his interpreter, a man named Newcomb. An eyewitness described Cochise as "a big Indian. He carried a fine rifle and two six shooters and rides as fine a horse as anybody."[42] Cochise, who undoubtedly perceived the volunteers as a threat to his people, must have been amused at Eyre's naïveté. Wrote the latter:

> We wished to be friends of the Apaches; that at present I was only travelling through their country and desired that he [Cochise] would not interfere with my men or animals; that a great Captain was at Tucson with a large number of soldiers; that he wished to have a talk with all the Apache Chiefs and to make peace with them and make them presents.

Cochise assured Eyre that his people were peaceful and agreed to return at sunset. This satisfied the officer, who issued presents of tobacco and pemmican. Cochise must have mocked Eyre's simplicity; his word given to the enemy when at war was disingenous. If Eyre was foolish enough to believe him, all the better for the Indians.[43]

After the conference, soldiers found the bodies of three soldiers: John Maloney, Albert Schmidt, and James Keith. All had been stripped, shot through the chest, and lanced through the neck. Eyre sent out a frenzied but fruitless pursuit of the Indians, who could be seen in the conical peaks overlooking the mesa, probably Helen's Dome and Boroce Peak. Eyre prudently moved his troops two miles east of Apache Pass and made camp. Later that night, Cochise's warriors fired a few rounds into the camp, wounding one man and killing a horse. The next day the command left for New Mexico and on July 4 occupied Fort Thorn.[44]

Thanks to Eyre's candor, Cochise made preparations to ambush the next party of soldiers traveling through Apache Pass. Perhaps it was at this time that he invited Mangas and his Bedonkohes and Chihennes to join him at the pass. He would not be disappointed; with the exception of a small force left behind at Tucson, Carleton had prepared a systematic march of his command to the Río Grande. On July 9, West ordered Captain Thomas L. Roberts, First Infantry, California Volunteers, to take a command of a 126-man detachment made up of 72 men of Company E, First Infrantry; 24 men of Company B, Second Cavalry, under Captain John C. Cremony; 20 men of Company E, First Infantry, under Lieutenant W. A. Thompson (his company manned the two howitzers); and 10 men of Company H, First Infantry, under First Lieutenant Alexander Bartholomew MacGowan. Like Eyre, Roberts was ordered to avoid "a collision with the Indians . . . and caution all of your men to do so until they become the aggressors." The 22 teams and 242 head of stock made an attractive target.

Roberts's command left Tucson at 4:30 A.M. on July 10 and marched twenty miles to the Cienega, arriving there at 6 P.M. The command rested the next day and resumed its trek in the early hours of July 12, halting at the San Pedro River, where horses and men were watered and rested. At this point Roberts, as instructed, left MacGowan's detachment and three cavalrymen to guard the supplies which were to be left for the next group of troops. Roberts further divided his command, taking sixty infantry, the howitzers, and eight troopers to Dragoon Springs. Captain Cremony, with the rest of the command, forty-five infantry and cavalry, remained with the train and cattle. At 8 A.M. on July 13 Roberts's detachment arrived at Dragoon Springs, remaining there until 5 P.M. the next day, July 14, when he and his sixty-eight men began their march to Apache Pass, which lay forty miles to the west.[45] There can be little doubt that Cochise and Mangas watched the command from the time it left Dragoon Springs. The dust kicked up by the whites would have been visible for miles. The two leaders had prepared an ambush with a body of warriors estimated to number between one hundred and a ridiculous eight hundred.[46] In addition to Cochise and Mangas, many of the Chiricahua leaders who became well known in the 1870s and 1880s were said to have been present, including, according to Apache accounts, Juh, Victorio, and Nana. Some of Francisco's Eastern White Mountain Apaches may have participated.[47]

Unfortunately, no detailed account from the Indians' point of view was recorded. In later years Cochise allegedly told a participant that when the Americans came "straggling into the pass" after a march of forty miles in nineteen hours with only a cup of coffee, he was confident "of killing everyone."[48] Asa Daklugie echoed Cochise's sentiments and told Mrs. Eve Ball that the Indians were confident of stopping the soldiers' attempt to reach the water.[49] The Apaches had superior numbers, secure positions, and the element of surprise in their favor, yet the volunteers prevailed, with both sides concurring that Thompson's howitzers, which fired forty shells, proved to be the key in averting a catastrophe.[50]

Most accounts agree that the soldiers reached Apache Pass about noon, although Private John Teal recalled that it was about 10:30 A.M. Cochise and Mangas allowed Roberts's command to reach the abandoned stage station. "Then just as the company halted and broke ranks at the station" the Indians, "well armed with rifles and pistols,"[51] attacked the train from the rear. The first volley, which came within eighty yards of the troops, killed one private and wounded a teamster. The fatigued and thirsty soldiers responded immediately, rushing back to support the rear guard and rescue the train. Here they fought off the Indians with the aid of a few well-placed shots from Thompson's "jackass battery." The Indians were routed and four killed here, according to military reports. The soldiers escorted the train to the stage station.

Yet they were still six or seven hundred yards from the spring and faced the same problems Bascom encountered seventeen months before. About 1 P.M., Captain Roberts deployed his men and proceeded cautiously up the narrow canyon toward water. The Apaches, probably led by Cochise, began firing from the "rocks and ravines on the hills on both sides of the spring [and] kept up a rattling fire." The Indians had constructed breastworks on the two hills which overlooked the springs and were invulnerable to rifle fire. Private Barr was killed and another man wounded. At this critical moment, Roberts acted decisively and it would be difficult to say how he

Battle of Apache Pass. Roberts placed his howitzers slightly to the left of center of this photo and shelled the Apache positions above the springs. (*Photo by Karen Hayes*)

could have done any better. He deployed his command, sent two parties of skirmishers into the hills and ordered Lieutenant Thompson to begin shelling the heights above the springs. Amid this fierce fighting, the howitzer began lobbing shell after shell, forcing the Chiricahuas to scatter "like quail in every direction," carrying their wounded and dead with them. During the fight an unlikely hero emerged: a dog named Butch, "who ran around the brush and chaparral, barking and scouting Indians before losing one toe during the fight, shot off by the Indians."[52]

The fight for the springs ended about 4 P.M. The official casualties for the whites were two killed and two wounded; Roberts estimated that the Indians had suffered a loss of at least nine dead.[53] In contrast, Cremony, who arrived the following day, claimed that he learned from a "prominent Apache who was present in the engagement, that sixty-three warriors were killed outright by the shells, while only three perished from musketry fire."[54] Cremony's propensity to overstatement is evident here. Conversely, Apache versions understate the incident, claiming that few, if any, were killed.[55] In truth, the number of Apache casualties cannot be determined with accuracy any more than the number of Indians engaged in the fighting. Dan L. Thrapp writes: "The Indians no doubt saw it as a happy chance for possible loot . . . and were very sure that they could break it off and get away when they chose; that was the nature of an Apache ambush."[56]

The fighting over, Roberts dispatched Sergeant Mitchell and five troopers to join Cremony, who was en route to Apache Pass with the government train of twenty-one wagons and the remainder of Roberts's command. The horse soldiers succeeded in getting through the pass but a few miles west of it twenty Apaches, reportedly under Mangas Coloradas, attacked Mitchell's party. The Indians killed two horses, wounded one man, and cut off Private John W. Teal, who had been leading his fatigued horse. Mitchell's party escaped, but Teal's fate seemed hopeless until "a lucky shot by me sent the chief off in the arms of his Indians."[57]

According to legend, the chief shot off his horse by Teal was none other than Mangas Coloradas. Legend also says that the wounded leader was taken to Janos, where a doctor saved his life. Both accounts are from the pen of Cremony, which leaves them open to suspicion, but the Apache version given to Mrs. Ball corroborated Cremony's account.[58]

Cochise continued the fight the next day, positioning his warriors behind breastworks on the two hills overlooking the springs. But the troops again dislodged the Chiricahuas, who scattered after a few shells landed in their vicinity. Soon after that, Cremony's cavalry occupied the breastworks, which "were skillfully arranged, being made of large rocks piled on each other, with convenient crennels for musket practice." The command moved on to San Simon the following day.[59]

Although the fight at Apache Pass was a virtual standoff, it had significant ramifications. Captain Roberts wisely recommended that a fort be established near the springs. "Otherwise every command will have to fight for the water, and . . . are almost certain to lose some lives." Carleton, who arrived at the pass about July 27, heeded Roberts's advice, judging it "indispensably necessary to establish a post in what is known as Apache Pass" because of the "hostile attitude of the Chiricahua Indians." Consequently, in General Order No. 12 he decreed that Fort Bowie would be situated at Apache Pass and garrisoned by one hundred men of Companies A and G, Fifth California Infantry, under Major Theodore A. Coult. The fort's main responsibility was to keep communications open on both sides of the Chiricahua Mountains. Apparently, Carleton's extreme Apache views were not yet completely formulated as is attested by his orders "to attack all Apaches" unless they bear flags of truce. In the months that followed he issued orders to reject any such overtures before attacking the Indians.[60]

Construction of the fort began on July 28, and by August 14 a wall surrounded it. Indians were lurking in the neighborhood and in early August ambushed and fatally wounded an unarmed soldier six hundred yards from the post. Cochise had not returned in force, and Coult felt that his camp was "pretty safe from any attack of Indians, unless they should come in overwhelming force and desperately storm the hill," which, he correctly pointed out, was "contrary to their usual mode of warfare." For the next several years Cochise appeared at Fort Bowie with his warriors but refrained from attacking it. It remained a permanent fixture in southern Arizona, much to the chagrin of both the Apaches and the soldiers stationed there. In fact, Major Coult went so far as to suggest the abandonment of the post during the winter because of expected heavy snowfall. Carleton disagreed, which abruptly put an end to the discussions.[61]

In late July, Carleton left Apache Pass for the Río Grande. Two miles east of the pass he found the bodies of nine white men who had left Pinos Altos on July 9 bound for California; on July 13, as they approached the pass, the Chiricahuas had ambushed them.[62] Cremony told how these unfortunate frontiersmen were surprised:

Two miles east of the pass, right in the clear and unobstructed plain, there is a gully . . . six to eight feet deep, a quarter of a mile long, three or four yards wide, and cannot be seen from horseback until the rider is within fifty yards of the spot. With consummate cunning a large body of the Apaches ensconced themselves in this gully, knowing that the travellers would be somewhat off their guard in an open plain. . . . The scheme proved eminently successful . . . the hardy miners rode forward with their rifles resting in the slings across the saddle bows, their pistols in scabbards, and their whole attention absorbed in the pass they were about to enter. When they had arrived within forty yards of the gully or ditch, a terrific and simultaneous fire was opened upon them by the concealed Indians, which killed one-half their number outright, and sent the remainder wounded and panic stricken to seek safety in flight. They were immediately pursued and massacred to a man.

These were the corpses that Carleton had stumbled upon. The Indians had burned one man at the stake, "the charred bones and the burnt ends of the rope" still visible.[63]

This was only the beginning of Carleton's journey through Apachería. The remainder of his march was marked by skeletons, skulls, graves, and charred wagons, all stark testimonials to the audacity and brutality of the Indians. Upon reaching Santa Fe to take command of the Department of New Mexico, he received more reports from the superintendent of Indian affairs, emphasizing the critical condition of the territory because of Apache raids. Furthermore, the Indians had gone unpunished, and this galled the stern officer. These frightening pictorials left Carleton with a vivid glimpse of Apache warfare. Thus he turned his attention, every bit of it, to the Indians because he knew no other way. Where his previous orders had been to avoid conflict with the Indians, in the fall of 1862 he redirected his enormous energy and indefatigable zeal against the Apaches.

Carleton was a disciplinarian, a martinet, and a highly principled man who imposed his morality and devotion to duty on his subordinates. A devout Christian, a good family man, and a gentleman, he was unwavering to those who dissented from his views. His main problem was his focus, his perspective. The view from his lens was too narrow, yet he carried out his duties with a zeal and energy which the Department of New Mexico had never seen. He became the absolute ruler of New Mexico during the Civil War; his decisions, based on his morals and convictions, were, of course, correct. He could not be dissuaded.

Carleton inevitably offended many people. His Apache philosophy can be summed up in one word: extermination. He would give no quarter, and during a time when many southwesterners had lost friends or relatives to Apache raids, where humanitarians were as scarce as supporters of Abraham Lincoln in Richmond, Carleton's rigid, unyielding policies toward Apaches were initially supported by most southwesterners. A decade later, General George Crook waged constant war against the Apaches to force their subjugation. He treated them with firmness combined with compassion and dignity when they capitulated. In contrast, Carleton accepted only unconditional surrender, and when some of the bands were ready to yield, instead of grasping this opportunity, he tried to stamp it out by imposing conditions that were totally unacceptable to the Indians. By that time, he had become obsessed with a psychopathic hatred of Apaches.

In the end it was Mangas Coloradas, not Cochise, who incurred the wrath of Carleton and his subordinates' antipathy toward the Indians. By October 1862 his extreme and militant Apache policy had evolved; he ordered his men to reject all flags of truce and to kill all male Indians capable of bearing arms.[64] Robert M. Utley writes that Carleton "brought a rare understanding of Indian warfare and a ruthlessness in applying it."[65] So it was that his extermination policy began. No matter how cruel, inhumane, and immoral it appears to have been to us armchair judges of the twentieth century, we must not overlook the fact that Cochise and Mangas practiced the same policy, yet the whites professed to be civilized and thus more understanding than the Indians and, considering themselves superior, were much more at fault than the Indians. Added to this was the fact that Cochise, Mangas, and other noted Apaches never thought of or practiced extermination or genocide, while that was what many Anglos persuaded themselves was a proper course.

After the fight at Apache Pass, Cochise and Mangas took their people to Mexico. In late July, Cochise was reported near Fronteras,[66] while Mangas allegedly was taken to Janos, where a doctor, under threats of death, extracted the ball from John Teal's carbine.[67] Mangas, now past seventy, soon returned to his beloved Pinos Altos and requested peace. Unfortunately for the Chihennes, Dr. Steck, whom they longed to see, was no longer agent and the army ruled the territory.

The new agent for the Gila Apaches was Fernando Maxwell. Little is known about his activities and his accomplishments, if any. He apparently remained in seclusion at Santa Fe until the following spring. In any event, his absence forced Mangas to deal with the military, who abruptly dismissed any thoughts of an armistice, Carleton writing, "I have no faith in him." [68]

The story of Mangas's death has been told many times and needs no in-depth analysis here. Suffice it to say that against the better judgment of his own people he went to Pinos Altos for a parley, was seized, and shortly afterward "killed while attempting to escape," a euphemistic way of saying he was executed. [69]

The capture and killing of Mangas, pernicious in every respect, naturally increased the antipathy between whites and the Chiricahuas. If death had come in battle, the Indians would have responded differently, but it had not. Thrapp puts it best: "The greatest tragedy of the affair was less the death of the aging chieftain than the lasting distrust generated on the part of Apaches toward white Americans and soldiers." [70] Mangas had been eager for peace, realizing that he could not defeat the Americans, so Chiricahua suspicion of whites now reached new heights. The Chihennes, led by Victorio, Nana, Loco, and Riñon, and the Bedonkohes, under an obscure chief named Luis, perhaps a son of Mangas, again joined forces with Cochise.

For Cochise, the loss of his father-in-law deeply grieved him. If his hatred of Americans had subsided since Coyuntura's death, Mangas's death reinvigorated it and reminded him that the Americans could not be trusted. To the Chiricahua tribe, the execution of Mangas was indeed "the greatest of wrongs." [71]

Chapter 11

COCHISE WILL NEVER BE FRIENDLY

After the Apache Pass fight of July 15, 1862, Cochise made straight as an arrow for the mountains southeast of Fronteras. He needed time to lick his wounds and to reflect upon what had happened. At the least his people were safe from American troops, for Cochise had no conception that his Chokonens were not Carleton's first priority. The battle had neither disabled nor taken the fight out of him; he remained bitterly opposed to any talk of peace, especially with Americans, even though his Chihenne allies under Mangas Coloradas felt otherwise.

About July 24, Cochise and "a party of Chiricahua broncos . . . passed by here [Fronteras] and have scattered by distant routes." The presence of over "300 of all sexes and ages" disturbed Fronteras authorities, who feared Cochise's Chokonens. Furthermore, the regular force at Fronteras numbered but thirty men, leaving the citizens "without security for their lives or interests." Captain Gabriel García came to the reluctant conclusion that he could not take any offensive measures; his force was too small and his artillery piece inoperable. Yet this minor crisis dissipated and Cochise caused no reported trouble at this time in Sonora.[1]

Their arrival troubled García, but it was not his only concern. In early July, Miguel Yrigóllen, Elías, and Aguirre led 156 Chokonens, including 28 men, and brought their followers in. They had been living near Janos when a group of Chihuahuan volunteers from

Guerrero destroyed their camp, capturing 11 of their band.[2] They joined the remnants of Remigio's group, whose ranks had been decimated by smallpox. Toward the end of that month Santiago, Delgado, and José Manda brought their people in, bringing the total living near Fronteras to 262 Chiricahuas, including 52 warriors. These leaders were all closely associated with Cochise and several probably participated in the Apache Pass fight.[3]

While Remigio and other chiefs worked hard at stabilizing relations at Fronteras, Cochise remained undisturbed in the Sierra Madre probably in the vicinity of the Teras Mountains. In August, Plume split from Cochise and brought his extended family group to Fronteras, and in late August *Estrella de Occidente* editorialized that the armistice has "produced good results" and succeeded in "reducing them to a social life [in which] their basic needs are satisfied."[4]

This optimistic report was intended to prepare the citizens of Ures for the arrival of a delegation of Chiricahuas under Remigio to discuss a formal treaty with Pesqueira.[5] The governor, embroiled in fighting off the French invasion of Sonora, promised to conclude a treaty as soon as possible.[6] Cochise, wary and suspicious of Sonora, refused to be a party to any agreement, his actions revealing his contempt for both the treaty and those Chokonens who would contemplate peace.

Pesqueira was delayed, and Apache raids inevitably increased in late 1862. He quickly promised to retaliate against the hostiles, who had "left a trail of blood" in their wake.[7] The situation worsened in January 1863 when Apaches, probably Chiricahuas, butchered a party of twelve Sonorans near Huasabas; only one boy escaped.[8] Pesqueira responded angrily and reinstated the scalp bounty, reinforced the garrison at Fronteras, and reestablished a force at Bacoachi. Furthermore, alarmed by reports that the Chiricahuas at Fronteras were raiding, he decided to go there and investigate.[9]

Pesqueira reached the presidio on the hill in late March 1863. His first step was to issue an edict prohibiting trade between Apaches and Mexicans, warning that harsh punitive actions would be taken against any citizen continuing this insidious practice.[10] He recognized that the Indians were depredating in both Mexico and the United States, perhaps responding to a charge that Major David Fergusson had made from Tucson the previous fall.[11] In response, the governor wrote Brigadier General West at Mesilla admitting that the Indians had been raiding across the line into the United States while implying that a similar state of affairs existed at Mesilla.[12]

Undoubtedly there was a semblance of truth about this age-old practice. Cochise had done so for much of 1861, and there was no reason to believe that he had ceased. In later years he conceded that "a great many of us were one time at peace at Fronteras and some of the Mexicans used to tell us to come up here and steal American horses, which are big and worth a great deal of money in Mexico."[13] One such raid occurred at Fort Bowie, only eighty miles north of Fronteras, in the fall of 1862. On October 5, Apaches attacked the herd at the fort. Two parties of troops unsuccessfully pursued the Indians west for ten miles, in all probability Cochise's Chokonens. Captain Hugh Hinds reported that "the Indians are getting hungry and bold but retreat before my scouting parties at all times. They appear to want the stock and care little about fighting for it." This was the essence and character of an Apache raid: minimum risk. No stock was worth a life.[14]

In any event, more than half the Chokonens agreed to a formal truce, the conditions of which were rigid and restrictive. Pesqueira concentrated on controlling the Chiricahuas through close vigilance and by placing responsibility in the hands of the chiefs. He demanded two roll calls per week and insisted that all arms be turned over to the military commander. Of course the Chiricahuas may have assented to this, but in practice it never took place and their best arms were cached for future use. The final demand, one tried unsuccessfully in past treaties and the one which would eventually undo this one, compelled the men to serve as scouts against hostiles, primarily Cochise's Chokonens. In return, Pesqueira agreed to issue rations of corn or wheat, tobacco, whiskey, and some clothing. At this time the Indians numbered 270 and were led by Santiago, Remiqio, Miguel Yrigóllen, and Taces.[15]

Cochise's absence tended to indicate that he was in Arizona, for it had been only a short time since the execution of Mangas Coloradas. Compounding this was the wounding of Mangas's wife, Tues-seh; the killing of one son, probably Seth-mood-a;[16] and the capturing of another. As a result, within a few days, Cochise's wife,

Dos-teh-seh lost her father and a brother killed by troops, a brother captured, and her mother wounded. Naturally revenge must be had.

In the days following Mangas's murder the remaining Bedonkohes joined Cochise, perhaps on a permanent basis.[17] According to Geronimo, they "retreated into the mountains near Apache Pass" although their intentions were not clear;[18] his recollections are corroborated by contemporary military reports. On February 16, 1863, some four weeks after Mangas's death, Indians suddenly appeared in the hills overlooking Fort Bowie. Displaying a flag of truce, six women eventually came into the post and the following day twenty more came in; one hundred warriors were visible in the hills. Unfortunately, no report has been found that would either identify the Indians or explain their motives. Cochise's emissaries may have been scouting the vulnerability of the eighty men garrisoned at the fort, which was too strong for an attack. In any event, troops scouted for Apaches on February 17 and 18 but failed to find any.[19]

Lieutenant John F. Qualey wrote Fergusson concerning the Indians' visit. His report has not been found, but Colonel David Fergusson's reply, as instructed by Brigadier General West, indicated that both officers knew of the Chiricahuas' talk of an armistice. From Tucson on March 12, Fergusson informed Qualey:

> I have been directed by the general commanding the District of Arizona to instruct you to order back all flags of truce presented by Indians. To do this instantly on their being presented and then to attack the party sending them and to endeavor to make their woman and children prisoners and to send your captives to Mesilla whenever an opportunity shall offer . . . also to war on the grown male Indians whenever and wherever found, without hesitation or exception.[20]

There would be clashes when the weather turned warm.

Geronimo's chronology is somewhat confusing, but he clearly recalled that his Bedonkohes joined Cochise shortly after Mangas Coloradas's death. This was probably in March 1863, when Cochise "took command of both divisions." Soon after that, "we were again attacked by another company of United States troops . . . we were repulsed and decided to disband."[21] Geronimo may have been referring to an incident which occurred on March 22, 1863. Apaches "supposed to have been Chiricahua and Gila Apaches" attacked the herd at Fort West[22] and ran off sixty horses. The boldness of the attack surprised the troops, for the horses were less than a mile from camp and were guarded by a sergeant and twelve men. That evening Captain William McCleave, one of the army's best Indian hunters; eighty-one men; and two guides, including Juan Arroyo, left with ten days' rations, vowing "either [to] retake the horses or Apache blood enough to pay for them."[23]

McCleave chased the raiders west for some seventy miles to the Black River, then struck the trail again. Believing a ranchería to be near, on March 27 he stumbled upon a camp situated along the Río Bonita, a tributary of the Gila River, said to have been a favorite camping place of Cochise. The soldiers attacked and routed the Indians, killing twenty-five Apaches in twenty minutes. The troops lost one man dead, Private James Hall. Whom McCleave attacked is not known. Bonita Creek was in White Mountain Apache country, where the Chokonens were to be found from time to time, and a report in early March saying that Chihennes had fled to Coyotero country leads to the possibility that the victims were Chiricahuas; the band, however, remains unknown.[24]

The Bedonkohes and Chokonens scattered, Cochise apparently moving south into the Chiricahuas, bound for Sonora. On April 25 a large band of Indians approached Fort Bowie from the north. Captain Benjamin F. Harrover gathered a force of twenty-five men and encountered the Apaches near the springs. Here a minor brush ensued before the Indians retreated, the whites in pursuit. The Apaches, armed with "many guns of large caliber also several rifle muskets," succeeded in wounding one soldier. Harrover thought several Indians were killed or wounded. From the report and the large body of Indians involved, West concluded that Cochise and his band were involved, and they probably were.[25]

By the second week of May, Cochise had shown up at Fronteras, ready to fight anyone in his way, whether be they citizens, troops, or peaceful Chiricahuas. His appearance had a frightening effect on everyone in the vicinity, where the peace consummated six weeks earlier was on the verge of collapsing.[26]

Problems had surfaced from the beginning because the treaty was a most unpredictable arrangement at best. Pesqueira had ordered two detachments to scout the mountains north and east of Fronteras for those Chokonens and Nednhis who had refused to come in. In compliance with the terms of the treaty, Remigio and four warriors guided a command of forty men led by Captain José Escalante to examine Batepito and Pilares. The Chokonen leader Santiago and five of his men scouted for the second command of seventy men led by Captain Angel Elías, who would reconnoiter the Arizona-Sonora boundary.[27]

Neither force accomplished much, but Elías's troops found a Chokonen ranchería in the Anibacachi Mountains twenty-five miles northwest of Fronteras near the Arizona line. It may have been the camp of Delgado, who had come in with Santiago the previous July, but one of Santiago's warriors, who probably had relatives in this local group, deserted the Sonorans and warned the encampment. Not everyone escaped; one child was captured and a Chokonen warrior named Gándara was killed and scalped. Meanwhile, Escalante's scout was uneventful, he and his men eventually scouting Turicachi before returning to Fronteras after a 360-degree journey.[28]

The desertion of the scout was the first sign that the armistice would be short-lived. Even more serious, Chiricahua raiding parties continued raiding in the interior while living under the pretense of peace. Two warriors returned to Fronteras with stock stolen from Sahuaripa; it was confiscated and two Apaches were imprisoned, which produced a volatile atmosphere. They escaped, and a few days later the small groups of Miguel Yrigóllen, Taces, and Lorenzo bolted in the direction of the Teras Mountains. Lieutenant Colonel Buenaventura led forty-five troopers in an attempt to overtake them but was unsuccessful.[29]

At this crucial stage Cochise arrived at Fronteras on a trading mission, his intent being to exchange loot for food, guns, and ammunition. Currently at war with the United States and with Chihuahuan troops scouting aggressively throughout the Janos area, he probably wished to maintain peaceful relations at Fronteras, yet some kind of difficulty ensued, probably because of Pesqueira's edict banning trade with Apaches. In later years Cochise recalled an incident that occurred at Fronteras in the early 1860s. Evidently it began when the Indians were disposing of American stock. "When [our] people came back there with" the stolen stock, the people of Fronteras "killed them and took the horses and saddles away."[30] This act, or something similar, touched off the explosion. Cochise returned with his men, killed several citizens, and the armistice disintegrated. The Chiricahuas, "incited by Chis," headed for the mountains. Once again Cochise was at war with all whites and Mexicans.[31]

For the remainder of 1863 and 1864, Cochise's activities become somewhat difficult to trace. We get glimpses of his whereabouts from escaped captives and occasionally from the Chiricahuas' actions. He returned to southern Arizona after the incident at Fronteras and his people spent the rest of the spring gathering, baking, and storing mescal. He remained in touch with his Chihenne and Bedonkohe relatives to the east and north and planned a summer campaign in southern New Mexico to avenge Mangas's death.

As it turned out, Cochise was fortunate to have avoided northern Chihuahua, where the scalp-bounty system was in full swing and the Nednhis were being systematically hunted down. Joaquin Terrazas and his volunteers were having a field day against the Carrizaleños, killing Cojinillín, whose scalp was worth five hundred pesos, a considerable sum in these days.[32] Finally, in early 1864, Zuloaga assisted Terrazas in capturing Felipe and forty-six others, which incapacitated the remaining Carrizaleños and virtually destroyed them as a distinct group.[33] Their remnants, under Gorgonio and El Zurdo, probably were absorbed into the Janeros unit of the Nednhi band, by this time led by Juh,[34] a heavy-set but first-rate war chief who fought side by side with Cochise throughout the 1860s.

Meanwhile, in the spring of 1863, West and Carleton began vigorously thumping their war drums. In mid-March, Carleton had reminded West: "I do not look forward to any peace with them, except what we must command. They must have no voice in the matter. Entire subjugation or destruction of all the men are the alternatives."[35] Truly, this policy of unconditional surrender as regards Cochise's people was a fiasco and served to exacerbate already poor relations.

Although Carleton had not mentioned Cochise, West in southern New Mexico recognized his importance. In late May he wrote Colonel David Fergusson, commander of the District of Western Arizona at Tucson, suggesting that he plan a campaign against Cochise and his band, believed to be living in the Chiricahua Mountains.[36] Nevertheless, in the summer of 1863 it was reported that the

"Apaches are quiet" in southern Arizona. Pressure from northern Mexico, plus some unfinished business (avenging Mangas's death) may account for the Chokonens, Bedonkohes, and Chihennes joining in the summer of 1863 to fight the whites; Cook's Peak would be their headquarters. The audacity and brutality of their attacks surprised West, who had discounted the Chiricahuas as too fragmented to take the offensive.[37]

The first of several hard fights took place about June 17 when Chiricahuas killed First Lieutenant L. A. Bargie and two other men opposite San Diego Crossing on the Río Grande. The Indians, "apparently pertaining to the parties of the chief (Mangas Coloradas) who was killed some time ago by the Californians near Pinos Altos," applied the same barbaric treatment to Bargie's body as the troops had to Mangas. The courageous officer was found with "his head cut off, his breast cut open, and his heart taken out."[38]

Captain Emil Fritz pursued the Indians west, thinking they were "Mimbres River Indians" or Mangas's Chihennes. West was incensed by the outcome of the fight and ordered Captain McCleave to put his Fort West command in the field against the Indians. West's fury may be inferred from his terse but explicit instructions to McCleave:

> This band of Meimbres [*sic*] River Indians must be exterminated to a man. At the earliest possible moment that the condition of your command will admit of it, you will undertake this duty. Use every available man. . . . Scour every foot of ground and beat up all their haunts.[39]

Cochise's Chokonens likely did not have a hand in Bargie's death, which was probably the work of Luis's Bedonkohes and Victorio's Chihennes. A few weeks later, however, he apparently joined these two leaders and they set up shop at Cook's Canyon.

On July 11 a small detachment of seven men under Sergeant E. V. Hoyt was escorting a supply train east to Las Cruces. At Cook's Canyon he was attacked by a large body of Indians, which resulted in the abandonment of three wagons and nineteen mules. Four soldiers were wounded and four Indians were killed, but Hoyt's party eventually reached Las Cruces with their lives.[40]

About two weeks later a detachment of California Volunteers

commanded by Second Lieutenant John Lambert left Las Cruces and entered Cook's Canyon at 5 A.M. on July 24. The allied Chiricahuas were ready and opened fire, wounding a sergeant and killing a private. After driving the Indians back, Lambert circled his wagons, which probably saved lives because the Apaches, estimated at between 150 and 250 warriors, were concealed in ambush. After five hours of skirmishing the Indians tried to set fire to the grass, which failed to ignite. Next, in a rare tactic for Apaches, they prepared an assault from three directions. This frightened Lambert. With his options dwindling fast, he abandoned two wagons, supplies, and twelve mules, hoping the Indians would not pursue; they did not. What Lambert did not realize was that Captain Chauncey R. Wellman and his command were approaching Cook's Canyon from the west. Wellman caught a quick glimpse of the retreating Apaches but thought that they were too strong to pursue; he overtook Lambert's command, and both arrived at Las Cruces about noon on July 25.[41]

There is some evidence that Cochise joined Victorio (they were said to be great friends, according to Mrs. Ball) in these hard fights, but there is no direct proof. Only Cochise could have gathered such a body of warriors, and the absence of Apaches in Arizona in the summer of 1863 tends to indicate that he may have been in New Mexico. The locality of Cook's Peak, the characteristics of the fight, and the fact that some of the stolen booty was recovered in the Chiricahua Mountains six weeks later points to his participation. In fact, the hostilities led to the establishment of Fort Cummings in Cook's Canyon on October 2, 1863.[42]

West, always ready to explode when it came to Apache victories, was initially irate over Lambert's actions. Later he grudgingly admitted that Lambert's judgment might have been correct, but "still it is a defeat and . . . has enabled the Indians to provide themselves with subsistance." Consequently, he issued Special Order No. 39, calling for an extensive campaign against the Apaches of southern New Mexico. He reiterated his belief that the Indians must be pursued until exterminated. In fact, he considered the situation so important as to go to Cook's Canyon himself. On August 10 he met Captain McCleave, who had established a base camp on the Mimbres from which he could campaign against the hostiles.[43]

Cochise returned to Arizona after the fight and focused his attention on the Americans living at Apache Pass. In late August a party of seventy-five Apaches stole every horse from Fort Bowie. The Indians had broken into three groups and the raid was efficiently and effectively carried out.[44] But these successes were not destined to continue.

On September 5, Captain James H. Whitlock discovered and destroyed an Indian camp in the Chiricahua Mountains. Three days later he found the Chokonens (likely led by Cochise, who was thought to be in the area) "in force [and] a very spirited fight for about 15 minutes" ensued in which two whites were wounded. Among them were Juan Arroyo, Whitlock's skillful guide, whose competence in the 1860s would have been rivaled only by the incomparable Merejildo Grijalva. More shots were exchanged the next day before the Indians vanished deeper into the mountains. Items taken from the Indian village were "sufficient evidence of the Indians being the same that attacked Lieutenant Lambert's party." Whitlock later said Luis, the Bedonkohe leader, was present.[45]

The Chiricahuas faced aggressive campaigning from below the border. Stung by its fruitless policy of pacification, Sonora declared that "peace with this class of enemy is a Utopia, an unrealistic project."[46] The intermittent Chiricahua-Sonora peace treaties between 1831 and 1863 were now a thing of the past, although Apache distrust and the enmity of Sonorans probably was the primary reason, rather than Sonora's official hard-line rhetoric.

During the summer of 1863, Bavispe and Bacerac had mobilized national troops to hunt Apaches believed to be living in the Animas Mountains, yet nothing of note occurred. In late September, Captain Eraclio Escalante led a scout from Fronteras and attacked Taces's Chokonens in the Pitaicache Mountains. The soldiers killed Taces and a woman and captured two others, one of whom escaped during the night and warned other Chiricahua rancherías, likely including Cochise, who was reported in the vicinity.[47] Eskinya, a Chokonen who figured prominently in events of the 1870s, succeeded Taces as leader of that small local group.

Once again the Chokonens scattered, some heading for the Chiricahuas, others to the Huachucas or Dragoons. Thanks to the testimony of an escaped Mexican captive, we have some insight as to Cochise's situation in the fall of 1863. The American and Mexican offensives had forced the Apaches to keep on the move; as a consequence "they were starving." Furthermore, the Chokonens had "been very unsuccessful in their late raids into Sonora in search of booty and that their arrows had become useless and their ammunition exhausted." This report was corroborated several months later by another former captive. The two posed immediate problems for the Indians, especially if they were willing to act as guides. Accompanied by Mexican and American miners, the escapee led them on a scout which succeeded in surprising a Chokonen ranchería near the San Pedro; five Indians were killed and another captured. Although the location of the Indian camp was not specifically identified, it was probably in either the lower Dragoons or the Huachuca Mountains.[48]

Mexican troops continued to make their presence felt in late 1863 and early 1864. In November 1863 the indefatigable Captain Eraclio Escalante and ninety men from Bavispe wiped out a Nednhi ranchería near Janos, killing twenty-one Indians, including six warriors, and capturing seven others. Their leader, Susopa, was among the dead.[49]

It was the Chokonens' turn in early 1864. Leaving Bacoachi, Captain Cayetano Silva led a force into southern Arizona, scouting the Mule and lower Dragoon mountains before crossing the Sulphur Springs Valley to the Chiricahuas. On February 12 his scouts discovered a ranchería, perhaps at Turkey Canyon, called by the Indians Tsetagolka, or Mound of White Rocks. Silva divided his troops into three groups: Lieutenant Manuel Gallegos, an experienced Apache fighter and 30 infantry to the right; Lieutenant Feliciano Ruiz with a force of nationals to the left; Captain José Escalante with the cavalry to the center. At daybreak the three commands converged on the village, which proved to be Santiago's and routed the unsuspecting Apaches. As in previous fights, no prisoners were wanted, but somehow 3 children survived and were not killed. Men, women, and children were cut down indiscriminately. Six warriors and 15 women and children were reported killed.[50] Five months later a Chokonen warrior named Ka-eet-sah admitted that the Sonorans had killed "about thirty in one day, among them all of his family."[51] By the time the news reached Tucson, the total dead in the fight had increased fivefold to 107 and it had occurred thirty to forty miles south at Fort Bowie.[52]

The surprise was so complete because the Chiricahuas had evidently decided to request peace at Fronteras. Emissaries had already been sent; in fact, these messengers may have actually entered the fort and held discussions before the attack. Captain Silva ordered out Captain José Jesús Escalante and fifteen dragoons to overtake and attack the Indians if possible. Near Fronteras, Escalante completed his mission, killing three Indians and capturing three more children.[53]

With northern Mexico on the offensive, Cochise had probably established his winter camp in the northern region of Chokonen country, trying to avoid white contact. Toward late February, only a few weeks after the annihilation of Santiago's group, the Bedonkohe leader Luis, three warriors from his band, and fifteen Chokonens from Cochise's band left the Gila country for a raid against their old antagonists, the miners at Pinos Altos. The Chokonen chief awaited the outcome, but if Luis had succeeded, "Cochise and his tribe would have come the next time." An Apache scouting party had appeared at Pinos Altos on February 13 and threatened the citizens, declaring they would return about February 25.

The miners sent word to Captain James H. Whitlock, who was in camp along the Mimbres. With twenty-one men he left the night of February 24 and arrived at Pinos Altos the next morning. Luis led the Bedonkohe-Chokonen party into Pinos Altos about noon; at dusk Captain Whitlock's command moved into town and, assisted by citizens, killed thirteen of the eighteen warriors, including Luis, his three Bedonkohes and nine Chokonens. Mexicans scalped the Apaches and brought the hair to Carrizal, Chihuahua, for the bounty.[54] Whitlock also retook a Mexican captive named Marijenia Figueira, who had been captured at Banamichi by Miguel Narbona in 1849.[55] Her testimony revealed the destitute condition of the Chiricahua hostiles:

All the Indians that came in with this party were living near the mouth of the Black River. We came by Fort West: have been eight days coming. The Navajoes are at war with all the other tribes that I know of. They took all our stock; left us very poor; very poor indeed. We have no stock except 3 ponies, and 1 of these soldiers got last night. We have no dried meat; have nothing to live upon except mescal. . . . Can occasionally kill a deer. Have no powder or guns. Our

guns are nearly all worn out . . . we have no clothing. We have to live
down in the valleys. We cannot live up in the mountains; it is too
cold. Runon [Riñon] and Victoria [Victorio] get powder and lead
from a man named Zuloaga, who lives in Corralitos Mexico. . . .
Zuloaga is always on friendly terms with us even when his government is at war with us.[56]

The Chiricahuas avenged Luis's death on March 22, 1864, running off seventy-two mules from a government train at Camp Mimbres.[57] Whitlock, now a battle-hardened Apache fighter, elected to
wait a few days before pursuing, hoping the raiders would relax
their vigilance. The command of seventy-two officers and men left
on March 27 and followed the trail west toward the mountains north
of Stein's Peak. Whitlock, however, decided to use a circuitous
route, moving north to the Gila River and cutting the trail near Safford or Solomonville, which led to a ranchería in the Graham Mountains. The Indians were woefully unprepared for the attack. The
troops "charged their camp," killed 21 "wretches," and looted the
village. Whitlock believed the ranchería contained 250 individuals
"supposed to be [of] the Chiricahua tribe," which, if true, meant
this was Cochise's camp, for no other Chokonen local group would
have been this size. It was probably Cochise who led the force of
poorly armed warriors who skirmished with the troops but soon
withdrew. The Chiricahuas lost their homes, property, and stock and
possessed but two or three guns.[58]

About one month later Cochise retaliated, apparently having been
joined by some Bedonkohes and Chihennes, for he showed more
strength than to have drawn only from his Chokonens. With a force
estimated at one hundred to two hundred warriors, the Chiricahua
war party lay concealed in ambush in the steep hills of Doubtful
Canyon near Stein's Peak. A detachment of sixty men under Lieutenant Henry Stevens rode into Doubtful Canyon early on May 4.
Although a notorious site for Apache ambush, the men did not anticipate danger and Juan Arroyo had failed to detect the Indians'
presence. Wrote one of the soldiers: "We did not know that there
was an Indian within 20 miles of us."

As the sun was coming up, Stevens's command passed the abandoned stage station near Stein's Peak and the Apaches launched their
surprise. The silence was broken by whoops from the rocks and

Doubtful Canyon. On May 5, 1864, Chiricahuas showered arrows on Stevens's command from both sides of the canyon. (*Photo by Dan Thrapp*)

crevices on both sides on the canyon. The first assault wounded four
men as the Chiricahuas, lacking guns and ammunition, "poured arrows into our ranks by the hundred." Undaunted, Stevens, whose
horse was killed in the opening assault, rallied his men in a manner
which would have made Hollywood proud. Ordering his troopers
forward, he "swung his hat around his head and encouraged the
men all he could while in the act of swinging, an Apache shot an
arrow through [it]." After a forty-five-minute fight the Indians, who
"had fought like devils," withdrew to higher positions in the mountains. Lieutenant Stevens reported that ten Apaches were "left dead
on the ground"; moreover, he thought, twenty or more were
wounded. The troops' losses consisted of one man missing in action, one mortally wounded, one with a broken arm, and three
others slightly wounded.[59] Carleton praised Stevens, gleefully passing the report on to Washington and describing the encounter as "a
handsome little fight."[60]

Cochise was probably at both Whitlock's and Stevens's fights. From Fronteras it was rumored that he had been killed in one of them, which would tend to support his presence in one or perhaps both engagements.[61]

Stevens's command was proceeding to Fort Bowie to participate in General Carleton's grand Apache campaign. Now that he had subdued the Navajos, Carleton turned his attention to the Apaches, determining to subjugate them. This would be "a serious war; not a little march out and back again." His objective was simple: "to hunt and destroy all but the women and children."[62]

In April he had begun making the necessary administrative and organizational plans, in which he excelled. He planned a pincerslike assault against the Apaches north of the Gila. Troops would be pulled in from everywhere, and Carleton urged ranchers, merchants, miners, and even the Pimas, Maricopas, and Papagos, the Apaches' traditional enemies, to take the field.[63] He envisioned that the Apaches would be defeated and forced to seek refuge in northern Mexico. To ensure their entrapment, he requested that Governors Pesqueira and Terrazas place troops along the border, where the fleeing Apaches could easily be ambushed.[64] He revealed his obsession with defeating the Apaches when he assured Captain Tidball at Fort Bowie that he would "do all that mortals can do to bring this Apache war to a speedy and final end."[65] He would whip them before Christmas, he said confidently.[66]

Public sentiment supported wholeheartedly his policy. A letter from Tucson in Janaury 1864 declared that Arizona was "virtually in the hands of Apaches." The Apache "must be hunted to his own secret strongholds and shot down like a wild beast whenever found."[67] Richard McCormick, secretary of Arizona Territory, concurred believing that popular opinion was in "favor of an utter extermination of the ruthless savages."[68]

Actually it was the Western Apaches, not the Chiricahuas, who absorbed the brunt of Carleton's offensive. U.S. soldiers scouted the White Mountains, where some three hundred warriors were reported, and Major Nelson Henry Davis did succeed in killing forty-nine and capturing sixteen near the confluence of the San Carlos and the Gila. Cochise, said to be on the Gila with Francisco's band, easily eluded the slow-footed troops, who were no match for the mobile Chokonens.[69]

Carleton's troops encountered one local group of Chokonens that summer, but Cochise was not among them. On July 10, Captain Thomas Theodore Tidball left Fort Bowie with fifty-eight men and twenty-two days' rations to scout the Chiricahuas; Merejildo Grijalva served as guide. The command marched southeast along the western slope of the Chiricahuas through country which few, if any Americans, had traveled. The first night, the command camped in the mouth of Bonita Canyon, where the Chiricahuas had fought the Sonorans twelve years before. The next day's march was a few miles southeast, and camp was made at Pino Canyon on the night of July 11. The next day, Tidball continued south along the western foothills, stopping at the mouth of Turkey Canyon. Finally, on July 14, the command penetrated the heart of the Chiricahuas to the summit, bivouacking near Fly's Peak. From here the command marched northeast for six or seven miles before striking an Indian trail, which led some seven miles to Cave Creek Canyon. Merejildo called this Río Ancho (Broad River), which coincided with the Apache name of Tu-n-tel-jin-li ("Water Broad Going").

Tidball immediately sent Sergeant Brown and twenty men to follow the trail. Shortly thereafter he encountered Plume, who stood his ground, perhaps protecting his own small group, which consisted of four or five warriors and about fifteen women and children. First, Plume began shooting arrows, without effect, and then, for devilment, began throwing rocks. This was condoned until he severely bruised a trooper; at this point the soldiers were forced to kill him. But old Plume had not died in vain, for the rest of his group escaped. His camp consisted of five wickiups on the side of a high mountain near the summit, which overlooked the San Simon Valley. It was probably near Portal Peak.[70]

The next day Tidball continued south along the eastern foothills and discovered more Chokonens. The Indians were too suspicious to approach but agreed to come in to Fort Bowie in eight days to make peace, a typical ploy to halt pursuit. Four days later Merejildo conversed with a warrior named Ka-eet-sah,[71] who decalred that his Apaches "belonged partly to Mangas' and partly to Chies'

[Cochise] bands and that they had a treaty and traded with the people of Janas [Janos]." As to Cochise's whereabouts, Ka-eet-sah disclosed that he was still on the Gila with the Coyoteros, probably meaning Francisco's Eastern White Mountain band. With the Apaches aware of his presence, Tidball marched across Sulphur Spring Valley to the Dragoon Mountains before returning to Fort Bowie on July 31.[72]

By this time Carleton believed that many of the Apaches had fled to Mexico and in spite of the inauspicious beginning he continued to believe that his troops could subdue the Indians by December.[73] This illusion was shared by few. He directed Major N. H. Davis to campaign against the hostiles living in northern Chihuahua. Davis moved his command into Chihuahua, scouting Alamo Hueco, Espuelas, and Boca Grande, but found no Apaches. To put to rest the rumors about José María Zuloaga trading with Apaches, Davis marched to Janos and Corralitos and talked with Zuloaga, who convinced the American that the complaints had no foundation. One wonders whether Davis, had he concluded that the charges were correct, would have executed Zuloaga as Carleton had advocated. But Davis, a thoughtful and pragmatic man, felt it best to dismiss the allegations and, fortunately for all concerned, Carleton's undistinguished plan was not implemented.[74]

While Davis was reconnoitering northern Chihuahua, other scouts were busy along the Gila, and a new post, Fort Goodwin, was established in Western Apache country. With such increasing American activity, Cochise may have left Coyotero country for the Chiricahuas or the Dragoons. In early August a war party of some eighty warriors swooped down on Cuquiarachi and stole one hundred head of stock. Their trail led to southern Arizona. In early October, Indians were prowling around Fronteras, their rancherías believed to be either in the Dragoon or Chiricahua mountains.

In November a force of eighty men left Fronteras, scouted the Mule Mountains, and found nothing before moving toward Cochise's stronghold in the Dragoons. They found Indians in the southern foothills, so Captain Manuel Gallegos and thirty men set out in pursuit. Suddenly a party of forty to fifty warriors appeared in the rear. Another force was dispatched but could not overtake the

Apaches—undoubtedly Cochise's for no other Apaches lived in this range. The troops returned to Sonora but left a force at Cuquiarachi because the Indians had threatened another attack.[75]

One month later, troops from Bacoachi, Fronteras, and Bavispe concentrated and took the offensive. In December, they struck a trail of stolen cattle in the Animas Mountains. On December 11 the combined force of 125 men remained in ambush but saw no Indians; the next day they saw smoke. Quickly, three divisions were formed: a force on each flank and one in the middle. The Sonorans surprised the camp, destroyed it, and killed 39 Apaches (9 warriors and 30 women and children). In addition, they captured 28 Apaches, including 3 babies who froze to death on the return march to Bavispe. It is not known which band was hit, but from the location it would appear to have been a Chokonen or Nednhi local group.[76]

In January 1865 came signs that four years of war had worn out the Chihennes, who, under Salvadora, Victorio, and the venerable Nana,[77] expressed a desire for peace. The issue was simple, the solution complex. Should the military commander (Carleton) or the superintendent of Indian affairs (now Dr. Michael Steck, the Chiricahuas' former agent) handle the negotations?[78] Carleton decided the military had sole jurisdiction and he of course could not be dissuaded. He alone would determine whether the Apaches should be considered pacified (sufficiently whipped) or hostile. And he wanted no interference from civil authorites.

Carleton's reservation policy would remain. All Apaches and Navajos who wanted peace would be required to move to Bosque Redondo on the Pecos River, a place hated by everyone concerned except Carleton. If the Indians refused, they faced extermination. Referring to Cochise, Carleton revealed his misconceptions, shared by most Anglos concerning Apache organization: "Cochise continued to hold out, when he falls the Pinal Apaches will succumb."[79] The Pinals were a band of Western Apaches and completely independent of Cochise's Chiricahuas.

The Chihennes fervently wished to see their old agent, Steck, whom they remembered fondly, and Steck wanted to see them. The obstacle was Carleton, who went so far as to deny Steck an escort to Pinos Altos. Thus the Apaches were forced to negotiate with the

Victorio. The great Chihenne chief who in 1865 said that "Cochise will never be friendly" to Americans. (*Courtesy National Archives*)

military; nonetheless, on March 20, Nana and thirty-three individuals (eighteen of them warriors) met Second Lieutenant John K. Houston near old Fort Webster. The talk ostensibly satisfied Nana. Four days later, Victorio arrived at the Mimbres River, claiming that he wanted peace if he were allowed to live on the Gila or the Mimbres; he even offered to fight hostiles and help recover stock. No matter how desperate, however, "he would not go to the Bosque or let his people." Cochise was a different story, admitted Victorio, declaring that he had attempted to convince him to make peace but the Chokonen leader "*does not wish it and will never be friendly more.*" [80] His country was still sparsely settled, and American troops had not yet come close to subjugating him.

Chapter 12

CATCH THE WILD FOX

The year 1865 was destined to be Cochise's most active since the first year of his outbreak. We can follow his trail easier today than did the army and civilians who were so anxious to put an end to Apache hostilities, Cochise's in particular. Cochise's war continued because hostilities between him and Americans had become normal relations. For the first eighteen months after Coyuntura's death he had taken the offensive, but after the Apache Pass fight, his war had become more of a defensive one. Perhaps even more important, it had become a way of life for Cochise.

There was precedent for his actions. In 1846, Mexicans murdered his father, which touched off a decade of war before friendly relations were reestablished at Janos and Fronteras in 1857 because the Chokonens feared the presence of American troops in their country. Cochise was a pragmatist, yet this side of him emerged only after he came to accept that war was a losing proposition. His people had never been completely subjugated by anyone, Mexican or American, and in the mid 1860s there was no reason to think that U.S. troops would prove otherwise.

In January 1865 there was a large body of Apaches between Fort Buchanan and the San Pedro River. On January 4, thirty Indians attacked the mail express between Fort Bowie and Tubac; the two men escaped to San Pedro Crossing, but the Indians took their horses and mail. Eight days later the Apaches struck again, ambushing a wagon within a mile of Tubac and killing one man and wounding another. Captain John L. Merriam reported the incident, vowing to make a campaign against the hostiles, who deserved "prompt and severe punishment."[1]

A month later Cochise swept into the same area with a war party of seventy to eighty Chokonens. On February 17 they ambushed three people near the Santa Rita mines, killing William Wrightson and Gilbert W. Hopkins and capturing a Mexican boy. Shortly afterward, "Cochise and some 20 of his best and bravest warriors" assaulted the Santa Rita hacienda but were driven back by the sharp-shooting of John T. Smith,[2] a former California volunteer, aided by a woman who later became his wife. As the besieged whites fired through loopholes, the "Indians began to drop off" and were driven back to the hills.[3] Swinging east, Cochise crossed the southern foothills of the Santa Ritas before moving north toward abandoned Fort Buchanan, where a vedette station had been established. On the afternoon of February 17 the war party thundered down on the station. Wrote Corporal Buckley:

> No signs of Indians for some time back. On the morning of attack one man went hunting (he is still missing), and in the afternoon two men went, as usual, to cut hay for the horses. I was sitting at the door of the house when an Indian shot me through the thigh. This was the first knowledge we had that the Indians were around. I drew my pistol and shot the Indian at the same time Private Berry shot another. The Indians now closed in large numbers (seventy or eighty) round the house, and soon had it on fire. We kept them off until the roof began to fall in . . . when I saw that the only chance for saving our lives was to force our way through the Indians. We broke from the house amidst a shower of arrows, . . . [we] kept them off till we got to the hills, when they gave up the chase, and we made it safely to Santa Rita.

The raiders made off with six horses, two carbines, 250 cartridges and about 200 rations.

The characteristics of the attack, the number of warriors involved, plus the fact that some of the plunder later was found in Chiricahua camps, leads to the probability of Cochise's presence.[4] Two days later, Apaches raided a ranch near Tubac but were repulsed with one warrior reportedly killed, which was of little consolation to the whites of that region. The Indians had driven everyone out only a few years before, and only within the past year had any semblance of mining and commerce been resumed.

Papago scouts told their agent, Mathias O. Davidson, that the Apaches were organizing a "force to strike a terrible blow in this vicinity." Davidson urged Carleton to send help in the form of arms and men, but by this time the general's responsibility no longer included Arizona and he was involved in a controversy with Dr. Steck, which merely prolonged the Apache war in the Southwest.[5]

After the vedette station raid, Cochise returned to the mountains along the border, and for the next month Chokonen and Nednhi bands invaded northern Mexico. Four raiding parties hit the Janos–Corralitos–Casas Grandes region, causing farmers to lose more than seven hundred total working days, according to José María Zuloaga. A garrison at Janos was sorely needed, he said. Little did he realize that matters would get worse.[6]

Toward the end of March, Cochise made plans for an expedition against Mexico, evidently to avenge relatives killed in the Animas Mountains the previous December. Runners were dispatched to Chokonen and Nednhi local groups, inviting them to join him in the Chiricahuas for a foray into Sonora. Since some of the troops from Bavispe were involved in the massacre at Dzisl-di-jole ("Round Mountain"), Cochise and probably Juh planned the ambush. Juan José Zozaya, an experienced observer on the Apache-Mexican scene, estimated the war party to number between 150 and 200 warriors, about the combined strength of Cochise's and Juh's bands.[7]

Cochise was almost certainly the leader of this war party because Victorio, who had sent a messenger to Cochise, reported the chief was absent "out on a scout."[8] This term could have meant that Cochise was out raiding with a few warriors or out with a major war party. The Chiricahuas designated both terms as "they are scouting about."[9] This time, he was at war.

They selected a site which lay along the road between Bavispe and Janos. The distance between these two towns was about sixty miles by road. The first twenty-five miles east from Bavispe traversed the northern tip of the great Sierra Madre—through innumerable canyons which offered the Indians ideal sites for ambush. In early April a party of eleven men left Bavispe for Janos. They followed the road east for about twelve miles to a place called Ta-

Location of Cochise's ambush, Sierra Madre

savare. Here the road turned north through Higueras Canyon to Carretas before veering abruptly east to Janos. At Tasavare the Chiricahuas, most of them on foot and many armed with rifles and revolvers, were concealed behind rocks on both sides of the pass. Ten men died instantly and one was captured.

About this time, Luis García's wagon train was moving west from Janos to Bavispe, unaware of danger. García had made the same trip on numerous occasions, but his party suffered the same fate as the first. On April 5 he reached the unoccupied Hacienda de Carretas and the next morning his party, consisting of eleven men, two women, and two children entered a place called Lagartos, still oblivious to the presence of Apaches. Here the Chiricahuas had set up another trap, with the first volley coming from the hills and then the second, from a hidden arroyo. All the men were killed and the women and children captured, probably with the intent of exchanging them for Apaches held in Sonora. The train was looted and sixty head of stock were captured.[10]

Meanwhile at Bavispe, seventeen nationals under Sergeant Juan Serraño had left on April 4 to meet and escort García's train. They reached Tasavare the next day and found the corpses from the previous day's massacre. Stunned but alerted, they pushed on to meet García's train but never reached it. At Higueras Canyon the war party attacked, and it was a virtual repetition of the two earlier attacks. Three men escaped, but thirteen lay dead and one wounded in Higueras Canyon. The three survivors fled east to Janos for reinforcements, which came in the form of Juan José Zozaya and twenty-three men. Zozaya's party cautiously scouted the site, concluding that every one of both Serraño's and García's parties had been killed by gunfire. The Indians' trail led north because Cochise crossed the border into Arizona after these engagements.[11]

Military affairs were changing in Arizona. On January 20, 1865, the District of Arizona was removed from Carleton's command and placed in the Department of the Pacific, commanded by Major General Irvin McDowell.[12] He immediately recommended Brigadier General John Sanford Mason,[13] who combined administrative skills with a good fighting record, as commander of the new District of Arizona. This approved, on February 20, McDowell, Mason, and John Noble Goodwin, Arizona's first governor, convened in San

Francisco. One of the items discussed was the Apache situation, and all concurred that Arizona's prosperity hinged on the Indians' subjugation. Whether they discussed Cochise is not known, yet shortly after Mason reached Arizona in May he recognized Cochise's importance by calling him "the very worst Indian on the continent." [14]

The new commander faced almost insurmountable problems. The number of troops was insufficient to conduct campaigns against the hostiles. Moreover, they lacked adequate clothing, supplies, and horses. Communication among the scattered military posts was sporadic and uncoordinated; consequently, few victories had been won. Yet Mason's arrival with reinforcements, plus the federal government's approval in raising volunteer troops, possibly averted another crisis in southern Arizona and may have turned the tide in Apache-Anglo relations, although no one could have realized it at the time. [15]

Mason reached Maricopa Wells on May 30 and confirmed recent reports that "the Indians really have possession of this Territory." He decided to view at first hand the situation in southern Arizona. On June 8 he arrived at Tubac, calling it a "worthless town" and apparently discussing the Apaches with citizens. He reported that the hostiles were living in the mountains north of the Gila, except for a few Indians in the Huachuca and Chiricahua mountains. [16]

By this time Arizona's new commander had formulated his Apache policy, one which reflected an understanding of the Indians and a willingness to provide for those truly subdued. He advocated a reservation policed by the military as the first step in controlling Indians who surrendered. The army would take the responsibility of feeding and clothing those who desired peace; for those who continued to resist, Mason advocated launching campaigns into their territory to destroy their rancherías and compel them to sue for peace. [17] As for Cochise, he continued to resist, moving his base of operations into northern Mexico when pressured to do so. He was not prepared to make peace as long as he could find refuge south of the border.

Mason continued his tour from Tubac, going to Fort Bowie, where "a salute in his honor [was] fired." Here he heard rumors that Cochise was camped north in the Sierra Bonita Range (Mount Graham), near the spot where Whitlock had surprised him the year before. Consequently, on June 26, Mason issued special orders instructing Lieutenant Colonel Clarence E. Bennett to take every available man and attack Cochise. Merejildo Grijalva would act as scout.[18]

Bennett departed that evening with forty-three men, three civilians, and two scouts, Merejildo and Lojinío, a tame Apache. Marching west out of the pass, the command turned north and followed an old Indian trail along the western foothills of the Dos Cabezas Mountains, called Nakibitci (Two Heads or His Two Tails) by the Chiricahuas. On June 29 the troops found a deserted ranchería which was thought to have been Cochise's; it had contained two to three hundred Indians. From here Bennett continued his march to Fort Goodwin, rested for a few days, and on the evening of July 2 set out to return to Bowie. En route, Merejildo discovered two more rancherías, one a Chokonen camp containing articles from the attack at Fort Buchanan five months before and the other belonging to Francisco, who after a skirmish had appeared in the mountains and "abused everybody, declared he would never make peace with the whites, and said the Apaches did not intend to." The command recovered twenty-seven beef cattle from Francisco's camp before arriving at Fort Bowie on July 6. Bennett recommended that "vigorous efforts should be made to annihilate the bands of Cochise and Francisco."[19]

In the meantime Cochise apparently had reached a decision. Sensing an American buildup of citizens, troops, and emigrants, he decided to move south into Sonora. In late June he and Francisco led a large war party of 150 warriors, which included recruits from the Western Apaches. His stay in the northern limits of Chiricahua country in 1863 and 1864 had gained him several allies, including Esh-kel-deh-silah, the influential White Mountain chief whom Cochise gave a Mexican captive.[20]

This war party, which apparently divided into two groups, wreaked much devastation throughout July 1865. On July 7 or 8, it attacked Ochoa's ranch, killing two women, three children, and one man. On July 11 it wiped out a German family named Amelung twenty-two miles east of Tucson at the Cienega and killed the mother, father, youngest child, and several Mexicans while capturing two boys. The booty from these attacks was supposed to be ten thousand dollars in gold plus several wagons and some stock.[21]

Cochise swung east and struck again two days later, this time against six soldiers southwest of present-day Willcox. This group had left Lieutenant Colonel Bennett, then en route to old Fort Breckenridge, to return to Bowie. It had gone but five miles when seventy-five Apaches waylaid them. The first volley killed a private, wounded two soldiers, and killed or wounded five of the six mounts. The soldiers fled, leaving the wagon, stock, and harness behind, and struggled on foot to the post, having suffered severely from thirst, and reached Fort Bowie on July 14. Captain Merriam vowed to avenge the attack, which he believed was committed by the Indians whom Bennett had fought a few weeks before. Yet his command was too dispersed: fourteen men were at Tubac, three at Fort Goodwin, three with the express, ten at San Pedro Crossing, and several were performing daily post duties. His morning report showed only ten privates on duty, and he feared that the Apaches would attack Bennett's command at old Fort Breckenridge.[22]

Bennett discovered a trail of one hundred Apaches on July 15, in all likelihood Cochise's party. Cochise, however, after attacking the troops near Croton Springs, plunged southwest against the ranches in the Santa Cruz county. During the next week he tried twice to run off the herd at the San Rafael ranch, a short distance north of the border, but was unsuccessful on both occasions.[23]

Unbeknownst to Cochise, Mason had ordered a "scout and exploration of the Huachuca Mountains and San Pedro Valley." In compliance, on July 19, 1865, Captain Hiram A. Messenger with thirty men, two citizens (Oscar Hutton and E. K. Brown), and two guides left the Mowry mines. What was to be a simple reconnaissance ended up in an encounter with an Apache war party led by Cochise himself. The first day out, Messenger found an Indian trail near Canelo Hills. On July 22 he followed it into Sonora, camping six miles south of the Arizona border near the deserted adobe presidio of Terrenate, some fifteen miles east of Santa Cruz. Late that day, two soldiers named Compton and Hicks went hunting. When they failed to return, Sergeant Kelly and Private Henry left to search for them. About 4 P.M. Compton and Hicks arrived at camp, reporting that ten Apaches had fired on them.

At once Captain Messenger took 15 men to search for Kelly and Henry. His small force came to a ridge; wisely, he deployed his troops before entering an ominous-looking canyon. At this point the Indians, estimated at between 100 and 150, fired on the troops, who fought a rear-guard action back to the main camp. The Apaches, "whooping like devils and pimping like bull frogs," surrounded the soldiers but respectfully stayed out of rifle range. The Apache leader (believed to be Cochise) was perched on a ridge and commanded by "motion of the hand to advance, retreat, close up or deploy." This continued for several hours until a heavy rain rendered the Apaches' bows ineffective. One soldier was wounded and the Indians suffered no reported casualties.

That night the Apaches moved north into the Huachucas and could be heard whooping and singing, evidently celebrating a victory. The next morning the bodies of Kelly and Henry were found stripped and lanced. Kelly had died instantly; Henry apparently made a good fight, as attested by the pools of blood found near him. For good measure the Indians had smashed his skull with a rock. The guides, Antonio and Marcial,[24] examined the arrows and pronounced them to be from the Chiricahuas (Chokonens), Pinals, Gilenos, Coyoteros, and Sierra Blancas, with the Chokonen arrows "much the greatest," indicating that Cochise had been joined by several Western Apaches in the fight. Marcial and Antonio, both of whom knew Cochise by sight, believed that he had led the war party and personally conducted the fight.[25]

News of Cochise's whereabouts soon was received by Captain Hiram Storrs Washburn,[26] who was in southern Arizona enlisting men for the Arizona Volunteers at the new Fort Mason.[27] Manuel Gallegos, a former Sonoran officer who had joined the volunteers with the rank of lieutenant, had just returned from a recruiting mission at Bacoachi with twenty-six Indian fighters. He probably brought word that Cochise was reported to be in the vicinity of Fronteras.[28]

The Arizona Volunteers were organized to fight Apaches. Although two companies were mustered in at Tubac, they never posed much of a problem to Cochise. Recruiting had begun in earnest about mid-July 1865, with the officers primarily Americans and the soldiers primarily natives of Sonora. Captain Washburn wrote Governor Goodwin and predicted that he would have his company prepared for "Apache hunting" by mid-August. He pointed out that he had enlisted eighty recruits, mainly Mexicans, which he believed would promote "amity and mutual confidence between the two nations." Moreover, he felt that their past experience in Apache campaigning boded well for the success of the volunteers.[29] His was not shared by all Americans. An Anglo who was well acquainted with the volunteers said "it was a mixed command a few white men [and] several of that variously tainted race called Mescican." Furthermore, some whites "looked upon these troops as scum."[30]

Sometime in August, Cochise notified authorities at Fronteras that he and his subordinate chiefs, Miguel Yrigóllen, Delgado, José Manda, Remigio, and Elías, would come in and make peace.[31] Four hundred Chokonens were expected. The Mexicans could not turn to the state government for help because the French had driven Governor Pesqueira and his supporters from Sonora. The invaders' army, situated at Hermosillo, had no intention of fighting Apaches, who, for most of 1865, found northern Sonora an "open, unprotected field . . . for their robberies and murders," according to an American living in Hermosillo.[32] Their options limited, the officials at Fronteras turned to the Arizona Volunteers for help.

Washburn realized that capturing Cochise would be a delicate mission, but the end would justify the means. Thus he had no compunction about using tactics which would have made Baylor or Carleton proud:

> Chicusa [Cochise] now that he is made rich from the robbery at the Cienega, July 11, wants to have a good spree and a few fancy articles of half civilized life. So as usual on occasions of a full treasury he has been in to Fronteras soliciting peace. Fronterans understand well the game, partly from fear, but chiefly from a desire to barter their mescal and other surplus articles for the coin, pistols and various other articles acquired by the Apaches jurisprudence, gave their consent and immediately sent word to me that the celebrated Apache general Choqueese will soon appear before them . . . with 400 Indians. . . . At first these warriors will be very suspicious and will only fall into the snare by the most careful and astute dissimulation, which with liberal portions of mescal will soon gentle them, so that by the most cautious and most careful concert on our part and that of the authori-

ties at Fronteras we may almost safely calculate in getting nearly the
whole of these Indians without the loss of a man.[33]

Subsequent developments forced a change in these plans.

Like most Americans, Washburn viewed Cochise as the key and
quickly became obsessed with either subduing or capturing him. He
became increasingly frustrated after receiving definite information
that Cochise was near Fronteras, but he was helpless to take action.
Washburn's enthusiasm waned as he became hamstrung by a lack of
money, clothing, guns, and supplies. On September 1 he reported
that neither arms nor supplies had been furnished and that every
man had become ill from "eating crude fruit and sleeping on the wet
ground without blankets." In addition, his company had not even
been formally mustered because the official documents had not arrived. More than anything, it seemed that the conscientious officer
feared that some other command would capture Cochise and deprive
him of credit.[34]

Perhaps had Washburn's command been equipped and turned
loose against Cochise, as it would be during the winter of 1866
against the Indians of central Arizona, the Chiricahuas could have
been routed and forced across the border. Instead, his volunteers remained inactive and Cochise moved farther east to the vicinity of
Janos. Here in late August two large bands, probably Cochise's
Chokonens and Juh's Nednhis, were encamped, which forced a
party of Americans to alter their route to avoid the Indians.[35]

By October, Cochise had returned to the Chiricahuas and Washburn inquired about reward money if he could capture him or any
other Apache leader. He claimed that Cochise's whereabouts was
"well known and my men can take him if they can get arms." He
seemed determined to orchestrate a dramatic success for himself,
having concluded that seizing Cochise would give him an excuse to
visit Washington, where he had personal business. He wrote Governor Goodwin on October 9, 1865: "I suppose if I will catch your old
Wild Fox Kechise, General Mason will give me an order to take him
to you in Washington."[36]

That fall several Apache leaders discussed peace, including Cochise, who was in the vicinity of Fort Bowie in late October. With
cold weather approaching, perhaps he was prepared to consider a

temporary cease-fire with the hope of living unmolested in the Chiricahuas. He was undoubtedly aware that his two dependable allies, Francisco's Coyoteros and Victorio's Chihennes, were also discussing terms at Fort Goodwin and Pinos Altos, respectively.

Cochise's unexpected arrival at Fort Bowie and his talk of a truce puzzled Major James Gorman, who had been ordered to make war, not talk peace. On October 30 many Chokonens were reported in the hills overlooking Fort Bowie; white peace flags and smoke signals were visible everywhere. The next day they reappeared and their leader, perhaps Cochise, "jabbered and howled industriously." Major Gorman, who shared the army's prevailing dislike of Indians, claimed that "he had no authority to make a treaty," actually believing that the Apaches deserved to be shot. Feelings had not changed much in four years.

Shortly after this, an officer and a civilian left the post and met the Chiricahuas, telling them to return in twelve days, at which time Major Gorman would have received orders from his superiors. Over the next two days, several Chokonen women entered the post and were fed and clothed. Unfortunately, no reports have been found to determine what transpired, but they were definitely identified as Cochise's people and he undoubtedly was in the neighborhood.[37]

Regardless of what was said to the Indians, Major Gorman decided to lead an expedition against them. He left on November 1 with thirty-four men for the Pinery, ostensibly to cut wood. Although Gorman failed to mention it in his report, a civilian eyewitness wrote that two large wagons, normally used for gathering wood, were concealed with soldiers so as not to arouse the Indians' suspicion. Evidently the strategy worked. The day after he left, five Apache women entered the post and remained all night.[38]

Meanwhile, Gorman marched through the Chiricahuas, camping by day and moving by night, perhaps trying to vindicate himself from past allegations of inactivity, incompetence, and drunkenness. Early on the morning of November 5, Merejildo Grijalva located a Chokonen ranchería, which he assumed was Cochise's because a sentinel had been posted on a high ridge and Cochise was one of the few Indians known to take this precaution. Preparations made, Gorman left eight men with his horses and took the remainder on foot toward the encampment. They succeeded in slipping past the lookout before he discovered them and warned the village. The Indians quickly scattered up the mountains, while the troops swept down on the ranchería and indulged in target practice against their foes. They found another ranchería about a half-mile away, but Gorman remarked disappointedly that "the Birds had flown leaving everything behind them." Seven Indians were killed and one soldier wounded in the fight, which reportedly took place sixty miles south of Fort Bowie. This is certainly wrong because that would place the engagement almost in Sonora. The fight occurred in the southwestern Chiricahua Mountains probably some thirty-five to forty straight-line map miles, which would be around sixty by trail.

Gorman's command captured many things which implicated Cochise's people in the raids of the previous winter and summer. Included were several items from the attack on the vedette station at Fort Buchanan on February 17; a saddle belonging to Mr. Wrightson, killed the same day; and several articles taken from the German family killed at the Cienega in July. Many native items were found and destroyed, including large quantities of mescal, dried meat, baskets, and cooking utensils. Merejildo believed this was Cochise's camp (and his opinion was rather conclusive evidence), as did Major Gorman, who contended that "Cochise and his band have committed more depredations than any other equal numbers of Indians in this part of the territory."[39]

Whether this was Cochise's local group is not important; the significance is how he might have perceived the attack. The Chokonen had made peace overtures, and admittedly it was highly improbable that anything meaningful could have been concluded. In all likelihood, a peace of any duration could not have been consummated, for Cochise had not been sufficiently whipped and the Americans would not have allowed him to use Arizona as a base to raid into Mexico. Yet an officer from Bowie had told the Indians to wait twelve days for a response to their proposals; instead, Major Gorman had seized this opportunity to make a campaign in which he killed seven Chokonens, some of them probably women and children. Gorman's campaign erased any thoughts that Cochise, if indeed he was sincere, might have harbored about an armistice.

Cochise also shared in the misunderstanding. He had waged a ruthless war against Americans for the previous five years and in the past year had been as hostile as ever, sparing neither women nor children. Now, with winter approaching and no assistance available from a French-controlled Mexico, he opted to give the Americans a try, perhaps hoping to camp in the Chiricahuas as he had done in the past.

Despite Gorman's success, Cochise remained encamped in the Chiricahuas during the winter of 1865–66. Although troops had scouted the mountains twice in the past sixteen months, they had not conducted a winter campaign, so Cochise could not have expected Mason to conclude that a major campaign against the Chiricahuas was warranted and necessary. Mason made plans for simultaneous operations both east and west of the Dragoons, hoping to deprive Cochise of using that area as sanctuary. In mid-December, Colonel Charles W. Lewis left Fort Mason for the Huachuca Mountains, where Cochise "the Chiricahua chief and famous rifleman" was reported to be living.[40] Three detachments scouted along the San Pedro and the Huachucas and Dragoons but found no Indians. Lack of good footwear forced one division to curtail its scout. The second force, under Captain Porfirio Jimeno, ambushed a group of hostiles at Sulphur Springs on December 24, killing one Indian and wounding two. The third command scouted the Dragoons and found a deserted camp in Cochise's west stronghold before returning to Fort Mason in late December. Replenishing their supplies, the troops returned to Sulphur Springs and united with Jimeno, whose force had been bivouacked for several days.

Next, Lewis decided to examine the Chiricahuas. He detoured to Fort Bowie, replaced Marcial Gallegos with Merejildo Grijalva, and on January 6 plunged south. But the Apaches were vigilant. Two days out the Americans found a large ranchería in the southern Chiricahuas, perhaps the vicinity of Rucker Canyon, where Gorman had found them two months before. It had been deserted two days before. Even so, sixty to seventy warriors could be observed in the high mountains; the women and children had fled into northern Mexico, with the men following the next day. Lewis followed the trail of these fleeing Chiricahuas into Sonora, halting at Fronteras, where he found the people destitute because the "Indians had robbed them of everything." He abandoned the pursuit and returned to Fort Mason. The command's disorganization and Captain Jimeno's lack of initiative "deprived us the pleasure of finding the whole Chiricahua tribe of Indians at home," lamented an officer, although Cochise's people probably would have detected the force even if Jimeno's command had been more aggressive. Very few could come up with Cochise when he was on guard. After Gorman's attack, he was not about to be surprised again.[41]

The winter campaign was over, a dismal military failure which did nothing to improve the Indian situation. Yet it was a moral victory in the eyes of General McDowell in San Francisco, who unrealistically claimed triumph because of "driving Cochise's band into Sonora."[42]

Other factors in late 1865 also muddied the waters. These further shaped Cochise's perceptions about Americans and certainly were instrumental in his decision to spend much of the next three years living in Mexico, beyond the reach of U.S. soldiers. He was beginning to lose some of his allies. First, on November 10 troops at Fort Goodwin gunned down Eastern White Mountain leader Francisco, allegedly while trying to escape. Francisco had been imprisoned for his part in the Cienega attack the previous summer. Moreover, a falling out of sorts had come between Cochise's Chokonens and the White Mountain and Pinal bands of the Western Apaches. Both were said to be "bitter against the Co Chise's band of Indians who were undoubtedly the perpetrators of all the emigrant road massacres" in the past few years.[43]

At Pinos Altos in late 1865, Victorio's Chihennes repeated their peace attempts of the previous spring, hoping for an alternative to Bosque Redondo or extermination. What followed became known as the Bean Treaty, either because the Apaches were served a dinner of beans or because of the presence of Sam Bean, an early settler at Pinos Altos. Several Chihennes ventured into Pinos Altos with peaceful intentions, and in a premeditated attack the Americans killed three Apaches while "drinking coffee in a house," with results which may be imagined very easily. According to one account, Victorio himself was "shot in the cheek." About three weeks later he avenged this attack, slaying four soldiers and wounding another near Fort Cummings.[44] Incidents like Gorman's attack, Francisco's execution, and the Bean Treaty convinced Cochise and Victorio that

Americans favored a continuation of the war and that the fighting must go on.

Driven out of Arizona, Cochise moved into northwestern Chihuahua to the vicinity of Janos, which a large number of Apaches had surrounded in mid-January 1866 and cut off communications. Word was somehow transmitted to Lieutenant Colonel Edward Willis at Fort Selden, situated on the east bank of the Río Grande twelve miles north of Doña Ana. Willis obtained permission from Mexico to enter Chihuahua "for the purpose of hunting Apache Indians." Taking forty-five men, he marched east to Fort Cummings and received reinforcements of twenty-five men. From here the command proceeded south to Janos, but the Apaches, whom Willis believed to be Mimbres (Chihennes) and other bands, detected them and fled to the mountains. Since the Chihennes were active in the Pinos Altos region at this time, the bands most likely involved were Cochise's Chokonens, freshly arrived from the Chiricahuas, and Juh's Nednhis, although there is no tangible proof.[45]

Meanwhile, in Arizona, Brigadier General Mason was being assailed from all sides. His lack of success against the Apaches had generated an expected uproar among citizens, the territorial press, and even within the military. All recognized that the Apache situation had not improved during the first year of Mason's stint, although the Arizona Volunteers had accomplished much against the Indians of central Arizona.[46] In the south, however, Cochise's Chokonens continued to raid. The troops were disparaged by remarks that they "cannot protect themselves much less than people. . . . Few or no Arizonians die a natural death."[47]

Everyone had a solution and most continued to advocate extermination. The military lacked resources and a penurious Congress, more concerned about Reconstruction, paid little attention to Arizona. One ingenious individual advocated a plan in which the United States would purchase from Mexico the lower peninsula of California for ten million dollars. The next step would require an expenditure of thirty million dollars to round up and drive all the Indians there. Finally, the government would place a cordon of forts to maintain order, similar to the Spanish presidio system of the 1700s. If the Apaches misbehaved, the government could withhold food and starve them to death. This policy was suggested by a writer in San Francisco, no doubt sensitive to Apache lifestyle and culture. Indeed, perhaps he should have proposed it to Cochise, who, if he could be found, might have jumped at the opportunity![48] Fortunately, this lamebrained scheme was not considered at department headquarters of the Military Division of the Pacific, commanded by Major General Henry Wager Halleck.[49] Yet Halleck conceded that Mason's winter campaign was a failure and "too extensive for his means." The general implied that Mason failed to understand the Apaches' mode of warfare, so he sent Brigadier General McDowell to Arizona to investigate and to recommend a solution.[50]

Other methods of dealing with the hostiles were considered, including using friendly Apaches. In early 1866 the Pinal and Coyotero Western Apaches continued friendly relations with the Americans at Fort Goodwin. In conference with Lieutenant Colonel Robert Pollock, they found it convenient to blame Cochise's followers as the "perpetrators of all the emigrant road massacres" of the past few years. In fact, Pollock believed he could induce these Indians to act as guides against the hostile Chokonens.[51] In Tubac, citizens went a step further, hiring tame Apaches as mercenaries against their incorrigible brethren and also, according to one report, paying them one hundred dollars for each scalp brought in.[52]

In early spring 1866, Cochise laid plans for a foray (originating from either northern Mexico or the Chiricahua Mountains) against the ranches in the Santa Cruz and Sonoita Valley. In April, after making several stock raids, the Chokonen war party besieged the San Rafael ranch, located a few miles southeast of the junction of Sonoita Creek and the Santa Cruz River. The owner of the hacienda, Rafael Saavedra, and his servants retreated to the main house at the first fire. The Apaches burned the smaller structures and captured a young woman who cried out, "For God's sake, save me." Against his family's objections, Saavedra heroically left the hacienda and somehow saved the woman but was killed in the process, or so the story goes. The ranch soon was abandoned. Thomas Yerkes lost sixty-six head of stock in this raid and claimed that Cochise's band was the perpetrator. Juan de López, a servant at the ranch, even identified Cochise, whom he believed was wounded slightly. It was but one more of the countless times Cochise was reported killed or wounded.[53]

Shortly after this raid Esteban Ochoa hired, armed, and equipped tame Apaches to track the hostiles. These Indians felt much antipathy toward their unpacified relatives, claiming their sole purpose in life was to avenge their own dead, killed by the wild Apaches. Accordingly, a party of twenty-five left Tubac in late April and picked up the hostiles' trail, reportedly Cochise's Chokonens. Somewhere in southeastern Arizona or northern Sonora, they found the ranchería of Cochise, "Chief of the Coyoteros de Chiricahuas," and attacked it the first week of May. When the fight broke out, one man, evidently a chief, tried to rally his warriors but was killed and scalped, as were three others. The ears were cut off, although one was left behind "for the devil to take to the dead Apache."[54]

Three weeks later Cochise retaliated. On May 31 he led at least 100 warriors (two other reports put the number at a ridiculous 260 and 300 to 400) and stole Camp Wallen's herd, which was grazing three miles from the garrison. This post, established only three weeks earlier on the north bank of Babocomari Creek, was situated just north of the Huachuca Range and south of the Whetstones. In theory, the post was supposed to "prevent hostile incursions of Sonora Apaches and the band of Cochise." Apaches swooped down from the east, south, and west and made off with fifty-seven horses, ten to twelve mules, and seventy-two head of cattle; only five horses remained at the post. Sergeant Henry I. Yohn and five others, joined later by a civilian, pursued the Apaches. Half a century later, Yohn recalled that the hostiles tried to surround his party but failed to do so. At this point, "Cochise was pointed out to me. He was commanding the Indians and rode a magnificient black horse."[55]

The next day, Captain Isaac Rothermel Dunkelberger, fifty-four troops, and sixteen tame Apaches left Fort Mason and arrived at Wallen on June 3. The scouts worked the trail for some fifty miles along the Arizona-Sonora line before the Indians scattered like quail. The scouts reported that the raiders were Cochise's band and numbered "eighty to one hundred warriors," a far cry from the three to four hundred estimated by Camp Wallen's commander.[56]

The large number of Apaches horrified the commander, Captain

William Harvey Brown, who, thought one soldier, "possessed very
few soldierly qualifications."[57] He dreaded an Apache assault on his
post, knowing that his men were unequipped to resist. Brown had
seventy-two men: sixteen without carbines, sixty without cartridge
boxes, and thirty-three without sabers. In a forceful letter to his superiors, he protested that "it is very wrong to expose men thus in an
Indian country,"[58] although one wonders whether he would have felt
the same way if his troopers had been sufficiently equipped. Brown
was also afraid that a large band of Apaches could easily overrun the
camp. His sincere concern reflected his lack of understanding of
Apache guerrilla warfare, for Cochise had neither the inclination,
nor the patience, nor the firepower necessary to put Wallen under a
prolonged siege. The camp had a quiet summer and fall.

Cochise had little, if any, contact with American troops for the
remainder of 1866. Mason's winter campaign had failed and the
Arizona Volunteers had been discharged during the summer. On
June 10, Mason was replaced by Lieutenant Colonel Henry Davies
Wallen, who relinquished command to Colonel Charles Swain
Lovell two months later. Lovell lasted only until November, when
McDowell decentralized the District of Arizona into five sub-
districts, hoping each would become more effective in fighting
Indians.[59]

These administrative changes had little effect on Cochise, who remained in northern Mexico for the rest of the year. Raids into the
United States furnished subsistence and trading material at Janos
and at Casas Grandes, where it was said that Apaches showed up
like clockwork every Saturday to trade plunder and even gold for
lead and bullets.[60]

In August, Cochise himself was seen by Francisco Martínez, a
Sonoran citizen, who was dumbfounded by the reception the Chiricahuas had received. He said Cochise, "with his entire band and a
great deal of stock," showed up at Janos and was treated "very
well" by the authorities. In fact, Martínez reported, they said they
"were very happy to see him." A friend of Martínez tried to buy his
own horse, which had been stolen by the Indians in Sonora, but they
refused to trade unless they were given powder or ammunition, both
of which reportedly flowed freely at Janos.[61]

Naturally Sonoran citizens became alarmed at the increase in illicit trade at Janos; they recalled the consequences of the treaties of 1842, 1850, and 1857. Just as predictably, raids into Sonora continued, and the Chokonens and Nednhis who were trading at Janos were blamed. A large band of Apaches swept through the streets of Fronteras on August 30, killed a man and a woman, and ran off some stock. Cochise may have been shot in the neck during this fight. On September 10 another raiding party, probably the same one, ambushed and killed two men near Cuquiarachi. Outcries from Sonoran officials followed, blaming the people at Janos for harboring the hostiles and for providing a market for trade. Sonora would suffer "double than what we had previously suffered" forecast an observer from Bavispe. In mid-November, seventy Apaches raided Bavispe, and the stock was believed to have found its way to Janos.[62]

Chihuahua also suffered at the hands of Apaches. In late August a war party said to number two hundred overran the town of Cruces in the district of Namaquipa. More than twenty people were killed, several wounded, and several captured.[63] Raids of this nature, combined with Sonoran complaints about fraudulent activities at Janos, ultimately prompted Chihuahua to act. In December Cayetano Ozeta led a group of volunteers from Guerrero, in southwestern Chihuahua in the foothills of the Sierra Madre. After a tedious scout they succeeded in surprising Cochise's camp on December 22 at the Espia Hill, some seven or eight miles southeast of the Boca Grande Mountains northeast of Janos. They killed five warriors and one woman and captured four others.[64] Even Cochise's sanctuary in northwestern Chihuahua was no longer safe, and his band once again scattered north into the Chiricahua and Animas mountains, hoping to steer clear of both American and Mexican troops. It would not be an easy task.

Chapter 13

TOO MANY MEXICANS

Throughout 1867 and 1868, Cochise maintained his pragmatic philosophy of avoiding Americans, living primarily in the mountains of northern Mexico, southeastern Arizona, and southwestern New Mexico. From these safe retreats Chokonen and Nednhi parties continued to raid southern Arizona, Sonora and, to a lesser extent, Chihuahua.

Of Cochise little was known. His encounters with Americans were fought only on his terms, and few lived to identify him, adding to the mystique which surrounded him. Many people wondered whether he was living, while others thought "he had taken up his abode in northern Mexico."[1] This uncertainty notwithstanding, practically every report, whether it originated from the army, the Bureau of Indian Affairs, newspapers or pioneers, concurred on one thing: Cochise was the most able, most intelligent, and most hostile of the Apaches. Subjugate him and only then would peace come to southeastern Arizona.

After the attack at Boca Grande in late 1866, Cochise's people scattered into the Animas and Chiricahua mountains. In January 1867 he organized a war party against Sonora, intending, according to a captive who was with the Apaches, "to make many prisoners in order to exchange for their own people captured by the troops of Chihuahua," obviously a reference to Cayetano Ozeta's triumph.[2]

In early February a large band of Chiricahuas, possibly led by

Cochise, attacked seven men near Cumpas, killing four and capturing two. One, a boy named Priciliano Rivera, inexplicably turned
up at Moctezuma six days later; somehow he had escaped or had
been turned loose by the Apaches. His story was interesting. He declared that the Apaches numbered fifty-five, were accompanied by a
citizen from Janos who helped "plan the campaign," and intended
to ambush travelers between Moctezuma and Granados. The unlikely presence of a renegade Mexican was a common occurrence
in the late 1860s and perhaps explained why the Indians had increased
their attacks on American mail riders. These cutthroats understood
the value of the money which the mail usually contained.[3]

With Sonora aware of his presence, Cochise diverted his operations to Arizona. In mid-February it was reported that "he was on
the warpath with his entire force and some of his men could be seen
daily from Fort Bowie." Undoubtedly they were responsible for the
death of mail carrier Charles Fisher on February 19, 1867, seven
miles east of Bowie.[4] Cochise's next target was the Mowry mines,
which contained a fine cache of weapons (thirty repeating rifles and
several Colt revolvers) plus an abundant supply of ammunition
stored in the main house. Several eyewitnesses reported that Cochise led the Apaches, who, according to various estimates, numbered between forty and eighty warriors.

On the morning of the fight, five Americans were at the mines:
Thomas Yerkes, Robert Reed, Richard Doss, Edward Marcy, and
Edward Hunting. Yerkes and Reed were visitors; the others were
employees at the mine. Early that morning Yerkes and Doss went
outdoors and saw two Indians with rifles aimed at them. They fled
toward the house; Yerkes made it safely, but Doss was wounded
"severely in the legs." This was the beginning of a brisk fight between the Indians and the five whites.

Within minutes the Chiricahuas surrounded the house, took possession of the corral, and climbed onto the roof. Edward Marcy was
"shot dead through a window." Yet the whites "had plenty of arms"
and, shooting from loopholes, "kept up a regular fight." Next Cochise tried to set the buildings on fire but failed. About ten o'clock
Oscar Buckalew, the mail contractor, arrived. He boldly penetrated
the Indians' line and dashed into the fortress, but not before the
Apaches killed his horse and shot him in the leg, a wound serious

enough to require amputation later. Soon afterward Oscar Hutton and another man approached and observed the fight. They fled for help at once, with the Apaches in hot pursuit for a few miles. Knowing they would bring soldiers, Cochise withdrew to a nearby hill, baffled by the firepower from the few whites in the house. Yerkes and Buckalew both heard the chief, whom they assumed was Cochise, deliberating with his men. Expecting reinforcements, Cochise broke off the engagement.

In the meantime, the two whites dashed into Santa Cruz, gathered a force of thirty-one citizens, and sent messengers to Camp Wallen. At once Captain William Harvey Brown collected forty-four men and launched a rather indifferent pursuit, earning him the disdain of McDowell at department headquarters in San Francisco. Learning the details of the encounter, Brown termed it "an unusual daring Apache fight." He concluded that Cochise undoubtedly was responsible because of the nature of the combat and "the large number of good arms" displayed by the Indians, although an eyewitness claimed that only one-fourth of the Apaches had firearms. Thomas Yerkes said he learned from other Indians that "Cochise himself was there." By the time reinforcements arrived, the main body had crossed the border into Sonora, and soon after that Cochise returned to his base camp in the Chiricahuas.[5]

During the spring of 1867, Mexican and American military leaders were drawing up plans to take the offensive against Cochise. No longer contending with the French, Sonora directed her energies against the Chiricahuas living in northern Mexico, with Pesqueira announcing that his soldiers would pursue and exterminate Apaches. With this in mind, he reestablished garrisons at Bavispe, Bacoachi, and Santa Cruz. Atypically, Chihuahua cooperated and the two states carried their campaigns into southeastern Arizona and southwestern New Mexico, an area which had been unscouted by American patrols and was off limits to Mexican troops.[6]

Concurrent with Mexico's offensive, the new commander at Tucson, Colonel Thomas Leonidas Crittenden,[7] designated Cochise public enemy No. 1 and laid plans to subdue him. His good intentions notwithstanding, he lacked officers and men in his district to keep continual patrols in the field. Those few penetrating Apachería were easily eluded by Cochise. Fort Bowie, the one post from which aggressive scouting might have paid dividends, was inadequately garrisoned throughout the mid-1860s, having an average of only one officer and forty-five men. The garrison was strengthened after a military inspector recommended in early 1866 that "the operations of Cochise and his band are the terror of the Southern country. It is my opinion that the troops here [Fort Bowie] could be employed to advantage in going for him."[8]

Even with the additional manpower, scouts were made typically in response to Apache raids and had only a minute chance of overtaking any hostiles.[9] Nonetheless, Crittenden succeeded in putting several detachments in the field, which, although not injuring Cochise, did force him south along the border, where he was vulnerable to Mexican campaigns.

The first victory over the Chiricahuas came in early April 1867 when Chihuahuan troops under Cayetano Ozeta, one of the most active of Mexico's Indian hunters, followed a trail into the southern Chiricahuas. Here they found a Chokonen or Nednhi local group headed by Tuscas and succeeded in killing or capturing the entire encampment. Ozeta's troops killed twelve (including eight warriors), captured twenty-six, and recovered a captive from Arispe. They also confiscated twelve horses and mules and recovered articles of United States mail, implicating this group in the death of mail carrier Charles Fisher some six weeks earlier a few miles east of Fort Bowie. This was a severe blow to Cochise, who was in the Chiricahuas but arrived too late to give Ozeta a fight.[10]

In late April Sonoran troops captured an Apache who admitted that he was en route to the Chiricahuas to join Cochise on a campaign. Cochise had sent runners to other Chiricahua groups calling for "a great reunion," which attracted not only his Chokonens but some of the Nednhis living in the Teras Mountains in Sonora. Many warriors flocked to his summons and joined him in a foray into Mexico to avenge Ozeta's victory.[11]

While most of the Chiricahuas were raiding in Mexico, the subdistrict commander at Tucson had Cochise on his mind. On May 10, 1867, Captain Brown, always sensitive to the opinion of his superiors, wrote Crittenden suggesting a "large party of troops at some suitable time to visit the Chiricahua or Guadelupe Mountains in search of Cochise and his band."[12] That June, Crittenden grumbled that he had hoped "to drive off or destroy Chiz [Cochise] and his band," yet his forces were incapable of an offensive. His only three company posts were needed to supervise the Western Apaches.[13]

While Crittenden contemplated taking the offensive, Cochise beat him to the punch. Having returned from Mexico, he led a party of seventy warriors on raids near Tubac. On June 13, Chiricahuas attacked a wagon train, killing one man, wounding two others, and running off sixty head of cattle. The next day they ran off the horses of the Papago scouts at Calabasas and raided a ranch in the vicinity.

Lieutenant Colonel Edward McGarry, commanding the Subdistrict of Santa Cruz, which had been created specifically to subjugate Cochise, ordered out detachments from Tubac and Camp Wallen. This unenlightened officer, who had a powerful friend (McDowell) at department headquarters and would soon be relieved of command because of public intoxication, authorized the unnecessarily harsh measure of hanging Indian captives. Fortunately, the scheme was not implemented and his superiors subsequently revoked his orders. In any event, the command from Wallen, guided by Merejildo Grijalva under Lieutenant Edward Johnston Harrington, started in hot pursuit and on June 21 overtook a small group of Indians in the southwestern Chiricahuas, killing three warriors and wounding one.[14]

Harrington's dogmatic scout was interesting because it proved that a U.S. command led by a tenacious officer with a skillful guide could damage Cochise. He reported:

> On the morning of Friday, the 21st . . . as the command was rounding a curve in the Chiricahuas an Indian on horseback was seen riding leisurely along . . . evidently unaware of our presence. The order was given to charge, but simultaneously the Indian discovered us and with a loud yell dashed away at full speed toward the rancheria which came in sight a moment later . . . The majority of our horses being barely able to strike a trot we were unable to catch up with them before they . . . escaped up the side of the mountains, which it was impossible for us to follow with any show of success. . . . [Yet] the chase was kept up with the result of killing three Apaches and wounding it is supposed mortally a fourth. . . .
>
> . . .The command withdrew to the rancheria. Here everything was destroyed. The lodges, twelve in number were found to be filled with the greatest abundance of everything used by an Indian. At least a five

month supply of roasted mescal was burned together with hundreds
of dressed skins and hides. . . . I would state that the force of Indians
that made this attack . . . numbered no less than seventy warriors and
belonged to the band of Cochise. . . . They did not, however, all keep
together but separated into different bands some making their way
into Sonora and the others, numbering about twenty, returning to
their rancherias which we attacked.[15]

Harrington's success led Crittenden to conclude that Cochise
could be found in the Chiricahua Mountains. If so, he believed that
troops could "probably get a fight," although first they had to find
him. With this in mind, in July he planned a pincerslike campaign
"to destroy Chachiz and his band" by converging on the Chiricahua
Mountains. He ordered McGarry to take a force from Tubac and
proceed east into the Chiricahuas; at the same time, he directed Captain Guido Ilges from Camp Grant to scout southeast and "if practicable to go as far as the Chiricahua Mountains." Ideally the two
commands would flush out any hostiles before they eventually
united.[16]

Cochise detected the commands and easily eluded the troops,
probably crossing the border into Sonora. As a frustrated soldier
tersely reported on the essence of Apache hunting: "Chase them and
they sink into the ground or somehow vanish, look behind and they
are peeping over a hill at you."[17] In spite of what Crittenden
thought, Cochise and his Apache guerrillas would fight only on their
terms unless they were cornered and given no alternative.

Once in Mexico the Chiricahuas faced a revitalized Sonoran army
led by the capable and indefatigable Lieutenant Colonel Angel
Elías, who had countered Apache inroads with regular patrols along
the border. On July 2, 25 mounted Indians surprised a small party
near Caguilloña and killed two men before fleeing north toward the
Chiricahuas.[18] A week later Elías headed a mixed force of 137 cavalry and infantry from Fronteras in a sweep for hostiles along the
line. After two weeks of uneventful scouting, the Sonorans cleaned
out a small ranchería north of Agua Prieta, probably in the Perilla
Mountains, killing 3 warriors and 6 women and capturing 6 children. Elías returned to Fronteras and, keeping the pressure on, sent
out another force of 104 men. It departed on July 19 and four days

later discovered Apaches and killed 2 more. Whether these were from Cochise's local group is unknown; the important consideration was that Sonora had taken the offensive.[19]

So would the Apaches. On August 2, Apaches "in great numbers" killed two men and three women along the road between Huepac and Arispe. Nine days later, forty-three Apaches attacked farmers near Bacoachi and murdered one man and wounded another. Two days later, on August 13, this same band ambushed another man near Bacoachi. On the last day of August a large group deprived Cumpas of its stock, although national troops recovered most of the animals. The Sonoran press labeled the hostiles "a mournful plague" and claimed that the state had been unable to drive them out or contain their incursions. North of the border, the *Alta California* in San Francisco, wrote that the Apaches, forced south by American troops, were overrunning Sonora. The country around Fronteras and Bacoachi was ravaged, according to an American observer. By that fall it was reported that Apache hostilities in Sonora were worse than at any other time since 1861.[20]

Typically, Sonora pointed its finger at others for its own inability to protect its people. A common charge heard along the frontier was that the Americans armed and provisioned the hostiles. While some of the Western Apaches probably raided from Fort Goodwin and some unscrupulous traders continued their clandestine traffic in guns and ammunition, those complaining should have scrutinized their own nation, particularly at Janos. Cochise had continued on good terms there, which was beneficial to him and to the citizens of Janos, who could travel, plant, and raise stock without fear of attack. That fall, investigators gathered testimony at Bavispe and Moctezuma from citizens who had observed the trade conducted at Janos.[21]

The inquiry focused on affairs between Janos citizens and the Chiricahua bands, an oft-repeated complaint. The commission concluded that an informal peace existed for the sole purpose of crooked trade, that the Apaches traded stolen Sonora livestock for guns and ammunition, and that these inhabitants went so far as to warn the hostiles of Mexican campaigns. Furthermore, a well-defined distribution network had been established to dispose of stolen stock, with the booty inevitably finding its way across the U.S. border to El Paso or New Mexico.

These charges echoed the allegations made by Elías González in 1844 and Carrasco in 1851; like those, they were certainly well founded. The investigation's results were forwarded to Chihuahua's government. In early 1868 it responded and regarrisoned Janos, which had not seen permanent troops since their withdrawal in early 1858. This action shut down one of Cochise's last reliable places to trade, at least for the time being.[22]

The importance of this action should not be overlooked or underestimated. The redeployment of troops at Janos abruptly interrupted the Chiricahuas' trafficking in Mexican and American booty in exchange for guns, ammunition, and liquor. This notorious market, characterized by one American officer as a den of thieves, had been accessible to Cochise throughout the 1860s. Its reoccupation was significant in that, combined with Sonora's aggressive campaigns, he would eventually be forced to seek refuge in Arizona.[23]

For part of the winter of 1867–68, Cochise camped at a place the Indians called Dziltilcil, or Black Mountain, otherwise known as Sarampion in the Peloncillo Range, long a favorite Chiricahua retreat. From here he may have had a hand in the parties that harassed Fort Bowie fifty miles to the northwest. On November 5, 1867, the commanding officer at Fort Bowie, Lieutenant John Cuthbert Carroll, and mail rider John Slater were decoyed into an ambush and killed a few miles west of the post. Second Lieutenant Edward Buckley Hubbard initially attributed the outrage to Apaches from Fort Goodwin. Although many warriors undoubtedly slipped away from time to time, some joining the hostile Chiricahuas, this deed probably was the work of Cochise's band. He was known to have been in the vicinity, and it took place in the heart of Chiricahua country. The days following the murders the Indians "were hooting and guying the soldiers from the clifts and boulders on the mountain sides . . . mostly in Spanish," which tends to point to Cochise's Chokonens, for normally they were the only Apaches who operated in that area.[24]

For the next month Indians lurked near Fort Bowie, looking for an opportunity to run off the herd. Lieutenant Robert Pollock re-

Fort Bowie, 1867. (*Courtesy Arizona Historical Society, Tucson*)

ported large numbers in the hills on December 10 and 11. Twelve brave warriors tried to run off the herd but were repulsed. Their presence alarmed Pollock; he feared an attack by the Indians, who were "growing very bold indeed."[25] Yet none came at this time and the Indians retired to their winter camps.

Sonora and Chihuahua continued to pressure the Chiricahuas in 1868. Joaquin Terrazas and Cayetano Ortiz, with a force of 250 volunteers, patrolled Chihuahua's northern frontier, exterminating Apaches whenever found. For the first time in many years the two Mexican states had cooperated to achieve their goal. The Chihuahuan troops crossed into Sonora and Sonoran troops entered Chihuahua without the petty bickering which had characterized past relations. In addition, both states ignored the U.S. boundary and trailed Apaches into southeastern Arizona and southwestern New Mexico.[26]

In early 1868, Cochise remained at Sarampion, no doubt feeling his band secure. Few American troops had scouted that section of the country, and Mexican troops normally did not trespass into American territory. By accident, his whereabouts would become known. Benigno Arvizu and a Chihuahuan force had reconnoitered northern Chihuahua during the first three weeks of February; no Apaches had been encountered. About mid-February a Chiricahua raiding party stole some horses at Casas Grandes; Arvizu seized this opportunity and followed the trail to Sierra Blanca, a small group of hills twelve miles northeast of Fronteras. About February 20 the Mexicans surprised a small camp, killed one Chokonen, and captured another. The prisoner said Cochise was camped at Sarampion, some forty miles northeast.

With a chance to strike Cochise or the *cabecilla* (used to denote a head chief), Arvizu sent forward his best mounted troops, sixteen in all, under Cayetano Ozeta. Crossing into Arizona near the San Bernardino ranch, they continued northeast toward the lower Peloncillos. Cochise apparently had not expected troops from Mexico, which may explain how, on that raw winter day, Arvizu was able to surprise Cochise's camp and wound several warriors. The Chokonens fought a brief rear-guard action before withdrawing. Arvizu's command succeeded in capturing a small boy and some stock. Cochise and a score of warriors from other camps harassed Ozeta's command all the way out of the mountains before the intruders wisely withdrew west into the San Bernardino Valley, having lost but one man wounded.[27]

Nothing more was heard of Cochise until May 13, 1868, when a hundred Apaches attempted to run off the herd at Fort Bowie but were foiled by "the use of the breech loading arms." The Indian trail led south into the mountains.[28] Other Chiricahuas were observed in the Stein's Peak area, where a traveler reported many Indian campfires.[29] Two weeks later they returned and waylaid a Cook and Shaw mail coach.

The ambush took place ten or twelve miles east of Apache Pass, with the Indians killing or capturing the entire party of four men (two soldiers and two citizens). After the first volley wounded the driver, John Brownley, Charles ("Tennessee") Hadsell grabbed the reins and reversed direction toward Fort Bowie. A brisk running fight ensured for six miles before the stage came to a stop. Then, for some reason, the whites apparently surrendered, although they were armed with rifles "and 40 rounds of ammunition and one or two pistols." The Indians took the wounded Brownley and "ripped off his clothes, scalped him and tied a rope to his feet, tied the rope to a saddle and drew him a quarter of a mile." Troops later followed the Indian trail south for fifteen miles into the Chiricahuas, where they discovered the bodies of the two soldiers. They had been "tortured and suffered such a death as only an Apache Indian can invent." Sonoran troops found Hadsell's body after attacking a Chiricahua ranchería a few months later. One of the soldiers lamented that it was "one of the most horrid affairs I have ever heard of."[30]

Meanwhile, in Mexico the Chiricahuas continued to be hounded by the dogmatic Sonorans, who launched successful scouts in the spring of 1868. In March troops attacked a ranchería, killing four and capturing three, in the Teras Mountains, probably a Nednhi unit. In June two more warriors were killed on the border. In July, Cochise, feeling pressure from all sides, resorted to his old ploy of soliciting peace at Janos; that would offer refuge in northern Chihuahua. Yet as six Chiricahuas negotiated with Ozeta, sixty Apaches rampaged through Casas Grandes, wounded a man, and stole more than fifty horses. When Ozeta heard this news, he promptly imprisoned the six peace emissaries.[31]

Troubles mounted for Cochise and the Chiricahuas, who had hoped to reestablish friendly relations with Chihuahua. They were living at Alamo Hueco and the Hatchet Mountains, which were home to a Chokonen local group called the Dzilmora people, although all three bands used the area as a base to raid into Mexico. The shutdown of the Janos trade forced some of the Chiricahuas to turn to a place they called Kegotoi (Dilapadated Houses), otherwise known as Cañada Alamosa and today called Monticello, a small settlement in New Mexico. Several parties of Apaches were reported trading there in mid-August when troops from Fort McRae encountered one hundred Indians south of Cañada Alamosa. The Apaches signaled that they wished to talk but after a short parley fired upon the whites, wounding two men before fleeing south toward Chihuahua.[32]

Cochise probably felt threatened from all directions by the late summer of 1868. Unexpected pressures arose from the north when in late August troops from Fort Cummings attacked a small camp in the Hatchet Mountains, due east of the Animas Mountains, killing two Indians and capturing two children. Two days later another skirmish resulted in another warrior's death and another child's capture. Later accounts reported that these prisoners were from Cochise's band, which had fled toward Janos and Alamo Hueco.[33]

In the summer and fall of 1868, Sonora continued its campaigns against Cochise's people. Governor Pesqueira's loyal commander, General García Morales, directed these, now that he had been able to suppress the Yaqui and Mayo rebellions in the southern part of the state. Beginning in May 1868, Morales directed his attention to the Apaches, who reportedly had killed 116 Sonorans during the past twenty-seven months. Consequently, Sonora declared another war based on extermination, which received the support of the federal government. By late summer Morales had sent a strong force into the field, a force which had the potential to inflict serious casualties on the Chiricahuas. He hoped the Indians would be kept on the run until they became exhausted and were forced to surrender unconditionally.[34]

The Chiricahuas felt the effects of this campaign immediately. In August a force from Bavispe crossed into Chihuahua and discovered a small ranchería in the Carcai Mountains (one of Juh's favorite campsites), where two warriors and two women were killed. In October, Captain Sacramento Monroy, recently appointed commander at Bavispe, struck the Indians, quite possibly Cochise himself. In early October, Indians stole some stock at Bavispe; Monroy and forty-three men picked up the trail and followed it north to the Enmedio Mountains. Three days later, on October 16, his persistence was rewarded. His scouts cut the trail and surprised a ranchería at Alamo Hueco, killing twelve persons (four warriors) and capturing nine others. This was definitely a Chokonen local group.

Chino, who was a brother of Posito Moraga and who had helped free Cochise at Fronteras in 1848, was at Janos soliciting peace at the time. Cochise was thought to have been in the vicinity, but no one knew for sure. After his victory, Monroy marched to Janos and demanded that the Apaches be turned over, but Ozeta refused.

Among Monroy's prisoners were members of Chino's family; he quickly produced two Mexican captives and exchanged them for his wife and child. Monroy returned to Bavispe, irate that Ozeta had not allowed him to attack Chino's group. He promptly fired off a report to General Morales, taking Ozeta to task for refusing to surrender the Apaches. As a result, Morales decided to investigate Ozeta's conduct and lead another scout.[35]

Clearly, for Cochise things were getting out of hand in Mexico. The military pressure was the primary reason he decided to move north to the Gila River and Mogollon Mountains, where he had not been seen for several years. Thus he fortuitously avoided Morales's next campaign, which left Bavispe on October 20 with the intent of striking Chiricahuas at Janos, as Elías González and Carrasco had done in years past. The next day, Morales camped eight miles west of Janos, having secreted himself in ambush. Two days later he detained and interrogated six citizens and on the basis of their statements sent Captain Francisco Toyos and forty men to attack the Indian villages in the neighborhood of Janos.

Again a Sonoran force caught the Apaches napping, several of whom were actually at Janos negotiating with Ozeta. Toyos's soldiers routed the band and killed twelve Chiricahuas, including Aguirre and Elías, two of Cochise's subordinates and longtime companions. Among the dead were two children and eight women; the Mexicans also recovered a captive from Guaymas.[36]

With any hope for peace gone, Ozeta threw his hat into the ring, moving to kill or capture as many Chiricahuas as possible. First, after Toyos's assault, he imprisoned the Chiricahua peace party of twelve individuals who were at Janos discussing terms. The next month he prepared his own offensive and attacked a ranchería north of Janos, killing twelve more Apaches, including José Mangas (brother of Mangas Coloradas), who may have been living with the Chokonens. In December, Ozeta marched triumphantly to Chihuahua City with twelve scalps and ten prisoners. After a short stay he returned to the frontier to continue his campaign.[37]

Although Cochise himself seems to have escaped these attacks, he certainly felt the losses. In February 1869 he admitted having lost more than one hundred of his band within the past year, although his

Dragoon Mountains. View from the ridge looking east into Sulphur Springs Valley. (*Photo by Karen Hayes*)

claim that many of them died of sickness is incomprehensible unless he meant lead poisoning.[38] Lieutenant Colonel Thomas Casimer Devin,[39] Arizona's new district commander, questioned whether Cochise himself had been injured by the Mexican campaigns but correctly added that "his band have just been well thrashed in Mexico."[40]

In November 1868 there surfaced definite information corroborating Cochise's relocation to Arizona. Solomon Barth, a trader with the Western Apaches, recalled that in late 1868 he unexpectedly ran into Cochise, who at the time was visiting the Coyotero chief Pedro near the future site of Fort Apache. According to Barth, Cochise stripped him and his six companions and confiscated their goods, leaving them with only their shoes. It was only through Pedro, who intervened because he knew Barth, that Cochise spared the Americans' lives. Reminiscences are sometimes suspect but on this occasion Solomon Barth's recollection was corroborated by a contemporary newspaper account of the incident. On November 11, 1868, the

Arizona Miner published a story about Barth's encounter with Cochise, but the newspaper doubted that the Chiricahua leader had participated because of the place where it had taken place:

> From Messrs. Young and Bryant who recently came through from
> New Mexico, we learn that while they were in camp at Zuni, Sol
> Barth [and] George Clinton, formerly of this county, with some
> Mexicans arrived at the villages from the White Mountains almost
> naked and in a starving condition. They had left Zuni but a short time
> previous with a pack train of some 20 head of animals and goods and
> trinkets specially suited to trade with the Indians. With them was an
> Indian guide. After crossing the Mogollon range . . . the members of
> the party were seized, one by one, by Indians, deprived of their arms,
> stripped of their clothing, and threatened with death and would have
> been murdered but for the interference of an Indian who knew Sol
> [Barth]. . . . Sol told Messrs. Bryant and Young that the Indians who
> robbed him belonged to Ca-Cheis' band, but we doubt this as Cacheis
> and his band live over 100 miles east of where he had been robbed.
>
> If what we heard of Sol Barth is correct, we do not pity him for his
> misfortune. It is believed here and in New Mexico that he has been in
> the habit of trading these Indians, powder, lead and guns.[41]

Albert F. Banta's version, which was obtained from two Mexican
captives, agreed with Barth's. Banta also met Barth when he returned to Zuñi.[42]

The *Miner,* which was skeptical of Cochise's presence in White
Mountain Apache country, represented what most Arizonians believed. After all, Cochise had been in southern Arizona or Mexico
for the past several years and there was no reason to think he would
abandon his homeland for Western Apache country. Yet in December there surfaced conclusive evidence that he was in the vicinity of Fort Goodwin and might come in to that post. A few Chokonens did stop in early that month and the commanding officer wrote
to Tucson for instructions. Devin ordered him to continue rationing
the Indians who remained on the reservation but to carry out expeditions against the "Coyotero, Chiricahuas and Pinal Apaches who
have not been permanent dwellers upon the reservation."[43] As for
Cochise, wrote Devin, "if he wants to come in he must surrender
himself and family or leave them as hostages."[44]

In late December an *Arizona Miner* correspondent writing from

Goodwin reported optimistically that Cochise was still expected in.[45] Nonetheless, for some reason, perhaps because of Devin's unrealistic terms or perhaps because of the prevalence of malaria at Fort Goodwin or perhaps because he felt the Americans would hold him accountable for past deeds (something he was acutely sensitive to), he failed to come in. Instead he headed for the Dragoon Mountains, where he hoped to spend the winter without trouble.

Devin began to have second thoughts about his inflexible conditions, realizing that they had been or would be rejected by Cochise. On January 25, 1869, he wrote:

> Cochise, the boldest and most enterprising Apache in the Territory, and who for the past seven years has been a terror in Southern Arizona, has sent me word that if I will allow him to return to his home (in the Chiricahua Mountains) and remain there, he will not only remain at peace but be responsible for the safety of the Overland road and the stock in its vicinity. All this he used to effect before the attempt to take him prisoner aroused him to make war. I have offered to meet him at Dragoon Springs if he will come in, and hear his proposal. He is undoubtedly the ablest Indian in Arizona, and could be made very useful if it were found that he could be trusted.[46]

Questions remain to be answered as to how Cochise communicated with Devin to make this remarkable offer. If he and Devin could have consummated an agreement at this time, several hundred lives and untold thousands of dollars could have been saved, yet neither party pursued these possibilities. After a brief, inconclusive meeting with Captain Frank Perry, Cochise once again vanished from American contact.

Although Cochise was beginning to feel the squeeze from the military on both sides of the border, he had not yet accepted that the old way of life was ending. That he even considered peace indicated that the reality of his situation had overwhelmed his intense antipathy toward Americans. His rage had subsided, and now it was time to seek a new path for his people, who were dwindling fast. He may have wanted peace, but not peace at the price of freedom. That would come later.

Chapter 14

THE AMERICANS ARE EVERYWHERE: WE MUST LIVE IN BAD PLACES TO SHUN THEM

On January 20, 1869, Captain Frank W. Perry ("a gallant and efficient officer," according to Devin)[1] left Fort Goodwin with a detachment of one officer, sixty-two soldiers, two guides, one surgeon, and a Coyotero Indian named Phillippi, "who said he would take them into Cochise's camp." After an unadventurous two-week march, they reached the Dragoons and bivouacked. The next morning, probably February 5, they "captured" two Chokonens. Later that day, Cochise himself met Phillippi and haughtily declared that "but for the fact he meant peace they should never go back." Surprisingly, he agreed to meet Captain Perry the next day, his first sincere face-to-face peace parley with Americans since the Bascom affair almost eight years earlier to the day. An attentive individual provided a good look at the powerful but aging chief: unfortunately, Perry's official report of the conference has not been located.[2]

An account of Perry's remarkable interview with the elusive Chiricahua was published in the *Arizona Miner* on March 20, 1869. The observer described Cochise as "about 6 feet 2 inches, strongly muscled, with mild, prominent features, hooked nose and looks to be a man that means what he says."[3] It would appear that Cochise had indeed accepted the inevitability of peace but still retained a profound distrust of Americans. An extract of the talk follows:

> *Cochise*—What are you doing out here, Captain?
> *Perry*—Come to see you and prospect the country generally.

Colonel Thomas Casimer Devin. A well-liked and much-respected officer in the Southwest, Devin vowed to "kill or capture" Cochise after the Stone massacre at Dragoon Springs. (*Photo from* Third Cavalry)

Cochise—You mean you come to kill me or any of my tribe, that is what all your visits mean to me. I tried the Americans once and they broke the treaty first, the officers I mean, this was at the Pass. If I stop in, I must be treated right, but I don't expect they will do all they say for us. I won't stay at Goodwin, it is no place for Indians. They die after being here for a short time. I will go in to Goodwin to talk to you, after I hear how you treat Indians there. I will send in two of my Indians who will let me know (he did send in two squaws). I lost nearly one hundred of my people in the last year, principally from sickness. The Americans killed a good many. I have not one hundred Indians now. Ten years ago I had 1000. The Americans are everywhere, and we must live in bad places to shun them. I can't give you any mescal, as there is another scout on the other side and we can't make any fires to roast it.[4] The Coyoteros are stronger than we are, and steal stock from us; some of them say you came to kill us but some Indians lie. My Indians will do no harm until I come in, which I may do inside of two months.

Perry—I heard you were wounded often but you walk all right.

Cochise—I was wounded twice. First near Santa Cruz, in the leg twelve years ago. I had a bad leg for some time afterward. Next near Fronteras, two years ago, in the neck. We are known as the Gamo Apaches. I would like some bread and tobacco and a blanket.

Captain Perry filled Cochise's request, "but the soldiers went hungry for about three days."

The detachment continued to Fort Bowie, having received no specific commitment from Cochise. He would not come in at this time, preferring the precarious life as a free Apache to the inherent restraints at Fort Goodwin, where smallpox and other sickness prevailed, or at Cañada Alamosa, where most of the Chihennes submitted to an unofficial truce. He would await further developments before deciding on a course of action.[5]

Meanwhile, having been unsuccessful in his quest to meet Cochise, Devin began active operations against the Apaches. His superiors egged him on, urging active and unrelenting warfare. In March he assembled his subdistrict commanders at Tucson and ordered them to begin campaigning. That spring, summer, and fall, troops scoured southern Arizona.[6] In particular, Captain Reuben Bernard led several successful sorties against the Chiricahuas, keeping them on the run and providing the troops with invaluable knowledge of the territory.

Despite a newspaper report that the troops in Arizona were "having a jolly time in sending Indians to the happy hunting ground," in reality the army could do very little to prevent depredations and to protect Arizona's nine thousand inhabitants.[7] Its fourteen military posts, garrisoned by twenty-one hundred troops, could not cover all areas of potential conflict. The army's strategy of subjugation centered on the dispersion-concentration theory. The dispersion concept, a defensive policy similar to Mexico's presidio system, provided for forts throughout Indian country. In theory, these would demoralize the Indians while affording protection to settlers and travelers. The concentration concept, an offensive policy, put posts at strategic points from which troops could be rapidly dispatched in response to hostilities.[8]

Neither policy worked, and combining them also failed, especially in Arizona, where the outposts were undermanned and too scattered to prevent hostilities. Similarly, offensive campaigns usually took too long to assemble and lacked coordination and communication with nearby posts. Rarely were troops from more than one post employed against Cochise. The few successful movements, typically in response to Apache depredations, had a common denominator: a successful guide or scout. Without one, the troops were virtually helpless.

As for Cochise, despite his peaceful expressions, Chokonen raids continued and actually increased in southern Arizona because the pressures from Mexico had forced him to establish his rancherías in the Dragoon and Chiricahua mountains. He led many of the raids and many of them were concentrated in the Sonoita Valley, one officer writing that the Indian trail usually led "in the direction of the Chiricahua Mountains . . . [where] a band composed of deserters from the other tribes live and is led by a chief known as Cochise."[9]

In 1869 and 1870, Cochise spent much of his time in southern Arizona. It was no coincidence that these years were two of the bloodiest in southern Arizona history. His people needed "to make a living" and that, of course, meant more raiding, much of it in Arizona but with an equal amount in Mexico. A pioneer recalled that "during the years of 1868, 69 and 70 in my opinion we suffered most from the cruelties of the Apaches."[10] The intelligent John Spring wrote that from "1868–1871 Cochise's band killed no less than thirty-four of my friends and acquaintances within a radius of 50 miles of Calabasas."[11] He could not have known for sure who was responsible for all of these depredations and murders, but many certainly could be traced to Cochise's wickiup.

The raiding continued in the spring of 1869. On April 21, Apaches overwhelmed a government train near Camp Crittenden, killing two soldiers and capturing twelve mules. One week later they swept down on John T. Smith's ranch near Tubac and ran off 130 horses. The intrepid Smith and fourteen Mexicans pursued, but the hostiles counterattacked and repulsed the whites.[12] These incidents and similar ones were reported to the superintendent of Indian affairs in Arizona, who wrote that "the conduct of the Indians throughout the Territory during the months of April and May is in no ways improved. From nearly every portion of the interior news of depredations committed by the wild Indians of the territory continue to reach me."[13]

The summer of 1869 was no different. Cochise, as he would do for the next three summers, made his headquarters in the Dragoons. From here small groups raided in all directions. Early that summer Apache raids threatened "to break up the entire settlements" of the Sonoita and Santa Cruz valleys. On June 9 the Indians attacked Yerkes's ranch and killed a man. In June also they killed "old man" Pennington and his son Green. On July 3 hostiles surprised the settlements on the San Pedro, killing three men and running off the stock.[14] And the Chiricahuas directed their attention to the vulnerable mail riders between Tucson and Mesilla. Three mails were captured during an eight-day period, shutting down the line.[15]

These raiding parties often led to more encounters, some of which were brisk engagements. In July a Chokonen party swept down on Imuris, Sonora, and ran off some stock. Fifteen nationals pursued them to Santa Cruz, where they enlisted seven more men and twelve presidio soldiers, all commanded by Lieutenant Florencio Ruiz. On July 16 the command struck the trail, which led north into Arizona and then east to the lower San Pedro. The next day the tenacious Mexicans overtook the Apaches about four miles south of the Dragoons and succeeded in recapturing the herd and killing two Indians. But the country was swarming with hostiles, and an hour later at least thirty Chokonens appeared from the Dragoons. Frightened, Ruiz wisely broke off the engagement and returned to Sonora.[16]

Throughout the summer of 1869, Mexican troops continued to threaten Chiricahua bands living in northern Mexico and southern Arizona. In July, probably while Cochise was skirmishing in the Dragoons, two Mexican patrols killed several Chiricahuas, including Cochise's old associate Chino, in the mountains of northern Sonora.[17] In August the indefatigable Cayetano Ozeta launched yet another offensive from Chihuahua. Finding no Apaches in northern Mexico, he cautiously decided to encroach into U.S. territory. At Guadalupe Canyon he encountered two Chiricahuas, one a warrior training a young boy in the art of making arrows. Ozeta's men wounded the man in the arm before capturing him and the boy. The man revealed that about four miles north there was a ranchería which contained sixteen warriors and one hundred individuals. Their leaders were "very well known in Janos by their savage raids," implying that either Cochise or Juh was in the vicinity.[18]

Ozeta, suspecting that the gunfire had alarmed the ranchería, hustled his force to the village but found it hastily abandoned; stock, saddles, and hides had been left behind. The Mexicans remained there for the night, observing a flurry of Chiricahua smoke signals, which alerted other groups to his presence. On September 7, Ozeta tried to lure the Chiricahuas into the open by retreating south into Mexico to the Enmedio Mountains, hoping the Indians would pursue. The ploy failed. Although a few Apaches had kept constant watch, they were much too cautious to attack. The Mexicans reached Janos on September 17 and Ozeta left for Chihuahua City on September 26, leaving troops behind to protect Janos.[19]

In September it was rumored in Sonora that the Chiricahuas were planning "a large campaign against Fronteras" in retaliation for Sonora's successful scouts of the previous summer.[20] Cochise was probably instrumental in organizing this war party, which even attracted warriors from the Western Apaches. Luckily for the people of Fronteras, it did not get below the border. In late September a band of Pinals led by Bob-chee-a-a set out to join Cochise. The Pinals had a minor brush with U.S. troops some twenty-five miles northwest of Camp Grant on September 28. From there Bob-chee-a-a's band headed for the San Pedro River and then the Dragoon Mountains, where it apparently joined Cochise.[21]

Evidently the allied Apaches intended to head south, skirting the Dragoons, before striking east to the Chiricahuas to pick up additional Chokonens and Nednhis. During the day on October 5 an eagle-eyed Apache on a high vantage point in the Dragoons saw a mail coach moving across Sulphur Springs Valley. This unexpected and fortuitous prospect of easy plunder was something Cochise could not pass up. Six white men were with the stage: Mr. Kaler (the driver), John Finkle Stone[22] (owner of the Apache Pass mine) and four soldiers of Company D, Twenty-first Infantry, who approached Dragoon Springs at sundown on October 5. They evidently felt secure because the Apaches rarely attacked after dark; furthermore, Kaler and Stone had made this same trip on numerous occasions. The Indians were waiting.

During the day Cochise had prepared an ambush similar to the one east of Apache Pass in July 1862. According to the report of Devin and the recollections of William Sullivan, who was with the relief party, the fight took place "near the forks of the Goodwin and Bowie roads opposite Dragoon Springs."[23] This would place it a few miles east of the Dragoon stage station. All accounts concur as to the circumstances. Cochise had placed his men in a small gully which ran parallel to the road. Covered by grass and soapweed and further obscured by darkness, the Indians lay completely concealed from the unsuspecting Americans. As the stage approached, the Apaches showered arrows and bullets on it and its escort, apparently killing the driver and three soldiers at the first volley. The stage turned from the road and galloped south before encountering mounted Indians, probably under Cochise, who overwhelmed Stone and the other soldier. The fight lasted only a few minutes and the six whites discharged only six rounds.

Cochise struck again at 10 A.M. on October 6 about twelve miles west of Sulphur Springs. Fifty to sixty warriors, accompanied by three white men (all concealed behind boulders), jumped a herd of 250 cattle owned by William Eastwood and George Scott. The American party, consisting of seventeen men, one woman, and two

John Finkle Stone. An Arizona entrepreneur killed at Dragoon Springs on October 5, 1869. (*Courtesy Arizona Historical Society, Tucson*)

children had left San Antonio bound for California. The cattle were strung out for about a mile when the Apaches, some dressed in the clothing of the murdered Stone party, made the first of three charges on the herd. The fight continued for more than three hours, with the Indians mortally lancing one man through the body and forcing five drovers to flee to Bowie. During the clash, Scott and a man named Smith Haile aimed a half-dozen shots at the leader, whom they believed to be Cochise. To their dismay, each missed its mark.[24]

Later that day a government train destined for Bowie found the remains of Stone's party. Again the Apaches attacked; twice they charged, but each time Sergeant Mack and his men of Company E, Twenty-first Infantry, staved off the agressors.[25]

In the meantime, one of the Texas cowboys, named Scott, dashed into Fort Bowie about 8 P.M. on October 6 and reported the details of the attack. With Captains Dunn and Bernard absent on patrol, Lieutenant William Henry Winters, the senior officer at the post, mounted every available man (twenty-five troopers) and, guided by Merejildo Grijalva, sped toward Sulphur Springs. En route, Winters received a messenger informing him of the Stone massacre. "Doubly enraged at the murder of his friend Stone," he forged on to Dragoon Springs, reaching there at 1 A.M. on October 7. He found six corpses and scribbled a message to Devin in Tucson, blaming Cochise and suggesting that troops from Camp Crittenden might head off the Apaches near Mule Pass on the Sonora line. Winters vowed to punish the hostiles: "Nothing can be done for the dead, I now start for the Indians and hope I may come up with them."[26]

After the assault on Mack's detachment, Cochise herded the cattle along the eastern foothills of the Dragoons before crossing the valley toward the lower Chiricahuas. At daybreak on October 7, Merejildo cut the trail, which, as he had predicted, would cross Sulphur Springs Valley to the Chiricahuas and then, he believed, lead into Mexico. Consequently, at nine o'clock, Winters sent another dispatch to Captain Bernard at Fort Bowie: "I am hot upon the trail and hope to be up with the cattle by daylight tomorrow. They are Cochees band and are returning by the Chiricahuas about fifty miles south of the post; if some men could run down the eastern side of the mountain, they may cut them off." It took the courier twenty-seven hours to get this information to Bernard, who was in the saddle

Legend

1. Stone Massacre, Oct. 5, 1869
2. Cochise attacks Texas cattle herd, Oct. 6, 1869
3. Winters overtakes Cochise, Oct. 8, 1869
4. Bernard fights Cochise, Oct. 19, 1869

Camp San Carlos

Fort Goodwin

location map

Arizona

Aravaipa Creek

Gila River

Pueblo Viejo

Whitlock's Cienega

Arizona / New Mexico

PELONCILLO MTNS.

Scale in Miles

0   10   20   30

Fort Grant

San Pedro River

Sulphur Springs Valley

San Simon River

Steins Peak

Railroad Pass

Playa

San Simon Station

DOS CABEZAS MTNS.

Croton Springs

Fort Bowie

Bernard

San Simon Agency

Tres Alamos

Apache Pass

Winters

Ewell Spr.

Pinery Agency

Dragoon Springs

Sulphur Springs

CHIRICAHUA MTNS.

East Stronghold

DRAGOON MTNS.

Winters

4

Tex Canyon Bernard

Cochise

Cochise

SWISSHELM MTNS.

Camp Wallen

PEDREGOSA MTNS.

3

HUACHUCA MTNS.

MULE MTNS.

CHIRICAHUA INDIAN RESERVATION

International Boundary 1872–1876

drawn by Don Bufkin   MEXICO

Guadalupe Pass

Southeastern Arizona, Battle of Chiricahua Pass

within an hour. If the message had been delivered sooner, Cochise might have been caught in the jaws of a trap.[27]

All that day Winters followed the hot trail like a bloodhound; he would not rest until he brought his quarry to bay. That night he pushed on and at 8 A.M. on October 8 the tenacious officer and his command, which had marched twenty-two hours without sleep, overtook the Indians on the east side of what he believed were the lower Chiricahua Mountains but probably were the Pedregosas. His fatigued men fired "upon the Indians as they advanced." This was the Apache rear guard, and three of five Indians were killed; Cochise and the mounted warriors were with the cattle some two or three miles to the east.

Although they were outnumbered two or three to one, the soldiers "rushed forward with enthusiasm." The vivid memory of their massacred friends at Dragoon Springs, plus Merejildo's recognition of Cochise, pushed these brave men forward. Winters immediately attempted to prevent the Indians on foot from reaching the mountains. Sensing this, Cochise led the mounted warriors on several assaults, diverting Winters's attention. Cochise was riding a gray horse and "giving orders as he always is known to do." Wrote Winters: "Many efforts were made to kill Cochise but without success, with his mounted warriors he several times charged the men in advance and although conspicious and special attention directed to him and many shots fired at him, he escaped." Merejildo also paid special attention to Cochise, who exhibited his skill on horseback, "but everytime he got a chance to shoot, Cochise would slip over to the side of the horse, hanging on the horse's neck." The fight lasted about ninety minutes, until the Indians on foot reached the foothills and Winters withdrew.[28]

Winters had scored an impressive victory: he recovered the entire cattle herd and most of the mail while inflicting severe damage on Cochise. He reported that his command killed twelve warriors, even noting which soldier had done the sharpshooting. The American loss was two wounded. Of course the proof would have been an actual body count; this is not to imply that Winters intended to overstate his accomplishments, for, as the *Arizona Miner* wrote, "Cochise, for the first time since 1861, has been badly whipped."[29]

Cochise had little but bitter experience to show for the Winters fight, yet for some reason he kept his band together, rejecting the usual option of scattering or crossing into Mexico, probably because of the ubiquitous Mexican patrols. Instead he moved north into the Chiricahuas, probably not expecting American troops to return; it was a miscalculation that cost him dearly. He had not counted on the determination of either Devin, bound "to kill or capture" him,[30] or Captain Reuben Bernard, a relentless and tireless campaigner from Fort Bowie who correctly believed that his primary responsibility was to disable Cochise and his band.

On October 9, 1869, Lieutenant Colonel Devin issued Order No. 23, in which he directed Bernard to follow Cochise's trail to wherever it might lead. Consequently, on October 16, Bernard began the first of what would be four patrols during the next month. Marching by night, he skirted the eastern face of the Chiricahuas and on October 18 arrived at the scene of Winters' fight. The next day he picked up the trail and followed it to the "top of the highest mountain in the vicinity," where he found a deserted village. A few hours later, Merejildo found the trail, which led west into Tex Canyon for another ten miles before he discovered fresh tracks. After a five-minute gallop, Bernard found another abandoned camp. He took a small force and continued into a canyon; Merejildo took five men and headed for a rocky mesa. About halfway up they were attacked from the heights by an estimated one hundred to two hundred Apaches, who opened fire "from all parts of the rocks above us." The Indians were close enough to use their accurate bows and in the initial attack succeeded in killing two men and wounding one.

For the next thirty minutes a desultory, ineffective fire continued. Bernard collected his force and decided to attempt to outflank and dislodge the Indians. But Cochise had anticipated this, positioning his warriors so that "every point on the mesa was well guarded." He allowed the troops to approach to within one hundred feet before unleashing a withering fire, which drove them back. Unperturbed, Bernard took thirty cavalry to the right; Cochise again responded and rebuffed the troopers.

The battle continued from a distance the rest of the day until near sunset, when Lieutenant John Lafferty was shot as he tried to recover the bodies of the men killed in the initial firing. The Apache bullet fractured and "carried away the greater portion of the lower

Reuben F. Bernard. A veteran of Arizona, Bernard was the most energetic and capable officer stationed at Bowie. (*Courtesy National Archives*)

jawbone." The mesa was carpeted with Indians, and Bernard concluded that the situation was hopeless for assault. He prudently withdrew, declaring that he would have needed twice as many men to dislodge the Apaches. Nonetheless, he believed that his men had punished Cochise severely: he reported eighteen warriors killed and several wounded. Like Winters's numbers, these are suspect and probably overstated; after all, Cochise enjoyed an advantageous position and there is no mention of actual bodies.

The fight took place in the southcentral Chiricahuas on very rough and broken ground covered with rocks, trees, and bushes. Although the exact location has not been determined, the evidence points to Tex Canyon near where Camp Rucker was later situated, both favorite strongholds of Cochise and Juh. The battle was supposed to have occurred twenty-five miles northwest of the Winters fight. This location was much more north than west, but the distance is about correct. It was also supposed to be about forty-five miles from Fort Bowie, which, by trail, is about right. The Apaches moved north after the fight, and Bernard noted that the last leg of his scout was in the northeast section of the Chiricahuas. Despite this, there was positive identification of another site as the battleground in the memoirs of Captain Frederick Elisha Phelps. He had an encounter with Chiricahuas in August 1872 at Horseshoe Canyon, where "some years before a desperate fight between Apaches and Lafferty's troop of our regiment had taken place." In any case, Phelps may have been referring to the Russell fight in October 1871, which definitely took place at Horseshoe Canyon.[31]

Bernard admired the Apaches' fighting skills and courage, respecting Cochise's conduct and strategy in particular. He reported that the Chiricahua warriors "were recklessly brave." As for Cochise, Bernard thought he was "one of the most intelligent hostile Indians on this continent." Even so, he vowed to leave again on October 24 "with every man I can mount."[32]

With definite information about Cochise's position, Devin in Tucson ordered reinforcements to Fort Bowie: one company from Camp Crittenden and two from Fort Goodwin. The fact that they were not sent earlier revealed that no one expected Cochise to remain in the Chiricahuas, at least the more accessible regions. Major Henry R. Putnam at Goodwin pointedly asked Captain Dunn why reinforcements had not previously been requested: "Had you given me definite information on the subject I should have had a sufficient force present with you before this time to have assisted in destroying that scoundrel and his band."[33]

Although the reinforcements had not arrived, Bernard left again on October 24, repeating his march of a week before and halting at the battleground on October 26. Surprisingly Cochise was still around. The next day, as the troops marched through a canyon, the Indians opened fire. There were no casualties, and Cochise withdrew to a spot where Bernard dared not venture. That evening a few Chokonens came down from the hills and conversed with Bernard's scouts, questioning what terms or conditions might be offered. Bernard's terse reply was unsatisfactory, for "if they wanted peace they could come in and accept such terms as would be given them." This was unacceptable to Cochise. The fact that he even considered capitulating indicated how desperately he must have perceived his situation to be.[34]

Reinforcements arrived the next day, Captain Thomas Searle Dunn and 19 infantry from Bowie, but not the cavalry troops from Goodwin that Bernard had requested. Dunn was responding to Bernard's plea that he had located Cochise "where I cannot hurt him. If troops have been sent to Bowie, please send them forward at once." Bernard sent him back to Fort Bowie with a six-man cavalry escort. Finally, on October 29, Captain Harrison Moulton, Lieutenant Albert John Garrett, and 31 men arrived from Crittenden, increasing Bernard's force to 118 men. In the early morning of October 30 the command marched in three columns to the top of the mountain, where the Indians had last been seen. The following day Bernard discovered Apaches and another skirmish occurred, with a couple more warriors reported killed. His troops exhausted, the persistent officer finally abandoned the pursuit. One participant wrote: "It was impossible to drive them from such a place, as they were armed." Bernard returned to Fort Bowie on November 2.[35]

By this time, troops had been pulled in from everywhere. First the reinforcements from Fort Goodwin arrived, swelling Bernard's force to 156 men, which also included detachments from Camp Crittenden and 21 Mexican cavalry from Fronteras. But Cochise had decided to avoid Bernard and led the soldiers "over the worst country [he] possibly could," finally splitting up into small groups to rendezvous at some prearranged point. Totally exasperated, the indefatigable officer gave up the scout, letting Cochise go "to some other mountain." He succeeded in killing a warrior, however, from whom he recovered a Springfield rifle taken during the Stone massacre.[36]

To Cochise the battle of the "rocky mesa" was at best a stalemate. Although he had countered and frustrated Bernard at every turn, compelling him to give up the chase on three occasions and finally to leave him alone, the several engagements were costly lessons; several good men had been killed. In the words of Dan L. Thrapp it was "a remarkable stand against overwhelming odds in opponent numbers and arms, and a sure mark of his skill and ability under pressure."[37]

Cochise had never faced American adversaries like the dogmatic, Apache-wise Bernard and Winters, who, guided by the consummate scout Merejildo Grijalva, were more than capable of following him over the roughest of country. Dr. Levi Dorr, who accompanied the troops from Camp Crittenden, summed up the situation in a letter to a friend: "Heretofore officers have not tried to fight Indians in such impregnable mountain passes but their late doings [Stone massacre] & it being Cachiese was a stimulus." In later years Cochise admitted that he refrained from attacking government mail coaches because he knew "all the soldiers would be ordered out to avenge [any] death[s]," a lesson he learned the hard way after the Stone massacre.[38]

For the remainder of 1869, Devin pushed his subordinates to keep the pressure on Cochise. Some Chokonens were reported to have fled to the Animas and Guadalupe mountains; Cochise and his own local group were believed to have retired north to the Burro Mountains. Devin heard this rumor and, hoping to punish him further, ordered Major Putnam to reconnoiter in the Burro Mountains in hopes of picking up Cochise's trail. Trying to motivate Putnam, Devin delivered a pep talk, declaring that "the officer who succeeds in destroying him [Cochise] will earn not only the highest encomiums from his superior but the gratitude of the people of Arizona as well."[39]

Cochise had indeed moved north, probably following the Peloncillo Mountains to the Gila country. Bernard's persistence compelled him to contemplate peace again. The chief was beginning to realize that peace was vital to prevent the extermination of his

people. He had two options: try Coyotero country near Fort Goodwin or await the results of Chihenne peace discussions at Cañada
Alamosa. Cochise had sent a message to Loco, a Chihenne chief,
that he would bring in his band once he was assured of the whites'
good intentions. Until then, he recuperated in the extreme northern
limits of Chiricahua territory, living near the Eastern White Mountain Coyoteros, with whom several Chokonens had intermarried.
Although this band had been close allies of Cochise in the early
1860s, they had "not banded with Cochise . . . for marauding for a
number of years, but frequently exchanged corn for the others
stock."[40]

In December 1869 and January 1870, Cochise camped along
Bonita Creek, a tributary of the Gila. Here he was safe from Mexican troops, and if he were pressured by U.S. troops he could easily
slip into the impregnable and relatively unexplored Mogollon
Mountains, considered sacred by the Chiricahuas. Authorities at
Fort Goodwin were unaware of his presence, or at least did not report that he was near. For his part, Cochise was discrete in his
movements. According to a captured Chokonen, he and his family
lived near Fort Goodwin and received "supplies from the Indians at
that post." The implications are not that startling; what this really
meant was that Cochise traded with Apaches who were receiving
rations at Goodwin. If he had come in, the officers at the post would
certainly have reported it.[41]

Major David Ramsay Clendenin, commander at Fort Goodwin,
was not aware that Cochise was in the vicinity, perhaps believing
that the hostiles had remained in southern Arizona. This may be inferred from correspondence in early 1870s. In early January at Fort
Bowie, Captain Thomas Dunn requested Western Apache scouts
from Fort Goodwin to "act in conjunction with the enlisted Indian
scouts and troops in scouting after Cochise." Devin concurred, as
did Clendenin, yet this concept of using an Apache to catch an
Apache was not employed against Cochise at this time.[42]

In mid-January 1870 some of Cochise's band left Coyotero country bound for the Dragoons. As a result, Captain Bernard, Merejildo, and sixty-three men from Fort Bowie marched west toward the
Dragoons. Merejildo cut their trail near the entrance of Cochise's
east stronghold and followed it south about eight miles along the

Cochise's west stronghold, Dragoon Mountains. Bernard attacked a Chiricahua camp a few miles south of here in January 1870. (*Photo by Karen Hayes*)

foothills. Here the trail turned sharply west to the top of a mountain (probably Black Diamond Peak), where they found a deserted ranchería overlooking Sulphur Springs Valley. Merejildo again struck the trail, which led northwest over "the roughest portions of the mountains" for ten miles, leading to the top of another hill, perhaps Dragoon Peak. Finally, on January 28, he found the Chokonen ranchería a few miles southwest of Cochise's west stronghold.

Bernard pushed his men forward, riding "over as rough a country as horses could possibly travel," and attacked the camp, killing thirteen and capturing two before the Indians melted into the rocks and hills, leaving behind all their possessions. The troops found a bar of gold taken from John Stone, plus some mail correspondence. The captives revealed that Cochise was in Coyotero country but had "turned the command over to two subchiefs named respectively Chackone[43] and Schogo."[44]

With the advent of spring in 1870, Cochise returned to his country, perhaps to the Chiricahuas, where Indians were reported in

March. That spring and summer there were more Chiricahua raids, destruction of property, and the inevitable murders on both sides of the border. Indians raided the Sonoita Valley in March, hitting Gardner's ranch once again and fleeing toward the San Pedro River. Troops from Camp Crittenden, accompanied by Gardner, followed the raiders (Cochise's "entire band was on the raid") and saw smoke signals in the Dragoons and Huachucas. Perhaps in the Dragoons, Gardner and the soldiers attacked a ranchería and claimed they killed several Chiricahuas.[45]

The severity of these raids induced the secretary of war to place 125 Spencer and Sharps rifles at Fort Lowell to be distributed to eager citizens.[46] In Mexico, Sonora maintained its two-hundred-peso scalp bounty, and Chihuahua, claiming that American troops had forced the Apaches south, mounted a major offensive of two hundred men under veteran Indian fighter Joaquin Terrazas.[47]

That spring Cochise was reported raiding in Sonora, which seems confirmed by his conspicuous absence in Arizona. In late March small raiding parties were detected near Bavispe and followed to the Arizona border. The Mexicans surprised the ranchería, killing five Indians, capturing three, and recovering two hundred head of cattle. Another Sonoran scout found a village of thirty wickiups in the Teras Mountains, but the Apaches were a step ahead and escaped into the hills. Additional U.S. mail was recovered, probably from the Stone massacre. Whether this was a Chokonen or Nednhi group was not clear; the significance was the relentless Mexican pressure.[48]

In June 1870 two raiding parties left the Dragoons. One killed a man and stole some stock from Thomas Gardner, who claimed that in 1873 and 1874 Cochise admitted he had led the raid. The Indians made a beeline toward the Dragoons.[49] Meanwhile, at Fronteras, a Chokonen raiding party ran off some stock. The presidio commander, Adrian Maldonado, and a company of troops followed the trail into the lower Dragoons, probably to the vicinity of Bennett Peak, where they discovered a ranchería in the early evening of June 26. Maldonado dismounted his command, leaving eight men with the horses while he and the remaining fourteen pushed forward to attack. The Chokonen had detected the Mexicans and a vigorous sixty-minute skirmish ensued, after which the Indians fell back out of range. Maldonado thought he had repulsed them, but the real reason for their withdrawal was the arrival of reinforcements, possibly under Cochise because the fight assumed a different flavor. There was a second Chiricahua assault, this time from the front and both sides; four marksmen were hidden among the rocks and their firing began to take a heavy toll. Decidedly outnumbered now, Maldoñado retreated, having lost two men killed and one wounded. He believed that he had killed five Indians.[50]

That summer, Apache war parties ravaged southern Arizona. Cochise's Chokonens, from their strongholds in the Dragoons, destroyed farms and ranches and ambushed solitary travelers and small parties. On July 17 a large Chokonen war party raided Blanchard's ranch, stealing his stock and burning the ranch to the ground. A week later the same party, it is supposed, attacked Tubac, whose thirty inhabitants watched helplessly as the Indians looted the town and drove away most of the stock. Afterward this band continued into Sonora, where Cochise was reported (erroneously) to have been killed in a skirmish near Dolores. The report delighted the *Arizonian,* which added that "the worst Indian who ever strung a bow or pulled a trigger is defunct."[51]

Raids continued in August and Cochise, guilty or not, was blamed. On August 7, some Apaches, thought to be under Cochise, surrounded two wagons at Davis Springs, about eighteen miles from Camp Crittenden. Two men were killed and one was missing and presumed dead. That evening the mail rider to Tucson discovered the grisly remains and reported the incident to Captain Moulton at the fort. The captain set out with twenty men and followed the Indians' trail northeast for forty miles. The Apaches, generously reported at two hundred, ambushed Moulton from a strong position behind some rocks. Moulton abandoned his chase and the Indians continued on to a ranch at the Cienega, killing two men and forcing its temporary abandonment.[52]

With the accounts of sanguinary Apache raids, destruction of property, and loss of life everywhere, Cochise's next move caught Arizonans by surprise. In early August he sent a messenger, perhaps his wife, Dos-teh-seh, to Camp Mogollon and requested peace. She conferred with Major John Green, saying that Cochise "wanted to make peace with the whites and was tired of war and that he would like to make arrangements to come in and see me himself." A stupefied Green did not know how to handle the possibility of dealing with the elusive Chiricahua chief. He wrote headquarters: "He is such an old offender, I thought it best to ask instructions from the Department Commander in regard to his case."[53]

No response from the new commander, Colonel George Stoneman, has been found, but we can deduce that Green received permission to parley with Cochise because at the end of August, Cochise showed up at Camp Mogollon. With winter approaching, the grass poor, his ponies thin, his sanctuary in the Dragoons invaded by Mexican troops, his country patrolled constantly by U.S. troops, he reluctantly decided to put aside his enormous distrust of Americans. As usual, the facts are in dispute, the Indians saying he came in as the conqueror and the whites claiming he arrived as the conquered.

Chapter 15

WE ARE ABOUT EVEN: COCHISE VISITS
TWO RESERVATIONS

Cochise came in to Camp Mogollon (soon to be renamed Camp
Thomas and then Fort Apache) about August 30, 1870, and met
with Major John Green, who had the thankless task of rationing and
containing some one thousand Western Apaches, primarily of the
two White Mountain bands. That he chose Camp Mogollon to test
the waters rather than another post indicated his continued distrust
of Americans. No doubt he felt that he could not go to Fort Bowie,
for that was where he had been betrayed, as he believed, by the
Americans and he would not risk it again. Fort Goodwin was un-
healthful and, he may have felt, too dangerous for him to enter, so
he chose the next-best place: distant Camp Mogollon, where, he believed, he might get a fair shake. The noteworthy conference took
place outside the post; Cochise refused to place himself completely
in the hands of the soldiers.

Although Green's report to department headquarters has not been
found, at least three versions of the parley exist, each written from
Camp Mogollon to newspapers. On September 17 the *Weekly Arizonian* published the first letter, which furnished an eyewitness account of the meeting. The *Alta California* published a letter November 14; it contained Green's version as well as the Apache side, both
recorded by Silvester Mowry two weeks after the parley.

The *Arizonian*'s letter presented a good description of Cochise
but offered nothing about his motives and little information regard-

ing the parley. Cochise "came in about the 30th of August . . . made peace . . . and said that Colonel [Major] Green was a good man and had treated him well, and that consequently he should return to his own country and put a stop to all hositilities. . . . He claims that he was treated very badly at Camp Bowie some years ago but thinks that he has killed about as many as he has lost and now that he is about even."[1]

In contrast, Mowry's revealing letter provided two accounts, one from Major Green and the second allegedly from the White Mountain Apaches. According to Green, Cochise

> was very respectful; said he had been fighting the Americans for thirteen years, and now was tired and wanted to sleep. The troops had worried him, killed almost all of his band. He thought we were about even, and would like to come on the reservation and be chief of the Bonito River Apaches and that he would protect the road from Camp Bowie to the San Pedro . . .

Furthermore, Cochise provided insight as to his influence among the Western Apaches and his ability to draw from their ranks for his war parties:

> He believed the Pinals would make peace if he did, as he was really the great war chief. . . . Whenever he wanted men for a large war party, he sent to all the tribes for volunteers, and they came. . . . He claimed that he did not begin the war thirteen years ago, and only fought for revenge and self defense.[2]

Mowry's alternate version, which he obtained from the Western Apaches, probably seemed more characteristic of the bloodthirsty Apaches envisioned by most white Americans. Accompanied by twelve well-armed warriors, Cochise arrived wearing "ostentatiously ivory handled revolvers and a gold chain recognized to have been Colonel Stone's." Furthermore, the story goes, he was "insolent to such a degree that the interpreter was afraid to translate." Cochise claimed "the troops were cowards and the Americans were liars. . . . He would go on killing as long as he pleased."[3]

This account, which differed dramatically from the two independent Anglo versions, might have been in character a decade before, but not in 1870. Cochise was no longer the arrogant Chiricahua, nor was he ostentatious. Instead, his tastes were simple, his demeanor dignified. From here on, in every discussion with Americans, he expressed a desire to stop the killing and showed a healthy respect for American troops. Certainly he might have arrived well armed and highly suspicious and might even have worn Stone's gold chain, although that seems dubious. His presence might well have unnerved the interpreter, a normal result considering the power, prestige, and influence Cochise held among the Apache people. The one certainty would seem to have been Cochise's sincere wish to be left alone and to live in peace. Pedro, a White Mountain chief, corroborated this in an interview with Colonel George Stoneman two weeks after the Cochise-Green conference.[4]

Green's actions stirred up the hornets, in particular the territorial press, which was incredulous that he let Cochise out of his grasp. Even worse, the officer had not made any promises that he could not keep, much to its dismay. Green hoped that he had taken the first delicate step in gaining Cochise's confidence, and he had handled an extremely sensitive situation in an admirable way. He had exercised restraint, and it is impossible to say what the eventual outcome might have been had he done otherwise. If he had tried anything duplistic or had he attempted to coerce Cochise to come in against his wishes, irreparable harm might have been done. Nonetheless, the press vilified Green because he had let Cochise out of his grasp. One ridiculous assertion was that Cochise had his warriors surround Green, instructing them "to fire if he [Green] said anything that did not please Cochise."[5] The *Arizona Citizen* espoused the opinion that was prevalent in Arizona, editorializing that the most effective way to control the Apaches "would be greatly facilitated and rendered lasting by prefacing it with a temporary shortage of food, arms, and ammunition and giving them generous doses of cold lead."[6]

For his part, Cochise had not promised to remain at Camp Mogollon because he apparently was uncomfortable in Western Apache country. Relations between the Chiricahuas and Western Apaches evidently had become strained, with Cochise's people uninvited intruders. So he decided to return south to his ancestral home in the Chiricahuas.

About this time, Colonel Stoneman[7] was traveling through southern Arizona on an inspection tour. He had commanded the District of Arizona since August 1869 and had assumed command of the new Department of Arizona the following May. He disliked the climate (he referred to Tucson as a "hot, sickly town"),[8] and his cavalier and condescending manner quickly alienated and antagonized most Arizonans. So did his policies, which showed little thought, no imagination or initiative, and a superficial understanding of the Apache problem.

Symptomatic of this was the issue of the location of department headquarters. Stoneman decided it would be at Prescott during the summer and at Drum Barracks, California, during the winter, where the weather was more benign than that of northern Arizona at that season. It was a grave mistake. Typically, he underestimated the resentment and uproar it would provoke in the press and among civilians. His justification was viewed as a bunch of nonsense. Stoneman believed it would "satisfy the people, prevent clamor, and obviate the embroilment of the civil authorities of Arizona with the Indians."[9] This statement demonstrated that he was as incompetent a forecaster as he was a department commander, for precisely the opposite occurred.

His military policies were just as frightening to Arizonans. Foremost was his position as a cost cutter: he centralized troops in strategic areas to combat the hostiles. To those Indians sincere for peace, the reservation system would continue. In one respect, Stoneman was an atypical military man in that he favored subjugation of the hostiles "by moral or religious influences, the field is open, the harvest is ready and awaiting the laborers," although his motives could perhaps be questioned.[10]

In the end it was his inactivity and his attitude that did him in. When his report for 1870 was published—he proposed that five posts, including Fort Bowie, be closed—Arizonans screamed bloody murder. Said the *Arizona Citizen:* "Never was a man less fit than he for high responsibilities."[11] Edgy from criticism, Stoneman responded by threatening the people of Tucson with a troop withdrawal unless they ceased their complaints.[12]

Stoneman had begun an inspection tour from Fort Whipple on August 30—about the time that Cochise and Green were parleying. Going northeast to the Little Colorado River, he followed it east near present-day Holbrook, then veered south to Camp Mogollon, arriving there on September 11 and meeting several White Mountain chiefs, who told him that Cochise wished to live in peace near Bonita Creek. How Stoneman perceived this offer and whether he understood its significance is not known, yet, according to one correspondent, he opposed giving Cochise sanctuary.[13]

The correspondent was none other than the ubiquitous Sylvester Mowry, who had accompanied the paymaster on his route through southern Arizona. Leaving Tucson on September 2, Mowry wrote several letters to the *Alta California* in San Francisco, published under the title "Arizona Notes by the Way." His first stop was Camp Crittenden, where he found but "two officers and two men fit for duty." The situation was so critical, he asserted, that if Cochise realized its "weakness he could at one blow wipe out everything here."[14] Of course Mowry knew better than to imply that Cochise, or any other Apache, would attack a fort and risk needless fatalities, but a smattering of white lies never hurt a story.

They next went to Fort Bowie and then on to Fort Goodwin. At the latter post he learned that Cochise had requested peace, so he added some color for his San Francisco readers, writing that [Cochise's] hands [were] reeking with the blood of his victims hardly cold in death." From here Mowry's route lay north to Camp Thomas (formerly Camp Mogollon), where he arrived on September 14 and obtained Green's version of the meeting with Cochise. In any event, noted Mowry, Green's plan was "only an experiment and if it failed on a years trial there was nothing left but extermination."[15]

While Mowry expounded on him, Cochise was in the Chiricahuas talking over the possibilities of relocating his band, particularly since cold weather was approaching. In the end his Chokonens rejected the move to White Mountain country, perhaps influenced by a message from Victorio or Loco,[16] whose peace experiment at Cañada Alamosa was beginning to bear fruit. An important council was to be held with a special agent from New Mexico who wished to confer with all the Chiricahua leaders.

Like Cochise, the Chihennes had also been at war since 1861, except for a few unsuccessful cease-fires in the mid-1860s. In May 1869, Loco and Salvadora[17] (a son of Mangas Coloradas) solicited peace at Cañada Alamosa, having determined that this course was vital if their people were to survive. Victorio concurred but was too

suspicious to come in. Shortly thereafter, Loco went to Fort Craig
and talked with Lieutenant Colonel Cuvier Grover, who assured him
that his band would be left alone if it remained quiet.

Meanwhile, William Clinton, New Mexico's superintendent of
Indian affairs at Santa Fe, had no Southern Apache agent and was
uncertain about the next step. He even considered moving the Indians to the Navajo Reservation—if the Navajos would have them.
While these behind-the-scenes negotiations went on, Loco settled
opposite Fort McRae on the Cuchillo Negro, named for the former
Chihenne leader, and received spartan rations. At Santa Fe the district commander, Colonel George Washington Getty, recommended
that "if possible an agent of the Indian Department be sent . . . to
induce them to remove to a permanent reservation."[18] Fortunately
for all parties concerned, on July 20, 1869, First Lieutenant Charles
Edward Drew[19] was appointed agent for the Southern Apaches, who
came to like and respect him.

Drew reached Chihenne territory in late August and found Loco
and his local group (only 17 warriors out of 150 people) camped ten
miles west of Fort McRae. Loco had visited McRae twice early that
month, although his sincerity and motives were questioned by Captain John Curtis Gilmore.[20] Loco told Drew he wanted "a good
peace and no lie," and Drew reported optimisitically that "they
appear willing to make peace and I think that with proper care
and by treating them honestly and justly the whole of the Apache
tribes may be brought in from the warpath."[21] Whether this included
Cochise was not clear; at the time he was occupied with Bernard's
troops in the Chiricahuas.

Drew continued to meet with the Apaches in September and October, performing his duties competently and skillfully and proving
to be in the words of one historian "one of the best [agents] the
Apaches ever had."[22] He earned the confidence and trust of the
Apaches, perhaps the most important ingredients in dealing successfully with recalcitrant Indians who had been at war for almost a decade. What Loco and Victorio really wanted was a reservation in
their own country with the government providing food and clothing,
hardly an inappropriate request. Drew passed their wishes on, but
his requests ran into red tape with his superiors, who failed to ac-
knowledge his efforts and neglected to forward instructions. This

was the precarious state of affairs in December when Cochise sent word to Loco that he would come in if the reservation experiment worked.

Cochise's message to Loco was prompted in part by the several hard fights with Winters and Bernard in the fall of 1869. Loco told Drew about Cochise's proposal. As usual the Chokonen chief was wary, citing past acts of treachery, yet just the hint of his coming in excited Drew. The agent recognized Cochise's importance among the Indians and wrote to Clinton:

> Cochise . . . the most daring robber and bloodthirsty of the Apaches, had said he would come in and join him [Loco] as soon as a treaty was made, but he wished to be satisfied that there is no treachery about it, and that if he comes in he will not be betrayed and killed as his people have been in times past.[23]

But Cochise stayed clear of Cañada Alamosa, mainly because Drew had encountered one obstacle after another and thereby failed to bring stability to the reservation.

Drew had inherited a no-win situation: the army had no faith in the Indians against whom it had waged war, and the Bureau of Indian Affairs had neither the funds nor the manpower to manage the Indians. The Apaches, desperate for peace, had been forced to put their destiny in the hands of whites they distrusted. Drew risked his life to obtain the Indians' confidence, yet the people he called on for support gave him no help. His communications to Santa Fe were not acknowledged; no visible aid, either in terms of emotional encouragement or in money for food and blankets, was forthcoming. Drew, who nowadays would be called a self-starter, managed his Indians in much the same style Tom Jeffords employed a few years later. He took an agency that had been vacant for eight years and appeased a race whose recent experiences with white Americans had been irrevocably hostile. Little by little he gained their confidence, but he still lacked tangible support from the Indian Bureau.

Compounding Drew's problems were other difficulties endemic to the history of the West, especially the Southwest. He encountered obstacles with whites, who were "strongly opposed to any attempt to make peace with the Apaches." "No doubt they have their own reasons," he said, alluding to the contraband trade at Cañada Ala-

Thomas Jeffords. Cochise's best-remembered white friend, Jeffords played a significant role in bringing peace to the Southwest and was the only agent of the Chiricahua reserve. (*Reproduced by permission of the Huntington Library, San Marino, California*)

mosa. Scalp hunters from Chihuahua, who had crossed into New Mexico and vowed to attack Loco's and Victorio's people, were another situation that needed to be addressed. District headquarters in Santa Fe ordered the commanders at Forts McRae, Cummings, Bayard, and Selden to arrest any armed Mexicans entering the United States. This served to deter most mercenaries. But the largest task Drew had was to rebut charges by two experienced frontiersmen turned Indian traders who were attempting to enhance their position with the Indians—a euphemistic way of saying they wanted more independence to turn a dollar. The accusers were none other than Elias Brevoort[24] and Tom Jeffords, who alleged that Drew had been furnishing liquor, among other illicit things, to the Indians.[25]

On Clinton's recommendation, Jeffords and Brevoort had been appointed traders "with the Mimbres and Gila River tribe" on December 20, 1869.[26] Clinton had been acquainted with both men at Santa Fe. In addition, he had received excellent references about them from several of Santa Fe's citizens, who attested to their good character. Jeffords "professed to be well acquainted with these Indians," implying that he had dealt with the Apaches before the fall of 1869. Clinton hoped Jeffords would assist the inexperienced Drew. In fact, the frontiersman may have been involved in Loco's first peace initiative the previous spring. In all probability, however, Jeffords's acquaintance with the Chihennes did not extend to Cochise's Chokonens at this time.

In late January the traders brought a stock of goods from Santa Fe to Cañada Alamosa. Within the next two months they had at least two meetings with Drew, who made sure the pair knew who was boss. When they found they could not intimidate him, Jeffords and Brevoort mounted a smear campaign to discredit him, hoping to get him removed. Jeffords may have been unofficially campaigning for Drew's position, as he would do more than once during the next few years, yet his and Brevoort's power play backfired. The investigation exonerated Drew and laid skepticism to their allegations. Instead the commissioner of Indian affairs in Washington, Ely Samuel Parker, a full-blooded Iroquois Indian, revoked their licenses.[27]

Thomas Jonathan Jeffords, enigmatic and controversial, was a "tall, spare man with reddish hair and whiskers of considerable length."[28] Little is known of his early life. He was born in 1832 on

Chautauqua Lake near Maryville in extreme western New York and came west before the Civil War. In the 1850s he was said to have been a sailor on the Great Lakes. It was at this time that he apparently received the title of captain, which he retained for the rest of his life. In 1858 he was employed in laying out the road between Leavenworth, Kansas, and Denver, Colorado, where he practiced law for a short time. He then drifted south to Taos, New Mexico, and prospected in 1859 and 1860. With the outbreak of the Civil War, he scouted for Brigadier General E. R. S. Canby, bringing dispatches to Tucson in July 1862, and was said to have guided Brigadier General James H. Carleton's California Column east into New Mexico.[29]

Jeffords's activities after the war are more difficult to trace. He did some prospecting and eventually became involved in mail operations. In October 1867, George W. Cook, a former officer in the New Mexico Volunteers who had been involved in peace talks with the Chihennes in early 1865, and John M. Shaw of Socorro, New Mexico, who became the Chihennes' agent in 1874, formed the Southern Overland U.S. Mail and Express Line and operated a line of passenger coaches between Santa Fe and El Paso, connecting at Mesilla for Tucson and Los Angeles. Jeffords became affiliated with this route as a "conductor on the mail line" between Santa Fe and Tucson, as reported in the *Santa Fe New Mexican* of July 28, 1868, although he was referred to as Jeffies. Any doubt about his identity was cleared up three months later with a statement that "George W. Cook and Captain Jeffords of the Southern Overland Mail are stopping at the Exchange Hotel [in Santa Fe]." According to Alice Rollins Crane, who interviewed Jeffords in 1895, his responsibility included the area between Socorro and Tucson.[30] He left this position in early 1869, did some prospecting, and moved into southern New Mexico to the vicinity of the Cañada Alamosa.

Exactly when Jeffords became acquainted with the Chiricahuas is not known with certainty. His first contacts, however, were almost certainly with the Chihennes and not Cochise's Chokonens and perhaps occurred as early as 1865 in the ill-fated peace parley near Pinos Altos. Jeffords was clearly acquainted with Loco and Victorio by the summer of 1869. A few months later, he and Brevoort applied for the position of Indian trader for the Southern Apaches (although one might speculate what materials the Apaches had to barter; the answer, of course, was stolen stock). Clinton recommended approval because Jeffords "professed to be well acquainted with these Indians. I told him . . . to assist the agent in every way he could."[31] Jeffords was clearly familiar with the Chiricahuas by the fall of 1869, and if we follow the traditionally accepted story, he had already gained Cochise's friendship.

Aside from his long life (he died in 1914 at eighty-two), Jeffords's activities are intriguing. Unlike many frontier characters, he was neither a braggart nor ostentatious; on the contrary, he was a reticent man who spoke little of himself and preferred to be left alone. Wrote historian C. L. Sonnichsen:

> Jeffords offered little help to those who wanted to know more about him. He talked with his pioneer friends about the early days but he made little attempt to get his extraordinary story on record and made no effort at all to correct the misstatements and mistakes that got into circulation.

Yet in spite of his reluctance to beat his own drum, he was a jovial and easygoing man who enjoyed good times and good company. S. W. Grant, a soldier stationed at Fort Bowie in the 1870s, recalled that Jeffords "was always jolly, rather witty and hard to confuse. I remember we used to have dances at the post now and then—just the laundry women and the soldiers. Once, one of the women complained that he stepped on her toe. With much apparent concern he asked, 'which toe, madam?'"[32]

Actually it was Jeffords who may have unwittingly created his own legend in his statements to Thomas Farish and Robert Forbes in the last few years of his life. The traditional story has Jeffords, at the time supervisor of the mail route, riding alone to Cochise's camp in 1867 to make a personal compact under which Cochise agreed to refrain from attacking his mail riders. Jeffords told this to Robert Forbes, and it has been reported so much that it is thought to be fact and history.[33]

Farish is the primary source dating Jeffords's first meeting with Cochise in 1867, yet he almost certainly and incorrectly deduced this. He quoted Jeffords as saying that he first met Cochise after "having been an Indian Trader under a commission from Mr.

Parker, Secretary of the Interior."[34] Parker assumed office in April
1869 and granted Jeffords's license on December 20, the latter receiving it in January 1870. This point cannot be overemphasized.
Clearly, if we use Jeffords's own recollections, his first meeting with
Cochise must have occurred no earlier than 1870. Although this in
itself is not conclusive evidence (Jeffords could have a faulty memory), it finds support in other reliable accounts.

Jeffords first acknowledged knowing Cochise in February 1871,[35]
which is, of course, not incontrovertible evidence. In November
1872 he told Arizona Governor Anson Safford that he had known
Cochise for three years, thereby placing their first meeting in 1869
or 1870.[36] Finally, the reliable Fred Hughes, who should have
known the facts, since he was Jeffords's assistant in the early 1870s,
declared that the pair first met at Cañada Alamosa, probably in the
fall of 1870,[37] which I believe is supported by the scant available
evidence.

Farish and Forbes differ concerning Jeffords's motives. Farish
stated that Jeffords aspired to gain Cochise's friendship. Shortly before his death in 1914, Jeffords apparently told Farish about his first
meeting with Cochise, although he failed to mention anything about
a compact to protect his mail riders. Jeffords said Cochise

> had killed twenty-one men to my knowledge, fourteen of whom were
> in my employ. I made up my mind that I wanted to see him. I located
> one of his Indians and a camp where he came personally . . . I went
> into his camp alone, fully armed . . . I spent two or three days with
> him, discussing affairs, and sizing him up. . . . This was the com-
> mencement of my friendship with Cochise and although I was fre-
> quently compelled to guide troops against him and his band, it never
> interfered with our friendship.[38]

In contrast, Jeffords had told Robert H. Forbes in 1913:

> In the early 1860s he had a contract for the carrying of mail be-
> tween Tucson and a point east, through dangerous Apache country.
> The delivery was by riders on horseback whom he paid liberally, but
> he rarely settled with them because they were killed enroute by the
> Apaches. He stated that he lost twenty men in this way and that he,
> himself, had the scars of Indian arrows on body.
>
> The situation became so bad that he determined upon a most
> dangerous contact with Cochise to make arrangements for the pas-

sage of his riders with mail through Indian country. Alone he rode into Cochise's camp in the Dragoon Mountain Stronghold and dismounting and laying aside his weapons, made his way to Cochise's wickiup where the astonished chief asked him if he expected to return. Jeffords, speaking the language, stated that he came to talk with a brave and honorable man about his riders passing through Apache territory. Cochise, admiring the bravery of a man who would dare to enter his camp, entered into conversation which resulted in the agreement which Jeffords desired.[39]

The Jeffords legend began here and was then romanticized and popularized by Elliot Arnold in his book *Blood Brother* and the motion picture *Broken Arrow*. I have not found any records predating 1913, either from Jeffords's contemporaries or from Jeffords himself, supporting what Jeffords told Forbes. If this incredible story were true, it certainly would have been known by some of his associates and perhaps even by some fo the Chiricahuas.

In contrast, some of Jeffords's contemporaries who knew about the relationship had other opinions concerning its origin. One Indian agent wrote that it began while "having been a trader with the Apaches for some length of time."[40] An army officer wrote that Jeffords met Cochise while "prospecting in the mountains in Cochise's country and was supposed to have effected friendly relations with Cochise"—virtually the same story related by Governor Safford in late 1872.[41] Frank C. Lockwood, whose book *The Apache Indians* stood as the best synthesis of the Apaches until the arrival of Dan L. Thrapp's works, concurred, writing that Jeffords had quit his job with the mail company and turned to prospecting. He visited Cochise to "see if some agreement could not be entered into so that he might pursue his *work* unmolested." By his work, Lockwood was referring to prospecting.[42]

There is another argument which substantiates my thesis that no such pact existed. A review of Apache ambushes on mail riders in Chiricahua territory reveals that several attacks occurred between 1867, the accepted historic date of the compact, and 1872, when Cochise finally made peace. In fact, near Apache Pass in May 1868, Cochise's Chokonens slaughtered a mail rider and tortured to death another, along with two soldiers. The mail riders were employed by Jeffords,[43] so any agreement between him and Cochise must have been consummated after this point and before the time Jeffords left Southern Overland, probably in early 1869. Yet Apache attacks on mail riders continued, with no discernable pattern, until Cochise's final peace in 1872.

The Apache version was told to Mrs. Eve Ball, their oral historian. Jeffords's visit was not a voluntary one but the result of his being captured by Cochise's men. The Apaches also say that Cochise spared his life because Jeffords displayed no fear. According to Asa Daklugie, their relationship began about ten years after the Bascom affair, placing the event about 1870–71.[44] Morris Opler wrote that his "informants had little to say about Jeffords . . . largely because of death taboos" but that his "best guess [was] that Jeffords became acquainted with Cochise in the capacity of a trader."[45]

After examining all the evidence, I believe the Jeffords-Cochise relationship began in the fall of 1870 when Cochise visited the Cañada Alamosa Reservation. As for Jeffords's alleged truce with Cochise to protect mail raiders, the only evidence we have is what Jeffords told Forbes in 1913. This finds no support in any previous statements or correspondence that would corroborate it.

Some contemporaries perceived Jeffords as a disreputable character and an opportunist who would sell anything to anyone in order to turn a profit. A number of army officers viewed him as a troublemaker, perhaps because of his complicity in the Drew controversy, perhaps because he used unconventional procedures to control the Indians, or perhaps because of conjecture that he sold guns and whiskey to the Indians, a charge made more than once. In fact, one officer claimed to have been present during a transaction[46] and another claimed he had witnesses who would testify against Jeffords.[47]

Jeffords was not a saint; if indeed he traded with Cochise when Cochise was considered hostile (and from October 1870 to October 1872, Cochise was on and off the reservation) and if indeed he pursued the job as Indian agent (evidence supports this, although he denied it), it should not overshadow or obscure the immense public service he performed. A historian has described him as "a rough self-reliant man able to cope with the times."[48]

Shortly after the Jeffords-Brevoort shakedown, Lieutenant Argalus Garey Hennisee, described as having "good talents, character and soldierly requirements," succeeded Drew as agent, the likeable officer having died of thirst after becoming lost in the mountains during a scout for hostile Mescaleros. Hennisee had served previously as agent for the Mescaleros, and in time he gained the confidence of Loco and Victorio.[49]

When Hennisee reached Chihenne country, he found 360 Chihennes but only 46 warriors present. This would change as word spread through Apachería that regular rations would be provided. With winter approaching, other bands came in. By late August 1870, some 540 Apaches were present, and Hennisee believed that more liberal rations would entice in more Apaches, perhaps even Cochise. He also requested farming implements, but this suggestion fell flat because Clinton's budget was used up. Hoping that Washington could offer help, Clinton wrote the Bureau of Indian Affairs; still no help came. Acting Commissioner of Indian Affairs William Cady ignored Clinton's plan with the standard bureaucratic response: "You are aware of the amount appropriated . . . [you] can decide how to allocate it." Clinton had other agencies to run, all with strained budgets, and could not accommodate unforeseen expenses.[50]

In October, William F. M. Arny,[51] a zealous religious reformer, arrived in Southern Apache country, eager to find a solution to the conflict which had raged throughout the 1860s. Appointed special agent the previous March, he had visited the Utes, Navajos, Zuñis, Hopis, and Pueblos. At Albuquerque in early October he met Hennisee, who agreed to gather the Indians at Cañada Alamosa for a council about October 22. Arny arrived in Apache country in mid-October. Here he met Victorio's and Loco's people and, to his pleasant surprise, found that Cochise had cautiously come in with thirty-four of his men—ninety-six Chokonens in all. Tom Jeffords was also in the vicinity.[52]

Cochise, committed to peace provided certain conditions were met, arrived on October 20. This excited Arny, who called him "the principal chief" of the White Mountain Apaches, Coyoteros, and Chiricahuas,[53] and Cochise immediately became the focus of attention. Hennisee and Arny, with Richard C. Patterson[54] interpreting, interviewed the reclusive chief.

The physical and emotional toll of a decade of war showed plainly

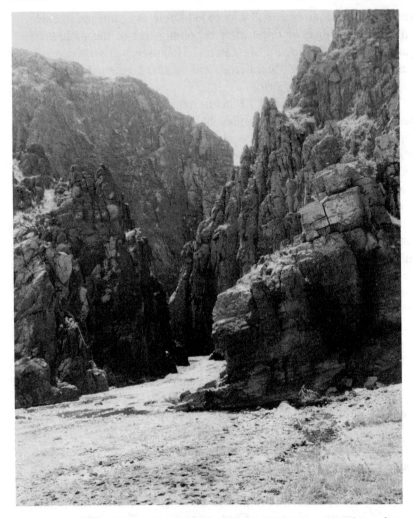

The canyon between Cañada Alamosa and Ojo Caliente, two active points in Cochise's time. (*Photo by Dan Thrapp*)

on Cochise's face as he spoke that first day. His speech was true to form. As he had with Perry and Green, he blamed the whites for beginning the war, at the same time admitting that his band had killed and robbed since that time; he had lost many men and now had more dependents than he could provide for. He carefully

avoided answering questions about specific past activities and refused to answer any questions which required a commitment of any
type. Arny and Hennisee judiciously failed to press him. Here are
excerpts from the interview as transcribed by Hennisee:

Arny—The Great Father wants to know what the Indians want so
as to keep peace.

Cochise—I have been to the White Mountains [Camp Thomas] to
learn how they talked and am now here to hear what you have to say
so that I can take the word back to my people at Chili Cowi
[Chiricahua Mountains].

Arny—This paper was written by the Great Father and I read what
he says to his children.

Cochise—I want to talk first, I have come to hear you talk. If the
government talks straight I want a good peace. My people . . . hide
in the mountains and arroyos and keep out of the way. I want the truth
told. A man has only one mouth and if he won't tell the truth he is put
out of the way.

Arny—The Great Father wants a good peace and they must stop
the killings and stealing and go upon a reservation or he will send
soldiers after them again and continue to do so until they are willing
to make peace.

Cochise—The Apaches want to run around like a coyote, they
don't want to be put in a corral.

Arny—The Great Father didn't want to put them in a corral. He
wants them to eat and dress like a white man, have plenty of everything and be contented, wants to know where they want to receive
their rations. . . . Talk it over among yourselves and tell me early
tomorrow what you want, where you want the rations issued. . . .

Cochise—We want it so that the whites and everybody can travel
where they please, build their fires at night, lay down and rest in
peace. . . . [I will] talk to all the tribes and learn what they want so
that I can talk straight. . . . I am going out to talk to the other Indians
and have them leave the roads clear.[55]

The conference ended the next day. Cochise explained that he
could not be held accountable for depredations committed by other
bands, for he was the leader only "in my own country," meaning
Chokonen territory. Yet he agreed to "send out for my people to
keep the roads clear." The Indians believed that their reservation
would be at a place they chose because that is what Arny had said to

them. Arny failed to anticipate the problems that this seemingly innocuous statement would create. He recommended that the government immediately provide food and clothing to the Apaches, whom
he characterized as "the most vicious, barbarous and uncivilized"
Indians in North America.[56]

Arny reached Albuquerque in early November and prepared a
thorough report to Parker, outlining six potential reservations for the
Apaches: Camp Thomas, Gila River, Mimbres River, Cañada Alamosa, Fort Stanton (east of the Río Grande in Mescalero country),
and Fort Tularosa, situated some fifteen miles north of the town
of Reserve above the Apaches' sacred Mogollons. After hearing
Hennisee's recommendations, Arny advocated Fort Tularosa as the
reservation site. It was a practical decision in that it removed the
Apaches from the "vile whiskey sellers" at Cañada Alamosa, had
good water and grass, and logistically supplies could be brought in
from the Río Grande at reasonable rates. Furthermore, Arny declared, "the Indians themselves, I believe would prefer it to any
other location," althought it is a mystery how he arrived at this conclusion. Finally, he recommended that no treaty be made until the
reservation had been established and the Indians relocated. Those
off the reservation would be considered hostile and the military
could deal with them.[57]

Cochise had remained at Cañada Alamosa, but not without notice. After receiving rations on October 21, 1870, he tried to live
quietly and renew old friendships with his Chihenne relatives and
probably became acquainted with Tom Jeffords, who was the subject of a complaint for trading whiskey to Apaches for a mule.[58] Yet
very few people believed that Cochise would stay put, such was his
reputation. At Fort Bowie a skeptical Bernard was perturbed that
Cochise was on a reservation, believing he would remain only till
"spring or as long as he can keep quiet and collect some ammunition."[59] Two days later, on November 25, he wrote the commanding
officer at Fort McRae:

> I hear that the chief Cochise and his band of Chiricahua Apaches is
> now on the reservation near your post. You will confer me a favor by
> forwarding this to the Indian agent in charge of the Indians. I wish
> him to let me know whether Cochise is on the reservation or not. I am
> charged with the duty of keeping him and his band from committing

depredations on the travellers on this road and settlers in this vicinity. If Cochise is now on the reservation, I feel confident that he will remain there only long enough to get us off the alert, when he will make an effort to take in some party. I . . . request that should he (Cochise) leave the reservation for any cause whatsoever, that I be notified of the fact at once so I may be on the look out for him. [When] he [Cochise] leaves to hunt . . . this will probably be his excuse to get away.[60]

Be that as it may, at the time of Bernard's request, Cochise had already left Cañada Alamosa for the Chiricahua Mountains to collect the remainder of his band. Leaving with Hennisee's consent, he took his brother-in-law, Salvadora, and two other men, telling the agent he would return with his people. On December 2, Captain George Shorkley responded to Bernard's letter:

In conversation with the agent yesterday he informed me that Cochise with 3 of his men left the reservation on November 16 with the declared intention of bringing upon the reservation all of his tribe and that this was to be done in five moons. The agent states that the remainder of the men Cochise brought in remain upon the reservation. From the pacific course pursued by Cochise it is believed that he desires a permanent peace.[61]

Hennisee confirmed Cochise's departure in a letter to Nathaniel Pope, who had succeeded Clinton as superintendent of Indian Affairs in New Mexico, and in anticipation of Cochise's return warned that immediate government aid must be sent or the Indians, whose patience was nearly exhausted, would leave at the first sign of spring.[62] Pope immediately fired off a letter to Parker, declaring that

Cachise is the most powerful and the most warlike chief of the Apaches and for a long time has been the terror to the citizens of southern New Mexico. His visit to Canada Alamosa . . . is considered a friendly demonstration and if he can be induced to settle upon the proposed reservation . . . I am sure that depredations . . . will cease in a short time.[63]

Cochise returned to the vicinity of Cañada Alamosa in early December but faced several fresh complications, a situation not conducive to controlling the heretofore hostile Chokonen. Hennisee acknowledged that "it will be several days before I learn whether or not it is true. [If so,] it is one of the most important events that ever happened to this territory."[64] Unfortunately for the suspicious Apaches, Hennisee was replaced by Orlando F. Piper,[65] who could not have come at a worse time. Cochise had met Hennisee and had shown trust in the agent by returning to Cañada Alamosa. Piper, a Presbyterian layman, was miscast as Hennisee's successor. These wild Indians required a strong but delicate hand; and Piper, according to an associate, "may have been a very good preacher but he was entirely out of his place as an agent."[66]

Cochise faced another obstacle upon his return. Washington had decided to move the Apaches from Cañada Alamosa to Fort Stanton in Mescalero country. Although many of the Chihennes maintained close relations with their Mescalero brethren, most did not wish to move east of the Río Grande, claiming they were unfamiliar with that country and unhappy with its cold winters. Cochise would never have considered moving. Piper quickly determined that the Indians would unanimously reject an order to locate at Fort Stanton: "It would be like beginning all over—they would resist, flee to the mountains." Cañada Alamosa offered "wood, water, pasture and good soil," reasoned Piper. "If the reservation is here there is no reason why they can't be satisfied."[67]

The government's inability to feed and clothe a thousand Apaches compounded the problem. Piper desperately needed one thousand blankets; Pope could send only two hundred. These significant shortages, combined with the new agent, plus the fear of removal, convinced Cochise to remain uncommitted. In mid-December someone, probably Tom Jeffords, told Piper that "Cochise is not at Canada Alamosa [but] that he could be brought in at a short time if sent for."[68] On December 23, Piper interviewed Loco, Victorio, and Nana and inquired of Cochise. They responded "he has gone after his people and will be back when the corn is up."[69] Fed up with the uncertainty about the future of the reserve, Cochise had returned to Arizona, probably taking those who had come in with him the previous October.

In Washington orders were issued for the War Department to supply subsistence to the Apaches, but Colonel Getty claimed he had barely enough beef to feed his own troops. Thus Nathaniel Pope, who had succeeded Clinton, was forced to cut funds for other agencies to buy supplies. For his part, Piper worked diligently throughout January 1871, urging the Indians to consider the proposed reservation at Fort Stanton. All attempts failed; "they positively refuse to go." [70] On the last day of January he recommended that the agency be located at Cañada Alamosa in anticipation of Cochise's return, which he believed was imminent. "Cochise would soon be in with his band," Piper said naïvely. In the end, the aging leader would return only if the situation at Cañada Alamosa stabilized. [71]

Chapter 16

NO REST, NO PEACE

Cochise began the winter of 1871 in southeastern Arizona, awaiting the results of affairs at Cañada Alamosa. Once the situation there settled down, he decided, he would return to the reservation. He was tired of war. Unfortunately, Cochise's plans went awry and he found himself embroiled in one conflict after another as American troops hounded him and his people from one place to another. During the first six months of 1871, he found it impossible to avoid collisions with citizens and troops and said of this period that the Americans allowed him "no rest, no peace."[1]

Agent Piper was also busy in early 1871, hoping that once the government discarded the ill-advised Fort Stanton idea, Cochise would return. Piper's wishes notwithstanding, little had been accomplished to alleviate Cochise's apprehension: rations were irregular and scarce, clothing and blankets had been issued in small quantities, and the question of removal to Mescalero country remained a distinct possibility. To make matters worse, Cochise became involved in a series of hard fights in which Apache blood was spilled. All in all, the first six months of 1871 must have been confusing and troubling for the once powerful chief.

The first three weeks of the year passed uneventfully for Cochise, who was thought to be camped in the Chiricahuas. Troops had examined these mountains in late December but found no signs.[2] In mid-January, small parties of Indians began making for the Chiricahuas. At about the same time, a group of fifteen prospectors left Ralston, New Mexico (near present-day Lordsburg), for the Chiricahuas, where, according to a captured Apache woman, gold could be found. On January 23 some thirty miles south of Apache Pass, Apaches ambushed the party, wounding two men named Robert Schell and Hugh O'Neil.[3] Two others fled to Fort Bowie and reported the incident to Captain Bernard, who dispatched Captain Gerald Russell, a hard-fighting Irishman who had risen through the ranks, and thirty troops to the scene of the attack. Bernard was convinced that the Indians "are without doubt the band of Cochise as no others ever visit this range . . . close watch will have to be kept up to prevent depredations." Russell's scout found no trails, for the Indians had moved deeper into the mountains and some moved north toward the Gila River.[4]

From their winter camps, small Chiricahua raiding parties went out to make a living, their objective primarily stock. Toward the end of January a few warriors pilfered every head of stock from travelers near Fort Bowie. Other raiders ventured toward Silver City and on February 5 stole fourteen mules and horses. Certain of pursuit, they headed west to the Gila before shifting direction to the southwest and their destinations in the Chiricahuas. If they were pursued, the troops would halt at the Gila, or so the raiders thought. It was unusual for New Mexican troops to enter Arizona, which was part of a different military district, although the Apaches may not have realized this.

When news of the raid reached Fort Bayard, Captain William Kelly; fourteen men of Troops C, Eighth Cavalry; one packer; and Juan Arroyo, a skillful guide who was in the same class as Merejildo, left in pursuit. Kelly proceeded first to Silver City, where he was joined by seven citizens under James Bullard, a confirmed Indian hater. They followed the raiders' trail to the Gila, where it abruptly turned south along Mangas Creek, then continued into the Burro Mountains. Here on February 8 a party of seven troops joined Kelly, increasing his force to thirty-one men. The march was resumed as Arroyo cut the trail, which veered southwest through the Peloncillos and then turned west into the Chiricahuas. By February 12, the troops had penetrated the eastern Chiricahuas, following "a well beaten trail to the summit." At 1 P.M. Bullard's citizens found the Indian camp, in all likelihood a few miles southeast of Chiricahua Peak some thirty miles southeast of Fort Bowie. That the pursuit from Silver City was unexpected may be discerned by the Indians' lack of a sentinel, a precaution Cochise usually employed. The whites quickly made preparations and in a blinding snowstorm poured a devastating fire on the bewildered Apaches. The fight ended abruptly as the Indians deserted their camp, leaving behind all of their possessions. The New Mexicans had achieved a complete victory: fourteen Apaches dead (the bodies were counted), an estimated twenty wounded, and one captured.

Next the Americans turned to the task of looting and burning the ranchería, which contained seventeen well-built wickiups. Among the confiscated property were two thousand five hundred pounds of beef and mule and horse meat, a priest's cassock, blankets, lead, two rifles, five revolvers, and American military papers dated May 1868, implicating this group in the attack on the Southern Overland U.S. Mail Company stagecoach at Apache Pass that month. Some of the stock stolen from Silver City also was recovered. The next day Kelly's party returned to the ranchería and found that the Indians had placed skins, manta, and other items around the body of their leader, which led at least one observer to speculate that Cochise was among the slain. Actually the band was either a local group of Cochise's Chokonens or quite possibly a Nednhi band wintering in the Chiricahuas. In fact, Geronimo may well have been involved because the results of Kelly's fight closely resembled what he later described in his autobiography. In any event, Cochise was neither present nor involved.[5]

While Kelly was hunting Indians, a Chiricahua raiding party from Cochise's group stole sixteen horses from Fort Bayard. On February 13 the post commander issued arms and provisions to thirty citizens so they could follow the Indians. Heading the posse was a noted Apache fighter, John Bullard (whose brother Jim was with Kelly). His command followed the trail on a northwesterly course and skirted the Mogollon Mountains to the San Francisco River country. About February 24, Cochise's camp was found in the nearby mountains. After dividing his command, Bullard unexpectedly encountered an Apache who was fleeing to raise the alarm. Then, according to the *Las Cruces Borderer,*

[Bullard's] companion fired first, wounded the Apache in the thigh. Bullard shot him through the chest. As he sank to the ground the Apache drew with both hands a revolver from his belt and aimed with deadly precision at the Captain's breast. Bullard was reloading, saw the movement, and spoke to his friend to fire quick, but alas; too late. Almost simultaneously the revolver of the Apache and the rifle of Bullard's companion fired. The top of the Apache's head was blown to atoms and Bullard sank slowly to the ground. As he rested upon the turf Bullard opened his shirt bosom and examined his wound, then sinking backward died without a groan.[6]

By this time, other civilians had taken positions around the ranchería and unleashed a withering fire, forcing the Apaches to fall back. Fourteen were left dead in the village, among them Salvadora, who had left the reservation with Cochise the previous November.[7]

Not long after the battle Piper obtained the Indian version of it, confirming that Bullard had run into Cochise. In his monthly report dated March 31 the agent wrote that

10 or 12 new Indians have come in within a few days. They are said to be from Cochise's band. They are so shy that I thought best not to talk to them at present. They were in the fight with Captain Bullard's party. Three Indians who left here last fall were killed in the same fight. One of them was a son [Salvadora] of the old chief Mangas Coloradas.[8]

That spring Cochise was involved in other skirmishes, forcing his people to move from one place to another. On March 17 a small group of Apaches returning to Arizona from a raid into Chihuahua, ran off two mules from Fort Bowie. Russell, eleven soldiers, and two guides followed the Indians to the mountains north of Stein's Peak. On March 21 they discovered a large Chokonen ranchería of thirty to forty warriors and in a brief skirmish reportedly killed three Apaches. After the fight he returned to Bowie for reinforcements.[9]

Two days later the relentless officer departed again with thirty men and three citizens. Marching by night, they reached Pedrocito Canyon in the Peloncillo Range and discovered a deserted ranchería which contained a "tress of auburn colored woman's hair carefully wrapped in paper, . . . a gentleman's glove and a small book." From the direction of their trail, he concluded that "it is almost certain that a portion of the Indians had just returned from Old Mexico, in which case it would seem that they had been implicated in the perfidious massacre of Mr. Charles Keerle and wife about the [1st of March]." [10]

Russell tenaciously continued the pursuit and on March 28 overtook the Indians near Duncan, Arizona. Dividing his force into three platoons, he easily routed the Chiricahuas, who left their entire camp and possessions in the hands of the soldiers. Debris littered the ground. Russell thought he had killed fifteen Apaches and lamented that he would have killed more except "that two thirds of my command were recruits, while the greater portion of the old soldiers were with the pack-train, as it required the most active and experienced men for packers." In closing his report, he echoed the frustrations of many army officers, declaring "that the number of troops at this Post is entirely inadequate to [perform] their multifarious duties." Russell had defeated a Chokonen group which had been at Cañada Alamosa because ration tickets signed by Lieutenant Hennisee were found in the ranchería. [11]

Kelly's, Bullard's, and Russell's triumphs compelled some Chiricahuas to seek refuge at Cañada Alamosa, where Piper had gradually begun to improve relations via increased rations, additional clothing, and the abandonment of the Fort Stanton option. There were reports that many wounded warriors had limped back to the reservation, but not Cochise. Both Piper and Pope understood that only humane treatment and consistent policies would bring him in. The solution, they agreed, was to offer liberal rations. Piper, who had advocated this policy to Pope, received unsolicited support from New Mexico's Governor William A. Pile. On March 18, 1871, Pope wrote Indian Commissioner Parker in Washington and explained that the hostile Apaches, led by Cochise, were off the reservation. To convince the wary chief to return, they needed to promise him rations, he believed. Yet even with this flurry of activity, the severe losses he had suffered, and the new military leaders in Arizona and New Mexico, who planned extensive campaigns to obliterate him, the chief was not prepared to come in. [12]

The same day Pope was writing Parker, the latter was thinking about Cochise. Perhaps a face-to-face meeting in Washington with the Great White Father would solve their differences, so Parker wrote Pope:

> You are instructed to request the Apache Chief Cochise and such other chiefs of that tribe as you may deem to be a proper person on account of his influence among the tribe to visit this city [to] confer with the Department in regard to the condition and welfare of their people.[13]

For the next year, well-meaning whites would try to persuade Cochise of the benefits of going East, but before they could do so he first had to be found.

On March 29, Pope instructed Piper to send out messengers to tell Cochise that he would meet him at any "such place as he might select."[14] The logical choice for this important and dangerous task was Tom Jeffords, who by this time was well known to Cochise. In February, Piper had informed Pope that

> there is a man by the name of Jeffries [Jeffords] living at Canada Alamosa that is well acquainted with Cochise having been a trader with the Apaches for some length of time. He informs me that he believed that he can induce Cochise and his band to come in and settle on a reservation and is willing to make the effort provided he can have assurance from the Indian Department that he will be liberally compensated for his time and trouble in case of success.[15]

Jeffords was either unavailable or Piper was unwilling to meet his terms for compensation. Instead, the agent enlisted José María Trujillo,[16] a short, dark-haired, fifty-one-year-old Mexican who was the justice of the peace at Cañada Alamosa, to head the search party because the Indians would not go alone, fearful of meeting troops. They left about April 11 and made for the Gila River and then Stein's Peak, where Cochise had last been reported, but they found no fresh signs. They returned to Piper ten days later, convinced that Cochise had moved south, either "to Chihuahua or Sonora . . . with most of the hostile Apaches to avoid the numerous scouting parties of troops from the different posts in Arizona."[17]

Cochise had left the Gila River country but had not yet reached Sonora. With most of his band, perhaps joined by a few Western Apaches, he had returned to southeastern Arizona for a raid into

Mexico. They rendezvoused in the Dragoons, where he had camped in relative obscurity the previous two summers. In mid-April he made his presence felt. On the evening of April 13, Indians stole some cattle from a ranch on the San Pedro River. Five cowboys pursued what they thought was a small raiding party. After proceeding about four miles, they were overwhelmed by a reported one hundred Apaches, who killed three of the cowboys and wounded the other two. Early the next morning the Indians jumped the eastern mail rider, Mark Revelin (better known as Brigham), killed him and, as with Keerle's victims, cut his body "into small pieces," obviously to avenge their losses of the previous months.[18]

Late on April 14 a mail driver discovered Indians at Sulphur Springs; he wisely refused to proceed and sent a message to Fort Bowie. Early the next morning Russell, thirty troopers, and Merejildo Grijalva were in the saddle. Marching all day, they arrived at Dragoon Pass that evening and bedded down for the night. They found Revelin's body early the next morning. Russell sent Merejildo

Western Dragoon Mountains. Russell retired to this valley after his fight with Cochise in April 1871. (*Photo by Karen Hayes*)

and six men to follow the trail, which led to one of highest points in the Dragoons. Here he turned back and joined Russell, who had entered the Dragoons from the west. The scout thought the Apaches numbered about one hundred: fifty on foot and an equal number on horseback. He believed the Indians were waiting in ambush in the heights above them. With darkness approaching, he decided to remove his force to the San Pedro Valley and continue the chase the following morning.

Cochise had anticipated Russell's move. The hostiles' trail ostensibly led into the canyon, but Cochise had opted to backtrack and position his warriors in Russell's rear on both sides of the hills. Just as Russell began to retire from the mountains, the war party opened fire. Russell recalled that "the attack was commenced by firing one shot, then a volley, then a yell from every direction." The troops were surrounded and heavily pummeled, although, miraculously, no one was hit. Under Russell's steadying hand, his men refused to panic. After his troopers dismounted and secured their horses, they gave the Indians a hot reception. As the Apaches were "completely entrenched," Russell ordered a retreat toward the valley after a twenty-minute fight. Neither party suffered any known casualties. Russell was sure that Cochise had led the Indians, stating "now this is one of Cochise's tricks for he is positively the only Indian in the country who waits for troops and resorts to this kind of strategy." Furthermore, Merejildo may have recognized either Cochise or his voice because Major Andrew Wallace Evans noted that the Apaches were commanded by "Cochise in person."[19]

Russell decided that "it would be a useless risk to go into the mountains after Cochise with so few men." Consequently, he sent a runner to Evans, requesting reinforcements. Shortly after, his force arrived at the San Pedro settlement, where he learned the details of the April 13 fight. He dispatched another courier to Fort Lowell in Tucson. On April 18 the reinforcements from Bowie reached Russell, swelling his force to sixty-three men. He marched back to the Dragoons and by early morning of April 19 had climbed to the highest point in the range, probably Mount Glenn, which was only a few miles north of Cochise's two strongholds. From here he could discern Chiricahua campfires.

Cochise had left a few scouts to watch Russell's movements. That night he slipped west to the San Pedro and followed the river south into the Huachucas, while others cut west toward the Whetstone Mountains. Russell tenaciously followed the hostiles for two days before he was forced to abandon the chase because of a severe attack of inflammatory rheumatism. He believed that Cochise "with his band can be found without fail" in the Huachuca Mountains.[20]

At Tucson, Captain Alexander Moore, an experienced officer in the Southwest, commanding Fort Lowell, organized a series of patrols against the hostiles south of the Gila. Feeling that Cochise might slip into Sonora, Moore wrote Governor Pesqueira of his intentions to protect the settlements by regular details along the border. Regarding Cochise, Moore pledged that he would "totally annihilate this band," which, he believed, was living in the Dragoons or Chiricahuas. If Pesqueira approved, Moore proposed to follow hot trails into Sonora.[21]

At the time, Pesqueira's troops were making inroads against the Apaches, prompted in part by the scalp bounty. The U.S. reservation policy had restricted the Apaches' ability to come and go as they pleased. Furthermore, attrition was taking its toll as Cochise's war headed into its second decade. Since the Sonoran offensive of 1867–68, the only Apaches who periodically remained in Mexico were Juh's Nednhis, although some Chokonens may have camped in Mexico from time to time. By early 1871 the Mexicans could sense that the tide had turned; no longer could large Apache war parties ravage the state and leave burned ranches and destroyed towns behind them.

Pesqueira probably appreciated Captain Moore's information concerning the Apaches along the border, though it came as no surprise. He had received reports from his subordinates that there were rancherías in the Huachuca and Mule mountains. A mid-April scout forced a Chiricahua group to abandon its village in the Sierra Madre and leave behind everything. Cochise's people were pressured no matter where they went.[22]

Cochise usually did not range as far west as the Whetstone or Huachuca mountains. He had been pushed from the Gila country into southern Arizona as U.S. troops made one patrol after another. By early May he had probably moved his camp back to the Dragoons, living at the very top of the mountains, from which he could observe the valleys on both sides. He soon learned of the Camp Grant massacre, one of Arizona's darkest moments, in which some one hundred Apaches were slain.[23] The details of this well-known affair will not be repeated here; suffice it to say that it rivaled, if it did not surpass in barbarity and savagery, any of the atrocities committed by Indians against whites. These same Tucson citizens, it was rumored, planned a similar action against Cochise in early May.[24]

In the meantime, Captain Moore had dispatched troops to southern Arizona in search of Cochise. One scout was led by Lieutenant Howard Bass Cushing, whose sole objective was to kill Apaches in general and Chiricahuas under Cochise in particular. Cushing stood five feet seven inches and had great determination; he seemingly possessed no fear and had boundless energy. Captain John G. Bourke remarked that Cushing was "the bravest man he ever saw,"[25] which was quite an accolade considering Bourke's long and distinguished service in the West. This flamboyant pair, Bourke and Cushing, had led several successful scouts against the Mescaleros and the Western Apaches, but there is no evidence to indicate that they had ever fought Chiricahuas. Cochise, to Cushing's dismay, had not been totally whipped.

Cushing had become obsessed with subjugating Cochise. The previous September he had discussed with Stoneman and Mowry the possibility of going out after him. According to Mowry, Cushing "was in great hopes and determination of capturing Cochise and his band."[26] With Cochise's whereabouts known, Captain Moore ordered Cushing to scout the Sonoita and Santa Cruz valleys. He scoured southern Arizona for one week before he was decoyed and killed by Chiricahuas near the Whetstone Mountains on May 5, 1871. Two other men died in the fight, and the Indians were believed to have suffered heavy losses.

Contemporary accounts attributed Cushing's death to Cochise, who was blamed for virtually every depredation in southeastern Arizona. Sergeant Mott described the Apache chief as a "thick, heavy set man, who never dismounted from a small brown horse during the fight." This description does not fit Cochise, and historian Dan L. Thrapp argues convincingly that the Apache leader Mott ob-

served was Juh, the prominent Nednhi leader. Mrs. Eve Ball's informants corroborated Thrapp's conclusions that Juh led the Apaches
who defeated Cushing.[27]

Cochise was probably in Mexico at the time. In May he led a war
party against Sonora in response to several recent Mexican campaigns. On April 24, Colonel Elías had scouted as far north as
Apache Pass and after a short stay at Fort Bowie started for home.
En route, his scouts located a small ranchería in the southern Chiricahuas. Elías quickly divided his force, surrounded the camp, and
easily obliterated the entire encampment of ten individuals (killing
four men and four women and capturing two children).[28] Word
spread quickly throughout Apache country. It was quite conceivable
that Cochise led the Sonora raid to retaliate for Elías's campaign. In
any event, his war party wreaked havoc in northern Sonora.

Cochise remained in Sonora for about two weeks before returning
to Arizona. From Santa Cruz came a report that one hundred
Apaches under him were raiding the state. On May 13 the Chiricahuas attacked a small party near Baviacori and captured Antonio
Ochoa. In an unusual ploy, the Apaches (perhaps Cochise) forced
Ochoa to write a letter to authorities in which they threatened to kill
their captive if they were pursued; if not followed, they offered to
sell him at either Santa Cruz or Fronteras. The Apaches felt threatened by the reinforcements of troops in northern Sonora, but
whether their proposal was considered by the Sonorans is not
known. There is no record that the Apaches returned their captive.[29]

On May 23, Cochise's war party, now estimated at sixty men, ambushed eleven men about a mile south of the border in the vicinity of
the Patagonia Mountains; the Indians killed two and wounded two.
The following day they attacked the Agua Fria ranch, wounding two
men, then hit Calabasas, killing J. B. Blanchard and George K.
Saunders. Both fights, which occurred on May 24, were hard
fought, with the boldness of the attacks characteristic of a Cochise
war party. One white man, John Petty, shot several Apaches, one of
whom might have been Cochise, who returned to camp slightly
wounded. The Apaches were well armed with "needle guns and
Henry Rifles, no arrows were used"—further evidence that this was
probably Cochise because his band was the best armed of all

Apaches. After these forays the hostiles fled east toward the San Pedro and then split, Cochise for the Dragoons and another party for the Huachucas and Chiricahuas.[30]

Cochise arrived at the west stronghold about May 24 or 25 and learned that José María Trujillo, with the assistance of a couple of Chihennes, had found his camp about May 15. Pope had sent Trujillo's mixed party of Apaches and Mexicans out on April 26 with orders not to return until they found Cochise. Although they discovered his camp, they could persuade only about a hundred Chokonens, primarily women and children with three leaders, to return to Cañada Alamosa. Cochise's own family and immediate followers refused to go until he returned from his raid in Sonora.[31] Shortly after his return, nine warriors departed to join their relatives at Cañada Alamosa. They arrived on May 31 and revealed that Cochise "has returned from his raid and is now at camp wounded." Thinking this might be an opportune time to bring him in, Pope tried to organize another party to "go to the camp and wait till Cochise returns but [I] find great difficulty in persuading or hiring persons to go for the trip is a very dangerous one."[32]

This time Tom Jeffords agreed to go, with Pope and Piper contracting to pay him one thousand dollars for his service. He left on June 7 with a good idea of where Cochise had last been seen. Besides himself, two Apaches and two Mexicans (Florentino Gonzáles and La Virgin Sánchez) comprised his party. Heading west, Jeffords reached the northeast end of the Chiricahuas on June 15. Here he left Gonzáles with the mules, and Jeffords, Sánchez, and the two Indian guides started for the Dragoons. The next day they found Cochise and delivered Pope's offer of rations, protection, and the invitation to visit Washington.

Yet even the influential Jeffords could not persuade Cochise to leave Arizona. The chief admitted that "he also desired peace and would be glad if his people were at Canada Alamosa but that his country was filled with soldiers and he was afraid to continue with his women and children." He might come in when "the troops were withdrawn" from his country.[33] Even Jeffords's letter of safe conduct guaranteeing him protection could not dissuade Cochise, who remained adamant, probably because of the recent Camp Grant mas-

sacre, or so Jeffords believed. Jeffords reluctantly left. He arrived at
Cañada Alamosa about June 26 and reported to Pope his conversation with Cochise.

For some reason, both Piper and Pope were somewhat dubious
about Jeffords's veracity. In his first report, dated June 28, Pope said
he was "disposed to credit" Jeffords's story because the facts were
"confirmed by the Indians who were with him." Shortly after that,
an impressionable Piper wrote that "it is the general opinion that he
did not see Cochise."[34] The whole matter was apparently drummed
up by a man named Coffman, who had wanted to accompany
Jeffords but was denied unequivocally because the Indians refused
to take a stranger along. This ruffled Coffman, who did not have to
look far to find others who would discredit Jeffords, always a controversial man. Hoping to clear up any misunderstanding, Jeffords
wrote Pope on July 24, sending affidavits of the two Mexicans who
accompanied him:

> Enclosed please find evidence complying on my part to the letter
> with our contract. After your leaving Canada [Alamosa] there must
> have arrizen a doubt in your mind of good faith on my part. Its cause I
> do not ask though if it is from anything that Mr. Coffman said to you
> when he went to Santa Fe I regret it.[35]

In 1872, Brigadier General Howard confirmed Jeffords's visit. "I
have indisputable proof that he [Jeffords] visited Cochise in these
same mountains . . . at the time you sent him. Ponce and chiefs separately told me where they saw him." By then Jeffords had received
half the money promised him.[36]

In the summer of 1871, Cochise tried to avoid troops until the
right opportunity to return to the reservation presented itself. He remained in southern Arizona fully two and one-half months after he
saw Jeffords and, except for a couple of encounters, successfully
avoided white contact. American troops were everywhere, and at no
place—not even the Dragoons, Chiricahuas, or Mexico—was he
safe from potential catastrophe. Although he tried to live as quietly
as possible (with some raiding into Mexico), he steadfastly avoided
hostilities in southern Arizona because he knew the military would
vigorously follow any of his parties. He was a prisoner in his own
country.

In spite of his isolation, Cochise was cognizant of the military buildup in southern Arizona, undoubtedly aware that a large column of troops had left Tucson in July under Lieutenant Colonel George Crook. Crook replaced Stoneman, who had been swept out in a wave of condemnation led by Governor Anson Safford. Once a staunch supporter, Safford turned on Stoneman after reading his recommendations to close five posts. The governor complained to the secretary of war and in April met with President Grant, who promised to find a suitable replacement. Crook was selected.[37]

Military activities were also heating up in New Mexico. The new commander, Colonel Gordon Granger, whose quarry also was Cochise, had drawn up plans for an extensive campaign involving two hundred troops. He intended to cooperate with the Department of Arizona "to scout the Chiricahuas" and effect the "destruction of this notorious Indian [Cochise]."[38] Yet even as these two military commanders made preparations to carry out their responsibilities, government officials in Washington had a change of heart. They were appalled at the Camp Grant massacre, and this influenced government policy regarding the Apaches for the next few years. A new policy was adopted, one based on deeply humanitarian notions.

This philosophical dichotomy prevailed not only in the Southwest but was found on the national level. Two letters published in the *Army and Navy Journal* a week apart represented two diverse solutions to the Apache problem. The first responded to the Camp Grant affair and the second was provoked by the death of the popular and dashing Cushing. The theme of both letters was the government's treatment of Apaches. Samuel Forster Tappen, respected and much admired for his courage and integrity, had been a member of several peace commissions to the Plains Indians. He skeptically pointed out that "speculators and adventurers in Arizona want an army there, and to get it an Indian war must be provoked at all hazards." Without knowing much about the Apaches, he emphatically condoned their mode of warfare, conceding that "if any people in the world were ever justified in making war and for the most excessive casualties upon their enemies, the Apaches were."[39]

Tappan's views were countered a week later by the ubiquitous Sylvester Mowry. Enraged by Cushing's death and disgusted with vacillating federal policy, he attacked the "pseudo philanthropists—

the Senators or members of Congress—who, from a maudlin sympathy, cry out for religion and blankets for the Indians, or vote the troops to put an end to their bloody orgies." Place these benevolent men in Arizona and they would empathize with southwesterners, bellowed Mowry. He advocated a simple solution: Give Crook adequate troops and "perfect freedom of action" and only then would the Apaches be exterminated or finally subjugated.[40]

Tappan and Mowry, both sincere in their convictions, typified the beliefs of two groups. The former spoke for the eastern humanitarians, philanthropists, and religious leaders who were appalled by government mistreatment of the noble red man. On the other side stood Mowry, speaking for most westerners, who had suffered from years of Indian raids, and the army, which was eager to rectify past criticism of inactivity and incompetence. The western press criticized the inconsistent government policies; The concerns of eastern humanitarians would vanish if they lived in Apache country, it said. For the most part, the southwestern press preached military force as the solution. The *Las Cruces Borderer* delightedly announced that the army's "good work was progressing—within one month some fifty Indians had been made 'good Indians.' "[41] A Tucson newspaper added that the Apaches must be "thoroughly subjugated by military power and any attempts to compromise before they are reduced to this condition is accepted by them as an acknowledgement of weakness and cowardice."[42]

At this stage in May 1871 arrived the best Indian fighter in the United States Army, a courageous man and a relentless campaigner who had sympathy and compassion for the Indians, George Crook. His reputation had preceded him, and if the advance notices were true, he would prove to be the very antithesis of the passive Stoneman. "Indian hunting is Crook's specialty," wrote a correspondent. "The fact is Crook is nothing but an Indian anyway . . . his mind, physiognomy and education are all Indian."[43] The *Arizona Citizen* noted that he was "a Lieutenant Colonel who would fight the Indians and know how to do it."[44]

Praise for Crook came from all quarters, while in the next breath came the qualifier: if the government would allow him to implement his policies. Wrote a correspondent from Fort McDowell: "Will the government aid him as he needs or will the Quaker policy still continue to rule and he go under like his predecessors?"[45] Another tersely predicted: "He will clean out the Apaches, provided the politicians leave him alone."[46]

In his autobiography Crook wrote that "he did not want the assignment" because he was "tired of fighting Indians." His feelings were assuaged because he believed the position was temporary, after which he could move on to something less challenging.[47] Yet his actions belied an ambivalent or apathetic attitude. After he arrived in Tucson on June 19 in his characteristically unpretentious, unobtrusive manner, his first step was to confer with citizens, scouts, and officers to learn all he could about the Apaches. He quickly assimilated this information and concluded that the hostiles must be defeated in their own terrain. Once this was accomplished, he would treat them in a fair and humane manner, establishing strict but compassionate policies. The consensus of those to whom Crook spoke, however, was that Cochise had to be defeated. It was therefore against Cochise that Crook planned his campaign:

> Ranging down into Mexico and New Mexico are what are known as Cochise's band. Their numbers being variously estimated at from 80 to 300 warriors. This chief has the reputation of being very smart and an uncompromising enemy to all civilization and has such an influence over the two other tribes [Pinals and Coyoteros] that their warriors are only too glad to join him in his numerous raids . . . it is against Cochise' band that I propose concentrating all my energies for the present.[48]

On July 11 Crook's column of 204 men left Tucson for Fort Bowie via the same trail used by Carleton's California Column nine years before. His avowed objective was to subjugate Cochise and his band. When his command reached Bowie, it struck north, Crook believing he was on Cochise's trail. But Cochise was in southern Arizona. After two weeks of unsuccessful scouting, Crook arrived at Fort Apache on August 12, 1871. There, to his astonishment, he discovered Trujillo and Loco, whom Piper had sent out to find Cochise. Crook was astounded that Trujillo was trying to find the same Indian he was trying to defeat. Totally exasperated, he ordered Trujillo to return to New Mexico, even instructing him which route to take, on the grounds that "two of this party were recognized by several of my men as being Cochise's worst men and whom they knew to be ringleaders in some of his past outrages." Crook added magnanimously that he did not arrest them (although he believed they were spies) because he did not want to "interfere with the policies of the Indian Department."[49]

By this time, much to Crook's consternation, the government had finally arrived at its Apache policy. On July 17 the War Department had issued orders instructing him to suspend operations until a new peace commissioner had an opportunity to seek a peaceful solution with the hostiles. Crook says he became aware of this order on August 27 when he arrived at Camp Verde. He suspended his campaign, albeit grudgingly, writing Washington that if authorized, "with my present arrangement and knowledge, I have not the slightest doubt of my ability to conquer" and secure "a lasting peace with the Apache race in a comparatively short space of time."[50] He was not boasting.

Crook's reaction was predictable. Despite his admirable qualities, he was at times intolerant of those who disagreed with his views and methods, including his superiors. The arrival of the new peace commissioner, Vincent Colyer, was not well received by Crook, who, with the benefit of hindsight, wrote caustically that he "had been sent out by the 'Indian Ring' to interfere with my operations . . . and was going to make peace by the grace of God."[51] As for Cochise, weary of life on the run, he was ready to bring his people to a reservation.

Chapter 17

CAÑADA ALAMOSA

Vincent Colyer, Quaker and humanitarian, had been sent by President Grant partly in response to the Camp Grant massacre and partly to persuade Cochise to visit Washington. As far as most southwesterners were concerned, particularly the partisan press, Colyer's humanitarian ways were egregiously misguided when applied to the Apaches; to them, he was an uninformed easterner who at best possessed a superficial understanding of the situation. To be fair, his mission would accomplish some good. Historian Dan L. Thrapp wrote that he established "a series of reservations which was to form the framework of the system for settling the Indians that is in existence to this day." [1]

Colyer's assignment incensed most southwesterners. First, his appointment as peace commissioner had suspended Crook's offensive; second, Colyer, edgy from scurrilous attacks on his character and motives, became openly critical of white treatment of the Apaches. The *Daily New Mexican* at Santa Fe referred to him disparagingly as an "old philanthropic humbug." The *Arizona Miner* went a step further and slandered his character, calling him a "cold-blooded scoundrel [and] a red-handed assassin." According to its editor, John Marion, Arizonans should "dump the old devil into the shaft of some mine, and pile rocks upon him until he is dead." Governor Anson Safford, whose position required impartiality, tried to give Colyer the benefit of the doubt and advised patience. He felt that

Colyer would eventually recognize the error of his ways and the situation then would be turned back to Crook for resolution.[2]

Colyer and a small escort of troops reached Cañada Alamosa in mid-August 1871. Here he met Piper, who he thought was "a discreet and able officer," yet he found few Apaches. They had stampeded after hearing a rumor that some whites from the Mimbres were planning a repetition of the Camp Grant massacre. A few days later, Piper convinced seventy-five Apaches to return; a few months earlier, he had fed one thousand. Colyer categorically blamed all of the problems on unreasonable citizens: "Is it not a shame that a few lawless white men can thus be allowed to overturn all the good work of the Government . . . [and] risk the bringing about of a costly war?"[3]

His conclusion was a classic example of the naïveté with which white peace commissioners approached the Indian problem. Colyer's analysis was an oversimplification in that he exonerated the government from any responsibility. Yet for the past two years the government had procrastinated in providing help and security for these same Indians. If it had adopted a consistent and humane position, practically every Chiricahua, including Cochise, would have settled on the reservation.

Meanwhile, as Colyer was en route to New Mexico, Pope and Piper continued to do all they could to locate Cochise and persuade him to come in. Although Trujillo's party was turned back by Crook in mid-August, other Apaches may have given Cochise Colyer's message. On August 14, Colyer wrote, "Cochise heard from," although no specifics were given.[4] Finally, on August 19 or 20, some forty Chokonens arrived at Cañada Alamosa, followed by Cochise's brother Juan and another seventeen on the twenty-first. Cochise had sent them, believing "they would find a good piece here" and that "they must come and stay." These Chiricahuas brought the first definite news about Cochise since Jeffords had returned in late June. Whether Cochise was responding to Colyer's invitations was neither known nor important. The bottom line was that he had decided to move back to the reservation. Arizona, he commented later, "was a bad place"; if he had remained, in all probability he eventually would have been captured or killed.[5]

These freshly arrived Chokonens brought news that Papagos had surprised Cochise's camp along the Arizona-Sonora boundary, scattering his band. Needing stock to move his people to New Mexico, Cochise's men had pilfered forty horses from Pagagos living in northern Sonora. The Papagos, led by a chief named Miguel, followed the trail into the coniferous Santa Rita Mountains in southern Arizona. At daybreak, Miguel's party caught the ranchería by surprise. The results, as published in the Sonoran press, were strikingly similar to what the Indians later told Colyer. According to the Papagos, the Apaches offered "little resistance, abandoned their horses and ran up the mountains." Some five or six Chokonens were killed and their ears cut off and turned in for the bounty. The Apache version was similar. They admitted to Colyer that some five or six had been killed before Cochise retired to the inaccessible part of the mountains, having first killed his horses for food. At the time of the attack Cochise was sick, either from a recent wound or from the illness which would claim his life some three years later. This incident took place in mid-August 1871.[6]

The rest in the Santa Ritas had been good for Cochise's people, but morale had to be deteriorating. Troops had hounded them ever since they left Cañada Alamosa; on both sides of the border, soldiers seemed omnipresent. It was time for Cochise and his men to think of the less-dangerous reservation life if they wanted to survive as a people.

While Colyer was conferring with the Chihennes about the site for a reservation, Cochise was making plans to leave Arizona. Yet he still needed mounts, and Camp Crittenden, being within easy striking distance, was a reasonable choice. There was little doubt that Cochise was present because some of the captured horses were later seen in his possession at Cañada Alamosa. In addition, the nature of the raid was characteristic of Cochise. It occurred about mid-morning on September 4, 1871, when twenty-five warriors charged the herd at Crittenden, which was guarded by one sergeant and seven privates. The surprise was complete and the Indians' appearance was "so impetuous and unexpected that many of the herders were panic stricken." In a moment, the entire herd of fifty-four horses and seven mules was in the hands of the Apaches. According to an unofficial account—which might explain the ease in which the attack was carried out—Cochise had dressed "six or eight of his most trusted men in the garb of the Papago hay cutters. They rode right through the parade grounds and on to the herds . . . when all of a sudden, the Indians gave the war hoop." Whatever the particulars, pursuit was fruitless. An officer tersely remarked that "infantry upon foot could accomplish nothing in rescuing a fleeing herd driven by well mounted Indians."[7]

While the Camp Crittenden raid was taking place, other Chiricahuas duplicated Cochise's feat by running off some eighty head of stock at Fronteras[8] before crossing into the United States. Cochise now had sufficient animals to move his people to Cañada Alamosa. Here the great Chiricahua chief, now past sixty and with his health deteriorating and his people decreasing in number, hoped to spend the rest of his days at peace with as little American contact as possible.

Once in New Mexico, Cochise found that Colyer's entourage had left, but not before setting aside a reservation northwest of Cañada Alamosa. On September 23 or 24, the chief turned to the one white he trusted and sent a runner to Tom Jeffords, then living at Cañada Alamosa. Cochise offered to "deliver him[self] up to the government in any manner he chose," thereby revealing the faith he placed in Jeffords and his futility of living as a free Apache. On September 26, Jeffords told Piper that Cochise was in the vicinity, saying it could take ten days to bring him in; later that evening he qualified the projection to either "tomorrow or the next day without fail." Piper at once wrote Pope, asking him to "get here with as little delay as possible" and recommending that Jeffords "be liberally compensated," for the scout had yet to receive any of the thousand dollars he had been promised.[9]

Still the old warrior remained suspicious, as was attested by the manner in which Jeffords was brought to his camp. W. H. Harrison was with Jeffords when Cochise's messenger showed up at 11 P.M. on September 27. Harrison recalled:

> We opened the door and our Indian courier came in and told the Captain to come over at once so we mounted and rode about three hours, came to his outpost, but the guide took us through alright to Cochise's camp, where, with about two hundred warriors, we drank Tissween and smoked an hour before we started for Canada Alamosa."[10]

On the morning of September 28, Cochise arrived at the agency and met Orlando F. Piper.

Piper was awestruck to meet the man he had heard so much about during the past ten months. He courteously invited Cochise into his quarters to talk. Cochise demurred, saying "no we talk out here," and his "Indians spread some blankets" while the chief's bodyguards scrutinized every movement. Piper was no match for Cochise, according to an eyewitness.[11] The agent's report was succinct:

> Cochise and his band came in on the 28th. He says that he wants peace, that his people are nearly all killed off. I have had several talks with him and gave him and his party presents and double rations. He expressed himself well pleased with the reception given him and was satisfied that I was acting in good faith. I feel satisfied that he is anxious for peace.[12]

Apparently Cochise was camped on the Cuchillo Negro, about twelve miles south of the agency, with thirty warriors and some two hundred members of his band.

Piper immediately wrote both Pope and Captain George Shorkley about Cochise, asking the latter, "Can't you come up and see the great warrior of the Age?" He felt that Cochise was a man of "great natural talents" who could be "of great advantage" to the agency if his confidence could be obtained.[13]

As expected, Cochise's arrival was greeted with much excitement. Nathaniel Pope rushed down from Santa Fe to meet him and try to persuade him to visit Washington. In early October he and Piper conferred with Cochise. More of Cochise's men had arrived, bringing his following to perhaps 60 men; soon, Chiva[14] (or Cheever) showed up with another 190 individuals. Chiva, a Bedonkohe or Chokonen chief, remained prominent throughout the Geronimo wars of the 1880s. Piper suggested that since Cochise was "very shy of soldiers . . . no troops should be sent here for a short time."

Cochise promised to remain at peace and agreed "to send runners to all roving bands to tell them what he had done and to advise them to go to the reservation at once." Most of the Chokonens would follow him in; nonetheless, there were some who "could not be induced to come in," and Cochise emphasized that he could not be held responsible for their actions. In return, Pope pledged to "feed, clothe and protect him and all his Apaches" and invited him to visit Washington.[15] Yet Cochise still feared treachery. It was reported "that a guard of his own men watch him and those who visit him at all times; his horse is saddled and placed near him nightly and for many nights he slept with the lariat in his hands." The suspicious chief would not consider leaving his country and place himself in the hands of any Americans.[16]

After the meeting, Cochise moved his group farther west along the Cuchillo Negro to the foothills of the Black Mountains, camping at a place later called Chise.[17] He wanted to be left alone, but his arrival had created a great deal of publicity. The press continued to view his presence with uncertainty and became increasingly skeptical when raids continued in southeastern Arizona, Cochise's normal stomping ground. One engagement in particular generated much controversy because it took place near Apache Pass, and the experienced officer involved suspected that he had fought Cochise. Of course he had no idea that Cochise was sitting in his wickiup some two hundred miles northeast at the time of the engagement.

On October 21, 1871, sixty Chiricahuas burned a ranch at San Simon, some twenty-five miles northeast of Fort Bowie. One man was killed and another was slightly wounded but managed to make his way to Bowie, arriving there the next day. The indomitable Gerry Russell took twenty-five men and marched to San Simon, finding the burned ranch and the body of Richard Barnes. Russell struck the trail and ascertained that because it came from the east, it must have originated from Cañada Alamosa, although one must question how he could have come to this absolute conclusion. He followed the trail along the eastern slopes of the Chiricahuas until it veered directly west into Horseshoe Canyon of the Chiricahua Mountains, northeast of the spot where Bernard had fought Cochise two years before. As his men halted to water their stock, the Apaches "from all directions with the most fiendish yells . . . opened a double crossfire." The first volley killed Russell's guide, a popular and athletic civilian named Bob Whitney.[18] The fight raged for four hours before the Apaches withdrew. Besides Whitney, Russell's command had one trooper wounded and two horses killed; the Apache losses were unknown, but as the soldiers had fired two thousand rounds "with great deliberation," Russell believed the Indians had been severely punished.[19]

Based on several factors, Russell honestly felt that Cochise had led the Indians, which naturally provoked another controversy because Cochise was supposed to be peacefully settled on the reservation. The press delightedly disparaged the peace policy, proudly claiming, "I told you so." Russell offered his well-reasoned explanation for identifying Cochise as the leader to the editors of the *Las Cruces Borderer,* who had interviewed Cochise in the Black Mountains on October 27, only three days after Russell's fight in the Chiricahuas. Russell explained:

> To say that Cochise was seen standing on a rock and identified is simply nonsense; I am sure I never said so and if any man of the party said so he was certainly mistaken. . . . But I did say that Cochise was there for the following reasons. The trail which I followed led into Horseshoe Canyon from the northside and left it on the southside; continuing down the valley at the same time the Indians were in the canyon waiting for me. Now this is one of Cochise's tricks. . . . The attack was commenced by firing one shot, then a volley and then a yell from every direction. Now I was attacked by Cochise when there was no doubt as to his presence in the Dragoon Mountains last April in precisely the same manner; . . . besides all this an Indian yelled Yo Cachise in plain English [and] Chivero.[20]

Chivero was a reference to Merejildo Grijalva, whom the Apaches had mistaken for Bob Whitney. Russell's argument was sound, but Cochise was not present. The fight was almost certainly the work of Juh's Nednhis, together with some of Cochise's Chokonens who had not made peace.[21]

Russell's attributing the raid to Cochise agitated the press and stirred up questions about Cochise's peaceful intentions. Word reached Vincent Colyer in Washington, and he immediately telegraphed Pope, asking "Has Cochise left Cañada Alamosa on warpath? When did you last hear from him?" Ten days later, Pope assured Colyer that "Cochise has not left the reservation," a fact that Tom Jeffords corroborated a few months later.[22]

It was this same widespread skepticism of Cochise's presence and his intentions which had prompted the editors of the *Las Cruces Borderer* to visit him. "Knowing the intense interest entertained by the people of southern New Mexico regarding the celebrated Apache Chief Cochise, . . . we determined for the benefit of the public to venture our scalp within reach of his blood stained hands." Accompanying them was Charles Coleman, a former Butterfield Overland Mail employee who had known Cochise at the Apache Pass stage station in 1860.

The editors went west to the agency, where they were joined by Piper, before proceeding to Cochise's ranchería fifteen miles southwest of the agency. Cochise was lying in his wickiup and came out when he recognized Piper's voice. After introductions, Coleman asked, "Do you know me Cochise?" Cochise thought for a moment and abruptly exclaimed, "Yes. Charley—Apache Pass, much time ago, put shoes on mules." Dos-teh-seh also recognized Coleman, as did many of the older warriors. Coleman commented that Cochise "had changed very little since 1860, except that he was not so fleshy and strong as then." [23]

Journalists by trade, the editors of the *Las Cruces Borderer* succeeded in obtaining the most revealing and insightful interview ever granted by Cochise, who may have opened up because they were not government officials. A relaxed Cochise carefully responded to the reporters' questions without the evasiveness which characterized most of his interviews with Anglos. Of course he refused to talk of past actions, undoubtedly fearing white retribution. The editors described him as a "tall and finely formed man . . . little indication of age. His hair is intensely black, his face smooth and slightly ornamented with yellow ochre. His mouth is splendidly formed and flexible, his nose prominent and his eye expresses no ferocity. . . . His countenance is pleasant . . . a sense of melancholy and thoughtfullness is clearly discernible." When asked why he had left Arizona, Cochise replied that he had been "allowed no rest the past year, that the people of Arizona would give him no peace, that the country was bad and everything there pinched him." In keeping with every other interview, Cochise blamed the war on the Americans. Now he wanted his views made public: "Tell the people that I have come here to make peace, a good peace, that I like this country and wish to spend the remainder of my life here at peace with all men." [24]

Cochise expressed two concerns during this talk. The first was that hostile Chokonens remained out in the Chiricahua Mountains (a local group which had not made peace), in southern New Mexico (a small group of Chokonens or Chihennes under Miguel Tuerto), and north and west of Lake Guzmán (Juh's and Geronimo's Nednhis). He thought his own Chokonens living in the Chiricahuas would eventually make peace, but the Nednhis would fight "until the last one was killed." He did not want to be held responsible for their actions.

The second point he emphasized dealt with the impending removal to the new reservation at Tularosa. The editors had quickly realized the importance of this delicate subject because Cochise's reply to every question was "coupled with a request that he might live and die here and not be removed to another reservation and in this expression Loco and Cheever joined with." The Indians' removal seemed to be the uppermost idea in their minds. The editors' last statement referred to the new reservation established by Vincent Colyer two months earlier a hundred miles northwest of Cañada Alamosa. It was a place where the Apaches were disinclined to live, and if they were compelled to go there, "one half to two-thirds will take to the mountains, and become more desperate than ever," warned the editors of the *Borderer*. For once the press was speaking from insight and not unfounded rumors. How right it would be.[25]

No one paid serious attention to these warnings. Colyer had inspected the proposed reservation during his whirlwind visit to the Southwest and had selected it because its mountainous location was remote from white settlements and was surrounded by "arable lands, good water and plenty of wood and game." His white man's logic was correct, but his understanding of the Chiricahuas was shallow. The Indians did not want to move; the area around beautiful and picturesque Cañada Alamosa was their home. They had countless reasons, some valid and others seemingly trivial: the Tularosa location was too close to the Navajos; swamplike conditions prevailed in the summer and it was too cold in the winter; the water was bad; the grass was unhealthy; and on and on. Although these arguments appeared frivolous to whites, they were real to Indians. Another factor in their refusal to move was the government's decision to establish a military post there, which upset the restive Apaches. Finally, perhaps their most significant objection was the remoteness from Cañada Alamosa, which had fast acquired the same reputation as Janos, where open market conditions prevailed and the Indians could unload their stolen stock and rations for whiskey and other sundries. This was perhaps the primary factor for their opposing the move to Tularosa. Some unscrupulous residents at Cañada Alamosa capitalized on these fears and undermined the goverment's policy by spreading rumors and lies about Tularosa.[26]

Loco and Victorio had been steadfastly opposed to Tularosa from the beginning. Cochise seemed indifferent at first and then became antiremoval. A few days after his arrival, Piper wrote that Cochise "does not make the selection of a reservation as a condition of peace," but in his next sentence it was evident that Cochise was against the idea. Piper continued: "I do not think that the objections he makes to going to Tularosa are on his account but on account of the desire of the chiefs that have been here some time." At no time did Cochise absolutely refuse to go to the new reservation, yet by the same token he never promised that he would move.[27]

Piper had at first been optimistic that his wards would move. On September 30, two days after Cochise's arrival, he wrote that he did not anticipate trouble and that the agency would be moved by October 20.[28] The first hint of a potential problem surfaced nine days later when he wrote a private letter to the Presbyterian board in Philadelphia admitting that he feared "trouble in getting the chiefs to consent to remove."[29] Three days later, Granger telegraphed Brigadier General John Pope of the Apaches' refusal and wondered whether he should "delay establishing a post."[30] Finally, on October 17, New Mexico's superintendent of Indian affairs, Nathaniel Pope, unable to delay any longer, informed his superiors in Washington that he had met with Cochise, Victorio, and Loco. They wished to remain at Cañada Alamosa but he felt they would follow the agency, at least "when they get hungry." Reluctantly he admitted that "it may be necessary to humor them until spring."[31]

Piper seemed to vacillate in his position, having the unenviable task of carrying out a policy which neither he nor the Indians desired. Throughout October, Cochise quietly supported Victorio and Loco, emphasizing that while he preferred Cañada Alamosa, he would consider moving if the two Chihenne leaders consented. Piper did all he could to convince Loco and Victorio, even offering them a horse as a bribe to go to Tularosa. On October 19 he suggested that they should not "delay the removal till spring" unless another reservation was under consideration. The next day he conferred with Cochise, Victorio, and Loco. Exasperated and enervated, Piper wrote Nathaniel Pope of the Apaches' defiant response to removal—almost certainly Victorio and Loco speaking with the tacit support of Cochise:

> I have used every argument in my power and made all the promises I could to induce the Indians to go to the new reservation. They positively refuse to go; saying that I may take the rations and give them to the bears and wolves.

In conclusion, Piper reversed his previous position and recommended that the Tularosa proposal be abandoned. If so, he felt that "thousands, probably millions of dollars" would be saved. To explain his change in heart, he offered to come to Washington to express the Apache view, a favorite ploy used by some agents to procure a trip to the East.[32]

This uncertainty prompted Brigadier General John Pope, Granger's superior, who commanded the Department of the Missouri, to dispatch Lieutenant Colonel Nelson Henry Davis from Leavenworth, Kansas, to New Mexico to "report as accurately as possible" on the state of affairs at Cañada Alamosa. Davis had met Victorio and other Chihennes in 1865 and had formed rigid, Carleton-like perceptions of Apaches. He described Cochise as "the terror and curse of the people of Arizona and New Mexico" and in a classic overstatement declared that the Chiricahuas were responsible for "the murder of more men, women and children and the loss of more property by theft than probably any score of chiefs." Although Davis apparently did not meet Cochise, he concluded that Cochise had come in only because many of his warriors and relatives were killed. Previously, asserted the inspector, Cochise had "declared that he would never make peace with the whites," failing to mention or consider that Cochise had made that statement some six and a half years earlier, when circumstances were much different.

Davis did recognize that the Indians "objected to going to Tularosa." Therefore, he suggested, the government should allow the "Indians to remain for the present at Cañada Alamosa as a matter of economy." His rationale, however, was not based on humane convictions but, rather, on his inherent distrust of Apaches. After all, he conceded, the reservation "is an experiment and I question whether thay are sincere in their profession of peace and will remain peacable longer than until spring and warm weather." Davis obviously felt that any effort to move the Indians would be a waste of time and resources, which, he reported, was also Granger's opinion.[33]

Meanwhile, as October drew to a close the Indians, perhaps sensing the whites indecisiveness, remained unyielding in their refusal to move. On the surface, Cochise's role may have appeared subservient to Victorio's and Loco's, but their position would have been untenable without his support. The day after Davis's report was received, the two arms of government in New Mexico sprang into action. Colonel Granger wrote Piper and inquired about the likelihood of removal and Piper replied that if coerced "they may flee to the mountains of Arizona."[34] At the same time, Nathaniel Pope told Washington that the "Apaches positively refuse to go" and added that "I don't think it wise or practicable to move them by force but if the department decides it would be better to do so now than in the spring." The chiefs had issued an ultimatum: the agency would remain at Cañada Alamosa or they would go to war. The error was in not moving the Apaches as soon as Cochise came in. If this had been done, the Indians probably would have gone and the whole controversy about removal would have been avoided, although the portended unrest may have occurred anyway.[35]

Pope's communication was passed along to the secretary of the interior, Charles Delano, who immediately decided to consult with Colyer, recently returned from "Apache country" and supposedly familiar "with their wants."[36] Thus on November 6, 1871, Colyer, Delano, Secretary of War William W. Belknap, and President Ulysses S. Grant discussed Tularosa. After Colyer briefed them on the situation, they concluded to allow the Indians to remain at Cañada Alamosa for the present. Colyer telegraphed the verdict to Pope, cautioning him to tell the Indians that their stay at Cañada Alamosa was "limited in duration and that they must prepare to move for Tularosa as soon as possible." Two weeks later, Delano decided that the transfer would occur as soon as practicable in 1872. Consequently, Lieutenant General Philip Sheridan issued General Order No. 8, ordering the removal to Tularosa and the establishment of a military post to be named Fort Tularosa.[37]

This decision reached Cañada Alamosa in early December. Soon afterward many Chiricahuas left for the mountains and others for Mescalero country east of the Río Grande. Among the latter were Nana and Horache, who were apparently responsible for the attack on Shedd's ranch on Christmas Day 1871 and for the killing of a man near the Organ Mountains.[38] As for Cochise, Piper typically misread his intentions, reporting that he and his Chokonens remained, seemingly content after the announcement postponing the removal.[39]

Granger realized that it would not be practical to relocate the Indians before spring. Besides requiring time to plan and organize the move, he would not contemplate this mission without the presence of Superintendent Pope, who was absent on personal business and would not return until February. Compounding this was the problem of a winter move. Consequently, Granger decided to delay the entire relocation until April 1, 1872, with the actual transfer to take place on May 1. His superior, Brigadier General Pope, concurred and the date was established.[40]

With the removal date fixed, Cochise grew even more unapproachable, although his name swirled around in several more controversies while he remained on the reservation. In December he requested permission to leave the reservation to hunt. Knowing that some of the Apaches had already fled and recalling that when Cochise left a year earlier he had not returned for ten months, Piper wisely refused.[41] On December 31 he completed his quarterly report, noting ominously that "Cochise and most of his band are here. They are very restless and suspicious." Citing the presence of Mexicans at Cañada Alamosa, Piper asserted that "evil disposed persons are continually circulating reports that troops are after them to drive them to Tularosa."[42]

Throughout December the agitators from Cañada Alamosa stirred up trouble. Early that month many Indians traded their rations for whiskey, leaving them "destitute of food" and starving. Fearing more trouble, Piper requested help from Fort McRae, which came in the form of a noncommissioned officer and nine men. On December 12 he issued blankets as the soldiers looked on to prevent any trading. The citizens at Cañada Alamosa, many of them masters of crooked devices, retaliated by arresting Piper later that day. Little wonder that Piper repeatedly commented about the deleterious effect these "evil disposed persons" had on the Apaches, referring to the Chihennes and not Cochise's Chokonens who remained in the mountains. Cochise's appearance at the agency became less and less frequent. He would send his family in for rations; he himself wanted to be left alone.[43]

That was virtually impossible. First, Crook was angry about the continuation of scattered raids in southeastern Arizona, either the work of Western Apaches, some of Cochise's own band who had refused to make peace, or Juh's Nednhis, still as incorrigible as ever. In any event, these activities enraged Crook, who was publicly dubious of Cochise's sincerity and inwardly angry that Cochise had escaped his grasp and deprived him of the satisfaction of subduing the great Chiricahua. He began his sniping in early December, writing to his superior in San Francisco, Major General John McAllister Schofield and suggesting that Cochise be forced to return to Arizona, "where he belongs," and that "he be required to show some sincerity in his professions of peace" by helping troops to subdue other Chiricahuas who had remained hostile. To the pragmatic Crook, Cochise "should control his people for good as effectually as he had heretofore for bad." Schofield forwarded Crook's request to Washington with this comment: "Whether it is practicable or not is another matter."[44]

Soon yet another issue entered the drama and added more fuel to Crook's discontent. In late November 1871, Charles Brown, a Tucson businessman, just in from southern New Mexico, reported to Captain Moore at Tucson that the horses stolen from Camp Crittenden "are now at Cañada Alamosa in the possession of Cochise." Moore immediately sent a note to Crook, inquiring whether he should try to recover the horses.[45] Eventually Nathaniel Pope received Moore's communication, which he forwarded to Piper, asking him to investigate. Piper soothingly replied that when Cochise arrived from Arizona, he "had in his possession three or four horses supposed to belong to the cavalry. Two of them had shoes on their feet. The brands had been so defaced that it was impossible to tell what they had been." Pope reluctantly concluded that the matter should be dropped.[46]

Military headquarters at Santa Fe thought otherwise, ordering Captain George Shorkley at Fort McRae to investigate. Shorkley was an officer with considerable experience, knowledge, and ability in dealing with the Chiricahuas. On April 6, 1872, he logically explained why the mounts could not be recovered:

> Cochise and his men are not now at or near Canada Alamosa . . . any efforts made by me to recover the animals would be futile and were the Indians at Canada Alamosa, no serious efforts could be made by me without alarming or offending the Indians as they were told at the time they came into the agency that all ordinary property there in their possession would be assured to them. It is believed that the animals are not now worth the effort necessary to recover them.

Shorkley's letter closed the matter, although it undoubtedly failed to mollify Crook.[47]

The editors of the *Las Cruces Borderer* added their own two cents' worth after Chiricahuas captured both the eastbound and westbound mail near Fort Bowie on January 25, murdering three men. The Apaches, dressed in army shirts and well armed with needle guns, probably headed south to their ranchería near Batepito, Sonora, which was fifteen to twenty miles below the border. After these atrocities the editors of the *Borderer* called for the mail company to hire Cochise and his warriors "to escort the mail . . . with enough warriors to accomplish the object. Himself and a half dozen warriors I think will be sufficient." How Cochise responded, or whether Piper even made the offer, is not known."[48]

In all likelihood, Cochise would not have been receptive. About this time Piper had written to Vincent Colyer about Cochise, who had become a recluse towards the whites:

> I do not know what to say of Cochise. . . . He does not seem disposed to place confidence in anything said to him. He has not been on to the agency since the order for their removal has been made public; he has regularly sent in for rations.[49]

Cochise was apparently going to bide his time on the reserve through the winter. In early January, Tom Jeffords told Captain Shorkley that Cochise was now camped in the forested San Mateo

Mountains, probably in the lower valleys near Vicks Peak (named for Victorio) twelve miles north of the agency. The chief "would come in for the big talk," according to Jeffords, who was referring to a conference to be held with Colonel Granger and Superintendent Pope. Until then, "fearing that the [agency beef] may be poisoned," he would remain in the mountains and hunt his own meat.[50]

Jeffords told Shorkley that "many of the Indians are dissatisfied with the agent Mr. Piper [including], Cochise and some of the captains." Shockley concurred, writing "that this dissatisfaction exists I have no doubt." With respect to the Tularosa removal, Shorkley believed that Jeffords "wants the Indians to go to Tularosa and took much pains to convince me of this. I am satisfied he thinks it will advance his interest very much if the Indians go peacefully."[51] Shorkley was right on target. Jeffords had made plans to construct a building at Tularosa, probably with the hope of being appointed post sutler, but the idea was vetoed by Colonel Granger. He informed Jeffords "that under existing orders no citizen can be allowed to settle or build on a government reservation without special permission from the Secretary of War."[52]

Throughout February, Cochise remained in the mountains and did not bother to visit the agency. Lieutenant Colonel Thomas Devin stopped briefly at Cañada Alamosa, hoping to see the Indian he had offered to meet three years before; Cochise, however, was "out in the mountains and could not be got in."[53]

Those who wished to see Cochise had to go to his camp. On the last day of February, Piper and Jeffords visited him and invited him to Washington. Again Cochise would not consider leaving, suspecting treachery if he placed "himself in the hands of Americans." Piper also reported dissension between Loco's Chihennes and Cochise's Chokonens, an inevitable occurrence with the camps in close proximity to each other. Recently the bands had "one or two pitched fights"; in all probability, either tiswin or whiskey was involved, which resulted in the death of two or three Apaches and the wounding of several others. This alone may have convinced Cochise that he had overstayed his welcome in Chihenne country.[54]

Finally, in mid-March, the plans for the big talk about Tularosa were made. The government's hope for calming the crisis and relocating the Apaches hinged on convincing the Indians of two things:

Gordon Granger. Commander of the district of New Mexico, Granger met Cochise in March 1872 at Cañada Alamosa and later boasted to Crook that "Cochise will go wherever I send him." (*Courtesy National Archives*)

first, that a trip to Washington to visit the Great White Father would be to their benefit; second, that Tularosa was their only choice. If they refused to move, the troops would be called out. As it turned out, neither option was attractive to Cochise, although Victorio consented to visit Washington, according to Piper. The government would rue the day that it adhered to this stupid, shortsighted policy of placing the Apaches at a place they came to detest. The wonder of it all was that those involved never learned their lesson.

Colonel Granger, who proudly boasted to Crook that Cochise "will go wherever I direct him," arrived in an optimistic mood. His first objective was to "do all I can to induce Cochise, Salvadora, Loco, and Victorio" to visit Washington, although he would have had a miraculous task in convincing Salvadora, considering that he had been killed in the Bullard fight more than a year earlier. Granger's entourage arrived at Cañada Alamosa on March 17. The following day, the Indians began arriving, and on the nineteenth Cochise appeared and the parley began. Granger and Nathaniel Pope tried desperately to persuade the chief to visit Washington, but to no avail, with Cochise declaring that he would rather talk on top of a mountain. Removal to Tularosa was next on the agenda, and May 1 was the assigned date on which it would occur. The Indians objected, which Pope summarily labeled as "unimportant and . . . frivolous," expecting that most of the Indians would follow the agency in need of provisions. He would be dead wrong.[55]

Cochise's responses were typically evasive because the presence of army officers usually inhibited his replies. A transcript of the meeting was published in the *Santa Fe Daily New Mexican* and reprinted by the *Arizona Miner*. Granger and Pope did all in their power to persuade him to visit Washington. His inherent distrust of Americans can be discerned from his remarks. After all, Bascom had arrested him for acts committed by other Apaches. What would happen if he went to Washington and "two or three of his warriors should steal while I am gone. It would make me look like a liar." Cochise's health was deteriorating, but the basic reason he declined to go seemed to be his profound distrust of Americans.

Cochise also was concerned about the Indians still at war, and he assured Granger that "this must look strange to you, but they are not my people. I would like to go to them and tell them of what you have said." Granger replied that "the Great Father will thank you very much if you bring about such a result."[56]

Two other eyewitnesses recorded fascinating descriptions of the aging chief. Assistant surgeon Henry Stuart Turrill wrote that Cochise "impressed me as a wonderfully strong man, of much endurance, accustomed to command and to expect instant and implicit obedience." Turrill felt that Cochise was "the greatest Indian that I have ever met," which was quite a compliment considering that he had been in contact with the Sioux and Cheyennes.[57] Dr. Anderson Nelson Ellis, post surgeon at Fort Craig, described Cochise as "five foot ten inches . . . lithe and wiry every muscle being well developed and firm. A silver thread was now and then visible in his otherwise black hair, which he wore cut straight around his head about on a level with his chin." Ellis also recorded Cochise's speech, which provided a vivid picture of the frustration of a man who realized that his time was passing, that his people were on the verge of extinction, swept over by the whites invading Apachería. Cochise made his feelings clear; he had no wish to leave Cañada Alamosa:

> My blood was on fire, but now I have come into this valley and drunk of these waters and washed myself in them and they have cooled me. . . . I speak straight and do not wish to deceive or be deceived. I want a good, strong and lasting peace.

While his attentive audience listened, Cochise referred to himself, uncertain as to the white's expectations. He continued:

> The white people have looked for me long. I am here! What do they want? . . . Why am I worth so much? . . . I am not God. I am no longer chief of all the Apaches. I am no longer rich; I am but a poor man. . . . I came in here because God told me to do so. He said it was good to be at peace—so I came! . . . God spoke to my thought and told me to come in here and be at peace with all. . . . The Apaches were once a great nation; they are now but few, and because of this they want to die and so carry their lives on their finger nails.

The chief ended his oratory by leaving no doubt about where he wanted to live:

> I want to live in these mountains; I do not want to go to Tularosa. That is a long ways off. The flies on those mountains eat out the eyes of the horses. The bad spirits live there. I have drunk of these waters and they have cooled me, I do not want to leave here.[58]

Cochise had never agreed to removal, yet his objections barely fazed Granger and Pope, who casually dismissed his importance and even granted him permission to leave Cañada Alamosa in order to communicate with the hostile Chiricahuas and "try to persuade [them] to go to Tularosa." The council ended on March 20. Within ten days Cochise left, with the consent of Granger and Pope, with only a slim chance of returning as long as the new reservation was to be at Tularosa.[59]

Chapter 18

DRINK THE SAME WATER, EAT THE SAME
BREAD: THE COCHISE-HOWARD TREATY

A few days after the Granger talk, Cochise left the reservation with
the stated intention of rounding up members of his band who had
remained hostile, yet clearly this was not his only reason for leaving. He had no desire to relocate at Tularosa, and he may have been
hoping that his departure would convince the Americans to cancel
or postpone the removal. According to an informed source, he
"could not have been induced to go there [Tularosa] under any
consideration." [1]

Even so, the new reservation was established and Cochise looked
for alternatives. Casting another glance at northern Mexico, he
again courted Janos, remaining near it for some time before pressure
from Mexican troops forced him to return to Arizona. During the
summer of 1872, his warriors resumed their old way of life: raiding,
torturing, and murdering, particularly in southern Arizona. Cochise
took no part in these hostilities, ostensibly remaining in camp to
protect his people from the seemingly omnipresent U.S. patrols. It
was in this setting that a new peace commissioner, General Oliver
Otis Howard, with Tom Jeffords's help, found Cochise in the fall
of 1872.

Cochise left Cañada Alamosa about March 30 or April 1 in typical Apache fashion: neither the military nor the Indian agent had
a definite idea of where he had gone. [2] Devin said he heard that

Cochise had returned to the Chiricahuas but was dubious because "I think he has had enough and only wants to be left alone."[3] In early April, Captain Shorkley at Fort McRae, responding to an inquiry from Crook, informed district headquarters in Santa Fe that neither "Cochise nor his men were at the reservation and are not likely to return."[4] Piper seemed bewildered and was unwilling to hazard a guess as to Cochise's whereabouts.[5]

Whether Cochise would return was a subject of debate among whites who knew him. Before leaving he reportedly told José García, a citizen from Palomas who occasionally supplied the reservation with beef, that he would be absent for about a month to "find members of his band" and bring them to the reservation.[6] Another person close to the scene wrote the *Missouri Republican* that Cochise "has gone off, by permission, to try to induce some more of his band to come in. . . . No doubt is entertained by those who know him of his being back by the time and at the place appointed. All fears in regard to Cochise may be at once dismissed."[7]

Once he was off the reservation and in the mountains he considered home, Cochise's decision was easily made. He had never been a reservation Indian and good weather was approaching; furthermore, he was unable to persuade all of his Chokonens to move to Tularosa. If the reserve had remained at Cañada Alamosa or if the agent had been Steck or Jeffords instead of Piper, Cochise might have returned. To avoid American troops, he made his way back into the mountains and again turned to Janos for refuge and supplies.

By mid-April 1872, some two weeks after leaving, Cochise sent a runner to Tom Jeffords informing him that he was moving farther west. Either for security or protection, he asked Jeffords to accompany him, leaving his options open in case he decided to return to New Mexico. Jeffords had to refuse; he had recently broken some ribs in a fall and was not up to the rigors of travel.[8]

In the meantime, plans were drafted in early April to move the Apaches from Cañada Alamosa to Tularosa. Piper eventually succeeded in relocating 350 Indians from Victorio's, Loco's, and Gordo's bands, to hated Tularosa,[9] assisted by Jeffords and Zebina Nathaniel Streeter.[10] By the end of May, Chiva brought his group of

60 or 70 Bedonkohes and/or Chokonens to Tularosa. Cochise had "told him to take his people to Tularosa, saying that he would follow if they were well treated at the agency." [11]

All involved in the move pronounced it a success despite the absence of a thousand Apaches who had fled Cañada Alamosa and were roaming southern Arizona and New Mexico. The previous October, Piper estimated that 1,900 Apaches were on the reserve, almost certainly an unintentionally inflated number. Of these, only 350 went to Tularosa, leaving more than 1,500 Indians to account for. Cochise's following, perhaps 300 individuals, had left for Arizona and northern Mexico. Another 400 had moved east of the Río Grande to the Mescaleros' reservation at Fort Stanton, where they were unwelcome visitors. The remainder were in southern New Mexico.

Many of the Apaches had gone to join Nana and his son-in-law Horache, both of whom had left Cañada Alamosa the previous December, at Fort Stanton. On May 1, Ponce,[12] a son-in-law of Cochise described as "about 35 years old [with] a stutter in his speech," and Escani took 305 Indians to Fort Stanton, hoping to remain there. Their appearance startled Captain James Franklin Randlett, who informed Devin: "They [Ponce and Escani] stated that the band had left Canada Alamosa about five weeks since . . . that Mr. Piper knew they were coming to visit their relatives here, that they would like to remain here until the rainy season." Randlett refused their request but was dismayed because the Mescaleros' agent, A. J. Curtis, had rationed the Apaches when they arrived.[13]

Once Tularosa was established, Devin had orders to round up all Indians off the reservation and force them in. Although he had enough troops to snap the whip at the laggard Chiricahuas, he had to do so without antagonizing those who were off the agency. The task required great delicacy and the implementation of a firm policy. The Indian Bureau and the military, however, were indecisive in their actions.

Devin faced a series of delays which postponed his military action. Originally he was to treat as hostile any Apaches not at Tularosa by April 29. On May 5 he arrived at Tularosa, where he lingered for a few days before moving to Fort Craig on May 9, where he received a request from Pope "that I commence no operations . . . until the Indians have a little more time—say June 1."[14] It was believed that every Chiricahua who intended to go to the reservation would be there by that time. The rest were spread throughout the territory, and scattered raiding had resumed in southern New Mexico. A correspondent for the *Missouri Republican* conceded that the policy was a failure because of delays in carrying it out. The program should have been implemented "vigorously and at once. It is sheer madness vacillating so long between the policy of Extermination and . . . Reservation."[15]

Throughout May, both Pope and Piper continued to think Cochise would return, but their hopes dissipated with reports of renewed Apache depredations in New Mexico and Arizona and rumors that Cochise had made peace at Janos. On the last day of May, Piper reported that "one of Cochise's men is here and it is thought that he has been sent to see how things were here."[16]

Chokonen raiders made Arizona aware of their presence. On May 1 at Fort Bowie the tracks of about thirty Indians were discovered near the post herd, but they were unable to steal it. Their trail continued south.[17] Three days later at the foot of Stein's Peak, a small group of Chiricahuas ambushed and killed mail rider Henry Abrahams, mutilated his body, and burned his buckboard. Merejildo Grijalva discovered the remains and determined that the Apaches had come from the Burro Mountains.[18] Later that month it was reported from El Paso that Cochise and about three hundred Apaches were at Janos; this was corroborated by eyewitnesses. He had clearly rejected Tularosa.[19]

By mid-May most of the Chokonen and Nednhi bands were in northern Chihuahua; the former had moved there to avoid U.S. troops, the latter to escape persistent Sonoran campaigns into the Pitaicache and Espuellas mountains, which had kept Juh's followers on the run. Eventually they moved into Chihuahua and Janos to elude the aggressors. In late April and early May, three Sonoran detachments scoured the usual Apache strongholds. Lieutenant Manuel Gallegos and forty men patrolled toward the Pitaicaches, Lieutenant Joaquin Samaniego and thirty men traversed the San Pedro along the Sonora-Chihuahua border, and Colonel Cayetano Silva with another force reconnoitered the mountains along the Arizona-Sonora boundary. This offensive compelled the truculent spirits led by Juh and Geronimo to enter Chihuahua and solicit peace at Janos. According to their messenger, they numbered thirty-three men and had been living in the Pitaicache Mountains. One of the warriors admitted that they had "suffered much from misery and hunger a consequence of the repeated Sonora campaigns. They are unable to prepare their mescal, that they are forced to live all their time in the hills; that recently two babies had died from hunger." Moreover, if peace were granted, Juh even consented to join Mexican troops against hostiles, which, considering his reputation, would indeed have been a sight to behold.[20]

Once the Nednhis opened negotiations, Cochise sent in two of his captains, Julian and Collali, and soon after that Remigio and Peñon[21] (probably the notorious Pionsenay). When convinced that no treachery was planned, he himself came in, undoubtedly to do some trading and renew old acquaintances. Since the civil authorities at Janos were not empowered to consummate a treaty, they instructed the Apaches to proceed to Galeana for further talks, but there were too many bad memories there and the Apaches stayed clear. In any event, Cochise was at Janos (at least two individuals told Devin they had seen him there) and remained in the vicinity for perhaps a month. He probably received reports about Tularosa and contemplated his next move.[22]

Devin feared that Cochise would use Janos as a base from which to raid on both sides of the border, and almost certainly this occurred to some extent. In late June, Cochise was again reported near Janos, where he probably remained until early July, when Sonoran troops crossed the border and destroyed Juh's ranchería in the Carcai Mountains. The entire camp was captured and ransacked. After this attack, Cochise crossed the border and returned to Arizona, probably to the southern Chiricahuas, before eventually returning to his beloved Dragoons.[23]

Once in Arizona, Cochise's captains were dispatched in different directions to make a living. He was through raiding and now spent his time planning and coordinating forays; he had groomed his son Taza, now in his late twenties, to succeed him. As his father had been, Taza was well trained for a leadership role. With Cochise's war chief, Nahilzay, Taza led many raids in the Sonoita Valley, which erupted in violence in the summer of 1872. The soldiers could do little to stop or even slow down the raiders. In mid-June a scout from Camp Grant examined the Dragoons but found no Indian sign. Late in the month another scout under Lieutenant Charles Bendire pursued Apaches into the Dragoons and recovered some twenty head of cattle; apparently this was a Chokonen group which subsequently moved northeast to the Stein's Peak area. Although Cochise's whereabouts were unknown, by midsummer 1872 he had returned to the Dragoons, from which he could either move to the Chiricahuas or slip back into Mexico.[24]

In late July, Devin's troops, scouting the Arizona–New Mexico border under Lieutenant William Stephenson, struck a Chokonen band in the upper Sulphur Springs Valley a few miles south of the lofty Graham Mountains. Climbing a steep mountain, the Americans spotted the Indians and charged the ranchería. The Apaches deserted their camp, making "but feeble resistance, firing a few shots." The troops killed one and "captured and burnt sixteen large lodges, together with several hundred pounds of mescal, all their camp equipage." Other confiscated material revealed that these Indians had been at Cañada Alamosa and had also "recently been trading with Mexicans," probably at Janos. This group numbered sixty individuals and was believed to be a "part of Cochise's that sent Colonel Bendire out of Dragoon Pass about a month ago."

Stephenson marched to Fort Bowie and while there met Merejildo Grijalva, who declared that the "bags, moccasins and beadwork captured . . . are the same as those made by the women of Cochise's band." From Bowie, Stephenson's command headed south and on August 6 destroyed a ranchería in the southeast Chiricahuas and succeeded in killing two Apaches, according to one report, before returning to Fort Bayard.[25]

With American troops swarming throughout their territory, some Chokonens (even Cochise himself, according to one report) apparently considered moving to Tularosa. At the end of August a band of White Mountain Apaches ran into some of Cochise's people, perhaps the same group Stephenson hit in Sulphur Springs Valley. They told the Coyoteros they "were going to Tularosa and that Cheis had already started to reach there that moon," which would have

meant early September. With winter approaching and Cochise's options fast dwindling, he might have considered Tularosa, but he remained in southern Arizona and Apache raids continued.[26]

Many of these were the work of Cochise's people. On August 27,
Lieutenant Reid T. Stewart, a popular young officer, left Camp Crittenden to attend a court-martial in Tucson. A small escort accompanied him but could not travel fast enough for the impetuous officer, so he took the buckboard and his driver, Corporal Joseph P. G.
Black, and pushed ahead of the escort. Black, who had carried the
mail over this same route for three years, protested but was overruled by Stewart, who had boasted, "I am not afraid of these
Apaches. I can lick a whole regiment of them."[27] About 11 A.M.
they entered Davidson Canyon, located between the Empire and
Santa Rita mountains. The Apaches were waiting. Possibly led by
Taza, they killed Stewart quickly with a bullet in the head. Black
attempted to escape but the Indians captured him, tied him to a tree,
and tortured him to death. The escort arrived too late and, finding
itself outnumbered, continued on through the canyon to Tucson.
That same day, Apaches murdered seven Mexicans in the Santa
Cruz and Sonoita valleys.[28]

These ferocious raids prompted many southwesterners, including
Crook, to doubt Cochise's sincerity about peace. Most Americans
were skeptical with good reason: Cochise had talked peace with
Perry in February 1869 and Green in August 1870 and had stayed at
and left Cañada Alamosa in the fall of 1871 and the spring of 1872.
Very few cared or understood why he had left and why he continued
raiding; what was clear was that his people had reverted to their old
way of life.

The situation became so hazardous in the Sonoita Valley that several farmers seriously considered abandoning their homes as soon
as they harvested their crops. Thomas Gardner, whom Cochise
wounded in the early sixties, declared that he would "willingly
make a fast, firm treaty . . . and give them [Apaches] one quarter of
all he raised."[29] All in all, Cochise's actions contradicted what he
had said the previous fall.

Like his predecessor, Vincent Colyer, Brigadier General Oliver
Otis Howard was a humanitarian and a deeply religious man. Born
in Leeds, Maine, in 1830, he entered West Point after graduating

General Oliver Otis Howard. He negotiated a final truce with Cochise in October 1872. Although the truce was flawed in some respects, it did bring peace to southeastern Arizona for the first time in over a decade. (*Courtesy National Archives*)

from Bowdoin College in 1850. He finished fourth in a class of
forty-six and taught mathematics at West Point until the outbreak of
the Civil War. In June 1861 he resigned his commission to become
colonel of the Third Maine Regiment. He saw action in several
major battles, losing his right arm at the Battle of Fair Oaks on May
31, 1862. By the end of the war, he had been promoted to brigadier
general of the army and major general of the volunteers. During the
war he became known as the Christian Soldier, which undoubtedly
helped him receive an appointment as commissioner of the Freed-
man's Bureau, an organization charged with supervision of roughly
four million liberated slaves; a more concerned man could not have
been chosen for a virtually impossible task, for Howard brought
honesty, compassion, and humane convictions. At the same time,
his lack of administrative skills, his idealistic and simplistic views,
and his universal trust in his fellow man set off a round of rampant
corruption.[30]

In February 1872, with the threat of renewed Apache hostilities
and recognition that Colyer's mission had not solved the Apache
problem, Secretary of the Interior Charles Delano concluded to send
the scrupulously honest Howard to Arizona and New Mexico to
"take such action as, in your judgement, may be deemed best for
the purpose of preserving peace with the Indians in these territories." Furthermore, wrote Delano,

> the Department invests you with full powers and a general discretion,
> to be exercised, as your own good judgement may dictate in carrying
> into effect its views in relation to these Indians. . . . The great object
> of the government is: *First* to preserve peace between the U.S. and
> these as well as all other tribes of Indians. *Second:* To induce them to
> abandon their present habits of life and go upon permanent
> reservations.[31]

Howard was acceptable to both church and humanitarian groups and
the military. He also would outrank every officer in the Southwest.
His main objective, he later recalled, was "to make peace with the
warlike Chiricahuas under Cochise."[32]

Crook was displeased about the arrival of another commissioner,
which once again forced him to delay military action. The fact that

Howard outranked him seemed to chafe him even more. Howard reached Arizona in April and on the fifteenth met with Crook, whom he thought was "a very fine officer ready to work heavily with me."[33] It was a cautious, correct courtesy call, but rapport did not develop. The pragmatic Crook did not reciprocate the same respect toward Howard. Questioning Howard's incessant piety, which to Crook seemed incongruous in Apache country, he incredulously complained that Howard was "clothed with even greater powers than those given Mr. Colyer."[34]

One of Howard's first requests of Crook was to meet Cochise, then thought to be at Cañada Alamosa. Accordingly, Crook wrote Granger and requested that Cochise be furnished an escort to Fort Apache. By this time, however, Cochise had left the reserve and an interview could not be arranged.[35]

Howard recalled that he heard only the phrase "kill em, kill em" as the solution to the Apache problem. In late May he reached Fort Apache and made several fruitless attempts to communicate with the Chiricahuas. He did succeed in appeasing Western Apache bands and took a delegation of Arizona Indians to Washington, where he arrived on June 20. After a short stay, countless interviews and speeches, and a meeting with President Grant, the delegation left Washington on July 10. Before returning to Arizona, however, they detoured to New York to visit Vincent Colyer and the Dutch Reform Society of New York before resuming the 2,500-mile journey west.[36] Howard's assistant this trip was a young and courageous officer of medium height with black hair and a heavy mustache. His name was Lieutenant Joseph Alton Sladen.[37]

Howard reached Santa Fe in early August and conferred with Nathaniel Pope, asking his advice about the best way to communicate with Cochise. Pope said Jeffords once delivered a message to Cochise and "that he was confident that the man had dealt honestly with him."[38] Howard's next stop was Fort Apache, where he made plans to communicate with Cochise, who was believed to be in southern Arizona. On August 12 he wrote his wife:

I find by rumors of depredations below here that Cochise and his band are likely to be reached from here as from Tularosa and so I may be delayed at this post longer than I had anticipated, starting from

Lieutenant Joseph A. Sladen. Howard's capable aide, he spent an interesting ten days in Cochise's camp and discovered that the Apaches were human beings after all. (*Carlisle Barracks Photo, Joseph A. Sladen Collection, U.S. Army Military History Institute, Carlisle Barracks, PA*)

here to meet Cochise if possible. I am trying to communicate with
Cochise. I find I cannot hurry and may be delayed some time.[39]

Two days later he reiterated these plans to Herman Bendell (superintendent of Indian affairs in Arizona) and dispatched Concepción (a
Mexican raised by Aravaipa Apaches) and George Stevens[40] to locate Cochise and procure an interview.

Howard waited for two weeks until Concepción and Stevens returned, unsuccessful in their mission. "Not ready to give up the
chase," he decided to make one last attempt to find Cochise through
the disenchanted Chihennes living at Tularosa. While at Fort
Apache he and Sladen had learned of "a mysterious white man
known to the Mescalero [Chihennes] who had visited Cochise frequently and was on friendly terms with him, and who could, if he
chose, find Cochise and carry to him any message."[41]

Before leaving Fort Apache, he tactfully wrote Crook and apologized for having interfered in Arizona affairs and "making such
radical changes, but . . . I feel assured that you know that my purpose is fixed to help you all I can." Crook was not convinced and
the letter only irritated him because he felt that Howard's sancti-
monious actions were insincere and unrealistic for the Arizona
frontier.[42]

Howard and his party started for Tularosa on August 30. The second day out they met a man named Milligan and quartered at his
ranch, "the only dwelling between Camp Apache and Fort
Tularosa," some seventy miles southeast of Fort Apache. Milligan
corroborated what Howard and Sladen had heard there, stating that
Jeffords was the only white man who could communicate with Cochise.[43] On September 4 while approaching Tularosa, Fred Hughes,
"the Tularosa interpreter," met the party with a letter from Piper
saying that the Chihennes "were fearfully discontented" and that
many had left the reservation; only three hundred remained. En
route, Hughes and Howard talked about Cochise, the former telling
the general that he had heard "from the Indians at Tularosa enough
to satisfy me that Cochise was ready to make peace." To accomplish
this, he also advised Howard to find "Captain Jeffords to take with
him on his mission as Jeffords had already met Cochise and the
latter had taken quite a liking to him."[44]

Reaching Tularosa, Howard dispatched Jake May, his Spanish interpreter, to Cañada Alamosa to bring Jeffords in. Next he met Agent Piper, who he thought "had a good heart . . . tried to do his duty and do right, but the Indians for some unknown reason do not like him." Shortly after that he held a council with Victorio, Loco, Nana, and Chiva. Howard was impressed with Victorio, whom he described as "a fine looking man . . . about five feet ten and well formed." But the leader who really caught his eye was Nana, a "very thick set [man] with a large head—much bigger than mine." The general sympathized with the Indians' main complaint: that they were forced from Cañada Alamosa to Tularosa over their objections.[45]

While Howard tried to placate the Chihennes, agreeing to visit Cañada Alamosa and inspect it, Jeffords arrived at Fort Tularosa on September 7. He had been out with troops trying to round up hostiles who had refused to move;[46] he had spent most of the summer in the vicinity of the reservation, renewing his request for permission to build a trading post. He was in Luther's store when General Howard approached and introduced himself. Jeffords later conceded that he had been skeptical of the general "on account of his well known humanitarian ideas, and to my mind, posing as a Christian soldier."[47]

After introductions, Howard asked Jeffords to find Cochise and bring him in for an interview. After "considerable deliberation," Jeffords responded: "General Howard, Cochise won't come. The man that wants to talk to Cochise must go where he is. . . . I'll tell you what I'll do, I will take you to Cochise. Will you go there with me, General, without soldiers?" Howard quickly replied, "Yes, if necessary." The frontiersman may have been testing the general, not believing that the latter would accept his offer, but Howard was determined to complete his mission and bring peace to the Southwest.[48]

For the next week Jeffords made preparations for the journey while Howard, Piper, and Pope met with the Chihennes, who used every argument they could think of to be returned to Cañada Alamosa. During the council the Indians' disrespect for Piper surfaced. Victorio said "the agent is getting old and he had better go home and see his children, and take care of them." [49] It was no coincidence that two days later Piper requested a leave of absence, which Howard granted, evidently believing that the diligent but miscast Piper and the restless Apaches would be better off without each other. On September 16 he issued Piper a thirty-day leave with permission to apply in Washington for an additional thirty days. In effect, this released Piper from his arduous duties. The general promised to use his influence to find Piper other employment with the Indian Bureau. [50]

On September 16, Howard, Jeffords, Loco, and Chie examined Cañada Alamosa, after which Howard acquiesced and decided that the government should scrap the ill-advised Tularosa and return the Apaches to Cañada Alamosa under the assumption that all of the Chiricahuas, including Cochise, would come in. At this time no one had any conception that the venerable chief might have other ideas.

Another important development took place that day. Evidently with Nathaniel Pope's support, Howard appointed Tom Jeffords agent for the proposed Cochise Reservation, which he planned to reestablish at Cañada Alamosa:

> For the special work of gathering the nomadic Apache Indians upon the 'Cachise Reservation' and of being their agent subsequently, subject to the regulations of the Indian Bureau, I hereby appoint Thomas J. Jeffords. He will report to the Supt. of Indian Affairs for New Mexico and be under instructions from here and higher authorities. [51]

This contrasts with the traditional version, as related by Jeffords, that Cochise insisted upon him as agent and that Howard had to persuade him to accept the job. As a matter of fact, Jeffords willingly accepted the position even before the historic pact was agreed to, although his appointment undoubtedly helped the final outcome. The boundaries of the proposed reservation were set:

> The Rio Grande to be the Eastern boundary—the northern line commencing at a point six miles on the Rio Grande north of the mouth of the Rio Canada and running direct to the summit of the south end of the San Mateo Mountains and thence westerly to include the springs known as "Canada de Alamo" . . . to a southerly direction along the summit of the Mimbres Mountains to a point known as "Mule

Springs" or "Oak Grove" a point about 14 miles north of Fort Cummings. South line to run in an easterly direction to the Rio Grande
just including Fort Thorn or as sometimes called "Santa Barbara."
Add to this the Sierra del Caballo.[52]

Who would have thought that Cochise might have other plans?

With affairs settled, Jeffords and Howard focused on the arrangements for locating Cochise. At Tularosa, Jeffords had convinced
Chie[53] to accompany the party, provided they could find Ponce, a
relative by marriage to Cochise, and procure his services. Howard
sent the supply wagon, driven by Albert Bloomfield, to Fort Craig.
Bloomfield, a Frenchman, had come to Arizona in 1861 and was
well known to Victorio's people. He was ordered to replenish supplies before proceeding to Fort Bowie. Jeffords also enlisted the
help of Zebina Streeter, the so-called White Apache, expanding the
party to five white men: Howard, Sladen, Jeffords, May, and
Streeter. Before leaving Cañada Alamosa, Howard bought a horse
for Chie in payment for his services.

They departed on September 18, 1872, to search for Ponce, who
had the "ability to guide us to the old chief's camp." They found
him and his band of fifty-nine, including notorious raiders Ramón
Chico and Sánchez, on the Cuchillo Negro River and persuaded him
to accompany the party. To do so, Howard provided him with a
horse and allowed his group to remain at Cuchillo, where they
would be furnished subsistence until their chief returned.[54]

On September 19, the party complete, Jeffords and his two
Apaches began the task of finding Cochise, who was believed to be
in the Chiricahuas.[55] Leaving the small settlement of Cuchillo, they
struck out southwest, probably rounding the Mimbres Mountains to
the south and reaching Fort Bayard on September 23. Supplies re-
plenished, the next day they resumed their search, continuing west
toward the Gila and halting at Silver City to have a horse shod.
Howard purchased two shirts for his Indian guides and hired a cook
named J. H. Stone. Before leaving, the general gave a speech on the
peace policy (which the hardy miners probably scoffed at) and then
resumed the march. About ten miles west of Silver City, the party
encountered a group of prospectors led by James Bullard, whose
brother John had been killed by Cochise's band in February 1871.

To the general's astonishment, Bullard wanted to kill the Indians, which Howard courageously prevented by stepping in front of Chie and Ponce, saying, "You will kill me first." Bullard left, "cursing the peace policy," although after Howard's success he acknowledged that he had been wrong and that the mission benefited the Southwest.[56]

They struck the Gila near Redrock before sweeping south toward the Peloncillos. In these foothills Chie and Ponce found signs indicating that "Cochise Apaches" had been in the vicinity. They astounded Sladen and Howard by announcing "the number of the party, the band which they belonged, and the time that had elapsed since they were here." Finally, about September 27, at a place Howard called Peracino Springs (several miles north of Stein's Peak), they succeeded in communicating with Nazee, a Chokonen leader, who soon brought his entourage of sixty into camp. This was probably the group Stephenson had struck in late July. One old woman, "wrinkled and haggard," was a wife of Cochise. Nazee revealed that the chief was in the Dragoon Mountains.

Nazee admonished the general to reduce his party if he wished to see Cochise.[57] This alarmed Sladen, but not an impervious Howard. Convinced of divine guidance, he sent Streeter, May, and Stone to Fort Bowie with a note to the commanding officer ordering him to "send out no scouts in this direction or in any, to interfere with the peace I am in a fair way of making." Streeter and company arrived at Bowie on September 29.[58]

Howard, Sladen, Jeffords, Chie, and Ponce entered the Sulphur Springs Valley "aiming for a depression in the Dragoon Mountains, a dozen of fifteen miles south of the Tucson Road called Middlemarch Pass."[59] They spent the evening of the twenty-ninth at the Sulphur Springs station. At midnight they departed, reaching the foothills of the Dragoons early the next morning, where they made a dry camp. At dawn, after only a few hours' sleep, they entered the Dragoons, with Ponce and Chie making smoke signals to indicate that their party had come in peace before going into camp.

Early that afternoon Chie left. A few hours later two young Indian boys appeared to guide them to the Apache camp. Taking a "long steep tiresome ride until the summit was reached," they finally emerged into the west stronghold. Here a few Chokonens under

Middlemarch Pass, Dragoon Mountains. Howard's party entered the mountains through this pass in search of Cochise. (*Photo by Karen Hayes*)

a warrior named Tygee were camped. To everyone's disappointment, Cochise was camped a few miles away and would not meet Howard's party until the next morning. The uncertainty about how he perceived their presence and his making Howard wait another day fostered an air of pessimism. Sladen was dubious of their prospects: "None seemed to know how he would react to them bringing two white men into his camp." Only Howard remained sanguine, believing that the major obstacles had been overcome.

Cochise had been watching their progress for several days. From the high peaks in the Dragoons, it has been said, his eagle-eyed scouts could discern troops as they left Apache Pass. Only through the presence of Jeffords and his two relatives had he allowed Howard access to his camp, which, as it turned out, made Howard a welcome visitor.

Early that morning (October 1), word spread through Tygee's camp that "he is coming." Immediately the Indians formed in a circle and spread blankets to receive their chief. Cochise's brother Juan, "a fierce looking Indian . . . short and thickset" arrived first, armed with a spear and bow and arrows. He dismounted, warmly embraced Jeffords, and was introduced to Howard. Moments later, Cochise arrived with his sister,[60] his youngest wife, and youngest son, Naiche. He "dashed to where we were gathered from his horse, and gave Jeffords the same warm greeting that Juan had accorded him." Next he turned to Howard, and Jeffords introduced him, saying to Howard, "This is the man." Cochise shook hands, responding, "Buenos días, Señor." After affectionately greeting Ponce and Chie, the chief was next introduced to Sladen: he shook Sladen's hand and repeated the welcome he gave Howard.

Before discussing business, Cochise spoke with Jeffords, Chie, and Ponce. He asked Jeffords whether the general would talk honestly and "do as they say they will." Jeffords replied, "Well, I don't know, I think they will but I will see that they don't promise too much." Next Cochise interrogated Ponce and Chie for about ten minutes, wanting to know everything about Howard: his history, status, and objectives.

As Cochise conversed with Ponce and Chie, Sladen carefully studied the chief, describing him as

> a remarkably fine looking man fully six feet tall, as straight as an arrow, and well proportioned, the typical Indian face, rather long, high cheek bones, clear keen eyes and a Roman nose. . . . A yellow silk handkerchief bound his hair, which was straight and black, with just a touch of silver.[61]

Satisfied with Ponce's and Chie's report, Cochise turned to Howard and asked the purpose of his visit. The general succinctly replied that "I have come from Washington to meet your people and make peace, and will stay as long as necessary." Cochise responded:

> Nobody wants peace more than I do. I have done no mischief since I came from Canada Alamosa, but I am poor, my horses are poor and I have but few, I might have got more by raiding on the Tucson Road, but I did not do it.[62]

Howard proposed to consolidate the Chokonens and the Chihennes and remove the Tularosa agency to Cañada Alamosa. To everyone's surprise, Cochise initially objected, declaring that he himself would go, "but I am sure it would break my band." Then he surprised Howard and Sladen by suddenly asking, "Why not give me Apache Pass? Give me that and I will protect all the roads. I will see that nobody's property is taken by Indians."[63] He refused to make a decision until he talked the matter over with his captains, who were out raiding—or, as Cochise euphemistically termed it, "making a living." Howard agreed to wait until the chief could gather his people.

At once runners were sent out to bring in his men. Fearing that his returning warriors might clash with troops, Cochise insisted that Howard ride to Fort Bowie to notify all troops that a "cease fire was in effect." At first the general demurred, proposing to send Sladen. Cochise objected, saying, "The soldiers may not obey Captain [Lieutenant] Sladen. They will obey you. I want you to go. Jeffords and Captain Sladen can stay here." In a way, the chief was testing Howard's sincerity, wondering whether the general would back his words with action. The general acquiesced and later that same day departed for Bowie with Chie as his guide.[64]

The pair traveled throughout the night, with the most arduous part of the journey spent crossing the Dragoons' "rugged heights and deep gulches." Howard tore his "coat in shreds, pricked my legs with thorns." Through Chie's perseverance and expertise, they finally reached the Sulphur Springs stage station about midnight, where Nick Rogers, the station keeper, took them on to Apache Pass. On October 2, Captain Samuel Storrow Sumner reported to General Crook:

> At 7AM this morning the general accompanied by one Indian reached this place. He had . . . met Cochise yesterday. General Howard left here at 2PM today on his return to the Dragoon Mountains. . . . He requested that no scouting parties be sent out from this point during the present position of affairs.[65]

Howard also telegraphed the commissioner of Indian affairs in Washington and instructed the commanding officer at Fort Lowell to notify "Crittenden and other posts near you and General Crook that they [Indians] may not be fired upon when doing no mischief."[66]

Sumner furnished Howard with supplies: two thousand pounds of corn, a sack of coffee, sugar, and flour plus some cloth purchased from the post trader. Sumner concluded optimistically that "there seems to be some liklihood of getting Cochise to go on a reservation," yet he was perplexed that Howard was considering including the area around Apache Pass.[67]

With provisions and accompanied by his entire party (Bloomfield, May, Streeter, and Stone), Howard started the forty-mile return trip to the Dragoons. They spent the first night (October 2) at the Sulphur Springs station. The next morning they cut through Dragoon Pass to the western side of the mountains, where they were met by Sladen, Jeffords, and several Indians. They learned that Cochise had relocated his camp a few miles northeast of the west stronghold the night before after one of his raiding parties returned and reported they had killed several whites. On September 30, these warriors had ambushed Sergeant George Stewart's party near Thomas Gardner's ranch, killing four of the six soldiers. Cochise said he didn't "think the troops can follow the trail of my Indians but if they do, they will be in here to-night and we will have a fight." No troops were near, but Cochise was not one to take chances, so he moved his camp into the inaccessible heights of the Dragoons, where the "entire band could at a moment easily conceal themselves behind boulders and crags."[68]

The next day, October 4, the ranchería was moved back to the west stronghold, where all awaited the return of Cochise's subchiefs to discuss peace. Howard and Sladen spent the next week in the stronghold, although Sladen apparently made one trip to Bowie. The two officers left behind interesting accounts of life in an Apache camp and furnished a good description of Cochise's character, intelligence, and the autocratic influence he held over his followers. On one of Sladen's first nights among the Chokonens, he witnessed a Chiricahua tiswin drunk: "Suddenly I heard sharp screams from Cochise's wife and sister and I saw them fleeing in terror from his bivouack. He was striking and scolding them and his voice was loud and harsh." Sladen was extremely relieved when Jeffords assumed control of the situation and calmed Cochise down.

Another incident described by Sladen illustrated Cochise's pragmatic ways. A wounded warrior had arrived at camp, probably from the September 30 fight near Gardner's ranch. He "was kept hidden away among the rocks" and the Americans could hear Cochise praying for his recovery "to the Great Father" and "the response of the assembly—for all the Indians had gathered around him." Because

Sladen had a medical background, Howard offered his services. "But Cochise would not consent to this. His reply was most sensible. The man was dangerously ill and might die . . . if he did die my people . . . would think that the Captain [Sladen] had given him bad medicine and they would want to kill him." Sladen agreed.[69]

Each day, one or more of Cochise's captains returned and reported to him. Sladen described the scene:

> Their return was always noticed with some formality. When they rode up they went at once to the stone where Cochise was seated, dismounted and sat down upon the ground, with great deliberation, and without any demonstration of emotion of any kind, they reported to the Chief; a short conversation ensued, in an ordinary tone, as if they had been present all the time, and then they retired to some hiding place to their own immediate family.[70]

As late as October 7, Howard continued to push for Cañada Alamosa as the reservation site.[71] The first captain to return was a thirty-five-year-old warrior named Nahilzay,[72] Cochise's brother-in-law, who strongly favored peace. But as more and more Apaches came in, many "rough and very troublesome," combined with Cochise's feeling that a reservation in Arizona would "cancel all old scores," the general gradually acquiesced to the chief's desires, rationalizing that it was the only way to keep them content.

On October 10 the last captain returned. He was "a short and stout man" who acted as Cochise's interpreter from Apache to Spanish. Sladen wrote that he was "a very important factor in the negotiations and the old chief often deferred to and referred important questions to him before deciding them." He was an obstreperous individual disliked by both Howard and Sladen. He "had been captured by the Mexicans as a child and had been a captive among them for many years." His identity is not definitely known but, given these descriptions, he may have been El Cautivo, the Captive, who was involved in the Dodge murder of 1856 and was with Cochise near Fronteras in October 1858. He was the last of Cochise's captains to return; only Taza and another leader were beyond recall, raiding in Sonora.[73]

The identity of the captains is somewhat in doubt because neither Howard, Sladen, nor Jeffords left behind a list of them. From piec-

ing together all of the available evidence, I believe the following Indians were captains in Cochise's band and possibly attended the
council. Strong cases can be made for Cullah (Collali), Remigio,
Julián, Peñon, Eskinya, Nahilzay, Nazee, Nasakee (Nah-zar-zee),
Tygee (Targash), Chacone, José Manda, and El Cautivo. Besides
these twelve Chokonens, two other warriors were up-and-coming
leaders within the Chokonen band: Chato and Chihuahua.

Cullah, Remigio, Julián, and Peñon had been with Cochise at
Janos in the spring of 1872. Cullah, born about 1825, had succeeded Yaque as chief of one group and survived the smallpox epidemic of 1862. He accompanied Taza to Washington in 1876 and
headed a small Chokonen group at San Carlos in 1877. Remigio
had succeeded Esquinaline in the early 1860s and had fought under
Cochise during the 1860s. Julián had succeeded Cochise's old friend
Elías as leader of a small extended family group in the late 1860s.
Pionsenay, or Peñon, was a first-rate Chokonen incorrigible whose
actions led to the closing of Cochise's reservation in 1876. Pionsenay's brother or half-brother was Eskinya, a member of Elías's and
Tace's group in the early 1860s. He was said to have been Cochise's
head medicine man and one of the more influential leaders within
the Chokonen band. As has been mentioned, Nahilzay was Cochise's war chief and was well known to both Fred Hughes and General Howard. He also appeared on the San Carlos census in 1880 as
a member of Naiche's band. In addition to these six, there were two
other old-time Chokonen leaders who might have been captains.
José Manda had been a subordinate of Cochise throughout the 1860s
and may have been with him at Cañada Alamosa in 1871–72.
Chacone, whose followers were attacked in the Dragoons by Bernard in January 1870, may have been present if he was still living.

The three Americans mentioned three other leaders: Nazee, a
prominent Chokonen man, went to San Carlos with Taza and was a
member of Naiche's band in the 1880 and 1884 censuses. Nasakee
was with Pionsenay in the 1876 outbreak. Tygee passed from the
scene by the mid-1870s.

Chato and Chihuahua, two Chokonen leaders of the 1880s, were
probably on Cochise's reservation, but whether they attended the
historic conference is not definitely known. In later years Chato
spoke openly about his life on Cochise's reservation and may have

Council Rocks. Located on the western slopes of the Dragoon Mountains, this was the probable location where Cochise and Howard met. (*Photo by Karen Hayes*)

accompanied Taza to San Carlos.[74] Fred Hughes recalled that Chihuahua was on Cochise's reservation, a fact corroborated by the informants of Mrs. Eve Ball. He accompanied Taza to San Carlos.[75]

Finally, there is the Indian I have identified as El Cautivo, Cochise's interpreter. In later years Sladen came to the logical conclusion that this man was Geronimo, based on his physical appearance and cruel and vindictive mannerisms. But he was almost certainly wrong. Sladen mentioned that this man had been a captive among the Mexicans, a description that does not apply to Geronimo. However, the evidence is equivocal regarding Geronimo's presence. Neither Howard nor Jeffords made any mention of him, and the reliable Fred Hughes claimed that Geronimo came to the reservation with Juh's Nednhis in November 1872; Charles T. Connell reported the same. Nonetheless, Geronimo claimed he was present and years later Captain Samuel Sumner confirmed this in a letter to Sladen.[76] Sumner should have known because he was at the council and also commanded Fort Bowie in 1872–73. In any event, if the notorious Geronimo was present, he played an inconspicuous role.

The Indians held a council among themselves the next day. Wrote Jeffords:

> General Howard wished to attend this pow-wow but I told him to stay where he was; that they would let us know if they wanted to make peace. After a while I knew by the noise in their camp that it was all right, and that they had decided for peace, and so told the general. Cochise then came up and told the general that they were ready to make terms of peace.[77]

The terms of the treaty were simple. Howard set aside the reservation Cochise wanted, saying later that "it was not the one I preferred but the only one I could get the Indians to agree to." He also "promised that the government would furnish the usual supplies of food and clothing." Finally, he agreed "that they should have Thomas J. Jeffords as their agent." The latter was a moot point, since Howard had appointed him special agent the previous month. In return, "Cochise and his captains promised to abstain from all unlawful acts they commit . . . what they call war," and Cochise pledged to "keep the roads in all that vicinity open."[78]

After these conditions were agreed to, Cochise declared poetically that "hereafter the white man and the Indian are to drink the same water, eat of the same bread, and be at peace."[79] To dispel his fears, Cochise insisted that the officers from Fort Bowie be present at the formal parley to be held the next day. Accordingly, on October 11, Howard sent Stone to Fort Bowie to request Captain Sumner's presence and cautioned Sumner to bring "two officers besides yourself, the doctor and a driver. . . . Do not take more men."[80] That same day he also wrote Crook, advising him that he had decided to give Cochise the Chiricahua Mountains as a reservation and declaring that the Indians would "cease from war and be contented." Consequently, "I have concluded to try them."[81]

Sumner was less than delighted about the prospect of riding all night to meet Cochise in council. Yet at 1 A.M. he, Captain Joseph Theodore Haskell, Lieutenant Charles Bird, and Dr. Edward Orr left Bowie and reached Sulphur Springs at six in the morning. Rest-

Treaty Peak, also known as Knob Hill. This peak had a white flag placed at its summit by Cochise to indicate to all that he had made peace. (*Photo by Karen Hayes*)

ing for two hours, they pushed on to Dragoon Springs and arrived there at 11:45, fifteen minutes before the conference was to begin.[82]

After formal introductions, the council began, with Cochise, his captains, and his warriors, some fifty in all, present. Naturally, Cochise dominated the conversation, reciting past acts of white injustice, treachery, and the unforgettable Bascom affair. He asked what his people had done to deserve such treatment and why the troops from Fort Bowie had been "down on him and his people." The officers listened courteously and explained that the troops' business was to pursue hostiles, but "as soon as he was willing to make peace, we were willing to do all we could to show him we wanted peace." Cochise replied that he was "getting old and would like to live at peace from this time on; but that if the white man would not let him do it, he would go away from here and fight him."[83]

While the council was in progress, Captain Haskell had a good opportunity to size up the chief. As were most other whites, he was impressed with what he saw:

The reports that we have had of Cochise have always given us to understand that he is old, used up, crippled from wounds and exposure, and of no account whatever as a leader or a chief. How mistaken we were! We met Cochise and thirteen of his captains, and Cochise is as different from the others of his tribe, as far as we saw, as black is from white. When standing straight he is said to be exactly six feet tall. I took a good look at him and made up my mind that he was only five feet ten inches. He is powerful, exceedingly well built, bright, intelligent countenance, and as fine an Indian as I ever laid my eyes on. . . . He was clean from head to foot. I looked at his scalp, his hair, face (painted fresh), neck, body, arms, and legs and he was clean. Most of the others were so filthy that you could scrape enough dirt off them to start a potato patch.[84]

After Cochise and one of his captains, probably El Cautivo, spoke for some three hours, the conversation finally turned to the terms of the treaty. The boundaries were confirmed:

Beginning at Dragoon Springs, near Dragoon Pass, and running thence northeasterly, touching the north base of the Chiricahua Mountains to a point on the summit of Peloncillo Mountains or Steins Peak range, thence southeasterly along said range through Steins Peak to the New Mexico boundary; thence due south to Mexican boundary, thence westerly along said boundary fifty-five miles; thence northerly following substantially the western base of the Dragoon Mountains to the place of the beginning.[85]

For his part, Cochise pledged to keep his Indians on the reservation and protect the Tucson road. After the conference concluded at 4 P.M., Howard's party prepared to leave for Tucson, but not before Cochise (whom Howard called "the most manly of all the chiefs") and the general had one brief final meeting, with Cochise saying good-bye in English.

That day, Howard traveled to the San Pedro River. The next day, a Sunday, he rested and caught up on his correspondence, writing Crook about the results and particulars of the reservation. He also wrote Jeffords, authorizing him to hire one clerk, one teamster, and two laborers and advising him that the agency "will be independent till I can see the Indian commissioner." For the time being, Jeffords was to draw whatever supplies he needed from Fort Bowie.[86]

Meanwhile, Sumner's party had returned to Fort Bowie, deeply concerned about the reservation site. On October 15, Sumner wrote that the location "may be unfortunate for both whites and Indians as the temptation to raid from there will be great." Furthermore, he added grimly, "I anticipate trouble in the reservation from Sonora, these Indians can slip across the border at any time . . . and return to their homes with stolen stock." He warned that problems were bound to occur because "the Mexicans will be likely to follow" raiding parties onto the reservation. He was right on target.[87]

The one-armed Christian general had carried out a courageous mission. Jeffords, not one to throw out unearned accolades, wrote: "I doubt if there is any other person that could have been sent here that could have performed the mission as well; certainly none could have performed it better."[88] Howard, with "Divine Help," had succeeded in making peace with Cochise, which Cochise kept faithfully for the remainder of his life. The problem with the treaty, as Sumner pointed out to Crook, was the proximity of the reservation to Sonora, with which Cochise had not made peace. As Cochise put it: "The Mexicans are on one side in this matter and the Americans on another. . . . I made peace with the Americans, but the Mexicans did not come to ask peace from me."[89]

Even if Sonora had requested peace with Cochise, it would not have mattered. Howard certainly did not grant Cochise permission to raid in Mexico. Although Cochise himself would not raid, he still considered his people at war with Mexico; thus he would make no efforts to prevent hostilities below the border. In fact, at this time it is doubtful that he even contemplated such. After all, who would the Chiricahuas raid if not the Mexicans? His Chokonens would find refuge and a market for their booty on the reservation.

Although the Howard-Jeffords-Cochise treaty brought peace and stability to southeastern Arizona for the first time since 1860, the same could not be said for Mexico. The Chiricahua Apaches continued their sanguinary raids below the border, with many originating from Cochise's reservation.

Chapter 19

THE CHIRICAHUA RESERVATION

The reservation established for the Chiricahuas was the subject of bitter controversy from the beginning. The press and Crook censured Howard because he seemingly gave in to all of Cochise's demands, in particular a reserve which was fifty-five miles wide, which adjoined Sonora, and which was independent from the military. Crook looked for justification to interfere and soon found plenty: incessant outcries from Sonora about the raiding from the new agency. He reprimanded Howard at every opportunity and even proposed sending troops to take over the reserve.

Cochise made no bones about his Indians raiding into Sonora; "I made peace with the Americans and not the Mexicans" was his standard reply. Although he apparently never left the reservation, during its first year of existence he made few, if any, attempts to restrain his people. By the same token, Jeffords proved somewhat insensitive to these charges, adopting a laissez-faire attitude and rationalizing that the Mexicans deserved whatever they received because of past mistreatment of the Chiricahuas.

Cochise sent out runners to gather the remainder of his people and to inform other Apaches that he had made peace. His Indians placed a pole with a white flag along the Tucson Road, a sign indicating to all travelers that they were at peace. Jeffords next began the task of organizing his agency. The most vital ingredient, rations, was furnished from Fort Bowie, where he received nine thousand pounds of

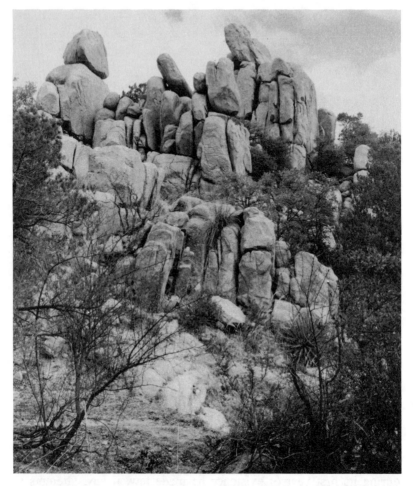

East stronghold, Dragoon Mountains. Cochise made his camp in this vicinity during the reservation years. (*Photo by Karen Hayes*)

corn, and at Tucson, where General Howard purchased some thirty-six hundred dollars' worth of supplies. On October 16, Jeffords rationed 450 Indians and set about, with Cochise's help, to bring more Indians to the reservation.[1] About October 20 he found the Stein's Peak band, probably with Chie's and Ponce's help, and brought them in. An observer numbered them at 60,[2] but a year later Jeffords reported 150.[3] This was a Chokonen group, quite possibly the local group of Chihuahua, who was said "to have been a very young chief when Cochise was very old," according to Mrs. Eve Ball, and "a leader during the last part of Cochise's life," according to Morris Opler.[4]

This accomplished, Jeffords sent Ponce, Chie, and Streeter to Tularosa. The guides, whom Jeffords compensated with cloth and tobacco, were expected to return to Arizona with their followers, along with Chiva and Gordo, yet for some reason, this did not happen. Streeter, meanwhile, had carried a message from Jeffords to Fred Hughes,[5] offering the latter a job as clerk of the reservation. Hughes consented and arrived on November 2.

He found the agency established at Sulphur Springs in a ten-by-twelve house rented from Nick Rogers for fifty dollars a month. The quarters were woefully inadequate. Jeffords, Hughes, and one worker had to live and work in this confining area. There was no space to store the Indians' rations. As a result, they were left in the open and a good quantity became spoiled. A few days later Hughes met Cochise:

> To show how suspicious the old fellow still was, he came accompanied by about fifty warriors. They made their camp about half a mile from the agency but within sight, they then commenced sauntering up to the agency building in squads of twos and threes until some fifteen or twenty had reached there, then seeing everything was all right they took Jeffords down to where Cochise was and he brought him up . . . [he] took me by the hand with both of his, told me he had heard of me before and that from this day on he was going to be my friend. He kept his word till the day of his death.[6]

In the meantime, Cochise had sent a runner to the Nednhis living near Janos, inviting them to partake of the truce.[7] Led by Juh, Geronimo, Nolgee, and Natiza, they had been on the run since the previous summer, keeping one step ahead of Sonoran scouts, before resuming friendly relations at Janos. They finally came in about November 20 and met Jeffords and Hughes at Pinery Canyon, some fifteen miles south of Apache Pass. Hughes recalled that this band "was under the command of a chief named Natiza and they were in reality Indians belonging to the government of Mexico."[8] The Nednhi population was variously placed at either two, three, or four hundred depending on who made the estimate. Hughes believed that this band of Apaches pretended indecision about peace and "wanted to be mean and were afraid of Cochise." Finally, after some procrastination, they assented to the same stipulations as Cochise's Chokonens.[9]

The Nednhis were a continuous source of trouble. What sort of relations they had had with Americans, if any, was not clear. Besides rations, the main reason they decided to live in Arizona was the security the reservation offered. From here they could easily slip undetected across the border to raid, then retreat to the sanctity of the agency. Cochise may have invited them knowing that raids into Arizona would continue unless he had them under his eye.

As Cochise had promised, Indian raids in southern Arizona ceased. Howard, who had been publicly abused by the press, began to receive the favor from many southwesterners. On November 1, Samuel Orr wrote the general from Fort Bowie that the citizens were "beginning to look upon the peace arrangement in a more favorable light." And the Apaches' apprehension subsided after visits to Sulphur Springs and Fort Bowie, where they had been treated well. Even so, concluded Orr, "the papers have ceased their howling for the present and all well meaning people give you credit for what you have done."[10]

Further evidence of Cochise's sincerity may be discerned from two letters written by men who previously had subscribed to the extermination policy. Thomas Hughes, who had settled on the Sonoita in 1868, had been victimized by several Apache raids. On November 23, 1872, he wrote Howard to express his "heart felt thanks for making peace with Cochise and his band of cut-throats." During the previous eighteen months, he had "lost nearly everything I could call my own except my life." Moreover, during that same period, "12 men have been killed by the Indians on my ranch which is only two miles from the military post of Camp Crittenden." Since the peace had been made, "everything has been going along very nicely . . . not one Indian sign has been seen in these parts since peace was made with Cochise."[11] A few weeks later another Arizona pioneer, Sidney Delong, one of the few whites who had participated in the Camp Grant massacre, wrote Howard and conceded that the armistice was working. "Thus far no cause for complaint has arisen and . . . you are entitled to the thanks of this people."[12] Delong, who operated the trading post at Bowie, had other reasons to be happy: the Indians were trading him the loot from their raids in Mexico.

Regardless of the armistice, the press continued to predict that the peace would not endure; after all, Cochise had come onto reservations before but eventually had left. But this reserve was in his country, and he trusted and respected the agent. On November 16 the *Arizona Miner* prognosticated that Cochise "will keep the peace but not beyond next summer."[13] Two weeks later the *Arizona Citizen* could not resist adding that "Cochise . . . so far has deported himself [well] . . . but, there is something in the genial sunshine of the spring months which usually overcomes his good resolves, and he is not responsible for climatic operations."[14]

Governor Safford visited Cochise in late November and was convinced that the chief wanted peace, yet he warned that "some real or imaginary cause may at any moment may set them again on the warpath."[15] Referring to Jeffords, Safford wrote: "I do not believe any other man living could now manage them, wild as they are." This unanimous skepticism on the part of Arizonans should not be casually dismissed as the sentiments of Indian-hating whites. Cochise had first made peace overtures in late 1868 and since that time his actions had shown he would do what he pleased unless he was content with government treatment. Almost predictably, the rations and supplies Howard had promised were slow in coming, and an exasperated Jeffords wrote letter after letter to obtain them, but without success.[16]

To begin with, Jeffords was disappointed with Washington's decision to put him in the Department of Arizona, reporting to Dr. Herman Bendell, superintendent of Indian affairs in Arizona. He had hoped to be assigned to the jurisdiction of Nathaniel Pope, whom Jeffords opined would "better understand the difficult position which I am placed."[17] Unfortunately, other views prevailed and on November 14, 1872, Jeffords was instructed by telegram to report to Bendell.[18] A communication problem surfaced immediately, with Bendell telling Jeffords how paperwork should be performed and how letters should be folded. On January 2, Bendell asked the agent to provide a list of the supplies that were required, promising that "every effort would be made to furnish them."[19] Jeffords had written Bendell on December 20 requesting "prompt action, for the present in all business pertaining to this agency," but he did not provide specifics. Four days later he again urged that supplies be furnished as "the government promised." Bendell asked for specifics, which failed to mollify Jeffords, who had only beef to issue the Indians and their patience was nearly exhausted.[20]

To be fair, Bendell was caught in a bind: in addition to budgetary problems, he had run into indifferent Washington bureaucrats who expected him to perform miracles without adequate funds. There was no deficit spending in the 1870s. Bendell was not discriminating against the Chiricahua Reservation; he treated the Fort Apache and Camp Grant Indians the same way he treated the Chiricahuas. His major problem was managing a superintendency on a budget which allowed for three agencies but now, after two peace commissioners, had seven. "How am I to contract debts in order to fulfill the promises made to the Indians . . . by the special commissioner? I have no funds on hand applicable for procuring food, shelter or transportation for the Indians."[21] The responsibility for this predicament lay with the Bureau of Indian Affairs and the secretary of the interior; it was their duty to ensure that sufficient funds were allocated to meet the government's commitments.

The situation could have exploded, but it did not. Cochise's health was failing, and he lacked the strength and will even to think of fighting another war. All he wanted was to be left alone. He had plenty of time to indulge in tiswin drunks, which perhaps dulled the pain of the disease which eventually took his life. Just as important, he had an agent he trusted and a reservation in his ancestral country. If rations were slow in coming, his people could sustain themselves by raiding into Mexico and by hunting and gathering, as they had done before the peace.

The indecisiveness perturbed Jeffords more than Cochise, who probably was not surprised that promises were not kept. The situation was exacerbated on January 24 when Bendell told Jeffords, as he had other agents, that his funds were exhausted: "Contract no debt without authorization from this office." Nine days later, Bendell allowed Jeffords to purchase small amounts of corn, but his creditors had to wait until the next fiscal year to be paid.[22] An incredulous Jeffords decided that he had had enough, so he turned to the one person who could get him some answers: General Howard.

Jeffords first complained to Howard about Bendell's "evasive replies" about when supplies would be furnished. He warned that his Indians might become unruly if food was not forthcoming—and quickly. Jeffords wondered what action he could take. The Indians, who now numbered 1,025, had complied with the agreement. "Not a single complaint has been made against them," yet the government's promises had not been carried out. Howard took immediate action, probably sending the letter to Charles Delano, secretary of the interior, who on March 5 telegraphed Bendell: "See that Chiricahua Reservation is furnished with all needful supplies. Don't neglect this duty." [23]

Bendell had recognized that the Chiricahuas "cannot be retained upon the reservation without being fed." Budget restrictions had forced him to provide with the resources on hand, and he had informed his superiors in Washington, who had ignored the problem and left Bendell without support. As frustrated with his superiors as Jeffords was of him, Bendell tendered his resignation on February 28, 1873, and it was accepted on March 24. [24]

In the meantime, he acted on Delano's orders, telegraphing Washington on March 11: "Chiricahua Reservation will be immediately supplied as directed." [25] That same day he also informed the Indian commissioner that the supplies should last until June 30. Three days later he advised Jeffords that he had ordered 23,000 pounds of corn, 1,820 pounds of coffee, 3,640 pounds of sugar, and 910 pounds of soap and salt. Although this problem was solved, Jeffords still had not received any funds to pay his creditors. While this crisis was averted, another one erupted. [26] It had been gathering momentum ever since the reservation was created: raiding into Sonora. The protagonists in this controversy were Crook versus Howard, Cochise versus Mexico, and Jeffords versus practically everyone else. The issue in each case was continued Chiricahuas forays from a U.S. government agency into a neighboring country. Jeffords, inclined to make excuses for his Indians, was criticized severely in some quarters, and with some justification.

As Captain Sumner had predicted, the savage and brutal raids into Sonora had continued, probably no more or no less than in previous years. The problem became magnified because of the reservation's proximity to Sonora's border. There was no doubt that much of the raiding could be attributed to the Chokonens and Nednhis living on the reservation, at times in conjunction with the Chihennes from Tularosa. Also, Western Apache bands from northern reservations made incursions, but these were decreasing each year as the government tightened its control of these bands. Experienced southwesterners understood the consequences of locating the reservation near the border. Perhaps Jeffords should have warned Howard, who failed to comprehend the intense hatred which had evolved from three centuries of Apache-Mexican conflicts. More than any other Apache band, the Chiricahuas had fallen victim to the Mexican machete and musket. Likewise, the Mexicans had fallen victim to the Chiricahua lance and bow.

Cochise himself had not understood the ramifications of raiding into Sonora, despite Howard's stern objection. After all, from 1858 to 1861, while living at Apache Pass, he had led large war parties into Mexico without objections from Americans. And while the Apaches living at Cañada Alamosa, their raiding parties occasionally slipped into Mexico with impunity. Furthermore, Cochise had raided into Arizona while living in Mexico, where the citizens of Fronteras and Janos encouraged the depredations because of the booty the Chiricahuas obtained. This had been a way of life along the border, but it must and would change. Cochise realized this, but he had not calculated that it would have to be so soon.

During the Indians' first four months on the reservation, there was heavy raiding into Sonora. The participants evidently were the younger Chokonen warriors and the turbulent Nednhis under Juh and Geronimo. To Cochise, the raiding was unimportant and he declined to halt it.

Sonora's complaints began a few months after the treaty. Each depredation was charged to Cochise, and article after article assailed Howard's character for allegedly permitting the Indians to cross the border. In mid-December 1872 the Sonoran representative in Mexico City complained bitterly to Porter C. Bliss, the U.S. consul, that Howard had granted Cochise permission to raid into Mexico and that the commander of Fort Bowie had orders to protect those who were blameworthy. On December 20, Bliss asked Washington for a response. Sonora's most prominent newspaper, *Estrella de Occidente*, reported that not only had Howard granted Cochise permis-

George Crook. Cochise eluded his grasp, which upset the commander of the department of Arizona. (*Courtesy Arizona Historical Society, Tucson*)

sion to raid below the border but had also furnished guns, saddles, and mounts. These ridiculous allegations were made repeatedly for the next eighteen months and were quite similar to American complaints against Fronteras and Janos in the 1860s.[27]

These charges were music to Crook's ears. He had only contempt for Howard,[28] whom he considered naïve and peace hungry. Moreover, Howard had unwittingly provoked Crook by innocently recommending that Fort Apache and Fort Bowie be transferred to the Military District of New Mexico—away from Crook's command. General Sherman, who deferred a decision until he heard from Crook and General Pope, noted that it "would much embarrass . . . Lt. Col. Crook."[29] The idea made little sense from a logistical point of view and ultimately was rejected. If anything, Arizona and New Mexico should have been one military department, especially since by this time the only real problems remaining were the Chiricahuas, who roamed over the southern parts of both states. Second, Colyer's and Howard's policies and actions were a joke as far as Crook was concerned. Before the Apaches would submit, they had to be defeated in battle; thus he had no empathy for either Howard or Cochise.

Looking for a legitimate reason to interfere (and the Chiricahua raiding into Sonora was), Crook determined that the "whole peace system had been a fraud" and struck upon a plan that would bring Cochise under his jurisdiction. His solution was a simple compliance with General Order No. 10, which, among other things, called for a daily roll call of all Indians on reservations.[30] If it were enforced, he believed it would accomplish two things: discourage depredations into Sonora and provide the military with some control over Cochise. Jeffords and Hughes both objected, predicting that Cochise would not submit to a daily count. They felt certain that if this policy were enforced it would drive "them to the warpath," something Hughes thought Crook wanted.[31] Their feelings were echoed by Colonel Delos Bennet Sacket (from the inspector general's office), who predicted that if they were forced to muster, Cochise and his whole band "would take to the mountains and we would have a second affair upon our hands."[32]

Crook's plans and strategy revolved around the Chiricahuas' refusal and subsequent outbreak; they would surely bolt for the mountains of Sonora. Consequently, he told Governor Pesqueira on January 9, 1873, that if the Chiricahuas refused the roll call, "I will commence hostilities against them without delay." He urged Pesqueira "to place strong detatchments along the border," to which the latter responded favorably, thanking Crook for his concern. Before Crook carried out these plans, however, he apparently had second thoughts and decided to send a party to confer with Cochise and obtain his preceptions of the treaty.[33]

What Crook really wanted was an excuse, or at least some justification, to intervene and implement his plans. In late January, Captain William Henry Brown, Lieutenant Charles Henry Rockwell, Lieutenant John Gregory Bourke, and a small escort arrived at Sulphur Springs and requested an interview with Cochise on behalf of Crook. From here Brown wrote Jeffords:

> General Crook has instructed me to have an interview with . . . Cochise and I am now here for that purpose. . . . General Crook has directed me not to enter the Indian camp with any armed men lest the presence of troops offend the Indians and tend to disturb the friendly relations which now exists and which General Crook is anxious to preserve in all its integrity. I shall be glad to meet Cochise and yourself at this place or any other place you may select.[34]

Jeffords arranged the meeting and on February 3, Brown's contingent met Cochise in the Dragoons.

The erudite Bourke recorded the interview, which probably occurred in the east stronghold. He described Cochise as "6 ft. in stature, deep chested, roman nosed, black eyes, firm mouth and a kindly and even somewhat melancholy expression. . . . He seemed much more neat than the other wild Indians." Interestingly enough, Cochise's youngest wife may have been the one individual who did not fear the chief. Envious of his oldest wife, she had bitten the chief on both hands and had left two scars, which caught the attention of Bourke. The interview was carried out in a businesslike manner, with Captain Brown directing the questions and Cochise responding:

> *Brown*—The General has sent me to Cochise to find out what he understands these terms [peace treaty] to be and, especially with reference to the movements of troops within the reservation.

John G. Bourke. An ethnologist and army officer, Bourke met Cochise in February 1873 in the east stronghold of the Dragoon Mountains. *(Courtesy Arizona Historical Society, Tucson)*

Cochise—The troops were to pass and repass by the road on the reservation the same as ever, according as the emergencies of the service might require but none were to come upon the reservation to live, nor were citizens to do so.

Brown—What stipulations, if any, were made in the treaty with regard to the people of Mexico?

Cochise (After first avoiding the question)—The Mexicans are on one side in this matter and the Americans on another. There are many young people whose parents and relatives have been killed by the Mexicans, and now these young people are liable to go down, from time to time and do a little damage to the Mexicans. I don't want to lie about this thing; they go but I don't send them.[35]

Brown told Crook about the interview and Crook must have been chagrined. It was clear to Bourke and Crook that Cochise did not think he had violated the agreement. This, plus the problem that no written treaty existed, forced Crook to cancel plans for a military takeover of the agency. He was compelled to write Pesqueira and concede that he had "encountered obstacles" and must await "further instructions from my government."[36]

During the first three months of 1873, Apache raiding in Sonora continued, much of it originating from the Chiricahua Reservation. A review seems to indicate they were no more severe than those of the previous two or three years. The Sonoran press blew the situation out of proportion and delightfully criticized U.S. handling of the Apaches. The situation was exacerbated with the printing of letters from Tucson—and even San Francisco—from individuals who were not aware of the facts. This led to slanderous and disparaging statements about Howard. If anyone should have been blamed, it should have been Tom Jeffords.

He maintained a remarkable influence with his wards. Not everyone concurred with his methods, yet all agreed that he was the only white man completely trusted by Cochise. Jeffords, although a public official, displayed a cavalier, unsympathetic, and insensitive attitude toward Mexicans. He had adopted the Apache belief that the Mexicans deserved what they received on the basis of past actions. He revealed his true feelings when he told a Mexican officer that "he did not consider it his duty to name those who had [raided] and when they returned he would ration them."[37] Even worse was his remark to the *Arizona Citizen* that "he did not care how many Mexicans his people killed . . . that for acts of treachery with those Indians, the Mexicans deserved the killings." Jeffords later acknowledged that this was his private belief and not his public stance.[38] Yet it was clear that he and Cochise did little to discourage the raids when they could have.

The depredations proved to be more than stock raids, as Jeffords had asserted. On Christmas Day 1872 a small party raided Imuris, stole some stock, and killed Paulino Armento. One week later, Chiricahua raiders ran off twelve horses and mules from Bacoachi. Soon after that, Apaches, perhaps the same band, ambushed and killed state mineralogist Juan García and a judge, Pablo Valencia, nine miles from Ures. In mid-January a party of twenty Indians murdered three citizens outside Ures; ten days later another citizen was ambushed near Ures. Toward the end of January along the road between Santiago and Ures, Apaches surprised Susano Valenzuela and his wife, killing both. According to *Estrella de Occidente,* seventeen Sonorans were killed between January 1 and February 7, 1873.[39] Although the Chokonens and Nednhis could not have had a hand in every killing, most of the perpetrators could probably be traced to the Chiricahua Reservation. Fatalities continued at this rate for the first six months of 1873, when, according to an informed estimate, Apaches had killed more than one hundred Sonorans.[40]

The Sonoran press lashed out at the government of Sonora and the United States for not protecting defenseless people. The solution, lamented *Estrella de Occidente,* was to make "each town, each village, each hamlet, and each congregation an encampment because the Apaches are everywhere." Reports from Santa Cruz, Magdalena, and Tucson stated that Cochise "the famous savage" had made peace only on the condition that "he be allowed to make war on Sonora" and use the reservation as protection after his forays into Sonora. *Estrella* conceded that it did not know whether Howard had acceded to this demand but it was certain "that the Apaches who are at peace in Arizona are permitted by the American leaders to make war on this state." The reference here was to Captain Sumner's inability to act because the reservation was independent of the military. In the end, doing nothing was almost as serious a violation as abetting the raiders.[41]

When asked about the raiding, Jeffords vacillated, answering in a manner intended to close the issue. On February 20 he admitted that his people did "only a small part" of the raiding.[42] A month later, responding to the commissioner of Indian affairs in Washington, he categorically rebutted the charges, insisting "that neither Cochise nor any of his subchiefs had left the reservation since they made peace." The agent's assertions notwithstanding, one must read between the lines of Jeffords's statements.[43] Although neither Cochise nor his subchiefs had left, this did not mean that his younger warriors or the unruly Nednhis had not.

In March an official from Sonora visited Fort Bowie with the dual purpose of delivering supplies and attempting to perfect a truce with Cochise. The delegation was headed by Juan Luna[44] and Cayetano Silva, officers in Sonora's National Guard. While at Apache Pass they met Jeffords, who helped arrange a conference with Cochise. The two officers, in the presence of Jeffords and Sidney Randolph Delong,[45] post trader at Bowie, extended an invitation for a permanent truce, but Cochise declared "he would not think of it." He staunchly denied having raided below the border, claiming that these incursions were the work of the Chihennes and the Nednhis.

Juan Luna offered a well-reasoned explanation of why he was convinced that some of the raiding originated from the Chiricahua Reservation:

> I was received courteously by Cochise and I am satisfied that he has not personally raided in Sonora since the peace . . . but . . . with what I did observe, I remain completely convinced that his Indians have committed depredations. . . .

Luna then enumerated the evidence he saw while in Cochise's camp and on the reservation: twelve horses stolen from Bacoachi; the rifle which belonged to Juan García, killed a few months before; clothing which belonged to Pablo Valencia, also killed a few months before. In fact, the truculent Nednhis were less than discreet about their raiding, one warrior boasting that they killed every Mexican they encountered and another admitting that a subchief had been killed along the Sonora River the month before. Luna concluded that prospects for a solution were dim. "The Apaches showed me a profound hatred" and "were against peace." Cochise even had to restrain a warrior who wanted to take Luna's horse in payment for his brother who had been captured by Mexicans.[46]

At this parley Delong invited Cochise to Fort Bowie for a visit. A few days later he came in, his first peaceful visit to Apache Pass since the Bascom affair twelve years before. His arrival generated much excitement. He entered the post on the morning of March 27, 1873, accompanied by his family and twenty warriors. Captain

Joseph Haskell observed his arrival and his encounter with his old captive and nemesis, Merejildo Grijalva, in a letter:

> On his arrival he met our post guide, Mary Hilda [Merejildo Grijalva] who, as you recollect, used to be a captain [captive] with Cochise. Mary Hilda offered him his hand before he dismounted, but Cochise told him he would not shake hands with him until he whipped him; so he got down off from his horse, and struck him two or three times with his whip and then they had a friendly embrace, and commenced to talk over old times.

Cochise met the officers, embraced Captain Sumner, and assured everyone that he was delighted with the peace. That afternoon he and his family (he had brought two wives, as well as his two sons, Taza and Naiche) had lunch at Delong's store before leaving at three o'clock. Captain Haskell concluded his letter by saying that "not a depredation of any kind has been committed by them since our peace agreement last October."[47]

This was the first of several visits by Cochise to Fort Bowie and Delong's store. Delong's clerk, Al Williamson, saw Cochise on several occasions and recalled that he was a stern and taciturn man. Occasionally he would bring in things to trade, such as deer skins, but his primary purpose for visiting was to assure everyone that he was satisfied with peace and to have a few drinks with the officers. As night approached, he would depart, having established strict rules that his people should leave before sundown.[48]

That spring Cochise moved his camp from the Dragoons to the Dos Cabezas Mountains fifteen miles north of Fort Bowie. As the Indians became more familiar with the whites, they began to visit the post more frequently, making Merejildo's "services at the post almost invaluable."[49] They continued to raid in Sonora, however, and Delong's store received additional merchandise and profits. Al Williamson recalled:

> I bought from one Indian, a silver mounted ivory handled pistol that he told me he had killed a Mexican officer, in order to get it. I saw seven Indians ride up to the store one day on seven Mexican ponies with silver mounted bridles and saddles. I asked them where they got them and they said Sonora. I have seen squaws come into the

store with their babies dressed with under garments trimmed with lace, all obtained in their raids.[50]

In mid-May a Nednhi-Chokonen group, reinforced by some Chihennes from Tularosa, organized a war party to Sonora and Chihuahua. Captain Sumner and Al Williamson had been hunting near San Simon when, on their return, they met fifty Indians, "well mounted and well armed . . . their bodies painted" and "naked except for loincloths." Sumner immediately wrote Jeffords that the Indians had told him they were going hunting but he took "this to be a blind" and hoped the agent would "take some action on the matter should the report be true." Jeffords investigated, but the Indains had already left.[51]

For Jeffords, matters could not have been much worse, it seemed, but they soon became so. Another letter from Indian Commissioner Edward P. Smith in Washington had arrived, requesting information on the raiding in Sonora. Jeffords again stated that neither "Cochise nor any of his sub chiefs have been engaged in raiding into Sonora" but conceded that "maybe some of the young people go." He was guilty of telling half-truths because as agent he was responsible for the acts of Juh's and Natiza's Nednhis, yet he had made no attempt to halt or to discourage them.[52]

Some of the Chiricahuas were raiding in northern Mexico and in early July 1873 returned to the reservation with a captive boy from Chihuahua. When informed, Jeffords dutifully proceeded to the ranchería in the Chiricahuas and found the boy, Panteleón Ignacio Rocha, in Geronimo's possession and brought him back to the agency. Rocha had been captured from Concepción, Chihuahua, about June 25. Captain Sumner offered to take responsibility for the boy's safe return, and Jeffords probably turned Rocha over to him.[53]

That summer the agent encountered more problems when the disenchanted Chihennes and Bedonkohes left Tularosa and came to Cochise's reserve. Tension between the Chihennes and whites had increased considerably during the first six months of 1873 and finally reached a climax that summer. The Indians longed for Cañada Alamosa but could not go there. As a result, sporadic raiding had begun in New Mexico that spring and some of the raiders sought refuge on the Chiricahua Reservation. By June, two to three hundred Chihennes had arrived and Jeffords rationed them, reasoning that if he did not, they would raid to subsist. This infuriated Major William Redwood Price, who was assigned the unpleasant duty of rounding up hostiles in New Mexico. He asked Sumner to drive them from the reservation back to New Mexico. Sumner demurred, noting that "I am not authorized to drive them off." [54] The reply incensed an already irate Price, who began a major smear campaign against Jeffords, uncharitably concluding that he was a "creature of Cochise's" who had attained his position through illicit trade. [55]

To be fair, neither Jeffords nor Cochise had encouraged these intrusions, both realizing that trouble would erupt eventually. By this time Cochise had come to understand that the raiding into Sonora had reached a critical stage and that he would have to take some action. The newcomers were led by Chiva, Gordo, and Sánchez; the first two had been close allies and were not the Indians that Cochise's people had quarreled with two winters before. Nonetheless, the prospect of interband conflicts, less distribution of rations, and more raiding into Sonora by a band over whom he had no control led Cochise to conclude that the fugitives should return to New Mexico.

The Chihennes' arrival increased the negative publicity the reservation was receiving. As expected, Price's allegations concerning Jeffords became the subject of an investigation undertaken by the commissioner of Indian affairs in Washington. Predictably, Howard and Crook put in their two cents' worth, with Howard staunchly defending Jeffords, saying that

> common rumor in New Mexico is not a good foundation for an opinion of character. Seldom did I find a man there speak well of another. So I did not reject the services of a brave man like Jeffords who periled his life to make peace because of slanders not proved . . . even if they came from a commissioned officer.

Furthermore, Howard suggested, if Sonora wanted peace, all it had to do was send a representative to Cochise, who would then grant a truce, or so Howard believed, revealing his naïve perceptions and simple solutions to an age-old and very complex problem. [56]

Crook confidently attacked every one of Howard's points, noting that Sonora had sent a representative, who was treated "with distain." He criticized everything associated with Cochise's reservation. He defended the character of Major Price, pointing out his fine war record, although he equally ignored Howard's distinguished career. Finally, almost as an afterthought, he fired one more shot and denounced the informality of Howard's peace with Cochise and the lack of a signed peace treaty. No other Apache bands had signed agreements, and Howard had not deviated from his orders.[57]

The acting Indian commissioner, H. R. Clum, reviewed the case and concluded that "as far as this office is concerned Cochise has with great fidelity kept his promise to refrain from marauding notwithstanding the promise of rations and assistance made to him by General Howard has been only partly fulfilled by the Government for want of funds." This hardly appeased Crook, who claimed that the special treatment given Cochise was having a demoralizing effect on other Apache bands.[58] According to Bourke, the Chokonens called the Western Apaches squaws because they were not "strong enough to insist on a reservation without soldiers."[59]

On September 16, 1873, Indian Commissioner Smith wrote Sonora's Governor Pesqueira to clear up misapprehensions regarding the Chiricahuas' agency. Smith emphasized that the Howard-Jeffords-Cochise agreement "never took the form of a treaty. No writing was drawn, no paper was signed." He assured Pesqueira that "General Howard did not grant Cochise the privilege of raiding into Sonora . . . [quite] the contrary." Quoting Jeffords, Smith said Cochise had "restrained members of his band who desired to raid into Mexico." Finally, he categorically denied that the government had issued arms, ammunition, horses, or saddles to the Apaches, as had been reported frequently in the Sonoran press.[60]

Unfortunately, Pesqueira did not receive Smith's letter. He became aware of it from John Hittell, editor of the *Alta California* in San Francisco, with whom he had carried on a running correspondence about the Apache problem. By this time Pesqueira had come to accept that Howard had not given Cochise permission to raid into Mexico, yet he asserted that the Apaches continued to show up with American horses, arms, and equipment, although one wonders how many eyewitnesses actually reported this. Pesqueira astutely pointed out that he was not concerned whether the Howard-Jeffords-Cochise treaty was in writing, for he correctly believed that

> the principal point is that the Department in question is responsible for the the acts of Cochise and his tribe, living on the Chiricahua reservation in peace, but who have made systematic incursions into Sonora to raid and murder Mexican citizens. . . . Neither local, civil or military authorities have attempted to impede these [incursions] . . . nor has anyone been authorized to intervene.

He pointedly asked: What if the situation were reversed? Would Americans tolerate it?[61] *Estrella de Occidente,* commenting on Jeffords's denial that Cochise was raiding, editorialized sarcastically: "Oh innocent Apaches! Oh Cruel whites! Oh distinguished officals! Who continues these murders in Sonora with impunity if Cochise tells his people that they should behave?"[62]

Jeffords had begun to feel the squeeze. By late summer 1873 he was being assailed from all sides—the Tucson press, the Sonoran press, military officers—and to top it all off, there was an investigation in Washington. No doubt he contemplated and came close to resigning. Finally, in late September, he admitted to Commissioner Smith that forty or fifty warriors were raiding in Sonora and justified it on grounds that the government had failed to furnish blankets for the coming winter, although raiding parties were usually organized for other reasons besides obtaining blankets.[63]

These pressures forced Jeffords and Cochise to address the consequences of continued raiding; finally, they determined to put a stop to it. In August a few Coyoteros stole some stock from the Patagonia mines. Cochise found them in the southern Dragoons and recovered three horses and a mule.[64] The next month, Jeffords and Cochise restored eight animals to citizens from Santa Cruz, Sonora,[65] and in October, Jeffords turned over some animals taken from Oquitoa, Sonora, which had been tracked to the agency.[66] Cochise understood that the raiding had to stop and, in the words of Jeffords's assistant, Fred Hughes, was "determined it shall be no longer."[67]

By this time, Cochise's health was deteriorating, but he still controlled his own band and was prepared to force the Chihennes and Nednhis to adhere to his wishes. In October 1873 he commented to inspector William Vandever that the whites should order the Chihennes to return to New Mexico. Vandever also reported that friction existed between Cochise and Natiza, probably because of the Nednhis' extensive raiding into Mexico.[68] Finally, in November 1873, Cochise decided to make his position clear. Jeffords was transferring agency headquarters from San Simon (where it had been since being moved from Sulphur Springs the previous August) to Pinery Canyon, mainly because San Simon had proved unhealthy: five children had died. Cochise took this opportunity to call a council of all the warriors and headmen and made it understood that this was his country and that those who wanted to remain in it must "refrain from raiding in Sonora [or] leave the reservation."[69]

From this point on, the raiding from the Chiricahua Reservation diminished significantly. It could not have happened at a better time. The commissioner of Indian affairs, Smith, had received requests from the War Department to turn the reservation over to Crook. After seriously considering this proposal, he refused but admonished Jeffords that he would do so unless the raids stopped. He wrote Jeffords: "Give Cochise distinctly to understand that unless the line between his reservation and Mexico can be thus guarded his reservation will be turned over to the military and he will be obliged to bring his men to a daily roll call."[70] By the time Jeffords received this message, he had already decided to resign. He was exhausted from his arduous duties, disillusioned by the lack of funds, and weary of the constant criticism.[71]

As 1874 dawned, Cochise clearly understood Smith's threat. He and Jeffords had "succeeded without trouble . . . in driving off all the Indians who did not belong to Cochise's band." The agent reassured Smith:

> I am happy to inform the department that it has been now over two months since any complaints whatever have been made against these Indians either by the citizens of this territory or by the people living on the other side of the Mexican line, and I have strong hopes that we have heard the end of this raiding in Sonora. . . . The Indians here have also appeared more settled and satisfied during the last two months than at any other time since peace was made.[72]

About the time Smith received Jeffords's letter, the government was considering yet another option: moving the Chokonens to New

Taza. Cochise's eldest son, he succeeded his father as chief. (*Courtesy Arizona Historical Society, Tucson*)

Chihuahua. This prominent Chokonen warrior was a group leader at the time of Cochise's death. (*Courtesy Arizona Historical Society, Tucson*)

Mexico. For his part, Cochise believed that he had remained faithful to the terms of the treaty and wondered why the government was so willing to break its word and force him onto a New Mexico reservation which had been closed two years before. Such talk was academic as far as he was concerned, for he knew his end was approaching. It would be Taza's and his headmen's decision.

Chapter 20

GOOD FRIENDS WILL MEET AGAIN

A few months after the San Simon council in which Cochise ordered a halt to the raiding into Sonora, Fred Hughes wrote a seemingly innocuous letter to the *Las Cruces Borderer* suggesting that Cochise's people could easily be consolidated with the Chihennes on a reservation in New Mexico. Believing that Vandever had officially advocated this as a solution, Hughes endorsed the idea and declared that it would "settle our Sonora difficulties." Moreover, only "a half dozen warriors" would object, or so he thought.[1]

Vandever had made no such recommendation, although privately he may have proposed it to Hughes or Jeffords. Hughes had not intended that his proposal become government policy. New Mexico's superintendent of Indian affairs, Levi Edwin Dudley, happened to read his letter and promptly forwarded it to Indian Commissioner Smith in Washington. Smith perceived that it might put a stop to the Sonora controversy and on March 19, 1874, ordered Dudley to proceed to the Chiricahua Reservation to ascertain Cochise's feelings about removal.[2] The transfer seemed logical to most Anglos. In the first place, it would consolidate two agencies into one, saving considerable expense. Even more important, it would remove the fighting Chokonens from the Sonoran border, thereby eliminating easy access into Mexico.

Leaving Santa Fe in early May, Dudley interviewed many citizens along the way; all were "universally opposed to removal" because they were apprehensive about disrupting relations. Dudley found that most whites praised Howard for his efforts: if the general returned to the Southwest, "he would find a warm welcome, and receive the thanks of the people." On May 21 he met Jeffords at Pinery Canyon and learned that Cochise, seriously ill, was in the Dragoons and that Juh and some of the Nednhis had left the reservation for Mexico.[3]

Some had gone the previous December, perhaps as a consequence of Cochise's edict. Others, including Juh, who had succeeded Natiza as leader of the Nednhis, had returned to Janos and resumed negotiations with Mexico. Juh claimed that "he never wanted to live in the United States." That spring he sent representatives to make peace at Janos and Galeana, where authorities asked Sonoran officials to suspend military operations for the time being. Although they were skeptical, they granted the request. Soon afterward a woman from Juh's band went to Ures to arrange a truce. The cease-fire had been in effect for only a few weeks before the Nednhis were charged with raiding and once again pushed into Arizona by Sonoran troops in late July. An old leader named Eligio (a relative of Coleto Amarillo) was captured at Janos by Sonoran troops and summarily executed. This terminated negotiations with Mexico.[4]

On May 22, Dudley and Jeffords started for the Dragoons to meet Cochise. Dudley recalled that

> the old Chief was suffering intensely and I at first thought he would not outlive the night. I found a ready welcome as soon as his son [Taza] explained who I was, for I had been expected; and when I gave him a photograph of General Howard and myself taken together my introduction to his favor was complete. The picture was frequently examined by the old chief during my stay and always followed by the warmest expression of feelings of affection for the general.

Dudley had a short conversation about removal, but within an hour Cochise became "much exhausted." Dudley left and returned to Fort Bowie, impressed with both Jeffords and Cochise.[5]

A few days later he returned to the Dragoons for another visit and found Cochise "still alive but failing rapidly." As to removal to New Mexico, Cochise declared he would leave the decision to his son Taza, but he made it clear that he preferred to remain in Ari-

zona. Dudley reported to Washington "that these Indians can be removed at any time. . . . Agent Jeffords said he could give me two
hundred and fifty who would return with me at once." Dudley digressed to express his view concerning Jeffords's unique influence
on the Indians:

> I am convinced that should you decide to remove these Indians
> Agent Jeffords can do so. . . . I have seen no man who has so com-
> plete control over his Indians as Agent Jeffords and I am sure that if
> they removed he would be the best man to make agent at Hot Springs.
> He does not answer all the requirements of an agent; none that I have
> seen do fill the bill in every particular. Jeffords can and does maintain
> discipline and he has the influence to bring Indians to his reservation
> and keep them there, and if they go away he generally knows where
> they have gone.[6]

His conclusion that Cochise's Chokonens might easily be relocated
was disputed by Hughes and Jeffords. Hughes now estimated that
only half would move, while Jeffords reported that any attempt
would result in renewed hostilities. "The government had not
enough troops to move them," claimed the Chokonens. Jeffords's
report convinced Smith to defer the decision on removal.[7]

Cochise's health had been deteriorating for several years. While
at Cañada Alamosa, he ate very little because of a stomach ailment
which was complicated when he made peace and had more time to
indulge in tiswin drunks. Nine months after his treaty, an officer
wrote that "Cochise is growing old and infirm . . . and is constantly
drunk on tiswin."[8] The following April, Lieutenant Colonel Roger
Jones reported that Cochise's death was imminent, "as it is known
he has been very sick for months past."[9] A few weeks later, Fred
Hughes arrived in Tucson and told the *Citizen* the Chiricahua leader
was "very sick" with "little hope of recovery."[10] Finally, on May
30, the *Citizen* reported that Cochise was dying, having been
"troubled by dyspepsia ever since he came on the reserve."[11]

With Cochise's death imminent, attention turned to who would
replace the man who had led the Chokonens for the past eighteen
years. Hughes said there were "three prominent aspirants: Cochise's
son [Taza], the big medicine man [Eskinya][12] and the war captain
[Nahilzay]. Another informed source labeled Cochise's captains

NA-CHISE, -- Son of Cochise,

Naiche. Cochise's youngest known son, he was the last hereditary chief of the fighting Chokonen. *(Courtesy Arizona Historical Society, Tucson)* "unmitigated scamps" (presumably alluding to Pionsenay, Eskinya, and El Cautivo) who "could not live without making mischief and trouble." [13] Hoping to ensure a smooth transition and a continuation of his policies, Cochise named Taza his successor. According to Asa Daklugie, Cochise had groomed Taza to succeed him, and his leading men, including Eskinya and the loyal Nahilzay, agreed to support Taza. Cochise's last instructions to his people were "to forever live at peace" with the whites and to "always do as [Jeffords] tells them." [14]

One of Taza's first acts was to find the Indian who had bewitched his father. If the spell was removed, the Indian would live; if Cochise died, the culprit would be burned at the stake. The alleged witch was found, but nothing could restore Cochise's health. Jeffords convinced Taza to spare the Indian's life. [15]

On the evening of June 7, 1874, Jeffords and Cochise had their final meeting. Cochise, who had been in and out of comas during the past few weeks, knew that death was near. As Jeffords was about to depart, Cochise asked him, "Do you think you will ever see me alive again?" Jeffords replied, "No, I do not think I will. I think that by tomorrow night you will be dead." Cochise agreed, saying, "Yes, I think so, too—about ten o'clock tomorrow morning. Do you think we will ever meet again?" Jeffords, surprised by the question, replied, "I don't know. What is your opinion about it?" Cochise responded that "I have been thinking a good deal about it while I have been sick here, and I believe we will; good friends will meet again—up there [pointing to the sky]." [16]

The next morning in the east stronghold, Cochise died, probably of dyspepsia or some form of stomach cancer. News of his death spread rapidly. There was tremendous sorrow throughout the rancherías. Fred Hughes recalled that "the howl that went up from these people was fearful to listen to [and] was kept up through the night until daylight next morning." [17]

According to custom, a close relative (probably either his wife Dos-teh-seh or his trusted sister) prepared Cochise for burial. This consisted of bathing his body, combing his hair, and dressing him in his best clothes—all done to prepare the deceased for afterlife. The burial probably took place later that day. Usually only close relatives were present: undoubtedly his sons, his three wives, a shaman,

Fort Bowie, 1874. The important post looked like this at the time of Cochise's death. (*Courtesy Arizona Historical Society, Tucson*)

and other members of his extended family group.[18] In this case, however, much of the Chokonen band was there, at least according to Jeffords, who wrote Indian Commissioner Smith:

> It is a custom among these Indians when one of their number dies to burn some clothing, blankets etc. at the grave of the deceased. . . . Upon the death of Cochise, I found that his whole band had stripped themselves of almost their entire clothing and burnt it at his grave for the purpose above described.[19]

A few days later, Jeffords gave an account of the burial to Al Williamson, who repeated it to historian Frank C. Lockwood:

> He was dressed in his best war garments, decorated with war paint and head feathers, and wrapped in a splendid heavy, red, woolen blanket that Colonel H. C. Hooker had given him. He was then placed on his favorite horse . . . [which] was guided to a rough and lonely place among the rocks and chasms in the stronghold, where there was a deep fissure in the cliff. The horse was killed and dropped

into the depths; also, Cochise's favorite dog. His gun and other arms
were then thrown in; and, last, Cochise was lowered with lariats into
the rocky sepulcher—deep in the gorge.[20]

The location of Cochise's grave was never revealed by his people or
by Jeffords, the only white man who knew. It was a secret the frontiersman carried to his grave.

So ended the life of one of the greatest Apache leaders of the
nineteenth century, one who had successfully eluded troops of four
states and two countries, a man who harbored intense hatred toward
the Mexicans who had killed his father and the Americans who had
hanged his brother and murdered his father-in-law. He had fought
back with all his strength, but in the end he realized his people
would have to live in peace or be exterminated. It was ironic that
this courageous Apache leader, who could always be found leading
his men into battle, died a natural death on a reservation.

Cochise's death created a tremendous void in Apache leadership.
No other leader, except perhaps Victorio, had faced the overwhelming onslaught of whites and Mexicans and had resisted until it was
no longer safe to be a free Apache. No other leader had succeeded in
obtaining a reservation in his country, one which was run by the Indians in conjunction with their agent without military interference.
Perhaps no other Apache chief exhibited more wisdom, courage,
fighting ability, and control of his followers than had Cochise.

The days, weeks, months, and years following his death were turbulent for his people. Had he lived, some of the problems might
well have been avoided. Suffice it to say that the Chiricahua Reservation was broken up almost two years to the day after Cochise's
death. Most of his local group followed Taza and Naiche to the
hated San Carlos Reservation. Some did not. Allied with their
Nednhi and Chihenne brethren, the remainder of the fighting Chiricahuas gave the Southwest a decade of intermittent war which culminated in the surrender of Naiche and Geronimo in September
1886 and the removal of almost every Chiricahua Apache to Florida. It was twenty-eight years before Cochise's people returned to
the Southwest. Ironically, those who chose to return settled on the
Mescalero Reservation in New Mexico, the very one Cochise rejected in 1870.

NOTES

Introduction

1. United States Army Military History Institute, Joseph Sladen Papers, Sladen to Alice Rollins Crane, October 26, 1896.

2. James Henry Tevis, *Arizona in the 50s*, 149.

3. *Boston Evening Transcript*, November 6, 1872.

4. Smithsonian Institution, J. B. White Manuscript No. 178.

5. Smithsonian Institution, N. S. Higgins Manuscript No. 180.

6. Anderson Nelson Ellis, "Recollections of an Interview with Cochise, Chief of the Apaches," *Kansas State Historical Society Collections*, 13 (1913–14), 391.

7. Frank C. Lockwood, *The Apache Indians*, 125.

8. Higgins Manuscript.

9. Oliver Otis Howard, *My Life and Experiences Among Our Hostile Indians*, 205.

10. National Archives and Records Center, Records of the Bureau of Indian Affairs, Record Group 75 (RG75), Microcopy T21 (T21), Roll 12 (R12), Hennisee to Clinton, October 31, 1870, Appendix A.

11. *Arizona Miner*, April 20, 1872.

12. Thomas Edwin Farish, *History of Arizona*, 229.

13. RG 75, T21, R12, Hennisee to Clinton, October 31, 1870, Appendix B.

14. Arizona Historical Society (cited hereafter as AHS), Fred Hughes Collection.

15. Sladen Papers, manuscript titled, "Making Peace with Cochise, Chief of the Chiricahua Apaches," 51. Copy in AHS.

16. John C. Cremony, "Some Savages," *Overland Monthly*, 8 (March 1872), 203–4.

17. Fred Hughes Collection.

18. Sladen, "Making Peace," 28, 52; Sladen Papers, Sladen to Crane, October 26, 1896.

19. Sladen, "Making Peace," 39–40.

20. Interview with Amelia Naiche, January 17, 1979.

21. Eve Ball with Norah Henn and Lynda Sanchez, *Indeh: An Apache Odyssey* (cited hereafter as Ball, *Indeh*), 23–24.

22. Sladen, "Making Peace," 44; John G. Bourke, *On the Border With Crook,* 235–36.

23. Fred Hughes Collection.

24. Morris E. Opler, *An Apache Lifeway,* 466–69.

25. Sladen, "Making Peace," 44.

26. Edward L. Keyes, "Some Recollections of Arizona and Cochise," *The United Service,* July 1890.

27. The Chiricahua Apaches consisted of four autonomous bands: Chokonens (Cochise's band), Chihennes, Nednhis, and Bedonkohes.

28. Henry Stuart Turrill, "A Vanished Race of Aboriginal Founders," *Publication Number 18 of the New York Society of the Order of the Founders and Patriots of America,* February 14, 1907, 22.

29. RG 75, T21, R17, Coleman to Acting Assistant Adjutant General (AAAG), District of New Mexico, October 18, 1872.

30. Turrill, "A Vanished Race," 21.

31. Fred Hughes Collection; *Arizona Citizen,* November 30, 1872.

32. Cremony, "Some Savages," 205.

33. White Manuscript No. 178.

34. Ball, *Indeh,* 23.

35. Lockwood, *The Apache Indians,* 106.

36. Tevis, *Arizona in the 50s,* 149; Cremony, "Some Savages," 203.

37. Levi E. Dudley, "Cochise, the Apache Chief, and Peace," *The Friend,* August 7, 1891.

38. Sladen, "Making Peace," 42.

39. Jeffords report dated July 20, 1874, Bancroft Library.

Chapter 1

1. Ralph Hedrick Ogle, *Federal Control of the Western Apaches 1848–1886,* 5; Frederick Webb Hodge, *Handbook of American Indians North of Mexico,* I, 63.

2. Ibid.; Jack Douglas Forbes, *Apache, Navaho and Spaniard,* xi–xxiii.

3. Grenville Goodwin, *The Social Organization of the Western Apache,* 1; Juan Nentvig, S.J., *Rudo Ensayo: A Description of Sonora and Arizona in 1764,* 21.

4. Opler, *Lifeway,* 1–2.

5. Ibid., 2.

6. Ibid.

7. Stephen M. Barrett, *Geronimo's Story of His Life,* 12–14; Ball, *Indeh,* 22; Angie Debo, *Geronimo: The Man, His Time, His Place,* 71.

8. Opler, *Lifeway,* 462–64.

9. Ibid. Harry W. Basehart, "Chiricahua Apache Subsistence and Socio-Political Organization," unpublished manuscript, University of New Mexico, 8–9.

10. Opler, *Lifeway,* 181.

11. Frank C. Lockwood, *Arizona Characters,* 62; Frank C. Lockwood, "Cochise, the Noble Warrior," *Arizona Highways,* February 1939, 6–7.

12. Samuel Woodworth Cozzens, *The Marvellous Country, or Three Years in Arizona and New Mexico,* 86.

13. Bernard John Dowling Irwin, "The Fight at Apache Pass," *Infantry Journal,* 32 (April 1928), 2.

14. *Arizona Miner,* March 20, 1869.

15. Ellis, "Recollections," 391.

16. *Arizona Citizen,* December 7, 1872.

17. Ball, *Indeh,* 23.

18. Gillet M. Griswold, "The Ft. Sill Apaches: Their Vital Statistics, Tribal Origins, Antecedents," unpublished manuscript, Field Artillery Museum, Fort Sill, Oklahoma, 24.

19. AHS, Robert Humphrey Forbes Collection.

20. John A. Rockfellow, *Log of an Arizona Trail Blazer,* 80.

21. Turrill, "A Vanished Race," 20.

22. Ball, *Indeh,* 22.

23. Tevis was born in Virginia in 1835, came to Arizona in 1857 or 1858, and soon afterward took employment with the Butterfield Overland Mail Company at the Apache Pass stage station. He became well acquainted with Cochise, and his memoirs, *Arizona in the 50s,* plus his letters to the *Weekly Arizonian,* provide information about Cochise during this period. Tevis left Apache Pass in late 1859 and eventually surfaced at Pinos Altos, New Mexico, in late 1860. He died in Tucson in 1905. Tevis, *Arizona in the 50s;* Dan L. Thrapp, *Encyclopedia of Frontier Biography,* 1411–12.

24. Tevis, *Arizona in the 50s,* 114–15.

25. *Arizona Citizen,* May 22, 1875.

26. James Kirker was born in Northern Ireland in 1793 and emigrated to the United States in 1810. He journeyed west in 1817, settling in St. Louis before finally moving to Santa Fe in 1824. In the late 1820s he moved to Santa Rita del Cobre in present-day southwestern New Mexico, where he became associated with the Chiricahuas. In the late 1830s, the governor of Chihuahua hired him to kill Apaches instead of beaver. His contract was canceled in 1840 but renewed in late 1845, and the following July his group slaughtered 148 Chiricahuas at Galeana. For a biography of Kirker, see William Cochran McGaw, *Savage Scene: The Life and Times of James Kirker, Frontier King.* David J. Weber, *The Taos Trappers: The Fur Trade in the Far Southwest, 1540–1846,* 221–25.

27. Relles (Reyes), a moderate Chokonen leader of the 1830s and 1840s, was well known in the Fronteras region. He participated in the August 1836 truce with Sonora and joined Pisago Cabezón in the peace treaty of 1842 at Janos. Hostilities resumed in 1844 and he joined raids into Sonora. He was the prime mover in the May 1846 truce at Galeana before falling victim to Kirker's scalp hunters in June 1846.

28. Pisago Cabezón, 1770(?)–1846(?), probably a Chokonen, succeeded his father when the latter died at the hands of Sonoran troops in the Enmedio Mountains about 1793. Pisago came into Janos about 1795 and remained during the presidio period, although at times he became disillusioned and bolted to the mountains. He had several wives and by the 1820s was the patriarch of an unusually large extended family group and perhaps had as many as thirteen children. Many of the noted Chokonen leaders of the 1840s and 1850s were members of his local group and probably were related to him. These included Tapilá, Carro, and Casimiro. Pisago passed from the scene in 1845 or 1846, possibly a victim of Kirker's massacre. University of Texas at El Paso, Janos Collection Roll 10 (cited hereafter as JA with roll number), de Gavo to Casanova, May 5, 1792.

29. James Hobbs, *Wild Life in the Far West,* 88.

30. Frederick Webb Hodge stated that Cochise succeeded his father, Nachi, as chief. The source for this statement is not known; it would appear, however, that someone confused the facts. George Wratten, interpreter and confidant of the Chiricahuas, read Hodges' statement and wrote the Bureau of American Ethnology, saying that Hodge should have said Nachi, son of Cochise, succeeded his brother Taza as chief of the Chiricahua Apaches. During the 1840s there was a minor leader named Naqui or Naque who lived near Janos and was a member of Pisago Cabezón's band. I think it unlikely that he was directly related to Cochise, given his relatively unimportant place in Chiricahua history. Hodge, *Handbook,* 317; Smithsonian Institution, George Wratten to Bureau of American Ethnology, May 4, 1907, copy in author's files.

31. Opler, *Lifeway,* 464–70, contains a good account of the role of a leader in Chiricahua society.

32. For an excellent summary of Apache-Spanish relations during the latter eighteenth century, see Max L. Moorhead, *The Apache Frontier: Jacobo Ugarte and Spanish-Indian Relations in Northern New Spain, 1769–1791.*

33. Kieran McCarty, *Desert Documentary: The Spanish years, 1767–1821,* 44–46.

34. Moorhead, *The Apache Frontier,* 123–29; Max L. Moorhead, *The Presidio: Bastion of the Spanish Borderlands,* 95–114.

35. Janos was founded as a presidio about 1691 to protect Mexico's northern frontier. It played a significant role in Chiricahua-Mexican relations for most of the eighteenth and nineteenth centuries. Moorhead, *The Presidio,* 21.

36. Moorhead, *The Presidio,* 101, *The Apache Frontier,* 126–28.

37. William B. Griffen, "Apache Indians and the Northern Mexican Peace Establishments," in *Southwestern Culture History: Collected Papers in Honor of Albert H. Schroeder,* 189.

38. Lockwood, *The Apache Indians,* 28–29.

39. Morris E. Opler to author, March 1, 1982. Opler points out that most Chiricahua names "tend to follow some physical or behavioral peculiarity of the individual bearing it or it refers to some well known event in which he was involved." Many Americans commented on Cochise's nose. For example, Al Williamson, who met him in 1873–74, described Cochise as "tall and straight . . . he had a Roman nose." Lockwood, *The Apache Indians,* 125. For an excellent discussion of the derivation of Apache names, see Goodwin, *Social Organization,* 522–35.

40. The source for the rest of this chapter, unless otherwise noted, is Opler, *Lifeway,* 13–18, 25–37, 67–75, 135–44.

41. Morris E. Opler and Harry Hoijer, "The Raid and War-Path Language of the Chiricahua Apache," *American Anthropologist.* 42 (October–December 1940), 617–34. This article contains a list of seventy-eight such words.

Chapter 2

1. Joseph F. Park, "The Apaches in Mexican-American Relations, 1848–1861," *Arizona and the West,* 3 (Summer 1961), 133–35; Joseph F. Park, "Spanish Indian Policy in Northern Mexico, 1765–1810," *Arizona and the West,* 4 (Winter 1962), 343–44.

2. Fronteras, about one hundred miles west of Janos and thirty miles south of present-day Douglas, Arizona, was established as a Spanish presidio about 1692 and remained an important frontier outpost for the next two hundred years. It was

an attractive target for Chiricahua raiders, Cochise in particular, from the 1830s through the 1870s. Moorhead, *The Presidio*, 22.

3. Santa Rita del Cobre is in southwestern New Mexico six miles northeast of Bayard. Situated in the heart of Chihenne country, the mines were discovered about 1800 by Apaches, who told Lieutenant Colonel José Manuel Carrasco, an officer at Janos, about them. Lacking funds, Carrasco sold out to Francisco Manuel Elguea, a Chihuahuan banker, who obtained a grant from Spain to establish a settlement and work the mines. By early 1804 they were evidently producing copper because troops were relocated from Casas Grandes to provide protection. The settlement came to depend on Janos for supplies and assistance. The mines were abandoned about June 1838 because of Apache hostilities and unprofitable operations. JA, R15, Salcedor to commander of Janos, February 3, 1804; *Mesilla Times*, October 18, 1860; Dan L. Thrapp, *Victorio and the Mimbres Apaches*, 18. John Russell Bartlett, *Personal Narrative of Explorations and Incidents in Texas, New Mexico, California, Sonora and Chihuahua* I, 227–28; T. M. Pearce, *New Mexico Place Names: A Geographical Dictionary*, 149.

4. Stuart F. Voss, *On the Periphery of Nineteenth Century Mexico: Sonora and Sinaloa, 1810–1877*, 48–49.

5. JA, R13, Barela to Vizcarro, December 23, 1821. William B. Griffen, *Apaches at War and Peace: The Janos Presidio, 1750–1858*, 124–25.

6. Juan Diego Compá (1772–1837), probably a Nednhi, was a brother of the more well-known Juan José Compá. He succeeded his father as chief after his father died of natural causes in 1794. He was generally at peace for the next forty years, although he was overshadowed by his better-known brother. He and his brother were killed in the Johnson massacre of April 1837. For an excellent discussion of the Compá family, see William B. Griffen, "The Compás: A Chiricahua Apache Family," *American Indian Quarterly*, 7 (Spring 1983), 21–49.

7. Fuerte (Spanish for "manly" or "strong") was one of the important Chihenne leaders from 1810 through 1840. The copper mines–Mimbres River area was his home base. One can speculate that he was in some manner related to Mangas Coloradas. It is also possible that since he passed from the scene about 1840 and Mangas Coloradas appeared suddenly about 1842, they were the same individual. William B. Griffen, who has done extensive work in this area, concurs with my conclusion. Griffen to author, December 26, 1986.

8. Mano Mocha was born about 1780 and one of his hands was maimed in a fight with a bear, hence his Spanish name. His Apache name was Tuin, and it is not clear whether he could have been a Bedonkohe leader, since his band territory was mentioned frequently as the Mogollon Mountains, or a leading man of the Chihennes. He dominated a local group for some thirty years and in his early years was reported to have been an important war leader. In the mid-1820s, James Ohio Pattie met him at the copper mines and was treated in a friendly manner. His actions in the 1830s and 1840s paralleled the more moderate faction of the Chiricahuas. He frequently participated in the peace discussions, but when he was dissatisfied he would lead his band to the mountains and war. He passed from the scene in the mid-1840s. James O. Pattie, *The Personal Narrative of James O. Pattie of Kentucky*, 120.

9. JA, R13, document entitled, "List of Apaches at Peace, December 1, 1821."

10. Matías, born about 1790, was a Chokonen leader with generally pacific views. Like Relles, he made his headquarters near Fronteras from the 1820s until

his death in the mid-1840s. On several occasions he became actively involved in peace negotiations, even traveling to Guaymas, Ures, and Chihuahua City to secure peace. After his death in the mid-1840s, his sons Pablo and Elías became group leaders but not on the band level because Cochise had arrived on the scene.

11. Teboca, a contemporary of Matías, was born about 1790 and led a local group of hostile Chokonens through the 1830s and 1840s. He had several sons who were associates of Cochise, among them Tullotte, Naquebre, Guero, Vicente, and Chiquito. Teboca passed from the scene about 1851, possibly killed in the Pozo Hediondo fight.

12. AHS, Film MC-6, Archivo General de Mexico, Roll 150, File 31, Eredia to Urrea, November 15, 1824; Villascueva to Urrea, July 24, 1824.

13. Ibid., File 32, Urrea to Secretary of War and Navy, November 16, 1824.

14. Ibid., Eredia to Urrea November 12, 1824.

15. JA, R16, Military Commander at Santa Rita del Cobre to the Military Commander 1st Sección, December 30, 1824.

16. JA, R21, Simón Elías to Commander at Janos, August 6, 1828; Commander at Janos to Military Commander of Chihuahua, December 28, 1828; various ration lists for 1828; AHS, Sonoran State Archives (cited hereafter as SA with roll number), Roll 12, Bustamente to Urrea, March 29, 1825; Muro to Elías González, April 25, 1831.

17. JA, R23, Melgar to Military Commander of Janos, February 6, 1830. Griffen, *Apaches at War and Peace,* 131-32.

18. Hermosillo, Sonora, Archivo Historico de Sonora, (cited hereafter as AHSH), Prefect of Arispe to Governor, January 13, 1830; Arvizu to Governor, February 17, 1830; Alcalde of San Ignacio to Governor, March 1, 1830.

19. JA, R24, Melgar to Military Commander at Janos, July 5, 1830.

20. JA, R23, Franco to Military Commander at Janos, December 21, 1830.

21. Turrill, "A Vanished Race," 19-20. JA, R4, various ration lists.

22. SA, R12, Simón Elías to Governor, June 28, 1831; AHSH, Commanding General to Governor, June 23, 1831; Governor to Commanding General, July 5, 1831.

23. Francisco R. Almada, *Diccionario de historia, geografía y biografía chihuahuenses,* 38.

24. SA, R12, Morales to Governor, February 23, 1832; Governor to Morales, February 26, 1832.

25. Juan José Compá (1786?-1837), a Nednhi leader, was the brother of Juan Diego Compá and the son of El Compá. In 1794 he attended the presidio school at Janos, which explains his literacy in Spanish. As Juan Diego Compá aged, Juan José assumed leadership of a local group but was never a dominant Chiricahua, as were Pisago Cabezón and Mangas Coloradas. A leading advocate in the peace treaties of 1832 and 1835, Juan José was killed in the Johnson massacre in April 1837. Griffen, "The Compás," 37-40.

26. SA, R12, Morales to Governor, March 27, May 9, 1832.

27. Ibid., Governor of Chihuahua to Governor of Sonora, document entitled, "Triumph over the Apaches," June 7, 1832.

28. Ibid.

29. Ibid., Arvizu to Madeno, June 27, 1832.

30. JA, R5, Conde to Justiniani, August 30, 1832.

31. Aquién was probably a Chokonen, but no other reference to him has been

found. William B. Griffen suggests that he perhaps could have been Matías, given the particular area assigned to him. Griffen to author, December 26, 1986.

32. Almada, *chihuahuenses,* 38. Unfortunately, no list of the twenty-nine leaders who agreed to the treaty has been located, although it probably exists somewhere in the archives of Mexico City.

33. Robert McKnight came to New Mexico in 1812. Soon after, suspected of being an American agent, he was arrested and imprisoned for nine years in Chihuahua and Durango. In 1826 or 1827 he and Stephen Courcier took over the operations of Santa Rita del Cobre, from which he was said to have made a fortune. He was involved in several Apache-Mexican treaties in the 1830s. Charges were brought against him in 1837 for illegal trade with the Indians. He resigned in early 1838, eventually resurfacing at Corralitos in the early 1840s. Bartlett, *Personal Narrative,* I, 228–29; Ross Calvin, ed., *Lieutenant Emory Reports: Notes of a Military Reconnaissance,* 98; Dwight L. Clarke, ed., *The Original Journals of Henry Smith Turner with Stephen Watts Kearny to New Mexico and California, 1846–1847,* 85–86; JA, R28, Zuloaga to Military Commander at Janos, March 7, 1838.

34. SA, R13, Elías González to Governor, July 6, 1834; JA, R6, Calvo to Ponce de León, December 15, 1835; *El Fanal de Chihuahua* (Alcance), November 4, 1834; Weber, *Taos Trappers,* 221–22.

35. Joseph F. Park, "The Assassination of Juan José Compá," unpublished manuscript in author's files, 15.

36. In a letter to Mexican officials, Juan José Compá furnished the Apache version: "The Apaches in Agua Nueva have risen in revolt, saying that one of them was killed and justice has not been done them. These Indians say they have killed several Christians and have stolen horses. Immediately thereafter they sent messengers to the Apaches in all places telling them they wanted to kill all Christians at Agua Nueva. Likewise the Apaches at Janos say they have been told the same by their neighbors at Janos. Moreover the chief Costilla has left Bavispe. He says the commander of the garrison told him they wanted to kill or sieze them." SA, R12, Arregui to Vice-Governor of Sonora, May 15, 1833.

37. Robert C. Stevens, "The Apache Menace in Sonora, 1831–1849" *Arizona and the West,* 6 (Autumn 1964), 215; Ralph A. Smith, "Indians in American-Mexican Relations Before the War of 1846," *Hispanic American Historical Review,* 43 (February 1963), 43.

38. Stevens, "The Apache Menace," 215–16.

39. SA, R13, Bustamente to Governor, January 8, 1834; Bustamente to Governor, January 14, 1834; Narbona to Governor, January 13, 1834.

40. Ibid., Bustamente to Escalente y Arvizu, April 26, 1834; Juan González to Escalante y Arvizu, April 5, 1834. Juan Elías to Governor, April 3, 1834.

41. Ibid., Ramírez to Commander at Tubac, July 3, 1834; Elías González to Governor, July 6, 1834; Elías to Governor, July 4, 1834.

42. Ibid., Villasquez to Governor, July 14, 1834.

43. Park, "The Assassination of Juan José Compá," 15.

44. SA, R13, Escalante y Arvizu to Bustamente, October 21, 1834.

45. Vivora, born in the late 1790s, had a long and fascinating life. His father was an important leader in the 1790s until his death in 1803 or 1804. Vivora's actions usually paralleled those of his close associate and band leader Pisago Cabezón. Like Pisago, he agreed to peace in 1836 at Fronteras and in 1842 at

Janos. He reportedly was present at the Juan José Compá massacre in 1837 but escaped unharmed. He also eluded the Kirker scalp hunters in 1846 but could not evade the white man's lethal disease of smallpox, to which he succumbed at Fronteras in early 1862.

46. SA, R14, Escalante y Arvizu to Bustamente, November 2, 1834; Mora to Bustamente, November 21, 1834; Governor of Chihuahua to Bustamente, November 18, 1834; Hubert Howe Bancroft, *History of the North Mexican States and Texas,* II, 654.

47. In the fall of 1834 several Chiricahua leaders had sent a messenger to Paso del Norte soliciting peace. The list sounds like a who's who of the 1830–40 chiefs; among them were Cuchillo Negro, Itán, Fuerte, Pisago Cabezón, Tapilá, Teboca, and Juan José Compá. *El Fanal de Chihuahua,* November 4, November 25, 1834.

48. JA, R28, Calvo to Justiniani, January 20, 1835; document entitled, "Conditions of the Preliminary Peace with Juan José Compá"; Justiniani to Calvo, February 12, 1835.

49. SA, R13, Rey to Escalante y Arvizu, May 9, 1835; Justiniani to Commanding General, Chihuahua, April 3, 1835.

50. Ibid.

51. Elías González was probably the most important military leader in Sonora during the 1830s and 1840s. He was born into a prominent family at Arispe in 1793, joined the military in 1809, and rose to captain in 1822. In 1827 he was named adjutant inspector for Sonora and Sinaloa. Seven years later he became commanding general of Sonora, succeeding Colonel Francisco Javier Arregui, whose presidio troops were in a mutinous state. In 1836 he negotiated a peace treaty with Chiricahuas at Arispe. In 1844 he led Sonoran troops against Chiricahuas living near Janos, who he thought were raiding into Sonora. In 1851 he retired in controversy. He was a capable leader who understood Apaches. Francisco R. Almada, *Diccionario de historia, geografía y biografía sonorenses,* 239–40; Voss, *On the Periphery,* 69, 85.

52. Stevens, "The Apache Menace," 217.

53. SA, R13, Elías González to Escalante y Arvizu, June 27, 1835; JA, R24, Justiniani to Military Commander at Janos, June 19, 1835.

54. SA, R13, Elías González to Villascuna, June 1, 1835; Elías González to Governor of Sonora, June 17, 1835.

55. Voss, *On the Periphery,* 69–70.

56. *El Noticioso de Chihuahua,* December 4, 1835.

57. JA, R6, Calvo to Ponce de León, December 15, 1835.

58. Ibid., Calvo to Military Commander at Janos, January 15, 1836; AHSH, Folder 74, Elías González to Governor of Sonora, December 19, 1835; Elías González to Governor of Sonora, January 19, 1836.

59. AHSH, Folder 75, Escalante to Governor of Sonora, April 2, 1836.

60. SA, R14 Elías González to Governor, February 10, 1836; *El Noticioso de Chihuahua,* April 22, 1836.

61. Stevens, "The Apache Menace," 220

62. Miguel Narbona, born in the early 1800s, was a Chokonen captured by Sonoran troops about 1812–14. He remained with the Narbona family for some ten years before he returned to the Chiricahuas. His role in the peace of 1836 was a minor one: he probably acted as interpreter in the discussions. In the 1840s and

1850s he became an inveterate raider. Cochise apparently became his second in command in the late 1840s and early 1850s. Miguel Narbona died about 1856.

63. *El Noticioso de Chihuahua*, November 25, 1836; AHSH, Folder 74, Elías González to Commanding General, October 1, 1836. Griffen, *Apaches at War and Peace*, 172.

64. Griffen, *Apaches at War and Peace*, 172.

65. Ibid.

66. JA, R27, Calvo to Ponce de León, October 11, 1836; JA, R27, Arze to Ponce de León, January 26, 1837.

67. Cañon de los Embudos (Canyon of the Funnels) was about fifteen miles south of the present Arizona-Sonora line below the San Bernardino ranch. It was the site of a historic conference involving Brigadier General George Crook and Geronimo in March 1886.

68. SA, R14, Elías González to Governor, February 12, 1837; AHSH, Folder 102, Escalante to Governor, February 26, 1837.

69. SA, R14; Elías González to Governor, February 26, 1837.

70. Ibid.

71. Jason Betzinez with William Sturtevant Nye, *I Fought with Geronimo*, 1.

72. *El Noticioso de Chihuahua*, May 26, 1837.

73. SA, R14, Escalante y Arvizu Proclamation, March 5, 1837; AHSH, Folder 102, García to Governor, March 3, 1837; Escalante to Governor, February 22, 1837.

74. John Johnson, a native of Kentucky and later a resident of Missouri, was a hatter by trade. He probably arrived at Oposura, Sonora, in 1827 and with a partner, José Antonio Aguirre, acquired title to a hacienda. From here, he made trips to Santa Fe and established trading contacts with other Anglos, among them Robert McKnight and James Kirker, and with several Apache leaders, including Juan José Compá. He died in 1852. Rex W. Strickland "The Birth and Death of a Legend: The Johnson Massacre of 1837," *Arizona and the West*, 18 (Autumn 1976), 257–86.

75. Antonio Pascual Narbona was an experienced Indian fighter who commanded Sonora's northern presidios during the early 1840s. It was his father who reportedly captured Miguel Narbona. He was well acquainted with the Chokonens, personally leading several campaigns into the Chiricahua Mountains, which eventually made him a marked man. The Chokonens finally killed him on the porch of his home at Cuquiarachi on December 23, 1847. *El Sonorense*, March 17, 1848.

76. Juan José's band probably captured Lautora García (evidently massacring her family) in early 1837. Her testimony at Moctezuma shows clearly that Johnson misrepresented some of the facts when he made his report at Janos. She later married into the Ramírez family and died at Oputo in 1879. Henry S. Brooks, "A Scrap of Frontier History," *California*, 2 (October 1880).

The Johnson account was pieced together from four primary sources. His official report, written at Janos two days after the massacre, was published May 5, 1837, in *El Noticioso de Chihuahua*. Johnson returned to Oposura on April 30 and again reported to local authorities, who interviewed Lautora García and obtained her important story. The report was sent to the governor, who commended Johnson's actions. AHSH, 102, Johnson's and Lautora García's testimony taken at Moctezuma, May 5, 1837. Henry Brooks's account, cited above, contains relevant material about Lautora García. Benjamin D. Wilson's account, in the Bancroft Library, is somewhat garbled and confused but does contain some important peripheral information.

77. AHSH, Folder 102, Johnson's account; Lautora García's account; *El Noticioso de Chihuahua*, May 5, 1837.

78. *El Noticioso de Chihuahua*, May 5, 1837.

79. Ibid.

80. Ibid.; SA, R14, Elías González to Governor of Sonora, May 10, 1837.

81. Strickland, "The Birth and Death of a Legend," 258.

82. *Condition of the Indian Tribes: Report of the Joint Special Commission*, 328.

83. Ball, *Indeh*, 22; Eve Ball, *In the Days of Victorio: Recollections of a Warm Springs Apache*, 46; Betzinez, *I Fought with Geronimo*, 1.

84. SA, R14, Governor to Ignacio Elías González, July 20, 1837.

85. Opler, *Lifeway*, 335.

Chapter 3

1. Park, "The Assassination of Juan José Compá," 27.

2. University of Texas at El Paso, Juárez Collection, Roll 8, Prefect of Galeana to Prefect del Paso, October 9, 1837; Varela to Prefect del Paso, October 26, 1837; *El Noticioso de Chihuahua*, December 11, 1837; July 19, 1838.

3. SA, R14, Elías to Escalante Y Arvizu, October 11, 1837.

4. José Ignacio Terán y Tato, born at Bacoachi in the early 1800s, was undoubtedly one of the wealthiest men in northern Sonora. During the late 1840s and early 1850s he personally financed and directed several campaigns against the Chiricahuas. He died in France in 1868. Almada, *sonorenses*, 784.

5. *El Restaurador*, January 30, 1838.

6. Ibid., February 6, March 10, 1838.

7. Tapilá, born in the late 1790s, probably was related to Pisago Cabezón, since he appears on the Janos ration lists from 1816 through 1819. In the early 1820s he probably married a woman of the Cide (Side) group, for he was included in Cide's camp at various times between 1822 and 1828. Likewise, in 1835 he was mentioned in a census taken at the Copper Mines, again as part of Cide's ranchería. He was mentioned on several occasions in the 1840s to the early 1850s, most of them involving hostile actions. He reportedly played a prominent role in the Pozo Hediondo fight of January 20, 1851. In November 1851 he was killed at Bavispe, where he had gone to discuss a truce and prisoner exchange.

8. *El Noticioso de Chihuahua*, April 12, 1838.

9. Ibid.; George W. Kendall, *Across the Great Southwestern Prairies*, I, 429.

10. *El Noticioso de Chihuahua*, June 21, 1838; JA, R27, Record of Events, July 1837. Griffen, *Apaches at War and Peace*, 176.

11. John C. Cremony, *Life Among the Apaches*, 32. Other writers, including Paul I. Wellman, have used Cremony's account. Wellman says "the three to four hundred souls who left Santa Rita were almost wiped out. Scarcely half a dozen ever reached Janos . . . the bleaching skeletons of all the rest sprawled on the road between." Paul I. Wellman, *The Indian Wars of the West*, 260. J. P. Dunn, *Massacre of the Mountains*, 315-16, cited Cremony's account, as did Stephen Longstreet, *War Cries on Horseback: The Story of the Indian Wars of the Great Plains*, 29-31. Mrs. Eve Ball offers an account from the Apache perspective: "Many set out for the border, but not one reached it. Not one." Again, evidence for this is

lacking, which leads one to speculate that some of her informants read Cremony's book. Ball, *In the Days of Victorio*, 46. There is gross exaggeration in almost every incident described by Cremony relating to Apache-Mexican or Apache-Anglo affairs. On the other hand, Bartlett, who traveled with Cremony and probably heard the same stories told at the same time, faithfully recorded each incident.

12. Frederick A. Wislizenus, *A Tour to Northern Mexico Connected with Col. Doniphan's Expedition in 1846 and 1847*, 57–58.

13. Bartlett, *Personal Narrative*, I, 228–29.

14. Bancroft, *History of the North Mexican States*, II, 656–59.

15. *El Restaurador*, August 28, 1838.

16. AHSH, Folder 96, Elías to Governor, June 19, 1839; Prefect of Bavispe to Governor, August 19, 1839.

17. Ibid., Folder 104, Gándara to Governor, December 3, 1839.

18. Ibid., Folder 110, Governor to Moreno, August 20, 1840.

19. McGaw, *Savage Scene*, 120–21; Hobbs, *Wild Life*, 81. It is ludicrous to suggest that Kirker entered this arrangement to protect the mining interests of his friends at Santa Rita del Cobre, Robert McKnight and Stephen Courcier, although legend says this was justification for his notorious deeds. At the time he was recruited, the mines had been deserted for ten months; moreover, evidence suggests that Kirker had collaborated with the Indians at exactly the time the mines were abandoned. In fact, Chihuahuan authorities accused him of directing the Apaches who attacked the wagon train at the end of March 1838. Perhaps he had advised the attack, but the Apaches told Gabriel Zapata that Kirker had recently traded them new firearms and at that time he was with Tapilá on a raid into Sonora. Not coincidentally, in mid-May, Kirker passed Socorro, New Mexico, en route to U.S. territory with a "large quantity of horses and mules together with his fellow countrymen." He had just left the Chiricahuas, whom, as Kirker later conveniently recalled, had taken him prisoner while trapping and forced him to accompany them. In any event, in July 1838, Chihuahua's governor wanted him arrested for "criminal and pernicious conduct."

20. Juárez Collection, Roll 9, de La Vega to Prefect District del Paso, April 2, 1839.

21. Park, "The Assassination of Juan José Compá," 24.

22. *El Antenor*, January 21, 1840.

23. McGaw, *Savage Scene*, 130–31.

24. AHSH, Folder 108, Morales to Secretary of the Department, September 21, 1840. *La Luna*, October 27, 1840.

25. AHSH, Folder 120, Pareda to Gándara, April 16, 1841; Folder 123, Cuesto to Governor, January 8, 1842.

26. JA, R30, Military Commander at Janos to Governor of Chihuahua, September 1, 1842.

27. Griswold, "Ft. Sill Apaches," 24, 32, 132. Griswold's biography has Dos-teh-seh born about 1838, which is clearly too late by about fifteen years. Taza, Cochise's oldest son, was born in the early 1840s, at which time Dos-teh-seh was in her late teens or early twenties. The name of Mangas Coloradas's wife was Tu-es-seh, according to Mrs. Eve Ball. Ball to author, June 5, 1978.

28. Keith Basso, letter to author, February 22, 1979.

29. Juárez Collection, Roll 11, Varela to Prefect del Paso, April 12, 1842; JA, R28, Ugarte to Madrigal, April 26, 1842. *La Luna*, April 19, 1842.

30. JA, R29, Aguirre to Military Commander at Janos, May 15, 1842.

31. JA, R29, Madrigal to Military Commander, Chihuahua, May 26, 1842. The Indians were referring to an incident in which several Apaches were killed. Josiah Gregg wrote that it occurred in the summer of 1839 when authorities enticed several Apaches into an ambush at Paso del Norte, where some twenty warriors were "treacherously dispatched in cold blood." Josiah Gregg, *Commerce of the Prairies*, 206–7.

32. JA, R29, Conde to Military Commander at Janos, June 9, 1842.

33. *La Luna*, June 28, 1842.

34. Ponce, born about 1810, was a literate Chihenne leader who was said to have been a good friend of Cochise. Like his contemporary Delgadito, he was a moderate leader who participated in the Janos agreements of 1842 and 1851 and signed treaties with Americans in 1852 and 1853. His group was on good terms with the Mescaleros, their neighbors east of the Río Grande. It was probably his son Ponce who guided General Howard to Cochise in 1872. The elder Ponce was killed by one of his own people "in a drunken frolic" in late June or early July 1854. RG 75, T21, R2, Steck to Meriwether, July 8, 1854.

35. *La Luna*, July 15, July 19, 1842.

36. JA, R30, Madrigal to Commander in Chief, September 1, 1842.

37. Esquinaline, a moderate Chiricahua leader born about 1800, headed one of the less-militant Chokonen local groups. A close associate of Cochise in the late 1850s, he was the Indian whom Tevis called Esconolea. During the late 1840s and early 1850s he was closely associated with Mangas, oftentimes uniting with the Chihenne leader for raids into Sonora. He was one of the leaders in the Chiricahua victory at Pozo Hediondo in January 1851. In the mid-1850s he saw his band dwindling and, with pressure from both American and Mexicans, tried to live in peace, first at Janos, then at Fronteras, and finally at Apache Pass with Cochise. In 1859, Samuel Cozzens described him as "a rather good looking specimen of an Apache, about sixty years of age and speaks Spanish, very imperfectly, however." He died in the early 1860s. *Missouri Republican*, August 29, 1859.

38. Yrigóllen was the dominant Chokonen leader from the early 1840s until his death at the hands of Sonoran troops at Janos in March 1851. His son, Miguel Yrigóllen, was a subordinate of Cochise in the early 1860s. Edwin R. Sweeney, "I Had Lost All: Geronimo and the Carrasco Massacre of 1851," *Journal of Arizona History*, 27 (Spring 1986), 35–52.

39. JA, R30, Janos ration lists of October 17, 24, and 31, 1842. AHSH, Folder 127, Elías González to Governor, January 26 and May 14, 1842.

40. *Revista Oficial*, February 7, 1843.

41. Ibid., April 18, 1843.

42. Griffen, *Apaches at War and Peace*, 199. JA, R30, Monterde to Madrigal, June 8, 1843; AHSH, Folder 134, Ignacio Elías to Governor, June 6, 1843.

43. JA, R30, ration lists of July 24 and July 31, 1843.

44. JA, R30, Monterde to Madrigal, August 18, 1843; SA, R14, Bozanigra to Governor of Sonora, December 6, 1843.

45. AHSH, Folder 134, Subprefect of Arispe to Governor, December 18, 1843.

46. SA, R14, Bozanigra to Governor of Sonora, February 8, 1844.

47. JA, R30, various rations lists, November 27, 1843, through January 15, 1844. Griffen, *Apaches at War and Peace*, 205–8.

48. Griffen, *Apaches at War and Peace*, 205–8.

49. Bancroft Library, Louis Alphonse Pinart Collection MM381, Documents 65, 69, and 72.

50. Chepillo drew rations at Janos from October 16, 1843, through December 4, 1843. In 1844 he joined Mangas and other Chokonens on raids into Sonora, later admitting that he killed a citizen near Fronteras. He became the leader of a Chokonen group in the early 1850s after the death of Yrigóllen and Tapilá. He was closely associated with Esquinaline, and both were reported to be living in the Chiricahua Mountains during the summer of 1856. Chepillo was involved in the peace negotiations at Fronteras in the summer of 1858 and probably was killed in the July 1858 massacre near that presidio.

51. Pinart Collection, Document 73; AHSH, Folder 146, Corella to Governor, May 3, 1844.

52. Ibid.; Park, "Apaches in Mexican-American Relations," 135; Alcance al número 35 de la *Revista Oficial,* August 28, 1844. *Revista Oficial,* September 24, 1844. Sonora conducted an investigation in order to justify its actions at Janos and Corralitos. The results can be found in the Pinart Collection at Bancroft Library. The probe focused mainly on the stolen Sonoran livestock and loot which Antonio Narbona and Elías González recovered in their attacks. It implicated, from the names of those involved, many influential civil officials at Janos and Corralitos. At Janos, Narbona confiscated stock, found in the Apache ranchería, which belonged to Sesario Corella, along with about six hundred pesos believed to have been stolen at the same time. He recovered the weapons of Francisco Alday and Arenito Vezinos, both of whom had been killed at Santa Cruz the previous month. Several head of stock were found in the possession of Janos citizens. Narbona found some in the possession of Juan José Zozaya, an influential citizen who served as peace commissioner to the Apaches in 1850; it had been stolen from Agustín Barela in June. Another Sonoran citizen, Seberiano Valencia, testified that he ransomed his own horse, stolen by the Apaches, from Zozaya at Janos for twenty pesos.

Results were similar at Corralitos. The owner of the mines, José María Zuloaga, had in his possession several horses and mules stolen in Sonora. Among them was stock from Sahuaripa, which infuriated Elías González because they had come from a raid led by Cigarrito in which nineteen people were killed. A horse belonging to Fernando Moreno was found in the possession of Angel Aguirre. Stock belonging to Sonoran citizens Bautista Valencia, Francisco Sicara, and Luis García was found, too. To top it off, Robert McKnight, former owner of the Santa Rita mines, now living at Barranco, had Sonoran livestock in his possession. Apache casualties numbered eighty to one hundred dead, with twenty or thirty killed at Janos and the remainder by Elías González's party near Corralitos.

53. Pinart Collection, Document 80, García to Elías González, January 1, 1845.

54. *Revista Oficial,* February 25, 1845.

55. Ibid., July 1, 1845. JA, R31, Ugarte to Janos Commander, June 20, 1845.

56. JA, R31, Conde to Padilla, July 20, 1845. JA, R28, Summary of Disbursements, July 1, 1845.

57. Láceris (Láceres, Pláceris) was a Nednhi leader of the Janeros group. He, too, matured in the presidio system and probably was related in some manner to the Compá family. He was born in the early 1800s and by 1842 had two wives and at least two children. He was at Janos from October 1842 through early 1844. From 1846 through the late 1850s, he was probably the most prominent Janeros leader of

the Nednhi band. A moderate, he generally preferred peace to war, although in the late 1840s he joined the Chokonens for many forays and was one of the ringleaders in the October 1849 capture of an American wagon train near Janos which resulted in the death of several Americans. Closely associated with Candelario, a son of Juan José, he was the leading Nednhi spokesman in the Janos treaties of 1850 and 1857. When affairs became brisk in northern Mexico, he migrated north, joining Delgadito and Mangas Coloradas in the peace with Americans in April 1853. He remained in New Mexico until the summer of 1856, when he returned to Chihuahua and began negotiating at Janos. He probably died in the late 1850s.

58. *El Provisional,* June 9, 1846.

59. Carro, a Chokonen leader of the late 1840s through the mid-1850s, had been, like so many of the Chokonen leaders, a member of Pisago Cabezón's group. He was a moderate leader, not as pacific as Esquinaline or as militant as Miguel Narbona, Tapilá, or Teboca. After the double-cross at Galeana, he, like most of the Chokonens, took to the warpath for the next decade. In July 1850 during a parley at Bacoachi he admitted that the permanent homes of his band were in the Chiricahua Mountains. In the summer of 1857 he made peace at Janos and died that fall, evidently killed by poisoned rations he received at Janos. SA, R16, Martínez to Governor, July 22, 1850.

60. *El Provisional,* July 7, 1846.

61. Ibid., July 14, 1846.

62. AHSH, Folder 160, Governor of Chihuahua to Governor of Sonora, July 6, 1846.

63. *El Provisional,* July 21, 1846.

64. George Frederick Ruxton, *Adventures in Mexico and the Rocky Mountains, 1846–1847,* 153–54; Mangas Coloradas's version was published in *Condition of the Indian Tribes,* 328; Betzinez, *I Fought with Geronimo,* 3. Betzinez put the massacre at a place called Kintal by the Apaches, which he believed was Ramos. He was wrong. Ramos was never more than a hacienda and at no time could it have eight hundred to a thousand inhabitants, as Betzinez asserted. Investigation reveals that the Chiricahua name for Casas Grandes was Kin-n-Teel ("house broad"), and the massacre occurred southeast of there at Galeana—further evidence that it was probably the incident described by Betzinez.

65. *El Provisional,* July 14, 1846.

66. Hobbs, *Wild Life,* 87–88.

67. Betzinez, *I Fought with Geronimo,* 1.

68. Ibid., 4–9.

Chapter 4

1. Born in 1794 in New Jersey, Kearny fought in the War of 1812 and several successive Indian campaigns before being named commander of the Army of the West in May 1846. He died in St. Louis in 1848. *Webster's American Military Biographies,* 212–13.

2. One chief told Kearny, "You have taken New Mexico, and will soon take California, go then and take Chihuahua, Durango and Sonora. We will help you. . . . The Mexicans are rascals; we hate and will kill them all." Calvin, *Lieutenant Emory Reports,* 100.

3. Philip St. George Cooke was born in 1809 at Leesburg, Virginia. He graduated from West Point in 1827 and saw action in the Black Hawk War of 1832, after

which he was promoted to first lieutenant. He was promoted to captain in 1835, saw more action in the Mexican War of 1846 and remained loyal to the Union in the Civil War, eventually reaching the rank of brigadier general. He wrote a manual on cavalry tactics and retired in 1873. He died in 1895. *Webster's American Military Biographies,* 79-80.

4. Pauline Weaver was born in Tennessee in 1800 to an American father and a Cherokee mother. He came west as a member of the Hudson's Bay Company and was one of the first whites to explore Arizona. He died in 1867 near Camp Lincoln (later Camp Verde), Arizona. Jay J. Wagoner, *Early Arizona: Prehistory to Civil War,* 254; Thrapp, *Encyclopedia,* 1525.

5. Antoine Leroux was a famous mountain man of the Southwest. Born in St. Louis, he came to New Mexico in the early 1820s and eventually settled at Taos. For the next twenty years he trapped and hunted throughout the Southwest. In 1852 he served as guide for Bartlett's boundary survey on its return from San Diego. He died in New Mexico in 1861. Thrapp, *Encyclopedia,* 848.

6. Manuelito, a Chokonen leader, was born in the 1780s. He received rations at Janos as early as 1810 as a member of Asquienalte's (Asquenitery) band, which had made peace in the 1780s. Manuelito was a leading spokesman during the peace of 1842, and it was his band that bore the brunt of Elías González's attack in August 1844. His influence had declined by the mid-1840s with the rise of Miguel Narbona and Yrigóllen. He died of exposure in the winter of 1849-50. *El Faro,* July 2, 1850; *Revista Oficial,* September 24, 1844; Alcance al número 35 de la *Revista Oficial,* August 24, 1844.

7. Philip St. George Cooke, *Exploring Southwestern Trails, 1846-1854,* 123, 129-30.

8. Ibid., 159-60.

9. Bancroft, *History of the North Mexican States,* II, 670.

10. AHS, Merejildo Grijalva, Hayden File.

11. *El Sonorense,* March 26, 1847; AHSH, Folder 175, Escalante to Governor, March 6, 1847.

12. AHSH, Folder 175, Justice of the Peace at Bacoachi to Governor, March 31, 1847; Folder 176, Cuesta to Governor, April 3, 1847.

13. Ibid., Folder 175, Escalante to Governor, April 6, 1847.

14. Ibid., Elías González to Governor, May 3, 1847.

15. AHSH, Folder 176, Escalante to Governor, May 6, 1847. AHSH, Folder 175, Escalante to Governor, June 14, 1847.

16. In fact, Western Apaches, reportedly Pinals, solicited peace at Tucson in August and October 1847, although no worthwhile agreement apparently was made. *El Sonorense,* October 8, 1847; AHSH, Folder 176, Military Commander at Tucson to Governor, October ?, 1847.

17. AHSH, Folder 175, Narbona to Prefect of Moctezuma, September 22, 1847; *El Sonorense,* October 8, 1847.

18. Bartlett, *Personal Narrative,* I, 273. *El Sonorense,* March 17, 1848; AHSH, Folder 199, Escalante to Governor, December 24, 1847; February 10, 1848.

19. *El Sonorense,* March 17, 1848; AHSH, Folder 199, Arvizu to Governor, March 1, 1848. The fate of these forty-two prisoners is uncertain. The young children probably grew up as Apaches and others may have been returned by the Chiricahuas in compliance with subsequent peace agreements.

20. Eusebio Gil Samaniego, a native of Bavispe, was well known to Cochise

and the Chiricahuas. Called Chato ("flat nose") by the Indians, he was a stern officer who led several campaigns against the Apaches. Evidently he was a man who asked no quarter and gave none.

21. SA, R14, Samaniego to Governor, June 21, 1848. The descendants of Cochise knew nothing of his having been captured at Fronteras. Granddaughter Amelia Naiche told me she had not heard of the incident. Neither had Mrs. Eve Ball, recorder of Chiricahua oral history. This is not surprising when one considers that very little historical information from the Indian perspective existed before 1870. In fact, none of Mrs. Ball's informants ever mentioned prominent Chiricahua leaders, such as Yrigóllen and Miguel Narbona. Interviews with Amelia Naiche, January 17, 1979, and Mrs. Eve Ball, January 17, 1979.

22. SA, R14, Calvo y Muro to Gándara, June 28, 1848.

23. Ibid., Calvo y Muro to Governor, August 19, 1848; Limon to Calvo y Muro, August 12, 1848.

24. Two years later Limon was killed by Apaches at Cocospera Canyon while serving as an escort for the Inez González party. Alan Radbourne, "Ambush at Cocospera Canyon," *English Westerners Tally Sheet,* (July 1979), 63–76.

25. *El Sonorense,* September 6, 1848.

26. Ibid., October 6, 1848.

27. Ibid., October 25, 1848. The Treaty of Guadalupe Hidalgo ended the United States–Mexican War of 1846. The United States agreed to restrain Indians from raiding into Mexico, to rescue any captives, and to extract compensation from the Indians for these raids. With respect to the Apaches, this was hopeless. The United States would have needed to establish forts along the Arizona and New Mexico border, and a penurious Congress was not about to approve additional expenditures. J. Fred Rippy argues convincingly that Mexico used all of her available resources to protect the northern frontier, but to no avail. J. Fred Rippy, "The Indians of the Southwest in the Diplomacy of the United States and Mexico, 1848–1853," *Hispanic American Historical Review,* 2 (August 1919), 363–96; Richard N. Ellis, *New Mexico Historical Documents,* 10–32.

28. Rippy, "Indians of the Southwest," 387–89.

29. *El Sonorense,* November 3, 1848.

30. SA, R14, Tuvera to Prefect of Ures, December 19, 1848.

31. Bartlett, *Personal Narrative,* II, 302.

32. SA, R15, Comadurán to Commanding General, December 14, 1848.

33. SA, R15, Comadurán to Elías González, January 26, 1849.

34. *El Sonorense,* April 15, 1850. This issue contains a summary of the individuals who emigrated to California. In all, 5,664 men departed Sonora, and this total included only five of the nine districts reporting.

35. SA, R15, Comadurán to Elías González, January 26, 1849.

36. Captain James Whitlock defeated a band of Chiricahuas near Piños Altos on March 1, 1864, killing thirteen warriors including Luis, a Bedonkohe chief probably related to Mangas Coloradas, and recapturing Marijenia Figueira. She provided details of the Banamichi raid, in which her mother and father were killed. She had been a servant for Luís and his family since that time. *The War of the Rebellion: A Compilation of the Official Records of the Union and Confederate Armies,* 34, Pt. 1, 122–23.

37. SA, R15, Cordova to the Prefect of Baviacora, March 9, 1849; Miranda to Prefect, March 13, 1849; *El Sonorense,* March 21, March 23, 1849.

38. SA, R15, Samaniego to Terán y Tato, April 24, 1849.

39. Juan Abad Telles, in his late fifties, was the grandfather of Mickey Free, who had a prominent role in Arizona history and the life of Cochise. It is ironic that Cochise, who probably participated in this attack, may have fought the grandfather of the boy who played such a prominent role in the Bascom affair in February 1861. My thanks to English historian Allan Radbourne for bringing this to my attention.

40. SA, R15, Limon to Elías González, May 1, 1849.

41. *El Sonorense,* June 1, 1849; SA, R15, Terán y Tato to Governor, May 29, 1849. The Chokonen prisoners were sent to Ures and Hermosillo for confinement. Among them were the wife and mother-in-law of Demos, a leading Chiricahua warrior who had an instrumental role in peace negotiations during the spring of 1850.

42. SA, R15, de Aros to Governor, May 24, 1849; de Aros to Secretary of War and Navy, July 13, 1849. Montoya was subsequently set free, while Romero was tortured to death over a period of several days. He left behind a wife and two young sons.

43. SA, R15, Terán y Tato to Governor, June 19, 1849; Elías González to Governor, June 22, 1849, *El Sonorense,* July 20, 1849. Duran's testimony was interesting. A war party of two hundred men was planning to raid along the Sonora River in late June. He also confirmed the increasing Apache activity at Janos, which illustrated the peculiar and precarious relationship between the Chiricahuas and Captain Baltazar Padilla, José María Zuloaga, and Juan José Zozaya, the leading military and public officials of the area. Duran confirmed that stolen Sonoran plunder was traded at Janos; furthermore, Zozaya had written a letter to Chief Babosa declaring that the people of Janos were his friends. Duran also revealed the Apaches' close contact with New Mexican traders, including a man named Armijo who supplied the Apaches with American rifles, powder, balls, cloth, and other provisions. According to him, the Chiricahuas feared the Americans and believed the latter were planning a campaign against them.

44. SA, R15, Elías González to Governor, July 12, 1849.

45. *El Sonorense,* June 1, August 3, 1849; SA, R15, Elías González to Minister of War and Navy, July 13, 1849; Elías González to Governor, July 15, 1849.

46. SA, R15, Elías González to Governor, October 30, 1849; document titled "Diary of Operations by Colonel José María Elías González in Pursuit of the Indian savages."

47. Ibid.

48. John Coffee ("Jack") Hays was born in Tennessee in 1817, became a captain in the Texas Rangers at the age of twenty-three, and led several successful scouts against Comanches. On April 11, 1849, he was named subagent for the Río Gila in New Mexico. Hays reached San Francisco in January 1850 and reported on an alternate route to Cooke's, that being through Puerto del Dado (Apache Pass), which saved more than 150 miles of travel. In all likelihood, Elías González told Hays about the more direct route. Thrapp, *Encyclopedia,* 634; *Alta California,* February 1, 1850.

49. Annie Heloise Abel, ed., *The Official Correspondence of James S. Calhoun While Indian Agent at Santa Fe and Superintendent of Indian Affairs in New Mexico,* 34.

50. SA, R15, Elías González to Governor, October 30, 1849.

51. JA, R32, Padilla to Commanding General of Chihuahua, March 22, May 26, 1849.

52. Ralph A. Smith, "The Scalp Hunt in Chihuahua—1849," *New Mexico Historical Review*, 40 (April 1965), 116–40. In the first few months the Carrizaleños were hit hardest. Their old chief, Jasquedegá, and twenty-two others were killed at Carmen on June 6, and in early July a son of Mano Mocha was killed at Corralitos. *El Faro*, June 23, August 14, 1849.

53. Missouri Historical Society, Solomon Sublette Papers.

54. Soquilla, born about 1800, was leader of a small Janeros local group. He had matured in the presidio system of the early 1800s and was a member of Asquienalte's band in 1816 through the mid-1820s. He figured prominently in the Janos peace of 1842, joined the Chiricahuas in the Sonora raids during 1844, and suffered the consequences when Elías González attacked his camp near Corralitos in August 1844. He had one wife and four children in the Janos census of 1843 and 1844.

55. JA, R32, Padilla to Inspector of the Colony, September 12, September 15, 1849.

56. Coleto Amarillo (Yellow Jacket) was, with Láceris, the dominant leader of the Nednhi band in the late 1840s and early 1850s. He was the leading spokesman for the Chiricahua bands in the peace consummated at Janos in June 1850. Sonoran troops killed him in April 1852 north of Lake Guzmán. His son, known by the same name, headed a small group through the early 1860s.

57. Arvizu, born in the late 1790s, probably was related in some manner to Manuel Chirimni. He was at Janos during the 1820s until the outbreak of 1831, participated in the Janos peace treaties of 1842 and 1850, and was killed at Janos by Sonoran troops under Colonel José María Carrasco in March 1851. Sweeney, "I Had Lost All," 52.

58. *Alta California*, May 16, 1850.

59. *Alta California*, May 16, 1850; *El Faro*, November 3, November 20, 1849; January 5, 1850. JA, R32, Padilla to Military Inspector, Chihuahua, November 6, 1849.

Chapter 5

1. Robert M. Utley, *Frontiersman in Blue, The United States Army and the Indians, 1848–1865*, 85.

2. Steen was born in Kentucky in 1800. Cited for gallantry in the Mexican War, he was wounded on August 16, 1849, in a fight with Chihennes near San Diego Crossing, which was on the Río Grande about ten miles southeast of present-day Hatch, New Mexico. In the late 1850s he was stationed at Fort Buchanan and might have met Cochise. Historic Stein's Peak was probably named after him. He retired with a rank of lieutenant colonel in 1863 and died in 1880. Thrapp, *Encyclopedia*, 1363; Francis B. Heitman, *Historical Register and Dictionary of the United States Army*, I, 919.

3. Thrapp, *Victorio*, 23.

4. AHSH, Folder 221, Martínez to Elías González, April 23, 1850. *Santa Fe Weekly Gazette*, March 19, 1853.

5. Jornado del Muerto, translated "journey of death," was a waterless stretch of about ninety miles from Rincon to San Marcial in south-central New Mexico. Pearce, *New Mexico Place Names*, 77.

6. AHSH, Folder 221, Martínez to Elías González, April 23, 1850; *Santa Fe Weekly Gazette,* March 19, 1853. According to Teofilo and Mateo Savanillo, Miguel's party suffered heavy losses.

7. Posito Moraga was a prominent Chokonen local group leader of the late 1840s and early 1850s. He probably died in the mid-1850s. His brother, Chino, was a subordinate of Cochise in the 1850s and 1860s.

8. AHSH, Folder 221, Elías González to Governor, February 13, February 28, 1850.

9. AHSH, Folder 221, Elías González to Governor, March 22, 1850.

10. Ibid.; AHSH, Folder 221, Ybarra to Elías González, March 22, 1850.

11. Ibid.,; *El Sonorense,* May 10, 1850.

12. *El Sonorense,* April 15, 1850.

13. SA, R16, Elías González to Governor of Sonora, May 13, 1850.

14. AHSH, Folder 221, Elías González to Governor, April 30, 1850.

15. *El Sonorense,* May 10, 1850; AHSH, Folder 221, Elías González to Governor, April 30, 1850.

16. *El Sonorense,* June 7, 1850. *El Faro,* June 25, 1850. AHSH, Folder 221, Elías González to Governor, June 25, 1850.

17. Rodolfo F. Acuña, *Sonoran Strongman: Ignacio Pesqueira and His Times* (cited hereafter as Acuña, *Pesqueira*), 8.

18. *El Faro,* July 2, August 17, 1850.

19. Ibid.; AHSH, Folder 221, Zozaya to Elías González, June 25, 1850.

20. *El Sonorense,* September 20, November 15, 1850. AHSH, Folder 221, Ramírez to Governor, August 30, 1850.

21. *El Sonorense,* November 15, 1850; AHSH, Folder 221, Terán y Tato to Governor, November 1, 1850; Elías González to Governor, November 11, 1850; SA, R16, Navamuel to Governor, October 5, 1850.

22. *El Sonorense,* January 31, 1851. Carrasco, born in 1813, reached the rank of lieutenant in 1833. He distinguished himself in the U.S.-Mexican War of 1846. He reached Sonora in January 1851 with forty troops and died in July 1851 of cholera. Almada, *sonorenses,* 146.

23. Pesqueira, born December 16, 1820, in Arispe, was educated in Europe. He returned to Sonora in 1839 and joined the local militia, or National Guard. By 1845 he had risen to captain and, as his biographer notes, "was suddenly catapulted from obscurity to statewide prominence" after the Pozo Hediondo fight. In 1857 he became governor of Sonora, a position he held throughout most of the 1860s and into the 1870s. He died on January 4, 1886. Acuña, *Sonora Strongman.*

24. *El Sonorense,* January 31, 1851; *El Correo,* February 11, 1851. In an issue dated May 30, 1851, *El Sonorense* charged that "Anglo scoundrels" had armed and led the Apaches, who were well armed with rifles and six-shooters. The Indians killed fifteen and wounded twenty-five from Bacoachi and killed eleven and wounded twenty-two of the fifty nationals from Arispe. AHSH, Folder 224, Villascusa to Governor, April 28, 1851.

25. Eduardo W. Villa, *Compendia de Historia del Estado de Sonora,* 242–44. Villa errs in dating the fight January 7.

26. AHS, Merejildo Grijalva, Hayden File.

27. Barrett, *Geronimo's Story,* 51–54.

28. For events leading up to Carrasco's campaign, see Sweeney, "I Had Lost All," 35–45.

29. *El Sonorense*, March 28, 1851.

30. AHSH, Folder 230, Flores to Quintana, August 15, 1851; Campo to Governor, July 21, 1851; *La Voz del Pueblo*, July 30, August 6, 1851.

31. San Simon was well known to Mexicans in the 1840s. At this time there was probably a running stream and at places the terrain was very marshy with willow groves, hence the name Cienega de Sauz (Willow Swamp). In 1859 the Butterfield Overland Mail Company established a stage station here, primarily for changing stock. Will C. Barnes, *Arizona Place Names*, 51.

32. *La Voz del Pueblo*, September 10, October 8, 1851.

33. AHSH, Folder 230, Flores to Governor, December 15, 1851.

34. *El Correo*, November 22, 1851.

35. *El Sonorense*, November 7, 1851.

36. Manuel Gallegos served as an officer in the Arizona Volunteers, 1865–66, and directed Sonoran campaigns against the Apaches in the early 1870s.

37. Bonita Canyon is in the Chiricahua Mountains some fifteen miles south of Apache Pass. Today it is under jurisdiction of the National Park Service and is a popular camping area.

38. SA, R16, Terán y Tato to Governor, April 2, 1852; *El Sonorense*, April 20, 1852.

39. SA, R16, Lozada to Blanco, April 12, 1852; *El Sonorense*, April 16, 1852.

40. Opler, *Lifeway*, 466.

41. *El Sonorense*, April 22, 1853; SA, R16, García to Governor, April 14, 1853; Thrapp, *Victorio*, 32–33.

42. SA, R16, Arvizu to the Justice of the Peace, Granadas, June 16, 1853; Lavadi to Commander of the Opatas, July 14, 1853.

43. SA, R17, Cota to Juzgado de Paces, Cumuripa, July 19, 1853.

44. Casimiro's daughter was one of twelve Chiricahuas captured by national troops under Flat Nose Samaniego in January 1854. The Chokonen chief succeeded in exchanging Mexican prisoners for his daughter, but during the ensuing negotiations Sonoran troops opened fire, killing Casimiro and two other warriors; the Indians retaliated by killing two of their hostages. In the following months the Chiricahuas avenged this incident by killing several of Samaniego's relatives and the son of Captain Reyes, the two Mexican leaders involved in the affair. SA, R17, Samaniego to Governor, February 2, 1854; Reyes to Governor, February 3, 1854.

45. SA, R17, Justice of the Peace, Alamos, to Governor, February 19, 1854; Terán y Tato to Governor, March 7, 1854; Samaniego to Governor, March 14, 1854; Padilla to Governor, February 17, 1854; Ballestero to Governor, February 21, 1854.

46. Costales was a subordinate of Delgadito who rose to prominence because of his fighting ability, even though he was not an Apache. Born at El Carmen, Chihuahua, he was captured as a youth by Apaches and was raised by the Chihennes. He was murdered by Mexicans on December 31, 1856, while on a mission for Dr. Michael Steck, agent for the Chihennes. Thrapp, *Victorio*, 5, 8, 52–53.

47. SA, R17, Prefect of Moctezuma to Prefect of Ures, May 24, 1854; SA, R18, García to Governor, June 24, 1854; Gándara to Governor, July 14, 1854.

48. The Gadsden Purchase was the result of the efforts of James Gadsden, minister to Mexico, who conducted the negotiations to purchase land below the Gila River in order to construct a transcontinental railroad along the Thirty-second Parallel. Gadsden agreed to pay Santa Anna fifteen million dollars, but the U.S. Senate

reduced the purchase price to ten million. Ellis, *New Mexico Historical Documents*, 41–46.

49. Bancroft, *History of the North Mexican States*, II, 693.

50. See, for example, SA, R18, Moreno to Governor, June 17, 1856; AHSH, Folder 283, Gomez to Governor, April 7, 1855; Pesquiera to Governor, November 3, 1855.

51. JA, R36, Padilla to Commanding General, Chihuahua, May 28, 1855.

52. Chiricahua bands had made treaties with the Americans in July 1852 and April 1853. Most of the Chihennes and the Janeros local group of the Nednhis participated; apparently, few of the Bedonkohes and none of the Chokonens were present. Under terms of the second treaty, the U.S. government agreed to feed the Apaches and to provide protection as long as the Indians abstained from depredations in Mexico. Neither party fully lived up to its part of the agreement; the Indians continued raiding in Mexico and the federal government furnished little food, seeds, or tools to farm, although the concept of Apaches' farming on a sufficient scale to feed themselves was a gross misconception on the part of well-meaning whites, indicating their lack of understanding of Chiricahua culture. Thrapp, *Victorio*, 27–34, 43–45.

53. Smith, "Indians in American-Mexican Relations," 39.

54. Steck was born in Pennsylvania in 1818 and graduated from Jefferson Medical College in Philadelphia about 1843. He went to New Mexico in 1849 as a contract surgeon with the army and in late 1854 was appointed agent for the Southern Apaches, essentially the Chiricahuas. He was an honest and able agent, trusted by the wild Chiricahuas. He died in 1883. Thrapp, *Encyclopedia*, 1361.

55. National Archives and Records Center, RG 393, Records of United States Army Continental Commands, 1821–1920, Letters Received, Department of New Mexico (cited hereafter as RG393,LR,DNM with citation), Eaton to Nichols, December 23, 1855.

56. Cochise had a brother named Juan, and this could have been him. But little is known of his activities and status, although as the son of a chief he might have been considered a minor leader. He was held in high esteem as a fighter and as a man.

57. Zimmerman Library, University of New Mexico, Michael Steck Papers, Box 2, Folder 2, document dated September 19, 1856.

58. RG393, LR, DNM, E10, 1856, Eaton to Nichols, March 17, 1856; Steck Papers, Box 2, Folder 1, Steck to Davis, February 17, 1856.

59. Thrapp, *Victorio*, 48–52, has a complete account of the events leading up to the Chandler attack and its ramifications; RG393, Entry 3179, Records Relating to Indian Affairs, Department of New Mexico. Testimony of Refugio Corrales to Captain Henry L. Kendrick near Zuñi, New Mexico. Corrales, who had been a prisoner for some sixteen months, supports my theory that the Chokonens and Mogollons (Bedonkohes?) were close allies at this time. In the spring of 1856 he had gone with his captors, whom he identified as Mogollons, to the Chiricahua Mountains to obtain agave, or century plant (mescal), one of the more important food staples in the Chiricahua economy.

60. *La Voz de Sonora*, May 30, 1856; SA, R18, Moreno to Governor, June 17, 1856; JA, R36, Padilla to Steck, November 3, 1856.

61. *La Voz de Sonora*, May 30, 1856; Almada, *sonorenses*, 76.

62. RG393, E3179, Records Relating to Indian Affairs in New Mexico; JA,

R36, Diary of Events, Padilla to Military Commander, August 1, 1856; *El Eco de la Frontera,* August 19, September 16, 1856.

Chapter 6

1. Yrinco, a minor Chokonen leader, was born in the early 1800s. A member of Pisago Cabezón's band, he appears on the Janos ration lists in 1842–44. His brother was Manuelito, the Chokonen leader who met Cooke's party at San Bernardino in the fall of 1846. Yrinco was a leading advocate for peace in the Chokonen negotiations with Sonora in 1850. He passed from the scene in the late 1850s.

2. Aguirre, a brother of Yrigóllen, was at Janos in 1842–43. He was an ally and subordinate of Cochise from the late 1850s until he was killed in October 1868 by Sonoran troops in the mountains near Janos.

3. Parte was a hostile Chokonen leader who was at Janos from 1842 to 1844. An associate of Cochise, he died at Fronteras in February 1862 of smallpox.

4. JA, R36, Padilla to Zuloaga, September 22, 1855; Zuloaga to Padilla, September 23, 1855.

5. Babosa, born about 1790, was a literate Chiricahua leader and was said to have been a good friend of Juan José Compá.

6. JA, R36, Diary of Events, June 1856.

7. Ibid., July 1856.

8. Thrapp, *Victorio,* 49–51, has a complete account of this unfortunate affair.

9. JA, R36, Zuloaga to Padilla, July 31, 1856. José María Zuloaga was born in the city of Chihuahua in 1804. He joined the military as *cadete* in 1816 and rose to the rank of captain before retiring in 1839. A controversial man intimately acquainted with the Chiricahuas, he was in the middle of the contraband trade for a quarter of a century. Beginning in 1844 there were countless accusations by Sonoran and American officials regarding his conduct. As late as 1864, James H. Carleton pointed an accusing finger at him. He died on June 31, 1868. Almada, *chihuahuenses,* 576.

10. JA, R36, Padilla to Steck, November 3, 1856; Zuloaga to Padilla, July 31, 1856.

11. National Archives and Records Center, RG75, Records of the Bureau of Indian Affairs, Records of the New Mexico Superintendency of Indian Affairs, 1849–80, T21, Roll 6 (cited hereafter as RG75, T21 with roll number), Steck to Meriwether, August 15, 1856.

12. *El Eco de la Frontera,* August 19, 1856.

13. Ibid., September 16, 1856.

14. JA, R36, Padilla to Steck, November 9, 1856; Padilla to Zuloaga, September 2, 1856.

15. JA, R36, Padilla to Zuloaga, September 3, 1856.

16. University of Texas at Austin, Janos Collection, Padilla to Governor, January 2, 1857.

17. *El Centinela,* September 15, 1855. *El Eco de la Frontera,* April 18, 1856.

18. JA, R37, Merino to Padilla, February 4, 1857; Merino to Padilla, February 25, 1857.

19. Ibid., Padilla to Merino, February 10, 1857; Rancherías at Peace, April 1, 1857; SA, R19, Merino to Governor of Sonora, March 14, 1857.

20. Steck Papers, Box 2, Envelope 4, Steck to Meriwether, March 14, March 15, 1857. The Bonneville campaign was intended to punish hostile Apaches, in

particular the Mogollon Apaches, but the Indians the offensive was intended to strike had slipped away into Mexico. Instead the White Mountain Western Apaches suffered the most: some forty warriors killed or wounded near Mount Graham. The important Chihenne chief Cuchillo Negro was also killed in another minor engagement. Utley, *Frontersmen in Blue*, 156–57.

21. New Mexican citizens followed a band of Apaches into the Florida Mountains in January 1857 and killed Flacon and his two sons. *Santa Fe Weekly Gazette*, February 14, 1857. On March 9, Lieutenant Alfred Gibbs pursued a party of raiding Chihennes to the northern slopes of the Mimbres Mountains, killing six and mortally wounding another. Gibbs himself was wounded. *Santa Fe Gazette*, January 22, 1858; Dale E. Floyd, *Chronological List of Actions etc. with Indians from January 15, 1837, to January, 1891*, 18; Heitman, *Historical Register*, II, 403; Nona Barrick and Mary Taylor, *The Mesilla Guard, 1851–1861*, 26.

22. Yaque, or Yaqui, was a first-rate Chokonen incorrigible. Born about 1820, he was one of the hostiles who, while living at peace at Janos in 1843–44 and 1850–51, led repeated raids into Sonora, even boasting about several murders he committed. He was probably the leader referred to by Tevis and Cozzens at Apache Pass in 1859–60 as Old Jack, probably a corruption of *Yaque*. Old Jack's belligerent personality seems to fit Yaque, who passed from the scene in the early 1860s. Tevis, *Arizona in the 50s*, 95–96; AHSH, Folder 234, Testimony taken by Colonel Carrasco at Janos; Pinart Collection, Documents 74, 79.

23. Henry Linn Dodge was captured in Zuñi country in November 1856 by raiding Chiricahuas and killed shortly thereafter, perhaps in retaliation for the unprovoked Chandler attack the previous spring. Thrapp, *Victorio*, 50–53. El Cautivo, an associate of Cochise, was one of the ringleaders.

24. JA, R37, Zuloaga to Padilla, February 25, 1857.

25. Steck Papers, Box 2, Envelope 4, Steck to Meriwether, March 15, 1857.

26. JA, R37, Padilla to Quintana, April 3, 1857.

27. AHSH, Folder 310, Zuloaga to Cruz, June 4, 1857; Norlega to Commander in Chief of Sonora, June 27, 1857.

28. SA, R19, Pesqueira to Municipal President of Huasabas, February 28, 1857.

29. Steck Papers, Box 2, Envelope 4, Steck to Bonneville, March 14, 1857.

30. SA, R19, García to Davila, July 6, 1857.

31. Ibid., Campuzano to Governor, July 26, 1857.

32. Ibid.

33. *Alta California*, December 24, 1857.

34. JA, R37, Rancherías at Peace, August 1, 1857.

35. SA, R19, Commanding General of Chihuahua to Governor of Sonora, July 15, 1857.

36. SA, R19, García to Governor, October 10, 1857.

37. Ibid.; Griffen, *Apaches at War and Peace*, 257.

38. SA, R50, Elías González to Governor, September 20, 1857.

39. SA, R19, Campuzano to Governor, September 29, 1857.

40. Acuna, *Sonoran Strongman*, 2.

41. *Alta California*, February 11, 1858.

42. SA, R19, Pesqueira to Corella, Instructions for Commander Rafael Corella regarding the Indians who have solicited peace at Fronteras, September 24, 1857. Almada, *sonorenses*, 76.

43. Ibid.
44. AHSH, Folder 304, Corella to Governor, October 15, 1857.
45. SA, R19, García to Prefect of Arispe, October 7, 1857.
46. Ibid., García to Governor, October 10, 1857.
47. Steck Papers, Box 2, Envelope 5, Steck to Collins, November 21, 1857.
48. *Conditions of the Indian Tribes*, 328.
49. SA, R19, Campuzano to Governor, November 16, 1857. Sylvester Mowry reported in early December that some six hundred Apaches had settled near Fronteras as a result of the Bonneville campaign. He heard they were under the control of Mangas Coloradas, but this seems improbable because no mention of Mangas can be found in Mexican documents. Furthermore, Mangas had returned to New Mexico by early December. National Archives and Records Center, RG75, Records of the Bureau of Indian Affairs, Letters Received, New Mexico Superintendency, M234, R548, Mowry to Mix, December 7, 1857.
50. SA, R19, Corella to Commander at Bavispe, November 5, 1857; García to Governor, November 30, 1857; García to Governor, December 16, 1857.
51. JA, R37, Padilla to Zuloaga, January 1, 1858.
52. *Alta California,* May 13, 1858.
53. AHSH, Folder 224, García to Governor, May 4, 1858.
54. *La Voz de Sonora,* June 18, 1858.
55. Ibid., May 28, 1858; June 18, 1858; July 2, 1858.
56. Edith Allen Millner, "Covered Wagon Experiences," unpublished manuscript in the Arizona Historical Society.
57. AHSH, Folder 224, García to Governor, July 13, 1858.
58. *La Voz de Sonora,* July 16, 1858; AHSH, Folder 224, García to Prefect of Arispe, July 25, 1858.
59. Ibid., July 23, 1858.
60. Opler, *Lifeway,* 349.
61. *San Diego Herald,* September 18, 1858; *Los Angeles Star,* October 2, 1858.
62. Thrapp, *Victorio,* 28.
63. RG75, LR,NMS, M234, R549, Mowry to Mix, September 14, 1858.
64. Opler, *Lifeway,* 336–39.
65. AHSH, Folder 322, Elías González to Governor, September 21, 1858. Manuel Sandomingo, *Historia de Sonora,* 373–74.
66. *Missouri Republican,* December 16, 1858.
67. SA, R50, Elías to Governor, October 22, 1858.
68. *La Voz de Sonora,* November 26, 1858.
69. Ibid., February 11, February 18, 1859. Note in Steck Papers (Feburary 1859?), Box 2, Folder 8.

Chapter 7

1. Dr. John B. White studied the Western Apaches in 1874 and found that the average Apache man was five feet six and a half inches tall and weighed 135 to 140 pounds. He described Cochise as follows: "This chief may be said to have been about the only one who really exercised control over any of the Apaches. He was a fine looking man, about five feet ten inches in height and well proportioned being about three and a half inches taller than the average Apache—of manly and martial appearance—not unlike our conceptions of the Roman soldier—possessing great

physical endurance, and one well calculated to command the respect of a band of savage warriors." White Manuscript No. 178.

2. Cozzens, *The Marvellous Country,* 86.

3. Tevis, *Arizona in the 50s,* 149.

4. Ewell was born in 1817 in the Georgetown section of Washington, D.C., graduated from the U.S. Military Academy in 1840, and earned a brevet for gallantry in the Mexican War of 1846. He served with distinction in both Arizona and New Mexico and was known affectionately as Old Baldy. Ewell resigned his commission at the outbreak of the Civil War and joined the Confederacy with the rank of lieutenant general. He died in Tennessee in 1872. Thrapp, *Encyclopedia,* 475–76; Heitman, *Historical Register* I, 410.

5. John Van Deusen Dubois, *Campaigns in the West, 1856–1861,* 20.

6. There is some uncertainty about where the attack took place, although I believe it occurred at Apache Pass on the basis on the following sources: The *Alta California* of November 7, 1857, reported that two men named Short and Irving were murdered at Doubtful Pass or Apache Springs, which could mean either Stein's Peak or Apache Pass. In a subsequent issue dated December 27, 1857, the *Alta California* reported that it occurred in a narrow pass near Dragoon Springs, about eighty miles from Fort Buchanan. If so, this would rule out Doubtful Canyon. The *San Diego Herald* published an account which stated that a party of immigrants had been attacked at Puerto del Dado (Apache Pass) by Apaches, who killed two men. *Alta California,* November 7, December 29, 1857. *San Diego Herald,* September 5, 1857.

7. *San Antonio Herald,* March 20, 1858; *The Butterfield Overland Mail Across Arizona,* 8–9. A four-year contract was awarded Birch on June 22, 1857, effective July 1, 1857, to carry two mails per month each way for $149,800 annually. The route was from San Antonio to San Diego, with stops in El Paso, Tucson, and Yuma Crossing. The trail followed known water holes through southern New Mexico and southern Arizona. The stations between Mesilla and Tucson were resting spots; no permanent structures were built until the Butterfield Overland Mail Company did so in 1858. Birch's operation lacked the necessary capital and was replaced by Butterfield. Wagoner, *Early Arizona,* 344–47.

8. *Alta California,* November 9, 1858; Diane M. T. North, *Samuel Peter Heintzelman and the Sonora Exploring and Mining Company,* 110. AHS, William H. Kirkland, Hayden File, contains Tom Jeffords's version. Contemporary accounts attributed this to the White Mountain Apaches, but, given Kirkland's and Jeffords's reminiscences, there is a good chance of Cochise's involvement.

9. Roscoe P. and Margaret B. Conkling, *The Butterfield Overland Mail, 1857–1869,* I, 128–31, 140–42; Leroy R. Hafen, *The Overland Mail, 1849–1869,* 86–89.

10. *Missouri Republican,* October 31, 1859.

11. Buckley employed six Americans to construct the Dragoon Springs station: Frank de Ruyther, William Brainard, James Laing, James Burr, Preston Cunningham, and Silas St. John. St. John, a native of New York, first worked for the Jackass Mail Route but severed his employment with Birch to accept a job with the Butterfield Overland Mail Company as construction foreman in Arizona and New Mexico. During the night of September 8, 1858, three Mexican laborers (Guadalupe Rameriz, Pablo Rameriz, and Bonifacio Miranda) brutally bludgeoned to

death Cunningham, Burr, and Laing while inflicting on St. John wounds which necessitated the amputation of his left arm by assistant surgeon B. J. D. Irwin of Fort Buchanan. Two stage stations were built in 1859: at San Simon, between Stein's Peak and Apache Pass, and at Ewell's Croxon Springs, between Apache Pass and Dragoon Springs. Conkling and Conkling, *Butterfield Overland Mail*, 142–45.

12. Tevis, *Arizona in the 50s*, 100.

13. *Weekly Missouri Democrat*, January 7, January 13, 1859.

14. Steck Papers, Box 2, Envelope 7, Steck to Collins, undated letter probably written in the fall of 1858.

15. Ibid., Steck to Collins, February 1, 1859. Abstract of Provisions, 1859. Steck's estimate of fifty warriors is far too low. At the time of his visit, two Chiricahua parties were raiding in Sonora. One returned about January 5 with fifty mules and two Mexican women; another party was reported to be out with Mangas Coloradas in Sonora. *Missouri Republican*, January 5, January 12, 1859. Geronimo might have been present. He recalled in his autobiography: "At Apache Pass I made a treaty with the post. This was done by shaking hands and promising to be brothers. Cochise and Mangas Coloradas did likewise. . . . This was the first regiment that ever came to Apache Pass. This treaty was made about one year before we were attacked in a tent [referring to the Bascom affair in February 1861]." Barrett, *Geronimo's Story*, 116–17.

16. Steck Papers, Box 2, Envelope 8, Steck to Collins, February 1, 1859.

17. *Weekly Arizonian*, March 31, 1859.

18. As mentioned before, this might have been Yaque. Tevis and Cozzens both referred to him as Old Jack, whose personality seems to fit Yaque's.

19. Tevis, *Arizona in the 50s*, 111–12.

20. Will C. Barnes, *Apaches and Longhorns: The Reminiscences of Will C. Barnes*, 51.

21. Francisco, a militant Eastern White Mountain Coyotero, was a Mexican captive who rose to prominence as a major war leader. Apparently he was a fine physical specimen, standing almost six feet tall. He once told Tevis that he would fight Mexicans "as long as he lived and had a warrior to follow him." Goodwin writes that the White Mountain bands living in the Eagle Creek and Graham Mountain area had some contact with the Chiricahua "up until 1870 or so." In Appendix I, Goodwin lists local groups and independent family clusters, with chiefs and subchiefs, from 1850 to 1875. A chief named Gotca-ha (Big One) was said to have been great friends with the Chiricahuas, and another chief, Na-ginit-a (He Scouts Ahead), also was said to have been close to the Chiricahuas. Na-ginit-a died in 1865 at the Goodwin Springs poisoning, which coincides with Francisco's death in 1865 from poisoning, although his was the lead variety. Another possibility is that Francisco was a Bedonkohe Apache, which Eugene St. John claimed in a letter to Frank C. Lockwood dated November 27, 1935. Mrs. Lori Davisson of the Arizona Historical Society has done extensive work on the Western Apaches and believes that Francisco was "most likely to have been an Eastern White Mountain Apache." (Letter to author February 27, 1980); *Weekly Arizonian*, July 14, 1859; Goodwin, *The Social Organization of the Western Apache*, 83–86, 661–62; AHS, Frank C. Lockwood Collection.

22. *Weekly Arizonian*, April 21, 1859.

23. Elías, a Chokonen leader, was a son of Matías. He should not be confused with Elías the Chihenne chief. A contemporary of Cochise, the Chokonen Elías

was involved in the Janos peace of 1842 and the bloody raids into Sonora in early 1844. He was with Cochise in 1861–62 near Fronteras and again in August 1865, at which time he was one of the leaders who were reportedly eager to make peace at Fronteras. He was killed near Janos by Mexican troops in August 1868. *La Estrella de Occidente,* December 4, 1868.

24. SA, R19, Military Commander at Fronteras to Prefect of Arispe, May 3, 1859.

25. Ibid. The Apaches told Tevis the Mexicans fired first. More likely, however, it was the Chiricahuas who instigated the combat; they were still smarting from the July 1858 massacre, and their revenge raid the previous September had been a bust. Furthermore, Cochise had the superior numbers and the whites hardly desired a fight. *Weekly Arizonian,* May 12, 1859.

26. *Weekly Arizonian,* June 9, 1859.

27. Ibid., July 14, 1859.

28. Bourke, *On the Border with Crook,* 119.

29. Farish, *History of Arizona,* II, 30.

30. Woodworth Clum, *Apache Agent: The Story of John P. Clum,* 33–34. Wellman, *Indian Wars,* 289; Ogle, *Federal Control of the Western Apaches,* 44; John Upton Terrell, *Apache Chronicle,* 216–19; Dan L. Thrapp, *Conquest of Apachería,* 14–17.

31. Clum, *Apache Agent,* 33–34.

32. *Missouri Republican,* September 16, 1859.

33. *Weekly Arizonian,* July 14, 1859.

34. RG 393, LR, DNM, R30, 1859, Reeve to Wilkins, July 20, 1859.

35. John Spring, *John Spring's Arizona,* 52.

36. RG 393, LR, DNM, R31, 1859, Reeve to Wilkins, July 21, 1859.

37. Spring, *Spring's Arizona,* 52; AHS, Fred Hughes Collection.

38. Higgins Manuscript 21–22.

39. *Missouri Republican,* August 29, 1859; *Weekly Arizonian,* August 18, 1859; Opler, *Lifeway,* 362–63; Basehart, "Chiricahua Apache Subsistence," 96–97.

40. Steck Papers, Steck to Collins, November 25, 1859.

41. RG393, LR, DNM, 57R, 1859, Reeve to Wilkins, November 27, 1859.

42. RG75, LR, 1824–61; Pima Agency SIA, 169M, 1860. Letter signed Yuma and sent by Sylvester Mowry, February 6, 1860.

43. Tevis, *Arizona in the 50s,* 168–69.

44. Rita Rush, "El Chivero, Merejildo Grijalva," *Arizoniana,* 1 (Fall 1960), 9.

45. *Missouri Republican,* December 23, 1859.

46. RG75, T21, R14, Walker to Collins, January 4, 1860.

47. Constance Wynn Altshuler, ed., *Latest from Arizona! The Hesperian Letters, 1859–1861,* 27–28.

48. Tevis, *Arizona in the 50s,* 137–40.

49. *Missouri Republican,* February 21, 1860.

50. Ibid.; RG393, LR, DNM, 4E, 1860, Ewell to Wilkins, February 1, 1860; Tevis, *Arizona in the 50s,* 170; Cremony, "Some Savages," 203–4. Apparently there was some uncertainty about whether the individual killed was an Apache or a Mexican captured by the Indians and raised as an Apache. Tevis, who was there, claimed José was a captive of Cochise.

51. RG393, LR, DNM, 4E, 1860, Ewell to Wilkins, February 1, 1860.

52. Ibid., 12E, 1860, Ewell to Wilkins, March 7, 1860.

53. *Missouri Republican*, May 8, 1860; *La Estrella de Occidente*, March 9, April 6, April 13, 1860.

54. *Missouri Republican*, May 2, 1860; Cozzens, *Marvellous Country*, 220–23.

55. *Missouri Republican*, June 3, 1860.

56. R6393, LR, DNM, 22E, 1860, Ewell to Maury, July 24, 1860.

57. Ibid.; Altshuler, *Latest from Arizona*, 102–5.

58. *Missouri Republican*, July 22, 1860; *Alta California*, July 4, 1860.

59. RG393, LR, DNM, 22E, 1860, Ewell to Maury, July 24, 1860.

60. *Alta California*, July 4, 1860.

61. *La Estrella de Occidente*, June 29, 1860. The *Alta California* of July 25, 1860, reported that Governor Pesqueira had "made a treaty with the Apaches and is to pay them 15,000 or 20,000 [in order] to abstain from further hostilities . . . also, that ten captains sued for peace at Corralitos." The Chokonen leaders who had left Apache Pass for Mexico included Chino, Yaque, and Miguel Yrigóllen. These leaders had their own followings distinct from Cochise's.

62. *La Estrella de Occidente*, June 29, July 6, 1860; *La Coalición*, September 4, 1860.

63. Ibid.

64. AHSH, Folder 354, Prefect of Arispe to Governor, September 2, 1860.

65. Ibid.

66. Ibid.; Prefect of Arispe to Governor, October 16, 1860.

67. RG75, M234, R550, Steck to Greenwood, May 11, May 15, 1860. The reservation would have included "the present communities of Gila, Cliff and Buckhorn, all northwest of Silver City, the boundary line going north almost to Shelly Peak, west to near Jackson on U.S. Highway 180 and its southern boundary would have touched Bald Knoll." Thrapp, *Victorio*, 65–66.

68. Altshuler, *Latest from Arizona*, 136, 147; RG393, LR, DNM, 46M, 1860, Morrison to Assistant Adjutant General, Department of New Mexico, October 27, November 10, 1860.

69. AHSH, Folder 354, Prefect of Arispe to Governor, December 23, 1860.

70. Higgins Manuscript, 20–21. Coyuntura (Kin-o-tero, Kin-o-tera), a younger brother of Cochise, was hanged at Apache Pass by Lieutenant Bascom in February 1861. Eve Ball identified him as Cochise's brother. This, the Higgins Manuscript, and Sonoran documents clearly identify Coyuntura as the Indian hanged at Apache Pass. Mrs. Ball said she "learned very little about him and that was from Ralph Chee, a grandson of Hugh Chee who was the son of Chie, a nephew of Cochise who would serve as a guide for General O. O. Howard." Based on this information, Chie (or Chisito) might have been the son of Coyuntura.

71. AHSH, Folder 354, Governor to Prefect of Arispe, December 28, 1860.

Chapter 8

1. Ball, *Indeh*, 22–30; Griswold, "Ft. Sill Apaches," biographies of Cochise, 24, Taza, 132, Naiche, 106, Dash-den-zhoos, 29, Naithlotonz, 110; AHS, Gatewood Collection, Box 1, Envelope 5.

2. Lockwood, *The Apache Indians*, 125.

3. Ball, *Indeh*, 25.

4. Opler, *Apache Lifeway*, 467.

5. Ball, *Indeh*, 25; Griswold, "Ft. Sill Apaches," 132; Katherine C. Turner, *Red Men Calling on the Great White Father*, 137–44.

6. Smithsonian Institution, Bureau of American Ethnology, George Wratten letter to W. Holmes, May 4, 1907.

7. Oury's account was published in the *Arizona Weekly Star* on June 28, July 5, and July 12, 1877. AHS, William Sanders Oury File. Policeman Oberly's recollections were published in an unidentified New York newspaper in 1886. A copy is in the files of the Arizona Historical Society. Captain Bernard J. D. Irwin's version was written in 1887 but published in 1928 in the *Infantry Journal*, 32 (April 1928); Daniel Robinson, "The Affair at Apache Pass," *Sports Afield*, 17 (August 1896), 79–84.

8. Driver A. B. Culver's account was published in *Arizonian* on February 9, 1861. A copy is in James Wallace's Hayden File in the AHS. William Buckley's version was reported in the *Alta California* issue of February 19, 1861. A copy is in Buckley's Hayden File in the AHS. The anonymous letter critical of Bascom was published in the *Missouri Republican*, December 27, 1861.

9. Benjamin H. Sacks, "New Evidence on the Bascom Affair," *Arizona and the West*, 4 (Autumn 1962), 261–78. Sacks cites Bascom's official reports, which can be found in NA, RG393, LR, Department of New Mexico, 1861.

10. Barrett, *Geronimo's Story*, 115–17; Betzinez, *I Fought with Geronimo*, 40–42; Ball, *Indeh*, 25; Ball, *In the Days of Victorio*, 155. Cochise's account, given to Arny at Cañada Alamosa, New Mexico, was reported in the *Santa Fe New Mexican* on November 1, 1870, and is in NA, RG75, M234, R557, Arny to Parker, October 24, 1870.

11. John Ward, born in Ireland about 1806, had come to Arizona from California in the late 1850s. By 1859 he had a ranch on Sonoita Creek and had taken in a widowed family: Jesúsa Martínez and two children, Félix and Teodora, ages twelve and ten, respectively. Ward and Jesúsa had five children before he died in 1867. Many accounts have vilified Ward, but he seems to have been an industrious farmer and family man who only wanted to rescue his stepson. Alan Radbourne, "Salvador or Martínez? The Parentage and Origins of Mickey Free," *English Westerners Society Brand Book*, 14 (January 1972), 2–26.

12. Ibid.; The Ward boy, known as Félix Ward and later in life as Mickey Free, spent the rest of his life with the Western Apaches. In the 1870s and 1880s he was a scout for the army against the Chiricahuas. He died on the Fort Apache Reservation in 1915.

13. George Nicholas Bascom, born in Kentucky about 1836, graduated from West Point in 1858 and reached Arizona in October 1860. He was killed by Confederates in the Battle of Valverde in February 1862. His courage was never questioned, but his judgment certainly could be. Heitman, *Historical Register*, I, 197.

14. *Los Angeles Star*, February 16, 1861, reprinted from the *Arizonian*. Copy in John Ward's Hayden File, AHS; Altshuler, *Latest from Arizona*, 165.

15. Altshuler, *Latest from Arizona*, 170.

16. Radbourne, "Salvador or Martínez?" 19.

17. National Archives and Record Center, M1072, Letters Sent, Department of New Mexico, R2, Wilkens to Reeve, September 11, 1859.

18. RG393, LR, DNM, E22, 1860, Ewell to Maury, July 24, 1860.

19. Irwin's account, 3–4; RG393, LR, DNM, Bascom to Maury, January [February] 14, 1861.

20. Irwin's account, 4.

21. Robinson was born in Ireland in 1830, immigrated to the United States in 1849, and enlisted in Company C, Seventh Infantry. He saw extensive duty in the post–Civil War campaigns in the West before retiring in 1889 with the rank of captain. He died in Iowa in 1911. Thrapp, *Encyclopedia,* 1230.

22. Robinson's account, 79–80.

23. Wallace, born in Massachusetts in 1828, was a stage driver for the Butterfield Overland Mail Company. He had married recently and owned a house in Tucson. *The Butterfield Overland Mail Across Arizona,* 19, 32; Altshuler, *Latest from Arizona,* 285.

24. Robinson's account, 80.

25. Both of Bascom's reports suggest that he met and captured Cochise's party on February 3. Benjamin Sacks, in his article "New Evidence on the Bascom Affair," uncovered the company returns for Company C for February 1861, which revealed that the prisoners were taken on February 4. Sacks, "New Evidence," 268. A. B. Culver, who arrived in Tucson on Friday, February 8, also dated the meeting February 4. James Wallace, Hayden File.

26. Robinson's account, 80; AHS, Nathan Benjamin Appel, Hayden File.

27. Robinson, who had a clear view of the participants, states that Ward shared Bascom's tent and acted as interpreter. If so, Ward probably was a Spanish interpreter because he knew no Apache. Robinson's account, 80; Oury recalled that Bascom's interpreter was Antonio, probably a Mexican who had been a captive of the Apaches. Antonio accompanied Bascom on other scouts, so it is conceivable that he was with the officer at Apache Pass, although I feel it more probable that Antonio, if present, arrived with one of the relief parties. Oury's account.

28. RG393, LR, DNM, Bascom to Maury, January 14 [February 14] and February 25, 1861 (cited hereafter as Bascom's reports).

29. Bascom's reports.

30. Culver's account in James Wallace's Hayden File.

31. RG393, LR, DNM, 65C, 1861, Chapin to AAG, Department of New Mexico, April 25, 1861.

32. Ball, *Indeh,* 25; Barrett, *Geronimo's Story,* 115; *Santa Fe New Mexican,* November 1, 1870. Turrill, "A Vanished Race," 14.

33. Robinson's account, 80–81.

34. Turrill, "A Vanished Race," 14–15.

35. Robinson's account, 80–81; Buckley's account; Oberly's account, 4; Oury's account.

36. Oberly's account, 4; *Missouri Republican,* December 27, 1861.

37. Robinson's account, 81.

38. Ibid. Irwin wrote that the parley was arranged by Bascom, who released one Indian woman. Irwin, however, was still 125 miles away when this took place. All other accounts agree that Cochise initiated the parley. Irwin's account.

39. Bascom's reports; Robinson's account, 81; Oury perpetuated the legend that Wallace was captured by Cochise immediately after his escape from Bascom on February 4. Actually, Wallace was captured the next day under different circumstance. Oury's account.

40. Oury's version was the only one which stated that Welch (or Walsh) was killed mistakenly by troops. One can infer from other accounts, however, that such was indeed the case. A. B. Culver stated that "Welch also escaped and got to the

corral of the station when he was shot dead." Buckley declared that the Indians "shot one and took one prisoner; the other man being shot at the station." This seems to suggest that the soldiers did the work. Bascom failed to mention who killed Welch; if his soldiers were responsible, it would hardly have been a credit to his record.

41. Bascom's reports; Robinson's account, 82. Mangas Coloradas may have been present, although Bascom's estimate of five hundred warriors is clearly too high. Probably they numbered one-third of that at best.

42. Robinson's account, 82.

43. Culver's account. A person speaking in normal tones in the canyon can be heard distinctly by anyone on Overlook Ridge.

44. Bascom's reports.

45. I don't believe Bernard marched with Bascom's command to Apache Pass. He probably arrived with one of the relief parties from either Fort Breckenridge or Fort Buchanan, probably the former. Benjamin Sacks concluded that Bernard, if indeed present, must have arrived with Lieutenant Moore on February 14 because Bernard was named on the muster rolls at Breckenridge before and after the affair. Sacks, "New Evidence," 273. It is unlikely that Bernard was with Robinson's detachment, as this command, like Bascom's, was stationed at Fort Buchanan.

46. Oury's account. He perpetuated the story that Bascom refused to trade because Cochise offered only Wallace for the Indians and would not include the other three white men taken on the late afternoon of the sixth. Oury's account (written in 1877 in response to Governor Safford's account, which was highly critical of Bascom) was easily the most confused of all those written some years after the incident. He defends Bascom's handling of Cochise. Interestingly enough, ten years earlier he was William A. Bell's source for the account published in *New Tracks in North America*. In it, if he is quoted correctly, he takes Bascom to task for the way he handled Cochise and inexplicably states that Bascom hanged the Indians before Cochise killed his white prisoners. William A. Bell, *New Tracks in North America*, 279–80.

47. Arizona Governor Anson Safford reported this version in the *Arizona Citizen* on December 7, 1872. In 1869 and 1870, Captain Reuben F. Bernard made reference to Wallace's fate. In one report, referring to Cochise, he claimed to know of fifteen whites killed by "putting lariats around their necks, tied their hands behind them and dragged to death." Don Russell, *One Hundred and Three Fights and Scrimmages: The Story of General Reuben F. Bernard*, 70–71. A similar version was furnished, possibly by Bernard, to Colonel George Stoneman's entourage in the fall of 1870. In this account, at a signal from Cochise, "the Indians started their horses on a run, the necks of the poor whites were broken, and their bodies dragged over sharp rocks." John H. Marion, *Notes of Travel Through the Territory of Arizona*, 35.

48. Culver's account.

49. The Chokonens captured this train after the Cochise-Bascom meeting of February 6, when Cochise offered to exchange Wallace for his family. Wallace returned later that evening with a note indicating that Cochise held three other prisoners. Buckley's stagecoach found the bodies in the early morning of the seventh. Buckley's account, Culver's account. The *Sacramento Daily Union* correspondent in Tucson wrote that the train was captured on February 6. *Sacramento Daily Union*, March 4, 1861.

50. Oury's account; *Mesilla Times,* February 21, 1861, quoted in *The Butter-field Overland Mail Across Arizona,* 24.

51. Buckley's account.

52. Robinson's account, 82; Barrett, *Geronimo's Story,* 117.

53. Dan Thrapp to author, March 28, 1985.

54. Bascom's reports; Robinson's account, 83; Culver's account; Buckley's account.

55. Robinson's account, 82.

56. Barrett, *Geronimo's Story,* 117.

57. Robinson's account, 82–83.

58. Ibid.

59. Bascom's reports; AHSH, Folder 364, Prefect of Arispe to Governor, March 9, 1861 Barrett, *Geronimo's Story,* 115–18.

60. Irwin's account.

61. Oury's account.

62. *Estrella de Occidente,* March 1, 1861.

63. Irwin's official report in Sacks, "New Evidence," 264–66.

64. AHSH, Folder 364, Corella to Governor, February 13, 1861.

65. Irwin's account.

66. Moore's report and Bascom's report, both cited in Sacks "New Evidence," 265–67.

67. Bascom's report; Moore's report. Irwin recalled incorrectly that there were six Americans, and Oury said there were three. Robinson remembered "Wallace and others." The official reports of Bascom and Moore seem to be correct. The *Mesilla Times* of February 21, 1861, also reported four victims.

68. In his report, Bascom clearly took responsibility for this decision. Oury, who was present, claimed that the men and soldiers voted unanimously to hang the prisoners. Bascom, however, objected, at which point Lieutenant Moore, the ranking officer, took command and assumed responsibility. Oury's account. Irwin suggests that he proposed the execution, claiming he would hang his three captives even if Bascom refused to execute his. Bascom then relented, probably under pressure from the other officers. The honest Robinson reported that "a council was held by the officers; and at this it was decided that the five [six] captive Apaches should die by hanging." It is interesting to note that the Apaches' version, as given by Betzinez and Mrs. Eve Ball's informants, insist that the whites killed their prisoners before the Apaches tortured theirs. This, of course, was wrong. Geronimo stated correctly that after Bascom refused to trade, "we killed our prisoners, disbanded, and went into hiding in the mountains." Barrett, *Geronimo's Story,* 117.

69. Bascom's reports.

70. Oberly's account.

71. Ibid.

72. *Mesilla Times,* February 21, 1861.

73. Robinson's account, 84; Oury's account.

74. Oberly's account. Cochise seems to have corroborated Oberly when he mentioned this to Arny in 1870. Oberly also claimed that the Indian prisoners' "fate . . . hung on a game of 7-up in which the side for mercy was beaten and the death sentence pronounced." Cochise's wife Dos-teh-seh was the only adult Indian to have witnessed the events and possibly leave behind an eyewitness account. *Santa Fe New Mexican,* November 1, 1870.

75. Moore's report, reprinted in Sacks, "New Evidence," 265.

76. Bascom's reports.

77. *Missouri Republican*, December 27, 1861.

Chapter 9

1. *Arizona Miner*, March 20, 1869.

2. *Alta California*, November 14, 1870.

3. RG75, LR, DNM, M234, R557, Arny to Parker, October 24, 1870.

4. Howard, *My Life and Experiences*, 208.

5. RG393, LR, DNM, 71C, 1861, Chapin to AAG, Department of New Mexico, May 18, 1861.

6. *Missouri Republican*, December 27, 1861.

7. Cremony, "Some Savages," 205.

8. Higgins Manuscript.

9. Bell, *New Tracks in North America*, 280.

10. RG393, Letters Sent, Subdistrict of Arizona, Devin to Sherburne, January 25, 1869.

11. Marion, *Notes of Travel*, 35.

12. Wellman, *Indian Wars*, 294.

13. Lockwood, *The Apache Indians*, 107.

14. Robert M. Utley, *A Clash of Cultures: Fort Bowie and the Chiricahua Apaches*, 23.

15. Clum, *Apache Agent*, 39.

16. See, for example, Barrett, *Geronimo's Story*, 118; Betzinez, *I Fought With Geronimo*, 41–42; Ball, *Indeh*, 25; Ball, *In the Days of Victorio*, 155.

17. James L. Collins, born in Kentucky in 1800, came to New Mexico in the mid-1820s and ran a mercantile business in Chihuahua until 1846. With the outbreak of the Mexican War, he relocated to Santa Fe, where he established the *Santa Fe Weekly Gazette*, which he published until 1858. He was appointed superintendent of Indian affairs for the Department of New Mexico by President James Buchanan, a position he held until early 1863. He was robbed and killed in Santa Fe on June 6, 1869. William A. Keleher, *Turmoil in New Mexico, 1846–1868*, 484.

18. RG75, LR, DNM, M234, R550, Collins to Greenwood, February 24, March 3, 1861.

19. RG393, Letters Sent, Department of New Mexico, AAG to Lynde, February 10, 1861.

20. Ibid., AAG to Lynde, February 25, 1861; *Mesilla Times*, March 16, 1861.

21. RG94, Records of the Adjutant General's Office, Loring to Townsend, May 19, 1861.

22. RG393, LR, DNM, 14L, 1861, Lynde to AAG, DNM, March 20, 1861; 18L, 1861, April 10, 1861.

23. Ibid.; RG393, LR, DNM, 7L, 1861, Buckley to Lane, February 16, 1861.

24. Barrett, *Geronimo's Story*, 118.

25. AHSH, Folder 364, Prefect of Arispe to Governor, March 19, 1861, Acuna, *Sonoran Strongman*, 70.

26. AHSH, Folder 364, Corella to Governor, February 13, 1861; Prefect of Arispe to Governor, March 19, 1861.

27. *Mesilla Times*, March 3, 1861.

28. Altshuler, *Latest from Arizona*, 182–83; *Missouri Republican*, December 27, 1861.

29. RG393, LR, DNM, 65C, 1861; Chapin to AAG, DNM, April 25, 1861; 22M, 1861, Morrison to AAG, DNM, February 28, 1861.

30. AHSH, Folder 364, Corella to Governor, May 6, 1861.

31. *Mesilla Times*, May 11, 1861.

32. Thrapp, *Conquest of Apachería*, 19. Hubert Howe Bancroft, *Scraps*, unidentified California newspaper item dated November 1863, copy in Arizona State University Library.

33. Emmie Giddings W. Mahon and Chester V. Kielman, "George H. Giddings and the San Antonio–San Diego Mail Line," *Southwestern Historical Quarterly*, 61 (Summer 1957), 238.

34. *Alta California*, June 22, 1861; *Sacramento Daily Union*, July 15, 1861; RG393, LR, DNM, 70C, 1861, Jones to Grant, May 4, 1861; Bennedict to Grant, May 4, 1861.

35. RG393, LR, DNM, 71C, 1861, Chapin to AAG, Department of New Mexico, May 18, June 3, 1861.

36. RG393, LR, DNM, 83C, 1861, Pesqueira to Chapin, June 5, 1861.

37. AHSH, Folder 364, List of Apaches at Peace, May 15, 1861; García to Governor, May 6, 1861.

38. Galindo, a contemporary of Cochise, was born about 1810. He was a member of the Janeros local group of the Nednhi band and was involved in the Janos peace of 1842–44. He succeeded Láceris as leader of the Janeros local group. Galindo was a major figure in the peace of 1860 at Janos and stayed at Fronteras through the summer of 1861. In late 1861 he and his brother Tonina began raiding in Sonora, primarily the districts of Sahuaripa and Alamos. He passed from the scene shortly thereafter.

39. AHSH, Folder 364, García to Governor, May 19, 1861; Prefect of Arispe to Governor, May 22, 1861.

40. Ibid., Prefect of Arispe to Governor, May 28, 1861.

41. *Missouri Republican*, July 6, 1861.

42. Raphael Pumpelly, *Travels and Adventures of Rafael Pumpelly*, 168.

43. NA, RG123. Pete Kitchen Indian Depredation Claim 6845.

44. RG393, LR, DNM, 81C, 1861, Bascom to Chapin, June 22, 1861; Chapin to AAG, DNM, June 23, 1861; AHS, W. M. Thompson manuscript, "The Fighting Doctor"; AHS, Frank C. Lockwood Collection; Constance Wynn Altshuler, "Arizona in 1861: A Contemporary Account by Samuel Robinson," *Journal of Arizona History*, 25 (Spring 1984), 62–63.

45. RG393, LR, DNM, 81C, 1861, Chapin to AAG, DNM, June 23, 1861.

46. Robert W. Frazer, *Forts of the West*, 4, 6.

47. *Alta California*, September 2, 1861.

48. As quoted in Wagoner, *Early Arizona*, 425.

49. James H. McClintock, *Arizona: Prehistoric, Aboriginal, Pioneer, Modern*, III, 182.

50. Turrill, "A Vanished Race," 20.

51. R. S. Allen, "Pinos Altos, New Mexico," *New Mexico Historical Review*, 23 (October 1948), 302–3.

52. Missouri Historical Society, Webb Collection.

53. Thrapp, *Victorio,* 68–71; RG393, LR, DNM, 35L, 1860, Lynde to AAG, December 18, 1860.

54. RG393, LS, DNM, M1072, R2, Frame 0287, Maury to Lynde, December 30, 1860; LR, DNM, 8L, 1861, Lynde to Maury, February 17, 1861.

55. Tully, born in 1824, was an important merchant in Arizona and New Mexico from the mid-1860s until 1880. Thrapp, *Encyclopedia,* 1445.

56. Steck Collection, Ochoa to Steck, March 26, 1861. Abstract of Provisions Issued.

57. *Missouri Republican,* December 27, 1861.

58. *Mesilla Times,* May 11, 1861.

59. RG75, M234, R550, Tully to Collins, June 2, 1861.

60. RG75, T21, R5, Labadie to Collins, June 2, 1861; *Missouri Republican,* July 6, 1861; *Santa Fe Gazette,* June 15, 1861.

61. *Mesilla Times,* June 15, June 30, 1861; *Missouri Republican,* July 6, 1861; *Estrella Occidente,* July 26, 1861.

62. RG75, M234, R550, Steck to Collins, July 15, 1861.

63. McClintock, *Arizona,* 180–81.

64. RG393, L5, DNM, Carleton to AAG, August 14, 1865.

65. *Santa Fe Gazette,* September 22, 1866; NA, RG393, E3161, Miscellaneous Letters Received, Department of New Mexico.

66. Arizona Historical Society, Diary of George Hand.

67. University of Arizona Library, Special Collections, AZ 300, Thomas Akers Diary.

68. As usual, accounts vary on the number of Indians involved. Billy Fourr estimated their number at 60, definitely too low, while Thomas Farish estimated them at 400 to 500, definitely too high. Mowry and Oury placed them at 200 and 300, respectively, the latter figure about the total number of warriors the two chiefs could have amassed. Two contemporary accounts provide insight. The white men who found the bodies estimated the number of Indians at 100 on the basis of their trail. An escaped Mexican captive claimed that Cochise had 180 fighting men at this time, which was too high for the Chokonens and must have included some Bedonkohes, Nednhis, and Chihennes. Arizona Historical Society, William Fourr manuscript. Farish, *History of Arizona,* II, 59–60. Mowry's account was in the *Arizona Miner,* November 7, 1868; Oury's account appeared in the *Arizona Daily Star,* July 27, 1879. The *San Francisco Evening Bulletin* of September 7, 1861, carried the account of the Americans who found the bodies. Bancroft, *Scraps,* contains the statement made by an escaped Mexican regarding Cochise's warrior strength. Unidentified California newspaper item dated November 1863.

69. *San Francisco Evening Bulletin,* September 7, 1861. *Arizona Daily Star,* July 27, 1879. W. W. Mills, *Forty Years at El Paso, 1848–1898,* 195–96.

70. *San Francisco Evening Bulletin,* September 7, 1861. Tevis, *Arizona in the 50s,* 229–30.

71. Fourr manuscript.

72. *Arizona Daily Star,* July 27, 1879.

73. New Mexico State University Library, Rio Grande Historical Collection, Keith Humphries File.

74. AHSH, Folder 364, Perez to Governor, November 4, 1861.

75. Moses Bradley Carson, born in 1792, was a successful trapper before he moved to New Mexico in 1826 and began a colorful forty-year career in the West. He died in 1868 at Eagle Flat, Texas, a mining camp northeast of El Paso. Thrapp, *Encyclopedia,* 235.

76. The primary source for the Ake party's retreat to New Mexico is *They Die But Once* by James B. O'Neil, in which one of Ake's sons relates his version. Although he claimed that "there were 47 men in the company all told when we pulled out from there (Tucson) seven women and sixteen children" he almost certainly meant forty-seven in all. This would put the number of men at twenty-four, which approximates the recollections of Tom Farrell (nineteen men); Robert Phillips, who recalled there were twenty-five to thirty men and boys; and Mariano Madrid, who said the Indians outnumbered the whites ten to one and he believed there were two hundred Indians in the fight, thereby putting the number of whites at twenty. In a later statement Ake indicated that only eight men escaped unharmed, which, if one takes into account the accepted casualties of four whites killed and five wounded, plus the seven men who bolted at the beginning of the fight, would mean that there were twenty-four men in the fight. James B. O'Neil, *They Die But Once: The Story of a Tejano,* 36–46; RG123, Indian Depredation File 3112, T. J. Cassner, Administrator.

77. O'Neil, *They Die But Once,* 41.

78. Ibid.; RG123, Indian Depredation File 3112.

79. University of Arizona Library, Special Collections, AZ 197, Palmer Manuscript.

80. O'Neil, *They Die But Once,* 41–43; NA, RG123, Indian Depredation File 3112.

81. George Wythe Baylor, *John Robert Baylor, Confederate Governor of Arizona,* 12.

82. W. Hubert Curry, *Sun Rising in the West,* 55.

83. Ibid.; Indian Depredation File 3112.

Chapter 10

1. *La Alianza de la Frontera,* October 10, 1861; AHSH, Folder 366, Sánchez to Governor, September 17, 1861.

2. AHSH, Folder 366, Sánchez to Governor, September 17, 1861.

3. Ibid., Folder 364, Perez to Governor, November 4, 1861.

4. Baylor was born in Kentucky on July 20, 1822, moved to Texas in 1840, and became an Indian fighter of some note, participating in several campaigns against the Comanches. In July 1861 he arrived in New Mexico with some four hundred Texas riflemen and by the end of the year was military governor of the territory. He died on February 8, 1894. Baylor, *John Robert Baylor.*

5. Ibid., 32.

6. Hurley is about ten miles southeast of Silver City. Pearce, *New Mexico Place Names,* 73.

7. Curry, *Sun Rising in the West,* 52–53.

8. As usual there is much disagreement about the number of Indians thought to be in the fight. The only contemporary account appeared in the *Mesilla Times* of October 3, 1861, which placed the Apaches at 250 to 300 warriors. One year later, Baylor reported the Indians at 400, while Carleton wrote in 1867 that some 500 Indians were involved. *Mesilla Times,* October 3, 1861; as quoted by James Collins

to W. P. Dole, October 8, 1861, 37 Cong., 2d sess., Pt. I. *Estrella de Occidente,* November 22, 1861, picked up the *Messila Times* account. Baylor's account can be found in *The War of the Rebellion,* 15, Pt. I, Baylor to Magruder, December 29, 1862, 916. *Santa Fe Gazette,* July 27, 1867. Mastin died on October 7, 1861, of blood poisoning. *Mesilla Times,* October 17, 1861.

9. Opler, *Lifeway,* 344–45.

10. Juárez Archives, UTEP, Roll 23, Ruiz to Ochoa, October 3, 1861; AHSH, Folder 364, Perez to Governor, November 4, 1861.

11. AHSH, Folder 364, Perez to Governor, November 4, 1861.

12. Ibid.

13. AHSH, Folder 366, Sánchez to Governor, December 3, 1861; December 16, 1861.

14. *Estrella de Occidente,* March 7, 1862.

15. *Missouri Republican,* November 29, 1861.

16. Charles Harkins, "A Scrap of Frontier History," *Overland Monthly,* 21 (March 1893), 266.

17. NA, RG94, Letters Received, Adjutant General's Office, M944, AGO, 1861, Mowry to Cameron, August 8, 1861.

18. *Santa Fe New Mexican,* June 15, 1866. Bancroft, *Scraps,* 48.

19. NA, RG94, LR, AGO, 1861, Mowry to Barlow, August 2, 1861: *Santa Fe New Mexican,* June 15, 1866.

20. Arizona State University, Tempe, Sylvester Mowry Files, Mowry to Sibley, December 14, 1861; NA, RG123, Indian Depredation File, 3358, Fritz Contzen Claim.

21. Lockwood Collection.

22. Bancroft, *Scraps,* 48.

23. Ibid.; *Estrella de Occidente,* March 7, 1862; J. Ross Browne, *Adventures in the Apache Country,* 201.

24. Hunter, born in Tennessee about 1824, had farmed along the Mimbres before the war. He joined Baylor's force in the summer of 1861 and was elected first lieutenant in Captain George Frazer's company of Arizona Guards. Boyd Finch, "Sherod Hunter and the Confederates in Arizona," *Journal of Arizona History,* 10 (Autumn 1969), 139–206.

25. NA, RG94, M619, R284, Mowry to West, June 28, 1862.

26. Mowry File, Hunter to Mowry, April 11, 1862.

27. Ibid.; Mowry to Editor, *San Francisco Call,* June 28, 1862.

28. Bancroft, *Scraps,* 48.

29. Mendibles, like most escaped prisoners, had an interesting story to tell. A band of White Mountain Apaches captured him in 1857 near San Xavier, Sonora. For the next seven years he lived in the White Mountain region until U.S. troops under Captain John S. Thayer recovered him from the Western Apaches in July 1864. *Alta California,* February 20, 1865; June 5, 1870.

30. Ibid.; *The War of the Rebellion,* (cited hereafter as *WOR Series*), 1, Pt. I, 1095. Edward Palmer, who was well acquainted with the Western Apaches, said Cochise led the Apaches. Palmer Manuscript.

31. Sibley, born in 1816 at Natchitoches, Louisiana, graduated from West Point in 1838 and was commissioned in the Second Dragoons. He fought with honor in the Mexican War and participated in the Mormon expedition of 1857–58 and the Navajo campaign of 1860. He resigned his commission when the Civil War started

and joined the Confederacy. In July 1861 he was appointed commander of the Department of New Mexico. He raised a regiment at San Antonio and marched to El Paso. After several battles with Union troops in New Mexico, Sibley withdrew to Texas in April 1862. He died at Fredericksburg, Virginia, in 1886. *Webster's American Military Biographies,* 388.

32. Baylor, *John R. Baylor,* 14–15; Baylor erred in writing that he followed the Indians to Carretas in Sonora. This hacienda was almost certainly deserted at the time. He meant Corralitos, Chihuahua, where the mines of José María Zuloaga were located. The Mexican account of Baylor's intrusion can be found in AHSH, Folder 378, Moreno to Governor, March 31, 1862.

33. *WOR Series,* 50, Pt. I, Baylor to Helms, March 20, 1862, 942.

34. West, born in New Orleans in 1822, was a captain of mounted volunteers in the Mexican War. He was named lieutenant colonel of the First California Infantry in August 1861 and became a colonel the following June. Like Carleton, he was a controversial figure in the Southwest. After the war he returned to his native state and in 1870 was elected to the U.S. Senate. He died in Washington in 1898. Thrapp, *Encyclopedia,* 1534–35.

35. Aurora Hunt, *Major General James Henry Carleton, 1814–1873, Western Frontier Dragoon,* 220–25.

36. Canby was born in Kentucky in 1817, graduated from West Point in 1839, and joined the Second Infantry. From 1839 to 1842 he fought the Seminoles in Florida. He was promoted to first lieutenant in 1846 and to captain in 1847. He saw extensive action in the Mexican War, receiving a brevet to lieutenant colonel. He participated in the Mormon expedition of 1857–58 and in 1861 was commissioned general of the Department of New Mexico. He was killed in 1873 during a peace conference with Captain Jack, a Modoc Indian leader. Thrapp, *Encyclopedia,* 218–19.

37. *WOR Series,* 50, Pt. I, 120.

38. Hunt, *Carleton,* 226.

39. Bancroft, *Scraps,* 193.

40. Ibid.

41. Ibid.; *WOR Series,* 9, Pt. I, 585–87; 50, Pt. I, 120–22.

42. Bancroft, *Scraps,* 193.

43. *WOR Series,* 50, Pt. I, 120–22.

44. Ibid.

45. Ibid., 128–31.

46. Accounts vary as to the number of Apaches involved. The *Sacramento Union* (August 14, 1862) and the *Santa Fe Gazette* (October 4, 1862) put the number at more than 100. Edward Palmer placed Cochise's strength between 200 and 300 warriors. Two participants, John C. Cremony and Albert J. Fountain, put Apache strength at 700 and 800, respectively, undoubtedly more than double the actual number of Indians involved. As was the case the previous summer, the allied Chiricahuas may have numbered 200 warriors. About a year after the battle at Apache Pass a captive who escaped from Cochise claimed he had mustered a following of 180 warriors, which must have included recruits from the Nednhis, Bedonkohes, and Chihennes. *Sacramento Union,* August 14, 1862; *Santa Fe Gazette,* October 4, 1862; Palmer Manuscript; Cremony, *Life Among the Apaches,* 161–67; Joseph Miller, ed., *Arizona Cavalcade: The Turbulent Times,* 30–35.

47. Ball, *Indeh*, 19–20; Eve Ball, "Cibicu: An Apache Interpretation," in Ray Brandes, ed., *Troopers West: Military and Indian Affairs on the American Frontier*, 123.

48. Miller, *Arizona Cavalcade*, 35.

49. Ball, "Cibicu," 123.

50. According to Lieutenant Fountain, Cochise told him that "you never would have whipped us if you had not shot wagons at us." Miller, *Arizona Cavalcade*, 35. Asa Daklugie told Eve Ball that "after they turned cannon loose on us at Apache Pass . . . my people knew that the Apaches were doomed." Ball, "Cibicu," 123. *Army and Navy Journal*, December 11, 1869, quoted a letter from Tucson which attributed the victory solely to the howitzers. It is interesting that Daklugie seemed to imply that the howitzers were some kind of secret weapon which they had never faced. Cochise had seen its awesome destructive capabilities at Fronteras on several occasions, and just nine months earlier these allied Chiricahuas had faced a cannon at Pinos Altos.

51. Asa Daklugie disputes this, having told Mrs. Ball that "most of the Indians were armed only with bows and arrows." Ball, *Indeh*, 20; Contemporary accounts are conflicting. Eyre, who had met with the Chiricahuas some three weeks before, reported they were well armed with six-shooters and single-barreled shotguns. *WOR Series*, 50, Pt. I, 120–22. The Indians probably had obtained many weapons from their victims and by trading in northern Mexico, but their most significant problem was keeping a dependable supply of ammunition. One year later an escaped captive declared that the Chokonens' ammunition was exhausted. Bancroft, *Scraps*, 48.

52. *WOR Series*, 50, Pt. I, 131; George Hand Diary. Ernest Marchand, ed., *News From Fort Craig, New Mexico, 1863*, 34. Henry P. Walker, "Soldier in the California Column: The Diary of John W. Teal," *Arizona and the West*, 13 (Spring 1971), 40. Konrad F. Schreier, Jr., "The California Column in the Civil War: Hazen's Civil War Diary," *Journal of San Diego History*, 22 (Spring 1976), 45.

53. *WOR Series*, 50, Pt. I, 128.

54. Cremony, *Life Among the Apaches*, 164.

55. Betzinez, *I Fought with Geronimo*, 42; Ball, *In the Days of Victorio*, 47.

56. Dan L. Thrapp, letters to author, December 5, 1975; December 16, 1981.

57. Walker, "Teal's Diary," 41.

58. Ball, *In the Days of Victorio*, 47; Cremony, *Life Among the Apaches*, 160; Ball, *Indeh*, 19–20.

59. Bancroft, *Scraps*, 196.

60. *WOR Series*, 50, Pt. I, 128–29, Pt. II, 40–41; 9, Pt. I, 565.

61. *WOR Series*, 50, Pt. II, 73–74, 146.

62. *Santa Fe Gazette*, October 4, 1862; *WOR Series*, 9, Pt. I, 565. The victims were Thomas Buchanon of Pennsylvania; William Allen of Illinois; Conrad Stark of Ohio; William Smith of Pennsylvania; David Berry of Iowa; James Burnes of Wisconsin; James Ferguson; and two Mexicans from Mesilla.

63. Ibid.; Cremony, *Life among the Apaches*, 174–75.

64. *WOR Series*, 15, 580.

65. Utley, *Frontiersmen in Blue*, 260.

66. AHSH, Folder 376, Prefect of Arispe to Governor, August 19, 1862.

67. Cremony, *Life Among the Apaches*, 176; Ball, *Indeh*, 20.

68. *WOR Series,* 15, 147–48.

69. For good accounts of Mangas's death, see Dan L. Thrapp, *Conquest of Apachería,* 21–23, and *Victorio and the Mimbres Apaches,* 82–84. West's duplistic report is in *WOR Series,* 50, Pt. II, 296–97. A reliable synthesis is Lee Myers, "The Enigma of Mangas Coloradas Death," *New Mexico Historical Review,* 41 (October 1966), 287–304. An eyewitness account can be found in Daniel Ellis Conner, *Joseph Reddeford Walker and the Arizona Adventure,* 34–42.

70. Thrapp, *Victorio,* 83.

71. Barrett, *Geronimo's Story,* 119–21.

Chapter 11

1. AHSH, Folder 376, Prefect of Arispe to Governor, August 19, 1862.

2. *La Alianza de la Frontera,* June 26, July 3, 1862. AHSH, Folder 372, García to Governor, July 6, 1862.

3. AHSH, Folder 372, García to Governor, July 31, 1862.

4. *Estrella de Occidente,* August 22, September 5, 1862.

5. Ibid.

6. Acuña, *Sonoran Strongman,* 75–79.

7. AHS, SA, R19, Pesqueira Circular dated January 2, 1863.

8. *Estrella de Occidente,* February 20, 1863.

9. *Uno de Tantos* (Ures), April 9, 1863.

10. *Estrella de Occidente,* April 3, April 10, 1863.

11. *WOR Series,* 50, Pt. II, 121. On September 15, 1862, Fergusson wrote Pesqueira: "I have been informed that several hundreds of Indians have been very lately in Fronteras, Sonora, making preparations for hostilities against the troops, citizens, residents, and travellers of Arizona, and that they even had the effrontery to send a deputation to Your Excellency [Remigio's party], with the hopes of obtaining a treaty of peace, in order that they might with more impunity commit their atrocities in this Territory."

12. RG393, LR, DNM, W120, 1863, Pesqueira to West, March 26, 1863.

13. Diary of John Bourke, entry dated February 3, 1873, copy in AHS.

14. RG393, Unregistered Letters Received, District of Arizona, Hinds to West, October 6, 1862.

15. *Estrella de Occidente,* April 3, April 10, 1863.

16. Seth-mood-a, born in the 1830s, was a son of Mangas Coloradas, hence probably a full brother of Dos-teh-seh. According to Griswold, he was killed in the Pinos Altos Mountains by Mexicans. I think it more probable that he was killed by U.S. troops. Griswold, "Ft. Sill Apaches," 123.

17. Debo, *Geronimo,* 71.

18. Barrett, *Geronimo's Story,* 121.

19. NA, Returns From Military Posts, Fort Bowie, M617, R129, February 1863.

20. NA, RG393, Letters Received, Fort Bowie, Fergusson to Qualey, March 12, 1863.

21. Barrett, *Geronimo's Story,* 123–24.

22. Fort West was established on February 24, 1863, by Captain William McCleave, First California Cavalry. It was on the east side of the Gila River in the Pinos Altos Mountains and was named for Brigadier General Joseph Rodman West.

It was abandoned January 8, 1864. Frazer, *Forts of the West,* 108.

23. RG393, LS, Fort West, Fritz to Bennett, March 26, 1863.

24. LR, DNM, B57, 1863, McCleave to Whitlock, April 8, 1863. *Santa Fe Weekly Gazette,* April 18, April 25, 1863.

25. *WOR Series,* 50, Pt. I, 213, Pt. II, 466.

26. *Estrella de Occidente,* June 12, 1863.

27. Ibid., April 10, April 17, 1863.

28. Ibid., April 17, 1863.

29. Ibid.

30. Bourke Diary, entry dated February 3, 1873.

31. *Estrella de Occidente,* June 12, 1863.

32. The volunteers killed Cojinillín and ten other men near Boca Grande in northwest Chihuahua in early May 1863. M619, R1410, Returns from Military Posts, Fort West, May 1863. *La Alianza de la Frontera,* May 29, June 6, 1863.

33. *La Alianza de la Frontera,* February 20, March 5, 1864.

34. Juh, born in the early 1820s, was undoubtedly one of the leading Nednhi warriors at this time. His Apache name, Tandinbilnojui (He Brings Many Things With Him), indicates his prowess and success as a warrior. According to Asa Daklugie, son of Juh, Cochise and his father were together during the 1860s and early 1870s. Physically, Juh was an atypical Apache, standing about six feet tall and weighing about 225 pounds. He headed the Nednhi band until his death in 1883. Grenville Goodwin, *Western Apache Raiding and Warfare,* 110; Ball, *Indeh,* 22–30. For a good biography of Juh, see Dan L. Thrapp, *Juh: An Incredible Indian.*

35. *Conditions of the Indian Tribes,* 105.

36. *WOR Series,* 50, Pt. II, 466.

37. *Alta California,* July 23, 1863. In late June a force from Fronteras scouted the Huachuca and Dragoon mountains without encountering recent signs of Apaches. *Estrella de Occidente,* July 17, 1863.

38. *Condition of the Indian Tribes,* 119. *Santa Fe New Mexican,* April 14, 1865. *WOR Series,* 50, Pt. II, 490. RG393, LR, DNM, Morrison to AAG, Department of New Mexico, June 24, 1863.

39. *WOR Series,* 50, Pt. II, 490.

40. Ray C. Colton, *The Civil War in the Western Territories,* 131.

41. RG393, District of Arizona, Unregistered Letters Received, Lambert to Captain ?, July 25, 1863.

42. Frazer, *Forts of the West,* 98.

43. *WOR Series,* 50, Pt. II, 571; RG393, LR, Department of New Mexico, West to McCleave, July 27, 1863; West to Whitlock, July 26, 1863.

44. Ibid., Pt. I, 233–34.

45. Ibid., 242; RG393, LR, DNM, S199, 1863, Shirland to West, September 9, 1863.

46. *Estrella de Occidente,* March 4, 1864.

47. Ibid., October 2, 1863; Bancroft, *Scraps,* 48.

48. Bancroft, *Scraps,* 48.

49. *Estrella de Occidente,* December 4, December 11, 1863.

50. Ibid., February 26, 1864.

51. *Santa Fe Gazette,* October 15, 1864.

52. *WOR Series,* 34, Pt. II, 593.

53. *Estrella de Occidente,* February 26, 1864.

54. *WOR Series,* 34, Pt. I, 122–23; University of Texas at El Paso, Carrizal Collection, Roll 8, document dated March 18, 1864.

55. See chapter 4, for an account of this raid.

56. *WOR Series,* 34, Pt. I., 123.

57. RG393, Letters Sent, Fort West, Whitlock to Smith, March 22, 1864.

58. *WOR Series,* 50, Pt. II, 826–29.

59. RG393, Unregistered Letters Received, District of Arizona, Stevens to Smith, May 5, 1864; Bancroft, *Scraps,* 209.

60. Bancroft, *Scraps,* 209. RG94, LR, AGO Main Series, Carleton to AAG, May 25, 1864.

61. *Estrella de Occidente,* June 24, 1864.

62. RG393, Unregistered Letters Received, District of Arizona, Carleton to Davis, April 1, 1864; *Condition of the Indian Tribes,* 172.

68.63. *Condition of the Indian Tribes,* 178.

64. Ibid., 177–78.

65. RG393, Letters Received, Fort Bowie, Carleton to Tidball, June 17, 1864.

66. *Condition of the Indian Tribes,* 178.

67. *Alta California,* March 1, 1864.

68. RG75, Records of Arizona Superintendency of Indian Affairs, M734, R1, McCormick to Poston, March 5, 1864.

69. *WOR Series,* 50, Pt. II, 869–72.

70. *Santa Fe Gazette,* October 15, 1864.

71. This was Caisca, a Chokonen who was on the Fronteras ration rolls of 1861 and 1862 as a member of Elías's and Miguel Yrigóllen's band.

72. *Santa Fe Gazette,* October 15, 1864.

73. RG393, LS, DNM, Carleton to Vickroy, July 3, 1864.

74. *WOR Series,* 41, Pt. I, 125–31.

75. *Estrella de Occidente,* August 19, 1864; January 20, 1865.

76. Ibid., January 13, 1865.

77. Nana, a Chihenne incorrigible from the word go, was born about 1800. His Apache name was Kas-tziden (Broken Foot). He had close ties with the Mescaleros throughout his lifetime, and was said to have been related to Delgadito, who had died recently, and he may have taken over the leadership of that small local group. Nana reportedly had five daughters, who were married to warriors of note, including Riñon, Horache, Vicente (a brother of Geronimo), and a Mescalero chief named Tomaso Palona. One of Nana's wives was a sister of Geronimo. Nana was a leading spirit in the wars of the 1880s. He died in 1896. Griswold, "Ft. Sill Apaches," 110–11; *Indian Raids as Reported in the Silver City Enterprise,* 38. For a good account of Nana's famous raid in 1881, see Stephen H. Lekson, *Nana's Raid: Apache Warfare in Southern New Mexico.*

78. Thrapp has a complete account of the Carleton-Steck fiasco, which eventually ended up being fought in the press by the two Santa Fe newspapers, the *Gazette,* and the *New Mexican.* Thrapp, *Victorio,* 87–91.

79. *Arizona Miner,* November 23, 1864.

80. RG393, LR, DNM, 42B, 1865, Houston to Burkett, March 22, 1865; italics mine.

Chapter 12

1. *WOR Series,* 48, Pt. I, 551.

2. John T. Smith came to Arizona with the California Volunteers. Discharged in November 1864, he went to the Santa Rita mines. He had several brisk encounters with Apaches in the late 1860s and early 1870s. Smith died on May 9, 1877, of heart disease. AHS, John T. Smith, Hayden File.

3. Bancroft, *Scraps,* 382.

4. *WOR Series,* 50, Pt. I, 402–3.

5. NA, RG393, E19, LR, District of Arizona, D48, 1865, Davidson to Carleton, February 22, 1865; *WOR Series,* 48, Pt. I, 552.

6. *El Republicano,* May 13, 1865.

7. Ibid.

8. RG393, LR, DNM, 98B, 1865, Davis to Cutler, May 3, 1865.

9. Opler, *Apache Lifeway,* 333–34.

10. *El Republicano,* May 13, June 3, 1865.

11. Ibid.

12. Irvin McDowell was born in Columbus, Ohio, in 1818, graduated from West Point in 1838, and was promoted to first lieutenant in 1842. Throughout the Mexican War he was an aide to General John E. Wool. In May 1861 he was promoted to brigadier general and in July of that year commanded Union troops in the First Battle of Bull Run, in which the North was soundly defeated. Charges were made against him but later were dropped. He also served in the Second Battle of Bull Run, though in a subordinate role. He was named commander of the Department of the Pacific in July 1864 and one year later became commander of the Department of California. He died in San Francisco in 1885. *Webster's Military Biographies,* 263.

13. Mason, born in Ohio in 1824, graduated from West Point in 1847. During the 1850s he served primarily in California, in 1862 becoming brigadier general of the California Volunteers. He died in Washington, D.C., on November 29, 1897. Constance Wynn Altshuler, *Chains of Command,* 258.

14. Altshuler, *Chains of Command,* 39–40; Report of the Secretary of War, 1866, 96–98.

15. RG75, M234, R3, Davidson to Dole, August 12, 1865; Altshuler, *Chains of Command,* 39–42; Hubert Howe Bancroft, *History of Arizona and New Mexico,* 555–56.

16. *WOR Series,* 50, Pt. II, 1247, 1263.

17. Ibid.

18. Miscellaneous Post Orders, Fort Bowie, 1865, in Fort Bowie files.

19. *WOR Series,* 50, Pt. I, 415–19.

20. Goodwin, *The Social Organization of the Western Apache,* 413.

21. *Alta California,* August 11, 1865; AHS, Hiram Storrs Washburn, Hayden File. Amelia Naiche, granddaughter of Cochise, told me a story in the presence of Mrs. Eve Ball that Cochise found a little white boy hidden under a wagon and put him on the back of his horse. Cochise then cared for the boy and reared him until, according to legend, he was released near Fort Apache. One wonders whether her story is connected with the July 1865 massacre at the Cienega. Interview with Eve Ball and Amelia Naiche, January 17, 1979.

22. RG393, LS, Fort Bowie, Merriam to Green, July 14, 1865.

23. RG393, E20, District of Arizona, 1862–70, Unregistered Letters and Orders Received, 1862–71, Higgins to Mason, August 1 [?], 1865.

24. This was Marcial Gallegos, who was captured by the Pinal band of the Western Apaches about 1843 and lived among them fourteen years, during which time he rose to prominence as a war leader. He left the Apaches in July 1857 after difficulty with a Pinal chief, returned to his family at San Ignacio, Sonora, and served as a scout for the United States Army against the Apaches. SA, R19, Aquilar to Governor, July 11, 1857.

25. RG393, E20, District of Arizona, Unregistered Letters, Higgins to Mason, July ?, 1865; Higgins Manuscript.

26. Born in Vermont in 1820, Washburn came to Arizona as a surveyor in 1857. After the volunteers were discharged, he moved to Washington, where he worked for the government for the rest of his life. Washburn, Hayden File.

27. Fort Mason, established August 21, 1865, at Calabasas on the Santa Cruz River, was named for Brigadier General John S. Mason. The Tubac post was abandoned and the garrison was relocated here. On September 6 it was renamed Camp McKee and abandoned on October 1, 1866, because of its unhealthy location. Frazer, *Forts of the West,* 11.

28. Arizona State Library, Territorial Records of Arizona, Military–Indian Affairs, voucher payable to Manuel Gallegos; Thrapp, *Apachería,* 34.

29. AHS, Washburn, Hayden File.

30. Palmer Manuscript, Pt. 2.

31. Washburn, Hayden File.

32. *Missouri Republican,* December 20, 1865.

33. Washburn, Hayden File.

34. Ibid.

35. Cornelius C. Smith, "Some Unpublished History of the Southwest," *Arizona Historical Review,* 5 (October 1932), 6 (January 1935), 45–64.

36. Territorial Records of Arizona, Washburn to Governor, October 5, October 9, 1865.

37. Smith, "Some Unpublished History of the Southwest" (6 January 1935), 49–53. M617, R129, Post Returns, Fort Bowie, October and November 1865.

38. Ibid.

39. RG393, LS, Fort Bowie, Gorman to Green, November 9, 1865; RG75, M234, R3, clipping from unidentified newspaper about Gorman's attack.

40. *Alta California,* December 31, 1865.

41. RG393, E29, Book of Scouts, District of Arizona, Codington to Lewis, February 11, 1866.

42. McDowell to Adjutant General, Washington, March 23, 1866, quoted in Pinckney Tully's Indian Depredation File 1515, RG123.

43. RG75, M234, R3, Pollock to Mason, November 11, 1865; RG393, E29, Book of Scouts, District of Arizona, Pollock to AAG, Subdistrict of the Gila, December 14, 1865.

44. *Missouri Republican,* February 24, 1866. AHS, Charles T. Connell manuscript titled "The Apaches Past and Present," chap. 14.

45. Frazer, *Forts of the West,* 102. RG393, Department of Missouri, Letters Received, 131W, 1866, Willis to De Forest, February 16, 1866; Brigadier General

Richard H. Orton, *Records of California Men in the War of the Rebellion, 1861 to 1867,* 78. In a letter to the author, Dan L. Thrapp suggests that "probably Juh led them, since Janos was largely [his] town, although Cochise was often there." Letter dated October 1, 1979.

46. Washburn's command in particular. See Thrapp, *Apachería,* 33–38; Altshuler, *Chains of Command,* 50–51, 53–55.

47. *Alta California,* May 6, 1866.

48. Ibid.

49. Halleck was born in New York State in 1815 and graduated from West Point in 1839. He resigned in 1854 and opened a law practice in San Francisco, becoming one of the most successful businessmen in California. In August 1861 he was commissioned a major general in the army and commanded the Department of Missouri in 1862. He displayed excellent administrative skills during the war, and these overshadowed his lack of military strategy. He commanded the Military Division of the Pacific from August 1865 to March 1869 before being transferred to the Division of the South. He died in Louisville, Kentucky, on January 9, 1872. *Webster American Military Biographies,* 158–59.

50. RG393, E19, LR, District of Arizona, Halleck to Scott, January 25, 1866.

51. RG393, E731, LR, Southern Subdistrict of the Gila, Pollock to Winchell, December 14, 1865.

52. Ogle, *Federal Control of the Western Apaches,* 60.

53. James M. Barney, *Forgotten Heroes of the Apache Wars,* 8–9. RG123, Indian Depredation File 9192, Thomas Yerkes File; AHS, Charles Shibell, Hayden File. Granger, *Arizona Place Names,* 317.

54. *Arizona Miner,* May 23, 1866; Report of the Secretary of the Interior, 39th Cong., 2d sess., House Ex. Doc. 1, Series II, 111–13.

55. AHS, Charles M. Wood Collection, interview with Henry I. Yohn, December 17, 1925; RG393, LS, Camp Wallen, Brown to Commander, Southern Subdistrict of the Gila, June 10, 1866; Spring, *Spring's Arizona,* 57–59; RG94, LR, AGO, R539, 1867, Report of Inspection by Major and Assistant Inspector General Roger Jones, May 18, 1867 (copy in AHS).

56. RG393, E29, Book of Scouts, District of Arizona, Dunkelberger to AAAG, Tucson, July 1, 1866.

57. Spring, *Spring's Arizona,* 55.

58. RG393, LS, Camp Wallen, Brown to Commander, Southern Subdistrict of the Gila, June 10, 1866.

59. Altshuler, *Chains of Command,* 61; Bancroft, *History of Arizona and New Mexico,* 556.

60. NA, RG59, M184, R2, Dispatches from U.S. Consulates in Ciudad Juárez, Pierson to U.S. Consulate, June 17, 1872.

61. AHSH, Folder 397, Toyos to Governor, October 13, 1867.

62. AHSH, Folder 390, Luna to Governor, September 12, 1866; Folder 391, Toyos to Governor, October 23, 1866. In February 1869, Cochise admitted that he had been wounded in the neck at Fronteras a few years earlier. This may have been the raid. *Arizona Miner,* March 20, 1869.

63. *El Boletin de Chihuahua,* September 15, 1866.

64. *La República,* February 22, 1867. The Apache prisoners told their captors this was the camp of Cusi, in all likelihood a corruption of the name *Cuchis.* Since

this Indian was later referred to as a *cabecilla* (big chief) instead of a *capitancillo* (little chief), plus the fact that he was known to have been in the area, I have concluded that this was probably Cochise's camp.

Chapter 13

1. *Army and Navy Journal*, December 11, 1869.
2. AHSH, Folder 397, Montana to Governor, February 12, 1867.
3. Ibid.; *Estrella de Occidente*, February 22, 1867.
4. RG393, LR, Fort Bowie, Eschenburg to AAAG, Tucson, February 28, 1867; *Santa Fe Gazette*, March 16, 1867.
5. RG393, LR, Subdistrict of Tucson, Brown to Toby, March 6, 1867; *Arizona Miner*, April 6, 1867; *Santa Fe New Mexican*, May 4, 1867; *Alta California*, October 22, 1873; RG123, Indian Depredation Files, Oscar Buckalew, File 8770, Thomas Yerkes File 9192.
6. *Estrella de Occidente*, March 8, 1867.
7. The son of U.S. Senator John J. Crittenden, Thomas Leonidas Crittenden was born in 1815 at Russellville, Kentucky, and fought in the Civil War on the Union side. On April 5, 1867, he succeeded Colonel Charles S. Lovell as commander of the Subdistrict of Tucson. Altshuler, *Chains of Command*, 73, 244.
8. AHS, Inspection Report of General Charles A. Whittier at Fort Bowie, February 27, 1866.
9. RG393, M617, R129, Post Returns, Fort Bowie, 1867–68.
10. *La República*, April 12, 1867; *Estrella de Occidente*, May 3, 1867.
11. *Estrella de Occidente*, June 21, 1867.
12. RG393, LR, Subdistrict of Tucson, Brown to AAAG, Subdistrict of Tucson, May 10, 1867.
13. RG393, LS, Subdistrict of Tucson, Crittenden to AAG, Department of California, May 8, 1867.
14. RG393, LR, Subdistrict of Tucson, McGarry to Ripley, June 16, 1867; 40th Cong., 2d sess., House Ex. Doc. 1324; Wood Collection; Spring, *Spring's Arizona*, 97–102; Floyd, *Chronological List of Actions*, 28. There is discrepancy as to the number of casualties. Spring did not recall any Indian fatalities. Floyd states that three Indians were killed and six captured. Opler may have heard the Chiricahua version, which admitted to two dead. Opler, *Lifeway*, 254.
15. 40th Cong., 2d sess., House Ex. Doc. 1324.
16. RG393, LS, Subdistrict of Tucson, Crittenden to McGarry, July 8, 1867; Crittenden to Ilges, July 11, 1867.
17. *Army and Navy Journal*, September 28, 1867.
18. *Estrella de Occidente*, July 19, 1867.
19. Ibid., August 16, August 30, 1867.
20. AHSH, Folder 397, Gallego to Governor, August 10, 1867; *Estrella de Occidente*, August 16, 23, 30, 1867; *Alta California*, October 28, 1867.
21. AHSH, Folder 397, Toyos to Governor, October 1, 1867.
22. Ibid.
23. RG393, LR, Department of Missouri, 15N, 1869, Russell to Post Adjutant, Fort Selden, December 10, 1868. Several complaints of this type were made by American officers. Brigadier General Edward Ord wrote Colonel George Washington Getty that at Janos, Apaches from Arizona traded powder, lead, and arms and

disposed of plunder obtained in Arizona. LR, DNM, M1088, R11, Ord to Getty, February 25, 1870.

24. RG393, LS, Fort Bowie, Hubbard to AAG, Department of California, November 8, 1867; Bell, *New Tracks in North America*, 282-85; Thomas Thompson Hunter, "Early Days in Arizona," *Arizona Historical Review*, 3 (April 1930), 105.

25. RG393, Fort Bowie, Pollock to Wright, December 17, 1867.

26. *La República*, April 17, 1868.

27. Ibid., March 13, 1868.

28. RG393, LS, Fort Bowie, Ripley to Wright, May 13, 1868.

29. Fort Bowie File, Shackleford Diary.

30. RG393, LS, Fort Bowie, Ripley to Commanding Officer, Ford Goodwin; May 28, 1868; Ripley to AAAG, District of Arizona, June 3, 1868; RG393, LR, Fort Bowie, Hubbard to Ripley, June 3, 1868; *Santa Fe Gazette*, June 20, August 1, 1868; *Alta California*, August 5, 1868; AHS, William Henry Larrabee File.

31. *El Republicano*, August 14, 1868; *Estrella de Occidente*, March 27, April 25, May 1, 1868.

32. RG393, LS, Fort McRae, Gilmore to AAAG, District of New Mexico, August 15, 1868.

33. RG393, LS, Fort Cummings, Moore to AAAG, District of New Mexico, September 4, 1868. These captured children were not Chihennes (Eastern Chiricahuas) because the following autumn (1869), Lieutenant Drew tried to return the prisoners to Victorio and Loco but no one knew who they were. One of them, later named Apache John, was adopted by William F. M. Arny, who claimed the Indian belonged to Cochise's band. Perhaps he discerned this after meeting Cochise in October 1870. Apache John died in December 1872 at Santa Fe. *Santa Fe New Mexican*, December 11, 1872.

34. Acuña, *Sonoran Strongman*, 100-101.

35. *Estrella de Occidente*, November 6, 1868.

36. Ibid., December 4, 1868.

37. *La República*, December 11, 1868.

38. *Arizona Miner*, March 20, 1869.

39. Devin, born in New York in 1822, served with distinction in the Civil War as a lieutenant colonel, Sixth New York Cavalry. He was appointed to the Eighth Cavalry on recommendation from Grant and Sheridan. He became involved with Cochise in New Mexico in 1872. Devin died in 1878. Thrapp, *Encyclopedia*, 400.

40. RG393, LS, Subdistrict of Tucson, Devin to Perry, December [?], 1868.

41. *Arizona Miner*, November 11, 1868.

42. AHS, Albert F. Banta File.

43. RG393, LS, Subdistrict of Tucson, Winters to Commanding Officer, Fort Goodwin, December 20, 1868.

44. RG393, LS, Subdistrict of Tucson, Devin to Perry, December ?, 1868.

45. *Arizona Miner*, January 30, 1869.

46. RG393, E13, LS, District of Arizona, Devin to Sherburne, January 25, 1869.

Chapter 14

1. LR, AGO, Main Series, M619, R737, 768P, 1869, Devin to Jones, August 26, 1869.

2. *Arizona Miner,* March 20, 1869. Many of Arizona's records from the days before it became a military department in 1870 were destroyed in the San Francisco earthquake of 1906.

3. Ibid.

4. This was probably a small patrol from Camp Wallen under Lieutenant William McK. Owen, who destroyed a deserted ranchería of twelve wickiups somewhere in the Dragoons about January 31, 1869. Post Returns, Camp Wallen, M617, R1348, January and February 1869.

5. *Arizona Miner,* March 20, 1869.

6. Ibid., March 6, 1869.

7. *San Francisco Daily Morning Call,* October 9, 1869.

8. Robert M. Utley, *Frontier Regulars: The United States Army and the Indians, 1866–1891,* 46–49.

9. RG393, LS, Camp Crittenden, Downey to Andrews, September 10, 1869; RG75, M734, R3, Downey to Andrews, September 10, 1869.

10. Samuel H. Drachman, "Arizona Pioneers and Apaches," *Arizona Graphics,* 1 (November 18, 1899), 7.

11. RG123, Thomas Yerkes Depredation File 9192.

12. Smith, Hayden File. *Weekly Arizonian,* April 24, 1869. Floyd, *Chronological List of Actions,* 39, places the fight on April 20, 1869, reporting one soldier killed.

13. RG75, M734, R8, Dent to Taylor, May 31, 1869.

14. RG393, LS, Camp Crittenden Whipple to Veil, June 11, 1869; *Weekly Arizonian,* June 19, July 17, 1869.

15. *Santa Fe New Mexican,* July 20, 1869.

16. *La Estrella de Occidente,* August 6 and 13, 1869.

17. Ibid.

18. *La República,* October 22, 1869.

19. Ibid.

20. *Estrella de Occidente,* October 1, 1869.

21. RG393, LS, Camp Grant, Green to AAG, District of Arizona, RG393, LR, Subdistrict of Tucson, Clendenin to Devin, February 24, 1870.

22. Stone, born in New York State in 1836, came to New Mexico in 1863 and served as a deputy U.S. marshal. In the late 1860s he developed the Apache Pass Mining Company. Thrapp, *Encyclopedia,* 1373–74. "Colonel John Finkle Stone and the Apache Pass Mining Company," *Arizona Historical Review,* 6 (July 1935), 74–80.

23. "Stone and the Apache Pass Mining Company," 77; LS, Subdistrict of the Gila, Devin to Sherburne, October 11, 1869.

24. *Army and Navy Journal,* December 11, 1869; LR, AGO, M619, R737, Winters to Devin, October 7, 1869; RG393, LS, Subdistrict of Southern Arizona, Devin to Sherburne, October 11, 1869; *San Francisco Daily Morning Call,* November 5, 1869; RG75, M234, R3, Andrew to Parker, November 9, 1869; RG123 Indian Depredation File Number 6875, William Eastwood File.

25. RG393, LS, Subdistrict of Tucson, Devin to Sherburne, October 11, 1869.

26. LR, AGO, M619, R737, Winters to Devin, 1 A.M. October 7, 1869.

27. Ibid., Winters to Bernard, 9 A.M., October 7, 1869.

28. Ibid., Winters to Devin, October 10, 1869; Grijalva, Hayden File.

29. LR, AGO, M619, R737, Winters to Devin, October 10, 1869; *Arizona Miner,* November 6, 1869.

30. *Arizona Miner,* November 20, 1869.

31. Frank D. Reeve, "Frederick E. Phelps: A Soldier's Memoirs," New Mexico Historical Review, 25 (April 1950), 118.

32. LR, AGO, M619, R737, Bernard to Devin, October 22, 1869.

33. RG393, LR, Fort Bowie, Putnam to Dunn, October 28, 1869.

34. LR, AGO, M619, R737, Bernard to Devin, November 2, 1869.

35. Ibid.; L. L. Dorr, "The Fight at Chiricahua Pass in 1869," *Arizona and the West,* 13 (Winter 1971), 377.

36. LR, AGO, M619, R737, Bernard to Devin, November 14, 1869.

37. Dan L. Thrapp, letter to author, March 28, 1985.

38. Dorr, "The Fight at Chiricahua Pass," 377; Sladen, "Making Peace," 34.

39. RG393, LS, Subdistrict of Southern Arizona, Devin to Putnam, October 22, 1869.

40. RG75, M234, R557, Shorkley to AAAG, District of New Mexico, December 25, 1869; Drew to Clinton, January 5, 1870. RG393, Green to AAAG, Department of California, December 6, 1869, copy in AHS.

41. RG393, LS, Fort Bowie, Bernard to Dunn, February 1, 1870.

42. RG393, LS, Fort Bowie, Dunn to Clendenin, January 4, 1870; RG393, LR, Subdistrict of Tucson, Clendenin to Devin, January 15, 1870; LS, Subdistrict of Southern Arizona, Devin to Clendenin, January 7, 1870.

43. Chackone, or Chacone, had been at Janos in 1843–44 and was with the hostile Chokonens under Miguel Narbona and Teboca in late 1850 and early 1851. He probably participated in the Pozo Hediondo fight. He died sometime in the 1870s.

44. RG363, LS, Fort Bowie, Bernard to Dunn, February 1, 1870.

45. RG123, Indian Depredation Files, Thomas Gardner File 8689.

46. *Alta California,* April 4, 1870.

47. *La República,* April 29, 1870.

48. *Estrella de Occidente,* May 13, June 18, 1870.

49. *Weekly Arizonian,* June 11, June 18, 1870; AHS, Thomas Gardner, Hayden File.

50. AHSH, File 434, Morales to Governor, July 15, 1870; *Weekly Arizonian,* July 23, 1870.

51. *Weekly Arizonian,* July 23, August 6, August 27, 1870.

52. Ibid., August 13, 1870.

53. RG75, M234, R4, Green to AAG, Department of Arizona, August 13, 1870.

Chapter 15

1. *Weekly Arizonian,* September 17, 1870.

2. *Alta California,* November 14, 1870.

3. Ibid.

4. Marion, *Notes of Travel,* 31–32.

5. *Arizona Citizen,* June 17, 1871.

6. Ibid., April 22, 1871.

7. George Stoneman was born on August 8, 1822, in Busti, New York. Graduating from West Point in 1846, he was commissioned in the First Dragoons and served as quartermaster with Cooke's Mormon Battalion. In 1855 he was promoted

to captain and in 1861 to major. During the Civil War, he earned several brevets and in July 1866 was promoted to colonel. He retired in August 1871 and served as governor of California from 1883 to 1887. He died in Buffalo, New York, on September 5, 1894. *Webster American Military Biographies,* 417–18. Heitman, *Historical Register,* I, 930.

8. RG94, LR, AGO, P734, 1870, filed with A551, Stoneman to AAG, Division of the Pacific, November 24, 1870.

9. Ibid.

10. RG94, LR, AGO, P801, 1871; Stoneman to AGO, Washington, February 17, 1871.

11. *Arizona Citizen,* May 6, 1871.

12. Ibid., May 13, 1871.

13. *Army and Navy Journal,* May 27, 1871.

14. *Alta California,* September 28, 1870.

15. Ibid., October 13, November 10, November 14, 1870.

16. Loco, born in the early 1820s, headed a local group of Chihennes. He was peacefully inclined, while his Chihenne contemporary Victorio was more militant. He lost an eye as a young man when he was attacked by a grizzly. I have not found any reference to Loco prior to 1868. He was considered to be a kind and friendly man respected by whites and Indians. He figured prominently in the affairs of the 1870s and 1880s and died in 1905 at Fort Sill, Oklahoma. See Thrapp, *Conquest of Apachería,* 231–50. Thrapp, *Victorio,* contains much information relative to Loco's life, and Ball, *Indeh,* 38–42, contains the Apache recollection of Loco. See also Griswold, "Ft. Sill Apaches," 87.

17. Salvadora was a son of Mangas Coloradas, hence a brother-in-law of Cochise. Born about 1830, he first came into the picture near Janos in 1854 when he and other Apaches attacked a wagon train in the Enmedio Mountains and afterward skirmished with Mexican troops. He was a voice in the ill-fated peace parleys in early 1865. The next year, he and Victorio led a war party of 125 Chihennes against Pinos Altos. By late 1868 he and Victorio were reported to be the leaders of the Chihennes. In the fall of 1870 he left Cañada Alamosa with Cochise and in early 1871 was killed in a battle with Americans in the rugged Mogollon mountain region. JA, R34, Padilla to Governor, February 23, 1854; *Santa Fe Gazette,* June 23, 1866; RG393, LR, DNM, 41S, 1865, Cook to Shaw, January 17, 1865, and 98D, 1865, Davis to Cutler, May 3, 1865; *Las Cruces Borderer,* April 13, 1871.

18. Thrapp, *Victorio,* 98.

19. Charles Edward Drew, a native of New Hampshire, was born in 1840. He enlisted in 1861 and became a lieutenant in the Twenty-sixth Massachusetts Infantry on September 23, 1861. In 1866 he transferred to the Regular Army and on July 20, 1869 was appointed agent for the Southern Apaches. Thrapp, *Victorio,* 342.

20. RG393, LS, Fort McRae, Gilmore to AAG, District of New Mexico, August 12, 1869.

21. RG75, M234, R556, Drew to Parker, September 3, 1869.

22. Thrapp, *Victorio,* 98.

23. RG75, M234, R557, Drew to Clinton, January 5, 1870.

24. Brevoort, born in Michigan in 1822, had been in New Mexico since the mid-1850s. He was at Fort Buchanan in 1857 as post sutler and was said to have been well acquainted with the Apaches. Thrapp, *Victorio,* 344; *Alta California,* October 15, 1857.

25. Thrapp, *Victorio,* 104–8.

26. RG75, M234, R557, "Traders with Gila Apache Indian License"; RG75, Miscellaneous Division, Traders' Licenses.

27. Thrapp, *Victorio,* 104–8.

28. Howard, *My Life and Experiences,* 187–88.

29. Farish, *History of Arizona,* II, 228; C. L. Sonnichsen, "Who Was Tom Jeffords?" *Journal of Arizona History,* 23 (Winter 1982), 388; RG123, Indian Depredation Files, Tom Jeffords File 9695. In testimony dated February 25, 1895, Jeffords said he came to Tucson in July 1862.

30. *Santa Fe New Mexican,* July 28, November 10, 1868. Alice Rollins Crane's article on Jeffords appeared in an unidentified Los Angeles newspaper. Copy in Huntington Library, San Marino, California.

31. RG75, M234, R557, Clinton to Parker, no date, probably April 1870.

32. Sonnichsen, "Who Was Tom Jeffords?" 382–83. AHS, "The Story of S. W. Grant."

33. Robert H. Forbes's account of his conversation with Jeffords was published in the *Journal of Arizona History,* 7 (Summer 1966), 87–88.

34. Farish, *History of Arizona,* II, 228–29. Actually Parker was the commissioner of Indian affairs, who reported to the secretary of the interior.

35. RG75, T21, R15, Piper to Pope, February 7, 1871.

36. *Arizona Citizen,* December 7, 1872.

37. Fred Hughes Collection.

38. Farish, *History of Arizona,* II, 228–29.

39. Forbes, letter to *Journal of Arizona History,* 87–88.

40. RG75, T21, R15, Piper to Pope, February 7, 1871.

41. Turrill, "A Vanished Race," 16–17; *Arizona Citizen,* December 7, 1872.

42. Lockwood, *The Apache Indians,* 112.

43. See chapter 13 for an account of this incident.

44. Ball, *Indeh,* 27–28.

45. Opler to author, August 29, 1979.

46. Henry Stuart Turrill, an assistant surgeon in the U.S. Army, claimed to have seen Jeffords trading contraband to the Apaches. According to Turrill, he "came upon Captain Jeffords with a half dozen of the most villainous-looking individuals. . . . They were arranging a lot of packs of powder and lead for transportation to the mountains." Turrill's account is unreliable at times and was written in 1907, thirty-five years after the alleged incident. "A Vanished Race," 16–17.

47. Major William Redwood Price, angry because the Chihennes from New Mexico were receiving shelter at Jeffords's Chiricahua reservation in Arizona, wrote that "I have witnesses here [Fort Tularosa] who will testify that Jeffords, the agent there, was a trader among them for several years before he was made their agent trading powder, lead and caps for their stolen stock." At district headquarters in Santa Fe, Colonel John Irvin Gregg endorsed Price's allegations, stating that information of a "similar character regarding Mr. Jeffords was received by Colonel Granger at the interview with Cochise in March, 1872." M666, R123, Price to AAG, District of New Mexico, August 1, 1873.

48. Dan L. Thrapp, letter to author, April 9, 1978.

49. Hennisee was born January 16, 1839, in Maryland. He fought in the Civil War for the First Eastern Shore, Maryland Infantry, and in 1867 joined the Regular Army. Thrapp, *Victorio,* 345.

50. RG75, T21, R11, Cady to Clinton, August 22, 1870; Hennisee to Clinton, August 31, 1870.

51. For a biography of Arny, see Lawrence R. Murphy, *Frontier Crusader—William F. M. Arny.*

52. RG75, T21, R12, Hennisee to Clinton, October 31, 1870.

53. RG75, M234, R557, Arny to Parker, October 24, 1870. Arny was clearly confused in making this statement, perhaps because Cochise had just been at Camp Thomas, the White Mountain Apaches' reservation. Cochise, of course, represented the Chiricahuas, whom Arny referred to as the Chillicorias.

54. Patterson, an able and conscientious interpreter, came to New Mexico in 1862 with the California Volunteers. At the end of his enlistment he settled at Cañada Alamosa, where he became acquainted with the Chiricahuas. Darlis M. Miller, *The California Column in New Mexico,* 64–65.

55. RG75, T21, R12, Hennisee to Clinton, October 31, 1870, Appendix A, Council held with Arny and Cochise.

56. Ibid.; RG75, M234, R557, Arny to Parker, October 24, 1870.

57. RG75, M234, R557, Arny to Parker, November 8, 1870.

58. Second Lieutenant Leverett Hull Walker was directed by Special Order No. 106, Headquarters Fort Craig, dated November 13, 1871, to "investigate the title" of two mules which were once in Jeffords's possession. By the time Walker reached Cañada Alamosa, he found the mules owned by a man named Arden, who had bought them from Jeffords. Walker investigated and concluded that Jeffords had traded whiskey to the Apaches for one mule in October 1870. He obtained the second from Apaches about March 1871. The Indians had stolen it in July 1870 from Mesilla. LR, District of New Mexico, M1088, R12, I82, 1871, Stafford to AAG District of New Mexico, November 17, 1871.

59. RG393, LS, Fort Bowie, Bernard to Stone, November 23, 1870.

60. Ibid., Bernard to Commanding Officer, Fort McRae, November 25, 1870.

61. RG393, LS, Fort McRae, Shorkley to Bernard, December 2, 1870.

62. RG75, T21, R12, Hennisee to Pope, November 30, 1870.

63. RG75, T21, R29, Pope to Parker, December 12, 1870.

64. RG75, T21, R12, Hennisee to Pope, December 8, 1870.

65. Piper hailed from Macomb, Illinois, and held a variety of civic positions throughout his life but was not suited to be an Indian agent. His appointment was sponsored by the Presbyterian Board of Foreign Missions. Thrapp, *Victorio,* 346.

66. Fred Hughes Collection.

67. RG75, T21, R12, Piper to Pope, December 31, 1870.

68. Ibid., December 16, 1870.

69. Ibid., December 31, 1870.

70. Ibid., January 26, 1871.

71. Ibid., January 31, 1871.

Chapter 16

1. *Las Cruces Borderer,* November 1, 1871.

2. RG393, LS, Fort Bowie, Russell to Stone, December 21, 1870.

3. *Alta California,* February 4, 1871.

4. RG393, LS, Fort Bowie, Bernard to Stone, January 24, 1871. Whether Cochise was present at this skirmish is not known. Bernard assumed that he was be-

cause he had no way of knowing that Juh's and Geronimo's Nednhis, who lived in the Chiricahuas at times, were distinct from Cochise's Chokonens.

5. *Alta California,* April 8, 1871; *Las Cruces Borderer,* April 27, 1871; RG393, LS, Department of Missouri, Kelly to Post Adjutant, Camp Bayard, February 19, 1871. Geronimo recalled that U.S. troops attacked his band, killing sixteen individuals and capturing his entire camp. Afterward he moved to New Mexico and joined Victorio's people before returning to Arizona and the Chiricahua Reservation. Barrett, *Geronimo's Story,* 124–26.

6. *Las Cruces Borderer,* March 16, 1871.

7. Ibid., *Alta California,* April 8, 1871.

8. RG75, T21, R15, Piper to Pope, March 31, 1871.

9. *Las Cruces Borderer,* April 13, 1871; RG393, Book of Scouts, 1869–94, Fort Bowie, Russell to Evans, March 25, 1871.

10. Thirty-five Chiricahua Apaches attacked an American group known as the Charles Keerle party on the morning of March 4, 1871, at Chocolate Pass, midway between Casas Grandes and Galeana. There were about eight Americans, including Keerle's wife. All were killed except one man, who managed to escape to Galeana and raise the alarm. Keerle was transporting a load of bacon from Chihuahua to Fort Bayard. The bodies "were horribly mutilated—the hands cut off and placed besides the bodies" and both Keerle and his wife were beheaded. Among the Americans murdered were Gus Hepner, Thomas Sunderland, and Charles Delard. *Las Cruces Borderer,* March 16, April 13, 1871; *Missouri Republican,* March 24, 1871.

11. *Las Cruces Borderer,* April 13, 1871; RG393, LR, Fort Bowie, 1862–71, Russell to Evans, April 4, 1871.

12. RG75, M234, R558, Pope to Parker, March 18, 1871; Piper to Pope, March 18, 1871.

13. RG75, T21, R13, Parker to Pope, March 18, 1871.

14. RG75, M234, R558, Pope to Parker, April 6, 1871.

15. RG75, T21, R15, Piper to Pope, February 7, 1871.

16. José María Trujillo was born in Carrizal, Chihuahua, in 1819 or 1820. He became a soldier at Janos, achieving a fine record, in the 1840s and 1850s before relocating in New Mexico. He became well acquainted with the hostile Chiricahuas while living at Janos. Trujillo was the justice of the peace at Cañada Alamosa in the early 1870s. JA, R30, R33, Record of Enlistments.

17. RG75, T21, R15, Piper to Pope, April 30, 1871; RG75, M234, R558, Pope to Parker, April 21(?), 1871.

18. *Las Cruces Borderer,* April 27, May 4, 1871; *Weekly Arizonian,* April 15, April 22, 1871.

19. RG393, LS, Fort Bowie, Evans to Russell, April 23, 1871; RG393, Book of Scouts, Fort Bowie, 1869–94, Russell to Evans, May 5, 1871. LS, Fort Bowie, Evans to Commissary General of Subsistence, August 14, 1871; *Las Cruces Borderer,* December 13, 1871.

20. Ibid.

21. *Estrella de Occidente,* May 19, 1871.

22. Ibid.

23. On April 30, 1871, an Anglo-Mexican-Papago party of 140 men led by William S. Oury attacked a band of Western Apaches ostensibly living at peace

near Camp Grant. Some of the raids into southern Arizona were blamed on these Apaches, many the work of other bands, of which the Chiricahuas were probably most accountable. Oury's party massacred over 100 Indians (mostly women and children), which prompted the government to send a peace commissioner (who turned out to be Vincent Colyer) to right the wrongs inflicted on both sides. See Thrapp, *Conquest of Apachería*, 79–94, for an unbiased account of the tragedy. See also Don Schellie, *Vast Domain of Blood: The Story of the Camp Grant Massacre*.

24. *San Diego Union*, copied from the *Arizona Citizen*, May 6, 1871.

25. Thrapp, *Conquest of Apachería*, 63.

26. *Army and Navy Journal*, May 27, 1871; Marion, *Notes of Travel*, 45.

27. Thrapp, *Conquest of Apachería*, 70–78; Ball, *Indeh*, 26–27.

28. *Estrella de Occidente*, May 5, May 12, 1871.

29. Ibid., May 19, 1871.

30. *Arizona Citizen*, May 27, 1871; *San Diego Union*, June 1, 1871; *Las Cruces Borderer*, June 8, 1871.

31. RG75, M234, R558, Pope to Parker, May 24, 1871; M234, R6, Piper to Hudson; RG393, LR, District of New Mexico, Pope to Granger, May 30, 1871; *Las Cruces Borderer*, June 8, 1871.

32. RG393, LR, District of New Mexico, Pope to Granger, May 31, 1871; RG75, M234, R558, Pope to Parker, May 24, 1871.

33. Cochise did not expect a troop evacuation. What he meant was that several patrols had remained active in southern Arizona since the Cushing fight. In fact, Captain Alexander Moore had twice attacked camps in the Huachuca Mountains, killing three Chiricahuas on June 2 and "scattering them in every direction through the mountains" on June 10. Afterward, Moore scouted the Whetstones and Dragoons and must have been in the vicinity when Jeffords found Cochise on June 16. Moore evidently reached the Dragoons on June 19 or 20, at which time Cochise either eluded detection or had moved south. RG94, Records of the Adjutant General, Muster Rolls, Third Cavalry, Company F, April 30–June 30, 1871.

34. RG75, M234, R558, Pope to Parker, June 28, 1871. RG75, T21, R15, Piper to Pope, July 23, 1871.

35. RG75, T21, R15, Jeffords to Pope, July 24, 1871.

36. RG75, Howard to Pope, October 11, 1872, copy in AHS.

37. Altshuler, *Chains of Command*, 196–97.

38. RG393, LS, District of New Mexico, M1072, R4, Granger to AAG, Department of Missouri, May 4, 1871.

39. *Army and Navy Journal*, May 20, 1871.

40. Ibid., May 27, 1871.

41. *Las Cruces Borderer*, April 13, 1871.

42. *Arizona Citizen*, January 14, 1871.

43. *Army and Navy Journal*, August 26, 1871.

44. *Arizona Citizen*, May 13, 1871.

45. *Army and Navy Journal*, July 15, 1871.

46. Ibid., August 26, 1871.

47. George Crook, *General George Crook: His Autobiography*, ed. by Martin F. Schmitt (cited hereafter as Schmitt, *Crook*), 160.

48. RG75, M234, R4, Crook to AGO, July 10, 1871.

49. RG75, M234, R558, Pope to Parker, August 26, 1871; Colyer to Pope, Au-

gust 21, 1871. *Peace with the Apaches of New Mexico and Arizona,* 44. RG75, M234, R4, Crook to AGO, September 1, 1871.

50. RG393, LS, District of Arizona, Crook to AGO, September 19, 1871.

51. Schmitt, *Crook,* 167.

Chapter 17

1. Thrapp, *Victorio,* 144.

2. Richard N. Ellis, *General Pope and U.S. Indian Policy,* 215. Lockwood, *The Apache Indians,* 185–86.

3. Colyer, *Peace with the Apaches,* 9.

4. Ibid., 44.

5. Ibid., 9–10.

6. Ibid.; AHSH, Folder 432, Tepeda to Governor, August 23, 1871; *Estrella de Occidente,* September 1, 1871.

7. RG393, LS, Fort Lowell, Mizner to AAG, October 8, 1871; Hunter, "Early Days in Arizona," 116–17.

8. *Arizona Citizen,* September 9, 1871.

9. RG75, T21, R15, Piper to Pope, September 26, 1871.

10. AHS, W. H. Harrison File, H3186.

11. Ibid.

12. RG75, T21, R15, Piper to Pope, September 30, 1871.

13. RG393, LR, District of New Mexico, Piper to Shorkley, September 27, 1871; Orlando F. Piper Collection at Presbyterian Historical Society, Philadelphia, Piper to Lowrie, October 9, 1871.

14. Chiva, Chivo, Cheever (ca. 1820–ca. 1887) was a friend of Cochise from the early 1840s, when both were at Janos. He was quite involved in Chiricahua affairs in the 1870s and 1880s and was one of the Apache leaders who did not go out with Geronimo in May 1885. He was removed to Florida in September 1886 and eventually died as a prisoner of war.

15. RG393, LR, District of New Mexico, Piper to Shorkley, October 19, 1871; RG75, M234, R558, Pope to Parker, October 19, 1871. Cochise is referring to members of his band who had not yet come in and who were, in all likelihood, going to remain at war. At least two Chokonen captains had refused to make peace, and then there were the Nednhis under Juh, Natiza, and Geronimo, who might depredate in southern Arizona, which Cochise realized would be charged to him.

16. Ibid., RG75, M234, R558, Davis to AAG, Department of Missouri, October 25, 1871. On several occasions Cochise refused this invitation to visit Washington, perhaps fearing he would never return. His son Taza had no such apprehensions, eventually journeying east in 1876, where he contracted pneumonia and died in the nation's capital.

17. Chise was a farming community about twelve miles southwest of Cañada Alamosa and twenty-four miles northwest of present-day Truth or Consequences, New Mexico. Pearce, *New Mexico Place Names,* 34.

18. Whitney, born in New York on January 9, 1840, had accompanied Captain Walker in his well-known mining expedition of 1863. After the Civil War he drifted back into New Mexico and was subcontractor for the mail between El Paso and Mesilla. He was described as standing six feet, four inches and was fluent in Spanish and some "Indian dialects." *Santa Fe Gazette,* January 2, 1869; *Alta California,* November 17, 1871; Thrapp, *Encyclopedia,* 1561.

19. RG98, Book of Scouts, Fort Bowie, 1869–94, Russell to Smith, October 27, 1871; James M. Barney, *Tales of Apache Warfare*, 22–24.

20. *Las Cruces Borderer*, December 13, 1871.

21. Historian Dan Thrapp points out that "Juh did a lot of the work that Cochise was blamed for, even in the Chiricahua Mountains, some of Russell's reports asserting that Cochise was the Indian he fought bear internal evidence suggesting that it was Juh, instead of Cochise." Juh never did come into Cañada Alamosa, at least as far as Mrs. Ball was told. Furthermore, the Nednhis and some Chokonens remained in the Chiricahua Mountains in the fall and winter of 1871–72. According to a captive who was freed near Fronteras in early January 1872, there was a large ranchería in the Chiricahuas. In February a Sonoran scout discovered a large camp near Batepito (probably Juh's) as northern Mexico exerted pressure on the Apache bands. In fact, one scout reported they had killed Cochise himself—one of the many times Cochise was killed by Sonoran troops. Thrapp to author, letter in author's file.

22. RG75, T21, R15, Colyer to Pope, November 6, 1871; Pope telegram reprinted in the *New York Times*, November 16, 1871. In January 1872, Jeffords told Captain George Shorkley that "Cochise had not left" the reservation. RG393, LS, Fort McRae, Shorkley to Devin, January 8, 1872.

23. *Las Cruces Borderer*, November 1, 1871.

24. Ibid.

25. Ibid.

26. RG75, Council with Mimbres Apaches at Fort Tularosa, September 11, 1872, copy in AHS.

27. RG75, M234, R558, Piper to Davis, September 30, 1871.

28. Ibid.

29. Piper Collection, Piper to Lowrie, October 9, 1871.

30. RG393, M1072, R4, LS, District of New Mexico, Granger to Pope, October 12, 1871.

31. RG75, M234, R558, Pope to Commissioner of Indian Affairs, October 17, 1871.

32. RG75, T21, R15, Piper to Pope, October 19, 20, 21, 1871.

33. RG75, M234, R558, Davis to AAG, Department of Missouri, October 25, 1871; RG94, M666, R24, Davis to AAG, Department of Missouri, October 25, 1871. Davis stated that Cochise refused to go to Washington but permitted his picture to be sent; whether a photograph was taken, however, is not known for sure.

34. RG393, LR, Department of Missouri, H300, 1871, Piper to Granger, October 30, 1871.

35. RG75, M234, R558, Pope to Commissioner of Indian Affairs, October 26, 1871.

36. RG348, Report Books of the Office of Indian Affairs, Clum to Delano, November 5, 1871.

37. RG75, M234, R558, Delano to Clum, November 7, 1871. *Army and Navy Journal*, December 9, 1871; RG75, T21, R15, Colyer to Pope, November 7, 1871.

38. RG393, M1088, R15, B1, 1872, Bennett to Granger, January 6, 1872.

39. *Las Cruces Borderer*, December 13, 1871.

40. LS, District of New Mexico, M1072, R4, Granger to AAG, Department of Missouri, December 11, 1871.

41. *Las Cruces Borderer*, December 13, 1871.

42. RG75, T21, R15, Piper to Pope, December 31, 1871.

43. Ibid., Piper to Pope, December 9, December 12, 1871; January 31, 1872.

44. RG, M234, R6, Crook to AAG, Military Division of the Pacific, December 7, 1871.

45. RG75, T21, R17, Moore to AAAG, Department of Arizona, November 29, 1871.

46. RG393, LR, District of New Mexico, Piper to Pope, March 11, 1872.

47. RG393, LR, District of New Mexico, Shorkley to AAG, April 6, 1872.

48. RG75, T21, R15, Editor of the *Borderer* to Piper, February 5, 1872; M234, R5, Smith to AAAG, Department of Arizona, January 25, 1872; *Arizona Miner,* February 10, 1872; RG393, LS, Fort Bowie, Smith to AAAG, Department of Arizona, January 25, 1872. This may have been the origin for the stories about Cochise's warriors' escorting the mail through hostile Apache country.

49. RG75, M234, R5, Piper to Colyer, January 27, 1872.

50. RG393, LS, Fort McRae, Shorkley to Devin, January 8, 1872.

51. Ibid.

52. RG393, LS, District of New Mexico, M1072, R4, AAAG, District of New Mexico to Jefferies [Jeffords], July 21, 1872.

53. RG393, LR, District of New Mexico, Piper to Shorkley, February 29, 1872.

54. Ibid.; RG75, T21, R17, Piper to Pope, February 29, 1872.

55. RG393, LS, District of New Mexico, Granger to Crook, January 27, 1872; Granger to AAG, Department of Missouri, March 16, 1872. RG75, M234, R559, Pope to Walker, March 18, March 20, March 28, 1872.

56. *Santa Fe New Mexican,* March 30, 1872; *Arizona Miner,* April 20, 1872.

57. Turrill, "A Vanished Race," 18.

58. Ellis, "Recollections," 391–92.

59. *Santa Fe New Mexican,* March 30, 1872. On March 28, 1872, Pope telegraphed Walker that "Cochise has renewed his promise made to me last fall to go in person and try to persuade roving Apaches to go to the reservation." RG75, M234, R559, Pope to Walker, March 28, 1872.

Chapter 18

1. Fred Hughes Collection.

2. RG75, M234, R559, Pope to Walker, April 29, 1872. RG75, T21, R17, Streeter to Pope, May 4, 1872; RG393, LR, District of New Mexico, Shorkley to AAG, April 6, 1872; Devin to AAG, District of New Mexico, April 13, 1872; Report of the Commissioner of Indian Affairs, 1872, 306.

3. RG393, LR, District of New Mexico, Devin to AAG, District of New Mexico, April 13, 1872.

4. RG393, LR, District of New Mexico, Shorkley to AAG, April 6, 1872.

5. RG75, M234, R559, Pope to Walker, April 29, 1872.

6. *Las Cruces Borderer,* May 1, 1872.

7. *Missouri Republican,* May 17, 1872.

8. RG75, T21, R17, Streeter to Pope, May 4, 1872.

9. There is a detailed account of the removal to Tularosa in Thrapp, *Victorio,* 144–54.

10. Born in New York State about 1838, Streeter led a fascinating and intriguing life. He was closely associated with the Chihennes and also was well acquainted with Jeffords as both assisted Piper in the move to Tularosa. Streeter accompanied

Jeffords and Howard on the historic visit to Cochise. In the late 1870s he allegedly turned renegade and was said to have participated in several raids against whites. He was killed in Sonora in 1889. Thrapp, *Encyclopedia,* 1378–79.

11. RG75, M234, R559, Pope to Walker, June 5, 1872.

12. Ponce, born about 1840, headed a small group of Chihennes in the 1870s. He was a heavy-set Indian with a tendency to stutter, and he and his followers spent much time in northern Chihuahua and southwestern New Mexico. He apparently married into Mangas Coloradas's family. His father also may have been named Ponce and perhaps was an influential chief, killed in the early 1850s, who was said to have been a literate, intelligent, and wealthy leader. The younger Ponce was one of the Indians captured with Geronimo by Clum in 1877. He passed from the scene shortly thereafter.

13. RG393, LS, Fort Stanton, Randlett to Devin, May 22, 1872; LR, District of New Mexico, Randlett to Devin, May 22, 1872.

14. RG393, M1088, R15, LR, District of New Mexico, Devin to AAG, District of New Mexico, May 9, 1872.

15. *Missouri Republican,* May 31, 1872.

16. RG75, T21, R17, Piper to Pope, May 31, 1872.

17. RG393, Returns from Military Posts, Fort Bowie, May 1872.

18. RG393, LS, Fort Bowie, Haskell to AAAG, Department of Arizona, May 10, 1872.

19. *Las Cruces Borderer,* June 5, July 10, 1872.

20. *Estrella de Occidente,* May 10, May 31, June 28, 1872; AHSH, Folder 443, Aragon to Governor, June 19, 1872.

21. Pionsenay, brother of Eskinya, "one of Cochise's war leaders," was a first-rate incorrigible in his own right. In April 1876 he led a small group of drunken warriors who attacked and killed Nick Rogers and O. O. Spence at Sulphur Springs. Two months later he was wounded by Taza and turned over to civil authorities by John P. Clum. Somehow he managed to escape and made his way into Mexico. For the next year and a half he was a hostile, raiding on both sides of the border before he was killed at or near Janos about December 1877. RG393, E204, Brief of Indian Affairs at San Carlos, 1878.

22. AHSH, Folder 443, Aragon to Governor, June 19, 1872; *Estrella de Occidente,* June 28, 1872; *La República,* May 24, 1872; RG393, LR, District of New Mexico, Devin to AAG, August 8, 1872. LR, Department of Missouri, Devin to AAG, District of New Mexico, July 29[?], 1872.

23. *Estrella de Occidente,* July 26, August 9, 1872.

24. *Arizona Miner,* July 13, July 27, 1872; Connell, "The Apaches Past and Present."

25. RG393, LR, District of New Mexico, Devin to AAG, August 8, 1872; LR, Department of Missouri, Stephenson to Granger, August 2, 1872; Reeve, "Frederick E. Phelps," 110–22; Floyd, *Chronological List of Actions,* 52.

26. Bowdoin College, Oliver Otis Howard Papers, Soule to Howard, September 11, 1872.

27. Connell, "The Apaches Past and Present." Reid T. Stewart graduated eighth in a class of forty-three from West Point in June 1871. Only twenty-two when he was killed, he was described as "genial and frank with a winning disposition." He grew up around Erie, Pennsylvania. His rifle was seen by Howard and Sladen in

Cochise's camp. Heitman, *Historical Register,* 925; *Army and Navy Journal,* September 21, 1872; Thrapp, *Encyclopedia,* 1368–69; Thrapp, *Apachería,* 115–16.

28. Thrapp, *Apachería,* 115–16; *Army and Navy Journal,* September 21, 1872; *San Diego Union,* September 7, 1872.

29. AHS, Petra Etchell File.

30. *Webster's American Military Biographies,* 185.

31. Howard Papers, Delano to Howard, February 29, 1872.

32. Howard, *My Life and Experiences,* 124.

33. Howard Papers, Howard to wife, April 15, 1872.

34. Schmitt, *Crook,* 169.

35. RG393, LR, District of New Mexico, Crook to Granger, April 20, 1872.

36. Howard, *My Life and Experiences,* 172–80.

37. Sladen, born in England in 1841, enlisted as a private in the Thirty-third Massachusetts Infantry in August 1862. He was awarded the Medal of Honor in 1895 for his actions in the Battle of Resaca, Georgia, on May 14, 1864. After the war he was commissioned a second lieutenant in the First Infantry. He became captain in 1888, retired in 1889, and went into insurance. He died in Oregon in 1911. Heitman, *Historical Register* 1, 890; Joseph Sladen Papers; Thrapp, *Encyclopedia,* 1319.

38. Howard, *My Life and Experiences,* 187.

39. Howard Papers, Howard to wife, August 12, 1872.

40. Stevens, a native of Massachusetts, was born about 1844 and came to Arizona in 1866. He married the daughter of a White Mountain Apache leader and later served as a scout for Crook and as sheriff of Graham County. Thrapp, *Encyclopedia,* 1366.

41. Sladen, "Making Peace," 2.

42. RG75, Howard to Crook, August 29, 1872, copy in AHS.

43. Farish, *History of Arizona,* II, 230; Howard Papers, Howard to wife, September 8, 1872.

44. Fred Hughes Collection; Howard Papers, Howard to wife, September 8, 1872.

45. Howard Papers, Howard to wife, September 8, 1872.

46. Ibid.

47. Farish, *History of Arizona,* II, 230–31.

48. Ibid.; Howard, *My Life and Experiences,* 188; Sladen, "Making Peace," 5.

49. RG75, Council of Mimbres Apaches at Fort Tularosa, September 11, 1872, copy in AHS.

50. RG75, T21, R17, Piper to Pope, September 13, 1872; Howard to Piper, September 16, 1872.

51. RG75, T21, R17, Howard to Pope, September 16, 1872.

52. Howard Papers, document originally dated September 16, 1872, and then changed to October 7, 1872.

53. Chie, Chee, or Chisito's identity is questionable. Jeffords, Howard, and Sladen all concurred that he was a nephew of Cochise. Mrs. Eve Ball's informants told her that Chie was a son of one of Cochise's sisters or brothers and also that Chie's father was believed to have been killed at Apache Pass, a fact corroborated by Howard. When he and Chie were in Apache Pass, the young Apache became distressed because this was where his father had been slain. Based on this, I believe

Chie was a Chokonen born about 1850, the son of Cochise's brother Coyuntura, who was hanged at Apache Pass in February 1861. After this, Cochise brought Chie up until the late 1860s, when Chie married a Chihenne, probably into Mangas Coloradas's family, and went to live with her people. It is also possible that Chie accompanied Cochise on one of his visits to Cañada Alamosa and remained there with the Chihennes. Chie remained at Tularosa and Cañada Alamosa even after the Chiricahua Reservation was established. He was killed in 1876 or 1877 by Apaches, probably in an incident involving alcohol. If Chie was Coyuntura's son, it is ironic that the death of his father ignited the war and the efforts of his son helped bring peace to Arizona.

54. RG75, T21, R17, Howard to Pope, September 19, 1872.

55. Howard Papers, Howard to Walker, September 15(?), 1872.

56. Howard, *My Life and Experiences,* 192–93; Sladen, "Making Peace," 13–15; RG94, General Howard correspondence relating to peace with Cochise, Howard to Commanding Officer, Fort Bowie, September 28, 1872; NA, RG217, Howard's accounts, 5911.

57. Ibid.

58. NA, RG94, Howard correspondence relating to peace with Cochise, Howard to Commanding Officer, Fort Bowie, September 28, 1872.

59. Unless specified, the sources for the Howard-Jeffords-Cochise treaty are Sladen's reminiscences at Carlisle Barracks; Howard's *My Life and Experiences* and "Account of His Mission to the Apaches and Navajos," published in the *Washington Daily Morning Chronicle* on November 10, 1872; and Tom Jeffords's account, which can be found in Farish, *History of Arizona,* II, 230–35, and in the AHS.

60. Cochise's sister was a widow about fifty years old and was described as "large and bony with strong marked features." The chief put much trust in her, placing her in charge of one of the outposts in the high Dragoons. Sladen, "Making Peace," 29.

61. Ibid., 27.

62. Ibid., 28.

63. Howard, *My Life and Experiences,* 207. Evidently, many of Cochise's band had no desire to live with the Chihennes in New Mexico, probably because of interband rivalries and disputes. Loco's and Cochise's bands had clashed the previous winter and the result was a couple of deaths. Cochise, with many relatives among the Chihennes, was more receptive than his other captains, who had no desire to leave their land in southeastern Arizona. Likewise, most of Victorio's and Loco's people had no wish to relocate to Cochise's reservation.

64. Ibid., 209.

65. RG393, LS, Fort Bowie, Sumner to AAAG, Department of Arizona, October 2, 1872.

66. RG75, M234, R560, Howard to Commanding Officer, Fort Lowell, October 2, 1872.

67. RG393, LS, Fort Bowie, Sumner to AAAG, Department of Arizona, October 2, 1872.

68. Farish, *History of Arizona,* II, 233. Sladen, "Making Peace," 42. This was probably the party which raided a ranch two miles from Camp Crittenden early on September 30, 1872, killed one Mexican, and ran off three horses. Second Lieutenant William Prebel Hall dispatched Sergeant George Stewart and five troopers to

warn Thomas Gardner, whose ranch was seven miles away. On their return trip the soldiers were attacked by "about 50 Indians who were lying in a little ravine." Stewart and three others were killed instantly. M234, R6, Hall to AAAG, Department of Arizona, October 1, 1872; *Arizona Citizen,* October 19, 1872.

69. Sladen, "Making Peace," 53–54.

70. Ibid., 40.

71. Howard continued to push for the Cañada Alamosa reservation as late as October 7, 1872, as is indicated by a document dated Dragoon Mountains, October 7, 1872, describing Cochise's reservation at Cañada Alamosa. Howard Papers.

72. Nahilzay (Ny-les-shizie) was considered by Fred Hughes and Charles T. Connell to be Cochise's war leader. He moved to San Carlos with Taza in 1876 and in late 1879 assisted in the delicate negotiatons to bring in Juh and Geronimo from Mexico to San Carlos Agency. He bolted with Naiche in the September 1881 exodus from San Carlos and was a leading man in the fight at Casas Grandes soon after that. He was captured at this time and sent to a Chihuahua prison, never to be heard from again. Fred Hughes Collection. Griswold, "Ft. Sill Apaches," 116.

73. Sladen, "Making Peace," 45–46.

74. AHS, Dan Williamson File.

75. Eve Ball to author, February 14, 1976.

76. Howard Papers, Alden to Howard, April 22, 1891.

77. Jeffords's account, copy in AHS.

78. NA, M666, R123, Howard to Commissioner of Indian Affairs, September 23, 1873.

79. Howard, *My Life and Experiences,* 220.

80. RG94, General Howard correspondence relating to peace with Cochise, Howard to Sumner, October 11, 1872.

81. RG75; AHS, Howard to Crook, October 11, 1872.

82. RG393, LS, Fort Bowie, Sumner to AAAG, District of Arizona, October 15, 1872.

83. *Boston Evening Transcript,* November 6, 1872.

84. Ibid.

85. Report of the Indian Commissioner to the Secretary of the Interior, 1872; Charles J. Kappler, *Indian Affairs, Laws and Treaties,* 802–3.

86. RG75, AHS, Howard to Sumner, October 13, 1872; Howard to Jeffords, October 13, 1872.

87. RG393, LS, Fort Bowie, Sumner to AAAG, October 15, 1872.

88. Report of the Commissioner of Indian Affairs, 1873, 292–93.

89. Bourke Diary, February 3, 1873.

Chapter 19

1. RG75, M234, R5, Orr to Howard, November 23, 1872; NA, RG217, Howard voucher for supplies purchased from Lord and Williams for Cochise, October 15, 1872; Report of the Commissioner of Indian Affairs, 1873, 291–92.

2. RG393, LS, Fort Bowie, Sumner to Nickerson, November 2, 1872.

3. Report of Commissioner of Indian Affairs, 1873, 291.

4. Chihuahua, born about 1822, succeeded his father as chief of a Chokonen local group which may have split from Cochise at this time. His Apache name was Kla-esch. Mrs. Ball was uncertain whether Chihuahua was present at the treaty signing but said he was on the reservation from time to time. In size, Chihuahua's

local group was "next in numbers to Cochise." He was one of the fighting leaders in the wars of the 1880s and was highly respected by both whites and Apaches. He died in 1901 at Fort Sill. Griswold, "Ft. Sill Apaches," 18; Opler to author, October 9, 1978; Ball to author, February 14, 1876.

5. Hughes was born in England in 1837 and came to Arizona with the California Volunteers in 1862. He provided much assistance to Jeffords and helped John Clum in the Indians' removal to the San Carlos Reservation in 1876. He was killed by lightning in 1911. Charles C. Colley, *Documents of Southwestern History,* 102. Miller, *The California Column,* 213. Fred Hughes Collection.

6. Fred Hughes collection.

7. Connell, "The Apaches Past and Present," 13.

8. Ibid., Fred Hughes Collection.

9. Hughes and Orr placed their number at 200. AHS, Fred Hughes Collection; Howard Papers, Orr to Howard, November 23, 1872. The *Arizona Citizen* of November 30, 1872, reported the Nednhit at 300; in his report for 1873, Jeffords wrote that they numbered 400. Report of Commissioner of Indian Affairs, 1873, 291.

10. Howard Papers, Orr to Howard, November 1, 1872.

11. Ibid., Thomas Hughes to Howard, November 23, 1872.

12. Ibid., Delong to Howard, December 20, 1872.

13. *Arizona Miner,* November 16, 1872.

14. *Arizona Citizen,* November 30, 1872.

15. Ibid., December 7, 1872.

16. Harry G. Cramer III, "Tom Jeffords, Indian Agent," *Journal of Arizona History,* 17 (Autumn 1976), 265–300. Cramer's excellent article documents the problems Jeffords faced.

17. RG75, T21, R17, Jeffords to Pope, November 26, 1872; T21, R17, Clum to Pope, November 14, 1872.

18. Ibid., Clum to Jeffords, November 14, 1872.

19. RG75, M734, R8, Bendell to Jeffords, December 7, 1872; January 2, 1873.

20. RG75, M734, R7, Jeffords to Bendell, December 20, 24, 1872.

21. RG75, M234, R7, Bendell to Commissioner of Indian Affairs, April 18, 1873.

22. RG75, M734, R8, Bendell to Jeffords, January 24, February 2, 1873.

23. RG75, M234, R8, Jeffords to Howard, February 11, 1873; M734, R7, Delano to Bendell, March 5, 1873.

24. RG75, M734, R8, Bendell to Commissioner of Indian Affairs, February 28, March 4, 1873; RG75, M234, R8, Delano to Acting Commission of Indian Affairs, March 24, 1873.

25. RG75, M234, R7, and M734, R8, Bendell to Delano, March 11, 1873.

26. RG75, M234, R7, Bendell to Commissioner of Indian Affairs, April 23, 1873.

27. *Estrella de Occidente,* March 14, 1873.

28. This was one opinion not shared by Crook's subordinate, John G. Bourke. Bourke believed that Howard's mission was completed at "great personal discomfort and no little risk." Bourke, *On the Border with Crook,* 235.

29. RG94, M666, R24, Delano to Belknap, December 10, 1872; Sherman to Belknap, December 17, 1872; Belknap to Delano, December 20, 1872.

30. Ibid. Crook to AAG, Military Division of the Pacific, February 11, 1873; *Estrella de Occidente*, July 4, 1873.

31. Fred Hughes Collection; *Alta California*, April 25, 1873.

32. RG159, Records of the Inspector General, D. B. Sacket Report on the Department of Arizona, June 30, 1873.

33. *Estrella de Occidente*, July 4, 1873.

34. RG393, E169, LS, Department of Arizona, Nickerson to Jeffords, January 29, 1873.

35. Bourke Diary, notation dated February 3, 1873.

36. *Estrella de Occidente*, July 4, 1873.

37. *Estrella de Occidente*, June 20, 1873; *Alta California*, April 25, 1873.

38. *Arizona Citizen*, November 29, 1873.

39. *Estrella de Occidente*, January 10, February 7, 1873; *Arizona Citizen*, February 15, 1873.

40. RG159, Sacket Report.

41. *Estrella de Occidente*, January 17, January 24, February 7, February 14, 1873.

42. *Arizona Citizen*, February 22, 1873.

43. M234, R8, Jeffords to Commissioner of Indian Affairs, March 21, 1873.

44. Luna, born about 1830, was in command of Sonora's National Guard. He was the only survivor of an Apache massacre near Fronteras in the fall of 1855. *Alta California*, May 13, 1873.

45. Delong, as did so many Arizona pioneers, came to Arizona with the California Volunteers in 1862. Born in New York State in 1828, he was a multitalented man. He was discharged from the volunteers in 1866 and went to work for Tully and Ochoa, noted merchants. He was appointed post trader at Fort Bowie on January 5, 1871. Four months later he participated in the Camp Grant massacre, which he later regretted. He died in 1914. For a biographical account of his life, see Randy Kane, "An Honorable and Upright Man: Sidney R. Delong as Post Trader at Fort Bowie," *Journal of Arizona History*, 19 (Autumn 1978), 297–314.

46. *Estrella de Occidente* June 20, 1873; Lockwood, *The Apache Indians*, 125–26; *Alta California*, May 13, 1873.

47. *Army and Navy Journal*, April 26, 1873.

48. Lockwood, *The Apache Indians*, 124–26.

49. RG393, LS, Fort Bowie, Sumner to Nickerson, April 22, 1873.

50. AHS, Al Williamson manuscript titled "Reminiscences of the Early Days of Arizona."

51. Ibid.; RG 393, LS, Fort Bowie, Sumner to Jeffords, May 14, 1873.

52. RG75, M734, R7, Jeffords to Smith, June 4, 1873.

53. RG393, LS, Fort Bowie, Sumner to Jeffords, July 12, 1873; *Arizona Citizen*, July 12, 1873.

54. RG393, LS, Fort Bowie, Sumner to Price, August 6, 1873.

55. RG75, M234, R9, Price to AAG, Department of Missouri, August 30, 1873; RG94, M666, R123, Price to Willard, August 1, 1873.

56. RG94, M666, R123, Howard to Commissioner of Indian Affairs, September 23, 1873.

57. Ibid., Crook to Adjutant General, Washington, December 8, 1873.

58. Ibid., Clum to Delano, September 26, 1873; Crook to Adjutant General, Washington, December 8, 1873.

59. LR, AGO, M689, R187, Bourke Report on the Apaches.
60. *Arizona Citizen,* October 11, 1873.
61. *Estrella de Occidente,* January 9, 1874.
62. Ibid., February 13, 1874.
63. RG75, M234, R8, Jeffords to Smith, September 25, 1873.
64. *Arizona Citizen,* August 23, 1873.
65. Ibid., October 4, 1873.
66. *Estrella de Occidente,* October 24, 1873.
67. *Arizona Citizen,* August 23, 1873.
68. RG75, M1070, R1, Vandever's Report, 1397, October 18, 1873.
69. *Estrella de Occidente,* November 21, 1873.
70. M666, R123, Smith to Jeffords, December 29, 1873.
71. M576, R16, Jeffords to Delano, January 1, 1874.
72. *Arizona Citizen,* February 28, 1874.

Chapter 20

1. RG75, M234, R563, Hughes to Editor, *Las Cruces Borderer,* February 11, 1874.
2. Report of the Commissioner of Indian Affairs, 1874, 300–2.
3. Ibid.
4. *Estrella de Occidente,* May 8, July 31, August 14, August 28, September 11, 1874; SA, R20, Ochoa to Governor of Sonora, August 26, 1874.
5. Report of the Commissioner of Indian Affairs, 1874, 300–2.
6. Ibid., 301.
7. Report of the Commissioner of Indian Affairs, 1874, 288; *Arizona Citizen,* May 16, 1874.
8. Sacket's Report.
9. Fort Bowie Files, Abstracts of an Inspection by Lieutenant Colonel Roger Jones of Fort Bowie, April 27, 1874.
10. *Arizona Citizen,* May 16, 1874.
11. Ibid., May 30, 1874.
12. Eskinya, born about 1820, appeared on the Janos ration rolls in 1843–44. He was also at Fronteras in the early 1860s and probably succeeded Taces as leader of a Chokonen local group in the mid-1860s. He and his brother Pionsenay sparked the uprising and ultimate closing of the Chiricahua Reservation in 1876. He was killed by Naiche in June 1876 during an interband fight. Fred Hughes Collection.
13. Sacket's Report.
14. RG75, M234, R10, Jeffords to Smith, June 10, 1874; Ball, *Indeh,* 25.
15. Fred Hughes Collection; Al Williamson, "Reminiscences."
16. Lockwood, *The Apache Indians,* 128–29.
17. Fred Hughes Collection.
18. Opler, *Apache Lifeway,* 472–78.
19. RG75, M234, R10, Jeffords to Smith, July 6, 1874.
20. Lockwood, *The Apache Indians,* 129–30. Other accounts of Cochise's death and burial are in *Army and Navy Journal,* July 11, 1874, which can also be found in Homer W. Wheeler, *Buffalo Days,* 349–50. Edward L. Keyes has a reliable account, reportedly obtained from Taza, which is similar to Williamson's. Keyes, "Some Recollections." See also Rockfellow, *Log of an Arizona Trail Blazer,* 84–85.

BIBLIOGRAPHY

Manuscript materials, Unpublished Documents, Collections

Archivo Historico de Sonora, Hermosillo, Sonora.

Arizona Historical Society, Tucson. Hayden Files or collections: Nathan Benjamin Appel, Albert F. Banta, Diary of John Bourke, William Buckley, Charles T. Connell manuscript "The Apaches Past and Present," Petra Etchell, Robert Humphrey Forbes, William Fourr, Thomas Gardner, Charles Gatewood, Merejildo Grijalva, Diary of George Hand, W. H. Harrison, Fred Hughes, William H. Kirkland, William Henry Larrabee, Frank C. Lockwood, Edith Allen Milner unpublished manuscript "Covered Wagon Experiences," Policeman Oberly's account of the Bascom affair, William Sanders Oury, Charles Shibell, Joseph Sladen, John T. Smith, W. M. Thompson manuscript "The Fighting Doctor," James Wallace, John Ward, Hiram Storrs Washburn, Charles A. Whittier, Al Williamson manuscript "Reminiscences of the Early Days of Arizona," Dan Williamson, Charles M. Wood.

———. Film MC-6, Archivo General de Mexico, Roll 150.

———. Sonora State Archives, Rolls 12–20, 49–50.

Arizona State Library, Phoenix. Territorial Records of Arizona.

Arizona State University Library. Benjamin H. Sacks Collection; Sylvester Mowry File; Copy of Hubert Howe Bancroft, *Scraps,* a collection of Arizona items clipped from California newspapers.

Ball, Eve. Interviews, correspondence with author, 1975–83.

Basehart, Harry W. "Chiricahua Apache Subsistence and Socio-Political Organization." A report of the Mescalero-Chiricahua Land Claims Project. Contract Research No. 290–154. University of New Mexico, March 1959.

Basso, Keith. Correspondence with author, 1978.

Bowdoin College, Brunswick, Maine. Oliver Otis Howard Papers.

Davisson, Lori. Correspondence with author, 1980.

Goodwin, Grenville. Collection at Arizona State Museum, Tucson.

Griffen, William. Correspondence, 1983–89.

Griswold, Gillet M. "The Ft. Sill Apaches: Their Vital Statistics, Tribal Origins,

Antecedents." Unpublished manuscript, Field Artillery Museum, Fort Sill, Oklahoma, 1970.

Huntington Library, San Marino, California. Alice Rollins Crane article on Tom Jeffords which appeared in an unidentified Los Angeles newspaper.

Missouri Historical Society, St. Louis. Webb Collection.

National Park Service. Fort Bowie Collection.

New Mexico State University Library, Las Cruces. Rio Grande Historical Collection, Keith Humphries File.

Opler, Morris E. Correspondence with author, 1979–82.

Park, Joseph F. "The Assassination of Juan José Compá." Unpublished manuscript in author's files.

Pinart, Louis Alphonse. Microfilm Collection. Bancroft Library, University of California, Berkeley.

Piper, Orlando F. Collection at Presbyterian Historical Society, Philadelphia.

Sladen, Joseph Alton. Papers. United States Army Military History Institute, Carlisle Barracks, Pa.

Steck, Michael. Papers. Zimmerman Library, University of New Mexico, Albuquerque.

Sublette, Solomon. Papers. Missouri Historical Society, St. Louis.

Thrapp, Dan L. Interviews, correspondence with author, 1975–89.

United States Government, National Archives and Records Center. Record Group 94, Records of the Adjutant General's Office (AGO), 1780s–1917: AGO, Microcopy 619, Roll 737, Report of Bvt. Col. Reuben F. Bernard relating to the engagement at Chiricahua Pass, Arizona, on October 20, 1869; AGO, Microcopy 666, Roll 24, correspondence relating to Vincent Colyer's mission to the Apaches; AGO, Microcopy 666, Roll 123, correspondence relating to the agreement with Cochise negotiated by General Oliver Otis Howard; AGO, File titled "General Howard correspondence relating to peace with Cochise"; AGO, Letters Received, 1850–76, Miscellaneous Letters Received concerning Indian affairs in Arizona and New Mexico.

———. Record Group 75 (RG75), Records of the Bureau of Indian Affairs: Microcopy 234, Letters Received, 1824–80, Arizona Superintendency, 1863–80, Rolls 3-12; Microcopy 234, Letters Received, 1824–80, New Mexico Superintendency, 1849–80, Rolls 546–64; Microcopy 734, Records of the Arizona Superintendency of Indian Affairs, 1863–73, 8 rolls; Microcopy T21, Records of the New Mexico Superintendency of Indian Affairs, 1849–80, Rolls 1–18; Miscellaneous Division, Traders' Licenses; Report Books of the Office of Indian Affairs, 1838–85.

———. Record Group 123, Records of the United States Court of Claims, Indian Depredation Division.

———. Record Group 159, Records of the Office of the Inspector General.

———. Record Group 217, Records of the U.S. General Accounting Office.

———. Record Group 148, Records of the Office of the Secretary of the Interior; State Department Territorial Papers, Arizona and New Mexico.

———. Record Group 59, Microcopy 184, Roll 2, Dispatches from U.S. Consuls in Ciudad Juárez (Paso del Norte), Mexico, 1850–1906.

———. Record Group 393, Records of United States Army Continental Commands, 1821–1920. *Arizona:* Letters Received, Department of Arizona, 1871–74; Letters Sent, Department of Arizona, 1871–74; Letters Received,

District oif Arizona, 1862–71; Unregistered Letters and Orders Received, District of Arizona, 1862–71; Book of Scouts, District of Arizona; Brief of Affairs at San Carlos, 1878; Letters Sent, District of Arizona, 1862–71. Letters Received, Southern Subdistrict of the Gila; Letters Received, Subdistrict of Tucson; Letters Sent, Subdistrict of Tucson; Letters Sent, Subdistrict of Southern Arizona. *Missouri:* Letters Received, Department of Missouri, 1865–72. *New Mexico:* Letters Received, Department of New Mexico, 1849–65; Letters Received, District of New Mexico, 1866–74; Letters Sent, Department of New Mexico, 1849–65; Letters Sent, District of New Mexico, 1866–74; Records Relating to Indian Affairs, Department of New Mexico.

Military Posts: Returns from Fort Bowie, Fort West, Camp Wallen; Fort Bowie, Letter Received, Letters Sent; Camp Crittenden, Letters Sent; Fort Cummings, Letters Sent; Camp Grant, Letters Sent; Fort Lowell, Letters Sent; Fort McRae, Letters Sent; Fort Stanton, Letters Sent; Fort Tularosa, Letters Sent; Camp Wallen, Letters Sent; Fort West, Letters Sent.

United States Government, Smithsonian Institution. Copy of letter from George Wratten to Bureau of American Ethnology; J. B. White Manuscript Nos. 178, 179, and 188 on the Apache Indians; N. S. Higgins Manuscript No. 180, historical notes on the Apaches.

University of Arizona Library, Tucson. Special Collections. AZ 300, Thomas Akers Diary; AZ 197, Palmer Manuscript.

University of Texas at Austin. Janos Collection.

University of Texas at El Paso. Carrizal Collection; Janos Collection, 1700–1899. 37 rolls; Juárez Collection, 1619–1893, 12 rolls; Periodico Oficial de Chihuahua, Rolls 1–8.

Wilson, Benjamin. Reminiscences. Bancroft Library, University of California, Berkeley.

United States Government Publications

Abel, Annie Heloise, ed. *The Official Correspondence of James C. Calhoun While Indian Agent at Santa Fe and Superintendent of Indian Affairs in New Mexico.* Washington: Government Printing Office, 1916.

Army and Navy Journal. Various issues, 1867–74.

Conditions of the Indian Tribes: Report of the Joint Special Commission. Washington: Government Printing Office, 1867.

Heitman, Francis B. *Historical Register and Dictionary of the United States Army from its Organization, September 20, 1789, to March 2, 1903.* 2 vols. Urbana: University of Illinois Press, 1965.

Hodge, Frederick Webb. *Handbook of American Indians North of Mexico.* 2 vols. Washington: Government Printing Office, 1907.

Kappler, Charles J. *Indian Affairs, Laws and Treaties.* Washington: Government Printing Office, 1903.

Orton, Brigadier General Richard H. *Records of California Men in the War of the Rebellion, 1861–1867.* Sacramento: State Printing Office, 1890.

U.S. Congress: 39th Cong., House Ex. Doc. 1; 40th Cong., 2d sess., House Ex. Doc. 1324.

United States Department of the Interior. Annual Reports Commissioner of Indian Affairs, 1869–74.

United States Department of War. Reports of the Secretary of War, 1866–67.

The War of the Rebellion: A Compilation of the Official Records of the Union and Confederate Armies. Series I, 53 vols. Washington: Government Printing Office, 1880–1901.

American Newspapers

Boston Evening Transcript
Las Cruces (New Mexico) *Borderer*
Los Angeles Star
Mesilla (New Mexico) *Times*
(Prescott) *Arizona Miner*
Sacramento Daily Union
San Antonio Herald
San Diego Herald
San Diego Union
(San Francisco) *Alta California*
San Francisco Daily Morning Call
San Francisco Evening Bulletin
Santa Fe Gazette
Santa Fe New Mexican
Silver City (New Mexico) *Enterprise*
(St. Louis) *Missouri Republican*
(St. Louis) *Weekly Missouri Democrat*
(Tucson) *Arizona Citizen*.
(Tucson) *Arizona Daily Star*
(Tucson) *Arizona Weekly Star*

Mexican Newspapers

Sonora (Bancroft Library, Berkeley)

(Ures) *El Sonorense*
La Estrella de Occidente
La Voz de Sonora
(Ures) *Uno de Tantos*

Chihuahua (University of Texas at El Paso Microfilm Collection, Oficial periodico de Chihuahua)

(Chihuahua City) *El Antenor*
El Boletin de Chihuahua
El Centinela
El Correo
El Eco de la Frontera
El Fanal de Chihuahua
El Faro
El Noticioso de Chihuahua
El Provisional
El Republicano
El Restaurador
La Alianza de la Frontera
La Coalición
La Luna

La República
La Voz del Pueblo
Revista Oficial

Books: Primary Sources

Altshuler, Constance Wynn, ed. *Latest from Arizona! The Hesperian Letters, 1859–1861*. Tucson: Arizona Pioneer Historical Society, 1969.

Ball, Eve. *In the Days of Victorio: Recollections of a Warm Springs Apache*. Tucson: University of Arizona Press, 1970.

———. with Nora Henn and Lynda Sanchez. *Indeh: An Apache Odyssey*. Provo, Utah: Brigham Young University Press, 1980.

Barnes, Will C. *Apaches and Longhorns: The Reminiscences of Will C. Barnes*. Ed. by Frank C. Lockwood. Tucson: University of Arizona Press, 1982.

Barrett, Stephen M. *Geronimo's Story of His Life*. New York: Garrett Press, 1969.

Bartlett, John Russell. *Personal Narrative of Explorations and Incidents in Texas, New Mexico, California, Sonora and Chihuahua, Connected with the United States and Mexican Boundary Commission During the Years 1850, '51, '52, and '53*. 2 vols. Chicago: Rio Grande Press, 1965.

Bell, William A. *New Tracks in North America: A Journal of Travel and Adventure Whilst Engaged in the Survey for a Southern Railroad to the Pacific Ocean During 1867–68*. Albuquerque: Horn and Wallace, 1965.

Betzinez, Jason, with Wilbur Sturtevant Nye, *I Fought With Geronimo*. New York: Bonanza Books, 1959.

Bourke, John G. *On the Border with Crook*. New York: Time-Life Books, 1980.

Browne, J. Ross. *Adventures in the Apache Country: A Tour Through Arizona and Sonora, 1864*. Ed. by Donald M. Powell. Tucson: University of Arizona Press, 1974.

The Butterfield Overland Mail Across Arizona. Tucson: Arizona Pioneer Historical Society, 1958.

Calvin, Ross, ed. *Lieutenant Emory Reports: Notes of A Military Reconnaissance*. Albuquerque: University of New Mexico Press, 1968.

Clarke, Dwight L., ed. *The Original Journals of Henry Smith Turner with Stephen Watts Kearny to New Mexico and California, 1846–1847*. Norman: University of Oklahoma Press, 1966.

Clum, Woodworth. *Apache Agent: The Story of John P. Clum*. Lincoln: University of Nebraska Press, 1978.

Colyer, Vincent. *Peace with the Apaches of New Mexico and Arizona, Report of Vincent Colyer, Member of Board of Indian Commissioners, 1871*. Tucson: Territorial Press, 1964.

Conner, Daniel Ellis. *Joseph Reddeford Walker and the Arizona Adventure*. Ed. by Daniel J. Berthrong and Odessa Davenport. Norman: University of Oklahoma Press, 1956.

Cooke, Philip St. George. *Exploring Southwestern Trails, 1846–1854*. Ed. by Ralph P. Bieber. Philadelphia: Porcupine Press, 1974.

Cozzens, Samuel Woodworth. *The Marvellous Country, or Three Years in Arizona and New Mexico*. Boston: Lee and Shepard Publishers, 1876.

Cremony, John C. *Life Among the Apaches*. Tucson: Arizona Silhouettes, 1954.

Crook, George. *General George Crook: His Autobiography*. Ed. by Martin F. Schmitt. Norman: University of Oklahoma Press, 1946.

Curry, W. Hubert. *Sun Rising in the West: The Saga of Henry Clay and Elizabeth Smith*. Crosbyton, Texas: Crosby County Pioneer Memorial, 1979.

Dubois, John Van Deusen. *Campaigns in the West, 1856–1861*. Ed. by George F. Hammond. Tucson: Arizona Pioneer Historical Society, 1949.

Ellis, Richard N. *New Mexico Historical Documents*. Albuquerque: University of New Mexico Press, 1975.

Goodwin, Grenville. *Western Apache Raiding and Warfare*. Ed. by Keith H. Basso. Tucson: University of Arizona Press, 1973.

Gregg, Josiah. *Commerce of the Prairies*. Ed. by Max L. Moorhead. Norman: University of Oklahoma Press, 1958.

Hobbs, James. *Wild Life in the Far West*. Glorieta, New Mexico: Rio Grande Press, 1969.

Howard, Oliver Otis. *My Life and Experiences Among Our Hostile Indians*. New York: Da Capo Press, 1972.

Indian Raids as Reported in the Silver City Enterprise. Silver City, New Mexico: William H. Mullane, 1968.

Kendall, George W. *Across the Great Southwestern Prairies*. 2 vols. N.p.: Readex Microprint Corporation, 1966.

Lang, Walter B. *The First Overland Mail: Butterfield Trail, St. Louis to San Francisco, 1858–1861*. Washington: n.p. 1947.

McCarty, Kieran. *Desert Documentary: The Spanish Years, 1767–1821*. Tucson: Arizona Historical Society, 1976.

Marchand, Ernest, ed. *News from Fort Craig, New Mexico, 1863: Civil War Letters of Andrew Ryan with the First California Volunteers*. Santa Fe: Stagecoach Press, 1966.

Marion, John H. *Notes of Travel Through the Territory of Arizona, Being an Account of the Trip Made by General George Stoneman and Others in the Autumn of 1870*. Ed. by Donald M. Powell. Tucson: University of Arizona Press, 1965.

Miller, Joseph, ed. *Arizona Cavalcade: The Turbulent Times*. New York: Hastings House, 1962.

Mills, W. W. *Forty Years at El Paso, 1858–1898*. El Paso, Texas: Carl Hertzog, 1952.

Nentvig, Juan, S.J. *Rudo Ensayo: A Description of Sonora and Arizona in 1764*. Translated, clarified, and annotated by Alberto Francisco Pradeau and Robert R. Rasmussen. Tucson: University of Arizona Press, 1980.

North, Diane M. T. *Samuel Peter Heintzelman and the Sonora Exploring and Mining Company*. Tucson: University of Arizona Press, 1980.

O'Neil, James B. *They Die But Once: The Story of a Tejano*. New York: Knight Publications, 1936.

Pattie, James O. *Personal Narrative of James O. Pattie of Kentucky*. Ed. by Timothy Flint. Chicago: Donnelley and Sons, 1930.

Pumpelly, Raphael. *Travels and Adventures of Raphael Pumpelly*. New York: Henry Holt and Company, 1920.

Rockfellow, John A. *Log of an Arizona Trail Blazer*. Tucson: Arizona Silhouettes, 1955.

Ruxton, George Frederick. *Adventures in Mexico and the Rocky Mountains, 1846–1847*. Glorieta, New Mexico: Rio Grande Press, 1973.

Spring, John. *John Spring's Arizona*. Ed. by A. M. Gustafson. Tucson: University of Arizona Press, 1966.

Tevis, James Henry. *Arizona in the 50's.* Albuquerque: University of New Mexico Press, 1954.

Wheeler, Homer W. *Buffalo Days.* Indianapolis: Bobbs Merrill Co., 1926.

Wislizenus, Frederick A. *A Tour to Northern Mexico Connected With Col. Doniphan's Expedition in 1846–1847.* Glorieta, New Mexico: Rio Grande Press, 1969.

Books: Secondary Sources

Acuña, Rodolfo F. *Sonoran Strongman: Ignacio Pesqueira and His Times.* Tucson: University of Arizona Press, 1974.

Almada, Francisco R. *Diccionario de historia, geografía y biografía chihuahuenses.* Chihuahua: Talleres Graficos del Gobierno del Estado. 1927.

————. *Diccionario de historia, geografía y biografía sonorenses.* Chihuahua: n. p., 1952.

Altshuler, Constance Wynn. *Chains of Command: Arizona and the Army, 1856–1875.* Tucson: Arizona Historical Society, 1981.

Bancroft, Hubert Howe. *History of Arizona and New Mexico.* San Francisco: History Company, 1889.

————. *History of the North Mexican States and Texas.* San Francisco: History Company, 1889.

Barnes, Will C. *Arizona Place Names.* Revised and enlarged by Byrd H. Granger. Tucson: University of Arizona Press, 1979.

Barney, James M. *Tales of Apache Warfare.* Privately printed by James M. Barney, 1933.

————. *Forgotten Heroes of the Apache Wars.* Phoenix: n.p., 1951.

Barrick, Nona, and Mary Taylor. *The Mesilla Guard, 1851–1861.* El Paso: Texas Western Press, 1976.

Baylor, George Wythe. *John Robert Baylor, Confederate Governor of Arizona.* Ed. by Odie Faulk. Tucson: Arizona Pioneer Historical Society, 1966.

Brandes, Ray, ed. *Troopers West: Military and Indian Affairs on the American Frontier.* San Diego: Frontier Heritage Press, 1970.

Colley, Charles C. *Documents of Southwestern History.* Tucson: Arizona Historical Society, 1972.

Colton, Ray C. *The Civil War in the Western Territories.* Norman: University of Oklahoma Press, 1959.

Conkling, Roscoe P., and Margaret B. Conkling. *The Butterfield Overland Mail, 1857–1869.* 3 vols. Glendale: Arthur H. Clark Co., 1947.

Debo, Angie. *Geronimo: The Man, His Time, His Place.* Norman: University of Oklahoma Press, 1976.

Dunn, J. P. *Massacres of the Mountains.* New York: Archer House, n.d.

Ellis, Richard N. *General Pope and U.S. Indian Policy.* Albuquerque: University of New Mexico Press, 1970.

Farish, Thomas Edwin. *History of Arizona.* 8 vols. San Francisco: Filmer Brothers Electrotype Co., 1915–18.

Floyd, Dale E. *Chronological List of Actions etc. with Indians from January 15, 1837, to January, 1891.* Fort Collins, Colo.: Old Army Press, 1979.

Forbes, Jack Douglas. *Apache, Navaho and Spaniard.* Norman: University of Oklahoma Press, 1971.

Frazer, Robert W. *Forts of the West.* Norman: University of Oklahoma Press, 1977.

Gerald, Rex E. *Spanish Presidios of the Late Eighteenth Century in Northern New Spain*. Santa Fe: Museum of New Mexico Press, 1968.

Goodwin, Grenville. *The Social Organization of the Western Apache*. Tucson: University of Arizona Press, 1969.

Griffen, William B. *Apaches at War and Peace: The Janos Presidio, 1750–1858*. Albuquerque: University of New Mexico Press, 1988.

Hafen, Leroy R. *The Overland Mail, 1849–1869*. Cleveland: Arthur H. Clark Co., 1926.

Hunt, Aurora. *Major General James Henry Carleton, 1814–1873, Western Frontier Dragoon*. Glendale, California: Arthur H. Clark Company, 1958.

Keleher, William A. *Turmoil in New Mexico, 1846–1868*. Introduction by Lawrence R. Murphy. Albuquerque: University of New Mexico Press, 1982.

Lekson, Stephen H. *Nana's Raid: Apache Warfare in Southern New Mexico*. El Paso: University of Texas at El Paso, 1987.

Lockwood, Frank C. *Arizona Characters*. Los Angeles: Times Mirror Press, 1928.

———. *The Apache Indians*. New York: Macmillan Company, 1938.

Longstreet, Stephen. *War Cries on Horseback: The Story of the Indian Wars of the Great Plains*. Garden City, New York: Doubleday & Company, 1970.

McClintock, James H. *Arizona: Prehistoric, Aboriginal, Pioneer, Modern*. 3 vols. Chicago: S. J. Clarke Publishing Company, 1916.

McGaw, William Cochran. *Savage Scene: The Life and Times of James Kirker, Frontier King*. New York: Hastings House, 1972.

Miller, Darlis M. *The California Column in New Mexico*. Albuquerque: University of New Mexico Press, 1982.

Moorhead, Max L. *The Apache Frontier: Jacobo Ugarte and Spanish-Indian Relations in Northern New Spain, 1769–1791*. Norman: University of Oklahoma Press, 1968.

———. *The Presidio: Bastion of the Spanish Borderlands*. Norman: University of Oklahoma Press, 1975.

Murphy, Lawrence R. *Frontier Crusader—William F. M. Arny*. Tucson: University of Arizona Press, 1972.

Ogle, Ralph Hedrick. *Federal Control of the Western Apaches, 1848–1886*. Albuquerque: University of New Mexico Press, 1970.

Opler, Morris E. *An Apache Lifeway*. Chicago: University of Chicago Press, 1965.

Pearce, T. M. *New Mexico Place Names: A Geographical Dictionary*. Albuquerque: University of New Mexico Press, 1977.

Russell, Don. *One Hundred and Three Fights and Scrimmages: The Story of General Reuben F. Bernard*. Washington: U.S. Cavalry Association, 1936.

Sandomingo, Manuel. *Historia de Sonora*. Agua Prieta, Sonora: n.p., 1953.

Schellie, Don. *Vast Domain of Blood: The Story of the Camp Grant Massacre*. Los Angeles: Westernlore Press, 1968.

Terrell, John Upton. *Apache Chronicle*. New York: Thomas Y. Crowell Company, 1974.

Thrapp, Dan L. *Al Sieber: Chief of Scouts*. Norman: University of Oklahoma Press, 1964.

———. *Conquest of Apachería*. Norman: University of Oklahoma Press, 1967.

———. *Juh: An Incredible Indian*. El Paso: University of Texas at El Paso, 1973.

———. *Victorio and the Mimbres Apaches*. Norman: University of Oklahoma Press, 1974.

————. *Encyclopedia of Frontier Biography.* 3 vols. Glendale, Calif.: Arthur H. Clark Co., 1988.

Turner, Katherine C. *Red Men Calling on the Great White Father.* Norman: University of Oklahoma Press, 1951.

Utley, Robert M. *Frontier Regulars: The United States Army and the Indians, 1866–1891.* New York: Macmillan Co., 1973.

————. *A Clash of Cultures: Fort Bowie and the Chiricahua Apaches.* Washington: National Park Service, 1977.

————. *Frontiersmen in Blue: The United States Army and the Indians, 1848–1865.* Lincoln: University of Nebraska Press, 1981.

Villa, Eduardo W. *Compendia de Historia del Estado de Sonora.* Mexico: Patria Nueva, 1937.

Voss, Stuart F. *On the Periphery of Nineteenth Century Mexico: Sonora and Sinaloa 1810–1877.* Tucson: University of Arizona Press, 1982.

Wagoner, Jay J. *Early Arizona: Prehistory to Civil War.* Tucson: University of Arizona Press, 1975.

Weber, David J. *The Taos Trappers: The Fur Trade in the Far Southwest, 1540–1846.* Norman: University of Oklahoma Press, 1971.

Webster's American Military Biographies. Springfield, Mass.: G & C Merriam Company, 1978.

Wellman, Paul I. *The Indian Wars of the West.* Garden City, N.Y.: Doubleday & Company, 1947.

Articles and Essays

Allen, R. S. "Pinos Altos, New Mexico," *New Mexico Historical Review,* 23 (October 1948), 302–32.

Altshuler, Constance Wynn. "Arizona in 1861: A Contemporary Account by Samuel Robinson," *Journal of Arizona History,* 25 (Spring 1984), 21–76.

Brooks, Henry S. "A Scrap of Frontier History," *Californian,* 2 (October 1880), 344–48.

Cramer, Harry G. III. "Tom Jeffords, Indian Agent," *Journal of Arizona History,* 17 (Autumn 1976) 265–300.

Cremony, John C. "Some Savages." *Overland Monthly,* 8 (March 1872), 201–10.

Dorr, L. L. "The Fight at Chiricahua Pass in 1869," ed. by Marian E. Valputic and Harold W. Longfellow, *Arizona and the West,* 13 (Winter 1971), 369–78.

Drachman, Samuel H. "Arizona Pioneers and Apaches," *Arizona Graphics,* 1 (November 18, 1899), 3–7.

Dudley, Levi E. "Cochise, the Apache Chief, and Peace," *The Friend,* August 7, 1891.

Ellis, Anderson Nelson. "Recollections of an Interview with Cochise, Chief of the Apaches," *Kansas State Historical Society Collections,* 13 (1913–14), 387–92.

Finch, Boyd. "Sherod Hunter and the Confederates in Arizona," Journal of Arizona History, 10 (Autumn 1969), 139–206.

Forbes, Robert H. Letter in *Journal of Arizona History,* 7 (Summer 1966), 87–88.

Griffen, William B. "The Compás: A Chiricahua Apache Family," *American Indian Quarterly,* 7 (Spring 1983), 21–49.

————. "Apache Indians and the Northern Mexican Peace Establishments," in *Southwestern Culture History: Collected Papers in Honor of Albert Schroeder,* ed. Charles H. Lange. *Papers of the Archaeological Society of New Mexico,* Vol. 10 (1985), 183–95.

Harkins, Charles. "A Scrap of Frontier History," *Overland Monthly,* 21 (March 1893), 265–76.

Howard, Oliver Otis. "Account of His Mission to the Apaches and Navajos," *Washington Daily Morning Chronicle,* November 10, 1872. Copy in Arizona Historical Society, Tucson.

Hunter, Thomas Thompson. "Early Days in Arizona," *Arizona Historical Review,* 3 (April 1930), 105–20.

Irwin, Bernard John Dowling. "The Fight at Apache Pass," *Infantry Journal,* Vol. 32 (April 1928), 1–8.

Kane, Randy. "An Honorable and Upright Man: Sidney R. Delong as Post Trader at Fort Bowie," *Journal of Arizona History,* 19 (Autumn 1978), 297–314.

Keyes, Edward L. "Some Recollections of Arizona and Cochise," *The United Service,* July 1890, 98–101.

Lockwood, Frank C. "Cochise, the Noble Warrior," *Arizona Highways,* February 1939, 6–7, 24–27.

Mahon, Emmie Giddings W., and Chester V. Kielman. "George H. Giddings and the San Antonio–San Diego Mail Line," *Southwestern Historical Quarterly,* 61 (Summer 1957), 220–39.

Myers, Lee. "The Enigma of Mangas Coloradas' Death," *New Mexico Historical Review,* 41 (October 1966), 287–304.

Opler, Morris E., and Harry Hoijer. "The Raid and War-Path Language of the Chiricahua Apache," *American Anthropologist,* 42 (October–December 1942), 617–35.

Park, Joseph F. "The Apaches in Mexican-American Relations, 1848–1861," *Arizona and the West,* 3 (Summer 1961), 129–46.

————. "Spanish Indian Policy in Northern Mexico, 1765–1810," *Arizona and the West,* 4 (Winter 1962), 325–44.

Radbourne, Allan. "Ambush at Cocospera Canyon," *English Westerners Tally Sheet,* 25 (July 1979), 63–76.

————. "Salvador or Martínez? The Parentage and Origins of Mickey Free," *English Westerners Society Brand Book,* 14 (January 1972), 2–26.

Reeve, Frank D. "Frederick E. Phelps: A Soldiers' Memoirs," *New Mexico Historical Review,* 25 (April 1950), 109–35.

Rippy, J. Fred. "The Indians of the Southwest in the Diplomacy of the United States and Mexico, 1848–1853," *Hispanic-American Historical Review,* 2 (August 1919), 363–96.

Robinson, Daniel. "The Affair at Apache Pass," *Sports Afield,* 17 (August 1896), 79–84.

Rush, Rita. "El Chivero, Merejildo Grijalva," *Arizonian,* 1 (Fall 1960), 8–9.

Sacks, Benjamin H. "New Evidence on the Bascom Affair," *Arizona and the West,* 4 (Autumn 1962), 261–78.

Schreier, Konrad F., Jr. "The California Column in the Civil War: Hazen's Civil War Diary," *Journal of San Diego History,* 22 (Spring 1976), 31–47.

Smith, Cornelius C. "Some Unpublished History of the Southwest," *Arizona Historical Review,* 6 (January 1935), 45–64, 5 (October 1932), 333–40.

Smith, Ralph A. "Indians in American-Mexican Relations Before the War of 1846," *Hispanic American Historical Review,* 43 (February 1963), 34–64.

————. "The Scalp Hunt in Chihuahua—1849," *New Mexico Historical Review.* 40 (April 1965), 116–40.

Sonnichsen, C. L. "Who Was Tom Jeffords?" *Journal of Arizona History,* 23 (Winter 1982), 381–402.

Stevens, Robert C. "The Apache Menace in Sonora, 1821–1849," *Arizona and the West,* 6 (Autumn 1964), 211–22.

————. "Colonel John Finkle Stone and the Apache Pass Mining Company," *Arizona Historical Review,* 6 (July 1935), 74–80.

Strickland, Rex W. "The Birth and Death of a Legend: The Johnson Massacre of 1837," *Arizona and the West,* 18 (Autumn 1976), 257–86.

Sweeney, Edwin R. "I Had Lost All: Geronimo and the Carrasco Massacre of 1851," *Journal of Arizona History,* 27 (Spring 1986), 35–52.

Turrill, Henry Stuart. "A Vanished Race of Aboriginal Founders," *Publication Number 18 of the New York Society of the Order of the Founders and Patriots of America,* February 14, 1907.

Tyler, Barbara Ann. "Cochise, Apache War Leader, 1858–61," *Journal of Arizona History,* 6 (Spring 1965), 1–10.

Utley, Robert M. "The Bascom Affair: A Reconstruction," *Arizona and the West,* 3 (Spring 1961), 59–68.

Walker, Henry P. "Solider in the California Column: The Diary of John W. Teal," *Arizona and the West,* 13 (Spring 1971), 33–82.

INDEX

with Sonoran troops, November 1864, 222–23; continues to hold out, 223; will never be friendly, 225; war becomes defensive conflict 226; leads war party against Americans, 227–28; receives message from Victorio, 228; returns to Arizona, 230; reported at Mount Graham, 231–32; his abandoned ranchería found, 232; leads Chiricahuas and Western Apache war party against Arizona and Sonora, July 1865, 232–34; skirmishes with American troops in Sonora, 233–34; reported near Fronteras, August 1865, 234–35; Washburn suggests trap, 235–36; moves near Janos, late August 1865, 236; returns to Chiricahuas, October 1865, 236; near Fort Bowie, 236–37; talk with officers, 236–37, 247; ranchería attacked by Gorman, November 1865, 237–38; remains in Chiricahuas, winter 1865–66, 239; eludes American troops, 239–40; loses allies, 240; Western Apaches bitter, 240; convinced that war must continue, 240–41; near Janos, early 1866, 241; attacks San Rafael ranch, slightly wounded (early 1866), 242–43; ranchería struck by "tame" Apaches, early May 1866, 243; attacks herd at Camp Wallen, 243–44; raids Fronteras, possibly wounded, 245; Chihuahuan troops attack camp near Boca Grande, December 1866, 245; war party against Sonora for captives, 246–47; attacks Mowry Mines, March 1867, 247–48; returns to base camp in Chiricahuas, April 1867, 248; object of Crittenden's thoughts, 248–50; vulnerable to Mexican campaigns, 249; arrives too late to fight Ozeta in Chiricahuas, 249; heads war party to Mexico to avenge Ozeta's victory, 249; raids near Tubac, 250; Harrington attacks his band in Chiricahuas, 250–51; American campaign, 251; Cochise moves into Sonora, summer 1867, 251; camps at Sarampion, winter 1867–68, 253; band kills Lt. Carroll near Ft. Bowie, 253; at Sarampion, 254–55; attacked by Chihuahuan troops at Sarampion, February 1868, 255; solicits peace at Janos, July 1868, band attacked in Hatchet Mountains, August 1868, 257; decides to move from Mexico to Arizona, 258; band defeated in Sonora, 259; strips Barth and companions, 259–60; Devin's terms for peace, 260–61; parleys with

Perry in Dragoons, 262–64; in Dragoon Mountains, summer 1869, 266; skirmishes with Mexican troops, 267; organizes war party, 267–68; massacres Stone's party, attacks Texas cattle herd, 268, 270; attacks Mack's party, 270; Winters fight, 272–73; moves into Chiricahuas, 273; fights Bernard, 273–77; retires to Burro Mountains, 277; sends message to Loco, 278; camps along Bonita Creek, 278; part of band returns to Dragoons, January 1870, 278–79; remains in Coyotero country, 279; returns to Chiricahuas, spring 1870, 278–79; ranchería attacked, 280; raids Sonora, 280; raids Gardner ranch, June 1870, 280, skirmishes with Mexican troops in Dragoons, 280–81; raids Arizona and Sonora, 281; erroneously reported killed near Dolores, Sonora, 281; talks peace with Major Green, Camp Mogollon, 281–85; influence with Western Apaches, 284; in Chiricahuas, 287; sends word to Loco, 289; relationship with Jeffords, 293–96; expected at Cañada Alamosa, 97; talks with Army and Hennisee at Cañada Alamosa, 297–300; leaves Cañada Alamosa, November 16, 1870, 300–301; Bernard's concerns, 300–301; returns to Cañada Alamosa, 301–302; decides not to stay at Cañada Alamosa, 302; Piper expects him to return, 303; Americans allow him no rest during first 6 months of 1871, 304; raiding party hits Fort Bayard, February 1871, 306; camp attacked near Mogollons, 306–307; invited to Washington, 309; believes in Mexico, 309; attacks Americans, engages Russell at Dragoons, 310–12; learns of Camp Grant massacre, 313; not involved in Cushing's death, 313–14; raids in southern Arizona, 314–15; returns to camp in Dragoons, meets Jeffords, June 1871, 315; tries to avoid American troops, 316–17; Crook's thoughts on him, 319–20; Colyer's mission, 321–23; sends his people to Cañada Alamosa, 322; Papagos attacked camp in Santa Rita Mountains, 322–23; reported sick, 323; decides to leave Arizona for Cañada Alamosa, 323–24; raids Camp Crittenden, 323–24; appears at Cañada Alamosa, 324–25; invited to Washington, 326; controversy over Horseshoe Canyon fight, 326–27; interview with editors of

GERONIMO

GERONIMO

The Man, His Time,

His Place

by Angie Debo

To the memory of *MARGUERITE HOWLAND*

whose competence with documents was equaled

by her ready helpfulness

The earliest known photograph of Geronimo, at about age sixty, taken by A. Frank Randall at San Carlos in the spring of 1884. "You never have caught me shooting." Courtesy National Archives and Records Service, Washington, D.C.

PREFACE TO THE FOURTH PRINTING

In my original preface I expressed regret over blank spaces in the record of Geronimo's life. Now I am glad to state that one small blank space has been filled by Dan L. Thrapp (ed.) in *Dateline Fort Bowie*, published by the University of Oklahoma Press in 1979, presenting the newspaper dispatches sent by the able Charles Fletcher Lummis from the Apache war zone in 1886. It gives me great satisfaction to rewrite my page 245 to include this detail regarding a previously unknown son of Geronimo.

ANGIE DEBO

Marshall, Oklahoma
August 17, 1986

PREFACE TO THE FIRST PRINTING

All my life I had heard about Geronimo. As a small child in northern Kansas I was told of the blanket of human scalps he was wearing when he was "captured" after his last "outbreak." (Scalping was not an Apache practice.) We children even gave his name to an especially cross-grained turkey gobbler. In Oklahoma, where I finished my growing up, incidents of his life as a prisoner of war at Fort Sill and of his appearance at various celebrations constantly filled the news. As late as 1916, seven years after his death, the Geronimo Motor Company was incorporated with great fanfare in nearby Enid. (The automobiles and trucks it turned out might have made the big time, except for a fire that burned down the plant and wiped out the investors.)

The supposedly factual story behind this sensationalism was that Geronimo, at the head of four or five hundred hostiles, had been captured after a successful military campaign and that the band had thereafter been held in captivity. The true account had appeared in a few specialized books, but these had not changed the accepted version. I myself assumed it was true and incorporated it briefly in two of my books, allowing it to stand in one I edited, repeating it in one I wrote.

Finally, in the 1950's I began to explore the life of Geronimo. After some reading and preliminary research in Apache history, I interviewed elderly members of the band who had known him and remembered the hiding, the raids, and the violent deaths of a hunted people's life-way. But my study was interrupted by other duties and other writing tasks, and my notes were filed away. Now in these last years I have returned to the subject, reinforcing these earlier insights by additional research.

The historical background at this time has been accurately established. Frank C. Lockwood's comprehensive account was published in 1938; Ralph Hedrick Ogle, after the most intensive research ever made in the field, published his study of government policy toward the related Apache tribes in 1940; and more recently Dan L. Thrapp's scholarly books and articles have presented special phases of the subject. All this work furnished the setting of Geronimo's life. There was no need for me to duplicate the research that has produced these findings. My task was to explore Geronimo's individual experiences, his motivations, his personal life and character. And he did not live in solitude against this background. He had a family and family ties extending to distant relatives. He had comrades and followers, friends and enemies, and among his associates were chiefs and leaders well known in Southwestern history. As far as possible I have presented all these people as actual human beings with their distinctive characteristics.

I wish I could believe that I have written a definitive biography. But too many times I have had to resort to "probably," "It seems that—," and "It is fairly certain that—," conjectures based on the best evidence obtainable, but still conjectures. Some of these may be wrong, but I doubt that evidence will ever be uncovered to establish all the facts beyond question. These Apaches were wild people, as wild as the deer that fleeted across the rocks and hid in the thickets of their mountains. The hunter might glimpse them, but that was all.

Still, even these glimpses of Geronimo are revealing. At a few conferences his words were recorded. Incidents of his life and impressions of his personality lingered in the memory of aged Apaches. Finally, during the twenty-three years of his captivity, his outward actions and his responses, though often misinterpreted, were observed and chronicled. He even dictated his reminiscences to a sympathetic listener. Thus he is seen not as a lay figure or a Wild West character but as an individual.

His energy, his determination, and his sturdy independence can be perceived as traits that distinguished him throughout his life. His strong economic sense is apparent, whether in supporting his family and providing for his band by hunting and raiding as a wild Apache or in setting up a profitable business of selling souvenirs and banking the money he acquired in his later days as a Wild West exhibit. He had an active intellectual curiosity and a capacity for original thought. He was hard-headed and practical-minded, ruthless in competition, stern and unbending in his judgments, unrelenting in his hatreds. But he was kind and affectionate to his family and constant in his friendships, and his love for his mountain homeland was the unchanging sentiment of his life. He and his white adversaries never arrived at the same definition of truth: to them he was simply a liar whose word could never be trusted; but if one can follow his reasoning, he is seen as a man of essential integrity. He was deeply religious, and when a promise was made with oath and ceremony—mere poetic trimmings to the white man—he kept his pledge. His suspicions were real, the instinctive distrust of any wild creature. And they were even well founded, based on acts of treachery he had seen. A lesser man could not have written his name so boldly on the history of the Southwest.

I have had much help in uncovering his story. When I visited the Mescalero Reservation in 1957 to interview Geronimo's son and granddaughter, I stopped at the nearby trading post of Mrs. Eve Ball. She willingly shared with me, a stranger, her unique knowledge of Apache personalities, and she has continued this assistance to the present day. Mr. Benedict Jozhe, long-time tribal chairman of the Fort Sill Apaches, has answered my questions and several times made the long drive to my home with Moses Loco, grandson of Chief Loco, to furnish needed information. In 1959 he brought the aged James Kaywaykla, thus giving me an opportunity to hear the story of the only surviving witness of the disaster that ended the career of the great Victorio.

Mr. John A. Shapard, Jr., of the Bureau of Indian Affairs, whose wife is a great-granddaughter of Chief Loco, has freely given me assistance and advice valuable beyond calculation. The late Colonel Ora E. Musgrove, who learned the true story of Geronimo's surrender when he was a young enlisted man at Fort Sill and followed it in his maturity by extensive research in the National Archives, made me a free gift of his findings. Mr. Dan L. Thrapp took much trouble going into his files to answer my questions. Dr. Berlin Basil Chapman, author of many scholarly books and articles about Oklahoma Indian history, loaned me his notes and some documents he had acquired during his research on a related project.

Mr. John M. Brown, stationed at the Naval Aviation Schools Command at Pensacola, put me on the track of material regarding Geronimo's imprisonment at Fort Pickens. Miss Jean Pitts of the Historic Pensacola Preservation Board conducted me on a tour of the area, and Mr. George D. Berndt, historian of the Gulf Islands National Seashore of the National Park Service, gave me specific identification of the sites and furnished me with contemporary newspaper accounts regarding the prisoners. Mr. Luis R. Arana, staff historian of the National Park Service's national monuments at Saint Augustine, first called my attention to Lenna Geronimo's meeting with her father at Saint Louis.

There are also the ever dependable archivists and curators in whose collections I worked. The late Marguerite Howland and her assistants in the documents department of the Oklahoma State University library guided me through many days of exploration. I could not have untangled Geronimo's family and tribal relationships except for the help of Mr. Gillett Griswold, curator of the

Army Artillery and Missile Center Museum at Fort Sill. Miss Jane F. Smith and Mr. Robert M. Kvasnicka of the National Archives and Records Service helped me solve many puzzling problems. And always I had the assistance of Mr. Jack D. Haley of the Western History Collections and Mrs. Alice Timmons of the Phillips Collection of the University of Oklahoma Library and of Mrs. Rella Looney, since retired, and of her successor, Mrs. Martha R. Blaine, Indian archivists of the Oklahoma Historical Society. Finally, in this age of electrostatic copies I am indebted to the archivists of collections I have not visited for making material available through the mail. I am also under obligation to owners of copyrights, who have given me permission to quote from published sources.

Most of all, I am grateful to my friends and neighbors, Hugh and Ramona O'Neill, who furnished transportation to places beyond my present driving radius. And when I employed Ramona to type the final copy of my manuscript, she carried on the work with a perceptive understanding that amounted to collaboration.

ANGIE DEBO

Marshall, Oklahoma

CONTENTS

ILLUSTRATIONS

MAPS

INTRODUCTION

On September 5, 1886, the great news from Fort Bowie, Arizona, flashed across the nation. The day before, in Skeleton Canyon near the Mexican border, the Apache warrior Geronimo and the chief Naiche, son of the great Cochise, had surrendered to Brigadier General Nelson A. Miles. With them were sixteen warriors, fourteen women, and six children.

"APACHE WAR ENDED!" "GERONIMO CAPTURED!" Never were so many headlines owed by so many to so few. From the time these Indians had broken away, five thousand men of the regular army, a network of heliograph stations flashing mirror messages from mountain to mountain, and false promises at the end were required to effect their "capture." The paper work flowed in rivers of telegrams from army posts to Washington; since then it has burgeoned into many books. The word *apache* has become the designation of underworld characters in Paris, and during World War II American paratroopers shouted the name "Geronimo" as they stepped off into the sky. What manner of man was this Geronimo?

He was a red-handed murderer who "ought to be hung," screamed the western newspapers. He was cruel, selfish, treacherous, and mendacious, with no virtues but courage and determination, said the best of the army men and Indian agents who tried to cope with him. He was "only a medicine man," was hated by all but a small faction of his own people, and owed his reputation to sensational advertising, said the scholars and historians.[1]

In Geronimo's old age when he was a prisoner of war at Fort Sill, Oklahoma Territory, in 1905, Stephen Melvil Barrett, superintendent of schools in nearby Lawton, tried to get permission from the military to let him tell *his* side of the story. But Lieutenant George A. Purington, the army officer in charge, bluntly refused— the old Apache deserved to be hanged, he said, instead of being spoiled by so much attention from civilians—and Barrett had to appeal directly to President Theodore Roosevelt. A series of communications through channels (five pages of fine print, ten endorsements, six weeks of time) finally gave the required permission with the condition that the manuscript be submitted to the army chief of staff before publication.[2]

Barrett then secured the services of Geronimo's "nephew" (actually his second cousin) Asa Daklugie, who had been trained in the famous Indian school at Carlisle, Pennsylvania, and the three worked together on the story. When it was finished, Barrett first submitted it to the president, who read it and pronounced it "very interesting" but suggested that Barrett "disclaim responsibility where the reputation of an individual is assailed." The army chief of staff also found it "interesting," but indicated "a number of passages which, from the departmental point of view, are decidedly objectionable." Barrett refused to back down on one incident—the event that drove Cochise to hostility—but tempered the other passages by footnotes stating that this was Geronimo's opinion, not his.[3]

As a factual account the book suffers from the old warrior's

---

1 See, for example, Frederick Webb Hodge, *Handbook of American Indians North of Mexico*, s.v. "Geronimo," and Ross Santee, *Apache Land*, p. 176.

2 S[tephen] M[elvil] Barrett, *Geronimo's Story of His Life*, pp. xiii–xx.

3 *Ibid.*, pp. xxiii–xxvii, 115n. 2, 116n. 3, 138n. 3, 139n. 1, 147n. 7, 179n. 1, 181n. 4. By a curious slip of the pen Barrett attributed the Cochise incident to Mangas Coloradas.

4

failing memory, especially in chronology, and also, perhaps, from his natural tendency to magnify his youthful exploits. Some imaginative editing is also apparent; one conspicuous example is the inclusion of scalping, which was not an Apache practice. But the book's spirit is unmistakably Indian, and it is the first account of the Apache wars from the inside looking out.

Two other such first-hand narratives have appeared in recent years. Jason Betzinez, whose mother was Geronimo's first cousin, had been out with the hostiles during 1882–83. During the long imprisonment following 1886 he had been sent to Carlisle, where he accepted its teachings and became a white man in all but blood. In his old age he wrote down his reminiscences in his careful penmanship, and Wilbur Sturtevant Nye, formerly stationed at Fort Sill, contributed some maps and helped with the organization. The resulting book, *I Fought with Geronimo*, was published in 1959. James Kaywaykla, who lived until 1963, retained his vivid childhood memory of flights and battles: "Until I was ten years old I did not know that people died except by violence." Eve Ball of Ruidoso, New Mexico, who has been closely associated with the band since 1949, took his story down in shorthand and published it in 1970 under the title *In the Days of Victorio*. It gives an intimate story of a closely knit group of individuals in their relations with each other and their reaction to tragedy. Like Geronimo's reminiscences, these two accounts reveal some confusion regarding details and sequence of events, but they show what it meant to be a hunted Apache.[4]

Other insights were gained from the studies of Morris Edward Opler, the ethnologist, who recorded the life-way of the people as

4 Incidentally, both these books refute Barrett's accounts of scalping. See *I Fought with Geronimo*, especially p. 86, where Betzinez says he never knew Geronimo to bring in a scalp, and *In the Days of Victorio*, pp. 13, 46, where Kaywaykla states, "I have seen hundreds of people killed but not one scalped." Scalping, however, did occur on rare occasions. In an interview (Apache, Okla., Jan. 26, 1955) Jason Betzinez told me he had heard of one incident when a woman took a Mexican's scalp in revenge for the killing of her son. And Asa Daklugie told Eve Ball that his band, the wildest of all Apaches, did occasionally take one scalp for use in the victory dance, but the man who performed the act had to undergo a four-day purification ceremony, during which he remained in isolation (Eve Ball to Angie Debo, December 20, 1960).

he worked among them during the 1930's. His informants not only described the primitive culture, but in some cases gave their recollections of events occurring during the wars. Finally, an immensely important unpublished compilation of the biographies of these Apaches has been made by Gillett Griswold, the civilian director of the United States Army Artillery and Missile Center Museum at Fort Sill. With the assistance of the aged survivors and their descendants and the examination of army records, he has collected statistical information—births, deaths, marriages, family relationships, and other data—as far as it can be determined, regarding 728 members of the band during the wars and the years of captivity.[5]

Thus, it is now possible to view the life of Geronimo in its native setting.

[5] This collection is hereafter cited as Griswold, "The Fort Sill Apaches."

CHAPTER 1

GOYAHKLA, THE CHILD

Geronimo placed his birth date in June, 1829, but he was almost certainly born a few years earlier. As the old warrior tried to organize the sequence of events, Barrett apparently attempted to arrange them according to the white man's calendar. Now, by matching his experiences with known historical dates, it is possible to construct a more accurate chronology. Jason Betzinez said that his mother and Geronimo grew up together as children. Her birth date can be fixed at approximately 1823 by her memory of Halley's Comet and "The Night the Stars Fell." It can also be established by contemporary evidence that Geronimo had a wife and three children in 1850 or earlier.[1]

To his birthplace Geronimo gave the Apache name of No-doyon Canyon and located it near the headwaters of the Gila River in what is now southeastern Arizona, then a part of Mexico.[2] At other times he stated simply that he was born in Arizona. But by modern nomenclature the Gila does not head in Arizona, for of the branches that unite near the present-day town of Clifton to form the main stream, one now carries the name into New Mexico.

[1] See Betzinez, *I Fought with Geronimo*, pp. 14, 15, 18; *infra*, pp. 34–35.
[2] Barrett, *Geronimo's Story of His Life*, p. 17. See also Betzinez, *op. cit.*, p. 14.

Daklugie accordingly moved the location upstream to the three forks of the river near the present Cliff Dwellings National Monument in southwestern New Mexico.[3] Geronimo could not have been mistaken about the site. Apaches regarded their birthplace with special attachment. The child was always told of the location, and whenever in its roving the family happened by, he was rolled on the ground there to the four directions. This observance took place throughout the growing years, and even adults sometimes rolled in this manner when returning to the spot where they were born.[4] But Geronimo or his editor could have been mistaken about the state. Even that seems improbable, however, for the Apaches soon became aware of such political subdivisions in dodging military forces. One can only say that Geronimo was born in the early 1820's near the upper Gila in the mountains crossed by the present state boundary, probably on the Arizona side near the present Clifton.

His father was Taklishim ("The Gray One"), the son of Chief Mahko of the Bedonkohe Apache tribe. His mother, although a full-blood Apache, had the Spanish name Juana.[5] Possibly she had been captured and enslaved by the Spanish. For centuries there had been a pattern of Apache raids on Spanish settlements and Spanish capture and enslavement and occasional escape of Apache women and children. As an adult, Geronimo spoke Spanish, which he might have acquired from his mother or which he might have picked up from his contacts with the Mexicans.

Geronimo never saw his grandfather, Mahko, who died when Taklishim was a young warrior. The chief had two wives, and after his death the principal one, whose name is not now remembered, continued to exert a strong influence within the tribe. She was the mother of five of his six children who grew to adulthood. One of these was Taklishim and another was a daughter whose daughter, Nah-thle-tla, became the mother of Jason Betzinez. Mahko's other

---

3 Eve Ball interview, July 26, 1971.
4 Morris Edward Opler, *An Apache Life-Way*, p. 10.
5 Griswold, "The Fort Sill Apaches," s.v. "Geronimo."

8

wife had one daughter, the mother of a notable woman named Ishton, the mother of Asa Daklugie.[6]

The grandchildren and great-grandchildren of Mahko were taught to revere his memory. Geronimo grew up listening to his father's tales of the chief's great size, strength, and sagacity, and of his wars with the Mexicans, at that time under Spanish rule.[7] Betzinez described another aspect of Mahko's life. He was peace loving and generous, raising much corn and owning many horses, which he traded with the Mexicans, and storing corn and dried beef and venison in caves, which he shared with the needy of his tribe.[8] Probably both characterizations are true. The Bedonkohes were relatively undisturbed in their mountain fastness during Mahko's lifetime, and at such periods trading relations might be established with the Mexicans, but there were traditions of old wars and raids. The young Geronimo thrilled to the stories of these exploits, while the gentle Betzinez listened to his mother's accounts of the chief's kindness and peaceable pursuits. Daklugie struck a fair balance. As he heard it, Mahko, although a great warrior, fought only when attacked, but there was one story of an epic battle with another Apache tribe.[9]

It is impossible to untangle completely the tribal divisions of the Apaches with whom the Bedonkohes were associated. Ethnologists have evaded the problem by classifying them all as Chiricahuas,[10] and this generalization has often been used in official records. In

[6] *Ibid.*, s.v. "Mahko." I have accepted the statements of Geronimo, Betzinez, and Daklugie and the genealogy worked out by Griswold. It should be noted, however, that some of the older Fort Sill Apaches believe that Geronimo was born in Old Mexico. They remember that he spoke with an accent different from that of their own people. It is possibly significant that Barrett identified Mahko as chief of the Nednai Apaches, who in later historic times lived in Old Mexico. See *Geronimo's Story of His Life*, p. 35n. But even if this is correct, it seems well established that in Mahko's time the band lived in the area designated as Geronimo's birthplace.

[7] Barrett, *op. cit.*, p. 15.

[8] Betzinez, *op. cit.*, pp. 2, 14–15, 39.

[9] Eve Ball to Angie Debo, June 25, 1973.

[10] One earnest attempt has been made by a student of ethnology to distinguish these tribes and their component bands. See the thesis by William Grosvenor Pollard III, "Structure and Stress: Social Change among the Fort Sill Apaches and Their Ancestors, 1870–1960," M.A. thesis, University of Oklahoma, Norman, 1965. Pollard is convinced that the Bedonkohes were identical with the Mogollon Apaches sometimes mentioned in official reports and by travelers.

Geronimo's home range

earlier times all who lived in the jumbled mountains of south-eastern Arizona and southwestern New Mexico had been called the Gilas, with no differentiation of tribes and bands.[11] But to Geronimo's people the Bedonkohe tribe was a well-defined unit, though apparently there was no successor to Mahko. Its members always kept their tribal affiliation distinct but made temporary connections with related tribes and intermarried freely with them so that only nine or ten full-blood Bedonkohes were living when Geronimo dictated his memoirs in 1905.

At least four tribes can be recognized among the Bedonkohes' close associates. East of them in southwestern New Mexico were two that often merged. The Mimbrenos (sometimes called the Coppermines) lived in the Santa Rita and Silver City region and the mountains to the southwest. The Warm Springs (Ojo Caliente) tribe, known as the Chihenne or Red People because of a band of red clay drawn across their faces, ranged between the Mimbrenos and the Rio Grande, but their heartland centered around the pleasant bathing pool and the clear stream that issued from San Mateo Peak on the canyon of the Alamosa River above the Mexican town of Cañada Alamosa, later known as Monticello.[12] South of the Bedonkohes in the fastnesses of the Chiricahua, Dos Cabezas, and Dragoon mountains were the Chokonens or true Chiricahuas, and south of the Chiricahuas in the Sierra Madre of Old Mexico were the Nednais, wildest of all Apaches.

These related tribes had occasional contacts with other Apaches of New Mexico and Arizona. East of the Rio Grande were the Mescaleros, with whom the Mimbrenos and Warm Springs people were acquainted. To the north were the Coyotero and White Mountain Apaches, with whom their relations were never very close and sometimes hostile; and joining the White Mountains and Coyoteros were the Navahos, a kindred people no longer regarded

11 Hereafter, to avoid repetition of the expressions "what is now Arizona" or "the present New Mexico" I shall follow the present state boundaries in identifying locations.

12 Dan L. Thrapp treats the Mimbrenos and the Warm Springs tribe as one tribe, which he designates as the Mimbres (Mimbrenos); see *Victorio and the Mimbres Apaches*. It is true that the two bands were always closely associated and eventually became united, but I have followed Apache custom in distinguishing them.

as Apaches, with whom they sometimes visited and traded. To their west were many tribes of Apaches, some of whom they knew but whom they regarded as inferiors. Their name for them was Bi-ni-e-dine, meaning "Brainless People." One of these with whom Government policy was to bring them into unhappy proximity was a small nomadic tribe known as the San Carlos, which lived in the area between the Gila and San Carlos rivers.[13]

Into this setting Geronimo was born. He was given the name Goyahkla, with the generally accepted meaning "One Who Yawns," why or under what circumstances is not known. One can guess that yawning was the habit of a sleepy baby, but no characterization could have been more inappropriate to the energetic spirit that marked his personality. Some aged Fort Sill Apaches suggest a name slightly different in pronunciation, with the meaning "intelligent, shrewd, clever." As an adult, he became known by the Mexicans as Geronimo, and this name was adopted even by his own people. The Spanish-Apache feud had been inherited by the Mexicans after their independence; and according to one story, in a battle with them he was fighting like a fiend, charging out repeatedly from cover, killing an enemy with every sally and returning with the dead man's rifle. Each time he emerged, the Mexicans began to cry out in terror, "Cuidado! Watch out! Geronimo!" (Perhaps this was as close as they could come to the choking sounds that composed his name, or perhaps they were calling on St. Jerome.) The Apaches took it up as their battle cry, and Goyahkla became Geronimo.[14]

Of his babyhood, he said, "I rolled on the dirt floor of my father's tepee, hung in my tsoch (Apache name for cradle) at my mother's back, or suspended from the bough of a tree."[15] Although one always thinks of the slight, brush-covered wickiup as the Apache dwelling, his mention of a tipi is probably correct. George Catlin

13 Barrett, op. cit., pp. 12–15; Ball, In the Days of Victorio, pp. xiv, 29–30; Betzinez, op. cit., pp. 2, 4, 9, 14–16, 43; Griswold, op. cit., s.v. "Mahko," and "Coloradas, Mangus"; Eve Ball to Angie Debo, June 26, 1973.
14 Woodworth Clum, Apache Agent, p. 29. Geronimo's own account of this battle is in Barrett, op. cit., pp. 51–54.
15 Barrett, op. cit., p. 10.

An Apache woman and child. "I hung in my tsoch at my mother's back, or suspended from the bough of a tree." Courtesy Mrs. Eve Ball.

14

An Apache village in the region of Geronimo's birthplace, painted by George Catlin about 1856. "As a child I rolled on the dirt floor of my father's tepee." Courtesy American Museum of Natural History, New York City.

painted tipis when he visited the Gila Apaches about 1856.[16] According to Daklugie, it was only when his people were closely pursued during the wars that they adopted the wickiup, which could be easily set up and abandoned. He said they used deer and antelope hides with the hair left on for the tipi covering. It was placed hair side out and so cut with the natural direction of the animal's coat that the hair lay downward—a device that must have added much to the waterproofing of the lodge.[17] Even at the

16 *Episodes from Life among the Indians and Last Rambles*, plates 138, 139, and 141. These paintings also show skin-covered A-frame structures interspersed among the tipis, but the type apparently did not survive. Catlin gave the date 1855, but he found war raging against the Apaches in New Mexico and the war did not begin until 1856. Catlin was notoriously inaccurate about dates.

17 Eve Ball interview, July 26, 1971. See also Ball, *op. cit.*, p. 17.

present time a tipi is ceremonially used in the girls' puberty rites, a strong indication of its former importance in Apache culture. But the wickiup also has a long history. In its best form in time of peace it was a substantial, comfortable, dome-shaped dwelling built on a framework of poles.[18] Even in its brush and straw form the Apaches stretched a skin covering over it when their location was relatively permanent.

In spite of their precarious existence, these Indians had a rich and complex ceremonial life. Geronimo's parents certainly must have employed a medicine man or perhaps a midwife to fashion his *tsoch* with prayers and ritual, placing amulets on it to guard him against early death. When he was four days old, or possibly a little later, he must have been placed in it with much ceremony in the presence of relatives and neighbors, after which all participated in a feast. The Apache child did not actually stay in his cradle until his neck became strong enough to support his head when he was a month or more old. Then he spent most of his time there until he became old enough to crawl around the camp. When the age of walking approached, perhaps after he was already walking, came the ceremony of putting on his first moccasins, again with a medicine man in charge, which was celebrated by songs, prayers, and dancing and feasting for relatives and friends. In the spring, usually the spring following this ritual, came the ceremonial cutting of his hair. All this Geronimo inherited as the child of a people who cherished their children.[19]

As soon as he was old enough to understand, he also inherited Apache traditions. His father related exploits of war and hunting and events of recent history. His mother told him the origin myths of his people. She taught him to pray to Usen, a nebulous and remote Supreme Being often called Life Giver. But "We never prayed against any other person, . . . we ourselves took vengeance. We were taught that Usen does not care for the petty quarrels of men." She told him the legends and exploits of supernatural beings,

---

[18] Oliver La Farge, *A Pictorial History of the American Indians*, p. 137. See also Opler, *op. cit.*, pp. 385–86.
[19] Opler, *op. cit.*, pp. 10–18.

especially of White Painted Woman and Child of the Water, all connected with the emergence of the Apaches as sentient persons, and of the beneficent Mountain Spirits, who lived in hidden caverns and whose ceremonials and customs the Apaches duplicated. He must have learned also of witches, men and women whose malevolent Power brought calamity to individuals or the group.[20]

His group comprised an extended family. He said he had three brothers and four sisters, but as far as is known only one of these was an actual sister, all the others being cousins. There was no word in the Apache language to distinguish cousins from siblings.[21] Indeed, a family of eight children was almost unheard of among the Apaches. Ideally, they spaced their children about four years apart by refraining from sexual intercourse until the previous baby was weaned at about age three (the same prohibition was observed to protect the unborn child during pregnancy). The man, of course, could have sex relations with another wife, but only the leaders could afford plural marriages. In the words of Opler's informants, he might "sneak around" and find "easy women," but throughout Apache society undue preoccupation with sex was regarded as a weakness.[22] It is apparent, however, from the Fort Sill birth records, that this family planning was frequently disregarded. Still, whether from conscious spacing or from the deaths of children weaned before they were ready for adult food, Apache families were small. Thus, it is typical that Mahko, with two wives, had, as far as is known, only eight grandchildren. All seven of these "brothers" and "sisters" of Geronimo can be traced, and among his "nephews," who in their turn were sometimes called his "brothers," were his most trusted warriors.[23] Throughout his life his family ties were very close.

"With my brothers and sisters I played about my father's home,"

20 *Ibid.*, pp. 196–200, 242–54, 267–72, 306–309; Morris Edward Opler, "Mountain Spirits of the Chiricahua Apache," *The Masterkey*, Vol. XX, No. 4 (July, 1946); Barrett, *op. cit.*, pp. 3–11, 18–19; Ball, *op. cit.*, pp. 68–70.

21 Opler, *An Apache Life-Way*, pp. 58–62.

22 *Ibid.*, pp. 5–6, 13, 141–42, 415; Ball, *op. cit.*, p. 8.

23 Griswold, *op. cit.*, s.v. "Mahko."

he said. This home was a cluster of dwellings. Usually when a man married he became a member of his wife's family, obligated to contribute to their economic support, but—since he was usually young with few possessions—he was entitled to use their property in time of need. The lodges of the daughters were built close to the parental abode, and intercourse was restricted only by the inconvenient courtesy of mother-in-law avoidance, which the Apaches, like many other Indians, were careful to observe. Sons, since they joined the families of their wives, might live at some distance, although their children shared in the affection of the paternal grandparents. But circumstances sometimes altered this residence pattern, and it seems fairly certain that all the sons and daughters of Mahko lived in close proximity.[24] Their children grew up in a time of peace, a condition rare in Apache history. As Geronimo recalled it, "During my minority we had never seen a missionary or a priest. We had never seen a white man. Thus quietly lived the Be-don-ko-he Apaches."[25]

In this undisturbed security the small boys and girls played together, imitating adult occupations, engaging in war games, hiding among the rocks and pines, making toys with great ingenuity or using those made by their parents, and hunting wild fruit and nuts. Geronimo seemed to remember with the greatest pleasure their excursions through the surrounding country.[26] Then, in accordance with Apache prudery, the sexes began to separate at the age of five or six, and the fathers began to train the boys, and the women the girls, in their specialized occupations.

The little girls began to assist in carrying water, bringing in wood, gathering and storing wild food plants, and cooking the meals; and they learned to dress the skins and make clothing, build the lodges, and weave the baskets. They were trained to be strong and vigorous, rising early and practicing the swift and tireless running upon which their lives might depend. The boys helped care for the horses, practiced much with the bow and arrow, and

24 Opler, *An Apache Life-Way*, pp. 18–19, 24–25, 55–58, 62–65, 163–69; Barrett, *op. cit.*, pp. 19–20; Betzinez, *op. cit.*, pp. 14–15.

25 Barrett, *op. cit.*, p. 34.

26 *Ibid.*, pp. 19–20, 22, 25; Opler, *An Apache Life-Way*, pp. 45–49.

learned to make weapons and tools. They were subjected to even more rigorous physical training than the girls, rising before sunrise and bathing in the creek even when ice had formed on the surface. They were required to race up the side of the mountain carrying water in their mouths and were made to spit it out on their return to show that they had breathed properly through the nose. They shot small game as soon as they could handle their weapons; by the time they were fourteen they hunted with the men. They were systematically trained for war—shooting, dodging, hiding, tracking, learning to map the terrain and find their way back to camp.[27]

The Apaches had many contests in which these skills were used —arrow shooting, racing, wrestling—and there were also games of chance. There were other games with complex rules in which teams played against each other. The most important game was the hoop-and-pole game, in which each contestant tried to slide a pole toward a rolling hoop so that when the hoop toppled over it would rest on the end of his pole. This game was sacred, having been handed down from the animals before the emergence of the human race. The hoop and poles were prepared with great ceremony, and only men could play; women were not even permitted to come near the ground. All these games, whether of skill or chance, were accompanied by excited betting, for the Apaches were inveterate gamblers.

They also spent much time in feasting and dancing. Some of these social gatherings were connected with a ceremonial or religious observance such as the womanhood rites for a girl attaining puberty. More were purely recreational. "I was always glad when the dances and the feasts were announced," Geronimo remembered. "So were all the other young people." Men and women danced as partners in these social dances, which thus furnished some discreet courting opportunities in a society where the girls were closely supervised in their relations with youths of the opposite sex.[28] Geronimo did not refer to the fierce intensity of the war

27 Opler, *An Apache Life-Way*, pp. 49–51, 65–76; Betzinez, *op. cit.*, pp. 30, 55.
28 Barrett, *op. cit.*, pp. 26–28; Opler, *An Apache Life-Way*, pp. 339–40, 444–48, 454–56.

The hoop-and-pole game. Note the rolling hoop and the two contestants with their poles. The photograph may have been taken at the San Carlos Reservation in 1884. *This game was sacred, having been handed down from the animals before the emergence of the human race.* Courtesy Smithsonian Institution, National Anthropological Archives, Washington, D.C.

dance preparatory to a war party or a raid. Apparently he had few such experiences in his sheltered youth. He would have many thereafter.

These isolated Apaches were a happy and self-sufficient people. They loved the wild jumble of canyons and mountains that was their homeland. They knew the use of every plant, the habits of every animal, the storing of every item of food—perfect adaptation to environment, by white man's reasoning. They viewed it differently. As Geronimo explained it in his old age: "For each tribe of men Usen created, He also made a home. In the land created for any particular tribe He placed whatever would be best for the welfare of that tribe.

"When Usen created the Apaches He also created their homes in the West. He gave to them such grain, fruits, and game as they needed to eat. To restore their health when disease attacked them He made many different herbs to grow. . . . He gave them a pleasant climate and all they needed for clothing and shelter was at hand."[29]

But the Apaches did not depend entirely on natural products. Whenever they were relatively undisturbed they practiced an extensive agriculture. As soon as Geronimo and his "brothers" and "sisters" were old enough, they helped their parents in the fields. In his tribe both men and women joined in the work. Each family had its own plot—his family had about two acres—in an extensive field in a valley. They broke the ground with crude wooden implements and planted their crops, the corn in rows, the beans among the corn, and the pumpkins in irregular order over the plot. They cultivated them as needed, and the whole group shared the burden of protecting the field against their ponies and the deer and other wild animals. In the autumn they gathered the pumpkins and beans in the large woven baskets made by the women, tied the ears of corn together by the husks, and carried the harvest on the backs of their ponies to their dwellings, where the corn was shelled. Then the entire store was placed in the caves frequently found in their mountains. They laid down a layer of rock and oak branches on the cave floor, put the containers with the food on top of that, and closed the entrance with rocks sealed with mud.[30]

29 Barrett, *op. cit.*, p. 15.
30 *Ibid.*, pp. 20–21; Opler, *An Apache Life-Way*, pp. 371–75. Geronimo included melons among the crops grown, but possibly his memory tricked him, recalling the melons he raised later at Fort Sill. For the extent of Apache planting, see Secretary of the Interior, *Annual Report*, 1869, pp. 102–103, in which an army officer describes a field of at least one hundred acres of fine corn that had been planted and tended with

The Apaches also made from their corn a fermented drink known as *tizwin*, prepared by the women with the help of the children. They may have learned the technique from the Indians in Old Mexico or from the Spanish-speaking Mexicans. First they soaked the corn overnight in water. They dug a long trench and lined it with grass, placed the soaked corn in the trench, and covered it with another layer of grass. Sometimes they covered the whole with earth or with a blanket. After sprinkling the corn with water morning and evening for ten days, during which it sprouted, they took it out, ground it with their grinding stones (mano and metate), and then boiled it for four or five hours. Finally, they strained off the liquid and set it aside. After about twenty-four hours, when it stopped bubbling, it was ready to drink.[31]

It had a relatively low alcoholic content, but the Apaches were efficient drinkers; after a preliminary fast they achieved a calculated debauch that threw the whole band into disorder. There were quarrels, fights, even killings, as all the latent violence of a primitive people came to the surface. Certainly such disturbances must have occurred in Geronimo's childhood, but he said only that the beverage "was very highly prized by the Indians." In this sheltered time, secure in the affection of an extended family, he may have been relatively untouched by these occurrences. It is also possible that during this undisturbed period in the history of his people some moderation was observed in the use of the intoxicant.

Thus, the child Geronimo labored in the fields with his parents and no doubt helped in storing the food and making the *tizwin*.

---

the crudest of implements and irrigated by *acequias* constructed with almost unbelievable industry. The Apaches concerned were of the White Mountain tribe. For the techniques of constructing the *acequias*, see Grenville Goodwin, "Experiences of an Indian Scout," *Arizona Historical Review*, Vol. VII, No. 1 (part 1, Jan., 1936), pp. 32–33. This narrative by an old Apache has recently been published in Keith H. Basso (ed.), *Western Apache Raiding and Warfare: From the Notes of Grenville Goodwin*, pp. 93–185, from the field notes left by Goodwin at the time of his death, but I have used his own published version except where his notes give additional information.

[31] Barrett, *op. cit.*, p. 22; Opler, *An Apache Life-Way*, pp. 369–70, 436.

Also, he began to hunt with the men—at the early age of eight or ten, he thought, looking back—but to him "this was never work." On the prairies that surrounded their mountains they found herds of deer, antelope, elk, and buffalo, which furnished much of their food supply. The buffalo were not plentiful, and the hunters had to travel some distance to find them. There is one record of a successful hunt northeast of Albuquerque.[32] The Apaches chased the big animals on horseback, riding close and killing them with arrows or spears. Their skins were used for tipi coverings and bedding. Geronimo said that it required more skill to hunt deer than any other animal. The hunters had to approach from downwind; sometimes if the animals were grazing in the open they had to spend many hours crawling long distances on the ground, keeping a weed or a bush before them to hide their approach. Deerskin, with the hair removed and tanned into softness by the women, was used to make their clothing. In the mountains were many eagles, which were hunted for their feathers. "It required great skill to steal upon an eagle," said Geronimo, "for besides having sharp eyes, he is wise and never stops at any place where he does not have a good view of the surrounding country." Fish abounded in the mountain streams, but although small boys sometimes threw stones at them or shot at them for practice with their bows and arrows, the Apaches had a strong taboo against eating them. "Usen did not intend snakes, frogs, or fishes to be eaten," said Geronimo.[33]

An equal revulsion existed against eating the bear, which, in a way not entirely clear, was supposed to be a sort of ancestor of the people. Or, as some Apaches said, a bear was like a person, could walk erect like a person, and might be the reincarnation of some evil individual. Grizzlies and black and brown bears were numerous in the mountains, and instances of ferocious attacks by them occurred often in Apache experience. The Indians defended them-

32 Opler, *An Apache Life-Way*, p. 327. Jason Betzinez, who belonged to the Warm Springs tribe, remembered a hunting trip on the High Plains beyond the Pecos River; see Betzinez, *op. cit.*, pp. 33–35. But it is doubtful that the Bedonkohes traveled as far east as that.
33 Barrett, *op. cit.*, pp. 31–34.

selves in these encounters, but if they were forced to kill the bear they let the carcass lie without eating any part of it.[34]

Geronimo came close to one such experience when in his early childhood he accompanied the women on a berry gathering expedition. One woman became separated from the others, and as she made her way on her pony through the thick undergrowth and pine trees with her small dog following, a grizzly bear rose in her path and attacked the pony. She jumped off, and the pony escaped. The bear then attacked her. She tried to fight him off with the long knife every Apache carried, and the dog distracted his attention by snapping at his heels. Finally he struck her over the head, tearing off almost the whole scalp. She fell but did not lose consciousness. As she lay on the ground, she struck him four good thrusts with her knife, and he left her. She bound back her scalp as best she could, then became so deathly sick she had to lie down. That night the pony came in with its loaded baskets. The Indians went out to hunt her but did not find her until the second day. They carried her home, and with the herbs and prayers of the medicine man she recovered.[35]

The Apaches, in fact, were very successful in treating wounds, for the Power of the medicine man (or woman), expressed through special songs and incantations, was reinforced by skillful treatment and a knowledge of the healing properties of native plants.[36] As Geronimo saw it, "The Indians knew what herbs to use for medi-

[34] Betzinez, *op. cit.*, pp. 32–33; John Russell Bartlett, *Personal Narratives of Explorations and Incidents in Texas, New Mexico, California, Sonora, and Chihuahua Connected with the United States and Mexican Boundary Commission during the Years 1850, '51, '52, and '53*, I, p. 321; Ball, op. cit., pp. 55–56. Once Mrs. Ball unwittingly served bear to Kaywaykla when in his old age he was a guest in her home. When he discovered what he was eating, his eyes became sharp points of fury, and he stalked out of the house. The next morning, his anger gone, he apologized. "I've been a member of the Reformed Church for sixty years," he explained, "but I've been an Apache much longer than that." Barrett apparently misquoted Geronimo as saying that bears were good for food and valuable for their skin. It is possible, however, that some of the western Apache tribes did not observe this taboo against bear meat. See, for example, Basso, *Western Apache Raiding and Warfare*, p. 187.

[35] Barrett, *op. cit.*, pp. 22–24.

[36] For an example of the healing of a badly shattered arm that the army surgeon wanted to amputate, see Britton Davis, *The Truth about Geronimo*, p. 168; for the practice of a woman with healing Power see Ball, *op. cit.*, pp. 16, 169–70.

cine, how to prepare them, and how to give the medicine. This they had been taught by Usen from the beginning. . . . In gathering the herbs, in preparing them, and in administering the medicine, as much faith was held in prayer as in the actual effect of the medicine." And he went on to say that some of the Indians were skilled in cutting out bullets and arrowheads from wounded warriors and that he himself had done much of that.[37]

The Apaches were also attacked at times by cougars, but they had no taboo against hunting the big cats. During his lifetime Geronimo killed several of them with arrows and one with a spear. The men carried them home on their horses, ate the meat, and used the skins. They valued the hide for making quivers for their arrows. "These were very pretty and very durable," said Geronimo.[38]

When Geronimo was still a young boy, a party of Nednai Apaches who had relatives in the band came up from Mexico to visit them. Among them was a youth named Juh,[39] the son of a chief or prominent leader. He was a stockily built boy who spoke with a stutter, strong-willed and at that age somewhat of a bully. When the Bedonkohe girls went into the woods to gather acorns, he, with some followers, would wait until they had completed their task and then snatch their filled baskets. Among the victims was Geronimo's favorite "sister," his cousin Ishton. One can perhaps recognize the tendency of a half-grown boy to make life miserable for a girl he admires (cf. Whittier, "the snowball's compliments."), but Mahko's widow did not make this allowance. She told Geronimo and some of his friends to waylay Juh and his companions and give them a good whipping. The one who told the story failed to follow up on the outcome, but knowing Apache obedience to elders, one can be sure that the matriarch's orders were carried out.

Later, after Juh had grown up and established himself as a war leader among the Nednais, he returned and married Ishton. Fol-

[37] Barrett, *op. cit.*, pp. 23–24.
[38] *Ibid.*, pp. 33–34.
[39] The explosive Apache syllable is pronounced more nearly like Ho or Who, and it is often spelled Whoa or Hoo.

lowing Apache custom, he became a member of her family, and he and Geronimo formed a friendship that was to endure throughout their lives—Juh "was as a brother to me," said Geronimo in his old age, looking back. But customs varied with circumstances, and after living for some time among the Bedonkohes, Juh took his wife and went back to join his people in the Sierra Madre.[40]

Some time after Juh's departure, Geronimo's father died, following a long illness. The relatives and friends dressed him in his best clothes, painted his face, wrapped a rich blanket around him, placed him on his favorite horse, loaded up all his belongings, and with crying and wailing bore him to a cave in the mountain. There they placed the body on the floor, with his possessions beside him, and sealed the entrance with rocks coated with mud so that it would be hidden. Only the close friends who performed an Apache burial knew the location, and they avoided the place thereafter. Even the name of the deceased was not spoken,[41] though strangely enough this taboo did not apply to Spanish nicknames.

Geronimo was not yet grown, but this was the end of his childhood.

[40] Betzinez, *op. cit.*, p. 15; Ball, *op. cit.*, pp. 123–26; Griswold, *op. cit.*, s.v. "Juh"; Barrett, *op. cit.*, p. 101. Pollard states that among the Mimbrenos and Warm Springs Apaches, as distinguished from the Chiricahuas, a married couple joined the husband's family after the birth of the first child, but he cites no authority, and his assumption that the same custom was observed among the Bedonkohes is not convincing. If he is correct, however, such a practice may explain the residence patterns of Geronimo and his associates; see Pollard, "Structure and Stress," p. 42.

[41] Barrett, *op. cit.*, p. 36; Betzinez, *op. cit.*, pp. 8n., 16; Opler, *An Apache Life-Way*, pp. 235–37, 472–76. In the account of Juh's visits and the death of Geronimo's father I have followed the order of events given by Betzinez and accepted by present-day Apaches. Barrett has Geronimo say that he was "a small child" when his father died, an obvious error in translation. He was a well-grown youth, old enough to assume the support of his mother.

CHAPTER 2

ADULT RESPONSIBILITIES

Juana never remarried after Taklishim's death, and young Geronimo assumed her support. Apparently by this time his sister, Nahdos-te, had married. (Her husband was a prominent Warm Springs leader named Nana, who was to figure largely in Apache history.) In their grief and loneliness Juana and Geronimo decided to visit Juh and Ishton and other relatives among the Nednais. It was a difficult journey, for they were unfamiliar with the terrain and the location of the water holes. More baffling was the absence of trails or any sign of camps and places where horses had been tethered. They were soon to understand that these wild Indians had learned to obliterate their tracks, conceal their camps, and keep their horses at a distance. But they finally reached Juh's stronghold in the Sierra Madre and were warmly welcomed by his people.[1]

Up to this time Geronimo had apparently not experienced the hostility between the Apaches and the Mexicans, but he had certainly been told of it. It went far back in Southwestern history. The Spanish conquistadores, who had reduced the settled Indians to

---

[1] Barrett, *Geronimo's Story of His Life*, pp. 36–37; Betzinez, *I Fought with Geronimo*, p. 16.

vassalage, had sent out slave-catching expeditions against the ranging Apaches. The Apaches retaliated, and the Spaniards incited the other tribes against them.[2] When the Comanches arrived in the Southwest, the Spaniards enlisted them also. Thus, the Apaches were driven into the mountains, and raiding the settled communities became a way of life for them, an economic enterprise as legitimate in their culture as gathering berries or hunting deer; and first the Spanish and then, after achieving independence, the Mexican government responded by systematic attempts to exterminate them by paying bounties for their scalps.[3]

This pattern had existed so long that even historians believed that the Apaches had always been a predatory race. And long experience had taught them all the tricks of survival. They knew the location of every water hole and hidden canyon. Men, women, and children could travel with incredible speed and secrecy, striking their enemies here today, a hundred miles away on the other side of the mountains tomorrow. If they had horses, they rode; if the going became too rough, they killed and ate their mounts and continued on foot. If attacked, they could scatter and fade into the surrounding rocks, traveling separately in order to leave no trail and collecting again in some predetermined place.[4] Incidents growing out of this age-old pattern formed the immediate background of Geronimo's career as a warrior and raider.

In 1835 the Mexican state of Sonora passed a law offering one hundred pesos (a peso was roughly equivalent to a dollar) for every scalp of an Apache warrior. Two years later the state of Chihuahua set a scale of one hundred pesos for a warrior's scalp, fifty for a woman's, and twenty-five for a child's. These offers even

2 These facts, as revealed in Spanish archives, have been presented by Jack D. Forbes in *Apache, Navaho, and Spaniard.* See especially pp. 24, 28, 120–21, 160–61, 207–208, 244–45, 281–85.

3 See Alfred Barnaby Thomas, *Forgotten Frontiers: A Study of the Spanish Indian Policy of Don Juan Bautista de Anza, Governor of New Mexico, 1777–1787,* especially pp. 187–94, 216–20, 253, 257–91, 312–38, for Spanish attempts to incite Comanches and Navahos against the Apaches and the payment of bounties for Apache scalps, ears, and heads.

4 Betzinez, *op. cit.,* pp. 6, 65.

attracted roving Americans who had wandered into Mexican territory, and they, too, took up the business of scalp-hunting.[5] Among these was one James Johnson, and his biggest haul was made in 1837 from the Mimbrenos.

In the heart of that tribe's territory were valuable copper deposits. (They are still being worked and may even have been worked in prehistoric times by Indians.) In 1804 a Mexican capitalist began extensive operations there. He brought in workmen; built a settlement, Santa Rita del Cobra (now Santa Rita), with a triangular fort and fifty or more adobe houses; and operated mule trains going out with packloads of ore to the city of Chihuahua and bringing back supplies. Some gold was also produced in the area—not in any spectacular quantity but enough to add to the profit from the copper mines. All the time he maintained an uneasy peace with the Mimbrenos.

Johnson had been operating a trading post in Sonora, and the Mimbreno chief, Juan José Compa, believed him to be his friend. Then Johnson came to Santa Rita with an accomplice and some relatively innocent mule buyers from Missouri, whom he had tricked into accompanying him. He laid out a generous supply of pinole and invited the Indians to help themselves. As they were eating, he fired into the crowd with a concealed blunderbuss (or perhaps a six-pounder) while his companion made sure of the chief. The surviving Indians counterattacked, killing some of the Missourians, but the archconspirators escaped. Estimates of the scalps they took vary from about twenty to four hundred, in either case a profitable day's hunting.

According to one story, the enraged Indians annihilated the mule train coming in with supplies and killed all the people in the settlement. Another account says that they overpowered the supply train, taking everything except one mule for each man to ride back to Mexico, and at the same time ensured the evacuation of the settlers by warning them that no more supplies would be permitted

[5] Dan L. Thrapp, *The Conquest of Apacheria*, pp. 8–9 and notes.

to reach them. It is certain that the mines and the settlement were abandoned in 1838.[6]

As far as is known, the Santa Rita massacre and its aftermath did not involve the Bedonkohes. Probably they knew of it, since they were closely related to the Mimbrenos. And Geronimo was certainly involved in the Apache-Mexican hostility that followed. When as a youth he joined the Nednais, he must have gone out with Juh on raids of Mexican ranches and pack trains, killing the men and carrying off the horses and loads of freight, for he said that he was admitted to the council of warriors at the precocious age of seventeen,[7] and this admission was granted only after rigorous training and apprenticeship.

First the youth was taught the rules of survival. Have the women pound enough meat and fat for a week's food, and take along a supply of water. Cross open flats by night, and reach a mountain and hide in the brush by day. Locate water holes by climbing to a high place and looking for green spots; but do not go to them by day, only at night. Do not sleep under a tree—that is the first place where an Indian, a Mexican, or an animal will look. Find a place in the open under a bush or grass, but where you can reach cover quickly. If you become lost and want to call for help, make a fire and send up a smoke signal, but put it out and run away to a place where you can watch and see if anyone comes.

After the youth had mastered these techniques, he might volunteer to join a hostile expedition. As an apprentice warrior, he conformed to certain ceremonies and was known as Child of the Water. "War is a solemn religious matter," said Geronimo. The older men watched out for him, but he and his fellow apprentices were required to perform all the work about the camp—caring for the horses, getting the water and wood, doing the cooking, serving on guard duty. If he showed courage and dependability on four

6 *Ibid.*, pp. 10–12; Ball, *In the Days of Victorio*, p. 46; John Carey Cremony, *Life among the Apaches*, pp. 30–32; Frank C. Lockwood, *The Apache Indians*, pp. 67–79; Bartlett, *Personal Narratives*, I, pp. 322–23.

7 Barrett, *op. cit.*, pp. 37–38. Geronimo, of course, could only guess his approximate age.

such expeditions (the Apaches, like other Indians, regarded four as a sacred number) he was accepted as a warrior, a man among men.[8]

Perhaps the greatest joy that Geronimo felt in thus attaining his majority was the privilege of marrying a slender, delicate girl of the Nednai tribe named Alope.[9] The two had long been in love. In spite of the barriers that Apache custom interposed, youths of the opposite sex were aware of each other's preferences, and their feelings were usually considered in the marriage arrangements made by their families. The proper formality was for the parents or other representatives of the young man to call on the parents of the girl to make the agreement and the economic settlement while he waited outside the lodge and she sat sedately within behind her mother, with neither permitted to speak.[10]

But according to Geronimo, he made the arrangements himself. It was the accepted practice for a mature man to carry on the negotiations, and even as a youth Geronimo showed an independent spirit. Perhaps he felt that he had carried enough responsibility to be on his own. By his account, "as soon as the council granted me these privileges [of manhood] I went to see her father concerning our marriage." He asked "many ponies for her. I made no reply, but in a few days appeared before his [lodge] with the herd of ponies and took with me Alope. This was all the marriage ceremony necessary in our tribe."[11] In his reminiscences he did not find it relevant to explain how he acquired the horses or how many Mexicans he had to kill in obtaining them.

It is evident that he soon left the Nednais and returned with his wife and his mother to his native mountains. Betzinez, who was not born until 1860, believed that he remained with Juh, but his own account clearly indicates that he established his home with his

---

[8] *Ibid.*, pp. 187–90; Opler, *An Apache Life-Way*, pp. 134–39.

[9] This is the name given in Barrett, *op. cit.*, p. 38, and according to Eve Ball it was used by Asa Daklugie (Ball interview, July 26, 1971). Its liquid syllables have none of the harsh consonants that usually characterize Apache names, but the name, Gee-esh-kizn, given in Griswold, "The Fort Sill Apaches," s.v. "Geronimo," seems to be a variant spelling of the name of Geronimo's second wife.

[10] Opler, *op. cit.*, pp. 77–81, 142–48; Betzinez, *op. cit.*, p. 18.

[11] Barrett, *op. cit.*, p. 38.

Bedonkohe kindred.[12] As he described his domestic arrangements: "Not far from my mother's tepee I had made for us a new home. The tepee was made of buffalo hides and in it were many bear robes [*sic*], lion [that is, cougar] hides, and other trophies of the chase, as well as my spears, bows, and arrows. Alope had made many decorations of beads and drawn work on buckskin, which she placed in our tepee. She also drew many pictures on the walls of our home. She was a good wife, but she was never strong. We followed the traditions of our fathers and were happy. Three children came to us—children that played, loitered, and worked as I had done."[13]

Meanwhile, in 1846 war broke out between the United States and Mexico. Apparently Geronimo was not affected by it in his remote mountains, but his Mimbreno relatives learned of it and heartily approved. The historian will remember that in the early summer of that year Brigadier General Stephen Watts Kearny set out from Fort Leavenworth, near Independence, Missouri, to take New Mexico and California. He occupied Santa Fe and then traveled south. On the Rio Grande near Valverde before he turned southwest he met his first Apaches. They came to his camp in a friendly spirit and furnished him with four young warriors as guides, and he made an appointment to meet their leaders near the copper mines. When he reached that place, he found it deserted, with adobe houses falling into ruins and ten or fifteen shafts of the unworked mines. He continued on west to Mangas Creek, a tributary of the Gila heading between the Big and Little Burro Mountains.

There, on October 20, he met the Mimbrenos. Their leader was Mangas Coloradas (Roan Shirt, Red Sleeves), a chief of immense physical stature and corresponding courage and ability whose influence extended to many of the Apache tribes of the area. His people were dressed in motley garb, mainly Mexican, an indication of their success in raiding. They were mounted on good

12 *Ibid.*, pp. 43, 46–48; Betzinez, *op. cit.*, pp. 16–17.
13 Barrett, *op. cit.*, pp. 38–39.

horses, and the soldiers noted their superb horsemanship, even the children being accustomed to riding from infancy. One of the chiefs—probably Mangas—offered to help the Americans if they would invade Chihuahua, Sonora, and Durango. He said the Mimbrenos hated the Mexicans and would kill them all, but any Americans could pass safely through their country. Kearny continued west to California, but later Colonel Alexander W. Doniphan passed through on his way to join Zachary Taylor at Monterrey, and he received—and declined—the same offer. The Americans' accounts of these contacts show their disdain for the Apaches. Even so, friendly relations were established.[14]

But although the Apaches approved of the war, they were less approving of the peace that ended it. The Treaty of Guadelupe Hidalgo, ratified in 1848, which conveyed the Spanish Southwest to the United States, contained a pledge that the American government would restrain the Indians in its newly acquired territory from raiding in Mexico and would repatriate any captives they might take on such raids.[15] The next year an Indian agent was sent to Santa Fe to establish relations with these tribes, and in 1850 Congress established a rudimentary government for a Territory of New Mexico, which included the present New Mexico, Arizona, and southern Colorado. The Mexicans, of course, were left to cope with the Nednais in the Sierra Madre.

Following the peace, a joint commission was appointed to run the new international boundary, with John Russell Bartlett to head the American commission and General Pedro Garcia Condé to head the Mexican. John Carey Cremony, a young Boston newspaperman who spoke fluent Spanish, was employed as Bartlett's interpreter, and Colonel Lewis S. Craig was in command of his military escort. The joint commission set up the initial monument with appropriate ceremonies on the Rio Grande near El Paso on April 24, 1851. Bartlett had decided to use the Santa Rita copper mines as his headquarters while the survey worked west. He had the

14 Thrapp, *Victorio*, pp. 20–21; Lockwood, *op. cit.*, pp. 75–79.
15 William M. Malloy, *Treaties, Conventions, International Acts, Protocols and Agreements between the United States of America and Other Powers*, pp. 1112–13.

triangular fort repaired for the use of the military and the crumbling adobe houses made livable for the officers of the commission.

He reached the place himself in early May and soon set off to northern Mexico for supplies, passing through the state of Chihuahua to Fronteras in Sonora and finally reaching Arispe on the Sonora River. He was a careful observer, and as he traveled through this Mexican frontier region he noted the devastation wrought by the Apaches—towns empty of inhabitants and a vacant countryside with dilapidated houses and abandoned fields and orchards.[16] At Fronteras Bartlett was told of an event that was the greatest personal tragedy of Geronimo's life and the dominant influence of his future career. The story came straight from General Carrasco, who commanded the frontier troops of Sonora.

The state of Chihuahua had decided to try peace with the Apaches. It invited them to trade in the towns, even furnishing them rations. Such trade had frequently taken place between the Indians and Mexican settlements with which they had established amicable relations. They exchanged animal hides and furs and other wild products for brightly colored cloth, knives, ornaments, and other articles. Often they raided one Mexican settlement and traded the plunder with another that was willing to connive in their depredations. Now they had a market in Chihuahua for the horses and mules they took in Sonora. But "lately"—this word fixes the date at 1850 or possibly a little earlier—Carrasco disregarded the state boundary and came suddenly upon a band of Apaches trading at Janos, killed about twenty-five, and captured about fifty or sixty women and children, whom he took into the interior and distributed as slaves. The military commander of Chihuahua was greatly incensed at this invasion, but when he reported it to the central government, it supported Carrasco.[17]

Geronimo and Betzinez later told the story from the Apache side. Betzinez fixed the date as the summer of 1850. Geronimo's

---

16 Bartlett, *op. cit.*, I, 206–207, 220–81.

17 *Ibid.*, I, 267–68; Thrapp, *Conquest of Apacheria*, p. 8; Betzinez, *op. cit.*, p. 2. Cremony heard the same story from Carrasco and related it with an exaggerated number of Apache casualties in *Life among the Apaches*, p. 39.

date, the summer of 1858, is clearly in error, for he said it occurred at about the time of the boundary survey. By this time Geronimo and his Bedonkohe adherents had come under the leadership of Mangas Coloradas. In that fatal summer, with the great chief leading, they started on a trading trip to Casas Grandes. On the way they stopped at a town they knew as Kas-ki-yeh. Betzinez identified the place as Ramos, but since he was not born until 1860 and heard the story from his elders, Carrasco's designation of Janos may be accepted as correct.[18] As Geronimo told it:

Since it was a peaceable expedition they had taken their women and children along. They made their camp just outside the town, and every day the men went in to trade, leaving their families, horses, weapons, and supplies in camp under a small guard. But in spite of the supposed good will of the Mexicans, they took the precaution of deciding on a place of rendezvous in a thicket by the river that passed the town.

Late one afternoon, as the men were returning to camp, they were met by a few distracted women and children with the news that "Mexican troops from some other town" had killed the guard, captured the ponies and supplies, and massacred many of their people. At this news they all quickly scattered, fading into the landscape in the Apache way. Then at nightfall they began to gather at the appointed meeting place:

Silently we stole in one by one: sentinels were placed, and, when all were counted, I found that my aged mother, my young wife, and my three small children were among the slain. There were no lights in camp, so without being noticed I silently turned away and stood by the river. How long I stood there I do not know, but when I saw the warriors arranging for a council I took my place.

That night I did not give my vote for or against any measure; but it was decided that as there were only eighty warriors left, and as we were without arms or supplies, and were furthermore sur-

18 Betzinez, *op. cit.*, p. 3; Barrett, *op. cit.*, pp. 43, 113.

rounded by the Mexicans far inside their own territory, we could not hope to fight successfully. So our chief, Mangus-Colorado, gave the order to start at once in perfect silence for our homes in Arizona,[19] leaving the dead upon the field.

I stood until all had passed, hardly knowing what I would do. . . . I did not pray, nor did I resolve to do anything in particular, for I had no purpose left. I finally followed the tribe silently, keeping just within hearing distance of the soft noise of the feet of the retreating Apaches.[20]

＊＊＊＊＊＊＊＊＊＊＊＊＊＊＊＊

This account does not indicate how Geronimo knew that the members of his family had been killed instead of captured. He could have learned it from survivors who saw them die, but it seems that he managed to steal back to the scene of the massacre. Years later at Fort Sill he told the artist, Elbridge Ayer Burbank, that he found them all dead, lying in a pool of blood.[21]

Jason Betzinez's secondhand version of the disaster varies in many particulars from Geronimo's. He said that during the trading the Mexicans had treated the Apaches to their fiery mescal (*aguardiente*), made by distilling the fermented juice of the agave (century plant), and that the Indians were sleeping off the effects in their camp when the soldiers came killing and scalping.[22] In view of a statement made in 1852 by Mangas Coloradas,[23] it is probably true that some of the people in camp were intoxicated when the enemy struck. At all events, the survivors had a sorrowful homecoming. As Geronimo told it:

＊＊＊＊＊＊＊＊＊＊＊＊＊＊＊＊

For two days and three nights we were on forced marches, stopping only for meals, then we made a camp near the Mexican

19 That is, the Bedonkohes, according to Geronimo, lived in Arizona; other members of the party lived in New Mexico.

20 Barrett, *op. cit.*, pp. 43–45.

21 E. A. Burbank and Ernest Royce, *Burbank among the Indians*, p. 33.

22 Betzinez, *op. cit.*, p. 3. Apparently Betzinez had read Barrett's book; thus, he told Geronimo's story briefly as a separate incident, p. 16.

23 See *infra*, p. 47.

border,[24] where we rested two days. Here I took some food and talked with the other Indians who had lost in the massacre, but none had lost as I had, for I had lost all.

Within a few days we arrived at our own settlement. There were the decorations that Alope had made—and there were the playthings of our little ones. I burned them all, even our tepee. I also burned my mother's tepee and destroyed all her property.

I was never again contented in our quiet home. I had vowed vengeance upon the Mexican troopers who had wronged me, and whenever I . . . saw anything to remind me of former happy days my heart would ache for revenge upon Mexico.

◇◇◇◇◇◇◇◇◇◇◇◇◇◇◇◇◇◇◇◇◇◇

This hatred of the Mexicans continued throughout Geronimo's life. Even at Fort Sill he said, "I am old now and shall never go on the warpath again, but if I were young, and followed the warpath, it would lead into Old Mexico."[25]

Through this experience Geronimo received a gift of the Power that was to figure prominently throughout the rest of his life. Unlike Indians of some other tribes, the Apache did not go off alone on a conscious spiritual quest. Power came suddenly and unexpectedly. It was the life force of the universe, and it sought individuals through which to work. Its nature and the manner of its coming varied from person to person. In many cases it is easy for the skeptic to identify the experience as a dream. For example, an Apache telling of his father's vision said: "This happened towards morning, and he was sound asleep. Something touched him and told him to awake for it had good things to tell him. He pushed the cover off his head, and there beside him sat a silver-tip bear." The one to whom it came might be given a special song and ceremony to bring it into action, but no man could aspire to leadership and no woman could exert influence without it.[26] To say, as

24 It should be noted that the Mexican border before the Gadsden Purchase was farther north than at present; hence, the long journey to reach it.

25 Barrett, *op. cit.*, pp. 46, 110. Barrett inserted a touch of pathos by mentioning Geronimo's visits to his father's grave, an action forbidden by Apache taboos.

26 Morris E. Opler, *Apache Odyssey: A Journey between Two Worlds*, p. 42; Opler, *An Apache Life-Way*, pp. 186–216, 255–57, 261–64, 280–81, 306–309.

some of Geronimo's detractors have said, that he was "only" a medicine man is to ignore a fundamental tenet of Apache faith. As the years passed, he acquired many kinds of Power, but as far as is known the one he received at the time of his bitter loss was his first endowment.

He had gone out alone and was sitting with his head bowed weeping when he heard a voice calling his name, "Goyahkla!" Four times—the magical Apache number—it called. Then it spoke. "No gun can ever kill you. I will take the bullets from the guns of the Mexicans, so they will have nothing but powder. And I will guide your arrows."[27] The fact that he was often wounded, but never fatally, strengthened his belief. As late as 1897 he told Burbank that no bullet could kill him.[28]

He needed all the assurance his Power could give him. As soon as the warriors had collected weapons and supplies, Mangas Coloradas called a council and found that all were willing to take the warpath against the Mexicans. Geronimo was sent to enlist the help of their relatives. He went first to the Chiricahuas, whose chief was the great Cochise. There he was sure of a sympathetic hearing, for Dos-teh-seh, a daughter of Mangas, was Cochise's principal wife. The chief called a council at early dawn. Geronimo told his story, and the warriors agreed to join the campaign. He went next to Juh and the Nednais, with the same success.

According to Geronimo, it was not until the following summer that the war party set out. (Betzinez said it was in late fall of the same year.) They traveled in three divisions: the Bedonkohes [and certainly their Mimbreno relatives] under Mangas Coloradas, the Chiricahuas under Cochise, and the Nednais under Juh. According to Betzinez, the Warm Springs contingent was led by their chief, Baishan, whose name, meaning "knife," was translated by the Mexicans as Cuchillo or—because of the Apache practice of blackening their weapons to make them less conspicuous— Cuchillo Negro. But no doubt the Bedonkohe, Mimbreno, and

27 Sam Haozous interview, January 27, 1955.
28 Burbank and Royce, *op. cit.*, pp. 30–31.

Warm Springs warriors traveled together and were dominated by Mangas Coloradas.

They went south through Sonora, following hidden ways along river courses and through mountains, to Arispe. (They seemed to know that the military force that had ravaged their camp was stationed there.) Troops from the city came out to meet them, and there was some skirmishing. The following day the whole Mexican force—two companies of cavalry and two of infantry—came out to attack. A pitched battle followed, a departure from the usual Apache ambush from a hidden position. Geronimo, because he had suffered so much from these same soldiers, was allowed to direct the fighting. (This is his story, and it may well be true.) He arranged his warriors in a crescent in the timber near the river, and the Mexican infantry advanced towards them and opened fire. Geronimo led a charge against them, at the same time extending his crescent to outflank and encircle them and attack from the rear. (At least, that seems to be his meaning.) The battle lasted about two hours, the Apaches fighting with bows and arrows and in close quarters with their spears. Many of them were killed, but when the fight ended they were in complete possession of a field strewn with Mexican dead.[29] It was here, according to tradition, that Goyahkla received the name Geronimo.

Barrett added some trimmings, not only about a scalping orgy that followed, but also about a battlefield promotion of Geronimo to "war chief of all the Apaches." The word *chief*, as used by the Apaches, was a term as technical as the rank of an army officer or the title of a government official in white society, and all the Apaches, including Daklugie, have insisted that Geronimo never held that position. Eve Ball once reminded Daklugie of the statement in the story he had interpreted. "He laughed and said that neither he nor Geronimo told Barrett that Geronimo was a chief, but that Barrett made one of his uncle."[30]

Betzinez gave an account similar to Geronimo's of the extensive

29 Barrett, *op. cit.*, pp. 47–54.
30 Eve Ball to Angie Debo, February 27, 1972.

preparation, the war party and its leaders, and the fierce fighting, but he located the battle in Chihuahua inside the city of Ramos. He also said that Baishan was killed by the first volley of the Mexican guns—an obvious error, for Cuchillo Negro appeared very much alive in subsequent Apache history. But Betzinez's impressions are true. He heard the story told and retold for years thereafter, always with pride in what his people regarded as the greatest of Apache victories. And they never relaxed their hatred of the Mexicans.[31]

It remained now for the Apaches to cope with the ancient enemy and to enter into relations with the new invaders.

[31] Betzinez, *op. cit.*, pp. 4–9.

CHAPTER 3

MEXICANS AND AMERICANS

Bartlett returned from Sonora and arrived once more at the copper mines on June 17, 1851. On that very day he was visited by Mangas Coloradas and some of his people, who had been strangely absent throughout the spring. Mangas said that he had followed Bartlett several days and had been near his camp several times. This presents the intriguing possibility that the avenging Apache war party and Bartlett's wagon train had gone into Sonora at about the same time, that the battle before Arispe had been fought shortly after Bartlett's departure, and that the fast-moving Apaches had caught up with him towards the end of his journey.

In any event, Mangas warned Bartlett of the risk he had run in traveling without adequate protection when so many bad Indians were about. He said that he was a friend of the Americans and spoke of his meeting with Kearny. Bartlett told him of the war and the peace and explained that he had come to mark the boundary. He assured the Indians that the Americans would protect them if they behaved, but he said that the treaty bound them to protect the Mexicans against depredations across the border. The chief strongly disapproved of this provision. He said that his people had always stolen mules and taken prisoners from the Mexicans, but he promised not to molest the boundary commission.[1]

Bartlett was fair-minded and humane, and he believed that if the Indians were treated justly they would respond. Cremony regarded them with contempt and was sure they plotted treachery.[2] But Mangas Coloradas loyally observed his promise, and the Warm Springs Indians, who camped that summer on the Mimbres River below the copper mines, were equally friendly. Survey parties scattered fifty miles along the line were not molested. Wagons with stores for the camps went out safely, unprotected. Members of the commission traveled in small parties or alone unharmed. The mules and horses and a herd of cattle brought for food grazed undisturbed.[3]

This idyllic relationship was soon endangered by the unresolved issue of Apache-Mexican hostility. Late that same June two half-grown Mexican boys, captives of the Apaches, sought refuge in Cremony's tent. Bartlett turned them over to General Condé, who subsequently restored them to their families, but the Indians were greatly aroused. Finally, a council was arranged, and Mangas Coloradas and several other leaders of the two tribes—Cuchillo Negro, of the Warm Springs, Delgadito, probably of the same tribe, and Ponce and Coletto Amarillo, whose tribal affiliations are unknown—came with about two hundred warriors to confer with the American officials. Mangas began by asking, "Why did you take our captives from us?" And he went on to state his position: "You came to our country. You were well received. Your lives, your property, your animals were safe. You passed by ones, by twos by threes through our country; you went and came in peace. Your strayed animals were always brought home to you again. Our wives, our children and women came here and visited your houses. We were friends. We were brothers! Believing this, we came among you and brought our captives. . . . We believed your assurances of

1 Bartlett, *Personal Narratives*, I, pp. 297–302.
2 For his final evaluation, see *Life among the Apaches*, p. 320.
3 Bartlett, *op. cit.*, I, pp. 320–22.

friendship, and we trusted them." And again he demanded, "Why did you take our captives from us?"

Bartlett tried to explain the relationship contemplated by the peace treaty: "I have no doubt but that you have suffered much by the Mexicans. This is a question in which it is impossible for us to tell who is right, or who is wrong. You and the Mexicans accuse each other of being the aggressors. Our duty is to fulfil our promise to both . . . to show to Mexico that we mean what we say; and when the time comes . . . to prove the good faith of our promises to you."

Ponce became very angry. Delgadito was more conciliatory, but he defended the rights of his tribesman: "He cannot lose his prisoners, who were obtained at the risk of his life and purchased by the blood of his relatives. He justly demands his captives . . . and as justice we demand it."

Bartlett realized that the Indians could make things difficult for the commission. The Mimbrenos were camped on one side above the copper mines, and the Warm Springs band was on the other side in the broad valley of the Mimbres where the commission's livestock were grazing. He accordingly found a way to circumvent regulations against ransoming captives and offered to pay for the boys. The Apache leaders then held a short consultation, after which Delgadito announced: "The brave who owns these captives does not want to sell. He has had one of those two boys six years. . . . He is as a son to his old age. He speaks our language, and he cannot sell him. Money cannot buy affection. His heart cannot be sold. He taught him to string and shoot the bow, and to wield the lance. He loves the boy and cannot sell him."

It was true that the Apaches took captured children into their families and loved them as their own,[4] but Bartlett was bound by the treaty, and besides this, there was the appeal of the boys, who chose their own people in preference to the Apaches. He finally persuaded the council to adjourn to the commissary's stores, where calicoes, blankets, and sheetings worth $250 were laid out and

4 See, for example, Ball, *In the Days of Victorio*, pp. 113–14, 134, 167.

43

accepted. Bartlett thought that ended the matter, but it is clear that the Indians were not satisfied with the settlement.[5]

A few days later a Mexican teamster in the employ of the American commission deliberately shot and fatally wounded an Apache.[6] The Indians were mollified to see him brought in chains to a hearing, but Bartlett, mindful of proper legal procedures, wanted to send him to Santa Fe for trial. Ponce demanded his immediate execution so they could see it. Bartlett promised to turn the murderer's wages over to the victim's mother. She said she wanted blood, not money. The affair was finally settled by giving her thirty dollars, then due the prisoner, and promising to pay her his wages, twenty dollars a month, thereafter while he worked in chains. Bartlett thought that this settlement pleased the Indians, but it is apparent that they accepted it reluctantly.[7]

Their good relations with the commission quickly deteriorated. Several of Colonel Craig's mules disappeared. He blamed the Apaches and set off with thirty soldiers to their camp to recover the animals. They said they would hunt the mules—as apparently they did, and brought them back—but their friendly attitude changed after this encounter. Meanwhile, about four hundred Navahos arrived and camped on the Gila. It was probably they who made two separate raids on Craig's herd in August, making off with about seventy-five mules and some horses. Bartlett sent back to Doña Ana on the Rio Grande for more soldiers, and forty dragoons arrived. The Indians then ran off all of Craig's remaining mules and horses and the eighteen mules that had hauled the wagons of the dragoons. This time the Mimbrenos or their Warm Springs friends, possibly both, were almost certainly guilty.

During this time a small party of American miners had come in and started working the gold diggings the Mexicans had abandoned thirteen years before. The reopening of the mines was an

---

[5] Bartlett, *op. cit.*, I, pp. 311–17. Cremony also recorded the minutes of the conference in *Life among the Apaches*, pp. 58–66.

[6] The Mexicans living in the ceded territory, of course, became American citizens, but it will be necessary to continue referring to them as Mexicans to distinguish them from the incoming Anglos.

[7] Bartlett, *op. cit.*, I, pp. 228–29; Cremony, *op. cit.*, pp. 80–81.

ominous circumstance that was to dominate the future of the Mimbrenos. Then a party, in which Delgadito was seen and recognized, ran off all the intruders' cattle. The miners and some volunteers from the commission overtook the raiders and recovered the herd. "Our place was now in a state of siege," as Bartlett expressed it. The surveying parties were called in, and guards were stationed around the camp. Altogether, the commission and its military escort had lost about 150 horses and mules.[8]

This whole experience of the first official contact between an Apache band and a United States government agency reveals the tangled threads that were to form the future pattern. It shows how difficult it was even for men of good will like Mangas Coloradas and Bartlett to understand each other. Cremony had his own theory to explain it: lacking enough men to attack the commission, the treacherous chief pretended peace until he could bring in Navaho reinforcements (as though Apaches ever needed help in raiding!); when they arrived, he joined them. The high-minded Bartlett eventually came to the same conclusion.[9]

Geronimo was not present at Santa Rita that summer of 1851, but the conflicts that emerged there were to form the setting of his life. His own contact with members of the survey was uneventful. The commission left the Santa Rita camp on August 24 and continued westward. On September 5 the party went through Apache Pass in Cochise's mountains and came out in the valley beyond.[10] Somewhere along this line Geronimo saw his first white Americans. As he related it:

>>><<<<<<<<<<<<<<<<<<<<<<

. . . we heard that some white men were measuring land to the south of us. In company with a number of other warriors I went to visit them. We could not understand them very well, for we had no interpreter, but we made a treaty with them by shaking hands and promising to be brothers. Then we made our camp near their

8 Bartlett, *op. cit.*, I, pp. 228–29, 317–18, 330, 343–53; Cremony, *op. cit.*, pp. 80–85.
9 Bartlett, *op. cit.*, I, pp. 326–29, 353–54; Cremony, *op. cit.*, pp. 48–51.
10 Bartlett, *op. cit.*, I, pp. 358, 373.

camp, and they came to trade with us. We gave them buckskin, blankets, and ponies in exchange for shirts and provisions. We also brought them game, for which they gave us some money. We did not know the value of this money, but we kept it and later learned from the Navajo Indians that it was very valuable.

Every day they measured land with curious instruments and put down marks which we could not understand. They were good men, and we were sorry when they had gone on into the west. They were not soldiers. These were the first white men I ever saw.[11]

The historian will remember that the boundary survey was never completed. Probably Bartlett had conceded too much to Condé in fixing the initial point, and American leaders committed to Manifest Destiny argued that it was not far enough south to include a level route for a transcontinental railroad. The dispute ended with the acquisition of another piece of Mexico by the United States through the Gadsden Purchase of 1853.[12] Incidentally, the treaty of purchase abrogated the pledge that bound the United States to restrain its Apaches from raiding in Mexico;[13] but of course each country had an international obligation to prevent hostiles from crossing the border—if it could.

Meanwhile, after the departure of the boundary commission in 1851, more prospectors were coming into the area around the Santa Rita copper mines, often denying all rights to the Apaches. The Apaches retaliated by numerous depredations and the killing of travelers. In July, 1852, John Greiner, then serving as Indian superintendent of New Mexico, called Mangas Coloradas and other leaders to Santa Fe and made a treaty with them. It committed the United States to give presents to the Indians and treat them well, to punish its citizens who wronged them, and to fix the tribal boundaries. Military posts and trading posts were to

11 Barrett, *Geronimo's Story of His Life*, pp. 113–14.
12 The whole story is told by Odie B. Faulk in *Too Far North; Too Far South*. It is clear that the survey of this new boundary was not the one that Geronimo encountered; see pp. 147–49.
13 Malloy, *Treaties, Conventions*, p. 1122.

be established in their territory. The Indians promised peace to the United States, with free passage of its citizens through their country, and committed themselves to make no more raids in Mexico.[14] They objected to this last provision. Greiner asked the reason, and Mangas Coloradas told of the recent massacre at "Kas-ki-yeh," and the one in 1837 at the copper mines.

"Some time ago," he said, "my people were invited to a feast; aguardiente, or whiskey, was there; my people drank and became intoxicated, when a party of Mexicans came in and beat out their brains with clubs. At another time a trader was sent among us from Chihuahua. While innocently engaged in trading . . . a cannon concealed behind the goods was fired upon my people, and quite a number were killed. . . . How can we make peace with such people?"[15]

Greiner concluded that "if half their statements are true, the Indians would be justified in seeking revenge."[16] Clearly they never intended to stop raiding in Mexico. Indianlike, they based the binding force of their commitments on their oral protests and not on the text of the final document. Geronimo gave Barrett a detailed account of his raids through the 1850's.[17] True, he was not a signatory to the treaty, but Mangas Coloradas was the leader in one of these raids and at other times shared in the spoils.

By this time the Bedonkohes seem to have become merged with the Mimbrenos, though they still retained their tribal distinction. Geronimo soon married a Bedonkohe girl named Chee-hash-kish. Jason Betzinez, who knew her well in later years, always characterized her as "a very handsome woman." She became the mother of a son, Chappo, and a daughter, Dohn-say (Tozey), afterwards known as Lulu, both of whom were to grow up to share in their father's wars and his captivity. Soon he took a second wife, also a Bedonkohe, named Nana-tha-thtith, who became the mother of

---

14 Charles J. Kappler, *Indian Affairs, Laws and Treaties*, II, 598–600.
15 Quoted by Thrapp in *Conquest of Apacheria*, p. 13.
16 Thrapp, *Victorio*, pp. 27–28.
17 This account gives the dates 1859 to 1868, but they do not fit known facts. For example, it had Mangas Coloradas leading a raid in 1867. Mangas was killed early in 1863.

one child.[18] This marriage indicates his rising importance in the tribe. Only a superior hunter and raider could support two wives.

Barrett must have recorded Geronimo's raids almost exactly as he reported them. There is little scalping, no sentimentality, no confusion of events and places, but a straightforward account in orderly sequence. In a culture in which a warrior's exploits were like so many academic honors, subject to check by his associates, they had to be accurately presented. Here one may see the logical working of Geronimo's mind and his essential integrity as he frankly admitted his failures and avoided self-glorification in his successes.

"All the other Apaches were satisfied after the battle of [that is, avenging] 'Kaskiyeh,'" he said, "but I still desired more revenge." He finally persuaded two other warriors—he carefully stated their names—to join him on a raid. They went on foot and carried three days' rations. He traced their route through the country to a small village—"I do not know the name of this village." There they found five horses tied, and they were attempting to steal them when the Mexicans opened fire from the town and killed his companions. Then they swarmed out and surrounded him. He ran and dodged and hid, sometimes shooting a Mexican from concealment, finally eluded them, and reached his home "without booty, without my companions, exhausted, but not discouraged." Some of the Apaches blamed him for the loss of the two men, "but I said nothing. Having failed, it was only proper that I should remain silent."[19]

A few months later he managed to persuade two other warriors to join him on another raid. Again, the account presents the same accuracy of detail. They selected a village which they planned to attack at daylight, but the Mexicans discovered their camp and fired into it, killing one warrior. In the morning the two survivors encountered a company of Mexican soldiers coming from the south, well mounted and carrying supplies for a long journey.

18 Griswold, "The Fort Sill Apaches," s.v. "Geronimo."
19 Barrett, *op. cit.*, pp. 55–57.

Geronimo and his companion followed them until they were certain that the Mexicans were on their way to invade the Apache range north of the border; then they hurried ahead and warned their people. The Mexicans arrived immediately afterward. The Apaches drove them back, killing eight, but they lost another warrior and three small boys.

Geronimo, with twenty-five men, followed the trail of the invaders into Mexico and ambushed a cavalry company in a mountain defile. The troopers dismounted and placed their horses on the outside for a breastwork; thus Geronimo had to lead a hand-to-hand charge. A soldier struck him over the head with the butt of his gun, knocking him senseless. The warriors succeeded in killing all the Mexicans, but a number of their own men were killed. They bathed Geronimo's head in cold water and restored him to consciousness, and he was able to walk back on his return, though his wound was long in healing and he carried the scar the rest of his life. His final summation: "In this fight we had lost so heavily that there really was no glory in our victory, and we returned to Arizona. No one seemed to want to go on the warpath again that year."[20]

The following summer, with twelve warriors, Geronimo made another raid into Mexico. They sighted a mule train loaded with provisions and attacked. The drivers fled, and the Apaches started back with the booty, but unknown to them, Mexican troops were in pursuit. As they were eating their breakfast one morning, careless of the usual precautions, the soldiers fired on them. Geronimo was struck near the eye by a glancing bullet, and as the raiders all scattered for cover he received a slight flesh wound in the side. They "returned home empty-handed" with "not even a partial victory to report. I again returned wounded, but I was not yet discouraged. Again I was blamed by our people, and again I had no reply."[21]

Geronimo remained at the home *rancheria* while his wounds

20 *Ibid.*, pp. 57–61.
21 *Ibid.*, pp. 61–63.

were healing. Many of the men went out on a hunt, and some of them went north to trade with the Navahos for blankets, leaving only about twenty in camp. One night three companies of invading Mexican troops surrounded the settlement. In the morning, as the women were lighting the fires (they used the primitive drill, twirling a stick in a notch in a flat piece of wood[22]), ready to prepare breakfast, the soldiers opened fire. Many women and children and a few warriors were killed, and four women were captured. Among the dead were Geronimo's wife, Nana-tha-thtith, and her child. There was no chance for defense. Geronimo managed to snatch his bow and arrows, and although his eye was still swollen shut he hit one of the officers. But all the survivors fled for safety in the rocks while the troopers burned their lodges and carried off their ponies, weapons, provisions, and blankets. A few warriors who had been able to secure their weapons followed the invaders back to Mexico but were unable to attack them.

The captive women were taken to Sonora as slaves. Some years later they managed to escape and were finding their way back through the mountains. One night when they were sleeping inside a brush wickiup they had built as a temporary shelter, they heard growling outside. Their campfire had burned low, and one of them, a girl of about seventeen, started to replenish it when a mountain lion crashed through the wall, sprang upon her, and dragged her some distance. She fought him as best she could, and the others came to her assistance, finally killing him with their knives. Then they stayed in the mountains for about a month and nursed the girl until she was able to walk. They finally rejoined their people, but she carried the scars throughout her life.[23]

During this same period, there was another invasion of American territory by Mexican troops, this time from Chihuahua. They struck the *rancheria* of Geronimo's cousin Nah-thle-tla, who was to become the mother of Jason Betzinez. She was married to a Bedonkohe warrior and was living with her husband and her two

---

[22] For a description of the method, see Opler, *An Apache Life-Way*, pp. 393–94.
[23] Barrett, *op. cit.*, pp. 63–67, 68n.

children in the mountains south of the present Lordsburg, New Mexico. Her husband had gone on a war expedition to Mexico, where they were joined by Juh. Near Namiquipa, in Chihuahua, the combined force attacked the Mexicans and, through Juh's brilliant generalship, defeated them, but Nah-thle-tla's husband was killed.

The women and children felt safe on the American side of the border, but the avenging Mexican force overran the defenseless camp, killing many of the people and capturing others, including Nah-thle-tla and her children. The captives were taken to the city of Chihuahua and distributed as slaves. Nah-thle-tla's children were taken from her, and she never saw them again. After several months of servitude there, she and another young woman were sold to a wealthy Mexican from Santa Fe. They were loaded into an ox cart, caged in with webbed rope and guarded by a vicious dog tied in front, and taken on the long journey, traveling past the familiar landmarks of their country on the way. In Santa Fe Nah-thle-tla worked at household tasks for her owners until she finally managed to escape and find her way home. She had traveled at least two hundred fifty miles through unknown mountains, eating piñon nuts, seeds, and berries and going on foot until she managed to steal a pony near the end of her journey.[24] Such epics of stamina and resourcefulness were repeated many times in Apache experience.[25]

Geronimo spoke bitterly of the fate of captives. Not many escaped, he said, and "Those who did not escape were slaves to the Mexicans, or perhaps even more degraded." But it appears from the stories of the women who managed to escape that most of them had not been unkindly treated in their servitude. Working with typical Apache energy and resourcefulness, they must have made valuable house servants. Geronimo contrasted their slavery with the Apache custom of adopting captive Mexican women and children as members of their tribes.[26] This was indeed true, but he

24 Betzinez, *I Fought with Geronimo*, pp. 19–24.
25 See, for example, *ibid.*, pp. 10–14.
26 Barrett, *op. cit.*, pp. 67–68.

51

failed to add that captive men were sometimes fiendishly tortured by the Apaches.

In the summer following the Mexican attack on his *rancheria*, Geronimo, with the death of another wife and child to avenge, enlisted eight men for a raid. They captured a long pack train loaded with blankets, calico, saddles, tinware, and loaf sugar. On their journey home, in the Santa Catalina Mountains of Arizona, northeast of the little adobe village of Tucson, they met an American driving a mule train. He fled, and they took his train. It was loaded with cheese, no doubt to supply the new boom towns of gold-rush California. At that time Americans traveling on the California Trail were comparatively safe from raids, but on this occasion the temptation had been too great for the Apaches to resist.

When the raiders returned home, Mangas Coloradas assembled the tribe, and there was feasting on mule meat, all night dancing, and distribution of the spoils. Mexican cavalry followed, reaching the place three days later, but this time the Apaches were prepared. The warriors went out in two divisions, one under Mangas and the other under Geronimo, hoping to surround and destroy the whole company and take their horses. But the Mexicans avoided the trap, although ten of their men were killed with the loss of only one Apache. They then retreated, and thirty Apache warriors followed them far into Mexico. "No more troops came that winter," said Geronimo. And for a long time the Apaches reveled in their supply of blankets, clothing, sugar, and cheese.[27]

The following summer Geronimo "selected three warriors" for his raid. They hid near a town and watched. At midday no one seemed to be stirring; thus, they chose the siesta hour for their attack. The people fled, and they looked through the houses, where they found many "curious things. These Mexicans kept many more kinds of property than the Apaches did." The raiders drove in a herd of horses and mules, loaded them, and returned safely to Arizona. There was more feasting and dancing and distribution of

27 *Ibid.*, pp. 69–71.

presents—enough supplies "to last our whole tribe for a year or more." Geronimo considered this "perhaps the most successful raid ever made by us into Mexican territory."[28]

The next year Geronimo went out with a larger party—twenty men. Before they left, they provided for the safety of their families. The whole band scattered, to reassemble about forty miles away. Thus "it would be hard for the Mexicans to trail them and we would know where to find [them] when we returned." In Sonora the raiders captured a pack train that proved to be loaded with mescal. At camp that night they "began to get drunk and fight each other. I, too, drank enough mescal to feel the effects of it, but I was not drunk." He tried to stop the fighting, but failed. He tried to put out a guard, but nobody would serve. He expected an attack from Mexican troops at any moment. Finally, the warriors stopped fighting, and sank into a stupor. Then he poured out the remaining mescal—this must have been a heart-breaking experience for an Apache—put out the fire, and removed the pack mules to a distance from camp. Next, he attended to those who had been wounded in the brawl, cutting an arrowhead from the leg of one, pulling a spear point from the shoulder of another, and guarded the camp through the night. The following day they loaded their wounded on the mules and started for Arizona. On the way they captured a herd of cattle and started to drive them home. This proved to be difficult—driving cattle on foot and caring for the wounded—but they arrived home safely and gave another feast on mule meat. Then they killed all the cattle, dried the beef, and dressed the hides. "These were the first cattle we ever had." They decided to capture more.[29]

During the next summer Geronimo went out with four warriors. All their previous raids had been on foot because of the necessity for concealment, but now they rode, for this time they were after cattle. They went down into Sonora as far south as the mouth of the Yaqui River and looked out on the Gulf of California—"a

28 *Ibid.*, pp. 71–73.
29 *Ibid.*, pp. 73–77.

great lake extending beyond the reach of sight," this mountain people's first view of the sea. They captured about sixty cattle and started home, grazing them in valleys on the way. They returned to more dancing, feasting, and butchering, drying, and storing of the meat.[30]

On the next year's raid, Geronimo, with nine warriors, collected "many" horses and mules, but Mexican troops followed and recovered the whole herd. The Apaches returned to Arizona with no booty. The following summer he went out with thirty mounted warriors, "collected all the horses, mules, and cattle we wanted," killing "about fifty Mexicans" in the process, and returned home with presents and feasting. The next year Mangas Coloradas led the raid with eight mounted warriors, including Geronimo. They found a herd of cattle, fought the *vaqueros*, killing two, and made off with the herd, but Mexican troops armed with rifles came upon them, recovered the cattle, and took out after the raiders. The Apaches, unable to reach them with only bows and arrows, left their ponies and sought cover in the timber. The Mexicans then abandoned the pursuit, collected the Indians' ponies, and drove the cattle back across the plains. The raiders returned home with no victory to report, with no spoils to divide, and without their own horses. "This expedition was considered disgraceful," said Geronimo. The members of the party "felt keenly the taunts of the other warriors" and wanted to return. Mangas would not lead them, but Geronimo set out with them and raided several settlements, returning with horses and mules loaded with provisions, saddles, and blankets. Again there was feasting, dancing, and dividing of the booty, but Mangas would not accept any of it.[31]

"About a year after this" Mexican troops again crossed the border and made away with all the horses and mules of the band. Geronimo took twenty warriors and trailed them. They found the stock at a cattle ranch in Sonora. They fought with the *vaqueros*, again killing two, and made off with their own animals and the

30 *Ibid.*, pp. 77–78.
31 *Ibid.*, pp. 79–83.

Mexicans' herd. Nine *vaqueros* followed their trail. Geronimo sent the stock ahead while he and three other warriors guarded the rear. One night near the Arizona line they saw the *vaqueros* camp for the night and picket their mounts. They stole into the camp, cut the horses loose, and silently led them away, leaving the *vaqueros* asleep. "What these nine cowboys did next morning I do not know. . . . I know they did not follow us, for we were not molested. When we arrived in camp at home there was great rejoicing in the tribe. It was considered a good trick to get the Mexicans' horses and leave them asleep in the mountains. It was a long time before we again went into Mexico or were disturbed by the Mexicans."[32]

Strangely enough, the American officials were apparently unaware of these frequent invasions of United States territory by Mexican troops, but they knew that the Apaches were raiding in Mexico. The relations of the Mimbreno and Warm Springs tribes with the Americans had improved dramatically since the treaty made in 1852. The Indians tried to observe the peace, even sometimes in the face of great provocation. Among several incidents was one leading to the death of Cuchillo Negro. Some Indians living to the north had killed the agent to the Navahos. In the spring of 1857 a military expedition sent out to punish them found it easier to attack the chief's *rancheria* near the upper Mimbres. Six or seven Apaches, including Cuchillo Negro, were killed, and nine women and children were captured. As far as can be determined, Cuchillo Negro was succeeded as chief of the Warm Springs tribe by Delgadito.[33]

In 1855 these Apaches were subjected to another pressure familiar in United States–Indian relations. Dr. Michael Steck had been appointed as agent to all the southern tribes from the Mescaleros to the Chiricahuas. He induced the Mescaleros and all the Warm Springs and Mimbreno leaders except Mangas Coloradas, who adroitly evaded him, to come to Fort Thorn on the Rio

32 *Ibid.*, pp. 83–85.
33 Thrapp, *Victorio*, pp. 51–52, 54–55; Betzinez, *op. cit.*, p. 9 and n.; Davis, *The Truth about Geronimo*, p. 111.

Grande and sign a land cession treaty. The Warm Springs tribe and the Mimbrenos ceded about twelve thousand to fifteen thousand square miles, retaining a reservation of about two thousand to twenty-five hundred square miles comprising their heartland. Steck was honest and hard working and sincerely interested in the welfare of the Indians, but his real sympathy was with the expanding white frontier. This reservation, he reported, contained the copper mines and the gold mine and deposits of iron, silver, and lead. He favored removing these Indians and the Mescaleros to the Gila; they would be better off living with the tribes of that region [these would include Geronimo and the Bedonkohes] far from white communities and travel routes, and at the same time "you throw open for settlement the finest and most desirable portion of New Mexico." The Senate, no doubt with this in mind, failed to approve the treaty,[34] leaving the Indians with no title to their homeland.

Meanwhile, traffic was increasing on the California Trail to the south, threading Doubtful Canyon southwest of the Mimbrenos' main settlements and Apache Pass in the country of the Chiricahuas, and small parties were constantly traveling it in safety. On September 16, 1858, the Butterfield Stage Line, carrying mail and passengers from Saint Louis to San Francisco, began its twice-weekly service on the route, with a station at each of those strategic places. On Christmas Day that year Steck set out on this trail for Apache Pass, where he held his first conference with the Chiricahuas. They had committed no depredations on the trail for the past two years, he said, but they raided regularly in Mexico. He held a friendly council with them and gave them some presents. By this time he had plans to remove them also to the Gila with the Mimbrenos, Mogollons (Warm Springs tribe), and Mescaleros.[35] This lightly expressed policy of uprooting tribes and crowding them together in one place was to have monstrous consequences in future years.

[34] Thrapp, *Victorio*, pp. 42–46.
[35] *Ibid.*, pp. 61–64; Secretary of the Interior, *Annual Report*, 1859, pp. 713–14.

Geronimo seems to have been present at this conference. As he told it, "One day during the time that the soldiers were stationed at Apache Pass I made a treaty with the post. This was done by shaking hands and promising to be brothers. Cochise and Mangus-Colorado did likewise. I do not know the name of the officer in command, but this was the first regiment that ever came to Apache Pass." There were no soldiers stationed at Apache Pass and no military post there until after a subsequent hostile encounter. His "soldiers" may have been a military escort with Steck, and the "post" may have been the Overland Mail station. And if his account does refer to the meeting with Steck, he was probably mistaken about the presence of Mangas Coloradas. But he placed the date with approximate accuracy, "about a year" before an event that occurred early in 1861, a very slight discrepancy in the memories of a long life remote from calendars and written records.[36]

An account showing the relative safety of travel through the Chiricahua and Mimbreno country at that time was written by Hank Smith, who later became a pioneer settler on the High Plains (the Llano Estacado) of West Texas. It seems to have been in the spring of 1859 that he was employed to drive twelve hundred head of cattle from Fort Buchanan, west of the Chiricahuas' range, to Fort Bliss at El Paso. He had twelve Mexican *vaqueros* to assist him, and a military escort of a sergeant and ten troopers accompanied him as far as Apache Pass. Large bands of Indians—fifty or a hundred warriors—met him, but always in a friendly spirit, making no attempt to scatter or steal the cattle. On two occasions they requested (and received) a beef to butcher and eat; at other times they conducted the drovers to water holes and assisted in watering the herd, asking a beef or two in payment. At the Mimbres River Mangas Coloradas' band was friendly and helpful. There the men rested the herd for two days, engaging in racing contests with the Indians. At Fort Bliss they turned the cattle over

---

[36] Barrett, *op. cit.*, p. 116.

to the commissary department, short only twenty head for the entire journey.[37]

The following October, Steck, with no military escort, set out again to the west. He met about eight hundred of the Gila bands and distributed presents to them. Geronimo may have been present at this meeting, though he did not mention it in his reminiscences. Steck continued on his way to the broad San Simon Valley east of Cochise's mountains, where he met that chief with about four hundred Chiricahuas and distributed more presents. Cochise delivered to him three stolen animals and promised to watch over the mail coaches and travelers on the California Trail.[38]

But such peaceable relations were not to last.

[37] Hattie M. Anderson, "Mining and Indian Fighting in Arizona and New Mexico— Memoirs of Hank Smith," *Panhandle-Plains Historical Review*, Vol. I, pp. 81–86.
[38] Thrapp, *Victorio*, p. 65.

CHAPTER 4

TOO MANY WHITE MEN

The trouble began with mining development and settlements around Santa Rita in the heart of the Mimbrenos' country. With Steck's encouragement and some assistance in breaking up the land and repairing their *acequias*, they and their Warm Springs friends were farming industriously in the Mimbres Valley and along the Alamosa River below the springs, but it was evident that they would soon be crowded out. In the summer of 1858 work was resumed on the abandoned copper mines. The next year thirty settlers started Mowry City in the wide valley of the Mimbres River below the mines, all on tribal land. Also in 1859 a rich gold strike was made in the mountains northwest of Santa Rita, and the mushroom town of Pinos Altos sprang up there.

The miners were lawless and violent, with no respect for the Indians whose lands they were invading. They also encouraged Mexicans to come in and grow food for their mining camps and feed for their horses. This policy was, of course, a direct affront to the Indians, who had never accepted peace with that hated people, and in the inevitable conflicts the miners supported their protégés. In 1860 the army established Fort McLane a few miles to the south, but the miners openly defied the military authorities when they attempted to protect the Indians.[1]

Steck's report for 1860 gave a gloomy picture of the Mimbrenos. They had become destitute through the loss of game in the area and along the California Trail and demoralized by the whiskey that flowed freely near the settlements. They had been accused of killing some of the settlers' cattle, but considering their destitution and the fact that these unwelcome immigrants were operating in the heart of their country, the complaints were surprisingly few. Anglo and Mexican horse thieves were active in the area, and the Indians were blamed for their depredations also.[2]

Steck was sincerely concerned at the prospect that they would soon be dispossessed and homeless. By this time he had their reservation on the Gila selected, a fifteen-mile-square area including Mangas Creek (then called Santa Lucia Creek) and Springs and the rolling grasslands surrounding it, a few miles northwest of the mining area. He encouraged the Indians to farm there, and in 1859 he reported a well-tended tract about three miles long extending down the valley. But he was not satisfied merely to find a home for the harassed Mimbrenos. He wanted to include in the settlement the Mescaleros from their country east of the Rio Grande, the Mimbrenos' Warm Springs relatives, and the untouched Chiricahuas secure in their mountains to the southwest.

The following year New Mexico Superintendent James L. Collins recommended that the unrelated Jicarilla Apaches from the distant mountains of northern New Mexico should also be concentrated there. "The proposed change," he said, "would bring the whole Apache tribe together. . . . When thus united they would form a nation of eight or nine thousand souls. . . . All cultivating more or less, they could in a short time, if favorably located, be made self-supporting. . . . They are certainly more inclined to labor

---

1 Hank Smith was in the party that made the gold discovery. His account of the strike, the ensuing gold rush, and the riotous life of the settlement may be found in Anderson, "Mining and Indian Fighting," pp. 87–93, 101, 114. For the date, see p. 88n. See also Secretary of the Interior, *Annual Report*, 1858, pp. 548–49.

2 Thrapp, *Victorio*, pp. 65–66.

than many of the other tribes." Nobody wondered how they could all support themselves on this tiny acreage. Commissioner of Indian Affairs A. B. Greenwood gave Washington's blessing to the plan, and the land was set aside that year. As for Geronimo, he did not know that he was included in this policy. It was never carried out, and the Gila reservation was restored to the public domain in 1867.[3] Apache history at this period was dominated not by Washington but by swiftly moving events in the Southwest. In them Geronimo was deeply involved.

Characteristically, it was the miners who sparked the smouldering hostility into open war. It was almost certainly in the spring or summer of 1860 that Mangas Coloradas, always trying to keep the peace, went alone on a friendly visit to the Pinos Altos camp.[4] As James Kaywaykla heard the story later, Geronimo and two Warm Springs leaders, Victorio and Loco, whose names would soon be household words in the Southwest, pleaded with him not to trust the miners. Their warnings were justified; the miners tied him to a tree and lashed him unmercifully with their bullwhips. This action was not only cruel but also stupid. Mangas Coloradas was the acknowledged leader of all the Apaches of southwestern New Mexico and the father-in-law of Cochise. Understandably he went on the warpath, and naturally he went to enlist Cochise.[5]

Cochise had observed his pledge to protect travelers on the trail, and he maintained friendly relations with the employees and drivers he met at the Butterfield station at Apache Pass. He even had a contract to supply the station with wood during the winter of 1860/61. But apparently he joined Mangas Coloradas in the war against the white intruders in the latter's country. The fight-

3 Secretary of the Interior, *Annual Report*, 1859, pp. 713–14; 1860, pp. 243, 385. See also Thrapp, *op. cit.*, pp. 63–66 and n. 16.
4 Hank Smith told of a visit the chief made to the mines in the spring; Anderson, *op. cit.*, p. 91 and n. The Indians went to war in September. The atrocity referred to above might have taken place on this spring visit or on a somewhat later one. It would have taken some time for the chief's wounds to heal and for him to collect his warriors. Clum gives the year 1858, which clearly places the event too early; the Apaches at that time were still keeping the peace. See Woodworth Clum, *Apache Agent: The Story of John P. Clum*, pp. 29–32.
5 Ball, *In the Days of Victorio*, pp. 46–47.

ing began on September 27, and a bloody war it was. The Apaches gathered the Mexicans' corn, drove off the Mexicans' sheep and the miners' horses, and attacked the settlements and supply trains. They overwhelmed an emigrant train on the California Road, killing sixteen men, burning the wagons, and making off with four hundred cattle and nine hundred sheep, with only the women and children escaping in a wagon drawn by a swift team. The miners retaliated with attacks on the Apaches' *rancherias*, and pitched battles were fought between miners and Mexicans on the one hand and Indians on the other.[6] Apparently Geronimo was engaged in this fighting. He may have been referring to it when he said, "I had not been wronged, but some of my people had been, and I fought with my tribe."[7]

Soon an arbitrary act of the military brought the war to the country of the Chiricahuas. An eleven- or twelve-year-old boy of uncertain antecedents, probably half Irish and half Mexican, disappeared with some cattle from a squalid ranch home west of the Chiricahuas' range. It is now known that he was taken by a tribe living on the Gila and given to the White Mountain Apaches.[8] Later, as an adult under the name of Mickey Free, he would become an army interpreter in dealing with the Chiricahuas and their associates. Now, in late January, 1861, Second Lieutenant George Nicholas Bascom was sent from Fort Buchanan with fifty-four men to Apache Pass to recover him. Cochise, unsuspecting, came with his wife and young son, a brother, and two nephews to deliver some wood. At a parley inside the army tent, Bascom demanded the stolen boy. Cochise truthfully protested his innocence of the kidnaping but promised to find him if possible. Bascom did not believe the chief and said he would hold him hostage until the boy should be recovered. Cochise then whipped out his knife, slashed the tent wall, and escaped, but Bascom held the other Indians as prisoners. Cochise then captured three men

---

6 Anderson, *op. cit.*, pp. 94–105, 111–15.
7 Barrett, *Geronimo's Story of His Life*, p. 114; Clum, *op. cit.*, pp. 29–32.
8 Goodwin, "Experiences of an Indian Scout" (part 2), p. 38. Goodwin's informant was the boy's Apache foster brother.

from the stage station and a passing wagon train and offered to exchange. Bascom refused unless Cochise would produce the boy.

As February dragged by, there was some fighting and maneuvering which can be only glimpsed. Bascom sent to Fort Buchanan for reinforcements and for medical assistance apparently to treat his wounded; seventy more soldiers arrived under First Lieutenant Isaiah N. Moore. The affair ended with Cochise killing his hostages and the two officers hanging theirs.[9] Cochise's wife and child were afterwards taken to Fort Buchanan and released. According to James Kaywaykla, the child was Naiche, destined to be Geronimo's closest associate in his wars and his imprisonment.[10] If this story is correct, the woman was Dos-teh-seh, the daughter of Mangas Coloradas.

At this time Geronimo and other Bedonkohes under his leadership were living among the Chiricahuas. It was probably at this period that he married a close relative of the Cochise family, a Chiricahua-Nednai woman named She-gha. Her brother, Yahnozha, was to become one of his most dependable warriors. Then at some undetermined date he took a third wife, a woman of his own Bedonkohe band named Shtsha-she.[11] Throughout Geronimo's life as a warrior he held to this pattern of two or sometimes three wives at once—"overlapping," as Daklugie expressed it—and Nana-tha-thtith had been killed some time before.

Geronimo was apparently not present when Cochise cut his way out of the tent, for his account is very confused, but he participated in the ensuing events and related them clearly. "In a few days

9 This story has been told many times. Good accounts with critical evaluation of all the sources may be found in Lockwood, *The Apache Indians*, pp. 100–107, and Thrapp, *Conquest of Apacheria*, pp. 15–18.

10 Ball, *op. cit.*, p. 155. Kaywaykla called the child an "infant," but Naiche was probably about five years old in 1861.

11 Griswold, "The Fort Sill Apaches," s.v. "Geronimo." The Apaches do not remember the name of the wife related to Cochise, but I found a wife named She-gha, who was probably she and who lived until 1887. It is possible that "She-gha" is simply another spelling for "Shtsha-she," but Miss Elaine Clark, a careful student of the Apache language, believes them to be different names; letter to Angie Debo, June 5, 1973. She concedes the possibility, however, that they may be identical, in which case I have confused the two throughout my narrative, for it would have been Shtsha-she who remained with Geronimo until 1887 while the sister of Yahnozha dropped out of sight before that time and is still nameless.

[after the tent episode]," he said, "we organized in the mountains and returned to fight the soldiers. There were two tribes—the Bedonkohe and the Chokonen [Chiricahua] Apaches, both commanded by Cochise. After a few days' skirmishing we attacked a freight train that was coming in with supplies for the Fort. We killed some of the men and captured the others. These prisoners our chief offered to trade for the Indians whom the soldiers had captured at the massacre in the tent. This the officers refused, so we killed our prisoners, disbanded, and went into hiding in the mountains. Of those who took part in this affair I am the only one now living."[12]

According to Jason Betzinez, the occurrence, which the Apaches characterized as the "Cut through the Tent" affair, aroused much indignation and interest even among bands distant from the Chiricahua country. "I have heard my parents as well as others discuss it many a time," he said.[13] Geronimo, to whom raiding was a way of life, described its effect with typical understatement: "After this trouble all of the Indians agreed not to be friendly with the white men any more. There was no general engagement, but a long struggle followed. Sometimes we attacked the white men—sometimes they attacked us. First a few Indians would be killed and then a few soldiers. I think the killing was about equal on each side. The number killed in these troubles did not amount to much, but this treachery on the part of the soldiers had angered the Indians and revived memories of other wrongs, so that we never again trusted the United States troops." But he put in a good word for Steck: "I do not think that the agent had anything to do with planning this, for he had always treated us well."[14]

At this very time events in the Southwest were controlled by the white man's Civil War. On February 8, while Cochise and the army officers were engaged in diplomatic and arrow-and-rifle

12 Barrett, *op. cit.*, pp. 115, 117. It was certainly Barrett's error to attribute the tent incident to Mangas Coloradas instead of Cochise. Geronimo could not have made that mistake.
13 Betzinez, *I Fought with Geronimo*, p. 41.
14 Barrett, *op. cit.*, pp. 116, 118.

skirmishing around Apache Pass, a government for the Confederate States of America was established at Montgomery, Alabama. With much of the Butterfield Stage route in Confederate or disputed territory, it was decided in late March to abandon the service. The transcontinental mail and stage traffic was shifted to the great Overland Trail through Nebraska and over the mountains by the South Pass in Wyoming. Butterfield employees began to dismantle the stations and move the equipment from New Mexico and Arizona. One party under General Manager McNees, bringing in this property from the west, was ambushed and wiped out near the Doubtful Pass station by Indians believed to be led by Cochise.[15]

During July the federal military posts in New Mexico and Arizona were being rapidly evacuated as an invading Confederate force of Texans under Indian-hating Colonel John Robert Baylor advanced up the Rio Grande from El Paso; and Steck found it necessary to abandon his agency. At the same time, the Indians swept away all the livestock from the area around the copper mines, and the mines were deserted. On September 27, according to a newspaper published at Mesilla on the Rio Grande, Mangas Coloradas' warriors even attacked the town of Pinos Altos and fought an all-day battle with its defenders. The gold miners abandoned the place, and the settlers in the Mimbres Valley fled, leaving their houses and growing crops. The triumphant Indians believed they had driven out the soldiers and cleared their country of white intruders.[16] Geronimo's name does not appear in reports of these events, for he had not yet risen to prominence on the American side of the border, but there is no doubt that he was an active participant.

On August 1 Baylor proclaimed himself the military governor of a "Territory of Arizona" comprising the southern half of the two present states, with his headquarters at Mesilla. He organized

15 Hattie M. Anderson, "With the Confederates in New Mexico during the Civil War —Memoirs of Hank Smith," *Panhandle-Plains Historical Review*, Vol. II, pp. 80–82.
16 *Ibid.*, pp. 65–69; Secretary of the Interior, *Annual Report*, 1861, pp. 732–33; Thrapp, *Victorio*, p. 75.

two volunteer companies, the Arizona Rangers and the Arizona Guards, to reopen the road from the Rio Grande to Tucson. On March 20, 1862, he sent the following instructions to the captain of the Guards at Tucson: "I learn from Lieut. J. J. Jackson that the Indians have been in to your post for the purpose of making a treaty. The Congress of the Confederate States has passed a law declaring extermination to all hostile Indians. You will therefore use all means to persuade the Apaches or any tribe to come in for the purpose of making peace, and when you get them together kill all the grown Indians and take the children prisoners and sell them to defray the expense of killing the Indians. Buy whisky and such other goods as may be necessary for the Indians and I will order vouchers given to cover the amount expended. . . . Say nothing of your orders until the time arrives. . . ."

This order was disavowed by President Jefferson Davis and Secretary of War George Wythe Randolph. Later Baylor wrote a letter defending it. He had learned of this "law," he said, from a newspaper article, supposed it to be authentic, "and feeling convinced (as I do still) that such a policy was the only one suitable to the hostile and treacherous tribes, I acted on it."[17]

The Apaches continued raiding and killing at will throughout Confederate "Arizona," but the Texans were soon driven out by the Colorado Volunteers. At the same time, the summer of 1862, a "California Column" of eighteen hundred Union men under Brigadier General James Henry Carleton was advancing from the west. The Apaches under Cochise and Mangas Coloradas prepared an ambush high in the rocks above Apache Pass. They selected a strategic site overlooking the abandoned stage station and the nearby spring that meant life or death to men and animals on the trail.

They allowed a reconnaissance detail to go through on June 25 without open resistance, professing friendship but killing 3 men who had strayed from the command. Perhaps they were not yet

17 George Wythe Baylor, *John Robert Baylor, Confederate Governor of Arizona*, pp. 12–15.

66

in position. Then on July 14 an advance party under Captain Thomas L. Roberts, with 122 men and two mountain howitzers, entered the pass. When the soldiers approached the ambush, the Indians from their hidden positions, began picking them off, killing one and wounding others. Then the troops set up the howitzers and trained them on the heights, and when the shells began bursting among the Indians they withdrew. Cremony said that one of them told him later, "We were getting along well enough until you began firing wagons at us."

Cremony, who had been living in San Diego, had enlisted in the California Column and was in command of the supply train that was slowly advancing toward the pass. Roberts sent six men back to warn him, and some mounted Apaches pursued them. They all escaped but a private, who was cut off and surrounded. As the Indians were circling him for the kill, he managed to wound the impressive looking warrior who was in command. It is now known that the man wounded was Mangas Coloradas. The Apaches then abandoned the pursuit and concentrated on helping their stricken chief. Roberts went back to protect the train, and although the Apaches attacked it from the heights, the howitzers were again brought into play and the loaded wagons came through. The main column under Carleton followed without incident. The Apaches had failed. Carleton then left a detail to build a fort commanding the spring. This was the beginning of Fort Bowie, destined to a prominent place in the life of Geronimo and the history of his people. The date was July 28, 1862.[18]

It is significant that in this engagement the Indians, or at least many of them, were armed with rifles, which came mainly from white men they had killed—an indication of the extent of their depredations on the American side of the border during the two

---

[18] Thrapp, *Victorio*, pp. 79–81; Lockwood, *op. cit.*, pp. 135–41; Martin F. Schmitt (ed.), *General George Crook: His Autobiography*, pp. 163–64 and n. 5; Ball, *op. cit.*, p. 47. Cremony told an exciting story of this fight in *Life among the Apaches*, pp. 144, 155–67, but his account is unreliable. For example, he said the howitzers killed sixty-three Apaches. Roberts, an army officer, no doubt inclined to overestimate enemy losses, reported only ten killed for the entire engagement; the Indians said that none of their warriors was killed, but that several were wounded.

years since they began their war.[19] The use of these weapons also brought a new dimension to their raids.

Strangely enough, the account of this fight at Apache Pass does not appear in Geronimo's dictated memoirs. Tradition says that he was there, and it is incredible that he would have failed to participate in an attack so carefully planned and involving his closest associates. Perhaps he simply forgot to mention it. He was intimately connected with the next incident.

After the battle in the pass, Carleton proceeded without difficulty to the Rio Grande, and on September 18 he assumed command of the Department of New Mexico. He at once began to issue orders to his subordinates to kill all Indian men wherever found. If they should attempt to treat for peace they were to be told that "you have been sent to punish them for their treachery and their crimes; that you have no power to make peace."[20] (The historian Dan L. Thrapp characterizes Carleton as "the Union Baylor.") Within the next few months he rounded up the Mescaleros, and within a year, the Navahos, and he placed them on a small tract on the Pecos River named the Bosque Redondo. There the two tribes fought each other and starved and suffered. He tried to do the same to the related tribes he classed as "Gilas." Their subjugation was entrusted to Brigadier General Joseph Rodman West, who fully shared his views.

West proceeded to the Gila and made his camp near Mangas Springs, on the short-lived Santa Lucia Reservation, in preparation for a campaign against Mangas Coloradas and his adherents.[21] But these Apaches, like other Indians, were unable to grasp the concept of an overall government entity. Every military command was a separate unit. Geronimo innocently described the establishment of this base in the heart of his mountains under orders of the enemy of Apache Pass: "About ten years [after the boundary survey of 1851] some more white men came. These were all

[19] For these depredations, see Secretary of the Interior, *Annual Report*, 1863, pp. 503–504.
[20] C. L. Sonnichsen, *The Mescalero Apaches*, pp. 98–99.
[21] Thrapp, *Victorio*, p. 83.

warriors. They made their camp on the Gila River south [actually southwest] of Hot Springs. At first they were friendly and we did not dislike them, but they were not as good as those who came first."[22]

Then he went on with his characteristic understatement, "After about a year some trouble arose between them and the Indians." Trouble indeed! It was the murder of Mangas Coloradas on January 18, 1863. There are several versions, but all agree that he was lured to his fate by a profession of peace. A party of gold seekers under the mountain man Joseph Reddeford Walker were traveling through the area on their way west and had camped at abandoned Fort McLane. It occurred to them that by capturing Mangas Coloradas and holding him as a hostage they would be ensured a safe journey; then if all went well, they would release him. Men from this party and a unit of the California Column accordingly got possession of the chief under a flag of truce at the abandoned Pinos Altos settlement. Then West appeared and took the prisoner. He placed him under guard with a strong indication of his wishes, and during the night the chief was shot by the guards "while attempting to escape." The army surgeon cut off his head, "boiled it in a great black pot," according to James Kaywaykla, and sent the skull to a phrenologist, who reported that it was larger than Daniel Webster's. It was afterwards used as a lecture exhibit.[23]

Geronimo characterized the murder of Mangas Coloradas as "perhaps the greatest wrong ever done to the Indians." His account shows the serious consideration they gave to what they thought was an opportunity to make peace. Apparently the chief and his followers had not left the Chiricahua country after the fight in the pass. There they received a report, perhaps as part of the plot, of the friendliness of Apache Tejo, a tiny settlement in the vicinity of their old home, now cleared of the miners and settlers who had

22 Barrett, *op. cit.*, p. 114.

23 Daniel Ellis Conner, *Joseph Reddeford Walker and the Arizona Adventure*, pp. 32–42; Thrapp, *Conquest of Apacheria*, pp. 20–23; Thrapp, *Victorio*, pp. 82–83; Ball, *op. cit.*, p. 48. Conner's eyewitness account seems to be the correct one.

driven them to war. The chief and three warriors "went to Apache Tejo and held a council with these citizens and soldiers. They told him that if he would come with his tribe and live near them, they would issue to him from the Government, blankets, flour, provisions, beef, and all manner of supplies." This sounded like the days of the absent Steck. The chief promised to return with his answer within two weeks.

"When he came back to our settlement he assembled the whole tribe in council." This, of course, included the Bedonkohes. "I did not believe that the people at Apache Tejo would do as they said and therefore I opposed the plan," said Geronimo, "but it was decided that with part of the tribe Mangus-Colorado would return to Apache Tejo and receive an issue of rations and supplies." If all turned out as represented, "the remainder of the tribe would join him and we would make our permanent home at Apache Tejo. . . . We gave almost all of our arms and ammunition to the party going to Apache Tejo, so that in case there should be treachery they would be prepared for any surprise." About half the tribe accompanied the chief, while the remainder remained in Arizona under the charge of Geronimo.[24]

But the arms and ammunition did not help the Apaches who went with Mangas Coloradas. Trustingly, he put himself in the power of the conspirators, thus forfeiting his life against any attempt at rescue. The next day, while his family and friends anxiously waited for word of his release, the soldiers attacked their camp, killing eleven or twelve, and, it is said, decorating the bridles of their horses with the scalps. Several fights followed, and two Apache camps were destroyed.[25]

Meanwhile, in Arizona the rest of the band with Geronimo was waiting for news of the chief and his party. "No word ever came to us from them. From other sources, however, we heard that they had been treacherously captured and slain. In this dilemma we

24 Barrett, *op. cit.*, pp. 119–20.
25 Conner, *op. cit.*, pp. 41–42; Lockwood, *op. cit.*, pp. 145–47; Thrapp, *Victorio*, p. 83.

did not know just exactly what to do, but fearing that the troops who had captured them would attack us, we retreated into the mountains near Apache Pass. . . . On this retreat, while passing through the mountains, we discovered four men with a herd of cattle. Two of the men were in front in a buggy and two were behind on horseback. We killed all four, . . . drove the cattle back into the mountains, made a camp, and began to kill the cattle and pack the meat." So much for the army's efforts to bring peace and order to the Southwest.

Before they finished their butchering, the Indians were attacked by cavalry, and one warrior, three women, and three children were killed. They had to fight with bows and arrows because most of their guns and ammunition were with the ill-fated band that had gone with Mangas Coloradas. They scattered, then reassembled at an appointed rendezvous about fifty miles away. Ten days later the same troops attacked again. The Indians retreated four miles back into the mountains, where they were joined by Cochise and some of his Chiricahua warriors, and he assumed command. A few days later more troopers attacked, and again they disbanded. This time the Bedonkohes "reassembled near their old camp vainly waiting for the return of Mangus-Colorado and our kinsmen. . . . Then a council was held, and it was believed that Mangus-Colorado was dead. I was elected Tribal Chief."[26]

One wonders whether this "election," like the previous one, was made up by Barrett. This time it might have occurred. The Bedonkohes had long followed the leadership of their great Mimbreno neighbor, Mangas Coloradas. Soon they were to become permanently merged with the Chiricahuas. If they did elect Geronimo as chief, his office ended with the separate existence of his tribe.

There was no successor to Mangas Coloradas. His son, Mangus, was young and lacked the drive required to establish authority over a people so strongly individualistic as the Apaches. The Mimbrenos united with their close relatives, the more numerous Warm

---

[26] Barrett, *op. cit.*, pp. 121–24.

Springs tribe. Delgadito was soon killed in a battle with Mexicans,[27] and Victorio and Loco became the Warm Springs chiefs.[28]

Victorio was to rise to a place of greatness in Apache history similar to that of Mangas Coloradas. He also was physically impressive—Kaywaykla, a Warm Springs child, always remembered his "majesty of form and bearing"—"I think he was the most nearly perfect human being I have ever seen"[29]—and he was to show military strategy approaching genius. His entire "foreign" policy revolved around his love for the secluded basin on the Alamosa River that enclosed the healing waters that gave the tribe its name. When allowed to remain in that area, he observed the peace; any attempt to relocate him brought war.

Loco, though a brave and able warrior, sought peace throughout his life. It was even said by the war party that his Spanish name Loco indicated that he was "crazy" enough to trust the white men.[30] A pleasanter explanation is that once, in a battle with Mexicans, he risked his life by running through a hail of bullets to rescue a wounded warrior; the Mexicans called him "that loco Apache," and the name stuck.[31] There was never any question of his courage and skill. Once he killed a grizzly bear singlehandedly, armed only with a knife. And Betzinez remembered seeing him send an arrow entirely through a beef on issue days during his later reservation experience.[32]

Another prominent Warm Springs leader was Geronimo's brother-in-law, the aged Nana. Although he appeared feeble and limped perceptibly from a "broken foot," he seemed indestructible. He was to become the most uncompromising of all Apaches in

[27] Davis, *The Truth about Geronimo*, p. 111. Davis was greatly confused about tribes and leaders, but he made this statement on the authority of Mangus and Loco.

[28] Modern Apaches are in disagreement about which of the two was the chief. Jason Betzinez, who grew up as a member of the Warm Springs tribe and knew both of them well stated that they were elected as dual chiefs (*op. cit.*, pp. 24–25, 49). This duality seems to fit the position they took in negotiating with government officials during the 1860's. Later the tribe became divided over war and peace, and it seems apparent that the war faction recognized Victorio and the peace party, Loco.

[29] Ball, *op. cit.*, p. 41.

[30] *Ibid.*, p. 28; but for tributes to his courage and integrity, see pp. 138–39.

[31] Ball interview, July 23, 1971.

[32] Betzinez, *op. cit.*, pp. 6, 33.

their wars against the white man, but to his people he was a wise, kind, grandfatherly figure. He was the granduncle of Kaywaykla, and the child revered him for his tenderness to the young, his consideration of the women, his courtesy to his fellow warriors, and his complete devotion to his tribe.[33]

Also in the band was Nonithian, who was probably the son of Delgadito but too young to succeed to leadership. He married Geronimo's widowed cousin Nah-thle-tla and was to become the father of Betzinez and a daughter later known as Ellen. Soon he was killed trying to separate two drunken, fighting relatives.[34] All these members of the Warm Springs band were to be closely associated with Geronimo in the troubled times following the murder of Mangas Coloradas.

The federal government now began to make plans for administering the area. A month after the chief's death—on February 24, 1863—Congress cut off the western half of New Mexico to form the Territory of Arizona, thus establishing the boundaries of the present states. Later that year Steck came back with elaborate plans for his Apache charges. Their reservation should be protected by a patent, military posts should be established nearby to control them and keep off white encroachment, and ample rations should be furnished for their subsistence. Military conquest was impossible, he believed, but even if it were accomplished, it would cost three million dollars annually, and the tribes could be fed for one-twentieth of that sum. They should be encouraged to accumulate property, and he warned against allowing them to perpetuate such "absurd" customs as destroying the property of the deceased. (The white people had not yet adopted the extravagant burial customs of a later century.) He also would curtail their numerous celebrations, especially the elaborate puberty ceremony for the girls, in which the parents impoverished themselves to feast the tribe and "make night hideous with their songs."[35]

[33] *Ibid.*, pp. 50–51; Ball, *op. cit.*, *passim.*
[34] Betzinez, *op. cit.*, pp. 9n., 24, 26, 38.
[35] Thrapp, *Victorio*, pp. 84–86.

This "womanhood" rite was, in fact, a beautiful celebration, free from the sadism that marks the puberty rites of many primitive people. The girl wore an elaborately trimmed buckskin dress and performed various rituals in and around an especially constructed tipi. She was advised of the duties and privileges of womanhood and was honored as the temporary embodiment of White Painted Woman. As one of the songs expressed it,

>≈≈≈≈≈≈≈≈≈≈≈≈≈≈≈≈≈≈

> You have started out on the good earth;
> You have started out with good moccasins;
> With moccasin strings of the rainbow,
>   you have started out;
> With moccasin strings of the sun's rays,
>   you have started out;
> In the midst of plenty you have started out.

>≈≈≈≈≈≈≈≈≈≈≈≈≈≈≈≈≈≈

Special dances were performed for her, especially the Dance of the Mountain Spirits by masked performers wearing fantastic pronged headdresses—a deeply moving spectacle. There was much use of *hoddentin*, the pollen of the tule rush or sometimes of corn, always sacred to the Apaches. Every detail of the complicated ritual was carried out with prayer and ceremonial exactness, and the girl's extended family shared in the preparations and the expenses.[36] Certainly it *was* expensive—as expensive as a daughter's wedding in modern white society.

The Apaches, of course, were unaware of Steck's well-meant designs against their culture. Victorio, Nana, Loco, and the sons and even the widow of Mangas Coloradas began to make cautious peace overtures to him. But he was unable to make any headway with them in view of Carleton's insistence that they should be caged up with the other prisoners on the Bosque Redondo.[37]

---

[36] Opler, *An Apache Life-Way*, pp. 82–134. I personally have been more stirred by the Dance of the Mountain Spirits than by any other performance I have ever seen.
[37] Thrapp, *Victorio*, pp. 88–91.

Masked dancers impersonating the Mountain Spirits, with the accompanying clown. The photograph may have been taken at San Carlos by A. Frank Randall in the spring of 1884. Note the wickiups in the background. *In spite of their precarious existence, the Apaches had a rich and complex ceremonial life.* Courtesy Smithsonian Institution, National Anthropological Archives.

Finally, the Mescaleros suddenly left one night in the fall of 1865; then, Apachelike, they vanished, not only from Carleton's searching, but also from the ken of present-day historians.[38] Even this disappearance did not change Carleton's determination to round up the Warm Springs band.

Such differences between the civilian agents and the military were to continue throughout the Apache wars. But as at other times, this disagreement lay more in a conflict of authority than in fundamental philosophy. Steck and his superiors had consolidation plans similar to Carleton's except that they lacked the power to carry them out.

[38] Sonnichsen, *op. cit.*, pp. 118–22.

Probably even more than the Indians, the white citizens were the victims of Carleton's intransigence. With the Civil War ended, settlers were returning to New Mexico. Gold miners were back at Pinos Altos; about three hundred were working the mines by 1868. That year silver was discovered a few miles southwest, and Silver City soon sprang up there. The Indians seemed to have everything their own way, raiding and killing at will. They even swept the horses away from the military posts, putting the troopers on foot. Citizens' complaints joined Steck's protests at Washington, and Carleton was finally transferred to another assignment in the fall of 1866.[39] Two years later a treaty with the Navahos permitted them to return to their homeland, but the Warm Springs Apaches vainly pleaded for a reservation that would allow them to live in their country at peace.[40] Their efforts finally enlisted Cochise.

That formidable Chiricahua had killed and raided unchecked. especially on the California Trail. Then came his strange pact with Thomas J. Jeffords. In the mid-sixties Jeffords had served for eighteen months as superintendent of mails on the route between Fort Bowie and Tucson, where he himself was wounded by arrows and fourteen of his drivers were killed. Then he went alone into Cochise's stronghold. It was the first time since that redoubtable chief became a hostile that a white man had seen him and lived. Somehow the chief was impressed, and the two became fast friends. He never violated his bond with Jeffords, but he continued his war against all other white men.[41]

These relations certainly involved Geronimo, although his name had not yet come into public notice. One incident of these hidden years touched him very closely. Juh was living, as he frequently did, with the Chiricahuas. In the winter of 1869/70, as nearly as Apaches can reckon dates, he had left his pregnant wife, the wise and capable Ishton, there in his camp while he raided in Mexico. When her time came, her labor was so painful and prolonged that

---

39 Thrapp, *Victorio*, pp. 91–93.
40 *Ibid.*, pp. 98–100.
41 Lockwood, *op. cit.*, pp. 110–12.

death seemed imminent. The Apaches had none of the taboos observed by the men of some Indian tribes against events in the female cycle. Geronimo hastened to the camp of his favorite "sister" and climbed a mountain to pray alone. Later Apache memories stretched the time of her labor to the mystical four days. On the fifth day at sunrise, as he lifted his hands and eyes towards the east, his Power spoke: "The child will be born and your sister will live; and you will never be killed with weapons, but live to old age." The infant was born that day and received the name Daklugie, meaning "Forced-his-way-through" or "One-who-grabs."[42]

Meanwhile, in the summer of 1869 Loco and Victorio, from their *rancherias* on the Alamosa and the parallel arroyo of the Cuchillo Negro, had begun to make tentative peace offers to the military at the posts on the Rio Grande. The superintendent of Indian affairs for New Mexico suggested that they be settled with the recently repatriated Navahos. The Mescalero agent, unable to contact his invisible tribe, wanted them sent across the Rio Grande to his vicinity. Their historian, Dan L. Thrapp, says that one may search through the thousands upon thousands of documents in the government records without finding a valid reason given for up-rooting them. All they ever asked was to remain at peace in their homeland.[43]

By that time, able and conscientious First Lieutenant Charles E. Drew had been appointed as agent to them and their relatives. (There was a brief period of appointing army officers to serve in this capacity, but the practice was soon forbidden by Congress because it removed an important area of patronage.) He managed to lure Loco, Victorio, and some other leaders to a council at Cañada Alamosa. The tribe maintained permanent peace with this Mexican town, trading stolen horses, mules, and cattle for whiskey, guns, ammunition, and food. At the council there they were vigilant and suspicious, bringing along forty fully armed warriors,

42 Ball interview, July 26, 1971; Eve Ball to Angie Debo, November 13, 1972.
43 Thrapp, *Victorio*, pp. 98–99.

maintaining lookouts on every hill, and keeping a guard over their horse herd.[44] Loco told Drew that not only the Warm Springs tribe, but Cochise and the Chiricahuas as well were willing to come in. But Washington took no action while the Indians patiently waited.

Drew died the following summer. At the same time, Cochise visited the new military post soon to be known as Fort Apache in the White Mountain area of east central Arizona and conferred with the commanding officer there. Finally, in October of that year (1870) the Indian Office sent Special Agent William Arny to study the situation. He and Drew's successor finally induced the Indians to meet them at their Warm Springs retreat. Present were twenty-two chiefs and leaders with 790 of their people, including Cochise with his family and 96 of his Chiricahuas. Cochise was coming to realize the attrition of his tribe; his losses, though smaller than those of the enemy, could not be recouped as easily by his small band. He said that he and his people had killed many white men, but if the government would furnish them with food and clothing he would bring in the whole tribe in peace. He did not like the White Mountain area, but was willing to consider the Alamosa.[45] Victorio said that within a month there would be 1,000 to 1,200 Indians collected there.

In his report Arny urged the establishment of a reservation for all of these related tribes. He suggested six different locations, but he did include in his list the Alamosa Valley and the Warm Springs. There were fifty-two families of white squatters living there, he said, referring to the Mexican settlement of Cañada Alamosa, but since they had no title to the land they could be removed by paying them eleven thousand dollars for their improvements. His own choice of the six locations was the Tularosa Valley, an uninhabited place in the mountains of western New Mexico east of Fort Apache. Meanwhile, he would allow them to remain in

[44] Secretary of the Interior, *Annual Report*, 1869, pp. 104–10. For the amicable relations between Cañada Alamosa (Monticello) and the Warm Springs Indians, see Betzinez, *op. cit.*, pp. 24, 26; Ball, *op. cit.*, p. 57; and Thrapp, *Victorio*, pp. 126–28.

[45] Thrapp, *Victorio*, pp. 104, 125–26, 129 and note 50. As far as I know, only Thrapp has uncovered these overtures by the supposedly unapproachable Cochise.

their Alamosa homeland until they could be persuaded or forced to remove.[46]

Geronimo mentioned this Warm Springs council only incidentally, as a preliminary to a visit he made to the area. Soldiers had attacked his camp, killed sixteen of his people, captured all their horses and supplies, and destroyed their lodges. "We had nothing left; winter was beginning, and it was the coldest winter I ever knew." Game was scarce, his people were suffering, and he decided to seek help.

"We had heard that Chief Victoria of the Chihenne (Oje Caliente) Apaches was holding a council with the white men near Hot Springs in New Mexico, and that he had plenty of provisions. We had always been on friendly terms with this tribe, and Victoria was especially kind to my people. . . . We easily found [him] and his band, and they gave us supplies for the winter. We stayed with them for about a year, and during this stay we had perfect peace. We had not the least trouble with Mexicans, white men, or Indians. . . . No one ever treated our tribe more kindly than Victoria and his band. We are still proud to say that he and his people were our friends."[47]

Contemporary accounts confirm his story of about a year of comparative peace on the Alamosa. Then the United States government finally came up with an Indian policy. It was to involve Geronimo and all the related tribes.

[46] *Ibid.*, pp. 130–31.
[47] Barrett, *op. cit.*, pp. 124–28.

CHAPTER 5

WASHINGTON HAS A POLICY

Something had to be done about the hostile Indians. Prospectors, miners, ranchers, adventurers of all types were coming in increasing numbers to New Mexico and Arizona. Towns were springing up—wild, lawless, stirring with ambition. And there was always the traffic on the trails. Thus, the area was becoming more and more vulnerable to Apache raids and more vocal in its outcries.

Nobody on the frontier admitted that the Indians also had their experience of wrongs and suffering, but the federal government was torn between benevolence and severity. President Grant had proclaimed his celebrated Peace Policy, and a Board of Indian Commissioners, made up of distinguished philanthropists, had been created to influence and evaluate Indian administration. The Department of the Interior, with its Indian Office, and the War Department fought each other from the cabinet level in Washington to the agencies and armies in the field. All this in its most intense form came to the Apaches, beginning in 1871.

Clearly, these Indians had to be assured of a place to live and some livelihood besides raiding. That year Congress appropriated seventy thousand dollars for "collecting the Apaches of Arizona and New Mexico upon reservations, furnishing them with subsistence and other necessary articles, and to promote peace and civilization among them . . . Provided, That this appropriation shall be expended only in behalf of those Indians who go and remain upon said reservations and refrain from hostilities."[1] The same year also marked the arrival of General George Crook,[2] who had been fighting Indians in the Pacific Northwest, to take command of the Department of Arizona, and of Vincent Colyer, secretary of the Board of Indian Commissioners, to establish reservations for the Apaches. All these developments were to have profound influence on the life of Geronimo.

Crook was the greatest Indian fighter ever produced by the United States Army, but he had much to learn about Apaches. He arrived in June and began a systematic inspection of all the military posts in the territory, crossing mountains over unmarked trails, listening to army personnel and civilians. He was honorable and humane in dealing with Indians, but at the time he heard only one side of the story and thought of Apaches simply as vermin to be exterminated. During his learning period he developed the tactics that were to prove the only successful method ever employed in subduing this elusive people. Discarding unwieldy supply wagons and putting his troopers on foot if necessary, he developed mule pack trains with such efficient attention to detail that his methods were still enployed during World War II in Southeast Asia and New Guinea. He enlisted Apache scouts—"the wilder the better," he said—for trailing and much of the fighting; he found their loyalty, once they had entered government service, a strange and moving thing.[3]

Crook's chiefs of scouts were men skilled in woodcraft who had a thorough knowledge of Indians. The most notable were half-Indian, half-Scot Archie McIntosh, whom Crook had brought from the Northwest;[4] Al Sieber, already an experienced frontiers-

1 United States, *Statutes at Large*, XVI, p. 546.

2 Brevet rank; he was serving as lieutenant colonel. He was promoted to brigadier general on October 23, 1873.

3 For Crook's own account, see Schmitt, *General George Crook*, pp. 162–73; for a balanced historical evaluation see Thrapp, *Conquest of Apacheria*, pp. 79–110, 120.

4 Dan L. Thrapp, *Al Sieber, Chief of Scouts*, pp. 88–89, n. 3.

man and scout in turbulent Arizona;[5] and Sam Bowman, part Choctaw in blood, who spoke Apache well enough to serve as interpreter in a pinch.[6] As his aide-de-camp the general had alert, able Second Lieutenant John Gregory Bourke, who proved his loyalty in many battles, became an interested observer of Apache customs, even learning their language, and by his brilliant writing preserved an invaluable record of the campaigns.[7]

When in his initial travels Crook reached Camp Apache (later Fort Apache), he was advised that the White Mountain Apaches and the related Coyoteros were friendly. (In this remote area they hunted through the mountains and tended their little fields in the valleys, undisturbed by the aggressions that had driven other tribes to war and raiding.) "It was difficult to realize that there could be any of the Apache tribe who were friendly to anybody," he said, but he conscientiously refrained from attacking them. From among them he enlisted his first Apache scouts. One was a young man named Noch-ay-del-klinne,[8] who was destined to set events in motion for one of Geronimo's later breakouts.

While he was there, three Indians and three Mexicans rode in with a letter from Warm Springs Indian Agent O. F. Piper stating that they were out to bring in the legendary Cochise. But "as two of this party were recognized as being Cochise's worst men . . . I felt very suspicious they were there in the capacity of spies." Since there was little they could discover, and since he did not want to interfere with the "Peace Department" (his scornful name for the Department of the Interior), he left them unharmed. Actually, one of the Apache messengers was Loco and one of the Mexicans was José Trujillo, the alcalde of Cañada Alamosa; they had been sent in preparation for Colyer's visit to contact Cochise and further the friendly relations already made with him. New Mexico Superintendent Nathaniel Pope still hoped to induce the Chiricahuas to

---

5 Thrapp, *op. cit.*, is the definitive biography of Sieber.

6 Davis, *The Truth about Geronimo*, pp. 36, 56.

7 John G. Bourke, *An Apache Campaign in the Sierra Madre*, pp. 6–13, introduction by J. Frank Dobie.

8 John G. Bourke, *On the Border with Crook*, p. 178.

settle with their Warm Springs relatives. But their mission failed because of their accidental meeting with Crook. He told them they had no business in Arizona and rudely ordered them home.[9]

By this time more than one thousand Indians had collected on the Alamosa, but they still had no title to their homeland. Every lawless act perpetrated by Indians, Anglos, or Mexicans was laid to their charge, and a large party of citizens of Silver City had recently made ready to wipe them out. Governor William A. Pile learned of the contemplated massacre and stopped it by "peremptory orders" backed up by troops. But the Indians learned of it and fled. Colyer reached Fort Craig on the Rio Grande on August 16 and went on up the Alamosa. He found hundreds of wickiups still standing, but no Indians. Finally, up the canyon in the vicinity of their springs he met Agent Piper, Loco, and Trujillo, but he decided that this area was too small and that it would be "preposterous" to buy out the three hundred or so Mexicans settled down the river. Looking around, he decided on the Tularosa Valley, formerly recommended by Arny.

Word was relayed to Washington, and on November 20 an order was issued setting the area aside. Then shortly after Colyer left, Cochise, even though he had failed to receive the messengers, came of his own accord with about thirty warriors and their families and settled on the Cuchillo Negro. Pope and Piper conferred with him, finding him anxious for peace but unwilling to go to the Tularosa. Victorio and Loco positively refused to go. The region was too cold, they said. Although the Apaches were mountain people, they required low valleys for their planting, and the altitude of the Tularosa was too high for comfortable winter dwelling or the maturing of their corn. It was finally decided to leave them undisturbed for the present.[10] Colyer did not subscribe to the plan of moving the Mescaleros across the Rio Grande to join them; instead, he recommended the establishment of a reservation for

---

[9] Thrapp, *Conquest of Apacheria*, pp. 99–100; Thrapp, *Victorio*, pp. 137–38.
[10] Thrapp, *Victorio*, pp. 133, 136–43.

them in their own mountains. This, their present reservation (with some changes in area), was set aside for them in 1873.[11]

Meanwhile, Colyer went on into Arizona, where he and his mission were subjected by press and citizens to all the strident vilification of a crude, new society. (Some of the epithets were "cold-blooded scoundrel," "red-handed assassin," and "treacherous black-hearted dog.") By this time Crook had his careful plans all made for a campaign against the Apaches. Then, as he expressed it, "I discovered from the newspapers that a Mr. Vincent Colyer had been sent out by the 'Indian ring' to interfere with my operations . . . and was going to make peace with the Apaches by the grace of God." He accordingly countermanded his orders and directed his subordinates to cooperate with the "peace policy." Colyer met with leaders of the different tribes—Apaches and other hostiles—and established reservations for them near the military posts in the vicinities of their various homelands. One of these areas, although subsequently pared down to satisfy miners and settlers, is still in existence—the Fort Apache Reservation for the White Mountain band and the Coyoteros, a large tract surrounding the military post of that name.

Thus, according to Crook, "Vincent the Good" traveled through the country "making peace as he went, and the Indians just immediately behind him left a trail of blood behind them from the murdered citizens." It was not quite as bad as that, but it was apparent that peace and good will would have to be supplemented by more drastic action. On November 5 in western Arizona a raiding party of Yavapais (known as Apache-Mohaves, but unrelated to the Apaches) Colyer had just settled on a reservation attacked and robbed a stagecoach, killing the driver and six of its eight passengers. Crook delayed his retribution for a time until their guilt was established,[12] meanwhile continuing his preparations for an intensive campaign against hostiles in general. He was supremely confident—"if this entire Indian question be left to

[11] Sonnichsen, *Mescalero Apaches*, p. 139.

[12] For the raid and the ensuing punishment of the raiders, during which Crook almost lost his life, see Thrapp, *Al Sieber*, pp. 90–103.

me . . . I have not the slightest doubt of my ability to conquer a peace with this Apache race in a comparatively short space of time."[13] Able as he was, he underestimated the fighting qualities of the Apaches.

In December he sent word to the bands that they must be on their reservations by mid-February to escape punishment; on February 7 he warned them that only nine more days remained. Then just as he was ready to start, he was notified, to his disgust, that Brigadier General Oliver Otis Howard was being sent out on another peace mission. Howard had a good Civil War combat record but an ostentatious piety that repelled fellow officers and westerners.[14] Indians, less reticent than white men in expressing religious feelings, liked and trusted him.

In late April, 1872, he arrived in Arizona, where he conferred effectively with the Indians and made some rearrangement of the reservations. Of these, the San Carlos Reservation, across the Salt River south of the Fort Apache Reservation, is still in existence, though with a reduced acreage. Both of these areas were formally set apart by executive order that year on December 14. Some of the Indians gladly settled down on these places of refuge, but Howard agreed with Crook that military force would be required to bring in the raiders.[15]

In July he met with the Warm Springs Apaches in New Mexico. The removal plans for that unhappy tribe had finally been carried out in the late spring of that year. An agency and a military post had been established on the Tularosa, and they had been ordered to settle there. By persuasion and threats Loco and Victorio had finally been induced to go, but only about three hundred of their people had joined them. The others, forced from their homeland, were widely scattered—and no doubt they raided. Howard visited the ones on the reservation, and they complained of the cold climate, impure water, much sickness, the death of their children, and a season too short for growing crops. Howard inspected their

13 Thrapp, *Conquest of Apacheria*, pp. 102–106; Schmitt, *op. cit.*, pp. 167–68.
14 Thrapp, *Conquest of Apacheria*, p. 106.
15 *Ibid.*, p. 111.

beloved Alamosa and frankly admitted that it was a more suitable location. He promised to have it set apart for them by corn planting time the following year. The relieved Indians failed to notice that this settlement was conditioned upon the consent of Cochise to join them there. For the present he advised the chiefs to remain where they were.[16]

Meanwhile, they assisted him to contact Cochise. Crook had been "intending to iron all the wrinkles out of Cochise's band . . . I already had my spies in his camp and intended moving on him with my whole force after night, and surrounding him by daylight in the morning and give them such a clearing out that it would end him for all time to come, as his band was recognized as the worst of all the Apaches." But to the general's chagrin, Howard arrived first.[17]

Since his return from New Mexico and his meeting with the federal officials there, Cochise had committed no hostile acts, although some of his people had done so. But Howard considered it necessary as well as prudent to obtain help in approaching him. Victorio arranged for the general to meet Thomas Jeffords and a young warrior named Chee (Chie), who was a nephew of Cochise and one of his most trusted men; they consented to accompany Howard. The general also enlisted Ponce, probably a son of Mangas Coloradas and thus Cochise's brother-in-law.[18] Ponce spoke Spanish fluently and therefore could act as interpreter. He was believed to be the head of a band of raiders and would be heard from thereafter. Howard found them innocently gathering corn, possibly planted by Mexicans, in the canyon of the Cuchillo Negro.

With these assistants, Howard and his party set out on their 350-mile journey. At Silver City, where they spent one night, they

16 Thrapp, *Victorio*, pp. 144–48, 151. See also Ball, *In the Days of Victorio*, p. 49.
17 Schmitt, *op. cit.*, pp. 176–77.
18 This identification of Chee and Ponce was given to Eve Ball by Asa Daklugie. Chee's descendants now live on the Mescalero Reservation. Regarding Ponce's relationship to Mangas Coloradas, Daklugie cited his father, Juh—"I think that is true. He was my father's *segundo* [second in command, or assistant, with the implication of the succession], and Juh should have known" (Ball to Angie Debo, June 25, 1973). Howard mistakenly attributed this relationship to Chee. There is no evidence that Ponce was related to the Ponce encountered by Bartlett.

were almost mobbed by its turbulent, Indian-hating citizens, but—
as Howard expressed it— "fortunately there were present several
sensible men" who protected them. Even so, he took the precaution
of setting out the next morning before the town awoke. A few
miles beyond they met a party of prospectors. One of them raised
his rifle to kill the two Indians, but Howard rode his horse in
between, and the bad man backed off from becoming embroiled
with official Washington. When the party reached Cochise's domain, there were smoke signals, the bark of a coyote, and cautious
reconnaissance by Chee before they were guided to the sheltered
valley enclosed by towering crags which was the chief's stronghold
in the Dragoons. Cochise finally rode in with his wife, his sister,
and his young son Naiche, who appeared to be about fourteen
years old. (His older son, Taza, was not present.) He greeted
Jeffords affectionately and cordially shook hands with Howard.
Howard described him as fully six feet tall and well proportioned,
with large, dark eyes and a pleasant expression.

He told how the trouble started with the capture and subsequent
hanging of his relatives at Apache Pass. "You Americans began
the fight," he said, "and now Americans and Mexicans kill an
Apache on sight. I have retaliated with all my might. I have killed
ten white men for every Indian slain." But he was now ready to
make peace, and he sent out messengers to call in his scattered
lieutenants. These must have included Geronimo, for the latter
participated in the negotiations and was a party to the settlement.

Howard remained there eleven days while the leaders were
gathering for the council. (He made friends with the Indian
children, even teaching young Naiche to write his name.) The
final agreement was made on October 13. Cochise would have
accepted Howard's suggestion that his people join their Warm
Springs relatives on the Alamosa, but he was not able to persuade
all of the leaders to consent to the removal. He therefore decided
against going. It would break up his band, he said; the ones who
remained would commit depredations in Arizona, while if he
stayed he could collect and control them all, protect the roads,

87

and observe the peace. He also laid down the condition that Jeffords serve as agent.

Howard accordingly agreed to set aside the Chiricahuas' homeland as their reservation. It lay on the Mexican border, extending fifty-six miles west of the New Mexico–Arizona line, and included the Chiricahua and Dragoon mountains and the intervening Sulphur Springs Valley. It was confirmed by executive order on December 14. Jeffords, busy with projects of his own, was reluctant to take the position of agent but was persuaded to accept.

Geronimo showed his pleasure with the agreement but was still suspicious. He went out of the mountains with Howard and Cochise to report to the military on the success of the meeting, he and Howard riding double on the general's horse. With true Apache agility he mounted by springing over the horse's tail, then reaching his place behind Howard with another spring. The two became friendly during the ride, but when they approached the soldiers Howard felt him tremble. At the same time Cochise put his warriors into skirmish order, ready for defense or flight. No doubt the Indians were remembering Mangas Coloradas and others lured to their death by a promise of protection. But the meeting passed off well. The agency, with Jeffords in charge, was established near Fort Bowie, and Geronimo entered into the peace that followed.[19] All his life he remembered Howard with affection and gratitude and expressed satisfaction with the agreement: "This treaty lasted until long after General Howard had left our country. He always kept his word with us and treated us as brothers. . . . We could have lived forever at peace with him. If there is any pure, honest white man in the United States army, that man is General Howard. All the Indians respect him, and even to this day frequently talk of the happy times when General Howard was in command of our Post.[20] After he went away he placed an agent

[19] Thrapp, *Victorio*, pp. 153–54, 350 n. 42; Lockwood, *The Apache Indians*, pp. 112–22; O. O. Howard, *My Life and Experiences among Our Hostile Indians*, pp. 186–225. Howard gave some additional details in a book he wrote for children, *Famous Indian Chiefs I Have Known*, pp. 112–36, 357. He made many errors in recording historical events, but his account of his own experiences appears to be accurate.

[20] By "our Post," Geronimo referred to the agency. Of course Howard was not in

at Apache Pass who issued to us from the Government clothing, rations, and supplies, as General Howard directed. When beef was issued to the Indians I got twelve steers for my tribe, and Cochise got twelve steers for his tribe."[21]

Geronimo may have exaggerated his own importance in saying that he and Cochise received equal portions for distribution, but his statement may well be true. He probably represented Juh and his band (because of his speech defect Juh usually let Geronimo speak for him) as well as all the homeless stragglers from the Warm Springs tribe. And one of Geronimo's outstanding traits in the later, better-known period of his life was his hard economic sense. Thus, it was typical that he should manage the distribution for these unrecognized participants.

As soon as Howard's conference with Cochise and his lieutenants in the Dragoons was over, Chee and Ponce reported back to the Warm Springs leaders on the Tularosa. Cochise's success in securing title to his homeland made them more dissatisfied than ever, and this dissatisfaction was increased when Howard's recommendation that they be permitted to return to *their* homeland was disallowed. Counting the three hundred unwilling transients on the Tularosa, and ignoring the exiled wanderers scattered—and no doubt raiding—from New Mexico to Sonora, the authorities reasoned that since Cochise had not consented to remove to the Alamosa the tribe was not numerous enough to warrant a reservation there. Early in 1873 Howard wrote from Washington to break the news to the disappointed leaders Ponce, Victorio, and Loco. "I am not the President or Great Father," he apologized. "I only obey orders."[22]

Meanwhile, as soon as Howard's peace mission was over, Crook began his twice-delayed campaign against the tribes in the mountains of western Arizona. It began on November 15, 1872. The winter that followed appears in army reports as a succession of

command there or at the military post, but he did have authority as a special agent of President Grant.
21 Barrett, *Geronimo's Story of His Life*, pp. 128–29.
22 Thrapp, *Victorio*, p. 149.

hardships, individual exploits, pursuits, and the destruction of *rancherias*, in all of which the Apache scouts demonstrated Crook's confidence in them as trailers and guerrilla fighters. By spring the defeated raiders began to come in and settle on the reservations. Some eventually broke away, but Crook continued to comb the mountains and canyons for them. After they surrendered, he treated them with fairness and compassion. The Apaches learned that Nantan Lupan (Chief Grey Wolf) was a relentless enemy, but that they could trust his word.[23]

The general still itched to get his hands on Cochise, but Howard's peace pact prevented operations against the Chiricahua chief. He did send a mission to the chief in February, 1873. The party included Jeffords, who served as interpreter; George H. Stevens, acting agent at San Carlos, a prominent Arizona rancher married to a White Mountain Apache woman; and Bourke. Bourke was impressed by Cochise's sincerity and his efforts to keep the peace with the Americans. But regarding the Mexicans, "he said he considered them as being on one side in this matter, while the *Americans* were on the other. The former had not asked for peace as the latter had done. He did not deny that his boys were in the habit of raiding on Mexico, but this he could not prevent as it was no more than was done from all the Reservations."[24]

Cochise's homeless Warm Springs relatives also found the Chiricahua Reservation a convenient place to leave their families while the warriors went on to raid in Mexico. Jeffords learned that whether or not he fed them, they stayed. Then when the warriors returned and joined them, they all came in to share the rations. Jeffords was in a quandary. If he should refuse to feed them, hunger would drive them to more raiding. He believed that rationing, by supplying their needs, at least reduced it.[25]

At the same time, Cochise guarded the trails and protected the ranches on the American side of the line, not only from his own

23 Thrapp, *Conquest of Apacheria*, pp. 119–43; Bourke, *op. cit.*, p. 112; Ball, *In the Days of Victorio*, p. 184.

24 Bourke, *op. cit.*, p. 235; Thrapp, *Conquest of Apacheria*, pp. 145–47.

25 Thrapp, *Victorio*, p. 166.

people but also from lawless raiders coming down from the north. But complaints were coming from the governor of Sonora to Governor Anson P. K. Safford of Arizona. On March 31, 1873, the harried Safford sent the communication to Crook. He added that "so far as the people of Arizona are concerned, I believe that Cochise has kept his word with us," but he feared that any attempt to halt the raids on Mexico would start another war with him.[26]

There is no record of Geronimo's actions during this period. It seems to have been a quiet interlude in his turbulent career. He may have been referring to it when he said, "It was a long time before we again went into Mexico or were disturbed by the Mexicans."[27] He was closely associated with Cochise (it may be, in fact, that it was at this time that he married She-gha), and Cochise did discourage, though he did not prevent, the Mexican raids. The chief's personal relationships with the white Americans can be glimpsed by the reminiscences of old Al Williamson, who as a youth of eighteen clerked in a trading post at Fort Bowie. There he often saw Cochise and his sons, Taza and Naiche. The chief was grave, never smiled, and, although he would drink with the officers, always left the post before sundown and required his people to do the same. Taza had a pleasant, smiling face, and like his grandfather, Mangas Coloradas, was very large. One day Al put him on the scales, and he weighed 199 pounds. Young Naiche resembled his father in his slender build and reserved manner.[28]

Cochise died in June, 1874. Before his death he called in his headmen and in their presence designated Taza as his successor. As the Apaches remembered it, he had carefully trained Taza for this responsibility. He exacted a promise from him and Naiche that they would preserve the peace. New Mexican Superintendent Levi Edwin Dudley had visited him in his stronghold during his last illness, hoping to persuade him to remove to the Alamosa. Later, Dudley hoped to persuade Taza.

In preparation for this removal the area had already been set

---

26 *Ibid.*, p. 165; Thrapp, *Conquest of Apacheria*, pp. 168–69.
27 Barrett, *op. cit.*, p. 85.
28 Lockwood, *op. cit.*, pp. 124–26. Lockwood talked with Williamson in 1934.

aside as a reservation by an executive order on April 9. But in any case, Dudley recommended the abandonment of the Tularosa Reservation (it had been a failure from the beginning, he said) and the location of the Warm Springs tribe in their homeland. To keep squatters from flocking there in order to claim reimbursement from the government, he issued an order reserving the tract, subject to approval. The approval was granted, and in July instructions came to remove the Tularosa Agency to that place. By the end of the summer, about four hundred Indians had assembled in the loved region.[29]

Thus, by a combination of Crook's efficient fighting methods and the overtures of peace commissioners, the Apache wars were in process of settlement. Of course, not all was sweetness and light on the reservations. Some of the agents placed in control were weak and unable to restrain their wild charges. Others were corrupt, entering into collusion with contractors to cheat on the quantity and quality of rations or even selling the Indians' supplies to the mining settlements. There were lawless spirits among the Apaches unwilling to settle down, and still more lawless white men, often leading citizens, who deliberately stirred up Apache wars in order to profit from fat army contracts—two million dollars annually to the Southwestern economy. But although there remained some police work by the army to bring in outlaws, and a more efficient management of the reservations by the civilian agents, Apache depredations no longer threatened normal development of the Southwest.

A demonstration of good reservation administration was furnished when John Philip Clum came on August 8, 1874, as agent on the San Carlos Reservation. This reservation had had a turbulent history, with seven hundred wild Indians, a succession of short-term agents, including a notorious swindler, and two companies of cavalry unable under the circumstances to keep order. The agency was a log hut with an earthen floor and canvas doors

[29] Thrapp, *Victorio*, pp. 165–68, 170, 352 n. 42. The feeling the Warm Springs Apaches had for the place is shown throughout the accounts by James Kaywaykla and Jason Betzinez (Ball, *op. cit.*, and Betzinez, *I Fought with Geronimo*).

situated on the gravelly, wind-swept flat above the junction of the Gila and San Carlos rivers. Clum immediately got rid of the soldiers and assumed control. He lacked three weeks of being twenty-three years old, but he was honorable, able, and efficient; and he had all of Crook's single-minded confidence that he could manage all the Apaches by himself if only the wicked rival service (in Crook's belief, the civilian "Indian ring"; in Clum's the army) would keep out of it.

Clum liked the Indians and treated them fairly, and they reciprocated. He set up crude but effective courts with the leading chiefs as a council of judges, and he enrolled and trained the warriors as police to enforce order. He called in the Indians for a regular count, not only to ensure against their straying, but also to give them an air-tight alibi when they were falsely accused of raiding. On every weekly ration day he issued three hundred pounds of beef, fifty pounds of flour, eight pounds of sugar, four pounds of coffee, one pound of salt, and two bars of soap for each hundred Indians. There, friends and relatives pooled their shares and made a gala social gathering of the occasion. Beyond this, Clum encouraged industry by buying supplies from their little farms and hiring them in the construction of adequate adobe buildings at the agency. He found them eager to work, and he observed that they took naturally to livestock raising. Thus, he looked forward to a time when their rations could be discontinued.[30]

By 1875 Apache-white relations were in the most hopeful state since the wars began in 1860. All the tribes had guaranteed titles to protected refuges, usually comprising their former heartlands. It had been demonstrated that a reservation could be managed for the welfare of its inhabitants and that good order and contentment could prevail there, with eventual self-support a not impossible goal. The army would still be needed—Clum to the contrary not-

---

[30] Thrapp, *Conquest of Apacheria*, pp. 147–54, 162–65; Clum, *Apache Agent*, pp. 132–40, 148–49, 163–64. John P. Clum was writing his reminiscences when he died suddenly in 1932, and his son, Woodworth Clum, completed the book from these unfinished notes. I agree with Thrapp, who finds his account "wildly inaccurate" but a valuable source if carefully checked.

withstanding—to search out "renegades" from their mountain hideouts, but Crook had developed the techniques. As he expressed it, "I knew if I were to permit a party, even if small, to remain out it would get accession to those on the reserve, who, in turn, would become dissatisfied, and it would not be long before they would be pretty much all out in the mountains again. So frequent expeditions were sent out, and destroyed several small parties."[31]

But in that same year of 1875 the Indian Office began to carry out the concentration policy so often recommended by planners and theorists. This cruel and stupid uprooting of barely tamed hostiles, so recently guaranteed a settled homeland "forever," was to bring about eleven more years of Apache wars with the most arduous military campaigns in American history, the death of hundreds of civilians in the United States and Mexico, and damage and suffering without reckoning to the Apaches.[32] As a direct result, Geronimo became a "renegade," and his career from this time on becomes an epic of the Southwest.

[31] Schmitt, *op. cit.*, p. 182. For these mopping-up expeditions see Thrapp, *Al Sieber*, pp. 117–55.

[32] For a historical evaluation, see Thrapp, *Conquest of Apacheria*, p. 166.

CHAPTER 6

GERONIMO IS BRANDED
A RENEGADE

Economy in administration was the reason given for consolidating the subdued hostiles of Arizona and southwestern New Mexico on one reservation. It cannot be argued that it was done to prevent the raids into Mexico; most of the tribes were moved *closer* to the border. The bureaucratic tendency to organize human beings into neat compartments no doubt had its influence. But it is fairly certain that land hunger was the underlying motive of even the most humane administrators, for the vacated reservations were regularly restored to the public domain.

The reservation chosen was the San Carlos, probably because it was convenient to the greedy contractors at Tucson, at that time the territorial capital. Clum welcomed all the new arrivals to his "happy family" (his words), ignoring the fact that during the transfer the less submissive invariably slipped away and became "renegades." Crook, who had rounded up many of the hostiles in the first place, strongly opposed the measure. Bourke later wrote, "It was an outrageous proceeding, one for which I should still blush, had I not long since gotten over blushing for anything the United States Government did in Indian matters." But the civilian administration was in control. In March, 1875, Crook was transferred to the northern plains to fight the Sioux and their Cheyenne and Arapaho allies. His successors, brevet Major General August V. Kautz and later brevet Major General Orlando Bolivar Willcox, were left to cope with the inevitable hostilities.[1]

Crook was still in command at the time of the first removal—that of some Apache and non-Apache tribes of western Arizona from their recently guaranteed reservation. Crook declined to use force, but Dudley, who had been placed in charge, pressured the Indians into consenting. They were launched on their journey on February 27, 1875. On the way they started fighting each other. Several were killed, and the battle was stopped only by the courageous intervention of Al Sieber. This was an earnest of what would happen when mutually hostile tribes were crowded together in one "happy family." Another ominous sign: of the 1,476 Indians who started out, only 1,361 were turned over to Clum at San Carlos. Some of the missing 115 could be accounted for, but most of them had fled into their old hideouts.[2]

The White Mountain and Coyotero tribes of the Fort Apache Reservation were the next to be uprooted. These Indians had even invited the military to establish the post in their homeland and had gratefully added the distributed rations to their hunting and farming economy.[3] But such a feud developed between the civilian agent and the army officer in command there that Clum was instructed to bring the Indians of that reservation to San Carlos. With sixty of his San Carlos Indians and George H. Stevens, then a trader at his agency, he rode up to Fort Apache "on a big white horse," showing a "paper" from Washington—as old John Rope, a member of the band, told it in later years—and induced those tribes to remove. They made the sixty-mile journey and arrived at their new location on July 31, 1875. A few remained, especially

[1] Thrapp, *Al Sieber*, pp. 158–59; Schmitt, *General George Crook, Autobiography*, pp. 183–84; Bourke, *On the Border with Crook*, pp. 216–17.

[2] For this removal, see Thrapp, *Al Sieber*, pp. 156–69.

[3] The account of their first meeting with white soldiers, the establishment of cordial relations, and the Indians' assistance in locating the post were related by John Rope, who was present throughout (Goodwin, "Experiences of an Indian Scout" [part I], pp. 36–40).

96

the families of scouts in army service at Fort Apache, but the agency was closed. This time the abandoned land was not restored to the public domain but was added to the San Carlos Reservation and administered by the San Carlos Agency, a consolidation that was to remain in effect until 1897. Clum now had forty-two hundred Indians of unrelated tribes, many hostile to each other, collected on one reservation.[4]

Next, in 1876, came the Chiricahuas. In their case an incident furnished the pretext for the move. It involved a warrior named Skinya and his brother and supporter, Pionsenay. According to Clum, Skinya, who had been one of Cochise's leading warriors, contested young Taza's position as chief. In any event, a factional fight broke out, and the tribe divided, with Skinya and about a dozen of his followers living in the Dragoons and the majority under Taza camped near the agency. Jeffords had warned the station keeper at Sulphur Springs on the California Trail near Skinya's camp that he would be removed from the reservation if he should sell whiskey to the Indians. He sold a supply, however, to Pionsenay. The brothers and their small band of followers became intoxicated and went on the warpath, killing the station keeper, his assistant, and another white man and stealing their horses and ammunition. Jeffords and the military trailed them to their Dragoon refuge but were unable to capture them.

An aroused public opinion then clamored for vengeance on the tribe. The *Arizona Citizen* of Tucson declared that "the kind of war needed for the Chiricahua Apaches, is steady unrelenting, hopeless, and undiscriminating war, slaying men, women, and children, . . . until every valley and crest and crag and fastness shall send to high heaven the grateful incense of festering and rotting Chiricahuas."[5] Governor Safford wired Washington demanding the abandonment of the reservation and the removal of the Indians.

---

[4] *Ibid.*, p. 41; Clum, *Apache Agent*, pp. 153–63; Thrapp, *Conquest of Apacheria*, pp. 166–67; Ralph Hedrick Ogle, *Federal Control of the Western Apaches, 1848–1886*, pp. 149–59.

[5] April 15, 1876. Quoted by Ogle, *op. cit.*, p. 166, n. 87.

97

Equally "undiscriminating" was the decision of the Indian Office to uproot the whole tribe for the deeds of this small, repudiated faction. Clum was instructed to carry it out. With a military force supplied by Kautz in the background, he arrived with fifty-four of his armed police at Sulphur Springs on June 4. On the same day the outlaws entered Taza's camp and tried to induce the tribe to join them. A fight ensued in which Naiche shot and killed Skinya, Taza wounded Pionsenay, and six other members of the small band were killed. The following day Clum met with Taza and Naiche at the agency and obtained their consent to the removal. But Jeffords informed him that another band under Geronimo, Juh, and a warrior named Nolgee were also living on the reservation, having been included in the settlement with Howard, and that these leaders wanted to meet with him.

This conference was accordingly held at the agency on June 7 or possibly June 8. Geronimo seemed to be the leader. (Clum did not know that he spoke for the band because of the impediment in Juh's speech.) He told Clum that he was willing to go to the San Carlos Reservation, but that his people were about twenty miles distant, and he asked permission to bring them in. Clum consented, but sent some of his police to shadow the two leaders. Upon reaching camp, the leaders gave brief orders, and the band killed their dogs to prevent their barking, broke camp, and fled— the first of Geronimo's many breakaways. By the time the scouts reported to Clum and Clum alerted the soldiers, the Indians were far on their way. Juh and Nolgee went to their Sierra Madre hideouts, but Geronimo had other plans. On July 21, with a party of about forty, he appeared on the Warm Springs Reservation.

Meanwhile, on June 12 the agent left Apache Pass with 325 good Chiricahuas for their new home on the San Carlos. These included 37 members, mainly women and children, of Pionsenay's small band, but their wounded leader himself escaped. There were, in fact, only 60 warriors in the entire party. Their more turbulent relatives were with the Nednais in Mexico; about 135, including Geronimo and his band, joined their Warm Springs friends on the

Alamosa; and an unreckoned number were hiding out in their ancestral mountains. Between the closing of the Chiricahua agency in June and the following October, they had killed—according to Jefford's official report—more than 20 people and had stolen 170 head of livestock.[6]

This was Clum's introduction to Geronimo. From that time on he became the elusive warrior's nemesis. In his lively writings he attributed every raid before and after this meeting to Geronimo. His solution to the whole Apache problem was simple: hang Geronimo. He attributed every reverse to, "If only Geronimo had been hanged———." Other Southwesterners adopted the same simplistic interpretation. Thus, Geronimo acquired a fame—or notoriety—far out of proportion to his deeds or misdeeds.

In his own account Geronimo touched briefly on the murder of the station keeper by "a band of outlawed Indians" and concentrated on the factions within the tribe. As he told it, "some Indians at the Post were drunk on 'tiswin,' which they had made from corn. They fought among themselves and four of them were killed. There had been quarrels and feuds among them for some time, and after this trouble we deemed it impossible to keep the different bands together in peace. Therefore we separated, each leader taking his own band. Some of them went to San Carlos and some to Old Mexico, but I took my tribe back to Hot Springs and rejoined Victoria's band." As for his flight from Clum, he reasoned, "I do not think that I ever belonged to those soldiers at Apache Pass, or that I should have asked them where I might go."[7]

Thus, by the closing of the Chiricahua Reservation a fairly compact tribal unit that had observed a precarious peace was dispersed through the mountains, impossible to contact or control. Clum knew that lawless spirits among them were committing depredations, which typically he blamed on Geronimo, but all

6 John P. Clum, "The San Carlos Apache Police," *New Mexico Historical Review*, Vol. V, No. 1 (part 2), pp. 79–80, and "Geronimo," *New Mexico Historical Review*, Vol. III, No. 1 (part 1), pp. 8–9, 13–19; Clum, *Apache Agent*, pp. 176–84; Lockwood, *The Apache Indians*, pp. 214–18; Ogle, *op. cit.*, pp. 164–68; Thrapp, *Victorio*, p. 180.
7 Barrett, *Geronimo's Story of His Life*, pp. 129–30, 132.

Naiche, "the tall, handsome son of Cochise," who came with his Chiricahuas to San Carlos. Photograph taken there by A. Frank Randall in the spring of 1884.

seemed serene on the San Carlos. He wanted to marry a girl in Ohio, and he conceived the hare-brained idea of paying his transportation by engaging in show business. With about twenty of his Indians, including Taza, he toured the East, visiting the Centennial Exposition at Philadelphia and ending at Washington. In Washington Taza died of pneumonia and was given an elaborate funeral with General Howard in attendance. There, Clum ran out of funds, and the commissioner of Indian affairs paid the way of the party back to Arizona. (Incidentally, Clum married the girl, and she became the only white woman on the reservation.)[8]

Naiche was decidedly hostile to Clum when he learned of the death of his brother. He appeared pacified when other members of the party told him of the burial ceremonies, and the agent did not suspect that for years thereafter the band believed that the young chief had been poisoned.[9] This belief contributed to the Chiricahuas' growing dissatisfaction with the new location and their resentment over the loss of their homeland.

Naiche was recognized as his brother's successor, but he never attained the stature of his father or other great chiefs of the Apaches. As it was told to Kaywaykla, "When Tahza was poisoned Naiche was too young to become the leader. He had not been trained for the place as had his brother because Cochise wanted his younger son to be loyal to Tahza."[10] As he grew older it was apparent that although he was a brave and able warrior, he was temperamentally unfitted to exercise authority. Some of the Apaches tried to explain it. Sam Kenoi, an elderly Nednai, characterized him to Opler: "He liked his Indian dancing, and he liked his fighting, and he liked his drinking. You could make a good soldier out of him, and that was all. He was always influenced by Geronimo."[11] Young Lieutenant Britton Davis, who knew him well on the reservation, gave a similar evaluation: "Nachite was a good warrior

8 Clum, "Geronimo" (part 1), p. 23; Clum, *Apache Agent*, pp. 185–98, 201–203; Howard, *My Life and Experiences*, p. 215.
9 Clum, *Apache Agent*, pp. 198–201; Ball, *In the Days of Victorio*, pp. 51–52.
10 Ball, *op. cit.*, p. 127.
11 Morris E. Opler, "A Chiricahua Apache's Account of the Geronimo Campaign of 1886," *New Mexico Historical Review*, Vol. XIII, No. 4 (Oct., 1938), p. 369.

with no peace scruples; but he was fond of the ladies, liked dancing and a good time generally, and was not serious enough for the responsibilities of leadership."[12]

Certainly he lacked the drive of Geronimo, the statesmanship of Mangas Coloradas, and the military genius of Cochise or Victorio. More serious to his tribesmen, he had no Power—no ceremony that would reveal enemy plans, deflect bullets, or cure sickness. But in his mature years as a prisoner of war, the officers in charge found him dependable and cooperative, affable and courteous in his manners, and possessing a quiet influence over his people. In the period of relatively normal living at Fort Sill he produced notable paintings and wood carvings.[13] In another culture he would have been a creative artist, but there was no place for one of his temperament under the hard conditions of Apache life.

Nevertheless, Naiche was the recognized chief, and Geronimo always deferred to him in that capacity. This deference can be seen even in the photographs, in which Naiche invariably is placed on the right. It was true, though, as Sam Kenoi said, that Geronimo dominated his more sensitive superior. At that time, however, they were separated, with Naiche on the San Carlos Reservation and Geronimo at the Warm Springs Agency.

The Warm Springs Reservation was under a very weak administration, and it was soon apparent that bands of "renegades" were using it as a refuge between raids while they carried on a lively business of stealing horses from Arizona and selling them to New Mexico ranchers or in the Mexican towns on the Rio Grande. The Warm Springs people were aware of what was happening, but they seemed unable to prevent it. As one of them explained it to Opler in later years:

We were on friendly terms with the towns around us and we

12 Davis, *The Truth about Geronimo*, pp. 71–72.
13 Hugh Lenox Scott, *Some Memories of a Soldier*, p. 198; Burbank and Royce, *Burbank among the Indians*, p. 34.

were causing no trouble there. But the [Chiricahuas] and the [Nednais] came around. They used to bring in horses stolen from the south and they got us into trouble.

Some of our leading men said, "There are too many [Nednais] and [Chiricahuas] here. They are bringing in horses. They will get us into trouble." But our leader, Victorio, wouldn't do anything about it. He said, "These people are not bothering us."

Then a bunch of them came with some horses from the south. There were about seven [leaders] in the bunch. They had stolen horses from the Pima Indians around Tucson.[14] [The Pimas were a sedentary, agricultural tribe, long-time enemies of the Apaches.]

Apparently Ponce and other well-known "renegades" were in the party with their followers, but probably Geronimo was the leader. (At least he got the blame.) On March 17, 1877, an army officer reported seeing him at the agency with one hundred horses, very indignant that he was not permitted to draw the rations he had missed during his absence. This brought matters to a head.

On March 20 the commissioner of Indian affairs wired Clum to "take Indian Police and arrest renegade Indians at Southern Apache [that is, the Warm Springs] Agency," remove them to San Carlos Reservation, "and hold them in confinement for murder and robbery." Clum called on General Edward Hatch, commander of the Department of New Mexico, and was notified that three companies of cavalry would meet him at the agency on April 21. He accordingly set out on the four-hundred-mile journey with about one hundred of his trusty police and arrived with an advance contingent of twenty-two on the evening of April 20. There he found a telegram saying the cavalry would be delayed until April 22. He knew that if he waited, the "rengades" would take flight. Reasoning that they knew of only the twenty-two men they saw

14 Opler, *An Apache Life-Way*, pp. 462–63. I have substituted the tribal names used by the Apaches for the terminology—Eastern, Central, and Southern Chiricahuas —of ethnologists.

The site of the Warm Springs (Ojo Caliente) Agency. Through the cleft in the center background the Alamosa River flowed down to the Mexican town Cañada Alamosa. Here on April 21, 1877, Geronimo for the only time in his life was "captured"—by a ruse. "We thought they wanted a council and rode in to meet the officers." Photograph by Dan L. Thrapp.

with him, he sent a courier to his chief of police, Clay Beauford, to bring up the others during the night.

The adobe buildings at Warm Springs faced a large parade

ground. On the west side was the agency, and about fifty yards to the south of it was a large vacant commissary building. Along the south side stretched a row of employee quarters. The east and north sides terminated in a deep ravine. The reserve police arrived at about four o'clock in the morning and were concealed in the commissary building. At daylight Clum sent a message to Geronimo and the other "renegade" leaders in camp about three miles away, summoning them to come in for a conference. They came, clearly not expecting a confrontation, for they brought their women and children. As Geronimo told it, "The messengers did not say what they wanted with us, and as they seemed friendly we thought they wanted a council and rode in to meet the officers."[15]

With Beauford and half a dozen of his police, Clum took a position on the porch of the agency building facing the parade ground. The others of his small force were lined along the parade ground on each side of him, half of them north towards the ravine, half south to the commissary building. The "renegade" warriors, fully armed, gathered in a compact group before him, with Geronimo, Ponce, and five (or six, as Geronimo told it) other leaders in front. He directed his charges mainly at Geronimo, but he spoke to the group. He accused them of killing men and stealing cattle in violation of the Howard-Cochise peace and of breaking their promise of the preceding year to come in to San Carlos; now, he said, he had come to bring them in. Geronimo answered defiantly: "We are not going to San Carlos with you, and unless you are very careful, you and your Apache police will not go back to San Carlos either. Your bodies will stay here at Ojo Caliente to make food for coyotes."

In later years Clum admitted that just at that time he would have liked to see the cavalry. He and Beauford and two agency employees were the only white men there. But he gave a prearranged signal; and the commissary doors burst open and the reserves emerged running, in single file, rifles at the ready, and formed a line along the south side of the parade ground. The "renegades"

15 Barrett, *op. cit.*, p. 131.

105

were caught between a threatened cross fire. A few stragglers started to move away, but were halted by Beauford's raised rifle. Thereupon a woman in the crowd sprang upon the chief of police, threw her arms around his neck and shoulders, and pulled down his gun. He threw her off, and by the time he raised it again, all the reserves were in place ready to halt any attempt at escape. (One would like to know the name of this Amazon. There were some women warriors among the Apaches who fought regularly alongside their men.[16])

Clum had been watching Geronimo's thumb creeping toward the hammer of his rifle. Now it moved back, and the agent realized that he had won. He handed his own gun to one of the police and ordered the "renegade" leaders to lay their rifles on the ground. They shuffled their feet and made no move to comply. Clum motioned to Beauford, and Beauford aimed his gun straight at Geronimo. Then Clum stepped down and disarmed him. To the end of his long adventurous life—for he was to become the founder of the *Tombstone Epitaph* and the mayor of that wild town in its heyday—Clum never forgot the concentrated hatred in Geronimo's face as he was relieved of his rifle. (With typical arrogance the agent kept it the rest of his life and handed it on as a family heirloom.) Beauford disarmed the other leaders, and their followers laid their rifles on the ground. Clum then asked Geronimo and "his sub-chiefs" to come up on the porch for a conference, and the main body—men, women, and children—dispersed in groups over the parade ground.

On the porch, as the leaders squatted around in the favorite Apache position, Clum again berated Geronimo for his flight the year before, informed them that they were prisoners, and ordered them to the guardhouse. Geronimo then leaped to his feet, "erect as a lodge-pole pine, every outline of his symmetrical form indicating strength, endurance, and arrogance." At the same time the other

---

16 See Ball, *op. cit.*, for the exploits of the famed woman warrior, Victorio's sister Lozen, and of James Kaywaykla's own mother in her service as a warrior fighting beside her husband.

six sprang to their feet, as did most of the warriors in front. Geronimo's hand crept toward the knife in his belt, and in his fierce eyes Clum read his indecision, whether to surrender or to draw the knife and die fighting. While he hesitated, one of the police sprang forward and snatched the knife, and the guns of the others clicked as they were pointed at the seven leaders. Geronimo flashed one defiant glance at his captors. Then he relaxed and said, "In-gew" ("all right").

Clum had forgotten that the agency had no guardhouse; therefore, he decided to use the corral. He had intended only to disarm and imprison the leaders, but Geronimo's attempt to draw his knife decided him to have them shackled. He marched them to the blacksmith shop while their followers looked on. Geronimo watched impassively while the irons were being heated. Did he expect to be tortured? Then the irons, connected by chains, were riveted on the ankles first of Geronimo, then of the others. When the shackling was completed, they were led to the corral, given beds of hay, blankets, and food, and placed under strict guard. Then Beauford, with twenty police, marched the band to their camp, made them gather up their belongings, and brought them back with their stolen horses and cattle before sunset.

This was the only time that Geronimo was ever captured, and then by a ruse. At the end of his career he could taunt the army with the undeniable fact that "you never have caught me shooting."[17]

The next morning Victorio and two other Warm Springs leaders came to the agency to see what was happening. Clum ordered them to bring in their people that evening for counting, explaining his reasons. Soon the cavalry arrived. Clum showed their commander around. He saw Geronimo and the other "renegade" leaders shackled and guarded in the corral and their followers, disarmed and with their guns locked up, gathered under the trees in groups fraternizing with the police. (Clum always believed that his police were effective in spreading propaganda about the happy situation on the San Carlos Reservation.)

17 Opler, "A Chiricahua Apache's Account," p. 379.

107

The only known photograph of Victorio, possibly taken in the unsettled period following his removal from Warm Springs in 1877. It is said that he had to be physically restrained and lost his headband in the struggle. "We should not have been driven from our homes. We were not to blame for what Geronimo did." Courtesy National Archives and Records Service.

The Warm Springs people were counted without incident. They numbered 343. Then the police started counting the "renegades." All was going smoothly until a young warrior named Nulah sat on the ground and refused to be counted unless Clum would take the chains off Geronimo. Clum ordered two of the police to take him to the corral and place him under guard. He wrenched free and sat down again. Victorio's people and Geronimo's people were watching, many of them laughing heartily, while the cavalry officers were sitting on the porch observing the spectacle. Clum had been a boxer and a wrestler in college. He jerked the Indian to his feet, parried a knife thrust, and finished his antagonist by a blow with his rifle barrel. Then the counting was resumed. The total, including the seven shackled leaders, was 110. The following evening Nulah was first in line while his companions watched with amused smiles. (One would like to know more about this courageous and loyal follower of Geronimo. If he survived the hazards of Apache life, he must have become a notable warrior under some other name.)

The next day a telegram from Tucson informed Clum that Ponce and Nolgee were raiding in southwestern Arizona. And Ponce was in irons in the corral! But Clum could not ignore the appeal; he immediately dispatched Beauford with seventy-five of his police to catch the real or imaginary raiders. At the same time he told the Indians, especially Ponce, about the telegram to make them realize the importance of having an alibi; there was no more objection to the daily count. Then a telegram from the commissioner of Indian affairs instructed him to remove not only the captured "renegades" but also the Warm Springs band to San Carlos. After all their wandering and pleading for a title to their homeland, this buffeted people had enjoyed secure possession only three years. Their removal could, of course, be justified on the ground that they had harbored the raiders, but it was not only cruel but unwise, and would bring terrible consequences. Clum talked with Victorio and secured his consent. Perhaps the chief was influenced by the good reports he heard from the police about San Carlos. Perhaps he simply reasoned, "What's the use?"

As late as the 1950's members of the tribe who were still living in Oklahoma insisted that their uprooting was unjust. Old Sam Haozous, great-great-grandson of Mahko and grandson of Mangas Coloradas, said with an intensity of feeling impossible to convey in print: "We were innocent and should not have been driven from our homes. We were not to blame for what Geronimo did. The United States didn't give this land to us. It was ours." And Jason Betzinez said with tragedy in his voice and tears in his eyes: "That was *our* country. It had always been our home."[18]

All of this was invisible to Clum as he made his energetic preparations for the journey. "There was no sadness," he said, only a band of "hopeful people." He decided that with his reduced police force he was warranted in accepting twelve troopers as an escort. Wagons were provided for the shackled leaders and for any who might become ill on the journey. The others were to walk, except that a few thrifty families with horses loaded their possessions on travois. (The ill-gotten herds of the raiders were, of course, confiscated.) Preparations were all completed by the morning of May 1. Then, just as they were ready to start, Clum found a very sick Indian sitting on a step in front of one of the employee quarters. The man had smallpox. Clum hastily improvised an ambulance from a wagon and put the patient in the charge of one of the police who had had the disease.

The journey was uneventful, even pleasant, as Clum described it. He found that even Geronimo had "become a most tractable prisoner and did not give his guards the slightest inconvenience during the long trek." (In later years, throughout all their captivity, army officers were to marvel at the docility of the Apache prisoners.) During the first days, the children romped, chasing lizards and playing tag, and the dogs ran after rabbits; then all quieted down to the daily march. Four babies were born en route. Clum ordered a baggage wagon to stand by and bring them in with their mothers. More cases of smallpox developed, and the pest

18 Haozous interview, January 27, 1955; Jason Betzinez interview, January 26, 1955.

wagon became crowded. The original patient recovered, but eight died. The long train reached San Carlos on May 20.[19]

This trip accomplished, the hanging of the shackled leaders came next on Clum's list of things to be done. In after years, he always wrote as though this were a mere matter of routine, but at the time he thought it was necessary to offer some hearsay evidence that he had collected from Apache gossip along the trail. He wrote officially to the sheriff at Tucson: "I have personal evidence against some of these prisoners, and will be glad to testify against them. Through my Apache police, and information they have obtained by fraternizing with the renegades, ample evidence is now available to convict each of the seven chiefs on many counts of murder. This evidence should be used while details are still fresh in the minds of witnesses." Half a century later he wrote of the "vast amount of expense, tribulation, distress and bloodshed" that would have been avoided if Geronimo's arrest "had been swiftly followed by prosecution, conviction and execution."[20]

Geronimo did not magnify his danger when in his old age he said of this imprisonment that it "might easily have been death to me."[21] And the suspicion growing out of this traumatic experience was to influence him throughout his life. Exasperated army officers, government officials, and Indian-hating frontiersmen—not to mention historians—never understood how strongly it entered into his subsequent flights.[22] At the same time, ever present but not so clearly expressed, was a deep-seated preference for the untram-

19 In this whole story I have followed Clum's account (Clum, *Apache Agent*, pp. 204–49), and Clum, "Geronimo" (part 1), pp. 26–39. He may have embroidered it a little for dramatic effect, but it seems, in the main, accurate. Eve Ball's informants discredit it as pure invention and deny that Geronimo was ever "captured." See Ball, *op. cit.*, p. 50. But they admit that Geronimo and the others were shackled, and until they explain how these warriors were induced to hold still for irons to be riveted on their ankles, Clum's account will have to stand. Also, it is supported by the testimony of John Rope, who got the story from a member of the police force. See Goodwin, "Experiences of an Indian Scout" (part 1), p. 42.

20 Clum, "Geronimo" (part 2), p. 125; Clum, *Apache Agent*, p. 250.

21 Barrett, *op. cit.*, p. 133.

22 In an analysis of Geronimo's character, Morris Edward Opler gives fear and suspicion as his motivation. See "Some Implications of Culture Theory for Anthropology and Psychology," *American Journal of Orthopsychiatry*, Vol. XVIII (Oct., 1948), pp. 617–19.

111

meled freedom, in spite of its dangers, of the old Apache life-way. He would settle down under pressure, but the wild urge was there; when his suspicion was aroused, it was easy to break away.

Clum kept the seven shackled leaders (eight, according to Geronimo) and twelve other prisoners locked in the agency guard-house. He told the rest of the band that they were free from arrest and might establish their camps anywhere on the reservation, and he instructed their leaders to bring them in once a week to be counted and receive the issues of food and clothing. He recruited four of them for his police force and added Victorio to his council of judges. But members of the band continued to die from small-pox. (Nobody seemed to think about vaccination.) When they brought the disease, the other tribes fled in terror to the mountain-ous areas of the reservation. Probably this fear added to the resent-ment that soon developed between them and the newcomers. The unaffected among the latter also sought refuge in the mountains. But the arid flats along the Gila, where a sub-agency was estab-lished for them, presented a disheartening appearance. "We were completely downcast over the prospect of having to live in this hot, desolate country," said old Jason Betzinez. "I well remember our feeling of indignation and helplessness over this ill turn in our fortunes."[23]

With Clum's good administration of the reservation they might have become reconciled to the change, but he was having his own frustrations. When he returned from Ojo Caliente, he found a company of soldiers camped just outside the agency under orders to inspect and manage his Indians. This raised his ever-present hostility against the army to the boiling point. He informed the commanding officer that *he* was in charge, and he fired off a tele-gram to the commissioner of Indian affairs at Washington. He had another grievance. During his three years' tenure he had con-solidated five Indian agencies into one, saving the government $25,000 on each, and his own responsibility had increased from

[23] Clum, *Apache Agent*, p. 249; Clum, "Geronimo" (part 1), p. 38; Goodwin, *op. cit.* (part 1), p. 42; Betzinez, *I Fought with Geronimo*, pp. 46–47.

the supervision of eight hundred to that of five thousand Indians, with no increase in salary. His telegram, dated June 9, read:

IF YOUR DEPARTMENT WILL INCREASE MY SALARY SUFFICIENTLY AND EQUIP TWO MORE COMPANIES OF INDIAN POLICE FOR ME, I WILL VOLUNTEER TO TAKE CARE OF ALL APACHES IN ARIZONA—AND THE TROOPS CAN BE REMOVED.

When this arrogant proposal became known, the War Department went into a tantrum equal to his own, and the Arizona newspapers joined in condemning him. But one of his friends, a leading Tucson merchant, revealed the real motive behind some of the attacks. "What are you trying to do?" he asked, "ruin my business? If you take the military contracts away from us, there would be nothing worth staying for. Most of our profit comes from feeding soldiers and army mules." The Indian Office rejected his overconfident offer, and he resigned in a huff, leaving at the end of July.[24]

James Kaywaykla's early childhood was a nightmare of flight and terror, the result of Clum's removal of the Warm Springs band, but he made a surprisingly perceptive evaluation of the agent. "As agents went, John Clum was one of the best," he said. "The Apaches conceded that; but they knew also that he was responsible" for the consolidation policy. (This policy, of course, did not originate with Clum; he only carried it out—with enthusiasm.) "And they knew, too, that his motive for attempting to bring all Apaches under his rule was an increase in salary." (They misjudged him here also; his motive was excess energy and the exhilaration of using it.) But—"They respected the arrogant young man in spite of that, for he was both courageous and honest. . . . They liked his using Indian police and Indian judges . . . [for] it was commendable to have a man who realized that our standards differed from theirs and felt that a man should be judged by the mores of his people."[25]

Meanwhile, Geronimo remained shackled in the guardhouse.

[24] Clum, *Apache Agent*, pp. 249–55; Clum, "The San Carlos Apache Police" (part 1), pp. 210–11.
[25] Ball, *op. cit.*, pp. xiii, 50–51.

The sheriff at Tucson failed to claim him, and soon after Clum left, the succeeding agent, Henry Lyman Hart, removed his shackles and set him free. Thus, according to Clum, he received no punishment for having murdered at least one hundred men, women, and children. And if he had been hanged, five hundred more human lives would have been saved, to say nothing of twelve million dollars and the most humiliating military campaigns in American history. His shackles "never should have been removed, except to permit him to walk untrammeled to the scaffold."[26]

Geronimo's own account of his arrest is more restrained. He told how after he was invited to come in, he was disarmed, and "Scouts conducted me to the guardhouse and put me in chains. When I asked them why they did this they said it was because I left Apache Pass." He made no mention of Clum's other accusation: that he had been on raids, killing people and stealing livestock. It is even possible that he had observed the peace as he interpreted it—applicable only to Anglos—and had confined his raids to Mexicans and Pimas. He was not the liar he was represented to be by his detractors. He sometimes used deception of an adversary for strategic purposes as he had done with Clum at Fort Bowie, but if one can untangle his wild logic, his account of events rings true. He went on to say: "I was kept a prisoner for four months, during which time I was transferred to San Carlos. Then I think I had another trial although I was not present. In fact I do not know that I had another trial, but I was told that I had, and at any rate I was released. After this we had no more trouble with the soldiers [that is, the police], but I never felt at ease any longer at the Post [the agency]. We were allowed to live above San Carlos at a place now called Geronimo. . . . All went well for a period of two years, but we were not satisfied."[27]

This unstable situation was to erupt in a succession of breakouts.

26 Clum, "Geronimo" (part 1), p. 34.
27 Barrett, *op. cit.*, pp. 132–33.

CHAPTER 7

A PATTERN OF BREAKOUTS IS SET

After Clum's departure, things went from bad to worse on the San Carlos Reservation under weak or corrupt agents.[1] The Warm Springs band, starving and poorly clothed, dying from smallpox, ill from malaria bred by the mosquito-infested Gila flats, and pining for their mountain homeland, became increasingly dissatisfied. At the same time, Pionsenay, having recovered from his wounds, was happily raiding with Nolgee in Mexico or hovering around the reservation making contacts with his Chiricahua friends. The miserable captives began saving up flour from their scanty rations and hiding away other supplies.

On the night of September 1, Pionsenay and his adherents came in rich with plunder and full of boastful tales of successful raiding. Early the next morning, with 22 of their women and children who had been living on the reservation, they headed back towards Mexico, and Victorio and Loco broke away with 323 of *their* followers and escaped into the mountains to the northeast, leaving 143 of their band, including some members of their families, at San Carlos. In comparison with subsequent Apache breakouts, the

[1] Details of their speculations are given by Ogle in *Federal Control of the Western Apaches*, pp. 194–213 *passim*.

Warm Springs fugitives at this time acted with restraint, fighting the soldiers only to cover the escape of their women and children and killing civilians only when necessary in obtaining supplies. Late in September the two chiefs appeared at Fort Wingate in the Navaho country of New Mexico and offered to bring in their people. They had not intended to go on the warpath, they said, but were only seeking a refuge. Assured of protection, most of their followers, who had been scattered through the mountains, collected there during October. Nana, however, with a small band joined the Mescaleros.

The refugees at Fort Wingate begged above all to return home, but they said they would go anywhere except back to San Carlos. Indian Inspector William Vandever came from his office at Santa Fe and conferred with Victorio and Loco. As he reported it, they complained of the hostility of the other tribes at San Carlos. "They said further that the water was bad . . . it made their people sick, and therefore they determined to go somewhere else to live. My reply to them was, that, they must learn to stay wherever the Government chooses to put them." He concluded that it was "wholly out of the question to yield to their desire to return to Ojo Caliente," and he recommended that they be permanently located in the Indian Territory (present Oklahoma), meanwhile being subsisted on the Mescalero Reservation until their removal.

The Washington officials decided that allowing them to return to Ojo Caliente would be "a sign of weakness" and "establish a bad precedent"; their short-lived reservation had been restored to the public domain in August, and the agency buildings were in process of being sold. But while the Indian Office wavered between driving them back to San Carlos or sending them to Fort Sill in the Indian Territory, the army permitted them to drift back to their beloved homeland. They remained there through the winter of 1877/78, carefully keeping the peace, while settlers, travelers, and prospectors were secure in their persons and property.[2]

[2] Thrapp, *Conquest of Apacheria*, pp. 177–78; Thrapp, *Victorio*, pp. 193–207; National Archives and Records Service, Inspectors File No. 1732, Vandever's Report, October 23, 1877. For Kaywaykla's account of the flight, see Ball, *op. cit.*, p. 52.

116

Naiche and most of the Chiricahuas remained on the San Carlos Reservation. Geronimo also did not go out with either his Warm Springs friends or Pionsenay. On the evening of September 23 (or possibly September 25) Hart held a conference with him and made him "captain" of the remaining Warm Springs band. Geronimo promised that he would not leave the reservation and would inform Hart of any contemplated breakouts. At the same time the Chiricahua leaders made the same promises.[3]

Some of Geronimo's close relatives were among the Warm Springs people who did not go out with their leaders. Among them were his widowed "sister," Nah-thle-tla, and her teenaged children, Betzinez and Ellen. They recognized Geronimo as "the senior member" of their family group and were "under compulsion" to follow his leadership. Apparently Nana's wife, Nah-dos-te, and their son also remained, probably for the same reason. Although a man of tribal prestige like Nana might become independent of his wife's family, the bond was still there.

The promises made by Geronimo and the Chiricahuas did not last long, as the dissatisfaction on the reservation continued to mount. The warriors began stealing guns and ammunition, preparing for a breakout, and Juh came up from Mexico to encourage it. Geronimo is credited with being one of the leaders in the plotting, but Betzinez gives an interesting personal reason for his immediate decision to leave. He and his family had been camping in the mountains north of the sub-agency. There, during a *tizwin* drink, he scolded his nephew—apparently the son of Nana and Nah-dos-te—"for no reason at all." The young man, with typical Apache sensitivity to disapproval, thereupon committed suicide. Geronimo, blaming himself for his relative's death, then left with Ponce and other noted irreconcilables for Mexico. The date was April 4, 1878.

Betzinez with his mother and sister remained on the reservation. He has left a revealing account of the indecision they felt as they were torn between their obligation to the head of their family group

[3] National Archives and Records Service, *loc. cit.*, enclosure, Hart to Vandever, September 24 (or 26), 1877.

117

and their own peaceable inclinations. Geronimo, of course, took his immediate family. According to Betzinez, he had two wives. These must have been Chee-hash-kish, with her two children Chappo and Dohn-say, and She-gha. If he had only two, he had not yet married Shtsha-she.[4]

As Betzinez told it, Geronimo and Juh were in command of the escaping band. They intercepted a wagon train, killing the drivers and obtaining food and ammunition. They were attacked by troops, but beat them off and reached the border. Once in Mexico, they joined the band of Juh and Nolgee in their Sierra Madre hideout, from which they set up a lively traffic in stolen goods with the conniving citizens of Janos.[5]

Another band of Apache raiders was soon loosed on the ranchers and travelers of New Mexico and Arizona. In the summer of that same year (1878) the Indian Office requested the army to drive the Warm Springs band to San Carlos. The officer in command at Ojo Caliente reported on their cooperative attitude and their earnest desire to stay, but the order went out. When the attempt was made to remove them, they fled to the mountains. Finally, the army collected twenty men, seventy-eight women, and seventy-five children, including the peaceable Loco, and delivered them to the Indian police at San Carlos in November. Among those who remained out were fifty irreconcilable warriors under Victorio. They began of necessity to rob and kill. Their hunted existence, with their flight from pursuing soldiers and their losses in killed and captured, as remembered by three-year-old James Kaywaykla, is an epic of courage and determination.

Finally, early in January, 1879, Victorio called down from the heights to the officer in command at Ojo Caliente and asked for a talk. The officer, unarmed, climbed the mountain with an interpreter for a conference. It was eventually decided that the band

---

4 Betzinez also said that he took along the young Mescalero girl Ih-tedda, whom he afterwards married, but this seems improbable. Not only in his book, but also in personal conversations I have found Betzinez confused about Geronimo's family.

5 Thrapp, *Conquest of Apacheria*, pp. 189–90; Betzinez, *I Fought with Geronimo*, pp. 47–49; Griswold, "The Fort Sill Apaches," s.v. "Nah-dos-te."

should settle with the Mescaleros. By late July the Mescalero agent reported that 145 had collected there, and arrangements were being made to permit their people who were at San Carlos to join them. Plans were even being considered to establish them once more at Ojo Caliente. But Victorio learned that indictments had been found against him in Grant County for horse stealing and murder. (It appears that Pionsenay was the actual culprit. And considering the murders and livestock rustling by white men in the contemporary Lincoln County War and throughout that lawless period, one wonders why the Apaches were picked out for prosecution.) Just then a party from Silver City, including a judge and the prosecuting attorney of Grant County, came to the reservation on a hunting and fishing trip. (Nobody ever considered that killing the game on the Indians' land was exactly the same as their killing the livestock of the ranchers.) Victorio thought they had come to arrest him, and the whole band fled, along with some lawless spirits among the Mescaleros. It was August 21, 1879.[6]

Now the killings and robbings on both sides of the border surpassed anything previously experienced in Apache raids. They began before Victorio was well out of the Mescalero Reservation when two Mexican sheep herders were killed and their horses were taken. Then came a dreary succession of wagon trains captured and livestock—horses, cattle, sheep—swept away from ranches, always with every defender killed. Even the cavalry mounts were captured, and the troopers were set on foot. Troops were pulled out from everywhere for the arduous campaigning, only to be lured into deadly ambushes while the Apaches melted away. The harassed white officials suspected that Juh and Geronimo joined Victorio, but this seems untenable. Understandably, when every rock exploded with death the soldiers saw too many Indians, more than Victorio alone could have had—a common miscalculation in Indian fights. But the keen-eyed child Kaywaykla never saw any

[6] Ball, op. cit., pp. 3–10, 52–53, 64–66; Thrapp, Victorio, pp. 208–20; Sonnichsen, Mescalero Apaches, pp. 161–71; Thrapp, Conquest of Apacheria, pp. 179–81. For an account of non-Indian murders and livestock rustling in contemporary New Mexico, see Lily Klasner, My Girlhood among Outlaws, pp. 169–91 and passim.

Geronimo's Mexican refuge and raiding range

of these supposed allies until they all gathered in Juh's stronghold the year after Victorio's death. No doubt some of the raids were separate exploits of Juh, possibly even of Geronimo, slipping up from the Sierra Madre. In some of the captures of wagon trains, teamsters were tortured by suspending them head-down over the burning wreckage.[7] This was the punishment reserved by Apache custom for their own witches after a trial and conviction by a council.[8] Extending it to white victims was the practice of some Apaches, but it was not the trademark of Victorio.

[7] Thrapp, *Conquest of Apacheria*, pp. 182–89; Thrapp, *Victorio*, pp. 220–48; Ball, *op. cit.*, pp. 71–73, 79–86.
[8] Opler, *An Apache Life-Way*, pp. 252–54.

"I was with Victorio until his death, with Nana for years, and Geronimo several months," said Kaywaykla. "I do not like to think of the things I witnessed." But he went on to say, "I have seen hundreds of people killed, but nobody tortured." He felt horror when a wealthy Mexican family—two men, a woman, and a little boy—were brought into camp and summarily executed; and his grandmother was shaking as she took him in her arms and tried to comfort him. He saw a small detachment of Mexican soldiers lured into a trap and exterminated. "The warriors walked among the bodies collecting rifles and ammunition belts . . . shirts and saddles," he said, but "The men were not tortured; the bodies were not mutilated. I know, for I lay on my belly and watched this thing happen." He went on to say, however, that mutilation of a body might occur after death to avenge such mutilation as was "perpetrated on the body of Mangas Coloradas."[9]

In the fall of 1879, while Victorio was slashing his bloody way across northern Chihuahua, Geronimo and Juh were holed up in a hidden camp at McIntosh Spring in the Guadelupe Mountains near the Arizona–New Mexico line. From this place they sent a runner to ask General Willcox to "be their friend." This envoy contacted the general's aide-de-camp, Captain Harry L. Haskell, then at San Bernardino conducting a scout in the southeastern corner of Arizona. Haskell, seeing the importance of this overture, decided at once to visit the hostiles' camp. They had imposed the condition that he bring no soldiers, and he went accompanied only by an interpreter, probably Jeffords. (In spite of the treachery the Apaches had experienced when they came under supposed safe conduct to confer with white men, they still observed their savage code of honor.) He held a conference with the leaders and then went back to San Bernardino while they considered his proposals. The next day they called him back, and he went with Jeffords and Archie McIntosh.

9 Ball, *op. cit.*, pp. 13, 46, 77–78, 119. For a historian's account of the annihilation of this Mexican force, see Dan L. Thrapp, *Juh: An Incredible Indian*, pp. 18–19. Thrapp believes that Juh participated and bases his conclusion on the report of the American consul at Chihuahua.

As he reported it, "The Indians say they have heard that General Willcox has always treated their people well and they have come to live at peace, that they shall not go on war-path nor break out from the agency, that they have not been with Victoria and do not know where he is." They asked that the scout companies be withdrawn while they collected their band, and that Haskell remain with them until they should be settled at San Carlos. They wanted to be located with their own people at the sub-agency (probably to avoid the hostility of the other tribes on the reservation) and asked that Nolgee, who had already gone in, might visit them there.

The agreement was made without difficulty, and the hostiles settled down on the reservation. It was in December, 1879, or perhaps the following January. The *Arizona Star* at Tucson hailed the good news. "These Indians belong to Cachise's old tribe—the worst in the deck. They deny having fought with Victorio and his band, but own up to having done deviltry under their own chiefs, Hoo and Geronimo. . . . We take it that the people of southern Arizona and Sonora are resting easier, since the surrender of these 'disturbing elements.' "

But the Mexican consul at Tucson was alarmed at the prospect that they would use the reservation as a safe base for more intensive raids into Mexico. Willcox assured him that "Hoo and his followers . . . will be kept at San Carlos, where they can harm neither Americans nor Mexicans, and like the rest of the Indians on the reservation will be treated friendly as long as they behave themselves and will be used as auxiliaries for the subjugation of hostile bands across the border."[10]

Everything indeed seemed at peace at San Carlos. Reuben Hood, who operated a trading post there, reported in late May that the hostiles were "perfectly content with their new home, and instead of being in sympathy with Victorio's band, they exhibit

10 Thrapp, *Juh*, pp. 19–21, citing Office of Indian Affairs, Letters Received, 1821–81, Roll 581, File No. W67–1880, Haskell to AAAG, December 14, 1879, and Roll 582, File No. W1354, Willcox to Prieto, November 8, 1879, and January 31, 1880; and *Arizona Star*, January 7, 1880.

hostile feelings towards them." He cited Jeffords as confident that they would not assist Victorio even if he should appear there.[11] In fact, some of Victorio's warriors had already reached them, possibly with the idea of enlisting assistance. Earlier that spring a dashing leader named Washington, said to be a son of Victorio, made a swift raid into Arizona with fourteen well-armed warriors. They reached a camp of Juh's and Geronimo's people, now good reservation Indians, and apparently skirmished with them. Then they were attacked and pursued by the soldiers, who suffered some casualties but inflicted no damage. Killing and pillaging as they went, the raiders returned to Victorio's camp in New Mexico without, as far as is known, losing a man.[12]

But by that time the great Apache was approaching the end of his career. On May 24 in a box canyon at the head of the Palomas River in the Black Range of New Mexico he was trapped by a force consisting mainly of Apache scouts and suffered his first tactical defeat. He lost about thirty of his people—men, women, and children—and according to the scouts was himself wounded. He set out for the border, killing everyone he met on the way, but on June 5 before he reached it, the army came up with him again, killing ten of his band and wounding three. (Every such loss reduced his small fighting force, while the army manpower seemed limitless.) One of the slain was Washington. In fact, Victorio lost three sons at one time or another during the wars, leaving only a small boy, Istee, hidden out in the Black Range with his mother. Mangus, who had married Victorio's daughter, also left his wife and little son, later known as Frank Mangus, in the same refuge. The child Kaywaykla was not so shielded. His father had been killed during a raid, but the rest of the family remained with the band.[13]

Now south of the border, Victorio raided deep into Chihuahua, once striking within thirty miles of the capital. Officials of the two

11 Thrapp, *Juh*, p. 21, quoting *Arizona Star*, May 27, 1880.
12 Thrapp, *Conquest of Apacheria*, pp. 198–99; Thrapp, *Victorio*, pp. 275–76.
13 Thrapp, *Victorio*, pp. 277–82; Thrapp, *Conquest of Apacheria*, pp. 199–203; Ball, *op. cit.*, pp. 15, 58–60, 113.

countries prepared for "the biggest manhunt in the history of the Southwest" (Thrapp's words), as military forces were put into action on both sides of the line. In September plans were developed for enlisting Juh and others in his band to aid in the operations.[14] Juh's response to the suggestion, had it been made, cannot be conjectured. It is impossible to believe that Geronimo, with his strong family and tribal ties to the Warm Springs band, could have been enlisted. There was also mention of approaching Naiche, who probably would not have responded either. But Victorio for once relaxed his vigilance and led his weary people to a supposed resting place at Tres Castillos, where three rugged hills rise above the plain far east of the protecting Sierra Madre.

There, a strong Mexican force under Colonel Joaquin Terrazas, a cousin of Governor Luis Terrazas of Chihuahua, lay hidden. It was October 14, 1880. When the Apaches started to relax and make their camps, Terrazas sprang the trap. The Indians were almost out of ammunition. Kaahteney, a popular young warrior soon to become prominent in Apache history, had been sent out with another man to capture some, but they had not yet returned. Everything was soon over. The Mexicans' casualties were only three killed and ten wounded. They killed and scalped for the bounty seventy-eight Indians, of whom sixty-two were warriors, the rest women and children; they captured sixty-eight women and children to be sold into slavery; they took 120 horses, 38 mules, and 12 burros; and they recovered two Mexican boy captives. They were given a triumphal entry into the city of Chihuahua with the seventy-eight scalps borne on poles and the captives following. It is said that the scalp bounty added up to fifty thousand dollars, but the cheering multitude thought the victory was well worth the price.

Only seventeen Apaches—men, women, and children—escaped the massacre. These included Nana, who was with the rear guard, and Victorio's son-in-law Mangus. Victorio was among the dead.

14 Thrapp, *Juh*, p. 21, citing Record Group 393, Records of U.S. Army Continental Commands, 1821–1920, Department of Arizona, misc. papers re Victoria's campaign, roll 36, 2715, Carr in the field at Bowie, to AG, Whipple, September 1, 1880.

Kaywaykla and his mother, Guyan, escaped, but his baby sister was lost; his grandmother and his young girl cousin Siki (Sy-e-konne) were among the captives. (Siki was a daughter of Loco. Her mother, Guyan's sister, had died and the girl had been brought up by her grandmother.[15]) A woman who was then, or who afterwards became, a wife of Mangus was also captured. Later, under the Spanish name of Huera, she was to figure largely in a crisis of Geronimo's life. A hunting party sent out before the attack and the two warriors on the ammunition raid eventually joined the survivors, but even so, it was a tragically diminished band.[16]

The white men of the American Southwest also had their losses to consider. In his report for 1881 William Tecumseh Sherman, the commanding general of the army, reckoning the price of the Victorio war in the hundreds of civilians slain and the millions of dollars expended, sarcastically remarked that while he did not know why the Interior Department had insisted on removing these Indians to Arizona, the reasons must have been very good to justify the cost to settlers and the government.[17]

In contrast, Juh and Geronimo and their followers were living quietly on the reservation. Even Clum, writing of that time, credited the two leaders with peaceable intentions.[18] It may have been at this period that Geronimo's daughter, Dohn-say, received some sort of Apache accolade as one of the three outstanding young women of their band. This must have pleased Geronimo, for he loved his family. (The other two were Betzinez' sister, later known as Ellen, and the young woman who became the wife of Geronimo's "brother," actually his second cousin, Perico.)[19]

But the survivors of Victorio's band did not come in to share the peace with their friends and relatives on the reservation. Nana

---

[15] Ball, *op. cit.*, p. 87.

[16] *Ibid.*, pp. 87–102; James Kaywaykla interview, July 29, 1959; Thrapp, *Victorio*, pp. 293–307, 310–11. Thrapp, who has examined the site of the massacre, is impressed by the accuracy with which the four-year-old Kaywaykla's memory fits the terrain.

[17] Thrapp, *Victorio*, p. 314.

[18] John P. Clum, "Apache Misrule," *New Mexico Historical Review*, Vol. V, No. 3 (July, 1930), pp. 226–27.

[19] Jason Betzinez interview, August 21, 1959.

gathered the broken fragments and led them to hidden places in the Sierra Madre to rest and recuperate.[20] The next year (1881) they made cautious overtures to return. In April Loco reported to the San Carlos agent that they had communicated with him, offering to come in and join his band and refrain from raiding if they could be assured of protection. Apparently the assurance was not given, although Loco said he would be responsible for their future good behavior. Then in July, according to the Mescalero agent, they made four attempts to contact *him*, hoping to settle there; but each time they approached they were driven back by the soldiers. Rebuffed, they went on the warpath.[21]

If it was Nana who initiated these overtures, one can hardly credit his sincerity. Kaywaykla, who heard all the adult conversation at the time and afterwards, represented him as implacably committed to vengeance for the disaster at Tres Castillos. "Nana . . . was not content with an eye for an eye, nor a life for a life. For every Apache killed he took many lives."[22] In either case, in late July, with fifteen warriors of his own band and about twenty-five Mescaleros who joined him, he began a series of slashing raids through the mountains of south central and southwestern New Mexico. Old and crippled as he was, he seemed tireless, riding as much as seventy miles a day, striking army units and citizens' posses, killing miners, herders, Mexican-Americans—every person encountered—and capturing horses and supplies. Altogether eight companies of cavalry, eight companies of infantry, and two companies of Indian scouts were called out to run him down, but his hostiles inflicted casualties and melted away unharmed. Finally, in late August they crossed the border, and "on positive orders from the government," said the official summary, "the chase was abandoned."[23]

Geronimo and Juh and their people on the reservation were not directly affected by Nana's raid, but the panic into which it threw

20 Ball, *op. cit.*, p. 113.
21 Thrapp, *Victorio*, p. 310; Secretary of the Interior, *Annual Report*, 1881, p. 5.
22 Ball, *op. cit.*, pp. 119–20, 123.
23 Thrapp, *Conquest of Apacheria*, pp. 212–16; Sonnichsen, *op. cit.*, pp. 191–94.

the government officials may well explain the irrational actions that were to drive these scarcely tamed bands into hostility. It all began, innocently enough, with one of those religious revivalist movements that have broken out spontaneously among frustrated Indians at various times and places, linked only by a fervent faith in the disappearance of the white man and the return of the old order.[24] This time the "prophet" was Noch-ay-del-klinne.

This frail, mild ascetic was living with his family on Cibecue Creek in the western part of the former Fort Apache Reservation. The Indians removed by Clum from this area had been permitted to return to their homeland by an effective temporary agent,[25] and many had gone there, preferring the opportunities for self-support in this bountiful region to dependency on government rations. There was a garrison at Fort Apache to keep them in order, but they remained under the authority of the distant San Carlos Agency. The Chiricahuas and their Nednai associates were still held there in the vicinity of the sub-agency farther up the Gila, and a few miles beyond that, off the reservation to the east, was Fort Thomas.

Released from close herd on the Gila, the White Mountain and Coyotero Apaches discovered the extent to which white intruders were overrunning their land.[26] The boundaries of the combined reservation had in fact been moved back several times to accommodate mining interests, and towns had sprung up on land thus lost to the Indians. Out of their frustration they turned to religion. By the spring of 1881 Noch-ay-del-klinne had convinced them (and probably had convinced himself) that he could commune with the spirits of the dead and even had the power to bring their dead chiefs back to life. He taught his followers a new dance, in which the performers were arranged like the spokes of a wheel, all facing inward, while he stood at the hub and sprinkled them with

[24] The historian will recall the Shawnee movement headed by Tecumseh's brother and the "ghost dance religion" that swept the Plains tribes in the 1890's. Less well known nativist revivals have occurred in other widely separated tribes.

[25] Ogle, *op. cit.*, p. 197.

[26] *Ibid.*, pp. 130, 203–204.

the sacred *hoddentin* as they circled around him.[27] The Indians flocked to him and danced with a religious ecstasy frightening to white observers. It was reported that he linked the return of the dead chiefs to the disappearance of the white men and foretold that the consummation would occur at the time of the corn harvest.

It is not known to what extent the hard-headed Geronimo was affected by these emotional orgies. Apparently he did at least visit the prophet. He must have been referring to him when he said later at Fort Sill, "Once while living in San Carlos Reservation an Indian told me that while lying unconscious on the battlefield he had actually been dead, and had passed into the spirit land." There he saw Indians he had known in life camped in a green valley with plenty of game, and "was sorry when he was brought back to consciousness."[28]

As he remembered it from his boyhood, Asa Daklugie stated that his father Juh and Geronimo were present when the religious excitement reached its tragic climax. He was probably mistaken about this. The army made an investigation of the incident, and no evidence of their presence was found. But Daklugie also said that Geronimo told him at Fort Sill shortly before his death in 1909 that he had never understood how he and Juh could have been influenced by the prophet's incantations. This is entirely typical of Geronimo's healthy skepticism. Nana apparently had greater faith. According to Daklugie, who as an adult knew that leader well at Fort Sill, Nana once visited the prophet, attended at least one prayer session, and on a misty predawn saw him call up Mangas Coloradas, Cochise, and Victorio. "The word of Nana could not be questioned," said Daklugie.[29] One may question his vision, but there is no need to question his visit. Nobody knew where the invisible Nana was except when he struck. While he was collecting his people and recuperating he could have taken a side trip to Cibecue.

[27] James Mooney, *The Ghost-Dance Religion and the Sioux Outbreak of 1890*, pp. 704–705.

[28] Barrett, *Geronimo's Story of His Life*, pp. 208–11.

[29] Dan L. Thrapp, *General Crook and the Sierra Madre Adventure*, p. 40 n.; Thrapp, *Juh*, pp. 21–25.

The dancing and the emotional fervor were at their height at the very time Nana was splashing blood over the map of New Mexico. Officials responsible for good order on the reservation and the safety of civilian lives outside were understandably nervous. White men have seldom sensed the meaning of such religious manifestations among unhappy Indians grasping at nostalgic memories of their past.[30] Joseph Capron Tiffany was the agent at San Carlos. According to inspectors sent out from Washington, he not only sold immense stores of goods supposed to be issued to the Indians, but also established a ranch where he put his private brand on issued cattle, fed them issued grain, and detailed an agency employee to herd them.[31] Certainly in the Cibecue emergency he exhibited ineptitude and lack of discernment. The commander at Fort Apache was Colonel Eugene Asa Carr,[32] who, though a competent officer, had no sympathy for Indians. He tried, however, to calm the situation. In a post order he issued on August 17 he said he had heard that "some silly or evil disposed soldiers" had been telling the Indians that the army was planning to attack them or drive them from the reservation, and he warned against such "foolish or wicked" boasts.[33]

As the excitement increased, even the enlisted scouts at Fort Apache demanded passes to attend the dances, and they returned as converts. Tiffany sent his Indian police to arrest the prophet, and they came back empty-handed, grumbling about white aggression. The prophet evaded summonses from both Tiffany and Carr to come in for a conference. Finally, after considerable vacillation, the agent on August 14 sent this demand to the officer: "I want him arrested or killed or both."

Carr accordingly set out on August 29 with 117 men, including 23 scouts. They arrested Noch-ay-del-klinne, who submitted quietly, but his followers attacked the troops, and even the scouts defected and joined them. The prophet, an estimated 18 other

30 For example, the massacre of the Sioux ghost dancers at Wounded Knee in 1890.
31 Ogle, *op. cit.*, pp. 211–13.
32 Brevet rank, major general.
33 Thrapp, *General Crook and the Sierra Madre Adventure*, p. 14.

Indians, and 8 of Carr's men were killed. Carr slipped away by night and reached Fort Apache, and the Indians then made a futile attack on the post. Small bands also struck out, killing several soldiers and civilians they found in the vicinity of the reservation. It is clear, however, that there was no plan for a general uprising; it was only that the Indians revered their prophet and were furious over his arrest and death. Major General Irvin McDowell, who commanded the Department of the Pacific, which included Arizona, came to this conclusion: "The fact of the troops finding the medicine-man and his people in their homes, where they had been planting corn,[34] shows that they were not then for war."

After their first angry reaction, the Indians settled back into disillusionment. Their prophet was dead. No miracles had intervened. Their dream was over. But the whole Southwest was unnerved by the fear of a general outbreak. General Willcox rushed all available Arizona military forces to the area. Reinforcements were sent in from New Mexico and California—cavalry, infantry, artillery—twenty-two companies in all. The huge consolidated reservation swarmed with armed men. The Indians involved in the Cibecue fight, including the mutinous scouts, began to surrender. Possibly the presence of the soldiers did hasten their submission. It had the opposite effect on the Chiricahuas and their relatives.

According to Tiffany's report, these bands had been "perfectly quiet during the whole White Mountain trouble," but there had been no soldiers in their area since Clum had informed the military in 1876 that he was in charge of the agency. Now soldiers were marching and countermarching all over the place. The Indians there, especially those like Geronimo and Juh, who were uneasily conscious of past depredations in Mexico, became nervous. About the middle of September they came to ask Tiffany "what was going on, and what so many troops meant about the agencies. I explained it to them and told them to have no fear, that none of the Indians who had been peaceable would be molested in any way. They said

---

34 He did not mean that they had been planting corn in August, but that they were a settled people with corn fields.

they had been on the war-path and had come in in good faith and were contented, that they did not want war or to fight. . . . They inquired if the movement of troops had anything to do with what they had done in Mexico. I assured them it had not. They shook hands, much delighted and went back" to the sub-agency.[35]

But two bands that *had* engaged in the fighting were in the area. One had five members, who are usually classed by historians as Chiricahuas but apparently were White Mountain Indians. Their leader was Benito (Bonito), who will be heard from hereafter.[36] The other was a White Mountain band of twenty-six under a leader known as George. On September 25 the two leaders came to Ezra Hoag, the employee in charge of the sub-agency, and surrendered. General Willcox, at Fort Thomas, then released them on parole, but five days later, for no discernable reason, it was decided to take them into custody. September 30 was ration day at the sub-agency, and all the Indians were assembled there in the happy confusion of the distribution. Suddenly three companies of cavalry appeared. George and Benito, not wanting to miss their rations, sent word that they would voluntarily appear later at Fort Thomas, but the commander deployed his troops and advanced on their people. The two bands then fled to the Chiricahuas and Nednais, the latter took flight, and seventy-four warriors under Juh, Geronimo, and the formerly peaceable Naiche set out with their families for Mexico. Among them were Benito and his tiny band.

Incidentally, George and his band also escaped. They bolted in the opposite direction and hid out in the northern part of the reservation, but they were eventually captured. Altogether, the army collected about one hundred suspects during the weeks following the Cibecue fight. A general hanging of the participants was at first contemplated, but through McDowell's influence all were eventually released except five scouts. The latter were court-

<hr>

[35] Department of the Interior, *Annual Report*, 1881, p. 5.

[36] For a biographical sketch of Benito as a White Mountain Indian, see Griswold, *op. cit.*, s.v. "Benito." But Willcox regarded him as a Chiricahua who had been planting with the Coyoteros living on Turkey Creek; Secretary of War, *Annual Report*, 1882, pp. 145, 148. Whatever his tribe, he became a member of the band in Mexico.

martialed; three were hanged, and two were sentenced to long terms in the army prison at Alcatraz.[37]

The army officers were completely baffled about the cause of the Chiricahuas' and Nednais' stampede, but the reason is evident. As Hoag said, they were "literally scared away." Even Geronimo-hating Clum passionately supported this judgment.[38] Few white men ever understood the fears of this volatile people, who had centuries of good cause to fear. Two and one-half years later, when the runaways had been brought back after a gruelling army campaign, Geronimo explained his reasons.

He said he "left on account of the trouble on the Cibecu. Some Indians from the White Mountains came to us when that trouble took place. A White Mountain Chief called 'George' came to us and told us a great many things and we left on that account. . . . We were treated very badly by the Agents here also, and that made us want to leave. We were given rations but not all that we should have had, not all that belonged to us. They gave us a little manta and cloth, but not enough. . . . We were not allowed to go to the mountains to bake mescal. [The large fleshy bulb of the century plant—the same plant from which the Mexicans made their fiery intoxicant—was steamed in pits over heated stones by the Apache women, and it constituted one of their most important foods.] . . . The manta they gave us was not enough to make a breech-clout. On account of these things we were dissatisfied."[39]

On their way to the border the fugitives killed everybody they encountered, picking up supplies and horses as they fled. The army pursued them, striking them twice in inconclusive actions but otherwise failing to catch up with them.[40] Their trail took them close to Tombstone, and Mayor Clum, with a posse, including

---

[37] Scholarly accounts of the entire Cibecue affair and its aftermath are in Thrapp, *Conquest of Apacheria*, pp. 217–30; Thrapp, *General Crook and the Sierra Madre Adventure*, pp. 3–50; and Ogle, *op. cit.*, pp. 203–209. For the Indian Office version, see Secretary of the Interior, *Annual Report*, 1881, pp. 5–7.

[38] Clum, "Apache Misrule," pp. 226–39, and "Geronimo" (part 2), pp. 126–30.

[39] National Archives and Records Service, 1601 AGO 1884, F/W 1066 AGO 1883, Geronimo to Captain Emmet Crawford, March 21, 1884.

[40] Thrapp, *Juh*, pp. 26–28. Geronimo's account of the flight is in Barrett, *op. cit.*, pp. 134–35.

three of the famous Earp brothers and other frontier notables, set out to follow them. Clum blamed Geronimo for the whole affair— even for being the source of Noch-ay-del-klinne's visions. Geronimo would not be set free this time, he said, but turned over to the authorities in a box with a paper lily on his chest. But that involved catching him, and the posse never came in sight of the speeding Indians.[41]

The life of Geronimo and his friends and relatives was now centered in the Sierra Madre.

[41] Clum, *Apache Agent*, pp. 265–67.

CHAPTER 8

THE BANDS GATHER IN
THE SIERRA MADRE

The observant child Kaywaykla has given a good description of the Apache leaders as he first saw them assembled in the Sierra Madre. He had a photographic memory of the physical appearance and character traits of the people he met, and these first impressions were reinforced by subsequent acquaintance. Juh and Geronimo had already settled in those mountains when Nana arrived with his small following. After his revenge raid in New Mexico, that incorrigible hostile had rested his people in hidden *barrancas* on the west side of the great uplift. Then, far to the south, they "camped near a stream at the foot of a mile-high mountain," where they could see a zigzag trail leading up to the flat top, which was Juh's fabulous stronghold. In that relaxed situation the meeting with Geronimo began with an expression of the broad Apache humor.

Juh first came riding in, "a powerful figure on a sturdy war horse. . . . He was very large, not fat, but stockily built." As he dismounted, he towered above Nana, who himself must have been close to six feet tall, and "his body was twice as thick. . . . His heavy hair was braided and the ends fell almost to his knees. His features differed from those of the Warm Springs. They were what people would now call Mongoloid." He and Nana greeted each other cordially. Soon Geronimo approached at the head of a party of horsemen. Juh suggested that they "play a joke on him." The fire was hastily covered, and all sought hiding places behind boulders and along the walls of the canyon. Geronimo rode un-observing into the trap, taking no precautions in that secure refuge. Then Nana emerged with good-natured banter.

Geronimo was not above a white lie in such a situation. "I knew all the time you were here," he countered. "You did not," said Nana. "And you the sly fox of the Apaches!" But warm greetings followed. Geronimo's "erect compact figure was smaller than that of Juh, but blocky and muscular," as Kaywaykla saw him. After him came "a tall stately young man . . . the tall, handsome son of Cochise."

Apparently the united band never climbed to the stronghold, but remained at the foot of the mountain for the days following. Kaywaykla observed them in their dances and councils. He watched Juh come to the dance at the head of his warriors, wearing only a breechclout and gorgeously beaded moccasins. On his head was "the tight-fitting skull cap of the Nednhi Medicine Man," from which "floated long streamers of eagle plumes that dangled almost to his heels." His speech impediment did not appear in his singing. "He had a soft, deep voice and was skillful in improvising rhythmic accounts of the exploits of his band."

Among Geronimo's warriors were his "brothers" Perico and Fun. The two were sons of the same father. Fun's mother was Geronimo's first cousin, who went by the Spanish name of Bonita. The name of Perico's mother is not remembered, and the ancestry that made him Geronimo's second cousin has not been traced. Possibly Geronimo had a fifth "sister," whom—following the Apache tendency to keep to the mystic number four—he did not mention.[1]

In subsequent events Perico was to appear as Geronimo's chief lieutenant, and even at this time "to many Apaches, Fun was the

[1] Griswold, "The Fort Sill Apaches," s.v. "Mahko," "Perico," "Fun."

bravest of all the band."[2] Kaywaykla also observed, "For the first time I saw Yanosha, another mighty warrior," Geronimo's brother-in-law. The members of this related group were to be with Geronimo at the time of his last break to the mountains and his final surrender.

Yahnozha "was followed by a small thin boy, little more than half-grown," an orphan named Kanseah. Through some unexplained relationship this youth was Geronimo's nephew, and Yahnozha, by an Apache custom not unlike the page-squire apprenticeship of nobles' sons in medieval Europe, was training him to be a warrior. Kanseah also was destined to be present when Geronimo's last holdout band reached the end of its tangled trail. Another boy noticed by Kaywaykla was Daklugie, who followed his father's warriors to the dance. Kaywaykla was already intimate with two boys of his own band. When Nana was collecting his people after the tragedy of Tres Castillos, he had picked up from the Black Range the wife and young son of Mangus, and Istee, the son of Victorio. Istee was "a handsome and intelligent lad about three years older than I," as Kaywaykla characterized him. Mangus' son was also slightly older than Kaywaykla. The eager child, aspiring to begin his warrior's training, had watched with longing as the two carried on their duties at camp or on the trail.

In this meeting of bands, Kaywaykla was impressed by the recognition given his "grandfather" (actually his granduncle, his grandmother's brother), the revered elder statesman Nana. And among the young warriors rising to prominence in Nana's following was Kaahteney, who had married the widowed Guyan.[3] Kaywaykla was delighted to learn that his adored stepfather had been chosen by Nana to succeed him as leader of the band. A few years later that spirited young warrior was to figure in a crisis of tribal history.

Although the boy's eager interest was centered on the warriors

[2] Other informants have made the same statement about Fun's courage.

[3] For the marriage, and Kaywaykla's happiness over the event, see Ball, *In the Days of Victorio*, p. 106.

and their sons, he was aware of the quiet influence exerted by Juh's favorite wife, Geronimo's "sister" Ishton, the mother of Daklugie. She was "not a warrior." (This was relevant to the child's experience, for Guyan had shouldered a rifle and fought by her husband's side until his death.) But in other ways Ishton was "powerful." It was believed that she suggested "much of the strategy employed" by Juh and Geronimo, but was "far too wise to admit it." Nothing is known of Juh's other wives, but Daklugie's older half-brothers, Delzhinne and Daklegon, had already attained the status of warriors.[4]

Thus, Kaywaykla saw his people as a child admiring the war leaders and loving his family elders and as an adult looking back with affection and understanding on a small, intimate group. But he was completely out of character in presenting one Chiricahua member of Geronimo's band, an "insolent young man" named Chatto, whom he saw as a greedy opportunist, scheming for position, treacherous, and thoroughly unreliable. Even Chatto's manners were bad—rude, pushing, devoid of respect for his superiors. It could only be said that he was a brave and able warrior, and for that reason he was tolerated.[5] He was to become a controversial figure in subsequent tribal history, and Kaywaykla's memory of his early impressions were certainly affected by that development.

The united bands soon decided in council to bring Loco's people from the reservation. According to Kaywaykla, Geronimo was the originator and leader of the movement, and this judgment seems to be correct. As the boy remembered it, the plan was purely a rescue mission to save friends and relatives from the sickness, starvation, and discomfort they would experience with the approaching summer if they remained penned up on the sun-scorched, malarial Gila flats with no means of self-support and cheated on their ration issues by a corrupt agent.[6] No doubt he did hear ex-

4 For Kaywaykla's characterization of the Apaches assembled below Juh's stronghold, see *ibid.*, pp. 113–14, 121–27, 136, 146. See also Griswold, *op. cit.*, s.v. "Yahnozha." For Juh's family I am indebted to Eve Ball, letter, July 13, 1973.

5 Ball, *op. cit.*, pp. 136–39.

6 *Ibid.*

pressions of sympathy for their plight, but rescue was scarcely the motivation. Geronimo was more realistic in assessing it: "In 1884 [1882] we returned to Arizona to get other Apaches to come with us into Mexico. The Mexicans were gathering troops in the mountains where we were ranging, and their numbers were so much greater than ours that we could not hope to fight them successfully, and we were tired of being chased about from place to place."[7] In other words, they wanted reinforcements, though in looking back he may have exaggerated the need at that particular time. And although most of Loco's people were women and children, according to army estimates there were thirty warriors in his band. Women and children were also valuable assets to a tribe in building up its strength. And as for the Mexican menace, it was soon to appear.

Several times during the winter the assembled bands in the Sierra Madre sent messengers to Loco urging him to join them, warning that if he should refuse they would use force. One such contact made in the middle of January, 1882, was reported to Willcox by an inspector of the Indian Office and the army officer in command at Fort Thomas, and he moved his forces to keep "a closer and more vigorous watch" on the border. Similar preparations were made by the army in New Mexico. All this military activity, however, caused no inconvenience to the invaders, who slipped invisibly past the defenses through the mountains on the western edge of New Mexico and crossed through the Steins Peak Range into Arizona. Apparently they traveled in small parties before assembling in the Apache manner for their final dash to the reservation.

According to the army officers, Juh, Geronimo, and Naiche were the leaders,[8] but since nobody saw them this is only a guess. In the Apache accounts, Juh is mentioned only by Kaywaykla, and that child, of course, remained in the Sierra Madre refuge. John Rope, who also was not present but who had talked with many

[7] Barrett, *Geronimo's Story of His Life*, pp. 105–106.
[8] Secretary of War, *Annual Report*, 1882, p. 72.

who were and who gave circumstantial details of the advance of the party, made no mention of him. Neither did Betzinez, who was one of the kidnaped band. This makes it extremely doubtful that Juh participated in the raid.[9] In either case it is apparent from all Apache accounts that Geronimo was in command. Nana remained in the Sierra Madre to care for the women and children.[10]

On the San Simon River northeast of Fort Bowie, according to Rope, two of the raiders (he gave their names) stole two good horses from some cowboys at a ranch and decided to take them back to Mexico before joining the party. Rope traced their route to "a little over towards Janos where there is a high mountain with pine trees on it." There they were captured by a Mexican army unit. Questioned by the officer (probably the notable Indian fighter Colonel Lorenzo García) they revealed the route of the expedition, which would require about four days to reach San Carlos and about twelve days to return to the vicinity of the Mexican camp. The officer held them captive with a promise to release them if their report should prove accurate and a threat to kill them if the return should fail to materialize. Then the Mexicans laid their trap,[11] with results that would be fatal to Loco's people.

Meanwhile, the other raiders continued on their way. Near Ash Flat, about twenty miles north of Safford, the united band came to a sheep ranch belonging to George Stevens, at that time the sheriff of Graham County with his home in Safford. There are four accounts of the massacre that followed. Three, all told at second or third hand, came from the eyewitness story of a well-known White Mountain Apache named Bylas, a close relative of Mrs. Stevens. Two of these—one told by Clum and the other told in his old age by Jimmie Stevens, the young son of George Stevens— are enlivened by dramatic touches and colored by the narrators'

[9] Dan L. Thrapp, whose judgment is entitled to great consideration, is convinced that he did. He bases this conclusion on the opinion of the army officers; the established fact that Juh was seen at Corralitos, near the Mexican border, a month before the party reached San Carlos; and the masterly conduct of the expedition, typical of Juh's tactics (Letter to Angie Debo, Dec. 8, 1972).

[10] Ball, *op. cit.*, p. 139. Britton Davis, who knew the Apaches well, also stated that Geronimo was the leader (*The Truth about Geronimo*, p. 142).

[11] Goodwin, "Experiences of an Indian Scout" (part 2), pp. 41–42.

hatred of Geronimo. The third, by Rope, who knew all the people involved, sounds like an exact report. In addition, there is a contemporary newspaper account quoting a grieving small boy who survived. The four stories differ widely in details, but all reveal the ruthless spirit of Geronimo and his absence of all faith and pity when dealing with Mexicans.

Stevens' foreman was a Mexican named Victoriano Mestas (or Bes-das) who had been captured in boyhood by Geronimo on one of his Mexican raids. Geronimo apparently had treated him well, as the Apaches regularly treated their adopted children, giving him a pony and saddle and supplying him with shirts, but soon he traded him off to a white rancher, and Mestas had grown up as a Mexican and had married a Mexican woman. As chief shepherd of Stevens' ten thousand sheep, he was in charge of nine (some stories say ten) Mexican and three White Mountain Apache herders. (Rope named the Apaches—names like Hac-ke-ha-da-dol-ni-he.) Bylas was also at the sheep camp with his wife and children and other White Mountain families. With the Mexican herders were Mestas' wife and three children and two other Mexican women.

The war party came riding up to the camp with Geronimo, Naiche, and Chatto in the lead. Jimmie Stevens also mentioned the leader of a small Chiricahua band who went by the name of Chihuahua—a warrior relatively unknown at the time, but destined to figure largely in later Apache history.[12] Stevens said there were seventy-six men in the party. The army guess was "about sixty."[13] Even if the number was exaggerated, it was a major expedition.

The raiders began killing Stevens' sheep, and because Geronimo liked horsemeat better than mutton he shot a sorrel pony belonging

[12] Juh was not present there, else he would certainly have been mentioned, but that fact does not entirely preclude the possibility that he was one of the leaders. The most direct army mention of him is a statement by the commander of Fort Apache that a Cibecue participant named Na-ti-o-tish "met Hoo according to agreement near Eagle Creek. . . . This information can be relied on" (Thrapp to Angie Debo, Dec. 8, 1972). That conference on nearby Eagle Creek, if it occurred, could have taken place while the main party was raiding the sheep camp.

[13] Ogle, *Federal Control of the Western Apaches*, p. 213.

to Jimmie Stevens, and they told the women to prepare the meal. Some of the stories indicate that Geronimo promised not to harm the Mexicans, that Mestas in particular trusted him, and that there was some talk and fraternizing. Mestas was wearing a fine shirt elaborately embroidered. Geronimo asked him for it, not wanting it to be bloodied, and Mestas tremblingly complied. Then at Geronimo's signal his men seized and bound the Mexicans— Mestas and his herders, his wife and two of his children, and the other women who had helped to cook the meal—and dispatched them by stabbing, clubbing, and shooting them or beating out their brains with stones.

Mestas' third child, a boy about nine years old, escaped by hiding behind Bylas' wife or under her long skirt. When he was discovered, it was Naiche, according to Clum, who protected him, even threatening to kill Geronimo if the woman were harmed; in Jimmie Stevens' account, it was an unnamed warrior of the band who braved the killer. It was this young Mexican boy's story that appeared in the newspaper account. He said that he saw his parents and brothers killed, his father after excruciating torture (the newspaper may have added this detail), and that he himself was saved through the pleas of Bylas' wife.[14]

The war party then resumed their journey. As a precaution against discovery they left two men at the sheep camp to guard the White Mountain women and compelled Bylas and the other White Mountain men to accompany them as far as the reservation. In the evening they camped on the south side of Ash Flat. There Geronimo sang four songs, consulting his Power to learn the situation at San Carlos, and was assured that the raid would be successful. His Power also helped the good work along by laying a deep sleep on Loco's people and the agency employees. By this time Geronimo's access to such supernatural aid was an important asset to his generalship. Fifty years later his followers told Opler that he would go through his ceremony and announce, " 'You should go here;

14 Clum's account is in Clum, *Apache Agent*, pp. 272–76; Jimmie Stevens' is in Ross Santee, *Apache Land*, pp. 167–71; Rope's is in Goodwin, *op. cit.* (part 2), pp. 42–46; and the newspaper story is in Thrapp, *Conquest of Apacheria*, pp. 237–38.

you should not go there.' That is how he became a leader."[15] No doubt, like superstitious people in white society, he and his warriors overlooked the occasions when the signs failed.

After this assurance, the party made a night ride to the reservation, arriving before dawn in the brush along the Gila east of the agency. They cut the telegraph wires connecting the agency with the sub-agency and with the nearby mining camp of Globe, just off the reservation to the west. It also appears that they sent agents to alert confederates in Loco's camps, for a rider with a Nednai accent came "long after midnight" to the tent where Betzinez lived with his mother and sister to ask directions to the lodge of Gil-lee. (This Gil-lee, or Zele, a Chiricahua, was to become prominent in the Apache wars as an associate of Chatto and Benito.) Geronimo, in fact, threatened to infiltrate the entire reservation. There were about forty police there, living at their homes scattered throughout the various camps, and he had said he would send three men into every camp to kill them all. Perhaps this was idle boasting, for he made no attempt to carry out his threat. While the band waited on the river for daylight, one of the men, using an Apache technique, threw a pebble into the air. It was visible, and thus they knew that dawn was approaching. At daybreak they crossed over to the Warm Springs camps.[16] It was April 19, 1882.

Loco and his people were living three miles east of the agency on the same gravelly bench between the Gila and San Carlos rivers. Except for some brush and scrawny cottonwoods along the streams, the area was bare of vegetation. The Indian agents regularly gave glowing reports of irrigation works and bountiful crops raised by their charges, but these stories can be discounted. Still, Loco had pledged his word to stay there, and he stayed. His people were at least at peace. Now at daybreak they heard shouting and saw a line of armed warriors between them and the agency, while others, swimming their horses, were approaching from across the river. One of the leaders was shouting, "Take them all! . . . Shoot

15 *An Apache Life-Way*, p. 200.
16 Goodwin, *op. cit.*, (part 2), pp. 46–47; Betzinez, *I Fought with Geronimo*, p. 55; Griswold, *op. cit.*, s.v. "Gil-lee."

down anyone who refuses to go with us! Some of you men lead them out."

"We did everything they told us to do," said Betzinez. They were driven away on foot with barely time to snatch up a few belongings. It is said that Loco was forced at gunpoint to lead the evacuation.[17] Geronimo went in front, guiding them east along the foot of the hills north of the Gila. Others stayed behind as a rear guard against any help that might come from the agency. Soon they heard shooting behind them. Chief of Police Albert D. Sterling, with one member of his Apache force, had ridden up to see what was happening. According to official reports the telegraph operator at the sub-agency had managed to repair the break in the wire and alert the agency; according to Rope the Warm Springs people had fired two shots to call him.[18] He and his Apache policeman were both killed.[19]

The killing of the policemen convinced Loco's people of their helplessness. "We told ourselves that our safety depended on keeping quiet and not trying to escape," said Betzinez. "We were filled with gloom and despair." Their captors herded them along the river for several miles, then turned northeast into the Gila Mountains. Near sunset they were given a short rest near a spring, then were started out on a night journey. Loco, a resourceful and brave warrior in spite of his peace policy, was admitted to the council of the leaders. Naiche, Chatto, and others were prominent, but clearly Geronimo was in charge. At midnight, during another brief rest, some volunteers were sent to a sheep camp for food with instructions as to the morning's rendezvous. At sunrise these raiders came with several hundred sheep, and the band ate and rested for two days.

There the leaders in council discussed plans to escape to Mexico with this great company and avoid combat with the troops, who

---

17 Thrapp, *Juh*, p. 30.

18 At least I think Rope meant that it was the Warm Springs people, not the invaders, who fired the signal shots.

19 Betzinez, *op. cit.*, pp. 56–57; Goodwin, *op. cit.* (part 2), p. 47; Thrapp, *Conquest of Apacheria*, p. 236.

were certainly scouring the country for them. There were probably about one hundred warriors and three to four hundred women and children[20]—a difficult number to conceal. They saw that they would have to make better time. It is in fact evident to one who reads Betzinez' firsthand account of their journey that they were showing little of the speed and endurance typical of Apache movements. Probably Loco's people had become soft during their enforced idleness on the Gila flats. Betzinez' mother had systematically trained him and his sister in physical fitness, but probably few had been so rigorously kept in condition. And although by his own reckoning he was twenty-two years old, he had received no training as a warrior, and he traveled with the noncombatants. Probably other young men did, also. After all, how could a youth serve the necessary apprenticeship while cooped up at San Carlos with no opportunity even to hunt? Thus, the abductors were burdened with hundreds of helpless people.

Several men were accordingly sent north up the San Francisco River to raid a ranch for horses and mules for the captives to ride. They came back driving the animals and spent another day or so breaking them to be ridden bareback or with improvised saddles made of bundles of reeds. Then men were sent to another ranch for more mounts while the main band waited out of sight on the other side of a hill. Just at that inconvenient time one of the girls reached puberty, and her womanhood ceremony was observed in an attenuated form while shots were heard from the ranch. By this time the ranging parties had killed more than fifty people—prospectors, wagon train drivers, ranchers, lone travelers, everyone they encountered on their raids. Loco's people were now deeply committed as hostiles.

Once mounted, the company set off for another night journey. The abductors surrounded their captives as they rode, but some managed to slip away and head for the Navaho country. By morn-

[20] The well-informed George Stevens estimated the number of warriors at 90. Crook, after careful calculation following the exodus, set the number at 176, and the total in the band is usually placed at 700—estimates that are probably too high. See Thrapp, *General Crook and the Sierra Madre Adventure*, p. 77, and *Al Sieber*, p. 237.

144

ing, completely exhausted, they stopped to rest at a spring in the rugged Steins Peak Range. From this place a dozen warriors were sent out on a scouting expedition while the rest of the party moved halfway up the mountainside. Lieutenant Colonel George A. Forsyth, out hunting the hostiles, discovered the trail of these scouts and sent his scouts to find them. The finding came the other way. The hostile scouting party ambushed Forsyth's scouts in the mountains and killed four of them. Then the officer came to the rescue with six companies of cavalry. There in a canyon—"I never saw a more rugged place," he reported—he attacked the whole hostile force while the noncombatants watched from the heights. Although he claimed to have "won" the engagement, he hastily pulled out, leaving the Indians in possession. He thought he had killed two. Later, Crook's careful investigation showed that the Indians had lost one warrior.[21]

After driving off Forsyth's vastly superior force, the hostiles made another long night march, moving down the mountainside and crossing the wide, open San Simon Valley to the southwest. Perhaps in this extremity Geronimo again summoned his Power—to delay the morning. Fifty years later one of his followers related such an event to Opler. Geronimo was crossing a level place and wanted to reach the mountains before the pursuing enemy could sight him, "So [he] sang, and the night remained for two or three hours longer. I saw this myself."[22] By morning they reached their assembly point in the Chiricahua Mountains southeast of Fort Bowie. There they rested during the day while some of the warriors stationed on a peak kept the post in view, half expecting to see troops coming out in search of them. But nothing happened, and after another night march through rugged arroyos and foothills along the east edge of the range and a recrossing of the San Simon Valley to the southeast, they entered Mexico. There in the Sierra de San Luis, just south of New Mexico, they rested another day. They had continued to leave a trail of blood behind them.[23]

21 Thrapp, *Conquest of Apacheria*, p. 248.
22 Opler, *An Apache Life-Way*, p. 216.
23 The inside story of their experiences is in Betzinez, *I Fought with Geronimo*, pp.

They had conducted their exodus with almost incredible skill and success, and now they believed themselves safe. They had escaped the American soldiers, and they never had much regard for the fighting qualities of Mexicans. In the evening their leaders summoned them to another night journey. This time it was a pleasant excursion free—they thought—from pursuit. They rode in bright starlight southeast across the Janos Plains, laughing, breaking into snatches of song, calling to companions, challenging each other to short races. Several times they stopped at springs to rest. By morning they reached the base of the Sierra Emmedio, "a very rough, small mountain in the middle of the Janos plains."[24] They camped on the west side at a fine spring, with the uplift rising behind them. Between them and the mountain was a rocky ridge overlooking their camp. To the south a jumble of rocks formed a small, round hill. Away to the west and south stretched the level plain. For two days they rested and relaxed, spending their nights dancing in celebration of their deliverance. The women even gathered the fleshy crowns of the mescal and placed them in pits for the prolonged cooking.[25] They had long been deprived of this food during their virtual captivity at San Carlos.

But unknown to them, Forsyth had decided to disregard international law and cross the border. With his large force of four hundred soldiers and fifty scouts he kept at a safe distance, but Captain Tullius C. Tupper was hot on the trail, picking it out through mountain and plain. He had thirty-nine troopers and forty-seven lynx-eyed Apache scouts under the indefatigable Al Sieber. On the night of April 27 they saw the fires of the hostiles' camp five miles ahead. Sieber and four of the scouts crept up to investi-

---

57–66. The civilian casualties and the army pursuit based on original sources is given in Thrapp's books: *General Crook and the Sierra Madre Adventure*, pp. 76–84, includes his study of the terrain, and excellent photographs of the localities in the Steins Peak Range follow p. 70; and a more detailed account is in *Conquest of Apacheria*, pp. 235–46.

24 The words of Al Sieber.

25 Ball, *op. cit.*, p. 141. Kaywaykla's account of the flight, which he received second hand, is confused and inaccurate. He said that the mescal roasting was interrupted by the fight in the Steins Peak Range.

gate. The Indians, with their guard relaxed in their supposed sanctuary, were dancing around their big fire, and the spies were undiscovered. They reported the lay of the ground to Tupper, and he brought his force—still undiscovered—into position during the night. The scouts were to man the ridge at the back while the cavalry was to advance on the plain in front to make a concerted attack on the unsuspecting camp. They arrived just before dawn. The Indians were still dancing. They might have annihilated the band except for the cooking mescal.

The scouts were taking their position on the ridge when a man and three women appeared within twenty-five feet of them, laughing and talking as they came to see about their mescal. Even in the dim light the officer in command recognized the man as the son of Loco. Knowing that discovery was imminent, he gave the order to fire. All four were killed, and the premature shots aroused the camp. So says the army account.

Kaywaykla told the same story as he heard it from the Indian man who was supposed to have been killed. He was not the son but the youthful grandson of Loco; his mother was Loco's daughter, and his father, who had been killed by Mexicans, had been a son of Mangas Coloradas. In later years he was known as Talbot Gooday. In spite of differences in detail, the two accounts of the incident as seen from opposite sides are striking in verisimilitude. As Gooday told it, the band planned to make an early start on their travels that morning if the mescal had finished cooking. His mother called him and two young women to go with her to inspect it. One of the girls stooped over to make the test when a shot rang out and she fell across the pit. The other girl started to run and was picked off. Gooday pulled his mother behind a rock. He had no weapon except a knife.[26]

At the sound of the shots the Apache camp sprang into action. The scouts fired down upon it from the ridge, and the troopers

---

[26] Gooday's account is in Ball, *op. cit.*, p. 141. For his biography, see Griswold, *op. cit.*, s.v. "Gooday (Talbot)." Kaywaykla cites Frank Gooday, a slip of his speech or of Mrs. Ball's pen—Frank Gooday was not born until years later at Fort Sill. Elsewhere, Kaywaykla's informant is correctly identified as Talbot Gooday.

The site of Tupper's attack on Loco's band, taken from the ridge from which the scouts fired on the Apaches, who fled to the rocky hill in the center. *Geronimo's venture to abduct Loco's people had indeed cost them dearly.* Photograph by Dan L. Thrapp.

attacked from the front, killing six warriors. The whole band made for the rocky hillock at the side, the warriors firing as they ran, but in their excitement they shot too high and inflicted little damage. There they took refuge, the women and children hiding in the rocks, the men firing from cover. Loco called across to the scouts, urging them to defect, but they answered with insults. He was slightly wounded as he leaned against a rock. Some of the warriors tried to save their horse herd but were driven off. Desultory firing continued for several hours, with Tupper unable to dislodge the Indians on the hill and the Indians unable to drive off the attackers.

Early in the afternoon four young warriors circled to the south and east, came up behind the scouts on the ridge, and began firing on them from the rear. The scouts then withdrew and joined the troopers on the plain, and the four warriors, ducking behind rocks, continued firing. This diversion gave the Indians on the hill a chance to escape to the east into the foothills that ringed the mountain. Possibly Tupper had already ordered the scouts to join him, for he withdrew his whole command. His men were exhausted and almost out of ammunition, and it was clearly impossible for his outnumbered force to encircle and destroy the Indians. Taking along the Indians' horses, he retired to his camp of the previous night. There, Forsyth finally arrived and assumed command.[27]

According to Crook's later investigation, the Indians lost fourteen men in the day's fighting.[28] At dusk they came out from the foothills and assembled for their flight to the south. They were in a desperate plight. The few scanty supplies—blankets, utensils, other necessities—they had brought when they left the reservation had been left behind that morning when they fled from their camp. Many of them were wounded, and they lacked transportation. They drank from a spring they found and distributed a little food that some of them had snatched up. Just before they started, some of the warriors came in with a few horses they had recaptured from the retreating soldiers, but most of them were on foot.

As they dragged themselves across the level Janos Plains they became so utterly exhausted that they had to rest and sleep for an hour or so. A few warriors who had horses, Naiche, Chatto, Kaahteney, and about a dozen others, did not stop but rode on. Early in the morning, according to Betzinez, they saw some Mexican soldiers, but they went on into the foothills without returning to warn the company. Betzinez may have been mistaken about their seeing the Mexicans, but their subsequent conduct is hard to

27 A summary of the army pursuit and the battle, with a careful description of the terrain, is in Thrapp, *General Crook and the Sierra Madre Adventure*, pp. 84–90, with photographs following p. 70; a more detailed account is in his *Al Sieber*, pp. 225–37. The Apache version, which harmonizes well with the army account, even in day-to-day incidents, is in Betzinez, *op. cit.*, pp. 66–69.
28 Thrapp, *Conquest of Apacheria*, p. 248.

explain. Meanwhile, the main band resumed their journey. By morning they were close to their chosen assembly point. They had traveled twenty-nine miles that night.[29]

With daylight the band was straggling in an irregular column about two miles long. They had reached a country of low hills and were paralleling Aliso Creek, a dry stream bed in a small arroyo. Visible ahead were the blue shapes of the Sierra Madre. A few warriors were out in front leading the way, but they stopped to rest, and the laboring column passed, unaware of danger from that direction. The other warriors were in the rear, guarding against possible pursuit by the American soldiers. Suddenly, García's men emerged from a ravine and struck the long line from the side. As Betzinez remembered it: "Almost immediately Mexicans were right among us all, shooting down women and children right and left. People were falling and bleeding, and dying, on all sides of us. . . . Those who could run the fastest and the farthest managed to escape. . . . my mother and sister and I were among them, being excellent runners. . . . I had no weapons of any kind, not yet having been made a warrior. We headed rapidly for the mountains. As we ran, my mother and I heard Geronimo behind us, calling to the men to gather around him and make a stand to protect the women and children. We learned later that thirty-two warriors responded to Geronimo, around whom some women and children assembled for protection."

The Mexicans fired on the ones who were fleeing, but a number ran over a hill and escaped. There, on the other side, sitting under a tree smoking, was the party that had ridden ahead. They had heard the shots but had made no move to return. Betzinez was a truthful witness, and Al Sieber, who examined the site the next day, found evidence that some "young bucks . . . put spurs to their horses and made escape."[30] Why did they do it? The three Betzinez named were warriors of undoubted courage. Had they quarreled with Geronimo and disassociated themselves from the expedition?

29 Betzinez, *op. cit.*, p. 70.
30 Thrapp, *General Crook and the Sierra Madre Adventure*, p. 92.

Had something occurred during the previous day's battle to alienate them? Were they disgusted by the rest stop in the night? Apaches were individualists in their wars; if they trusted their leader, they carried out his orders, but he could not enforce obedience.

Betzinez called to the fugitives, and they came from hiding places until a considerable band was collected. Then they moved to the rendezvous point on the steep side of a mountain, where other fugitives had preceded them. Meanwhile, Geronimo and Chihuahua and the warriors they had assembled, with a few women and children, had taken their stand in the dry creek bed. There the real battle was fought as the Mexicans made repeated efforts to dislodge them. There are three accounts of this fight—all remarkably similar—by Geronimo himself; by Kaywaykla, who got the story from Talbot Gooday; and by Betzinez, who heard it when the participants rejoined the fugitives on the mountainside.

The women dug holes in the banks for shelter, and the men cut footholds so they could step up and fire. By digging in the sandy soil they found water to drink. When their ammunition ran low, a woman ran out in a hail of bullets and retrieved a bag that had been dropped a few yards away. As the Mexicans charged, the officers rallied their soldiers with the hated name of Geronimo. The Indians understood their Spanish: "Geronimo is in that ditch. Go in and get him!" and the taunt, "Geronimo, this is your last day!" This time the Indians' marksmanship was steady. They killed three officers and eighteen or nineteen men and wounded many more of García's 250-man force.

The battle continued until dark. Then somebody set the grass on fire. (The Indians did it, said Geronimo, in order to drive off the Mexicans; the Mexicans did it, said Betzinez and Kaywaykla, to smoke out the Indians.) The Indians prepared to slip out unseen. And then, according to Gooday, Geronimo called out to his men, "If we leave the women and children we can escape." Fun, who had been the bravest of the brave throughout that hard-fought day, was unable to believe his ears. He asked the leader to repeat it.

Geronimo gave the order to go, and Fun raised his rifle. "Say that again and I'll shoot," he said. Geronimo climbed to the top and disappeared.[31]

This incident is as hard to explain as the desertion of the mounted warriors in the morning; even Geronimo's most severe detractors conceded his courage.[32] But could it be a significant revelation of his practice in extremity? Three times in battle he lost, or was to lose, wives and children while he escaped. Was this merely a series of coincidences? It should be pointed out, however, that Gooday was not an impartial witness. Throughout his long life—he died in 1962—he held a strong resentment against Geronimo for the death of his Warm Springs relatives because of Loco's forced exodus. But Kaywaykla was convinced of the truth of his story,[33] and it gained some credence throughout the tribe. Opler heard it in garbled form in the 1930's.[34]

And some groups creeping to safety did abandon the babies. Betzinez said that the warriors "asked the consent" of the women to choke them "so that they wouldn't give away their movements by crying," and he implies that it was done. Sam Haozous told of one mother who strangled her baby rather than leave it to grow up in Mexican slavery. But Fun was credited with holding off the Mexicans until the babies in his sector could be carried out.

The party on the mountainside suffered much from cold. Since it was unsafe to build fires, they pulled grass for covering. There was no help for the wounded and no food. Throughout the night the sound of wailing and mourning for lost relatives was heard. In the morning they looked far into the valley and saw the Mexican and American armies come together. They expected a fight, but nothing happened. Their leaders gave orders for them to move, and halfway down the mountain they met Geronimo and his

31 Ball, *op. cit.*, pp. 144–45.

32 See, for example, Santee, *op. cit.*, p. 167, for a statement by the ardent Geronimo-hater, Jimmie Stevens.

33 He told it to me as a fact without mentioning the source: "Geronimo wanted to desert the women and children and Fun said he would shoot him if he did" (interview, July 29, 1959).

34 "A Chiricahua Apache's Account of the Geronimo Campaign of 1886," p. 368 and n. 12.

party. There was much excited conversation and comparison of experiences. Then Geronimo gave the order to resume the march.[35]

When the Apaches observed the meeting between the Mexican and American forces they were vaguely aware of the international issues involved. Forsyth, as he admitted later, "had strict orders in my possession not to enter Mexican territory," but when he came up with Tupper's force and learned of the Sierra Emmedio battle he decided to continue the pursuit. The following morning he reached the site and found the Indians gone. He followed their trail across the plain and camped for the night not far from the place where García had attacked them that very day. The next morning García confronted him, demanded his authority for invading Mexico, and peremptorily ordered him to leave. Forsyth said he was following orders to exterminate the hostile Apaches. García informed him the job was already done and showed him over the battlefield. It was a ghastly sight, strewn with the bodies of nineteen soldiers (García in his report said eighteen) and three officers of the Mexican force and seventy-eight Indians. In addition, the Mexicans had captured thirty-three women and children, one of the women, it is said, being a daughter of Loco. Of the Indians killed, only eleven were warriors; most of the others were victims of the first attack before the warriors came to their rescue. In fact, the Indians afterwards told Crook that they had won the real battle, the fight on Aliso Creek.

The two commanders parted amicably, and Forsyth returned to the United States. Washington was not informed that its armed forces had invaded Mexico. Forsyth's report was stopped by his immediate superior with the advice that "the less said about it the better." Tupper located his fight in the mountains of New Mexico, and so it appears in the War Department's *Annual Report.*[36]

[35] For the Apaches' account of the ambush and the fight on Aliso Creek, see Betzinez, *op. cit.*, pp. 71–75; Ball, *op. cit.*, pp. 143–45; and Barrett, *op. cit.*, pp. 106–109. Geronimo's story of the fight is accurate and detailed, but the rest of his account is confused—probably by Barrett. Haozous's taped interview is in the Duke Oral History Material in the Western History Collections of the University of Oklahoma Library.

[36] For the army's account of the García fight, see Thrapp, *Al Sieber*, pp. 236–41 and nn. 26 and 32; Thrapp, *General Crook and the Sierra Madre Adventure*, pp. 92–95 and photograph after p. 70; Secretary of War, *Annual Report*, 1882, pp. 72, 148–50.

To the Indians the meaning of all this was that Forsyth was on his way back to the border and that García lacked the resources to follow them into the mountains. Their day's journey after their night on the mountainside took them through successive ranges of hills. They had to travel slowly because of the many wounded, who had to be helped or carried. Geronimo, meanwhile, had sent some men out to distant ranches to steal cattle, and these foragers came driving beeves to the next rendezvous. Thus, they had their first good meal since the night before Tupper's attack three days before. They rested there for two days.

When they resumed their journey, three badly wounded members of the band, a woman and two men, remained at the camp to recover. The identity of the woman is not known, but one of the men was Tsoe (Tzoe), a young White Mountain Apache married to two Chiricahua women, both of whom had been killed in the García fight,[37] and the other was Kayihtah (Kieta), a cousin of Yahnozha. Each of the men was destined to play a decisive role in ending Geronimo's career. Geronimo sent a man back the following evening to help them, but he proved to be unreliable and reported that the place was occupied by the Mexicans. The company moved on in great anxiety, but the three managed somehow to sustain themselves, and a month later, fully recovered, they rejoined their people.

Meanwhile, the main body soon reached the camp of Juh's Nednais. These people were not at their fastness deep in the Sierra Madre, but, moving about as their custom was, they had established their base high in the mountains about thirty miles southwest of Casas Grandes. When Loco's people arrived, destitute and defeated, carrying their wounded, they found many strangers, but there were some happy reunions with friends and relatives in the two bands. "They gave us food and blankets and by talking to us cheerfully tried to take our minds off our losses," said Betzinez. Geronimo's venture to abduct Loco's people had indeed cost them

[37] At least that was what Crook understood him to say when he subsequently became a captive (Bourke, *Apache Campaign*, p. 31; Thrapp, *General Crook and the Sierra Madre Adventure*, p. 121). He seemed a little young to have two wives.

dearly—twenty-six fighting men out of about one hundred and great destruction inflicted on Loco's women and children. Still, the largest number of these related Apaches that had come together in many years were now assembled in one camp, and among them were many experienced warriors.[38] And their mountain refuge had never been invaded by an enemy.

Mexico and the southwestern United States could well beware.

[38] Betzinez, *op. cit.*, pp. 75–77.

CHAPTER 9

LIFE IN THE SIERRA MADRE

The united band under the leadership of Juh and Geronimo soon moved to a new location close to the San Miguel River, where they were joined by a party returning from a successful raid. There, Loco's peaceable people saw a victory dance performed by the honored raiders surrounded by a circle of their women—a new experience to Betzinez and probably to other young members of the group.[1]

After a few days of relaxation and recreation, the leaders held a council and decided to take a trading trip to Casas Grandes. About one-third of the band joined the expedition. Juh had established fairly constant peaceable relations with this Mexican town,[2] which no doubt furnished a market for the spoils of his raids. But this understanding was not recognized by the state of Chihuahua, and after the Indians had reached an intoxicated condition, the Mexicans struck. Betzinez attributed the act to treachery on the part of Casas Grandes, but Geronimo said that "two companies of Mexican troops from another town attacked us." Probably

[1] Betzinez, *I Fought with Geronimo*, p. 77.
[2] Kaywaykla said that after Victorio's survivors joined Juh's band Nana was very careful not to raid Casas Grandes in deference to this relationship. See Ball, *In the Days of Victorio*, pp. 129–32.

they were state troopers from the town of Galeana, about twenty miles southeast. Juh, in fact, did not hold Casas Grandes responsible, for he continued his peaceable trading relations with that community.

"We fled in all directions," said Geronimo. He and Juh escaped, and among others who got away were the fleet-footed Betzinez and his mother and sister. Some of the warriors—probably led by Juh and Geronimo—fought the attackers, but the rout was complete. The Mexicans killed many of the Indians (twenty, said Geronimo) and carried thirty-five into captivity. Among the captives were the wife and two children of Chatto and Geronimo's beautiful wife Chee-hash-kish, the mother of his teenaged son and daughter. In after years Chatto made vain attempts to recover his family, and Geronimo never saw his wife again, although word drifted back to the Apaches that she married a fellow captive.[3]

The band waited at their camp four days for their missing people to come in. Then they moved southwest into the heart of the Sierra Madre and made their camp on the brink of an immense canyon through which flowed a branch of the Yaqui River. But they soon became restless and started moving west towards Sonora. It required a whole day for even the sure-footed Apaches to make the perilous descent into the awesome depth of the canyon and the difficult climb to the opposite side. They continued on through the mountains, crossing another branch of the Yaqui River and then the river itself. Coming out in less rugged country, they planned a raid on a Sonora town. There, Geronimo asked Betzinez to become his assistant. Thus the young man entered his apprenticeship. Several such warriors in training were in the party. Among them was a youth later known as Lot Eyelash. Geronimo's son Chappo was there also; probably he, too, was an apprentice

[3] The most detailed account of the Casas Grandes massacre is in Betzinez, *op. cit.*, pp. 77–80. Briefer references are in Barrett, *Geronimo's Story of His Life*, pp. 103–104, and Ball, *op. cit.*, p. 133. The story that reached the American side of the border is in Thrapp, *Conquest of Apacheria*, pp. 263–64 and notes 31 and 32. Mention of the fighting by some of the warriors is in Griswold, "The Fort Sill Apaches," s.v. "Ny-ith-shizeh," and the fate of Chee-hash-kish is in *ibid.*, s.v. "Geronimo." It was unusal for an adult male captive to be spared, but this did sometimes occur. See Ball, *op. cit.*, pp. 20–21.

and not a recognized warrior. As it happened, the raid was abandoned because too many soldiers were in the vicinity,[4] but other raids were to follow.

It was probably during this time when all the bands were united, even more probably after the loss of Chee-hash-kish, that Geronimo married a diminutive Nednai girl named Zi-yeh, whose father seems to have been a white captive, an Apache in all but blood, and whose mother was related in some way to Kaywaykla's mother, Guyan.[5] Later, she was to share Geronimo's captivity, and his affectionate concern for her and their young children was evident throughout the Fort Sill period.

But the consolidation of the bands was short-lived. An amicable difference of opinion arose among the leaders, and in typical Apache fashion they separated. Juh and his Nednai followers turned back into their heartland, while Geronimo, Chihuahua, and Kaahteney, with their contingents of Warm Springs and Chiricahua relatives totaling about eighty men, women, and children, went on to raid in Sonora. Betzinez and his mother and sister were, of course, in the latter group. Apparently a child was born to one of Geronimo's wives during this time, for at one stage of the journey she and her baby rode Betzinez' big mule—the only ones who rode, a probable concession to a recent delivery.[6]

Their raids took the band south almost to Ures and north to the bend of the Bavispe not far from the Arizona line. While the warriors went out to plunder villages, drive in cattle, horses, and mules, and capture pack trains, the women were safely hidden in the mountains, where they dried beef, gathered and stored wild products, and made clothing from the bolts of cloth abundantly supplied by their men. If one did not consider the feelings of the Mexicans, it was an idyllic life, requiring hardihood and caution, filled with adventure but not too much danger, and enlivened by

---

4 Betzinez, *op. cit.*, pp. 81–83, 106; Griswold, *op. cit.*, s.v. "Eyelash, Lot."

5 Griswold, *op. cit.*, s.v. "Zi-yeh." For Zi-yeh's father, see *infra*, pp. 182–83, 187.

6 Betzinez, *op. cit.*, p. 86. Betzinez told me he did not remember which wife this was. It would have solved a subsequent identity problem if he had known (interview, August 21, 1959).

victory dances. For his part, Geronimo *did* consider the feelings of the Mexicans. Betzinez, who was closely associated with him during this period, said that he was still motivated by bitterness against the state of Sonora for the massacre of his family.

There were garrisons in the towns, but the raiding parties easily evaded them or drove them off. They observed the usual precautions—posting lookouts, obliterating their trails, concealing their camps, planning rendezvous ahead—but the military made no attempt to hunt them out. Only once a hidden Mexican soldier killed a warrior who was charging past. They labored over some rough terrain, but in other places they "traveled slowly, enjoying the trip and the pleasant surroundings." As Betzinez remembered it, much of the country "looked as though it belonged to us." At the northern end of their journey in the late summer or early fall they "settled down for an indefinite stay. It was just like peacetime. We had plenty to eat, good clothing taken from the stolen stocks, and no enemies nearby."[7]

There was only one disturbance, but this indicates that not all the Indians brought from the reservation in April were reconciled to their forced membership in the band. While close to the border, a San Carlos man and his Chiricahua wife started to run away. The girl's father was so enraged that he told the men to hunt them down and kill them, but the couple evaded their pursuers and made their way back to the reservation.[8]

This proximity to the border gave an opposite idea to the band. The warriors held a council and decided to invade southern Arizona for ammunition. Their guns were of late American make, and the Mexican cartridges did not fit. They hid their women and children at the foot of a mountain under the care of the apprentice warriors and, no doubt, of the older men. The raiders soon rejoined them, bringing great quantities of ammunition and "many articles useful for camp life," but their success was shadowed by the loss of a young warrior who died from wounds received on the raid.[9]

[7] Betzinez, *op. cit.*, pp. 83–88.
[8] *Ibid.*, p. 88.
[9] *Ibid.*, pp. 88–89.

159

Thus, with the man killed by the Mexican soldier, the expedition cost the band two warriors. And the Apaches always regarded such losses seriously.

Strangely enough, the raid into Arizona seems to have been largely overlooked in army reports and the usually volatile Arizona press.[10] Possibly the party made one fortunate haul, such as wiping out a freight train, with little other disturbance. And probably attention was focused on a circumstance unknown, but ominous, to the Apaches: General Crook had been recalled from the North to the Department of Arizona, arriving at his headquarters, Whipple Barracks outside Prescott, on September 4. Convinced that raids of this kind would continue as long as the Indians remained in Mexico, he began making plans for invading their sanctuary.

Meanwhile, the band started back to their interior fastness. On the way Geronimo's Power served them well. When they were close to Oputo he told them that some Mexican soldiers were on their trail, and he predicted the exact time and place of their appearance. Thus forewarned, his warriors attacked and captured all the Mexicans' horses and supplies. At the victory dance that followed, a young warrior and a woman companion caused much merriment by a comic impersonation of a Mexican couple, he as a soldier with a gun over his shoulder and she as a simpering senorita.

Without further incident the party returned laden with spoils to the "great canyon." Juh's band soon appeared on the opposite side, and they heard the beating of each other's tom-toms across the gorge. Finally, Geronimo's band made the difficult crossing to rejoin their friends. "It was a very happy time for us all, exchanging presents and reminiscences," said Betzinez.

Juh also had a story to tell. With a skill typical of his military genius he had won a battle with Mexican soldiers. For two days his warriors had skirmished with the pursuing troops until their ammunition was exhausted. He then led them up a steep mountain,

10 The easiest explanation is that Betzinez confused this raid with a widely publicized one made the following spring, but his account is carefully written, and the details of the two are at variance.

leaving a plain trail, and concealed them just above a section that ran parallel to the ascent. There he had them roll a line of big rocks into position. When the Mexicans reached that stretch of trail, the warriors rolled the rocks down on them. Not many escaped from the falling boulders and the trees uprooted by the descending mass. Then the Apaches gathered up the guns and ammunition. They had not lost a single warrior.[11]

After camping several weeks beside the "great canyon," the leaders held a council and decided to attack Galeana, probably in revenge for the massacre at Casas Grandes. Also, the Apaches may have known that the commander of the garrison there was the hard-bitten Indian fighter Juan Mata Ortiz, who had been second in command of the force that destroyed Victorio, for the ever-vengeful Nana, who had not been at the Casas Grandes disaster, joined the expedition. The party traveled by easy stages, holding dances on the way, and formed a camp with their women and children on the mountain range that overlooked the town. There they held another council and planned their strategy. This battle was not in the usual Apache style, for they used the tactic common to many other Indian tribes of decoying the enemy into an ambush. "Everything went according to plan," said Betzinez. Its faultless execution furnishes striking proof of the discipline observed under the leadership of Juh and Geronimo.

Warriors were placed in groups along a ravine that paralleled the highway that connected Galeana with Casas Grandes, and the main body was concealed in a depression beyond this ambush. Some volunteers rode up close to the town and started driving several Mexican horses up the road. A small body of Mexican cavalry rode out in pursuit. The Apaches fled, keeping just out of range until they reached the hidden warriors ahead. Suddenly the pursuers encountered a withering fire from the front, and at the same time the warriors concealed in the ravine sprang out and attacked them from the rear. The Mexican commander then swerved off the road to a rocky hill a short distance away, where

11 Betzinez, *op. cit.*, pp. 89–92.

Cerrito Mata Ortiz, the rounded hill on the right, where Geronimo and Juh annihilated a small Mexican force. "Everything went according to plan." Photograph by Dan L. Thrapp.

his men dismounted and began piling up rocks at the apex to form a breastwork.

The Indians rode to another hill close by and turned their horses over to the apprentice warriors, of whom Betzinez was one. They then stole invisibly to the base of the hill which the Mexicans were fortifying, encircled it, and began crawling up the slope, each rolling a stone in front of him as a shield. Geronimo, Juh, Nana, and others of the older men and some of the best marksmen, including Kaahteney, took a sheltered position near a lone cedar tree at the base and fired a few shots to distract the enemy's attention. Finally, at the very summit, the Apaches sprang to their feet and charged the works in a hand-to-hand fight. They lost two of their warriors but killed the officer and twenty-one men, all but one of the Mexicans. To their immense gratification they found that the officer was Ortiz. (The hill is still known as Cerrito Mata Ortiz, and the little plaza in Galeana is called by his name.[12])

As the Mexican survivor fled towards the town, Geronimo shouted, "Let him go. He will tell the rest of the soldiers and they will come out and we can kill more." Soon another Mexican force did emerge. The Apaches mounted and rode towards them, and the soldiers started digging in. Since it was nearly sunset, the Indians decided not to attack. They watched them dig until dark, then joined their women and children on the mountainside.[13]

There was no victory dance. The band was too deeply grieved over the loss of their two warriors. That same evening word came to them that Mexican soldiers were on the way from Casas Grandes to attack them, and they fled into the mountains. After camping there in security several days, the band again divided, Juh going back to his stronghold and Geronimo and Chihuahua establishing a base camp on the headwaters of the Bavispe River.

After staying some time in this pleasant place of good water, firewood, and abundant game, Geronimo and Chihuahua decided to acquire some needed supplies by another raid into Sonora. This

12 Thrapp, *Victorio*, pp. 311–12. Thrapp has visited the site and examined the terrain.

13 News of this fight reached the United States, and a garbled account was published in the Albuquerque *Star* of December 8, 1882 (Thrapp, *Conquest of Apacheria*, p. 262). There are two eyewitness narratives—one by Betzinez, who saw it from the hill where he was holding the horses, told in *I Fought with Geronimo*, pp. 93–96, and the other by the child Kaywaykla, who watched it from the camp on the mountainside, in Ball, *op. cit.*, pp. 134–35. Kaywaykla added some conversation of the leaders, which he could not have heard. For Kaahteney's skill with the rifle, see Ball, *op. cit.*, p. 142.

time they left the women and children in camp while the warriors and the young apprentices made a rapid dash across the Bavispe and circled the area to the west where the pack trains passed through on their way to Ures. Butchering cattle and acquiring horses as they went and slipping undetected around the towns, they succeeded in capturing a pack train heavily loaded with dry goods and other supplies. During the journey Betzinez was greatly pleased by a compliment from Chihuahua on his handling of the captured animals, and in the victory dance upon the return he was included with the warriors in the center of the circle.[14] But although he was capable and dependable in carrying out such responsibilities, it is clear that he had no liking for the life of a warrior, and he was never to attain that status.

The band remained in the area for several months, then went back to the camping place on the brink of the "great canyon." Juh's party finally joined them there. They had suffered a great misfortune. The Mexicans had attacked them, killing some of their people and capturing many women and children. Juh's wife, Ishton, and his four-year-old daughter had been killed, and his older daugther, Jacali, was severely wounded.[15] This loss of his favorite "sister" was, indeed, a grief to Geronimo.

The remnants of Victorio's band had been with Juh at the time, and the child Kaywaykla carried throughout his life a flashing picture of the encounter. The camps of Kaahteney's and Juh's families were close together near an arroyo. When the soldiers attacked, Kaahteney fought them off while Guyan went for the horses, calling to Kaywaykla to run down the arroyo. When he passed Juh's camp, he saw Ishton and the two girls fall, the boy Daklugie kneeling beside his mother, and an older brother standing over them firing at the soldiers. As he fled down the arroyo, he heard hoofbeats behind him. His step-father raced past, sweeping him to a place on the saddle before him, and the family reached the mountain in safety. Three days later, when the scattered mem-

14 Betzinez, *op. cit.*, pp. 96–101.
15 *Ibid.*, pp. 101–102. Betzinez did not mention the little girl.

bers of the band assembled, Juh's two older sons were carrying their sister on a stretcher made by fastening a blanket to two lances. She had been wounded in the leg and was a cripple thereafter.[16]

After Juh arrived at the "great canyon," the united bands, in spite of their losses, included more than eighty fighting men. They remained there until spring. Then two new raids were planned, one into Sonora for pack trains and the other into Arizona and New Mexico for ammunition. Juh and his people did not join these parties. They had become demoralized by their misfortunes, and their band was breaking up in mutual ill feeling.[17] As nearly as can be determined, Juh, his three sons, and his few followers struck out on their own while Jacali, probably because of her wound, remained with the main body,[18] which established its base camp for the women and children on the headwaters of the Bavispe. That place was a natural amphitheatre surrounded by towering mountains with a sparkling stream running through.[19]

With their families settled, the men made the usual careful preparations for the raid—cleaning and greasing their rifles, making new moccasins (Apache warriors took good care of their moccasins), plaiting good rawhide ropes, sharpening their knives, even washing their hair with the saponaceous roots of the yucca.[20] Then they set out on the familiar raiding trail into Sonora.

After the first night's stop, Chatto and Benito, with twenty-six warriors, turned north towards Arizona. Chatto was in command. In the party were the youthful Naiche, Tsoe, and Tsoe's close friend Beneactiney, the son-in-law of Chihuahua. Beneactiney was

[16] Ball, *op. cit.*, pp. 146–47. Daklugie also told this story in more vivid detail to Mrs. Ball (Eve Ball to Angie Debo, July 13, 1973). The Fort Sill records identify a woman named Ish-keh who died at Fort Sill in 1897 as the same person as Ishton, but this identification is certainly an error. Kaywaykla could have been mistaken about the identity of the woman he saw fall, but Daklugie saw his mother killed by Mexican bullets.

[17] Betzinez, *op. cit.*, p. 102; Secretary of War, *Annual Report*, 1883, p. 176. These statements are supported by Tsoe, who told Britton Davis that only three men and five women remained with Juh; quoted by Thrapp, *Conquest of Apacheria*, pp. 272–73. See also Bourke, *Apache Campaign*, p. 95.

[18] This is surmised on the basis of where they were when they next appeared.

[19] Bourke, *op. cit.*, p. 79; Thrapp, *General Crook and the Sierra Madre Adventure*, map in back pocket made from field notes of an army engineer.

[20] Bourke, *op. cit.*, pp. 39–40, 62; Betzinez, *op. cit.*, pp. 85, 102.

Betzinez' cousin and was regarded as the head of the family of the widowed Nah-thle-tla, since Betzinez had not attained warrior's rank.[21]

The main body, said to number eighty men,[22] warriors and apprentices, continued west into Sonora. This time they penetrated far into enemy territory, passing through a well-settled region to a point one hundred miles southwest of Ures. They committed the usual depredations, plundering the towns, taking cattle and horses, and killing the people they encountered (most of the Mexicans stayed out of reach), but they failed to find a pack train.

There were diverting incidents. Once they approached a walled town, "riding in column of twos just like cavalry, with Geronimo and Chihuahua at the front." Two mounted Mexicans saw them coming and galloped madly back to warn the inhabitants. Then Geronimo placed his warriors in a line outside to jeer at the people cowering on their flat rooftops. At another time there was the incident of the traveling saddle. On a dark night they had stopped to rest until moonrise. Chappo unsaddled his horse and laid the saddle on a rock. When the moon came up and the band was preparing to start, both saddle and rock were gone. Finally they were found in the bushes, the "rock" an armadillo still carrying the saddle on its back.[23] Chappo was subjected to much laughter and teasing by his young friends.

On their return journey the raiders did find and capture a pack train. It was loaded with dry goods, blankets, and other needed articles, but it also contained mescal. At the camp that night many of the older men got drunk, but the young apprentices stood guard and no enemy appeared. Before they reached the base camp two messengers met them with the news that Beneactiney had been killed. He had been the special protector of Betzinez. Chihuahua

---

21 Betzinez, *op. cit.*, pp. 88, 97, 107, 116. The participation of Naiche rests on a statement later made by Tsoe, given in Thrapp, *Conquest of Apacheria*, p. 273. Some writers have credited Chihuahua with the leadership, but Betzinez, a reliable witness, gives several instances of his presence on the Sonora raid.

22 Tsoe's statement.

23 The Apache saddles, of course, were not the heavy stock saddles used by Southwestern frontiersmen.

came over and laid his hand on the shoulder of the grieving young man, urging him not to mourn too deeply, for "He was a very brave warrior." The party soon reached the base camp, where Betzinez found his mother and sister saddened by the death of their relative. A few days later Chatto and Benito came in from their successful raid with guns and ammunition and a small white boy they had captured.[24]

The raiders had indeed been busy on the American side of the line. On March 21 they struck a charcoal camp near Tombstone, killing three of the four men they found there. Next, at a second camp they killed one man and fired into a tent. When no one responded, Beneactiney and Tsoe ran towards it, and a man inside shot and killed Beneactiney. The next victims of the raiders were three miners. They raced on, killing a lone man here, a small party there, stealing fresh horses to replace their worn-out mounts. All the border country was in an uproar, with violent newspaper editorials and futile pursuits by army units and citizens' posses.

The reservation braced itself for an invasion. It had been transferred from civilian control to the military when Crook was sent back to Arizona. He had put able Captain Emmet Crawford in charge, with headquarters at San Carlos. Among Crawford's subordinates were the experienced Second Lieutenant Charles B. Gatewood at Fort Apache and young, ardent Second Lieutenant Britton Davis in command of the scouts at San Carlos. Now there was the prospect of another kidnaping of reservation Indians by hostiles or perhaps some voluntary recruitments to swell their number. Davis saw his Indians guarding their camps with guns and ammunition he had not suspected them of having and even establishing outposts in the neighboring hills.

But the raiders did not reach the reservation. They sped north along the San Simon Valley to the Gila and turned east to enter New Mexico north of Steins Peak. They traversed the Burro Mountains and then on the road between Silver City and Lordsburg they came upon a buckboard carrying Federal Judge H. C.

24 Betzinez, *op. cit.*, pp. 102–108.

McComas and his wife and six-year-old son, Charlie. They killed and stripped the two adults and took the child along. This was the boy Betzinez had seen; his fate would become for many years an unsolved mystery of the Southwest. The prominence of these latest victims shocked the nation. The judge was a well-known jurist, and Mrs. McComas was the sister of Eugene F. Ware, the Kansas historian and poet who later served as pension commissioner.

After this it was believed that the raiders were heading west and would shortly attack San Carlos. Instead, they bore south, dodged their pursuers, and escaped into Mexico. In a foray lasting only six days they had ridden fully four hundred miles, sometimes traveling seventy-five or one hundred miles a day, and had killed twenty-six persons. They had not even been sighted except by their victims and a few intended victims who escaped. Members of the band later told Davis that Chatto slept only on horseback, standing vigilantly on guard while the others snatched brief pauses for rest.[25] But one member defected, with results that may well have been the determining factor in Crook's subsequent success in invading their refuge.

As Betzinez told the story, which of course he heard at second hand, Tsoe had been deeply grieved by the death of Beneactiney at the charcoal camp. Shortly afterwards, when the party stopped on a high mountain, he started crying as he looked off towards the reservation where his mother and other relatives lived. He told his companions that he could not go on. They gave him some supplies and wished him well, and he set off alone. But Tsoe later told Crook that he had been taken to Mexico against his will and now took the opportunity to steal away from the raiding party during the night. Both stories may be true. Tsoe and Chatto were close friends, and Chatto might have helped him to leave without the knowledge of the rest of the party.[26]

But the reunited band in the Sierra Madre was unaware of the consequences of his defection. Fifteen volunteers soon went out

25 The whole story of their raid is in Thrapp, *Conquest of Apacheria*, pp. 267–71. For Davis' experience, see *The Truth about Geronimo*, pp. 34–35, 56.
26 Betzinez, *op. cit.*, pp. 116–18; Ball, *op. cit.*, p. 175; Bourke, *op. cit.*, pp. 30–32.

towards Oputo and returned with one hundred cattle. There was a busy day of butchering followed by a feast and a victory dance. Then at this camp a fire broke out and spread through the tall, dry grass, sending a great cloud of smoke high above the mountains and marking the locality for any Mexican soldiers who might be following the raiders. Apparently Juh also had joined the band by this time, for Betzinez stated that he and Geronimo were in command. They sent back sentinels who reported that Mexican soldiers were indeed following the broad trail made by the cattle. The Indians then crossed a deep canyon and established a camp beyond it while the warriors prepared an ambush. Some, armed with guns, were posted on the ridge along the gorge, the best fighting men were deployed astride the trail, and still others were sent to a steep slope at the nearby head of the canyon to roll rocks down on any of the enemy who might attempt to climb up there to outflank them.

The soldiers descended into the gorge while the hidden warriors waited impatiently. Finally they emerged on the ascent. When they reached the brink, the warriors posted along the trail ahead opened fire. The Mexicans retreated and ran into the ambush, while rocks were rolled down on them from the head of the canyon. They rallied and fought bravely, making several attempts to dislodge the Indians, but they eventually withdrew after serious losses. In the melee the Apaches shot one of their own men, their only casualty. They sent out parties to shadow the movements of the retreating enemy, but the Mexican withdrawal was complete.[27]

It is enlightening to read the official Mexican report of this battle. The able García was in command, marching from Moctezuma with eighty-six federal troops and fifty auxiliaries and absorbing another force of auxiliaries on the trail. On April 25, deep in the mountains at "a point whose name is unknown," they found the Indians "in two positions in impregnable points and difficult of access." They divided and made a frontal and a flanking assault (here one remembers the warriors with rocks at the head

---

[27] Betzinez, *op. cit.*, pp. 110–11.

of the canyon) and drove off the Indians, killing eleven and wounding many "according to the bloody tracks they left."[28]

After the battle the Apaches, unaware of their reported casualties, traveled on and made their camp in a pleasant location under the pines on a very steep mountain. There, secure from enemies and with plenty of meat, they relaxed for a time. Then the principal men held a council and decided to make a raid on Chihuahua to take Mexican prisoners to exchange for their people captured at Casas Grandes and in the attack on Juh's camp. A party of thirty-six volunteers accordingly set out with Geronimo as leader, traversing the mountains and coming out on the plains to the east. They crossed the main highway south of Galeana, walking on their heels in the dust to leave little round holes not recognizable as human tracks. Continuing east, then turning north, killing cattle for food and all the time watching the roads for travelers, they finally sighted a party of two men and six women near the village of Carmen, not far from the Mexican Central Railroad. They killed the men and captured the women, one of whom was carrying a nursing baby. The women were the wives of soldiers stationed at one of the towns.[29] Geronimo told them not to be afraid, that they would not be harmed, but understandably they were terrified. He sent the oldest one to the officials to report his purpose for an exchange of prisoners. Meanwhile, the raiders continued on their way, watching for other travelers.

One evening all were gathered around the fire eating. Geronimo was sitting next to Betzinez with a knife in one hand and a chunk of beef Betzinez had cooked for him in the other. Suddenly he dropped the knife and exclaimed, "Men, our people we left at base camp are in the hands of U.S. soldiers. What shall we do?"

"This was a startling example of Geronimo's mysterious ability to tell what was happening at a distance," said old Jason Betzinez,

---

28 Thrapp, *General Crook and the Sierra Madre Adventure*, pp. 141–42 and note 21, quoting the official Mexican report.

29 Betzinez said their husbands were stationed at Casas Grandes, but this statement must have been a slip of his pen.

looking back. "I cannot explain it to this day.[30] But I was there and saw it. No, he didn't get the word by some messenger. And no smoke signals had been made."

In response to Geronimo's question, every man replied that they should return to their base camp immediately. They were at least one hundred and twenty miles away and completely out of touch with it. They started that very evening and traveled all night. Their captives slowed them down. "We tried to help the women and get them to walk faster but we really didn't expect Mexican women to walk as far and as fast as Apache women."

Before they again reached the road south of Galeana, the men captured some cattle to drive back. The last night out Geronimo made another prophecy. He said that on the following day's journey a man standing on a hill to their left would report the capture of their camp. It came out exactly as he had predicted. In the middle of the afternoon a man hailed them from a hilltop and then came down the rocks to report that Crook had indeed captured their camp and had taken their people into custody. They held another council and decided to investigate. Abandoning their captives and their stolen cattle, they made their stealthy way to the summit of a high mountain overlooking Crook's camp. There Geronimo disposed them in firing positions among the crags.[31]

Would there be a battle or a conference there in the mountains?

30 Neither can I. One can usually attribute Geronimo's Power to a lucky guess and the tendency of superstitious people to disregard all adverse evidence. But Jason Betzinez in his old age was entirely free from superstition. He simply told what he saw.

31 Betzinez, *op. cit.*, pp. 112–16; Bourke, *op. cit.*, p. 109; Secretary of War, *Annual Report*, 1883, Crook's report to the Military Division of the Pacific, July 23, 1883, p. 178. Crook obtained his information from the Mexican women captives. See also Goodwin, "Experiences of an Indian Scout" (part 2), p. 67.

CHAPTER 10

THE SANCTUARY IS INVADED

The capture of the Indians' camp was the culmination of developments on the American side of the line of which they were blithely unaware.

As soon as he arrived in Arizona, Crook began in his systematic way to study the situation. First, he held conferences with the reservation Indians. As he reported it, "The simple story of their wrongs, as told by various representatives of their bands, under circumstances which convinced me they were speaking the truth, satisfied me that the Apaches had not only the best of reasons for complaining, but had displayed remarkable forbearance in remaining at peace."

Even their life, such as it was, seemed insecure. Their reservation had been cut down five times to satisfy intruding miners and ranchers. The western boundary had been moved back because of the discovery of silver and later of copper in that area, and the riotous mining towns of Globe and McMillenville had sprung up there. On the east, where their reservation had once extended to the New Mexico line, a large strip had been cut off for the benefit of copper mining interests, and the town of Clifton had developed as the center of the industry. Now white exploiters were eyeing

172

their remaining land, and the Apaches "were constantly told . . . that they were to be attacked by troops on the reservation and removed from the country."

Four thousand of them were confined to the pestilential flats near the agency at San Carlos, wholly dependent upon the scanty supplies left after the grafters had taken their share. A more fortunate fifteen hundred, living in the mountains around Fort Apache, were nearly self-supporting, killing game, collecting and storing wild products, and tending their little fields in the valleys. Crook gave the others permission to choose their own locations, and they began to move out and settle in bands and family groups under the direction of their leaders.[1]

There were no depredations of any kind by the reservation Indians after Crook took over, but he had no illusions about the bands in Mexico. As he went about enlisting scouts and organizing pack trains to invade their stronghold, Chatto's raid confirmed his analysis. But he must have wondered how he would find their hide-out. Then came his lucky break.

On the night of March 28 a telegram came to San Carlos with the report of the McComas outrage and the belief that the raiders were headed towards the reservation. As it happened, Captain Crawford had been called away to assist Crook, and Davis was in charge. The young officer watched in suspense for a repetition of the Loco kidnaping, possibly even the massacre of all the whites at the agency. Five trusty Indians had been enlisted there as "secret scouts"—actually spies—to report to the officers any indication of unrest or hostility so that potential disturbances might be nipped in the bud. Now close to midnight on March 30 one of them slipped noiselessly into Davis' bedroom. "Chiricahua come," he whispered. (By this time all the related bands were known as

1 Secretary of War, *Annual Report*, 1883, Crook to Military Division of the Pacific, September 27, 1883, pp. 160–64; Davis, *The Truth about Geronimo*, pp. 32–34, 41–44, 48; Ogle, *Federal Control of the Western Apaches*, pp. 130–31, 189; Lockwood, *The Apache Indians*, p. 258. The changes in reservation boundaries are shown in Charles C. Royce, "Indian Land Cessions in the United States."

Chiricahuas.) He reported that the hostiles were in the camp of a White Mountain or Coyotero leader named Nodiskey twelve or fourteen miles away. (Nodiskey was regarded as a bad Indian.) It was believed that there were fifteen or twenty of them. That would mean Chatto's whole party.

Davis had thirty scouts under Sam Bowman to keep order on the reservation. He and Bowman hastily collected them and with a few other Apache volunteers, set out through the night, and cautiously approached the camp. At daylight from a hidden position they called on the occupants to surrender. Thus they captured the entire force—the unruffled, smiling Tsoe. He said he had come to the camp to get news of his relatives, and he talked freely about the raid and the location of the various bands in the Sierra Madre. Davis wired Crook, Crook instructed him to find out whether the Indian would act as guide for the invasion, Tsoe readily consented, and Davis sent him on to the general.[2]

All Crook needed now was permission to enter Mexican territory to search out the hostiles. He traveled by train to confer with the officials and military commanders of Sonora and Chihuahua, and reached a cordial understanding with them. The Mexicans were unable to protect their people and Chatto's raid into the United States showed that the Americans were equally helpless so long as the band remained in their refuge.[3]

Crook then set out on the Mexican campaign, crossing the international boundary on May 1. Captain Bourke as usual served on the General's staff and kept a day-by-day diary of the expedition. In the carefully selected force were 9 officers, 42 enlisted men, and 193 Apache scouts; and it had five pack trains of 266 mules with 76 civilian packers. A few of the scouts were Chiricahuas, but most of them belonged to White Mountain and other reservation tribes unfriendly to the outlaw band. Al Sieber served

[2] Davis, *op. cit.*, pp. 16, 56–59; Thrapp, *Conquest of Apacheria*, pp. 272–73, and *General Crook and the Sierra Madre Adventure*, pp. 118–21.

[3] Secretary of War, *Annual Report*, 1883, Crook to Military Division of the Pacific, September 27, 1883, p. 163; Thrapp, *General Crook and the Sierra Madre Adventure*, pp. 123–27.

as chief of scouts with Archie McIntosh and Sam Bowman as his assistants; and Crawford, assisted by Gatewood and another officer, was in command. Mickey Free and a Mexican named Severiano, captured in youth and brought up as an Apache, were the interpreters. Accompanying the expedition was A. Frank Randall, a correspondent of the *New York Herald*. He carried photographic equipment that would have preserved a pictorial record of the confrontation in the Sierra Madre, but it was destined to be destroyed when the mule carrying it rolled over a precipice.[4]

Besides Bourke's diary, there is a scout's-eye view of the campaign given by John Rope—"we were scouts in order to help the whites against the Chiricahuas because they had killed a lot of people," he said.[5] Tsoe proved to be a congenial spirit, truthful, reliable, and cooperative throughout, and his knowledge of the terrain was invaluable. He was given the sobriquet of "Peaches," because although he was considered a full-blood Apache, he had a fair complexion and rosy cheeks, probably inherited from some forgotten captive white ancestor. "He was one of the handsomest men physically, to be found in the world," wrote Bourke. "He never knew what it meant to be tired, cross, or out of humor."[6]

Bourke was equally impressed by the scouts as they fanned out ahead, each one an individual working independently, "the perfect, the ideal, scout of the whole world," with eyes keen as a hawk's, tread as stealthy as a panther's, ears that heard everything. An artist might call them undersized, he said, but otherwise they were physically perfect. "Their chests were broad, deep, and full; shoulders perfectly straight; limbs well-proportioned, strong and muscular, without a suggestion of undue heaviness; hands and feet small and taper [sic] but wiry; heads well-shaped, and countenances often lit up with a pleasant good-natured expression." On the march they laughed and joked. At night they washed their hair;

4 Thrapp, *General Crook and the Sierra Madre Adventure*, pp. 128–29, 137, 139; Bourke, *op. cit.*, pp. 56–57; Secretary of War, *Annual Report*, 1883, Crook to Military Division of the Pacific, July 23, 1883, pp. 174–75.

5 Goodwin, "Experiences of an Indian Scout" (part 2), p. 56.

6 Bourke, *op. cit.*, pp. 52–53.

Mickey Free, the interpreter with Crook's Sierra Madre expedition and on the reservation. He was mistrusted by the Apaches as "the coyote whose kidnapping had brought war to the Chiricahuas." Courtesy Arizona Historical Society, Tucson.

Tsoe ("Peaches"), who guided Crook to Geronimo's sanctuary in the Sierra Madre. Photograph taken by A. Frank Randall at San Carlos in the spring of 1884. "He was one of the handsomest men physically to be found in the world." Courtesy National Archives and Records Service.

177

cut sections of cane and made pipes for smoking or flutes with which they produced a weird music; or built an air-tight hut, poured water on hot stones, and took a sweat bath.[7]

But concerning the health and stamina of the scouts, a few ominous indications may be worth noting. Years later, as prisoners of war, the Apaches were to die in appalling numbers from tuberculosis. The physical examination given these scouts at the time of their enlistment may be significant. Said Rope, "They felt my arms and legs and pounded my chest to see if I would cough. That's the way they did with all the scouts they picked, and if you coughed they would not take you." One of them was to die of an unspecified cause after they reached their destination in the Sierra Madre, and a few days later Bourke recorded that two others "were so far gone with pneumonia that their death was predicted every hour."[8] Tubercular pneumonia had not at that time been identified by medical science. Could this infection have been present in their native state, but held in check somewhat by their outdoor living?

Such possible weakness was unmarked, however, as the expedition moved down the San Bernardino River, then up the Bavispe. "For three days," said Crook, "we did not see a human being. The whole country had been laid waste by the Apaches and much land of value and formerly cultivated had grown into a jungle of cane and mesquite." They threaded the canyon of the Bavispe past the river towns of San Miguel, Bavispe, Bacerac, and Huachinera. "The condition of these little Mexican communities was deplorable," said the General. "Apache attacks were to be looked for at any moment. No man would venture away from the vicinity of his own hamlet." The "inhabitants welcomed us with exuberant joy."[9] This was the other side of Betzinez' lighthearted narrative.

Crook camped near Tesorababi, a former ranch abandoned because of Apache raids, and on May 8 turned southeast into the

7 *Ibid.*, pp. 38–40, 46, 51–52, 62–64.

8 *Ibid.*, pp. 120–21; Goodwin, "Experiences of an Indian Scout" (part 1), p. 43, and (part 2), p. 69.

9 Secretary of War, *Annual Report*, 1883, Crook to Military Division of the Pacific, July 23, 1883, p. 175; Bourke, *op. cit.*, pp. 56–74.

heart of the hostiles' mountain sanctuary. Here was a complete picture of their life-way. The whole area was an extensive complex of crisscrossing trails beaten by the feet of hundreds of stolen animals, and recently occupied camps on the mountains and along the streams. Only the planted fields that typically marked Apache settlements were missing; for these Indians' sole support came from gathering wild products and raiding, with their main dependence on the latter. Cached in trees or strewn along the trails with the prodigality of affluence were dried meat, mescal, buckskin, horse-hides, cowhides, and articles taken from the Mexicans—cloth, clothing, saddles, flour, even letters. The camp remembered by Peaches in the natural amphitheater had been abandoned. The invaders made a "terrible" climb up a nearby mountain, where on the summit were forty lodges in one place, thirty in another, two or three in every protected nook—all likewise abandoned. Then after a slide down the face of a bluff they came to an open space also dotted with the frames of dismantled wickiups. At these places were the ashes of fires, the straw of unused beds, play-grounds of the hoop-and-pole game, dance grounds, mescal pits, stones for grinding acorn meal—all the paraphernalia of an active society. Everything seemed secure, but Peaches said the hostiles never relaxed their vigilance, keeping sentinels posted and extinguishing their fires at night; and it was apparent that they frequently changed their campsites.

Travel was difficult almost beyond endurance for the white men, and pack mules rolled down precipices and were dashed to pieces in the chasms below. (One of these mules, alas, carried Randall's photographic equipment.) But the scouts climbed up the heights "like deer." They accordingly held a conference with Crook and suggested that they advance on their own. Crook agreed, and Crawford with 150 scouts started out ahead, sending back messages directing the rest of the command to favorable routes and camping places as it cautiously followed. He believed that the hostiles were unaware of their presence.[10]

10 Bourke, *op. cit.*, pp. 74–91.

While the main body was waiting for these directions, some of the packers and scouts made a side trip into the adjoining mountains and found evidence of a recent battle between Mexicans and the hostiles. This was the fight in the canyon described by Betzinez and reported by García. Their examination of the battlefield gave a remarkable confirmation of Betzinez' account. They concluded that the Apaches had ambushed the Mexicans, killed a number with bullets and rocks, and had put the rest to flight. They even found the grave of one Apache warrior, the one Betzinez reported as killed by their own crossfire.[11]

Meanwhile, on May 15 the advance party of scouts discovered the *rancheria* of the hostiles on the side of a mountain across an intervening valley.[12] In some army accounts it was designated as the camp of Chatto and Benito; in others, as that of Chihuahua. It did, indeed, contain the people of those leaders, but it was the main camp of the entire body of related tribes except Juh's few followers, and Geronimo, at this most influential stage of his career, was the overall leader.[13]

The scouts attempted to surround the *rancheria*, some of them fired prematurely, and the hostiles fled, but they killed at least nine of them and captured five children, three girls and two boys, rounded up the horse herd, and occupied the camp. Chihuahua and other men of the band had just returned with many cattle from a successful raid. They had been butchering, and meat was spread out everywhere on the bushes to dry. Also, there was a quantity of mescal, freshly cooked or drying. The scouts looted the camp and set it on fire.[14]

Meanwhile, a courier from Crawford had reached Crook, who

---

11 *Ibid.*, pp. 76, 86.

12 There is some confusion in Bourke's book about dates, but this accords with the official map of the expedition reproduced by Thrapp in *General Crook and the Sierra Madre Adventure*, back pocket.

13 Geronimo's leadership is apparent throughout. See, for example, the statement of Loco's family cited in *ibid.*, p. 173.

14 Goodwin, *op. cit.* (part 2), pp. 58–63. Rope's account is circumstantial and personal, with such details as, "The [captured] girl had lots of beads made from Yo-il-tchine, the roots of a kind of bush that grows down there. She had four strings of them," and "I saw someone's heels sticking out of a clump of bushes. I grabbed this person and pulled him out"; it was a little boy with "no blood on him."

came up quickly but did not arrive until the fighting was over. The victorious scouts came into his camp bringing their captives and with their horses grotesquely loaded with plunder—prizes such as gold and silver watches, even some photograph albums, and much American and Mexican money. While they gloated over their wealth, Crook questioned the captives. They "behaved with great coolness and self-possession, considering their tender years." The oldest was a well-grown girl, a daughter of Benito. She said that her people had been dismayed to find their stronghold discovered and would be still more disconcerted when they learned that Tsoe, who knew every hidden fastness, was guiding the invaders. Most of the warriors were out on raids—some had gone out that very day—but she was sure that Loco and Chihuahua would be glad to return to the reservation. She was not so sure about Geronimo and Chatto. Juh was defiant, but his band had been destroyed. Most important of all, she said that a small white boy named Charlie, captured by Chatto on his recent raid, had been in the *rancheria* and had run off with the women. She believed that if she could contact them, she could bring in the whole band, including this boy.

Crook sent her and the older of the boy captives back with a conciliatory message. The next day women carrying white rags as flags of truce began to venture in. Among these, according to Rope, was a sister of Geronimo. This was probably Nah-thle-tla, the mother of Betzinez, although Geronimo had other "sisters" in the camp.[15] She said that Chihuahua wanted to come in and was trying to gather up his people, who had been scattered by the fight. He did come in the next day, "a fine-looking man, whose countenance betokened great decision and courage." He said he wanted to surrender and had sent runners to the bands that were out raiding. No doubt it was one of these couriers that would soon

---

15 Bourke called her the sister of Chihuahua, but Rope was more careful than any white man in identifying Indians. The band that was raiding with Geronimo in Chihuahua had taken their families along and settled them in a temporary camp on the way, but they had started back in advance of their men and could have reached the base camp by this time.

hail Geronimo's party from the hillside. By nightfall that day (May 18) forty-five men, women, and children had come in. The women "showed the wear and tear of a rugged mountain life," wrote Bourke. But the "children were models of grace and beauty."[16] By the next day the number of surrendered hostiles had swelled to an even one hundred. The women tore up flour sacks, tied them on poles, and set them all about the camp to signal to the returning warriors that all was peace. There were indications that Chihuahua was not entirely ready to surrender, and they warned the scouts that the combined forces might attack. "We piled rocks and pine logs up to lie behind," as Rope recalled it, and they held their arms in readiness.

Geronimo's thirty-six raiders did, in fact, arrive that night and took their positions among the rocks a thousand feet above Crook's camp. The women called up to them "and told them not to shoot . . . that they did not want any fighting" but only to make friends. At daybreak (May 20) Geronimo sent down two messengers (two old men, said Betzinez; two old women, said Bourke) to find out the general's intentions. If they should fail to return, he planned to attack. There were some other communications back and forth. Geronimo's "sister" went up to the raiders, and they sent her back to request some of the scouts to meet with them. The scouts sent relatives of the raiding party—a brother-in-law of Chatto and a relative of Geronimo's father-in-law Dji-li-kine.[17]

Although Geronimo, with his six marriages, must have had several fathers-in-law, Dji-li-kine was almost certainly the father of Zi-yeh. He was a white man by blood, but had been captured in boyhood by the White Mountain Apaches and brought up as a member of that tribe. He was "like one of us," as John Rope expressed it. Then he had married a Nednai woman and joined her people, "and was just like one of them." According to Rope, he was "not as tall as an old-fashioned long musket," but he was

---

16 The children of their descendants are still remarkably beautiful.

17 Bourke, *op. cit.*, pp. 91–100; Goodwin, *op. cit.* (part 2), pp. 63–66; Betzinez, *I Fought with Geronimo*, p. 116.

"about the best fighter of any of [the band] . . . and they usually did what he advised."[18]

These messengers told the raiders that hostilities had been suspended to give Chihuahua time to bring in his people and the captured Charlie McComas. Finally, the men began to drop down from the mountainside and enter the camp by twos and threes. "In muscular development, lung and heart power, they were, without exception, the finest body of human beings I had ever looked upon," Bourke reported. "Each was armed with a breech-loading Winchester; most had nickle-plated revolvers of the latest pattern, and a few had also bows and lances."

But Geronimo and the other leaders still stayed out. Crook decided to contact them by the most supremely courageous act of his adventurous career. (He suppressed this story, and so did the other officers; it was not known until Rope's reminiscences were published in 1936.) He took his gun and left the camp ostensibly to shoot birds. The hostile leaders confronted him, "grabbed his gun away and took the birds he had shot." Then Mickey Free and Severiano came to interpret. "They all sat on the ground and talked. After about two hours" the general and his former enemies came into the camp together.[19]

Then and in the ensuing days Crook and Geronimo had several conferences. Although the general must have realized that his position was precarious, he professed indifference about whether his antagonist should surrender or fight it out. But he reminded the Apache that his mountain fastness was not impregnable and warned him that Mexican forces also would be coming in to invade it. Geronimo said he had always wanted to be at peace. He had been ill-treated at San Carlos (Crook could hardly deny that in view of his own appraisal of conditions there), and driven away (even Clum conceded that). As for the Mexicans, they were treacherous, made war on his women and children, and ran like

18 Basso, *Western Apache Raiding and Warfare*, pp. 110, 165–67.
19 Goodwin, *op. cit.* (part 2), pp. 66–67; Bourke, *op. cit.*, pp. 100–102. Rope's account of Crook's bird-shooting stroll is glimpsed in the reminiscences of another scout. See Basso, *op. cit.*, p. 200.

coyotes from his warriors. He said he was even then trying to arrange an exchange of prisoners. But he admitted that he could not cope with united American and Mexican soldiers assisted by Apache scouts. If he could not make peace, he and his warriors would die in the mountains fighting to the last. Crook remained remote and unconcerned.[20]

The following morning (May 21), Geronimo, Naiche, Chatto, and a leading warrior named Tcha-nol-haye joined Crook at breakfast. "They all seemed to be in a pleasant humor and consumed with relish the bread, beans and coffee set before them; pork they would not touch."[21] Geronimo said he had sent some of his young men out to collect his scattered people. Meanwhile Chihuahua's messages were having their effect, as increasing numbers of "all ages and both sexes" continued to come in; "most of them were mounted on good ponies, and all drove pack and loose animals before them." During the day Kaahteney arrived with his band of thirty-eight, "mostly young warriors . . . driving steers and work animals and riding ponies and burros. All were armed with Winchester and Springfield breech-loaders, with revolvers and lances whose blades were old cavalry sabres. The little boys carried revolvers, lances, and bows and arrows."

Feeding so many Indians was making serious inroads on Crook's supplies. He told them to help out by killing their own cattle and ponies, and the young men began butchering. Bourke watched the process with fascination. Standing within five or six feet of a steer, a young Apache would strike it with a lance immediately behind its left shoulder, and with one short bellow the animal would fall forward upon its knees, dead.[22]

On May 22 the Mexican women captives arrived at the camp, hysterical with relief and gratitude. Although they had not been mistreated by Geronimo, they had suffered much from terror and

[20] Bourke, *op. cit.*, pp. 101–104, 111–12.
[21] The Apaches had a deep-seated aversion to eating pork. It may have been an undefined taboo. See Barrett, *Geronimo's Story of His Life*, p. 62 and n.
[22] Bourke, *op. cit.*, 104–105; Thrapp, *General Crook and the Sierra Madre Adventure*, p. 159.

the hardships of the journey and their three days of wandering through unknown mountains and canyons after being abandoned by their captors. The sympathetic officers ministered to their needs, and when the expedition returned to Arizona they were sent back to their people. Thus, there was no exchange of prisoners, and Geronimo's wife, Chatto's family, and other victims of Casas Grandes remained in slavery.[23]

Perhaps it was the arrival of these captives that inspired the hostiles that night to hold a victory dance, which according to custom was followed by a social dance. By this time the scouts "mixed with [them] like friends," as Rope expressed it; thus, they were invited to the dance. Bourke gave a lively description, saying that "they danced together in sign of peace and good will," but he may have been mistaken, for Rope said that Sieber forbade the scouts to participate. One disobeyed and found himself in an embarrassing predicament. By Apache etiquette the women chose their men partners for these night-long social dances, and at the close each man was expected to give a substantial present to his lady. This time the scout's partner demanded twenty cartridges, and he complied. When the other scouts reported, "the officer [Sieber, no doubt] made him go back and get the cartridges." How he made it up to the woman is not recorded. But in spite of this breach of discipline, the scouts, for all their fraternizing, never relaxed their vigilance, keeping their rifles and cartridges always at hand.[24]

On the following morning (May 23) Crook issued rations to 220 hostiles in his camp. Soon after, Nana came in with 17 of his people. "He has a strong face, marked with intelligence, courage, and good nature, but with an understratum of cruelty and vindictiveness," was Bourke's impression. (This last was never shown to his adoring followers.) He "limps very perceptibly in one leg." He reported that the hostiles were coming in by every

23 Bourke, *op. cit.*, pp. 107–11; Thrapp, *General Crook and the Sierra Madre Adventure*, p. 160; Goodwin, *op. cit.* (part 2), pp. 67–68; Secretary of War, *Annual Report*, 1883, Crook to Military Division of the Pacific, July 23, 1883, p. 178.

24 Bourke, *op. cit.*, pp. 114–15, 117; Goodwin, *op. cit.* (part 2), p. 68.

185

trail and that all would go to the reservation as soon as they could collect their families.[25]

The next day the expedition, with the surrendered hostiles, started back, traveling only a short distance and making camp about noon at a pleasant place on the Bavispe, where they remained several days while the women gathered and steamed a supply of mescal for the return journey. There Loco joined them with a small band. It was probably at this time that he told Crook that some of his people had become separated from the main body during the recent fight with García and had taken the opportunity to return to the reservation. One of them had gone back to bring him, but the aged chief felt unequal to the journey and advised them to go on without him. The party, comprising Loco's immediate family and a few others, totaling six men and fourteen women, had started before Crook entered the Sierra Madre. At this very time they were nearing Fort Apache, where they surrendered to the military. Loco told Crook that he also wanted to return "and obtain a little farm, and own cattle and horses, as he once did."[26]

During this stop, Bourke amused himself by observing the Indians. The scouts gambled with the hostiles, winning hundreds of dollars in gold, silver, and paper money. The women and children bathed in the stream, disporting themselves with "agility and grace." He commented on the "modesty of the Apaches of both sexes, under all circumstances." He thought the leaders—he named Geronimo, Loco, Chatto, Nana, Benito, Chihuahua, Mangus,[27] Kaahteney and Gil-lee (Zelé)—were "men of noticeable brain power, physically perfect and mentally acute—just the individuals to lead a forlorn hope in the face of every obstacle."

He watched some little boys, tired of swimming, who played at fighting Mexicans. Three, representing the enemy, ran, dodged, and hid, trying to elude their pursuers, "who trailed them to their covert, surrounded it, and poured in a flight of arrows." They

25 Bourke, *op. cit.*, p. 115.
26 Bourke, *op. cit.*, pp. 115–16; Thrapp, *General Crook and the Sierra Madre Adventure*, pp. 162–63, 172–73.
27 Mangus had probably come in with Kaahteney.

186

"killed" one and seized the others, carrying them into captivity. In the excitement the "corpse" rose up to watch. "In such sports, in such constant exercise, swimming, riding, running up and down the steepest and most slippery mountains, the Apache passes his boyish years. No wonder his bones are of iron, his sinews of wire, his muscles of India-rubber."[28]

Geronimo urged Crook to remain in the mountains a week longer so he could finish collecting his people. At this time he had not actually surrendered, although according to Crook and Bourke he was fairly begging for the privilege of doing so.[29] But Crook may have overdone his pose of indifference and aroused the deep-seated fears of the wild warriors. According to Rope, they held a council and planned a desperate attack on the expedition. They would invite the scouts to join their girls in a social dance. Then they would start killing their guests. "It didn't matter if they themselves got killed." But because many of the scouts were White Mountain people, Dji-li-kine dissented, saying "the White Mountain people are like relatives of mine." Geronimo argued with him. "My father-in-law, tonight we mean to do as we told you. Whenever we have gone to war before, you have gone with us." But he still refused. "You chiefs don't mean anything to me," he said. "I have been with you many times and helped you kill lots of Mexicans and whites, and that's the way you got the clothes you are wearing now. I am the one who has killed these people for you, and you have just followed behind me. I don't want to hear you talking this way with me again." And he walked away from the council.

But the council went ahead with plans for the dance. Al Sieber may have learned of the plot, or he may have objected to the fraternizing on general principles as he had done before. He knew his Apaches, a people ever mindful of the proprieties. One of the scouts had died that day, and he accordingly sent word for them

---

[28] Bourke, *op. cit.*, pp. 116–20.

[29] *Ibid.*, pp. 103–104, 112–13, 118; Secretary of War, *Annual Report*, 1883, Crook to Military Division of the Pacific, July 23, 1883, pp. 176–77.

to stop the dance, and they did.[30] Thus, by a thread the expedition was saved. The hostiles could not have wiped out Crook's force, but if they had sprung their trap there would have been one more indecisive battle with Apaches, the whole band would have scattered, and the general would have returned from another futile pursuit. There is no indication that he or any of his officers ever knew how near they came to disaster. Apparently the plot was never revealed until Rope's story was published in 1936.

On Crook's last day in this camp, May 27, an excited scout came in with a story to tell. He had gone out hunting some distance to the north and had discovered a large body of Mexican soldiers driving back the cattle Geronimo had abandoned when he made his hasty return to the captured camp. Crook sent a small party out to communicate with them, but they failed to make contact. By this time the mescal had finished roasting, and on May 28 the expedition broke camp and started back. Late that night Geronimo, Chatto, Kaahteney, and Chihuahua joined them, bringing in 116 of their people. These leaders held a conference with Crook, and again they asked for a few days' delay. Crook admitted the reasonableness of their request, but said his dwindling supply of rations made delay impossible. Geronimo said that if Crook would travel slowly they would try to overtake him at the border; if not successful in that, they would move through the mountains to San Carlos. Crook consented, but warned them "that if they could not catch up with the troops they must take their chances of being killed by any Mexicans or Americans they might encounter."[31]

Loco, Nana, Benito, and Kaahteney remained with Crook,[32] while the other leaders turned back. Geronimo was no doubt sincere in requesting time to collect his people. The charge, often made, that this was a scheme to enable him to continue raiding is untenable; he could not have raided successfully in "a few days" or "a week" with Crook present and watching. Rope even said that

30 Goodwin, *op. cit.* (part 2), pp. 68–69.

31 Bourke, *op. cit.*, pp. 120–21; Secretary of War, *Annual Report*, 1883, Crook to Military Division of the Pacific, July 23, 1883, p. 177.

32 Davis, *op. cit.*, pp. 69–70.

188

the hostiles asked Crook's permission "to gather a lot of horses from the Mexicans" and that Crook consented and told them to meet him at the border.[33] This is not credible. Geronimo would not have revealed such a plan to Crook; Crook would not have approved it; and in any case Rope would not have been present at the conference. No doubt Rope did hear gossip to that effect around the camp. And after the hostile leaders turned back and found themselves free once more, the opportunity to raid was too good to pass up.

Crook had received the surrender or the promise of surrender of all the leaders except Juh, who with his few remaining followers was in his old stronghold far to the south on the headwaters of the Yaqui. The general continued his journey with 325 captives, 52 men and 273 women.[34] Many of them were glad to return. Betzinez characterized their feeling as "a great relief. . . . No more worries, no more sleepless nights, fearing attacks by an enemy."[35] It is, in fact, apparent that the group forcibly brought to Mexico the previous year had been prevented from returning. Sam Haozous, who had been a boy at the time, recalled in later years that "Geronimo wouldn't let us get back."[36] It is also apparent that the women were tired of the rugged life. It was they who took the initiative in the surrender.

But little Charlie McComas was not present on the return journey. The Indians told Crook, and he believed them, that they had been unable to locate the child after he ran into the brush at the time of the scouts' attack on their camp.[37] For many years his fate was an unsolved mystery, and there were constant reports of his appearance. As late as 1938 a news story stated that an archeological expedition into Mexico had discovered a "lost" Apache tribe

[33] Goodwin, op. cit. (part 2), p. 69.

[34] Secretary of War, Annual Report, 1883, Crook to Military Division of the Pacific, July 23, 1883, pp. 176, 178.

[35] Betzinez, op. cit., p. 116.

[36] Interview, January 27, 1955.

[37] Bourke, op. cit., p. 128.

never brought back to the United States, whose red-haired, blue-eyed leader was thought to be Charlie McComas.[38]

The Apaches knew all the time, but they were protecting one of their people from possible punishment. Old Sam Haozous said in 1955, "All the people are dead now, so I can tell how Charlie McComas died." Jason Betzinez, who of course was raiding at the time, published the story in his book as he had heard it later from a fellow student at Carlisle. An old woman in the camp was wantonly shot by the scouts during the attack when she was begging to be taken captive. Her son, in grief and anger, then picked up a stone and beat the child on the head. But, according to Sam Haozous, the wound was not fatal. It must have been the following day that Haozous' mother and aunt, making their way down the mountainside through rocks and brush to Crook's camp, came across the boy and found him still living. The aunt was greatly attached to the child. Sam Haozous' voice was very tender and compassionate as he quoted her: " 'Poor little fellow. We can't let him die here. Let's take him along.' But my mother said, 'If we bring him in, the soldiers will blame us.' So they left him. Nobody else went that way, so no doubt he died there."[39]

Crook did not return by way of Sonora, but struggled east through the mountains on the Chihuahua side of the line. Then the expedition descended and camped where "a broad, perfectly distinct trail" led towards Casas Grandes. There, carved on the trunk of a tree they found the message in Spanish, "The 11th Battalion Passed Here 21st of May '83."[40] This reinforced the warning Crook had given to Geronimo. It was the third instance of the Mexicans' penetration of the mountains during the previous six weeks. Although they had not reached the Apaches' inner sanctu-

38 Federal Writers' Program, *New Mexico: A Guide to the Colorful State,* pp. 417–18.

39 Goodwin, *op. cit.* (part 2), p. 63; Betzinez, *op. cit.,* pp. 118–19; Sam Haozous interview, January 27, 1955. Betzinez said it was Ramona, the daughter of Chihuahua, who told him the story, but she afterwards denied knowing anything about it (Eve Ball to Angie Debo, February 27, 1973). His informant must have been some other girl.

40 Thrapp, *General Crook and the Sierra Madre Adventure,* p. 167; Secretary of War, *Annual Report,* 1883, Crook to Military Division of the Pacific, July 23, 1883, p. 178.

ary, they were approaching it. Meanwhile, Crook chose a route remote from inhabited areas to avoid meeting any Mexican force that might send his prisoners fleeing to the mountains.

On the way, the expedition passed close to Aliso Creek, where García had attacked Loco's weary people and their abductors the year before. There, some of the scouts braved Apache avoidance of the dead. "We shouldn't have gone to look at this place, but we did it anyway," said Rope. It was a ghastly sight. "There were many bleached-out bones, pieces of women's dresses, and lots of beads scattered on the ground." "Human bones, picked white and clean by coyotes," said Bourke.[41]

Before reaching the international boundary, the expedition entered Sonora. On June 10 it crossed the line and reached Silver Springs near the present Douglas, Arizona, where Crook had established a base camp. From there the Southwest and the nation at large received the first news of the campaign since he had passed out of communication three weeks before. The officers also found their first newspapers. They were full of inflammatory telegrams saying that the government would hang all the men of the hostiles and parcel out the women and children among the tribes of the Indian Territory. Somehow this "news" got to the prisoners, and Bourke believed that it drove the leaders who had promised to follow and surrender back into the mountains. The clamor for their removal, in fact, became so serious that Crook issued a warning against it in his official report. "The glibness with which people generally speak of moving them would indicate that all we have to do is to take them from their camps, as you would chickens from a roost, without reflecting that to attempt their removal would bring on the bloodiest Indian war this country has ever experienced."[42]

The general took no chances. The prisoners and the scout contingent were escorted to San Carlos by Captain Crawford with four companies of cavalry picked up at the border. They arrived on June 23. As Rope remembered it, "All the people at San Carlos

41 Goodwin, *op. cit.* (part 2), p. 70; Bourke, *op. cit.*, pp. 125–26.
42 Bourke, *op. cit.*, pp. 126–27; Secretary of War, *Annual Report*, 1883, Crook to Military Division of the Pacific, September 27, 1883, p. 169.

knew that we were coming that day and waited for us. Right on top of Copper Reef we stopped to line up. From here we could see lots of looking glasses flashing signals to us from San Carlos. . . . Now they put one hundred of us scouts in front, then all the Chiricahuas, then the rest of the scouts, then the soldiers, and last of all the pack train. . . . Sieber rode in front. There was a crowd of Indians on both sides, watching us. . . . All the scouts went to the right and camped. All the Chiricahuas went to the left, and the pack trains were brought to the center. We cooked in eight lots. All our relations came to see us. . . . The second day after that all of us scouts were discharged and got our pay."[43]

Not only to the scouts, but also to some of the 325 former hostiles it was a homecoming. And if Crook had any misgivings about the leaders who still remained out, he refused to admit them. On July 23 he closed his report of the campaign by saying that the fact that they had not yet arrived was "of no significance. Indians have no idea of the value of time."[44]

He would settle the ones he had and wait for the others. The future was to prove him right.

[43] Goodwin, *op. cit.* (part 2), p. 72.
[44] Secretary of War, *Annual Report*, 1883, Crook to Military Division of the Pacific, July 23, 1883, p. 178.

CHAPTER 11

BACK TO THE RESERVATION

The surrendered hostiles were located temporarily at San Carlos until all their people should be assembled. Captain Crawford, again in overall command, was stationed there with Davis as one of his assistants, while Gatewood was back at Fort Apache. Feared and hated by the other reservation Indians, the newcomers turned to the officers for reassurance and sympathy. Then, as Davis expressed it, "we began to find them decidedly human," with a keen sense of humor and full of fascinating tales of their years of warfare.[1]

But not all of the band entered into these friendly relations. This was the first reservation experience for the popular young warrior Kaahteney, and he was dissatisfied and suspicious. He haunted the officers' quarters, standing outside an open window or a door, silent and watchful. Reports reached them through their "secret scouts" that he regretted coming in and was plotting a break as soon as he could collect a sufficient following. They could not arrest and punish him lest Geronimo learn of it and be afraid to return. All they could do was to watch him closely. And al-

[1] Davis, *The Truth about Geronimo*, p. 72. Betzinez also wrote of the hostility of the other tribes (*I Fought with Geronimo*, pp. 122–23).

though they gave no thought to Nana—army officers always disregarded him because of his age and apparent feebleness—one can be certain that he was hand in glove with Kaahteney. The boy Kaywaykla, who heard all the family conversations, understood that the surrender was only a temporary concession to Crook's invasion of their stronghold.[2]

Another member of the party who attracted the attention of the officers was Juh's crippled daughter, Jacali, then about eighteen years old. Her wound had never healed, but had remained a running sore. The leg below it had shriveled to skin and bone "as immovable as a rod of iron," and she "was hardly more than skin and bones herself." But she had ridden the long journey up from the Sierra Madre in that condition. At the reservation the army surgeons persuaded her with some difficulty to submit to an amputation, and she was restored to health.[3] But probably she did not live long, for her subsequent history is unknown.

The friends and relatives of these first arrivals were in no hurry to join them. A little news drifted back of hard-fought battles in which the Mexicans went into the mountains after them but were always driven off.[4] Geronimo later stated that two of his people had been killed.[5] Probably he counted Dji-li-kine as one of these two, for that elusive warrior had remained with the raiders in Mexico and had been shot in the head—so they reported—by a Mexican while they were stealing horses.[6] It was also learned that Juh had died. The reports varied: they agreed that he had got drunk on mescal at Casas Grandes but after leaving the town had

2 Davis, *op. cit.*, pp. 70, 73, 113; Secretary of War, *Annual Report*, 1885, Crook to Division of the Pacific, September 9, 1885, pp. 175–76; Ball, *In the Days of Victorio*, pp. 148, 150. Kaywaykla was completely confused about the events of the surrender, and he implicated Geronimo in a scheme to draw rations on the reservation during the winter and break away in the summer. This does not fit the time of year when Geronimo subsequently came in, but Kaywaykla probably reported correctly the spirit of his own family elders.

3 Davis, *op. cit.*, p. 70.

4 Bourke, *Apache Campaign*, p. 127.

5 National Archives and Records Service, 1601 AGO 1884, F/W 1066 AGO 1883, Geronimo to Captain Emmet Crawford, March 21, 1884.

6 Goodwin, "Experiences of an Indian Scout" (part 2), p. 71. Rope doubted their story—he suspected that they had killed him themselves because of his refusal to join the plot to attack the scouts—but it seems entirely plausible.

fallen off his horse from a cliff or in a stream and had broken his neck or drowned. He may have been drinking, but according to Daklugie, who was present, he must have died from a heart attack or a stroke.

Juh had, indeed, been trading in Casas Grandes. Perhaps Mangus had joined him at this time, for he had a considerable party with him. He sent his men ahead with the supplies he had purchased, while he, with his three sons, remained in the town to ensure that none was left behind. Then he sent Daklegon to deliver a message to his warriors while he followed with Delzhinne and Daklugie. Several miles out, his horse fell into the river. "The banks were not high, the water was not deep, and both boys reached him quickly. He lay in shallow water, apparently stunned by the fall." The two boys were unable to lift him, heavy as he was, to the overhanging bank. Daklugie held his head above water while Delzhinne rode after the warriors for help. He was still alive when they returned. "They built a shelter for him and tried to save his life, but he died shortly after. They buried him beside the river."[7]

"After the deaths of my father and mother I was a very lonely child," said Daklugie in his old age to Mrs. Ball. But his brothers were sympathetic, saying he should always be with them. The three were in Mangus' band, although they sometimes encountered Geronimo and spent some time with him. Geronimo personally directed the training of the young boys of his band, and Daklugie retained a lively recollection of his strict discipline. During the winter in the high sierras, when ice was formed on the streams, he used to have them build a fire on the bank and time after time alternately warm themselves and plunge into the water. He stood there with a stick in his hand, which, however, he never found it necessary to use. Daklugie adored his "uncle" and would have preferred to stay with him, but Geronimo never gave him permission, saying he should remain with his brothers. In after years Daklugie wondered if Geronimo might have foreseen that the boy would be the last of his line and felt that he would be safer with

[7] Ball, *op. cit.*, p. 148. Kaywaykla got this account from Daklugie.

the less aggressive Mangus.[8] If Geronimo's Power gave him that forewarning, it was soon realized; Daklegon and Delzhinne were captured by Mexican cavalry and taken to Mexico City, where they died.[9]

Meanwhile, the promise the hostiles had made to come in to the reservation seemed all but forgotten. Finally, in October Crook sent Davis to the border with a pack train and a company of scouts recruited partially from the members of their band who had come in at the time of the surrender. His purpose was to encourage the others to join them and to guard them on their way to the reservation. Although it should have been evident to even the most virulent Apache-hater that as long as they remained in their Mexican sanctuary raids like Chatto's would continue, the newspapers were abusing Crook for bringing some of them back to Arizona and inciting citizens to attack any others that might try to come in. One such occurrence, and the whole band would have fled, with disaster piled on disaster.

Suddenly, eight warriors with five women and children appeared at Davis' camp. Then in late October Naiche and Gil-lee, with nine other warriors, arrived with about twice their number of women and children. On November 16 Chihuahua and Mangus, with about ninety of their people, came in. (No doubt the orphaned Daklugie was in this group.) Other small bands followed. By the end of November, 423 of the former hostiles, including eighty-three warriors, were on the reservation. Another party came on December 20. Chatto and nineteen others arrived on February 7, 1884.[10]

Some of them made their own way back to the reservation, slipping invisibly through the mountains. Davis brought up two companies. Since he was a regular army officer and the scouts were enlisted men, even the most turbulent Arizonans might have hesitated

[8] Eve Ball to Angie Debo, July 13, 1973.
[9] Griswold, "The Fort Sill Apaches," s.v. "Juh."
[10] Davis, *op. cit.*, pp. 73, 77, 79–80; Thrapp, *General Crook and the Sierra Madre Adventure*, pp. 175–76, citing Crook's papers. Davis placed Chatto with Mangus, but his memory probably tricked him.

to attack them; but even so, he kept away from traveled routes, avoided towns and ranches, and made rapid marches of forty or fifty miles daily. The returning wanderers were by no means a beaten people. As they sped uphill and down with their tireless, effortless stride, the young officer marveled at their physical perfection. "The thought of attempting to catch one of them in the mountains gave me a queer feeling of helplessness, but I enjoyed a sensation of the beautiful in watching them." If a baby chanced to be born along the route, the mother soon caught up with the party and moved on.[11]

Geronimo did not arrive until late in February. He had improved his time well. Davis had been sending scouts out daily to patrol the border watching for his arrival. One day they reported that he was approaching. Davis sent two of them down to meet the party and explain his own presence—they "were as wary and suspicious as so many wild animals"—while he rode his mule to the border and waited. He saw a long line of Indians coming up the valley, and following them two or three miles behind was a great cloud of dust.

Geronimo rode up on his white pony. He was in a bad humor. Without checking his mount until its shoulder bumped the shoulder of Davis' mule, he angrily demanded the reason for escorting his people to the reservation. He had made peace with the white men; why did he have to be protected against them? Davis explained that it was bad white men he feared. They might come out of the towns full of whiskey and try to cause trouble, but the scouts were now American soldiers, and if such ruffians should kill one they would be hanged. Geronimo was mollified and shook hands with the young officer.

Davis inquired about the dust cloud. Geronimo spoke to the point. "*Ganado*," he said in Spanish. And indeed they were—about 350 head of beeves, cows, and half-grown calves. That meant slow travel along regular roads with access to water, giving opportuni-

11 Davis, *op. cit.*, pp. 80–81, 85; Secretary of War, *Annual Report*, 1884, Crawford to Assistant Adjutant General, Whipple Barracks, p. 134.

ties for citizens to organize and attack. Now at the outset Geronimo demanded a three-day halt for his cattle to rest and graze. To avoid Mexican pursuit he had driven them too hard. Davis consented to rest that day but insisted on starting out the following morning. They traveled eighteen or twenty miles each day, and every evening Geronimo came to the officer's tent protesting that the long marches were running all the fat off his cattle. When they reached Sulphur Springs, long a favorite Indian camping ground because of its fine water and grass, Geronimo balked. Davis could go on if he wanted to, but *he* was going to stay there a few days to rest his herd. Davis had to consent to one day's halt.

Sulphur Springs was then the headquarters of a small ranch. An adobe wall four or five feet high enclosed the springs and a low adobe ranch house with a porch on the front. A small gate in the wall before the house formed the entrance to the enclosure. On all sides the valley stretched away as level as a floor. The pack train camped outside about fifty yards from the gate, the scouts a little way beyond. Several Apache families had made their camping places along the wall running in front of the house, two of them close to the gate on either side. The other families were scattered about the ranch. The cattle, mules, and ponies had been watered and were grazing half a mile away with three mounted Indians on herd to prevent their mixing with the ranch cattle.

Davis had just pitched his tent and was awaiting the cook's call to supper when two men dressed in civilian clothes came out of the ranch house. One, showing his badge, informed the officer that he was the United States marshal for the Southern District of Arizona; the other announced himself as the collector of customs from Nogales, the Arizona port of entry from Mexico. They said they had come to arrest Geronimo and his warriors for the murder of Arizona citizens and to take possession of the cattle smuggled across the border. Davis said he would not obey such orders except from Crook, and the marshal then subpoenaed him as a United States citizen to help in the arrest. He added that in the morning he would subpoena the packers and the five cowhands at the ranch, and if they should refuse to assist him he would go to the village of Willcox, about forty miles north, and organize a posse with every available man in town. "I am going to have those Indians," he said, "and then I am going to see that you answer to the federal court for your refusal to obey my order."

This meant a fight. Davis had orders from Crook to escort Geronimo and his band to the reservation, and he was determined to throw in his lot with them. He could expect no help from the military; Fort Bowie, the nearest post, was thirty miles away to the east, and Camp Grant was still farther to the north. But it would take the marshal some time to collect his posse. If Davis could persuade Geronimo to start at once, they could make some distance on the journey. Then the women and children could continue their flight to the reservation while Geronimo and his warriors and Davis and his scouts would stand off the marshal and his men. But would Geronimo cooperate? He might break back for the border, to be followed by his relatives on the reservation, with the usual bloody trails on the way.

Then came relief. Davis' West Point friend, Second Lieutenant J. Y. F. Blake, was stationed at Fort Bowie. Davis had sent word for Blake to meet him at Sulphur Springs and spend the night, but in his excitement he had forgotten the invitation. Just then Blake rode up. The two young officers began scheming. Blake had graduated a year before Davis and thus was technically his superior. If the Indians would move out, he would be their escort while Davis would remain in obedience to the subpoena. (It is uncertain even now whether the credentials of the civilian "officers" were real or fraudulent, but Davis accepted them as authentic.)

The two young men had just finished supper when the marshal and the collector joined them to do a little gloating. Blake had brought along a quart of whiskey. He offered it to the two civilians and saw hospitably that they drank most of it. They had a good laugh at Davis' expense and went back to the ranch house. One of them brought his bedding outside and settled down to sleep on the porch not more than ten feet from the Indian families by the gate. But his deep breathing was reassuring.

Now all depended on Geronimo. Davis sent his scout first sergeant to call him from his bed. The other scouts had sprung up from somewhere and were awaiting orders. Geronimo's warriors joined the tense circle. Davis did not tell him the whole truth. If he had learned of the plan to try and hang him, he would have fled with his people back to the Sierra Madre, and the ensuing campaign to search them out would have been more difficult than the one before. Davis simply said that the customs man had come to collect one thousand dollars on the cattle, and if the payment were not made he would take them. Thus, in order to avoid trouble, the herd should be started for the reservation immediately. His "brother" (Blake) would go along while he himself would stay at the ranch to throw the officers off the trail.

Geronimo angrily refused to start. Staring straight into the eyes of the lieutenant, his lips twitching, and shifting his rifle from arm to arm, he said he had come in for peace but had found nothing except trouble. If those men wanted to take his cattle let them try it. He was going back to bed, and he would take the promised layover. Just then the sergeant, who belonged to a tribe that hated Geronimo and his people, added some rapid words of his own. Davis never knew what he said. Mickey Free had been interpreting, but the moment was too tense for him to interrupt. Whatever it was, it caused Geronimo to wilt. He looked around at his men and the scouts, but found no support. Then Davis slyly suggested that probably he would not be able to get away undiscovered by the men at the ranch. This touched the Apache's pride: "His people could leave me standing where I was and I would not know that they were gone." Davis then reminded him of what a good joke it would be on the officers if they woke in the morning and found that the Indians with all the cattle and ponies had got away. Geronimo almost smiled, looked at his men, and saw that they agreed.

Davis went to the pack train and woke the packmaster, and he started the train silently on its way. When the officer came back to the gate, the Indians had all vanished from their sleeping places along the fence. Geronimo's young nephew Kanseah retained a vivid memory of what happened. As he told the story in his old age, he and his mentor, Yahnozha, who knew many English words, had scouted around and listened. "One man said he was from the Customs and he wanted to take our cattle because we had not paid any tax on them. Our cattle! He hadn't stolen those cattle; why should he get them?" They heard Davis talking to Geronimo. Of course, he said, it would be impossible to move all those people without waking the men. "Dogs would bark, children would cry. . . . If any people knows how to be quiet it is the Apache. . . . We shook with laughter as we got everything ready to move. It did not take ten minutes. Not a dog barked. Not a baby cried. We tied children's feet together under the bellies of the horses. We tied small children to adults. And we started. At first we moved slowly, very slowly. We had to, because of the cattle. But after we got out of hearing we put boys with lances to keep the cattle moving, and we made time. By morning we were far north of that spring. . . ."[12]

Davis took up a lonely vigil by the gate, sitting on an empty box and holding his saddle mule by the bridle. In the morning he saw the man on the porch stir and sit up. Then in great excitement the man ran into the house and called his companion. They climbed to the roof and scanned the horizon through field glasses. There was not even a cloud of dust in sight. They demanded an explanation from Davis. He told them that a superior officer had come, had taken command, and had left with the outfit. He could not say whether they had gone east towards Fort Bowie or north towards Camp Grant or whether, followed by Blake, they had bolted for Mexico, but he was there in obedience to the marshal's orders. There was nothing they could do. The Indians were close to sanctuary in one of three places. Davis then struck out, and after two days of hard riding he overtook Blake a few miles south of the reserva-

12 Ball, *op. cit.*, pp. 152–53 and note 3. Mrs. Ball here represents Kaywaykla as the narrator, but she informed me, as her footnote also indicates, that it was actually Kanseah (to Angie Debo, February 27, 1973).

tion line, and they delivered their charges to Crawford without further incident.[13]

But Geronimo lost the cattle he had worked so hard to accumulate to set his people up in ranching. Although all the parties coming up had been riding stolen horses, Crook had overlooked it, but he could not overlook a theft of this magnitude. The cattle were taken by the agency and ultimately sold, and the proceeds were turned over to the Mexican government to undertake the task of sorting out the claimants. Geronimo protested in outraged innocence. He was still protesting twenty years later at Fort Sill: "I told him [Crook] that these were not white man's cattle, but belonged to us, for we had taken them from the Mexicans during our wars. I also told him that we did not intend to kill these animals, but that we wished to keep them and raise stock on our range. He would not listen to me, but took the stock."[14]

In the company that came up with Geronimo were twenty-six warriors and some seventy women and children.[15] Geronimo's three wives and his children were, of course, in the group. One young son, of whom nothing further is known, had died on the journey. Geronimo told Crawford that there were "twenty-five men women and children still out. . . . They said that at the end of the next moon they wanted some of their people to be sent to the line after them."[16] Possibly these were the remnants of Juh's family and his few followers. A small party did arrive in April, and Crawford could truly say that "for the first time since the establishment of the reservation all the tribes of the Apache nation in their entirety were upon it."[17]

13 The whole story may be found in Davis, *op. cit.*, pp. 82–101.
14 Thrapp, *Conquest of Apacheria*, p. 294; Barrett, *Geronimo's Story of His Life*, p. 135.
15 Davis, *op. cit.*, pp. 84, 90.
16 National Archives and Records Service, 1601 AGO 1884, F/W 1066 AGO 1883, Geronimo to Crawford, March 21, 1884.
17 Secretary of War, *Annual Report*, 1884, Crawford to Assistant Adjutant General, Whipple Barracks, undated but subsequent to August 21, p. 134. Crawford, of course, was referring only to the Arizona Apaches and their relatives. Crook reported that the last party arrived on May 15, but Crawford, who was in charge, stated specifically that they came in April.

202

Plans were being made for their permanent settlement even before the arrival of this last small, belated band. On March 21 Geronimo made a formal statement of their position to Crawford for forwarding to Crook. It is apparent that the leaders had held a council, had decided on a policy, and were present indicating their agreement when it was submitted. But although Geronimo voiced a group consensus, this first recorded expression of his views reveals his practical, logical mind, his sense of responsibility, and his sound economic planning—along with considerable adroit diplomacy. (Clearly he had not yet learned that he would lose his cattle.) His statement began: "Geronimo said: That he has come here with the understanding that everything he asked for was to be granted him. When the General was in the Sierra Madre, he met the General and remembers everything that the General then told him."

He went on to attribute supernatural powers to Crook, a form of address often used by Apaches to officials they wished to conciliate.[18] At this distance it is impossible to determine whether this was simply a convention of Apache etiquette or an attempt at flattery, or whether warriors who believed themselves to be the recipients of Power attributed corresponding Power to white men. In any case, Geronimo's statement reveals his shock at finding his sanctuary invaded: "When he saw General Crook then he told the General that he thought he was a God. That he did not believe he was an American, for he did not believe that an American could go there. He was much astonished to see General Crook there and thought that he was so powerful that he could command the sun the moon and everything."

He told of his decision to come in and stated frankly the reason for his long delay: "As soon as he saw General Crook he thought that he would leave the mountains and come to live at peace on the reservation. . . . Now he is very much pleased to be here. He thinks that it is better to live here than among the rocks and thorns in the mountains down there. He remained in the mountains so long

18 Crook, who heartily disliked General Howard, was very scornful of similar compliments paid that officer by an Apache chief, but he failed to mention the instances when he himself had been thus addressed. See Schmitt, *General George Crook*, p. 171.

because he wanted to get some horses and cattle to bring here. He was poor and did not think that he would have friends here to give him these things." Apparently referring to Crook's scouts, who had talked with him when he was wavering in his mountain stronghold, he said that "all the Indians told him that they went to bed early and got up late and had nothing to fear, here all the Indians have nothing to excite them, and it is good for him; he likes it. All the men who were sent to him told him that . . . everybody here was good to the Indians, and only kept them from doing harm."

He wanted the past to be blotted out. (This theme would recur in his subsequent surrenders.) "He wants everything to be done straight. He is saying that so that everything may be forgotten. All made new, so that they can begin again. Before, here in San Carlos, everything was wrong with the Indians and the people here. But now it is all being carried on straight, and he wants it to continue. He will never think again as he used to think before; now he thinks, that the Americans on the reservation want him to live here, and have cooking utensils &c and not run around in the mountains cooking their meat on sticks before the fire."

He realized that it would not be easy for his people to take up "civilized" pursuits: "They are all here now like brancho mules, which it is necessary to teach little by little, until they are all tamed. And he thinks that they are all to be treated well until they all are living well. He feels now as if he were in a big hole and covered up as far as his chest, while he is at San Carlos. He has surrendered entirely, and any orders given him he will obey without thinking of resisting them. . . . If in future some one tells anything bad about him he wants to know right away who it is that is telling bad things about him."

His main concern was in finding a suitable homesite, and he saw no reason for reservation boundaries. "Here in San Carlos it does not seem to him that it is very well, because there is no grass, no good water, and there is some sickness here too. He would like to live where there is lots of water, lots of land, and lots of wild animals. He knows where there is such a place. He wants to know where they are to live. Whether they will have enough land to live all together. He wants this line around the reservation to be taken away. Now that there is no war, there should be no line, except the line at San Bernardino, the Mexican line."

Here, as related above, he told of the small band still out. Then he went into the heart of his message, an earnest appeal to settle on Eagle Creek:

There is plenty of land, plenty of grass and his people can all live there. Those Americans who live on Eagle Creek, can't their land be bought from them and given to the Indians? They take great interest in good land, as they want to farm and live like white men, and think that Eagle Creek would be good for them. Now that they are here, and you [Capt. C.] have them [the Indians] in your power,[19] you can do as you please with them, and ought to let them do what they wish to. . . . All of them have the same things as white men, hands, legs, arms &c, just as white men, and are surprised that they are not given the same things as white men when they ask for them. This peace they promised was a legal peace and they expect to get the land they want on account of having made this peace.

He used every means he could summon to gain his object— entreaty, adequate presentation to Crook, the united support of his people, justice as he argued it, and the practical advantages:

He begs you [Capt. C.] as if you were his father,[20] and asks you to give him what he asks for. He wants that this paper be well written, so that the General will give them this land. All these Indians who [are here] around me knew what I have said, and are very anxious to get this land. They want General Crook to know this so he will give it to them. At Camp Apache it is not good to live as there is

19 Brackets in original.
20 Brackets in original.

no game around there, and he has heard that the Indians around there have come here for rations, and learning that the ground there is not sufficient to live on. There are many of us, and there is not enough land around Camp Apache for us . . . for we want to plant melons, squashes, corn and everything. . . . If we go to Camp Apache we will starve to death there. He is afraid that after he had raised one or two crops, the land will be taken from him. There is no mescal to bake around Camp Apache. . . . He wants to live on Eagle Creek, and if they think that he is going to steal anything, soldiers can be put to watch him. He thought that everything he wanted to do in this country he would be able to do, and he is much astonished to find that he cant get Eagle Creek. . . . When the General was in the Sierra Madre the interpreter told them that the General said they could live on Eagle Creek or on the creeks that come out of the Mogollon Mts.[21] If we cant go to Eagle Creek we want to go to Ash Creek [on Ash Flat] and see how the country is there.

∞∞∞∞∞∞∞∞∞∞∞∞∞

There was the ever-present concern about the captives in Mexico. These, of course, included Geronimo's wife, and possibly Juh's two sons were still alive. He had made another attempt to free them after Crook left the Sierra Madre: "I went to Case Grande and talked with an Officer about the Indian captives the Mexicans have. There were no Americans there. I was not actually in the town, but out near it and two Mexican soldiers came out and talked to me." He returned to the subject later in his statement: "We want all our captives here. They are in Mexico and we believe that General Crook can get them for us. We believe that he can do anything."

He gave the reasons—previously quoted[22]—for the breakaway from the reservation after the Cibecue fight. He said that although

---

21 Crook certainly had not told them that. The general's unbreakable rules were: never lie to an Indian, and never promise an Indian anything you can't carry out. The interpretation may have been faulty, and Geronimo probably heard what he wanted to believe. He must have been sincere in his statement, for it was addressed to Crook.

22 *Supra*, p. 132.

he had heard of "a little white boy" about whom the general inquired, he had never seen him. He ended by stating the objective of his band to choose a place to live apart, away from the unfriendly tribes on the reservation: "If these Indians around San Carlos come here after I leave and talk about me, I don't want you [Capt. C.] to believe them.[23] We are going out to look for some land to farm, and we dont want any [of these] Indians around here with us. We want to be alone, and have no Indians but Chiricahuas with us.[24] Where we are going to live we would like to have a store, so that we can buy what we want in the way of manta &c. We only want a little one just for ourselves."[25]

The large party that had come up with Crook must have had a weary wait, especially during the summer on the sun-scorched flats around the agency, until the arrival of the rest of their people made it possible to locate them. But Crook was not unmindful of their welfare. In January he persuaded them to let him send forty-seven of their boys and five of their girls to the school recently established by Captain Richard H. Pratt at Carlisle. Among the boys were a son of Loco, afterwards known as Dexter Loco, and two sons of Benito.[26] Also, after Crawford took over under Crook's directions, the cheating on supplies was ended. To Britton Davis was assigned the duty of issuing the rations, and he corrected sickening frauds on the Indians.[27]

But the reform of the system was not as easy as a simple change from civilian to army control. There were good men and bad men in both services. The good men, whether civilian agents or army officers, followed identical practices. Besides cleaning up the graft, they recognized the authority of the tribal leaders, maintained

23 Brackets in original.
24 By this time all these related tribes were known officially as Chiricahuas, and that designation accordingly appeared in Crawford's transcript of Geronimo's statement.
25 National Archives and Records Service, 1601 AGO 1884, F/W 1066 AGO 1883, Geronimo to Captain Emmet Crawford, March 21, 1884.
26 National Archives and Records Service, Record Group No. 75, Bureau of Indian Affairs, Letters Received 1881–1907, Secretary of War Robert T. Lincoln to Secretary of the Interior, January 25, 1884; Griswold, "The Fort Sill Apaches," s.v. "Benito" and "Loco, Dexter."
27 Davis, op. cit., pp. 32–35, 41–46.

order by a native force (of police by agency terminology, of scouts in army parlance), and for the trial of offenders set up native courts not very different from the Apaches' own practices.[28] They also made a careful distinction between peaceable Indians and hostiles. At the same time, in both services were men insensitive in their treatment of the Indians and corrupt men who robbed them. But the able Crook, who was close at hand, was more adept in checking irregularities than the distant Indian Office at Washington. This was graphically shown at San Carlos after Davis was sent to the border in October to shepherd in the late arrivals.

Crawford then assigned the rationing to Archie McIntosh. This trusted scout was well liked by the Indians, and his wife, an Apache woman, was related to Chihuahua and others of the band. He had served Crook with unfailing dependability for twenty years, and his hardihood and courage in tight places had sometimes meant the difference between success and disaster, but he failed in this test of integrity. On March 28 Crawford received a tip that he was stealing supplies and hauling them to a ranch he owned on Pinto Creek off the reservation near Globe. Although this report, as Crawford said, "has taken me back entirely," he investigated and found it to be true. Then, as he reported to Crook: "I sent for all the Chiefs & told them about it. They all said they wanted Archie kept. They said it made no difference if he took half of their rations he was a good man & could have them. I sent for Archie & he acknowledged that [the accusation] was true & he had the impudence to tell me that it was done at every Military Post in the Dept.[29] The Chiefs tell me to telegraph you & say they wanted him kept but if you said discharge him all right."

Chihuahua, Kaahteney, and two or three others then left, but Geronimo, Chatto, and Mangus remained for a private word: "They said that they thought what I had done was right, that their women & children ought to have that ration[,] that they received

[28] For trials under primitive Apache custom, see Barrett, *op. cit.*, pp. 185–86, and Opler, *An Apache Life-Way*, pp. 252–54. For the Apaches' adaptation to the jury system, see Davis, *op. cit.*, pp. 48–49, and Bourke, *On the Border with Crook*, p. 446.

[29] There was probably more truth in this than Crawford was willing to admit.

208

enough themselves. Archie I think has been feeding up the Chiefs & principal men but cutting down the rest."

Crawford told McIntosh he was fired, but said he might telegraph an appeal to Crook. McIntosh then resorted to a technique as old as federal-Indian relations: he collected the leaders and induced them to make the appeal. The telegram read: "We the undersigned after a council yesterday—we all have said we want Archie McIntosh to stay with us. You put him over us and he is our friend. He gives us all we want to eat and he is good. Capt Crawford told us that Archie stole our provisions from us. . . . We all saw what was taken away in the wagon—We want you to come to us right away to straighten things out for us. He brought us back with you and we want to talk to you." It was supposedly signed with the names of Geronimo, Kaahteney, Benito, Loco, Chihuahua, Chatto, Mangus, Naiche and Gil-lee. The operator would not send it until he could consult Crawford. Crawford read it and ordered McIntosh off the reservation with the warning "that if he ever attempted to again call the Indians together for the purpose of breeding discontent I would put him in irons." In reporting the incident, Crawford said he suspected it was McIntosh who put Geronimo up to requesting a store, hoping to get the lucrative job of running it.[30] The whole episode is typical of the complex forces that made honest administration of Indian affairs virtually impossible.[31]

Geronimo did not get his store. Neither did he get the location he had earnestly requested for his people. All the lower course of Eagle Creek was in the area subtracted from the Indians' holdings. Geronimo was aware of that; hence his suggestion that reservation boundaries be wiped out. This, of course, was impracticable, and as for extending those boundaries and buying out the settlers, that would have reversed the entire course of frontier history. But Crook permitted the Indians to choose any location on the reservation. Apparently they rejected Ash Creek. They selected an area around Turkey Creek, about seventeen miles southeast of Fort

30 Thrapp, *Al Sieber*, pp. 290–93.
31 See Ogle, *Federal Control of the Western Apaches*, pp. 194–96, 201, 210–13.

Apache and close to the settlement of the White Mountain bands, with which some of them had marriage or other connections. It was a beautiful region of tall pines, clear streams, abundant game, and for these mountain people an ideal summer climate, but it lacked extensive farmland and sufficient water for irrigation. Most of the good land on the reservation had, in fact, been taken already by other tribes.

Crawford and Davis favored furnishing these former hostiles with breeding stock for cattle and sheep raising (Geronimo's idea exactly). And they could have planted their usual small patches in the valleys. But the Indian Office was committed to the farming methods of the eastern United States. Crawford himself had ordered two hundred plows, two hundred harrows, four hundred sets of plow harness, and one hundred wagons, but these were no doubt intended for the tamer, already settled tribes. The army had been buying corn and barley for its animals from these Indians, who had to prepare the ground with shovels and harvest their barley with knives.[32]

But distant Washington decreed a uniform pattern, and it was the job of Davis to carry it out. Along with some picks and shovels and some seed, which they truly appreciated, his charges received a dozen light wagons, a dozen plows, and a dozen sets of double harness. Two weeks were spent on the San Carlos river bottom training the wild ponies and wilder Indians in the use of this farm machinery. It was a hilarious experience, with the Indians whooping and laughing as their ponies pulled the plows at a gallop and with the plowman barely holding to the handles and the point only occasionally cutting into the soil.[33]

The former hostiles were engaged in another activity that spring at San Carlos. It is not mentioned, as far as is known, in army or agency reports, but it is of great interest to the historian. A. Frank Randall, now settled at Willcox, brought his photographic equipment and made portraits of the leaders against a contrived background of desert plants. Their poses show that they were willing,

[32] Davis, *op. cit.*, pp. 102, 137; Secretary of War, *Annual Report*, 1884, Crawford to Assistant Adjutant General, Whipple Barracks, pp. 135–36.
[33] Davis, *op. cit.*, pp. 102–104.

Apache family at their wickiup. Probably photographed by A. Frank Randall at San Carlos in the spring of 1884. Courtesy National Archives and Records Service.

even cooperative subjects, and the resulting portraits have found their way into many books.[34]

In general, these photographs convey the impression that the spring of 1884 was a time of relaxation and wellbeing for the assembled bands. Then in late May all arrangements were completed, and the entire company set out with Davis in charge for what was hoped would be their permanent home on Turkey Creek.[35]

34 Some of these pictures are marked with the name of the notable Southwestern photographer Ben Wittick or attributed to the Army Signal Corps, but Richard Rudisill of the Museum of New Mexico at Santa Fe, who is an authority on Wittick's work, states that Wittick copied and claimed the work of other photographers and that the Army Signal Corps simply collected photographs from many sources in the early 1900's with little attempt to record data. He is convinced from his own studies that the well-known picture of Geronimo kneeling and holding his rifle in the Wittick Collection was originally made by Randall; Rudisill to Angie Debo, July 17, 1972, and July 8, 1975. This finding would put all others with an identical or similar setting in the same category. In addition, copies of seven of these photographs are in the records of the Army Signal Corps in the National Archives and Records Service, and they carry the notation, "Copyright, May 16, 1884, A. F. Randall." The date fits, for the spring of 1884 marks the only occasion in their history when all the Apaches depicted in these photographs were together.

35 Crawford's report said "in May"; Davis remembered it as "about the first of June." Secretary of War, *Annual Report*, 1884, p. 135; Davis, *op. cit.*, pp. 103, 106.

211

Naiche with his wife, Ha-o-zinne, as identified by her daughter, Amelia Naiche. This and the following seven photographs were taken by A. Frank Randall in the spring of 1884. Courtesy Smithsonian Institution, National Anthropological Archives.

Dos-teh-seh, daughter of Mangas Coloradas, wife of Cochise, and mother of Taza and Naiche. Courtesy *Chronicles of Oklahoma*.

213

Chihuahua, the leader of a small Chiricahua band, who rose to prominence among his people. Courtesy *Chronicles of Oklahoma*.

Loco. *Though a brave and able warrior, he sought peace throughout his life.* Courtesy Smithsonian Institution, National Anthropological Archives.

215

Mangus. He lacked the drive necessary to succeed his father. Courtesy Museum of New Mexico.

Nana. *Army officers always disregarded him because of his age and apparent feebleness.* Courtesy U.S. Army Artillery and Missile Center Museum, Fort Sill.

217

Kaahteney, his wife, Guyan, and the child Kaywaykla. Courtesy Museum of New Mexico.

Gil-lee and his wife, Tzes-ton. Courtesy Museum of New Mexico.

219

CHAPTER 12

PEACE WITH SUSPICION ON
TURKEY CREEK

As the emigrating party moved up to their new home, they came to the Black River in flood. Davis managed the crossing with the wagons as boats and the energetic Indian men and their ponies as motive power. It furnished the Indians almost as much fun as had their agricultural training. They numbered 521, of whom 127 were men and boys capable of bearing arms. Soon they were joined by some Coyoteros and some of the White Mountain band so that they numbered more than 550.

Crook came to see them immediately after their arrival and was much amused when he learned of the techniques used in the river crossing. They scattered among the trees and streams and began at once to erect their clusters of wickiups. They were pleased with their new homesite. Kaywaykla, with the discomforts of the previous summer of waiting at San Carlos fresh in his mind, found the new place a pleasant contrast: "There was an abundance of good water, wood, and game. There was good grazing. There were no mosquitoes, few rattlesnakes, and no cavalry. There were poles and brush to make shelters, and even the canvas of old tents for covering until hides could be secured. The only use I remember for wagons was to place the beds on the side toward the wind for shelter. In addition, we planted rows of evergreens around the [wickiups] to serve as windbreaks."[1]

Davis was in sole charge. He pitched his tent in a little glade under the pines, with a large tent nearby in which to store the rations. He had Mickey Free as his interpreter, and Sam Bowman served as cook and general camp helper. To keep order he had a company of scouts enlisted entirely from the recently hostile bands. Chatto he made first sergeant. "One of the finest men, red or white, I have ever known," was the young officer's characterization of him. Certainly Chatto never violated the pledge of peace he had given Crook in the Sierra Madre, and his loyalty was proved in many tight places. Of Geronimo's relatives, his "brother" Perico became second sergeant,[2] and young Chappo requested and received the job of Davis' "striker" (that is, servant, with pay of five dollars a month more than that of the ordinary scout). Less conspicuous in the officer's entourage were two "secret scouts," a man and a woman he had brought with him from San Carlos.[3]

Geronimo and Naiche, with their people, chose their campsite several miles away from Davis' tent. So did Kaahteney's followers, but the young leader himself settled on a ridge just above Davis, where he could keep the officer under surveillance. Nana was there also, unregarded by Davis but still dominating the friends and relatives of Victorio. The camps of Chihuahua and Mangus were only a short distance away. The fatherless boys Daklugie and Istee lived in Mangus' family. Daklugie was in some way related to Mangus, and Istee, as a son of Victorio, was, of course, a young brother of Mangus' wife. Kaahteney undertook their training as warriors along with that of his step-son Kaywaykla.[4]

The Indians liked Davis. He was honest and fair and treated them as individual human beings. He consulted Chatto daily re-

[1] Davis, *The Truth about Geronimo*, pp. 104–107; Ball, *In the Days of Victorio*, p. 156.

[2] Perico may have been known here as Juan, or possibly he soon succeeded an Indian named Juan. See Davis, *op. cit.*, pp. 106, 150; and Ball, *op. cit.*, pp. 156–57.

[3] Davis, *op. cit.*, pp. 38–39, 106.

[4] *Ibid.*, p. 107; Ball, *op. cit.*, pp. 156, 158–59. I have followed Kaywaykla's locations because the boy's memory of sites was more accurate than that of Davis.

garding general conditions in the camp and the needs of the scouts.
Loco, Benito, and Gil-lee came frequently to his tent for friendly
or business talks. Mangus was cooperative and with Loco often
backed him in controversies with other leaders. Geronimo, Naiche,
Chihuahua, Nana, and Kaahteney held aloof. The officer knew
that there was an undercurrent of suspicion stirring in the band,
and he believed Kaahteney to be the leader of the discontented
faction.[5]

Kaywaykla, looking back, described the situation from their
side. They distrusted Davis' helpers. Illogically, they blamed
Mickey Free for being the innocent cause of Cochise's trouble—
"the coyote whose kidnapping had brought war to the Chiricahuas"—and they believed he interpreted falsely to put all they said
to Davis in a bad light. They trusted Bowman, but Davis usually
employed Mickey Free. He knew of their suspicions, but as he said,
"He may have fooled me on occasion, but if he did it was done so
skilfully that I never found it out." They regarded Chatto as a
traitor to his people who had become a turncoat because he had
failed to obtain the leadership of the band. The bitter rivalry between him and Kaahteney may well have been the basis of the
hostility. They hated Chatto's friend Tsoe because he had guided
Crook to their sanctuary. Tsoe had remained with the scout company at San Carlos, but he was often sent with messages to Fort
Apache. They knew about the "secret scouts," and they were
convinced that Chatto was one of them. In this they were mistaken,
but no doubt Chatto did inform Davis of things he observed or
imagined in the band, coloring his reports by his hatred of Kaahteney. Through it all, they hoped that Davis would eventually
discover the treachery of his trusted adherents, but meanwhile
they watched—Kaahteney from his camp on the ridge, Perico and
Chappo from the scout company.[6]

They had more open grievances: the making of *tizwin* and the

5 Davis, *op. cit.*, pp. 111, 115, 139–40.

6 Ball, *op. cit.*, pp. 154–57, 162–65, 175; Davis, *op. cit.*, p. 37. Kaywaykla believed
that Geronimo placed his relatives near Davis for that purpose, but apparently they
enlisted in good faith.

control of their families. Crook had issued rules regulating these matters as soon as he first came to Arizona and began settling hostiles on reservations. Now Davis called the chiefs together and laid down the law. Disobedience would land them in jail. They were nearly unanimous in their opposition. Chihuahua was especially outspoken; Kaahteney was silent and surly.

Although *tizwin* drinking unquestionably threw the camps into disorder and violence, they had logical reasons for their stand. They said they had promised Crook that they would keep the peace with white Americans, Mexicans, and other Indian tribes, and they were observing this agreement. The white officers and soldiers, and all white men and Mexicans drank something "to make them feel good," and why should the same thing be forbidden the Indians? They had always made *tizwin*, and they did not want any of their people put in jail for following the tribal custom.[7]

Family discipline involved the punishment of a wife for adultery. This must be understood against the background of the Apaches' culture. The woman occupied an honored and secure place in their society. Typical is the advice given a young married couple by the father of the bride:

〰〰〰〰〰〰〰〰〰〰〰〰〰

I talked to that boy her husband. I said, "I'm talking to you. . . . Every day means that you should bring in something to eat. . . . If you have nothing to eat, your wife cannot cook anything for you. . . . Look at her clothes. Many things rest on you. It's a man's duty to bring in the meat and clothes. You can't expect the woman to do that. . . ."

I said, "My daughter, it is your [duty] to keep . . . everything neat about your place. Keep yourself neat the way you were when I was raising you. Keep your husband's clothes clean. Keep your fire going all the time. . . . Don't fuss at each other."

And I said to the boy, "A woman must be treated well because she feeds you; she's the only friend you have. Your mother and father can't treat you better than your wife does. That's the way I

7 Davis, *op. cit.*, p. 123.

Nal-tzuk-ich (Cut Nose), believed to be one of Crook's spies in the Sierra Madre campaign. Photograph taken by A. Frank Randall at San Carlos in the spring of 1884. Courtesy Museum of New Mexico, Santa Fe.

224

feel about my wife." I told him, "She's the mother of the whole thing, this life you have to go through, and you may have a long life."[8]

>>>>>>>>>>>>>>>>>>>>>>>>>

If a man abused his wife, the fact that he had become a member of her family gave them the right to intervene and protect her.[9] If she was lazy or a nagger, there was nothing he could do except to scold her in private. But she was expected to be chaste. Most Apache women were, but there were occasional exceptions, and the husband was obligated to vindicate the family honor by cutting off the end of his wife's nose. If he failed to take action, he lost face in the band. A few women were seen—one was even photographed —with this disfigurement. Crook sternly banned the practice on all reservations he controlled. Possibly for this reason beating was substituted. In some cases the man even killed his wife and then himself in his grief and humiliation,[10] and no wronged husband could ever be induced to complain. His shame was too great.[11]

Now the leaders, as upholders of public morals as well as law and order, told Davis that neither family discipline nor *tizwin* drinking had entered into their agreement with Crook. The meeting broke up with no acceptance of the general's orders on the part of the leaders and no wavering by Davis in his determination to enforce them.[12]

Soon after that, Davis, on a turkey hunt, was following a trail up a mesa when he heard a gobble in the creek bottom behind him. He turned back and shot a turkey. He always hoped it was not the one that gobbled, for he believed that the gobbler had saved his life. That evening a pebble hit the wall of his tent, the signal of a "secret

8 Opler, *An Apache Life-Way*, p. 169.
9 Opler, *Apache Odyssey*, pp. 14–15.
10 Opler, *An Apache Life-Way*, pp. 408–10.
11 Ball, *op. cit.*, p. 176. I myself know of a case where a modern descendant of these Apaches punished his wife for flagrant unfaithfulness. Brought to trial, he gave no justification. Asked if he had any reason to complain of his wife's conduct, he finally admitted that he had—"She wouldn't get up and cook my breakfast"—and he accepted his prison sentence with no further defense.
12 Davis, *op. cit.*, pp. 123–24.

scout." It was his woman spy. As he told it, Mickey Free was with her, but he wrote elsewhere that he always spoke to his "secret scouts" directly without an interpreter because they were afraid Mickey Free would reveal their identity. Possibly Davis confused this incident with another related by Kaywaykla, probably occurring the same evening, in which Chihuahua lay hidden outside and heard Chatto and Mickey Free "fabricate" a story of a planned uprising by Geronimo and Kaahteney.

In any event, the woman told Davis that the good spirit of one of his ancestors was in that gobbler. Kaahteney and his adherents had been having a *tizwin* drink on top of the mesa, and when they saw the officer coming with his gun they thought he was on his way to arrest them and were lying in wait ready to shoot him when he should reach the top. Then they would incite as many more of the Indians as possible and make a break for Mexico.[13]

Davis felt that this called for a showdown. He sent to Fort Apache for four troops of cavalry, about 140 men, to arrive at sunrise. At the same time he sent the scouts to summon all the leaders to his tent. The outcome was uncertain. Kaahteney had thirty-two followers, the most reckless of the young warriors. Chatto, Benito, Loco, Mangus, and Gil-lee could be counted on to oppose the young dissenter. Geronimo and Naiche seemed uncommitted, and Davis typically failed to reckon with Nana. He thought that if the sentiment of the majority was for peace, he would win; if they sided with Kaahteney, let it be war now. And there was the uncomfortable reminder of what had happened at an attempted arrest fewer than three years before at Cibecue.

The dramatic confrontation occurred early that morning of June 22, with the cavalry dismounted and ready, Kaahteney and his followers defiant, twenty of the chiefs and principal men assembled in the tent, and other warriors surrounding it with not a woman or child in sight. All the men were armed. Crook, in fact, had strong convictions against disarming Indians. First, he considered it impossible; they always found ways of concealing their weapons.

13 *Ibid.*, pp. 39, 124–25; Ball, *op. cit.*, pp. 162–63.

Then there were plenty of unscrupulous dealers who would supply them in spite of regulations. And significantly, only by being armed could they protect themselves from "the disreputable class of white men" ready to commit depredations against them and their property on the reservation.[14]

But never before had the leaders come armed to a meeting with Davis. There was a tense moment when Kaahteney's followers fanned out and advanced toward the tent, cocking their leveled weapons. But the scouts stood firm, ready to support Davis even at the risk of their lives, and he arrested Kaahteney without incident. Benito and one of the scouts promised to be Kaahteney's sureties if he were not disarmed. He went quietly with them to San Carlos, where he was tried by an Indian jury and convicted of threatening to start an uprising.

Was he guilty as charged? Kaywaykla passionately insisted throughout his life that his step-father was the victim of malicious lies told by Chatto, Mickey Free, Tsoe, and Davis' spies. It should be noted, however, that Kaahteney had been surly and uncooperative during all the months that Chatto was still in Mexico, and even if his words were "twisted" by a hostile interpreter, his manner was his own. Even Kaywaykla said that Davis had urged him to enlist as a scout and he had refused.[15]

Crawford sentenced him to serve three years in irons in the military prison on Alcatraz Island.[16] But Crook recognized the potential of the energetic young warrior and recommended that "he be kept in irons at hard labor for one month and his confinement then relaxed, and he be permitted to go about the island and the city of San Francisco so that he may observe and become acquainted with the manner of living of the whites and thus learn something which may be of benefit to his people when he is re-

14 Secretary of War, *Annual Report*, 1883, Crook to Military Division of the Pacific, July 23, 1883, pp. 177–78; and September 27, 1883, pp. 168–69.

15 Ball, *op. cit.*, pp. 157, 162.

16 The army's account of his arrest and trial is in Davis, *op. cit.*, pp. 125–30; and Secretary of War, *Annual Report*, 1884, Crawford to Assistant Adjutant General, Whipple Barracks, p. 135. Davis said he was sentenced to five years in prison, but Crawford's contemporary report is no doubt correct.

turned to the reservation."[17] In October Crook suggested to the Indians that he be allowed to return if they would be responsible for his good conduct, but Geronimo and (of course) Chatto opposed the plan, saying that he kept the other Indians stirred up.[18] Crook did have him released after about eighteen months, and he returned willing to cooperate with the military and even able to read and write a little.[19]

But this outcome was not foreseen by Kaahteney's grieving family at the time of his arrest. "Mother made no sound," said Kaywaykla, "but I buried myself in my blanket and tried to stifle my uncontrollable shaking and sobbing. Grandfather . . . sat beside me with head bowed and hand on my shoulder. I knew that Kaytennae was as his right hand, and that he suffered as did mother and I." Soon Kaywaykla was sent to pick up the family's share at a ration issue, and there Chatto told him that Kaahteney was "chained on a rock so far from land that no man could swim across that water." When the boy reported to Nana, he was reassured. Nana "had traveled far and seen all the rivers in the land" and there was no water so wide that Kaahteney could not swim across it. Also Nana had gone to a mountain to pray and Usen had told him that Kaahteney would return. But the fear persisted that he had been put to death, and that Geronimo, Naiche, Chihuahua, Nana, and Mangus would be the next victims. Every time one of these leaders appeared, Chatto and Mickey Free would draw their hands significantly across their throats.[20] The Apaches were, of course, aware of instances when Crook had sent his scouts to bring in the heads of incorrigible hostiles.[21]

Meanwhile, Davis was trying to start his Indians in farming. It was late in June by the time all were settled—too late for intensive planting, they told him, for snow would kill the crops before

17 Quoted by Thrapp, *Conquest of Apacheria*, pp. 308–309.
18 Secretary of War, *Annual Report*, 1885, Crook to Assistant Adjutant General, Division of the Pacific, September 9, 1885, p. 176; *Senate Exec. Doc. 88*, 51 Cong., 1 sess., p. 13.
19 Bourke, *On the Border with Crook*, pp. 472–73, 478, 480.
20 Ball, *op. cit.*, pp. 165–68, 175, 177.
21 See, for example, Thrapp, *op. cit.*, pp. 160–61.

maturity. But Kaywaykla remembered, "All cultivated little open glades and planted corn and vegetables." Crawford reported that they raised that year an estimated forty-five thousand pounds of corn, a considerable amount of barley, and "many melons, pumpkins, and other vegetables" so that he was able to reduce "certain portions of their rations." He said that the work was not "by any means" confined to the women, and he credited Geronimo and Chatto with being the best farmers in the group. Davis, however, thought that the best was not very good.[22]

In his zeal the young officer overlooked the small beginnings. "We especially liked roasting ears," Kaywaykla remembered. "Then there was another food, an oblong thing larger than a turkey egg, and covered with thin brown skin. Mother roasted it in the ashes. We liked potatoes. And how we enjoyed watermelon!" Once his mother sent him to Davis with a melon she had raised, and he received a can of tomatoes in return. His mother also collected Davis' empty cans, cut them into strips, then wrapped them around a tapered stick to make cone-shaped bells which were suspended from buckskin thongs on ceremonial garments to jingle as the wearer walked. The Apache women were still cutting up tin cans to make bells with which to trim their baskets when they were prisoners at Fort Sill.[23]

But these wild people found many problems in adapting themselves to the unfamiliar life-way. Apparently Davis had been using a brand of deviled ham with a well-known trademark. Kaywaykla brought his mother a flat container upon which was pictured "a tall thin man with hooves and a tail. The officer had been eating man meat! My people had been told that sometimes White Eyes [that is, white men] practiced cannibalism, and here was the proof. No more collecting of discarded cans! Nana made Medicine for me and I suffered no ill effects."[24]

When fall came, the Indians prepared to follow their immemorial custom of moving to a lower altitude. Except for their fear

22 Secretary of War, *Annual Report*, 1884, Crawford to Assistant Adjutant General, Whipple Barracks, pp. 135, 136; Davis, *op. cit.*, pp. 107–108, 122–23.
23 Lucy Gage, "A Romance of Pioneering," *Chronicles of Oklahoma*, Vol. XXIX, No. 3 (Autumn, 1951), p. 306.
24 Ball, *op. cit.*, pp. 157–58.

of betrayal, they had spent a good summer. They had raised crops and gathered wild food; killed deer, dried the venison, and tanned the skins for clothing and wickiup covers; and ground acorn and corn meal. They held a big dance and feast to celebrate the end of the season and then moved their camps down to the valley of the White River near Fort Apache. Davis' tent was pitched about three miles from the post, and the Indians camped in the surrounding foothills or along the streams. From his large tent nearby he issued the flour, coffee, sugar, and other groceries to them, while their meat ration was issued at the slaughterhouse at the post.[25]

While there, the survivors of Tres Castillos had a happy experience. Crook had indeed responded to Geronimo's appeal on behalf of their people held in Mexican slavery. He urged Washington to act, pointing out that all the Mexican captives held by the Indians had been returned.[26] The administration did make representations to the Mexican government, all without result. The Mexican officials refused to admit that they dealt in Apache slaves, and they even sent photographs of the captives to Crook to show that they were happy and free and could return to their people if they wished.[27]

But five of the captives of the Tres Castillos disaster managed to escape—Kaywaykla's grandmother, his cousin Siki, Huera, and two other women. They had been shipped to Mexico City, where they were purchased by the owner of an extensive hacienda in the vicinity. There they served for more than three years, the older woman caring for the children of the family, the others working in the fields, before they found a chance to slip away. Their journey of more than one thousand miles on foot, hiding out, living off the country, with one knife and one blanket their only equipment, is an Apache odyssey of courage, hardihood, and skill in woodcraft. After reaching the United States they were taken by the army and

25 *Ibid.*, pp. 175–76; Davis, *op. cit.*, pp. 130–33, 135–36.
26 Secretary of War, *Annual Report*, 1884, p. 134. For the return of two Mexican boys captured by Kaahteney and adopted into his family, see Ball, *op. cit.*, pp. 113, 158–59, 165, 167.
27 *Senate Exec. Doc. 35*, 51 Cong., 1 sess., p. 42.

restored to their rejoicing relatives. The officers at Fort Apache tried to enlist Huera as an interpreter because of her fluent knowledge of Spanish, but she refused to serve. For some reason she was hostile and never came near Davis, even sending someone to draw her rations. Possibly it was because of the ban on *tizwin*. Just as some women in other cultures are notable cooks, she was a skilled *tizwin* maker, and her product was in great demand.[28]

Also, now that they were settled near Fort Apache, suspicious members of the band found good cause to distrust the army. This distrust was explained to Opler half a century later by Sam Kenoi, who had been a small boy at the time. At the post the soldiers would point to them, asking, "Which is Geronimo? Which one is Naiche?" Then "when the officer wasn't looking," some private with rough humor would pass his hand across his throat. Late at night they would hold secret councils. "They would say to each other, 'That white soldier . . . might be a good man trying to let us know just what they are going to do to us.' . . . They would think that white soldier was a kind fellow, that he was telling them that they were going to have their heads cut off." Then they would listen, trying to find out more. One with a little understanding of English would hear a soldier say, "Those Indians ought to go to jail," or, "Those Indians ought to be killed," and he would report his findings to the others. As Kenoi said, "those Indians were wild. They didn't know any better."[29] Nodiskey, who had joined the band because his wife was a Chiricahua, was especially active in spreading these rumors. Davis believed that he was a disturbing influence but could never find any positive evidence against him. Huera also warned Geronimo that he and Mangus were to be arrested and jailed.[30]

Davis never knew of these fears and of the harassment that

28 Ball, *op. cit.*, pp. 168–84; Davis, *op. cit.*, p. 140. Because the women were brought in by a military conveyance, Davis assumed that the American government had secured their release in exchange for the returned Mexican captives.

29 Opler, "A Chiricahua Apache's Account," pp. 365–66. Kenoi stated this as a hypothetical case, but it was based on actual experience. Other informants told Opler of these attempts of the soldiers to terrorize them.

30 Davis, *op. cit.*, pp. 140–41, 202.

Huera, the wife of Mangus. "Huera told me that they were going to seize me and put me and Mangus in the guard-house, . . . and so I left." Courtesy Arizona Historical Society, Tucson.

aroused them. As soon as spring approached (the spring of 1885), he and his Indians moved from the unfriendly vicinity of the post back to Turkey Creek. It fell to Bowman to instruct them in farming. Davis was not impressed by their exertions. He thought Geronimo's efforts were typical. One day the reformed raider came to him, proudly exhibiting a small blister on his palm, and asked him to visit his "farm." Davis went there a day or two later. He found Geronimo sitting in the shade with one of his wives fanning him while the other two were hoeing a patch of sickly corn.[31] But Geronimo may have been ill on that occasion. He and Betzinez did plant a field of barley that spring. The patterns might vary, but whether in raiding, ranching, or farming, Geronimo's economic drive was a constant. In a different culture he would have been a captain of industry.

Whether or not their farming accomplishments were satisfactory, the former hostiles were loyally observing the peace they had made with Crook two years before in the Sierra Madre. There had not been one act of Apache violence in all the Southwest—not one horse stolen, not one man killed. Crook could truthfully say in his 1884 report that "for the first time in the history of that fierce people, every member of the Apache tribe is at peace." But with the apparent end of hostilities the civilian administration began to assert its authority, and the old feud broke out between the War and Interior departments.

The army had been in control of the Indians on the reservation ever since Crook's arrival in Arizona in 1882. Now at San Carlos Crawford and the Indian agent issued conflicting orders regarding farming practices, the arrest and punishment of offenders, and the purchase of cattle. Crook asked to be relieved of his responsibility unless he could have undivided control. His request was not granted, but Crawford, in disgust, asked and received permission to rejoin his regiment, and Crook appointed Captain Francis E. Pierce to succeed him. None of this conflict extended to Turkey Creek, but the band knew of the departure of Crawford, and this

[31] *Ibid.*, pp. 136–37.

made them uneasy; they were constantly asking Davis whether Nantan Lupan had gone also. Geronimo, in particular, needed continual reassurance. Also they probably knew of the breakdown of authority at San Carlos, and this may have made them bolder in asserting their own independence. That, at least was Davis' interpretation, although it does not appear in subsequent Indian analyses of the situation.[32]

Whatever the cause, wife beating and *tizwin* drinking reappeared that spring among Davis' charges. A young woman came to him with an arm broken in two places, her hair matted with blood, and her shoulders a mass of welts and bruises. The post surgeon patched her up, and Davis arrested her husband and gave him a sentence of two weeks in the jail at Fort Apache. Several of the leaders came and demanded his release, but Davis refused. Next, he arrested and jailed an Indian responsible for a *tizwin* drink. That afternoon Chihuahua and Mangus came to his tent to protest. He was not surprised at the attitude of Chihuahua, who was a constant protestor against the regulations, but he was puzzled at the attitude of Mangus. That night one of his "secret scouts" told him about Huera and the reason for Mangus' concern. Whether she had been his wife before her capture, or whether he had married her after her return, he was now upholding her interest.[33]

The leaders held a council and decided on concerted action. They prepared themselves by an all-night *tizwin* drink. Then before sunrise on the following morning, Friday, May 15, they assembled with about thirty of their followers before Davis' tent. Many of them were armed, and no woman or child was in sight. The scouts were standing around in groups, all under arms. When Davis came out, the leaders said they had come for a talk. All of them but Chatto, who remained with the scouts, then entered the

32 For the entire history of the conflict between the civil and military administration, see Ogle, *Federal Control of the Western Apaches*, pp. 221–31. For the army account, see Bourke, *op. cit.*, pp. 457, 460–63; Davis, *op. cit.*, pp. 34, 138–39, 146–47; and Secretary of War, *Annual Report*, 1885, pp. 170–75, 179–85. For Betzinez's interpretation, see *I Fought with Geronimo*, p. 129.

33 Davis, *op. cit.*, pp. 139–41, 202.

tent and squatted in a half-circle in front of the young officer. Loco began quietly to present their case. Chihuahua, who was plainly intoxicated, sprang to his feet and interrupted him. He repeated the old arguments. They had agreed on peace, but "nothing had been said about their conduct among themselves; they were not children to be taught how to live with their women and what they should eat or drink. . . . They had complied with all they had promised to do when they had their talk with the General in Mexico; had kept the peace and harmed no one. Now they were being punished for things they had a right to do so long as they did no harm to others."

Davis tried to explain the reasons for the regulations. When he got to wife beating, Nana got up, made an angry remark to Mickey Free, and limped out of the tent. Mickey tried to avoid interpreting, but Davis insisted. These were his words: "Tell the *Nantan Enchau*[34] that he can't advise me how to treat women. He is only a boy. I killed *men* before he was born."

Chihuahua went on: "We all drank tizwin last night, all of us in the tent and outside, except the scouts; and many more. What are you going to do about it? Are you going to put us all in jail? You have no jail big enough even if you could put us all in jail."

Davis answered that this was too serious for him to decide. He would wire the general and let them know the answer. Benito and Gil-lee started to say something, but Chihuahua cut them off. The council was over. Neither Geronimo nor any of the others had spoken, and only Chihuahua showed the effects of the previous night's drinking.

Davis worded his telegram to show that it was intended for Crook, but following army practice he sent it to his immediate superior, Captain Pierce, at San Carlos. Pierce had come to his command of the reservation with no knowledge of Apaches, and he was accustomed to ask advice from the experienced Al Sieber. But Al had proved the Apaches' point by spending that same night

[34] Stout Chief. Davis was stockily built, in contrast to the lanky Gatewood and Crawford.

gambling and drinking the much more potent white man's *tizwin* and was sleeping it off. Perhaps the sequel proved Crook's point of its harmful effects. When Pierce woke him up and showed him the telegram, he said, "It's nothing but a tizwin drunk. Don't pay any attention to it. Davis will handle it," and he went back to sleep. Pierce returned to his office and pigeonholed the telegram.

The rest of Friday passed with no answer. Saturday came and went; so did most of Sunday. Davis saw the Apache leaders every day, but he had nothing to tell them. Rumors spread through the camp. The leaders would be hanged or have their heads cut off. Probably that had been done to Kaahteney. The whole band would be arrested and taken away somewhere. Davis kept in touch with the scouts. And he waited. It never occurred to him that his message had not reached Crook; he supposed the general was making preparations to deal with the situation and would communicate his orders when he was ready. He and Crook always believed that if that message had gone through, the affair would have been settled as a minor incident. Its neglect was to have tragic consequences to the army, to civilians of the Southwest, and, most of all, to the Apaches.

On Sunday, May 17, Davis was at Fort Apache waiting for a reply to his telegram. At about four o'clock in the afternoon Chatto and Mickey Free came to him with the alarming news that a number of the Indians had broken out from the reservation and were on their way to Mexico. He attempted at once to telegraph Pierce, but the line was dead. The Indians had cut the wire in several places where it passed through the forks of trees and had fastened the severed ends with buckskin thongs. This was Nana's idea, said Kaywaykla; formerly they had torn out a section of wire, and the break was easily found and repaired. This time the damaged places were not located until the following day.

The commander of the troops at the post immediately prepared to take the field while Davis hastened to his camp to summon his scouts to accompany them. He formed the company in front of his tent and prepared to issue ammunition, but fearing that some might be disloyal he ordered them to ground arms (rifle butts on the ground) while Chatto and two others stood ready to shoot any man who raised his gun. Perico, Chappo, and one other then slipped out of ranks and melted into the brush. Afterwards, he was told that they had planned to kill him and Chatto, and he believed that his order to ground arms had prevented it. Later Crook accused Geronimo of planning the killings. Geronimo denied that accusation and appealed to White Mountain witnesses, never his friends, to support his denial. Crook ignored his defense; to him, Geronimo was a liar, and that settled it. But according to Kaywaykla, the three disaffected scouts had remained behind to divert suspicion, intending to overtake the others as soon as the breakout should become known. This seems the more logical explanation. It was to the interest of the runaways to escape unnoticed and put as much distance as possible between themselves and the soldiers. They would hardly have risked a probable fight with the scouts, loyal as those scouts were to Davis. These three defections were the only ones during the campaign that followed.

It was dark by the time the cavalry arrived and set out with Davis and his scouts to pursue the fleeing hostiles. They marched all night, and the next morning they came out on the crest of a ridge. Across a wide valley they saw the dust raised by the Indians' ponies ascending another ridge fifteen or twenty miles away. Davis, with Chatto and ten other scouts, then turned back. At Fort Apache he reported to Crook on the now functioning telegraph and went to his camp to assess the extent of the breakout. He called up all the Indians and counted them. Thirty-five men, eight boys old enough to bear arms, and 101 women and children were missing. Among the men were the leaders, Geronimo, Chihuahua, Naiche, Mangus, and Nana. Among the boys were Geronimo's nephew, Kanseah,[35] and Mangus' protégés, Istee and Daklugie. Three-fourths of the band remained, under Loco, Benito, Gil-lee, and (of course) Chatto.[36]

[35] The presence of Kanseah in the party is shown by subsequent events.
[36] Davis, *op. cit.*, pp. 144–52, 206–207; Secretary of War, *Annual Report*, 1886, pp. 147–48; Ball, *op. cit.*, pp. 175–77.

By this time the ominous message, "The Apaches are out," was burning up the wires and screaming in newspaper headlines throughout the Southwest. Exposed settlers, travelers, and prospectors grouped or fled for safety, often too late. Army units— twenty troops of cavalry and probably two hundred Indian scouts —crisscrossed the mountains, guarded the border and the water holes, and wore themselves out in futile pursuit, while the hostiles, killing as they went, helped themselves to horses and goods, once capturing three wagonloads of army supplies and ammunition.[37]

On the reservation Benito and Chatto were very bitter against the hostiles,[38] and in the ensuing campaign most of the men served as scouts.[39] But some who remained had close ties to the runaways. Nana had decreed that his sister, the "Grandmother" of Kaywaykla's narrative, and her daughter, Kaywaykla's mother, should stay, although his wife, Geronimo's sister, accompanied him. Siki had married Toclanny, a dependable scout who had never been a hostile, and remained with her husband.[40] Betzinez was torn between his peaceable inclinations and his duty to Geronimo. Returning home that Sunday evening from planting barley in the field he and Geronimo were farming together, he was told of the outbreak. With his mother and sister he started out to catch up with the fleeing hostiles. Then, "As I hurried along . . . through the dark moonless night, my thoughts were very troubled. I came to the conclusion that it would be foolish to throw away what I was just beginning to learn of a better way of life." He told his mother and sister of his decision, and they all managed to return to the reservation without being discovered. He shed some tears when he arrived and saw that not one of his young cousins or friends had remained. It did not help his feelings to find that "some greedy Indians" had appropriated all the horses Geronimo's party had left behind. Chatto even claimed the barley field, but Davis supported Betzinez' ownership.[41]

37 Thrapp, *Conquest of Apacheria*, pp. 315–26.
38 *Ibid.*, p. 315.
39 Davis, *op. cit.*, p. 151.
40 Ball, *op. cit.*, p. 177; Griswold, "The Fort Sill Apaches," s.v. "Toclanny, Roger."
41 Betzinez, *op. cit.*, pp. 129–30.

Benito. Although he was largely responsible for the breakaway in 1881, he settled down peaceably after surrendering to General Crook in the Sierra Madre. Photograph taken by A. Frank Randall at San Carlos in the spring of 1884. Courtesy U.S. Signal Corps, National Archives.

Looking back, Davis tried to analyze the causes of the breakout. He attributed it to the dissatisfaction of three factions, totaling no more than twelve or fifteen men, led by Geronimo, Chihuahua, and Mangus. The two last, he thought, had not expected the trouble to go so far. They opposed the wife-beating and *tizwin* prohibitions, the first on general principles, the second on personal grounds—Huera's right to make it and Chihuahua's right to drink it—but they did not plan a breakout. Davis believed it was Geronimo who planned it and took advantage of their dissatisfaction. He had not been active in the wife-*tizwin* controversy. His motivation must have been pure depravity; he was "a thoroughly vicious, intractable, and treacherous man. His only redeeming traits were courage and determination."[42]

Apparently Davis was right in charging Geronimo as the moving spirit in the breakout, but he never understood the wild leader's reasons. Geronimo himself later made a clear and logical explanation to Crook, but to army officers and civilians alike this only indicated his mendacity.[43] Their exasperation is understandable. This was his fourth breakaway, to say nothing of his kidnaping of Loco, and there would be one more before his final capitulation. But every time he had cause—as he saw it.

It is certain that he had come in the year before with every intention of settling down. His loss of the cattle had been a disappointment, but he had observed the peace. He tried to trust Crook, and yet there might be truth in the taunts of soldiers and scouts and the warnings of his associates. And how could he be sure that Crook would not be replaced as Crawford had been? Somehow he learned that the newspapers were clamoring for his death. He knew how close he had come to that death when Clum was in charge. And there was the uncertainty over what had been done to Kaahteney. In the spring he had started to plant his barley, hoping to harvest it. Now, in the crisis, with some unknown punish-

42 Davis, *op. cit.*, pp. 142–43.
43 *Ibid.*, pp. 200–207.

240

ment about to descend, he consulted his Power. Naturally, in his suspicious state of mind it confirmed his worst fears.[44]

Later, the Apaches that remained on the reservation told Davis and Crook that Geronimo and Mangus induced Chihuahua and Naiche to break out by telling them that they had killed Davis and Chatto and that troops were coming to arrest the whole band and send them away. As soon as these leaders discovered the deception, they threatened to kill Geronimo and Mangus, and the runaways broke up. Mangus and his few followers left for Mexico and never rejoined the others. Naiche collected his family and tried to return, but they ran into some of Davis' scouts and joined Chihuahua. Chihuahua's people then hid out in the mountains north of the Gila, intending to slip back, while Geronimo went on to Mexico. Then, ten days later, Davis and his scouts came to the place where the trail forked and followed Chihuahua's. They came up with the band, and some shots were exchanged. Chihuahua was now committed.[45]

A hide-and-seek pursuit by the soldiers ensued through the mountains of southeastern Arizona and southwestern New Mexico, with the hostiles breaking up into small parties and dashing out to kill and rob. The soldiers seldom glimpsed them, but the bodies of at least seventeen civilians and about 150 horses and mules worn out and killed or abandoned marked their passing. By June 10 most of them had crossed the international border. Lieutenant Davis, following one party, found two newly born, dead babies on the trail. They had traveled ninety miles on stolen horses without a pause until they camped in Mexico.[46]

It is impossible now to determine the truth of the story Davis heard of conflict among the leaders. There is no mention of it in any of their subsequent recorded statements. It is apparent that after they reached Mexico they operated for a time as separate

44 Opler, "A Chiricahua Apache's Account," p. 367 and n. 8. Sam Kenoi did not state that the warning from Geronimo's Power occurred at this exact time, but certainly it did.

45 Davis, *op. cit.*, pp. 152, 205, 209; Thrapp, *Conquest of Apacheria*, pp. 316–18, citing an article Davis published in the *Army-Navy Journal*, October 24, 1885.

46 Davis, *op. cit.*, p. 153; Thrapp, *Conquest of Apacheria*, pp. 318–26.

bands under Chihuahua, Geronimo, Naiche, and Mangus; but except for Mangus and his party they soon united with no evidence of bad feeling.[47]

Once in Mexico, their raids there went unrecorded, but there could be no peace on the American side of the border as long as they remained at large. This meant that their sanctuary had to be invaded.

47 Ball, *op. cit.*, p. 181.

CHAPTER 13

HISTORY REPEATS ITSELF
FOR GERONIMO

On June 11 a force under Captain Crawford followed the hostiles into the Sierra Madre. Another command, under Captain Wirt Davis, entered Mexico on July 13. At the same time Crook stationed troops at strategic points on the American side of the boundary in an attempt to seal it off or to pursue any bands that might slip across. To the army the campaign meant hardships that approached the limit of human endurance against an enemy that melted away unseen.[1] To the Indians it was the old story of "run, ride, fight, hide, then ride and fight again."[2] In the 1930's Opler attempted to explore Apache dreams to determine their religious revelations. One informant told him that his dreams had no such meaning, but ran "on the order of war" when the scouts were on the trail of his band. "I dream they are making a raid on my people and I am trying to get away from them."[3] After more than forty years it was still his nightmare.

1 Crook's summary is given in Secretary of War, *Annual Report*, 1886, pp. 147–51; Thrapp's carefully researched account is in *Conquest of Apacheria*, pp. 326–32.
2 Eve Ball, "On the Warpath with Geronimo," *The West*, Vol. XV, No. 3 (August, 1971), p. 62. Mrs. Ball's informant was describing another campaign, but the experience is typical.
3 Opler, *An Apache Life-Way*, p. 191.

Confused reports of the campaign came back to Crook of encounters in the mountains of Mexico—inflated accounts of Apache losses by young officers eager for promotion or uncertain about what actually happened among the rocks and canyons. On June 23 Crawford's scouts under Chatto discovered Chihuahua's camp in the Bavispe Mountains northeast of Oputo. They failed to surround it, and most of the band escaped, but they killed one woman, captured fifteen women and children, and brought back a number of horses and much plunder. Among the captives were a son and a daughter of Chihuahua later known as Eugene and Ramona.[4] On July 29 Captain Davis' scouts ambushed four hostile warriors in the Haya Mountains and killed two. On August 7 a picked detail of seventy-eight of his scouts under an army officer struck Geronimo's camp in the mountains a little northeast of Nacori. They "killed" Nana, three other warriors (one the son of Geronimo), and one woman; "wounded" Geronimo and trailed him some distance by the blood; captured fifteen women and children, among them "three wives and five children of Geronimo's family" and Huera, the wife of Mangus; and overran the camp, acquiring thirteen horses and mules besides saddles, blankets, dried meat, and other articles. Only two warriors and one woman escaped.[5]

The "dead" Nana and Chappo and the "wounded" Geronimo went on their way unharmed. The other "deceased" warriors seem to have survived also. In Crook's final report the casualties had shrunk to "1 squaw and 2 boys."[6] According to Geronimo, "One boy was killed and nearly all of our women and children were captured."[7]

The captives, indeed, were real and may even have been counted

---

[4] Lieutenant Britton Davis, who was serving with Crawford, gives the details of this encounter in *The Truth about Geronimo*, pp. 166–69. The Apache account, as remembered by Eugene and Ramona Chihuahua, is told in Ball, *In the Days of Victorio*, p. 178.

[5] National Archives and Records Service, Consolidated File 1066 AGO 1883 [referred to hereafter as Consolidated File], Crook to AAG Division of the Pacific, August 17, 1885.

[6] Secretary of War, *Annual Report*, 1886, p. 150.

[7] Barrett, *Geronimo's Story of His Life*, p. 136.

correctly. Geronimo lost his entire family except for his warrior son. It is known that his wives Zi-yeh and She-gha were captured. If a third wife was captured, Shtsha-she must still have been living. If so, she soon dropped out of sight, for she does not appear in any later accounts of his family. As for the five children, there was Zi-yeh's infant son, afterwards known as Fenton[8]; a three-year-old girl whose exact identity is not established (was she the baby carried on Betzinez' mule during the Sonora raid in 1882?); and a two-year-old son who died shortly thereafter in captivity at Fort Bowie, and whose grave marker in the post cemetery carried the un-Apache name, "Little Robe."[9] Nothing is known of the two other children reported. Dohn-say may have been counted or even her children (at some unreported date she married a young warrior named Dahkeya). Also among the captives was Hah-dun-key, the wife of Geronimo's "brother" Perico, and their children.

Geronimo had indeed suffered a grievous loss, as had the entire hostile band. In the two encounters they had lost fully one-third of their women and children. (Revised figures of the breakout after some stragglers slipped back indicated that ninety-two women and children were absent from the reservation.) Apaches were devoted to their families. Also, in their well-structured division of labor a man without a wife to prepare food and clothing was as seriously handicapped economically as was a woman without a male provider. Stories of lone outlaws hiding in the mountains who slipped back to steal wives appear frequently in Apache history. The women accepted the situation, and there are cases of stable marriages formed in this way.

Thus, through economic necessity as well as sentiment Geronimo and four of his followers set out to bring back their families, or—if necessary—to steal wives. They slipped through the cordon of troops guarding the international border and worked their way through the mountains to the reservation. Their people who had not joined in the breakout had been moved to the vicinity of Fort

[8] Fenton Geronimo's tombstone at Fort Sill gives 1882 as his birth date but he was born later. See his photograph made no earlier than 1895, *infra*, p. 376.

[9] Charles Fletcher Lummis, *Dateline Fort Bowie*, pp. 83, 87–88.

245

Apache and were closely guarded for their own protection. The captives had not been confined at the post, but had been permitted to live with them. The White Mountain Apaches were patroling the country, but the five coming on foot singly from the east managed to evade them. They picked up some White Mountain horses, and, finding a White Mountain woman alone, compelled her to take them to the camp of Geronimo's family, reaching it at one o'clock on the morning of September 22. They managed to recover his wife She-gha and his three-year-old daughter and to steal another woman. Scouting parties were sent out immediately in pursuit, but the raiders separated and faded into the mountains to the east.[10]

Perico, unsuccessful in recovering Hah-dun-key, took the stolen woman as his wife. Her name was Bi-ya-neta Tse-dah-dilth-thlilth. (Bi-ya-neta should be sufficient for identification hereafter.) The two were to live harmoniously together in the mountains of Mexico, through the succeeding years as prisoners of war, and after their final release. Three of their five children are buried at Fort Sill; descendants of the other two are probably still living.[11]

On their way back from the raid on the reservation, Geronimo and his party captured some Mescalero women as wives. The Mescalero Charlie Smith, who died at a great age in 1973, has told the story. Although he was a young child at the time, he remembered how a party of his people were permitted to leave their reservation to gather piñon nuts and hunt piñon-fattened deer in the mountains of southwestern New Mexico. While the men hunted, the women divided into small groups gathering the nuts. With Charlie and his mother, Cumpah (afterwards known as Sarah), were a woman with a baby and an unmarried girl who later received the name Ih-tedda (Young Girl). Suddenly horsemen swooped down upon them. Charlie started to run for the

---

10 Rutherford B. Hayes Library, George Crook Letterbook I (No. 234, L.S. 2320), pp. 227–28, copies furnished me by Dan L. Thrapp. The raid is mentioned in *Senate Exec. Doc. 35*, 51 Cong., 1 sess., p. 50.

11 Griswold, "The Fort Sill Apaches," s.v. "Tse-dah-dilth-thlilth, Bi-ya-neta." It seems fairly certain that Bi-ya-neta was the woman stolen at this time.

brush, and a bullet struck him in the calf of the leg. (He carried the scar throughout his life.) The two women (one carrying her baby), the girl, and the small boy were scooped up, and each one was placed on a horse behind a captor and taken to Geronimo's camp.[12]

Geronimo took Ih-tedda, and the two older women became wives of other members of the band. The boy lost track of the woman with the baby. He could never be brought to reveal the name of the one who took his mother. This man was kind to his captured wife and seriously undertook the training of his stepson in the skills of a warrior. "I really liked my step-father, and was proud when I learned that he was considered one of the bravest of the Apaches. . . . I could not understand why in his absence my mother cried. And she did not explain."

He was not so appreciative when Geronimo undertook the training of the boys that winter in the Sierra Madre, especially when he was forced to plunge repeatedly into icy streams. Later, as an adult, he was to develop a great admiration for Geronimo for holding out after most of the Apaches accepted peace and reservation life, but in his childhood, "There were times when I just hated him."[13] After the band became prisoners of war, Cumpah and her son were reunited with the boy's own father.[14]

Meanwhile, Geronimo's raid on the American side of the line was closely followed by others during that same fall of 1885. On September 28 a band of about twenty hostiles crossed into southeastern Arizona. They were so closely pursued by the troops through the Chiricahua and Dragoon mountains that they killed "only" three men. They then captured the horse herd of the cattlemen of the area who were gathered for their fall roundup, and, superbly mounted on these crack cow ponies, they escaped into Mexico. Early in November came the most spectacular raid of all.

---

[12] This must have occurred *after* the raid near Fort Apache, for the men had horses, and Charlie Smith remembered that Geronimo had a wife with him.

[13] Ball, "On the Warpath with Geronimo"; Eve Ball to Angie Debo, May 31, 1973. Charlie Smith's account of these experiences is apparently based on vivid childhood impressions. In tribal and family history I have found his memory unreliable.

[14] Consolidated File, report of Major William Sinclair, August 25, 1887.

247

It was led by Jolsanny (Josanie), often known as Ulzana, a brother of Chihuahua.

With ten warriors he entered New Mexico, and they made for the mountains, killing as they went, while troops swarmed over the area without sighting them. On November 23 they appeared near Fort Apache and struck the Indians who had remained on the reservation, objects of their hatred because the men had joined the army as scouts. There, by the best count obtainable, they killed five men and boys, eleven women, and four children and captured six women and a child. The next day they killed two herders in charge of the reservation beef cattle and made away with Benito's horses. A party from the post, with Chatto and eighteen scouts, pursued them, but they slipped away. A reservation Indian came back with the head of one raider, but that was their only known casualty.

Troops were alerted all over the Southwest, and Lieutenant General Philip H. Sheridan, who had succeeded Sherman as commander in chief of the army, even came out from Washington to confer with Crook at Fort Bowie. They decided to make a stronger effort to break up the hostile base in Mexico, and the commands of Captains Davis and Crawford were accordingly reorganized and reoutfitted for the invasion. Meanwhile, on the American side of the border Jolsanny and his nine warriors continued to evade the armed forces. At the end of December, mounted on excellent horses, they escaped into Mexico. As Crook summarized their raid, they had "traveled probably not less than one thousand two hundred miles, killed thirty-eight people, [and] captured and wore out probably two hundred and fifty head of stock."[15]

Meanwhile, Crawford crossed the line with his pack train and his scouts on November 29. Entering the Sierra Madre and laboring through its jumble of towering peaks and yawning gorges, they reached the Aros (or Haros) River about sixty miles south of Nacori. This was apparently the area of Juh's legendary stronghold, never before breached by a hostile force. There they found trails, campsites, and other evidences of Apache occupation. On

15 Thrapp, *Conquest of Apacheria*, pp. 332–39; Secretary of War, *Annual Report*, 1886, pp. 150–51.

the evening of January 9 the scouts reported that they had found the hostile *rancheria* ten or twelve miles away on a rugged eminence well calculated for defense. It was decided to make a night march and surround it. "It was a dark and moonless night," as Lieutenant Marion P. Maus, who was second in command, reported it. They followed a trail "over solid rock, over mountains, down cañons so dark they seemed bottomless."

Just before dawn they saw the dim outlines of the hostiles' position and were stealthily moving to encircle it when some burros in the camp started braying and its defenders sprang to arms. Shots were exchanged without damage to either side, and the occupants slipped out, sped down the mountainsides, and melted into the rocks below. The invaders took possession of the camp, acquiring the entire horse herd and stores of provisions. Later they had reason to appreciate its strong defensive position.

Soon a woman came in to report that Geronimo and Naiche wanted a conference. It would be interesting to know her identity, for some of the women were very influential in the band. Confused Apache tradition indicates that she may have been Tah-das-te (Dahteste), a sister of one of Chihuahua's wives, or Lozen, a sister of Victorio who never married and became famous in the band as a warrior and possessor of Power.[16] Crawford agreed to meet them the following day (January 11) on the river below the camp. The whole band was there except Mangus' small party, and it is apparent that Geronimo, with his usual deference to Naiche, was the leader. He afterwards said that the appearance of Crawford's force convinced him that no refuge was safe from invasion.

Even the scouts in Crawford's command were exhausted from the night march and the difficult days that had preceded it. When night came, they threw themselves among the rocks in the captured camp to sleep. Then, in the early dawn of a cold, foggy morning, some of them called out an alarm. At once a volley of rifle fire struck the camp. One of the scouts, still sleeping, was seriously wounded, two others slightly. They started to return the fire, but

16 Ball, *In the Days of Victorio*, pp. 151, 182.

Crawford checked them. It was now seen that the attackers were Mexican irregulars, volunteers serving without pay except the plunder they might collect. Apparently they had at first mistaken Crawford's command for the hostile camp, but when Maus and the interpreter, Tom Horn, called out to them in Spanish, and Crawford sprang on a rock waving his handkerchief, they deliberately shot Horn, wounding him slightly, and fatally wounded Crawford. They could not have mistaken these men for hostile Apaches. When Crawford fell, the enraged scouts returned the fire, killing all the Mexican officers and wounding five of the men.

The Apache band by this time had assembled on the height on the other side of the river, from which they had a good view of the encounter. "Geronimo watched it and laughed," said old Sam Haozous with an emphasis impossible to convey in print.[17] The Mexicans apparently found the American force too strong for them to overrun, but they remained in the vicinity, showing their hostility. Maus, now in command, decided to withdraw. He was short of ammunition and supplies and was separated from his pack train, which he feared the Mexicans might capture. He also saw no opportunity for his conference with the Apache hostiles while the Mexicans were near; a woman, in fact, came from the band that afternoon saying they feared to come in. Accordingly, on the following day he started back. In camp that night a woman again came to him from Geronimo requesting a conference.

The meeting was held on the second day after, on January 15. No doubt, although he did not say so, the officer was accompanied by Concepcion, a sergeant of the scout company, a Mexican captured in his boyhood and adopted by the Apaches, who served as interpreter. The hostile leaders had stipulated that Maus come unarmed. (There were too many instances of Indians coming to a meeting with army officers only to be seized and killed.) He found Geronimo, Naiche, Nana, and Chihuahua with fourteen men assembled for the conference. They sat in a circle nearly surrounding Maus, with Geronimo in the center. Every one had his rifle

17 Interview, January 27, 1955.

250

upright, and every belt was full of ammunition. Maus considered this a breach of faith and was understandably apprehensive. He did not know that never once in his turbulent career did Geronimo violate his wild code of honor. There was silence for fully a minute. Then, looking the officer straight in the eye, Geronimo asked, "Why did you come down here?"

"I came to capture or destroy you and your band," said Maus.

The direct answer seemed to please Geronimo. He rose, walked over to Maus, and shook his hand, saying he could trust him to report accurately to Crook. He then told the story of his grievances —"all of which were purely imaginary or assumed," Maus reported. (They were "imaginary," but not "assumed." No white man ever believed that Geronimo was sincerely convinced of an official plot against his life.) But the band was ready to discuss terms. Their relatives captured the previous summer were still in army possession, and now their fastness had been invaded. Geronimo, as spokesman, designated nine members of the band he would send back with Maus, and he promised to meet Crook near the border in "two moons to talk about surrendering. With this understanding," Maus reported, "I returned to camp."

Geronimo soon sent in the nine "prisoners," as Maus now designated them. He listed them as follows: "Nana and one buck . . . the wife and child of both Geronimo and Natchez [Naiche], and one boy, also the sister of Geronimo and one other woman."[18] Geronimo's sister was, of course, the wife of Nana, who accompanied her husband. The wife he surrendered was the young Ih-tedda.[19] He retained his older wife, She-gha. His child was the unidentified

18 This list was furnished me by Dan L. Thrapp, who found it in the Rutherford B. Hayes Library, Crook's Annual Report, 1886, Appendices I and K. Men and women were usually listed as "bucks" and "squaws" in army records.

19 This is contrary to the statements made by the Apaches, but I began to question the accuracy of their memory when I learned that the wife with Geronimo at the time of his final surrender was estimated to be thirty-five years old. This could hardly have been the "Young Girl" he had kidnaped. Then, considering that Ih-tedda was pregnant at the time of the meeting with Maus, I doubted that in view of Apache sex prohibitions he would have chosen her to remain with him. The final proof came in the birth of Ih-tedda's baby in a Florida prison at the very time Geronimo and the wife he had retained were held in captivity at San Antonio, Texas.

251

little girl. Was she the captive Zi-yeh's daughter who had somehow become separated from her mother and would now be returned to her? It seems more probable that she was the child of Shtsha-she and that Shtsha-she had indeed been captured with the rest of Geronimo's family and had since died. The wife Naiche surrendered was his oldest wife, Nah-de-yole, and the child was probably her son afterwards known as Paul. His other wives, E-clah-heh and Ha-o-zinne, remained with him.[20] (More will be heard of them hereafter.) The identity of the "one buck," "one boy," and "one other woman" is not known. It is fairly certain that they formed one family.

Although the word was not used, these "prisoners" were, in effect, hostages—given as a pledge of the promised meeting. One would like to know the reasons behind the selection. Perhaps there was a wish to protect them from the precarious existence of the hunted band. Nana was old and crippled. Ih-tedda was pregnant, and the Apaches, whenever it was possible, were careful of their pregnant women.[21] The health of Geronimo's little girl at that time is not known, but soon the army surgeon was to report her condition as "very feeble." In any case, their separation from the band was to last only "two moons."[22] Maus returned without further incident, and his "prisoners" were placed under guard at Fort Bowie. At some undetermined time the earlier captives were also brought there.[23] Now there would be no rescue.

On February 5 Maus was sent back across the border to await the arrival of the main band. He established his camp in northern Sonora about ten miles south of the Arizona line. The hostiles met their schedule; on March 15 they signaled their approach, and by March 19 all had arrived. Maus could not induce them to cross

20 For Naiche's family, see Griswold, *op. cit.*, s.v. "Naiche (Christian)," and "Naiche, Paul."

21 Opler, *op. cit.*, pp. 5–6.

22 For Maus's report of the expedition, see Secretary of War, *Annual Report*, 1886, pp. 155–64. Another account by Maus is in Nelson A. Miles, *Personal Recollections*, pp. 450–67.

23 Ball, *In the Days of Victorio*, p. 179 and note 5; Bourke, *On the Border with Crook*, p. 472.

The hostiles' camp at Cañon de los Embudos "in a lava bed, on top of a small conical hill surrounded by deep ravines." Note the sentinel with a gun. This and the following three photographs were taken by C. S. Fly, March 25–27, 1886. Courtesy U.S. Army Artillery and Missile Center Museum.

the border. They chose a strong position in the Cañon de los Embudos, and Maus established his camp one-half mile away. He had reported their presence to Crook as soon as he received their first message; now Geronimo came to his camp almost daily to ask when the general would arrive. It is apparent that the wild leader had staked everything on this meeting.

Crook set out from Fort Bowie, eighty-four miles away. Preceding him was his inevitable pack train. To soften up the hostiles, he brought along the reformed Kaahteney, now released from Alcatraz, the dependable scout Alchise, and "a couple of old Chiricahua squaws. . . . with all the latest gossip from the women prisoners at Bowie." Probably one of these women was Nah-dos-te, for provision was made for Nana to take his place among the leaders at the conference. There was a good complement of interpreters, and

253

Eighteen Apaches lined up by Fly for a photograph. Naiche is in the front row, center; Fun is in the second row, standing second from left; Yahnozha is mounted at the back, far right. Warriors of Geronimo's band often drew a line of paint across their faces to distinguish them. *All were in superb physical condition, and well dressed, well armed, and well mounted.* Courtesy Smithsonian Institution, National Anthropological Archives.

Bourke served as the general's aide. There were several other officers and civilians in the party. C. S. Fly, a Tombstone photographer, received permission to join them—a fortunate circumstance, for his photographs constitute an important record. Later, at the meeting place, Bourke, was to note the offhand manner in which Fly requested the hostiles—"as fierce as so many tigers," according to Crook's report—to change positions or turn their faces to improve his portrayal. On the way down Kaahteney demonstrated the marksmanship that had distinguished him among Victorio's warriors. The scouts took off after a drove of peccaries, and he shot one through the head while his horse was going at full speed.

The party settled at Maus's camp, "a strong position on a low mesa." The *rancheria* of the hostiles "was in a lava bed, on top of a

Geronimo with three of his warriors. From the left: Yahnozha, Chappo, and Fun. Soon all four were to break back into the mountains. Courtesy U.S. Artillery and Missile Center Museum.

small conical hill surrounded by deep ravines." Between the two camps were "two or three steep and rugged gulches which served as scarps and counter-scarps." Geronimo and other leaders came into Crook's camp, but only half a dozen at a time, while "the others were here, there, and everywhere, but all on the *qui vive*, apprehensive of treachery and ready to meet it." All were in superb physical condition and were well dressed, well armed, and well mounted—an indication that they had employed their "two moons" to good advantage since Maus had despoiled their camp.

The conference was held on the afternoon of March 25 under some large cottonwood and sycamore trees. Geronimo, Naiche, Chihuahua, and an otherwise unidentified leader named Kutli (Catle or Cayetano) participated, while twenty-four armed warriors listened in the background ready to fire if any attempt should be made to seize them. Geronimo was the spokesman. He pre-

The confrontation. Geronimo is near the left of the picture facing the camera; Crook is second from the right, facing Geronimo, with his gloved hand resting on his knee. Nana can be recognized at the right of Geronimo. Lieutenant Maus with a mustache and wearing a slouch hat is in the angle. Note the vigilant Apaches in the background. "The sun, the darkness, the winds are all listening to what we now say." Courtesy University of Oklahoma Library, Western History Collections, Norman.

sented his case with deadly seriousness; great beads of sweat rolled down his temples and over his hands, and he clutched nervously at a buckskin thong he held. Crook, always honorable in dealing with Indians, had Bourke record every word. Thus, one can follow Geronimo's logic and understand his motivation. First he chose his interpreter. (No more Mickey Frees!) Then he began:

꧁꧂꧁꧂꧁꧂꧁꧂꧁꧂꧁꧂꧁꧂

I want to talk first of the causes which led me to leave the reservation. I was living quietly and contented, doing and thinking of no harm, while at the Sierra Blanca [White Mountains]. I don't know what harm I did to those three men, Chatto, Mickey Free,

256

and Lieutenant Davis. I was living peaceably and satisfied when people began to speak bad of me. I should be glad to know who started those stories. I was living peaceably with my family, having plenty to eat, sleeping well, taking care of my people, and perfectly contented. . . . I hadn't killed a horse or man, American or Indian. I don't know what was the matter with the people in charge of us. They knew this to be so, and yet they said I was a bad man and the worst man there . . . I did not leave of my own accord. . . . Some time before I left an Indian named Wadiskay [Nodiskey] had a talk with me. He said, "they are going to arrest you," but I paid no attention to him, knowing that I had done no wrong; and the wife of Magnus, "Huera," told me that they were going to seize me and put me and Magnus in the guard-house, and I learned from the American and Apache soldiers [scouts], from Chatto, and Mickey Free, that the Americans were going to arrest me and hang me, and so I left. . . . I want to know now who it was ordered me to be arrested. I was praying to the light and to the darkness, to God and to the sun, to let me live quietly there with my family. . . .

I have several times asked for peace, but trouble has come from the agents and interpreters. I don't want what has passed to happen again. . . . The Earth-Mother is listening to me and I hope that all may be so arranged that from now on there shall be no trouble and that we shall always have peace. Whenever we see you coming to where we are, we think that it is God—you must come always with God. . . . Whenever I have broken out, it has always been on account of bad talk. . . . Very often there are stories put in the newspapers that I am to be hanged. I don't want that any more. When a man tries to do right, such stories ought not to be put in the newspapers. There are very few of my men left now. They have done some bad things but I want them all rubbed out and let us never speak of them again. . . . We think of our relations, brothers, brothers-in-law, father-in-law, etc., over on the reservation, and from this on we want to live at peace just as they are doing, and to behave as they are behaving. Sometimes a man does something and men are sent out to bring in his head.

I don't want such things to happen to us. I don't want that we should be killing each other. . . .

I have not forgotten what you told me, although a long time has passed. . . . I want this peace to be legal and good. Whenever I meet you I talk good to you, and you to me, and peace is soon established; but when you go to the reservation you put agents and interpreters over us who do bad things. Perhaps they don't mind what you tell them, because I do not believe you would tell them to do bad things to us. . . . I want to have a good man put over me. While living I want to live well. I know I have to die some time, but even if the heavens were to fall on me, I want to do what is right. I think I am a good man, but in the papers all over the world they say I am a bad man; but it is a bad thing to say so about me. I never do wrong without a cause. Every day I am thinking, how am I to talk to you to make you believe what I say; and, I think, too, that you are thinking of what you are to say to me. There is one God looking down on us all. We are all children of the one God. God is listening to me. The sun, the darkness, the winds, are all listening to what we now say.

To prove to you that I am telling you the truth, remember I sent you word that I would come from a place far away to speak to you here, and you see us now. Some have come on horseback and some on foot. If I were thinking bad, or if I had done bad, I would never have come here. If it had been my fault, would I have come so far to talk to you! . . . I am glad to see Ka-e-a-tena. I was afraid I should never see him again. That was one reason, too, why I left. I wish that Ka-e-a-tena would be returned to us to live with his family. . . . Now I believe that all told me is true, because I see Ka-e-a-tena again . . . as I was told I should.

〰〰〰〰〰〰〰〰〰〰〰〰

Thus he finished his apologia. Crook bluntly told him he was lying. It would have required more objective reasoning than even this high-minded soldier possessed at the time to see that his wild adversary, from his own standpoint, spoke the truth. Geronimo had promised to live at peace on the reservation; he had broken his promise and had gone out and killed innocent people; therefore, his word was not to be trusted. A dialogue followed, with charges and recriminations between the two.

Geronimo began, "I want to ask who it was that ordered that I should be arrested." Crook answered, "That's all bosh. There were no orders for any one to arrest you." Geronimo suggested that perhaps the orders had come from somebody else, and he continued to seek the source of the plot against him. He appealed to Crook: "There is no other captain so great as you. I thought you ought to know about those stories, and who started them." When Crook still accused him of lying, he said, "If you think I am not telling the truth, then I don't think you came down here in good faith."

In this exchange there is some indication of the surrender terms Crook was considering. He ignored Geronimo's assumption that he could return to the reservation and start anew. "You must make up your own mind whether you will stay out on the warpath or surrender unconditionally. If you stay out, I'll keep after you and kill the last one, if it takes fifty years." Then the general's mind passed immediately to Kaahteney and to the beneficial effect of his punishment. He accused Geronimo of insincerity in expressing relief at seeing Kaahteney unharmed and well, reminding him that "over a year ago I asked you if you wanted me to bring Ka-e-a-tena back but you said no." (This had occurred before Geronimo had become suspicious; now he was truly reassured to see that Kaahteney had not been harmed.)

Crook then tried by cross-questioning to show that Geronimo had frightened the other Indians into leaving the reservation. He asked which ones had been threatened. Geronimo said that all of them were, and "If you don't want to believe me I can prove it by all the men, women, and children of the White Mountain Apaches." Crook then pinned him down to: "They wanted to seize me and Magnus."

"Then why did Natches and Chihuahua go out?" Crook asked.

"Because they were afraid the same thing would happen to them," answered Geronimo.

"Who made them afraid?" Crook persisted, and he wanted to know what Geronimo told them.

"The only thing I told them was that I heard I was going to be seized and killed, that's all," was Geronimo's answer.

Crook next tried to establish the validity of Davis' account of the breakout. He asked why Geronimo had sent some of his people to kill Davis and Chatto. Geronimo denied sending them and offered evidence; if it were true, "these Indians [Naiche, Chihuahua, and Kutli, who were present at the council] would say so." Crook continued: ". . . and you reported that they were killed and that is the reason so many went out with you." Geronimo then referred to the White Mountain Indians present (scouts, in general unfriendly to the hostile band), who would establish his innocence. Finally, he said, "Well, here is a White Mountain sergeant, a man like that won't lie; ask him." Crook ignored these prospective witnesses; he and Davis had got the story from members of the band at Fort Apache, and he was convinced.

Geronimo made one last attempt at justification. "Whenever I wanted to talk with Lieutenant Davis, I spoke by day or by night. I never went to him in a hidden manner. May be some of these men know about it. Perhaps you had better ask them." Crook's reply was to close the conference: "I have said all I have to say. You had better think it over to-night and let me know in the morning."

"All right, we'll talk to-morrow," said Geronimo; "I may want to *ask* you some questions, too, as you have asked me some."

But there was no "talk to-morrow" with Crook. The leaders spent the day in their volcanic fastness in serious discussion. Kaahteney and Alchise circulated among them breaking down their resistance. A few messages passed back and forth between them and Crook. The general had been instructed to insist upon unconditional surrender, but he had been given some latitude, which he interpreted to mean that he should obtain the best terms he could. The Indians at first would consider only a return to the reservation, but the time had passed for such easy forgiveness. Remembering Kaahteney, Crook finally stipulated that all the warriors except the supposedly senile Nana should be imprisoned in the East for not more than two years with such members of their families as might choose to accompany them. No doubt he had old Fort Marion at Saint Augustine in mind; seventy-two hostile warriors of the South Plains had been sent there as prisoners eleven years before and had come back willing to observe the peace.

Chihuahua was the first to break, but Crook left him in the camp so that he might influence the others. Geronimo was the last holdout. Crook's emissaries feared even to mention surrender to him. Finally, after much agonizing, the same four leaders came to Crook at about noon on March 27 and said they "wanted to talk." As Bourke told it, Nana "toddled after them, but he was so old and feeble that we did not count him." Again they sat down under the sycamores.

Chihuahua spoke first. His submission was complete: "I am anxious to behave. . . . I surrender myself to you because I believe in you and you do not deceive us." And he gave Crook some of the fulsome compliments that formed the ultimate expression of Apache good will: "You must be our God. . . . You must be the one who makes the green pastures, who sends the rain, who commands the winds. You must be the one who sends the fresh fruits that appear on the trees every year. . . . Everything you do is right." He asked only that "you send my family with me wherever you send me. . . . I ask you to find out if they are willing to go or not." (Through all the years of their subsequent imprisonment, Chihuahua seemed to grieve the most of any of the band about the separation from his children.) Naiche spoke next, expressing the same submission: "When I was free I gave orders, but now I surrender to you. . . . You now order and I obey. . . . Now that I have surrendered I am glad. I'll not have to hide behind rocks and mountains; I'll go across the open plain. . . . There may be lots of men who have bad feelings against us. I will go wherever you may see fit to send us, where no bad talk will be spoken of us. . . . I surrender to you, and hope you will be kind to us. . . ."

Then Geronimo spoke. He had finally concluded to trust Crook, but he was more restrained than were his associates. "Two or three words are enough," he began. "We are all comrades, all one family, all one band. What the others say I say also. . . . Once I moved about like the wind. Now I surrender to you and that is all. [Shakes hands with General Crook.]²⁴ . . . My heart is yours, and I hope yours will be mine. . . . Whatever you tell me is true. We are all satisfied of that. I hope the day may come when my word shall be as strong with you as yours is with me. That's all I have to say now, except a few words. I should like to have my wife and daughter come to meet me at Fort Bowie or Silver Creek."

Geronimo had two wives and two daughters in army captivity. Probably he was referring to Zi-yeh, with her baby, and his grown daughter, Dohn-say, who had been captured by Wirt Davis' scouts the previous August and whom he still believed to be in the vicinity of Fort Apache. Crook promised that the meeting would occur and advised Geronimo to pay no more attention to unfriendly talk. "There are some people who can no more control their talk than the wind can." (Crook knew what it meant to be abused by a violent population and a frontier press.)

Geronimo then called on Alchise and Kaahteney "to speak a few words. They have come a long way and I want to hear them speak." Kaahteney pleaded a sore throat, but Alchise, secure in Crook's favor, made an earnest appeal on behalf of the hostiles: "They have surrendered. I don't want you to have any bad feelings towards them. They are all good friends now . . . because they are all the same people—all one family with me; just like when you kill a deer, all its parts are of the one body. . . . No matter where you send [them] we hope to hear that you have treated them kindly. . . . I have never told you a lie, nor have you ever told me a lie, and now I tell you that [they] really want to do what is right

²⁴ Brackets in original.

and live at peace. . . . I want you to carry away in your pocket all that has been said here to-day."

Crook told them that he would go on ahead to Fort Bowie and that they would follow with Maus and the scouts. Chihuahua promised to send on word to him every day. Crook said, "All right. Ka-e-a-tena can write your letters for you."[25] The next morning he set out early to telegraph the goods news to Washington.[26]

The Apache wars were ended. Or were they?

[25] The transcript of the conference is printed in *Senate Exec. Doc. 88*, 51 Cong., 1 sess., pp. 11–17. It may also be found in Davis, *op. cit.*, pp. 200–212. Bourke's account is in *On the Border with Crook*, pp. 472–79; Crook's report is in Secretary of War, *Annual Report*, 1886, p. 153.

[26] The telegram is on pp. 2–3 of the Senate document and on pp. 199–200 of Davis, *op. cit.*

CHAPTER 14

GERONIMO BRINGS DISASTER TO HIS PEOPLE

The night after the surrender, the scarcely tamed hostiles went on a drunken debauch. They had obtained the makings from a bootlegger named Tribolett, who operated just on the Mexican side of the border. All through the night Maus heard the sound of shots being fired in their camp. The next morning before daylight Alchise and Kaahteney, apparently sent by Chihuahua, awakened Crook with the news that Naiche was lying on the ground unable to stand and that others were in nearly the same state. They asked permission to take a squad of scouts and guard the bootlegger. But the mischief was already done. It was worse than bootlegging.

Tribolett apparently belonged to that class of scoundrels who profited from the Apache wars and intrigued to foment them. The wars brought not only army contracts, but also the shadier business of smuggling and trading with the raiders for their stolen livestock and other plunder. He was probably well known to the hostiles and trusted by them. Now he convinced the ever suspicious Geronimo that plans had been made to hang him as soon as he should cross the border. He may have been in the pay of profiteers at Tucson known collectively as the "Indian ring."[1] As Crook once

[1] This is the conclusion expressed by Thrapp in *Conquest of Apacheria*, pp. 346–47.

said, "With them, peace kills the goose that lays the golden egg."

Unaware of this sinister influence working among the surrendered hostiles, Crook set out that morning for Fort Bowie, leaving Maus to bring them in. Their intoxication was apparent. Near their camp, as he passed it, were saddled mules wandering around without riders, while Geronimo, Kutli, and three other warriors were grouped on two of the other animals—"all drunk as lords," in Bourke's words.[2]

Maus waited for the band to move, but they were slow about starting and traveled only a short distance that day, still watchful and keeping scattered in small groups. Geronimo advised Maus to go on with the scouts or he would not be responsible for his life. When they camped, the officer "went into their camp and found trouble. Natchez had shot his wife, and they were all drinking heavily." During that night, March 28, Maus heard a few shots fired, and the next morning he learned that Geronimo and Naiche, with twenty men, fourteen women, and six children, had slipped away in the night, taking only two horses and one mule from their herd, "and not a soul as far as I could ascertain, knew anything of the time they had gone, or that they intended to go."

The small band that broke away was made up largely of family groups. With Geronimo were his son Chappo and Chappo's young wife; three second cousins, including his "brothers" Perico and Fun; his brother-in-law Yahnozha; and his orphaned nephew, Kanseah. With Naiche were his wife Ha-o-zinne and several of her relatives: her parents, her half-brother, and her first cousin. Thus, eight of the twenty warriors, not counting the youth Kanseah, were related to the two leaders. Many of them were in their teens or early twenties.[3]

This time nobody could accuse Geronimo of starting a mass stampede. Secret plans for the flight must have been made during the day of March 28, for it was at that time that Naiche shot his wife, E-clah-heh. Present-day Apaches remember the incident well

2 *On the Border with Crook*, p. 480.
3 For names and descriptions of members of the band, see *infra*, pp. 304–306.

in their traditions. E-clah-heh, as was often the case with the women, dreaded the hard life of the hostiles. She started running to join the soldiers, and Naiche thereupon shot her to prevent a general defection. (His intoxicated state probably contributed to his action.) She was wounded in the leg. Thus unable to travel, she, with her young daughter, afterwards known as Dorothy, remained behind. She was a great-granddaughter of Mahko, hence a second cousin of Geronimo and a first cousin ("sister") of Fun and Betzinez.

Maus detailed an officer and some of his scouts to escort the main body of surrendered hostiles to Fort Bowie. These included the leaders Chihuahua, Jolsanny, Nana, and Kutli. With his remaining scouts he followed the trail of the fugitives some distance into the Mexican mountains, but he never came in sight of them. On his return he was joined by two of the runaway warriors. They had heard people leaving during the night, and, supposing something was wrong, had gone along. In the morning, when they understood the situation, they had turned back.[4]

Years later, at Fort Sill, Geronimo gave a concise account of the breakaway. He told how "with all our tribe" he started to go "back to the United States, but I feared treachery and decided to remain in Mexico. We were not under any guard at this time. The United States troops [mainly scouts] marched in front and the Indians followed, and when we became suspicious, we turned back. I do not know how far the United States army went after myself, and some warriors turned back before we were missed, and I do not care." He was still convinced of Crook's treachery. Probably his trust in Tribolett was based on a long experience of profitable transactions in stolen goods and mescal sales. He told of the argument between himself and Crook at the conference and his final decision to accept Crook's denial of any intention to arrest him. But—"It was hard for me to believe him at that time.

4 For the incidents of the breakaway, see Bourke, *op. cit.*, pp. 480–81, and Maus in Miles, *Personal Recollections*, pp. 468–70. Crook's summary is in Secretary of War, *Annual Report*, 1886, p. 154. A brief biography of E-clah-heh is in Griswold, "The Fort Sill Apaches," s.v. "E-clah-heh."

Now I know that what he said was untrue, and I firmly believe that he did issue the orders for me to be put in prison, or to be killed in case I offered resistance." He was convinced that Crook's death, which occurred four years after the surrender conference, "was sent by the Almighty as a punishment for the many evil deeds he committed."[5]

In after years, the more conciliatory Naiche also told the story of the flight. On January 2, 1890, Crook came to interview the prisoners, who were then held at Mount Vernon Barracks, Alabama. "How did you come to leave that night?" he asked. "I was afraid I was going to be taken off somewhere I didn't like," Naiche answered, "to some place I didn't know. I thought all who were taken away would die. Since then I have found out different. . . . Nobody said anything to me that night; I worked it out in my own mind."

"Didn't the Indians talk about [it] among themselves?" asked the general.

"We talked to each other about it," said Naiche. "We were drunk."

"Why did you get drunk?" inquired the general.

"Because there was a lot of whisky there and we wanted a drink, and took it," was the chief's logical answer. Then he went on, "The other[s] didn't want to go out. I don't know why the others didn't know of it; I thought they all did."[6]

Meanwhile, on that same March 29 Crook reached Fort Bowie and sent out his telegram telling of the hostiles' surrender and stating the terms. Sheridan answered the following day. Citing the highest authority—President Cleveland—he rejected these conditions, instructing the general "to enter into negotiations on the terms of their unconditional surrender, only sparing their lives." He should prevent their escape and "insure against further hostilities by completing [their] destruction, unless these terms are

---

5 Barrett, *Geronimo's Story of His Life*, pp. 137–40. See also pp. 135–36 regarding his flight from the reservation to escape Crook's designs against his life. It required two footnotes for Barrett to disclaim responsibility for these "exact words of Geronimo."

6 *Senate Exec. Doc. 35*, 51 Cong., 1 sess., p. 33.

acceded to." These instructions were, of course, impossible to follow. Sheridan was thousands of miles removed from the conditions of Apache fighting. Crook, for once departing from his aboveboard method of dealing with Indians, decided to conceal from the hostiles the rejection of the surrender terms. The certainty that they would all scatter to the mountains was too appalling.

A courier from Maus informed the general on the same day, March 30, of the flight of Geronimo and Naiche with their small party. He relayed the bad news to Sheridan, and Sheridan replied in an angry telegram, blaming him for laxity. Crook tried to explain; then, failing, he asked to be relieved of his command. On April 2 Sheridan ordered his transfer to command the Department of the Platte and directed Brigadier General Nelson A. Miles to succeed him in Arizona. The next day he ordered Crook to ship the prisoners to Fort Marion "under the terms directed by the President in my telegram of March 30." Two days later he found an excuse for the breach of faith. The settlement had been rejected by both parties— "The present terms not having been agreed to here, and Geronimo having broken every condition of surrender, the Indians now in custody are to be held as prisoners and sent to Fort Marion without reference to previous communications and without in any way consulting their wishes in the matter."[7]

Crook disarmed these new prisoners and conducted them and the prisoners taken previously to Bowie Station on the railroad a few miles north of the post. They numbered seventy-seven— fifteen men, thirty-three women, and twenty-nine children. Among them were two wives and three children of Geronimo then in army hands; two wives, two children, the mother, and other relatives of Naiche; and families or relatives of all the other warriors who remained at large. They reached Fort Marion on April 13.[8]

Miles came to relieve Crook on April 12. He was an experienced

---

7 These telegrams are in *Senate Exec. Doc. 88*, 51 Cong., 1 sess., pp. 2–10; they were also published by Miles in *Personal Recollections*, pp. 471–75.
8 Secretary of War, *Annual Report*, 1886, pp. 49, 154–55.

Indian fighter, but was given to glorifying his exploits; he lacked Crook's quiet dedication, his understanding of the Apaches, and—most important of all—his integrity. Crook had said he could not use more than three thousand regular soldiers to advantage.[9] Miles acquired five thousand, one-fourth of the entire army, in his campaign against eighteen warriors with Geronimo and Naiche and a smaller party with Mangus. Rejecting Crook's reliance on Apache scouts, he discharged all of them except a few he used as trailers. First he tried cavalry. When the horses proved unable to climb the mountains, he dismounted his troopers. But only a few of them could stand up to the hardships accepted as a matter of course by Apache women and children. He set up heliograph stations to flash messages from mountain to mountain, a system of communication the Apaches had long been using, having shifted from smoke signals to mirrors.

In his *Personal Recollections*, which covered his whole lifetime, Miles devoted one-sixth of his space to the Apaches, one-tenth (fifty-six pages) to his own military campaign against them. In his account the campaign was a series of difficult pursuits, occasional encounters, heroic exploits—and complete failure. To do him justice, it may be noted that if the enemy had been more numerous he might have had better success in finding them. Mangus remained out of sight. Naiche and Geronimo first struck at points in Sonora, then on April 27 they entered the United States and raided at will, even around Fort Apache and San Carlos. Characteristically, Miles reported this raid as a victory for the army: "They have killed but fourteen persons in the Territories of the United States, the last one June 5, and were on our soil but twenty-three days before they were driven out." On the other side of the border they killed even more Mexicans.[10]

Later, at Fort Sill, Geronimo gave his version of this raid. Pursued by American and Mexican soldiers,

9 *Ibid.*, p. 8.
10 For Miles's official report, see *ibid.*, pp. 164–76; for his evaluation of Geronimo's raid across the border, see *Senate Exec. Doc. 83*, 51 Cong., 1 sess., p. 10.

269

〰〰〰〰〰〰〰〰〰〰〰〰〰〰〰

we finally decided to break up into small bands. With six men and four women I made for the range of mountains near Hot Springs [Warm Springs], New Mexico. . . . We ranged in the mountains of New Mexico for some time, then thinking that perhaps the troops had left Mexico, we returned. On our return through Old Mexico we attacked every Mexican found, even if for no other reason than to kill. We believed that they had asked the United States troops to come down to Mexico to fight us.

. . . We were reckless of our lives, because we felt that every man's hand was against us. If we returned to the reservation we would be put in prison and killed; if we stayed in Mexico they would continue to send soldiers to fight us; so we gave no quarter to anyone and asked no favors.[11]

〰〰〰〰〰〰〰〰〰〰〰〰〰〰〰

There is no doubt that Geronimo killed Mexicans wantonly because he liked to see them die, but the killings on the American side of the border were a necessary part of raiding. The raiders killed to obtain supplies, and they killed every person they met to prevent his reporting their presence. In his 1890 interview Crook asked Naiche why they killed people, and the chief answered: "Because we were afraid. It was war. Anybody who saw us would kill us, and we did the same thing. We had to if we wanted to live."[12]

And as far as the American army was concerned, they continued to live. They did lose one warrior by desertion, a man named Massai, who was destined to become famous in Western legend.[13] They lost another through Mexican treachery. A courier from the officials at Casas Grandes brought the news to Britton Davis, who had resigned from the army to manage a ranching and mining enterprise at the nearby hacienda of Corralitos. According

[11] Barrett, *op. cit.*, pp. 140–41.

[12] *Senate Exec. Doc. 35*, 51 Cong., 1 sess., p. 33.

[13] Betzinez, *I Fought with Geronimo*, pp. 143–44; Secretary of War, *Annual Report*, 1886, p. 168; Davis, *The Truth about Geronimo*, pp. 220, 222. According to Davis, the deserter was Kayihtah, and Miles so implied, but this is certainly a mistake. Betzinez knew Massai well, and there is no indication that Kayihtah was ever with the war party.

270

to this report, the hostiles had sent three men to transact some of their periodic business there, and the Mexicans "stood them up before an adobe wall, and made 'good injun' of them." Two must have escaped, for only one was killed.[14]

But Miles, for all his efforts, did not kill or capture a single hostile. He finally decided to proceed against some Apaches he could catch—about four hundred of them who had remained at peace on the reservation, making a start at farming, accumulating livestock, cutting hay to sell at the post, and serving the army as scouts against the hostiles. But they were hated by the white citizens of Arizona—to whom all Apaches looked alike—and disliked by the other tribes on the reservation. On July 3 Miles suggested to Sheridan that they should be removed and located elsewhere. This policy had been frequently advocated by both the War and Interior departments (in unaccustomed accord),[15] but with bureaucratic insensitivity none of the officials had ever given a thought about where these displaced people should be settled. Crook had objected to their removal, and at first Sheridan also opposed it, citing the disastrous Victorio wars resulting from the uprooting of the Warm Springs band. But now, upon the recommendation of Miles, it became the official policy.[16]

One cannot resist the suspicion that, failing to apprehend the eighteen hostiles with their women and children, Miles needed some "captives" to show. Naturally, he advanced a different reason. He had made "a very careful examination into the condition of the Chiricahua and Warm Springs Apaches . . . and a more turbulent and dissipated body of Indians I have never met." *Tizwin* drinks with "riots and bloodshed" were frequent, "and the stillness of the nights was often broken by the discharge of rifles and pistols in their savage orgies. The indolent and vicious young men and boys were just the material to furnish warriors for the future." He

14 Davis, *op. cit.*, pp. 194, 218. Other reports mention the death of only one hostile, and the loss of three cannot be reconciled with the known number remaining in the band.

15 See, for example, Secretary of War, *Annual Report*, 1882, p. 186; 1886, pp. 6–7.

16 *Senate Exec. Doc. 83*, 51 Cong., 1 sess., pp. 2–3.

asserted that the band "had been in communication with the hostiles, and some of them had been plotting an extensive outbreak."[17]

Nevertheless, Miles, in spite of his faults, had humane intentions. Seven years before he had any experience with the Apaches he had denounced as "cruel" the removal of hardy, mountain Indians to a warm, malarial climate.[18] Now he pointed out that the prisoners recently sent to Florida "would in a short time most likely die" because of the low altitude if left there. Therefore, the two bands should be relocated on a new reservation. There, they should be started in farming and stock raising, and "most of their children [should be] scattered through the industrial Indian schools." He had a place picked out for them near the Wichita Mountains in the Indian Territory where they would find a healthful climate and fertile soil.

This plan would have placed them in the vicinity of Fort Sill on the reservation owned by the Comanches, Kiowas, and a small tribe closely connected with the Kiowas which bore the misleading name Apaches. Miles had conducted military operations against these South Plains tribes, but he had never learned anything about them. The Comanches were long-time enemies of the real Apaches of the Southwest, and their Kiowa allies shared this hostility. And although the Kiowa-Apaches had a distant linguistic relationship with the true Apaches, they had come down from the north with the Kiowas and had no tradition of any connection with the Southwestern bands. Miles assumed that the two tribes were an identical people and would accept each other as relatives. Nothing could have been more unrealistic.

There was, however, some available land in other parts of the Indian Territory, which comprised all of present Oklahoma except the Panhandle. Although many tribes of Indians driven from their homelands before the advancing frontier had been placed on reservations there, a considerable area remained unassigned. But people of the adjoining states, especially the Kansans, constantly

17 Secretary of War, *Annual Report*, 1886, pp. 170–71.
18 Nelson A. Miles, *Serving the Republic*, p. 204.

intrigued to have it opened to white settlement; hence, they opposed any addition to the Indian population. In 1879 Congress, at
their urging, had adopted an amendment to the Indian Appropriation Bill prohibiting the location there of Apaches or other Indians
from New Mexico or Arizona.[19] The administration informed
Miles that it would be "impossible" to have this prohibition re-
pealed. He then suggested the present Oklahoma Panhandle, a
High Plains tract cut off from Texas by the Compromise of 1850
and left out in forming subsequent state boundaries. This was
clearly impracticable. The level, treeless grassland lacked all the
resources required for Apache self-sufficiency. (Even for the white
man its agricultural productiveness had to wait until the development of large-scale mechanized wheat farming.)

But even with no place in sight to replant them, Miles continued
his plans for uprooting the Apaches. Believing that "their consent
would be advisable and desirable," he selected ten of their leaders
to go to Washington to negotiate the removal. Chatto headed the
delegation. Among the other members were Kaahteney, Loco, and
a dependable scout named Noche, and three of their women accompanied them. Miles placed Captain Joseph H. Dorst in charge.
He wanted them to be shown the Indian Territory as a home site,
and they left with that expectation. The administration vetoed this
suggestion, but permitted them to go on to Washington.[20] There,
they stood as a unit against removal.

Chatto was the spokesman. His appeal to Secretary of War
William C. Endicott at a conference held on July 26 reveals the
deep currents of Apache feeling. His words, translated first into
Spanish and then into English by Concepcion, Mickey Free, and
Sam Bowman, were presented in the third person. Captain Bourke,
who was in Washington working on ethnological studies for the

---

[19] U.S. *Statutes at Large*, XX, 313, February 17, 1879. This was a compromise. The
land seekers had tried to close the area against *all* further Indian relocations. They
argued that the Indians would attack the settlements in the surrounding states, but their
real motivation appears in the debates. See *Congressional Record*, VIII, 311 ff.

[20] *Senate Exec. Doc. 35*, 51 Cong., 1 sess., pp. 35, 36, 41, 44, 48; *83*, pp. 4–5, 8, 10,
13; Secretary of War, *Annual Report*, 1886, p. 14.

Chatto at Washington, July, 1886. The picture was by a Smithsonian Institution photographer. "He came here to ask for his country; to ask for his land, where he lives now; to ask that is why he has traveled so far." Courtesy U.S. Army Artillery and Missile Center Museum.

government, [21] was present to assist in the interpretation. Chatto told Endicott:

�..

What he came to look here for was good words, good advice—he is looking for the words as if God is speaking. He has come, too, because he wants to take a paper with him, so as to remember the words that have been told him here. . . .

He came here to ask for his country; to ask for his land, where he lives now; to ask that is why he has traveled so far. At Camp Apache what he plants grows up very well; the water that runs there is very good; that is why he wants to stay there. . . .

The favor he wants to ask of you, is to ask for his land as if he was asking a favor from God, and he hopes that you won't forget his words. It is to him . . . as if God had said that he and you had come together to exchange words; and he thinks now that God is listening to what he says.

〠..

Then he went on to speak of his personal problem, of his family in Mexican slavery: "You may have some children. Everybody loves his son, loves him dearly; holds him in his arms and to his heart. . . .

"He says he has a wife and two children in Chihuahua; that Captain Bourke knows it; that he has seen their pictures over there; and he asks . . . that these children may be given back into his hands, so he can take them to his heart again, and have them with him at Camp Apache. He has feelings just like white people, and for that reason he wants to have his people once more with him. He can not make big houses like this, but can only take small sticks and make a house; but still, even if his hands ache, he wants to live that way."

Bourke explained Chatto's meaning: "In speaking of his house, Chato means that no matter how poor a man is, his home, when it is the best he can offer, is the place for his wife and children to be.

21 Bourke, *Apache Campaign*, pp. 6, 10–12.

"When he says I have seen their pictures, he is speaking of the photographs which were sent by the Mexican authorities to General Crook to induce Chato to believe that his wife and children were better off where they were in Chihuahua than they were on the reservation."

Chatto continued: "He says he has had his picture taken here [it had been taken by a Smithsonian photographer], . . . and he wants to have some of them sent to the man with whom his family is in Chihuahua. . . . He wants to have his name, Chato, put on the picture, so that his wife will know."

Endicott promised to give him some copies to send, and Bourke explained that the best way to accomplish this was to send them to Crook for forwarding. He said that Crook had been in correspondence with persons in Chihuahua and knew exactly where Chatto's people were.[22] But if this was done, the appeal was futile. Chatto was never to see his wife and children again.

The secretary gave Chatto the "paper" he had requested, a simple statement that he had been in Washington. He also gave him a silver medal. To the delegates this meant that their mission to save their homeland had succeeded. It was far otherwise. Throughout the month of August the telegraph wires between Washington and Arizona were clogged with conflicting orders to prevent the return of the delegates lest they complicate the scheme for removing their people. They were taken first to Carlisle to visit their young relatives (including Loco's son) in school there, and then on their way west they were detained at Fort Leavenworth, Kansas.[23]

Miles, hoping to succeed where Washington had failed in obtaining their consent to removal, entrusted his plan to Dorst, who was still in charge of the delegation at Fort Leavenworth. First, the Indians were told that the white citizens of Arizona and New Mexico were demanding their removal and that the civil authorities were ready to proceed against them for murders they had

22 *Senate Exec. Doc. 35*, 51 Cong., 1 sess., pp. 41–43.
23 *Ibid.*, *83*, pp. 10–26.

committed in past raids. Dorst then presented a draft agreement granting them a reservation of six hundred square miles where they would be reunited with the Fort Marion prisoners and possibly with the still hostile bands of Geronimo and Mangus. Each family would receive six hundred dollars' worth of farm equipment and domestic animals, and fifteen of their leaders would be paid salaries varying from twenty to fifty dollars a month, besides being given "comfortable abodes" and other "valuables." If they would accept these terms, and if the government should ratify them, they would become *"treaty Indians"* living on this reservation; otherwise, they would be treated as prisoners of war. All ten members of the delegation thereupon "touched the pen," and an army officer witnessed their signatures.

Later, President Cleveland asked Dorst "why General Miles wished to give the chiefs and head men money for moving. I replied that it was because it had been the policy of the Government in other cases to purchase the influence of such men." Probably the proposed bribe *was* a consideration in obtaining the consent of the delegates, but it was not the determining one. Chatto, Kaahteney, and Noche talked to Crook freely about it in 1890. "We thought it was good to get $20 to $50 a month," said Chatto. But it is clear that fear of Arizona vengeance and the attractive features of the mythical reservation described by Dorst caused them to agree to the removal.[24]

Throughout the blizzard of telegrams Miles tried to bring them back to influence their people,[25] but Washington was adamant. And no consideration was ever given to the draft agreement they had signed. With the Indian Territory closed against them, there was no other such tract of land available. Miles had suggested that until a homesite should be found for the displaced band, they should be kept on the military reservation at Fort Riley, Kansas, a healthful region of smooth, grass-covered hills. This proposal also received no consideration, and one can imagine the violent objec-

---

24 *Ibid.*, *35*, pp. 34–36, 48–50; *83*, p. 17.
25 See especially *ibid.*, *35*, p. 48.

tions of the Kansans against having these supposedly dangerous people set down in their midst. The administration decided on Fort Marion as "the place of confinement" for these additional "prisoners of war." This ancient defensive work, built by the Spaniards as the Castillo de San Marcos, was a subpost of Saint Francis Barracks at Saint Augustine. The War Department wired Lieutenant Colonel Loomis L. Langdon, the commanding officer of the small garrison there, asking if he could accommodate four or five hundred more prisoners. He replied that he could take seventy-five, but he recommended against sending any.[26]

Langdon explained more fully by letter, incidentally revealing the conditions under which his prisoners lived. The small parade ground inside the old fort, he said, was surrounded by walls in which were casemates once occupied by the garrison, but the terreplein above had become so dilapidated that water leaked down into them, rendering them uninhabitable. Therefore, he had pitched tents—eighteen in all—on the terreplein to shelter the prisoners. He could put up twenty more tents to take possibly eighty additional persons, "but the sanitary conditions will be bad." The small military reserve was so closely surrounded by the town that it was impracticable to quarter any of them outside. He warned against the assumption that a camp could be built on the beach or on nearby Anastasia Island. Both these places "are liable to overflow every fall and winter," and "besides the danger of getting drowned" the prisoners would "have to face the diseases peculiar to the low grounds of such localities." He suggested sending the ones he had to the military reservation at Carlisle so that their children might attend school there. Then he could prepare for the new arrivals, possibly accommodating two hundred. Sheridan's endorsement on this letter reads: "The conditions stated by Col. Langdon need not interfere with sending the remainder of the Chiricahua and Warm Spring Indians to Fort Marion."[27]

26 *Ibid., 83,* pp. 17–18.
27 National Archives and Records Service, Consolidated File 1066 AGO 1884, telegrams August 21 and letter August 23, 1886.

Sheridan probably did not know that Langdon's humanitarian protest was being reinforced by a commercial one in favor of Fort Pickens near Pensacola. An article in the *Pensacolian* of September 18 told of the expected arrival of "all of the Apaches of Geronimo's tribe" to the state, pointed out the lack of facilities at Fort Marion, and went on to indicate the efforts made by ambitious city builders to secure the prisoners for the local tourist business: "A move has been set on foot to have some of these red devils sent down to this place and incarcerated at Fort Pickens. Congressman Davidson has been consulted and he has sent a strong recommendation in favor of the scheme to the proper authorities in Washington. If Bob succeeds in this he can point with pride as having been instrumental in giving Pensacola an attraction which will bring here a great many visitors."[28] In their wars the Apaches had been an asset to the economy of Arizona through army contracts; now they were eagerly sought to bring prosperity to Florida.

There is no indication that the Pensacola bid was considered by the administration. The only problem was to plan the removal of the Indians cautiously lest they take to the mountains. Then on September 12 the order went out that the delegation detained at Fort Leavenworth should also be sent to Fort Marion "for confinement with other Indian prisoners now there."[29]

Thus, peaceable people living quietly on their reservation, tending their little farms and striving in all ways to conform to government policy were changed by bureaucratic semantics into "prisoners" to be "confined." But as long as they remained unsuspecting, they could be induced to assist the government. During those same early days in July when Miles was advising Sheridan to remove them, he called their leaders together at Fort Apache and enlisted Kayihtah and his cousin and close associate, a Nednai named Martine, to take a message to the hostiles with Geronimo and Naiche to induce them to surrender. Probably it was at this time that Miles chose his Washington delegation. It seems clear that

28 *Pensacolian*, September 18, 1886.
29 *Senate Exec. Doc. 117*, 49 Cong., 2 sess., p. 73.

Noche advised him in selecting the messengers to the hostiles,[30] believing that only these two men could approach Geronimo and live. Kayihtah's cousin, Yahnozha, was known to be in Geronimo's band, and Martine had been in training with Geronimo's close friend, Juh.[31]

Miles placed Lieutenant Gatewood in charge, with authority to call upon any officer for a military escort. Gatewood did not share Bourke's and Davis' liking for the Apaches or their confidence in the scouts, but the Indians knew and trusted him as a man of integrity. He had even learned to speak their language, but as interpreter he took along George Wratten, who, as a young boy, had worked as a clerk at a trading post on the reservation and had acquired greater fluency.[32] (Wratten was destined to remain with the Apaches for many years.) A packer and a courier completed the party.[33]

This mission was the real test of Miles's policy. It had been easy to plot against the peaceable Indians on the reservation and to hold the trusting Washington delegation in captivity, but the only hope of ending the war rested on the shoulders of one army lieutenant and two Apaches who had volunteered to help.

[30] Conflicting stories are told of their enlistment and of the rewards promised them. Betzinez, *op. cit.*, pp. 135–36; Opler, "A Chiricahua Apache's Account," pp. 371–73; and Ora E. Musgrove, "A Belated Reward for the Surrender of Geronimo," from National Archives and Records Service, statements by Noche, Kayihtah, and Martine at Fort Sill, May 2, 1911. See also Lockwood, *The Apache Indians*, p. 329, and Thrapp, *Conquest of Apacheria*, p. 364.

[31] Statements by Kayihtah, Martine, and Daklugie furnished me by Eve Ball.

[32] James Kaywaykla, Benedict Jozhe, and Moses Loco, interview, July 29, 1959.

[33] Charles B. Gatewood, "An Account of the Surrender of Geronimo," manuscript in Gatewood Collection, Arizona Pioneers' Historical Society, Tucson.

CHAPTER 15

"THIS IS THE FOURTH TIME I HAVE SURRENDERED"

Mounted on mules, and with a three-mule pack train, Gatewood's little party crossed the border into Mexico.[1] They joined the command of Captain Henry W. Lawton, who had been combing the mountains in the Aros River vicinity far to the south in a futile attempt to find the hostiles. Then came word that Geronimo had put out peace feelers to the Mexican officials at Fronteras, only thirty miles from the border. By this time it was the middle of August. The entire command moved north by forced marches, Gatewood's little party with an escort of six men arriving first. There he learned that two of the hostiles' women—one of them is said to have been Geronimo's trusted envoy, Tah-das-te[2]—had recently come there with overtures of surrender. They had been permitted to trade and had left with three extra ponies laden with food and mescal.

---

[1] Gatewood, "Account of the Surrender of Geronimo," p. 5. Here, and in the following pages, except where I have indicated otherwise, I am following Gatewood's narrative. Although it was not written until 1895, it is painstakingly accurate, and it is supported by a statement made by George Wratten at Washington, March 5, 1905 (S. M. Huddleson, "An Interview with Geronimo and His Guardian, Mr. G. M. Wratton").

[2] Statement by Kayihtah and Martine recorded by Asa Daklugie and furnished me by Eve Ball.

Neither side had been negotiating in good faith. Geronimo afterwards said he had had no intention of surrendering but had talked peace only to obtain supplies. The Mexicans, for their part, were concentrating soldiers in the town, intending to lure the Apaches there and massacre the whole party.[3] The municipal president insisted that Gatewood should not follow the women. The lieutenant accordingly started south, ostensibly to join Lawton, then circled north and struck their trail. He followed them for three days into the mountains, "with a piece of flour sack to the fore as a white flag" carried "high on a century plant pole." But, as he said, "that doesn't make a man bullet proof." He camped in a canebrake on the Bavispe River. The next day—August 23—he sent the two Apache messengers to the hostiles, who "occupied an exceedingly rocky position high up in the Torres Mountains" about four miles away.[4]

As it happened, the half-grown Kanseah was on guard. Through his field glasses—with which the hostiles were abundantly supplied —he saw the two moving dots on the trail. He reported to Geronimo, Geronimo called his warriors, and they seated themselves in council. By this time Kanseah recognized Martine and Kayihtah, carrying a white flag. He told Geronimo who they were.

"It does not matter who they are. If they come closer they are to be shot," ordered Geronimo.

"They are our brothers," protested Yahnozha. "Let's find out why they come. They are brave men to risk this." When Geronimo argued, Yahnozha said, "We will not shoot. The first man who lifts a rifle I will kill."

"I will help you," said Fun.

Then Geronimo grunted, "Let them come."[5]

The envoys came in and delivered their message. Probably Kayihtah was the spokesman. "The troops are coming after you

3 Dan L. Thrapp, "Geronimo's Mysterious Surrender," *Brand Book*, Los Angeles Corrall, Vol. XIII (1969), reconciles the varying accounts in Mexican and American sources.

4 Gatewood, *op. cit.*, pp. 5–8.

5 Ball, *In the Days of Victorio*, pp. 185–87. Mrs. Ball got the story directly from Kanseah.

from all directions," he said. Their "aim is to kill every one of you if it takes fifty years." He reminded them that "everything is against you. . . . If you are awake at night and a rock rolls down the mountain or a stick breaks, you will be running. . . . You even eat your meals running. You have no friends whatever in the world." He innocently assumed that they could return to the reservation, and he described the happy situation there: "I get plenty to eat. I go wherever I want, talk to good people. I go to bed whenever I want and get all my sleep. I have nobody to fear. I have my little patch of corn. I'm trying to do what the white people want me to do. And there's no reason why you people shouldn't do it."[6]

They agreed, and Geronimo sent Martine back to Gatewood to ask for a conference, while Naiche sent the officer an additional message assuring him of safe-conduct. There was nothing but the honor of soldiers like Gatewood to assure safe-conduct to the hostiles. On that very day President Cleveland telegraphed the War Department: "I hope nothing will be done with Geronimo which will prevent our treating him as a prisoner of war, if we cannot hang him, which I would much prefer."[7]

Martine arrived at Gatewood's camp in the canebrake just before sundown, while Kayihtah remained that night in the hostiles' *rancheria*. Meanwhile, Gatewood had sent a courier back to Lawton, and Lawton's scouts had already reached his camp, while the rest of the command was not far behind. The next morning Gatewood, with the scouts, started for the hostile camp. They were met by three armed warriors with a message from Naiche that the scouts should turn back and that the officer should meet the hostiles at a designated bend of the river. Gatewood and his small party accordingly proceeded there, unsaddled their mules, and turned them out to graze. The hostiles came in a few at a time and turned out their own mounts. Geronimo was one of the last to arrive. He laid down his rifle and came over to shake hands with

6 Opler, "A Chiricahua Apache's Account," pp. 375–77. Opler's informant, Sam Kenoi, was not present, but his account seems accurate except for a spiteful charge of cowardice against Martine, which is plainly untrue.

7 *Senate Exec. Doc. 117*, 49 Cong., 2 sess., p. 4.

Gatewood. The lieutenant passed around tobacco, and soon all were smoking cigarettes rolled in the Apache way, in oak leaves. (Apaches did not use the peace pipe, but they valued tobacco and used it on ceremonial occasions or as a special luxury.[8])

Geronimo opened the council by announcing that the warriors had come to hear General Miles's message. Gatewood gave it to them straight: "Surrender, and you will be sent to join the rest of your friends in Florida, there to await the decision of the President as to your final disposition. Accept these terms or fight it out to the bitter end." All listened attentively, and a long silence fell upon the group. Then Geronimo passed a hand across his eyes, extended his arms, making his hands tremble, and asked for a drink. They had just been on a three days' drunk, he said, on the mescal the women had brought from Fronteras. "The Mexicans expected to play their usual trick of getting us drunk and killing us," he explained, "but we have had the fun." Their spree had passed off happily "without a single fight," but "now I feel a little shaky." Gatewood answered that he had brought no liquor. Geronimo then got down to business.

He said that he would leave the warpath only on the condition that the band could return to the reservation and live as before. Gatewood said that Miles's message was final. Geronimo then "narrated at length the history of their troubles," while Gatewood remained unimpressed. The warriors then "withdrew to one side in the cane brake, and held a private conference for an hour or so." When they returned, they all ate a noon meal, probably supplied by Gatewood's packer. After it, they resumed their places, and the council continued. Looking Gatewood square in the eye, Geronimo delivered his ultimatum, the result of their deliberation: "Take us to the reservation or fight." Surrounded as he was by armed enemies, the officer was decidedly uncomfortable, but Naiche, who had said very little so far, spoke up to assure him "that whether they continued the war or not," his party "would be allowed to depart in peace." Gatewood then informed the

[8] Opler, *An Apache Life-Way*, pp. 441–43.

hostiles that they had no reservation to return to, that their people had been sent to join Chihuahua in Florida. This removal had not yet occurred, but Gatewood supposed that it had. The news was a real blow. The Apaches withdrew for another private council. After they reassembled, Geronimo announced that they would continue the war, but that they wanted to kill a beef and remain in conference through the night. The tired Gatewood had to consent, but to his relief they found no beef to kill.

Then, after some smoking and general conversation, Geronimo asked Gatewood what kind of man the new general was. He wanted to know his age and size, the color of his hair and eyes, whether his voice was harsh or agreeable. Did he talk much or little, and did he mean more or less than he said? Had he many friends among his own people, and did they generally credit his word? Did the soldiers and officers like him? Had he had experience with Indians? Would he keep his promises? They all listened intently to Gatewood's answers. Even at this distance of time and culture one can sense the desperate earnestness of the Indians and how much depended upon the quality of the man in whose hands they were asked to place their lives. Geronimo summed up their conclusions: "He must be a good man since the Great Father sent him from Washington, and he sent you all this distance to us."

Toward sunset Gatewood suggested that his party repair to the camp of Lawton, who had arrived that day (August 24), while the hostiles should continue their discussions. To this they agreed. Then Geronimo, out of their anguished indecision, made a strange appeal to the enemy soldier: "We want your advice. Consider yourself one of us and not a white man. Remember all that has been said today, and as an Apache, what would you advise us to do?"

"I would trust General Miles and take him at his word," Gatewood answered. At this, "They all stood around looking very solemn," as the lieutenant remembered it, "and no further reference was made to the matter, except Geronimo said he would let me know the result of their council in the morning." Only the future would reveal the extent to which Gatewood had unwittingly betrayed them.

Before he left, they asked him to go alone or with one man to the nearest army post to communicate with Miles in an attempt to gain a modification of his terms. They would send several of their warriors as a hidden escort to protect him from Mexicans or others. He told them that the general had made up his mind and would not change it. Then, "After shaking hands all around, we bade them a solemn good-bye and rode to Lawton's camp." On the way young Chappo overtook them, and after riding along for a mile or so, Gatewood asked him where he was going. "With you," he replied, "I'm going to sleep close to you to-night, and tomorrow I'll return to our camp," and he added, "I have my father's permission to do so." Gatewood, knowing the unfriendly attitude of the scouts toward Geronimo's band, feared that some of them would stick a knife in Chappo during the night, with fatal consequences to the mission. He explained his fear to Chappo, and the youth reluctantly returned. Later, Gatewood learned that his action had made a favorable impression on the hostiles.

The following morning in Lawton's camp, the scout pickets passed in a call for Bay-chen-daysen (Long Nose; that is, Gatewood). The lietutenant came out and met Geronimo and several of his warriors a short distance away. As he approached, they dismounted and unsaddled their ponies, and all but Geronimo, who wore a large pistol in front of his left hip, laid their arms on the saddles. He told Gatewood that they had decided on surrender.

Betzinez, who heard the story from his close relatives in the band, told of this final weakening. It was Perico who said, "I am going to surrender. My wife and children have been captured. I love them, and want to be with them." Then a second and a third of Geronimo's "brothers" expressed similar decisions. One of them, of course, was Fun. The other was Ahnandia, a second cousin of Geronimo by a different line of descent from Mahko. (His wife was Geronimo's messenger, Tah-das-te.)

At these defections "Geronimo stood for a few moments without speaking. At length he said slowly, 'I don't know what to do. I have been depending heavily on you three men. You have been great fighters in battle. If you are going to surrender, there is no use my going without you. I will give up with you.' "[9]

The deadly seriousness of the band was apparent throughout their conferences with Gatewood; they well knew that everything in their lives hung on the issue. And the deliberations of these eighteen wild warriors in a mountain hideout indicate the strength and stability of Apache institutions. There was the democratic manner of reaching decisions, and the influence, but never the despotic power, of their leaders. Every time Geronimo spoke to Gatewood, he expressed a conclusion they had reached in council.

They had worked out the conditions of their surrender before they presented themselves at the army camp. They would travel armed to the United States and surrender to Miles, provided Lawton would accompany them to protect them from Mexican and American troops. Gatewood should remain with them and, when convenient, sleep in their camp. Gatewood consented, Lawton approved the agreement, and the whole band—men, women, and children—moved close to the army camp. Miles was informed of the arrangement, and Skeleton Canyon, the rugged, age-old raiding route between Old Mexico and the Arizona mountains, was chosen as the place of meeting.[10]

The cavalcade then started for the border, the Indians with Gatewood and Wratten traveling independently in front, Lawton's command following. On the third day out a Mexican force of about two hundred infantry appeared from the direction of Fronteras. While the command remained to parley with them, the Indians, with Gatewood, raced on through brush and rocks, protected by flankers and a rear guard under Naiche. After an hour's run, they halted to see if there would be a fight between the Ameri-

[9] Betzinez, *I Fought with Geronimo*, p. 138. Ahnandia was Betzinez' first cousin. The two had been "raised together, just like brothers," according to Betzinez' identification of a photograph in the Fort Sill collection.

[10] Gatewood, *op. cit.*, pp. 8–14. Gatewood always referred to twenty-four warriors. Actually there were only eighteen, the whole band of men, women, and children numbering thirty-eight. Lawton gave the correct number in his report to Miles.

can and Mexican soldiers, in which case the warriors intended to join the Americans.

Soon a courier from Lawton informed them that the Mexican commander demanded a meeting with Geronimo in order to be assured that the Indians indeed intended to surrender. It was arranged that a meeting should take place close to the Indian position far from the Mexican force, with each of the principals to be accompanied by seven armed men. The Mexicans arrived first and were received by the American officers with due formality. Then Geronimo and his party came through the bushes, Geronimo dragging his rifle and with his six-shooter in place. Gatewood introduced the two principals, and they greeted each other. Then the Mexican officer shoved his revolver around to his front. Instantly, Geronimo "drew his half way out of the holster, the whites of his eyes turning red and a most fiendish expression on his face." The Mexican hastily put his hands behind him, and Geronimo dropped his hand to his side.

The Mexican asked Geronimo why he had not surrendered at Fronteras. Geronimo retorted that he did not want to be murdered. The Mexican then asked, "Are you going to surrender to the Americans?" Geronimo answered, "I am, because I can trust them. Whatever happens, they will not murder me or my people."

"Then," said the Mexican, "I will go along and see that you *do* surrender."

"No," retorted Geronimo, "You are going south and I am going north. I'll have nothing to do with you or any of your people." A Mexican soldier was finally permitted to go along with the command, and after the surrender was consummated he took back an official statement from Miles to that effect.[11]

The journey was resumed without further incident. At one time Gatewood and his Indians became separated from Lawton's pack train. That night Perico's wife—the stolen Bi-ya-neta—was preparing "a toothsome repast" of newly killed venison and "flour, sugar, and coffee the thrifty woman had brought with her." Perico,

11 Gatewood, *op. cit.*, pp. 14–15.

288

"with considerable grace and dignity," invited Gatewood and two other officers with him to share the meal. Bi-ya-neta "made everything clean, the edibles were well cooked, and it pleased her to see us eat so heartily."[12]

One of the officers was the surgeon, young Dr. Leonard Wood, who was destined for future fame in Cuba and the Philippines. That evening Geronimo became interested in Wood's gun, a model new to him, and asked to examine it. Wood was a little apprehensive, but he handed it over with some ammunition and explained the mechanism. Geronimo shot it off, barely missing one of his men. He thought that was very funny, saying "good gun" between bursts of laughter.[13]

A day or so later they came to Guadelupe Canyon on the American side of the line. The Indians had killed some of Lawton's troopers in a fight there, and now they were uneasy, fearing the army would seek revenge. As it happened, Lawton was absent most of the day, communicating with Miles, and the trigger-happy officer who was second in command expressed an inclination to attack them and settle the surrender right there. When they learned of this, they mounted their ponies and broke out of the canyon, the women and children at the front. Gatewood caught up with Geronimo and rode along with him, while the troops followed slowly. Geronimo asked the lieutenant what he would do if the soldiers opened fire. Gatewood said that he would ride back to stop them, if possible; otherwise, he would run away with the Indians. Naiche, who had joined them, then said, "You must go with us, for fear some of our men might believe you treacherous and try to kill you." The two leaders proposed that they should all run into the mountains near Fort Bowie and that the Indians would remain there while Gatewood would go down to the post and confer with Miles. Gatewood advised against it; he knew that Miles was not at Fort Bowie, and he was afraid that before he

---

12 *Ibid.*, p. 15.

13 Wood's story of the campaign is included in Miles, *Personal Recollections.* See pp. 513–14 for the account of this incident.

could reach there some army unit would attack the band and drive them back into the Sierra Madre.

They camped a few miles farther on. Lawton joined them, but they spent an uneasy night. Several young officers were suggesting that Geronimo should be murdered. This talk was enough if he should hear of it to put him to flight again, and neither Lawton nor Gatewood wanted to risk what had happened to Crook. Gatewood attempted to leave, saying he had carried out his mission. Lawton, his superior in rank, ordered him to stay, and he stayed.[14]

The glory-seeking Miles was in the worst quandary of all. He ardently wanted credit for Geronimo's "capture," but if the elusive raider should slip away again, he did not want to bear Sheridan's censure. For six days, from August 28 to September 3, messages raced back and forth by courier, heliograph, and telegraph wire, with Lawton desperately entreating the general to come and accept Geronimo's surrender and with Miles stalling and demanding reassurance. On August 31 Miles suggested that Lawton "secure the person of Geronimo and Natchez . . . by any means, and don't fail to hold them beyond the possibility of escape." In a second communication that same day he explained the "means." Lawton could "send for them saying you have a message from me and from the President." Then, having lured them into his camp, he could disarm and hold them, "or you can do whatever you think best." Clearly, this last hinted at murder. A third message that same day was more emphatic: "You will be justified in using *any* measures." As for Miles's meeting the hostiles, "If you have any guarantee or hostages . . . I will go down, but if they are going to put their camp in the hills it might result as other talks have." And he said in his third message, "I am ready to start but not unless I am sure it will do good."

Geronimo then sent his "brother" Perico with George Wratten as interpreter to Fort Bowie to tell Miles that the band indeed wanted to surrender. The general now had his hostage, but even when he learned of this—he was still not at Fort Bowie—he con-

14 Gatewood, *op. cit.*, pp. 15–17.

tinued to express his doubts. Lawton replied on September 2, explaining that the Indians were "alert and watchful, and to surprise them is simply impossible. I could by treachery perhaps kill one or two of them, but it would only make everything much worse than before." Truly, such an act would have set off a bloody vengeance that would have made previous Apache wars seem mild. That day the Apaches again proposed to Gatewood that they make a dash for the vicinity of Fort Bowie and wait there for Miles, but on the same day Miles finally started for Skeleton Canyon after protecting himself by reporting to his superiors that he did not "anticipate any favorable result. They are still in the mountains and not within the control of our forces." Late on the afternoon of September 3 he arrived at the rendezvous.[15]

Geronimo immediately rode down unarmed from his camp high in the rocks to greet him. Dismounted, he approached the general, shook hands with him, "and then stood proudly before the officers," waiting for the conference to start.

"General Miles is your friend," the interpreter began.

"I never saw him, but I have been in need of friends," said Geronimo. "Why has he not been with me?"

When this was interpreted, general laughter broke out among the officers.[16]

Miles was impressed by his wild antagonist. Although he had no scruples against winning Geronimo's confidence through treachery, and tricking and deceiving him, it is apparent that after he had him in his power he respected his strength and regarded him with good will. As the general saw him, "He was one of the brightest, most resolute, determined looking men that I have ever encountered. He had the clearest, sharpest, dark eye I think I have ever seen, unless it was that of General Sherman when he was at the prime of life. . . . Every movement indicated

15 These messages may be found in Odie B. Faulk, *The Geronimo Campaign*, pp. 139–45.

16 Barrett, *Geronimo's Story of His Life*, p. 172. The account comes from W. T. Melton, who was employed at a ranch in the vicinity.

power, energy and determination. In everything he did, he had a purpose."[17]

His purpose now was surrender. Miles stated the terms. The hostiles would be sent to Florida, but he emphasized the part that concerned them most: "Lay down your arms and come with me to Fort Bowie, and in five days you will see your families now in Florida with Chihuahua, and no harm will be done you." He drew a line on the ground, saying, "This represents the ocean." Then, putting a small stone beside the line, he said, "This represents the place where Chihuahua is with his band." He picked up another stone and placed it a distance from the first and said, "This represents you, Geronimo." Next, he placed a third stone, saying, "This represents the Indians at Camp Apache." Then, picking up the last two stones, he placed them with the one representing Chihuahua, with the words, "That is what the President wants to do, get all of you together."[18]

It was probably at that moment that Geronimo turned to Gatewood, smiled, and said in Apache, "Good, you told the truth." He kept close to Miles as if afraid he might be left behind.[19] No doubt he knew that he was surrounded by soldiers and civilians who thirsted for his blood. He told the general of the imaginary plot by Chatto and Mickey Free that had caused him to leave the reservation. For once he found an officer who would listen. Miles not only listened but apparently was convinced.[20]

Meanwhile, Naiche remained out in the hills with most of the band, mourning for his "brother" who had gone back into Mexico to look for a favorite pony and, it was feared, had been killed by the Mexicans. Naiche, of course, had no brother; the missing warrior may have been his brother-in-law, Zhonne, the half-brother of Ha-o-zinne. The next day, at Geronimo's suggestion, he

17 Miles, *Personal Recollections*, pp. 520–21. To most army officers Geronimo's eyes expressed cruelty and low cunning.
18 *Senate Exec. Doc. 117*, 49 Cong., 2 sess., pp. 22, 29.
19 Gatewood, *op. cit.*, p. 17.
20 At least he so reported it. See Secretary of War, *Annual Report*, 1886, p. 173. He may have used it as his justification for making prisoners of Chatto and the other scouts.

and Gatewood went out to talk with Naiche. They explained that the big white chief had arrived and that even in this time of grief it would be discourteous to keep him waiting. Naiche, ever mindful of the amenities, consented, and later Geronimo rode out and brought him in.[21] He impressed Miles as "a tall, slender young warrior, whose dignity and grace of movement would become any prince."[22] The same terms were presented to him, and he also surrendered. It was now late in the afternoon of September 4.

Miles made the ceremony impressive. As Geronimo told it in later years, "We stood between his troopers and my warriors. We placed a large stone on the blanket before us. Our treaty was made by this stone, and it was to last till the stone should crumble to dust; so we made the treaty, and bound each other with an oath." As he said, "We raised our hands to heaven and . . . took an oath not to do any wrong to each other or to scheme against each other." Lawton then built a monument on the spot—of rough stone ten feet across and six feet high. Some cowboys later tore it down and found only a bottle containing a sheet of paper with the names of the officers present. Even so, it lasted longer than the agreement did. But looking back nineteen years, Geronimo could truly say, "I do not believe that I have ever violated that treaty."[23] Few white men ever understood how seriously the Apaches took such pledges.

By the following morning, September 5, all the hostiles had come into the camp. Early that day Miles, accompanied by a military escort, started out with Geronimo, Naiche, and three other leaders in his ambulance for Fort Bowie,[24] leaving the rest of the band for Lawton to bring in. He made the sixty-five-mile journey in one day. On the way, Geronimo looked out towards the familiar Chiricahua Mountains and remarked, "This is the fourth time I have surrendered." "And I think it is the last time," answered Miles.[25] Upon their arrival, the general flashed his exultant mes-

21 *Ibid.*; Gatewood, *op. cit.*, pp. 17–18.
22 *Serving the Republic*, pp. 228–29.
23 Barrett, *op. cit.*, pp. 145–47, 173–74.
24 So said his telegrams. In other places he reported four. Perhaps he included Perico, who was already at the post. But army officers were never able to count Apaches.
25 Miles, *Personal Recollections*, pp. 526–27.

Fort Bowie in 1886. In the extreme rear angle is the commanding officer's quarters, occupied by both Crook and Miles. Courtesy Arizona Pioneers' Historical Society.

sages across the country. He waited until the following day to wire the secretary of the interior: "The indians surrendered as prisoners of war on sept fourth. I returned here last night bringing Geronimo Natchez hereditary Chief and three others Lawton will bring in the remainder tomorrow about forty in all—Indians are perfectly submissive and will do whatever I say—I intend to ship them to Florida in a few days unless otherwise ordered— Geronimo says reason he broke out was that Chatto and micke free had laid plot to kill him That statement is Confirmed by others and not disproved by [illegible]."[26]

At Fort Bowie, Miles continued his friendly reassurance to the leaders, again using graphic figures. Extending one hand horizontally with the open palm towards them he traced the lines with the

[26] National Archives and Records Service, Record Group No. 75, Bureau of Indian Affairs, Letters Received 1881–1907, 27984—1886.

294

finger of the other hand, saying, "This represents the past; it is all covered with ridges and hollows"; then rubbing it with his free palm, he said, "This represents the wiping out of the past, which will be considered smooth and forgotten." Again clearing a piece of ground with the back of his hand, he told them that "everything you have done up to this time will be wiped out like that and forgotten, and you will begin a new life." He held out the prospect of a happy reunion of the whole band: "Leave your horses here, maybe they will be sent to you; you will have a separate reservation with your tribe, with horses and wagons, and no one will harm you."

Questioned about those promises later, Geronimo and Naiche said that they "did not believe Crook because he talked ugly" to them, but that "Miles talked very friendly to us, and that we believed him as we would God." Looking back after nineteen years as a prisoner, Geronimo summed it up: "I looked in vain for General Miles to send me to that land of which he had spoken; I longed in vain for the implements, house, and stock that General Miles had promised me."[27]

Miles, of course, knew that his promises to the Indians would not be kept. He probably hoped that things would work out that way eventually. He had indeed argued with the administration throughout July and August trying to find a home for the displaced tribes, or, failing that, a Western place of detention for them. As late as September 2 he had made a last-ditch attempt to have the reservation Indians sent to Fort Riley and Fort Leavenworth in Kansas, but the following day—the very day when he met Geronimo in Skeleton Canyon—a peremptory order from the War Department directed him to send them to Fort Marion.[28] As for the hostiles with Geronimo, it was the consensus reached at Washington on September 7 that Miles should hold the men as "close prisoners" at some point in Arizona, "subject to such trial and punishment as may be awarded them by the civil authorities of

27 *Senate Exec. Doc. 117*, 49 Cong., 2 sess., pp. 22, 30; Barrett, *Geronimo's Story of His Life*, pp. 144–47, 178.
28 *Senate Exec. Doc. 117*, 49 Cong., 2 sess., p. 36.

the Territories of Arizona and New Mexico. The women and children of his party should go to Fort Marion."

Nothing would have pleased the local authorities more than to get their hands on the hostiles. One can understand their feelings, considering the killings and robbings these raiders had inflicted, but any trial, as Miles pointed out to his superiors, would have been "simply a mockery of justice." To his wife he wrote that the Apaches had "surrendered like brave men to brave men," and "we were in honor bound not to give them up to a mob or the mockery of a justice where they could never have received an impartial trial."[29]

Unaware of all this, the six hostile leaders at Fort Bowie serenely awaited the arrival of the rest of their party. They even did some shopping at the trader's store, purchasing boots and other finery with the ample funds involuntarily furnished by the Mexicans, or, as another story has it, receiving them as a gift from the government by the grace of Miles. In either case, the new garments were worn proudly in contemporary photographs.

Lawton arrived with the rest of the band on the morning of September 8. They had one new member. The evening before they started, a baby girl was born to the young wife of Chappo. Her husband carried the child, but that was the only concession made to the mother; she mounted her horse unaided and traveled with the others. But, as Crook had learned, even surrendered Apaches were hard to hold. During the last night out, three men, three women, and a boy crept from Lawton's camp and escaped.[30] They were reported killed by Mexican forces—in some accounts it was the American army that wiped them out—but like other "deceased" Apaches, they continued to raid. A year later, on October 7, 1887, Britton Davis reported that they had made away with some horses from the Corralitos Ranch. They were joined from time to time by a few outlaws from the San Carlos Reserva-

29 *Ibid.*, pp. 8, 10, 21, 44; letter quoted by Faulk in *The Geronimo Campaign*, p. 170.
30 This is the army's story. But Wood said that in the darkness an officer rode suddenly down on the camp and stampeded the band, and when daylight came, the seven were missing. See Miles, *Personal Recollections*, p. 514.

Geronimo and Naiche at Fort Bowie after their surrender to Miles on September 4, 1886. Notice the new boots and other finery. Courtesy University of Oklahoma Library, Western History Collections.

tion, and their descendants probably still live in some hidden retreat of the Sierra Madre.[31]

But Miles's immediate problem was to spirit the hostiles in his possession out of Arizona and the jurisdiction of its courts before

[31] *Senate Exec. Doc. 117*, 49 Cong., 2 sess., pp. 12, 44; W. T. Melton in Barrett, *Geronimo's Story of His Life*, pp. 173–76; National Archives and Records Service, Consolidated File 1066 AGO 1883, brief from Adjutant General's Office, October 21, 1887; Betzinez, *op. cit.*, p. 145. Miles failed to include the boy in his report of the hostiles' escape, but he was with them.

an order from Washington could stop him. Misleading as his promises to them had been, he had his own way of keeping faith. As soon as the main party arrived, he placed them all in wagons under heavy guard and set out immediately for Bowie Station. When they left the post, the military band broke into "Auld Lang Syne." They wondered why the soldiers laughed. The train left Bowie Station at 2:55 that afternoon. Lawton was in charge of the detail that guarded them. Kayihtah and Martine were sent along with the "other captives" (their official designation from this time on), and George Wratten accompanied them as interpreter. They were to travel by way of El Paso, San Antonio, and New Orleans to Florida.[32]

It would be hard to find a more mendacious summary of a campaign than that which Miles presented in his official report of their surrender: "The hostiles fought until the bulk of their ammunition was exhausted, pursued for more than 2,000 miles over the most rugged and sterile districts of the Rocky and Sierra Madre Mountain regions, beneath the burning heat of midsummer, until, worn down and disheartened, they find no place of safety in our country or Mexico, and finally lay down their arms and sue for mercy from the gallant officers and soldiers, who, despite every hardship and adverse circumstance, have achieved the success their endurance and fortitude so richly deserved."[33]

But regardless of the means by which the result had been achieved, the various bands were on their way to twenty-seven years of captivity.

[32] *Senate Exec. Doc. 117*, 49 Cong., 2 sess., pp. 30, 34; *35*, 51 Cong., 1 sess., p. 36; Miles, *Personal Recollections*, pp. 527–28.
[33] Secretary of War, *Annual Report*, 1886, p. 174.

CHAPTER 16

ALL TRAILS LEAD TO PRISON

As soon as Miles shipped out the band with Geronimo and Naiche, he started north immediately to check on the removal of the reservation Indians. He had been assured by Lieutenant Colonel James F. Wade, then the commander at Fort Apache, that they were "under good control." On September 5 Wade called the unsuspecting Indians on a pretext to the post, where they were surrounded and disarmed. Looking back seventy-three years, Kaywaykla remembered it thus: "Gooday and my mother told me how the army enlisted scouts when Geronimo went out. They had them line up under the flag and had them raise their hands and swear. They explained, 'If you see your own kin out with Geronimo, kill them.' Then after Geronimo surrendered, they lined the scouts up under the same flag and disarmed them. Then they threw them in with Geronimo's bunch."[1] Wade herded the men into one of the buildings and sent the women and children to pack their belongings. Massai tried to stir up the men to revolt, but none of this peaceable band responded. Their situation was in fact hopeless. They were without arms and surrounded by soldiers, while their families were in army hands.

1 Interview, July 29, 1959.

On the morning of September 7, the day before Miles shipped out his surrendered hostiles, Wade loaded the evacuees into wagons and conducted them under close guard to Holbrook, ninety miles north on the railroad. They reached it on September 12. The next morning the loading began. Most of the Indians had never seen a train before. Some of the old men and women even prayed to it as it approached whistling, and the terrified children fled to the brush. The soldiers caught the women and children and threw them on it, and the men followed. It pulled out at noon on September 13.[2] Miles, who was then at Albuquerque, reported that the ten carloads of Indians passed that place at 2:30 the following morning.[3]

At the front and rear of the train were cars for the military escort. Wade was in charge of the eight officers and eighty-four enlisted men.[4] On the platforms between each two carloads of prisoners, four of the soldiers stood on constant guard. One of the officers, a man who regarded Indians with disdain, in later years described the conditions within the cars. The heat was intense as they crossed the arid reaches of the Southwest, and all the doors and windows were fastened shut. Once he had to pass through the whole train, and "When I think of that trip, even at this time, I get seasick." It was "not possible for any human being, other than an Indian," to endure the stench. It never occurred to him that the army, not the Indians, was responsible for this state. The Apaches were a clean-living people, accustomed to breathing pure mountain air, bathing in clear streams, and frequently changing their campsites. It is possible that the tubercular infection that was to decimate them during their captivity began on this journey. If there was any source of contamination on the train, all were exposed.[5]

The Apaches fully expected to be killed, and the soldiers in-

[2] Senate Exec. Doc. 117, 49 Cong., 2 sess., pp. 15–16; Betzinez, I Fought with Geronimo, p. 141; Opler, "A Chiricahua Apache's Account," pp. 381–82. Opler's informant, Sam Kenoi, was about ten years old at the time.

[3] Senate Exec. Doc. 83, 51 Cong., 1 sess., p. 28.

[4] National Archives and Records Service, Consolidated File 1066 AGO 1883 (hereafter cited as Consolidated File), telegram by Loomis L. Langdon, September 20, 1886.

[5] His account is quoted by Faulk in Geronimo Campaign, pp. 164–65.

creased their terror by that significant motion of the hand across the throat. Massai decided to escape. He patiently worked the fastenings loose on a window, and as the train was pulling slowly up a grade before reaching Saint Louis, he dropped out and rolled into the brush. "He was just an average Apache," said Betzinez, using average Apache skills. He traveled undetected through an unfamiliar land of closely settled farms and towns, finding food along the way, and finally reached his mountains. Because his family had remained on the train, he slipped down and stole a Mescalero woman for a wife. He lived many years as an outlaw, stealing out occasionally from his remote hideout to take cattle or waylay a lone traveler. Finally, he was killed, and his widow took the children and returned to the Mescaleros, but the story of the "Broncho Apache" passed into Western legend.[6]

The rest of the prisoners arrived at Fort Marion on September 20. They numbered 381—278 adults and 103 children. Chatto's delegation of ten men and three women were brought there the same day.[7] But the hostile band of Geronimo and Naiche did not join them. As soon as it was learned that Miles had shipped them out, all his superiors jumped on him through channels from Washington on down. Why had he acted "in *direct contravention*" of Sheridan's order of September 7 *"to hold them in close confinement at Fort Bowie"* until the president should decide on their disposition? He answered that they were already gone before it reached him. But why the hurry to ship them without authority? His answer was that he *was* carrying out orders received from March 30 on—to place them "beyond the reach of escape." There was no such safe place in Arizona; hence, he had sent them to a more secure place of confinement.[8]

On September 10 the War Department ordered Brigadier Gen-

---

6 Betzinez, *op. cit.*, pp. 144–45. Betzinez was in the same car with Massai at the time he slipped from the train, and in 1911 he talked with his widow at Mescalero. The story of his escape and a somewhat idealized account of the family life has been told by his daughter, Alberta Begay, in "Massai—Broncho Apache," *True West*, Vol. VI, No. 6 (July–August, 1959).

7 *Senate Exec. Doc. 117*, 49 Cong., 2 sess., p. 75.

8 *Ibid.*, pp. 7–13, 16, 30–32.

Geronimo waiting at San Antonio while Washington was debating his fate. His expression shows the strain of this uncertainty. He fully expected to be killed. Courtesy University of Oklahoma Library, Western History Collections.

Other prisoners waiting at San Antonio. From left: Bi-ya-neta, Ha-o-zinne, Fun, Naiche, and Nah-bay. Courtesy National Anthropological Archives, Smithsonian Institution.

eral D. S. Stanley, commanding the Department of Texas, at San Antonio, to stop the train, take charge of the prisoners, and hold them until he received further orders. The train arrived the same day, and they were accordingly taken off and held there under strict guard.[9] But it soon began to dawn on Washington that the hostiles, "instead of being captured, surrendered, and that the surrender, instead of being unconditional, was, contrary to expectations here, accompanied with conditions and promises." Now the question filled many more telegrams: What terms had been given them? Miles evaded a direct answer, and Stanley was directed to ask the prisoners. By then it was September 29.

Stanley questioned Geronimo and Naiche separately in the

[9] *Ibid.*, pp. 13–14.

presence of the post commander. They told him a consistent story, it was confirmed by George Wratten, and he was convinced of its accuracy. They said they had never thought of surrender until Gatewood and the two scouts came to them. They told of Miles's graphic presentations, moving the stones together and sweeping away the past; of his assurance that within five days they would see their families; and of his promise of a reservation.[10]

Stanley was then (on October 11) directed to give statistical data regarding the individual prisoners and to report on their character and conduct. He complied with a census that fixes definitely—against confused Apache memories[11]—the personnel of this last-ditch band of hostiles. The list follows:

Geronimo, about forty-seven, and wife, about thirty-five; [Geronimo was much older than that, but the estimate indicates his sturdy good health. The wife was She-gha. Zi-yeh, captured the year before by Wirt Davis' scouts, was now in Florida. Ih-tedda, sent back with Maus to Fort Bowie by Geronimo, was also in Florida.]

Natchez [Naiche], about thirty-five, and wife, about seventeen; [This wife was Ha-o-zinne.]

Perico, first cousin of Geronimo, about thirty-seven, and wife, about twenty-eight; [Perico was Geronimo's second cousin, usually designated as his brother or half-brother. His wife was the stolen Bi-ya-neta.]

Fun, first cousin of Geronimo, about twenty, and wife, about nineteen; [Fun, a half-brother of Perico, was Geronimo's second cousin, often designated as his brother.]

Ahwandia [Ahnandia], about twenty-six, and wife, about twenty-one; [Ahnandia was also a second cousin of Geronimo and

10 *Ibid.*, pp. 17–22, 29–30.
11 It is a revealing experience to read the lists of names furnished by conscientious old-time Apaches—Daklugie, Kaywaykla, Kanseah, Betzinez, and Charlie Smith—to Eve Ball and Gillett Griswold. Every one of these lists contains errors. Too many years had passed.

a first cousin of Betzinez. He too, was often called a brother of Geronimo. His wife was Tah-das-te, who is said to have served sometimes as Geronimo's messenger.]

Napi [Nah-bay or Nahba], about forty-five, and wife, about thirty-five; [Nothing further is known about this couple. Their two-year-old daughter was with them.]

Yahnozha, about thirty-two, and wife, about twenty; [Yahnozha was Geronimo's brother-in-law, probably the brother of She-gha. He was closely related to Naiche.]

Fishnolthtonz [Tissnolthtos or Tisnolthtos; the printer misread the initial letter *T*], about twenty-two, and wife, about fourteen; [A daughter born years later at Fort Sill married Charlie Smith and is still living.]

Bishi [Beshe], about forty, and wife, about thirty-five; [The wife was named U-go-hun. The two were the parents of Naiche's wife, Ha-o-zinne. Beshe was probably older than this estimate, for later at Fort Sill he was one of the oldest members of the band. He was known as "Old Man Beshe."]

Chapo [Chappo], about twenty-two, and wife, about sixteen; [The name of Chappo's wife was Nohchlon.]

Lazaiyah [La-zi-yah], brother of Napi, about forty-six, and wife, about thirty-seven; [Nothing further is known about this couple.]

Motsos [Moh-tsos], about thirty-five, unmarried; [His wife and children were in Florida.]

Kilthdigai, about thirty-five, unmarried; [Nothing further is known about this warrior. He may have been called by another name.]

Zhonne, about twenty, unmarried; [Zhonne was the son of U-go-hun, thus a half-brother of Naiche's wife, Ha-o-zinne.]

Lonah [Hunlona], about nineteen, unmarried. [Hunlona was a nephew of Beshe, hence a cousin of Ha-o-zinne.]

Children: Three boys, Skayocarne, twelve years; Gardiltha [Garditha], ten years; Estchinaeintonyah, seven years; and three girls, Leosanni, six years, parents in San Augustine; Napi's infant, two years; Chapo's baby, one month. Chapo is Geronimo's son.[12]

〜〜〜〜〜〜〜〜〜〜〜〜〜〜〜〜〜〜

The boy listed as Skayocarne must have been Kanseah, who was unquestionably in the group. Kanseah was about fifteen years old, but undersized even by Apache standards, and white men regularly underestimated the age of the small, nimble Apache children. The child given the name of Estchinaeintonyah may have been Charlie Smith, who always asserted that he and his mother and her abductor were there. If his memory is correct, his mother and stepfather must have been one of the less well known couples. The boy, Garditha, was an orphan, according to Betzinez. He was a brother or a cousin of Leosanni, certainly the latter if she had parents at Saint Augustine. (There is no indication as to how this little girl became separated from her parents.)

This description of the band members is supplemented by a photograph showing them resting on the railway embankment outside the train at a stop on the way to San Antonio. The picture shows all but one of the warriors, the two boys Kanseah and Garditha, and four of the women. Unfortunately, not all of them have been accurately identified. Eve Ball and Gillett Griswold have made an earnest attempt to fix their names, and aged Apaches with fading memories and failing eyesight have cooperated, but all of them have located persons in the picture who were not present. Even so, the photograph is a striking representation of that small, valiant band that maintained itself undisturbed against the utmost efforts of a powerful government.

Although Stanley was able to name and describe the members, he was unable to comply with Washington's request for information regarding their character and conduct. "The Indians will not inform on each other," he said, and when he inquired of Wratten,

---

[12] *Senate Exec. Doc. 117,* 49 Cong., 2 sess., pp. 25–26; Griswold, "The Fort Sill Apaches," biographical sketches. There is no possible doubt of the accuracy of Stanley's list. The warriors' names—with some variations in spelling—check exactly with a list made independently by Langdon when they came under his supervision as prisoners in Florida. See Consolidated File, report of Loomis L. Langdon, March 24, 1887.

A rest stop on the way to San Antonio. Identified without question: front row, from left, Fun, Perico, Naiche, Geronimo, Chappo, and the boy Garditha; second row, Jasper Kanseah on the left. Probably correct in second row: Yahnozha next to Jasper Kanseah; fourth from left, Ahnandia; extreme right, Beshe. The women at the back, as identified by Jason Betzinez: from left, Ha-o-zinne, wife of Naiche; Bi-ya-neta, stolen wife of Perico; Nohchlon, wife of Chappo; Tah-das-te, wife of Ahnandia. It is known, however, that Betzinez made some errors in identifying the warriors. Courtesy U.S. Army Artillery and Missile Center Museum.

the interpreter told him that "he knows of the character of a few only, and that their character is good." Their conduct "since they have been here has been excellent," he found (Clum's experience exactly). He then reported on "the two enlisted scouts—Kayehtah, about thirty-eight; Martine, about twenty-seven. Character of both is good. Wives of both in Florida."[13]

Eight days later President Cleveland finally announced his decision regarding the band, and the War and Interior departments expressed their concurrence. There was some sense of obligation to honor Miles's promise that their lives would be spared and that they would be sent to Florida. This precluded turning them over to the civil authorities of the two territories.[14] His other promise—that the tribe would be reunited, with the distant prospect of a reservation—did not count. On October 19 Secretary of War Endicott sent the instructions to Sheridan:

By direction of the President it is ordered that the hostile Apache adult Indians [then followed the names of the warriors] be sent under proper guard to Fort Pickens, Florida, there to be kept in close custody until further orders. These Indians have been guilty of the worst crimes known to the law, committed under circumstances of great atrocity, and the public safety requires that they should be removed far from the scene of their depredations and guarded with the strictest vigilance.

The remainder of the band captured at the same time, consisting of eleven women, six children, and two enlisted scouts, you are to send to Fort Marion, Florida, and place with the other Apache Indians recently conveyed to and now under custody at that post.[15]

The cynical mendacity of the wording here is worth noting. Strictly speaking, Geronimo and the warriors of the band had not been "captured," but induced by false promises to surrender; now to Endicott's bureaucratic mind even the scouts had been "captured at the same time."

When Stanley broke the news to Geronimo and Naiche, they

[13] *Senate Exec. Doc. 117*, 49 Cong., 2 sess., pp. 25–26.
[14] *Ibid.*, p. 18.
[15] *Ibid.*, p. 26.

protested that they had been promised reunion with their absent relatives instead of separation from those in the band. Stanley forwarded their statement up through army channels along with his own conclusion that it was correct. At the same time, Wratten tried to obtain special clemency for Ahnandia; he had known him in reservation days as "a sober and industrious man." He also had a personal reason for his concern. Once while he was carrying out his official duties another Indian had tried to kill him, and Ahnandia had saved his life. Wratten said that Ahnandia had left the reservation only through fear that he himself would be killed, had remained in Mexico, and had refrained from raiding across the border. Now as a prisoner he and his wife had worked together, producing articles for sale. He had bought an elementary reading book and had been "studying English very hard," acquiring some proficiency in reading and writing. He and his wife were "very much attached to each other," and Wratten was confident that they would have a good influence on the Indians at Fort Marion if they were permitted to join them there.[16]

Stanley forwarded the appeal with his endorsement that "so far as the good conduct and industry of the indian [*sic*] and his squaw are concerned," it was "perfectly true to my own knowledge." It worked its way up through channels to Sheridan and the War Department, where it was marked "Disapproved." His endorsement of the statement by Geronimo and Naiche was similarly treated. He had to carry out the order, dividing the prisoners into two groups and placing them in different cars for the journey. The train left on October 22.[17]

The news that the notorious Geronimo and the other warriors were destined for Fort Pickens brought rejoicing to Pensacola promoters.[18] (Apparently their congressman *had* got in some good work.) The prisoners arrived at 2:00 A.M. on October 25.

16 Consolidated File, George M. Wratten to Assistant Adjutant General, Department of Texas, October 20, 1886.

17 *Senate Exec. Doc. 117*, 49 Cong., 2 sess., pp. 28–30; Secretary of War, *Annual Report*, 1886, pp. 13–14.

18 *Pensacolian*, October 23, 1886.

At 8:30 a steamer ran alongside the railroad wharf, and they were loaded aboard for the short trip across the bay to Fort Pickens on Santa Rosa Island. A crowd had gathered to see them. It was noticed that Naiche "seemed much amused" by the staring, pushing onlookers. During the passage "one old brave"—this must have been "Old Man Beshe"—was "delighted" in watching the "dolphins" disporting themselves in front of the boat. The island lay before them, a gleaming stretch of white sand with sparse vegetation growing on its wind-piled drifts. At one end were a few shrubs and scrubby trees, and there stretched a low, rambling structure, its walls of solid brick masonry discolored by time and weather, the old fortification "from which place," opined the local press, "they will never emerge, unless they are taken out feet foremost." It was said that as they were leaving the boat, one of them was heard to remark in a plaintive tone, "Won't see Mexico no more."[19] (The speaker must have Ahnandia, using his conscientiously acquired English.) Meanwhile, the train was carrying their wives and children three hundred miles across the state to Fort Marion, where they arrived the same day.

Mangus and his band were still to be brought in. The army had searched for them in Mexico, but no trace of them had been discovered. Seventy years later, Daklugie told their story. They hid in the foothills with the high sierras close by in case of need. Once they went as far south as the great Canyon de Cobra. They lived largely on deer killed with the bow and arrow to avoid the betrayal of gunfire, but they killed Mexican livestock when necessary. Mangus avoided conflicts with Mexicans, but had some trouble restraining the almost grown boys, his son Frank and Daklugie. After the capture of Dalzhinne and Daklegon, he had only two recognized warriors, an aged Mescalero named Fit-a-hat and a very young man named Goso.

Early in October, while Geronimo and his band were waiting at San Antonio, Mangus started north for New Mexico. Crossing the plain, the two boys, without Mangus' consent, drove off the

19 *Ibid.*, October 30, 1886.

mule herd from the Corralitos Ranch. Davis followed the trail and found they were heading north. He telegraphed Miles, and Miles sent Captain Charles L. Cooper out from Fort Apache to find them. In the mountains east of the post Mangus discovered Cooper's camp and sent Daklugie to make overtures of surrender.[20] It was the capture of the mule herd that had decided him to come in. As he told it in 1894, "I didnt want to do any harm to anybody so I took a bee line for camp apache [sic] but before I reached there—I met some soldiers who took us in."[21]

On October 19, three days before Stanley shipped out Geronimo's band, Cooper arrived at the post with his "captives": Mangus and his two warriors; three women, one of whom was Mangus' wife, the daughter of Victorio; five children, including the two well-grown boys; and the mule herd, which Miles in due course returned to Davis. Cooper also brought a heroic story of pursuit and capture, which found its way into army reports.

The prisoners were started out from the post on October 30 and placed on the train at Holbrook. The aged and feeble Fit-a-hat died while they were passing through New Mexico and was buried at Fort Union. In Colorado Mangus managed to open a window and escape from the train. He was stunned by the fall, so he was easily captured although he was not seriously injured. He and Goso arrived at Fort Pickens on November 6. The women and children were taken on to Fort Marion.[22]

Summing it up, Miles reported that his victorious campaign had closed the Apache wars, ending "the terrible depredations which the Chiricahuas and Warm Springs Indians had for so many generations instigated"; permitted the discharge of over four hundred Indian scouts and the transfer of army units to the departments

20 Eve Ball to Angie Debo, July 13, 1972.
21 Consolidated File, Hugh Lenox Scott's report to M. P. Maus, August 29, 1894.
22 Ibid., O. O. Howard, October 20, 1886, and Loomis L. Langdon, March 24, 1887; Davis, The Truth about Geronimo, pp. 231–32; Senate Exec. Doc. 117, 49 Cong., 2 sess., pp. 75–77; Secretary of War, Annual Report, 1886, pp. 14, 49; 1887, pp. 156, 158. Typical of the army's inability to count Apaches is Miles's manipulation of these figures. Learning that two of the children were "large boys capable of bearing arms," he added them without subtracting them from the "children." Thus he had "2 large boys" and five children.

of California, Texas, and the Platte; and reduced military expenses in Arizona *"more than one million dollars per annum"* [italics his].[23]

The cost to the Apaches would appear in the years ahead.

[23] Secretary of War, *Annual Report*, 1887, p. 158.

CHAPTER 17

THE APACHES SETTLE DOWN AS PRISONERS

Langdon, a humane officer, had done the best he could with Chihuahua's band at Fort Marion. He had been placed in charge there on June 16. Up to that time the prisoners had been camped on the beach. Although the agency of mosquitoes in malarial infection had not yet been discovered, the unhealthfulness of such localities was generally known, and it was also believed that the water there was contaminated. One man had already died of malaria ("remittent fever") complicated by dysentery, and a number of others were infected. But a well was being drilled at Fort Marion, and Langdon was able to move the prisoners there on June 19.[1]

In his first report, on July 4, he recommended the adoption of measures "for the education of the children and the placing of the adults in permanent homes." And even before he had been asked to add the reservation evacuees to his crowded enclosure, he had begun to think of Carlisle. In his communication of August 23, previously referred to, he drew up a careful statement recommending the transfer of all the present captives to that place, where

[1] National Archives and Records Service, Consolidated File 1066 AGO 1883 (hereafter cited as Consolidated File), Langdon's report, July 4, 1886.

313

they could live on the reserve while their children attended school. He pointed out that it was unwholesome to keep these formerly active people in indefinite idleness. The women had some light duties preparing their simple meals and—with the assistance of charitable ladies of the town—making their clothing, but the men had nothing to do beyond policing the place, although they would willingly work if given the opportunity. They had been confined long enough to learn the power of the government, and they were entirely docile. Two sisters of the local Convent of Saint Joseph had been coming in for an hour each day to teach the children, but these youths needed vocational training.

He did not recommend sending them to Carlisle unless the whole party, or at least those with children, should be sent. They were in constant dread of having their children taken from them. Even a present of clothing to a half-clad child excited their mistrust—"it looks to them like preparing them for a journey, a separation from their parents." There would be no problem of guarding the band on the reserve, "if there is a reserve of any size at Carlisle."[2] The fourteen men prisoners under the command of Chihuahua would be sufficient, "as the only object of having a guard is to keep the white people away from the Indians."[3]

When this recommendation worked its way up to Sheridan, Langdon was informed "that the final disposition of these Indians will doubtless be determined by the Interior Department and in the meantime all that is expected of him is to hold them as prisoners of War."[4] The Interior Department gave no consideration to such "final disposition," then or later, but suggestions had already been made for placing the children in an industrial boarding school. When Captain Pratt was consulted, he showed some decent hesitation about taking them without the consent of their parents. He proposed sending young Benito to live with them for a few

2 It comprised only about thirty acres (John J. Slonaker, Research Historian, Carlisle Barracks, to Angie Debo July 9, 1973). Probably all of this area was used by the school. Even so, it offered more space than the enclosing walls of Old Fort Marion.

3 Consolidated File, Langdon's report, August 23, 1886.

4 *Ibid.*, Sheridan's endorsement, September 3.

weeks in order to tell them about conditions and opportunities at the school and overcome their reluctance.[5] (This boy was probably the one known as Lorenzo Benito. Benito's other boy died at Carlisle. Benito himself as a White Mountain Apache was to escape the roundup of the reservation Indians.[6]) As far as is known, Pratt's suggestion was not followed.

Meanwhile, the prisoners were marking time at Fort Marion. By the end of August three of their young children had died. One of these was the four-year-old daughter Geronimo had sent back from the Sierra Madre with Maus. She had been "very feeble" when she came, and the best efforts of Langdon and the post surgeon in furnishing her with milk and other special food as well as medical care failed to restore her health. In general, the group seemed cheerful and contented. This typical conduct of Apache prisoners grew out of their experience as a hunted people. From earliest childhood they had been trained to accept hardships and disappointments without complaint.[7] They were allowed to go out in small parties under the escort of a guard to make purchases in the stores of the town.[8] They developed a brisk traffic in the sale of beadwork and other articles made by the women and bows and arrows fashioned by the men, and it is evident that the people of Saint Augustine were friendly and sympathetic.[9]

On September 20 Langdon was swamped by the arrival of the 381 evacuees from the reservation and the thirteen members of the Washington delegation. He put up tents and packed them into the space as best he could. Young Sam Kenoi remembered the place well:

We arrived . . . at night, moonlight, about ten or eleven o'clock. It's a big place made out of cement and stones. It has a great dungeon under it. . . . There is a big place about fifteen yards wide

5 *Senate Exec. Doc. 73*, 49 Cong., 2 sess., pp. 4–5, 10, 12.
6 Griswold, "The Fort Sill Apaches," s.v. "Benito."
7 See, for example, Ball, *In the Days of Victorio*, pp. 6, 73, 91.
8 Consolidated File, Langdon's reports, August 20, 23, 1886.
9 See, for example, Betzinez, *I Fought with Geronimo*, p. 146.

all around on top, with a cement wall about four feet high so you couldn't fall over. On each corner of that wall is a square, a little tower made out of stone and concrete with windows on each side. It was a lookout tower, I believe. On that run-around they had been setting up army tents thick. We were up there on a cement floor, and we had no privilege to move our tents. We had to stay right there.

And they had a big gate down there where they brought us in, and it was guarded by soldiers. The Indians were not allowed to leave that gate without permission. . . . Wood was given, a little, and a place to cook was provided in one of the dungeons below. We had to sleep on the hard cement floor. It was warm there in Florida. . . . Many died . . . . We were not used to the climate.[10]

〰〰〰〰〰〰〰〰〰〰〰〰〰

Eighteen of them died there before the year was over.[11] But that was only the beginning.

Of the 394 new arrivals, 70 were adult men, 221 were adult women, 41 were children between the estimated ages of five and twelve, and 62 were under age four.[12] Among them were fourteen scouts whose enlistments had not expired. Langdon asked whether they should continue to draw pay or be mustered out. The latter, said Washington. They were mustered out on October 8, becoming prisoners like the others. Of the interpreters who had accompanied the Washington delegation, Sam Bowman and Concepcion were employed for a time at the post; Mickey Free was returned to Arizona.[13]

Langdon's report of October 1 is eloquent of the patient endurance of the prisoners. Although the place was "excessively crowded," the Indian men, as sanitary police, kept it "scrupulously

10 Opler, "A Chiricahua Apache's Account," pp. 384–85. See also Betzinez, *op. cit.,* pp. 145–46.

11 *Senate Exec. Doc. 35,* 51 Cong., 1 sess., p. 37.

12 Consolidated File, Telegram by Langdon, September 20, 1886. I have added to his figures the number in the Washington delegation. Obviously he classed all over twelve as "adults," and the children "under age four" included the four-year-olds.

13 *Ibid.,* Langdon to Adjutant General, September 29, 1886, and endorsements. Washington had a hard time figuring out who these scouts were.

clean." Two bath tubs (provided for 469 persons) were "in constant use." There had been no instance of disturbance or disobedience during their confinement, and all seemed "harmonious in
their relations with each other." There had been seventy-six cases
of illness treated during the previous month, of which sixty were
of "intermittent fever," and one aged woman had died.[14] (Langdon
believed the malaria had been contracted in Arizona, but in this he
was almost certainly mistaken.)

An ominous circumstance barely mentioned in the October 1
report was to contribute to the lowered vitality of the prisoners.
They had been receiving the regular army ration; then, on September 22 a drastic reduction had been made by the War Department
upon the recommendation of the commissary general of subsistence. Langdon protested that the amount was insufficient, but
new regulations issued on December 11 and April 23 were to have
the effect of cutting it further.[15]

For the time, however, the number of prisoners remained constant, for one birth was recorded for the month—a daughter to
Geronimo's wife, Ih-tedda, on September 13. Langdon named the
child Marion,[16] but somehow she acquired the name of Lenna, by
which she would be known throughout her life. Geronimo, still at
San Antonio, was, of course, unaware of this addition to his family.

During that same month of October the Interior Department
formulated plans for educating the youthful prisoners. Carlisle
was selected to receive those between the ages of twelve and
twenty-two, and the possibility of local schooling for the younger
children was being considered. A count indicated twenty-four boys
and fifteen girls in the older group, forty boys and sixteen girls in
the younger.[17] The War Department thereupon rounded up the

14 *Ibid.*, October 1, 1886. This report is also found in *Senate Exec. Doc. 73*, 49 Cong.,
2 sess., p. 8.
15 Consolidated File, Report of Adjutant General R. C. Drum, June 15, 1887; report
of Major William Sinclair, September 30, 1887.
16 Information compiled by the National Park Service, Tallahassee, Florida.
17 Probably the imbalance in numbers between girls and boys was due to the girls'
early marriages, and the officers may have underestimated the age of the boys they
placed in the younger group.

317

older youths for delivery to Carlisle. The selections were made by Lieutenant Stephen C. Mills, who had been placed in direct charge of the prisoners, and the post surgeon examined the youths for physical fitness. Mills later said that the separation of these children from their families was the most disagreeable task he had ever performed. The desperate parents tried to hide them, and in one case they succeeded. It was a puzzle how they managed to secrete their children in this crowded place on this and other occasions. Years later it was revealed that the women concealed them—probably the smaller ones—under their long full skirts.[18]

They would have been still more unwilling to part with them if they had known that Carlisle was a death trap, an even more deadly center of tubercular infection than the crowded camp at Fort Marion. Pratt had founded the school in 1879 with young South Plains Indians who had completed their sentences at Fort Marion as its first students; and it is known that some of them were infected with tuberculosis when they came.[19] The school was, of course, well administered, and sanitary principles as understood at the time were observed. The infection probably was spread in the dormitories and classrooms. Certainly it was rampant there before the arrival of the Apache prisoners.[20]

Four of the youths at Fort Marion were not well enough to go with the first contingent. The others reached the school on November 4. The boys' hair was shorn, and all were dressed in conventional clothing. They received the given names by which they have been subsequently known. Among them was Jasper Kanseah, separated less than two weeks before from his Uncle Geronimo at San Antonio. Enough adventure had already been packed into his short life to fill several biographies. Then, two days later, on November 6, the children of Mangus' band arrived

18 Consolidated File, Eli D. Hoyle, Post Adjutant, October 26, 1886; Stephen C. Mills, October 29, 1886; and R. B. Ayres, November 2, 1886. David Michael Goodman, "Apaches as Prisoners of War, 1886–1894," Ph.D. diss., Texas Christian University, 1968, p. 135 and note 113, citing Bourke's diary; Benedict Jozhe interview, September 16, 1969.

19 Karen Douglas Peterson, *Plains Indian Art from Fort Marion*, pp. 102, 258.

20 Consolidated File, Report of John J. Cochran, July 1, 1889.

at Fort Marion. They, with the ones who had missed the first enrollment, required a second shipment, which reached the school on December 8. Among them were Asa Daklugie, Ramona Chihuahua, and Dorothy Naiche. The total number at Carlisle was now forty-four.[21]

On January 1 the Indian Office made a contract with the Bureau of Catholic Indian Missions for the schooling of the younger children at Saint Joseph's Convent. For Sam Kenoi it was not a happy experience: "In the morning they strung out those poor children, and without trying to dress them up . . . they sent them to the Catholic school in the city. They wore their loin cloths, wore rags around their heads, and were bare-legged. . . . [They] were turned in as prisoners every evening." Probably he remembered being subjected to some ridicule by the other children. James Kaywaykla took an opposite view: the "Catholic Sisters undertook to teach the children a little English, and provided baths, clothing, and sometimes medicine. . . . I will never forget the kindness of those good women, nor the respect in which we held them. For the first time in my life I saw the interior of a church and dimly sensed that the White Eyes, too, worshipped Ussen."[22]

James Kaywaykla's experience at the day school was brief, for he was taken to Carlisle in the next roundup, which occurred in April, 1887. Captain Pratt came down, bringing along an Apache student to persuade his young relatives to enroll. They were unconvinced; Pratt was forced to have them lined up so he could make his selections. Benedict Jozhe, the long-time chairman of the Fort Sill Apaches, relates the capture of his mother, a granddaughter of Loco. She was playing on the beach and had taken off one of her shoes. The soldiers snatched her up so quickly that she was unable to retrieve it, and she traveled to Carlisle with one bare foot.

[21] *Senate Exec. Doc. 73*, 49 Cong., 2 sess., pp. 2, 11–16; U.S. Army Artillery and Missile Center Museum, "Names &c. of Chiricahua Indian Children at Carlisle Indian School."

[22] *Senate Exec. Doc. 73*, 49 Cong., 2 sess., pp. 2–3; Opler, "A Chiricahua Apache's Account," p. 384; Ball, *op. cit.,* pp. 196–97.

Apache students at Carlisle Indian School about 1887. Back row: fourth from left, Asa Daklugie; fifth from left, Jason Betzinez; in front of Asa and Jason, Ramona Chihuahua, whom Asa afterward married; in front and slightly right of Ramona, Viola Massai, afterward married to Eugene Chihuahua; small boy in front of Viola, James Kaywaykla. *The boys' hair was shorn and all were dressed in conventional clothing.* Courtesy Mrs. Eve Ball.

Pratt selected sixty-two students from the lineup: thirty-two children, five older girls, twelve married couples, and twenty-seven-year-old Betzinez. Among them were Benedict Jozhe's father, also named Benedict Jozhe, who was the youngest brother of Fun; fifteen-year-old Charles Istee, the only surviving son of Victorio; another young brother of Fun named Burdett Tsisnah, with his wife, Lucy; and Talbot Gooday, grandson of Mangas Coloradas and Loco, with his wife, whose name is not remembered.[23]

Thus, Langdon's hopes for the education of the Apache youths at Carlisle were realized, though not in the way he had recommended. He did not see their painful separation from their parents. Sometime in October, before the first group was selected, he was

[23] Consolidated File, telegram from Romeyn B. Ayres to Adjutant General, April 26, [1887]; Betzinez, *op. cit.*, pp. 149, 151–53; Benedict Jozhe interview, September 16, 1969; Griswold, *op. cit.*, individual biographies.

320

Fort Pickens, Florida, the entrance to the two casemates in which the warriors were quartered. Author's collection.

transferred to Pensacola to command Fort Barrancas on the mainland and Fort Pickens, which was regarded as its subpost, on the island. He was there when Geronimo and Naiche and their thirteen warriors arrived on October 25. Less than two weeks later, Mangus was brought there with Goso.

Fort Pickens had not been occupied since the Civil War. Not only the parade ground and ditch but also the masonry itself was overgrown with weeds, grass, and good-sized trees. A pine tree was even growing out of one of the chimneys. Langdon put the prisoners to work for six hours a day, five days a week, clearing up the place under the immediate command of an officer and the interpreter, George Wratten. On Saturdays and Sundays they were free, except that they were required to attend to the washing and mending of their clothing on Saturday. Two of the casemates were made habitable to become their quarters. In these rather spacious

The leaders at Fort Pickens. From left: Geronimo, Naiche, and Mangus. The first two were painted for the occasion. Courtesy University of Oklahoma Library, Western History Collections.

rooms they ate and slept and spent their leisure hours. In each of them one prisoner was detailed as cook, and the food was prepared at the open fireplace. (It is easy now to identify their living quarters, for only two of the casemates show fireplaces.) Their beds were rough bunks, but they had plenty of blankets and bedsacks, which they filled once a month with fresh straw. They were amply supplied with clothing of the kind worn by enlisted men on fatigue duty.[24]

Two weeks after their arrival, a local newspaper reporter with a party was permitted to visit them, and he recorded his impressions of different individuals. "Of all the Indians at the Fort," he wrote, "Geronimo and Lona [the youthful Hunlona] have the most cruel countenances. Geronimo's face is expressive of inteligence, but he has the coldest eye we have ever beheld in the face of a human being. Natchez is very tall and straight with an air of superiority

[24] Consolidated File, Langdon's reports, January 7, June 28, and August 9, 1887.

about him," as though upholding "the dignity of his chieftainship. He was very reticent, not deigning to notice in any way the presence of visitors. . . . Mangus, strange to say, has rather a pleasant face, in fact he is the mildest mannered man that ever burnt a cabin or cut a throat. . . . Geronimo is not a chief, being the Big Medicine Man or rather the brains of the tribe, and is obeyed implicitly by the others. He is a great beggar and will ask for anything that strikes his fancy."[25]

Langdon found the prisoners to be "neat and orderly in person, rooms and cooking." The officer in direct charge of them reported that "not once has the least sign of discontent or insubordination been shown. They perform all that is required of them with cheerfulness, alacrity and intelligence." They remained in excellent health, a condition Langdon attributed to their work in the open. In his opinion they "really suffered at first owing to the smallness of the ration. The only one who complained, however, was Geronimo, (the medicine man) and for this he was rebuked by Natchez the chief. The latter is a very manly fellow and exercises a good influence over the others." But although Sheridan had been insensitive to the feelings of the Apaches, starving them was something else. He issued an order, and by the time of Langdon's report of January 7 they were being adequately supplied with food.[26] (Apparently nobody became concerned about the hungry Indians at Fort Marion.)

In this and subsequent reports Langdon urged that the prisoners' wives and children be sent to them. The place was healthful and there were ample accommodations. He knew they longed for their families, but he was unaware of the undercurrent of desperation beneath their outward cheerfulness. In any characterization of them he always designated Geronimo as the "medicine man" of the band. One can glimpse here the constant, fervent appeals to the Power that had apparently failed him and his people.

Meanwhile, the public was becoming aware that something was

25 *Pensacolian*, November 13, 1886.
26 Consolidated File, Langdon's reports January 7, June 28, and August 9, 1887.

wrong with the government's whole policy of dealing with the prisoners. Langdon had done his best for them without result, but now disturbing reports from public-spirited citizens reached the Indian Rights Association of Philadelphia, and Herbert Welsh, its executive secretary, took up their cause in earnest. Other Indian interest organizations were enlisted, and General Crook and Captain Bourke told of the indiscriminate punishment of Apaches who had not joined the hostiles. To Bourke, Geronimo was "a depraved rascal whose neck I should like to stretch," but there was "a marked difference" between his case and that of the scouts who had brought about his surrender.[27] Bourke and Welsh finally pressured the War Department into granting them permission to visit Fort Marion. They made their inspection early in March, 1887.

Sheridan also ordered an investigation that month. On March 16 he wrote to Colonel Romeyn B. Ayres, then in charge at Fort Marion, to learn how many of the men had served as scouts. Ayres reported "that of the eighty-two adult male Indians, confined in Fort Marion, Sixty-five, Served the Government as scouts during the whole or a portion of the time that Geronimo was out, viz. from the Spring of 1885, until the fall of 1886." And of the remaining seventeen he named four subchiefs, too old to be enlisted, who had been influential in keeping their people quiet on the reservation. Of the 365 women and children confined in the fort, 284, as nearly as he could ascertain, "make up the families of the scouts and the four friendly indians [*sic*] mentioned above." His last sentence is of sinister significance: "Care has been taken, in collecting these points, that they be not public."[28]

But the army could not conceal everything. Welsh published his report in April, and it created a sensation. There were also newspaper articles and speeches, and letters from prominent people to government officials. It finally began to dawn on President Cleve-

---

27 *Senate Exec. Doc. 35*, 51 Cong., 1 sess., pp. 52–53.
28 Consolidated File, March 25, 1887. This would leave only thirteen hostile warriors, and it is known that there were fifteen in Chihuahua's band. But at least one and perhaps others had died by the time Ayres made the investigation. In any case, the discrepancy is small.

land that peaceable Indians were being punished, that all were living under subhuman conditions at Fort Marion, and that even the holdout hostiles at Fort Pickens had been separated from their families in violation of the conditions of their surrender. He had been exasperated at the breakouts and raids with the robbings and killings and the extensive military campaigns, and he had been told on good authority that the whole body of related tribes was involved. Now he began to learn the facts. And even Secretary of War Endicott began to wilt before an outraged public opinion.[29] This agitation was to continue throughout the weary years that followed.

Although the public outcry did not bring immediate deliverance to the captives, it did bring some amelioration of their situation. During March the War Department considered transferring the entire band at Fort Marion to Fort Pickens. An inspector reported favorably on March 11, and when his recommendation was submitted to Ayres and Langdon they both approved. They contrasted the crowded conditions, the enforced idleness, and the proximity to the town at Fort Marion with the healthful situation and greater space on an almost uninhabited island at Fort Pickens.

Incidentally, the comments of these two officers reveal the extent to which the captives had justified the hopes of the tourist promoters. The sight of these wild people caged was a sensational experience. On their way east every time their trains stopped, staring crowds awaited them, pushing and shoving for the best views, while the escorting troopers formed a cordon around them; and San Antonio had held a Roman holiday, with hawkers selling photographs and souvenirs, while Geronimo's band was detained there.[30] Now at Saint Augustine Ayers complained that they had no opportunity for normal exercise outside the walls; when they were taken out, they were "swarmed about by the curious and idle, making annoying comments, . . . disinclining them often to fresh air and exercise." Even more significant was a suggestion from Langdon at

29 Goodman has told the whole story in "Apaches as Prisoners of War," pp. 84–111.
30 *Ibid.*, pp. 7, 51, 58, 64–65.

Fort Pickens that if it should be decided to remove them from Fort Marion "it would be well to keep [the intention] as secret as possible, because all the railroad interests of Eastern Florida and the influential men of that region will make the most strenuous endeavors to prevent it by beseiging the War Dept. with petitions and remonstrances against the change which will divert a great deal of travel from that country and cause a loss to the railroads and hotels in that side of the state."[31] At the same time, visitors were flocking to Fort Pickens. Langdon began admitting them early in February. He required them to apply to him at Fort Barrancas for a pass so that he might judge their reliability. By the end of March they were coming in great numbers—rarely fewer than 20 a day, on one day reaching 457 (this must have been a planned excursion), and numbering 40 on the day he wrote.[32]

The War Department decided to remove the prisoners from Fort Marion, but chose to bring only the families of the Fort Pickens prisoners to join them there while sending the main body on to Mount Vernon Barracks, a military post in Alabama on the west side of the Mobile River about thirty miles north of the city of Mobile. On April 19 Langdon was notified by telegram to prepare for his contingent.[33] The train passed through Pensacola on April 27, and the families of the Fort Pickens prisoners were removed and taken by launch to the island. They numbered twenty women and eleven children.[34] The families of two or three of the men chose to go on with the main body. It is safe to assume, however, that Geronimo's three wives and their children were among those who joined their men. Geronimo was thus reunited with his little son Fenton, captured with his mother Zi-yeh in the Sierra Madre almost two years before, and for the first time he saw his infant daughter, Lenna. Probably he learned only then of the death of the little girl he had sent back with Maus in anticipation of the

31 Consolidated File, R. Jones, Inspector General, March 11, 1887, with endorsements by Langdon and Ayres.
32 *Ibid.*, Langdon's report, March 24, 1887.
33 His answering telegram is in *ibid.*, April 23, 1887.
34 *Ibid.*, Assistant Adjutant General (signature illegible), April 20, 1887.

surrender he failed to carry out. Chappo's young wife went on to Mount Vernon. Her name appears in a list of the prisoners there in 1887 or early 1888.[35] Probably her baby had died by this time. She herself must have died shortly after. Dohn-say, of course, went to Alabama with her husband, but Geronimo must have received news of her and of other family members and friends in the band. He always showed a surprising ability to keep in touch with relatives and associates from whom he was separated.

One can be sure that Naiche was reunited with his three wives and that Dilth-cley-ih, the daughter of Victorio, also joined her husband, Mangus. Huera came, too, but apparently Mangus did not welcome her. An especially well informed observer who visited the prisoners later referred to her as Mangus' divorced wife, with whom, however, the kindly Mangus did not quarrel although she was "confined within the same precincts." This perceptive visitor found Naiche gentlemanly, though dignified and reticent; he "responds to summons, smiles gravely, shakes hands cordially," ignoring the stares and comments of the curious with studied indifference. He found Mangus "more genial, smiles broadly" in friendly greeting, while "Geronimo steals up unannounced—sly and silent as a mountain lion. Feline is his eye." But he observed that even Geronimo, as well as Naiche, was a good husband and father, and that the affection of the mothers for their children was plainly apparent.[36]

The general public, accustomed to think of Apaches as sub-human, had no conception of what it meant to the Fort Pickens prisoners to be reunited with their families. A letter written the following year by a tourist is revealing: "I had good luck today. . . . Saw Geronimo. . . . He is a terrible old villain, yet he seemed quiet enough today nursing a baby."[37] The baby, of course, was Lenna. Now he could hold her in his arms.

[35] U.S. Army Artillery and Missile Center Museum, Archives.

[36] Richard Wheatley, "The Caged Tigers of Santa Rosa," *Pensacola Historical Society Quarterly*, Vol. II, No. 2 (April, 1966).

[37] B. F. Crary, "Historical Museum Letter," *Pensacola Historical Society Quarterly*, Vol. II, No. 2 (April, 1966).

Langdon settled the families in the dilapidated casemates formerly used as officers' quarters. Thus, each family had a separate apartment. (The men without families were grouped together as before in the company quarters at the opposite end of the structure.) The women performed the household labors while their men worked outside—clearing the ditch of a dense growth of wild indigo, digging and cleaning wells, and clearing a new parade ground and planting it with Bermuda grass. This division of labor accorded with Apache custom, which did not differ materially from that observed in white society; but Langdon, holding the stereotype of Indian women serving as "slaves" doing all the work, while "the men hunt, smoke, and loaf," was amazed that "there has never been a word of remonstrance on the subject."

There had, in fact, been "no occasion to reprimand, much less to punish a single one of these Indians since their arrival here." Their good conduct went beyond an enforced submission. Langdon commended them "for their cheerfulness of demeanor, for their prompt alacrity in obeying orders and for the zeal and interest shown in the duties assigned to them." But upon a return to more normal living with the presence of their wives and children they were emboldened to express hopes for their future. Two or three of them—no doubt Naiche, Geronimo, and perhaps Mangus—went to Wratten and asked him to tell Langdon that "they were very desirous of going into permanent homes on lands they could cultivate as their own."

Langdon was not ready to encourage even such timidly expressed demands. He sent back the stern message "that they had had that chance" once and had "lost it deservedly." Their lives had been "spared by a strong but merciful government and they should be thankful" to be forgotten for a while. Otherwise, "it might be remembered they had not as yet been punished for their crimes." After that warning, as Langdon reported it, "nothing more has been said about farms."[38] So *he* thought! They got Wratten to write to General Stanley at San Antonio asking him how much

[38] Consolidated File, Langdon's reports, June 28, August 9, 1887.

longer they would have to stay in prison and when they would get the good land Miles had promised them.[39] It would be twenty-six more weary years before their hopes would be realized. "I am an old man now," said Naiche at Fort Sill, and he still asked for "homes to ourselves where we can be to ourselves."[40]

Langdon, of course, was unware of these promises, and it was undeniable that these warriors had raided and killed. He did, however, try to salvage the youngest of them. Very soon he became interested in Goso, whose age he estimated at seventeen, and recommended that he be sent to Carlisle. Afterwards he sought the same opportunity for Chappo. His recorded impressions give the only known characterization of this tragic warrior son of Geronimo. In his first list of prisoners Chappo stood out as "a very intelligent young Indian." More than a year later, in recommending him for Carlisle, the officer gave this description: "Chappo. Age 23. This Indian is unusually intelligent; has learned considerable English and is ambitious to improve his mind and study subjects that will [be] of use to him in the future."[41] No doubt his father concurred. Throughout his later life Geronimo advocated equipping the youth of his band with the white man's techniques.

Sheridan gave his immediate approval to Langdon's first request regarding Goso. And eventually four of the young warriors were selected for educational training, but the red tape was not untangled until after the prisoners were removed from Fort Pickens. And now, with the arrival of their families, Langdon found three of their children who needed schooling. One was a son of Naiche, almost certainly the boy known as Paul. He was eventually sent to Hampton Normal and Agricultural Institute, the famous Virginia school for the training of Negroes, which at that time also accepted Indian students. The others were a brother and a sister (or possibly cousins) of Hunlona, orphans with no other relatives: a fifteen-year-old girl known as Katie and a small boy called Mike.[42]

39 Goodman, *op. cit.*, p. 334.

40 Berlin Basil Chapman, "Notes—Apaches."

41 Consolidated File, Langdon's reports, March 24, 1887, and April 6, 1888.

42 *Ibid.*, Langdon's reports, December 30, 1887, and April 23, 1888; Griswold, *op. cit.*, s.v. "Naiche, Paul."

Langdon soon became disturbed about Katie. An observance celebrated by the band in early June was unquestionably her womanhood ceremony. The Indians had wanted to hold it earlier, but Langdon, cooperating with the local tourist business, set a later date and invited visitors. About three hundred spectators joined the excursion, arriving on two steamers from Pensacola the evening of June 10. They thought they were seeing a Corn Dance designed to keep evil spirits from damaging the crop—a custom foreign to Apache practice—but in spite of his gross misinterpretation the reporting journalist unwittingly gave a clear description of the puberty rites. The party arrived late and missed part of the ceremony. No mention was made of the ritual involving the girl— it is even possible that the Indians managed to carry it out in private —but the Dance of the Mountain Spirits was clearly depicted.

A huge fire was blazing in the center of the parade ground so that even the interior of the extensive old fortress was lighted. A large buffalo robe had been placed on the ground with the skin side up, and Geronimo, Naiche, and about eight other men with switches in their hands formed a circle around it. In front of one of the men was a rude drum. As the spectators waited, they were startled by a strange cry rising in unison from the women inside the fortress—a reverent imitation, if they had known it, of the cry of White Painted Woman when her son, Child of the Water, returned from slaying the monsters of Apache mythology. As the reporter described it, "It was a peculiar cry, commencing very low and rising until it became very shrill, then dying away with a low wailing sound."

This was the signal for the men in the circle to begin "a wild kind of chant" accompanied by rhythmic beating on the hide and drum. Then two masked dancers appeared wearing the ceremonial costumes and pronged headdresses of the Mountain Spirits and performed the rite of "worshiping the fire"—to the undiscerning spectators, "a mimic warfare with the evil spirits." They were accompanied, as always, by a clown, whose actions were designed to create merriment but who at the same time was supposed to be invested with curative Power.

After about two hours the visitors returned to the city, but the Indians continued through the night. To the spectators it had been an entertaining exhibition of savage customs. In actuality, it can be seen as a moving revelation of the Apache spirit. Circumscribed as they were, these prisoners, far from their mountains and facing an unknown future, living in a grim old fortress on a narrow strip of sand with the sea closing them in, were still true to their ancient faith.[43]

As for Katie, she was now eligible for marriage. Although Langdon did not report his making an exhibit of the prisoners, he expressed his concern about her "in the interest of morality." He stated that Ahnandia, "who is living in the fort with his present wife wants to marry Katie—and her people [these would include Hunlona's relatives in Naiche's family] are said to be not averse to the 'marriage' so called." After a year of struggle with official regulations, he succeeded in sending her to Carlisle. She arrived on April 22, 1888, and died a year later—on May 27, 1889.[44]

Eventually, the four young warriors were also sent to Carlisle. Ira Goso, Chappo Geronimo, Eli Hunlona, and Calvin Zhonne entered the school on July 8, 1888. With them was Hunlona's young brother, who was enrolled as Bruce Patterson.[45] He remained there until 1898, when, having developed tuberculosis, he was transferred to the Indian service school at Albuquerque in the hope that the change of climate would benefit him. But he died there after slightly more than a month from a hemorrhage of the

43 *Pensacolian*, June 11, 1887.

44 Consolidated File, Langdon's reports, December 30, 1887, February 18, 1888 (with enclosed letter from Captain Pratt, February 13, 1888), and April 23, 1888; Acting Secretary of War (signature illegible) to Secretary of the Interior, March 8, 1888; and National Archives and Records Service, Record Group No. 75, Bureau of Indian Affairs, Records of the Carlisle Indian Industrial School, student record card of Katie Dionta.

45 U.S. Army and Missile Center Museum, "Names &c. of Chiricahua Indian Children at Carlisle Indian School."

Chappo Geronimo (left) and Jason Betzinez (right). The photograph was taken at Newtown, Pennsylvania, where Jason and possibly Chappo worked on farms between school sessions at Carlisle. Courtesy U.S. Army Artillery and Missile Center Museum.

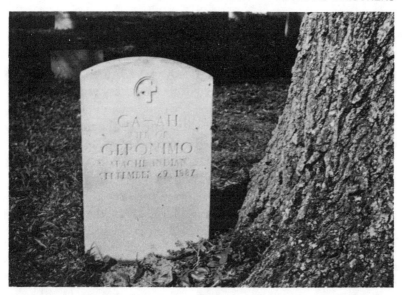

The grave of Geronimo's wife, She-gha, under a tree in Barrancas Military Cemetery. *Geronimo's travels were marked by the graves or the mutilated corpses of the members of his family.* Author's collection.

lungs, at about the age of seventeen.[46] Three of the four young warriors were also to succumb to the tuberculosis that lay in wait for them at Carlisle. Hunlona was to die at the school, Goso was to end his life while working on a Pennsylvania farm during vacation, and Chappo Geronimo was to rejoin his band to die with his family.[47] Five out of six was an unusually high death rate even for Apache youths at Carlisle.

But at Fort Pickens the prisoners, including the children, continued in good health. The post surgeon visited them at least twice a week and found few cases of illness. There was one exception. Geronimo's wife She-gha had been "very ill" when she came, and

[46] National Archives and Records Service, Record Group No. 75, Bureau of Indian Affairs, Letters Received, 1881–1907, No. 42481–1898; and Records of the Carlisle Indian Industrial School, student record card of Bruce Patterson.

[47] Biographical sketches of the four warriors are in Griswold, *op. cit.*, which, however, mistakenly places Goso in Geronimo's band instead of the band of Mangus.

333

she never recovered her health. She died on September 28. Geronimo and a few other Indians were permitted to accompany the body across the strait to Fort Barrancas, where it was buried in the post cemetery. The cause of her death was ascribed in a current news account to Bright's disease, but the cemetery records show it to have been pneumonia. In June a woman who may have been She-gha had been reported as ill with "cold or rheumatism in the chest." It seems probable that she had become infected with tuberculosis at Fort Marion. Hers was the only death that occurred during the entire period at Fort Pickens.[48]

Finally, the War Department decided to remove this party also to Mount Vernon Barracks. On May 13, 1888, they were taken across the bay to Pensacola and placed on the train. They reached their destination on the same day, leaving the train at the railway station in the small town of Mount Vernon, one-half mile from the military post. Thus, they got their first view of the locality that was to become drearily familiar to them in the ensuing years.

The post was built on a ridge in a location considered healthful. Its buildings, constructed in the 1830's, were of brick, and it was enclosed by a massive brick wall. The military reservation of 2,160 acres and the surrounding land were covered with small pine timber growing on sand ridges interspersed with low-lying swales and swamps. The soil was unsuited for agriculture, and the region was sparsely populated, with here and there a log cabin occupied by a poor white or black family supported by working at a sawmill or by gathering turpentine.[49]

The newly arrived prisoners, with Geronimo leading, were taken up the hill to the post. There, in front of one of the gates of the barracks wall, they were grouped, sitting on their baggage awaiting orders and looking down on the village that had been

48 Consolidated File, Langdon's reports March 24 and June 28, 1887, and March 17, 1888; Goodman, *op. cit.*, p. 66, quoting from *Army and Navy Journal*, XXV (October 15, 1887), p. 223. The date on the grave marker, where her name appears as Ga-ah, is September 29, but this apparently indicates the date of burial.

49 *Senate Exec. Doc. 35*, 51 Cong., 1 sess., pp. 38–39, Report by Guy Howard, December 23, 1889; Joseph K. Edgerton, "A Glimpse of the Sunny South," *Plattsburgh Republican*, February 25, 1893.

built to house their compatriots. For some obscure reason these friends and relatives had not come out to meet them. This may have been a formal decision. Sam Kenoi remembered a council in which some members, blaming the holdout band for their own plight, objected to their return.[50] But this tribal division, if it occurred, was soon to disappear.

At the time, Geronimo advanced a few steps and surveyed the encampment. Not a soul was in sight. Finally, a woman emerged from a distant dwelling and came toward him with slow steps and bowed head. It was his daughter Dohn-say. Still following Apache convention, he appeared to be oblivious to her approach. But when she came close, her feelings overcame her. She ran to him, threw her arms around his neck, and burst into wild weeping. Not a muscle of his face relaxed, but his emotion must have been as deep as hers.[51]

Other reunions as keenly felt took place throughout the group. Except for the exiled youths at Carlisle, the band was one. But the years ahead would be bleak.

[50] Eve Ball furnished me notes of her interview with Sam Kenoi.
[51] Walter Reed, "Geronimo and His Warriors in Captivity," *The Illustrated American*, Vol. III (August 16, 1890), p. 232. Reed's knowledge of history and Apache character was faulty, but he gave a careful account of events he witnessed.

CHAPTER 18

LIFE AT MOUNT VERNON
BARRACKS

Mount Vernon Barracks had a small garrison of infantry commanded by Major William Sinclair, who thereby became responsible for the Apache prisoners. When the main body arrived from Fort Marion on April 28, 1887, he marked their lassitude and attributed it to their scanty rations. They had been able to buy some food in Saint Augustine with the money they earned from the sale of souvenirs to tourists, but even so they had been hungry. Now they had lost even that market. A few still had some money they had brought along, and with it they bought cattle and sheep to butcher, but it was soon exhausted.

The post surgeon, J. H. Patzk, put it bluntly. On June 30, reporting on the health of the prisoners, he stated that he had found "a degree of debility perceptible in many of them and probably the cause of some deaths. I consider this condition due to previous hardships, privations and especially insufficient feeding." One man and two women had died since their arrival. Strictly speaking, they had not died from starvation. Two of the deaths had been caused by tuberculosis and one from debility, probably unrecognized tuberculosis.[1] Throughout their imprisonment the medical

[1] National Archives and Records Service, Consolidated File 1066 AGO 1883 (hereafter cited as Consolidated File), Patzk's report, June 30, 1887.

336

officers were baffled by this infection, the causes of which were not understood at the time, but this period of semi-starvation must have contributed to the Indians' susceptibility.

On May 5, only a week after their arrival, Sinclair began a single-handed fight on their behalf against the intrenched power of the War Department.[2] Some sharp exchanges took place between him and his superiors in the months that followed.[3] He was backed up by Dr. Walter Reed, destined for future fame, who came on August 15 as post surgeon.[4] Finally, a report Sinclair wrote on September 30 worked its way up to Sheridan. In it he told how the prisoners were selling or trying to pawn their possessions for food. Sheridan quoted it with this comment: "It is certainly a disgraceful condition of affairs . . . when the prisoners are compelled to part with their private effects; the blankets required to keep them warm, and their crosses and other religious articles [probably given them by the nuns at Saint Augustine] to obtain sufficient to eat." This time the War Department listened and sent out an order on October 27 authorizing the issuance of full army rations.[5]

But the prisoners continued to die. Although Reed, after the manner of army and Indian service personnel, wrote optimistic reports, the improvement he expected did not occur. By the end of the year two men, ten women, and nine children had died out of the 352 prisoners committed to the post eight months before. The causes of death were even more ominous: ten from "consumption," five from "debility from old age . . . most probably affected with latent disease of the lungs," one from pneumonia, and one from tubercular meningitis. There were also "readily observed manifestations of diseases of a scrofulous type," at that time not known to be tubercular in origin.[6] Wherever or however they had picked it up, the disease had fastened itself upon the prisoners. Even the

2 *Ibid.*, Reports of May 5, 21, and 26, 1887.
3 For example, *ibid.*, Report of August 24, 1887, with comments by commissary general of subsistence.
4 *Ibid.*, Reed's reports, August 31 and October 31, 1887.
5 *Ibid.*, Sinclair's report with endorsements by Sheridan and the War Department.
6 *Ibid.*, Report of Walter Reed, December 31, 1887.

The first Apache village at Mount Vernon Barracks. *The site was in a hollow surrounded by thick timber, cutting off the air and sun.* Courtesy Alabama Department of Archives and History, Montgomery.

relatively high birth rate—sixteen during the same eight months—could not take up the slack.

The prisoners were no longer subject to the crowding they had experienced within the ancient walls of the Castillo de San Marcos. At first they lived in army tents just outside the barracks walls.[7] Then in September the men were put to work cutting down trees and constructing log cabins to form a village near the gate of the post. The cabins were completed and occupied as the winter progressed—thirty-five during January, twenty-seven during February, and so on. Additional housing was required when Geronimo and his band arrived from Fort Pickens in May. The work was virtually finished during June.[8]

Each dwelling had two rooms, each ten feet square, with a covered open space between like the settlers' double log cabins

[7] Ibid., Isabel B. Eustis to "Mrs. Hemenway," January 5, 1888.
[8] *Ibid.*, monthly reports by Sinclair.

(exactly suited to Geronimo's family—Zi-yeh and Fenton in one room, Ih-tedda and Lenna in the other). They had earthen floors and no furniture. The Indians slept on the ground or on boards, cooked over open fires, and sat on the ground. The spaces between the logs were chinked with clay, and a Sibley stove and a circular hearth with no chimney provided some heat. The site was in a hollow surrounded by thick timber, cutting off the air and sun.[9] The dwellings were cold and damp in winter, hot and close in summer, probably less conducive to health than the easily moved native wickiups. Still, anything was an improvement over Fort Marion. Reed was able to report a decline in the death rate during the year 1888—only thirteen, of which only four were from "consumption," while during the same period there had been thirteen births. He began to hope that the mortality had been checked by "the healthfulness of the location" and the fact that the prisoners had been "well housed and properly clothed and rationed."[10]

But philanthropic friends of the Indians still worked to improve their unproductive captivity. In December, 1887, the Massachusetts Indian Association, a women's society of Boston, sent two women experienced in teaching Indians at Hampton to investigate and report. As interpreter they brought along fourteen-year-old Parker West, one of the young boys sent to Carlisle from San Carlos by Crook four years before.

They found the Apaches "a keen and intelligent people." Also, "As we went about their camp they seemed to us a kindly gentle folk, and their affection and confidence were not hard to win. . . . An intense love of their children is their most striking characteristic. . . . Our only obstacle came from [their] fear that we had come to take more of their boys and girls from them. . . . The arguments and appeals that were made to us on this account made us glad that this was not our errand. . . . They kept letters and reports from Carlisle which were months old wrapped in pieces of cloth they had embroidered."

9 *Ibid.*, Report July 25, 1892, by Lieutenant W. W. Wotherspoon, then in charge of the prisoners; Goodman, "Apaches as Prisoners of War," pp. 122–24.
10 Consolidated File, Reed's report, December 31, 1888.

339

The visitors believed that the work the men did in building cabins furnished training in industry, and in their judgment the final solution of the Apaches' problem lay in settling the families capable of self-support on farms of their own, preferably in the vicinity of Hampton or Carlisle. They talked with the leading men about their hopes for their future. It was apparent that "Arizona is a country which the Apaches almost worship," but realizing the enmity of the people there, they were reconciled to remaining in the East if some opportunity were offered for themselves and their children. "Only old Nana refused to be reconstructed." When he joined the conference, "the other men waited with reverence while he talked long and eloquently." The young interpreter faltered, then said "with great emphasis 'he wants to know Do you *love* your own HOME?' " One of the women showed him a globe of the world and explained that it was covered with people, so the Indians could no longer roam widely, but they and the white men must live and work together like brothers. "The old chief sat with his head buried in his hands and said with a heavy sigh, . . . 'I'm too old to learn that.' "

In reporting on their visit, the two women pointed out the need of a "missionary teacher" to carry on social and religious work among the prisoners, but they made no attempt to influence government policy regarding the Indians' final settlement.[11] Crook was more aggressive. He went to Washington and presented their case to President Cleveland and Secretary of War Endicott, and he rode over to Hampton and inspected a farm in the area that might serve as a reservation for them until they could be removed to Fort Sill.[12] But no official action was taken, and Cleveland was defeated for reelection that year. This meant a new administration unfamiliar with the situation.

Meanwhile, the Massachusetts Indian Association raised the money and with the permission of the War Department sent two "missionary teachers" to conduct a school for the children.

[11] *Ibid.*, Report of Isabel B. Eustis to "Mrs. Hemenway," January 5, 1888. See also Reed, "Geronimo and His Warriors in Captivity," p. 235.
[12] Goodman, *op. cit.*, pp. 130–32.

The teachers arrived on February 14, 1889. These two or their successors, Sophie and Sylvia Shepard, continued this work as long as the prisoners remained at Mount Vernon. They used a one-room building furnished by the post for the eighty-or-so children until the fall of 1892, when an additional room was added. It is apparent that the children enjoyed the school and loved their teachers.[13]

Geronimo was an enthusiastic supporter of the school. Always practical-minded, he recognized the importance of the white man's skills of learning, just as in earlier days he had replaced the bow and arrow with the gun and had sought to acquire a start in cattle raising. Apparently self-appointed, he brought in the children and spent much time with them, training them with the same strict discipline he had once used in preparing the boys to become warriors, policing the schoolroom with a stick in his hand to intimidate any youngster who might be tempted to misbehave. His interest was noticed by General Howard, now in command of the Division of the Atlantic, who came in April to inspect the prisoners. Remembering the meeting in Cochise's stronghold and the good years following, Geronimo ran and threw his arms around the general and broke into excited Apache. Then he found an interpreter and began to tell him about the school. "We have fine lady teachers," he said. "All the children go to their school. I make them. I want them to be white children." Later the mild-mannered Chihuahua was assigned to work as janitor and to "maintain order," a change that must have been welcomed by the pupils.[14]

Geronimo's son Fenton became old enough to attend the school before the prisoners were removed from Alabama. Also of school age were his granddaughter and probably a grandson, Nina and Joe Dahkeya.[15]

[13] Consolidated File, Report by Sinclair, February 28, 1889; by Wotherspoon, October 13, 1891, July 25 and September 30, 1892, and October 1, 1893.

[14] *Ibid.*, Report of Wotherspoon, July 25, 1892; Norman B. Wood, *Lives of Famous Indian Chiefs*, p. 550; Schmitt, *General George Crook*, p. 293; Howard, *Famous Indian Chiefs I Have Known*, pp. 358, 361–62; Edgerton, "A Glimpse of the Sunny South."

[15] I am estimating the ages of Fenton and Nina by a photograph made in 1895. The age of Joe is not known. He died in 1899. See biographies in Griswold, "The Fort Sill Apaches."

Although he loved his family, Geronimo at that time deprived himself of the companionship of one wife and child. The Mescaleros had been importuning the government to return some of their people who had been caught in the roundup of reservation Indians at Fort Apache, and early in 1889 the War Department consented to send them home. Geronimo saw this as an opportunity to release Ih-tedda, as a member of that tribe, from the hopeless status of the prisoners. According to present Apache memories, she loved her husband and protested against leaving him, but he pointed out that the people were dying around them and that this was the only chance to save her life and Lenna's. Then she consented to go. The party, numbering twelve, left in February. Among them were Charlie Smith and his parents. His father, Askadodilges ("Hides His Foot," that is, "conceals his trail"), also named Charlie Smith, was the leader of the party. Thereafter, on the Mescalero Reservation he was known as "Alabama Charlie."[16]

A son, Robert, was born to Geronimo after Ih-tedda's return to New Mexico probably on August 2.[17] Through a reunion with Lenna fifteen years later, Geronimo received news of the family. As he told the story to Barrett, "So many of our people died that I consented to let one of my wives go to the Mescalero Agency in New Mexico to live. This separation is according to our custom equivalent to what the white people call divorce, and so she married soon after she got to Mescalero. She also kept our two small children, which she had a right to. The children, Lenna and Robbie, are still living at Mescalero, New Mexico."[18]

The sequel was to vindicate Geronimo's judgment in sending Ih-tedda back to their mountains. Her children were the only ones who were to live to perpetuate his family. Before the year 1889 was over, Reed had to admit that his hopes that the prisoners

16 Consolidated File, Reports of Sinclair, August 25, 1887, and February 28, 1889; Eve Ball, interview, July 23, 1971.
17 Robert Geronimo interview, August 7, 1957. He told me this was his birth date, but Apache dates are uncertain.
18 Barrett, *Geronimo's Story of His Life*, p. 178. For Geronimo's meeting with Lenna, see *infra*, pp. 412–14.

"were at last shaking off the disease which has been such a scourge to them" had been "premature and not well founded." On November 18 he reported that during the previous four months three of their wives, "all strong young women when my former report was made," and a girl of thirteen had died of pulmonary consumption and that three men and three women were ill with the same disease, "and within 90 days not one of these will be alive." Once contracted, it had proved "incurable"—"not one case has shown any improvement under treatment." He regarded the mortality as "simply appalling; this too amongst a people who, in Arizona, were remarkably exempt from lung troubles." (In this Dr. Reed was writing from his own experience; he had been stationed at Fort Apache and knew the Indians in their native surroundings.[19]) He could have added that nine of their children had recently been brought from Carlisle to die, the beginning of many such sad homecomings. And a compilation of school statistics made on July 1 that year showed that 27 of their original 112 had died there, 25 from tuberculosis, and that 2 of the remaining 76 were ill with scrofula (one of these last was Ira Goso).[20]

Without taking account of Carlisle, Reed attributed the trouble to the change from the dry air of the prisoners' homeland to "the excessive atmospheric moisture" of the coastal areas. Their transfer to Hampton, he felt, would be "very inadvisable." There had been a suggestion that a tract of land be purchased for them in the North Carolina mountains, where a holdout band of Cherokees had maintained themselves ever since the main body of that tribe had been driven to the Indian Territory half a century before. He was not prepared to say whether the high altitude and the distance from the coast of this region might make it a suitable location, but he was certain "that a dry climate must be the first consideration. I cannot urge this too strongly."

He said that the number of fatalities had caused "anxiety and alarm amongst the Indians." And adding to this "mental depres-

19 Ogle, *Federal Control of the Western Apaches*, p. 194 note 83.
20 Consolidated File, Report of John J. Cochran, July 1, 1889.

sion" was their conviction "that the Government does not propose, in the near future, to improve their condition." He said that Howard had told them during his visit in April that he was authorized by the president to find them a home. Then others, including Captain Bourke, had come to confer with them regarding a location. (They told these visitors that they would need good land, pasture, timber, and a start in livestock, and they especially wanted to go where a river flowed and where it snowed.[21]) These conferences, said Reed, had given them a hope for deliverance, but as the months passed "with nothing accomplished, as far as they can see, this feeling of hopefulness is rapidly subsiding."[22]

Nevertheless, efforts were still being made in their behalf. Later that year General Howard sent his son, Lieutenant Guy Howard, to investigate. The younger Howard reported on December 23 that he had found the camp at Mount Vernon "as good as a prison camp can be, but [it] can not be made a home." He presented the appalling mortality statistics—eighty-nine deaths in the camps and thirty at Carlisle, almost one-fourth of the total population in the three and one-half years since the first party came with Chihuahua in the spring of 1886. The men were put to work regularly, but "their labor is prison labor" without personal incentive. He recommended that Congress be advised to set them up in farming on "a suitable tract of land" by the following spring. "Another year's delay would be criminal."[23]

His report was duly forwarded to Secretary of War Redfield Proctor, who sent Crook on another investigation. Crook inspected the North Carolina tract late that same December and came on to Mount Vernon early in January, 1890. He arrived at the post unannounced and went at once to the home of the commanding officer. There, a young Indian spotted him and spread the news, and soon Chihuahua and Kaahteney appeared, overjoyed to see him. They all started to walk over to the Indian village, and outside the gate of the post they found a crowd wait-

21 Goodman, op. cit., pp. 156–58.
22 Consolidated File, Reed's report, November 18, 1889.
23 Senate Exec. Doc. 35, 51 Cong., 1 sess., pp. 37–39.

344

ing. Chatto came up to shake hands with the general, and with his other hand made an instinctive motion as though to clasp him about the neck, then withdrew it, remembering rank. "It was a touching sight," said Crook's aide. Other Apaches crowded around, delightedly shaking hands with the general, while more came running to join in the greetings.

Soon the general settled down for a council with the headmen. Geronimo, accustomed to leadership, pressed forward to speak, but Crook said to Wratten, "I don't want to hear anything from Geronimo. He is such a liar that I can't believe a word he says."[24] He questioned Naiche, as related in a previous chapter, as to his reasons for breaking away after surrendering to him. Then he asked why this runaway band had finally decided to come in. Their response wrecked Miles's claim that he had conquered them. As was his custom, Crook had every word recorded. The colloquy follows:

General CROOK. How did you come to surrender. Were you afraid of the troops?

NATCHEZ. We wanted to see our people.

General CROOK. Did troops force you to surrender?

NATCHEZ. We were not forced to do it. We talked under a flag of truce.

Wratten then told how the surrender had been accomplished.

"Could the surrender have been made without the scouts?" asked Crook.

"I do not think so," said Wratten.

Members of the group then related their experiences: their observance of the pledge they had made to keep the peace, their losses when they were taken from their small economic ventures on the reservation, their ever-present hope for a viable future.

Chatto took from his breast the medal given him at Washington,

24 Schmitt, *op. cit.*, pp. 292–93.

345

and, holding it out, he said, "Why did they give me that to wear in the guard-house? I thought something good would come to me when they gave me that but I have been in confinement ever since I have had it." He told how he had left everything to make the trip: "I was working on my farm and had one field planted in wheat and another in barley. . . . I had a wagon and could make a good deal of money with that hauling hay, supplies, etc. I didn't leave these of my own accord. I had sheep, about thirty head, that were increasing all the time; I had to leave them. I made money by shearing them and selling the wool; I had horses and mules which were worth a good deal of money. . . . You told us about farms; I got a plow and took good care of everything."

Others told of the property they had been forced to abandon on the reservation. Some of their livestock had been gathered up and sold, and the army, with much paper work, had kept account and doled the money out to them in five-dollar monthly payments,[25] but all had suffered losses. Noche said he had been paid for his horses but not for ninety cords of wood he had piled up for sale. Kaahteney said he had lost his crop and his wagon. Chatto gave figures to show that the payment for the livestock was grossly inadequate. Humble beginnings, but important to them, had been wiped out.

Kaahteney reminded Crook of how he had used his influence to induce the hostiles to surrender at the Cañon de los Embudos— "I talked your talk to them and your mind to them." He went on to say, "I never did anything wrong and never went on the warpath since I saw you. I tried to think as you told me to and was very thankful to you, and was very glad to see you again this morning; all the Indians were, even to the little children." He described his unproductive labor in the prison camp: "I help build roads, dig up roots, build houses, and do work all around here. Leaves fall off the trees and I help to sweep them up. I was working this morning

---

25 These payments were recorded in the reports of the post commanders until the last one was made on May 1, 1890. See, for example, Consolidated File, reports by Sinclair, December 5, 1887, and Major W. L. Kellogg, May 1, 1890.

346

when you came here. I don't know why I work here all the time for nothing. . . . I have children and relatives, lots of them, and I would like to work for them before I get too old to work. I'd like to have a farm . . . long enough to see the crops get ripe."

Chihuahua also said he would like to have a farm "and go right to work so that my children can have plenty to eat. . . . I have a daughter away at school and two other near relatives. I want to see them soon. Won't you make it so I can see them very soon?" And with the smothering pines surrounding him, thinking of the wide vistas of his homeland, he ended his appeal: "There are trees all about. I would like to go where I can see."

In his report Crook asserted that by the "most ordinary justice" those Indians who had served the government should not be held as prisoners: "Their farms have been taken from them, and others should be given to them. I cannot too strongly urge that immediate steps be taken to secure a reservation for them," where they could "work for themselves" and receive "the full benefit of their labors." Their mortality, he thought, was "due to home-sickness, change of climate, and the dreary monotony of empty lives."

He did not recommend sending them back to Arizona. If any trouble should break out so that they would again take the war-path, "it would be utterly impossible ever to get them to surrender again," and the cost in lives and property would be enormous. But he was convinced that no matter where they were placed they would be as law-abiding as any community in the country. He thought the North Carolina region the most suitable of any locality in the eastern United States, but he preferred the Indian Territory as more nearly like their homeland. Finally, he said he considered it a mistake to send their children to Carlisle, "a place which, from whatever cause it may be, proves so fatal to them. . . . Apaches are fond of their children and kinsfolk, and they live in terror lest their children be taken from them and sent to a distant school."

The secretary of war immediately recommended to the president that the prisoners be settled in one of the two suggested locations. Either would be satisfactory, but the Indian Territory seemed the better choice provided Congress could be induced to repeal the prohibition of 1879.[26]

Neither Crook nor Proctor understood the significance of recent events in the Indian Territory. The barrier that had reserved it for Indians had been broken the previous April when a tract in its heartland had been opened to white settlement. The very session of Congress that would be urged to admit the Apaches was creating a Territory of Oklahoma to embrace the new frontier, and plans were rapidly being pushed to break up all the Indian reservations there in preparation for additional land openings.[27] A resolution to put Proctor's Indian Territory plan into effect was introduced in the Senate and hotly debated, but there was never any chance of its passage. Crook, who had been leading the fight, died of a heart attack on March 21, but his death scarcely affected the outcome.[28] The prisoners remained in Alabama.

The War Department then attempted to "improve their condition where they now are located and are likely to remain." In June Lieutenant William W. Wotherspoon was sent to take special charge of them. He initiated plans for converting a mess hall and kitchen into a makeshift hospital. Eventually, the War Department constructed an adequate hospital and staffed it. Wotherspoon managed to use money from savings on the regular rations to buy milk, eggs, and other special foods for the patients.[29]

Even during the first lean days Major Sinclair had been able to hold out and sell some less needed supplies from the rations and buy potatoes and onions, which he hoped would protect the prisoners against scurvy. Then they were put to work clearing land and planting a garden. In spite of the poor soil, this plot produced enough vegetables for their own use and some for sale, besides making more surplus available from the rations. The money thus

26 *Senate Exec. Doc. 35*, 51 Cong., 1 sess., pp. 29–36.

27 The rapidity with which the former Indian Territory was settled and developed by white homesteaders and city builders is a familiar story. Oklahoma had a population of 1,414,177, of which Indians constituted only 5.3 per cent when it was admitted to statehood in 1907.

28 See Schmitt, *op. cit.*, pp. 294–300, for the fight over the measure.

29 Consolidated File, Wotherspoon's reports, November 30, 1890, and February 28 and April 30, 1891.

accumulated became a special fund used for their benefit—the payment of "salaries" of about ten dollars a month to those performing such services as supervising the gardening and washing the hospital linens, and the purchase of such household conveniences as cooking utensils and knives, forks, and spoons, and even prizes and Christmas treats for the school children.[30]

The gardening was done by the women and older men. The able-bodied men worked six days a week about the post or in improving their own village. George Wratten served not only as interpreter but also as superintendent of the labor crew. He married a young Apache girl, and their two daughters, known as Amy and Blossom White, became the mothers of some of the most gifted of present-day Apaches.[31] Geronimo, for some reason, disliked Wratten,[32] but it is apparent that most of the Apaches trusted him, and it is certain that he presented their case effectively to army officers.

Although the prisoners worked industriously at this forced labor, Wotherspoon believed that their final salvation lay in individual incentive. He held the current theory that Indians in general should disappear as Indians and merge into the general population; and applying this to the Apaches, he hoped that it would end their unproductive status as prisoners. Thus he released them from his labor gang and encouraged them to take employment for wages cutting wood or working on farms. By the following February four of them were working on a farm fifteen miles from the post. They were allowed to take their families along and were prospering.[33]

But Secretary Proctor had another plan for distributing Indians throughout the general population. His idea was to enlist them in the army, and he decided to begin with the Apaches, who

[30] The meticulously kept records of these transactions can be traced in all the reports of the officers in charge.

[31] See biographical sketches in Griswold, *op. cit.* Wratten and his Apache wife separated shortly before they left Alabama, and he subsequently married a white woman.

[32] Barrett, *op. cit.,* p. 179.

[33] Consolidated File, Wotherspoon's reports, July 31 and August 31, 1890, and February 28 and March 31, 1891.

349

had certainly demonstrated their qualifications as fighters. This canceled out Wotherspoon's policy of civilian employment. The able-bodied men responded eagerly; forty-six enlisted in May, 1891, leaving only twenty-eight men remaining in the camp. Some of their young men from Carlisle soon joined them. An additional thirty-one young men from various Apache tribes on the San Carlos Reservation also enlisted and were brought from Arizona. (Three of these last contracted tuberculosis immediately, although they had had very little contact with the prisoners in the village.[34]) These Apache soldiers formed Company I of the Twelfth Infantry. They were put to work at once building barracks. They lived under the same conditions as other enlisted men, receiving the same pay, and were subject to the same regulations.

Besides their regular drills they received an hour of instruction in English every day. They wore army uniforms, had their hair cut, and received given names, by which they were known thereafter. Among their noncommissioned officers were Sergeant Burdett Tsisnah and Corporal Larry Fun. Other members of the company were such well-known former hostiles as Naiche, Ahnandia, and Mangus. The company had field work with bridge building, scouting, trailing, and skirmishing (they must have enjoyed this).[35] They also spent much time building houses.

A better site had been selected for a new village on a sand ridge about three-fourths of a mile from the post, and the War Department furnished the building material. The work began early in 1891 while the men were still prisoners and was continued after their enlistment as soldiers. The army employed one or two skilled carpenters to instruct them, and they showed great aptitude and mechanical ability. They built about eighty small, snug houses, painted outside and finished within, floored, and set on adequate foundations, very different from the hovels in which they had

[34] *Ibid.*, Report of Post Surgeon W. C. Borden, July 25, 1892. By this time two had died and the other was near death.

[35] *Ibid.*, Wotherspoon's reports, May 31 and December 5, 1891, with attached summary, and September 2 and November 1, 1892; Report by D[avid] J. Baker, October 31, 1891. See also Edgerton, *op. cit.*, for the impression these Indian soldiers made on an observant visitor.

Geronimo at Mount Vernon Barracks. "Geronimo is the leading character among these people. He is no longer a savage in appearance or
dress." Courtesy U.S. Army Artillery and Missile Center Museum.

351

formerly lived. Each house was furnished with a cooking range and with bedsteads, tables, and chairs made by the men. The women kept their houses neat and showed their pride by adding decorative touches.[36]

Geronimo lived in one of these houses with Zi-yeh, their small son Fenton, and a cherished baby daughter, Eva, born September 23, 1889.[37] An intelligent observer who visited the post in February, 1893, wrote a lively description of him and his family:

Geronimo is the leading character among these people. He is no longer a savage in appearance or dress. I have met him often. He gave me a call a Sunday or two ago, with his wife, quite a young squaw, and their child. All had a holiday look, and the Chief, a man of 60 or more years, instead of compelling his squaw to carry the baby, a clean, good looking one, in the usual papoose cradle or hamper, on her back, was hauling it himself, in a child's little express wagon, and seemed quite proud of his employment. [Eva was three years old at the time.] G. is a large, well formed man, with a good head and strong Apache features, with a keen and crafty look in his eyes, and a certain dignity of bearing, indicating a man of authority and self respect.

The prisoners had complete freedom about the post and the reservation "and are daily met coming and going between their village and the trading stores at Mount Vernon, where they are both sellers and buyers." There was no tourist trade in the area, but passengers arriving on the train furnished a market for their craft articles, some of which this observer characterized as "very handsome and ingenious." Geronimo was very active in this business.[38] The visitor continued:

[36] Consolidated File, Wotherspoon's reports, April 30, June 30, and December 5, 1891, and Baker's report, October 31, 1891.

[37] This date is given in Griswold, *op. cit.*, s.v. "Godeley, Eva Geronimo." It seems to be an exact record rather than an estimate.

[38] See, for example, Howard, *op. cit.*, p. 358.

〰〰〰〰〰〰〰〰〰〰〰〰

Geronimo has an eye to thrift and can drive a sharp bargain with his bows and arrows, and quivers and canes, and other work, in which he is skillful. He prides himself upon his autograph, written thus, G E R O N I M O, which he affixes to what he sells, usually asking an extra price for it. He had a curious head dress, which he called, and Mr. Wratten says was his war bonnet. It is a sort of skull cap of buckskin, profusely and tastefully adorned with beads, and thirteen silver ornaments, representing the sun, moon and stars, and surmounted by a beaded cross, between two horn-like ornaments. . . . He seemed to value this bonnet highly, but finally, in his need or greed for money, offered it for sale for $25—his wife strongly objecting. [Probably her clever hands had fashioned it.] I finally bought it for a much less price, with a large bead necklace, which goes with it. . . . I asked him to write his name in the bonnet, and offered him a pen for the purpose, but he declined the pen, and went out and cut a small, dry twig, which he sharpened to a fine point, and then very slowly, and with much pains-taking, printed his name with the stick dipped in ink. This is the extent of his writing. . . . Adorned with his war bonnet and necklace, the old Chief is a picturesque figure, and has his share of personal vanity.[39]

〰〰〰〰〰〰〰〰〰〰〰〰

Thus, the prisoners tried to achieve a normal life in captivity. All their supervisors reported on their good conduct, their cheerfulness, their industry. But the women *would* gamble, and too many of the men had no resistance to the intoxicants supplied by a low class of whites and blacks just outside the military reservation. They were sober most of the time, but it was a sobriety enforced by the vigilance of the army officers and the prosecution of the bootleggers.[40] Soon after assuming charge, Wotherspoon appointed Geronimo as a "judge" or "justice of the peace" to try minor

[39] Edgerton, *op. cit.*
[40] This is a recurring theme in Wotherspoon's reports. See, for example, Consolidated File, January 31, June 30, and August 31, 1891, and October 1, 1893.

offenses at a monthly "salary" of $10.50 or $10.80 paid from his special fund.[41] Geronimo was very severe at first, sentencing one offender to six months in the guardhouse for getting drunk and imposing one hundred years imprisonment in another, more aggravated, case. But given some instruction and training, he learned to assess more reasonable penalties.[42]

Once Wotherspoon, after the manner of officials in charge of Indians, reported an improvement in their moral condition. He referred, of course, to sexual morality, not realizing that Apaches were more strict in this regard than contemporary white society. He was thinking of their polygamy and their informal divorce practices. Four of them had recently been married according to white customs at their own requests.[43] It is apparent that by the time they left Alabama they had abandoned polygamy except for the marriages already in existence. Geronimo never had but one wife at a time after he sent Ih-tedda back to her people.[44]

There were two cases of marital difficulty during the seven and one-half years the prisoners were kept at Mount Vernon. One that affected the family of Geronimo occurred in March, 1892, when Fun, becoming jealous of his young wife, shot her and killed himself. She, being only slightly wounded, recovered.[45] Two years later, in April, 1894, another man shot his wife and then himself.[46] There were also two cases of drunken quarrels between men that resulted in violent deaths.[47] But generally, the Apaches, in spite of their turbulent past, observed harmonious relations with each other.

Always a religious people in their native culture, they were now coming under the influence of Christianity. During at least part of

41 This expenditure appears in Wotherspoon's reports from October 31, 1891, and was continued through 1894. The "judge" is not named, but it is fairly certain that Geronimo served throughout. See, for example, mention of "the Indian Judge Geronimo" by Wotherspoon's successor, C. C. Ballou, in his report of April 18, 1894.

42 Edgerton, *op. cit.*

43 Consolidated File, Report, February 28, 1891.

44 Barrett, *op. cit.*, p. 179.

45 Consolidated File, Wotherspoon's report, March 31, 1892.

46 *Ibid.*, Report, C. C. Ballou, April 18, 1894.

47 *Ibid.*, Report of Wotherspoon, June 1, 1893; Report of Allyn K. Capron, June 23, 1894.

354

the period, the post chaplain conducted two services for them on Sundays—a Sunday school in the morning for their children and a service for the men and women in the afternoon. Both services were well attended.[48] Also the two women "missionary teachers" must have given the school children religious instruction along with the three R's. And some of the Indians apparently retained the impression made by the Catholic nuns at Saint Augustine. In July, 1890, Geronimo's wife Zi-yeh and the baby Eva were baptized in the Catholic Church at Mount Vernon.[49] This may explain the cross on the old warrior's headdress.

Meanwhile, the school was having a problem unrelated to religious instruction. Some of the children had grown up to the age at which they needed a different type of education. Wotherspoon tried to give the older boys some vocational training by taking them out of school half of each day to work at carpentry, but he recommended sending them to Carlisle or Hampton.[50] The War Department took no action, but the Massachusetts Indian Association raised enough money to support four of the older girls at Hampton.

By this time, Wotherspoon had become an aide to General Howard, and his successor, Lieutenant Charles C. Ballou, encountered the objection of their parents. He warned that if the girls remained at home they would soon marry and produce more children to grow up "in a camp of three or four hundred compulsory paupers." But the post commander hesitated "to sever family ties . . . where no crime is alleged," and the question worked its way up to Howard. Wotherspoon's advice to the general is a classic example of heartless official mendacity. He said it was simply a question whether the Indians' future should "be shaped by those in authority, who look" to their "ultimate good" or "by those old squas and men who have only personal motives and slight affection to guide them. . . . Knowing that it is Indian custom for the

48 *Ibid.*, Report of W[illiam] H. Pearson, December 31, 1891.
49 Goodman, *op. cit.*, p. 196 and note 8. The story was sometimes told that Geronimo himself had been baptized five times, but there is no reason to credit it.
50 Consolidated File, Reports, November 1, 1892, and July 1, 1893.

355

mothers to practically sell their daughters" he could understand their "aim in opposing their education." He had learned "to place little reliance upon Indian family-affection." The War Department agreed, and the girls were sent.[51]

It must be admitted, however, that the Carlisle and Hampton graduates, with a very few exceptions, did not merge into the general population but returned to their people.[52] In this same report Ballou expressed his perplexity regarding the status of three young men recently returned from Carlisle. The acting secretary of war instructed him to tell them that they were "free to live and seek employment wherever they prefer," but they would not be "permitted to remain with the prisoners of their tribe." Since the government had furnished them "ample opportunity to secure an education and learn a trade they must henceforth support themselves." But the order lapsed. At least two of the three remained,[53] and the Carlisle graduates continued to merge with the prisoners.

The officers in charge were also perplexed about the status of the men they had enlisted in the army. Before Wotherspoon left, he reported early in 1894 that the three years' service of most of them would soon expire. Would they revert to the status of prisoners, or would they be free to return to Arizona, leaving their wives and children still in captivity?[54] The War Department decided that they were free, but all but two unattached young men chose to join their prisoner families.[55]

Thus, the War Department was stuck with the prisoners. Its plan

[51] *Ibid.*, Report of Ballou, March 31, 1894, with endorsements; Report of Allyn K. Capron, July 5, 1894. Two years before this, Wotherspoon had written to an Indian interest group, "In his home the Indian is a good and faithful husband, a tender and affectionate father" (quoted by Goodman, *op. cit.*, p. 205). One is tempted to discredit all of Wotherspoon's reports, but they fit into the general pattern, which is in the main trustworthy.

[52] This is evident in the biographies in Griswold, "The Fort Sill Apaches." Although a few worked for a time in the industrial plants of Pennsylvania and New York, nearly all eventually joined the prisoners. For Jason Betzinez' satisfactory experience in a steel mill and his final return, see *I Fought with Geronimo*, pp. 159–61, 164.

[53] See biographies of the three—Knox Nostlin, Oswald Smith, and Leonard Kanesewah—in Griswold, *op. cit.* Not much is recorded here of Knox Nostlin; he probably died in Alabama.

[54] Consolidated File, Report, January 25, 1894.

[55] Griswold, *op. cit.*, s.v. "Jose Second" and "Jim Miller."

to find a home for them in the Indian Territory had been rejected by Congress. Next, its intention of dispersing them through educational training, outside employment, and army service had failed. Attempts to check their mortality by adequate housing and hospital care also failed. True, there was less sickness caused by unsanitary living conditions, but the hoped-for decline in tubercular infection had not occurred. In 1892 Wotherspoon concluded that this disease was due mainly to their "hereditary and physical degeneracy."[56] (The "hereditary and physical degeneracy" of Apaches!) Post Surgeon W. C. Borden was more scientific. His reports show serious consideration of the factors involved, and in the following year he published a comprehensive analysis of the prisoners' health problem based on a sympathetic understanding of their culture and the history of their confinement.[57]

The vital statistics from 1891 on are misleading because the frequent deaths of enlisted men were not included and because forty-six unrelated Apache prisoners from Arizona were added to the village population.[58] But a list of deaths by months from January 1, 1893, through July, 1894, shows a dreary pattern of pulmonary tuberculosis, tubercular meningitis, lupus, and intestinal tuberculosis.[59]

By that time, however, the continued efforts of philanthropic friends of the Indians had once more set the War Department to seeking a different location for the prisoners. This was to result in their removal from Alabama.

[56] Consolidated File, Report, July 25, 1892. His conclusion accords with general medical theory at the time as recorded under "Phthisis" in the ninth edition of the Encyclopedia Britannica. For sanitary regulations and problems, see the report of Surgeon-General C. Sutherland in Secretary of War, *Annual Report*, 1892, pp. 501–504.

[57] Borden, "The Vital Statistics of an Apache Indian Community."

[58] These consisted of the celebrated Eskiminzin and his band. I have told their story briefly in *A History of the Indians of the United States*, pp. 268–71, 281–82.

[59] Consolidated File, Report of Attending Surgeon Charles LeBaron, August 1, 1894.

CHAPTER 19

THE PRISONERS ARE BROUGHT
TO FORT SILL

Late in 1893 the War Department began a second attempt to relocate the prisoners. In December, Wotherspoon, accompanied by Captain Pratt, was sent for another inspection of the North Carolina mountains. He reported that the arable land was insufficient, either in the Cherokee tract or in the area adjoining it. But as he observed the industrious and self-supporting Cherokees he was convinced that a similar opportunity should be provided the prisoners. He thought it unnecessary that the farms furnished them "be contiguous, or, indeed, even in the same vicinity. The more these people are broken up, and the sooner they are thrown into association with the whites, the better."

In his endorsement the post commander, Major George D. Russell, suggested that they be located "even in divided bands if necessary" near prosperous farming or manufacturing communities in New England or the Middle States: "The women and children are naturally deft of hand, and some might make fair factory operatives." General Howard proposed sending them "in small parties, to different western reservations," or posssibly land could be found on some reservation for all of them. General John M. Schofield, Sheridan's successor as commander in chief of the army,

358

suggested one limitation, that they be not sent to Texas, New Mexico, or Arizona.[1]

The War Department worked on Congress, and on August 6 the following year it obtained an amendment to the Army Appropriation Act authorizing their transfer to any military reservation under its control.[2] The War Department then considered a plan to distribute them in various locations throughout the country. It was referred to Miles, then commanding the Department of the Missouri, which embraced the eastern half of the Western posts. Although Miles had been largely responsible for the plight of the prisoners in the first place, he had the grace to oppose this policy emphatically, saying it would be "gross injustice and refined cruelty" to separate these families and friends. He again suggested Fort Sill, now in his department, and ordered Lieutenant Hugh Lenox Scott, who was stationed there, to go with Captain Maus, at that time on his staff, to Alabama to confer with the Apaches.[3]

Before Scott left, word of the contemplated move got out. The Comanches and their Kiowa and Kiowa-Apache allies heard of it and held a council, then came to consult with the lieutenant. They knew and trusted him. He had been associated with Indians in war and peace ever since he went out from West Point to serve in the Seventh Cavalry just after its disastrous defeat under Custer on the Little Bighorn; he had become an expert in the sign language; and with tact and understanding he had contained the ghost dance excitement on the South Plains at the very time an inept handling of the situation in the North had culminated in the massacre at Wounded Knee. Now the Indians told him they had never liked the Apaches, but they consented to let them come if they would remain on the military reservation. Even this consent was a concession granted out of typical Indian sympathy for a homeless people, for the post was built on their land, which would revert to them when

1 National Archives and Records Service, Consolidated File 1066 AGO 1883 (hereafter cited as Consolidated File), Wotherspoon's report, December 14, 1893, and endorsements.

2 U.S., *Statutes*, XXVIII, 238.

3 Consolidated File, Miles to Major George W. Davis, Office of the Secretary of War, September 3, 1894.

it should be abandoned.[4] (Its permanent development as an artillery and missile center was not then envisioned.)

Maus and Scott held their conference with the chiefs and leaders of the prisoners on August 29. Second Lieutenant Allyn K. Capron, who was then in charge of them, was present, and Wratten served as interpreter. Scott recorded the proceedings. The Apaches were questioned "concerning their wishes to be removed to some other locality." Geronimo gave their answer. His unadorned statement—Geronimo lacked eloquence—is an accurate summary of their feelings:

I am very glad to hear you talk—I have been wanting for a long time to hear somebody talk that way. I want to go away somewhere where we can get a farm, cattle, and cool water.

I have done my best to help the authorities—to keep peace & good order to keep my house clean—God hears both of us and what he hears must be the truth. We are very thankful to you— these poor people who have nothing and nothing to look forward to—what you say makes my head and whole body feel cool—we are all that way—we want to see things growing around our houses, corn and flowers—we all want it—we want you to talk for us to Gen'l Miles in the same way you have talked to us—

Young men old men women and children all want to get away from here—it is too hot and wet—too many of us die here—I remember what I told General Miles— . . . I told him that I wanted to be a good man as long as I live and I have done it so far. I stood up on my feet and held up my hands to God to witness what I said was true—. I feel good about what you say and it will make all the other Indians feel good—Every one of us have got children at school and we will behave ourselves on account of these children, we want them to learn   I do not consider that I am an Indian any more   I am a white man and w'd like to go around and see different places   I consider that all white men are my brothers

4 Hugh Lenox Scott, *Some Memories of a Soldier*, pp. 182, 184.

Apache leaders at Mount Vernon Barracks in 1893. From left: Chihuahua, Naiche, Loco, Nana, and Geronimo. "Only old Nana refused to be reconstructed." Courtesy National Archives and Records Service.

and all white women are now my sisters—that is what I want to say.

This last assertion that he had taken up white ways and had come to accept white people would have been characterized by Crook in his day as more of Geronimo's lying, but the ensuing fifteen years were to prove his sincerity.

Maus wanted to be sure Geronimo spoke for the group. "I understand it to be your opinion that all of you want to go somewhere," he said.

"We all want to go everybody," Geronimo answered.

He was followed by Chihuahua, Naiche, Nana, Chatto, an Indian named Ruby (he was the son-in-law of Loco, and his young daughter at Carlisle was to become the mother of the future tribal chairman, Benedict Jozhe), Kaahteney, Mangus, and Loco.

361

Geronimo had indeed expressed the sentiments of the group; evidently, they had held a meeting of their own and had formulated their position. Several reminded Maus of their previous meetings with him and told of their changed attitude and their acceptance of the white man's way. Naiche said, "We live just like white people, have houses and stoves just like them and we want to have a farm just like other white people—we have been here a long time and have not seen any of us have a farm yet." Chihuahua said, "God made the earth for everybody & I want a piece of it—I want to have things growing——." And referring to the enclosing timber, he continued, "I want the wind to blow on me just as it blows on everybody else—I want the sun to shine on me and the moon just as on everybody else." Even Nana made one concession; although he was "too old to work," he wanted "to see all the young men have a farm and I could go around and talk to them and get something to eat."

Chatto said, "If anything I could say would hurry up the farms I wish it would—You can find some of the old people yet—the grandfathers and grandmothers, but most of them are dead—that is why I do not like it here. I want to hurry—I want you to tell Gen'l Miles to get them away from here in a hurry." Kaahteney expressed the same desperate concern: "I had lots of friends— cousins brothers & relatives when you saw me but since coming to this country they have all died— . . . I have children here and am all the time afraid that they will get sick and die——." Loco said that "it is just like a road with a precipice on both sides—they fall off on both sides—nobody killed them—sickness did it——."

Chihuahua spoke as usual of his scattered children: "I went to Carlisle to see them [as far as is known, there is no record of this trip] and it made my heart feel good to see them in the white mans road——." But even so, "I want to have all our children together where I can see them," and "I want my children wherever I go——." And thinking of the time Maus brought him back as a hostile, he assured the captain, "I want you to look at me and see that I am not like what I was when you saw me before——."

Mangus told of his life in hiding, of his voluntary surrender (very different from the army tale of his "capture"), and of his being brought to Fort Pickens: "When I got there I have been up to this time a good man and have never stepped of [*sic*] the good path (Lt Capron in charge of prisoners here stated, this man has the best record of any man in Co "I" 12th Infantry) While walking around I always want to look pleasant at everybody———." As for the place where they lived, "here we are in this little bit of a reservation—there are lots of trees here yes—they give shade but when you put your foot on the ground it burns you———."[5]

As Scott remembered it later, some of the prisoners told him the reservation was no larger than a thumbnail and that the trees were so thick one had to climb to the top of a tall pine to see the sun. He assured them that they would be sent to a place where they could not only look up at the sun but see mountains.[6]

Miles sent their statements along with his recommendations to the War Department, and it was officially decided that they would be sent to Fort Sill. They would still be prisoners of war; Oklahoma was no longer an "Indian Territory" with unassigned land out of which a reservation could be carved for a homeless tribe.

The post commander at Fort Sill, angry at the prospect of having to take the prisoners, planned to build a palisaded pen and corral them there under guard. Scott managed to pass the word to Miles, and Miles went over the commander's head and appointed Scott to take charge of them. The commander was soon transferred to the East. Scott believed that if he had remained at Fort Sill he would have driven the prisoners into running away. The resulting war in hunting them out of their native mountains would have been worse than anything that had gone before.[7]

All was now ready for their removal. But before they left, Geronimo suffered a personal bereavement. Chappo, the "unusually bright young Indian," who had been "ambitious to improve his

[5] Consolidated File, Verbatum report of the conference, Scott to Maus, August 29, 1894.
[6] Scott, *op. cit.*, pp. 182–83.
[7] *Ibid.*, pp. 187–88.

mind and study subjects that will [be] of use to him in the future" was sent from Carlisle in the last stages of tuberculosis to die with his people; he died on September 9. His body was placed on the train for the short journey to Mobile and, with a sergeant from the post in charge, was buried in the national cemetery there. Geronimo went along "with two of his wives, one the Mother of Crappo [*sic*]," according to a contemporary newspaper.[8] Geronimo had only one wife, and Chappo's mother, if she still lived, was in Mexican slavery. The woman besides Zi-yeh was probably the young man's sister, Dohn-say.

Thus, Geronimo's travels were marked by the graves, or in some cases by the mutilated corpses, of the members of his family. First, he buried his father in peace near the quiet headwaters of the Gila; next, through the violent years, the bodies of his mother, wives, and children were strewn along his bloody trails through Old Mexico and Arizona; then there were the graves of his little girl at Saint Augustine and his wife at Pensacola; and now the son upon whom he had set his hopes lay buried in the cemetery at Mobile. And he, himself, was bound for a last resting place where other graves would surround his own in the prisoners' cemetery at Fort Sill.

The plans for the removal were soon made. The able and humane Capron was in charge of the prisoners during the journey. Early in October they were placed on a special train which brought them by way of New Orleans and Fort Worth to Rush Springs, Oklahoma. At stops on the way Geronimo, in particular, received the usual ovations, to the great disgust of Oklahomans at such honors to a "murderer"—"The old devil should have been hung fifteen years ago." At Rush Springs wagons waited to take them the thirty miles to Fort Sill.[9] They arrived on October 4, a bedraggled looking party numbering only 296.[10] (This was not their entire

---

8 *Mobile Daily News*, September 12, 1894; article furnished me through the courtesy of Mr. John A. Shapard, Jr.

9 W[ilbur] S[turtevant] Nye, *Carbine and Lance*, p. 380.

10 Secretary of War, *Annual Report*, 1895, p. 34. I believe this is the correct number. Army figures in other places vary because of the inclusion of unrelated prisoners or the omission of the enlisted men.

population; about forty-five of their youths were still at Carlisle or Hampton or in a very few cases living and working in the East.) They had no livestock, not even a dog or cat. They had a few trunks and boxes, but most of their meager possessions had been destroyed by a fire in a railroad freight shed at New Orleans.[11]

Hundreds of Kiowas and Comanches, their enmity forgotten, came to meet them. They tried to talk with them in the sign language, but these mountain people were unfamiliar with this universal system of Plains Indian communication. Scott took some Kiowa-Apaches to see them, but the dialects were too dissimilar for mutual understanding. They called this Plains band "half Apaches" because they could understand only half of what they said. Finally, both sides produced Carlisle boys, and they communicated through the English language.[12]

Capron remained to assist Scott in supervising the prisoners, and Wratten continued as their interpreter. As at Fort Pickens and Mount Vernon Barracks, the men worked under army command. When they arrived, it was too late in the season to build houses; thus, they put up wickiups in the brush along a creek, using army canvas in place of skins for the overall covering. Soon after they came, they learned that mesquite trees grew in southwestern Oklahoma. Beans from these trees were among their favorite foods, but they had not tasted any since leaving their homeland. The nearest grove was forty-five miles away, but they asked Scott for permission to gather beans there. He said they could go if they would leave after noon on Saturday and be back for work by 7:00 A.M. on Monday. They took along a few horses to carry tents, supplies, and beans. They gathered about three hundred bushels of beans, trotted the ninety-mile round trip, and were ready for work Monday morning.[13]

Meanwhile, schooling had to be provided for their children. The Shepard sisters had been willing to accompany them, but the War Department refused to pay their salaries, and their sponsors

11 *Ibid.*, p. 298.
12 Scott, *op. cit.*, pp. 188–89; Nye, *op. cit.*, p. 380.
13 Scott, *op. cit.*, p. 197.

An Apache wickiup at Fort Sill, winter, 1894/95. The prisoners arrived on October 4, too late in the season to build houses. Courtesy U.S. Army Artillery and Missile Center Museum.

decided against sending them. Now arrangements were made with the Indian Office to place the children in the boarding school established for the Plains tribes near their agency at Anadarko, thirty-three miles away. Scott assembled the parents and told them that the wagons would be ready in four days and that he wanted the children to be clean and neat and prepared to start. His announcement was received in complete silence. He asked Chihuahua if he had anything to say. Chihuahua replied that of course they did not want the children to go, but they had been there long enough to know that the officer's orders were carried out. During the term the mothers would buy candy or some other treat for their children and trot the sixty-six miles to present it.[14]

At the same time, the adult men were learning the techniques of the range cattle industry. Congress had appropriated money to buy

14 *Ibid.*, pp. 197–98.

Geronimo and Naiche as cowhands. *The adult men were learning the techniques of the range cattle industry.* This autographed photograph was probably given to Scott during one of his later visits to Fort Sill. It was found in his effects after his death. Courtesy National Anthropological Archives, Smithsonian Instittuion.

367

White Wolf
Mountain

Medicine Bluff Creek

Mount Hinds

Signal
Mountain

Four Mile
Crossing

VILLAGES

1 Geronimo's
2 Perico's
3 Chihuahua's
4 Kayihtah's
5 Noche's
6 Kaahteney's

animals to start the herd, but it had to be used at once or it would go back into the treasury. The military reservation was unfenced, and there was no time to fence it or raise winter feed. But if the cattle were allowed to stray on to the surrounding Kiowa-Comanche land it would create bad feeling. That meant that they had to be herded on the grassland and that the Apaches had to be trained as cowboys. Scott and Capron were kept on constant duty. They had been advised against sleeping in the Apaches' camp—the Indians would cut their throats and escape—but the two officers found it necessary in managing the cattle, and they slept there as safely as in their own beds at the post.[15]

15 *Ibid.*, pp. 193, 195–96.

7 Mangus'
8 Toclanny's
9 Loco's
10 Chiricahua Tom's
11 Chatto's
12 Naiche's

Apache villages and cultivated fields, Fort Sill, 1897

There was much public apprehension that the Apaches would break away for their mountain homeland; and even Scott feared that if some of them should get drunk and commit a crime ("they were homicidal monomaniacs who would kill anybody when intoxicated") they might run away to escape punishment. He consulted a Mescalero who was living with the Comanches and knew all the trails and waterholes along the seven hundred miles to the Mescalero Agency; then he had a good map drawn and sent copies to Miles so the general would be prepared for instant action. He also kept twenty days' rations and a pack outfit in readiness. He told his prisoners of these preparations and warned them that the Comanches, who knew the Plains, were his friends and not theirs

369

Geronimo's house at Fort Sill. Here he lived with Zi-yeh and then children and entertained the artist E. A. Burbank and the writer S. M. Barrett. Courtesy Oklahoma Historical Society, Oklahoma City.

and would join in pursuing them. But they never even considered breaking away.[16]

Various Apaches who had not surrendered were still on the loose, committing depredations in Old Mexico and the American Southwest. The army was chasing them with the usual poor success[17]—"like chasing deer with a brass band," was Scott's opinion. He devised a plan for catching them and obtained Miles's approval. He had made friends with Naiche, Toclanny, and Kaahteney, who knew all their strongholds in Mexico and were willing to search them out. At the same time, their families in Fort Sill would be hostages for their loyalty. He planned to take about fifteen officers and men with the three Indians and set out ostensibly to shoot deer in the Sierra Madre. But the Mexican authorities refused permission, and the plan was dropped. Years later, in 1913, when Scott,

16 *Ibid.*, pp. 186, 193.
17 Secretary of War, *Annual Report*, 1896, p. 4.

370

Leaders of the old days. From left: Geronimo, Chihuahua, Nana, Loco, and Jolsanny. From S. M. Barrett, *Geronimo's Story of His Life*.

Surviving Bedonkohes. From left: Toclanny, a loyal scout; Nah-dos-te, Geronimo's sister, the wife of Nana; Nah-thle-tla, Geronimo's cousin, the mother of Jason Betzinez; Perico, Geronimo's "brother" (second cousin). From *Geronimo's Story of His Life*.

then a brigadier general, was in command on the border, Pancho Villa told him he knew where the Apaches were, but "there were then far worse outlaws on every side of us," and the Apaches were not molested.[18]

As soon as the first winter passed, Scott (now Captain Scott) set his Indians to building houses, using picket construction (upright posts set in a frame). These dwellings were distributed in small villages over the reservation, kindred groups clustered together according to the old Apache custom. (Plural wives were given separate houses closely placed.) A headman was appointed to supervise each village. Since the army had no provision for such officers, they were enlisted for the first three-year period as soldiers, entitled to wear the army uniform and draw the pay of privates, although many of them had passed the age of active service. Their names indicate that they owed their position to natural leadership instead of some white official's artificial selection. The list also indicates the increasing adoption of given names: Geronimo, Martin Kayihtah (later succeeded by Charles Martine), Leon Perico, Chihuahua, George Noche, Jacob Kaahteney, Carl Mangus, Roger (or Rogers) Toclanny, Chief Apache Loco, Christian Naiche, Alfred Chatto, and Chiricahua Tom (or Tom Chiricahua).[19] All these, except the last, had been prominent in Apache history. When one of them died, his son was usually chosen as his successor.

Then, in 1897 a scout detachment was activated, consisting of sixteen men entrusted with special duties such as the supervision of the cattle herd. Finally, in 1911 Noche, Kayihtah, and Martine were enlisted as an act of belated justice for their past services. George Wratten helped them present their claims: Noche's service as sergeant major of scouts under captains Wirt Davis and Crawford (and under Maus after Crawford's death) through the entire 1885–86 campaign, and the rewards Miles promised Kayihtah and Martine for making contact with Geronimo. These claims required

18 Scott, *op. cit.*, pp. 193–95.
19 Betzinez, *I Fought with Geronimo*, pp. 167–68. I have corrected his list slightly.

Kayihtah (left) and Martine (right) at Fort Sill. From *Geronimo's Story of His Life.*

twenty-eight endorsements, moving up and down through channels and filling eight crowded, single-spaced, typewritten pages
before the three were enlisted. Since the men were unable to meet
the physical requirements, they were placed on the payroll as
scouts, with no responsibilities. After their three-year enlistment
expired, they were again forgotten.[20]

Although Geronimo was the headman of his village, the army
was careful to cut him down to size. Like Crook, Bourke, and
Britton Davis before him, Scott disliked the hard-headed old
warrior. He described him as "an unlovely character, a cross-
grained, mean, selfish old curmudgeon, of whom . . . I never heard
recounted a kindly or generous deed." On the other hand, he found
Naiche "a straightforward, reliable person. When he was in charge
of the cattle herd I could depend on him completely in every
weather, and he never disappointed me." And "Old Chihuahua
was called the Apache Chesterfield, from his polite manners."[21]
But in spite of Scott's dislike of Geronimo, the energetic old
warrior was probably one of his best farmers. With mules the
officer had been able to acquire as army surplus when Fort Supply
in Oklahoma was abandoned, Scott directed the Apaches in breaking out land and placing it under cultivation. Each man had a plot
of his own planted to garden and field crops. They raised more
than 250,000 melons and canteloupes on the virgin soil that first
year. They ate what they could and sold the surplus at the post.
Scott's nine-year-old daughter stationed herself at their wagons
and helped them in bargaining and making change. A well-known
picture of Geronimo and his family in his melon patch was almost
certainly made that season. One doubts that *he* needed any help
in making sales.

Scott had seen corn planted by the Kiowas and Comanches
under the tutelage of their conscientious civilian agent grow rank

20 Musgrove, "A Belated Reward for the Surrender of Geronimo." Colonel Musgrove was a young noncommissioned officer at Fort Sill serving as recruiting sergeant.
Thus, he prepared the enlistment papers of the three. Later, in his mature years, he
found the entire record and the official correspondence in the National Archives and
Records Service.

21 Scott, *op. cit.*, p. 198.

Chihuahua and his family during the Fort Sill years. Apparently the older girl is Ramona. "Old Chihuahua was called the Apache Chesterfield, from his polite manners." Courtesy U.S. Army Artillery and Missile Center Museum.

Geronimo and his family in his melon patch at Fort Sill. With him are his wife Zi-yeh; his daughter Eva, standing next to him; his son Fenton; and probably his granddaughter Nina Dahkeya. *The Apaches raised more than 250,000 melons and canteloupes on the virgin soil that first summer.* Courtesy U.S. Army Artillery and Missile Center Museum.

and green and then crumple under the scorching Southwestern wind. Therefore, he introduced kafir corn, the new grain sorghum that was proving a boon to homesteaders on the Plains, the first grown in that part of Oklahoma. The fodder furnished feed for the Apaches' own livestock, and the surplus was sold to the cavalry at the post. They also cut and baled the hay from the rank prairie grass and sold it to the government. They cut posts and purchased wire and built a fence around the reservation, also enclosing their villages. They then had no need to keep their cattle under herd, but they became adept at roping, branding, and treating the animals for heel-fly, screwworms, and anthrax. Their cattle

376

soon became their chief means of support, with their hay coming second.[22]

Scott remained in charge of the Apaches until 1897. He said that during the whole time they never broke a promise they made him. His successors continued his policy. Everything was so peaceable that when the Spanish-American War broke out in 1898 all the troops were ordered away from Fort Sill except a detachment of twenty men. Then a wild rumor circulated to the effect that the Apaches were plotting an uprising. Panic spread through the post families, who expected a massacre, and troops were hastily sent there. Geronimo, Naiche, and other leaders were questioned. They were incensed at having their loyalty doubted. "I am a U.S. soldier," said Geronimo. "I wear the uniform and it makes my heart sore to be thus suspected." The Kiowas and Comanches were equally incensed; they were able and willing to protect the post against any Apache attack.[23]

Thus, the prisoners were settled, as far as the army could accomplish it, into what seemed to be a good life. They could look at the sun and moon in a big Western sky; they walked on clean grass and breathed pure air; and they saw mountains—not the rugged mountains of their homeland, but mountains. Still, they died. It is enlightening to select a few of their families at random and trace their births and deaths in the Fort Sill records.[24] Small children apparently died from improper feeding after too early weaning, but many deaths came at a usually safe age—of children past infancy, teenagers, returned Carlisle students, and men and women in the prime of life.

The cause was as baffling as it had been to the army surgeons at Mount Vernon Barracks. Jason Betzinez, returning to his people in January, 1900, after working in a Pennsylvania steel mill, blamed the traditional dances. It was bad enough, he thought,

---

22 *Ibid.*, pp. 186, 191–92, 198–99; Betzinez, *op. cit.*, pp. 168–70, 178. A clear-cut summary of the first two years' work is in Oklahoma Historical Society, Indian Archives, 47403—1896, Scott's report to Adjutant General, October 31, 1896.

23 Scott, *op. cit.*, pp. 197–98, 219–30; Nye, *op. cit.*, pp. 382–83.

24 Griswold, "The Fort Sill Apaches."

for the spectators in the dead of winter to sit on the frozen ground; but for the thinly clad dancers, streaming with perspiration, to drop down there exhausted was highly dangerous, to say nothing of the masks they wore, which they interchanged with each other. (By this time the nature of the infection was known.) He worried about this and then spoke to the officer in charge of the prisoners. The officer, with an understanding rare in white "civilizers," hesitated to interfere with a native custom, but Betzinez pointed out recent funerals which he attributed to exposure at the dances. The officer then forbade them during the cold weather.[25] The family records and the dates on the headstones indicate that this did not work, either.

"We are vanishing from the earth," said Geronimo, "yet I cannot think we are useless or Usen would not have created us." And as they saw their numbers dwindle, always they begged to go home. Geronimo diagnosed their sickness by a reasoning typically Indian. He told how it was "in the beginning: the Apaches and their homes each created for the other by Usen himself. When they are taken away from these homes they sicken and die. How long will it be until it is said, there are no Apaches?"[26]

All this, then, was the background of Geronimo's closing years. In this setting his personal characteristics, barely glimpsed in earlier times, became well known.

25 Betzinez, *op. cit.*, pp. 175–77, 179, 183.
26 Barrett, *Geronimo's Story of His Life*, pp. 15–16. By "Apaches" Geronimo referred to his own related tribes.

CHAPTER 20

GERONIMO IS SEEN AS A PERSON

In the publicity that marked his arrival at Fort Sill, Geronimo appeared as the bloody stereotype of the savage Indian. Among the more lurid tales that floated about was the story that when he was "captured" after his last "outbreak" he was wearing a blanket made of one hundred (sometimes it was ninety-nine) white scalps he had collected during that last fling. The account even found its way into serious publications, and writers in search of material sometimes puzzled the old warrior by asking to see the fabulous garment.[1]

But one of these early interviewers had the perception to see the human individual behind the lurid representations. In 1897, Edward E. Ayer, president of the Field Museum in Chicago, sent his artist nephew, Elbridge Ayer Burbank, to Fort Sill to paint a portrait of the fierce raider.[2] With the screaming headlines in mind, Burbank was glad that the "bloodthirsty savage" was in prison so that he could safely paint him behind bars. Arriving at the post, he learned that the captive lived in his own house and enjoyed the freedom of the reservation. A small Indian

[1] Howard B. Hopps, "Lawton," *Chronicles of Oklahoma*, Vol. XXIII, No. 3 (Autumn, 1945), p. 294; Betzinez, *I Fought with Geronimo*, p. 198.

[2] Since writing this book I have learned from the records of Burbank's family that he visited the Fort Sill prisoners in 1897, 1898, and 1899. Clark Hansell, interview, November 14, 1982.

boy, probably Joe or Thomas Dahkeya, helped him locate it. Geronimo was out hunting his horses. He soon came riding up, "an elderly Indian . . . short, but well built and muscular. His keen, shrewd face was deeply furrowed with strong lines. His small black eyes were watery, but in them there burned a fierce light." That face, "so gnarled and furrowed," appealed to the artist as "a wonderful study."

He greeted the old man courteously as "Chief Geronimo." Later he learned that this was fortunate; the soldiers at the post had nicknamed him "Gerry," a name he detested. The boy interpreted the conversation that followed. Geronimo asked the artist where he came from and then wanted to know all about Chicago. Finally he said, "Come," and Burbank followed him into the house. He pulled a photograph of himself out of an old trunk, handed it to the visitor, and said, "One dollar." Burbank meekly paid. This picture gave him the opportunity to ask the old Indian to sit for his portrait. He readily consented, and Captain Scott gave the required permission.

The following morning Burbank found Geronimo ready and eager to pose, but the artist had hardly started when the Apache signaled him to stop, and, calling a little girl—probably Eva—who was playing nearby, he asked her to interpret.

"This man wants to know how much you are going to pay him," she said.

"Ask him how much he wants," Burbank answered.

"You get much money for that picture," said Geronimo. "Maybe five dollars. I want half."

Burbank told him that if he would sit for two pictures, he could have all of the five dollars. The bargain was made.

For that first portrait Geronimo sat on the bed and Burbank on a box. There was no chair in the house until Geronimo inveigled the artist into buying him one. One day a man came by with a sack of grain for sale. Burbank perforce bought that also—for Geronimo's horse. But the Indian was a good sitter, although the habit of vigilance developed in his hunted life was still with him; at the least sound of approaching man or horse he would rush to the door and look out. Sometimes he became nervous from the long sitting, and then Burbank would let him rest. He would lie on his back on the bed and sing in his deep, rich voice—songs "of great beauty," according to the artist. One of them went:

O, ha le
O, ha le
Through the air
I fly upon a cloud
Toward the sky, far, far, far,
O, ha le
O, ha le
There to find the holy place
Ah, now the change comes o'er me!
O, ha le
O, ha le.

Burbank regularly brought his lunch when he worked at Geronimo's house, and he usually brought some extra food to share with his subject. Once during those first sittings Geronimo invited him to take dinner with him. Zi-yeh prepared the meal, which consisted of meat, bread, and coffee. The food was "clean and good," and she served it on a board placed on the ground before the two men. They ate with their fingers, there being no knives, forks, or spoons. Two years later Geronimo again invited the artist to dinner. This time he sat with Geronimo, Zi-yeh, and Eva at a well-set table covered with a linen cloth to an excellent meal topped with dessert.

Zi-yeh was in poor health—no doubt with the tubercular infection that was to lay her low—and Geronimo did all the housework, washing the dishes, sweeping the floor, keeping the place immaculate. Once Burbank tracked in some mud, and the sour look the old warrior gave him as he took a broom and swept it out taught the artist to be more careful in the future. Geronimo idolized Eva. "Nobody could be kinder to a child than he was to her." In spite of his notable thrift in his relations with outsiders, anything in the trader's store was hers for the asking. A small "nephew" also was "invariably about the house." This must have been his grandson, Thomas Dahkeya, the only survivor of Lulu's family. The little girl, Nina, had died in 1895; Lulu herself followed in 1898; and her warrior husband, Mike Dahkeya, and their son Joe died in 1899.[3] No doubt Thomas was living with his grandfather at the time of the artist's later visits. Burbank made no mention of Fenton. This last son of Geronimo's (except for the absent Robert) died in 1897, either before the artist's first visit or before he became acquainted with the family.

As Burbank saw Geronimo in his home, he found it hard to visualize him "as the leader of a band of ravaging savages. To me he was a kind old man." He taught his ponies to come at his shrill note,[4] and he never left the house without putting out a saucer of milk for his cat. (For some reason Burbank could never fathom, he always kept the cat's whiskers closely clipped.) Through the artist he dictated letters to friends in the old home-land, usually requesting that certain native "medicines" be sent to him and invariably closing with the words, "If you are in need, let me know and I will send you money."[5]

Others who knew him at this time testified to his kindly spirit. Oscar Brousse Jacobson, who later became head of the Art School at the University of Oklahoma, commented on Burbank's evalua-tion of him as "very gentle to his family and kind and generous to his tribesmen": "This is the same impression I had of Geronimo, gathered from several conversations I had with [him]."[6] Miss Ruth Hammond, retired librarian of Oklahoma State University, still remembers him as he appeared to her in her childhood when he

---

[3] These family records may be found in Griswold, "The Fort Sill Apaches," and also on the gravestones of the Apache cemetery on the military reservation.

[4] Barrett, *Geronimo's Story of His Life*, p. 123, n. 2.

[5] Burbank and Royce, *Burbank among the Indians*, pp. 17–22, 27–31.

[6] O. B. Jacobson and Jeanne d'Ucel, "Art in Oklahoma," *Chronicles of Oklahoma*, Vol. XXXII, No. 3 (Autumn, 1954), p. 276.

came to sell bows and arrows at the officers' quarters when her father was the post chaplain at Fort Sill. "He talked with my father. He did not seem to me like a fierce person, just a kind old man. He spoke a little English, enough to carry on his sales. He charged fifty cents extra for printing his name on the bow."[7]

But one day Burbank saw this kindly Indian turn into a ferocious savage. A magazine editor offered the artist a considerable sum of money if he would get the story of Geronimo's life. Geronimo consented if he were paid half the proceeds. Burbank went to his house, and the old man lay on the bed and began. But as he told of the massacre of his family by the Mexicans, he sprang up in such fury that he was unable to continue. The boy who was interpreting became almost as excited. "He is telling you the truth," he said, "for my father tells me the same story."[8] Apparently the article was never written.

Gambling also brought out Geronimo's latent fierceness. Once he invited Burbank to accompany him to a sports meet, probably the annual Fourth of July field day observed at the post, with horse races and other contests between the soldiers and the Kiowas and Comanches.[9] There he joined a game of monte, dealing the cards expertly with his small, quick hands and shouting at the top of his voice as he raked in his winnings. As they were leaving for home, a white man proposed that they race horses for a ten-dollar wager. Geronimo liked nothing better than horse racing, but his weight was a handicap. Often he pressed his small wife into service; the Apaches long remembered how she tied her hair in a tight knot when she rode.[10] This time he looked around for an Apache boy and found him at bat in a baseball game. He hit a homer just as Geronimo arrived. The old man raced after him all around the diamond and caught him at home plate. The horse race that

7 Interview, March 11, 1973.
8 Burbank and Royce, *op. cit.*, pp. 32–33. Burbank's account of the massacre is understandably confused.
9 Descriptions of these field days are given in Scott, *Some Memories of a Soldier*, p. 199; and Nye, *Carbine and Lance*, p. 375.
10 James Kaywaykla, Moses Loco, and Benedict Jozhe interview, July 29, 1959.

followed was close, but Geronimo's pony won, and he was wildly exultant.[11]

He would, in fact, bet on anything. One time he challenged Burbank to a marksmanship contest with a .22 caliber rifle, in which each man would pay his opponent ten dollars for every successful shot. The artist looked at the old man's watery eyes and was inclined to accept, but Geronimo showed so much eagerness that he said, "No, we'll shoot for fun." It was well for him that he did. Geronimo took a piece of paper about the size of a quarter and pinned it to a tree several yards distant. He hit the target at every shot and once hit the pin. Burbank missed it every time.[12]

Once he came to see Burbank at the post in a peculiar mood. He said that no one could kill him, or Burbank either if he willed it so. He bared himself to the waist, and Burbank was astounded to see the number of bullet holes in his body. Some of them were large enough to hold small pebbles, which he picked up and placed in them as he imitated the sound of a gun. He ended by shouting, "Bullets cannot kill me!"[13] Thus he trusted his Power. Even in his horse racing he relied as much on his "medicine" as on the speed of his favorite sorrel pony. He was in fact, an untamed Apache. His qualities of gentleness and ferocity were those of his native society.

Burbank met other members of this society on his third visit to Fort Sill. He came upon Geronimo riding through the woods with Eva and the little "nephew" on the horse with him. "You make heap money painting my picture," was his greeting to the artist. "You pay me so much," and he clasped and unclasped his hands to indicate twenty-five dollars. Burbank told him he had come this time to paint other chiefs. He persuaded Naiche, Chatto, Chihuahua, Mangus, and Loco to pose for him, and he painted a charming portrait of Eva.[14]

He had been anxious to meet Naiche, and when the meeting

11 Burbank and Royce, *op. cit.*, pp. 24–25.
12 *Ibid.*, p. 23.
13 *Ibid.*, pp. 30–31.
14 Eva's portrait is dated 1898.

Geronimo's daughter Eva at age nine, painted by Burbank, 1898. "Nobody could be kinder to a child than Geronimo was to her." Courtesy Butler Institute of American Art, Youngstown, Ohio.

occurred it was typical of the chief's artistic interests. One day, when the artist was sketching, he noticed "a tall fine-looking Indian" intently watching. He asked him where Naiche could be found. The Indian laughed. "I am Naiche," he said.[15] After that meeting, when Burbank was painting, Naiche used to watch him all day; and Burbank explained his techniques and later sent the

15 He dated Naiche's portrait 1899.

385

native artist a full set of colors from Chicago. Naiche presented Burbank with a cane he had carved, "beautifully executed, then as finely painted." Burbank wanted to purchase for the museum one of Naiche's paintings done in the Indian way on deerskin, and the chief set the price at three and one-half dollars. Then he learned that the unworldly Indian had paid three dollars for the skin, and he accordingly raised his payment to ten. Later, when the French artist Jean Baptiste Millet visited the museum, he pronounced it "the most beautiful decorative thing he had ever seen." Ayer gave it to him, and he took it back to France.

Although in his subsequent travels to many reservations Burbank saw and appreciated the work of numerous Indian artists, he always regarded Naiche as "by far the best" of all he had known.[16] But he considered all Indians as "essentially artistic." Even the hard-headed Geronimo "had a fine eye for line and color." Geronimo liked Burbank's portraits of him—"You heap savvy," was his judgment—and the two developed a real affection for each other. Their last parting was "quite sad," for both realized that they would not meet again.[17]

This had been Geronimo's first opportunity to form a friendship with a civilian white man. Soon, however, his white contacts were enormously increased. The government had continued its policy of breaking up the Indian reservations in Oklahoma and opening them to white settlement. The Kiowas, Comanches, and Kiowa-Apaches had resisted, but they had finally lost their fight. Each received an individual "allotment" of land, and in 1901 the remainder was given to white homesteaders. This meant a settler on every 160-acre tract, with towns springing up throughout the area and feverish construction of railroads to span it. The city of Lawton came into lusty existence just outside the military reservation and four miles from the post. This development had its bad side for Geronimo: it increased his opportunities to obtain forbidden alcohol. On such occasions he was confined in the post

16 Burbank and Royce, *op. cit.*, pp. 33–34, 207, 223.
17 *Ibid.*, pp. 22, 38, 205.

386

guardhouse until he sobered up. One of his grievances—a violation, as he saw it, of the peace he had made with Miles—was that "I have been arrested and placed in the guardhouse twice for drinking whisky."[18] At the same time the settlement of the area ended his isolation; the public began to see him as a human being instead of a caged tiger.

In April, 1905, the historian Norman S. Wood, in collecting material for his book on Indian chiefs, came to meet Naiche and especially Geronimo. He first interviewed Lieutenant Purington and then set out to find the old war leader. As he was passing the railroad station, the agent called out to him that Geronimo was there waiting for a train. He was on his way to the nearby town of Cache to visit Quanah Parker, the noted Comanche chief and former hostile, with whom he had formed a friendship. Wood was not a sensational writer expecting to see Geronimo wearing a blanket of human scalps, but he did have to change some of his preconceptions. "I found the noted chief on the platform of the depot; he took my proffered hand with a smile and a hearty 'How!' and pulled me up on the platform. I had expected to see a grey-haired, sour-visaged, skinny-looking old Indian, with a scowl on his face and nervous twitching fingers as if eager to shed blood. But instead I saw a smiling, well-kept, well-dressed Indian about five feet nine inches tall, with square shoulders and deep chest . . . He was dressed in a well-fitting blue cloth suit of citizen's clothes." As Wood was soon to learn, he had an open-faced silver watch in his vest pocket.

The writer found that "while he was quick to understand much that was said to him, he spoke but a few words of English." Wood therefore suggested by signs that they go to Wratten's house, about a quarter of a mile away across the prairie. Geronimo looked up the track and inquired of the station agent, "How much?" The agent pulled out the Indian's watch and ran his finger around the dial and half around again to indicate an hour and a half. "Good," said Geronimo, and the two started off. On the way was a little

18 Nye, *op. cit.*, p. 386; Barrett, *op. cit.*, p. 146.

387

stream, a good jump across. Wood had excelled in jumping in his college days and saw a chance to test Geronimo's agility by a running leap over this creek. To his surprise Geronimo vaulted across and landed a foot beyond his mark. At Wratten's house he obtained some more information, and with what he had learned from the lieutenant he wrote an accurate sketch of Geronimo's life and experiences at Fort Sill.[19]

All these increased white contacts were good for Geronimo's business. Wood, in fact, had bought one of his bows and arrows at the post sutler's store and brought it to him to autograph. No doubt many others did. And it was through a business contact that he was given the opportunity to present the Indian side of the Apache wars. Lawton School Superintendent Barrett first met him in the summer of 1904 when he was called upon to interpret Geronimo's Spanish and a prospective purchaser's English in fixing the price of a war bonnet. After that, Geronimo always had a pleasant word for Barrett when they met, but it was only after he learned that the educator had once been wounded by a Mexican that he came to visit him and express his hatred of Mexicans. Other visits followed in Barrett's home and Geronimo's. Once the superintendent brought along a Kansas City guest, who mentioned in conversation that he was a friend of General Howard. Geronimo instantly became cordial. "Come," he said, and he led the way to a shade, had seats brought, put on his headdress, and served big chunks of watermelon, all the time talking freely.

By this time Barrett had heard enough tales of Geronimo's adventures that he wanted to publish them. Geronimo said that if Barrett would pay him he would tell the whole story of his life. After the educator finally obtained permission by his direct appeal to President Roosevelt, he began with the help of Asa Daklugie to take down the old warrior's dictation. Daklugie was the ideal interpreter. He had returned from Carlisle in 1895, equipped with the white man's learning but wholly committed to Apache traditions and loyalties. He was Geronimo's main dependence and

19 *Lives of Famous Indian Chiefs*, pp. 550–59.

Asa and Ramona Daklugie and their children. *The home they established was a model of stability and permanence.* From *Geronimo's Story of His Life.*

Geronimo dictating his memoirs, with Daklugie interpreting and Barrett taking notes. "Write what I have spoken." From *Geronimo's Story of His Life.*

chosen successor, and after many councils the band had recently—in January, 1905—elected him as acting "chief."[20] (Naiche was still the chief; Daklugie succeeded to Geronimo's position as the power behind the throne.) He had married capable, level-headed Ramona Chihuahua, and the home they established was a model of stability and permanence.

With this help Barrett began early in October, 1905, and the three worked through the following winter, sometimes at Geronimo's home, sometimes at Daklugie's, or seated under the trees in some sheltered nook, even riding at a swinging gallop across the prairie. Geronimo refused to accept the presence of a stenographer to take shorthand notes, and Barrett and Daklugie had to

[20] *Lawton Constitution-Democrat* (weekly edition), February 18, 1909.

remember and record his statements as best they could. Every day he had in mind what he would tell and told it "in a very clear, brief manner." He refused to be questioned about details or to add another word; he simply said, "Write what I have spoken." But he would agree to come later to Barrett's study in Lawton or to some other meeting place and listen as Daklugie read it back to him in Apache, and then he would answer questions and contribute additional information.

He soon became tired of the whole proceeding and would have abandoned the task except that he had agreed to complete it. Barrett found that "when he once gives his word, nothing will turn him back from fulfilling his promise." (It would have surprised Crook to hear that!) His good faith was strikingly demonstrated on one cold day in January when he had agreed to come to Barrett's study. Daklugie came alone with the report that the old man was very ill with a cold or, as he feared, pneumonia, and that they must set another date. Just then Geronimo arrived, riding furiously on his exhausted horse. Entering the study, he said in a hoarse whisper, "I promised to come. I am here." Barrett explained that he had not expected him to keep the appointment on such a stormy day, and that, ill as he was, he must not try to work. He stood there for a time, then turned away without a word and mounted his pony for the eight-mile ride against the north wind back to his home.[21]

Geronimo's home that winter was in a state of flux. Zi-yeh had become "a chronic invalid" from tubercular lupus and had died in 1904.[22] On Christmas Day in 1905 Geronimo married again. According to newspaper accounts the woman was an Apache named Sousche or Mrs. Mary Loto, a widow, aged fifty-eight, with a grown son. It was said that the marriage was unknown to even his closest friends until he brought his wife home two or three weeks later.[23] Present-day Apaches know nothing about her, and

21 Barrett, *op. cit.*, pp. xi-xiii, xx-xxii.

22 Oklahoma Historical Society, Indian Archives, Chilocco—Fair, Farrand Sayre to S. M. McCowan, September 20, 1903.

23 *Beaver Journal*, January 13, 1906; *Mangum Star*, January 18, 1906; *Muskogee Times-Democrat*, November 8, 1906.

her name stirs no memory. Apparently she was not a member of their band. They are inclined to think that she may have been a Mescalero or perhaps a White Mountain or other Apache from Arizona, for members of those tribes sometimes visited the Fort Sill prisoners, and she could have been in such a party.

In any case, the marriage did not last long. Mention is made of Geronimo's wife in a letter written on April 11, 1906,[24] but before he had finished dictating his memoirs that spring she had gone. He dismissed the brief episode laconically: "Since the death of Eva's mother I married another woman (December, 1905) but we could not live happily and separated. She went home to her people—that is an Apache divorce."[25]

He had only his daughter Eva with him, he said. She was then sixteen years old, and he had given her an elaborate womanhood ceremony just before he started working with Barrett. Probably Ramona Daklugie helped with the woman's part of the arrangements. He invited all the Apaches, and many Kiowas and Comanches, as well as his friend Barrett. A level place was selected by the south bank of Medicine Bluff Creek near Naiche's village, and the grass on a large circular space was closely mowed. The celebration began on the first night of the full moon in September. For the womanhood rites Naiche led the singing, and Geronimo, with the assistance of the medicine men in charge, directed the dancing. The all-night celebration that closed the observance began with a social dance in which the whole group joined hands and danced in a circle around the fire. Then when the moon began its descent the music changed from the beating of the tom-toms to the plaintive sound of the flageolet. Most of the older people withdrew, and the "lovers' dance" began. The young men formed a circle close to the fire, and the girls formed an outer circle surrounding them. One after another a girl would dance to the inner circle and select a partner, and the two would dance together through the rest of the night. With these young couples this was often preliminary to

24 National Archives and Records Service, Record Group No. 94, AGO 1119665, from 445841, Pawnee Bill to Lieutenant General John C. Bates.
25 Barrett, *op. cit.*, p. 179.

The site of Eva Geronimo's womanhood ceremony. Naiche's village is on the right, the smooth tract on the left is the tilled field belonging to the village, and far in the middle distance Chatto's village and the trail leading to it can be glimpsed. Courtesy U.S. Army Artillery and Missile Center Museum.

the more businesslike marriage arrangement carried out with the parents of the girl.

When the moon was going down and the sun was rising, the dancing stopped. The gifts were then presented and some betrothals were announced. Soon the gathering broke up. Geronimo and Barrett were among the last to leave. As Barrett remembered it, Geronimo at that time told him that Eva had chosen her husband. If so, she did not marry him. Perhaps Geronimo did not consent. If Asa Daklugie's memory can be trusted, Geronimo hoped she would not marry, fearing that she would not survive childbirth.[26] Possibly the tuberculosis that was to bring her to an early grave was already sapping her vitality.

With the party over and the crowd dispersed, Barrett and

26 Eve Ball to Angie Debo, March 8, 1971.

393

Eva Geronimo (right), aged sixteen, wearing the costume of her womanhood ceremony. With her is Ramona Daklugie, who probably served as her attendant, wearing her own womanhood costume. Apache women still preserve these dresses throughout their lives. From *Geronimo's Story of His Life*.

A womanhood ceremony painted on buckskin by Naiche at Fort Sill. Note the girls, each with her older woman attendant, the dancers "worshiping the fire," the clown, the musicians, and the spectators. Courtesy Oklahoma Historical Society.

Geronimo prepared to leave. They mounted their horses, Barrett using the stirrup, Geronimo still agile enough to vault into the saddle in the Apache way. As his pony struck a canter, the old warrior started out for home singing his favorite "riding song."

Dorothy Kaywaykla, the daughter of Naiche and E-clah-heh, posed in her womanhood costume. From *Geronimo's Story of His Life*.

Later, in dictating his story, he thoughtfully summed up his reactions: "Perhaps I shall never again have cause to assemble our people to dance, but these social dances in the moonlight have been a large part of our enjoyment in the past, and I think they will not soon be discontinued, at least I hope so."[27]

During the same period when his cherished Eva was inducted into the responsibilities of womanhood, Geronimo was able to establish contact with his Mescalero children. The previous year, as will be recounted in the next chapter, Lenna had joined him at the Saint Louis fair. Then the following year—on September 12, 1906—Robert, who had been attending the Indian service school at Mescalero, entered Chilocco, a nonreservation boarding school in northern Oklahoma. The next year Eva also entered the school, and the half brother and half sister became well acquainted. Thomas Dahkeya was already there, having entered at least as early as the spring of 1904; Captain Farrand Sayre, at that time in charge of the prisoners, characterized him as "a promising boy."[28]

After Robert came to Chilocco, he spent his vacations with his father. By this time Geronimo had married again, a widow called Sunsetso or "Old Lady Yellow" by the Apaches who still remember her, or by the Spanish name of Azul (they have forgotten why the colors were different). She had been a Mexican captive, but had escaped. The couple did not live in Geronimo's house but with a family named Guydelkon in Perico's village. There the mother, her niece, had died, and the family consisted of the father and his two sons, her grandnephews. Close by was the home of the Jozhe family. Geronimo used to come over to their house for breakfast and hold their baby, the future tribal chairman (Geronimo liked babies).[29] When Robert came home during vacations, Geron-

27 Barrett, *op. cit.*, pp. 192–96; S. M. Barrett, *Sociology of the American Indians*, pp. 54–56.

28 Oklahoma Historical Society, Indian Archives, Chilocco—Deserters, Sayre to Superintendent, March 21, 1904; Frank J. Self, Acting Superintendent, to Angie Debo, February 12, 1973; undated application (probably 1909) by Robert Geronimo to enter Carlisle, furnished me by Eve Ball from Mescalero Agency Records.

29 Benedict Jozhe and Moses Loco interview, September 16, 1969; Griswold, *op. cit.*, biographies of Azul and the Guydelkons.

Geronimo and his last wife, Azul. The couple lived with Azul's relatives in Perico's village. Courtesy U.S. Army Artillery and Missile
Center Museum.

imo settled him first with the Daklugies and then with Eugene Chihuahua, who had married a daughter of Massai.[30] Probably the Guydelkon house was too crowded, even by Apache standards of sharing, to take him in.

Thus, Geronimo was seen in his day-by-day experiences in his home and with his people. But his fame had traveled far, and it attracted visitors interested mainly in sensation. One such incident was remembered by Carlisle-trained Jesse Rowlodge, an Arapaho born in 1886 on the reservation of his tribe, which bordered that of the Kiowas and Comanches. He had relatives among the Comanches in the Fort Sill area and as a young man often visited them, thus becoming acquainted with Geronimo. As he told the story: "Geronimo, he likes to play poker, you know, and montie . . . and a bunch of Comanche boys and myself used to go over there just to be with him. We used to like to play cards. And one frosty morning just as we came out of Ft. Sill into that timber, I picked up a hawk feather that had shed from a hawk. It was about five or six inches long." They found Geronimo at home building a fire. "He was all ready. We said, 'Hello, Geronimo.' 'Ho, ho, making fire,' he said in Comanche. He spoke pretty fair Comanche."

They spread out a piece of canvas, sat down around it, and started to play. Meanwhile, they stuck the feather in the hat Geronimo was wearing. Soon a buggy drove up with a local man and two visitors, a man and a woman from Baltimore. The woman wanted to know whether Geronmo had anything to sell her, and the Comanche boys interpreted. Then "one of those Comanche boys said, 'How's that feather on your hat?' He took his hat off. 'How much you want for that, Geronimo? How much you want for that?' The Comanche boy told him, 'Tell them five dollars.' 'Five dollars,' he said. That lady opened her purse and gave him five dollars. Just for a old feather! Just because he was Geronimo!"[31]

And just because he *was* Geronimo he became a major exhibit in Oklahoma and throughout the nation.

30 Eve Ball to Angie Debo, March 10, 1973.
31 Julia A. Jordan, "Oklahoma's Oral History Collection," *Chronicles of Oklahoma,* Vol. XLIX, No. 2 (Summer, 1971), pp. 167–68.

CHAPTER 21

GERONIMO ON EXHIBITION

During the Fort Sill years Geronimo became a commercial property, an exhibit to ensure the success of a celebration. If other Indians accompanied him, they fell into the background. His conduct on these occasions was a lasting demonstration of the code of courtesy and good breeding the Apaches had managed to retain even as hunted outlaws. He appeared self-possessed, alert, and not unfriendly to the people who crowded around him, and all the time he was observing, learning, marking down everything with his fresh curiosity and his active mind. At the same time, he used every opportunity he found to plead for a return to his homeland. Also, being Geronimo, he kept an eye open for business.

His first major experience of this kind was at the Trans-Mississippi and International Exposition held at Omaha from September 9 to October 30, 1898. A number of men, women, and children, including Naiche, his wife Ha-o-zinne, and their two small children, were selected from the Fort Sill prisoners, but Geronimo proved to be the main attraction. When the train stopped at stations on the journey, he cut buttons from his coat and sold them for twenty-five cents each to the eager spectators, and for five dollars he would sell his hat. Between stations he diligently sewed

Geronimo posed for a photograph wearing his ceremonial headdress.
Courtesy U.S. Army Artillery and Missile Center Museum.

Geronimo at Trans-Mississippi Exposition in Omaha, 1898. Courtesy Kansas State Historical Society, Topeka.

Naiche with Ha-o-zinne and two of their children at Omaha, 1898. Photograph by F. A. Rinehart of the Bureau of American Ethnology. Amelia Naiche, the baby in the picture, is still living on the Mescalero Reservation. Courtesy National Anthropological Archives, Smithsonian Institution.

403

Tah-das-te, said to have served in the old days as Geronimo's messenger. Photograph taken for the Bureau of American Ethnology by F. A. Rinehart at Omaha, 1898. Courtesy National Anthropological Archives, Smithsonian Institution.

more buttons on his coat and equipped himself with a new hat from a supply he had thoughtfully provided.[1]

During the fair he carried on a big business selling pictures of himself. But he did not forget the theme that throughout his imprisonment was the major purpose of his life. The story was told by Jimmie Stevens, then grown to young manhood, who had been sent to accompany a party of Apaches from the San Carlos Reservation to the exposition. His account is colored by his hatred for the raider who had killed and eaten his pony at the sheep camp in 1882. (The killing of the Mexicans that day did not seem to count with Jimmie.)

General Miles had come to the exposition to add his official presence to its Army Day, and its promoters saw that a meeting between him and Geronimo would bring good publicity. A crowd gathered to watch and listen. Stevens had been asked to serve as interpreter. At first he demanded that Geronimo pay him fifty dollars for the pony, but he finally decided that his enemy's discomfiture would be sufficient reward. Through all the years since the encounter in Skeleton Canyon, Geronimo had hoped for such a meeting with Miles, but now he trembled, the sweat rolled down his face, and he stuttered until he could not speak. According to Stevens, Naiche taunted him (this is probably not true), and then the words poured out.

First, he accused Miles of having lied in the assurances he gave to induce the surrender. Miles smiled broadly. He admitted that he had lied, but had learned lying "from the great nantan of all liars—from you, Geronimo. You lied to Mexicans, Americans, and to your own Apaches, for thirty years. White men only lied to you once, and I did it." Geronimo then made his plea to return to Arizona: "The acorns and piñon nuts, the quail and the wild turkey, the giant cactus and the palo verdes—they all miss me. . . . I miss them, too. I want to go back to them." When this was interpreted, Miles chuckled again: "A very beautiful thought, Geronimo. Quite poetic. But the men and women who live in

1 Burbank and Royce, *Burbank among the Indians*, p. 23.

Arizona, they do not miss you. . . . Folks in Arizona sleep now at night, have no fear that Geronimo will come and kill them." And he mimicked the old warrior's style, repeating his enumeration: "acorns . . . palo verde trees—they will have to get along as best they can—without you."[2]

One must make allowance for Stevens' bias. Miles had his faults, but he would not have ridiculed a fallen foe even before an audience on an occasion so gratifying to his ever present self-glorification. But there certainly was a confrontation between the two in which Geronimo's appeal failed. Later, however, when Miles visited Fort Sill, Geronimo asked to be released from the prisoners' enforced labor on account of his age, and again reminded the general of the promises made at the surrender. Miles granted this request, and Geronimo was dropped from the work detail. He continued, however, to help with the haying and the care of the cattle, "for, although I am old, I like to work and help my people as much as I am able."[3]

But his sturdy resourcefulness failed him during one amusing episode at Omaha. On Sundays, when they were free, he and Naiche and other Apaches used to get Jimmie Stevens to hire a livery team and take them through the countryside. One cloudy day, as they followed one road after another across the flat land checkerboarded with farms and fields of tall corn, every one exactly like the others, they became lost. "No mountains," said Geronimo, "nothing but corn." They were supposed to return before night, but darkness came with no stars to guide them. Finally, Stevens found a telephone and reported to the officer in charge of the Indians, and he came out and brought them in. They were almost twenty miles from town. Probably this was the only time in his adventurous life that Geronimo was lost.

They returned to find everyone braced for an Indian scare. Geronimo had talked to newspaper reporters about his longing to return to Arizona. Now it appeared that the Indians were headed

2 Woodworth Clum, *Apache Agent*, pp. 287–90; Santee, *Apache Land*, pp. 171–74.
3 Barrett, *Geronimo's Story of His Life*, p. 182.

for their mountains, with the usual bloody trail on the way. The city was alerted, farmers barred their doors, telegrams went out. When the lost party arrived, newsboys on the streets were selling extras with screaming headlines:

GERONIMO AND NACHEE ESCAPE
APACHE MURDERERS THOUGHT TO BE ON
THEIR WAY BACK TO ARIZONA

Jimmie read the story to the Indians under a street lamp, then hurried them to their camp.[4]

Geronimo's next public appearance was at the Pan-American Exposition at Buffalo in the summer of 1901. For this he was paid $45.00 a month and was allowed to select the party that accompanied him. Among them was eleven-year-old Thomas Dahkeya. The others probably were his old-time companions—"a lot of bummers" was the disgusted characterization of Captain Sayre.[5] But for once Geronimo's presence attracted little attention. Greater events dominated the headlines. In Oklahoma on August 6 was the opening of the Kiowa-Comanche and an adjoining reservation, and homeseekers from all over the United States rushed there to participate. Following that came the news of a new country aflame with economic and social development. Then, at the exposition on September 6 President McKinley was fatally shot by an assassin, and the whole nation was torn by suspense and grief. One can only assume that Geronimo sold photographs and took note of his surroundings with his detached but unfailing interest.

Even so, his appearance at Buffalo must have given ideas to commercial promoters. On the following March 8 the general manager of Pawnee Bill's Wild West Show, which was owned by the Oklahoman Gordon W. Lillie ("Pawnee Bill"), applied to the War Department for permission "to take Geronimo and party"

---

4 Clum, *op. cit.*, pp. 290–91; Santee, *op. cit.*, pp. 174–76.
5 Oklahoma Historical Society, Indian Archives, Chilocco—Fair, Sayre to S. M. McCowan, September 20 and October 5, 1903.

for a seven months' tour. But the War Department refused.[6] Requests to exhibit him at Madison Square Garden and similar places were also refused.[7]

At the same time, he became a drawing card at Oklahoma celebrations. The procedure was simple. The promoter simply obtained his consent and the consent of the officer in charge of the prisoners, and the officer wrote out a pass permitting his attendance.[8] The first of these appearances probably was in Lawton at its first Fourth of July celebration in 1902, when a group of Apaches with Geronimo at the head participated in the "monster street parade."[9] The following fall, thirteen-year-old Oklahoma City, the self-proclaimed "metropolis" (population, about ten thousand) of the territory, initiated an annual fair and racing meet. An "immense crowd" of about thirty-five hundred people was in attendance. For the first night's entertainment "Geronimo, the famous Apache chief, and his band of Indians, prisoners of war at Fort Sill, . . . gave an exhibition"—probably a dance—in front of the grandstand.[10] It was probably the next year that he helped to celebrate the Fourth of July in the new town of Anadarko, which had sprung up in the vicinity of the Indian school and agency on the day of the land opening. An existing photograph shows him and City Marshal J. F. Hefley riding together at the head of the parade. Here he is seen sitting his horse with proper dignity, wearing citizen's clothes except for the characteristic Apache headdress of a close-fitting cap with a streamer of eagles' feathers.[11]

In appearances outside Oklahoma the War Department made a distinction between purely commercial exhibitions and official celebrations. Thus, Geronimo was taken to the Louisiana Purchase

[6] National Archives and Records Service, Record Group No. 94, AGO 429518, from 445841, O. J. Krause to Adjutant General, March 8, 1902; statement by Arthur Guydelkon furnished me by Berlin Basil Chapman. The request made more publicity than the refusal, hence the frequent statement that Geronimo traveled with the show.

[7] Nye, *Carbine and Lance*, p. 385.

[8] Wood, *Lives of Famous Indian Chiefs*, p. 553.

[9] Institute of the Great Plains, "Lawton," p. 6, reprint from *Daily Republican*, July 5, 1902.

[10] *Oklahoman*, September 10, 1902.

[11] University of Oklahoma, Western History Collections.

Geronimo riding in a parade at Anadarko. *During the Fort Sill years Geronimo became a commercial property.* Courtesy University of Oklahoma Library, Western History Collections.

Exposition at Saint Louis in 1904. Congress made an appropriation of forty thousand dollars plus a supplemental twenty-five thousand dollars for the Department of the Interior to use in an exhibit showing aboriginal Indian culture and current educational methods.[12] S. M. McCowan, the capable superintendent of the Chilocco school, was placed in charge.[13]

But the mere thought of an Indian exhibit was enough to stir up the usual sensationalism. Promoters sought concessions from the management of the exposition to open Wild West shows featuring

12 U.S. *Statutes*, XXXII, 445; XXXIII, 207.
13 Oklahoma Historical Society, Indian Archives, Chilocco—Fair, W. A. Jones, July 24, 1903.

Indians on the midway ("pike"). Officers of the local government at Lawton wrote to recommend Geronimo, who, "as you know, has between eighty-five and one hundred white scalps . . . also a vest made of the hair of the whites whom he has killed." There was the promise of a kickback; if the scheme should succeed, "you will be cared for."[14]

The Washington officials managed to keep such designs under reasonable control, but it was inevitable that Geronimo would be chosen to join the Fort Sill contingent. Captain Sayre stipulated that he could attend only under McCowan's supervision, and the other members of the group were hand-picked for their steady character. They were scheduled to leave on May 10 with George Wratten. Geronimo was promised payment, probably a dollar a day, but some promoter got to him with an offer of one hundred dollars a month. On May 9 the hard-headed old man informed the captain that he would not go, and the others went on without him. **The exasperated McCowan wrote to Sayre, "You and I agree fully that Geronimo is not more than a blatant blackguard, living on a** false reputation." The wily bargainer probably learned that he could attend the fair only on the War Department's terms. He then told Sayre that he had been "badly advised" and was willing to go even without pay.[15] Geronimo glossed over these negotiations somewhat in his own account: "When I was at first asked to attend the St. Louis World's Fair I did not wish to go. Later, when I was told that I would receive good attention and protection, and that the President of the United States said that it would be all right, I consented."[16]

He lived in the "Apache village," one of the many clusters of typical native dwellings near the Indian Building. This building

[14] *Ibid.*, N. F. Shabert and W. R. Haynes to Commissioners of the Louisiana Exposition, April 25, 1903; McCowan's office to Frederick J. V. Skiff, October 26, 1903.
[15] *Ibid.*, Sayre to McCowan, September 20 and October 5, 1903, May 9, 24, 1904; [McCowan] to Sayre, May 28, June 3, 1904. Regarding the payment offered Geronimo, see Sayre to McCowan, September 7, 1903, and [McCowan] to Sayre, March 24, 1904. McCowan was willing to pay Quanah Parker $1.00 a day; [McCowan] to D. W. Haddon, April 18, 1904.
[16] Barrett, *Geronimo's Story of His Life*, p. 197.

410

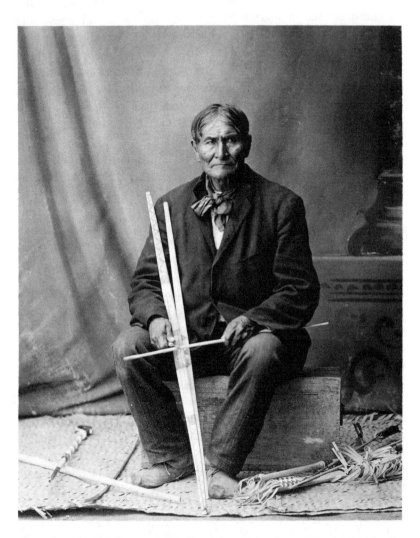

Geronimo in business at the Louisiana Purchase Exposition in St. Louis, 1904. "The old gentleman is pretty high priced, but then he is the only Geronimo." Courtesy National Anthropological Archives, Smithsonian Institution.

was divided by a wide hallway into two long apartments. One of these housed a model school with pupils of all ages—the smaller ones to show the teaching methods, the older ones to demonstrate their vocational skills—and the other contained booths where the old-time Indians worked at their native crafts. Geronimo had a booth to himself between that of Pueblo women grinding corn and making bread and that of Pueblo pottery makers. There he worked industriously at his bows and arrows, for which he found a ready sale, along with his photographs and autographs.[17] Orders even came to McCowan by mail. After quoting the prices—ten cents for an autograph, fifty cents to two dollars for a photograph—McCowan commented to one of these customers, "The old gentleman is pretty high priced, but then he is the only Geronimo."[18] He also entertained the spectators by singing and dancing. McCowan found him "an agreeable, amiable old man," usually "as happy as a bird."[19]

In the Apache village he probably renewed contacts with old reservation friends—and enemies—from Arizona.[20] More important to him was the presence of Thomas Dahkeya, who had been brought to the demonstration school with other students from Chilocco. And he must have been greatly surprised when Lenna arrived from Mescalero about July 14. New Mexico, like Florida in earlier years, was capitalizing on Geronimo's fame for its tourist business. Her transportation was paid by the railroads, with the understanding that a portion of her time would be spent in the New Mexico building distributing pamphlets about the Cloudcroft resort and other attractions. Truly, it would have been good business to present this slender, pretty girl with the refined and quiet manner as the daughter of the notorious Geronimo. But she

[17] Oklahoma Historical Society, Indian Archives, Chilocco—Fair, [McCowan] to John A. Buntin, February 2, 1904; to Sayre, April 25, 1904; to Charles M. Harvey, May 21, 1904; to J. W. Haddon, June 7, 1904; Haddon to McCowan, April 22, 1904; [McCowan], "The Government's Indian Exhibit at the Louisiana Purchase Exposition"; *Vinita Chieftain*, July 28, 1904.

[18] Oklahoma Historical Society, [McCowan] to G. E. Follansbee, October 4, 1904.

[19] *Ibid.*, [McCowan] to Sayre, July 1, 1904; to George A. Purington, September 5, 1904.

[20] *Ibid.*, [McCowan] to C. W. Crouse, March 9, 29, 1904.

Lenna Geronimo, probably photographed at the Louisiana Purchase Exposition, St. Louis, 1904. Note her "sore eyes." Courtesy U.S. Army Artillery and Missile Center Museum.

413

was suffering so severely from "sore eyes" (no doubt trachoma) that she was incapacitated from any duties at the school or the New Mexico exhibit.[21]

Geronimo and his teenaged children probably lived together as a family in his wickiup in the Apache village. Strangely enough, he did not mention the reunion with Lenna in dictating his memoirs to Barrett, but the accurate details he gave regarding his Mescalero family must have been based on what he learned from her. And it is apparent that he kept up the contact after her return, for he was aware of her subsequent marriage.[22] It is even possible that Robert's decision to enroll at Chilocco the following year was the result of this meeting.

Geronimo's two children were sent away from the fair at the end of the summer—Lenna about August 24 in time to enter school at Mescalero and Thomas to Chilocco on August 27.[23] It was certainly no coincidence that just at this time, becoming "tired of the crowds" and "homesick," Geronimo asked permission to go back to Fort Sill for a two or three weeks' visit. This was not granted, but he was allowed to return permanently a month later. He started back on October 2. McCowan sent him by way of Chilocco "because he was anxious to see his nephew [sic] Tommy once more. He says he thinks more of Tommy than all other things in the world." He was to remain there "as long as he desires" before being taken on to Fort Sill.[24] This was probably his first visit to Chilocco, but other visits were remembered by an elderly former student, who said the superintendent encouraged them as a help to the morale of the young Apaches there.[25]

21 *Ibid.*, A. N. Brown to James A. Carroll, July 1, 1904; Carroll to Sayre, July 11, 1904; to McCowan, July 13, 1904; [McCowan] to Carroll, July 23, August 6, 1904.

22 *Ibid.*, Sayre to McCowan, September 20, 1903; *Vinita Chieftain*, July 28, 1904; Barrett, *Geronimo's Story of His Life*, p. 178.

23 Oklahoma Historical Society, Indian Archives, Chilocco—Fair, Irving McNeil to McCowan, August 24, 1904; Chilocco—Enrollment, McCowan to W. N. Sickels, August 27, 1904.

24 *Ibid.*, Chilocco—Fair, George A. Purington to McCowan, August 28, 1904; [McCowan] to Purington, September 5, 1904; to Sayre, October 3, 1904; *Perkins Journal*, October 14, 1904.

25 Garland J. Blaine to Angie Debo, August 21, 1974, quoting the former student.

McCowan had indeed changed his opinion of Geronimo during the summer's association. He reported to Captain Sayre: "He really has endeared himself to whites and Indians alike. With one or two exceptions, when he was not feeling well, he was gentle, kind and courteous. I did not think I could ever speak so kindly of the old fellow whom I have always regarded as an incarnate fiend. I am very glad to return him to you in as sound and healthy condition as when you brought him here."[26]

The fair had been an interesting experience for Geronimo. Although he was under strict supervision, he was taken to see the shows and try out the amusement devices on the pike, and his comments on what he saw reveal the workings of his keen, if unsophisticated, intelligence.

Most of all, he was interested in the races of men: "There were many other Indian tribes there, and strange people of whom I had never heard." He saw Turks—"strange men with red caps" and "peculiar swords"—and watched their use of these scimitars in a sham battle. His expert judgment: "They would be hard people to kill in a hand-to-hand fight." He saw Igorots from the Philippines:

>>>>>>>>>>>>>>>>>>>>>>>>>>><

little brown people . . . that United States troops captured recently on some islands far away from here.

They did not wear much clothing, and I think that they should not have been allowed to come to the Fair. But they themselves did not seem to know any better. They had some little brass plates, and they tried to play music with these, but I did not think it was music —it was only a rattle. However, they danced to this noise and seemed to think they were giving a fine show.

I do not know how true the report was, but I heard that the President sent them to the Fair so that they could learn some manners, and when they went home teach their people how to dress and how to behave.

[26] Oklahoma Historical Society, Indian Archives, Chilocco—Fair, [McCowan] to Sayre, October 3, 1904.

≈≈≈≈≈≈≈≈≈≈≈≈≈≈≈≈≈≈≈≈

To him the sleight-of-hand performances were demonstrations of Power. He saw a man put a woman in a basket, cover it with red calico, and thrust a sword through in all directions: "I heard the sword cut through the woman's body, and the manager himself said she was dead; but when the cloth was lifted from the basket she stepped out, smiled, and walked off the stage. I would like to know how she was so quickly healed, and why the wounds did not kill her." He saw a Negro tied with ropes who slipped out free, leaving the ropes still tied. "I do not understand how this was done. It was certainly a miraculous power, because no man could have released himself by his own efforts."

He was taken to a puppet show. "In front of us were some strange little people who came out on the platform." They "did not seem in earnest about anything they did; so I only laughed at them. All the people around where we sat seemed to be laughing at me." He watched a performance by a trained bear. "I have never considered bears very intelligent, except in their wild habits," but here was a bear "as intelligent as a man. He would do whatever he was told—carry a log on his shoulder, just as a man would; then, when he was told, would put it down again." Here he gave another expert opinion: "I am sure that no grizzly bear could be trained to do these things."

He was treated to a ride on the Ferris wheel. His guards took him "into a little house that had four windows." Apparently he did not notice that the cars were attached to the revolving wheel. When he looked out, he saw that "our little house had gone high up in the air, and the people down in the Fair Grounds looked no larger than ants." He was given "a glass to look through (I often had such glasses which I took from dead officers in Mexico and elsewhere), and I could see rivers, lakes and mountains." Close as he was to the sky, he started to explore that, but he could see no stars, and the sun was too bright to examine. "Finally I put the glass down, and as they were all laughing at me, I too, began to laugh." Back on the ground, he "watched many of these little houses going up and coming down, but I cannot understand how they travel."

He was fascinated by the process of glass-making. "I had always thought that these things were made by hand, but they are not. The man had a curious little instrument, and whenever he would blow through this into a little blaze the glass would take any shape he wanted it to. I am not sure, but I think that if I had this kind of instrument I could make whatever I wished. . . . But I suppose it is very difficult to get these little instruments, or other people would have them. . . . I bought many curious things in there and brought them home with me." (Probably most of them went to Eva.)

His final summary: "I am glad I went to the Fair. I saw many interesting things and learned much of the white people. . . . I wish all my people could have attended the Fair." The trip was profitable in another sense important to him. He told how he sold his photographs at a profit and "wrote my name" for a price "and kept all of that money. I often made as much as two dollars a day, and when I returned I had plenty of money—more than I had ever owned before."[27]

The next year he was taken to Washington to ride in Theodore Roosevelt's inaugural parade. This also was good business. Just before he left, Lieutenant Purington handed him a check for $171. He took it to a Lawton bank, deposited $170, and started off with only $1 in his pocket. Whenever the train stopped at a station, people crowded around the car windows and bought his autographs for fifty cents each as fast as he could print them. When he changed trains, George Wratten, who went along as interpreter, had trouble getting him from one station to another through crowds of eager purchasers. He bought a trunk, filled it with good clothes, and returned with money in his pockets.[28]

Supposedly, this part of the inaugural parade was a "before" and "after" demonstration of the ability of Indians to acquire

27 Barrett, *Geronimo's Story of His Life*, pp. 197–206.
28 Wood, *op. cit.*, p. 550.

417

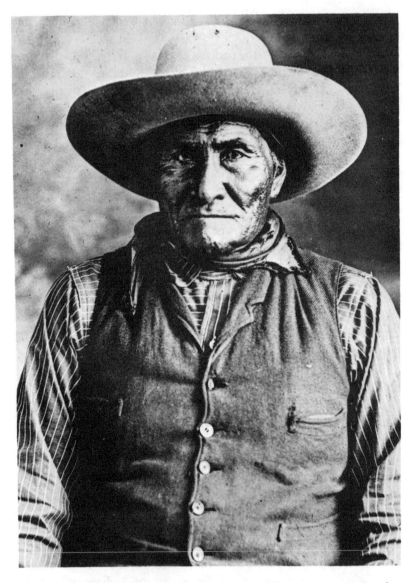

Geronimo as an alert observer at St. Louis. "I saw many interesting things and learned much of the white people." Courtesy Kansas State Historical Society.

"civilization" and the success of the government in guiding the process. Six "wild" Indians of the old order were to ride ahead, resplendent in their native costumes, to be followed by a unit of well-dressed, disciplined Carlisle cadets. If the ebullient "Teddy" was indulging his boyish fascination for the Wild West, that motivation was not mentioned.

The party was made up at Carlisle. Besides Geronimo there were Quanah Parker, Comanche; Little Plume, Piegan Blackfoot; Buckskin Charley, Ute; Hollow Horn Bear, Brulé Sioux; and American Horse, Oglala Sioux. A photograph made there shows them mounted, wearing their tribal accouterments.[29] Nobody thought to take a picture of the Carlisle contingent. Nobody, in fact, observed them in the parade, and even the other "wild" Indians went relatively unnoticed. Geronimo stole the show. Only the president attracted more attention.

The parade moved along Pennsylvania Avenue between packed masses of cheering citizens with Roosevelt in the lead, doffing his silk hat and smiling his big-toothed smile. Next came the army band. And then the Indians! The six came riding abreast. Geronimo was on his favorite pony, carefully shipped there for the occasion. He held himself erect, completely calm and self-possessed, while men threw their hats into the air and shouted, "Hooray for Geronimo!" "Public Hero No. 2," said the disgusted Woodworth Clum. This son of the Apache agent, hating Geronimo with all the intensity of his father, had been a member of the inaugural committee, and Roosevelt's request for Geronimo's presence had been made to him. Now he was privileged to stand near the president as he reviewed the parade in front of the White House, and he took the opportunity to ask, "Why did you select Geronimo to march in your parade, Mr. President? He is the greatest single-handed murderer in American history."

"I wanted to give the people a good show," answered the irrepressible Teddy.[30]

[29] Smithsonian Institution, Photograph No. 44356.
[30] Woodworth Clum, *Apache Agent*, pp. 291–92; John P. Clum, "Geronimo," pp. 254–55; Katherine C. Turner, *Red Men Calling on the Great White Father*, pp. 182–84, 192–93.

Interviewed at his hotel the next day, Geronimo unlocked his suitcase, "patted it with his slender, small, aristocratic looking fingers (he had a beautifully shaped hand)," and drew out his headdress. It was of skin ornamented with gold beads. He donned it and smilingly showed how he had worn it in the parade. The streamer "was as long as he was tall; he flaunted it in the air, drew himself up to his full height, and made every individual feather in it quiver as though alive."[31]

But Geronimo saw more than public acclaim or even financial profit in his trip to Washington. Four days later, on March 9, he and the other old-time warriors were taken to see the president. It was the first opportunity he had ever had to appeal to the highest authority for a return to Arizona. He had brooded over it so deeply that his plea, as interpreted by Wratten, rose to unaccustomed eloquence.

He began by the conventional Apache invocation to a personage invested with divinity: "Great Father, I look to you as I look to God. When I see your face I think I see the face of the Great Spirit. I come here to pray you to be good to me and my people." He told how he had fought to protect his homeland: "Did I fear the Great White Chief? No. He was my enemy and the enemy of my people. His people desired the country of my people. My heart was strong against him. I said that he should never have my country. . . . I defied the Great White Chief, for in those days I was a fool."

He made the hard admission that he had had "a bad heart":

I ask you to think of me as I was then. I lived in the home of my people. . . . They trusted me. It was right that I should give them my strength and my wisdom.

When the soldiers of the Great White Chief drove me and my people from our home we went to the mountains. When they

---

31 S. M. Huddleson, "An Interview with Geronimo and His Guardian, Mr. G. M. Wratton." Wratten must have been carried away by the events of the parade, for he claimed to have taught Geronimo all he knew of civilized deportment.

followed us we slew all that we could. We said we would not be captured. No. We starved but we killed. I said that we would never yield, for I was a fool.

So I was punished, and all my people were punished with me. The white soldiers took me and made me a prisoner far from my own country. . . .

Great Father, other Indians have homes where they can live and be happy. I and my people have no homes. The place where we are kept is bad for us. . . . We are sick there and we die. White men are in the country that was my home. I pray you to tell them to go away and let my people go there and be happy.

Great Father, my hands are tied as with a rope. My heart is no longer bad. I will tell my people to obey no chief but the Great White Chief. I pray you to cut the ropes and make me free. Let me die in my own country, an old man who has been punished enough and is free.

The president answered him with understanding and compassion: "I have no anger in my heart against you. I even wish it were only a question of letting you return to your country as a free man." But he told of the enmity that existed in Arizona against the band, and the prospect of trouble: "I should have to interfere between you. There would be more war and more bloodshed." Thus, he concluded that "it is best for you to stay where you are." He promised to confer with the commissioner of Indian affairs and the secretary of war "about your case, but I do not think I can hold out any hope for you. That is all I can say, Geronimo, except that I am sorry, and have no feeling against you."[32]

It was the following summer that Roosevelt gave Barrett permission to record Geronimo's story after that permission had been refused by the military. One wonders if the meeting following his inauguration may have influenced him to grant the request. The closing words of that book are, in fact, Geronimo's apologia and a

32 Wood, *op. cit.*, pp. 556–59. This appeal was published in many Oklahoma newspapers. See, for example, *Vinita Chieftain*, April 20, 1905.

continuation of his appeal. Barrett may have improved the language somewhat, but they accord with the sentiments expressed throughout his prison years: "I'm thankful that the President of the United States has given me permission to tell my story. I hope that he and those in authority under him will read [it] and judge whether my people have been rightly treated. . . . In the treaty with General Miles we agreed to go to a place outside of Arizona and learn to live as the white people do."

He went on to say that they had learned agricultural methods that would enable them to live on a smaller acreage than before. They were willing to accept this reduction, but there was "no climate or soil . . . equal to that of Arizona," and they longed to return to

that land which the Almighty created for the Apaches. It is my land, my home, my father's land, to which I now ask to be allowed to return. I want to spend my last days there and be buried among those mountains. If this could be I might die in peace, feeling that my people, placed in their native homes would increase in numbers rather than diminish as at present, and that our name would not become extinct.

I know that if my people were placed in that mountainous region around the headwaters of the Gila River they would live in peace and act according to the will of the President. They would be prosperous and happy in tilling the soil and learning the civilization of the white men, whom they now respect. . . . If this cannot be done during my lifetime . . . I hope that the remnant of the Apache tribe may, when I am gone, be granted the one privilege which they request—to return to Arizona.[33]

No doubt the president was moved when he read this plea, but his decision stll stood. Meanwhile, shortly after his trip to Wash-

---

[33] Barrett, *Geronimo's Story of His Life*, pp. 213–16.

422

ington, Geronimo participated in an event that was, more frankly than the inaugural parade, a Wild West promotion.

Frank Greer, an influential newspaper publisher at the Oklahoma territorial capital of Guthrie, had been able to bring the National Editorial Association to his ambitious young city for its annual meeting in 1905. His inducement was a visit to the 101 Ranch operated by the Miller Brothers, who had leased an immense tract of land from the Ponca Indians in northern Oklahoma. The ranch had not yet entered the show business that was to affect its subsequent history, but it had top cowhands accustomed to winning riding, roping, and bulldogging contests held informally with other outfits. Provision was accordingly made for excursion trains to bring the visiting editors to the ranch for one day's entertainment on June 11, and the Millers exerted every effort to make the occasion memorable. This included the presence of Geronimo, usually billed at such exhibitions as "the tiger of the human race" or "the Apache terror."

Lieutenant Purington had already received the request from the Millers when Norman Wood interviewed him in April, and he was inclined to grant it. "Out of the fifty or sixty thousand people expected on the ground that day," he told Wood, "it is thought that at least ten thousand will come purposely to see Geronimo." The promoters agreed to pay the old warrior his own price, but the amount he exacted is not recorded.

The day came, and so did Geronimo, and so did an estimated sixty-five thousand spectators ranged in grandstands built for the occasion. The Millers had bought some buffalo from Colonel Charles Goodnight's celebrated JA Ranch in the Texas Panhandle, and the main feature of the morning was "the last buffalo hunt," in which Geronimo would kill one of the animals to be butchered and served to the visitors at the noon meal.

The shooting was done from an automobile owned by a Chicago visitor, but from there on the stories differ. According to one account, Geronimo shot and wounded the buffalo, but failed to hit a vital spot, and a Miller cowhand had to finish the job. This could be true. The promoters, as usual, had confused their Indians. Geronimo was not a Great Plains hunter, accustomed to riding a horse especially trained to approach a buffalo on a dead run and swerve at precisely the right instant while the rider launched his arrow at the exact spot for the kill. By the other story, it was the Chicago visitor who wounded the buffalo, and it was Geronimo, riding in the automobile, who sprang out and "finished the animal with neatness and dispatch." Again, this could be true. Geronimo could have used an authentic Apache technique, which astounded Bourke when he saw captured cattle butchered in the Sierra Madre. In either case, the visitors saw Geronimo in action and were treated afterwards to a dinner of buffalo meat. But he did not steal the show that day. The afternoon was filled with feats of skill by the Miller cowhands and was closed by a grand finale in which three hundred obliging Poncas rode yelling from over the hill and engulfed a wagon train.[34]

Lurid accounts of the day's performance were published by the visitors in their home newspapers. As President Roosevelt heard it, Geronimo had participated in a public buffalo hunt in company with army officers. There he drew the line; he wrote an angry letter demanding that whoever at Fort Sill was responsible for this "disgraceful exhibition" should be disciplined. But as it turned out, only two officers had been present, and merely as spectators on leave in civilian clothes.[35]

Geronimo had no qualms about participating in a Wild West spectacle if he could make it pay. As Blaine Kent, an aged Iowa Indian, expressed it: "Old Man Geronimo, well he has good sense just like anybody else in putting on a show. And a lot of people was really scared of him you know." He remembered such an appearance at the 101 Ranch, probably on another occasion (he gave the date as 1906): "He was sitting there. . . . They had a table with a lot of pictures of him and postcards. . . . And they had a ball and chain on him down around the ankle. . . . But then there's guards

34 Wood, *op. cit.*, pp. 553, 559; Fred Gipson, *Fabulous Empire*, pp. 224–31.
35 Nye, *op. cit.*, p. 385.

424

behind him with guns, too. He was sitting there and people come by. . . . He don't say a word. Just look right at them. Don't smile. Don't laugh or nothing. Somebody will come along, look at his picture, and throw down a dollar bill, maybe a five dollar bill, and he grabbed that and stick it in a pocket. Won't even give them any change back. Then the man says. Ladies and gentlemen go on by, don't bother him none. (Mr. Kent chuckled at this point.)"[36]

It is safe to surmise that President Roosevelt was unaware of such exhibitions. And if the date 1906 is correct, Geronimo may have taken a side trip in an entirely different character to nearby Chilocco to meet the newly arrived Robert. The Apaches have a tradition that the first meeting between father and son occurred in this way.

Meanwhile, the success of such staged appearances encouraged Pawnee Bill to make another try. On April 11, following the meeting of the Editorial Association, he again applied for permission to take Geronimo with his show, strengthening his request by using House of Representatives stationery and attaching a supporting letter from his fellow townsman, Bird McGuire of Pawnee, Oklahoma's delegate to Congress. The showman stated that he had already made satisfactory arrangements with the old warrior, who requested that his wife and daughter accompany him. (The daughter, of course, was Eva, and the wife was the mysterious Mary Loto.) He promised to give all of them the best of care, protection from intoxicants, "and the benefit of whatever education may be had." This request was also refused.[37]

Geronimo continued however, to make headlines. In 1907 he got into all the Oklahoma newspapers when he disappeared after attending a Fourth of July celebration at Cache. In the evening he apparently started back to Fort Sill, but turned south instead and hid in the timber along a creek. Probably he had simply imbibed too freely at Cache, but it was widely reported that he was on his

36 Martha R. Siegel, "Field Notes," Perkins, Oklahoma, 1965. Used by permission.
37 National Archives and Records Service, Record Group 94, AGO 1119665, from 445841, Pawnee Bill to Lt. Gen. John C. Bates, April 11, 1906; Statement by Arthur Guydelkon furnished by Chapman; Oklahoman, April 22, 1906.

way to Old Mexico to join the Apaches still in hiding there. The soldiers found him the next day and brought him back to the post. Thus, another scare story ended without incident.[38]

But although he made no attempt to break away, Geronimo never relaxed his efforts to move the president. Later that same month he went to Lawton, called on a photographer, and ordered a picture of himself to be made. His words, certainly spoken through an interpreter, were rendered by a reporter in the jargon supposed to represent Indian English: "Me want good picture to send to my good friend, President Roosevelt. . . . May be so some time President say: 'Go, good old Geronimo; you killed heap white folks, but Jesus man made you good; be good man all time and war men [that is, the army] hold you no more." The photographer had him sit for the picture, and he went back to the reservation in better spirits than he had shown in many days.[39] This appeal also failed.

In October that year, the old warrior was permitted to attend a big Indian gathering held by the Shawnees at their ceremonial grounds close to the new railroad town of Collinsville, northeast of Tulsa. He went as the guest of his friend the well-known Shawnee leader Spybuck. The *Oklahoman* of Oklahoma City had just installed a new press that had received so much publicity in newspapers of the territory that even Geronimo had heard of it, and when his party passed through the city he expressed a wish to see it operate. As usual, he was keenly interested, but he also saw in the new equipment an opportunity to forward his plea to the president. His words were apparently recorded by the same reporter: "In the paper, write a letter to the great white father in Washington. Say to him: 'Geronimo got religion now. Geronimo fight no more. The old times, he forget.' Geronimo want to be prisoner of war no more. He want free. Tell the great white father that. Tell him in the paper." The *Oklahoman* did write the letter to the "great white father in Washington," and did "write it in the paper,"[40] but the

---

38 The identical news item appeared in a number of papers. See, for example, *Beaver County Democrat*, July 18, 1907.

39 *Oklahoman*, July 26, 1907.

40 *Ibid.*, March 1, 1953.

426

reasoning the president explained to Geronimo two and one-half years before still held.

The old man went on to Collinsville, leading the way to the ceremonial grounds in a red automobile. There, about fifteen hundred Indians of different tribes were assembled, wearing the traditional paint, feathers, and blankets they had put on for the occasion. Geronimo addressed them briefly in his native Apache, and interpreters translated it into the various languages. Barrett, always sympathetic to Indian culture, was present and recorded his words: "Brothers, I am glad to see so many of you and see you playing the old games. I shall not keep you long, but you have asked for my advice. Our way of life is gone. Your children must travel the white man's road. Schools and churches will help you and them. I have spoken."

When darkness fell, the grounds were lighted by many camp-fires, and the dances continued through the night.[41] Geronimo must have thought again that such dances "have been a large part of our enjoyment in the past, and I think they will not soon be discontinued."

His mention of the Christian religion in these later statements indicates the presence of a new Power in his personal experience. This was to lead to an inner conflict that was never resolved.

[41] *Ibid.*, October 18, 1907; Barrett, *Sociology of the American Indians*, p. 132.

CHAPTER 22

GERONIMO FINDS HIS POWERS
IN CONFLICT

The Christian missionary work among the Fort Sill Apaches was carried out by the direct descendant of the Dutch Reformed Church, the Reformed Church in America. This denomination sent its first missionary, the gifted Choctaw minister Frank Hall Wright, to the Indians of southwestern Oklahoma in 1895, but for a time the army authorities forbade him to work among the recently arrived Apaches. When this ban was finally lifted, Wright and Dr. Walter C. Roe, who had established a mission among the Cheyennes, called a council of the prisoners and with the cooperation of Lieutenant Francis Henry Beach, then in charge of them, presented the plan for a mission. There it was decided to concentrate on a school for the children. Geronimo rose and expressed the consensus of the group: "I, Geronimo, and these others are now too old to travel your Jesus road. But our children are young and I and my brothers will be glad to have the children taught about the white man's God."

The War Department then gave its permission for the construction of mission buildings on the reservation. The site chosen was a sheltered hollow known as the "punch bowl" about two miles northwest of the post. The first building erected was a small frame

428

Apache Mission of the Reformed Church, attended by Geronimo during his brief Christian commitment. *The conflict between his two life philosophies was to appear in his last hours.* Courtesy U.S. Army Artillery and Missile Center Museum.

schoolhouse with a room for the teacher's residence. Miss Maud Adkisson came in August, 1899, as the first worker with combined duties as teacher, nurse, and home visitor. The first winter fifty-five or sixty children were enrolled in the school. This was a great relief to the parents who would no longer be separated from their small children. The older pupils, however, were still sent away to boarding school, usually to Chilocco.

Religious services were conducted in the same building with Wright and Roe as the ministers. A Sunday school and a Christian Endeavor Society were also organized there. Every summer a camp meeting was held on the grounds. A large tent was set up for the services, and the Indian families camped in smaller tents surrounding it. Eventually, five buildings were constructed. Besides the schoolhouse, now enlarged, there was a church, a teachers' home, and an orphanage with two large buildings used as boys' and girls' dormitories.

Regarding the orphanage, the missionaries apparently did find two or three neglected children from undisciplined homes who needed this shelter, but the Apaches in general did not need assistance in caring for their many orphans. Through their losses, first by war, then by disease in captivity, they had had much experience in rearing parentless children by taking them into the homes of friends and relatives. But it was the educational theory of the time to make Indians into white people by keeping them in boarding schools away from native influence; thus, by assuming the support of the orphans, the missionaries had pliable material. The boarding facilities were also a convenience for young children whose village homes were too distant for day school attendance.[1]

Between thirty and forty children were day school pupils, and twenty-four lived in the dormitories. The mission staff increased to a superintendent, two teachers, two dormitory matrons, and several laborers. The pastor lived at the Comanche Mission, off the reservation between Fort Sill and Lawton, and ministered to both tribes.[2] During the first winter an elderly medicine man named Harold Dick set up such a strong opposition with his dances and ceremonies that attendance at the mission services dropped almost to zero,[3] but interest gradually revived.

The loyal scout Noche, although embittered by the injustice done him by the government, was the first convert among the leaders. He was followed by Chihuahua and finally by Naiche. (The last took the name Christian Naiche.) The unhappy Chatto, still hated by Kaahteney and his band, also became a convert. To the missionaries he appeared to be "a bright and interesting man, . . . frequently the spokesman of the people . . . who does his work

1 Amelia Naiche told me that her father was unwilling for her to attend as a boarding school pupil; thus, she made a six-mile walk, there and back, every day.
2 Richard H. Harper, "The Missionary Work of the Reformed (Dutch) Church in America, in Oklahoma," *Chronicles of Oklahoma*, Vol. XVIII, No. 4 (December, 1940), pp. 329–32; Elizabeth M. Page, *In Camp and Tepee*, pp. 73–75, 130–35; The Women's Missionary Boards of the Reformed Church in America, "The Story of the Apache Prisoners," *Missionary Lesson Leaflet*, Vol. VII, No. 2 (June,, 1906). This last publication has some startling historical errors.
3 Betzinez, *I Fought with Geronimo*, pp. 172–73.

well, and neither drinks nor gambles."[4] Less influential at the time, but adding to the stability of the congregation, were several returned Carlisle students who had become Christians at school. Among them were Jason Betzinez, the Benedict Jozhes, and James Kaywaykla and his wife, the former Dorothy Naiche. The strong-willed Asa Daklugie remained steadfast to the native religion, but Ramona was an earnest Christian, and Asa, whose love for her had begun in youth across the barriers of Apache etiquette and was to continue unchanged through a life extending beyond their golden wedding anniversary, accompanied her to all religious services.[5]

Geronimo, with his influence slipping, felt left out. He retreated in silence to his village but worked against the mission. Then, at the camp meeting in the summer of 1902 it was noticed that Zi-yeh had set up a tent on the grounds. On Sunday, the last day of the meeting, Geronimo appeared. Wright sought him out, talked to him earnestly, and won his promise to attend the evening service. He came and took a seat in the front row, sitting motionless with his hands folded in his lap until near the close. Then he sprang to his feet and made an impassioned speech, declaring that the Jesus road was best, and ending, "Now we begin to think that the Christian white people love us."

The missionaries encouraged him but did not admit him to church membership because of "a vein of self-importance in his talk." (Crook and numerous army officers would have agreed.) A year passed, in which periods of humility and gentleness alternated with arrogance and drinking sprees. Then in July, 1903, the camp meeting was held in an oak grove on Medicine Bluff Creek. Geronimo had been thrown from Zi-yeh's pony and had been severely injured. He was not present when the meeting started in the morning, but during the hot afternoon he arrived, riding slowly, barely able to sit his horse. He came into the tent, and Naiche came and

4 Page, *op. cit.*, pp. 136–40; The Women's Missionary Boards, *op. cit.*

5 The minutes of the Christian Endeavor Society, kept by Asa Daklugie as secretary, are in the Western History Collections at the University of Oklahoma. Other facts about the religious affiliation of these individuals are known to me through personal acquaintance.

sat beside him. He spoke in Apache, and Benedict Jozhe interpreted: "He says that he is in the dark. He knows that he is not on the right road and he wants to find Jesus." At this, as the missionaries remembered it, "Naiche's fine, strong face blazed with joy." During the succeeding days, they spent much time with Geronimo, explaining the tenets of their faith, and at the last service he accepted it. "I am old," he told them, "and broken by this fall I have had. I am without friends for my people have turned from me. I am full of sins, and I walk alone in the dark. I see that you missionaries have got a way to get sin out of the heart, and I want to take that better road and hold it till I die."

Dr. Roe examined him and found that under his apparent indifference he had long been listening and learning. He was baptized a week later. After the ceremony his people crowded around him. Naiche embraced him, and the women and children clung to his hands. As the missionaries told it afterwards, his face softened and became bright with joy.[6]

Thus, his emotions were deeply stirred as he made this commitment. But as he told it to Barrett two years later, he revealed the working of his independent mind. He had always been religious; now he compared his old beliefs with the new, finding much common ground. Barrett may have improved the wording, but the thought is pure Geronimo:

In our primitive worship only our relations to Usen and the members of our tribe were considered as appertaining to our religious responsibilities. [Although he did not state it then, even Christianity did not apply to Mexicans.[7]] As to the future state, the teachings of our tribe were not specific. . . . We believed that there is a life after this one, but no one ever told me as to what part of man lived after death. I have seen many men die; I have seen many human bodies decayed, but I have never seen that part that is

6 Page, *op. cit.*, pp. 142–46.
7 Barrett, *Geronimo's Story of His Life*, p. 110.

called the spirit; I do not know what it is; nor have I yet been able to understand that part of the Christian religion.

We held that the discharge of one's duty would make his future life more pleasant . . . We hoped that in the future life family and tribal relations would be resumed. . . . [He went on then to tell of the man he had known on the San Carlos Reservation, probably Noch-ay-del-klinne, who had told of seeing the spirits of departed friends.] Many Indians believed this warrior, and I cannot say that he did not tell the truth. I wish I knew that what he said is beyond question true. But perhaps it is as well that we are not certain.

Since my life as a prisoner has begun I have heard the teachings of the white man's religion, and in many respects believe it to be better than the religion of my fathers. However, I have always prayed, and I believe that the Almighty has always protected me.

Believing that in a wise way it is good to go to church, and that associating with Christians would improve my character, I have adopted the Christian religion. I believe that the church has helped me much during the short time I have been a member. . . . I have advised all of my people who are not Christians, to study that religion, because it seems to me the best religion in enabling one to live right.[8]

Thus, Geronimo did not discard his primitive beliefs, but supplemented them. It is clear that he found no discrepancy between Christian worship and his people's sacred observances such as the womanhood ceremony he had just celebrated for Eva. (In this belief he was probably more liberal than the missionaries.) His words, "I believe that the Almighty has always protected me," indicate that he still trusted his Power, although he gave it a Christian expression. It was no longer necessary for him to use it to deflect bullets, delay the daybreak, or reveal the location of the enemy; but illness believed to be caused by malevolent influences still afflicted his people, and to that it was applicable.

8 *Ibid.*, pp. 207–12.

It seems impossible to discover whether he used his "curative" ceremonies during his Christian interlude—if he did, the missionaries probably were not aware of it—but it is known that he did practice them during the Fort Sill period. Some of Opler's informants described the procedure as they had observed it in their boyhood. Geronimo permitted these young visitors to be present if they would remain quiet and observe his personal taboo against scratching. (One who scratched himself would immediately experience a choking sensation.)

One informant described a ceremony he had observed for an elderly man suffering from "coyote sickness," a disease caused by any contact with a coyote, a wolf, or a fox—even with the tracks of these animals or the ground where they had lain. This ceremony was held in an arbor outside Geronimo's house, beginning as soon as darkness fell. There a fire burned, with Geronimo and his patient on the west side, Geronimo facing east with the patient stretched out before him. There were several adults present, mainly relatives of the sick man, sitting in a semicircle in the back of the shelter, with an open space towards the east.

In front of Geronimo was a basket tray, holding an eagle feather, an abalone shell, and a bag of pollen. He began his ceremony by rolling a cigarette and sending a puff of smoke towards each of the four cardinal points, beginning at the east. Next, he rubbed certain parts of the patient's body with the pollen, praying to each direction as he did so. Each of his prayers referred to Coyote. Then he started to sing, accompanying his songs by beating on a drum with a curved stick. There were many of these songs, all relating to Coyote: how he was a tricky fellow, hard to see and find; how he had given these characteristics to Geronimo so that he also could make himself invisible; and how he helped Geronimo in curing. The singing continued until the evening star was halfway between the horizon and the zenith—the Apache midnight. The ceremony lasted four nights, each one a repetition of the first.

Another of Geronimo's patients at Fort Sill was an old woman who was helping her dog to follow a wolf; when the wolf ran into a hole, she seized its leg to pull it out. Then she became violently ill, with her body shaking, her lips twisted, her eyes crossed. Geronimo sang over her and cured her. (Anybody familiar with nervous disorders would conclude that *this* cure, at least, was real.) There is another case of his treating a patient for ghost sickness.[9]

Possibly these treatments took place during the early years at Fort Sill before he reached the age when his Power had sinister implications. For while the Apaches admired and trusted the possessor of Power, they feared its ultimate use. As the time of death approached, he might transfer the fatal summons to another person, especially a relative.[10] As Geronimo lived on while others fell away, no doubt such dark suspicions existed regarding him, but if he was aware of them he gave no sign, and certainly they never entered his own thinking. To him, whether pagan or Christian, Power was the central fact of his life.

He would have resolved his scientific-religious conflicts as like-minded men of other cultures have done through the ages, but his favorite amusements were something else. For a time after his conversion he probably refrained from gambling, horse racing, with its feverish wagers, and drinking, but he eventually returned to those forbidden pleasures. (There is reason to believe that some of his contemporaries also had their lapses, but they managed to keep them quiet.[11]) The Reverend Leonard L. Legters, who had become the pastor of the church in 1906, remonstrated with him; and he said that the rules were "too strict" and returned to the uncomplicated faith of his fathers. He was then suspended from membership in the church. This occurred about 1907.[12]

Throughout most of his life Geronimo seemed to be all of one piece—a completely integrated personality—but it is clear that this religious episode brought a spiritual cleavage that was never

9 Opler, *An Apache Life-Way*, pp. 40–41, 224–31, 260. For more details of the symptoms and cure of coyote sickness, see Goodwin, "Experiences of an Indian Scout," Part 2, pp. 33–34.

10 Opler, *op. cit.*, p. 256.

11 Betzinez, *I Fought with Geronimo*, p. 182.

12 *Lawton Constitution-Democrat* (weekly edition), February 18, 1909.

435

closed. At the same time his Power, the sustaining force of his long life, seemed to be breaking down.

As he approached what was probably his ninth decade, it was natural that he would have seen his contemporaries drop off. Old Nana, still unreconstructed, had died in 1896, and his widow, Geronimo's sister Nah-dos-te, in 1907; Chihuahua, the courtly gentleman and earnest Christian, in 1901; Mangus, never very fierce even when a hostile, also in 1901; and Loco, always mild and well disposed, in 1905, with the closing comment that he felt as though he had no country.[13]

But Geronimo's losses went beyond this common experience of old age. He had seen two wives die during his captivity. One by one he had seen his children die—Chappo in Alabama and, within the first five years at Fort Sill, his small son Fenton and his daughter Lulu, with all of her family but Thomas. His feeling for this orphaned grandchild was very strong. At Chilocco the "promising boy" had become "a good student and worker" selected to learn the painter's trade because of his excellent health and vitality.[14] As Geronimo saw him growing into young manhood, all his hopes were centered on this grandson as the remaining scion of his family. (When he finally established contact with his Mescalero son, Robert, the two never became very close; they had spent too many years apart.) Then on March 11, 1908, Thomas died at the age of eighteen. It was a heavy blow to the old man, and he reacted in three ways, all typical.

He retained his clear-cut judgment—and his business acumen. Three days after the youth's death, a Lawton attorney wrote to the War Department, saying that "Chief Geronimo" was "greatly distressed in spirit and brooding over the loss of an only grandson, that was very close and dear to him" and that a "move is on foot to get him a ninety day release" with "a change of scenery." If some promotion scheme was back of this story, it never emerged. The

---

13 Lockwood, *The Apache Indians*, pp. 324–25; Griswold, "The Fort Sill Apaches," biographies.

14 Oklahoma Historical Society, Indian Archives, Chilocco—Enrollment, [McCowan] to George L. Puirrington [*sic*], November 21, 1906.

letter traveled to Washington and back to the post commander, who then questioned the old Indian. Geronimo told him "that he does not feel depressed, but does feel the loss of a grandson as any other man would." He said that he had never talked to any person in Lawton about his feelings and that the request had been made without his knowledge. Asked whether he would like to take a trip for a while, he said "he would, if he could get in with some good show where he could make some money." The post commander went on to explain to the War Department that contrary to the implication of the letter, Geronimo was not "held in confinement" there—"he goes and comes at will, with nothing to do but eat and sleep."[15] That ended the matter.

But Geronimo had begun to suspect that some evil influence was destroying his family. By this time his cherished Eva was showing symptoms of debility. In his desperation he sought the cause in the ancient beliefs of his people. The post records and the cemetery headstones show the same succession of fatalities in other families, but he was thinking of his own. Surely someone had "witched" Thomas and probably had "witched" the other children. He called a dance to discover the culprit, with Lot Eyelash in charge. After three or four songs, the dancing stopped, and Lot called out his findings: "YOU DID IT! So you could live on."[16] Geronimo's feelings can only be imagined. He knew, of course, that he was not guilty. But among the more conservative Apaches the suspicion persisted even into recent times that Geronimo indeed used his Power to divert death from himself to his children.[17]

It was probably this crisis in his faith that caused the old man to consider again the Christianity he had renounced. At the camp meeting the following summer he talked to the missionaries, indicating that he wanted to start again, but at the same time he was engaging in his old habits and telling his tribesmen that he held to

---

[15] National Archives and Records Service, Record Group No. 94, AGO 1354977, from 445841, B. M. Parmenter to War Department, March 14, 1908, with endorsements; Assistant Secretary of War Robert Shaw Oliver to Parmenter, April 21, 1908.

[16] James Kaywaykla, interview, July 29, 1959.

[17] Eve Ball to Angie Debo, December 10, 1957.

the old religion.[18] As it happened, it was the most persistent of these old habits that was to lead to his death, while at the same time the collision between his two life philosophies was to appear in his last hours.

[18] *Lawton Constitution-Democrat* (weekly edition), February 18, 1909.

CHAPTER 23

GERONIMO'S FINAL SURRENDER

As Geronimo's years piled up to the winter of 1908/9, his rugged body began to show signs of breaking down. He was not well that fall, and his sturdy figure had shrunk. His activity was slowing. He had become increasingly absent-minded. To the amusement of his young friends, he would hunt for his hat while he was wearing it. One of them recalled an incident of these last years. Geronimo was fashioning a bow—his deft fingers never lost their skill—when he started to look for his knife, which he was holding in his hand. He asked his wife to hunt it for him. As the amused visitors watched, she refused, saying, "You're old enough to look for your own knife." He became angry. "Boys, you see how she is!" he said, "I advise you not to marry." Finally he saw it in his hand. "Why, I'm nothing but a fool," was his embarrassed admission.[1]

On a cold day in February, 1909 (February 11, according to the local newspaper), he rode to Lawton and sold some bows and arrows. There, he asked Eugene Chihuahua to get him some whiskey. It was illegal to sell liquor to an Indian, but the method of obtaining it was easy. Eugene simply asked a soldier to go into the

[1] *Lawton Constitution-Democrat* (weekly edition), February 18, 1909; Opler, *An Apache Life-Way*, p. 402.

saloon and buy it for him. The young man was to regret his part in the transaction to the end of his long life. Geronimo became intoxicated and, in attempting to ride back after dark, had almost reached his home when he fell off his horse and lay there all night. The next morning Mrs. Jozhe saw the horse standing saddled on the bank of the creek. She and others investigated, and found Geronimo lying partly in the water and partly on the ground. He contracted a severe cold, which became worse.

For three days his friends and family cared for him. Then one of the scouts (probably Benedict Jozhe) reported his illness to the post surgeon, who sent an ambulance to bring him to the little Apache hospital at the post. But the ambulance detail found him surrounded by about a dozen women, no doubt including his wife, and they refused to let him go. So many Apaches had died in the hospital that they called it "the death house" and feared to enter it. The surgeon reported to Lieutenant Purington, and that officer ordered a scout to accompany the ambulance and bring the old man in. By this time he was critically ill with pneumonia. It was Monday, February 15.

Now in these last hours was compressed the totality of Geronimo's life and character. The post surgeon expected him to die that night, but he asked that Robert and Eva be brought from Chilocco and was determined to live until they should arrive.[2] Purington summoned them by letter instead of by wire.[3] Thus, they did not come for two days. Geronimo had many grievances against the army, and this failure to bring his cherished Eva and his newly discovered Robert to his deathbed closed the circle.

Eugene Chihuahua stayed by him through the day, and Asa Daklugie, who was even more than a son, kept the night vigil. During those hours the old man relived the youthful tragedy of the massacre of his first family and his hatred of Mexicans. He talked

2 *Lawton Constitution-Democrat* (weekly edition), February 18, 1909; Eve Ball to Angie Debo, March 8, 1971; Betzinez, *I Fought with Geronimo*, pp. 179, 198; Musgrove, "A Belated Reward for the Surrender of Geronimo"; Benedict Jozhe, interview, September 6, 1969—"I've often heard my mother tell this story."

3 Oklahoma Historical Society, Indian Archives, Kiowa—Geronimo, Purington to John R. Wise, February 15, 1909.

of the men who were with him on his last war trail. He entrusted Eva to the care of the Daklugies and warned against her marriage. Asa promised to take her into their home.[4]

One experience of this last illness, as he told it to the Apaches at his bedside, indicates how deeply he had been affected by his unresolved religious struggle. Nat Kayihtah, the young son of the scout, had been a schoolmate and friend of Thomas Dahkeya. He had been permitted to go to the Mescalero Reservation to work and had died there of pneumonia on February 10, only the day before Geronimo made his fatal ride to Lawton. Apparently Geronimo had been told of his death. Now in his feverish imaginings, the two youths appeared to him and urged him to become a Christian. He refused, saying he had been unable "to follow the path" in his life, and it was now too late, but he asked why they had not come earlier. They answered that he had had the missionaries and had refused to listen to them.[5]

Throughout his second day in the hospital, his strong spirit staved off death in the hope of seeing his children. Then when night came, and they still had not arrived, he gave up and quietly sank away. His sturdy body held out until 6:15 the following morning, February 17. "I was sitting beside him holding his hand when he died," said Asa Daklugie.[6] This time his surrender was final.

As soon as he died, his widow rushed to his favorite horse, his well-known sorrel racing pony, and would have killed it, but other Indians prevented her. All day long grieving old women, groaning, weeping, and praying, filed in and out of the little stone building where his body lay, while men, dry-eyed and stricken, stood without, silently watching. The funeral was arranged for the following afternoon at three o'clock, and at their request the army gave all the men a half holiday so they could attend.[7]

---

[4] Eve Ball to Angie Debo, July 13, 1973.

[5] *Lawton Constitution-Democrat* (weekly edition), February 25, 1909. The Biblical analogy in this last sentence was certainly remembered from a missionary exhortation.

[6] National Archives and Records Service, Record Group No. 94, AGO 1490310, from 445841, telegram [Colonel Henry M.] Andrews to Adjutant General, February 17, 1909; Eve Ball to Angie Debo, July 13, 1973.

[7] *Lawton Constitution-Democrat* (weekly edition), February 18, 1909.

But while Geronimo's body waited in an elaborately decorated Lawton hearse, even his funeral had to be postponed for the arrival of Robert and Eva from Chilocco. They came on the train shortly after three o'clock obviously grief-stricken, and the procession started immediately to the cemetery where so many of the prisoners were buried. His grave had been dug beside that of Zi-yeh, and surrounding it were the graves of the other members of his family. The services were held there, Christian services conducted by the Reverend Leonard Legters. Virtually the entire tribe and many white people from Lawton were present. His funeral furnished an occasion for giving advice to his tribesmen, with his life used to point the moral.

Naiche, tall, erect, intelligent-looking, standing at the very edge of the grave, spoke first, briefly but impressively in Apache. He recalled incidents of the warpath, lauded Geronimo's bravery and skill as a war leader, and told how loyally he had adhered to the peace he made at the surrender. But he had refused to accept Christianity, thus being an utter failure in the chief thing in life. He closed by urging the assembled people to profit by his example.

The missionary, speaking through Eugene Chihuahua as interpreter, then conducted the formal service. He used the parable of the wise and foolish virgins to urge the Apaches to prepare for their own summons. Geronimo, he said, had probably been the greatest war leader the red men had ever known, but he had failed to conquer the pleasures of the body, and like all men he had been unable to conquer death. He told his hearers they might never become as great leaders as he had been, but they could conquer self so as to be ready for this last unconquerable experience. Then, just before the grave was filled, the relatives of the dead leader solemnly placed his riding whip and blanket in it.[8] Before he died, he had told them to tie his horse to a certain tree and to hang up his belongings on the east side of his grave, and in three days he would come and get them, but his widow decided to bury his

[8] *Ibid.*, February 25, 1909.

Robert Geronimo at his father's grave in the Apache Cemetery at Fort Sill, January 13, 1964. Courtesy U.S. Army Artillery and Missile Center Museum.

possessions with him.[9] (Regarding his possessions, it was said that the balance to his account in his Lawton bank was more than ten thousand dollars at the time of his death.[10])

An impressive rock monument surmounted by a stone eagle was erected at his grave by the Field Artillery School at Fort Sill

9 James Kaywaykla, interview, July 29, 1959.
10 Burbank and Royce, *Burbank among the Indians*, p. 24.

443

in 1931. Later, small headstones were set to mark all the graves in this tragically populous cemetery. Near the entrance a sign points out that the burials there form the "roll call" of "the most famous names in Apache history": Geronimo, Loco, Nana, and Chihuahua; and the sons and grandsons of Mangas Coloradas, Victorio, Cochise, Naiche, and Juh, and of such noted scouts as Kaahteney, Chatto, Kayihtah, and Martine.

All this history was in the minds of the Apaches that gathered that February day at the graveside of Geronimo. And the question persisted: Would this be the end of their trail, too?

EPILOGUE

Robert Geronimo never returned to Chilocco after his father's death, but transferred to Carlisle. Eva went back and finished the term, but that was the end of her schooling.[1] She came home and lived with the Daklugies. Although they tried to dissuade her, she soon married Fred Golene, a young member of the band who had been one of her fellow students at Chilocco. A daughter, Evaline, born to them on June 21, 1910, lived scarcely two months, dying on August 20. They buried the child close to Geronimo, but left a space between. Eva followed within a year, dying of tuberculosis on August 10, 1911, the last of Geronimo's prisoner descendants.[2] She was buried between her father and the baby, with her mother on the other side of the old war leader and her brother Fenton nearby. Not far away are the graves of her half sister, Lulu Dahkeya, and her family.[3]

Robert Geronimo rejoined his mother and step-father on the Mescalero Reservation after spending several years at Carlisle.

[1] Frank J. Self to Angie Debo, February 12, 1973.

[2] Oklahoma Historical Society, Indian Archives, Chilocco—Enrollment, [M. S. McCowan] to George L. Puirrington [sic], November 21, 1906; Chilocco—Students Returning Home, [McCowan] to Puirrington, September 30, 1907; *Beaver Herald*, August 17, 1911.

[3] Visit to cemetery, August 16, 1971.

By that time many of the former prisoners were living there. Several considerations had brought about their release from captivity and their settlement with the Mescaleros. When they were brought to Fort Sill, it was expected that the post, like other frontier posts of Indian war days, would soon be abandoned, leaving the reservation available as a permanent home for the prisoners. This policy was expressed officially as late as 1904.[4] And the Apaches themselves, in spite of the relative comfort in which they lived, still held an unchanged longing for freedom. Typical is a statement made by Asa Daklugie in answer to a questionnaire sent out by Captain Pratt to check on the welfare of the Carlisle graduates. He gave the requested information regarding his marriage, work record, housing, and so on, but to the final question, "Tell me anything else of interest connected with your life," he answered in his sturdy penmanship: "The 'interesting thing in my present life' is That, I wished to see, that 'Apaches people' get a freedom, from being a prisoner of War, under the Government. 'So they can have they own home.'"[5]

At the same time, friends of the Indians were still urging some provision for them. As time passed, an increasing proportion of them had been born in captivity or had been young children at the time of the wars of which they were supposedly prisoners. The death of the notorious Geronimo, who received most of the popular and official blame for the hostilities, increased the force of this argument. But ironically, it was the needs of the military that brought matters to a head.

Fort Sill, of course, had been a cavalry post during the Indian wars. Following that came a long period of inactivity. Then the War Department, because of the extensive and varied terrain of the reservation, began from 1902 on to recognize its importance for the training of artillery; and in 1910 it was selected as the site of the artillery school of fire. But the Apache prisoners, with their

4 U.S., *Statutes*, XXXII, 467, Act of June 28, 1902; XXXIII, 26, Act of February 18, 1904.

5 National Archives and Records Service, Record Group No. 75, Records of the Carlisle Indian Industrial School, Student Folder No. 72.

446

villages, their grazing cattle, their hay meadows, and their cultivated fields, were all in the way of the big guns. "These so-called
prisoners of war have more rights than free men," reported the
disgusted officer in charge of drawing up regulations for the
school.[6]

In 1911 their old friend Hugh L. Scott (then Colonel Scott),
was brought to Fort Sill for the special duty of making permanent
provision for them. He and another officer held a council with
them at the post. Naiche was the spokesman. "All we want is to be
freed and be released as prisoners," he said, "and given land and
homes that we can call our own. This is all we think about. We
are thinking the same today as the last time, and that is why we
are here now, to say these things. . . . Half or more than half of these
people talk English. Half or more than half can read and write;
they all know how to work. You have held us long enough. We
want something else now."[7]

A law releasing them was passed by Congress the following
year on August 24, 1912.[8] It made an appropriation of two
hundred thousand dollars for their settlement on lands to be
selected for them by the secretaries of war and the interior, and a
supplemental appropriation of one hundred thousand dollars was
made in 1913. A search for a suitable location indicated that the
Mescalero Reservation was the most desirable. (Arizona was completely out of the question because of the feeling against them
there.) A delegation from the prisoners was taken to visit the
Mescaleros, and they expressed their willingness to accept the band
on equal terms. But some of the prisoners wanted to remain in
Oklahoma, and it was decided to purchase individual farms for
them from the heirs of deceased Comanche, Kiowa, and Kiowa-
Apache allottees. They were allowed to choose between the two
locations, and numerous councils were held with them to deter-

---

6 Nye, *Carbine and Lance*, pp. 399–405.

7 Chapman, "Notes—Apaches," quoting National Archives and Records Service,
AGO 1808991B, Box 3142, 1912.

8 U.S., *Statutes*, XXXVII, 534.

mine their individual decisions.[9] Wratten, however, did not serve as their interpreter and did not assist in closing out their affairs. He had died on June 23, 1912, after almost twenty-six years of close association with them.

By this time, their number had declined to 261, of whom 183 chose to go to Mescalero and 78 decided to remain in Oklahoma.[10] Their cattle, about six thousand head, said to be the finest herd in the state, were sold, and they were compensated for the fence they had built around the reservation. The proceeds, $165,000, was placed to their credit to assist them in settling.[11]

The personal property of the Mescalero party—horses, mules, wheeled vehicles, household goods—was shipped to the reservation. They themselves were taken there on a special train under the escort of an army officer, arriving on April 4, 1913. Among them was Geronimo's widow with her young grandnephew, Paul Guydelkon, and his father.[12] All the surviving warriors of the last holdout band that surrendered to Miles were in the party with their families. There were Naiche, his wife, Ha-o-zinne, and five of his children; his old mother, Dos-teh-seh, daughter of Mangas Coloradas and widow of Cochise; his two half sisters, daughters of Cochise; and Ha-o-zinne's parents, Beshe and U-go-hun, and her half brother, Calvin Zhonne. The chief left in the Fort Sill cemetery the graves of his wives Nah-de-yole and E-clah-heh and eight of his children; and Dorothy, the wife of James Kaywaykla, remained in Oklahoma. Ahnandia had died of tuberculosis in Alabama. His wife, Tah-das-te, had remarried and went with her husband to Mescalero. Geronimo's "brother" Perico also went there with his stolen wife, Bi-ya-neta, and several of their children. His first wife, Hah-dun-key, had died at Fort Sill, and so had his half brother,

9 Oklahoma Historical Society, Indian Archives, Kiowa—Apache Prisoners of War, Colonel Hugh L. Scott and Kiowa Superintendent Ernest Stecker to Adjutant General, October 5, 1912.

10 Secretary of the Interior, *Annual Report*, 1913, p. 36; 1914, p. 58. This number varies slightly in official reports. A few babies born before the final settlement was made were added to the totals, and some who died before receiving land in Oklahoma were dropped from the record (Benedict Jozhe, interview, April 12, 1971).

11 Benedict Jozhe, interview, July 29, 1959.

12 Eve Ball to Angie Debo, January 18, 1973.

Burdett Tsisnah. The warrior La-zi-yah also had died at Fort Sill. Geronimo's nephew Jasper Kanseah joined the Mescalero group; and so did his brother-in-law, Yahnozha.

The betrayed scouts, Chatto, Noche, Kayihtah, and Martine, went there with their families, as did Toclanny and Siki with their children. So did Kaahteney, but he had buried Guyan at Fort Sill. Asa Daklugie and his wife, Ramona, and their children were also in the Mescalero party. There, the capable, independent-minded Daklugie became one of the strong leaders of the band. Eugene Chihuahua and his wife were in the group. Two daughters went with them, but they left the graves of six children at Fort Sill. The early Carlisle student Dexter Loco also chose Mescalero.[13]

Two of the missionaries went with the band to their new home. (The Fort Sill Mission, of course, was closed.) On the first Sunday eighty-seven of the band united by letter with the Reformed Church there.[14] They settled down quietly on the reservation in a locality of their own, good workers living in good houses, somewhat apart from the Mescaleros, but joining in reservation activities. The historian Frank C. Lockwood paid them several visits during the 1930's and made a careful study of the ones who had figured in their turbulent past, interviewing those still living, checking records, and questioning the former agency superintendent O. M. Boggess and the Reformed missionary Richard Harper. Then Mrs. Eve Ball came to live in nearby Ruidoso and began the friendly association with members of the band that was to lead to recording their reminiscences.

One glimpses in these experiences the steady character of these once wild people. Lockwood met Chihuahua's "two remarkable children," Eugene, "an industrious and successful farmer," and Ramona Daklugie in her "tidy, well-furnished little home," both proudly showing enlarged, framed photographs of their father. Naiche had died, but the missionary and the agency farmer told of his "earnestness of character," his good influence among his

[13] Griswold, "The Fort Sill Apaches," various biographies.
[14] Harper, "The Missionary Work of the Reformed (Dutch) Church in America, in Oklahoma," pp. 330–31, 334.

people, and his satisfaction with the life at Mescalero in contrast to the hardships of the warpath. Harper remembered Kaahteney as so mild and cooperative that it was hard for him to credit the army accounts of his rebellious past. Lockwood found Kayihtah and Toclanny genial and friendly, strangely unembittered by their unjust treatment. Martine, old and feeble in mind and body, seemed more resentful.[15]

Chatto had suffered most of all from the official ingratitude. He had greatly admired Crook and had committed himself completely to his new allegiance. No doubt when he found himself in favor he had lorded it over the bellicose members of the band. Then he had been given the same punishment. He brooded over this injustice, and he felt the resentment of the tribal members who regarded him as a turncoat. Boggess, who knew him well, considered him an excellent citizen with a satisfactory home life, and Harper characterized him as a man of striking bearing and dignity of character. But the factional hatred, held in check while the prisoners were under military control, now asserted itself so strongly that he and his family made their home apart from the Fort Sill settlement. In 1934 he and some others had been drinking together up in a canyon, and on their way down their automobile left the road and turned turtle in a creek. Chatto was so badly injured that he died. For many years his medal and his treasured copy of Davis' book were kept in the agency safe.[16] Perhaps they are still there.

Jasper Kanseah, the boy in Geronimo's band, lived until 1959. He could look back to a childhood memory of the great Cochise, retained a vivid impression of events on the warpath, and was the last surviving eyewitness of Geronimo's final surrender. After that came Carlisle, the prison experiences at Fort Sill, and the placid years at Mescalero telling and retelling the turbulent episodes of his people's history.[17]

Charles Istee, the only surviving son of Victorio, also joined the

15 Lockwood, *The Apache Indians*, pp. 325–43.
16 *Ibid.*, p. 326; Eve Ball, interview, July 25, 1971.
17 Ball, *In the Days of Victorio*, pp. 51, 152–53 and n. 3, 185–87. If Charlie Smith was with Geronimo's band until the last, he retained no memory of the surrender.

Mescalero party with his wife. Their son, Evan Istee, born shortly after their arrival, still lives on the reservation with his family.[18] So do the descendants of Geronimo. Lenna died young but left descendants. Robert, the mild son of the fierce raider, lived until 1966.[19] His four children, with their families, were still living on the reservation at the last report.

Meanwhile, as this band was settling into life with the Mescaleros, the government officials were purchasing farms for their relatives who chose to remain in Oklahoma. Most of this land was in a rich agricultural area north of Fort Sill centered around the town of Apache, which still perpetuates their name. They had to adjust to a more difficult life-way than did their kinsmen on the reservation, supporting themselves by farming and trades and establishing social relationships in a predominantly white society. In general it was the more progressive ones of the band, especially the Carlisle graduates, who made this choice.

Several of them were relatives of Geronimo. Among them were Jason Bètzinez and his mother, Nah-thle-tla. His sister's family had all died at Fort Sill, the five children one by one, then Ellen herself and her husband, Ambrose Chachu, in 1899. Nah-thle-tla, active and sturdy, lived to the remarkable age, as nearly as it could be determined, of 110 years, dying in 1934. Jason worked at the blacksmith trade he had learned at Carlisle and tended his eighty-acre farm. Late in life he married a Chicago woman who had served the prisoners at the Reformed Church Mission and brought her to his neat little house. Every Sunday he drove his automobile to Lawton, twenty miles away, to attend church. The two lived until 1960, Jason dying at the age of one hundred as the result of an automobile accident. They had no children.

Sam Haozous also remained in Oklahoma and became a successful farmer and good community citizen. He died in 1957, but his wife, the half-Apache daughter of George Wratten, an attractive woman much younger than her husband, continued until

[18] I met him and his much younger wife at the Reformed Church service there on July 24, 1971, and was struck by the remarkable beauty of their little boy.
[19] *Newsweek*, November 7, 1966.

recently to live at the old home. On the walls of the pleasant farmhouse hung many paintings by their gifted son, Allan Houser, who now teaches in the Institute of American Indian Arts at Santa Fe. Three of their four children who grew to adulthood graduated from college.

The Jozhes also settled on their land, where Jozhe became a successful farmer and Mrs. Jozhe won many prizes at the county fair for her canned fruit and vegetables. Their son, who was to serve more than forty years as tribal chairman, graduated from the American Indian Institute of Wichita, Kansas, a Presbyterian school headed by the well known Indian educator, Henry Roe Cloud. A great-grandson through his mother of Chief Loco, and a descendant through his father of the great Mahko, he is a nephew of Geronimo's "brothers," Perico, Fun, and Tsisnah. Gifted with a keen mind and a reflective disposition, he has become an authority on tribal history, genealogy, and present legal problems.

The Kaywayklas also made their living and reared their children on their farm. Dorothy died in 1946, but James lived until 1963, the last of his people who remembered Victorio and the disaster at Tres Castillos. Their descendants still live in Oklahoma. John Loco, the son of the chief, who had served as the head of Loco's village after the death of his father, also chose to settle in Oklahoma. In his later years he sometimes preached in a Reformed Church near Apache. He died in 1946.[20] His sons still live in the neighborhood.

But the members of the band who remained in Oklahoma have shown more of a tendency than have their Mescalero relatives to "enter the mainstream of American life"—to quote a shibboleth of early-day educators—finding their living elsewhere and even marrying non-Indians. One of John Loco's grandsons, married to a white woman, is a tool designer in Detroit. A granddaughter lives in a suburb of Washington, and her white husband, John A. Shapard, Jr., a historical legislative research analyst in the Indian

20 *Oklahoma City Times*, August 29, 1946.

452

Bureau, has done extensive independent research and writing in Apache history. Harry Perico, the son of Geronimo's lieutenant, sold his land and used the money for a college education. Then with his Chilocco-taught printer's trade he began working for the *Arkansas City (Kansas) Traveler,* and for many years until his recent retirement he served as foreman of its commercial printing department. For more than fifty years he was a member of the municipal band, and for three years he was the city golf champion. Arthur Guydelkon, whose brother accompanied Geronimo's widow to Mescalero, remained in Oklahoma. He and his young wife, a daughter of Talbot Gooday, lived for a time on their farm. Then they sold it, and he took a position in the civil service. They made their home in Lawton. Throughout his long life—he died in 1967—he was an important source of information regarding the life of Geronimo.[21]

Thus, the released prisoners have found their living in their separate ways. Like all ethnic groups, they range in character from the upright to the profligate. Their numbers have increased since they were freed from captivity. (Perhaps Crook was not far wrong when he cited "the dreary monotony of empty lives" as a contributing factor in their mortality.) No one is living now of the generation that remembered the raids, the hunted existence, and the bloody encounters with the military forces of two nations, but their descendants still have a strong sense of tribal solidarity. The Oklahoma and Mescalero bands maintain their contacts through frequent visits, and even the scattered members of the group cherish the traditions of their elders.

At a recent conference a son of John Loco, born a Fort Sill prisoner, smilingly held up his smooth wrists, saying, "See the scars of the fetters."[22] He was joking, of course. The prisoners were

---

21 Griswold, "The Fort Sill Apaches," various biographies; Benedict Jozhe, James Kaywaykla, and Moses Loco, joint interview, July 29, 1959; Benedict Jozhe, "A Brief History of the Fort Sill Apache Tribe," *Chronicles of Oklahoma,* Vol. XXXIX, No. 4 (Winter, 1961/62); *Arkansas City (Kansas) Traveler,* June 17, 1970.

22 At Anadarko, Oklahoma, August 27, 1973.

never chained, certainly not the small children, and any scars left on the souls of the captives are likewise invisible. But the experience may have given a special character to their descendants. And through their collective memories the story of Geronimo lives on.

BIBLIOGRAPHY

Source Material
I. Manuscript Material

Fort Sill, Okla. United States Army Artillery and Missile Center Museum. Archives.

Fremont, Ohio. Rutherford B. Hayes Library. George Crook Letter-book I.

Gatewood, Charles B. "An Account of the Surrender of Geronimo." Tucson, Arizona Historical Society, Gatewood Collection. Manuscript, 1895.

Huddleson, S. M. "An Interview with Geronimo and His Guardian, Mr. G. M. Wratton." Tucson, Arizona Historical Society, Gatewood Collection.

Norman, Okla. University of Oklahoma Library, Western History Collections; Phillips Collection.

Oklahoma City, Okla. Oklahoma Historical Society. Indian Archives.

Tallahassee, Fla. National Park Service.

Washington, D.C. National Archives and Records Service.
Consolidated File 1066 AGO 1883.
Inspectors File No. 1732.
Record Group No. 75, Bureau of Indian Affairs, Letters Received 1881–1907; Records of the Carlisle Indian Industrial School.

Record Group No. 94, AGO 445841.

II. Government Documents

Annual Reports of the Secretary of the Interior, 1858–69, 1881, 1913, 1914.

Annual Reports of the Secretary of War, 1882–87, 1890, 1892, 1894–96.

Kappler, Charles J. *Indian Affairs, Laws and Treaties. S. Doc. No. 452*, Vol. II, 57 Cong., 1 sess., 1904.

Malloy, William M. *Treaties, Conventions, International Acts, Protocols and Agreements between the United States of America and Other Powers. S. Doc. No. 357*, 61 Cong., 2 sess., 1910.

U.S., Congress, *Senate Executive Documents, Nos. 73, 117*, 49 Cong., 2 sess.; *Nos. 35, 83, 88*, 51 Cong., 1 sess.

U.S., *Congressional Record*, Vol. VIII (1879).

U.S., *Statutes at Large*, Vols. 16, 20, 28, 32, 33, 37.

III. Books and Articles

Anderson, Hattie M. "Mining and Indian Fighting in Arizona and New Mexico—Memoirs of Hank Smith," *Panhandle-Plains Historical Review* (Canyon, Texas), Vol. I (1928).

————. "With the Confederates in New Mexico during the Civil War—Memoirs of Hank Smith," *Panhandle-Plains Historical Review*, Vol. II (1929).

Ball, Eve. *In the Days of Victorio: Recollections of a Warm Springs Apache*. Tucson, University of Arizona Press, 1970.

————. "On the Warpath with Geronimo," *The West*, Vol. XV, No. 3 (August, 1971).

Barrett, S [tephen] M[elvil]. *Geronimo's Story of His Life*. New York, Duffield and Company, 1906.

————. *Sociology of the American Indians*. Kansas City, Mo., Burton Publishing Company, 1946.

Bartlett, John Russell. *Personal Narratives of Explorations and Incidents in Texas, New Mexico, California, Sonora, and Chihuahua Connected with the United States and Mexican Boundary Commission during the Years 1850, '51, '52, and '53*, Vol. I. New York, D. Appleton, 1854.

Basso, Keith H. (ed.). *Western Apache Raiding and Warfare: From the Notes of Grenville Goodwin.* Tucson, University of Arizona Press, 1971.

Begay, Alberta, as told to Eve Ball. "Massai—Broncho Apache," *True West*, Vol. VI, No. 6 (July–August, 1959).

Betzinez, Jason. *I Fought with Geronimo.* Ed. and annotated by Wilbur Sturtevant Nye. Harrisburg, Pa., Stackpole, 1959.

Bourke, John G. *An Apache Campaign in the Sierra Madre.* New York, Charles Scribner's Sons, 1958.

———. *On the Border with Crook.* New York, Charles Scribner's Sons, 1891.

Burbank, E[lbridge] A[yer], and Ernest Royce. *Burbank among the Indians.* Caldwell, Idaho, The Caxton Printers, Ltd., 1946.

Catlin, George. *Episodes from Life among the Indians and Last Rambles.* Ed. Marvin C. Ross. Norman, University of Oklahoma Press, 1959.

Clum, John P. "Apache Misrule," *New Mexico Historical Review*, Vol. V, No. 3 (July, 1930).

———. "Geronimo," *New Mexico Historical Review*, Vol. III, No. 1 (part 1, January, 1928), and No. 2 (part 2, April, 1928).

———. "The San Carlos Apache Police," *New Mexico Historical Review*, Vol. IV, No. 3 (part 1, July, 1929), and Vol. V, No. 1 (part 2, January, 1930).

Clum, Woodworth. *Apache Agent: The Story of John P. Clum.* Boston, Houghton, Mifflin, 1936.

Conner, Daniel Ellis. *Joseph Reddeford Walker and the Arizona Adventure.* Ed. and annotated by Donald J. Berthrong and Odessa Davenport. Norman, University of Oklahoma Press, 1956.

Crary, B. F. "Historical Museum Letter," *Pensacola Historical Society Quarterly*, Vol. II, No. 2 (April, 1966).

Cremony, John Carey. *Life among the Apaches.* San Francisco, A. Roman & Company, 1868. Reprinted by Rio Grande Press, Glorieta, N.M., 1969.

Davis, Britton. *The Truth about Geronimo.* New Haven, Yale University Press, 1929.

Edgerton, Joseph K. "A Glimpse of the Sunny South," *Plattsburgh Republican*, Plattsburgh, N.Y., February 25, 1893.

Gage, Lucy. "A Romance of Pioneering," *Chronicles of Oklahoma*, Vol. XXIX, No. 3 (Autumn, 1951).

Goodwin, Grenville. "Experiences of an Indian Scout," *Arizona Historical Review*, Vol. VII, No. 1 (part 1, January, 1936), and No. 2 (part 2, April, 1936).

Hopps, Howard B. "Lawton," *Chronicles of Oklahoma*, Vol. XXIII, No. 3 (Autumn, 1945).

Howard, O[liver] O[tis]. *Famous Indian Chiefs I Have Known*. New York, The Century Company, 1907.

————. *My Life and Experiences among Our Hostile Indians*. Hartford, Conn., A. D. Worthington & Company, 1907.

Institute of the Great Plains. "Lawton." Lawton, Okla., 1971, reprint of early newspaper articles.

Jacobson, O[scar] B[rousse], and Jeanne d'Ucel. "Art in Oklahoma," *Chronicles of Oklahoma*, Vol. XXXII, No. 3 (Autumn, 1954), Jacobson's impressions of Geronimo.

Jordan, Julia A. "Oklahoma's Oral History Collection," *Chronicles of Oklahoma*, Vol. XLIX, No. 2 (Summer, 1971).

Klasner, Lily. *My Girlhood among Outlaws*. Ed. and annotated by Eve Ball. Tucson, University of Arizona Press, 1972.

Miles, Nelson A. *Personal Recollections*. Chicago and New York, The Werner Company, 1897.

————. *Serving the Republic*. Freeport, N.Y., Books for Libraries Press, 1971.

Opler, Morris E[dward]. "A Chiricahua Apache's Account of the Geronimo Campaign of 1886, *New Mexico Historical Review*, Vol. XIII, No. 4 (October, 1938).

Reed, Walter. "Geronimo and His Warriors in Captivity," *The Illustrated American*, Vol. III (August 16, 1890).

Santee, Ross. *Apache Land*. New York, Charles Scribner's Sons, 1947, Chapter 17, Jimmie Stevens' reminiscences.

Schmitt, Martin F. (ed.). *General George Crook: His Autobiography*. Norman, University of Oklahoma Press, 1960.

Scott, Hugh Lenox. *Some Memories of a Soldier*. New York and London, Century Company, 1928.

Thomas, Alfred Barnaby (ed.). *Forgotten Frontiers: A Study of the Spanish Indian Policy of Don Juan Bautista de Anza, Governor of New Mexico, 1777–1787*. Norman, University of Oklahoma Press, 1932.

Wheatley, Richard. "The Caged Tigers of Santa Rosa," *Pensacola Historical Society Quarterly*, Vol. II, No. 2 (April, 1966).

The Women's Missionary Boards of the Reformed Church in America. "The Story of the Apache Prisoners," *Missionary Lesson Leaflet*, Vol. VII, No. 2 (June, 1906).

Wood, Norman B. *Lives of Famous Indian Chiefs*. Aurora, Ill., Indian Historical Publishing Company, 1906.

IV. Interviews

Betzinez, Jason. Apache, Okla., January 26, 1955; August 21, 1959.

Geronimo, Robert. Mescalero, N.M., August 7, 1957.

Hammond, Ruth. Stillwater, Okla., March 11, 1973.

Haozous, Sam. Apache, Okla., January 27, 1955.

Jozhe, Benedict. Marshall, Okla., July 29, 1959; September 16, 1969; April 12, 1971.

Kaywaykla, James. Marshall, Okla., July 29, 1959.

Loco, Moses. Marshall, Okla., July 29, 1959; September 16, 1969.

Naiche, Amelia. Mescalero, N.M., July 23, 1971.

V. Contemporary Newspapers and News Magazines

Arkansas City (Kansas) Traveler. Arkansas City, Kans., June 17, 1970.

Beaver County Democrat. Beaver, Okla., July 18, 1907.

Beaver Herald. Beaver, Okla., August 17, 1911.

Beaver Journal. Beaver, Okla., January 18, 1906.

Lawton Constitution-Democrat (weekly edition). Lawton, Okla., February 18, 25, 1909.

Mangum Star. Mangum, Okla., January 18, 1906.

Muskogee Times-Democrat. Muskogee, Indian Territory, November 8, 1906.

Mobile Daily News. Mobile, Ala., September 12, 1894.

Newsweek. November 7, 1966.

Oklahoma City Times. Oklahoma City, Okla., August 29, 1946.

Oklahoman. Oklahoma City, Okla., September 10, 1902; April 22, 1906; July 26, October 18, 1907; March 1, 1953.

Pensacolian. Pensacola, Fla., September 18, October 23, 30, November 13, 1886; June 11, 1887. Typed articles furnished by National Park Service, Gulf Islands National Seashore, Gulf Breeze, Fla.

Perkins Journal. Perkins, Okla., October 14, 1904.

Vinita Chieftain. Vinita, Indian Territory, July 28, 1904; April 20, 1905.

Secondary Material
I. Manuscript Material

Chapman, Berlin Basil. "Notes—Apaches." In possession of Dr. Chapman, Orlando, Fla.

Goodman, David Michael. "Apaches as Prisoners of War, 1886–1894." Ph.D. dissertation, Texas Christian University, Fort Worth, 1968.

Griswold, Gillett. "The Fort Sill Apaches: Their Vital Statistics, Tribal Origins, Antecedents." U.S. Army Artillery and Missile Center Museum, Archives. Fort Sill, Okla.

Musgrove, Ora E. "A Belated Reward for the Surrender of Geronimo." Unpublished article in possession of Angie Debo.

Pollard, William Grosvenor, III. "Structure and Stress: Social Change among the Fort Sill Apache and Their Ancestors, 1870–1960." M.A. thesis, University of Oklahoma, Norman, 1965.

Siegel, Martha R. "Field Notes." In possession of Martha R. Blaine, Oklahoma City, Okla.

II. Government Publications

Hodge, Frederick Webb (ed.), *Handbook of American Indians North of Mexico. Bureau of American Ethnology, Bulletin No. 30.* Washington, Government Printing Office, 1907–10.

Mooney, James. "The Ghost-Dance Religion and the Sioux Outbreak of 1890," *Bureau of American Ethnology Fourteenth Annual Report.* Washington, Government Printing Office, 1896.

Royce, Charles C. "Indian Land Cessions in the United States," *Bureau of American Ethnology Eighteenth Annual Report*, Part 2. Washington, Government Printing Office, 1899.

III. Books and Articles

Baylor, George Wythe. *John Robert Baylor, Confederate Governor of Arizona.* Ed. and annotated by Odie B. Faulk. Tucson, Arizona Pioneers Historical Society, 1966.

Borden, W. C. "The Vital Statistics of an Apache Indian Community." Boston, Damrell & Upham, 1893. Reprint from *Boston Medical and Surgical Journal*, July 6, 1893.

Debo, Angie. *A History of the Indians of the United States*. Norman, University of Oklahoma Press, 1970.

Faulk, Odie B. *The Geronimo Campaign*. New York, Oxford University Press, 1969.

———. *Too Far North: Too Far South*. Los Angeles, Westernlore Press, 1967.

Federal Writers' Program. *New Mexico: A Guide to the Colorful State*. New York, Hastings House, 1953.

Forbes, Jack D. *Apache, Navaho, and Spaniard*. Norman, University of Oklahoma Press, 1960.

Gipson, Fred. *Fabulous Empire*. Boston, Houghton Mifflin Company, 1946.

Harper, Richard H. "The Missionary Work of the Reformed (Dutch) Church in America, in Oklahoma," *Chronicles of Oklahoma*, Vol. XVIII, No. 4 (December, 1940).

Jozhe, Benedict. "A Brief History of the Fort Sill Apache Tribe," *Chronicles of Oklahoma*, Vol. XXXIX, No. 4 (Winter, 1961/62).

La Farge, Oliver. *A Pictorial History of the American Indian*. New York, Crown Publishing Company, 1956.

Lockwood, Frank C. *The Apache Indians*. New York, The Macmillan Company, 1938.

Nye, W[ilbur] S[turtevant]. *Carbine and Lance*. Norman, University of Oklahoma Press, 1937.

Ogle, Ralph Hedrick. *Federal Control of the Western Apaches, 1848–1886*. Albuquerque, University of New Mexico Press, 1970.

Opler, Morris Edward. *An Apache Life-Way*. Chicago, University of Chicago Press, 1941.

———. *Apache Odyssey: A Journey between Two Worlds*. New York, Holt, Rinehart, and Winston, 1969.

———. "Mountain Spirits of the Chiricahua Apache," *The Masterkey*, Vol. XX, No. 4 (July, 1946).

———. "Some Implications of Culture Theory for Anthropology and Psychology," *American Journal of Orthopsychiatry*, Vol. XVIII (October, 1948).

Page, Elizabeth M. *In Camp and Tepee*. New York. Chicago, Fleming H. Revell Company, 1915.

Peterson, Karen Douglas. *Plains Indian Art from Fort Marion*. Norman, University of Oklahoma Press, 1971.

Sonnichsen, C. L. *The Mescalero Apaches.* Norman, University of Oklahoma Press, 1958.

Thrapp, Dan L. *Al Sieber, Chief of Scouts.* Norman, University of Oklahoma Press, 1964.

———. *The Conquest of Apacheria.* Norman, University of Oklahoma Press, 1967.

———. *General Crook and the Sierra Madre Adventure.* Norman, University of Oklahoma Press, 1972.

———. "Geronimo's Mysterious Surrender," *Brand Book*, Los Angeles Corral, Vol. XIII (1969).

———. *Juh: An Incredible Indian. Southwestern Studies, Monograph No. 39.* El Paso, Texas Western Press, 1973.

———. *Victorio and the Mimbres Apaches.* Norman, University of Oklahoma Press, 1974.

Turner, Katherine C. *Red Men Calling on the Great White Father.* Norman, University of Oklahoma Press, 1951.

IV. Interviews

Ball, Eve. Ruidoso, New Mexico, July 23–28, 1971.

V. Letters

Ball, Eve. December 10, 1957; December 20, 1960; March 8, 1971; February 27, November 13, 1972; February 27, March 10, June 25, 26, July 13, 1973.

Blaine, Garland J. August 21, 1974.

Clark, Elaine. June 5, 1973.

Rudisill, Richard. July 17, 1972; July 8, 1975.

Self, Frank J. February 12, 1973.

Slonaker, John J. July 9, 1973.

Thrapp, Dan L. December 8, 1972.

INDEX